MW01195535

Reading Jonathan Edwards

Reading Jonathan Edwards

AN ANNOTATED BIBLIOGRAPHY
IN THREE PARTS, 1729-2005

M. X. Lesser

WILLIAM B. EERDMANS PUBLISHING COMPANY

GRAND RAPIDS, MICHIGAN / CAMBRIDGE, U.K.

© 2008 M. X. Lesser

All rights reserved

Published 2008 by

Wm. B. Eerdmans Publishing Co.

2140 Oak Industrial Drive N.E., Grand Rapids, Michigan 49505 /

P.O. Box 163, Cambridge CB3 9PU U.K.

Printed in the United States of America

14 13 12 11 10 09 08   7 6 5 4 3 2 1

Library of Congress Cataloging-in-Publication Data

Lesser, M. X.
    Reading Jonathan Edwards : an annotated bibliography in three parts, 1729-2005 /
M. X. Lesser.
        p. cm.
    Includes bibliographical references and indexes.
    ISBN 978-0-8028-6243-3 (cloth : alk. paper)
    1. Edwards, Jonathan, 1703-1758 — Bibliography.   I. Title.
    Z8255.5.L485 2008
    [BX7260.E3]
    016.2858092 — dc22

                            2007033338

www.eerdmans.com

Contents

Preface

"Shall we read Jonathan Edwards?" a friend asked the Rev. Robert E. Neighbor — he had been rereading *Freedom of the Will* — and, as he wrote in *Review and Expositor* for January 1918, made "an affirmative answer": it would be "decidedly advantageous" for ministers and laymen alike. Not all readers agreed. Sixteen years earlier, the Rev. Joseph H. Twichell lent *Freedom of the Will* to his friend Mark Twain: Edwards is a "drunken lunatic," Twain wrote after a night of reading, a "resplendent intellect gone mad — a marvelous spectacle. . . . By God I was ashamed to be in such company."

This compilation of reader response to Edwards over 276 years includes a reprint of two earlier works — *Jonathan Edwards: A Reference Guide* (1981) and *Jonathan Edwards: An Annotated Bibliography* (1994) — and the publication of a third, a gathering of commentary from 1994 to 2005, prominent in it the celebration of the tercentenary of his birth. About a hundred entries have been added to the first work and a third as many to the second; the last adds another 700 to the whole. The text preserves the pattern of arranging items alphabetically within a given year — added items are interleaved, identified by small caps — and of recording cross-references — 1765.2, for Samuel Hopkins's biography of Edwards, 2003.59, for George M. Marsden's. Unexamined items are indicated by an asterisk preceding the entry; essays in a collection follow the order of the editor(s), annotated serially, not alphabetically. Each of the three sections is self-contained: an introduction, tracing in detail the direction of criticism, and an annotated bibliography of articles, books, parts of books, dissertations, fugitive references, reviews, and reprints. A chronology of Edwards's works, listed by date and by short title and long, precedes the entire work; a comprehensive index of authors and titles, another of subjects, and one of additions closes it.

My debts, of course, are to those in the text, only somewhat less so to a stack of librarians the country over, none more generous and patient than Yves Hyacinthe, of Snell Library, Northeastern, and Jon Lanham, of Lamont Library, Harvard. I owe a debt to Francis Blessington for his gift of tongues; David F. Coffin, Jr., for sharing his bibliography prior to its publication; Wilson H. Kimnach for a privately published commemorative he edited; Mason I. Lowance, Jr., for two hard-to-find articles, and Robert E. Davis for five; and to Kenneth P. Minkema, *The Works of Jonathan Edwards,* for manuscripts, texts, and encouragement. For care and comfort through my years at Northeastern my thanks go to Ava Baker, Joseph DeRoche, Ivy Dodge, Maureen Godino, Gary Goshgarian, and, most especially, Mary Mello.

Like so much else, this is dedicated to the "uncommon union" with my Sarah, Lee.

Swampscott, Massachusetts   M.X.L.
September 10, 2006

Chronology of Works

1731   *God Glorified*
God Glorified in the Work of Redemption, By the Greatness of Man's Dependence upon Him, in the Whole of it. A Sermon Preached on the Publick Lecture in Boston, July 8. 1731. Boston: S. Kneeland and T. Green.

1734   *Divine and Supernatural Light*
A Divine and Supernatural Light, Immediately imparted to the Soul by the Spirit of God, Shown to be both a Scriptural, and Rational Doctrine. In a Sermon Preach'd at Northampton. Boston: S. Kneeland and T. Green.

1737   *Faithful Narrative*
A Faithful Narrative Of The Surprizing Work of God In The Conversion Of Many Hundred Souls in Northampton, and the Neighbouring Towns and Villages of New-Hampshire in New-England. In a Letter to the Revd. Dr. Benjamin Colman of Boston. Written by the Revd. Mr. Edwards, Minister of Northampton, on Nov. 6, 1736. London: John Oswald.

1737   *A Letter*
A Letter to the Author of the Pamphlet Called an Answer to the Hampshire Narrative. Boston.

1738   *Discourses*
Discourses on Various Important Subjects, Nearly concerning the great Affair of the Soul's Eternal Salvation. Boston: S. Kneeland and T. Green.

1741   *Sinners in the Hands of an Angry God*
Sinners In The Hands of an Angry God. A Sermon Preached at Enfield, July 8th 1741. At a Time of great Awakenings; and attended with remarkable Impressions on many of the Hearers. Boston: S. Kneeland and T. Green.

1741   *Resort and Remedy*
The Resort and Remedy of those that are bereaved by the Death of an eminent Minister. A Sermon Preached at Hatfield, Sept. 2. 1741. Being the Day

of Interment of the Reverend Mr. William Williams, the aged and venerable Pastor of that Church. Boston: G. Rogers.

1741   *Distinguishing Marks*
The Distinguishing Marks Of a Work of the Spirit of God. Applied to that uncommon Operation that has lately appeared on the Minds of many of the People of this Land: With a particular Consideration of the extraordinary Circumstances with which this Work is attended. A Discourse Delivered at New-Haven, September 10th 1741. Being the Day after the Commencement. Boston: S. Kneeland and T. Green.

1743   *Great Concern*
The great Concern of A Watchman For Souls, appearing in the Duty he has to do, and the Account he has to give, represented & improved. In A Sermon Preach'd at the Ordination Of the Reverend Mr. Jonathan Judd, To the Pastoral Office over the Church of Christ, in the New Precinct at Northampton, June 8. 1743. Boston: Green, Bushnell, Allen.

1743   *Some Thoughts*
Some Thoughts Concerning the present Revival of Religion In New-England, And the Way in which it ought to be acknowledged and promoted, Humbly offered to the Publick, in a Treatise on that Subject. In Five Parts. Boston: S. Kneeland and T. Green.

1744   *True Excellency*
The true Excellency of a Minister of the Gospel. A Sermon Preach'd at Pelham, Aug. 30. 1744. Being the Day of the Ordination Of The Revd. Mr. Robert Abercrombie To The Work of the Gospel Ministry In that Place. Boston: Rogers and Fowle.

1746   *Church's Marriage*
The Church's Marriage to her Sons, and to her God: A Sermon Preached at the Instalment of the Rev. Mr. Samuel Buel As Pastor of the Church and Congregation at East-Hampton on Long Island, September 19. 1746. Boston: S. Kneeland and T. Green.

1746   *Religious Affections*
A Treatise Concerning Religious Affections, In Three Parts. Boston: S. Kneeland and T. Green.

1747   *Humble Attempt*
An Humble Attempt To promote Explicit Agreement And Visible Union of God's People in Extraordinary Prayer For the Revival of Religion and the Advancement of Christ's Kingdom on Earth, pursuant to Scripture-Promises and Prophecies concerning the last Time. Boston: D. Henchman.

1747   *True Saints*
True Saints, when absent from the Body, are present with the Lord. A Sermon Preached on the Day of the Funeral of the Rev. Mr. David Brainerd, Missionary to the Indians, From the Honourable Society in Scotland, for the Propagation of Christian Knowledge, and Pastor of a Church of Christian Indians in New-Jersey; Who died at Northampton in New-England, Octob. 9th. 1747, in the 30th Year of his Age. Boston: Rogers and Fowle.

1748   *A Strong Rod*
A Strong Rod broken and withered. A Sermon Preach'd at Northampton, on the Lord's-Day, June 26. 1748. On the Death of The Honourable John Stoddard, Esq. Boston: Rogers and Fowle.

1749   *Life of Brainerd*
An Account of the Life Of the late Reverend Mr. David Brainerd, Minister of the Gospel, Missionary to the Indians, from the honourable Society in Scotland, for the Propagation of Christian Knowledge, and Pastor of a Church of Christian Indians in New-Jersey. Boston: D. Henchman.

1749   *Humble Inquiry*
An Humble Inquiry Into the Rules of the Word of God Concerning The Qualifications Requisite to a Compleat Standing and full Communion In the Visible Christian Church. Boston: S. Kneeland.

1750   *Christ the Great Example*
Christ the great Example of Gospel Ministers. A Sermon Preach'd at Portsmouth, At the Ordination of the Reverend Mr. Job Strong, To the Pastoral Office over the South Church in that Place, June 28. 1749. Boston: T. Fleet.

1751   *Farewell Sermon*
A Farewel-Sermon Preached at the first Precinct in Northampton, After the People's publick Rejection of their Minister, and renouncing their Relation to Him as Pastor of the Church there, On June 22. 1750. Occasion'd by Difference of Sentiments, concerning the requisite Qualifications of Members of the Church, in compleat Standing. Boston: S. Kneeland.

1752   *Misrepresentations Corrected*
Misrepresentations Corrected, And Truth vindicated, In A Reply to the Rev. Mr. Solomon Williams's Book. Boston: S. Kneeland.

1753   *True Grace*
True Grace, Distinguished from the Experience Of Devils; In A Sermon, Preached before the Synod Of New-York, Convened at New-Ark, in New-Jersey, On September 28. N.S. 1752. New York: James Parker.

PART I

1729–1978

Introduction

During his stay at the Allen Tates' in the autumn of 1942, Robert Lowell was hard at work on a biography of Jonathan Edwards, "heaping up books," he recalls, "and taking notes" (1968.13). After a while his enthusiasm flagged, "getting more and more numb on the subject, looking at old leatherbound volumes on freedom of the will and so on, and feeling less and less a calling." So together with Tate he began to collect poems for an anthology of English verse, and he abandoned Edwards. Not quite: over the next several years Lowell turned what he had found in Edwards into a pair of splendid poems, "Mr. Edwards and the Spider" and "After the Surprising Conversions" (1946.3), borrowing from him on spiders and suicides, unacknowledged. Then, many years later, Lowell wrote two more poems, "Jonathan Edwards in Western Massachusetts" (1964.14) and "The Worst Sinner, Jonathan Edwards' God" (1973.19), contemplative now and quite touched by the Stockbridge exile — "I love you faded, old." It is a cautionary tale.

Over the last 250 years, attitudes towards Edwards, or what may be wrung from him, have changed considerably, yet some fairly well-marked continuities remain. Biographies of Edwards, for example, were useful as "pious memorials" against the challenge to orthodoxy launched in the eighteenth and early nineteenth centuries, when the lives of ministering saints were summoned for defense; later in the century, when his kind of strenuous belief waned, his life became largely irrelevant or of only passing interest; now his life is useful again but as a clue to his time and place, hardly tutorial or, for that matter, inconsequential. In another way, as discomfort about necessity and imputation rose in the nineteenth century, the readers of *Freedom of the Will* and *Original Sin* came chiefly to damn Edwards; those in the twentieth century — with notable theological exceptions — to neglect him. And his style, considered so wretched that some of his nineteenth century editors recast his prose to rescue him, becomes in recent years the unitive instrument of his thought and the signal fact of his art.

Yet some things about Edwards do not change, or change ever so slightly. A troublesome, and largely unresolved, duality haunted Edwards from the start — mystic and rationalist, philosopher and theologian, poet of the divine and scourger of the wicked — and hangs on even now, though in our less dramatic age, there appears little need to color him tragic. The habit of reading the American experience as a quarrel between Edwards on one side and Franklin on the other, first noted sometime in the nineteenth century, becomes for twentieth-century cultural critics (and popularizers) a recurrent, if not wholly rewarding, theme. There is a list of his inadvertences — his antinomianism, his liberalism, his pantheism, his republicanism — to reckon with from the eighteenth century on. And there is, for Americans, the abiding question of his importance to their history, their religion, their society, their thought.

1

The first life of Edwards was published within months of his death. The anonymous "Brief Account," a ten-page preface to *Original Sin* (1758.4) ascribed to Samuel Finley and later reprinted as "A Contemporaneous Account" (1903.24), derives the essential facts of Edwards's life and much of the praise from the "public Prints," the obituaries published in Boston and New York newspapers and Gilbert Tennent's eulogy in the *Pennsylvania Gazette* (1758.5). Seven years later the second and perhaps the most frequently pirated biography appeared, Samuel Hopkins's *The Life and Character of the Late Reverend Mr. Jonathan Edwards, President of the College of New-Jersey* (1765.2). Not only is this account more thorough than Finley's — it is, after all, ten times as long — it is more intimate, for as a student in the Edwards home in Northampton, Hopkins reports as an eye-witness and a friend, a disciple and a just remembrancer.[1] Hopkins transcribes and interleaves extracts from Edwards's "Resolutions" and "Diary," the whole of *Personal Narrative*, and several letters in a detailed history of his forebears and his family, his habits of mind, the conduct of his ministry and the occasion of his dismissal, his removal to Stockbridge, and his death at Princeton; a bibliography of his manuscripts and publications; and brief lives of his daughter Esther Burr and his wife Sarah. Still valuable for its primary materials — *Personal Narrative*, for example, is more reliable here than in later redactions — and for its sympathetic understanding, the *Life* fulfills Hopkins's intention to render a "faithful and plain narration of matters of fact" about Edwards and to offer him to the public as a model of Christian piety, "the *greatest* — best — and *most useful* of men."

For the next sixty years the Hopkins life was variously edited, revised, enlarged, or corrected, always recognizable, if seldom attributed. Erasmus Middleton, for instance, dramatizes Hopkins's account of the Northampton troubles — "*Dismiss him! Dismiss him!* was the universal cry" — but closely follows his un-

---

1. For the Edwards-Hopkins relationship, see papers by Edwards Amasa Park (1852.8), Oliver Wendell Elsbree (1935.1), and David S. Lovejoy (1967.19).

named source (1786.1); the anonymous compiler of another life in the preface to a London imprint of *History of Redemption* (1788.1) closely follows Middleton, again unnamed. Edward Williams and Edward Parsons, editors of the first collected Edwards, the eight-volume Leeds edition (1806.1), "improve" upon an acknowledged Hopkins by adding Middleton; but Samuel Austin, editor of the first American, or Worcester, edition of the complete Edwards two years later (1808.3), acknowledges and prints Hopkins without change. At a farther remove, John Hawksley adds "numerous verbal emendations" to Williams and Parsons, in a separately published and attributed Hopkins (1815.1).

It was left to Sereno Edwards Dwight and his 766-page *Life of President Edwards,* the first of the ten-volume New York, or Converse, edition of the complete Edwards (1829.4), to incorporate Finley, Hopkins, and Williams and Parsons in what would become the standard biography for more than a century. The chief advantage the Dwight life enjoys is bulk: it collects and publishes for the first time the juvenilia, the "Miscellanies," and countless letters (especially to and from Scots ministers), and it reprints and expands the texts in Hopkins. Thus Dwight's 150-page account of Edwards's dismissal includes, *pari passu,* a history of the changes in communion practice; Hopkins's narration; Edwards's version of his differences with his congregation, as noted in his journals and explained in his letters; Joseph Hawley's belated recantation; and Dwight's review of the matter and his recommendations. But, here as elsewhere, Dwight must be approached with care. He so encumbers his narrative with indiscriminate detail and with a ponderous style that he makes it hard going indeed; more important, he silently alters his manuscript sources, deleting here, correcting there. It is a troublesome book but, until the Edwards manuscripts are edited, a necessary one.

Criticism during the first hundred years centers on Edwards's role in the early Northampton revivals and the Great Awakening — more accurately, on his reporting and defense of those events — and sometime later on *Freedom of the Will* and his treatises on sin and virtue. In their preface to the first publication of *Faithful Narrative* (1737.1), Isaac Watts and John Guyse recommend Edwards to their London readers as the "pious" recorder of the "astonishing" work of God in Northampton, though they are less pleased with his choice of Abigail Hutchinson and Phebe Bartlet as suitable examples of the conversion experience.[2] Within a year the preface and text were translated into German (1738.5), within three into Dutch (1740.1). Two years later John Willison offers Edwards's *Distinguishing Marks,* another conversion testimony, to his Scots readers as an American analogue to the Cambuslang revival (1742.3).

Though Benjamin Franklin urged his sister to read Edwards's justification of

---

2. Anne Stokely Pratt recounts the difficulties Watts had in securing the Edwards manuscripts (1938.3), drawing upon the Watts correspondence published by the Massachusetts Historical Society (1895.11); see also Arthur Paul Davis (1943.4).

the revival in *Some Thoughts* (see 1840.3), Charles Chauncy detected in it few instances of genuine religious experience and in the whole of the Awakening "a bad and dangerous tendency" to excess. In his celebrated attack, *Seasonable Thoughts on the State of Religion in New-England* (1743.2), Chauncy called upon Edwards to denounce itinerant preachers and to impose strict church discipline upon his congregation, to return to proper religious practice, to distinguish passion from affection.[3] The unchecked enthusiasm Chauncy saw in the revivals was just as plain to William Rand (1743.3), who thought Edwards a dupe of Satan, unable to distinguish true from false marks of the spirit. Edwards, of course, was convinced of the soundness of his evangelical position, and, together with his overseas correspondents and some American friends, urged a universal concert of prayer in his *Humble Attempt* (1747.1). Later in the century the founders of the Baptist Missionary Society would testify to the singular influence Edwards exerted upon them, especially through his *Humble Attempt* and *Life of Brainerd,* an influence greater than that of either George Whitefield or John Wesley (see 1942.8).

Except for such commentary on his revivalist pieces and the partisan debate over his Northampton difficulties — for example, the exchange between Robert Breck (1751.1) and William Hobby (1751.2) on the conduct of the church council that dismissed him or the attack of Solomon Williams (1751.3) on his admission practices that precipitated it — public remarks about Edwards are rare during his lifetime. Of course, *Original Sin* was issued in 1758, the year of his death, *True Virtue* and *End of Creation* seven years later, and *History of Redemption* nine years after that. Still, *Freedom of the Will* garners little notice and few pages before 1770, fully sixteen years after it was first published. Then an anonymous writer charges Edwards with blasphemy and atheism in a bitter, brief polemic (1770.1), and James Dana issues the first of two full-length examinations (1770.2), an event warmly greeted by a correspondent of Edwards's Yale tutor, Samuel Johnson (see 1929.6). Dana originally deals with Edwards from a practical and experiential point of view, assessing his principles of volition and causation, charging him with atheism; three years later he focusses upon Edwards's "false" distinctions between natural and moral necessity and his "injurious misrepresentations" of God as the author of sin (1773.1). Stephen West defends Edwards against Dana's perceived errors in his earlier work (1772.2), and then, more than twenty years later, returns to Dana's second examination in a sixty-five-page rebuttal (1794.3). Three years later Edwards's son and namesake carefully analyzes the meanings of liberty and necessity, fixing the free-will controversy upon the question of causative or fortuitous volition, in the most sustained defense of the doctrine (1797.1). But the attacks go on, variously. Joseph Priestley challenges Edwards's notion that sin is a withheld act (1777.1); Elias Smith argues the legitimacy of the Arminian contention (1793.6);

---

3. Chauncy's reaction to Edwards is most completely described by Edward M. Griffin in his unpublished dissertation (1966.16).

Samuel West twice tries Edwards for his confusion of antecedent and consequent necessity and his connection of motive and action (1793.7 and 1795.2); Isaac Taylor charges Edwards with a violation of scientific reasoning in mixing metaphysics with Scripture (1827.5); and Thomas Tully Crybbace, at one with Edwards for revealing the "absurdities" of his antagonists, dismisses him for his failure to clarify liberty and necessity (1829.3). Beyond the strictly theological argument, the response is mixed. Samuel Taylor Coleridge thinks *Freedom of the Will* "destroys all will" (1829.2); James Boswell, who had read it, reports Dr. Johnson, who hadn't, as saying, "All theory is against the freedom of the will; all experience for it" (1791.1); William Godwin admires its "great force of reason" (1793.5), William Hazlitt its "closeness and candour" (1829.5); and Alexander Hamilton reportedly exclaimed that "nothing ever came from the human mind more in proof that man is a reasoning animal" (see 1968.35). As an English reviewer put it, his regret was that such intellectual rigor as Edwards had was in the service of "theological chimeras" (1762.1).

Attitudes about the other Edwards seem more evenly balanced, if, at times, equally vitriolic. So William Hart assails the "arbitrary" relationship between virtue and benevolence in *True Virtue* (1771.2), and Samuel Hopkins defends its necessity (1773.2). The younger Edwards values a newly produced *History of Redemption* (1774.3), only to have a reviewer find it full of "pious conundrums" (1775.1). One commentator discovers not the "remotest semblance" of physical depravity in *Original Sin* (1824.2), another points to its obvious, unequivocal, and total presence (1825.2).

About Edwards's style, there is no balance — it is all bad. His language is mysterious (1750.2), negligent (1758.4), uncouth (1808.5), vulgar (1811.2), inelegant (1822.4), repellent (1824.1). So pervasive is the view that his is one of "the most remarkable specimens of bad writing" of the time that one nineteenth-century editor of *Religious Affections* abridges the text to rid it of ambiguities and tautologies (1817.1), and another writes *Sinners in the Hands of an Angry God* in "other language" for the modern reader (1826.1). For all that, criticism during the first century is given over to frequent and studied denunciations of Edwards on the will.

Little of that bitterness touches the man. On Solomon Stoddard's death, there is every hope that Edwards will inherit his grandfather's mantle (1729.1 and 1731.1); at his own death, he is mourned as the "greatest pillar" of America's Zion (1758.3). Gilbert Tennent, the evangelist preacher, calls him a "great Divine" (1758.5); Isaac Backus, the New England Baptist, considers him "one of the best divines" of his age (1767.2). An anonymous poet eulogizes "Great EDWARDS — dead!" (1758.2), and two of the Connecticut wits sing his name: Joel Barlow launches him into "the realms of light" (1778.1), and Timothy Dwight extols him as "that moral Newton, that second Paul" (1788.3). Overseas, Edwards wins similar praise. John Erskine, his Scots editor, writes in 1758 of the "irreparable" loss: "I do not think our age has produced a divine of equal genius or judgment" (see 1818.3).

And, as an American, he wins even more. John Ryland, the English Baptist, finds him "the greatest divine that ever adorned the American world" (1780.2), and Dugald Stewart, the Edinburgh philosopher, ranks him a peer of "any disputant bred in the universities of Europe" (1822.6). Such high praise would not come to Edwards again until, a generation later, George Bancroft warns that "he that will know the workings of the mind of New England in the middle of the last century, and the throbbings of its heart, must give his days and nights to the study of Jonathan Edwards" (1856.1). Except for a few academic theologians, the nineteenth century thought better of it.

2

"Next after the Bible, read and study Edwards," Dr. Lyman Beecher tells his son at Yale (see 1865.1), but, unlike some of the men in the Beecher family (1868.1), the women will have none of it. His wife flees his reading of *Sinners in the Hands of an Angry God* (see 1934.7); his daughter Catherine refutes Edwards in order to save her beloved from eternal damnation (see 1962.1); and, in *The Minister's Wooing* (1859.7), his daughter Harriet characterizes Edwards's sermons as a "refined poetry of torture."[4] The sermons are just as trying to other women later in the century. The heroine of Frank Samuel Child's *A Puritan Wooing* (1898.3) collapses upon hearing Edwards at Northampton on sin, only to recover converted. Less fortunately, the mother of the heroine in Paul Leicester Ford's *Janice Meredith* (1899.5) turns to stoney silence after hearing Edwards at Princeton on infant damnation. At a distance, John Greenleaf Whittier hears Edwards forging "the iron links of his argument" in a wilderness church (1866.2), as later in a Harvard commemorative ode Oliver Wendell Holmes thinks he hears Edwards's "iron heel" fall upon Princeton (1887.4).

The sound of the stern preacher of sin and damnation reverberates throughout early studies of American literature, though often it is muted by speculation of what Edwards might have been. Thus William Ellery Channing remarks at the beginning of the period that Edwards's mind was "lost" to literature by "vassalage to a false theology" (1830.2); at the end of the period, Walter C. Bronson regrets that so capable a writer was bound to a theology of any kind (1900.9). Edwards "might have been one of the first poets of his age," Edwards Amasa Park notes, "had he not chosen to be the first theologian" (1839.7). Even the redoubtable Moses Coit Tyler believes Edwards might have been "one of the world's masters" of imaginative literature but for his calling, or of the sciences for that matter (1878.7). He might

---

4. For the details of Harriet Beecher's struggle with Edwards's theology, see Charles Foster, *The Rungless Ladder* (1954.7), and Alice Crozier, *The Novels of Harriet Beecher Stowe* (1969.10); for the men in the family, see Robert Meredith, *The Politics of the Universe* (1968.15).

have been "another Newton," according to Benjamin Silliman, the editor and founder of the *American Journal of Science and Arts* (1832.6), or a naturalist of "brilliance," according to Henry C. McCook, a noted arachnologist (1889.9 and 1890.6). That Edwards might be compared to Benjamin Franklin becomes part of the popular assessment — favorably, in Eugene Lawrence's *A Primer of American Literature* (1880.7), or unfavorably, in Brander Matthews's *An Introduction to the Study of American Literature* (1896.10) — and persists, with little change, well into the next century.

As persistent — and derivative — are biographical studies of Edwards during those seventy years. Both *The Life of President Edwards* (1832.1), issued by the American Sunday School Union, and Samuel Miller's "Life of Jonathan Edwards" (1837.1), part of Jared Sparks's *The Library of American Biography*, rely heavily upon Hopkins and Dwight; both are directed to the young — young readers in the first, young ministers in the second. Neither merit much attention, nor does the overly long evaluation of Edwards as "intellectual athlete" by Henry Rogers (1834.4).

Other lives, abbreviated and standard, appear with some frequency and concentrate predictably on the "tragedy" of Edwards's dismissal, citing one cause or another. James Wynne, for instance, attributes Edwards's intemperate handling of the bad-book episode to his envy of Samuel Buell's success with his young parishioners, a point, Wynne argues, avoided by the overly solicitous Hopkins and Dwight (1850.6). Joseph Clark indicts the "mischievous notion" that a Congregational church council is like an ecclesiastical court and holds it, and Edwards's participation in the Robert Breck affair, responsible for his troubles (1858.7). One commentator traces the cause of his dismissal to the opposition of neighboring churches (1867.2), another to his opposition to bundling (1892.2). And Arthur Latham Perry, closer to fact, discovers his difficulties at Northampton and at Stockbridge in the antagonism of the Williams family, a "selfish cabal" (1896.11) and the subject of a novel sometime later (1967.27).

More comprehensive, though far more questionable, views depend upon psychological or genetic analyses. In "Jonathan Edwards: A Psychological Study" (1890.3), Joseph Crooker diagnoses Edwards a "theological monomaniac," suffering from genetic "delusional insanity," obvious early in his *Personal Narrative* and continuing virulent in the unrealistic treatises of his mature years, a hopeless case. Edwards, according to Crooker, contributes "absolutely nothing" to an understanding of man in history, nature, or society. A bit more sanguine is the pseudonymous Felix Oldmixon (1895.5), who observes that a strong will and spirit checked incipient madness in Edwards only to crop up in his grandson Aaron Burr, a clinical view somewhat at odds with the diagnosis that Burr inherited Edwards's courage but not his conscience (1900.15). The most extensive study of the genetics of the matter is Albert Winship's *Jukes-Edwards* (1900.20), which concludes not unexpectedly that, aside from minor divagations, the Edwards clan represents the "midday" of eugenics. Though thirty years late, that would have come as no surprise to the hundreds gathered in Stockbridge in September of 1870 for a two-day reunion of the Edwards family, rendering tributes to its founder and congratulations to his heirs (1871.5).

As in the earlier period, the documents of the Great Awakening and *Freedom of the Will* command critical attention, but increasingly other works emerge and still other doctrines are examined as the question of the relationship of Edwards to the Edwardseans becomes more and more a matter of debate. Joseph Tracy's pioneer study of the Awakening (1842.6) gives Edwards and his Northampton revivals of the 1730s a central place in the larger movement of the 1740s and claims that his dismissal "disposed the pious to be on his side" here and abroad. Not everyone agreed: Charles Hodge earlier remarks Edwards's failure to check the unrestrained emotion and excitation the revival engendered, even though it pumped "new life" into the Presbyterian church (1839.5); William Henry Channing considers Edwards the true, albeit unlovely, exemplar of the revival and of the Protestant emphasis on individualism and sinfulness (1847.2). At the end of the period, Samuel Perkins Hayes details the "unstable" social and religious conditions that gave rise to the revivals, reports the theological struggle, and examines the "paradox" of Edwards, in an uncritical history appearing in the *American Journal of Psychology* (1902.5).

No such neutral ground exists for *Freedom of the Will* and, as Horace Bushnell notes, even the ground shifts in time (1858.6). Patrick Campbell MacDougall praises Edwards on the will, notwithstanding his "verbal ambiguity," and chastises Isaac Taylor and his failed case on necessity (1831.2). William Hazlitt considers Edwards's exhaustive study "one of the most closely reasoned, elaborate, acute, serious, and sensible among modern productions," comparing Joseph Priestley's *Philosophical Necessity* unfavorably with it (1836.1). Jeremiah Day defends Edwards twice (1831.1 and 1841.3), the second time in an elaborate analysis of his language and structure to prove that Edwards is best understood when read "as a whole." In a frequently cited letter, Thomas Chalmers remarks that there is "No book of human composition which I more strenuously recommend" than Edwards's *Freedom of the Will* (see 1857.4), and Thomas Huxley, no less fulsome, finds Edwards's argument "has never been equaled in power, and certainly has never been refuted" (1879.7). And in his dissertation at Leipzig, William Harder Squires, with singular and sustained conviction, relates Edwards's determinism to Schopenhauer's metaphysics of the will and Wundt's psychology of voluntarism and fixes his place in American intellectual history (1901.10).

Still, *Freedom of the Will* suffers at the hands of many. Henry Philip Tappan expends more than a thousand pages (1839.8, 1840.6, and 1841.4) refuting Edwards logically, psychologically, and ethically on matters of causality, consciousness, and moral agency. Albert Taylor Bledsoe's *Examination* (1845.2) consigns Edwards to dialectical perdition for his atheism, delusion, and imprecision — "he does not reason at all, he merely rambles." More than thirty years later, an unrelenting Bledsoe, now editor of the *Southern Review,* reprints his assault serially from October 1877 to the following October. Rowland Hazard exposes the "fallacies" of Edwards's argument in a 350-page addendum to his *Freedom of the Mind in Willing* (1864.3), and D. D. Weedon faults Edwards's "intellective conclusions" and those of his Princeton advocates in a broad-based argument on responsibility and accountability (1864.5). And George Park Fisher in his brief and incisive "The Philosophy of Jonathan Edwards" (1879.4) concludes that the "iron network" of his doctrine of necessity fails to satisfy "the generality of mankind." Less restrained critics call *Freedom of the Will* a "monstrous deformity" (1842.2), "pantheistic" (1860.2), a "quibble and logomachy" (1862.4). William Ellery Channing thinks it "pernicious" (1841.2) and Charles Grandison Finney an "injurious monstrosity and misnomer" (1851.2). A young Emerson — he was twenty at the time of the journal entry — is ambivalent about *Freedom of the Will* (see 1909.1), but an old Mark Twain is decidedly not: Edwards is a "drunken lunatic. . . . By God I was ashamed to be in such company" (see 1917.6).

No less caustic are critics of *Original Sin* and Edwards's doctrine of imputation: it is "revolting" to one (1858.4), "most revolting" to another (1868.4), just "strange" to a third (1872.1). Yet one writer defends Edwards against contemporary distortions (1831.1), and George Park Fisher considers his doctrine of a piece with Aquinas and Augustine (1868.2). Frank Hugh Foster examines Edwards's doctrine of the punishment of sin and its effect upon the eschatology of his disciples (1886.1), though unlike recent scholars he argues the theological rather than the social or political implications of it. In Edinburgh, James Iverach lectures on the "unspeakable importance" of *True Grace* in the Edwards canon, finding in it the key to all the major works and to his evangelical thought (1884.2) as will others much later (1975.5 and 1978.23). At Harvard, William James in *The Varieties of Religious Experience* (1902.6) contends that Edwards's empirical method in *Religious Affections* is the only way to know Christian virtue.

The question of Edwards's theological "improvements" and his successors proposed by his son in the latter's collected works (see 1842.3) and argued in its reviews (1843.1 and 1844.5), becomes the point of dispute over the years in the leaden, sometimes angry pages of *Bibliotheca Sacra* (Andover), *Biblical Repertory* (Princeton), and *The New Englander* (Yale) and is, perhaps, best summarized by Edwards Amasa Park of the first and Lyman H. Atwater of the second. In "New England Theology" (1852.9), Park holds that that strain of theology, by whatever name, is a natural outgrowth of Edwards's doctrines and that those doctrines are retained by Edwardseans but in a slightly altered form. In "Jonathan Edwards and the Successive Forms of the New Divinity" (1858.2), Atwater argues that, except for the doctrines of mediate imputation and true virtue, Edwards is a strict Calvinist and that there are "broad and irreconcilable differences" between him and those calling themselves his successors. Particularly divisive was the reaction to Edwards's doctrine of the atonement, in one instance fairly disdained by the Edwardseans for its imprecision (1859.5) and in another heartily endorsed by others for its orthodoxy (1860.4). Perhaps the most reliable treatment of the whole problem during the period — after it ceased to be one — is George Nye Boardman's *A History of New England Theology* (1899.2), which concludes that while both parties speak of God as sovereign, New England Theology celebrates the glory of man, Edwards the glory of God.

Claims of influence, or the lack of it, on Edwards's thought spread during the period, especially conjectures about the source of his idealism. In his *L'Idealisme en Angleterre* (1888.2), Georges Lyon devotes a chapter to Edwards and immaterialism in America, discovering in Edwards similarities to Bishop Berkeley and positing his Yale tutor Samuel Johnson as the conduit. But, as Egbert Smyth points out, Edwards could not have known Berkeley through Johnson because Johnson first read Berkeley after he left Yale (1896.12); an examination of Edwards's shorthand notes confirms it (1902.14). John Henry MacCracken's *Jonathan Edwards Idealismus* (1899.6), a Halle doctoral dissertation, suggests Arthur Collier rather than Berkeley as the source, with no more real evidence than Lyon's study. Berkeley's editor, Alexander Campbell Fraser, takes an untenable middle position, claiming that Edwards "adopted" some of Berkeley though acknowledging that there is no proof that he ever read him, still less that he ever met him (1871.2, 1881.1, and 1901.5). The most balanced and convincing view, based on a careful reading of the juvenilia, is that of H. N. Gardiner in "The Early Idealism of Jonathan Edwards" (1900.12). Gardiner discounts the Berkeley evidence as "entirely internal" and defines Edwards's idealism as an "original expression of personal insight," influenced by the general direction of contemporary thought and sustained in a modified form throughout his later work.

That body of work grows with Tryon Edwards's edition of *Charity and Its Fruits* (1852.4), Alexander Grosart's *Selections from the Unpublished Writings of Jonathan Edwards of America* (1865.4), and Egbert Smyth's publication of Edwards's trinitarian views (1880.10). All are derived from manuscript sources — Grosart's was the only volume published of a projected complete Edwards so derived — and each speculates about the importance of them, a matter lent even more weight by Franklin B. Dexter's careful enumeration of the Yale holdings (1901.3) and Smyth's physical analysis of some early texts (1895.10). Sometime before, the manuscript problem erupted in a spate of suspicion and accusation about Edwards and the Trinity: it was alleged that the keepers of Edwards suppressed a manuscript testifying to his heretical, unitarian views. Horace Bushnell early (1851.1) and Oliver Wendell Holmes late (1883.4) cried heterodoxy, which the published manuscripts and denials of Smyth (1880.10) and Park (1881.2) did little to still. Only with the publication of George Park Fisher's *An Unpublished Essay of Edwards on the Trinity* was the matter finally settled (see 1903.26).

Yet even without a definitive *Trinity* or a complete Edwards — the *New York Times* felt it was a patriotic necessity to publish one (1900.2) — critics in the nineteenth century began to take a studied look at Edwards's thought as a whole, seeking out connections rather than isolated clues. Gardiner's essay on Edwards's idealism (1900.12) and Fisher's analysis of his philosophy (1879.4) represent deliberate efforts to evaluate Edwards without partisan rancor or wonted praise, to steer, as Joseph Thompson remarks (1861.3), between "unquestioning veneration" and "empirical judgment." Popular assessments continue to run to form. Oliver Wendell Holmes is precious and iconoclastic in his rejection of "the unleavened bread" of Edwards (1880.6), though he seems to have tasted of it himself (1886.2); Principal Fairbairn is respectful and adulatory in his acceptance (1896.5). Occasionally, a more balanced, if still highly critical, view emerges in the general press, for example, Leslie Stephen's influential piece in *Fraser's* (1873.2). Stephen discovers irreconcilable tensions in Edwards between the "gentle mystic" and the "stern divine." T. F. Henderson's "contradictory qualities" echoes Stephen's observation (in the ninth edition of the *Britannica*, 1875.3), as does George Angier Gordon's "radical inconsistency" a quarter of a century later (1900.14). Williston Walker notes similar tensions in his extended study of Edwards as one of *Ten New England Leaders* (1901.14). Walker had already reserved a special place for Edwards as "the greatest theologian" of American Congregationalism (1894.5) — Baptist (1839.4), Presbyterian (1868.4), and Methodist (1885.1) claims notwithstanding — for his modifications and departures from historic Calvinism. But the later study juxtaposes Edwards's formidable intellect against his transforming vision and concludes that "this remarkable man" will be "reverenced" more for his spirit than his intellect. To F. B. Sanborn that intellect is even more suspect because derivative, and Edwards remains, for all his acuteness, "our Puritan Schoolman, our Father Jonathan of Connecticut" (1883.6), the medieval mind of later critics.[5] Even so sympathetic a reader as Adam Leroy Jones, who places Edwards in the forefront of early American philosophy (1893.5), is forced to admit that Edwards's considerable reasoning suffers from "imperfect analysis" and his prose from intellectual isolation, the "speculative recluse" of Leslie Stephen's analysis.

The only full-length study of Edwards during the period agrees. Alexander V. G. Allen's *Jonathan Edwards* (1889.1) characterizes Edwards's style as "thinking aloud," the speculative thought of his Stockbridge years as an exercise "in confusion, if not failure." That Allen was ill-suited theologically to deal fairly with Edwards as some reviewers claimed (1890.12, for instance), may be simply the carping reaction of the defense. Nevertheless, Allen does indict Edwards for the "great wrong" of his doctrine of divine sovereignty, for his dogged belief in original sin, for the "false premises" of his theology. As is often the case at the close of the century, the mystical Edwards is the valuable Edwards: Allen isolates his God-consciousness as the "imperishable element" in him and the saving remnant of his

---

5. See especially Vincent Tomas (1952.12), Peter Gay (1966.14), and, earlier and more briefly, Percy Boynton (1936.2).

faith. In fact, in his tribute to Edwards on the sesquicentennial of his Northampton dismissal, Allen underscores the mystical and poetic in Edwards, remarking "the deepest affinity" between him and Dante, not Calvin.

That paper, "The Place of Edwards in History," formally opens *Jonathan Edwards, A Retrospect* (1901.6), a "serious attempt" by six scholars — Allen, Smyth, Gordon, Fisher, Henry T. Rose, and Gardiner — to gauge Edwards's thought and influence, to discover what in him is "temporary and accidental," what essential and permanent. To a man the very occasion of his dismissal is all but forgotten in a celebration of his gentleness, and the irreconcilable tensions Stephen noted twenty-five years earlier are all but relieved. By the turn of the century Edwards found a permanent niche in the American pantheon: on the first ballot, he was elected to the Hall of Fame, outdrawing Hawthorne by eight votes (1900.17).

3

Even so, twenty-six years would pass before the Charles Grafly bust of Edwards would be unveiled (1926.4), a time roughly matching a pause in the serious study of Edwards, a time of consolidation, and just a few years before a remarkable burst of creative scholarship about him. Though he takes on unexpected roles here and there — as a symbol for troubled times to President Roosevelt (not "a touch of the mollycoddle about him," 1916.6) or as a figure of comparison with that other Northampton celebrity, President Coolidge (1937.1) — Edwards remains for many readers, to borrow the unhappy phrase of Henry Bamford Parkes, "the fiery Puritan" (1930.10). Parkes portrays Edwards's times as those of "religious lunacy," his theology as "a blight upon posterity, . . . repulsive and absurd," and his person as "most tragic" and "not truly an American," in a biography short on insight and long on prejudice. In that, Parkes simply expands upon earlier sentiments and generally sums up the first three decades of the period: in order, a novelist scores Edwards as the "hoarsest of the whole flock of New World theological ravens" (1903.1); a freethinker vilifies him as the purveyor of "the worst religion of any human being who ever lived on this continent" (1918.3); and a writer for the *Forum* decries his "false, harsh, and artificial" morality (1926.6). Others take Edwards's fire and his dogma somewhat differently: his great-great-grandson ranks *Sinners in the Hands of an Angry God* "second only" to the Sermon on the Mount in a privately printed short biography and poetic tribute (1922.2), and Gilbert Seldes in *The Stammering Century* (1928.8) finds his imprecations sufficient cause for the reformist cults and widespread madness of the nineteenth century. Some few feel his fire not at all: the "real Edwards," according to I. Woodbridge Riley, is not the "sulphurous" Calvinist but the "philosopher of feeling," the typical mystic undergoing the traditional stages of the mystical experience (1908.2 and 1915.3).

That attitude, far less prominent during the first thirty years than that of

Parkes, informs two of the three major addresses delivered at the Edwards bicentennial celebration held at Andover Theological Seminary in early October of 1903 (1904.14). John Winthrop Platner discounts Edwards's energetic Calvinism as chiefly necessary to his "un-theological" times and recommends Edwards's "beatific vision" to his own; Egbert C. Smyth considers "the innermost meaning and the climax" in Edwards's theology to be his "vivid sense" of the immediacy and mutuality of God's communicated love; but Frederick J. E. Woodbridge dissents. Edwards fails the early promise of his mystical pantheism and, more important, fails to resolve the "intellectual duality" of his philosophical speculations and his theological convictions, a point repeatedly raised by nineteenth-century critics. Edwards's influence is now "largely negligible," Woodbridge goes on, because he lacks "philosophical thoroughness," probably a result of the "unanalyzed" and disruptive emotions of his conversion experience, a new point.

The many other celebrations — far fewer, however, than the Emerson centennials earlier that year — sought less to understand Edwards than to praise him. At Stockbridge, the seven ministers of the Berkshire Conferences speak in one voice of the spirituality and righteous effect of the "modern" or the "other" Edwards (1903.17); at Berkeley, though the principal speaker notes a "deep, happy inconsistency" between Edwards's logic and his intuition, he celebrates him as a "prophet of God" (1904.10); and in Columbus, Ohio, the speaker forecasts Edwards's influence to "millennial times" (1903.35). In Utica, New York, a preacher begs for a "duplicate" Edwards to again fill the air with "Calvinistic ozone" (1903.33), while in Brooklyn, another preacher, not to be outdone, contemplates a world in which "everyone of us were a Jonathan Edwards!" (1903.28). Such singleminded rhetoric prevails at Yale, at Hartford, and at Northampton (1903.13). Only at the dedication of the Edwards memorial gateway to the South Windsor cemetery a quarter of a century later is there the familiar caveat. Charles Andrews, anticipating Perry Miller by twenty years, characterizes the story of Edwards as "less the history of a life than the analysis of a mind," a mind, Andrews adds, at war with itself, intellect against emotion, logic against mysticism (1929.7).

Woodbridge had described that conflict before in slightly different form, and so had Henry Churchill King. Edwards was both a "theistic idealist" and a "mystical ethical Calvinist," argues King, a pairing that brings about inconsistencies in his thought and almost "anti-Protestant" doctrines in his theology (1903.34).[6] No more sanguine than King are Lewis Mumford, who sees Edwards impaled upon the horns of beauty and determinism (1926.5), and James Truslow Adams, who remarks the unavailing struggle in Edwards between the sweetness of his spirit and the pains of his doctrine (1927.1). Those contradictions, so much a

---

6. Later Henry Bamford Parkes would go King one better: Edwards's conversion experience, for instance, is "Catholic and not Calvinist"; his nineteenth-century followers deny "the Catholic solution" to nature and grace (1932.12).

part of the popular assessment of Edwards, also help define either New England Theology as a whole, according to a writer for the *American Journal of Theology* (1920.1), or the native philosophical tradition, according to a German writer on American thought (1928.10).

But the history of Edwards's life and times rather than an analysis of his mind, crowded with real or imagined contradictions, is the proper stuff of the period, and the definitive life, published at its close, is simply the last, best example of that predilection. An early, ninety-five-page book prizes the man at the expense of his worthless theology (1903.21); a four-page article extols the eugenics of the Edwards clan rather than his mostly unread books (1903.49) — Clarence Darrow, of course, would have neither man nor books (1925.2). An historian of Princeton doubts that Edwards would have made a successful president (1914.2); another of Yale doubts that he would have made a successful professor (1916.4). But all these are partial portraits. Only in Ola Elizabeth Winslow's definitive biography (1940.21) does Edwards the man emerge whole. Winslow explores the "inner curve of spiritual experience" to fasten on the essential Edwards — solitary and dignified, contentious, mystical leaning and ruthlessly logical, "neither Puritan nor fiery." Not an original mind, Edwards earns greatness by "initiating and directing" the Great Awakening and developing New England Theology, acts of "far reaching" consequences. Thus Winslow gathers together the facts of his life, gleaning information from the manuscripts and from a wide range of sources, early and late — from Thomas H. Johnson's first published work on Edwards describing his catalogue of books (1931.11) and from his second discovering the title of the bad book of Edwards's dismissal (1932.7), for instance. And Winslow arranges the whole of it with a fine narrative hand. But the analysis of Edwards's thought is left languishing in imprecision and in unrewarding speculation, in what is obviously an attempt to deal fully with the person and less thoroughly with his mind. In less than ten years Perry Miller's study will more than right the balance.

There was, of course, some important preliminary, even conclusive, work going on during the first thirty years of the century. Francis Albert Christie suggests that it was an Anglican rather than an Arminian threat that Edwards perceived in the 1730s (1912.3), the "myth" of Arminian-Calvinism a writer would call it a half century later (1968.12); Frank Hugh Foster defines Edwards's vital role in New England Theology in his *Genetic History* (1907.3), a valuable study eclipsing Boardman's earlier one (see 1899.2); and I. Woodbridge Riley usefully summarizes Edwards's development as a philosopher in sixty pages of his *American Philosophy: The Early Schools* (1907.6). Especially important is the full-length examination of Edwards's theology by the Dutch analyst Jan Ridderbos (1907.5). Edwards departs from the Reformed consensus both publicly and privately and, according to Ridderbos, develops a form of speculative thought at variance with "pure" Reformed theology, a point at issue from Miller on down. No less exceptional, if more eccentric, is *The Edwardean, A Quarterly Devoted to the History of Thought in*

America (but actually devoted to Edwards) published, edited, and, as far as can be determined, written by William Harder Squires from October 1903 to July 1904. Squires's argument, derived from his Leipzig dissertation two years earlier, is that an "adequate" understanding of Edwards's philosophy can rest only on voluntaristic principles, a system of thought indigenous to America, free of European cant and "error," central to all worthwhile modern philosophers. And Squires is at pains to prove it, by shrill repetition. In a year's time the journal ceased publication, leaving his patent clue to Edwards unexamined for almost seventy years (1972.9). These investigations aside, there remain only minor revisions of earlier attitudes, framed neatly enough by the Edwards entries in the eleventh and fourteenth editions of the *Britannica:* the assertion that Edwards was "the most influential religious thinker in America" (1910.4) yields in twenty years to the question of his "potent" influence and his "perpendicular piety" (1929.4).

Early, then, Edwards was broadly felt to have influenced the development of American philosophy or religious thought, for better or for worse, even by a few foreign critics (1904.16) and 1905.4). The collapse of New England Theology was attributed to his "morally incredible" view of man (1908.1), yet it was as well a "provincial" theology he lent little more than his name to (1914.6). Elements of Kant abound in Edwards (1906.2), elements of Einstein (1920.2), and of Freud (1920.6); he is likened to John Wesley (1913.3), thought "the very Doré of the pulpit" (1921.4). Josiah Royce ranks him with Emerson and William James (1911.2), Santayana with no one: he was "the greatest *master* in false philosophy" in America (1920.5). And three cultural historians continue the nineteenth-century habit of dividing America between Edwards and Franklin now between high-brow and low-brow (Van Wyck Brooks, 1915.1), spirituality and practicality (Carl Van Doren, 1920.7), and God and man (William Lyon Phelps, 1922.4). In his important essay in *The Cambridge History of American Literature* (1917.3), Paul Elmer More regrets Edwards's dogmatic theology kept him from literature; in his thoroughly wrongheaded one in *Main Currents in American Thought* (1927.2), Vernon Louis Parrington brands Edwards "an anachronism" but later goes on to suggest that his evangelism gave rise to democratic impulses among the people and that he was "the intellectual leader of the revolutionaries." Even earlier, in two of several studies of the Great Awakening, Edwards was singled out for his largely inadvertent help in creating "a conscious national unity" (1904.11) and "the foundation" for the separation of church and state in the emerging Republic (1905.2).[7]

Except for Paul Elmer More's extended reading of *Freedom of the Will* in his Cambridge essay, critical remarks about Edwards's most widely debated treatise

---

7. A few years earlier Sanford Cobb had concluded much the same thing in his study of religious liberty (1902.2); many years later Alan Heimert would explore the problem in greater detail and deeper controversy (see 1966.17). Winfield Burggraaff, *The Rise and Development of Liberal Theology in America* (1928.2), contends that Edwards's modified Calvinism ends in the "decidedly un-Calvinistic" doctrines of his successors, which contributes to the rise of religious liberalism.

seem obligatory and redundant, and attention turns to other work to reclaim something of value. Williston Walker, the Congregational historian, believes *True Virtue* rather than *Freedom of the Will* to be the "most influential" of Edwards, especially as it affected missionary zeal (1908.3), and William Wallace Fenn, the Harvard theologian, concurs, calling it Edwards's "pre-eminent" contribution to New England thought (1925.3). But two Dutch scholars, following Ridderbos on Edwards and Reformed theology, regard *True Virtue* as a "thorough modification" of Calvinism and an error (1913.2 and 1928.9). And another critic, sifting the permanent from the passing in Edwards, tosses *True Virtue* (and a good deal more) into the dustbin of mistaken theology, and with particular insight salvages for a more responsive age Edwards's "penetrating and comprehensive" doctrine of grace (1903.50). George Park Fisher's *An Unpublished Essay of Edwards on the Trinity, with Remarks on Edwards and his Theology* issued the same year (1903.25) is another act of reclamation. With the quarrel about Edwards's "suppressed" essay all but over, Fisher recounts its history — as will a later observer (1959.15) — and concludes that Edwards was a theist, believing in the personality of God, and a trinitarian, teaching tripersonalism.

Little more was done during the period to establish texts — H. N. Gardiner reprints six sermons and an unpublished seventh (1904.7) — until Clarence H. Faust and Thomas H. Johnson publish their *Representative Selections* (1935.3), an important addition to the American Writers Series in the thirties and a signal contribution to Edwards scholarship since. Not only do they publish several letters from diverse manuscript sources and reprint selections of the best texts from the Austin, Dwight, and 1858 editions, they also spend over a hundred, closely argued pages on Edwards as man, thinker, and writer. The middle section of this introduction, by far the longest of the three sections and derived from Faust's Chicago dissertation (1935.2), deals serially with Edwards's psychological analysis of the Great Awakening, the major issues of the free-will controversy, and the coherent nature of his doctrines of sin, virtue, and grace. All of this, Faust shows, rests upon Edwards's "exalted and mystical" rendering of divine sovereignty, first experienced in conversion and later explained through logical constructs. Such rigorous forms, Johnson points out later, may account for the "severe, undilated" style of the treatises, a style unlike that of the sermons, where clarity of expression and supple prose cadences make up for the want of "conscious artistry."

Representative Selections was only part of perhaps the most fruitful — certainly, the most promising — decade for Edwards studies. With the tercentennial of the Massachusetts Bay at hand and the tercentennial of Harvard hard upon it came a renewed, if more temperate, interest in Puritanism that led inevitably to Edwards as its intellectual exemplar. In 1932, Rufus Suter wrote "The Philosophy of Jonathan Edwards," the first dissertation at Harvard on Edwards.[8] Like others be-

---

8. The first American doctoral dissertation on Edwards, "The Philosophy of Jonathan Edwards and its Relation to his Theology," by Clement Elton Holmes, completed in 1904 at Boston University, is

fore him, Suter found Edwards torn between the opposing forces of his Calvinism and his Neoplatonism and concluded that the unresolved conflict created in Edwards a "deadlock." Shortly afterwards, Suter published two papers about Edwards — one about his ethics and aesthetics in the *Journal of Religion* (1934.8) and another about the problem of evil in *Monist* (1934.9) — and he continued publishing about Edwards well into the sixties (see 1961.14 and 1967.28). Less than a year before Suter's dissertation, Harvey Gates Townsend, who was to spend a lifetime editing and explaining Edwards, addressed the Seventh International Congress on Philosophy on an alogical element in Edwards's epistemology and metaphysics, calling the theory thus engendered "unique in our history" (1931.16). And in the same year of Suter's dissertation, Arthur Cushman McGiffert, Jr., published a sympathetic study of Edwards for Harper's Creative Lives Series (1932.10).

To McGiffert, Edwards is a "philosophically minded" scholar rather than a practical minister, a thinker relentlessly curious about the vexing problems of his day. Edwards begins with a theologically sovereign God but through mysticism moves on to pantheism and from it to personalism, all "with no apparent jolt," all of it standard fare. McGiffert favors Edwards's early work — *Religious Affections,* especially — rather than the "static" thought of his late years and believes him to be an early example of "modern-mindedness." Finding Edwards more American than modern, H. Richard Niebuhr discovers less change than McGiffert in his doctrine of divine sovereignty — Niebuhr calls it the "explicit foundation" of Edwards's thought (and his own) — and places it at the heart of his conversion experience, his imprecatory sermons, his evangelical ardor, and his millennial hope, at the heart, in short, of "the kingdom of God in America" (1937.7). Although Herbert W. Schneider in his *The Puritan Mind* (1930.13) also locates the source of Edwards's thought in his doctrine of divine sovereignty, he does not take it and its millennial consequence as integral to a native American tradition as Niebuhr does. On the contrary, Schneider considers Edwards's love of God an "individual analogue" of an earlier theocracy, devoid of public and social concerns, far "too sentimental and pathological" to be of much use in his America or ours. The following year brings three exceptions: Henry Seidel Canby includes Edwards among his "classic Americans," a symbol of intellectuality and the first of a long line of native "strenuous uplifters" (1931.4); Frederic Carpenter explains Edwards's "radicalism," founded upon his deep-grained mysticism, and draws parallels to later American writers (1931.5); and

---

apparently lost. What survives in print is an article by Holmes in *Zion's Herald* on Edwards and Northampton (1903.31). Other firsts include Charles G. Bauer on Edwards and New England Theology at Temple (1912.1), also ascribed to Howard F. Pierce (1912.6); Ralph Orin Harpole on the atonement, Yale (1924.1); Henry Bamford Parkes on the Awakening, Michigan (1929.10); Joseph G. Haroutunian on piety and moralism, Columbia (1932.4); George Noel Mayhew on Edwards and penology, Chicago (1932.11); and Rebecca D. Price on Edwards as educator, New York (1938.4). The first dissertation in English outside America was a study of Edwards's determinism by John Newton Thomas at Edinburgh (1937.9).

Francis Albert Christie enshrines our "first great philosophic intelligence" in the *Dictionary of American Biography* (1931.7).[9]

For all of Christie's praise and Riley's early analysis there remains the nineteenth-century reluctance to acknowledge Edwards as a philosopher. His high tribute aside — "the first and perhaps greatest philosophical thinker in America" — Harvey G. Townsend's chapter on Edwards in his *Philosophical Ideas in the United States* (1934.10) is a useful counter to that attitude. Townsend considers Edwards an ethical aesthetic indebted to the Cambridge Platonists — Clarence Gohdes had earlier thoroughly examined that source of his idealism (1930.6) — and encompassed by a belief that men love God because He is beautiful, a perception that will gain full expression a generation later (see 1968.8). Still, the editors of *Philosophy in America from the Puritans to James* (1939.1), though they include Edwards, consider him a working theologian for whom philosophy was a "spendthrift luxury" or merely a means to solve theological puzzles. Of course, historians of religion had no difficulty with such semantic dilemmas: Edwards was a theologian. He may lack a fully developed social gospel (1940.2); he may be more separatist than Calvinist (1930.7); but he is clearly a theologian of significance, especially to the American experience — for Jacob Meyer (1930.9.) and for William Warren Sweet (1930.14 and 1937.8), if not to the same extent for Lawrence Brynestad (1930.2). It is precisely as an influential theologian that Joseph Haroutunian treats Edwards in the standard interpretation of New England Theology, *Piety versus Morality* (1932.5), a study supplementing Foster (1907.3). Haroutunian traces the degradation of Edwardsean thought to the shift from Edwards's theology of "empirical piety" to the social morality of the Edwardseans as they responded to the ameliorating forces of social and political change in mid-century. Edwards was, as the title of an essay by Haroutunian had earlier described him, "a study in godliness," a type of theocentric Calvinist of "comprehensiveness, cogency, and profundity" (1931.10).

Other readings of Edwards gain a hearing now. Canby had dubbed Edwards a "born man of letters," an observation Thomas H. Johnson would explore in his doctoral dissertation (1934.4) — the second at Harvard in as many years — and the results of which he would add to *Representative Selections*. In another reading, Clarence H. Faust notes a "definitely theological tinge" to Edwards's scientific investigations and questions the legitimacy and spirit of such inquiries, in an essay in the first volume of *American Literature* (1930.4). That the new science doubtlessly affected Edwards's theology rather than the other way around is the point of three studies at the close of the period. In the first, Theodore Hornberger attributes Edwards's use of science to his desire to save

---

9. Not everyone agreed that year. Charles Angoff thought Edwards a "colossal" tragedy of American culture whose influence upon "enlightened American thought is nil" (1931.1). Apparently, Angoff had a change of heart: forty years later he officially welcomed a symposium on Edwards to Fairleigh Dickinson University (1975.2).

God from seventeenth-century scientific materialists, saturating all but his evangelical work (1937.4); in the second, James Tufts traces the influence of Newton's *Principia* and *Opticks* upon Edwards's idealistic and relational designs of nature and suggests that he "went beyond" Newton in uniting a world of atoms and a world of ideas in the Idea and Will of God (1940.20); and in the third, Townsend demonstrates Edwards's continuing, mature interest in natural science by making available for the first time the index and some items in *Images or Shadows* (1940.19). In yet another reading, two doctoral candidates examine Edwards's sermons, one at Iowa for his oratorical technique (1936.8), the other at Hartford for his doctrine of saving grace (1937.5). But of immediate significance to the growing cadre of Edwards students was the publication of bibliographical materials during the decade.

Compared to earlier listings of between twenty-five (1905.5) and seventy items (1902.10), the Edwards bibliography by John J. Coss for *The Cambridge History of American Literature* (1917.1) of over 150 items of biography and criticism and a compilation of the locations and holdings of manuscripts represents a qualitatively important increase. But in 1934, the Library of Congress issued a twenty-nine-page typescript listing more than 400 Edwards items found in its main reading room and including accession numbers (1934.11). In 1935, as part of their *Representative Selections,* Faust and Johnson appended an annotated bibliography of over a hundred Edwards items, adding a short list of primary sources and a longer one of background materials. (That valuable compilation was made even more so by Stephen S. Weber's addition of another fifty items to the section on biography and criticism for the paperback reissue twenty-seven years later, 1962.2). And in 1940, in addition to Winslow's extensive manuscript listing in her biography, Johnson published *The Printed Writings of Jonathan Edwards 1703-1758: A Bibliography* (1940.7), a descriptive bibliography of 346 numbered items instrumental for estimating Edwards's reputation and popularity. Just calculating the number of editions produced in Great Britain and translated on the continent during the eighteenth century reveals, among other things, that Edwards was "possibly better known abroad than at home."

In December of 1940 Perry Miller published his first essay on Edwards. He had, of course, studied Edwards in preparation for his extraordinary analysis of American intellectual history in 1939: Edwards's theology was "the supreme achievement of the New England mind," he remarked then (1939.5); more Calvinist than covenantal theologian, he had said in passing a few years earlier (1935.6). But only in "From Edwards to Emerson" (1940.9) did he concentrate on Edwards's particular vision, plotting the continuities between his "implicit" pantheism and mysticism and Emerson's transcendentalism. In time, Miller would concentrate on Edwards even more, so that the eighteenth-century philosopher-theologian came to dominate the twentieth-century intellectual historian. And, in time, Miller's labors in behalf of Edwards came to dominate the labors of others.

4

One field Perry Miller barely worked during that very productive season between 1941 and 1964 was biography, believing perhaps that Ola Elizabeth Winslow's life of Edwards was fairly well planted (1940.10). Except for some few scattered remarks, scholars apparently agreed. There was, of course, the system of countless references to Edwards in Clifford K. Shipton's continuation of Sibley's *Harvard Graduates* (1942.9) and Roland H. Bainton's account of Edwards's college days in *Yale and the Ministry* (1957.1). Pages in the life studies of those Edwards knew at Yale and elsewhere link him to David Brainerd (1950.5), the Williamses (1954.16), Thomas Clap (1962.17), and Ezra Stiles (1962.8). There was a fifty-page "Memoir" to a selection of his work that uses the standard biographical facts (1958.16); a 160-page novel, *Consider My Servant* (1957.5), that takes "some liberty" with many of those facts; and a ninety-five-page satire that prefers "ghostly" interviews to any facts whatsoever (1959.2). There were some few public honors — Princeton with showcases of Edwards memorabilia (1953.1) and Yale at the college named after him (1953.2) celebrate his birth, and H. Richard Niebuhr preaches in Northampton on the bicentennial of his death (1958.3) — but they are pallid memorials of turn-of-the-century tributes. Others celebrated the bicentennial of *Humble Attempt* (1948.3), an early instance of ecumenism, according to one (1958.5). Ernest A. Payne notes Edwards's influence on the London missionary movement (1941.10), and many more write of his influence upon revivalism: it is the subject of articles in Congregational (1943.8), Presbyterian (1961.9), and Baptist (1963.5) quarterlies; its lasting effects are seen in England (1956.2), Scotland (1944.2), and Wales (1960.18); and its adverse effects on William Ellery Channing (1952.6) and Charles Grandison Finney (1960.12). Indeed, the life of Edwards during this period is largely defined by his role in the revivals, part of a general reappraisal of the Great Awakening then underway, but readers are cautioned about whether he was the first of revivalists.

That accolade belongs to Theodorus Frelinghuysen and pietism, not Edwards and Calvinism, according to the religious historian William Warren Sweet, though Edwards forged the Northampton revivals and, through *Religious Affections*, the theological and intellectual basis for later ones (1942.10 and 1944.4). There was "a continuity" between the revivals of 1734 and 1741, argues Edwin S. Gaustad (1954.8), through the action of Edwards's personal piety upon the theological defenses of indwelling grace and public emotion, a view Gaustad elaborates later, especially as it touches the Edwards-Chauncy dispute (1957.6). To the old argument that through the Awakening Edwards unwittingly fostered religious liberty though he "cared little" for politics, as Anson Phelps Stokes repeats it (1950.18), or that Edwards may have been the intellectual leader of the Awakening but "not really of it," as Max Savelle puts it (1948.10), Perry Miller had a ready answer in "Jonathan Edwards' Sociology of the Great Awakening" (1948.8). Discovering hints of a social theory in three unpublished sermons probably composed between 1734 and 1741, Miller maintains that saving grace for Edwards operates within a social context as well as a personal or psychological one. Sometime later Miller contributed an essay to *America in Crisis* (1952.4) broadening the thesis. Edwards was not only a "formulator" of political and social theories of governance, he was also the ministerial embodiment of them. His endorsement of experiential religion and of the need for pastoral accommodation, Miller insists, paved the way for leaders responsive to the public welfare and the perceived threats to it. For Miller and for others after him, Edwards and the Awakening and the Revolution were fully joined.

Science and Edwards, far more thoroughly documented in the thirties than his role in the Awakening, is again looked into during the forties and after. A natural history bulletin of the State of Connecticut cites Edwards as the first recorder of ballooning spiders in America (1948.6); in *Scientific Monthly*, Rufus Suter cites his geometric method of inquiry and his deductive or contradictive method of proof and mourns an "American Pascal" lost to science (1949.15). One observer regrets that Edwards's atomic theories of steric hindrance gave way to a "sterile" theology (1961.5); at much the same time, another reader finds that Edwards grasped and used the fundamental implications of science throughout his theology (1961.13). One historian remarks the coincidence of Edwards's explanation of lightning and Franklin's (1941.2), a matter apparently explained when another historian uncovers a source common to both (1950.2). But Franklin enters more importantly as one of two "archsymbols," as Miller calls them in *The New England Mind: From Colony to Province* (1953.10), who divide American culture between them, though sometimes a third — John Woolman (1948.2) or Thomas Jefferson (1955.9) — is added to muddle things. It is Miller again, now in an introductory essay to selections of Edwards and Franklin in *Major Writers of America* (1962.7), who comprehends these "pre-eminently eloquent linked antagonists" in their mutual disinterestedness and who plumbs the "basic and sundering theme" of our literature and our intellectual heritage manifest in the "irreconcilable" division between Edwards and Franklin. A year later, David Levin reprints selections from both writers to illustrate *The Puritan in the Enlightenment,* but there is none of that disdain implicit in earlier pairings: here they simply share the world (1963.14).

Other familiar activities go on. Critics again try those tensions basic to earlier analyses, but they do it much less frequently now and with little of that characteristic agonizing. A British writer on American Protestantism points out the "unusual" blend of mysticism and logic in Edwards, thinks him a "Calvinist romanticist," and recalls his figure in the stained glass chapel window at Mansfield College, Oxford (1949.4). Edwards's idealism, at one time a crucial problem for critics, reduces itself to a slight, comparative issue in Floyd Stovall's *American Idealism* (1943.9), or, a bit more fully, to the standard American pattern of Locke and Newton before the "more sophisticated" German theories of the nineteenth century in Joseph Blau's *Men and Movements in American Philosophy* (1952.2). Only in Harvey G. Townsend's questionable claim for unity and coherence in the juvenilia and selected "Miscellanies" included in his *The Philosophy of Jonathan Edwards from his Private Notebooks* (1955.10) does a substantial argument rest upon Edwards's "radical" idealism. A better argument could be made that it is immaterialism rather than idealism that connects the juvenilia to later refinements in Edwards's mature work, as Wallace E. Anderson does (1964.2).

About divine sovereignty, there is no such argument, even if reasons differ. It explains everything: for Joseph Haroutunian, theocentricism is the "clue" to Edwards, grounded in the distinction between creator and created and manifest in his aesthetic view of man (1944.1); for Ralph Barton Perry, it is his one expression of "authentic" Puritan piety harmonizing the whole of creation (1944.3); for Herbert W. Schneider, it is his "master passion," enlisting empiricist and Platonic notions in its service (1946.5); for Carl J. C. Wolf, its fusion with experimental religion is one of the "true secrets" of revivalism (1958.29); for Henry Stob, it is his "determinative intellectual conviction," the very source of his ethics (1964.24); for H. Richard Niebuhr, according to his eulogist, Edwards's theocentricism is the sometime "key" to his own (1963.2; see also 1971.27). But the other side of Edwards's theocentricism has to do with covenantal relations, a point Miller had raised — and later despaired of — in "The Marrow of Puritan Divinity" (1935.6 and 1956.8) and which he addressed again in an essay about Solomon Stoddard (1941.7). The old man, Miller claims, "freed" his grandson from covenant theology and taught him revivalism, but he continued as a spectral presence in Northampton, inhibiting the younger man and finally overtaking him. Not so, Thomas A. Schafer says: Edwards was far more independent of Stoddard than that, even though he seems to follow the "general outlines" of his grandfather's evangelical theology. Edwards's conversion experience, Schafer notes, differs markedly from the Stoddard pattern, and his major work is an attempt to resolve the dichotomy inherent in Stoddard's formula of "preparation by man and conversion by God" (1963.19). Earlier, Peter Y. DeJong laid the "final eradication" of the covenant idea in New England, if not the end of the traditional church itself, to Edwards's attack on qualifications (1945.1); C. C. Goen called his insistence upon parental profession "a curious blindness to history" (1962.3). Still, Edwards's sense of the visible church as "the means" to God's society is, for Schafer, integral to the rest of his thought, especially in his fusion of the covenant of grace and the covenant of redemption (1955.7), a particularly sound defense.

There are a few desultory remarks about Edwards on original sin and imputation at this time (1955.5 and 1957.13) and a fine piece by Schafer on the ambiguity of justification by faith in his thought (1951.17). *True Virtue* revives the old polarities — it is "pious blasphemy" (1942.6) or an "important" contribution to American theology (1960.13) — as well as more serious inquiries. Alfred Owen Aidridge details William Godwin's debt to Edwards (1947.1) and, turnabout, Edwards's debt to Francis Hutcheson (1951.2). H. Richard Niebuhr and Waldo Beach, editors of *Christian Ethics* (1955.3), contend that Edwards's "primary" concern was ethical, that he agrees and disagrees with both realistic and idealistic formulations of historical Christian ethics in a radical way. (Niebuhr would later number *True Virtue* fourth among ten books that shaped his life, 1962.12.) Rufus Suter argues that the stark sense of reality in Edwards's ethics renders his universe "strange" to contemporary liberal theologians (1961.14); William K. Frankena, in his introduction to the University of Michigan edition of the text, believes it is just that sense in Edwards that appeals to contemporary moral philosophers (1960.4).

Freedom of the Will undergoes a similar transformation. There are still the certain cries of outrage (1942.3), though they are heard less often now, and there are still the expected notes about influences and sources — on Nathaniel Taylor (1942.7), in William Ames (1959.14) — but there are more revealing studies, too. Conrad Wright in the *Harvard Theological Review* traces the "tangle of verbal misunderstandings" between Edwards and the Arminians to their similar analyses of mind (1942.13); Harvey G. Townsend in *Church History* characterizes Edwards's struggle over the will and the understanding as "perennial" and his resolution in terms of natural law and natural order as "realistic and objective" (1947.6); W. P. Jeanes in the *Scottish Journal of Theology* discriminates between the conviction of man in the Edwards moral system and the sentiment of man in the Arminian one (1961.7); and three readers in the *Review of Metaphysics* debate limited and unlimited determinism in Edwards (1962.9, 1962.13, and 1962.15). In his *History of American Psychology*, A. A. Roback discovers "psychoanalytical adumbrations" in Edwards as he follows the labyrinth of comment on *Freedom of the Will* in the nineteenth century (1952.8). The most elaborate analysis of all, however, was a 128-page introduction to a new edition of the text.

In 1957, Yale University Press published the first volume of what has become the definitive Edwards (then under the general editorship of Perry Miller), Paul Ramsey's painstaking edition of *Freedom of the Will* (1957.14). In his prefatory essay, Ramsey traces in grave detail its provenance; the theological issues; the still-unresolved philosophical arguments; Edwards's "actual" debt to Locke and the major points of his antagonists, matters given "insufficient attention" in the past; and the effective and eloquent style of his refutation. But Arthur E. Murphy questions Ramsey's premises. In an important twenty-page commentary in *Philosophical Review* (1959.13), Murphy claims that Ramsey confounds Edwards by confusing voluntary action with the act of volition and that Edwards confounds himself by confusing "the language of mental causation with that of moral appraisal and justification." Still, Ramsey's thorough knowledge of the problems and his skillful editing of the text makes it a work of inestimable value and a model for succeeding volumes. Two years later the Yale *Religious Affections* appeared with an eighty-three-page introduction by John E. Smith (1959.18). No less precise in his historical and textual analysis than Ramsey, Smith provides as well commentary on the place of the affections in contemporary religious practice and on the "remarkable literary power" of the work, useful to a text that will become increasingly important in later evangelical estimates of Edwards. *Religious Affections,* Smith claims, restored religion to life, understanding to experience, order to piety, and, through its methodology, vitality to American Protestantism. That is high praise indeed (and perhaps excessive) for a text that, as Clyde A. Holbrook points out, was Edwards's "most discouraging and thankless job" (1960.9).

Other texts were produced, or rather built, during the period: Townsend's *The Philosophy or Jonathan Edwards from his Private Notebooks,* already noted; James A. Stewart's *Jonathan Edwards: The Narrative,* an edition of *Faithful Narrative* interspersed with scraps of biography, the Great Awakening, and conversion testimonies (1957.17); Ralph G. Turnbull's *Devotions of Jonathan Edwards,* select passages for weekly devotions (1959.20); and Leon Howard's *"The Mind" of Jonathan Edwards: A Reconstructed Text* (1963.13), a major contribution. Howard not only proves Edwards's early commitment to philosophical idealism and logical determinism, to conversion and Calvinism, but he also shows the "developing pattern" in Edwards of a mind that balances the power of logic and the power of emotion. Earlier Perry Miller had reprinted Observation No. 782 from the "Miscellanies" on the sense of the heart as evidence for his convincing and influential article on the relationship of spiritual knowledge and "radical" empiricism in Edwards (1948.8). Miller proposed that the sense of the heart, rooted in sensation and distinct from the understanding, is "a sensuous apprehension of the total situation" and makes possible for Edwards eternal salvation "in the midst of time." Two years later in another important essay, "Edwards, Locke, and the Rhetoric of Sensation," Miller pushed Edwards's psychology of sensation further still (1950.13). Edwards was a "revolutionary artist," Miller asserted, for accepting Locke's theory of language and then going beyond. To Edwards, an idea was "a unit of experience" sensibly apprehended, and grace was a new simple idea learned "only from experience" and realized in rhetoric. (This essay and four others touching Edwards are reprinted in *Errand into the Wilderness,* 1956.8.). Of even greater significance for future scholarship than these was the publication about the same time of Miller's edition of *Images or Shadows,* a text of 212 entries of types and tropes (transcribed from manuscript), and his forty-one-page introduction to it (1948.7). Edwards's typological use of nature is "a revolution in sensibility," Miller insists, profound in its implications because it accommodated, as earlier typologists could not, the world of Newton and the world of Locke. Thus Edwards sought a coherence of nature, Scripture, history, and mind, a revelation of the divine intention in the things of this world. Miller's large claim for Edwards, nay-sayers aside — I. A. Richards, for example, indicts Miller, Edwards, and typology for underwriting a "self-destructive" form of metaphor (1949.12) — , grows larger still in the work of others. In *Symbolism and American Literature,* Charles Feidelson calls Edwards a "philosophical symbolist," exploiting nature and anticipating Emerson (1953.5); in *The Shaping of American Religion,* Daniel D. Williams detects in Edwards's typology the "interplay of challenge and adjustment," the very mode of experience in America (1961.16); and in the *Journal of the History of Ideas,* Edward H. Davidson considers Edwards "the first native American symbolist," tracing his debt to Locke's "Of Words" and examining his distinctive theory of language (1963.7), as Miller had earlier suggested. With Ursula Brumm's *Die Religiose Typologie in Amerikanischen Denken* (1963.4, translated 1970.2), Edwards's types take a decidedly different turn. Brumm emphasizes the typological connection Edwards makes between his evangelism and his eschatology: he converts types to symbols in a program of hope for the kingdom of God in America, expectation and then fulfillment.

Some years before, Miller had remarked in "The End of the World" that the "hidden point" of *History of Redemption* was Edwards's placing of the millennium before the apocalypse, making possible the fulfillment of the Christian hope in America before its destruction (1951.12). There had been some mention of Edwards's *History* five years earlier — see L. E. Froom's *The Prophetic Faith of Our Fathers* for Edwards's dating of the Antichrist (1946.2) — but speculation about his eschatology begins with Miller in this period and continues into the next. It is a salient feature of Peter Kawerau's seventy-four-page treatment of Edwards and missions in his *Amerika und die Orientalischen Kirchen* (1958.13) and a contentious one in James P. Martin's briefer appraisal in *The Last Judgment in Protestant Theology from Orthodoxy to Ritschl* (1963.15). For Martin, it is Edwards's New Testament biblicism rather than Miller's Locke and Newton that explains his eschatology. The fullest explanation for the time, however, is C. C. Goen's "Jonathan Edwards: A New Departure in Eschatology" (1959.5), and it follows Miller. Edwards's theory that a golden age would precede the coming of Christ is "a radical innovation," according to Goen, and a real departure from commonly held Protestant thought. He was, Goen claims, America's "first major post-millennial thinker," and he provides a religious context to manifest destiny and radical utopianism — questionable assertions, as it later turns out (1977.8 and 1977.17).

There are a few other new departures, a good many returns, and some that seem to partake of both. Pride, according to one reader, is the key to Edwards's thought and action (1949.13); his doctrine of the will is the "mainspring" of Emily Dickinson's creative activity, according to another (1961.15). In *The American Adam,* R. W. B. Lewis compares Edwards to the elder Henry James and Horace Bushnell, assigning the three to a third party between the party of hope and the party of memory (1955.5); Clyde A. Holbrook divides detractors of Edwards into two parties, those who think him an "evil force" and those who think him a "tragic figure," in a rapid survey of 200 years of Edwards criticism (1953.8); and William S. Morris, as a party of one, points to the first volume of the Yale Edwards as the "first evident sign" of a reappraisal of Edwards, in an even shorter survey

(1957.12).[10] There are many more returns to earlier views. Edwards is still America's "first" philosopher (1952.7) and its "greatest," except for two or three others (1959.1); he is a saint to Austin Warren (1956.13), again to Randall Stewart (1958.23), and a tragedy to Chard Powers Smith (1954.13); he is still "thoroughly" Calvinistic, even if his successors are not (1957.7). And there are returns to familiar territory but with a difference. Edwards's style, the focus of so much apology early in the nineteenth century and of wishful thinking at its end, again becomes the subject of inquiry. Although Thomas H. Johnson had dealt with Edwards's style in *Representative Selections*, it was Edwin H. Cady in "The Artistry of Jonathan Edwards" who helped determine the shape of later studies (1949.1). By isolating a particular work (or genre) — *Sinners in the Hands of an Angry God*, in this instance — Cady was able to demonstrate that Edwards achieves an "organic oneness" wherein thought and experience and language (homely images and kinesthetic ones) blend to move audiences — the "objective correlative" of T. S. Eliot. So Robert F. Sayre isolates *Personal Narrative* and finds a new form of autobiography there (1964.21); and Edward H. Davidson isolates sentences of Edwards and Emerson to examine a new metaethics (1964.9). In other studies, Ralph G. Turnbull locates the source for Edwards's style in William Perkins and the English Puritans (1958.24), and Paul R. Baumgartner questions the view that Edwards, and Puritan writers generally, used rhetorical devices reluctantly (1963.3). Taking new and old together, there are several worthwhile summary statements: Thomas H. Johnson's in *Literary History of the United States* (1948.5) on literary continuities; Virgilius Ferm's in his edition of selections, *Puritan Sage* (1953.6), on his life; Sydney E. Ahlstrom in *The Shaping of American Religion* (1961.1) on his theology; and Loren Baritz in *City on a Hill* (1964.3), the most extensive of the four, on his effect on American culture and intellectual history.

At the beginning of the period, Max Otto feared that the attention lavished on Edwards in the thirties augured a general return to religious conservatism (1941.8); near the end of the period, a religious conservative believed it had come to pass (1957.2). Of course, nothing of the kind occurred, or rather the renascence of Edwards had nothing to do with it if it did. There were still those who would cite *Sinners in the Hands of an Angry God* and little else: a sociologist who saw Edwards as the "scourger of the wicked" (1964.4), a poet who saw his God as "the Holy Terror" (1960.11), clinicians who diagnosed him a "spiritual quack" (1950.6) or a Stalinist brain-washer (1957.15). There were others who would cite only his evangelical sermons — for their "pure gold" of Scripture (1952.13), for the minister who "really means business" (1957.4) — and publish thirty-five "choice" sermon outlines to celebrate the bicentennial of his death (1958.19). And there was Ralph G. Turnbull's *Jonathan Edwards the Preacher* (1958.25), a sometime analysis

---

10. That seems a curious (and misleading) comment. The reappraisal of Edwards was evident at least twenty years earlier; the Yale Edwards is only a late product of it.

of over 1100 manuscript sermons classified by type — dogmatic, imprecatory, evangelistic, ethical, memorial, vocational, and pastoral — and recommended to ministers and seminarians as the work of an "evangelical mystic." Turnbull says, cryptically, that "whereas Edwards was a staunch Calvinist on his knees, he was like an Arminianist on his feet." Two years later, John H. Gerstner published the most extended investigation of Edwards's evangelism from a pastoral point of view, *Steps to Salvation* (1960.5). Limited both in scope and value — Edwards is a "both/and" theologian who preaches "insistently and repeatedly" the evangelical message of "seeking" — Gerstner's book is but another indication of the considerable hold Edwards has on evangelical America.

Yet though he remains very much alive in that tradition even now — an academic theologian narrates three personal encounters with Edwards (1978.17) — the published work on Edwards continues to belong more to the study than to the pulpit. Nothing dramatizes that more than the direction taken by the six books devoted exclusively to Edwards (the earlier noted novel and satire excepted). Of them, two are evangelical and paradigmatic — Turnbull and Gerstner — the other four are theological or philosophical and thematic. Arthur Bamford Crabtree's sixty-four-page thoughtful examination, *Jonathan Edwards' View of Man: A Study in Eighteenth-Century Calvinism* (1948.1), was published by the Religious Educational Press in England a year before Perry Miller's study. In it Crabtree delves into Edwards's ideas of sovereignty, satisfaction, and grace and concludes that he fails to solve the problem of human responsibility in a determined universe. Though Edwards proves that inability to do evil and human responsibility are compatible, Crabtree stresses, he does not prove the more important proposition that inability to do good and human responsibility are compatible.

Perry Miller's *Jonathan Edwards* (1949.9) in the American Men of Letters series is the longest of the studies (363 pages); the most provocative: Edwards is "the most modern man of his age," a philosopher "infinitely more" than a theologian, a "major" artist; and the most novel: the history of Edwards's mind is interleaved with the facts of his life. Edwards becomes for Miller representative man, generalizing his experience into "the meaning of America," borrowing from and going beyond Newton and Locke, and finally, late in life, discovering that the central problem was history, that God's infinite judgment was renewed moment by moment and realized in beauty. That Miller overstated some facets of Edwards (his modernity, for instance) and neglected others (his Christianity, for instance) some readers were quick to point out. The best of that distressed (and often vituperative) lot are Vincent Tomas in "The Modernity of Jonathan Edwards" (1952.12): he "takes orders" from Scripture; and Peter Gay in *Loss of Mastery* (1966.14): "Far from being the first modern American, . . . he was the last medieval American — at least among intellectuals." Still, Miller's book was then, and remains now, the best single statement of the quality of Edwards's mind and the drama of his ideas. And just as Edwards became a "center of consciousness" for

Miller, as Alan Heimert put it (1964.12), so Miller became a center of consciousness for others.

Though half its length, neither as extravagant nor yet sympathetic, Alfred Owen Aldridge's *Jonathan Edwards* (1964.1) in the Great American Thinkers series is the only other study to approach Miller's. Aldridge begins where Miller does, but he stays put: for Aldridge, the eighteenth century explains Edwards, his success and his failure, his rigid Calvinism and the logic in its service, his inability to tailor his thought to common experience. Reason, for Edwards, became an instrument to reveal that reason itself was inadequate to moral truth or inferior to it. But for books of specialist concern or thematic nicety later on, Aldridge's study remains a fair complement to Miller's, intelligent and readable. The last of the book-length studies, unlike Aldridge's, is both sympathetic and questionable. Douglas J. Elwood's *The Philosophical Theology of Jonathan Edwards* (1960.3) correlates Edwards's theology to his philosophy in a synthesis of theism and pantheism, a "third way" through the "mutual immanence" of God that is panentheism or "mystical realism." Edwards's mysticism, according to Elwood, is an "extension" of his Puritan piety in the "continuous sacrament" of history; his doctrine of divine immediacy is a product of "his own direct experience" and important to contemporary theologians. That much of this begs examination is clear and forthcoming. Robert C. Whittemore carefully explains that Edwards is a Christian Neoplatonist, a "classical" theist, and a theologian of the sixth way — God is real and the universe is God's image or shadow — and goes on to characterize him as "an important philosopher" as well as "an anachronism" (1966.35).

While these books indicate the direction of Edwards scholarship, they cannot suggest its volume; other work may. From 1904 to 1938, doctoral candidates in America wrote seventeen dissertations concerning Edwards; from 1943 to 1964 they wrote thirty-nine.[11] Put another way, during the earlier period, a dissertation on Edwards was written once every two years; during the later period, a dissertation was written once every six months. Early, they were written chiefly at Boston, Temple, Yale, Chicago, and Harvard; later, word spreads: though Yale and Chicago each turn out five dissertations, Harvard four, Temple three, and Boston one, they are joined by Illinois with three, and Brown, Duke, Minnesota, and Southern California with two each. Significantly, the number of academic degrees exceeds the number of seminary degrees, perhaps thirty-two to seven, or by a ratio of more

11. The span of years represents the actual awarding of degrees and so does not conform to my artificial divisions. Richard S. Sliwoski lists 124 dissertations on Edwards to 1978, including foreign ones (1979.31). Over the same period I account for 139, including eleven foreign ones: 1899.6, 1901.10, 1937.9, 1957.9, 1958.14, 1966.25, 1967.26, 1972.14, 1973.34, 1975.4, and 1976.11. The difference lies in the standards for inclusion. My list is either more generous or less rigorous than his — I include Conrad Wright's paper on Arminianism, for example, for its early and frequent references to Edwards (1943.10). Whatever the criteria or the arithmetic, the outpouring of academic interest in Edwards remains great.

than four to one. Beyond the figures lies an impressive range of subjects (taken at random): Edwards's views on the atonement (1945.6), redemption (1949.5), the Trinity (1962.14), and election (1963.23); his anthropology (1952.1) and his ontology (1951.16), his Calvinism (1950.1) and Neoplatonism (1963.22), mysticism (1947.2) and idealism (1961.2); his ethical theory (1945.2) and his theory of the will (1948.4). Some few are published as books, more are squeezed into journals, others bear silent witness to an extraordinary outpouring of interest in Edwards. Over the next several years, the number and the range of dissertations would testify to an interest even greater.

5

From 1965 to 1978 doctoral candidates in America wrote seventy-two dissertations concerning Edwards. Compared to the preceding period, that is almost twice as many in about two-thirds the time, or five dissertations a year on average rather than two. Forty American institutions sponsored that work, twice as many as before. Six foreign institutions joined them: Gottingen, Pontifical Gregorian, Munich, McGill, Amsterdam, and St. Michaels. A good handful are clearly the work of seminarians; the rest come from a variety of disciplines, reflecting something of the breadth of interest. Again, at random, studies include Edwards on faith (1965.4) and Christ (1968.33), on glory (1965.14) and grace (1973.40); his typology (1967.20) and his teleology (1969.15); his social theories (1968.21), his educational (1973.25) and psychological ones (1974.5); studies of continuities in the Edwardseans (1972.25) and in Emerson (1976.33), comparisons with Chauncy (1966.16) and with Stoddard (1970.39); and, following earlier investigations, studies of his rhetoric (1967.7), his literary techniques (1971.18), his symbolic system (1972.41), and his style (1973.11). No fewer than eleven dissertations have to do with Edwards's millennialism and its consequences, an earnest of future publication.

Thus each of the decades since 1940 has seen almost a doubling of the number of dissertations on Edwards over the previous one. As much as that may be a stark reminder of the growth of doctorates in the last generation, it speaks as well to the general tendency and redirection of Puritan scholarship — more particularly, here, of Edwards scholarship — over that time. And if there would be something new and challenging in all this, there was as well the comfort of old arguments, probably no better realized than in the timely chore of ferreting out sources and influences. There was the inevitable study of the "antithetical figures" of Edwards and Franklin — apparently only one and that quite derivative, published abroad (1967.21) — and a veritable Homeric catalogue of relationships: Edwards and the abolitionist John Brown (1970.28), the determinist Thomas Chalmers (1971.25), the empiricist John Dewey (1975.12), the voluntarist Timothy Dwight

(1971.30), the evangelist Charles Grandison Finney (1969.19), the immaterialist Samuel Johnson (1971.7), the radical monotheist H. Richard Niebuhr (1976.41), the consistent Calvinist Edwards Amasa Park (1974.6), and the founding Methodist John Wesley (1966.26). Edwards's habit of mind is likened to Emily Dickinsons's "New Englandly" way of seeing (1966.15), his orthodoxy to Emerson's (1968.32), his "spiritual tension" and tone to Hawthorne's (1973.22) and 1976.18), his determinism to Melville's "Bartleby" (1969.28 and 1976.19), his "emblematic reading" of nature to Poe's (1972.35), his visionary temper to Whitman's (1976.2), his public profession to Mailer's (1978.2). Edwards exercised a "preponderant and perplexing" influence over Robert Lowell for three decades (1974.13) and fascinated Jorge Borges (1972.6); his sensationalist psychology and rhetoric recalls Mrs. Rowlandson's *A Narrative of the Captivity* (1973.31) and his account of his conversion recalls Adam's in *Paradise Lost,* Book X (1969.34). Joseph P. Schultz detects "remarkable" similarities between Edwards and the Habad masters of Hassidism in their psychology of the religious experience (1973.29), and Patricia Wilson-Kastner finds Edwards's theology "more comprehensible" as an adaptation of Gregory of Nyssa's Christian Neoplatonism (1978.24). Closer home, Hyatt Waggoner explores similar patterns of grace in Edwards, Emerson, Hawthorne, and Thoreau (1969.33); Mason I. Lowance extends to Thoreau the pattern of the perception of nature and the symbolic expression of it that Miller had found common to Edwards and Emerson (1973.18); and William H. Parker uncovers a countervailing pattern to rationalism in Edwards, Emerson, William James, and Reinhold Niebuhr (1973.26). More broadly, Ellwood Johnson in *American Quarterly* (1970.16) links Edwards's theory of perception to the individualism expressed by Emerson, William James, Mark Twain, and Whitman, a case of cultural continuity in America; and Sydney E. Ahlstrom in *Church History* (1977.1) considers Edwards a "proto-Romantic" in his reformulation of Calvinist doctrine in a natural context, part of the romantic religion revolution world wide.

Though the hell-fire preacher dies hard — two early studies of his "totalitarian" theology breathe little life into him (1965.1 and 1965.13) — the tragic figure of inner conflict shows even fewer signs of being abandoned, though reasons differ. One study attributes the antagonism between his mystical and rational selves to the disjunction of historic Puritanism and Cambridge Platonism (1967.8); another solves the paradox by examining his method of preaching (1967.9), what still another study calls the "double-edged form" of his rhetoric, a fusion of the rhetoric of sensation and the rhetoric of intellect (1969.8). Far more convincing than these is David C. Pierce's explanation of the two "fundamentally contrasting" forms of God and piety found in *Personal Narrative* — first, a God of order and restraint, arising from Edwards's devotion to divine sovereignty of orthodox Calvinism; the second, a God of space and variety, arising from his delight in the divine immediacy of contemporary natural enthusiasts (1968.22). Again, the division in Edwards's successors, long an academic quibble, is now laid to a split in Edwards himself as his early experimental piety fell victim to his later rational metaphysics (1974.4). John E. Smith returns to an equally old theme — Edwards as philosopher or theologian — in an important analysis in the *Review of Metaphysics* (1976.43). Smith neatly solves the "imposing enigma" set by Edwards's biblical absolutism and his philosophical speculation by demonstrating that he "never" rested his arguments on the Bible "alone" but "repeatedly" clinched them with philosophical concepts, the mark of "a major philosophical theologian." Perhaps neater yet is Morton White's resolution to the duality of his work, the logic and the emotion: Edwards is in the "middle band" of philosophy (1972.46).

The sixty-year-old issue of Edwards as covenantal theologian, first raised by Jan Ridderbos and later by Perry Miller, gets a careful reading at the beginning of the period and another at its end. Conrad Cherry argues persuasively that Edwards "definitely adhered" to covenant theology — the unequal contract between man and God as all Puritans understood it — even though he sought, unhappily, to mitigate the problematic nature of faith by distinguishing between the covenant of redemption and the covenant of grace (1965.5). A year later Cherry elaborates that thesis in *The Theology of Jonathan Edwards: A Reappraisal* (1966.9), remarking at the outset that Edwards is a Calvinist "first and last," that faith and love are "central" to his thought, that his is a "promise-making, promise-keeping God, . . . a covenant partner; not the God of an inscrutable hinterland." Edwards may have stretched Calvinism, Cherry points out, but he never broke with it; theologized on occasion, but invariably returned to the meaning of faith and the covenant of grace; sensed God immediately, but was hardly a mystic. In short, Edwards was nearly everything Miller said he was not. Cherry's well-documented argument, like Aldridge's two years earlier, tempers Miller's enthusiasm and excess in complementing his study. Five years later, in his introduction to an edition of Edwards's *Treatise of Grace* (1971.15), Paul Helm reiterates much of what Cherry claimed: the concept of grace was a "pivotal notion" for Edwards and worked "quite explicitly" within the covenantal framework of Calvinism. But the matter did not end there. Patricia Wilson-Kastner compares Edwards's view of individual salvation and historic redemption with that of his forebears and concludes that he rejects the covenantal theology of the Puritans for the determinist theology of Calvin. It is precisely the doctrine of divine grace that Edwards considers the "sole determining factor" for salvation; human autonomy in individuals or in history finds no place in his scheme (1977.34). In her book, *Coherence in a Fragmented World: Jonathan Edwards' Theology of the Holy Spirit* (1978.23), Wilson-Kastner carries the argument of grace one step farther: from each man's personal relationship with God comes his sense of integral community and from that, in turn, the notion that America is destined to be "a servant of God's glory in the world." Such theological chauvinism finds little room in Carl W. Bogue's *Jonathan Edwards and the Covenant of Grace* (1975.5), but the problem raised by Cherry does. Bogue agrees to the overwhelming importance of the covenant of grace but argues that

Edwards correlates it to his doctrine of redemption, treating both as temporal aspects of the unabrogated covenant of works — redemption is eternal, grace is becoming. Divine sovereignty and human responsibility meet there, and, according to an unduly hopeful Bogue, resolve the conflict and contradiction in Edwards.

About Edwards and the half-way covenant, there seems to be more clarification than debate. Edwards rejected his grandfather's system in owning the covenant, thus ending the revival of sacramental piety in New England (1972.16); he reverted to public profession either in a desperate effort to moderate the excesses of the Great Awakening (1968.23) or as a response to the "radical deviation" from covenant theology the revivals fostered (1970.23); he failed to distinguish between conversion and regeneration in Stoddard's "ingenious" scheme, an "injustice" to his grandfather and a "disservice" to himself (1972.40). Certainly, his dismissal hinged upon the changed qualifications he imposed; that it was the result of a shift from a belief in the covenant of grace to the covenant of works that apparently took place in his congregation (and in America), as one writer claims, is far from certain (1977.4).

On matters of earlier importance — his idealism, for instance, or his scientific pursuits — there is still occasional commentary but the emphasis changes. In one of the few mentions of it, George Rupp details Edwards's "alleged" idealism: Edwards goes beyond Newton, Locke, and Berkeley in stressing the dependence of every thing, being, and event on divine energy and in connecting his physics (especially his notions of solidity) to his metaphysics, but he fails to differentiate sufficiently between objects and ideas. Withal, there is still a "measure of coherence" to his metaphysics (1969.30). Another measure of coherence can be traced in his metaphors of light derived from Newton's *Opticks* and, according to Ron Loewinsohn, of greater importance for Edwards than the epistemology he derived from Locke (1973.17). That epistemology, another reader insists, was hardly affected by the new science, for in it, as in his theology generally, Edwards was "embarrassingly conservative" (1973.20). While his "sophisticated" scientific principles of causality may compare favorably with formulations of modern physicists (1970.18), his paper on flying spiders is simply a "felicitous and precocious" example of a well-established genre in natural philosophy, not a unique performance as is often claimed (1971.33). Even so, the Jonathan Edwards College Press issues a handsome text of "Of Insects," transcribed from the manuscripts by Wallace E. Anderson (1974.2), editor of the scientific papers for the sixth volume of the Yale Edwards published in 1980.

Edwards's empiricism and Locke's, from the beginning a study in similarities, becomes more and more an inquiry into differences. David Lyttle's standard argument that Edwards's idea of saving grace as a sixth sense derives ultimately from Locke's notation of a new simple idea finds careful emendation later on (1966.19). In fact, any characterization of Edwards's account of the religious experience or of the sixth sense as Lockean, Paul Helm justly remarks, is subject to "important qualifications," for Edwards uses Locke's empiricism as "a *model*" not a theory of that experience (1969.16). Lyttle, for his part, had pointed out that the sixth sense was "utterly different" from the natural senses, though unified with them and not empirical. But Claude A. Smith contends that Edwards is forced "to strike out on his own" to explain divine revelation, that he goes beyond Locke in his "more active view" of the mind, that he insists man actively judges and orders in aesthetic categories the data of experience and thereby gains "access" to the materials of revelation (1966.30). Sang Hyun Lee elaborates upon that point in his study of Edwards's theory of imagination (1972.23). Habit for Edwards, "drastically" different for Locke, becomes "a mediating principle" between the activity of the mind and the sensations it passively receives, and, without resorting to rationalist explanations, he can describe the indwelling of the Holy Spirit in a "fresh way." That all this may be more readily accounted for by the Reformed tradition of which he was "utterly captive," according to Sydney E. Ahlstrom (1972.2), or by the "standard lexicon" of Calvinist piety, as Terrence Erdt puts it (1978.7), was the point of J. Steven O'Malley's twenty-five-page article in the *Drew Gateway* (1970.29). Still, Dennis M. Campbell insists that it "knocked the props out from under" hierarchal authority and civil governance in its reliance upon internal awareness rather than Scripture or tradition (1976.14); and, carrying on from there to the particular conditions of the Connecticut Valley, Patricia J. Tracy claims that Edwards's dismissal from his Northampton pastorate resulted from just such a change in the traditional sources of authority and in the social order (1977.31).

So the suggestion of Edwards's not inconsiderable effect upon the changing social order, with its hint of rebellion, is published afresh, and his role in the Great Awakening continues to be a matter of first importance. Now, though, the very extent of the enterprise separates current work from earlier periods. In his controversial *Religion and the American Mind from the Great Awakening to the Revolution* (1966.17), Alan Heimert asserts that the evangelical religion of the Awakening, not the reasonable faith of eighteenth-century liberals, stirred men to rebellion and that Edwards helped provide "a radical, even democratic, social and political ideology" for it. *Some Thoughts* becomes, for Heimert, "the first national party platform"; *Freedom of the Will*, "the Calvinist handbook of the Revolution." Aside from such distressing hyperbole, Heimert's acknowledged practice of going "through and beyond the lines" of his myriad texts to contrary implications infuriates most readers (see, for instance, Edmund Morgan's review, 1967.25, or Sidney Mead's, 1968.14) if only because it so undermines the real contributions of the Edwardseans to the founding of the Republic (1967.22). Better for appraising Edwards's role is Heimert's joint editorship with Perry Miller of *The Great Awakening: Documents Illustrating the Crisis and Its Consequences* (1967.15): forty-eight pages of reiterated claims introduce a valuable compendium of source material about the revivals, much of it from Edwards.[12] Five years later, a good deal more of Edwards on the revivals finds its way into an important text: the fourth volume of the Yale edition gathers Edwards's tracts and occasional pieces together in accurate transcription and opens it with a ninety-five-page essay by C. C. Goen (1972.11). The editor details the changes both in Edwards and in his times from his clinical observations in *Faithful Narrative* to his accommodation in *Distinguishing Marks*, from his "most ambitious" defense in *Some Thoughts* to his self-confessed failure in the preface to Joseph Bellamy's *True Religion*. But, as Conrad Cherry notes in his review article, Goen slights Edwards's central function as evangelical preacher for that of dialectical theoretician, emphasizing theology at the expense of affections and perpetuating, however unintentionally, a split in Edwards remarked so frequently before (1973.4). As Thomas A. Schafer had pointed out (1969.32), Edwards affected American religious practice through his pastoral role by embodying both doctrinal correctness and vital piety, by demonstrating (at Stockbridge) the importance of missions, by promoting ecumenism (and a new eschatology for it), and by supporting voluntarism in his rejection of the half-way covenant. His "chief" role, Schafer concludes, may very well lie in the theological ethics of *Religious Affections* and *True Virtue*, not *Freedom of the Will*, a perception amply borne out in the work of the following decade.

Other references to Edwards and the Awakening — and there are quite a few — deal with the general historical importance of his role in the movement (1965.9); his "monomania" about the devil during it (1972.31); his effect upon American education (1970.7 and 1973.30) and upon the publication of Thomas Prince's *Christian History* (1966.33); and the parallels between his Northampton and John Cotton's Boston (1976.10) or William Williams's Hatfield (1978.10). Three writers mention Edwards's particular appeal to the young (1968.2, 1977.30, 1978.8), but in a useful statistical analysis, Cedric B. Cowing shows that his preaching had wider appeal, to men especially (1968.4). He serves as an example to evangelicals ministering to the urban masses (1966.7), of the Congregational way (1966.32), and for old Calvinism (1973.12). In two studies, Edwards emerges as a "moderate": in one, his emphasis upon the new birth at first seems radical to some, though in time opposition fades (1967.5); in the other, when he abandons steps to salvation for numbers of signs, he breaks sharply with an orthodox past and threatens his own position (1976.12). For one critic, the break-up of theological unity occasioned by Edwards's practice and defense of revivalism brings about the alternatives of modern American theology (1966.5); for another, his departure from Puritan practices of preparation generates "a new system" of New England

12. Other collections of source material on the Great Awakening include an uneven selection from Edwards and comments to match: see 1970.4, 1970.5, 1972.30, and 1977.26. Two readers evaluate the Heimert thesis with restraint (1971.5 and 1977.23), one without it (1973.38), and a fourth as the subject of a dissertation (1976.11).

theology (1966.23). On a related matter, Mary C. Foster skillfully defends Edwards's belief that his sermons on justification in November 1734 precipitated the revivals in Northampton a month later — Martin Marty still thinks it a surprise and the Great Awakening "accidental" (1977.22) — and she suggests, with reason, that the justification controversy was "much more fundamental" to the theological divisions following the Awakening than the more publicized debates on free will and original sin (1974.11). At the inauguration of a chaired professorship in South Africa, Edwards's role (through Brainerd) implies "the most shattering" social fact of divine grace: the elect could be men and women of Northampton and Stockbridge, colonist and Indian (1971.4). And Monroe Stearns suggests that Edwards brought the "unloved," the financially and politically oppressed of New England, to dignity through revival (1970.36), lifting them out of what Larzer Ziff calls their "inconsequential provinciality" (1973.42). By focussing on the shift in psychic make-up rather than on a rearrangement of social institutions, Ziff explains, Edwards developed the "characteristic pattern" of American rebellion against oppressive daily life.

That Edwards's psychic make-up was as much responsible for the Awakening as was his concern for the disenfranchised is the burden of the really important biographical studies during the period. There were, of course, derivative lives of Edwards, for the young (1968.35), in the Congregational tradition (1965.10), in the heroic colonial one (1966.3), or, less satisfactorily, amid the "friendly mountains" of the Connecticut Valley (1966.31). And there were local variations of it: Austin Warren plumbs Edwards's autobiographical writings for the conscience of a New England saint (1966.34); Leon Howard combs his undergraduate writings — he rejected Ramus for the Port-Royal logic — to prove him a "student rebel" (1971.17); and Richard Warch in his *School of the Prophets* thinks him at least a nonconformist at Yale (1973.36). There were, as well, discoveries about his financial difficulties with Northampton's elders (1967.13) and his personal difficulties with Robert Breck (1978.13); the publication of the long-awaited diary of Ebenezer Parkman with its Edwards jottings (1974.16) and the publication of a newly found letter of Thomas Cutler with its disturbing picture of Edwards: "very much emaciated, and impair'd in his health" (1973.32). There was a fictional treatment of his problems with the Williamses of Stockbridge (1967.27) and a "parable for the befuddled woman," a life of Sarah and Jonathan, neither fiction nor fact (1971.6). But it was Richard L. Bushman's two studies that add to the biographical Edwards in suggestive and significant ways, through standard Freudian concepts in one, "Jonathan Edwards and Puritan Consciousness" (1966.6); through Ericksonian ones in the other, "Jonathan Edwards as Great Man" (1969.5). In the first, Bushman traces Edwards's cycles of depression and exhilaration, particularly during his conversion experience, to infant-mother separation and union and to an unresolved Oedipal crisis, warning his readers against reductive errors. In the second, Bushman discovers in the "emotional congruities" of Edwards and the Great Awakening —

what Cushing Strout would later call a "notable conjunction" of private and public needs (1974.28) — Erik Erickson's model of the great man, the natural leader. Edwards's "exceedingly aggressive" conscience, a consequence of his father's traits and paternal demands, is sublimated in his conversion experience and corresponds to the pattern of larger motions of public anxiety at the time, a fortunate coincidence (and a provocative thesis). Not nearly as useful an explanation of Edwards's distinctiveness in the Great Awakening or elsewhere is Philip Greven's study of the Protestant temperament and child-rearing practices (1977.16). Here Edwards typifies the evangelical in his abasement of self, submission to authority, sublimation of hostility, and denial of masculinity. But the parental role is much more complex than that, and, as William J. Scheick points out, the family motif in Edwards is the environment for conversion and the symbol of the integrated self (1974.18).

Personal Narrative, a text that figures prominently in such readings, gains a different analysis in other hands. Daniel B. Shea's "The Art and Instruction of Jonathan Edwards's *Personal Narrative*" (1965.18) considers his autobiography "a mature articulation" of his spiritual experience, coherent, affecting, and artistic, governed by "heightened paradox" and by a narrative technique that joins analyst to actor, public instruction to private account. Shea's essay is first-rate, and, like Bushman's study of Edwards as great man, frequently (and justly) reprinted. In other studies of *Personal Narrative,* David L. Minter argues that Edwards altered the pattern of Puritan spiritual autobiography in a "radical sense," combining the interpretation of his conversion with the divine judgment of it (1969.26); Norman S. Grabo discovers a pattern of four concentric circles and an unconventional use of time in the structure of his conversion (1969.13); and David L. Weddle, using Erikson again, remarks the connection between the primary language of identity there and the secondary language of ideology in his treatises and finds, in the balance and synthesis Edwards achieves, that "religious autobiography is a form of theological argument" for him (1975.21). Earlier, Shea had taken the "interrelatedness of things" to be the hallmark of Edwards's thought, having traced an idea through the disparate forms of autobiography, narrative, polemic, and analysis to discover shifts in perspective, not in substance. Such coherence both within and without his personality shows that Edwards understood history in "multiple dimensions," and, as Shea suggests, that he contributed significantly to the "history of American consciousness" (1972.36).

Perusing many of the same texts, especially *Religious Affections,* a writer in the *Journal of Psychology and Theology* (1978.11) concludes that Edwards's analysis betrays an "integrated experience of seizure," a less useful observation than that it is "clearly informed" by melancholy, as Gail Thain Parker noted a decade earlier (1968.20). Yet for the most part, *Religious Affections* continues to be read as a manual for the uncertain Christian. The "real" Edwards for evangelicals can be found, for example, in the second sign (1966.11); the "very core" of pastoral theology (and personality theory) is there (1976.47); and, though contemporary theologians may have trouble with it, the problem of saving faith and history is solved there (1978.16). In a sense, John E. Smith's study of *Religious Affections* and its effect upon "all forms" of religion in America claims even more for it: by furnishing objective criteria to test genuine religion, Smith contends, Edwards pushed empiricism to pragmatism and made it possible to publicly assess private experience. Unwittingly, then, Edwards "opened the door" to an American religion of morality and good works, one following the practical bent of the American mind (1974.24).

Claims for *Freedom of the Will* during this period are less grand and border on the eccentric; *Original Sin* fares somewhat better, probably helped by the publication of the Yale text in 1970; but the critical importance of both continues to drop. One study of *Freedom of the Will* links Edwards's determinism to Karl Marx (1974.25), another to Friedrich Engels (1974.20), a third to B. F. Skinner (1974.22), and a fourth as a failed counter to Godel's proof, Chomsky's grammar, and D. M. McKay's model of free choice (1975.19). And in their introduction to a paperback edition of *Freedom of the Will,* Arnold S. Kaufman and William K. Frankena examine Edwards's defense of the compatibility theory, based on common sense rather than metaphysical usages of words, and find that, though he shows "immense skill" and modernity, he nevertheless fails to solve the nagging question of authority (1969.20). Another unresolved question, this on the relevance of original sin today, ends Clyde A. Holbrook's study of the comparative views on punishment, imputation, and identity in Edwards and his antagonist John Taylor (1965.8), views Holbrook traces more fully five years later in his 101-page introduction to *Original Sin,* the third volume of the Yale Edwards (1970.15). There he carefully follows the New England controversy, the sources, the provenance of the text, and the "mixed" reaction to it, and concludes that Edwards was "haunted" by Taylor and so buried him "under an avalanche of criticism" — another instance of the thorough, if unexceptional, introductions to the basic texts in the series. Finally, the problem of identity and individuation central to Edwards's theory of the imputation of original sin is examined once more to good effect, this time by David Lyttle, who points out that Edwards rejects man's uniqueness for his generic immateriality and his common relationship to God (1972.28); the problem of sin (and salvation) in an American context is again argued, this time by Alice Cowan Cochran, with less effect (1976.15). And David L. Weddle suggests that the organic metaphor of a tree Edwards uses to describe the solidarity of sinners (and saints) differs "significantly" from the biological and juridical metaphors of tradition in that he identifies the common disposition of man as a moral act in history (1974.29). That common disposition and the modified penal theory furnished to deal with it is the subject of Dorus Paul Rudisill's *The Doctrine of the Atonement in Jonathan Edwards and His Successors* (1971.26). Edwards abandons the traditional quantum measure of Christ's suffering and substitutes for it the nature of the suffering Christ, an effective function of God's chief attribute — love. "It would be scarcely possible," Rudisill concludes, "to glorify the suffering of Christ more than Edwards does." Even without that single-mindedness, Harold P. Simonson's *Jonathan Edwards: Theologian of the Heart* (1974.23) comes to much the same conclusion, less effectively. A "heart-felt pietism" lies at the core of religious experience for Edwards, and transcends sense, reason, understanding, and aesthetics. Only through the sense of the heart, through Christ, can man "come to possess all things" — nothing new in that.

In a posthumous essay, Perry Miller had characterized *True Virtue* as a "disturbing tract" for American Protestantism (1967.24), and it seems to have become just that, especially as scholars began to regard the ethical problem as an aesthetic or a political one. Beauty, insists Roland André Delattre in his pioneer work on aesthetics and ethics, explains more about Edwards than particulate studies and provides the "central clue" to the nature of reality for him, manifest and encountered as good in forms of primary beauty of consent and as being in forms of secondary beauty of proportion and harmony. Each of these forms, Delattre goes on, correlate and coordinate with each other and with the order of sensibility, so that beauty becomes the "formulative, structural, inner first principle" of existence, of man's perception, and of God's communication. *Beauty and Sensibility in the Thought of Jonathan Edwards* (1968.8) is quite demanding — a better start might be his adaptation for *Soundings* that year (1968.9) — and it may impose too formulaic a scheme on Edwards. Still it is, by all counts, a basic study and, as Delattre carries on the argument a decade later, a continually intriguing one. In "Beauty and Politics: A Problematic Legacy of Jonathan Edwards" (1977.9), Delattre discovers in Edwards's concept of beauty, expressed in *True Virtue* and *End of Creation,* a pattern of divine governance appropriate to human governance, a political order derived from a personal one of virtue. Men govern responsively in beauty, moving through history toward the kingdom of God. Five years earlier, Ernest W. Hankamer in his published Munich dissertation (1972.15) traced Edwards's "wahre Politik" through his anthropology and his ethics, basing his findings not so much on the aesthetic but on the moral fact of *True Virtue, Humble Inquiry,* and some sermons. Edwards regards the essence of man's freedom to be moral rather than social, says Hankamer, rooted in God's grace rather than secular guarantee. Taking it one step further or back (to Miller), Paul J. Nagy considers Edwards's thought to be "essentially social," though the cornerstone to it is "authentic" individualism (1971.23); Gerhard T. Alexis attributes Edwards's lack of concern for the social order of the theocratic ideal to be his otherworldliness (1966.2); and Robert B. Westbrook, returning to the center, finds Edwards's social criticism "self-consciously normative," part of his conviction that the imperfect society would yield in time to the community of saints, but such a possibility ended with the Great Awakening (1976.51).

The other major work, *The Ethics of Jonathan Edwards: Morality and Aesthetics* (1973.13), by Clyde A. Holbrook, takes the position that Edwards's ethics of "spontaneous virtue" can be best understood as an expression of theological objectivism rendered in "aesthetic rhetoric." Just as the Trinity represents "beauty in relationships," so moral beauty arises from consent of Being to being. Just so, Edwards in his radical theocentricism brings Calvinism and Neoplatonism together in a world of "beauteous evidences of God's presence." Though Holbrook's study is less formidable than Delattre's, it is also less exciting, for his "adventurous thinker" never gets beyond divine sovereignty — the "objective criterion" of an earlier statement (1967.16) — and Edwards's ethics and aesthetics, despite his title, are not nearly as congruent. That others find "an outstanding coherence and consistency" in Edwards is, however exaggerated, more to the point. Paul K. Conklin does in his *Puritans and Pragmatists* (1968.3), citing the fusion not only of ethics and aesthetics but of piety and sensationalism, "temperamental determinism" and holy affections — a "highly original" work of art. What is "highly original" to Paul J. Nagy is the fusion of Edwards's theories of the sense of the heart and consent to being, resulting in a unified view of man, nature, and God, "a new and interesting triad" (1970.26). For William A. Clebsch in his *American Religious Thought* (1973.5), Edwards's concept of unified experience rests on "turning the sense of duty to the sense of beauty," stamping the Puritan moral imagination with native American aesthetics. David L. Weddle thinks that Clebsch (and Delattre) confuse moral and aesthetic categories, for faith is consent to beauty (1976.48); Sang Hyun Lee thinks all of it a function of the integrating habit of mind (1976.32). As for sources, Charles Reynolds cites Edwards as the first to take Francis Hutcheson's ideal observer theory to strictly theological ends (1970.32) and Emily Stipes Watts numbers Thomas More's *Enchiridion Ethicum* an important Neoplatonic basis for his ethics (1975.20).

If, as Miller said, *True Virtue* was a disturbing tract, then *History of Redemption* is a challenging and fascinating one. Of course, Peter Gay had taken Miller to task for his large claims for Edwards and had used *History of Redemption* as obvious proof: "reactionary and fundamentalist" it was, a calculus of mystery and myth (1966.14). But to others, *History of Redemption* became the *vade mecum* of the seventies and its explication and its relationships the hard work of many hands. In *Redeemer Nation* (1968.28), Ernest Lee Tuveson places Edwards's scheme with those native plans for the redemption of society, marking his theory of continuous apocalypse and recurrent regeneration in America a radical and a profound change. Only later in as comprehensive a study as Tuveson's, *The Sacred Cause of Liberty* (1977.17), does Nathan O. Hatch offer a corrective. Edwards's apocalyptic expectations differ from the civil millennialists of the Revolution in this: Edwards looked not for religious liberty but for religious piety, a thoroughly apolitical millennium. Between these limiting propositions several scholars — Sacvan Bercovitch, Mason I. Lowance, John F. Wilson, and Stephen J. Stein come to mind — have worked imaginatively and quite impressively. Bercovitch links Edwards's "gradualistic apocalypticism" to seventeenth-century jeremiads, finding in both the necessary counterparts to the divine work of redemption but seeing in Edwards a "new angle" of temporal progression that, inadvertently, secularizes millennial hope into political destiny (1970.1). In his essential *Puritan Origins of the American Self* (1975.3), Bercovitch explores the peculiarly American cast to the eschatology of Edwards — one of the "solitary keepers" of the American dream — and his penchant for American figures. And in "The Typology of America's Mission" (1978.4), Bercovitch remarks that Edwards "drew out the implications" of the seventeenth-century millennialists of America's errand, differing only in his post-millennial idea of progress of that corporate mission. Lowance traces the "graduated" development of Edwards's typological exegesis to the remarkable *Images or Shadows*, wherein Edwards endows natural objects with allegorical significance leading to spiritual truth, and suggests that such a process may account calling him a mystic or a pantheist (1970.20). Sometime later, Lowance examines Edwards's unpublished writings on typology and *History of Redemption*, uncovers an "original epistemology" — nature, Scripture, prophecy, and millennialism in one — , and sees in his apocalyptic dating a "radical justification" for the Great Awakening and for an emergent nationalism (1977.20). That year saw two articles by John F. Wilson on *History of Redemption:* history for Edwards, as for church historians generally, is the "basic modality of individual and collective existence," founded upon the crucial redemptive process and couched in scriptural types and prophecies, neither modern nor medieval in character (1977.32); internal evidence in the notebooks Edwards used to prepare *History of Redemption* reveals the latter to be a synthesis of interest, his letter to the Princeton trustees a genuine expression, and his proposed work an extraordinary possibility (1977.33). Probably the most extensive scholarship, beginning with his dissertation in 1971 and culminating in the fifth volume of the Yale Edwards six years later, is that of Stephen J. Stein's investigations of the apocalypse. His thorough and readable ninety-three-page introduction to *Apocalyptic Writings: "Notes on the Apocalypse" and An Humble Attempt* (1977.28) traces the tradition, theory, and sources of Edwards's apocalyptic thought, finding in it a persistent interest, "intriguing and complex, but sometimes contradictory" attitudes, and a mix of public and private records. Stein had gone over some of this material earlier in the *William and Mary Quarterly* (1972.39); but before the publication of the Yale edition he had examined Edwards both on the Antichrist, showing that anti-Catholicism continued unabated through the Revolution (1974.26), and on the covenant of the rainbow, revealing a "delightfully different" Edwards who combines science and theology in the traditional four-fold exegesis (1974.27). That "multiplicity of levels" informs his biblical hermeneutics, Stein discovers in an examination of Edwards's "Blank Bible," emphasizing the spiritual as well as the literal understanding of a text and coming from efficacious grace (1977.29). Later, Stein takes issue with the growing scholarly sentiment about Edwards's eschatology, warning against "a monothematic portrayal" and offering providence as a "richer" construct than millennialism

(1978.18). Not providence, as Stein suggests, but Scripture as a whole is the key — the prism, rather — that Edwards used to show "coherence of vision and variety" in history, according to Karl Dieterich Pfisterer in his published Columbia dissertation (1975.13). As the historian of the revival, Edwards used Scripture to integrate the past; as the historian of redemption, Edwards used Scripture to conceptualize history "ontologically as well as historically."

Others comment on the aesthetics in his eschatology (1971.24) and the non-traditional, asymptotic element in it (1976.27); the Lurianic strand in his gradualist millennialism (1974.19); his growing sense of himself as a prophet of "God's grand architectural design" (1975.14); and his formulation of types and antitypes common to nineteenth-century American writers (1977.18). In his detailed study of millennial thought in eighteenth-century New England, James West Davidson holds that Edwards's model of the apocalypse combines both hope and gloom in typical fashion, that external affliction and inner conviction were "inseparable" parts in his scheme of redemption, and that, though his *History of Redemption* was New England's "greatest summary," its impact was "simply apolitical" (1977.8). But it did have another, deeper impact: inasmuch as the goal of missions is millennial realization, Edwards's history found a significant audience here in America (1965.15) and, together with *Humble Attempt,* abroad, especially in Scotland (1971.10) and England (1977.21).

Texts getting belated attention during the period — the coming publication of the manuscript collection should help[13] — are the sermons, and the focus is generally on style. "Future Punishment," for example, reveals Edwards as a conscious artist, weaving Lockean sensationalist imagery upon a Puritan plain style, according to James C. Cowan (1969.9); if not that, his art in the sermons can be explained as a "peculiarly heavy kind of pacing" upon the restraint of Puritan practice, according to Willis J. Buckingham (1970.3). Annette Kolodny finds "conscious artistic manipulation" in the cumulative arrangement of Edwards's figurative language to "force" listeners to respond (1972.20), and Robert Lee Stuart uncovers an "element of comfort" in his much-maligned Enfield sermon (1972.40). But it is Wilson H. Kimnach, in three separate and diverse studies, who has obviously set the direction of future work on the form. In "Jonathan Edwards' Sermon Mill" (1975.11), Kimnach concludes his inspection of 600 sermons with the observation that Edwards was an "ingenious manipulator" of the materials he kept "carefully inventoried" in files and index; in "The Brazen Trumpet: Jonathan Edwards's Conception of the Sermon" (1975.2), Kimnach traces the development of Edwards's sermonic form from the imitations of his father and grandfather's styles to his distinctive mature style evident even in his major treatises; and in "Jonathan Ed-

---

13. See the schedule of publication outlined by John E. Smith, general editor of the Yale Edwards (1979.32): the first volume of the early sermons is expected "in the near future." Aside from the costs and the editorial decisions involved, some of the delay can be attributed to the enormous task of transcribing Edwards's difficult hand, as Thomas A. Schafer noted earlier (1968.25).

wards' Early Sermons: New York, 1722-1723" (1977.19), Kimnach discovers in those early sermons clear promise of a later form and a growing concern for experiential religion. To all this, Harold P. Simonson demurs: Edwards was "first and last a Christian theologian, not a literary artist," and was rooted in a theory of the imagination consistent with revelation (1975.17). It is difficult to see why Edwards cannot be both theologian and artist. Perhaps it may be too much to claim, as John F. Lynen does, that Edwards is the artificer of a "perfect harmony" between present time and eternal time by means of a single point of view, or that he construes theology in a world he defines "poetically" (1969.23). Still, it seems reasonable (and demonstrable) that Edwards was both theologian and artist.

In fact, a unified view is just what Edward M. Griffin achieves in his forty-six-page *Jonathan Edwards,* one of the University of Minnesota pamphlets on American writers (1971.13). Griffin isolates three aspects of Edwards — "man, spokesman, and symbol" — to find Edwards complete, discovering in the "odd turns" of his life and the "radical distinction" between God and man at the core of his work, the symbolic figure of "an American artist." So Edwards, in this useful prolegomenon, shares with Melville and Hawthorne a mind that strikes the "uneven balance" between good and evil, and he is the dramatic realization of the struggling, hopeful pilgrim. Longer by a hundred pages or so and less successful is Edward H. Davidson's *Jonathan Edwards: The Narrative of a Puritan Mind* (1966.10), reporting in a cumbersome style the uneven battle between orthodox Calvinism and the new philosophy for the mind of "a Puritan baroque." Davidson traces the structure of Edwards's mind as it comes to grips with the sense and disposition of light — "a metaphor of the mind" — and the symbolic value of language, charting his progressive turning away from facts to ideas, in a dense survey of his work from the juvenilia to his mature treatises. A lack of cogency or clarity pervades Davidson: the intellectual triumphs over the poet in Edwards, he remarks, because of "that inevitable wastage of sensual delight"; *Religious Affections* is "deceptive" because "it assumes a brute, mechanistic universe — and proves the spiritual autonomy of God." By contrast, James Carse's *Jonathan Edwards and the Visibility of God* (1967.6) shares none of Davidson's faults, though it is a novel, not a standard, reading. Carse takes the central fact of Edwards's thought and ministry to be his rejection of the "principle of private judgment" in religious and ethical matters for the "principle of visibility," namely, that the greatest good for man lies in the visible Christ and that some men, through the effects of divine grace, are made visible to others. Thus the church, the "smaller society" of the redeemed, becomes a community of saints in the vanguard of "the long journey toward the ultimate society." Edwards preached "radical this-worldliness," but he failed as every other "great American prophet" must. Although some charges against Carse make sense — he builds a social activist minister, C. C. Goen says (1968.11); he neglects the supernatural, Norman Grabo adds (1969.14) — he does develop a coherent Edwards and a real one.

That too is the aim of William J. Scheick's *The Writings of Jonathan Edwards:*

Theme, Motif, and Style (1975.16), and he succeeds almost to the extent that Carse does but without his clarity and with an argument diametrically opposed. Scheick explores the "progressive interiorization" of Edwards's concerns and the many implications of it for his theology, his identity, and his art, by tracking the natural and familial images Edwards uses to explain the inner and outer selves. That the mainspring to Edwards's thought is his conversion experience and the uncertainty that marks it leads Scheick to conclude that his "entire career pivoted on this inner turmoil." At best, such a claim slights a later Edwards for an earlier one, the treatises for the narratives; but the book remains useful as an alternative, comprehensive reading. Somewhat more limited — he simply attempts less — is William S. Morris in his valuable thirty-five-page contribution to *Reinterpretation in American Church History*, "The Genius of Jonathan Edwards," (1968.17) wherein he discovers the essential Edwards to lie in his union of the rational and the empirical, the logic of Burgersdycke (not Ramus) and the sensationalism of Locke. Edwards's logic is "severely" metaphysical and his philosophy and theology one of "spiritual realism." And, as Morris aptly points out, Edwards is "a man of his age," accepting the importance of reason but insisting it be "the subject and not the cause of man's enlightenment," a view of Edwards shared variously by Henry F. May in brief — he was a paradox (1976.37); and by Donald H. Meyer at greater length — a "significant representative figure" of the American Enlightenment (1976.38). More limited still than Morris but fashioning another kind of unity is John H. Gerstner's four-part series on Edwards's apologetics appearing in successive issues of *Bibliotheca Sacra* (1976.22-25). Gerstner argues the orthodoxy of Edwards's views — he was well within the "general" tradition of Bible and church — in his defense of faith against the assaults of nationalism, pantheism, and deism, and sustains it in tightly-knit theology. Limited even further are estimates of Edwards the "great American master of the creative paradox" of Margaret Wiley (1966.36) or the "pious frontier intellectual" of Richard Hofstadter (1971.16). Better than these are the larger, though vaguer, pronouncements of Edwards's "depth and dimension" in Ola Elizabeth Winslow's *Basic Writings* (1966.37) or his "cosmic sweep" in Thomas A. Schafer's *Britannica* piece (1974.17).

In the same year appeared David Levin's *Jonathan Edwards: A Profile* (1969.21) and John Opie's *Jonathan Edwards and the Enlightenment* (1969.27), estimates of Edwards from Samuel Hopkins to Robert Lowell — and a good deal of important scholarship in between — with serial comments by the compilers. Longer (and more valuable) comments in bibliographic essays have kept pace. In his two-part essay for *A Critical Bibliography of Religion in America* (1961.4), Nelson R. Burr divides comments between Edwards's role in the Awakening and his reconstruction and defense of Calvinism; divides his intellectual life into periods of "youthful speculation," theology, and "systematic writing," and warns that it would be "misleading to judge him solely by any one." Winfield J. Burggraaff in the *Reformed Review* (1965.3) notes Edwards's "rehabilitation" by scholars and claims that nothing new has emerged since Perry Miller's "classic"; Thomas Werge, in a supplement to Burggraaff five years later in the same journal (1970.40), agrees with him on Miller and adds that important new work on Edwards will benefit from the general movement toward "defining the continuity" of Puritanism; and Gerald W. Gillette includes dissertations on Edwards in his checklist of doctoral work on Presbyterian and Reformed subjects from 1912 to 1965 (1967.12). But it is Everett Emerson's evaluation of bibliographies, editions, biographies, and criticism about Edwards over the last seventy-five years in *Fifteen American Authors before 1900* (1971.8) that is of first importance in its completeness and fairness. Daniel B. Shea complements Emerson with his worthwhile study of the first two hundred years of Edwards criticism and of its later echoes,[14] and Donald Louis Weber unravels the history of the image and meaning of Edwards for American culture from the "guardians" of the eighteenth century to the restorers of the twentieth, in a different sort of bibliographic essay (1978.20).

Everett Emerson's call for a "general book" on Edwards, issued at the close of his essay almost a decade ago, remains unanswered. It may just be, as an anonymous writer for *Zion's Herald* noted during the Edwards bicentennial, that "the time is not yet fully ripe for a final estimate" of him (1903.11). Perhaps with the schedule of the Yale Edwards more firmly fixed and with much of the manuscript collection then available at large, a synoptic book is possible. Recalling the plight of Robert Lowell a generation ago, perhaps not. Still, for some "wisely and skillfully searching professors," as Edwards said on taking his leave, there will always be a hope, and a judgment later.

---

14. Professor Shea kindly sent me a typescript copy; see 1980.41.

An Annotated Bibliography, 1729-1978

1729

1 Anon. Obituary. *Boston News-Letter,* 13-20 February, pp. [1-2].
   Hopes that Edwards will prove a worthy successor to his grandfather, that "the Mantle of Elijah may rest upon Elisha," in an obituary of Solomon Stoddard.

1731

1 Prince, T[homas], and W[illiam] Cooper. "To the Reader." In *God Glorified in the Work of Redemption by the Greatness of Man's Dependence upon Him. A Sermon Preached on the Publick Lecture in Boston, July 8, 1731. And Published at the Desire of Several Ministers and Others, in Boston, Who Heard It.* Boston: S. Kneeland & T. Green, pp. i-ii.
   Recommends Edwards's first published sermon for its "Strength and clearness" and hopes that Yale will produce many more like the young minister — he was twenty-seven — and that Solomon Stoddard's principles will "shine" in his grandson.

1736

1 Anon. Appendix to *The Duty and Interest of a People,* by William Williams. Boston: S. Kneeland & T. Green, pp. 1-19.
   Reprints part of Edwards's letter to Benjamin Colman, explains what occasioned it, and solicits subscriptions for publishing the whole of it (as *Faithful Narrative*).

1737

1 Watts, Isaac, and John Guyse. Preface to *A Faithful Narrative of the Surprizing Work of God in the Conversion of Many Hundred Souls in Northampton, and the Neighbouring Towns and Villages of New Hampshire in New-England.* London: John Oswald, pp. [iii]-xvi.
   Recommends Edwards's narrative of the "astonishing" work of God in Northampton and its

"pious" recorder, but questions the aptness of Abigail Hutchinson and Phebe Bartlet as significant illustrations of the conversion experience. Perhaps Edwards chose the first because she had died, the second because of the "stronger impression" a child might make on his audience. Even so, "Childrens Language always loses its striking Beauties at second-hand."

1738

1 Sewall, Joseph, et al. Preface to *A Faithful Narrative of the Surprising Work of God*. Boston: S. Kneeland & T. Green; D. Henchman, pp. [i]-v.
   Praises Edwards for publishing this "particular and distinct Account" of the work of God and reports that it was well received in London.

2 Watts, Isaac, and John Guyse. Preface to *A Faithful Narrative of the Surprising Work of God*. Edinburgh: Thomas Lumisden & John Robertson, pp. iii-xii.
   Reprints 1737.1.

3 ———. Preface to *A Faithful Narrative of the Surprising Work of God*. Second Edition. London: John Oswald, pp. [iii]-xvi.
   Reprints 1737.1.

4 ———. Preface to *A Faithful Narrative of the Surprising Work of God*. Third Edition. Boston: S. Kneeland & T. Green, pp. [i]-viii.
   Reprints 1737.1.

5 ———. Preface to *Glaubwürdige Nachricht* [*Faithful Narrative*]. Magdeburg: C. Leberecht, pp. [x]-xxx.
   Reprints 1737.1. Adds a history of soul-saving in Germany and New England by Johann Adam Steinmetz. (In German.)

1740

1 Watts, Isaac, and John Guyse. Preface to *Gelooofwaardig Historisch* [*Faithful Narrative*]. Amsterdam: Hendrik Van Bos, pp. 45-62.
   Reprints 1738.5. (In Dutch.)

1741

1 Cooper, W[illiam]. "To the Reader." In *The Distinguishing Marks of a Work of the Spirit of God, Applied to the Uncommon Operation that has Lately Appeared on the Minds of Many of the People of this Land: With a Particular Consideration of the Extraordinary Circumstances with which this Work is Attended*. Boston: S. Kneeland & T. Green, pp. i-xviii.
   Recommends Edwards's *Distinguishing Marks* for his scriptural, reasonable, and experiential arguments free of enthusiasm and sectarianism.

2 Sims, Stephen. *A Sober Reply in Christian Love to a Paragraph in Jonathan Edwards's Discourse, Delivered at New Haven, September 10th, 1741.* New London, Conn.: [Timothy Green], p. [1].

Attacks Edwards for his slur upon Quakers in his *Distinguishing Marks,* in a broadside affirming scriptural sanction for their true light of witness.

1742

1 Cooper, W[illiam]. "To the Reader." In *The Distinguishing Marks of a Work of the Spirit of God.* London: S. Mason, pp. [iii]-xii.

Reprints 1741.1.

2 ———. "To the Reader." In *The Distinguishing Marks of a Work of the Spirit of God.* Philadelphia: Benjamin Franklin, pp. [iii]-xvi.

Reprints 1741.1.

3 Willison, John. "Preface to the Scots Reader." In *The Distinguishing Marks of a Work of the Spirit of God.* Glasgow: T. Lumisden & J. Robertson, pp. v-vi.

Considers Edwards's book "a most excellent, solid, judicious, and scriptural Performance" and compares the revival in Northampton to that in Cambuslang.

1743

1 Anon. Letter to the Publisher. *Boston Evening Post,* 13 June, p. [2].

Notes the publication of Edwards's *Some Thoughts* in which he describes "Disorders, Delusions, Errors and Extravagances" that attended the revival.

2 Chauncy, Charles. *Seasonable Thoughts on the State of Religion in New-England: A Treatise in Five Parts.* Boston: Rogers & Fowle, xxx, 18, 424 pp.

Attacks "a bad and dangerous tendency" to excess and disorder in the current revivals and admonishes the ministers fostering and sanctioning them — Edwards is cited for the first time about a sixth of the way through — in an historical investigation of the Great Awakening through attestations, newspapers, and books. Edwards's *Some Thoughts* produces only a few instances of genuine religious experience, "though he had the whole *Christian World* before him," and many instances of uncontrolled passion. Only as Edwards ("so often refer'd to") and other ministers actively oppose these excesses by condemning itinerant preaching, imposing strict church discipline, and testifying to misconduct can there be any remedy or relief.

3 [Rand, William]. *The Late Religious Commotions in New-England Considered. An Answer to the Reverend Mr. Jonathan Edwards's Sermon, Entitled "The Distinguishing Marks of a Work of the Spirit."* Boston: Green, Bushell, & Allen, 60 pp.

Follows Edwards's method point by point in his defense of revival practices only to conclude that all of it strongly implies the contrary. Rather than evidences of the work of the spirit of God that Edwards discovers, his observations confirm enthusiastic and "gross" irregularities and errors. Edwards bas been duped by Satan.

1744

1 Anon. "Some Serious Thoughts on the Late Times." *Boston Evening Post*, 30 January, pp. [1-2].

Cites Edwards's description of "bodily Impressions" among his congregation following Samuel Buell's departure from the Northampton pulpit.

2 [Prince, Thomas]. "Accounts of the Revival of Religion in Boston." *Christian History* 2 (2 February): 390-91.

Notes Edwards's "natural Way of Delivery," free of agitation and full of solemnity.

1745

1 Clap, Thomas. *A Letter from the Reverend Mr. Thomas Clap, Rector of Yale-College at New-Haven, to a Friend in Boston.* Boston: T. Fleet, 8 pp.

Claims that Edwards told him that he overheard George Whitefield declare his intention of turning out "the generality" of ministers from their pulpits and defends himself against Edwards's denial.

2 ———. *A Letter from the Reverend Mr. Clap, Rector of Yale College in New Haven, to the Rev. Mr. Edwards of North-Hampton.* Boston: T. Fleet, 11, [1] pp.

Argues that Edwards contradicts himself in his earlier denial about George Whitefield and cautions him about his "bitter Manner." (Edwards had denied Clap's charge in *Copies of the Two Letters*, 1745, and pursued the matter further in *An Expostulatory Letter*, 1745.)

3 Willison, John. Preface to *Sinners in the Hands of an Angry God. A Sermon Preached at Enfield, July 8th 1741. At a Time of Great Awakenings; and attended with remarkable Impressions on many of the Hearers.* Edinburgh: T. Lumisden & J. Robertson, pp. iii-vi.

Acknowledges Edwards's "very alarming Title," but insists that men need not only the invitation and promise of the Gospel but the "Threats and Whips of the Schoolmaster" as well. Besides, Edwards knew Enfield and "judged it proper" to waken the lethargic souls with fire.

1747

1 Sewall, Joseph, et al. Preface to *An Humble Attempt to Promote Explicit Agreement and Visible Union of God's People in Extraordinary Prayer for the Revival of Religion and the Advancement of Christ's Kingdom on Earth, pursuant to Scripture Promises and Prophecies concerning, the Last Time.* Boston: D. Henchman, pp. [i-iv].

Offers "this exciting Essay" of Edwards to the people at a time of the outpouring of prayers. (The preface is signed by Joseph Sewall, Thomas Prince, John Webb, Thomas Foxcroft, and Joshua Gee.)

1749

1 Prince, Thomas, et al. Preface and Appendix to *An Humble Inquiry into the Rules of the Word of God Concerning the Qualifications Requisite to a Compleat Standing and Full Communion in the Visible Christian Church*. Boston: S. Kneeland, pp. vi, 1-16.
   Considers Edwards "singularly qualified" to argue the terms of the communion and defends his break with his grandfather's practice. In an appendix, Thomas Foxcroft answers Edwards's request for information about the communion practice of Protestants generally and Presbyterians in Scotland and Dissenters in England particularly by assuring him that his view is consonant with theirs.

1750

1 Breck, Robert, et al. *An Account of the Conduct of the Council which Dismissed the Rev. Mr. Edwards from the Pastoral Care of the First Church of Northampton*. [Boston], 8 pp.
   Recounts the events and admission practices leading to Edwards's dismission in an "impartial and just Relation." The Council could find "no proper Expedient" to resolve the differences between Edwards and his congregation on the matter of qualifications. Of the 229 "certified" members of the church, only twenty voted to retain Edwards.

2 First Church of Christ, Northampton, Mass. *The Result of a Council of Nine Churches Met at Northampton, June 22, 1750, with a Protest against the Same by a Number of the Said Council*. [n.p.] 8 pp.
   Records the proceedings of the church council recommending Edwards's dismission because of congregational opposition to his communion practice and the protest lodged against that action.

3 Frothingham, Ebenezer. *The Articles of Faith and Practice, with the Covenant, that is Confessed by the Separate Churches of Christ in General in this Land*. Newport, R.I.: J. Franklin, pp. 33-51, 411-32.
   Recommends "heartily" Edwards's *Humble Inquiry* for questioning the right to communion and for disavowing the half-way covenant, but finds fault with its view of Separatists and with its "misterious" [*sic*] language. Edwards errs about the visibility of saints and "opens a door wide enough for all moral hypocrites to come into the Church that can parrot or say over a form of Christian experience." His writing appears "in such different shapes" that it is often difficult to know what he means.

1751

1 Breck, Robert, et al. *A Letter to the Reverend Mr. Hobby in Answer to his Vindication of the Protest, Against the Result of an Ecclesiastical Council, Met at Northampton*. Boston: S. Kneeland, 28 pp.
   Refutes point by point William Hobby's *Vindication* (1751.2), but asserts that his "Representation of the case fully justifies us in dismissing Mr. Edwards."

2 Hobby, William. *A Vindication of the Protest Against the Result of the Northampton Council.* Boston: S. Kneeland, 19 pp.

Attacks Robert Breck's *Account* of Edwards's dismissal (1750.1) as "very partial, defective and unjust" and cites Solomon Stoddard's changed attitude on admission, the selection and division of the Council, the nature of the protestations, and so on, in a sometimes witty, page-by-page rebuttal.

3 Williams, Solomon. *The True State of the Question Concerning the Qualifications Necessary to Lawful Communion in the Christian Sacraments.* Boston: S. Kneeland, vi, 144 pp.

Refutes Edwards's *Humble Inquiry* point by point and page by page and upholds Stoddard's view of the communion as a converting ordinance. The "whole Controversy" turns upon the visibility of saints and the necessity of sanctifying grace prior to lawfully attending the Lord's Supper. Despite Edwards's reasoning, Stoddard's arguments — and the scriptural support for them — remain in "full force." (Williams does not expect to help Edwards stay on at Northampton because of his stand on qualifications.)

1753

1 Ashley, Jonathan. Preface to his *An Humble Attempt to Give a Clear Account from Scripture, How the Jewish and Christian Churches were Constituted, and What Sort of Saints is Necessary in Order to Be a Communicant at the Lord's Table.* Boston: S. Kneeland, pp. i-iv.

Recounts an invitation extended by the Northampton congregation to preach the Stoddardean way of communion after Edwards was dismissed and reprints the sermons he delivered.

1757

1 Anon. [A Memorial to Aaron Burr]. *Boston News-Letter,* 20 October, p. [1].
Notes that Edwards will succeed Aaron Burr as president of Princeton.

1758

1 Anon. Obituary. *Boston Gazette,* 10 April, p. [3].
Notes the death of Edwards, "a most rational, generous, catholick and exemplary Christian."

2 Anon. Obituary. *New York Mercury,* 10 April, p. [1].
Ends a column-length encomium on the life and death of Edwards with a ten-line poem that begins,

> Great EDWARDS dead! how doleful is the sound?
> How vast the Stroke! how piercing is the Wound?

3 Bostwick, David. "Self Disclaimed, and Christ Exalted: a Sermon Preached at Philadelphia, before the Reverend Synod of New York, May 25, 1758." In *Peace and Union Recommended*, by Francis Alison. Philadelphia: W. Dunlop, pp. 47-50.

Considers Edwards's death the loss of the "greatest pillar in this part of Zion's buildings" and reprints Gilbert Tennent's obituary (1758.5).

4 [Finley, Samuel]. "A Brief Account of the Book and its Author." In *The Great Christian Doctrine of Original Sin Defended; Evidences of its Truth Produced, and Arguments to the Contrary Answered. Containing, in Particular, a Reply to the Objections and Arguings of Dr. John Taylor, in his Book, Intitled, "The Scripture Doctrine of Original Sin Proposed to Free and Candid Examination, &c."* Boston: S. Kneeland, pp. [i]-x.

Recounts Edwards's life — derived from "public Prints" — and finds his intellect to be uncommon and his language to have "a noble Negligence" about it.

5 [Tennent, Gilbert]. Obituary. *Pennsylvania Gazette*, 6 April, p. 1.

Notes the death of Edwards, "a person of Great Eminence, both in respect of Capacity, Learning, Piety, and Usefulness; a good Scholar, and a great Divine," in a laudatory tribute.

1759

1 Bostwick, David. *Self Disclaimed, and Christ Exalted.* London: T. Field, pp. 31-33; London: E. Dilly, pp. 32-34.

Reprints 1758.3.

1760

1 Bellamy, Joseph. *A Careful and Strict Examination of the Covenant.* New Haven: Thomas & Samuel Green, p. 184.

Considers Edwards's *Religious Affections* "one of the best books . . . on experimental religion and vital piety since the days of inspiration."

1762

1 Anon. Review of *Freedom of the Will. Monthly Review* 27 (December): 434-38.

Regrets that Edwards's acuteness, dexterity, and subtlety of argument was in the service of the "theological chimeras of calvinistical orthodoxy."

2 [Bellamy, Joseph]. *A Dialogue on the Christian Sacraments.* Boston: S. Kneeland, 81 pp.

Presents a dialogue between Orthodoxus and Hereticus on the occasion of Edwards's dismission from the Northampton pulpit for denying communion to non-professing congregants. Orthodoxus converts to Hereticus's view of Edwards's doctrinal and practical soundness when confronted with an array of quotation from notable Puritan divines, from Richard Baxter to Isaac Watts.

3 ————. *An Essay on the Nature and Glory of the Gospel of Jesus Christ.* Boston: S. Kneeland, p. 191.

> Refers to Edwards's work for "the Solution of Difficulties" about original sin.

4 Gordon, William. "The Preface of the Compiler of this Abridgement." In *A Treatise concerning Religious Affections.* London: T. Field, pp. ix-xii.

> Finds Edwards's certain and judicious handling of religious affections a result of his being an eye-witness to the revivals, and charges Palaemon plagiarized from Edwards in his *Letters on Theron and Aspasio.*

1765

1 Anon. Preface to *Two Dissertations, I. Concerning the End for which God created the World. II. The Nature of true Virtue.* Boston: S. Kneeland, pp. [i]-iii.

> Finds these late pieces to be designed for "the learned and the inquisitive" rather than the common reader and typical of the play of Edwards's genius.

2 [Hopkins, Samuel]. *The Life and Character of the Late Reverend Mr. Jonathan Edwards, President of the College of New Jersey: Together with a Number of his Sermons on Various Important Subjects.* Boston: S. Kneeland, 291 pp.

> Transcribes and interleaves extracts from Edwards's *Resolutions* and *Diary,* the whole of *Personal Narrative,* and several letters, in a detailed history of his forebears and his family, his habits of mind, the conduct of his ministry and the occasion of his dismissal, his removal to Stockbridge, and his death at Princeton; a bibliography of his manuscripts and publications; and brief lives of his daughter Esther Burr and his wife Sarah. In its sympathetic understanding and eye-witness account, the *Life* fulfills Hopkins's intention to render a "faithful and plain narrative of matters of fact" about Edwards and to offer him to the public as a model of Christian piety, "the *greatest* — best — and *most useful* of men." (Reprinted in 1969.21.)

1767

1 Anon. Review of *Original Sin. Monthly Review* 36 (January): 17-21.

> Considers Edwards on original sin the "most important defense" against John Taylor (1694-1761) but doubts he has the advantage over him or that his work generally will be intelligible or useful to the "bulk of the people."

2 Backus, Isaac. *True Faith Will Produce Good Works.* Boston: D. Kneeland, pp. 67-71.

> Notes that Edwards's changed views on public profession led to the dismissal from the Northampton pulpit of "one of the best divines that his age has seen."

3 Hemmenway, Moses. *Seven Sermons on the Obligation and Encouragement of the Unregenerate.* Boston: Kneeland & Adams, pp. 34-35.

> Notes, contrary to Edwards in *True Virtue,* that a moral sense need not arise from self-love.

1768

1 [Finley, Samuel]. "A Brief Account of the Book and its Author." In *The Great Christian Doctrine of Original Sin Defended*. Dublin: Robert Johnson, pp. iii-xvi.
   Reprints 1758.4.

2 ———. "A Brief Account of the Book and its Author." In *The Great Christian Doctrine of Original Sin Defended*. Glasgow: Robert Urie, pp. iii-xiv.
   Reprints 1758.4.

1770

1 Anon. *A Preservative against the Doctrine of Fate: Occasioned by Reading Mr. Jonathan Edwards against Free Will, in a Book, Entitled A Careful and Strict &c.* Boston: Z. Fowle & I. Thomas, 31 pp.
   Calls the doctrine in *Freedom of the Will* "false and blasphemous" because Edwards fails to find sin repugnant to God nor responsibility available to man. Edwards contradicts common sense, overthrows morality, and encourages atheism.

2 [Dana, James]. *An Examination of the Late Reverend President Edwards's "Enquiry on Freedom of Will": More Especially the Foundation Principles of his Book, with the Tendency and Consequences of the Reasoning therein Contained.* Boston: Daniel Kneeland, xi, 140 pp.
   Deals with Edwards's *Freedom of the Will* from a "*practical* view," not from a speculative or abstract one, and discovers it to be "false, so far as our experience reacheth," in a detailed examination of the connection between volition and motive, cause and effect, liberty and necessity.

3 Hart, William. *A Letter to the Rev. Samuel Hopkins, Occasioned by his Animadversions on Mr. Hart's Late Dialogue, in which Some of his Misrepresentations of Facts, and Other Things, are Corrected.* New London, Conn.: T. Green, pp. 11-12.
   Calls Edwards's views on true virtue and on primary and secondary beauty "wrong, imaginary, and fatally destructive of the foundations of morality and true religion."

4 Holly, Israel. *A Letter to the Reverend Mr. Bartholomew of Harwinton: Containing a Few Remarks upon Some of his Arguments and Divinity. . . .* Hartford: Green & Watson, pp. 3-4.
   Urges repeatedly any who would discuss the halfway covenant or determine communion participants to "*Read Edwards!*"

5 Hopkins, Samuel. *Animadversions on Mr. Hart's Late Dialogue; in a Letter to a Friend.* New London, Conn.: T. Green, pp. 15, 17.
   Recommends Edwards's *True Virtue* to William Hart as a necessary corrective to the fallacies in the latter's *Brief Remarks*.

6 Mather, Moses. *The Visible Church in Covenant with God, Further Illustrated.* New Haven, Conn.: Thomas & Samuel Green, pp. 36-39.

Ascribes to Edwards in *Religious Affections* the notion that the implanting of grace in regenerate man results in physical change — a sixth sense — and that it becomes an unexamined assumption of New Divinity men.

1771

1 [Finley, Samuel]. "A Brief Account of the Book and its Author." In *The Great Christian Doctrine of Original Sin Defended*. Wilmington, Del.: James Adams, pp. iii-xi.
   Reprints 1758.4.

2 Hart, William. *Remarks on President Edwards's Dissertations concerning the Nature of True Virtue*. New Haven: T. & S. Green, 52 pp.
   Insists that Edwards's notions of true virtue overthrows Arminianism "and genuine Calvinism too," in a polemic on Edwards's definitions, doctrines, and inconsistencies found in *True Virtue*. To consider benevolence as the root of true virtue, as Edwards does, is "imaginary and arbitrary" and contrary to *"true divinity."*

1772

1 Hemmenway, Moses. *A Vindication of the Power, Obligation and Encouragement of the Unregenerate to Attend the Means of Grace*. Boston: J. Kneeland, pp. 12-22.
   Considers Edwards's distinction between natural and moral inability in *Freedom of the Will* to be "neither plain nor sufficient" and couched in language contrary to Scripture, "dark and indeterminate."

2 West, Stephen. *An Essay on Moral Agency; Containing Remarks on a Late Anonymous Publication Entitled "An Examination of the Late President Edwards's Inquiry on Freedom of Will."* New Haven: Thomas & Samuel Green, 255 pp.
   Defends Edwards's *Freedom of the Will* against James Dana's *Examination* (1770.2) by showing in detail that Dana fails to explain or refute "that very masterly tract."

1773

1 Dana, James. *The "Examination of the Late Rev'd President Edwards's Enquiry on Freedom of Will," Continued*. New Haven: Thomas & Samuel Green, vii, 161 pp.
   Examines again (1770.2) and more thoroughly Edwards's denial of moral liberty, his distinction between natural and moral necessity, and his discriminations of the nature and cause of evil discussed in *Freedom of the Will*. The whole controversy is reducible to this: Edwards's scheme of necessity can be defended only by positing God as the author of sin. From such "injurious representations" the moral character of God must be vindicated.

2 Hopkins, Samuel. *An Inquiry into the Nature of True Holiness, with an Appendix containing an Answer to the Rev. Mr. William Hart's Remarks on President Edwards's Dissertation on the Nature of True Virtue: and Brief Remarks on Some Things the Rev. Mr.*

Mather has Lately Published. Also an Answer to the Rev. Mr. Hemmenway's Vindication. Newport, R.I.: Solomon Southwick, pp. 81-160, 211-13.

Answers William Hart's *Remarks* (1771.2) on Edwards's *True Virtue* point by point on benevolence, secondary beauty, natural conscience, and the essential nature of virtue; remarks on passages in Moses Mather's *The Visible Church* (1770.6) about *Religious Affections,* the selfish heart, and the new divinity; and answers Moses Hemmenway's *Vindication* (1772.1) on moral inability in Edwards.

1774

1 Anon. Review of *The Justice of God in the Damnation of Sinners. Monthly Review* 51 (September): 246-47.

Considers Edwards's sermon a "curious system of pious abuse" unnecessary to good Christians.

2 [Calkoen, Hendrik]. Preface to *Een Bepaald en Nauwkeuurig Onderzoek* [*Freedom of the Will*]. Utrecht: Gisbert Timon van Paddenburg, pp. [7-23].

Offers a brief life of Edwards and a short appraisal of the free-will argument. (In Dutch.)

3 Edwards, Jonathan, the younger. Preface to *A History of the Work of Redemption, Containing Outlines of a Body of Divinity, in a Method Entirely New.* Edinburgh: W. Gray, pp. [iii]-v.

Explains his father's imaginative plan to offer a body of divinity in historical form to show all recorded "remarkable" events as part of the work of redemption and identifies the source as a series of sermons Edwards preached in Northampton in 1739. John Erskine has shaped the manuscript materials, obviously never intended for publication in that form, into a "continued treatise" without changing "sentiments or composition."

4 Hemmenway, Moses. *Remarks on the Rev. Mr. Hopkins's Answer to a Tract Intitled, "A Vindication of the Power, Obligation and Encouragement of the Unregenerate to Attend the Means of Grace."* Boston: J. Kneeland, pp. 28-29, 39, 44, 150-51 passim.

Claims Edwards's ideas on self-love in *True Virtue* led him into embarrassment and error about human nature and gave impetus to graver confusion in Samuel Hopkins. Hemmenway's extended quarrel is with Hopkins, not Edwards, whom he regards highly.

1775

1 Anon. Review of *History of Redemption. Monthly Review* 52 (January): 117-20.

Reviews Edwards's *History of Redemption,* finds it a "dull, confused rhapsody," and thinks it better suited to a less sophisticated age of "pious conundrums."

1777

1 Priestley, Joseph. *The Doctrine of Philosophical Necessity Illustrated.* London: J. Johnson, pp. 122-24.

Challenges Edwards's "not well founded" argument in *Freedom of the Will* that sin is a with-held act, not a positive one, and that, therefore, God is not the author of sin: causation is the same irrespective of the nature of the act.

1778

1 Barlow, Joel. *The Prospect of Peace.* New Haven: Thomas & Samuel Green, p. 8.
Addresses a long poem on the coming glory of America to the Yale class of 1778 and includes this couplet:

> While Metaphysics soar a boundless height,
> And launch with EDWARDS to the realms of light.

1780

1 Edwards, Jonathan, the younger. Preface to *Sermons on the Following Subjects.* Hart-ford: Hudson & Goodwin, pp. [iii]-v.
Attributes the delay in publication of ten of Edwards's sermons to the British invasion of New Haven. Although the disadvantages of posthumous publication are many, the chosen ser-mons still retain their "pungency."

2 Ryland, John. Preface to *The Excellency of Christ: A Sermon Preached at Northampton, in New-England, In the Time of the Wonderful Work of Grace there, in the Year 1738.* Northampton, England: Thomas Dicey, pp. [3]-6.
Recommends this sermon of Edwards, "the greatest divine that ever adorned the American world," especially to promote religious knowledge among the poor.

1781

A Brown, John. *The Christian, the Student, and Pastor, Exemplified.* Edinburgh: Gavin Alston, pp. 290-95.
Abridges *Personal Narrative* for some "brief hints" of Edwards, "a man of uncommonly close application," in sketches of nine religious leaders, three each in Scotland, England, and America.

1782

1 Edwards, Jonathan, the younger. Preface to *A History of the Work of Redemption.* Boston: Draper & Folsom, pp. [v]-viii.
Reprints 1774.3.

1785

1 Chauncy, Charles. *Five Dissertations on the Scripture Account of the Fall; and its Con-sequences.* London: C. Dilly, pp. 191-99, 260-64.

Claims Edwards's doctrine of imputation in *Original Sin* is "utterly inconsistent" with reason or revelation and a "base slander" on a good God, and quotes extensively from Edwards's text to prove it.

2 [Hopkins, Samuel]. *The Life and Character of the Late Reverend, Learned, and Pious Mr. Jonathan Edwards.* Glasgow: James Duncan; London: C. Dilly.

Reprints 1765.2.

1786

1 Middleton, Erasmus. "Jonathan Edwards, D.D." In his *Biographia Evangelica; or, An Historical Account of the Lives & Deaths of the Most Eminent and Evangelical Authors or Preachers, Both British and Foreign.* London: W. Justin, 4:294-317.

Derives a life of Edwards from the Hopkins account, with dramatic touches — "*Dismiss him, dismiss him,* was the universal cry" — and British aplomb — the vote to deny Edwards his pulpit was one of "the blessings of an absolute democracy!"

1787

1 [Hopkins, Samuel]. "The Life of the Reverend Mr. Jonathan Edwards." In *A Treatise concerning Religious Affections.* Elizabethtown, N.J.: Shepard Kollock, pp. [25]-116.

Reprints 1765.2.

1788

1 Anon. "The Life and Experience of the Reverend Jonathan Edwards." In *A History of the Work of Redemption.* London: T. Pitcher, pp. [3]-34.

Derives a life of Edwards from Middleton (1786.1).

2 Brem, Cornelis. Preface to *Verhandeling Over Gods Laatste Einde* [*End of Creation*]. Amsterdam: Martinus de Bruyn, pp. 3-6

Offers a brief introduction by the translator. (In Dutch.)

3 Dwight, Timothy. *The Triumph of Infidelity: A Poem.* "Printed in the World," p. 22.

Calls Edwards "That moral Newton, and that second Paul," in a mock-epic of the progress of Satan in America.

4 Edwards, Jonathan, the younger. Preface to *A History of the Work of Redemption.* Edinburgh: M. Gray, pp. [iii]-v.

Reprints 1774.3.

5 ———. Preface to his *Observations on the Language of the Muhhekaneew Indians.* New Haven: John Meigs, pp. [i-ii].

Recalls the Edwards family removal to Stockbridge, his facility with the local Mahican dialect, and his father's sending him to live among the Six Nations when he was ten to learn their language in the hope of becoming a missionary to them.

1789

1 Burhham, Richard. *Pious Memorials; or the Power of Religion upon the Mind, in Sickness and at Death: Exemplified in the Experience of Many Divines and Other Eminent Persons at those Important Seasons.* London: A. Millar, W. Law, & R. Cater, pp. 416-33.
Summarizes the standard life of Edwards and quotes at length from *Personal Narrative*.

2 Clark, George. *A Vindication of the Honor of God, and of the Rights of Men. In a Letter to the Rev. Mr. De Coetlogon, Occasioned by the Publication of Mr. Edwards's Sermon, on the Eternity of Hell Torments.* London: J. Johnson, 25 pp.
Abhors the "awful language" of Edwards's *Eternity of Hell Torments* for asserting that the torments of the damned glorify God, in a point-by-point refutation of that sermon, and concludes that it is better to leave men unconverted than to "blacken" God's righteous character.

3 Sutcliff, John. Preface to *A Humble Attempt to Promote Explicit Agreement and Visible Union of God's People in Extraordinary Prayer.* Northampton, England: T. Dicey, pp. vii-x.
Reprints the Edwards text to promote an agreement of Baptist ministers, meeting in Northampton and Leicester (England), to unite in prayer each month. "By re-publishing the following work, I do not consider myself as becoming answerable for every sentiment it contains. An author and an editor are very distinct characters."

4 [Winchester, Elhanan]. *A Letter to the Rev. C. E. DeCoetlogon, A.M. Editor of President Edwards's Lately-Revived Sermon, on The Eternity of Hell-Torments, by the Author of "Dialogues on the Universal Restoration."* London: [Winchester], 36 pp.
Prepares a "short answer" to Edwards's view of endless damnation and endless misery in his *Eternity of Hell Torments* by showing his texts and arguments to be "insufficient" to prove the case and by suggesting that etymologically *aionion* need not mean "endless."

1790

1 Anon. "Advertisement." In *An Humble Inquiry into the Rules of the Word of God.* Edinburgh: William Coke, pp. [iii]-iv.
Recommends Edwards's *Humble Inquiry,* despite current prejudice against it, and reprints Thomas Foxcroft's essay on British admissions practices (1749.1).

2 Watts, Isaac, and John Guyse. Preface to *A Faithful Narrative of the Surprising Work of God.* Elizabethtown, N.J.: Shepard Kollock, pp. [iii]-xiii.
Reprints 1737.1.

1791

1 Boswell, James. *The Life of Samuel Johnson.* London: Charles Dilly, 2:227-28.
Quotes Samuel Johnson's oblique remark on Edwards's *Freedom of the Will,* which he had not read: "'All theory is against the freedom of the will; all experience for it'" (15 April 1778).

2 [Hopkins, Samuel]. *Het Leeven van den Weleerwaarden en zeer Geleerden Herr Jonathan Edwards.* [*Life of Edwards.*] Translated by Englebert Nooteboom. Utrecht: Willem Van Yzerworst, xvi, 222 pp.

    Translates 1765.2 into Dutch.

3 Watts, Isaac, and John Guyse. Preface to *A Faithful Narrative of the Surprising Work of God.* Elizabethtown, N.J.: Shepard Kollock, pp. [iii]-xiii.

    Reprints 1737.1.

1792

1 Edwards, Jonathan, the younger. Preface to *A History of the Work of Redemption.* Worcester: Isaiah Thomas, pp. [iii]-v.

    Reprints 1774.3.

1793

1 Anon. "The Life and Experience of the Reverend Jonathan Edwards." In *A History of the Work of Redemption.* New York: T. & J. Swords, pp. [3]-34.

    Reprints 1788.1.

2 Austin, Samuel. Preface to *An Account of the Life of the Reverend David Brainerd.* Worcester, Mass.: Leonard Worcester, pp. [3]-7.

    Vouches for the authenticity of Edwards's *Life of Brainerd* because it was published by a learned, pious man.

3 Edwards, Jonathan, the younger. Preface to *A History of the Work of Redemption.* Edinburgh: M. Gray, pp. [iii]-v.

    Reprints 1774.3.

4 Erskine, John. Preface to *Miscellaneous Observations On Important Theological Subjects, Original And Collected.* Edinburgh: M. Gray, pp. [i-ii].

    Values the "solid reasoning" of these fragments of Edwards even though they lack "the beauties of eloquence."

5 Godwin, William. *An Enquiry Concerning Political Justice.* Dublin: Luke White, 1:279.

    Praises Edwards's *Freedom of the Will* for its "great force of reasoning."

6 [Smith, Elias]. *An Essay on the Fall of Angels and Men; with Remarks on Dr. Edwards's Notion of the Freedom of the Will, and the System of Universality.* Wilmington, Del.: Brynberg & Andrews, 76 pp.

    Attacks Edwards's *Freedom of the Will* as a work against reason, Scripture, and salvation, and argues that free agency does not lead to atheism but to Arminianism, a doctrine Christ and the apostles taught.

7 West, Samuel. *Essays on Liberty and Necessity; in which the True Nature of Liberty is*

Stated and Defended; and the Principal Arguments Used by Mr. Edwards, and Others, for Necessity, are Considered. Boston: Samuel Hall, 54 pp.

Questions Edwards's distinction between moral and natural necessity, his confounding of antecedent with subsequent necessity of volition, and his "absolutely denying that foreknowledge is an essential attribute" of God, in three essays on liberty and necessity.

1794

1 Austin, David. Preface to *The Millennium; Or, The Thousand Years of Prosperity, Promised to the Church of God,* by Joseph Bellamy. Elizabethtown, N.J.: Shepard Kollock, pp. [iii]-viii.

Explains that Edwards's *Humble Attempt* is joined to Joseph Bellamy's *The Millennium* in the same text in the hope that the first might bear upon the promise of the second. Edwards's call for concerted prayer remains an "invaluable tract" today.

2 Linn, William. *Discourses on the Signs of the Times.* New York: Thomas Greenleaf, pp. 174-75.

Approves the plan for a concert of prayers proposed by a group of ministers in *Circular Letters* (1798.1) to carry out Edwards's *Humble Attempt.*

3 West, Stephen. *An Essay on Moral Agency.* Second Edition. Salem, Mass.: Thomas C. Cushing, 313 pp.

Reprints 1772.2 and adds a sixty-one-page appendix to refute James Dana's continued examination of Edwards's *Freedom of the Will* (1773.1).

1795

1 [Smith, Elias]. *An Essay on the Fall of Angels and Men.* Providence: Enoch Hunt.

Reprints 1793.6.

2 West, Samuel. *Essays on Liberty and Necessity; in which the True Nature of Liberty is Stated and Defended; and the Principal Arguments Used by Mr. Edwards, and Others, for Necessity, are Considered.* Part Second. New Bedford, Mass.: John Spooner, 96 pp.

Questions Edwards again (see 1793.7) on liberty and necessity, refuting the "infallible connection" between motive and action, as Edwards had argued, and maintaining the self-determining power of the mind, in four essays on action and volition, moral agency, and God and the cause of sin.

1796

1 [Smith, Elias]. *An Essay on the Fall of Angels and Men.* Middleton, Conn.: Moses H. Woodward.

Reprints 1793.6.

1797

1 Edwards, Jonathan, the younger. *A Dissertation Concerning Liberty and Necessity; Containing Remarks on the Essays of Dr. Samuel West, and on the Writings of Several Other Authors, on Those Subjects.* Worcester, Mass.: Leonard Worcester, 234 pp.

   Defends Edwards against West's attack (1795.2) in an elaborate argument touching natural and moral necessity, inability, liberty, self-determination, motive, volition, foreknowledge, and responsibility. A central problem concerns the proper definitions of key words like *liberty* and *necessity,* and the "whole controversy" turns on the question of causative or fortuitous volition.

1798

1 *Circular Letters Containing an Invitation to the Ministers and Churches of Every Christian Denomination in the United States to Unite in their Endeavours to Carry into Execution the "Humble Attempt" of President Edwards.* Concord, N.H.: Geo. Hough, 32 pp.

   Urges a periodic concert of prayer like that "worthy" Edwards supported about fifty years ago in his *Humble Attempt.*

2 Middleton, Erasmus. *Evangelical Biography.* Philadelphia: John McCulloch.
   Reprints 1786.1.

1799

1 Edwards, Jonathan, the younger. Preface to *A History of the Work of Redemption.* Edinburgh: Alexander Jardine & Edmund Whitehead, pp. [iii]-v.
   Reprints 1774.3.

2 [Hopkins, Samuel]. *The Life and Character of the Late Reverend Mr. Jonathan Edwards.* Edinburgh: Alexander Jardine.
   Reprints 1765.2.

1800

1 Hall, Robert. *Modern Infidelity Considered with Respect to its Influence on Society.* Cambridge: M. Watson, pp. 62-63.

   Notes that "many fashionable infidels" have adopted Edwards's definition of true virtue, as has William Godwin.

2 Williams, Edward. *The Christian Preacher, or, Discourses on Preaching, by Several Eminent Divines.* Halifax: J. Fawcett, p. 474.

   Recommends Edwards as "a most excellent writer, both practical and controversial."

1801

1 Douglas, N[eil]. Appendix to his *An Antidote Against Deism.* Edinburgh: John Taylor, pp. [259]-65.

Rejects Edwards's notion, that eternal punishment is consistent with divine perfection, that misery will continue without end, and that good will come from the punishment of the wicked, found in *Hell Torments* by pointing out linguistic difficulties with the argument and its scriptural source.

2 Godwin, William. *Thoughts Occasioned by the Perusal of Dr. Parr's Spital Sermon, Preached at Christ Church, April 15, 1800. . . .* London: Taylor & Wilks, pp. 50-51.

Acknowledges a debt to Edwards, "from a spirit of frankness," because Edwards led him into a particular "train of thought" in *Political Justice.*

3 Watts, Isaac, and John Guyse. Preface to *A Faithful Narrative of the Surprising Work of God.* London: C. Whittingham, pp. [i]-xii.

Reprints 1737.1.

4 Wesley, John. "To the Reader." In *A Treatise concerning Religious Affections.* London: G. Story, p. 3.

Justifies an abridgement of Edwards's *Religious Affections:* "much wholesome food is mixt with much deadly poison."

1803

1 Hughs, J. Preface to *The Marks of a Work of the True Spirit.* Pittsburgh: John Israel, pp. iii-viii.

Compares the revivals of Edwards's Northampton, recorded in *Distinguishing Marks,* to those in Kentucky and the West today and can "readily discover" similarities between them.

2 Miller, Samuel. *A Brief Retrospect of the Eighteenth Century.* New York: T. & J. Swords, 2:30-31.

Calls Edwards's *Freedom of the Will* "the greatest work which the century produced" on moral necessity but regrets that some of the uses of the doctrine have been carried to extremes unintended by Edwards and have been "illegitimately drawn."

1804

1 [Hopkins, Samuel]. *The Life and Character of the Late Reverend Mr. Jonathan Edwards.* Northampton, Mass.: S. & E. Butler.

Reprints 1765.2.

1806

1 Williams, Edward, and Edward Parsons. "Editors' Preface." In *The Works of President Edwards, in Eight Volumes.* Leeds: Edward Baines, 1: [iii]-vi.
    Recommends Edwards as minister and writer of numerous and valuable theological works of "uncommon strength" of intellect, in the first collected edition of Edwards, including the Hopkins life (1765.2) slightly revised by the editors and using Middleton's remarks (1786.1).

1807

1 Middleton, Erasmus. *Evangelical Biography.* London: I. Stratford.
    Reprints 1786.1.

1808

1 Anon. "An Account of the Author's Life and Writings." In *A History of the Work of Redemption.* Edinburgh: John Walker, pp. [vi]-xvi.
    Derives a life of Edwards from Hopkins (1765.2).

2 Anon. "Life and Character of Rev. Jonathan Edwards." *Connecticut Evangelical Magazine and Religious Intelligencer* 1 (May): 161-78; (June): 201-12.
    Depicts the standard life of Edwards and reprints part of *Personal Narrative.*

3 Austin, Samuel. "Editor's Address to the First American Edition." In *The Doctrine of Original Sin Defended.* Worcester, Mass.: Isaiah Thomas, Jr., pp. [371-72].
    Advertises the forthcoming first American edition of Edwards's *Works,* from which young ministers may learn that "conclusive arguing is as applicable to morals as to mathematics."

4 Fawcett, J., and W. Steadman. "Advertisement." In *A Faithful Narrative of the Surprising Work of God.* Halifax: Holden & Dawson, pp. [i-ii].
    Reprints 1737.1 in an edition of Edwards's "very remarkable" account of divine grace for circulation among the poor.

5 [Foster, J.] "Edwards's *Faithful Narrative.*" *Eclectic Review* 4 (June): 548-50.
    Reviews a reprinted (1808) London edition of Edwards's *Faithful Narrative* and finds it still deserving of publication, even with its language of "theological uncouthness."

6 [Hopkins, Samuel]. "The Life and Character of Jonathan Edwards." In *The Works of President Edwards.* Worcester, Mass.: Isaiah Thomas, Jr.
    Reprints 1804.1.

7 Styles, John. Preface to his *The Life of David Brainerd, Missionary to the Indians, with an Abridgement of his Diary and Journal. From President Edwards.* London: Williams & Smith, pp. [iii]-iv.
    Rewrites Edwards's "copious" *Life of Brainerd* because it is redundant, filled with "much unimportant and exuberant" material, and presents it to "this age of antinomian delusion."

1809

1 Allen, William. "Edwards (Jonathan)." In his *An American Biographical and Historical Dictionary.* Cambridge, Mass.: William Hilliard, pp. 264-69.
Focusses upon the causes and results of Edwards's dismissal in a brief biography.

1811

1 Austin, Samuel. Preface to *An Account of the Life of the Rev. David Brainerd.* Newark, N.J.: John Austin Crane, pp. [3]-8.
Reprints 1793.2.

2 Osgood, Samuel. "A Review of Locke's Chapter on Power, and Edwards on the Freedom of the Will." In his *Three Letters on Different Subjects.* New York: Samuel Whiting & Co., pp. [173]-293.
Examines Edwards's use of terms such as *power, will, liberty,* and *necessity* in *Freedom of the Will* and finds that he appeals to the "vulgar sense of words" to further his cause at the expense of the truth. Edwards's argument is often self-contradictory and absurd because the critical terms he uses are as often destitute of meaning.

1812

1 Anon. "Mant's *Bampton Lectures.*" *Quarterly Review* 8 (December): 356-74.
Charges that Edwards's argument in *Freedom of the Will* rests upon the ambiguity of the word *necessity,* logical quibbles, and evasion.

2 [Smith, Elias]. *Essay on the Fall of Angels and Men.* Boston: True.
Reprints 1793.6.

3 Styles, John. Preface to *The Life of David Brainerd, Missionary to the Indians, with an Abridgement of his Diary and Journal. From President Edwards.* Boston: Samuel T. Armstrong, pp. [i-ii].
Reprints 1808.7.

1814

1 Brown, Francis. *A Sermon Delivered before the Maine Missionary Society at their Annual Meeting in Gorham, June 22, 1814.* Hallowell, Maine: N. Cheever, p. 13.
Notes the disparity between Edwards's interest in a concert of prayer and his failure to distribute translations of the Bible to the Indians or to establish missions among them.

2 Burder, George. Preface to *United Prayer for the Spread of the Gospel, Earnestly Recommended.* London: R. Williams, pp. [3-4].
Notes Edwards's role in the concert of prayer, in an abridgement of his *Humble Attempt.*

1815

1 Hopkins, Samuel. *Memoirs of the Rev. Jonathan Edwards, A. M., President of the College in New Jersey.* Edited by John Hawksley. London: James Black, 278 pp.
    Reprints 1765.2, with "numerous verbal emendations" by John Hawksley.

2 Williams, Solomon. *Historical Sketch of Northampton, from its First Settlement.* Northampton, Mass.: W. W. Clap, pp. 20-21.
    Notes Edwards's Northampton pastorate, from the invitation to assist his grandfather on 21 August 1726 to his dismissal on 22 June 1750.

1816

1 Middleton, Erasmus. *Evangelical Biography.* London: W. Baynes.
    Reprints 1786.1.

1817

1 Ellerby, W. "The Editor's Preface." *The Treatise on Religious Affections, by The Late Rev. Jonathan Edwards, A.M., Somewhat Abridged, by the Removal of the Principal Tautologies of the Original; and by an Attempt to Render the Language throughout More Perspicuous and Energetic.* London: Longman, Hurst, Rees, Orme, & Brown, pp. [iii]-vii.
    Defends his abridgement because Edwards's style was "ambiguous and verbose" rendering his ideas "feeble" and "obscure" amid a "monstrous profusion of words." Granted the style of many religious works is not good, probably Edwards affords "the most remarkable specimens of bad writing" of his time.

2 [Hopkins, Samuel]. "The Life and Character of Jonathan Edwards." In *The Works of President Edwards.* London: James Black & Son, 1:[6]-119.
    Reprints 1806.1.

3 White, William. "An Analysis of the Rev. Jonathan Edwards's Interpretation of the Last Ten Verses, in the Fifth Chapter of the Epistle to the Romans." In his *Comparative Views of the Controversy between the Calvinists and the Arminians.* Philadelphia: M. Thomas, 1:373-97.
    Finds it "remarkable" that Edwards's *Original Sin* and its articulate defense of imputation is not celebrated as widely as *Freedom of the Will* among Calvinists, in an examination of his use of Romans 5:12-21.

1818

1 Fuller, Andrew. Letter to John Ryland, 28 April 1815. In *Life and Death of the Rev. Andrew Fuller,* by John Ryland. Charlestown, Mass.: Samuel Etheridge, pp. 332-33.

Remarks that if his detractors "preached Christ half as much as Jonathan Edwards did, and were half as useful as he was, their usefulness would be double what it is," in a last letter of the founding secretary to the Baptist Missionary Society.

2 Trumbull, Benjamin. *A Complete History of Connecticut, Civil and Ecclesiastical.* New Haven: Maltboy, Goldsmith & Co., 2:145 passim.
   Offers an eye-witness account of the Enfield congregation by Rev. Eleazar Wheelock of Lebanon during the delivery of Edwards's *Sinners in the Hands of an God* and quotes at length from *Faithful Narrative*.

3 Wellwood, Henry Moncreiff. *Account of the Life and Writings of John Erskine, D.D.* Edinburgh: Archibald Constable & Co., pp. 196-226.
   Recounts the correspondence between Edwards and several Scottish clergymen, especially John Erskine, his editor in Scotland, and reprints a letter, 4 August 1758, expressing the "irreparable" loss through Edward's death. "I do not think," Erskine writes, "our age has produced a divine of equal genius or judgment."

1820

1 Anon. "Ellerby's Abridgement of Edwards." *Eclectic Review*, n.s., 13 (March): 271-75.
   Welcomes any republication of Edwards, even in abridgement, but questions Edwards's views on self-love and gratitude in *Religious Affections*.

2 Burnham, Richard. *Pious Memorials.* Bungay, England: J. & R. Childs.
   Reprints 1789.1.

3 Styles, John. Preface to *The Life of David Brainerd, Missionary to the Indians, with an Abridgement of his Diary and Journal. From President Edwards.* Second Edition. London: A. J. Valpy, pp. [v]-viii.
   Reprints 1808.7.

1821

1 Anon. Review of *The Works of President Edwards,* edited by Samuel Austin. *Christian Spectator* 3 (June): 298-315; (July): 357-65.
   Sketches the "prominent features" of Edwards as theologian, controversialist, and preacher by focussing upon his sermons and their affecting power.

2 Chalmers, Thomas. *The Christian and Civic Economy of Our Large Towns.* Glasgow: William Collins, 1:318-22.
   Finds Edwards ideally suited by temperament and ability to discern the genuine from the counterfeit in conversion experiences in particular and in Christianity in general.

3 Ellerby, W. "The Editor's Preface." *The Treatise on Religious Affections.* Boston: James Loring, pp. [i]-viii.
   Reprints 1817.1 and adds extract from *Eclectic Review* (1820.1).

4 [Middleton, Erasmus]. "A Sketch of the Life of President Edwards." In *A Treatise concerning Religious Affections*. Philadelphia: James Crissy, pp. [v]-xxviii.
Reprints 1786.1.

5 Styles, John. Preface to *The Life of David Brainerd, Missionary to the Indians, with an Abridgement of his Diary and Journal. From President Edwards*. 2nd American ed. Boston: Samuel T. Armstrong; Crocker & Brewster, pp. [v]-viii.
Reprints 1808.7.

1822

1 Anon. "Edwards on the Religious Affections." *Christian Disciple,* n.s., 4 (September): 445-63.
Commends Edwards's *Religious Affections* for its "real piety" and genuine concern, but denounces the "radical error" that runs through and deforms it. Edwards insists, unfortunately, that the religious affections are "altogether supernatural" and are not under man's control or direction. Such a view is but another instance — *Freedom of the Will* is the foremost — of Edward's "misdirected ingenuity."

2 Dwight, Sereno Edwards. "Advertisement by the Editor." In *Memoirs of the Rev. David Brainerd*. New Haven, Conn.: S. Converse, pp. 4-10.
Gives a history of Edwards's text and the abridgements of John Wesley (1801.4) and John Styles (1808.7). Perhaps the explanation for Edwards's method of alternate sources, that is, using Brainerd's diary for some days and his journal for others, lies in his "delicate integrity." Edwards did not wish "to subject his subscribers to the necessity of purchasing the same matter a second time," for parts of the journal had already been published. The text here restores the whole diary.

3 Dwight, Timothy. *Travels in New-England and New-York*. New Haven: Timothy Dwight, 4:323-28.
Counters the charge of the *Edinburgh Review* that America has contributed nothing to human knowledge by citing the example of Edwards's work. His major treatises, clear and precise and sublime, rival those of England and Scotland.

4 Green, Ashbel. *Discourses, Delivered in the College of New Jersey; Addressed Chiefly to Candidates for the First Degree in the Arts; with Notes and Illustrations, Including An Historical Sketch of the College, from its Origins to the Accession of President Witherspoon*. Trenton: E. Littell, pp. 313-26.
Reproduces extracts of minutes and other records of the trustees of Princeton in appointing Edwards president, offers a "memoir" of his life and work, and recounts his stay at the college before his death. Though his logic and scriptural knowledge were unequaled in his time, Edwards's style lacked elegance and harmony, his language was unselective and repetitive.

5 H. "Original Letter from President Edwards." *Evangelical and Literary Magazine* 5 (July): 365-69.
Prefaces a letter from Edwards to Joseph Bellamy, 25June 1750, recounting (and reprinting) the ministerial council's deliberations and noting his congregation's approval — "most . . . voted

for my being dismissed with great alacrity" — with an indictment of the liberals responsible for it.

6 Stewart, Dugald. *A General View of the Progress of Metaphysical, Ethical, and Political Philosophy, Since the Revival of Letters in Europe: First Dissertation.* Boston: Wells & Lilly, part 2:124-25, 256-57.

Suggests that Anthony Collins, *A Philosophical Inquiry concerning Human Liberty* (1715), anticipates Edwards, *Freedom of the Will* — an outline of the plan of the first could serve as a preface to the second — and makes this observation (often cited): "There is, however, one metaphysician of whom America has to boast, who, in logical acuteness and subtility, does not yield to any disputant bred in the universities of Europe. I need not say, that I allude to Jonathan Edwards."

1823

1 Anon. Review of *The Injustice and Impolicy of the Slave Trade,* by Jonathan Edwards [the younger], D.D. *Christian Spectator* 5 (January): 39-48.

Draws "remarkable" parallels between the two Jonathan Edwardses, father and son: both were graduated early; both spent two years as tutors; both settled early as ministers; both were dismissed for religious opinions; both resettled in retired positions; both became college presidents; and both died shortly thereafter.

2 Watts, Isaac, and John Guyse. Preface to *A Faithful Narrative of the Surprising Work of God.* Bungay, England: J. M. Morris, pp. [i]-xi.

Reprints 1737.1.

1824

1 Orme, William. *Bibliotheca Biblica: A Select List of Books on Sacred Literature, with Notices, Biographical, Critical, and Bibliographical.* Edinburgh: Adam Black, pp. 164-65.

Summarizes briefly Edwards's work and asks for perseverance and attention to overcome his repellent style.

2 R., T. "Edwards's Views of Original Sin." *Christian Spectator* 6 (November): 567-75.

Explicates Edwards on original sin to counter claims that he believed in physical depravity. The propensity to sin results from man's "innocent appetites and passions," not from a "substantial property or attribute." For Edwards, man's sinfulness, the root of which is self-love, is natural, native, or moral and bears not the "remotest semblance" to physical depravity.

1825

1 Eupoius. "On a Resolution of President Edwards." *Christian Spectator* 7 (January): 14-17.

Cites Edwards's Resolution 18 (somewhat misquoted) as an occasion for thinking of the importance of prayer.

2 [Tappan, Henry Philip]. *Views in Theology, No. III: President Edwards' Doctrine of Original Sin: the Doctrine of Physical Depravity*. New York: F. & R. Lockwood, 104 pp.

Contends that Edwards's "obviously and unequivocally" teaches the doctrine of physical depravity "uniformly" throughout the text, in a detailed refutation of T. R.'s contrary view (1824.2).

3 [Walker, James]. "Edwards's Doctrine of Original Sin." *Christian Examiner* 2 (May): 207-29.

Reviews and approves Henry P. Tappan's pamphlet on Edwards's *Original Sin* (1825.2) and attacks T. R.'s paper (1824.2) as a specious defense of Edwards's language. Edwards believed in physical depravity, a view explicit and uniform "throughout his work."

4 Young, David. "Introductory Essay." In *A Treatise concerning Religious Affections*. Glasgow: Chalmers & Collins.

Reckons Edwards "this great moral atomist," who demonstrates in *Religious Affections* the "reality" of the Christian experience and the "facts" of history and vindicates its "phenomena from the charge of enthusiasm."

1826

1 Clark, Daniel A. Preface to *"Sinners in the hands of an angry God," By The Venerated President Edwards, Rewritten, So As To Retain His Thoughts In A Modern Style*. Amherst: Carter & Adams, p. [2].

Attributes the unwarranted neglect of Edwards to his style, and so offers *Sinners in the Hands of an Angry God* in "other language."

1827

1 Bradley, Charles, ed. *Select British Divines*. Jonathan Edwards, 27. London: L. B. Seeley & Son, pp. [v]-vii.

Offers a biographical sketch of Edwards and considers *Religious Affections* (reprinted) unsurpassed in "discrimination and solidity."

2 Grinfield, Edward William. "Appendix II: Review of Edwards's History of Redemption." In his *The Nature and Extent of the Christian Dispensation, with Reference to the Salvability of the Heathen*. London: C. & J. Rivington, pp. 427-58.

Deplores Edwards's notions of the salvability of the heathen and the "absurdity and extravagance" of some of his observations, in a detailed review of *History of Redemption*.

3 M., E. "President Edwards's View of Original Sin." *Christian Spectator*, n.s., 1 (December): 625-29.

Questions T. R.'s understanding of imputation in Edwards on original sin (1824.2). Edwards held that man's sinful nature is not a consequence of imputation but antecedent to it. The first sin imputed to Adam was the same sin imputed to Adam's posterity: it was not Adam's sin; it was their own. In his anxiety to prove that Edwards does not believe in physical depravity, T. R. batters down Edwards's "stronghold."

4 [Porter, Noah]. "President Edwards on Revivals." *Christian Spectator,* n.s., 1 (June): 295-308.

Summarizes the points Edwards makes in *Some Thoughts* and concludes that his arguments are still pertinent to current revivals. Edwards insisted on the scriptural basis of revivals; he urged the elucidation and application of evangelical doctrines; he counseled awakened sinners to seek immediate repentance; and he emphasized practical and social duties.

5 Taylor, Isaac, ed. "Introductory Essay." In *The Modern Prevailing Notions Respecting That Freedom of Will Which Is Supposed To Be Essential to Moral Agency, Virtue and Vice, Reward and Punishment, Praise and Blame.* Liverpool: Edward Howell, pp. [xvii]-clxiii.

Argues the inapplicability of abstract propositions to questions of Christian doctrine, in a sometime examination of *Freedom of the Will.* Though Edwards's essay is justly celebrated for its analytical and logical powers, regarded as a "scientific treatise" it violates argumentation by mixing metaphysics with Scripture, moral truths with physiological facts. And though Edwards routed the sophistical Arminians, he fell before his "crushing engine of dogmatical exposition."

6 [Walker, James]. "The Revival under Whitefield." *Christian Examiner* 4 (November): 464-95.

Recounts Edwards's role in the Northampton revival and the Great Awakening, in a review of Charles Chauncy's *Seasonable Thoughts* and Thomas Prince's *Christian History.*

7 Wesley, John. "Thoughts upon Necessity." In *The Works of the Rev. John Wesley.* 1st American edition. New York: J. & J. Harper, 9:457-71.

Notes that the "whole mistake" of the "good and sensible" Edwards is his holding man responsible for necessary acts.

1828

1 Parr, Samuel. *The Works of Samuel Parr, LL.D.* Edited by John Johnstone. London: Longman, Rees, Orme, Brown, Green, 2:487-97.

Contrasts Edwards's idea of gratitude in *True Virtue* and William Godwin's comments on it in *Political Justice.* Edwards and Godwin apply the term *virtue* to different subjects, and so their ideas of gratitude, which both deny to virtue, have "little or no resemblance."

2 R., T. "Edwards's Views of Original Sin: Reply to E. M." *Christian Spectator,* n.s., 2 (January): 16-18.

Corrects E. M.'s supposition (1827.3) that Edwards ascribes to Adam's posterity double guilt, guilt of Adam's sin and guilt of a corrupt heart. If, as Edwards argued, Adam knowingly sinned from a heart having no sin in it and all men acted in Adam's act, then all men knowingly sinned from an uncorrupt heart.

1829

1 [Beecher, Lyman]. "Letters on the Introduction and Progress of Unitarianism in New England." *Spirit of the Pilgrims* 2 (March): 121-28.
   Agrees with "the judicious Edwards" about the sources and consequences of the Great Awakening, the good and the bad.

2 Coleridge, S[amuel] T[aylor]. "Aphorisms on that which is Indeed Spiritual Religion." In his *Aids to Reflection.* Edited by James Marsh. Burlington, Vt.: Chauncey Goodrich, pp. 105-107.
   Rejects Edwards's *Freedom of the Will* because it "destroys all will" and meaning and goes beyond even Calvin.

3 Crybbace, Thomas Tully. "Review of President Edwards's Account of the Freedom of the Will." In his *An Essay on Moral Freedom.* Edinburgh: Waugh & Innes, pp. 221-47.
   Argues that Edwards's *Freedom of the Will* establishes the universality of moral causation and moral freedom and "literally nothing" about liberty and necessity and that its value lies chiefly in demonstrating the "fantastic mass of absurdities" of his opponents.

4 [Dwight, Sereno Edwards, ed.] *Life of President Edwards. The Works of President Edwards,* 1. New York: S. Converse, 766 pp.
   Traces the life and times of Edwards, a solitary thinker who has "changed the course of human thought and feeling," in the first extensive biography, derived in part from Samuel Finley (1758.4) and Samuel Hopkins (1765.2), with brief asides on his work and including notebooks, letters, and miscellaneous manuscripts (often carelessly transcribed) — "The Mind," "Notes on Natural Science," "Resolutions," "Diary," *Personal Narrative,* and *Farewell Sermon.* Edwards's dismissal, "one of the most painful and surprising events" in New England church history, takes up one-quarter of the text (exclusive of appended reprints) and examines in order, the "facts" of Edwards's disagreement with Stoddardean communion practice, Hopkins's rendering of the event, Edwards's account in his journal and letters, Joseph Hawley's recantation, and Dwight's estimate: providentially, Edwards's dismissal helped reform church practice in New England and gave posterity the great works of his Stockbridge years. (Frequently reprinted.)

5 [Hazlitt, William]. Review of *Sermons and Tracts,* by William Ellery Channing. *Edinburgh Review* 50 (October): 125-44.
   Praises Edwards's reasoning, his "closeness and candour" and firmness in *Freedom of the Will,* in a review of Channing and other American writers.

6 Jones, Thomas. Preface to *Hanes Gwaith Y Prynedigaeth* [*History of Redemption*]. Bala, Wales: Robert Saunderson, [iii]-xii.
   Offers the standard life of Edwards and reprints parts of *Personal Narrative.* (In Welsh.)

7 Knapp, Samuel L. *Lectures on American Literature with Remarks on Some Passages of American History.* New York: Elam Bliss, pp. 82-83.
   Offers a brief life of Edwards and a confession that *Freedom of the Will* is abstruse.

8 Smith, John Pye. "Introductory Essay." In *A Narrative of the Revival of New England.* Glasgow: William Collins, pp. [iii]-xliv.

Notes that the times demand Edwards's "judicious and comprehensive" observations — out of print for forty years — in a detailed survey of revivals, and reprints the Watts-Guyse preface (1737.1).

1830

1 Anon. "Interesting Conversions: Jonathan Edwards." *Religious Monitor and Evangelical Repository* 6 (February): 414-16.
    Reprints part of *Personal Narrative* as testimony to Edwards's language of the new man.

2 [Channing, William Ellery]. ["Remarks on National Literature."] *Christian Examiner* 7 (January): 269-95.
    Calls for a national literature and cites Edwards as "one of the greatest men of his age, though unhappily his mind was lost, in a great degree, to literature, and we fear to religion, by vassalage to a false theology."

1831

1 B., A. "Edwards on the Imputation of Original Sin." *Christian Advocate* 9 (March): 131-35.
    Asserts that in *Original Sin* Edwards attributed both depravity and imputation to the covenant union between Adam and posterity, but denies that he ever taught the "monstrous absurdity" that men actually or personally sinned before they were born.

*2 MacDougall, Patrick Campbell. "Edwards on Free Will." [Edinburgh] *Presbyterian Review* 1 (September).
    See 1852.7.

3 [Porter, Noah]. "Review of the Works of President Edwards." *Quarterly Christian Spectator* 3 (September): 337-57.
    Praises, summarizes, and quotes from the Converse edition, especially from the first volume, Sereno Dwight's *Life* (1829.4).

4 [Taylor, Isaac], ed. "Introductory Essay." In *An Inquiry into the Modern Prevailing Notions Respecting That Freedom of the Will*. London: James Duncan, pp. [xvii]-clxvi.
    Reprints 1827.5.

5 Watts, Isaac, and John Guyse. Preface to *A Faithful Narrative of the Surprising Work of God*. Boston: James Loring, pp. [iii]-x.
    Reprints 1737.1.

1832

1 American Sunday School Union. *The Life of President Edwards.* Philadelphia: American Sunday School Union, 143 pp.

Derives a life of Edwards from the accounts of Samuel Hopkins (1765.2) and Sereno Dwight (1829.4); advises the young to emulate Edwards's mental discipline and habits of thought; and reprints parts of *Personal Narrative,* all of "Resolutions," and some of the juvenilia.

2 Brownlee, James. "Memoir." In *A History of the Work of Redemption.* Edinburgh: Stirling & Kenney, pp. [ix]-lvi.

Recounts Edwards's career in the standard fashion.

3 Colton, Calvin. *History and Character of American Revivals of Religion.* London: Frederick Westley; A. H. Davis, pp. 48, 126-27.

Presents Edwards and the revivals to English readers, his narratives of some of those "disagreeable" events characterized by the "artless simplicity of the child" but judged to be honest, exact, and sound.

4 Gregory, Olinthus, ed. *The Works of the Rev. Robert Hall, A.M.* London: Holdsworth & Ball, 1:58-60; 6:99, 121.

Cites Robert Hall's "undiminished pleasure" in Edwards's writings for "full sixty years." Yet in a recorded conversation Hall claims that Edwards found the distinction between liberty to will and liberty to act "buried" in the works of John Owen; thought it useful to "frighten" Arminians with; and "instead of smothering it, he nursed it" in *Freedom of the Will.*

5 Mackintosh, James. *A General View of the Progress of Ethical Philosophy, Chiefly during the Seventeenth and Eighteenth Centuries.* Philadelphia: Carey & Lea, pp. 108-10.

Questions Edwards's use of the word *being* in his ethical theory found in *True Virtue* and *End of Creation.* The term is a "mere incumbrance," cloaked in mystery and mysticism, obscuring his "really unmeaning" assumption that there are degrees of existence.

6 Silliman, Benjamin. "Juvenile Observations of President Edwards on Spiders." *American Journal of Science and Arts* 21 (January): 109-15.

Speculates that had Edwards devoted himself to science he might have become "another Newton" and quotes from his early observations of spiders to support it.

7 [Spaulding, Charles]. "Introductory Remarks." In *Edwards On Revivals.* New York: Dunning & Spalding, pp. [ix]-xvi.

Recommends Edwards's *Faithful Narrative* as a discriminating record of Northampton revival of 1734, reviews *Some Thoughts* section by section as a practical and profound analysis of the Great Awakening, and reprints both for "the present revived state of things."

8 [Taylor, Isaac]. *Essay on the Application of Abstract Reasoning to the Christian Doctrines: Originally Published as an Introduction to Edwards on the Will.* Boston: Crocker & Brewster.

Reprints 1827.5.

1833

1 Anon. "J. E. to M. S." *Christian Examiner* 14 (May): 236-40.

Concludes a fictional note from Edwards to Professor M. Stuart on the "invincible propensity" to evil by suggesting that men (and children) may more keenly feel their sinfulness as the "ungrateful abuse" of God's kindness and favor than as the result of imputation.

1834

1 Anon. "Works of President Edwards." *Eclectic Review,* 3d ser., 12 (September): 181-98.

Reviews the London edition of Edwards's *Works* (1834) and praises Henry Rogers's analysis (1834.4) and Sereno Dwight's biography (1829.4).

2 Bancroft, George. *History of the United States.* Boston: Little, Brown & Co., 3:399; 4:154-58.

Praises Edwards's concept of universal history found in *History of Redemption* as superior to that of Vico and Bossuet and uses briefly the major works to comment upon New England religion.

3 Pond, Enoch. "Review of Edwards on the Will." *Literary and Theological Review* 1 (December): 523-39.

Praises Edwards's *Freedom of the Will* as a "noble work," in a clarification of its major points.

4 Rogers, Henry. "An Essay on the Genius and Writings of Jonathan Edwards." In *The Works of Jonathan Edwards.* Edited by Edward Hickman. London: F. Westley & A. H. Davis, 1:i-lii.

Analyzes the "chief peculiarities" of Edwards's character and his chief productions, especially *Freedom of the Will,* in a discursive, double-columned essay on genius and "the most perfect specimen of the intellectual athlete the world has ever seen." Edwards's mind was logical, abstract, and deductive, "ill-adapted" to scientific inquiry; his style was "most repulsive," prolix, inverted, "barbarous and uncouth." *Freedom of the Will* is "stupendous" but lacks originality and contains logical defects; *Original Sin* is inferior in "vigour and subtilty" to it; *True Virtue,* the "most profound" of all of Edwards is as well the "least satisfactory"; and *Religious Affections* is one of the "most valuable" works on experimental piety "ever published."

5 Todd, John. "Address at Laying the Corner Stone of the Edwards Church, July 4, 1833." In his *The Pulpit — Its Influence upon Society. A Sermon, Delivered at the Dedication of the Edwards Church in Northampton, Mass., December 25, 1833.* Northampton, Mass.: J. H. Butler, pp. 47-56.

Predicts that the works of Edwards — "a wonderful man!" — will "mould and shape individual and national character, as long as the English language is spoken," though "[n]o denomination of christians dares claim Edwards as its leader," in an address by the pastor of the Edwards church.

6 Upham, Thomas C. *A Philosophical and Practical Treatise on the Will.* Portland, Me.: William Hyde, pp. 128-29.

Agrees with Edwards that his "learned and able" discussion of the will is hardly exhaustive, limited as it is to freedom, and ranks him intellectually with Joseph Butler and John Locke.

1835

1 Anon. "Life of the Rev. Jonathan Edwards, President of Princetown [*sic*] College, New Jersey." In *Christian Biography, Containing the Lives of Rev. George Whitefield, Rev. John Wesley, Rev. Augustus Hermann Francke, Rev. Jonathan Edwards.* London: Religious Tract Society, pp. 1-72.
   Offers a life of Edwards "selected" from the Hopkins (1765.2) and Dwight (1829.4) biographies.

2 Anon. "Miscellaneous and Literary Notices." *Biblical Repository and Quarterly Observer* 5 (April): 486-87.
   Reprints, in part, Henry Rogers's introduction to Sereno Dwight's London edition of Edwards (1834.4).

3 [Brazer, John]. "Essay on the Doctrine of Divine Influence." *Christian Examiner* 18 (March): 50-84.
   Quotes several passages from *Religious Affections* and *Personal Narrative* only to reject Edwards's doctrine of the supernatural influence of the Holy Spirit in the conversion of the sinner.

4 Mackintosh, James. "Dissertation Second: Progress of Ethical Philosophy, Chiefly during the Seventeenth and Eighteenth Centuries." In *Dissertations on the History of Metaphysical and Ethical, and of Mathematical and Physical Science.* Edinburgh: Adam & Charles Black, pp. 340-41.
   Reprints 1832.5.

5 Reed, Andrew, and James Matheson. *A Narrative of the Visit to the American Churches.* New York: Harper & Brothers, pp. 248-50.
   Suggests that Edwards asked "too much at once," in altering the communion practice of his congregation, but that neither he nor his congregation is to blame for his dismissal.

1836

1 Hazlitt, William. "On Liberty and Necessity." In his *Literary Remains.* London: Saunders & Otley, pp. 170-228.
   Compares Edwards in *Freedom of the Will* and Joseph Priestley in *The Doctrine of Philosophical Necessity Illustrated* (1777) and finds the first earnest and scrupulous and the other evasive and cavalier. Edwards exhausts the subject of necessity in "one of the most closely reasoned, elaborate, acute, serious, and sensible among modern productions" and anticipates Hazlitt's own remarks. Extensive quotations show Edwards's "usual truth of feeling" for clear, unambiguous definitions of key terms.

1837

1 Miller, Samuel. "Life of Jonathan Edwards." In *The Library of American Biography,* 8. Edited by Jared Sparks. Boston: Hilliard, Gray, & Co., pp. [1]-256.

Recounts Edwards's pastoral career and comments upon his work, in a full-length biography, derived chiefly from Samuel Hopkins (1765.2), Sereno Dwight (1829.4), and published estimates, of a ministerial model "exemplary, luminous, and useful."

1838

1 Day, Jeremiah. *An Inquiry Respecting the Self-Determining Power of the Will; or Contingent Volition.* New Haven: Herrick & Noyes, viii, 200 pp.

Uses Edwards's passing remarks in *Freedom of the Will* as an occasion to elaborate and prove that there is no contingent volition, for it is inconsistent with scriptural accounts.

1839

1 [Alexander, James Waddel, and Albert B. Dod]. "Transcendentalism." *Biblical Repertory and Princeton Review* 11 (January): 37-101.

Notes the important distinction between Edwards and the "false" theology of his successors, in an attack on the German influence on American thought and the "nonsense and impiety" of Emerson's Divinity School address.

2 Anon. "Jonathan Edwards's Later Life." *Hampshire Gazette,* 30 October, p. 1.

Recounts briefly Edwards's Northampton years.

3 Anon. Review of *A Review of Edwards's "Inquiry into the Freedom of the Will,"* by Henry Philip Tappan. *American Biblical Repository,* 2d ser., 2 (July): 257-58.

Remarks Tappan's "veneration" for Edwards though he assails his *Freedom of the Will.*

4 Backus, Isaac. *Church History of New England from 1620 to 1804.* Philadelphia: [Baptist] Tract Depository, pp. 149-69.

Notes, from a Baptist point of view, the controversy that Edwards engaged in with Charles Chauncy and others over revival religion. Some of Edwards's work has, perhaps unwittingly, a Baptist turn. In "On the Right to Sacraments," Edwards quotes from Romans 2:29, Philippians 3:3, and Colossians 2:11, 12, and "though he did not design it, yet many others have been made Baptists by the same scriptures, and the same ideas from them."

5 Hodge, Charles. "The Great Revival of Religion, 1740-45." In his *The Constitutional History of the Presbyterian Church in the United States of America.* Philadelphia: William S. Martein, Part II, pp. 13-122.

Traces Edwards's role in the Great Awakening — and that of the important revivalists, George Whitefield, the Tennants, Samuel Blair among them — and regards him "much less sensible" to the dangers of unrestrained emotions, bodily excitation, and nervous disorders than he was to become. His dismissal proves the "low state" of his congregation. and reveals "something wrong" with the Awakening "from the beginning": even under Edwards, spurious conversions and false religion flourished. Nevertheless, the revivals pumped "new life" into the Presbyterian Church, and it is still felt within it.

6 James, John Angel, and William Patton, eds. "Introductory Preface[s]." In *Edwards on Revivals.* London: John Snow, pp. [iii]-xii.

Recommends *Faithful Narrative* and *Some Thoughts* as the work of a "sober" eye-witness, not a "mere speculatist," in a survey of revivals from apostolic days to the Reformation and the ministry of Edwards.

7 Park, Edwards A. "Duties of a Theologian." *American Biblical Repository,* 2d ser., 2 (October): 347-80.

Eulogizes Edwards as a master theologian (with Augustine and Calvin) but wishes he had been "more of a brother" as well as the "father" of New England theology. Edwards had "a rich imagination, and might have been one of the first poets of his age, had he not chosen to be the first theologian."

8 Tappan, Henry Philip. *A Review of Edwards's "Inquiry into the Freedom of the Will."* New York: John S. Taylor, 300 pp.

Begins a detailed refutation of Edwards's *Freedom of the Will* by restating its doctrine, by following its "legitimate" consequences, and by examining arguments against self-determination, in a formidable exercise in logic. If Edwards's psychology is right, then a self-determining power of the will is the "greatest absurdity possible"; if his doctrine of necessity is right, then folly, for instance, may be a necessary act, a consequence of infinite wisdom yet opposed to it — a manifest absurdity. And his argument of the interminable series of cause and effect makes the whole notion of causality "equally absurd." Edwards's system is Lockean and utilitarian, pantheistic and atheistic. When Edwards keeps to religious matters like salvation, he seems "one of the old preachers of the martyr age"; but when he turns to matters philosophical, he falters. (For the continuing and concluding arguments, see 1840.6 and 1841.4.)

1840

1 [Atwater, Lyman H]. "The Power of Contrary Choice." *Biblical Repertory and the Princeton Review* 12 (October): 532-49.

Uses the occasion of the publication of a new edition of *Freedom of the Will* to call attention to the current discussion of the power of contrary choice and Edwards's "safe and prudent" study of it.

2 Campbell, John. *Maritime Discovery and Christian Missions, Considered in their Mutual Relations.* London: John Snow, pp. 159-60.

Refers to Edwards's powerful contribution to the union of prayer through his *Humble Attempt.*

3 Franklin, Benjamin. Letter to Mrs. Jane Mecom, 28 July 1743. In *The Works of Benjamin Franklin.* Edited by Jared Sparks. Boston: Hilliard, Gray, & Co., 7:8-9.

Recommends Edwards's *Some Thoughts* to his sister.

4 Quincy, Josiah. *The History of Harvard University.* Cambridge, Mass.: John Owen, 2:54-66.

Cites Edwards's doctrinal basis for revivalism, his insinuation that colleges "should, in fact, be nurseries of piety" in *Some Thoughts*, and Charles Chauncy's attack on enthusiasm and defense of Harvard in *Seasonable Thoughts*. Although Harvard was not "drawn into the vortex" of revivalist controversy until the arrival of George Whitefield, Edwards's "bold and uncompromising" metaphysics prepared the way.

5 Robe, James. *Narrative of the Revival of Religion at Kilsyth, Cambuslang, and Other Places, in 1742*. Glasgow: William Collins, p. 6.

Notes the popularity of Edwards's *Distinguishing Marks* in Scotland before the revivals of 1742.

6 Tappan, Henry P. *The Doctrine of the Will, Determined by an Appeal to Consciousness*. New York: Wiley & Putnam, 327 pp.

Continues a detailed refutation of Edwards's *Freedom of the Will* by testing his doctrine by an "appeal to consciousness," in a psychological investigation of reason, sensitivity, and will. Edwards confounds necessity and contingency, though they are opposite ideas, and collapses reason, sensitivity, and will into one, though they are separate faculties. There are two elements of necessity in the mind and one of freedom, acting harmoniously to "conditionate" one another. Hence motives, contrary to Edwards, are "phenomena of the reason and sensitivity conditionating the will." (For the beginning and concluding arguments, see 1839.8 and 1841.4.)

1841

1 Anon. "A Review of *An Examination of President Edwards's Inquiry on the Freedom of the Will*, by Jeremiah Day. *American Biblical Repository*, 2d ser., 5 (April): 500-504.

Finds Jeremiah Day's defense (1841.3) "labored" though "indispensable" to those who do not have the patience to go through Edwards.

2 Channing, William E[llery]. *Works*. Boston: James Munroe & Co., p. 1:xiii.

Considers Edwards's *Freedom of the Will* "pernicious" if taken seriously, but adds that no one does.

3 Day, Jeremiah. *An Examination of President Edwards's Inquiry on the Freedom of the Will*. New Haven: Durrie & Peck, xii, 340 pp.

Analyzes the language of Edwards's argument in *Freedom of the Will* section by section and definition by definition in an attempt to prove his thesis, confound his critics, and establish a categorical defense. There is in Edwards "a degree of negligence" about his style — the structure of his sentences, the position of relatives — and a lack of "nice precision" about his definitions. Edwards must be read "as a whole," checking earlier parts of the argument for consistency and determining the different meanings of key terms throughout the text. And that is the stuff of the inquiry: the definitions and relationship of will, volition, motive, necessity, contingence, inclination, inability, liberty, self-determination, indifference, foreknowledge, accountability, virtue, vice, fatalism, and common sense.

3A [Sears, Barnas]. Review of *A Treatise concerning Religious Affections*, by Jonathan Edwards. *Christian Review* 6 (December): 492-506.

Recommends *Religious Affections* — "the most useful, if not the ablest production" of Edwards — as a manual for young pastors to "diminish" hypocrisy, "purify" religion, and "increase" experimental preaching.

4 Tappan, Henry P. *The Doctrine of the Will, Applied to Moral Agency and Responsibility.* New York: Wiley & Putnam, ix, 348 pp.

Concludes a detailed refutation of Edwards's *Freedom of the Will* by examining the doctrine in connection with moral agency and responsibility and by exposing the "futility of the distinction" between moral and natural ability. "The mere natural ability as a constituted connexion between volition and voluntary action cannot contain freedom, if the volition itself be not an act of freedom." Contrary to Edwards, freedom does make man responsible though not independent of God. Man is made in God's image and the "more perfectly" he knows himself — his reason, his emotions, his freedom — the "more perfectly" he grows in knowledge. Man thus interprets the world through his own self-consciousness.

5 Vail, Eugene A. *De la Littérature et des Hommes de Lettres des États-Unis d'Amérique.* Paris: Charles Gosselin, pp. 205-11.

Surveys briefly Edwards's life and work. (In French.)

1842

1 Anon. "The Great Awakening." *Methodist Quarterly Review* 24 (October): 594-615.

Claims Edwards perceived that Methodists and Moravians held the "true doctrine" of justification, in a review of Joseph Tracy's *The Great Awakening* (1842.6). Edwards's sermons of "greatest effect" during the Awakening were Arminian or Methodistic.

2 Cheever, George B. "Review of Professor Tappan's Works on the Will." *American Biblical Repository,* 2d ser., 7 (April): 411-41.

Attacks Edwards's *Freedom of the Will* as contrary to the common consciousness and experience of man and to the common language of Scripture, in an essay-review of Henry Tappan's analysis (1839.8; 1840.6; and 1841.4). Edwards is like a "Boa Constrictor" in logic, his doctrines a "monstrous deformity."

3 Edwards, Jonathan, the younger. "Remarks on the Improvements Made in Theology by his Father, President Edwards." In *The Works of Jonathan Edwards, D.D.* Edited by Tryon Edwards. Andover, Mass.: Allen, Morrill & Wardwell, 1:481-92.

Lists in summary form ten important theological contributions Edwards (and his followers) made. Edwards "shed much light" on the question of the end of creation; made "important improvements" on the doctrines of liberty and necessity; "happily" offered his "original" scheme of true virtue; clarified the origin of moral end; illustrated experimental religion; explained disinterested affection; described the "new sense" doctrine of regeneration; and, through his disciples, examined the doctrines of atonement and imputation and the state of the unregenerate.

4 Emmons, Nathanael. "The Treasures of a Good and Evil Heart." In *The Works of Nathanael Emmons.* Edited by Jacob Ide. Boston: Crocker & Brewster, 5:139-40.

Disagrees with Edwards in *Religious Affections* that religion consists of a good heart and of good affections flowing from it: religion consists of a good heart which is good affections.

5 Mackintosh, James. "A General View of the Progress of Ethical Philosophy." *Encyclopaedia Britannica,* 7th ed., 1:340-41.
   Reprints 1832.5.

6 Tracy, Joseph. *The Great Awakening: A History of the Revival Time of Edwards and Whitefield.* Boston: Tappan & Dennet, pp. 1-18, 213-30 passim.
   Recounts Edwards's role in the Great Awakening, the "immediate occasion of its commence-ment" being his series of sermons on justification in 1734. "Edwards, indeed, had done more than any other man to awaken the ministry and the churches in the first instance, and to produce the movement" of the 1740s, a time of "nervous diathesis." His indulgence about bodily agitation and unrepressed feeling so in evidence at Enfield became even more pronounced as he remarked his wife's "visitation" and her subsequent "improvement in practical holiness." His dismission from Northampton drew sympathy for his views on conversion both here and abroad and "dis-posed the pious to be on his side."

7 Uhden, Hermann F. *Geschichte der Congregationalsten in Neu-England bis zu den erweckungen um das Jahr 1740: Ein Beitrag zu der kirchengeschichte Nordamerika's.* Leipzig: L. H. Rosenberg pp. 213-38.
   Describes the religious declension in New England and Edwards's hand in the revival of 1734, which is detailed in *Faithful Narrative.* (In German; translated as 1858.11.)

1843

1 Anon. "Review of Tappan on the Will." *Christian Review* 8 (September): 367-402.
   Claims Henry Tappan misconceives Edwards on the will and thus is "fighting a shadow," in an essay-review of Tappan's three-part study (1839.8, 1840.6, and 1841.4).

2 [Atwater, Lyman H]. "Dr. Edwards's Works." *Biblical Repertory and Princeton Review,* n.s., 15 (January): 42-65.
   Compares the thought of the elder Edwards with the "improvements" of the younger and finds the latter wanting, in a review of the *Works* of the son.

2A [Robinson, Edward]. Review of *Works,* by Jonathan Edwards. In *Bibliotheca Sacra; or Tracts and Essays on Topics Connected with Biblical Literature and Theology.* Edited by Edward Robinson. New York: Wiley and Putnam, pp. 391-92.
   Recounts the publication history of the collected Edwards and the editorial liberties taken with his language, "which, although some may count them improvements, are nevertheless not what Edwards wrote," in a review of the revised Worcester edition (1843).

1844

1 Anon. "An Account of the Author's Life and Writings." In *A History of the Work of Redemption.* Edinburgh: Thomas Nelson, pp. [vii]-xxvii.
   Offers the standard life of Edwards.

2 Baird, Robert. *Religion in America, or, an Account of the Origins, Progress, Relation to*

the State, and Present Condition of the Evangelical Churches in the United States. New York: Harper & Brothers, pp. 197-99, 273-74.

Characterizes Edwards's preaching just before the 1734 revival, like all preaching that prepares the way for awakenings, as "doctrinal" on matters of grace, justification, redemption, and so on.

3 [Dod, William Armstrong]. *History of the College of New Jersey, from its Commencement A.D. 1746, to 1783.* Princeton: J. T. Robinson, pp. 13-15.

Recounts, in a short memoir, Edwards's time at Princeton and translates his Latin epitaph.

4 P[ark], E[dwards] A[masa]. "Original Letter of President Edwards." *Bibliotheca Sacra* 1 (August): 579-91.

Reprints a letter from Edwards, dated 18 November 1757, in Stockbridge to Joseph Hawley, a cousin who actively sought his dismissal and later publicly recanted, and remarks its candor and rectitude and the power clergymen formerly held over the aristocracy.

5 Pond, Enoch. Review of *The Works of Jonathan Edwards, D.D., late President of Union College; with a Memoir of his Life and Character,* by Tyron Edwards. *American Biblical Repository,* 2d ser., 12 (October): 373-91.

Compares the two Edwardses, father and son: the father is more imaginative, inventive, and emotional, more effective a preacher, more profound an investigator than the son; but the son was a better polemical theologian than the father.

5A [Tholuck, August]. Review of "A Review of Edwards's "Inquiry into the Freedom of the Will," by Henry P. Tappan. *Methodist Quarterly Review* 26 (January): 61-85.

Considers Henry P. Tappan's study (1839.8) "the best refutation" of Edwards on the will to appear in print, in an essay-review of both Tappan and Edwards.

1845

1 Anon. "Edwards as a Sermonizer." *Christian Review* 10 (March): 32-53.

Claims the "cumbersome and unwieldy" structure of Edwards's sermons are "defective" models for candidates for the ministry to imitate. Even though his mode of sermonizing was "purely his own," Edwards uses language clearly and precisely, orders evidence consecutively and cumulatively, and ranges widely in subject and tone.

2 Bledsoe, Albert Taylor. *An Examination of President Edwards' Inquiry into the Freedom of the Will.* Philadelphia: H. Hooker, 234 pp.

Examines *Freedom of the Will* in a detailed analysis of volition, cause and effect, indifference, action and passion, foreknowledge, free agency, self-determination, virtue, liberty, and necessity, and concludes that Edwards's "whole scheme . . . is founded in error and delusion." Following Edwards on moral necessity destroys moral obligation and responsibility; applying his principle of first cause leads "directly to Atheism." He uses definitions with confusion and imprecision, finding a "common nature" in a term like *necessity* where there is "only a common name." For all his "gigantic power," Edwards is bound to the "treadmill of a merely dialectical philosophy," a philosophy "essentially shallow and superficial," and in his defense of his system, "he does not reason at all, he merely rambles."

1846

1 Anon. "Life and Genius of Leibniz." *Edinburgh Review* 84 (July): [1]-47.
   Compares Leibniz and Edwards, that "great Transatlantic Divine," on the rigor of their attack on indifference in free will.

1A Anon. Review of *An Examination of President Edwards' Inquiry into the Freedom of the Will,* by Albert T. Bledsoe. *Methodist Quarterly Review* 28 (October): 598-614.
   Regards Albert T. Bledsoe's work (1845.2) "a full, direct, and incontrovertible refutation" of the "celebrated" *Freedom of the Will* of Edwards, "one of the greatest of metaphysicians," in an essay-review.

2 Edwards, Jonathan, the younger. Preface to *History of the Work of Redemption.* Philadelphia: Presbyterian Board of Publication, pp. iii-viii.
   Reprints 1774.3.

3 Mahan, A[sa]. *Doctrine of the Will.* New York: J. K. Wellman, pp. 228-31 passim.
   Accuses Edwards of a "fundamental error" in philosophy — he confounds will with sensibility — and convicts him of faulty logic — his argument on the will is circular; his argument on necessity begs the question; and his argument on divine foreknowledge is based on a false assumption, neither rational nor scriptural.

1847

1 Albro, John A. *The Life of Thomas Shepard.* Lives of the Chief Fathers of New England, no. 4. Boston: Massachusetts Sabbath School Society, pp. 318-19.
   Calculates Edwards's debt to Thomas Shepard to be substantial inasmuch as 65 of 132 quotations in *Religious Affections* come from his *The Parable of the Ten Virgins.*

1A Anon. "The Divine Prescience Not Inconsistent with the Free Agency of Man." *Quarterly Review of the Methodist Episcopal Church, South* 1 (April): 161-75.
   Argues, *contra* Edwards, that inasmuch as God knows events absolutely and intuitively, so he foreknows future contingent or necessitated events, and thus divine prescience is "reconciled" with man's free agency.

2 C[hanning], W[illiam] H[enry]. "Edwards and the Revivalists." *Christian Examiner* 43 (November): 374-94.
   Explains revivalism as the product of the general Protestant emphasis on individualism, "a lonely pilgrimage over deserts of sin to the tomb of the Redeemer," and Edwards as an exemplar of it. His profound sense of his own sinfulness resulted in a "conscious longing" for salvation that he translated at large. Edwards "out-Lutherized Luther and out-Calvinized Calvin" in his depiction of the infinite sins of the finite man; he classified, examined, and treated sin-sickness like a clinician. But Edwards, who might have been a poet or a saint in another time, failed to see holiness as love, God as loving.

3 Griswold, Rufus Wilmot. *The Prose Writers of America.* Philadelphia: Carey & Hart, pp. 55-56.

Offers a biography and criticism of Edwards, accounting his style "uncommonly good," suitable and precise but lacking harmony. After reading Samuel Richardson's *Charles Grandison*, Edwards tried to write more gracefully and succeeded in part in *Freedom of the Will* and *Original Sin.*

4 Martin, Benjamin. "Bledsoe's Examination of Edwards's Inquiry." *New Englander* 5 (July): 337-47.

Finds Albert T. Bledsoe's study (1845.2) a mixture of good and bad: though some of the analyses are vigorous and acute, the tone is discourteous and ungracious to Edwards, contemptuous to his advocates.

5 Stearns, W. A. "The American Pulpit — Its Ends, Its Means, and Its Motives," *Bibliotheca Sacra* 4 (May): 247-70.

Compares briefly Edwards and George Whitefield, in a survey of American pulpit orators. Edwards was eloquent and logical, more solid and solemn than Whitefield but not as passionately appealing.

1848

1 Greene, W[illiam] B. *Remarks in Refutation of the Treatise of Jonathan Edwards, on the Freedom of the Will.* West Brookfield, Mass.: Cooke & Chapin, 30 pp.

Examines, sentence by sentence, the second section of the second part of Edwards's *Freedom of the Will* by question and answer, quotation and comment, an concludes that *"all our volitions are produced and determined by our will"* but that the will does not possess self-determination.

2 MacClelland, George. *Predestination and Election Vindicated from Dependence on Moral Necessity, and Reconciled with Freewill and a Universal Atonement: Preceded by an Answer to the System of Edwards.* Edinburgh: Bell & Bradfute, pp. 1-56 passim.

Considers Edwards's influence on Thomas Chalmers in his treatment of moral necessity and predestination to be profound and "destructive to the true faith" but finds the contrary views of the Arminians equally repugnant.

3 O[sgood], S[amuel]. "Jonathan Edwards." *Christian Examiner* 44 (May): 367-86.

Traces the course of Edwards's life and work, "a theologian great as Calvin, a logician not inferior to Spinoza."

1849

1 Anon. "The Life and Experience of the Author." In *History of the Work of Redemption.* London: George Virtue, pp. [3]-24.

Offers the standard life of Edwards.

2 Belcher, Joseph. *The Clergy of America: Anecdotes Illustrative of the Character of Ministers of Religion in the United States.* Philadelphia: J. B. Lippincott, pp. 163-65, 201-202.

Recounts anecdotes about Edwards and particularly the reaction of a young man to one of his sermons on redemption. "He waited with deepest and most solemn solicitude, to hear the trumpet sound and the archangel call; to see the graves open, the dead arise, and the Judge descend in the glory of his Father, with all his holy angels; and was deeply disappointed when the day terminated, and left the World in its usual state of tranquility."

1850

A Anon. "President Edwards and New England Theology." *Panoplist* 1 (October): 386-97; (November): 430-36.
Denies that Edwards shares the views of the New School on innate depravity, as "accredited organs" of that theology claim, by quoting from *Original Sin* and *Freedom of the Will* and by showing that Edwards "teaches to the contrary."

1 Beecher, Edward. "Man the Image of God." *Bibliotheca Sacra* 7 (July): 409-25.
Questions Edwards's concept of time and space as illusions of the imagination set forth in *End of Creation*. By denying reality to time and space, Edwards compromises rational man's ability to know God and subverts the chief end of his being.

2 Blakey, Robert. "Dr. Jonathan Edwards." In his *History of the Philosophy of the Mind.* London: Longman, Brown, Green, & Longmans, 4:492-519.
Deals with Edwards's theological system as found in *Freedom of the Will* chiefly and insists that it is based upon a mistaken theory of causation. To argue that nothing can exist without cause is to deny the existence of God and the "obligatory nature of moral distinctions." Edwards had the power of sustained reasoning but he lacked "logical comprehension." An acute philosopher, he was not a great one.

3 Fichte, Imanuel Hermann. *System der Ethik.* Leipzig: Dyk'sche Buchhandlung, 1:544-45.
Finds an abbreviated version of *End of Creation* "excellent" and Edwards, that "solitary thinker" in America, at the very center of the principle of morals: universal benevolence is the bond of love "uniting all to and in God." (In German.)

4 Osgood, Samuel. "Jonathan Edwards and the New Calvinism." In his *Studies in Christian Biography: or, Hours with Theologians and Reformers.* New York: C. S. Francis & Co., pp. 348-77.
Traces Edwards's career sentimentally and estimates his work principally as that of a deductive logician remorselessly pursuing Calvinist doctrines "in all their intrinsic repulsiveness." But beneath Edwards the metaphysician lies the poet; hence, his theology is more nearly "the creature of his intellect, working at the bidding of his emotions."

5 Wisner, William C. "The End of God in Creation." *American Biblical Repository,* 3d ser., 6 (July): 430-56.
Argues against Edwards's view of the God of creation in order to establish his own doctrine. The "ultimate objective end" of God in creating the universe was not, as Edwards held, a celebration of his attributes and perfections but was to "secure the greatest possible amount of creature holiness and happiness." Edwards's position ends in "absurdity"; his language and sentiment "savor much of pantheism."

6 Wynne, James. "Rev. Jonathan Edwards." In his *Lives of Eminent Literary and Scientific Men of America*. New York: D. Appleton & Co., pp. 134-67.

Offers the standard life of Edwards but dwells "at greater length" on the bad-book episode because Samuel Hopkins (1765.2) and Sereno Dwight (1829.4) "in their solicitude for [his] good name" avoid the real cause. Edwards was in a "jaundiced state of mind," irritated at the success Samuel Buell had with the young people of Northampton in his pulpit appearances before them. Edwards, "aware of the absurdity" of the charge of licentious reading against them, acted out of pique in his ringing condemnation. Thus began the end of "one of the ablest reasoners and profoundest thinkers of his age," but a writer whose style was "hideous and deformed."

1851

1 Bushnell, Horace. *Christ in Theology*. Hartford: Brown & Parsons, p. vi.

Notes that he was denied access to a newly discovered Edwards manuscript on the Trinity because of its questionable orthodoxy.

2 Finney, Charles G. *Lectures on Systematic Theology*. Edited and revised by George Redford. London: William Tegg & Co., pp. 479-500.

Rejects Edwards's views on natural and moral ability and inability and the "injurious monstrosity and misnomer" *Freedom of the Will,* in three lectures. Edwards made a "capital error" in adopting Locke's sensationalism.

1852

A Alexander, Archibald. *Outlines of Moral Science*. New York: Charles Scribner, pp. 168-70.

Avoids "any distinct remarks" on Edwards's "strange" definition of virtue since Samuel Hopkins adopts it as his "radical principle."

1 Anon. "President Edwards on Charity and its Fruits." *New Englander* 10 (May): 222-36.

Reviews Edwards's *Charity and its Fruits,* gives a history of the manuscript and outline of the contents of his "favorite" topic, and likens his sweetness of thought to that of Washington Irving.

2 Anon. "Retrospective Survey of American Literature." *Westminster Review* 57 (January): 288-305.

Praises Edwards, "a missionary at Northampton," for his subtlety and understanding and compares him to William Ellery Channing, in a survey of American writers of philosophy and literature.

3 Cheever, George B. "The Manuscripts of President Edwards." *Independent* 4 (23 December): 208.

Examines the Edwards manuscripts in Tryon Edwards's study and finds them "deeply interesting" as clues to his method of composition and evidence of his biblicism.

4 Edwards, Tryon. "Introduction." *Charity and Its Fruits; Or, Christian Love as Manifested in the Heart and Life.* London: James Nisbet & Co., pp. [iii]-vi.

Speculates that Edwards's habit of note taking and committing his thought to paper makes his manuscripts an incomparable record of his intellectual life. The series of lectures reprinted here was delivered at Northampton in 1738 and was "written in full," readied for publication. The treatise will rank with the best of Edwards.

5 Hamilton, William T. *The "Friend of Moses"; or, A Defence of the Pentateuch.* New York: M. W. Dodd, p. 282.

Remarks the fecundity of the Edwards clan.

6 Hanna, William. *Memoirs of the Life and Writings of Thomas Chalmers.* Edinburgh: Thomas Constable & Co., 1:16-17.

Quotes a manuscript letter from Thomas Chalmers to his mother, 26 February 1821, acknowledging his debt to Edwards on the will twenty-four years earlier.

7 MacDougall, Patrick Campbell. "Edwards on Free Will." In his *Papers on Literary and Philosophical Subjects.* Edinburgh: Johnstone & Hunter, pp. 66-138.

Welcomes the 1831 edition of Edwards's *Freedom of the Will,* with an introductory essay by Isaac Taylor, as an opportunity to praise Edwards and chastise Taylor. Though Edwards may rely too heavily upon conceptions independent of external things rather than upon the actual things themselves and though he may be guilty, at times, of verbal ambiguity," these are but passing flaws. Taylor's view of Edwards on liberty and necessity is inconsistent, self-contradictory, and just "wrong." His case against Edwards fails. (Reprints 1831.2.)

8 Park, Edwards A., ed. "Memoir." In *The Works of Samuel Hopkins, D.D.* Boston: Doctrinal Tract & Book Society, 1:9-266.

Traces Samuel Hopkins's personal relationship and theological debt to Edwards, from September 1741 when he heard Edwards deliver *The Trial of the Spirits* at Yale to his editorial labors following Edwards's death. Hopkins believed that, had Edwards lived, the two would have been "firmly united" in faith and in "essentially the same theories."

9 ———. "New England Theology; with Comments on a Third Article in the *Biblical Repertory and Princeton Review,* Relating to a Convention Sermon." *Bibliotheca Sacra* 9 (January): 170-220.

Defends Edwards and the Edwardseans against the attacks of Charles Hodge and the Princetonians and defines New England Theology. Variously called New Light Divinity, New Divinity, Edwardsean, Hopkinsian, Berkshire Divinity, and American Theology by the British and New England Theology by Americans, it stands "firm for the 'three radical principles,' that sin consists in choice, that our natural power equals, and that it also limits, our duty." Commentators err in dividing the elder Edwards and Joseph Bellamy from the younger Edwards, Nathanael Emmons, and Stephen West, for all these theologians bear witness to a systematic orthodoxy marked by "strong, practical common sense," a Calvinism in substance old, in form new. By 1796, two hundred ministers subscribed to the tenets of New England Theology.

10 ———. *New England Theology; with Comments on a Third Article in the Princeton Review, Relating to a Convention Sermon.* Andover, Mass.: Warren F. Draper.

Reprints 1852.9.

1853

1 Anon. "Dr. Alexander's Moral Science." *Bibliotheca Sacra* 10 (April): 390-414.
   Takes Archibald Alexander to task for confounding the opinions of others with those of Edwards in his "illustrious" *True Virtue.*

2 Anon. "Jonathan Edwards and John Wesley." *National Magazine* 3 (October): 308-11.
   Finds Edwards and John Wesley in agreement on every important aspect of theology except the abstract questions of liberty and necessity.

3 Anon. "President Edwards's Dissertation on the Nature of True Virtue." *Bibliotheca Sacra* 10 (October): 705-38.
   Defends Edward against charges (1853.4) that he and Joseph Bellamy disagreed on the nature of virtue by citing Edwards's public endorsement of Bellamy's theory, by answering Edwards's principal critics, and by examining *True Virtue* in detail.

4 [Atwater, Lyman II.] Review of *Outlines of Moral Science,* by Archibald Alexander. *Biblical Repertory and Princeton Review* 35 (January): 1-43.
   Calls *True Virtue* "a new adamantine barrier" that Edwards erected against a tide of selfish religion and argues that Joseph Bellamy followed him except when he moved "eccentric to his main orbit," in a survey of practical ethics.

5 Beecher, Edward. *The Conflict of Ages, or the Great Debate on the Moral Relations of God and Man.* Boston: Phillips, Sampson & Co., pp. 90-95 passim.
   Praises Edwards for avoiding the "sinful propensity to self-admiration" in his *Farewell Sermon.* He still suspected himself of tendencies to sinfulness, but he should have realized that their source "preceded his consciousness and choice."

6 ———. "The Works of Samuel Hopkins." *Bibliotheca Sacra* 10 (January): 63-82.
   Uses the occasion of a review of Hopkins's work to trace New England Theology to the revivals and Edwards, whose regeneration was produced "not at all by Locke" but by the Bible, and to attack the Princeton divines.

7 Bledsoe, Albert Taylor. *A Theodicy; or, Vindication of the Divine Glory, as Manifested in the Constitution and Government of the Moral World.* New York: Carlton & Porter, pp. 61-72, 98-110, 114-26 passim.
   Contends that Edwards's necessitarian views deny responsibility to man, make God the author of sin, and cloud moral distinctions, and posits a theodicy in which the goodness of God is consistent with the suffering of man, in a serial discussion of *Freedom of the Will, Original Sin,* and *True Virtue.*

8 Brown, John. "Prefatory Notice." *Theological Tracts, Selected and Original.* Edinburgh and London: A. Fullarton & Co., 2:293-94.
   Offers a brief life and longer praise of Edwards and reprints *End of Creation.*

9 [Cheever, George B.] "The Manuscripts of President Edwards." *Littell's Living Age* 36 (21 January): 181-82.
   Reprints 1852.3.

10 H., E. "Preface." *Spiritual Pride, Its Deceitful Nature and Evil Fruits.* London: Ward & Co., pp. [iii]-x.

 Justifies an abridgement of Edwards's *Some Thoughts* — an "endeavour to bring it forth from under a bushel of much circumstantial and prolix matter" — for the benefit of the Aged Pilgrim's Friend Society.

11 Jamieson, Robert. *Cyclopaedia of Religious Biography: A Series of Memoirs of the Most Eminent Characters of Modern Times, Intended for Family Reading.* London: John Joseph Green & Co., pp. 178-80.

 Offers a life of Edwards and speculates that he probably preferred to remain an academic at Yale than become a minister at Northampton.

1854

1 [Atwater, Lyman H.] "Modern Explanations of the Doctrine of Inability." *Biblical Repertory and Princeton Review* 26 (April): 217-46.

 Insists that Edwards's moral inability in *Freedom of the Will* is real inability, "invincible by the sinner," and that this view is "essentially" that of his predecessors, hardly the "novelty" some claim it to be.

2 Bledsoe, Albert Taylor. *A Theodicy.* New York: Carlton & Phillips.

 Reprints 1853.8.

3 E., T. "Samuel Davies and Jonathan Edwards." *Presbyterian Magazine* 4 (November): 512-15.

 Reprints a letter, dated 4 July 1751, from Samuel Davies (1723-1761) beseeching Joseph Bellamy to urge Edwards to take a position in Virginia and adds how different theology in America would have been had Edwards complied.

4 Jones, Electa F. *Stockbridge, Past and Present: or, Records of an Old Mission Station.* Springfield, Mass.: Samuel Bowles & Co., pp. 154-61.

 Charts Edwards's career both before and during his years among the Mahicans at Stockbridge.

1855

1 Allen, William. *An Address, Delivered at Northampton, Mass., on the Evening of October 29, 1854, in Commemoration of the Second Century since the Settlement of the Town.* Northampton, Mass.: Hopkins, Bridgman & Co., pp. 16-17.

 Offers a brief biography of Edwards and two causes for his dismission, his rejection of Solomon Stoddard's communion practice and his rigidity in matters of discipline.

2 Anon. "Familiar Sketches of Connecticut Valley: Rev. Jonathan Edwards." *Hampshire Gazette*, 10 July, p. 1.

 Provides a short, derivative life of Edwards.

3 Duyckinck, Evert A., and George L. Duyckinck. *Cyclopaedia of American Literature.*
New York: Charles Scribner, 1:92-95.

    Offers the standard short biography of Edwards, the "finest product" of American Puritan-
ism.

4 O'Callaghan, E. B., ed. *Documents Relative to the Colonial History of the State of New
York.* Albany: Weed, Parsons & Co., 6:907.

    Reproduces a letter from Thomas Cutler to Dr. Secker (28 August 1754) recommending Ed-
wards on election and reprobation but adding that he was "odd in his principles, haughty and
stiff and morose."

5 Tyler, William S. "Genius." *Bibliotheca Sacra* 12 (April): 283-312.

    Places Edwards's genius with that of Shakespeare, Bacon, and Washington.

1856

1 [Bancroft, George]. "Jonathan Edwards." In *The New American Cyclopaedia.* New
York: D. Appleton & Co., 7:11-20.

    Concludes a life of Edwards and an estimate of his work with this frequently reprinted enco-
mium: "he that will know the workings of the mind of New England in the middle of the last
century, and the throbbings of its heart, must give his days and nights to the study of Jonathan
Edwards."

2 Bledsoe, Albert Taylor. *A Theodicy.* New York: [Carlton & Porter].

    Reprints 1853.8.

3 Campbell, John McLeod. *The Nature of the Atonement.* Cambridge: Macmillan &
Co., pp. 49-112 passim.

    Attacks Edwards's (and John Owens's) idea of a limited atonement and his view that mercy
and love are arbitrary, not necessary. Not only does this imply that Christ died for the elect
rather than all men, it also substitutes a legal for a filial standing of Christ. Edwards, unlike later
Calvinists, eschews moral excellence through grace and clemency for the "fiction" of legal or penal imputation.

4 Chauncy, Charles. Letter, 16 March 1742/43. *New England Historical and Genealogical
Register* 10 (October): 332.

    Reprints a letter noting Charles Chauncy's preparation of an "antidote" to Edwards's *Some
Thoughts.*

5 Fish, Henry C. *History and Repository of Pulpit Eloquence.* New York: M. W. Dodd,
2:394-95.

    Reprints *Sinners in the Hands of an Angry God* and compares Edwards as a preacher to the
apostles in thought, argument, and effect.

6 Vaughan, Robert Alfred. *Hours with the Mystics.* London: John W. Parker & Son,
1:174.

Faults Edwards's *Religious Affections* for teaching that regeneration gives a new power rather than a new disposition to the mind, thus isolating one man from another.

1857

1 Ellis, George E. *A Half Century of the Unitarian Controversy.* Boston: Crosby, Nichols, & Co., pp. 98-99.
   Remarks the unnecessary contention about Edwards and the doctrine of physical depravity when it is clear that he believes in it.

2 Hollister, G[ideon] H. *The History of Connecticut from the First Settlement of the Colony to the Adoption of the Present Constitution.* Hartford: Case, Tiffany & Co., 2:587-94.
   Recounts Edwards's life in East Windsor amid an adoring family and a congenial natural environment.

3 Lossing, Benson J. *Eminent Americans.* New York: Mason Brothers, pp. 177-79.
   Offers a brief life and a favorable appraisal of Edwards.

4 Sprague, William B. *Annals of the American Pulpit.* New York: Robert Carter & Brothers, 1:329-35.
   Recounts Edwards's life and concludes with this from Thomas Chalmers's letter to "Dr. Stebbins of Northampton" (frequently reprinted): "There is no European divine to whom I make such frequent appeals in my class rooms as I do to Edwards. No book of human composition which I more strenuously recommend than his *Treatise on the Will,* — read by me forty-seven years ago with a conviction that has never since faltered, and which has helped me more than any other uninspired book, to find my way through all that might otherwise have proved baffling and transcendental and mysterious in the peculiarities of Calvinism."

5 Uhden, Hermann F. *Geschichte der Congregationalsten in Neu-England.* Berlin: Heinrich Schindler.
   Reprints 1842.7.

1858

1 Anon. Review of *History of the Church of Christ in Yale College,* by George P. Fisher. *New Englander* 16 (May): 434-49.
   Praises Yale for what it has done to promote theology through Edwards and his successors.

2 [Atwater, Lyman H.] "Jonathan Edwards and the Successive Forms of the New Divinity." *Biblical Repertory and Princeton Review* 30 (October): 585-620.
   Challenges George Fisher's account of New England Theology (1858.9) by arguing that, except for his doctrine of mediate imputation and his "eccentric" theory of true virtue, Edwards holds to concepts of Old Calvinism as his successors surely do not. There are "broad and irreconcilable differences" between Edwards and Hopkins, Emmons, Smalley, Taylor, Dwight, and the younger Edwards, though all have been "adroitly linked" to his name. But for the logical or illog-

ical ends to which they take his ideas of imputation, atonement, and virtue, these New Divinity men show little indebtedness to Edwards.

3 Bacon, Leonard. *A Commemorative Discourse on the Completion of Fifty Years from the Founding of the Theological Seminary at Andover.* Andover, Mass.: W. F. Draper, pp. 8-12.

Celebrates the fiftieth anniversary of the Andover Theological Seminary and suggests that Edwards's at-home study with Joseph Bellamy, Samuel Buell, and especially Samuel Hopkins constituted the "earliest germ" of those private schools for theological instruction that arose after the Great Awakening.

4 Baird, Samuel J. "Edwards and the Theology of New England." *Southern Presbyterian Review* 10 (January): 576-92.

Attacks Edwards's fundamental doctrine of causation, chiefly argued in *Original Sin,* which dishonors God and denies imputation. Edwards's "revolting fatalism" ends in an "inadequate" view of sin and corruption and prepared the way for the outbreak of Pelagianism and Socinianism at Yale.

5 ———. "Edwards and the Theology of New England." *British and Foreign Evangelical Review* 7 (July): 544-62.

Reprints 1858.4.

6 Bushnell, Horace. *Nature and the Supernatural.* New York: Charles Scribner, pp. 47-50.

Notes the change in fortunes of Edwards's *Freedom of the Will* from its original defense of the divine order to its current defense of the irresponsibility of the "moral outcast" and argues against Edwards's a priori knowledge of the strongest motive in choice.

7 Clark, Joseph S. *A Historical Sketch of the Churches In Massachusetts, from 1620-1858.* Boston: Congregational Board of Publication, pp. 155-59, 178-90.

Explains in some detail Edwards's role as a Congregationalist in the Great Awakening and focusses upon the "unreasonable and un-Congregational" handling of his dismission, attributing it to the "unsettled hostility" of some churches to revivalism and its results. At the heart of the problem lay the "mischievous notion" that a church council was like a church court to which congregants could appeal for swift, unchallenged action. Such a council, functioning in a judiciary not an advisory way, was "contrary to all rule and precedent" and assured, in its "tyrannical proceedings," Edwards's condemnation. Ironically, Edwards himself "lent sanction" to a judicial council in the much-disputed Robert Breck case some years before.

8 [Cunningham, William]. "Sir William Hamilton on Philosophical Necessity and the Westminster Confession." *British and Foreign Evangelical Review* 7 (January): 199-252.

Maintains, contrary to Sir William Hamilton's view, that the philosophical necessity of Edwards, and of Thomas Chalmers as well, is consistent with the Westminster Confession.

9 Fisher, George P. *A Discourse Commemorative of the History of the Church of Christ in Yale College, during the First Century of its Existence.* New Haven: Thomas A. Pease, pp. 36-37, 80-82 passim.

Notes that Yale College has trained many important New England divines and that they all share theological affinity with Edwards, the first of them.

10 Parton, J[ames]. *The Life and Times of Aaron Burr.* New York: Mason Brothers, pp. 25-30, 626.

Traces Edwards's career and records Aaron Burr's observation that his grandfather was "'the clearest head of America. How the race has degenerated,' he would say, with a humorous shrug." Edwards's chief contribution was to render irreconcilable church and state at a time when they were beginning to "mingle."

11 Uhden, Hermann F. *The New England Theocracy.* Translated by H. C. Conant. Boston: Gould & Lincoln.

Translates 1842.7.

1859

1 Anon. "Copy of Libel Against Jonathan Edwards." *Hampshire Gazette,* 29 March, p. 2.

Reprints a libel, recorded in January 1735/36, by Bernard Bartlet, of Simsbury, that Edwards was "as Great an Instrument of the Devil had on this side Hell to bring souls to Hell."

2 [Atwater, Lyman H.] "Jonathan Edwards and the Successive Forms of the New Divinity." *British and Foreign Evangelical Review* 8 (April): 267-96.

Reprints 1858.2.

3 [Byington, Ezra Hoyt]. "The Theology of Edwards, as Shown in his *Treatise Concerning Religious Affections.*" *American Theological Review* 1 (May): 199-220.

Claims that there is no "higher authority" than *Religious Affections* to deduce Edwards's theology, that it is practical and scientific, and quotes at length from it.

4 Marvin, A. P. "Three Eras of Revivals in the United States." *Bibliotheca Sacra* 16 (April): 279-301.

Remarks three periods of revivalism — 1740, 1797, and 1830. The first, the era of Edwards, was marked by the justification by faith and the doctrine of the new birth; the second by the doctrine of divine sovereignty; and the third by a sense of "personal duty to love and serve God." The country was saved from "total corruption" by the "Reformation of 1740."

5 Park, Edwards A. "The Rise of the Edwardean Theory of the Atonement: an Introductory Essay." *The Atonement: Discourses and Treaties by Edwards, Smalley, Maxcy, Emmons, Griffin, Burge, and Weeks.* Boston: Congregational Board of Publication, pp. xi-xxxix passim.

Charts Edward's modifications of the older Calvinist theory of the atonement as they affect "directly or indirectly" the more modern Edwardsean scheme proposed by his son. Edwards "exalts" the sovereignty of God rather than the atonement of Christ; urges a distinction between threat and promise, penalty and merit, but denies one between active and passive obedience; gives a "previously unwonted prominence" to love; and uses a "peculiar nomenclature" to argue his case. This loose, vague, seemingly inconsistent language not only has led opposing theologians to claim him their own but also has forced his successors to a deliberately precise language.

6 Smith, Henry B. *History of the Church of Christ in Chronological Tables.* New York: Charles Scribner, pp. 70, 73.

Lists, under New England polity, Edwards's vindication of original sin and divine sovereignty through a scriptural and rationalistic defense of Calvinism. Edwards's system has had a profound effect upon the theology of the churches.

7 Stowe, Harriet Beecher. *The Minister's Wooing.* New York: Derby & Jackson, pp. 332-38 passim.

Scatters comments about Edwards, quotes "Sarah Pierrepont" and regards his sermons on sin and suffering as "refined poetry of torture."

8 Taylor, Isaac. "Logic in Theology." *Logic in Theology and Other Essays.* London: Bell & Daldy, pp. 1-76.

Reprints 1827.5 (revised).

1860

1 Anon. "Religious Revivals." *Quarterly Review* 107 (January): 148-68.

Reviews books about the Irish revivals of 1857, cites the American counterparts of 1734 and 1741, and discusses Edwards's role in them.

2 Baird, Samuel J. *The Elohim Revealed in the Creation and Redemption of Man.* Philadelphia: Lindsay & Blakiston, pp. 47-50, 103-12, 160-64 passim.

Considers Edwards "unscriptural," "pantheistic," and "antinomian," and attributes much, if not all, to his false theory of causation. In *Freedom of the Will,* Edwards failed to recognize in the distinctive nature of the soul an efficient cause of its volitions and so promulgated a system hostile to his doctrine of grace. His doctrine of identity, which depends upon his theory of causation, is irreconcilable with his doctrine of imputation.

3 [Byington, Ezra Hoyt]. "The Theology of Edwards, as Shown in his *Treatise Concerning Religious Affections.*" *British and Foreign Evangelical Review* 9 (January): 119-36.

Reprints 1859.3.

4 Cooke, Parsons. "Edwards on the Atonement." *American Theological Review* 2 (February): 97-120.

Attacks Edwards A. Park's study of the atonement (1859.5) for its distortions, which pits Edwardseans against Edwards in a conflict of principles and subjects Christian doctrine to the "cramping-irons" of rationalizing metaphysics. Edwards has always been "an index" of orthodox Calvinism on the atonement as on other matters, but now by a skillful "play upon figurative language" a new system of Edwardseanism has sprung up opposed both to Calvin and Edwards.

5 [Porter, Noah]. "The Princeton Review on Dr. Taylor, and the Edwardean Theology." *New Englander* 18 (August): 726-73,

Asserts that Edwards should be "properly regarded as the founder of a new school" and that the Edwardseans are both his successors and "important" contributors to Christian theology. The "leading peculiarity" about Edwards was that he was both philosopher and divine: he brought current philosophical thinking into the Calvinistic system when possible and rejected it on "philosophic grounds" when it proved inconsistent. The Princetonians, on the other hand, "believe in the absolute perfection of the old metaphysics. The Edwardseans believe in their imperfection, and try to improve them."

6 Sherman, D[avid]. *Sketches of New England Divines.* New York: Carlton & Porter, pp. 138-82.
Reckons Edwards the "mightiest mind" in modern times and the "apostle of a new dispensation," in a biographical account fulsome in its praise and casual in its details.

7 Taylor, Isaac. "Logic in Theology." *Logic in Theology and Other Essays.* New York: William Gowans, pp. 7-69.
Reprints 1859.8.

1861

1 [General Association of Congregational Churches, Connecticut]. *Contributions to the Ecclesiastical History of Connecticut.* New Haven: William L. Kingsley, pp. 197-98.
Describes Edwards's role in the Great Awakening (and the ripple effect upon Connecticut towns) and documents the terms of the Bolton settlement, which he rejected for Yale.

2 Lawrence, E[dward] A. "New England Theology: The Edwardean Period." *American Theological Review* 3 (January): 36-68.
Examines the immediate legacy of Edwards's thought found in New England Theology by returning to the *"genuine"* theology of the chief productions of its "master-mind," both in a logical and a chronological order. Some may disagree with one part of the "construction" or another, as they are in the "right or left wing" of New England Theology, the New Divinity or the Old, the Old Calvinists or the New. Yet it is clear that in those major works — *Freedom of the Will, End of Creation, Original Sin,* and *True Virtue* — Edwards gave "deliberation and explicitness" to a doctrine and a theology that "entitle his words to be taken without attenuation or apology."

3 Thompson, Joseph P. "Jonathan Edwards, his Character, Teaching, and Influence." *Bibliotheca Sacra* 18 (October): 809-39.
Mediates between "unquestioning veneration" and "empirical judgment" of Edwards's character in an attempt to study the whole man, his life and his thought, and concludes that his theology is a "liberalized, rationalized, and harmonized" Calvinism affecting New England theology, Congregationalism, and Christendom.

1862

1 Frothingham, W. "The Edwards Family." *Continental Monthly* 1 (January): 11-16.
Journeys through the Edwards family to Judge Ogden Edwards, of Staten Island, New York, and stops to extol the "enviable greatness" of his grandfather Jonathan.

2 ———. "Jonathan Edwards and the Old Clergy." *Continental Monthly* 1 (March): 265-72.

Recounts tales and anecdotes about the clergy of New England and about its "great light," Edwards. With all his care and frugality, Edwards was still "the largest consumer of paper and ink in New England."

3 Maurice, Frederick Denison. *Moral and Metaphysical Philosophy*. London: Griffin, Bohn & Co., 4:469-75.

Claims that Edwards forsakes the very Puritans and Reformers he is heir to by exchanging a supremely righteous God for a supremely happy one. *Freedom of the Will*, however original or important it may still be, had a "debasing" effect on religious morality.

4 Pleus, Robert. "Man's Moral Freedom." *The Rev. C. H. Spurgeon and his Brethren, Drs. Payne and Wardlaw, President Edwards, and Others, in the Crucible; or the Peculiarities of Calvinism Tested*. London: G. J. Stevenson, pp. 80-105.

Analyzes the "false and stupid" philosophy of Edwards in *Freedom of the Will* from the title-page onward and attacks his "usual habit or crincumism" in moral matters. Edwards's book is a "quibble and logomachy, and, indeed, nonsense" and another example of perverse Calvinism.

1863

1 Lawrence, Edward A. "The Old School in New England Theology." *Bibliotheca Sacra* 20 (April): 311-49.

Compares "Old School" theology of Edwards and Bellamy with the "improvements" of Hopkins and Taylor on anthropological doctrines, sin, moral agency, ability and inability, regeneration, atonement and justification, divine sovereignty, and theodicy, in an attempt to reconcile them by clearly stating their positions.

1864

1 [Atwater, Lyman H.] "Whedon and Hazard on the Will." *Biblical Repertory and Princeton Review* 36 (October): 679-703.

Refutes D. D. Whedon (1864.5) and Rowland G. Hazard (1864.3) in their attack upon Edwards and suggests that such assaults on *Freedom of the Will* simply add to its fame and notoriety, demonstrate its considerable influence, and prove the "futility of all replies" to its basic arguments, notwithstanding some flaws in Edwards's logic and infelicities in his language.

2 Gillett, E[zra] H[all]. *History of the Presbyterian Church in the United States of America*. Philadelphia: Presbyterian Publication Committee, 1:122-23.

Notes Samuel Davies's offer to Edwards of a pastorate in Virginia and quotes the latter's approval of Presbyterian polity in a letter, 5 July 1750.

3 Hazard, Rowland G. "Review of Edwards on the Will." *Freedom of Mind in Willing; or, Every Being that Wills a Creative First Cause*. New York: D. Appleton & Co., pp. 173-435.

Exposes "the fallacies" of Edwards's *Freedom of the Will* in an extended argument on liberty, necessity, self-determination, causation, indifference, contingence, understanding, motive, and foreknowledge.

3A Stowe, C. E. "Sketches and Recollections of Dr. Lyman Beecher." *Congregational Quarterly* 23 (July): 221-35.

Remarks Edwards's influence on New England Congregationalists at the turn of the century: he became "Bible, Pope, Council of Trent, and all, so far as the authoritative decision of disputed points in theology was concerned."

4 Waterbury, J. B. "Rev. Jonathan Edwards." *Sketches of Eloquent Preachers*. New York: American Tract Society, pp. 151-62.

Attributes Edwards's effectiveness as a preacher not to his graceful delivery, musical voice, or practical rhetoric, all of which he seriously lacked, but to God-inspired power.

5 Whedon, D. D. *The Freedom of the Will as a Basis of Human Responsibility and a Divine Government Elucidated and Maintained in its Issue with the Necessitarian Theories of Hobbes, Edwards, the Princeton Essayists, and Other Leading Advocates*. New York: Carlton & Porter, 438 pp.

Refutes the doctrine of the will of Edwards (and others) on the basis of human responsibility and accountability, in an exhaustive analysis that first defines the terms; then considers the necessitarian argument in its causational, psychological, and theological aspects; and finally states the positive arguments of consciousness, morality, responsibility, freedom, and theodicy. Edwards succeeds in demonstrating the necessity of volition in action, but he fails signally to square moral intuitions with "intellective conclusions." His is not a judicial mind, but a forensic one, given to advocacy, not considered thought.

1865

1 Beecher, Lyman. *Autobiography, Correspondence, Etc., of Lyman Beecher, D.D.* Edited by Charles Beecher. New York: Harper & Brothers, 1:384 and 469-71; 2:237-38.

Mentions Edwards in several letters, most prominently in one to his son George at Yale, 5 November 1830, recommending "Next after the Bible, read and study Edwards."

2 Fiske, D[aniel] T. "Discourse Relating to the Churches and Religious History of Essex North." In *Contributions to the Ecclesiastical History of Essex County, Mass.* Boston: Congregational Board of Publication, pp. 280-81.

Asserts that Edwards did not oppose the half-way covenant so much as the Stoddardean form of it.

3 ———. "New England Theology." *Bibliotheca Sacra* 22 (July): 467-512; (October): 568-88.

Traces the shifting names and central doctrines of New England Theology — the nature of virtue, the nature of sin, original sin, natural ability, regeneration, atonement, and decrees — from Edwards through Hopkins to Emmons, in an historical rather than critical estimate of "modified" Calvinism.

4 Grosart, Alexander B. "Introduction." *Selections from the Unpublished Writings of Jonathan Edwards of America*. [Edinburgh]: Printed for Private Circulation, pp. 11-16.

Recounts plans to publish (with Tryon Edwards) a complete Edwards based upon available manuscripts — the project was interrupted by the "deplorable" Civil War — and briefly explains the contents of the texts printed here for the first time. The "Treatise on Grace" ranks with *Religious Affections* in its "rapturous exultation"; "Annotations on Passages of the Bible" is "more richly experimental" than the previously published "Notes on the Bible"; "Directions for Judging of Persons' Experiences" served as a testing-guide during the Awakening; and the eight sermon-notes refute the charge that Edwards read his sermons.

5 Hazard, Rowland G. "Review of Edwards on the Will." *Freedom of Mind in Willing.* New York: D. Appleton and Co.

   Reprints 1864.3.

6 Potwin, L. S. "Freedom of the Will: — Edwards and Whedon." *New Englander* 24 (April): 285-302.

   Reviews Edwards's *Freedom of the Will* and D. D. Whedon's *Freedom of the Will* (1864.5), compares their definitions of will and freedom and their causational and psychological arguments, and concludes that Whedon fails "most strikingly" to overturn Edwards.

7 Thomas, Robert. Preface to *Ymchwiliad Gofalus A Manwl. . . .* [*Freedom of the Will*]. Caernarfon: H. Humphreys, pp.[iii]-xxix.

   Offers a life of Edwards and commentary on *Freedom of the Will.* (In Welsh.)

1866

1 Hazard, Rowland Gibson. "Review of Edwards on the Will." *Freedom of Mind in Willing.* New York: D. Appleton &Co.

   Reprints 1864.3.

2 Whittier, John Greenleaf. "The Preacher." *The Poetical Works of John Greenleaf Whittier.* Boston: Ticknor & Fields, 2:386-97.

   Pictures Edwards forging "the iron links of his argument" in a wilderness church, in a poem about George Whitefield and the Great Awakening.

1867

1 Anon. Review of *The Works of President Edwards. Congregationalist and Boston Recorder,* 28 November, p. 242.

   Reviews a reissue of the 1843 edition of Edwards and calls for the release of some manuscripts preventing a "properly" edited text.

2 Gillett, E[zra] H[all]. "Jonathan Edwards, and the Occasion and Result of his Dismission from Northampton." *Historical Magazine,* 2d ser., 1 (June): 333-38.

   Recounts the problems raised by Edwards's views on qualifications of church membership, the council of ministers met to solve them, and the resulting course of his dismission. *Humble Inquiry* produced a "feeble impression" in Northampton and opposition in most of the neighboring churches; abroad it was thought "decisive" on the question. His dismission a year later brought attention to his views throughout New England, and within fifty years, "one by one," the churches adopted Edwards's scheme.

3 ———. "[Note on] the Clerical Members of the Council that Dismissed Jonathan Edwards from Northampton." *Historical Magazine*, 2d ser., 2 (September): 183.

Confirms an earlier attempt (1867.2) to list the ministers on both sides of the question of Edwards's dismission and asks for further information from readers.

4 Gridley, A. D. "Diary and Letters of Sarah Pierpont." *Hours at Home* 5 (August): 295-303; (September): 417-25.

Presents an "inside view" of the lives of Sarah and Jonathan Edwards through a fictionalized diary and letters, with observations such as this: "What has set my heart into a flutter today? Is it the air, the birds, the flowers, or the sight of tutor Edwards?"

5 Hoyle, Edward. *An Inquiry into the Truth of Christianity, and the Doctrine of Necessity.* London: Austin & Co., pp. 4-5, 14-17, 45-49, 76-82 passim.

Believes Christianity and the doctrine of necessity to be incompatible and cites Edwards's *Freedom of the Will*, early and frequently, as a principal source of the necessarian argument. Edwards's idea of the necessary relation between cause and effect is "false" and his insistence on necessity is at odds with man's responsibility. If divine foreknowledge is true, then man is not a free agent; if man is a free agent, then Christianity is "not true." Christianity is not from God.

1868

1 Beecher, Henry Ward. *Norwood: or, Village Life in New England.* New York: Charles Scribner & Co., p. 326.

Compares Edwards to Dante in remarks on New England theologians.

2 Fisher, George P. "The Augustinian and the Federal Theories of Original Sin Compared." *New Englander* 27 (July): 468-516.

Finds that Edwards "fell back" to the doctrine of original sin of Aquinas and Augustine and that his original speculations — for example, on the "first rising" of sinful inclination — do not "materially" modify those old ideas.

3 G[illett, Ezra Hall]. "[Note on] the General Council that Dismissed Jonathan Edwards from Northampton." *Historical Magazine*, 2d ser., 3 (January): 53.

Notes that ministers of the Council that judged Edwards were "equally divided": Edward Billings, William Hobby, David Hall, Jonathan Hubbard, and Robert Abercombie for Edwards; Joseph Ashley, Chester Williams, Timothy Woodbridge, Robert Breck, and Peter Reynolds for the Church.

4 Halsey, L. J. "Great Preachers and Pastors, or Retrospect of the Presbyterian Pulpit in America for One Hundred and Fifty Years: Jonathan Edwards and George Whitefield." *North-Western Presbyterian*, 16 May, p. 1.

Cites the contemporaneous influence Edwards's published treatises on the will, the affections, and original sin had on the "forming period" of the Presbyterian Church. Though a Calvinist in doctrine and a Congregationalist in practice, Edwards was a "thorough" Presbyterian in polity.

5 Lecky, W[illiam] E. H. *History of the Rise and Influence of the Spirit of Rationalism in Europe.* New York: D. Appleton & Co., 1:368, 387.

Ranks Edwards's *Original Sin* "one of the most revolting books that have ever proceeded from the pen of man."

1869

1 Eggleston, Nathaniel H. *In Memoriam. A Discourse Preached November 1st, 1868, on the Occasion of the Erection of Tablets in the Old Church at Stockbridge, Mass., in Memory of its Former Pastors: John Sergeant, Jonathan Edwards, Stephen West, and David D. Field.* New York: Baker & Godwin, pp. 19-24.

Recounts Edwards's Stockbridge years, the contrast between the man and the place.

2 Lawrence, M. W. "Old-Time Minister and Parish." *Putnam's Monthly Magazine,* n.s., 4 (August): 166-68.

Waxes sentimental about Edwards's birthplace, his father's ministry, and the "rustic bower" of his meditations.

3 Magoun, George F. "President Edwards as a Reformer." *Congregational Quarterly,* n.s., 1 (April): 259-74.

Reviews the life and times of the "saintly" and "Miltonic" Edwards, an "eminent" practical, theological reformer.

4 Stowe, Harriet Beecher. *Oldtown Folks.* Boston: Fields, Osgood, & Co., pp. 229, 363-65, 376-78, 458-59 passim.

Comments briefly and serially upon Edwards's rationalistic methods and suggests that the "average" New Englander combines the materiality of Franklin and the spirituality of Edwards.

5 Tarbox, Increase N. "Jonathan Edwards." *Bibliotheca Sacra* 26 (April): 243-68.

Details the facts of Edwards's early life and concludes that with so little to stimulate his intellectual growth (even at Yale), he was "the best possible refutation of Locke's philosophy, that the mind has 'no innate ideas.'" Central to Edwards's theology is his attempt to give "fuller recognition" to man in a scheme of divine sovereignty. Thus did he turn theology into "new channels and in the right direction."

1870

1 Anon. "Some Notes upon the Late Edwards Meeting." *Congregationalist and Boston Reporter,* 13 October, p. 2.

Relates the social side of the recent Edwards meeting in Stockbridge.

2 B., L. D. "The Edwards Clan." *New York Times,* 5 September, p. 2.

Announces a gathering of the Edwards's clan in Stockbridge on the next two days to "do honor to the memory of their great ancestor," gives the program for "the great event," and offers a brief life, appraisal, and list of descendants.

3 Irenaeus. "Gathering of the Tribe of Jonathan Edwards." *New York Observer,* 15 September, p. 290.

> Summarizes the papers and events of the Edwards gathering at Stockbridge. Mention of Edwards's New York pastorate draws questions and comments from readers on 29 September (p. 309) and 22 December (p. 403).

4 Magoun, George F. "Unpublished Writings of President Edwards." *Congregational Review* 10 (January): 19-27.

> Reviews and quotes from two items — a treatise on grace and "Directions for Judging of Person's Experiences" — in Alexander B. Grosart's Selections (1865.4), finding both cogent.

5 P[ark], E[dwards] A[masa]. "Edwards, Jonathan." In *Cyclopaedia of Biblical, Theological, and Ecclesiastical Literature.* Edited by John McClintock and James Strong. New York: Harper & Brothers, 3:63-67.

> Offers a life of Edwards and an estimate, principally the differing views on the questions of natural or moral inability in *Freedom of the Will* and the question of identity in *Original Sin.* In *True Virtue* and *End of Creation,* "like many of his other essays," Edwards sought "to reconcile reason with faith."

6 T., S. E. "Jonathan Edwards." *New York Times,* 8 September, p. 1.

> Reports the program and the speakers at the Edwards reunion at Stockbridge, including a "large number of outsiders," and discusses biographies, estimates, and portraits of him. A book about the reunion is to be published (1871.5).

7 Tarbox, I[ncrease] N. "Antiquities of Stockbridge." *Congregationalist and Boston Recorder,* 20 October, p. 1.

> Recounts briefly the Edwards family stay in Stockbridge.

8 ———. "The Edwards Meeting." *Congregationalist and Boston Recorder,* 15 September, p. 1.

> Reports the events and papers of the Stockbridge meeting of Edwards's descendants.

9 ———. "The Old East Windsor Burying-Ground." *Congregationalist and Boston Recorder,* 22 September, p. 2.

> Describes the meetinghouse, dwelling, and burial ground of the Edwards family in East Windsor, Connecticut.

1871

A C[handler], P. W. "Jonathan Edwards." *New Jerusalem Magazine* 43 (March): 593-602.

> Faults Edwards for a theological faith based on "intellectual powers alone," in a brief comparison with Emanuel Swedenborg.

1 Eggleston, N[athaniel] H. "A New England Village." *Harper's New Monthly Magazine* 43 (November): 815-29.

Sketches a history of Stockbridge and of Edwards's missionary work among the Mahicans, performed there "almost in secrecy and silence."

2 Fraser, Alexander Campbell, ed. *The Works of George Berkeley, D.D.* Oxford: Clarendon Press, 1:179.

Notes Edwards's affinity to Berkeley's immaterialism and their physical proximity: "when Berkeley was in Rhode Island, Edwards was settled in Massachusetts."

3 Simons, M. Laird. *Sunday Half-hours with the Great Preachers.* Philadelphia: Porter & Coates, p. 266.

Introduces and reprints selections from Edwards's "Wrath upon the Wicked."

4 Wakeley, J. B. *The Prince of Pulpit Orators: A Portraiture of Rev. George Whitefield, M.A., Illustrated by Anecdotes and Incidents.* New York: Carlton & Lanahan, pp. 274-78.

Describes the relationship between Edwards and George Whitefield. Edwards was uncertain of Whitefield's feeling for him; Whitefield "winced" at Edwards's criticism of his attitude toward "impulses." The two men parted amicably though, and Whitefield left with a deep affection for Sarah, mutually shared.

5 [Woodbridge, Jonathan Edwards], ed. *Memorial Volume of the Edwards Family Meeting at Stockbridge, Mass. Sept. 6-7, A.D. 1870.* Boston: Congregational Publishing Society, 206 pp.

Gathers together the more than twenty-five tributes to Edwards delivered during a two-day family meeting in Stockbridge, including a serial life by I. N. Tarbox, E. A. Park, John Todd, Mark Hopkins, and others, and verse lines about his descendants ("While honorables, D.D.'s, and LL.D.'s,/Lie 'mong us like the leaves in autumn breeze") by Sarah Edwards Tyler Henshaw, and about him ("an iceberg on Time's ocean") by Frank D. Clark.

1872

1 Hodge, Charles. *Systematic Theology.* New York: Charles Scribner & Co., 2:217-21.

Objects to Edwards's "strange" doctrine of original sin, for it is contrary to Scripture, intuition, and reason. Edwards agrees with the realists that Adam and man are identical, but he differs from them in denying the numerical sameness of substance.

1873

1 Blaikie, William Garden. *For the Work of the Ministry: A Manual of Homiletical and Pastoral Theology.* London: Strahan & Co., pp. 223, 325-26.

Discovers beneath the calm manner of Edwards's preaching a "deep fountain" of emotion and recommends his *Faithful Narrative* as the single most intelligent view of the "whole subject" of revivals.

2 Stephen, Leslie. "Jonathan Edwards." *Fraser's Magazine,* n.s., 8 (November): 529-51.

Accounts Edwards's effort "to live constantly" under an absolute and infinite God the source of the irreconcilable tensions within him — the "gentle mystic" of *Personal Narrative* as well as the "stern divine" of *Original Sin* — in a study of his life and major work. Edwards's theological system rests upon the "fundamental" doctrine of the light of God imparted to man; his metaphysical system, upon the "existence of absolute a priori truths." His style is "heavy and languid," natural in a "speculative recluse." His theory of morality is "ennobling"; his theory of the universe, "elevated." There is in Edwards "genuine metal," then, "no less unmistakably than the refuse."

1874

1 [Bledsoe, Albert Taylor]. "Foreknowledge and Free Will." *Southern Review* 15 (July): 91-109.
   Reprints Section XI of his *Examination* (1845.2).

2 Dwight, Benjamin W. *The History of the Descendants of John Dwight of Dedham, Mass.* New York: John F. Trow & Son, 2:1037-50.
   Offers a brief biography of Edwards and a genealogy.

3 Porter, Noah. "Jonathan Edwards." In his "Appendix I: Philosophy in Great Britain and America" to *History of Philosophy from Thales to the Present Time*, by Friedrich Ueberweg. New York: Scribner, Armstrong, 2:443-48.
   Examines briefly Edwards on the will, virtue, sin, and affections and notes the published arguments of both his friends and his critics. Edwards's work exerted a "powerful" influence on his successors and "trained" generations of Americans to "pronounced speculative tastes and habits."

4 Stephen, Leslie. "Jonathan Edwards." *Littell's Living Age* 120 (24 January): 219-36.
   Reprints 1873.2.

1875

1 Anon. "Jonathan Edwards." *Presbyterian Monthly Record* 26 (August): 232-35.
   Renders fulsome praise to Edwards the man and the preacher and traces his singular influence on a multitude of theologians here and abroad.

2 Bledsoe, Albert Taylor. "The Relation of the Will to the Feelings." *Southern Review* 17 (April): 435-48.
   Reprints Section VIII of his *Examination* (1845.2).

3 Henderson, T. F. "Edwards, Jonathan." *Encyclopedia Britannica*, 9th ed., 7:688-91.
   Traces Edwards's career and estimates the work of "the most distinguished metaphysician and divine of America." Edwards had the "contradictory qualities" of the mystic and the logician and in his isolation and retrospection was untouched by helpful and modifying influences of his time. His *Freedom of the Will*, a skillful structure, "inevitably collapses" under the weight of irreconcilable principles.

1876

1 Atwater, Lyman H. "The Great Awakening of 1740." *Presbyterian Quarterly and Princeton Review* 5 (October): 676-89.

Derives an account of the Great Awakening from Joseph Tracy (1842.6) and Edwards's *Some Thoughts*.

2 P[ark], E[dwards] A[masa], ed. "Jonathan Edwards' Last Will, and the Inventory of his Estate." *Bibliotheca Sacra* 33 (July): 438-47.

Reprints Edwards's will and inventory from records in the Probate Office at Northampton and finds them illustrative of the style of living of clergymen then.

3 Stephen, Leslie. "Jonathan Edwards." *Hours in a Library,* 2d ser. London: Smith, Elder, & Co. pp. 44-106.

Reprints 1873.2. (Frequently reprinted in this form.)

4 Stewart, J[ames] G. *Freedom of the Will Vindicated; or, President Edwards' Necessarian Theory Refuted.* Glasgow: David Bryce & Son, 75 pp.

Refutes Edwards's arguments on both the self-determining power of the will and the determining power of motives in *Freedom of the Will* and dismisses them as sophistical and unintelligible.

1877

1 Anon. "Studies and Conduct, Second Series, I. Jonathan Edwards — Resolutions for a Holy Life." *American Journal of Education* 27 (October): 721-28.

Recounts a brief life of Edwards, man thinking.

2 Bledsoe, Albert Taylor. "President Edwards' Inquiry into the Freedom of the Will." *Southern Review* 22 (October): 376-404.

Reprints the introduction and Sections I-III of his *Examination* (1845.2).

3 Maclean, John. *History of the College of New Jersey, from its Origin in 1746 to the Commencement of 1854.* Philadelphia: J. B. Lippincott & Co., 1:169-91.

Documents the appointment and administration of Edwards as president of Princeton and offers a standard biography. "Probably no man ever connected with this institution has contributed so much to the reputation of the College, both at home and abroad."

4 Smith, Henry B. *Faith and Philosophy: Discourses and Essays.* Edited by George L. Parentis. New York: Scribner, Armstrong & Co., pp. 149-51, 383-86 passim.

Praises Edwards's work, the center of which is man's relation to divine grace.

5 Thompson, Charles L. *Times of Refreshing: A History of American Revivals from 1740-1877, with their Philosophy and Methods.* Chicago: L. T. Palmer & Co., pp. 37-40.

Singles out Edwards's *Justification by Faith Alone* as a bulwark against the drift into spiritual lethargy in the 1730s and as vital to experimental religion.

1878

1 Anon. "Jonathan Edwards." *Hampshire Gazette,* 30 April, p. 1.
Recounts Edwards's career in Northampton.

2 Bledsoe, Albert Taylor. "President Edwards' Inquiry into the Freedom of the Will."
Southern Review 23 (January): 5-33.
Reprints Sections I-VII of his *Examination* (1845.2).

3 ―――. "President Edwards' Inquiry into the Freedom of the Will." *Southern Review*
23 (April): 338-89.
Reprints Sections VIII-XI of his *Examination* (1845.2).

4 ―――. "President Edwards' Inquiry into the Freedom of the Will." *Southern Review*
24 (July): 64-93.
Reprints Sections XII-XIV of his *Examination* (1845.2).

5 ―――. "President Edwards' Inquiry into the Freedom of the Will." *Southern Review*
24 (October): 344-72.
Reprints Sections XV-XVIII of his *Examination* (1845.2).

6 Northampton, Mass., First Parish. *First Parish, Northampton: Meetinghouses and
Ministers from 1653-1878.* Northampton, Mass.: Gazette Printing Co., pp. 15-17.
Details the salary and land given Edwards during his pastorate in the second meetinghouse.
After Edwards's dismissal in 1750, Judah Champion was offered the church but refused; later
John Hooker accepted and was ordained 5 December 1753.

7 Tyler, Moses Coit. *A History of American Literature.* New York: G. P. Putnam's Sons,
2:177-92.
Traces Edwards's career, quotes mainly from the juvenilia, analyzes the method of *Sinners in
the Hands of an Angry God,* and regrets his calling. Though "unsurpassed" as a dialectician, Edwards could have been "one of the world's masters" in physical science or in imaginative literature, for he had all the virtues of a writer — clear expression, bold imagery, and keen wit.

1879

1 Aldrich, P. Emory. "Report to the Council." *Proceedings of the American Antiquarian
Society* no. 73 (April): 9-39.
Remarks Locke's influence upon Edwards and through him to "every school of theology" in
the country, in a survey of the influence of Locke upon philosophy, politics, and religion in
America.

2 Anon. "Jonathan Edwards." *Hampshire Gazette,* 11 February, p. 1.
Reprints a report from the *Providence Press* of an address to the Historical Society by Abraham Payne on Edwards's career.

3 Eastman, Z. "Jonathan Edwards and About his Elms." *Hampshire Gazette,* 19 August, p. 1.

> Describes Edwards's career in Northampton, his house on King Street, and the elms that still stand before it (by a Chicago correspondent).

4 Fisher, George P. "The Philosophy of Jonathan Edwards." *North American Review* 128 (March): 284-303.

> Examines Edwards's major work, particularly *Freedom of the Will,* and concludes that the "iron network" of his doctrine of necessity is too confining and exclusive to satisfy "the generality of mankind." Edwards borrows the psychology of choice from Locke, but his failure to identify and distinguish voluntary and involuntary inclinations is his own and his philosophy of the will as a whole is "not consonant" with that of most Augustinian theologians. So, too, in *True Virtue,* he obviously knows Francis Hutcheson, but much of the "scientific construction" of theory is original with Edwards and his exchange of moral right and obligation for spiritual beauty is "most questionable."

5 Hageman, John Frelinghuysen. *History of Princeton and its Institutions.* Philadelphia: J. B. Lippincott & Co., 2:249-53.

> Notes Edwards's short stay at Princeton but claims he lent more honor to the College than any president before or since.

6 H[umphreys], Z[ephaniah] M. "Jonathan Edwards." In *Lives of the Leaders of Our Church Universal.* Edited by Ferdinand Piper and translated and edited by Henry Mitchell MacCracken. New York: Phillips & Hunt, pp. 547-57.

> Lauds Edwards's life and work, in superlatives.

7 Huxley, Thomas Henry. *Hume.* English Men of Letters. London: Macmillan & Co., pp. 194-95.

> Finds "curious" Edwards's handling of the authorship of sin in *Freedom of the Will,* an unavailing struggle between the theologian and the logician. But Edwards's orthodox, necessarian argument "has never been equaled in power, and certainly has never been refuted."

1880

1 Anon. "As to Jonathan Edwards." *Congregationalist,* 7 July, p. 4.

> Awaits the publication of Edwards's manuscript on the Trinity but, unlike Holmes (1880.6) and the *Hartford Courant* (1880.2), believes in Edwards's orthodoxy and quotes Egbert Smyth to prove it.

2 Anon. "The Injustice to Jonathan Edwards." *Hartford Courant,* 23 June, p. 2.

> Implores Edwards A. Park (see 1881.2) to publish a "suppressed" Edwards's manuscript on the Trinity so that the matter of his alleged unitarian views might be settled.

3 Chadwick, John W. "In Western Massachusetts." *Harper's Magazine* 61 (November): 873-87.

> Remarks Edwards's affection for his wife-to-be and reprints "Sarah Pierrepont."

4 Fisher, George P. "The Philosophy of Jonathan Edwards." *Discussions in History and Theology.* New York: Charles Scribner's Sons, pp. 227-52.
Reprints 1879.4.

5 ————. "The Religious Spirit of Jonathan Edwards." *Hampshire Gazette,* 25 May, p. 1.
Counters Boston critics of Edwards as a man hard and cold with citations of his kindness from *Personal Narrative* and his ministering to the Indians.

6 Holmes, Oliver Wendell. "Jonathan Edwards." *International Review* 9 (July): 1-28.
Sketches Edwards's life and major work, much of it like "the unleavened bread of the Israelite: holy it may be, but heavy it certainly is." His theological system itself is "barbaric, mechanical, materialistic, pessimistic"; his life's work "neglected" or "repudiated"; his intellect a compendium of "disorganizing conceptions." Edwards had come under the "misguiding influence" of the doctrine of the imputation of Adam's sin to man and the notion that a just God sanctions it. Such absurdities doomed him.

7 Lawrence, Eugene. *A Primer of American Literature.* Harper's Half-Hour Series. New York: Harper & Brothers, pp. 32-39.
Compares Edwards and Benjamin Franklin in a brief biography and notes that Edwards's fame is "once more rising."

8 Pond, Enoch. *Sketches of the Theological History of New England.* Boston: Congregational Publishing Society, pp. 22-48.
Sketches the influence of Edwards and his followers upon "improvements" in theology, especially on the nature and evidence of regeneration. On the will and original sin Edwards still offers the most cogent defense.

9 Sargent, Mrs. John T., ed. *Sketches and Reminiscences of the Radical Club of Chestnut Street, Boston.* Boston: James R. Osgood & Co., pp. 362-75.
Records the reactions of several members of the Radical Club in Boston to Oliver Wendell Holmes's "brilliant" essay on Edwards (reprinted). Wendell Phillips complains that the portrait is incomplete, that there are other sides to Edwards; James Freeman Clarke praises Edwards as a "Protestant saint" and suggests that "a little healthy Concord mysticism" such as Edwards's is not a bad thing for New England.

10 Smyth, Egbert C. "Introduction." *Observations concerning the Scripture Oeconomy of the Trinity and Covenant of Redemption.* New York: Charles Scribner's Sons, pp. [3]-18.
Attests to Edwards's "not unorthodox" trinitarian views and to the genuineness of the manuscript, reprinted here after considerable debate about its suppression and alleged heterodoxy. The text is the "Miscellanies" no. 1062, a late, "elaborately reasoned" piece, in which Edwards emphasizes, as do Puritans generally, the divine covenant or social aspect of the Trinity. Though the paper is hardly a treatise on the Trinity, it anticipates modern Christology and indicates Edwards's "peculiar genius."

1881

1 Fraser, A[lexander] Campbell. *Berkeley.* Philadelphia: J. B. Lippincott & Co., pp. 138-41.

Claims Edwards "adopted" Berkeley's ideas, though he may not have read him. On the spiritual substance of the universe, their views "coincide"; on causation, they "fundamentally differ."

2 Park, Edwards A. "Remarks of Jonathan Edwards on the Trinity." *Bibliotheca Sacra* 38 (January): 147-87; (April): 333-69.

Introduces and reprints, from Alexander B. Grosart's *Unpublished Writings* (1865.4), Edwards on the Trinity to answer current (and unfounded) charges of heterodoxy. Even though Edwards's language here is "approximate rather than complete, analogical rather than exact, initiatory rather than plenary, rudimental rather than perfected," it is clear that he believes in the "special mysteriousness" of the Trinity. Nowhere in his 500 manuscripts can be found a sentence expressing "any doubt" about that doctrine, though he will at times give more prominence to the simplicity than the triplicity of the divine mind.

3 ———. *Remarks of Jonathan Edwards on the Trinity.* Andover, Mass.: W. F. Draper.

Reprints 1881.2.

4 Phelps, Austin. *The Theory of Preaching: Lectures on Homiletics.* New York: Charles Scribner's Sons, pp. 560, 587-88.

Notes the incongruity in Edwards's preaching between his "subdued" delivery and his vehement words.

1882

1 Boardman Geo[rge] Nye. *The Will and Virtue: Two Essays.* Chicago: F. H. Revell, pp. 58-59, 120-25.

Treats briefly Edwards's "triumphant refutation" of self-determinism in *Freedom of the Will* and his "unwarranted distinction" between justice and holiness and his degradation of conscience in *True Virtue.*

2 Clark, Solomon. *Antiquities, Historicals and Graduates of Northampton.* Northampton, Mass.: Gazette Printing Co., p. 263.

Notes that Northampton is known for Edwards and the number of women marrying ministers.

3 Nichol, John. *American Literature: An Historical Sketch, 1620-1880.* Edinburgh: A. & C. Black, pp. 52-55.

Presents Edwards as a example not only of dated, grim Calvinism but also of "pure Colonial Puritan prose."

1883

1 [Foster, W. E.] "The Speculative Philosophy of Jonathan Edwards." *Monthly Reference Lists* 3 (December): 42.

   Lists books and parts of books about Edwards's philosophy and quotes briefly from them as a short annotated bibliography.

2 Hazard, Rowland G. *Man a Creative First Cause: Two Discourses.* Boston: Houghton Mifflin & Co., pp. 16-18.

   Deplores Edwards's "defective definitions" of will and freedom, in which choice and preference, to will and to choose are "identical." Based on that assumption, Edwards "logically infers that we are not free in willing."

3 Holmes, Oliver Wendell. "Jonathan Edwards." *Pages from an Old Volume of Life.* Boston: Houghton Mifflin & Co., pp. 361-401.

   Reprints 1880.6.

4 ———. "The Pulpit and the Pew." *Pages from an Old Volume of Life.* Boston: Houghton Mifflin Co., pp. 402-33.

   Questions whether Edwards's suppressed manuscript on the Trinity has in fact been published, believing it to be more extensive than Egbert Smyth's text (1880.10) and hoping that it will be recovered to prove that Edwards was capable of heresy or "writing most unwisely" and to reduce the "validity of his judgment" on matters like infant damnation.

5 Phelps, Austin. *English Style in Public Discourse with Special Reference to the Usages of the Pulpit.* New York: Charles Scribner's Sons, pp. 31-32.

   Calls the meaning Edwards gives to the word *necessity* in *Freedom of the Will* a "pure invention," neither English nor popular.

6 Sanborn, F. B. "The Puritanic Philosophy and Jonathan Edwards." *Journal of Speculative Philosophy* 17 (October): 401-21.

   Characterizes Edwards as "the most acute and inflexible" of American Puritans, the "clearest manifestation" of a derivative philosophy that, happily, yields to democracy and to the philanthropists like Benjamin Franklin. Edwards's "noble error" was to approach philosophy from received theology and to attempt speculative thought ignorant, for the most part, of Plato and Aristotle, the Schoolmen and Catholic theologians since Augustine. Although he shows an uncommon "subtlety of mind" and an awareness of the intellectual currents of his time, Edwards remains "our Puritan Schoolman, our Father Jonathan of Connecticut."

7 Stoughton, John A. *"Windsor Farmes": A Glimpse of an Old Parish.* Hartford: Clark & Smith, pp. 76-85.

   Recaptures the life of Edwards at Windsor Farms, from his boyhood to his rejection of the Bolton calling, and concludes with an encomium to a "brilliant light."

1884

1 George, E. A. "Jonathan Edwards." *Yale Literary Magazine* 50 (October): 7-11.

Studies Edwards's life and catches the two-fold nature of his character — his gentleness and his sternness — in his effeminate face and virile mind.

1A Hunnicutt, William Littleton Clark. "Freedom Human and Divine." *Quarterly Review of the Methodist Episcopal Church, South,* n.s., 6 (October): 702-12.

Calls Edwards's argument from cause in *Freedom of the Will* "a remarkable instance" of begging the question, in a study of God's freedom and man's.

2 Iverach, James. "Jonathan Edwards." In *The Evangelical Succession: A Course of Lectures Delivered in Free St. George's Church, Edinburgh, 1883-84.* Third Series. Edinburgh: MacNiven & Wallace, pp. 109-43.

Argues the "unspeakable importance" of *True Grace* for the "right apprehension" of Edwards's ideas; interprets his major works through his "ruling idea" of the sovereign grace of God; and places him, the equal of William Ames and John Owen, in the evangelical succession. So Edwards explores the problem of man without grace in *Original Sin;* the relationship between divine sovereign grace and man in *Freedom of the Will;* the behavior of those who have grace in *Religious Affections;* the outcome of grace in *True Virtue;* the action of grace in human history in *History of Redemption;* and the "supreme justification of the ways of God to man" in the *End of Creation.* Still some difficulties remain. For instance, in *Freedom of the Will* his abstractness renders "meaningless" the "concrete realities" of life; his determinism contradicts his doctrine of continuing creation; his philosophical disposition "unfortunately" cannot answer the "great question" of divine sovereignty and human agency. For all that, Edwards never fails to raise important questions about any topic he treats, to set "old doctrines in new light," to offer "fresh" points of view.

3 Sherwood, J. M. "Preface to the Present Edition." *Memoirs of Rev. David Brainerd, Missionary to the Indians of North America, Based on the Life of Brainerd Prepared by Jonathan Edwards, D.D., and Afterwards Revised and Enlarged by Sereno E. Dwight, D.D.* New York: Funk & Wagnalls Co., pp. xxv-xxvi.

Attributes Edwards's mission to the Stockbridge Mahicans to Brainerd's influence and a world-wide missionary zeal to the reading of Edwards's *Life of Brainerd.*

4 Tarbox, I[ncrease] N. "Jonathan Edwards as a Man; and the Ministers of the Last Century." *New Englander,* n.s., 7 (September): 615-31.

Recounts the career of the "superlative" Edwards as an illustration of the life of the minister in eighteenth-century New England.

5 Walker, George Leon. "Jonathan Edwards and the Half-way Covenant." *New Englander* 43 (September): 601-14.

Traces the history of the half-way covenant from Massachusetts Bay to the Connecticut Valley and the place it had in Edwards's dismission. Stoddard's church was "fully leavened" with his view of the Lord's Supper as a converting ordinance; his grandson, replacing him, seems to have accepted it "without hesitation." But in time "scruples" arose in his mind, and by 1749 he published *Humble Inquiry,* "a masterpiece of virile, subtle, comprehensive argument." It is clear that Edwards had "already before his dismission broken with the whole half-way covenant system, and not simply with the Stoddardean development of it."

1885

1 Briggs, Charles Augustus. *American Presbyterianism; Its Origin and Early History.* New York: Charles Scribner's Sons, pp. 259-61.

Defines Edwards as the "real" theologian of Methodism, though he influenced nineteenth-century Presbyterianism and Congregationalism in Scotland, England, and America as well.

2 Dexter, Franklin Bowditch. *Biographical Sketches of the Graduates of Yale College with Annals of the College History October, 1701-May, 1745.* New York: Henry Holt & Co., pp. 218-26.

Sketches Edwards's life at Yale, "the most eminent graduate of the College, the greatest theologian of his century, the ablest metaphysician of the period between Leibniz and Kant." Edwards earned "the highest rank" in his graduating class, continued two more years in theology, was tutor from 21 May 1721 to September 1726, and, "owing to the vacancy in the Rectorship for the whole of this period, his position was one of special responsibility."

3 Porter, Noah. *The Two-Hundredth Birthday of Bishop George Berkeley.* New York: Charles Scribner's Sons, pp. 71-72.

Insists that Edwards had not read Berkeley before writing "The Mind."

1886

1 Foster, Frank Hugh. "The Eschatology of the New England Divines." *Bibliotheca Sacra* 43 (January): 1-32.

Explains Edward's views on the punishment of sin and his contribution to the development of the eschatological doctrines of his followers, notably his son and Joseph Bellamy. As a matter of practical experience, Edwards held to the reality of eternal punishment because of an "extreme sensitiveness of his soul to sin, and his profound conviction of the utter inexcusableness and vileness of the sinner." Such punishment was, therefore, proportional (infinite offense to an infinite God merits infinite punishment), proper (a perfect God demands proper punishment), and suitable (God hates sin and expresses it eternally). As in so many other instances of doctrine, the sovereignty of God was "sufficient explanation" for Edwards.

2 Richardson, Charles F. *American Literature, 1607-1885.* New York: G. P. Putnam's Sons, 1:139-46.

Thinks that Edwards, as the "mouthpiece" of New England Calvinism, is superior in style, breadth, and value to Cotton Mather. His *Freedom of the Will* tries, unsuccessfully, to solve the problem of man's free will and God's foreknowledge and bears little upon practical life. Yet in his "Mechanism in Thought and Morals" that staunch anti-Calvinist Oliver Wendell Holmes "sometimes seems to join hands" with Edwards.

3 Strong, Augustus Hopkins. *Systematic Theology: A Compendium and Commonplace Book Designed for the Use of Theological Studies.* Rochester, N.Y.: E. R. Andrews, pp. 26, 287, 588 passim.

Extols Edwards as the "holiest man of his time" in an elaborate text of quotations by and about him and his theology.

1887

1 Bascom, John. "Books that have Helped Me." *Forum* 3 (May): 263-72.
   Cites *Freedom of the Will* as the "best thing" in his library as a youth, though not a trace of Edwards remains in him now.

2 Beers, Henry A. *An Outline Sketch of American Literature.* New York: Chautauqua Press, pp. 41-44.
   Finds art and intensity in Edwards — though he writes theology, not literature — in a style simple and direct and contrasts him to Franklin.

3 Fisher, George Park. *History of the Christian Church.* New York: Charles Scribner's Sons, pp. 524-27, 611-12, 650-51.
   Notes that Edwards "mingled" logic and mysticism in a piety "profound and sincere," founded New England Theology, and was "cordial" to the Great Awakening.

4 Holmes, Oliver Wendell. "Poem." In *A Record of the Commemoration, November Fifth to Eighth, 1886, on the Two Hundred and Fiftieth Anniversary of the Founding of Harvard College.* Cambridge: John Wilson & Son, pp. 237-49.
   Proclaims that "Harvard's beacon" will shed its reflected light upon Princeton, "Where mighty Edwards stamped his iron heel," in a poem celebrating Harvard's 250th anniversary.

5 Minto, William. *A Manual of English Prose Literature.* Boston: Ginn & Co., p. 434.
   Relates Edwards's limited appeal to his "dry" style.

1888

1 C., S. "Jonathan Edwards." *Hampshire Gazette*, 2 October, p. 3.
   Finds no evidence that Edwards ever said, "Heaven is being paved with infants' skulls," and demands an end to such slander.

2 Lyon, Georges. "L'Immatérialisme en Amérique — Jonathan Edwards." *L'Idéalisme en Angleterre au XVIIIe-Siecle.* Paris: Ancienne Librairie Germer Baillière et Cie, pp. 406-39.
   Compares Edwards's idealism with that of Malebranche and Berkeley — made available to Edwards by his Yale tutor, Samuel Johnson — and finds striking similarities, in a short life and longer examination of "The Mind." (In French.)

3 Shedd, William G. T. *Dogmatic Theology.* New York: Charles Scribner's Sons, 2: 203-209.
   Explains that Edwards's argument of identity in *Original Sin* extends the notion of inclination in *Freedom of the Will* to man's sinful disposition and guilt.

4 Strong, Augustus H[opkins]. "The New Theology." *Baptist Quarterly Review* 10 (January): 1-29.
   Characterizes Edwards's doctrine of the imputation of original sin as idealist, not traducian, for the unity of Adam and posterity was constituted by the idea and will of God, not by historical

descent. Edwards's "radical" error lies in his denial of substance, and his doctrine of continuous creation leaves man without freedom, guilt, or responsibility. There is no need for the New Theology, for "the old is better."

5 ————. "The New Theology." *Philosophy and Religion.* New York: A. C. Armstrong & Son, pp. 164-79.
Reprints 1888.4.

1889

1 Allen, Alexander V. G. *Jonathan Edwards.* American Religious Leaders. Boston: Houghton Mifflin & Co., xi, 401 pp.
Examines Edwards, the "father of modern Congregationalism" and the "greatest preacher of his age," as parish minister, revivalist, and philosophical theologian in a full-length study, "not ... devoid of sympathy" yet concluding, "The great wrong which Edwards did, which haunts us as an evil dream throughout his writings, was to assert God at the expense of humanity." Thus the speculative thought of his last phase — *Freedom of the Will, Original Sin, True Virtue,* and *End of Creation* — ends "in confusion, if not failure," and his work on the Trinity, however modern it seems is "weakened, if not neutralized," by his tenets of original sin and predestination and by his lack of interest in the humanity of Christ. The whole of Edwards suffers from the limits of his "solitary life" and occasions a style akin to "thinking aloud," a prose inelegant and difficult to interpret. The one "imperishable element" of this mystic and rationalist, when the "false premises" and "negative side" of his theology are discarded, is his deep-seated God-consciousness, the reality and revelation of the divine existence.

2 ————. *Life and Writings of Jonathan Edwards.* Edinburgh: T. & T. Clark.
Reprints 1889.1.

3 Anon. "Jonathan Edwards." *The Nation* 49 (October 17): 314-15.
Faults Alexander V. G. Allen's study (1889.1) for being "too apologetic" and not critical enough of Edwards.

4 Byington, E[zra] H[oyt]. "Rev. Robert Breck Controversy." *Papers and Proceedings of the Connecticut Valley Historical Society* 2 (February): 1-19.
Remarks Edwards's role in the Breck affair.

5 C., S. "Have the Teachings of Jonathan Edwards Ceased to Exert an Influence on Religious Sentiment?" *Hampshire Gazette,* 12 February, p. 3.
Claims Edwards's teachings still live and will continue to.

6 ————. "Jonathan Edwards, Senior, and Jonathan, Jr. — Resemblances." *Hampshire Gazette,* 16 April, p. 3.
Parallels the careers of Edwards and his son.

7 Hazard, Rowland G. "Review of Edwards on the Will." *Freedom of Mind in Willing.* Boston: Houghton Mifflin & Co.
Reprints 1864.3.

8 Lathe, H. W. "Historical Discourse: At the Rededication of the Fifth Meeting House of the First Church of Christ, Northampton, Mass., Nov. 24, 1889." *Hampshire Gazette*, 26 November, p. 2.

Recounts Edwards's career at Northampton.

9 McCook, Henry C. *American Spiders and Their Spinningwork*. Philadelphia: Henry C. McCook, 1:68-69; 2:280-82.

Acknowledges that Edwards anticipated his original findings about spider webs by 160 years and Pierre Latreille's foundation principle of the classification of spiders by a century.

10 Martineau, James. *A Study of Religion*. Oxford: Clarendon Press, 2:260-62.

Observes that while Scripture supports Edwards's view of determinism in human actions, reason does not, in a brief examination of Edwards on divine prescience.

11 Melden, C. M. "Jonathan Edwards." *Hampshire Gazette*, 27 August, p. 7; 10 September, p. 6.

Traces Edwards's career in Northampton, focussing on "two notable events," the revivals and his dismissal, and concluding that he is now "little more than a memory."

12 Richards, C. A. L. "An American Religious Leader." *Dial* 10 (November): 166-67.

Reviews Alexander V. G. Allen's *Jonathan Edwards* (1889.1) and finds it unexpectedly balanced.

13 White, L. "Edwards on the Will." *Methodist Review* 71 (January): 9-25.

Examines Edwards's *Freedom of the Will* with an eye to proving anew the Arminian faith in the freedom of moral agency and its rejection of theistic necessity. Edwards was "right" in treating the question of freedom theologically, noting the "plausible advantages" of necessity, claiming for God perfect providence, refusing the self-determination of the will, restricting freedom to doing, and insisting on man's dependence. But all this does not justify Edwards's conclusions that deny man responsibility.

1890

1 Allen, Alexander V. G. *Jonathan Edwards*. American Religious Leaders. Boston: Houghton Mifflin & Co.

Reprints 1889.1.

2 Anon. "Jonathan Edwards." *The Spectator* 64 (January 11): 58-59.

Reviews Alexander V. G. Allen's *Jonathan Edwards* (1889.1) and finds the author, at odds with Edwards's views, often dominating the theological argument.

2A Anon. Review of *Jonathan Edwards*, by Alexander V. G. Allen. *Methodist Review* 72 (January): 162-63.

Appreciates Alexander V. G. Allen's "well-done" study (1889.1), though Edwards's thought is "mistaken" and his theology "a thing of the past."

3 Crooker, Joseph H. "Jonathan Edwards: A Psychological Study." *New England Magazine,* n.s., 2 (April): 159-72.

   Examines Edwards psychologically and diagnoses him a "theological monomaniac" afflicted with a species of "delusional insanity," inherited from his grandmother and nurtured by his "rigid and arbitrary" father, resulting in an irrational dogma of divine sovereignty. *Personal Narrative* shows "incipient" symptoms of the disorder — he should have engaged in "healthy" sports and thoughts — and his later work, except for the "uncorrupted" *True Virtue,* bears little connection with reality. All in all, Edwards contributed "absolutely nothing" to the understanding of man in history, nature, or society.

4 Fisher, George P. "The Philosophy of Jonathan Edwards." *Discussions in History and Theology.* New York: Charles Scribner's Sons.

   Reprints 1874.4.

5 ———. Review of *Jonathan Edwards,* by Alexander V. G. Allen. *New Englander and Yale Review* 52 (January): 85-88.

   Questions the view that Edwards was inconsistent on divine sovereignty, in a review of Alexander V. G. Allen's study (1889.1).

6 McCook, Henry C. "Jonathan Edwards as a Naturalist." *Presbyterian and Reformed Review* 1 (July): 393-402.

   Examines, as an arachnologist, Edwards's paper on flying spiders to compare it to recent investigations, to test its scientific value, and to rank its priority. Although Edwards made some expected mistakes — matters more of speculation than of observation — he showed "brilliance" as a young naturalist.

7 Palfrey, John Gorham. *History of New England.* Boston: Little, Brown & Co., 5:5-7.

   Characterizes as "unimpassioned obstinacy" Edwards's pursuit of the doctrines of justification by faith and the sovereignty of God that led to the revival of 1734 and quotes from *Faithful Narrative.*

8 Smyth, Egbert C. "The Flying Spider — Observations by Jonathan Edwards When a Boy." *Andover Review* 13 (January): 1-19.

   Dates the observations recorded in "Of Insects," by external allusions and internal evidence, to a time "not later than the summer and early autumn of 1715," and reprints the text and the "apologetic epistle" Edwards wrote to his father's English correspondent.

9 ———. "Professor Allen's 'Jonathan Edwards.' With Extracts from Copies of Unpublished Manuscripts." *Andover Review* 13 (March): 285-304.

   Uses the occasion of a review of Alexander V. G. Allen's "stimulating and fascinating" study (1889.1) to reprint *Miscellaneous Observations* in order to examine and clarify Allen's "inner connections" of Edwards's thought.

10 Stearns, Lewis French. *The Evidence of Christian Experience.* New York: Charles Scribner's Sons, pp. 84-87 passim.

   Calls it an "evil day" for theology when Edwards sought to bolster the doctrine of grace with the doctrine of determinism, when he compromised the Christian experience of *Religious Affections* and the moral inability of *Freedom of the Will.*

11 Weeden, William B. *Economic and Social History of New England, 1620-1789.* Boston: Houghton Mifflin & Co., 2:700-706.

Compares Edwards and Benjamin Franklin as contributors to the social and political development of eighteenth-century America. Though Edwards was hardly political, his pulpit affected the politics of the next generation: men who were ruled by an absolute divine sovereign were unlikely "to submit kindly" to a temporal viceregent.

12 Wellman, J. W. "A New Biography of Jonathan Edwards." *Our Day* 5 (March): 195-219; (April): 288-307.

Berates Alexander V. G. Allen's study (1889.1) as the work of a scholar whose "nondescript" pantheism is "violently and even bitterly" opposed to Edwards's theology. This new biography, filled as it is with misstatements and misrepresentations, "should never have been written."

1891

1 Allen, Alexander V. G. *Jonathan Edwards.* American Religious Leaders. Boston: Houghton Mifflin & Co.

Reprints 1889.1.

2 Clark, Solomon. *Historical Catalogue of the Northampton First Church, 1661-1891.* Northampton, Mass.: Gazette Printing Co., pp. 40-67.

Lists church members and notes that Edwards's pastorate was "attended with uncommon success," though few conversions occurred when the Church "went into a dark cloud" at the end of his stay.

2A Girardeau, John L. *The Will in its Theological Relations.* Columbia, S.C.: W. J. Duffie, pp. 92-122 passim.

Asserts that determinism can be neither "adjusted" to Calvinism theologically nor answer the "grand inquiry" of man's present moral condition philosophically, regardless of what Edwards, the "mighty master of metaphysical argumentation," proposes to the contrary, in a examination of *Freedom of the Will* and *Original Sin*.

3 Holmes, Oliver Wendell. *Over the Teacups.* Boston: Houghton Mifflin & Co., pp. 249-50.

Imagines a nursery scene with Edwards, Sarah, and their three-year-old to suggest her tempering effect upon his stubborn doctrine of infant damnation and the possibility of "moral parricide."

1892

1 Hazard, Rowland G. "Review of Edwards on the Will." *Freedom of Mind in Willing.* Boston: Houghton Mifflin & Co.

Reprints 1864.3.

2 Stiles, Henry R. *The History and Genealogies of Ancient Windsor, Connecticut.* Hartford: Case, Lockwood & Brainard Co., 2:195-98.

Recounts Edwards's life and suggests the cause of his dismissal lay in his opposition to bundling.

3 Thomas, Reuen. *Leaders of Thought in the Modern Church.* Boston: D. Lathrop Co., pp. 7-24.

Charts the life of Edwards and claims that he "retired from his post" to the mission at Stockbridge rather than "tolerate" the obscene books discovered among the young at Northampton.

4 Tupper, Kerr B. "Jonathan Edwards." *Seven Great Lights.* Cincinnati: Cranston & Curtis, pp. 117-39.

Examines the life and times of Edwards, in effusion and in comparison to Mozart and Homer, among others.

5 Walker, Williston. "The Half-Way Covenant." *New Englander and Yale Review* 56 (February): 93-117.

Notes that Edwards's opposition to Stoddardeanism and the half-way covenant ultimately prevailed in New England, in a history of the doctrine from its beginning.

6 Wendell, Barrett. "Some Neglected Characteristics of the New England Puritans." In *Annual Report of the American Historical Association for the Year 1891.* Washington: Government Printing Office, pp. 245-53.

Notes that in Edwards's attempt to revive orthodoxy, American Puritan theology reached its "highest point."

1893

1 Davidson, J[ohn] N[elson]. *Muh-he-ka-ne-ok: A History of the Stockbridge Nation.* Milwaukee, Wisc.: S. Chapman, pp. 12-14.

Recalls Edwards's political and theological years at Stockbridge among the Mahicans. "Though he made their language the subject of a treatise, he never learned to preach in it."

2 Turpie, David. *Jonathan Edwards: An Address Delivered at Kenyon College, June 29, 1893.* Columbus, Ohio: Nitschke Brothers, 31 pp.

Points to Edwards's career as an historical exemplar and praises his work for its candor, good faith, and justice. Although the harsh doctrine of election no longer obtains in the form he gave it, it can be found in the theory of evolution and its "survival of the fittest."

3 Underwood, Francis H. *The Builders of American Literature: Biographical Sketches of American Authors Born Previous to 1826.* First Series. Boston: Lee & Shepard, pp. 40-44.

Recounts Edwards's career and considers his prose to be logical, idiomatic, and bald, marked by a "beautiful simplicity beyond the reach of art."

4 Walker, Williston. *The Creeds and Platforms of Congregationalism.* New York: Charles Scribner's Sons, pp. 283-85.

Remarks Edwards's opposition to Stoddardeanism and the half-way covenant in a "subsidiary" paragraph in his *Humble Inquiry*. To Edwards, the corporate experience of the half-way covenant is at odds with his emphasis on individual experience.

5 ———. *Three Phases of New England Congregational Development*. Hartford Seminary Publications, 28. Hartford: Hartford Seminary Press, pp. 12-14.
  Places Edwards in the second phase of New England Congregational development, the Great Awakening. Edwards marked a shift from discussions of polity to ones of doctrine and, hence, to divisions within the church.

1894

1 Bascom, John. "Jonathan Edwards." *Collections of the Berkshire Historical and Scientific Society* 2, Part 1: 1-25.
  Recounts Edwards's career, especially in Stockbridge, and hopes that his theology will perish with his time and his character will remain forever. Edwards suffered a "total misapprehension" of the nature of man.

2 Dunning, Albert E. *Congregationalists in America*. Boston and Chicago: Pilgrim Press, pp. 235-41, 261-64.
  Cites Edwards's "brilliant logic and fervent appeals" as vital and singular instruments in the Great Awakening, the results of which have been profound and extensive. Edwards "determined" the course of religious life and thought in New England, challenging the half-way covenant and separating church from state. Though he favored Presbyterian polity after his dismission, in fairness he remains "the father of modern Congregationalism."

3 [Kneeland, Frederick Newton]. *Northampton, the Meadow City*. Northampton, Mass.: F. N. Kneeland & L. P. Bryant, pp. 29-34.
  Prints pictures of the Edwards houses and memorials in Northampton with facts and observations of his life there.

4 Lowell, James Russell. Letter to Leslie Stephen, 15 May 1876. In *Letters of James Russell Lowell*. Edited by Charles Eliot Norton. New York: Harper & Brothers, 2: 165.
  Acknowledges "a great sympathy" with Edwards, except in his notion of a physical hell, on the occasion of the publication of *Hours in a Library* (1876.3).

5 Walker, Williston. *A History of the Congregational Churches in the United States*. American Church History Series, no. 3. New York: Christian Literature Co., pp. 253-59, 280-86 passim.
  Considers Edwards "the greatest theologian" of American Congregationalism, the founder of New England Theology, "the only original contribution of importance given by America to the development of Christian theology." Edwards championed Calvinism, not out of devotion to tradition but out of a religious experience, like Calvin's, rooted in divine sovereignty. But Edwards generally "modified" Calvinism by stressing man's responsibility and by fostering emotion and a "sense of immediate communion" between God and man. In particular, he emphasized four positions "essentially a departure" from historic Calvinism: that man had natural ability to do the will of God; that virtue consisted of disinterested benevolence; that both salva-

tion and damnation arise from a single, wise benevolence to the whole universe; and that the identity and unity of an individual is an effect of the constantly creative activity of God.

1895

1 Anon. "Art Treasures in Connecticut." *New York Times*, 14 January, p. 17.
Gives an account of the Edwards family and reprints a letter, 10 May 1716, from Jonathan to his sister Mary, whose embroidered apron "of great beauty" remains one of the handiwork "treasures" of the Connecticut Historical Society.

2 Beers, Henry A. *Initial Studies in American Literature.* Cleveland: Chautauqua Press, pp. 84-86.
Recasts 1887.2.

3 Gordon, George A. Preface to his *The Christ of Today.* Boston: Houghton Mifflin & Co., pp. v-viii.
Seeks a return to Edwards's "original principle" of the absolute sovereignty of God — the only insurance of continuity and progress in American Christianity — by following a theological tradition which "dates" from him.

4 L., C. B. A. "Genealogy of a Famous Family." *New York Times*, 27 January, p. 28.
Corrects some "surprising statements" about the Edwards family which appeared in an article on New Haven treasures in the *Times* two weeks earlier (1895.1). Sarah Pierrepont was not Jonathan Edwards's mother.

5 Oldmixon, Felix [pseud.]. "Old Colonial Characters: I. Jonathan Edwards." *Connecticut Quarterly* 1 (1): 33-38.
Traces the ancestors of Edwards and his grandson, Aaron Burr, in order to discover what "strain of blood" could account for such different men. Insanity, checked in Edwards by a strong will, spirit, and mind, crops up again in his "profligate, vicious and licentious" son, Pierpont, and his grandson, Aaron.

6 ———. "Old Colonial Characters: II. Edwards and Burr." *Connecticut Quarterly* 1 (2): 155-59.
Continues the Edwards genealogy (1895.5) and presents a brief life of America's greatest theologian, "at least of the last century."

7 Rankin, J[eremiah] E[ames]. "The Jonathan Edwards Letters." *Independent* 47 (28 November): 1603.
Offers corrections to some of his earlier notes to Edwards's letters (1895.8), principally that Harry is "not a horse, but a man, a slave."

8 ———. "New Memorials of President Edwards." *Independent* 47 (22 August): 1121.
Reprints an unpublished letter from Edwards to his daughter Esther, 20 November 1757, which offers a rare glimpse of his "tender and graceful domestic character."

9 ———. "The Second Letter of President Edwards." *Independent* 47 (5 September): 1185.

> Reprints Edwards's letter to his son-in-law, Aaron Burr, 14 March 1756, on the birth of his son Aaron, "who was to make the name of Burr so sadly infamous." This letter is "not so vivacious" as another already published (1895.8).

10 Smythe Egbert C. "Some Early Writings of Jonathan Edwards. A.D. 1714-1726." *Proceedings of the American Antiquarian Society,* n.s., 10 (October): 212-47.

> Recovers and reprints some early writings from the Edwards manuscripts — "The Soul," "Of the Rainbow," "Of Being," and "Colors" — and, through an analysis of the paper, ink, spelling, punctuation, and style, attempts to date and place them in his intellectual development as idealist and determinist.

11 Watts, Isaac. "Letters of Dr. Watts." *Proceedings of the Massachusetts Historical Society,* 2d ser., 9 (February): 331-410.

> Reprints letters from Isaac Watts to Benjamin Colman concerning the London publication of Edwards's *Faithful Narrative,* 28 February 1736/37; 2 April 1737; 3 October 1737; 31 May 1738; 7 June 1738; and 22 September 1738. See 1938.3 for a continuous narrative of their exchange and that of Edwards.

1896

1 Allen, Alexander V. G. *Jonathan Edwards.* American Religious Leaders. Boston: Houghton Mifflin & Co.

> Reprints 1889.1.

2 Byington, Ezra Hoyt. "The Case of Rev. Robert Breck." *Andover Review* 13 (May): 517-33.

> Claims Edwards's work in the revivals of 1734-35 in Northampton kept him from entering "very fully" into the Robert Breck affair, though he signed the ministerial petition opposing his settlement in Springfield.

3 Curtis, Mattoon Monroe. "An Outline of Philosophy in America." *Western Reserve University Bulletin* 2 (March): 3-18.

> Surveys Edwards's career to find his "objectification" of Calvinism and the stimulation he gave to intellectual life in America historically significant.

4 Faibairn, A. M. "Prophets of the Christian Faith, VIII — Jonathan Edwards." *Outlook* 53 (23 May): 930-32.

> Characterizes Edwards not only as America's "greatest" thinker but also as "the highest speculative genius" of the century, whose remarkable achievements, carried out in intellectual isolation from European culture and literary elegance, speak to us "in a strange tongue." Edwards is a "monotheistic idealist," combining intense spirituality and intense rationality with Locke's "imperfect" psychology. So in *Freedom of the Will,* Edwards advocates an "alien" doctrine and abandons his own philosophy, returning to the "exhausted charms" of Locke's empiricism.

5 ———. "Jonathan Edwards." In *The Prophets of the Christian Faith,* by the Rev. Lyman Abbott et al. New York: Macmillan Co., pp. 145-66.
Reprints 1896.4.

6 F[ield], H[enry] M. "'Plain Living and High Thinking.'" *The Evangelist* 68 (21 May): 10-11.
Cites terms of Edwards's settlement in Stockbridge where he wrote books "immortal" in American history: thirty-five dollars a year and a hundred sleigh loads of firewood. "Plain living and high thinking indeed!"

7 ———. "Plain Living and High Thinking." *New York Times,* 8 June, p. 5.
Reprints 1896.6.

8 Fisher, George Park. *History of Christian Doctrine.* International Theology Library. New York: Charles Scribner's Sons, pp. 395-410.
Examines Edwards's major works in a historical survey of great theologians and metaphysicians. His "rare mingling" of intellect and insight, logic and mysticism resemble Augustine, Anselm, and Aquinas.

9 Halliday, S[amuel] B[ryam], and D[aniel] S[eely] Gregory. *The Church in America and its Baptism of Fire.* New York: Funk & Wagnalls, pp. 9-15.
Finds the source of the Great Awakening to be Edwards's series of sermons on the justification of faith. His writings guided the course of this remarkable religious movement and tempered its excesses.

10 Matthews, Brander. *An Introduction to the Study of American Literature.* New York: American Book Co., pp. 18-20.
Recounts a short biography of Edwards, compares him to Franklin, and concludes that Franklin was the "more important" of the two.

11 Perry, Arthur Latham. "Jonathan Edwards and Ephraim Williams." *Origins in Williamstown.* Second Edition. New York: Charles Scribner's Sons, pp. 633-41.
Details the history of doctrinal and political contention between Edwards and the Williams family, especially the Ephraim Williamses, father and son, in both Northampton and Stockbridge. In a letter to Jonathan Ashley, 2 May 1751 (reprinted), the younger Williams, founder of Williams College, remarks, "'I am sorry that a head so full of Divinity should be so empty of Politics,'" and then lists his objections to Edwards's presence in Stockbridge — his coldness, his bigotry, his age, and "'his principles.'" The "whole selfish cabal" to dismiss Edwards from his pastorate, which had succeeded in Northampton, fails in Stockbridge.

12 Smyth, Egbert C. "The 'New Philosophy' Against Which Students at Yale college were Warned in 1714." *Proceedings of the American Antiquarian Society,* n.s., 11 (October): 251-52.
Denies Edwards got his idealism from Berkeley. A catalogue of books read by Samuel Johnson, Edwards's tutor, since leaving Yale shows he did not know Berkeley until 1728.

13 ———. *Some Early Writings of Jonathan Edwards, A.D. 1714-1726.* Worcester, Mass.: Charles Hamilton.
Reprints 1895.10.

1897

1 Bacon, Leonard Woolsey. *A History of American Christianity*. New York: Christian Literature Co., pp. 155-59, 169-72.
   Assesses Edwards's career in the revivals of the Connecticut Valley and finds his serenity in the "agitated scene" necessary to distinguish true from spurious affections.

2 DeWitt, John. "Princeton College Administrations in the Eighteenth Century." *Presbyterian and Reformed Review* 8 (July): 387-417.
   Notes the "great advantage" and celebrity Princeton gained from Edwards, his association and his name.

3 Grosart, Alexander B. "The Handwriting of Famous Divines: Jonathan Edwards, M.A." *Sunday at Home* 31 (May): 458-60.
   Reprints Edwards's letter of 13 July 1751 to William Hogg, Edinburgh, about his settlement in Stockbridge; reproduces the closing lines in Edwards's handwriting; and suggests, contrary to received opinion, that Edwards was compassionate as evident in the many tear-stained manuscript pages of *Sinners in the Hands an Angry God*.

4 Mitchell, Donald G. *American Lands and Letters*. New York: Charles Scribner's Sons, l: 58-70.
   Comments breezily upon Edwards's life and work: *Freedom of the Will* is not "a popular book for a circulating library — nor yet one for the boudoir."

5 Painter, F[ranklin] V. N. *Introduction to American Literature*. Boston: Leach, Shewell, & Sanborn, pp. 51-58.
   Offers a derivative biography of Edwards and remarks his "defective" style.

6 Smyth, Egbert C. "Jonathan Edwards." In *Library of the World's Best Literature*. Edited by Charles Dudley Warner. New York: R. S. Peale & J. A. Hill, 9: 5175-79.
   Notes, in a short bibliographical essay, the "incompleteness" of the definitive edition of Edwards (and the possibility of misconstruction) and quotes passages from his work.

7 ———. "Jonathan Edwards' Idealism with Special Reference to the Essay 'Of Being' and to Writings not in his Collected Works." *American Journal of Theology* 1 (October): 950-64.
   Considers Edwards's early idealism "a fitting philosophical counterpart" to his doctrine of the divine and supernatural light "variously and intimately connected" to his theory of the Trinity, and a view of the universe "he never lost," and quotes extensively from "Of Being" and the "Miscellanies."

8 Walker, George Leon. *Some Aspects of the Religious Life of New England with Special Reference to Congregationalists*. Boston: Silver, Burdett & Co., pp. 104-12 passim.
   Compares Edwards's *Personal Narrative* to Thomas Hooker's *The Soul's Preparation* in an attempt to explain the later intellectualization of the theology of conversion. Hooker was content

with the "vivid announcement" of truth and saw no need to justify or explain it; Edwards felt constrained to make truth of whatever kind intellectually coherent. Systematic doctrinal theology was born in the Great Awakening and matured into New England Theology.

1898

1 Anon. "Doorstone Given to Forbes Library." *Hampshire Gazette*, August, p. 6.
> Reports the memorial gift of the doorstep from Edwards's King Street home to the Forbes Library, Northampton.

1A Anon. Review of *Jonathan Edwards*, by Alexander V. G. Allen. *Methodist Quarterly Review* 47 (November): 767-70.
> Considers Alexander V. G. Allen's Edwards (1889.1) "a foundation study in New England theology."

2 Byington, Ezra Hoyt. "Jonathan Edwards and the Great Awakening." *Bibliotheca Sacra* 55 (January): 114-27.
> Calls Edwards the "moving spirit" of the Great Awakening and explains his role as preacher, counselor, and apologist in it.

3 Child, Frank Samuel. *A Puritan Wooing: A Tale of the Great Awakening in New England*. New York: Baker & Taylor Co., pp. 103-14 passim.
> Tells the tale of Esther Hardy, a second cousin of Sarah Pierrepont, who attends one of Edwards's imprecatory sermons, falls ill at the Edwards home, and converts under the warm affection and guidance of Sarah, in a novel of romance during the Great Awakening.

4 DeWitt, John. "Historical Sketch of Princeton University." In *Princeton Sesquicentennial Celebration 1746-1896*. New York: Charles Scribner's Sons, pp. 366-67.
> Records that seventeen of twenty trustees present voted for Edwards to be the second president of Princeton, a short though advantageous association for the College.

5 Jones, Adam Leroy. *Early American Philosophers*. New York: Macmillan Co., pp. 46-80.
> Examines Edwards's psychology, idealism, ethics, and will in a survey of early American philosophers: of his contemporaries only Samuel Johnson is treated comparably. His psychology, derived from Locke, develops beyond him into a formulation of the association of ideas, anticipating Hume and indicating "independence and originality." His idealism was worked out "early in life" ("The Mind"), and though it was "never formally renounced," it played "a very small part" in his mature thought. His ethical system rests upon the notion that perfection is the end of conduct, his doctrine of will on necessity and its relationship to moral agency. In all his philosophical speculations, Edwards's considerable reasoning suffers from "imperfect analysis" and his turgid style from "his isolation and his lack of experience in oral discussion."

6 Pancras, Henry S. *An Introduction to American Literature*. New York: Henry Holt & Co., pp. 63-67.
> Finds the "same strange contrast" between life and work in Edwards and in Michael

Wigglesworth, the same mix of strengths and weaknesses in colonial literature generally in Edwards.

7 [Smellie, Alexander]. "Introduction." *A Treatise Concerning the Religious Affections.* London: Andrew Melrose, pp. ix-xxxiii.

Defends Edwards against the extravagant "indictment" of the style of *Religious Affections,* in a fulsome review of his life, times, and work. Despite some "ruggedness" and haste, Edwards's style in the text is tender, strong, and "melodious."

8 Starr, Mary Seabury. "The Home of Timothy and Jonathan Edwards." *Connecticut Quarterly* 4 (January): 33-43.

Offers a short history of Edwards's birthplace in South Windsor, his father's role in the community and at home, and a sketch of this "poetical, dreamy lad." (Illustrated).

9 Stowe, C. E. "Jonathan Edwards." In *Realencyklopädie für Protestantische Theologic und Kirche.* Edited by Albert Hauck. Leipzig: J. H. Hinrichs, 5:171-75.

Sketches Edwards's career, thought, and influence upon his successors. (In German.)

1899

1 Allen, Alexander V. G. *Jonathan Edwards.* American Religious Leaders. Boston: Houghton Mifflin & Co.

Reprints 1889.1.

2 Boardman, George Nye. *A History of New England Theology.* New York: A. D. F. Randolph Co., pp. 32-70 passim.

Traces the history of New England Theology between 1730 and 1830, from Edwards, its "radiating centre," to its successive forms and modifications. The first, or Edwards, phase (1730-1760) provides a "permanent element" of orthodoxy and evangelicalism to the scheme through his influence in practical theology, metaphysical speculation, and dogmatics; through his revivalism and his pastoral policies, his theism of "the prevalence of the Infinite Will" and his ethics of true virtue, and his opposition to Arminianism in *Freedom of the Will* and to Pelagianism in *Original Sin.* Yet a basic difference exists between Edwards and New England Theology: though both hold that God is the "primal source of power," the new theology "seems to make the end of creation the glorification of humanity," not the glorification of God.

3 Brewer, David J., ed. *The World's Best Orations from the Earliest Period to the Present Time.* St. Louis: F. P. Kaiser, 5: 1976-84.

Introduces and reprints selections from three imprecatory sermons.

4 Byington, Ezra Hoyt. "Jonathan Edwards, and the Great Awakening." *The Puritan as a Colonist and Reformer.* Boston: Little, Brown & Co., pp. 273-305.

Follows the career of Edwards, "this representative Puritan pastor," as a revivalist of permanent influence and a theologian of modified Calvinism.

5 Ford, Paul Leicester. *Janice Meredith: A Story of the Revolution.* New York: Dodd, Mead & Co., 1: 57.

Refers to two sermons on infant damnation Edwards delivered at Princeton and the profound effect it had on the heroine's mother, in a novel on the Revolution.

5A Hendrix, Eugene Russell. "The Catholicity of American Methodism." *Methodist Review* 81 (July): 513-31.

Parallels the lives and ministries of Edwards and John Wesley, in a short history of the "phenomenal career" of Methodism in America.

6 MacCracken, John Henry. "Jonathan Edwards Idealismus." Ph.D. dissertation, University of Halle.

Published as 1899.7.

7 ———. *Jonathan Edwards Idealismus.* Halle: C. A. Kaemmerer, 82 pp.

Discounts Berkeley as a source, with Locke and Newton, of Edwards's idealism and suggests a more likely influence to be Arthur Collier's *Clavis Universalis.* (In German; see 1902.7 for an English version.)

7A Means, Oliver William. *A Sketch of the Strict Congregational Church at Enfield, Connecticut.* Hartford: Hartford Seminary Press, pp. 15-24.

Adds to the standard account of Edwards's visit to Enfield (1821.2) remarks from the manuscript diary of Rev. Stephen Williams, first pastor of the Congregational Church in Longmeadow, Massachusetts.

8 Minton, Henry Collin. "President Jonathan Edwards." *Presbyterian Quarterly* 13 (January): 68-94.

Traces the life and work of the thrice-great Edwards (thinker, preacher, man); more a theologian than a philosopher, more a polemicist than an apologist; a pantheist, a mystic, a reformer; guilty of "philosophical idiosyncrasies," innocent of the "libel" that he fathered what is now called New England Theology.

1900

1 Addison, Daniel Dulany. *The Clergy in American Life and Letters.* New York: Macmillan Co., pp. 39-40.

Perceives in Edwards the theologian a genuine style that makes him a "literary force" in America.

2 Anon. "An American Philosopher of the Eighteenth Century." *New York Times*, 11 June, p. 6.

Calls for a new edition of Edwards's work and a "less critical and more human" biography than Alexander V. G. Allen's (1889.1). Inasmuch as standard texts exist for Franklin, Locke, Berkeley, and others, so one should be published of the mystical and saintly Edwards, if only as "a matter of patriotism." (An editorial.)

3 Anon. "The Edwards Commemoration." *Outlook* 65 (30 June): 476-77.

Calls the memorial tablet unveiled 22 June necessary to Northampton, not to Edwards, and goes on to praise Edwards for his rationalism, transcendentalism, and influence upon the Beechers, Horace Bushnell, and Phillips Brooks.

4 Anon. "Exercises at First Church and Unveiling of Memorial Tablet." *Hampshire Gazette,* 23 June, pp. 1, 8.

Reports the commemoration of the 150th anniversary of Edwards's dismissal, with program notes, pictures, and annotations.

5 Anon. "The Jonathan Edwards Memorial." *Harper's Weekly* 44 (23 June): 574.

Considers the "serious error" Northampton made in dismissing Edwards to be corrected with the erection of a tablet in his honor at the First Church.

6 Anon. "Tablet to Jonathan Edwards." *New York Times,* 23 June, p. 7.

Reports the unveiling in Northampton of a tablet to Edwards in exercises "impressive in their simplicity."

7 Barnes, Lemuel Call. *Two Thousand Years of Missions before Carey.* Chicago: Christian Culture Press, pp. 412-13.

Notes Edwards's mission to the Mahican at Stockbridge.

8 Bridgman, S. E. "Northampton." *New England Magazine,* n.s., 21 (January): 582, 585-86.

Includes a brief life and portrait of Edwards.

9 Bronson, Walter C. *A Short History of American Literature.* New York: D. C. Heath & Co., pp. 33-34.

Offers a brief biography of Edwards and keen regret that his powers were wasted on theology.

10 Cole, Bertha Woolsey Dwight. "Not Jonathan Edwards's Son-in-Law." *New York Times,* 13 June, p. 6.

Corrects the confusion about Aaron Burr, father and son, in a *Times* editorial on Edwards (1900.2). The father, not the son (the vice-president), was married to Edwards's daughter Esther.

11 Downes, R. P. "Thinkers Worth Remembering: Jonathan Edwards." *Great Thoughts* 6 (September): 296-98.

Recounts a brief life of Edwards, a man of genuine piety and "morbid self-introspection."

12 Gardiner, H[arry] N[orman]. "The Early Idealism of Jonathan Edwards." *Philosophical Review* 9 (November): 573-96.

Traces Edwards's idealism to his earliest speculations on nature and the mind, "first crudely" expressed and defended in "Of Being" and then in "Existence," "Substance," and "Excellence," an "original expression of personal insight" sustained throughout his work though in a somewhat altered form. Edwards was influenced directly by Locke, Newton, and Cudworth; less directly by Descartes, Norris, and Malebranche; and not at all by Berkeley (the evidence to the contrary is "entirely internal"). From the beginning, Edwards tends toward a "comprehensive" idealism in which God is all in all, communicating himself by immediate illumination in an "uninterrupted exercise of glorious will." With that "deeper" idealism in the making, it is unnecessary to look for "precise expressions" of Edwards's early speculations in his later work.

13 [Gardiner, H. Norman]. "Honoring of Jonathan Edwards." *Hampshire Gazette*, 28 March, p. 1.

Appeals for funds for the Edwards commemorative plaque.

14 Gordon, George A. "The Significance of Edwards Today." *Congregationalist* 85 (28 June): 944-46.

Likens Edwards's significance today to Dante's: both live, despite their obsolete thought, error, and imperfections, through the "majesty" of their imaginative appeal. Edwards is guilty of a "radical inconsistency." The absolute love, being, and excellence he attributes to God "discredits" his doctrines of man's depravity and election; his "glorious" theology contradicts his "inadequate" and "incredible" anthropology.

15 Johnson, William Samuel. "Where Burr Got His Mental Force." *New York Times*, 15 June, p. 6.

Claims that Aaron Burr, the vice-president, inherited from his grandfather Edwards his "tremendous" though "conscienceless" mentality and his "always unshaken courage." This must be true unless "in heretical defiance of his great ancestor's thesis, we maintain that perhaps Aaron Burr had a will of his own."

16 M., G. P. "In Honor of Jonathan Edwards." *Congregationalist* 85 (28 June): 958.

Recounts the celebration and summarizes the five speeches at the dedication of the Edwards bronze memorial tablet in the First Church at Northampton, 22 June.

17 MacCracken, Henry Mitchell. "The Hall of Fame." *American Monthly Review of Reviews* 22 (November): 567-66.

Records the votes of the first twenty-nine great Americans elected to the Hall of Fame: Edwards got eighty-one to Washington's ninety-seven and Hawthorne's seventy-three. (Illustrated.)

18 [Mead, Edwin D.] "Editor's Table." *New England Magazine*, n.s., 23 (December): 475-80.

Reviews Albert E. Winship's *Jukes-Edwards* (1900.20) and finds the Edwards family an inspiring example of the "contagious nature of moral health."

19 Wendell, Barrett. *A Literary History of America*. The Library of Literary History. New York: Charles Scribner's Sons, pp. 83-91.

Accounts Edwards's distance from things practical and political a decided and negative influence on his theology. His view of sinful man arises not from an American experience he dimly knew but from a "densely populated, corrupt" society he imagined. By mid-century, American religious thought had "divorced itself from life almost as completely as from politics."

20 Winship, A[lbert] E. *Jukes-Edwards: A Study in Education and Heredity*. Harrisburg, Pa.: R. L. Myers & Co., 88 pp.

Contrasts the 1,400 descendants of Edwards with the 1,200 descendants of Max Jukes, the "midday and midnight" of eugenics, in a study of the heredity of intelligence, morality, and character.

1901

1 Anon. "The Life and Theology of Jonathan Edwards." *Presbyterian Quarterly* 15 (April): 222-37.

Recounts the career and theology of Edwards, "a born metaphysician," and doubts whether he "understood" his people.

2 DeNormandie, James. "Jonathan Edwards at Portsmouth, New Hampshire." *Proceedings of the Massachusetts Historical Society,* 2d ser., 15 (March): 16-20.

Expresses disappointment with the banal and tedious *Christ the Great Example of Ministers,* an installation sermon Edwards delivered for Job Strong in Portsmouth, N.H., 28 June 1749. Such a sermon delivered today would "greatly discourage" any candidate for ordination.

3 Dexter, Franklin B[owditch]. "The Manuscripts of Jonathan Edwards." *Proceedings of the Massachusetts Historical Society,* 2d ser., 15 (March): 2-16.

Traces the progress and disposition of the Edwards manuscripts — from the time of his death to August 1900, when Yale acquired them — and describes the contents. The collection includes "a major part" of the folios and quartos mentioned in Edwards's will and inventory, especially the "immense" number of sermons, between 1100 and 1200 items or probably a third of the sermons he may have written on any scrap paper that came to hand — bills and letters, prescriptions and copybooks, and, quite frequently, the thin soft paper his wife and daughters used in making fans to support the family. Edwards's style here is of "great simplicity and directness, . . . unexpected freshness and modernness" and suggests not an aloof metaphysician but a very human pastor.

4 Eggleston, George Cary. "Jonathan Edwards." *The American Immortals.* New York: G. P. Putnam's Sons, pp. 337-49.

Offers a life of Edwards (and of others in the Hall of Fame) and judges him in the light of a time that took authority without question and Scripture without criticism. Edwards was born and lived through an "extraordinary medley of contradictions which constituted [his] creed."

5 Fraser, Alexander Campbell. "Appendix: Samuel Johnson and Jonathan Edwards." *The Works of George Berkeley.* Oxford: Clarendon Press, 3: 390-98.

Argues that Edwards's concept of causation on power, differing from Berkeley's, ends in a God whose omnipotence outweighs his goodness and whose creation becomes increasingly and endlessly sinful and irresponsible. Edwards seems "unappalled" by this nor aware of the "agnostic pessimism" latent in such a view. (See also 2: 21-22, for similarities between Edwards and Berkeley's *Alciphron* on the sense perception of the visible world.)

6 Gardiner, H. Norman, ed. *Jonathan Edwards, a Retrospect; Being the Addresses Delivered in Connection with the Unveiling of a Memorial in the First Church of Christ in Northampton, Massachusetts, on the One Hundred and Fiftieth Anniversary of his Dismissal from the Pastorate of that Church.* Boston: Houghton Mifflin & Co., xvi, 168 pp.

Publishes the papers (with an introduction) delivered at the unveiling of a memorial to Edwards's dismissal from his church.

Gardiner, H. Norman. "Introduction," pp. v-xvi. Considers Edwards "so great, so representative, so influential" that a broad retrospective is necessary to account for and interpret the crisis and conflict in New England religious life that "more than any other man" he created. The work of this volume is "a serious attempt" to assay his character and his influence, his theology and his philosophy, to discover what was "temporary and accidental," what essential and permanent.

Allen, Alexander V. G. "The Place of Edwards in History," pp. 1-31. Remarks "the deepest affinity" between Edwards and Dante — their idealized women and their idealized worlds; their intellectual, poetic imaginations; their banishments and exiles — such that *Divine and Supernatural Light, Distinguishing Marks,* and *Religious Affections* are likened in "spirit and purpose" to the *Divine Comedy.*

Smyth, Egbert C. "The Influence of Edwards on the Spiritual Life of New England," pp. 33-48. Characterizes Edwards's influence upon New England as indirect, as "a witness unsurpassed" of intellectual power addressing the spiritual life of man, as a "synthesist, even more than an analyst" of the sweet sense of God's glory and harmony and love. The traits that mark New England theology — independence, truth, intellect — were his.

Gordon, George A. "The Significance of Edwards To-Day," pp. 49-74. Reprints 1900.14.

Fisher, George P. "Greetings from Yale University," pp. 75-79. Ranks Edwards "foremost in the long list" of Yale graduates and celebrates the genius and holiness of "the Saint of New England."

Ormond, Alexander T. "Greetings from Princeton University," pp. 80-86. Considers Edwards a "moulding" force on Princeton, and the College a "residuary legatee" of his fame, in a short biographical sketch.

Rose, Henry T. "Edwards in Northampton," pp. 87-111. Traces Edwards's career in Northampton and concludes that he was "not a model pastor." He was lonely and cold, tactless and humorless, a martyr and a mystic, but he was a "man for the hour" at the time of Northampton's spiritual declension.

Gardiner, H. Norman. "The Early Idealism of Edwards," pp. 113-60. Reprints 1900.12.

7 MacCracken, Henry Mitchell. *The Hall of Fame.* New York: G. P. Putnam's Sons, pp. 213-18.

Offers a brief life of Edwards for the young, transcribes the inscription at the Hall of Fame, and suggests that Edwards's idealism derives from Arthur Collier's *Clavis Universalis* (1713).

8 McKenzie, Alexander. "Remarks." *Proceedings of the Massachusetts Historical Society,* 2d ser., 15 (March): 23-24.

Ascribes Edwards's "most unhappy" reference to spiders in *Sinners in the Hands of an Angry God* to his "early and persistent" interest in them rather than to bad taste.

9 Rankin, Jeremiah James. *Esther Burr's Journal.* Washington, D.C.: Howard University, 100 pp.

Constructs a journal attributed to Edwards's daughter but almost thoroughly of Rankin's devising. Typically, Esther "writes" this about her father: "I have just come back from a most wonderful ride with my honored father, Mr. Edwards, through the spring woods. He usually rides alone. . . . Though father is usually taciturn or preoccupied — my mother will call these large words, — even when he takes one of us children with him, today, he discoursed with me of the awful sweetness of walking with God in Nature. . . . Going home, my father pointed out to me the habits of a flying spider, that sallies forth on his thread as upon wings."

10 Squires, William Harder. "Jonathan Edwards und seine Willenslehre." Ph.D. dissertation, University of Leipzig.

Published as 1901.11.

11 ————. *Jonathan Edwards und seine Willenslehre.* Lucka: Berger & Behrend, 53 pp.
Considers the doctrine of the will central to Edwards's thought and to his place in American intellectual history, in an examination of *Freedom of the Will* and a comparison to Schopenhauer's pure metaphysics of the will and Wundt's psychology of voluntarism. Edwards teaches an absolute determinism in his speculations on universal will, but he postulates a moderate determinism in his treatment of the human will. Edwards, Schopenhauer, and Wundt represent three important stages in the development and investigation of the problem of the will. (In German.)

12 Stagg, John W. "Three Maligned Theologians." *Presbyterian Quarterly* 15 (January): 1-53.
Defends Calvin, Edwards, and William Twisse against misrepresentations of their views on infant baptism. Edwards, for instance, "exempts infants dying in infancy from Adam's sin, the only cause of condemnation against them, and makes the exemption an argument for the certainty of their guilt under original sin."

13 Stiles, Ezra. *The Literary Diary of Ezra Stiles, D.D., LL.D., President of Yale College.* Edited by Franklin Bowditch Dexter. New York: Charles Scribner' Sons, 2: 337; 3: 275.
Praises Edwards as a linguist, logician, and metaphysician, but thinks his "valuable writings" will be forgotten in another generation and his reclusive temperament was unsuited to the labors of a college president.

14 Walker, Williston. "Jonathan Edwards." *Ten New England Leaders.* New York: Silver, Burdett & Co., pp. 217-63.
Juxtaposes Edwards's formidable intellect and voiced "terrors of the law" against his transforming vision and "mystic conception" of God and claims that the beauty of his spirit will be more "reverenced" than the qualities of his mind "respected," in a life and estimate of "this remarkable man" and his work.

1902

1 Bacon, Edwin M. *Literary Pilgrimages in New England.* New York: Silver, Burdett & Co., pp. 433-40.
Paraphrases Oliver Wendell Holmes's sketch of Edwards (1880.6) and adds biographical notes.

2 Cobb, Sanford H. *The Rise of Religious Liberty in America, a History.* New York: Macmillan Co., pp. 484-8.
Attributes to Edwards, "more than any other man," the separation of church and state in America. By insisting on its dignity and purity, its divine charter and divine grace, Edwards fashioned a church greater than the state and hence beyond its control. Yet there is "no proof that he meant to do anything of the kind."

3 Cooke, George Willis. *Unitarianism in America: A History of its Origins and Development.* Boston: American Unitarian Association, pp. 38-41.
Remarks Edwards's running battle with Arminianism and his role in the Robert Breck affair.

4 Fiske, John. *New France and New England.* The Historical Writings of John Fiske, no. 9. Boston: Houghton Mifflin & Co., pp. 222-26, 231.

Gives a short life and estimate of Edwards, "probably the greatest intelligence that the western hemisphere has yet seen."

5 Hayes, Samuel Perkins. "An Historical Study of the Edwardean Revivals." *American Journal of Psychology* 13 (October): 550-74.

Traces the history of American revivals, attributing them to "unstable" conditions and religious apathy; reports the theological struggle of the Great Awakening between the New Lights and the Old; notes the "paradox" of Edwards, insisting on both man's innate depravity and his duty to seek regeneration; and counters Edwards's defense of the "positive basis" of conversion with Charles Chauncy's analysis of abuses, excesses, and disorders. Revival activity from 1735 to 1742, in which Edwards played so important a part, was followed by "a half century of popular indifference."

6 James, William. *The Varieties of Religious Experience.* New York: Longmans, Green, & Co., pp. 20, 228-29.

Considers Edwards's empirical method in *Religious Affections* the only way available to know Christian virtue — its roots are "inaccessible" — and finds his "rich and delicate" descriptions of supernatural grace identical with those of an "exceptionally high degree of natural goodness."

7 MacCracken, John Henry. "The Sources of Jonathan Edwards's Idealism." *Philosophical Review* 11 (January): 26-42.

Proposes Arthur Collier's *Clavis Universalis* (1713) as the "intermediate link" between Locke and Edwards in the latter's development towards idealism. "A careful comparative study" reveals that "there are sufficient grounds for supposing that it was Collier and not Berkeley who turned the mind of the youthful Edwards in the direction of idealism."

8 McCulloch, James E. "The Place of Revivals in American Church History." *Methodist Review* 84 (September): 681-97.

Ascribes the pattern of revivals in America to the "law of ebb and flow of spiritual life" and finds Edwards responding to the lethargy, skepticism, heresy, and schism of New England. Edwards was "providentially sent" to restore Christ to his people in the first era of revivals (1734), as were Timothy Dwight and Charles Grandison Finney in the second (1797), and Jeremiah C. Lamphier and Dwight L. Moody in the third (1858).

9 Mallary, R. DeWitt. *Lenox and the Berkshire Highlands.* New York: G. P. Putnam's Sons, pp. 246-48 passim.

Recounts Edwards's seven years at Stockbridge ministering to the "benighted heathen" in the heart of his beloved Berkshires.

10 Moulton, Charles Wells, ed. "Jonathan Edwards." In *Library of Literary Criticism of English and American Authors.* Buffalo, N.Y.: Moulton Publishing Co., pp. 380-95.

Quotes from more than seventy texts commenting upon Edwards's life and work.

11 Sears, Lorenzo. *American Literature in the Colonial and National Periods.* Boston: Little, Brown & Co., pp. 91-94.

Remarks the direct, plain, and clear diction of Edwards's sermons compared to the "hard and dismal" style of the treatises, in an estimate of Edwards and Franklin as transitional figures.

12 Stagg, John W. *Calvin, Twisse, and Edwards on the Universal Salvation of Those Dying in Infancy.* Richmond, Va.: Presbyterian Committee of Publication, pp. 123-42 passim.

Balances Edward's views on infant reprobation with those of his on Christ's redemption: "All anyone can say is, that Edwards has made sin to appear exceedingly sinful, but that likewise he has made redemption to appear exceedingly glorious." (A partial adaptation of 1901.12.)

13 Trumbull, James Russell. *History of Northampton, Massachusetts, from its Settlement in 1654.* Northampton, Mass.: Gazette Printing Co., 2: 41-51, 195-234.

Details Edwards's years in Northampton; his financial, political, and ministerial difficulties; and the occasion of his dismissal; and tempers the indictment against the townspeople with this: at the time of his dismissal, Edwards was the pastor of "an obscure country parish," not America's greatest theologian.

14 Upham, William P. "Shorthand Notes of Jonathan Edwards." *Proceedings of the Massachusetts Historical Society,* 2d ser., 15 (February): 514-21.

Deciphers shorthand entries appended to "Notes on Natural Science," in which Edwards lays down rules he should observe in writing about philosophy and natural science. Inasmuch as no "special secrecy" seemed needed, Edwards, like other ministers then, probably used shorthand to "save time, space, and paper." The notes also make clear that Edwards did not borrow his idealism from Berkeley, for "he was not at that time acquainted with Berkeley's publications."

1903

1 Allen, James Lane. *The Mettle of the Pasture.* New York: Macmillan Co., p. 128.
Calls Edwards the "hoarsest of the whole flock of New World theological ravens," in a novel set in Kentucky.

2 Anderson Wilbert L. "The Preaching Power of Jonathan Edwards." *Congregationalist and Christian World* 88 (3 October): 463-66.
Attributes Edwards's powerful preaching to his reason, his passions, and his will, to his "skilled indirection" and speculative daring.

3 Anon. "Churches Celebrate 200th Anniversary of Edwards's Birth." *Hampshire Gazette,* 5 October, p. 4.
Compares the current flurry of praise for Edwards with the earlier vilification of him and reports church celebrations of his birth in Northampton.

4 Anon. "The Edwards Bicentennial." *Journal of the Presbyterian Historical Society* 2 (December): 166-69.
Summarizes "careful accounts" of celebrations of the Edwards bicentennial appearing in the *Congregationalist* (1903.13) and furnishes an index to some "important" periodical literature.

5 Anon. "Edwards's Bi-Centennial." *Springfield Daily Republican,* 6 October, p. 7.

Notes celebrations of Edwards's bicentennial at South Windsor and Yale.

6 Anon. [The Edwards Bicentennial]. *Yale Daily News,* 6 October, p. 1.
Reports the Edwards bicentennial celebration at Yale on 5 October, details the program, and quotes from Williston Walker's address.

7 Anon. "Edwards's Birthday." *Springfield Daily Republican,* 6 October, pp. 6-7
Details the celebration at Stockbridge commemorating Edwards's birth and quotes at length from the major speeches on the occasion.

8 Anon. "Honor Edwards's Memory." *Congregationalist and Christian World* 88 (17 October): 531.
Hopes the praise lavished upon Edwards now will sustain his memory in years to come.

9 Anon. "Jonathan Edwards." *Journal of the Presbyterian Historical Society* 2 (December): 157-60.
Suggests that there is "enough of Edwards for both" Congregationalists and Presbyterians. Though born a Congregationalist, Edwards "began and ended" his ministry a Presbyterian, in New York and in Princeton. (An editorial.)

10 Anon. "Jonathan Edwards." *Outlook* 75 (3 October): 248-51.
Praises Edwards's intellectual courage and vivid imagination, summarizes his theology for reluctant readers, and dismisses it as having only an "historical existence."

11 Anon. "Jonathan Edwards." *Zion's Herald* 81 (30 September): 1234-35.
Compares Edwards to Emerson and Wesley only to suggest that "the time is not yet fully ripe for a final estimate" of Edwards. There is some gold in the "vast quarry" of his works, but much dross. Even so, he is a "major prophet" of Christianity, akin to Calvin, Dante, and St. Francis.

12 Anon. "The Jonathan Edwards Bicentennial." *New York Daily Tribune,* 4 October, Part 2: 7.
Dwells on the personal aspects of Edwards's life, principally during the seven "troublesome" years in Stockbridge, to counter the popular notion of him as an "ecclesiastical machine." (Illustrated.)

13 Anon. "Jonathan Edwards Celebrations." *Congregationalist and Christian World* 88 (17 October): 537.
Describes in detail the celebrations at Andover, New Haven, Hartford, South Windsor, Stockbridge, and Berkeley of the 200th anniversary of the birth of Edwards.

14 Anon. Review of Edwards's Unpublished Essay on the Trinity. *Nation* 77 (12 November): 384.
Welcomes the long-delayed publication of Edwards's trinitarian views and finds them thoroughly orthodox and "singularly juiceless."

15 Anon. "Story of the Great Preacher." *Hampshire Gazette,* 10 October, p. 2.
Recounts Edwards's career but glosses over his Northampton dismissal: Edwards went to Stockbridge on the death of John Sergeant.

16 Anon. "Why Revive Edwards." *Congregationalist and Christian World* 88 (3 October): 454.

> Believes Edwards was "not a storehouse of truth but a dynamic force" whose theology is outdated but whose spiritual teaching is not.

17 [Berkshire County, Mass., Congregational Churches]. *Jonathan Edwards: The Two Hundredth Anniversary of his Birth. Union Meeting of the Berkshire North and South Conferences, Stockbridge, Mass., October Fifth, 1903.* Stockbridge, Mass.: Berkshire Conferences, 68 pp.

> Publishes the papers delivered at the Stockbridge bicentennial celebration of Edwards's birth.
>
> Hopkins, Henry. "Introduction," pp. 5-7. Acknowledges the greatness of Edwards's intellect and the importance of his influence as well as the limits of his formal reasoning and the failure of some of his theology.
>
> Porter, Elbert S. "Address of Welcome," pp. 8-11. Characterizes Edwards as a "student of deep things" and a prodigious user of writing paper.
>
> Andrews, George Wakeman. "The Edwards Family," pp. 12-18. Studies the Edwards family for its righteous effect upon the country through learned and virtuous descendants, and concludes that the Reformation rendered an "important service" by rescuing the clergy from celibacy.
>
> Smart, T. Chipman. "The Modern Note in Edwards," pp. 19-23. Notes that Edwards's belief that God "comes straight to the mind" as a spiritual light is one shared by people today.
>
> Rowland, Lyman S. "The Other Side of Edwards," pp. 24-33. Discovers another side to Edwards's preaching, "a Calvary as well as a Sinai, a Paradise as well as an Inferno," *Divine and Supernatural Light* as well as *Sinners in the Hands of an Angry God.* Edwards was poetic and aphoristic like Emerson, like Pascal.
>
> DeWitt, John. "Jonathan Edwards: A Study," pp. 34-58. Considers Edwards's "regnant, permeating, irradiating" spirituality the clue to the quality of his life and to the unity of his work. From spirituality Edwards concluded that aesthetic emotion was rooted not in material beauty but in holiness; through spirituality he stressed the inward state of man "in nature and in grace." Thus Edwards effected a shift in American theology by emphasizing the conversion experience.
>
> Park, William Edwards. "Edwards at Stockbridge," pp. 59-67. Recounts Edwards's Stockbridge years.

18 Chapell, F. L. "Jonathan Edwards and the Movement in New England." *The Great Awakening of 1740.* Philadelphia: American Baptist Publications Society, pp. 42-66.

> Records Edwards's role in the Great Awakening — the scenes of his ministry and the consequences of his career — from a Baptist point of view.

19 Clark, Irene Woodbridge. "A Wifely Estimate of Edwards." *Congregationalist and Christian World* 88 (3 October): 472-73.

> Reprints (for the first time) a letter by Sarah Edwards to the council at Northampton, 22 June 1750, on the controversy surrounding public profession. She insisted that "what might seem a sudden caprice on her husband's part was in reality the first public action based on a conviction long held, which time was continually strengthening."

20 Cone, Kate M. "Jonathan Edwards." *Outlook* 75 (3 October): 255-66.

> Relates the "true story" of Edwards's career by highlighting the women in his life, from his mother, who envisioned his destiny as he lay "a rosy baby on her breast," to his wife, who "exquisitely" illustrated an emotional side denied to her intellectual husband.

21 Crook, Isaac. *Jonathan Edwards.* Cincinnati: Jennings & Pye, 95 pp.

Prizes Edwards the man, not the theologian — "Thousands of pages are not worth the paper on which his disputations are written" — in a desultory reading of his life and work.

22 Crothers, S. M. "Jonathan Edwards." *Christian Register,* 22 October, pp. 1263-64.

Focusses on the moral philosophy of *True Virtue* — the "positive element" in Unitarianism — not the "repellent" Calvinism of *Sinners in the Hands of an Angry God,* and finds a "natural and inevitable" development from Edwards to Samuel Hopkins, William Ellery Channing, and Ralph Waldo Emerson. Edwards gave them (and us) an ethics impersonal and universal in which the love of Christ yields to the love of being in general.

23 Edwards, William H., comp. *Timothy and Rhoda Ogden Edwards of Stockbridge, Mass., and their Descendants: A Genealogy.* Cincinnati: Robert Clarke Co., pp. 6-16.

Derives a brief life of Edwards from standard biographical sources; reproduces portraits, photographs, letters, and the family coat of arms; and concludes that Edwards was "a child in the affairs of this world."

24 [Finley, Samuel]. "A Contemporaneous Account of Jonathan Edwards." *Journal of the Presbyterian Historical Society* 2 (December): 125-35.

Reprints 1758.4.

25 Fisher, George P. *An Unpublished Essay of Edwards on the Trinity, with Remarks on Edwards and his Theology.* New York: Charles Scribner's Sons, pp. vii-xv, 1-74.

Recounts the history and debate concerning the "heterodox" views of Edwards on the Trinity (see especially 1865.4 and 1881.2); concludes that the unpublished essay reprinted here is "one of the ablest arguments in behalf of fundamental positions of the Nicene theology"; and provides an abbreviated life of Edwards, a seriatim reading of his work, and appraisal of his influence upon New England Theology. At the heart of Edwards's philosophy and theology is the "doctrine of the Absolute," giving rise to doctrines of being, necessity, and causation, and to his early formulations of idealism and immanence, with its hints of pantheism. But Edwards was a theist, believing in the personality of God, and a trinitarian, teaching tripersonalism — the priority of the father and the coequality of the persons.

26 ———. "The Value of Edwards for Today." *Congregationalist and Christian World* 88 (3 October): 469-71.

Counts Edwards's value two-fold: as a model to ministers of a believer and thinker; as an "indispensable" source to investigators of religious thought and speculation in New England. Like Thomas Aquinas, Edwards is *Doctor Angelicus.*

27 Gardiner, H. Norman, et al. "Tributes to Jonathan Edwards from Careful Students of His Writings." *Congregationalist and Christian World* 88 (3 October): 458.

Offers tributes to Edwards by H. Norman Gardiner (his "attractive and tonic power"), by William Newton Clarke ("a hero in strife"), and by Egbert C. Smyth ("an entire consecration of genius and greatness to the promotion of Christian faith").

28 Gregg, David. *Jonathan Edwards, a Gift of God to the American People.* Brooklyn, N.Y.: Eagle Press, 20 pp

Reprints the first of three sermons — the others (unavailable) are "The Man, His Theological

Creed and Its influence" and "Practical Odds and Ends from the Age of Edwards; Or the Religion for Our Day" — preached at the Lafayette Avenue Presbyterian Church, Brooklyn, on successive Sundays, beginning 4 October 1903. The sermon elaborates upon a text from Matthew 23:24 in praise of prophets and wise men and concludes, "Think what it would be . . . if every one of us were a Jonathan Edwards!"

29 Harper, William Hudson. "Edwards, Devotee, Theologian, Preacher." *Interior* 34 (1 October): 1272-74.

Offers a brief life of Edwards, a man of "profound" devotion and "lurid" sermons, and quotes from the latter.

30 Higginson, Thomas Wentworth, and Henry Walcott Boynton. *A Reader's History of American Literature.* Boston: Houghton Mifflin & Co., pp. 19-23.

Considers Edwards's *Sinners in the Hands of an Angry God* a "form of insanity," but his description of Sarah Pierrepont "the high-water mark of Puritan prose."

31 Holmes, C[lement] E[lton]. "Edwards and Northampton." *Zion's Herald* 81 (30 September): 1238-42.

Culls some anecdotes and observations about Edwards's career in Northampton, from his planting of elms to the hiring of a horse — $2.23 to Boston and back — in a desultory account.

32 Hopkins, Samuel. "Edwards's Habits and Tastes." *Congregationalist and Christian World* 88 (3 October): 471.

Reprints selections from 1765.2.

33 Humphrey, G. H. *Jonathan Edwards: An Address Delivered in Utica, N.Y., on the 200th Anniversary of His Birth, Oct. 5, 1903.* n.p., 32 pp.

Recounts the life and thought of Edwards, a minister entirely free of "pulpitish cant, or tabernacular drawl," and begs for a "duplicate" Edwards to again fill the air with "Calvinistic ozone."

34 King, Henry Churchill. "Jonathan Edwards as Philosopher and Theologian." *Hartford Seminary Record* 14 (November): 23-57.

Considers Edwards "a thorough-going theistic idealist" in philosophy and "a mystical ethical Calvinist" in theology, in a study of the sources and parallels, strengths and weaknesses, and "great" inconsistencies of his thought. His "blinding vision" of a sovereign, arbitrary God denies man moral initiative, makes God the author of sin, and distorts Christ's role of love. Edwards is less than "absolutely loyal" to his principle of benevolence in *True Virtue*, almost "anti-Protestant" in his distinction between common and special grace, "unjustifiably pantheistic" in *End of Creation.* Still American theology owes him "a debt unsurpassed."

35 Morris, Edward Dafydd. *Jonathan Edwards; His Contribution to Calvinism, to Evangelical Theology Generally, to Christian Ethics and to Practical Religion.* A paper read before the Ministerial Association of Columbus, Ohio. [n.d., 15 pp.]

Praises Edwards for his "precious" contributions to Calvinism, evangelism, Christian ethics, and practical religion that will continue to "millennial times." Edwards improved Calvinism by making possible "the ultimate salvation of the whole human race" and bringing it in "closer affiliation" with Anglicanism, Lutheranism, and Wesleyan Arminianism. His contributions to evangelical theology rests principally in his concept of the Trinity and his rejection of the half-way covenant; to ethics in his *True Virtue;* and to practical religion in his *Religious Affections.*

36 Morris, George Perry. "The Edwards Manuscripts." *Journal of the Presbyterian Historical Society* 2 (December): 169-70.

Reprints the note on the Edwards manuscripts in his "The Human Side of Edwards" (1903.37).

37 ———. "The Human Side of Edwards." *Congregationalist and Christian World* 88 (3 October): 461-62.

Calls for a biography of Edwards that studies him not only as a theologian and writer of "noble English prose" but also as a lad and parent, an exile-evangelist and a "pioneer in industrial education."

38 Orr, James. "Jonathan Edwards; His Influence in Scotland." *Congregationalist and Christian World* 88 (3 October): 467-68.

Estimates Edwards's influence upon John McLeod Campbell to be "really profound," even though few outside of "serious circles" in Scotland — or New England, for that matter — ever heard of Edwards.

39 Palmer, B. P. "'No Grander Life Since Plato's.'" *Boston Sunday Globe,* 4 October, p. 44.

Recounts Edwards's career, with quotations and pictures, and catalogues his descendants.

40 Pattison, T. Harwood. *The History of Christian Preaching.* Philadelphia: American Baptist Publishing Society, pp. 354-59.

Asserts that Edwards begins the "powerful era" of preaching in America and that his greatness lies in a "rare combination" of insight, imagination, logic, will, intellect, and feelings to glorify God and save souls.

41 Rankin, Jeremiah Eames. *Esther Burr's Journal.* Washington, D.C.: Woodward & Lothrop.

Reprints 1901.9.

42 Sellers, Montgomery P. "New England in Colonial Literature." *New England Magazine,* n.s., 28 (March): 100-107.

Places Edwards "far above" all others in colonial letters, including Anne Bradstreet and Cotton Mather, even though his theology was "artificial" and his influence will rest upon his "wonderful personality."

43 Simpson, Samuel. "Jonathan Edwards — A Historical Review." *Hartford Seminary Record* 14 (November): 3-22.

Offers "in rapid review" the events of Edwards's career, derived from Sereno Dwight's *Life* (1829.4), and "hurried side glances" of social and religious conditions important to it.

44 [Squires, William Harder]. *The Edwardean, A Quarterly Devoted to the History of Thought in America.*

Examines (and endorses) voluntarism in a periodical devoted exclusively to Edwards and written by the editor, William Harder Squires, professor of philosophy at Hamilton College, Clinton, New York. *The Edwardean* was published quarterly for a year, from October 1903 to July 1904, and includes serially the following articles in the first (October) issue:

"The Edwardean," pp. 1-3. Intends to write a history of philosophy in America by reviewing with "modified prejudice" the voluntarism of Edwards, a theism reflecting the religious spirit of its people.

"Glimpses into Edwards' Life," pp. 4-12. Calls Edwards "the foremost thinker [America] has ever produced," a mystic, a pantheist, an "open-minded" man, in a short biography.

"The Seventy Resolutions," pp. 13-23. Defends Edwards's "Resolutions" against charges that they are the "weird creations of a morbid imagination" by reprinting the text of this "sane, inquisitive, and conscientious inquirer."

"President Edwards as Thinker," pp. 24-31. Praises Edwards's thought, arising as it does from the isolation of a "primitive wilderness," and centered as it is on the "idea and being" of God.

"Some Estimates of President Edwards," pp. 32-50. Cites and quotes from a variety of commentators here and abroad and concludes that Edwards is Hume, Kant, Schopenhauer, and Wundt "in one."

"Edwards' Metaphysical Foundations," pp. 51-64. Contends that an "adequate" understanding of Edwards's metaphysics can rest only upon pure voluntarism. Edwards is a "volitional pantheist, and the absolute monist." (Continues as 1904.15)

45 Thompson, Robert Ellis. "A Centenary View of Jonathan Edwards." *Sunday School Times* 45 (3 October): 494.

Judges Edwards's greatness as a pious man and strenuous Christian to have "disentangled" itself from a past of doctrinal and sectarian dispute.

46 W[alker], W[illiston]. "Edwards's Recovered Treatise." *Yale Alumni Weekly* 13 (4 November): 106-107.

Reviews George Fisher's *An Unpublished Essay of Edwards on the Trinity* (1903.25), recounts the provenance of the manuscript, and concludes that Edwards shows not a "hint" of heterodoxy. Indeed, Edwards seems more orthodox, more Athanasian in his trinitarian views than had been suspected.

47 Ward, William Hayes. "Jonathan Edwards." *Independent* 55 (1 October): 2321-27.

Proclaims Edwards the "broadest, grandest" man of the American pulpit, in a tribute of like superlatives.

48 Winship, Edith A. "The Descendants of Edwards." *Journal of the Presbyterian Historical Society* 2 (December): 170-71.

Summarizes 1903.49.

49 ———. "The Human Legacy of Jonathan Edwards." *World's Work* 6 (October): 3981-84.

Marvels at the 1,400 descendants of Edwards, among them college professors and presidents, writers and preachers, doctors and lawyers, judges and businessmen, and public officials — mayors, governors, congressmen, senators, ambassadors. Though Edwards's theology is "dead, and his books are unread," he lives in his descendants.

50 Zenos, Andrew W. "The Permanent and the Passing in the Thought of Edwards." *Interior* 34 (1 October): 1274-75.
    Delineates Edwards's influence on American theological thought as either permanent or passing. His doctrines of original sin and freedom of the will no longer hold their places, his doctrine of virtue only negatively. But his "penetrating and comprehensive" doctrine of salvation, exemplified in *The Satisfaction of Christ,* will continue its profound effect, for it best accounts for "Scripture facts."

1904

1 Anon. "Jonathan Edwards." *New York Times,* 6 August, p. 540.
    Reviews both Edwards's *Sermons* (1904.7) and the bicentennial *Exercises* at Andover (1904.14).

2 Bacon, Leonard Woolsey. *The Congregationalists.* The Story of the Churches. New York: Baker & Taylor Co., pp. 117-21, 135-39.
    Remarks Edwards's role in the Great Awakening and in the founding of New England Theology, a "distinctly American" theodicy.

3 Beardsley, Frank Grenville. *A History of American Revivals.* New York: American Tract Society, pp. 22-29 passim.
    Evaluates Edwards's role in the revivals of the Connecticut Valley and traces the "first manifestation" of the revival impulse in the 1730s to his sermons on justification, damnation, excellency, and duty.

4 Candler, Warren A. *Great Revivals and the Great Republic.* Nashville: Publishing House of the M. E. Church, South, pp. 43-47, 90.
    Quotes from *Faithful Narrative* marking the beginning of the Great Awakening but sees Edwards's role in it as secondary to George Whitefield's. Edwards became president of Princeton, "the child of the revival," because he was an evangelist.

5 Cole, Samuel Valentine. "A Witness to the Truth." *New England Magazine,* n.s., 29 (January): 583-86.
    Reprints 1904.14.

6 DeWitt, John. "Jonathan Edwards: A Study." *Princeton Theological Review* 2 (January): 88-109.
    Reprints 1903.17.

7 Gardiner, H. Norman. "Introduction." *Selected Sermons of Jonathan Edwards.* New York: Macmillan Co., pp. vii-xxix.
    Considers Edwards as preacher — his "chief public work and his chief reputation in his lifetime" — and reprints six of ten sermons published during his lifetime and an unpublished seventh, in a brief biography and estimate. Edwards's sermons are "singularly clear, simple and unstudied" in style, of value as history, as personal expression, and as literature.

8 Hazlitt, William. "Of Persons One Would Wish to Have Seen." In *Collected Works.* Edited by A. R. Waller and Arnold Glover. London: J. M. Dent & Co., 12: 26-38.

> Lists six metaphysicians of modern times — Hobbes, Berkeley, Butler, Hartley, Hume, and Leibniz — "and perhaps Jonathan Edwards, a Massachusetts man."

*9 Holmes, Clement Elton. "The Philosophy of Jonathan Edwards and Its Relation to His Theology." Ph.D. dissertation, Boston University.

> Cited in *Comprehensive Dissertation Index 1861-1972*, 32: 379.

10 Kingman, Henry. *Jonathan Edwards: A Commemorative Address in Observance of the Bicentenary of His Birth, at the First Congregational Church, Berkeley, California, October 5, 1903.* E. T. Earl Lecture Foundation, no. 1. [San Francisco:] Pacific Theological Seminary, 22 pp.

> Offers a biography of Edwards and estimates his significance to be less as a theologian or philosopher than as a "prophet of God." There was in Edwards a "deep, happy inconsistency" between his dialectical thought and his spiritual intuition.

11 Miller, Edward Waite. "The Great Awakening and its Relation to American Christianity." *Princeton Theological Review* 2 (October): 545-62.

> Surveys the Great Awakening, the changes it wrought on American Christianity, and Edwards's role in it, accounting his ministry simply a return to the "themes and style" of earlier Puritan preachers. Edwards showed "singular insight" in understanding the critical nature of the revival for America if not its profound effects, the destruction of unified New England Congregationalism and the creation of "a conscious national unity," a change in church and state.

12 More, Paul Elmer. "The Solitude of Nathaniel Hawthorne." *Shelburne Essays.* First Series. New York: G. P. Putnam's Sons, pp. 22-50.

> Relates Hawthorne's "Ethan Brand" and the abject loneliness of the guilty to Edwards's *Sinners in the Hands of an Angry God* and his "extravagant sense" of the individual soul.

13 Ormond, Alexander T. "Jonathan Edwards as Thinker and Philosopher." *Philosophical Review* 13 (March): 183-84.

> Summarizes a paper delivered at a meeting of the American Philosophical Association at Princeton University, 29-31 December 1903. The "key" to Edwards's philosophy lies in the 58th section of his "treatise on Decrees and Election" where he discusses God and the ideal and real worlds. Edwards "anticipates" Rudolf Hermann Lotze in his *Metaphysik* (1841) and denies to God and man "the freedom of indifference."

14 [Platner, John Winthrop], ed. *Exercises Commemorating the Two-Hundredth Anniversary of the Birth of Jonathan Edwards, Held at Andover Theological Seminary, October 4 and 5, 1903.* Andover, Mass.: Andover Press, 191 pp.

> Publishes the papers delivered at the Edwards bicentennial celebration at Andover and appends some unpublished miscellanies.
>
> Platner, John Winthrop. "Religious Conditions in New England in the Time of Edwards," pp. 29-45. Sketches the religious surroundings in which Edwards lived and thought and preached. Edwards found New England "morally decadent" and "untheological," church discipline "relaxed" under the half-way covenant; he "redeemed" the church from secularization, overthrew the half-way covenant, awakened men to conviction and conversion, and left New England with

"all the apparatus for an energetic theological life." But it is not his Calvinist theology that serves now; it is his spirituality and mysticism and "beatific vision."

Woodbridge, Frederick J. E. "The Philosophy of Jonathan Edwards," pp. 47-72. Reckons Edwards's influence "largely negligible" now, though he dominated New England thought for 150 years, and accounts his work a failure "not through refutation, but through inadequacy," through the lack of "philosophical thoroughness." Edwards was a thinker of promise and originality — see the mystical pantheism of his "The Mind" — who never developed his possibilities. He failed to link his philosophical speculations to his theological convictions, failed to resolve his "intellectual duality," even though his late work on teleology and virtue reveals a conscious effort to simplify and unify. Clearly, the "unanalyzed" and "potent" emotions of his conversion experience so disrupted Edwards intellectually that philosophy and theology were "almost completely divorced and unrelated."

Smyth, Egbert Coffin. "The Theology of Edwards," pp. 73-93. Discovers the core of Edwards's theology in his "vivid sense" of the reality, immediacy, and peace of God, made intelligible for him in the Trinity and manifest in the creation. God's absolute perfection implies "self-impartation, reciprocity, mutual Love"; he creates out of plenitude in order to communicate. As the glory of God is to give, so the end of man is to give himself to God. This is "the innermost meaning and the climax" of Edwards's theology.

Cole, Samuel Valentine. "A Witness to the Truth," pp. 95-103. Praises Edwards as "This Dante of New England" in a poem of 166 lines.

Orr, James. "The Influence of Edwards," pp. 105-26. Attributes Edwards's powerful influence to the "inseparable union" of intellectual power and spiritual perception, even though there were "strange contrasts" within him.

15 [Squires, William Harder]. *The Edwardean, A Quarterly Devoted to the History of Thought in America.*

Continues the examination of Edwards's thought, especially his voluntarism (see 1903.44) and includes serially the following articles:

"Jonathan Edwards as Philosopher," (January) pp. 65-77. Considers Edwards's voluntarism the "natural product" of his time, linked to the political philosophy and spirit of America, and the "prototype" of all succeeding systems. As a speculative philosopher — there is no desire to resurrect his theology — Edwards is "teacher" to all modern philosophers. The "exalted" theme of his philosophy is the unified will of nature, man, and God.

"A Revival of Edwards," pp. 78-83. Rejoices that the bicentennial celebration signals the revival of Edwards's philosophy, which will "emancipate" American thought from European "error," and gives renewed attention to his theology, "free from the hamperings of a pulpit prejudice."

"Edwards' Psychology of the Will," pp. 84-108. Validates *Freedom of the Will*, Edwards's "great masterpiece of his life," in contemporary psychological terms and proposes that his theological argument is simply "confirmatory" of the metaphysical and psychological arguments. Edwards replaces the "fatalistic element" in the volitional processes of traditional Calvinism with psychological motives of character, habit, disposition, prior conduct, and present circumstance, and makes them efficient causes of volitional processes of consciousness.

"Edwards' Relation to Voluntarism," pp. 109-15. Claims that all of Edwards's work, whether philosophical or psychological, ethical or theological, gives "minute expression" to voluntarism.

"A Glance at Edwards' View of Reason," pp. 116-28. Calls Edwards an "uncompromising rationalist" though a "consistent voluntarist," anticipating Kant in the limits he places on reason and fostering rationalism in America by giving reason priority in his philosophy.

"Edwards as Theologian," (April) pp. 129-61. Rescues Edwards's theology from the "New

Phariseeism" of liberal religionists and reprints parts of *End of Creation*. Edwards must be viewed both as a metaphysician of the absolute will of God and as a "practical teacher" and psychologist of the will of man. Thus his metaphysical theology leads to the "elimination of the will of man from the problem of human and divine relation," and results in his being considered "the most cordially hated thinker" of all time.

"Edwards's Inferno," pp. 162-74. Compares Edwards's hell to Dante's and Milton's, suggests his health and his hell were "interrelated facts," acknowledges the dramatic impact of his description, but questions its literalness for him (it would involve grave contradictions).

"A Passage from Edwards' Speculative Metaphysics," pp. 175-92. Reprints parts of "Of Being," comments upon Edwards's ideas of nothing and space, and concludes that he "affirms the objective reality and validity of space." The foundation of the visible universe is God, the only, absolute, and ultimate reality, "the first and last idea" of his metaphysics.

"Edwards' Philosophy of History and Religion," (July) pp. 193-256. Reprints parts of *History of Redemption;* compares Edwards's theistic philosophy of history and religion to the "psychophysical," the "individualistic," and the "gastro-centric"; finds it not only superior in its Christocentricity but of a piece with his "plain and voluntaristic system"; and concludes the final issue of the journal with this: "The philosophy of Jonathan Edwards is America's first and grandest contribution to the thought of the world. . . . Edwards has come nearest of all the world's metaphysicians to reconciling philosophy and religion."

16 Van Becelaere, [Edward Gregory] L[awrence]. *La Philosophie en Amérique depuis les Origine jusqu'à nos Jours (1607-1900)*. New York: Eclectic Publishing Co., pp. 33-48.

Notes Edwards's importance to the development of American philosophy — he introduced philosophical elements into Calvinist doctrine and inaugurated an era of intellectual speculation in America — in a general treatment of his life and work. (In French.)

17 Watkins, Walter Kendall. "English Ancestry of Jonathan Edwards." *New England Historical and Genealogical Register* 58 (April): 202-203.

Verifies a family tradition that Edwards's great grandfather William Edwards, of Hartford, was brought to New England in childhood by his mother, Ann, wife of James Cole.

18 Woodbridge, Frederick J. E. "Jonathan Edwards." *Philosophical Review* 13 (July): 393-408.

Reprints 1904.14.

1905

1 Anon. "Edwards Tablets." *Hampshire Gazette,* 6 October, p. 3.

Reports the gift of a memorial tablet at the Edwards home on King Street by the Betty Allen Chapter of the Daughters of the American Revolution and the reception following.

2 Davenport, Frederick Morgan. "The New England Awakening Originating with Jonathan Edwards." *Primitive Traits in Religious Revivals: A Study in Mental and Social Evolution*. New York: Macmillan Co., pp. 94-132.

Traces sociologically the "abnormal development" of religious emotion in New England and the role of Edwards, the "ardent apologist" for terror during the Great Awakening. Generally, New Englanders are dogmatic types capable of outbursts of emotions; Edwards, a mixture of

Celtic and Saxon strains, shows traits of "oriental imagination" and practical common sense. Such a person in such a place and time was bound to produce "much mental and nervous disorder" and must bear responsibility for it. Still, Edwards's attack on the half-way covenant, as part of his revival activity, "laid . . . the foundation" for the separation of church and state for the emerging Republic.

3 Greene, M[aria] Louise. *The Development of Religious Liberty in Connecticut.* Boston: Houghton Mifflin & Co., pp. 245-48, 302-304 passim.

Recounts Edwards's role in the Great Awakening and notes that the doctrinal change he brought about resulted from a fusing of his conservative theology to his restless evangelism.

4 Macphail, Andrew. "Jonathan Edwards." *Essays in Puritanism.* London: T. Fisher Unwin, pp. 1-52.

Considers that superstitious and immoral New England was "ripe" for Edwards, a "preacher of righteousness," who "never was able to distinguish between thought and emotion," in a general estimate of his career and the development of English and American Puritanism. His philosophical writings are part of "the rubbish of libraries," their subjects "strange," their method "obscure," their conclusions "unintelligible," their style "involved." Edwards "knew little" of this world, still less of people; an intuitive and apocalyptic thinker, there is something "irresistibly comic" in the idea of Edwards among the Housatonics.

5 Rand, Benjamin. "Edwards, Jonathan (1703-1758)." In *Dictionary of Philosophy and Psychology.* Edited by James Mark Baldwin. New York: Macmillan, 3:188-89.

Offers an Edwards bibliography of primary sources and over twenty-five critical items.

1906

1 Bacon, Edwin M. *The Connecticut River and the Valley of the Connecticut.* New York: G. P. Putnam's Sons, pp. 434-47.

Describes Edwards's birthplace and his genealogy.

2 Curtis, Mattoon Monroe. "Kantean Elements in Jonathan Edwards." In *Philosophische Abhandlungen: Festschrift für Max Heinze.* Berlin: Ernst Siegfried Mettler & Sohn, pp. 34-62.

Compares Edwards and Kant on morality and religion, sin and grace, God and man, God and Christ, church and state, nature and history, and concludes that they either "agree" or have "essentially the same" doctrines or concepts, in a point-by-point examination of Edwards's work. They differ in this: Kant is "more cold, formal, and schematic," less feeling than Edwards; so too, Edwards has a more "overwhelming" sense of the sovereignty of God than Kant.

3 Lowell, D. O. S. "The Descendants of Jonathan Edwards." *Munsey's Magazine* 35 (June): 263-73.

Traces Edwards's descendants and finds fourteen college presidents — of Amherst, Carnegie, Columbia, Hamilton, Johns Hopkins, Princeton, Rutgers, Union, University of California, and Yale — in six generations, "a remarkable instance of intellectual heredity."

1907

1 Anon. "The Edwards Memorial." *Hampshire Gazette,* 7 October, p. 6.

Dedicates the site of Edwards's house on King Street as the home of the Northampton Historical Society and reprints an address by President Seelye of Smith.

2 Anon. "The 'Narrative' of Jonathan Edwards." *Chautauquan* 49 (December): 124-25.

Praises Edwards's "spiritual insight" and quotes from *Personal Narrative.*

3 Foster, Frank Hugh. *A Genetic History of the New England Theology.* Chicago: University of Chicago Press, pp. 47-103 passim.

Details Edwards's contributions to the development of New England Theology, in an examination of the systematic and thematic connections in theology over two centuries — in the work of Bellamy, Hopkins, and Taylor; in questions of eschatology, atonement, and will; in controversies of unitarianism and universalism; in schools of theology at Yale, Oberlin, and Andover. Not only did Edwards try to solve the problem of divine sovereignty, the doctrine central to New England Theology, but he exerted considerable influence through his practical work as revivalist and pastor and through "the temper of his mind," independent and restless and daring. His *Freedom of the Will,* a "classic" of the Theology, engendered a series of treatises, each trying to prove agreement; his *Original Sin* bears the marks of a leader, one who "innovates as he writes"; and his *True Virtue,* slow to be appreciated, gave rise to a school of ethics and theology.

4 Hoskins, John Preston. "German Influences on Religious Life and Thought in America during the Colonial Period." *Princeton Theological Review* 5 (January): 49-79.

Numbers Edwards's *Faithful Narrative* one of the "immediate" sources of John Wesley's evangelism, German pietism a latent source.

5 Ridderbos, Jan. *De Theologie van Jonathan Edwards.* The Hague: Johan A. Nederbragt, iv, 329 pp.

Contends that Edwards diverges from the Reformed consensus and develops an unusual form of Reformed theology, in a study of his life and work. The source of Edwards's difference with the tradition is both public and private: he was a born Congregationalist (and remained one) and he was independent-minded, an original thinker. An analysis of his rationalism, ambivalence, and individuality, and a careful examination of his work on the will, virtue, grace, and the Trinity indicate serious qualifications to "pure" Reformed theology. (In Dutch.)

6 Riley, I. Woodbridge. "Jonathan Edwards." In his *American Philosophy: The Early Schools.* New York: Dodd, Mead & Co., pp. 126-87.

Traces Edwards's idealism and mysticism, their sources, phases, and relationship; connects these internal developments to his external career and to his published works; and concludes that though he was "a precocious idealist and a profound mystic, he was not a consistent philosopher." Edwards moves through the idealism of his years at Windsor and at Yale, to the determinism of his Northampton ministry, to the "tentative" pantheism of his Stockbridge thought, when a return to his early idealism results in "an almost monistic" immanency. Through it all runs the "common element" of his mysticism, affecting each state in a characteristic way. His idealism, rooted in his intuition more than his logic or his learning — he did not know Berkeley — , finds "precocious convincement of insubstantiality" in "Of Being," "tentative expression of a kindred immaterialism" in "The Mind, "rational advocacy of the mystical principle of intuitive apprehension" in *Divine and Supernatural Light,* and "laboured vindication of the dialectic of the heart" in *Religious Affections.* Edwards's later work, *Freedom of the Will* and *True Virtue,* suffers from ambiguity, from an unresolved dualism of Calvinism and pantheism, his theology overshadowing his philosophy.

1908

1 Gordon, George A. "The Collapse of the New England Theology." *Harvard Theological Review* 1 (April): 127-68.
   Ascribes the collapse of New England Theology to a "structural defect" in the system: the humanism of Edwards's God is "external, subordinate, temporal." Edwards was a "speculative genius" with a mind of "uncommon acuteness, massiveness, and depth," but his philosophy of man's world is "morally incredible." Neither Edwards nor his successors ever gained "the least insight" into the nature of revelation or reason in the Bible.

2 Riley, I. Woodbridge. "The Real Jonathan Edwards." *Open Court* 22 (December): 705-15.
   Suggests that the "real Edwards" is not, as is commonly held, the "odious" and "sulphurous" Calvinist theologian, but a "philosopher of feelings, a fervent exponent of the dialect of the heart," a poet, a mystic. In *Personal Narrative* Edwards details the traditional stages of the mystical experience, the purgative, the illuminative, and the unitive. But in the *End of Creation,* "the most boldly imaginative" of his work, Edwards embodies and enlivens the thoughts of the mystic and idealist in figures and metaphors.

3 Walker, Williston. *Great Men of the Christian Church.* Constructive Bible Studies: Advanced and Supplementary Series. Chicago: University of Chicago Press, pp. 339-53.
   Ranks Edwards as "the ablest theologian and most powerful thinker that colonial New England produced," in a brief biography and estimate of his work. *True Virtue,* though not as famous as *Freedom of the Will,* was probably the "most influential" of his work in New England because it taught disinterested love, the motive spirit of evangelism. "No wonder that the earliest American foreign missionaries came from the ranks of Edwards' disciples."

1909

1 Emerson, Ralph Waldo. *Journals.* Edited by Edward Waldo Emerson and Waldo Emerson Forbes. Boston: Houghton Mifflin Co., 1:286-87.
   Recounts a conversation with William Withington, a classmate, on 5 October 1823, about Edwards's error in *Freedom of the Will* of including the proposition to be proved with the definition. Emerson, however, praises Edwards's clarity in opening up the truth of the subject and wonders that "it ever was disputed."

2 Foster, Frank Hugh. "Jonathan Edwards." In *The New Schaff-Herzog Encyclopedia of Religious Knowledge.* Edited by Samuel MacCauley Jackson. New York: Funk &Wagnalls, 5:80-82.
   Traces the career of Edwards.

3 Powell, Lyman P. *Heavenly Heretics.* New York: G. P. Putnam's Sons, pp. 1-29.

Marks the scene, the manner, and the effect of Edwards's *Sinners in the Hands of an Angry God* at Northampton in June 1741 and accounts him "orthodox from first to last" for he lacked originality. Out of the pulpit this passionate revivalist exemplified piety and humility, as his life reveals.

1910

1 Davenport, Frederick Morgan. "The New England Awakening Originating with Jonathan Edwards." *Primitive Traits in Religious Revivals.* New York: Macmillan Co.

Reprints 1905.2.

*2 Ellis, C. G. "The Ethics of Jonathan Edwards." Ph.D. dissertation, New York University.

Cited in *Comprehensive Dissertation Index, 1974 Supplement,* 4:713.

3 Foster, Frank Hugh. "New England Theology." In *The New Schaff-Herzog Encyclopedia of Religious Knowledge.* Edited by Samuel MacCauley Jackson. New York: Funk & Wagnalls, 8:130-40.

Traces the development of New England Theology, "originating" with the constructive theology of Edwards in 1734 and ending with the Andover summaries of Edwards Amasa Park in the 1880s.

4 Gardiner, Harry Norman, and Richard Webster. "Jonathan Edwards." In *Encyclopaedia Britannica,* 11th ed., 9:3-6.

Traces Edwards's career and estimates the work of "the most able metaphysician and the most influential religious thinker in America." Edwards's philosophy is mixed with his theology in a way that is "never thoroughly combined" and with the result that, for example, the pantheism of his philosophy is never reconciled with the individuality of his moral theology. His *Freedom of the Will* is "defective" in its abstract concepts.

1911

1 Brown, W. Adams. "Covenant Theology." In *Encyclopaedia of Religion and Ethics.* Edited by James Hastings. New York: Charles Scribner's Sons, 4:223.

Suggests that Edwards's interest in the "eternal law of things" kept him from the covenant idea.

1A McGiffert, Arthur C. *Protestant Thought Before Kant.* New York: Charles Scribner's Sons, pp. 175-85.

Considers Edwards a "profound" theologian, subtle and dialectical, more than the generally remembered evangelical Pietist or rigid Calvinist. His last works, especially *True Virtue* and *End of Creation,* are unequaled in modern theology for their significance and intelligence.

2 Royce, Josiah. *William James and Other Essays on the Philosophy of Life.* New York: Macmillan Co., pp. 3-8.

Ranks Edwards with Ralph Waldo Emerson and William James as one of only three representative American philosophers and the first in order of time. Edwards articulated ideas fundamental to our religious life by discovering the nature of man and God in his profound religious
experience.

3 Smith, Frances M. "Historic Lineages in America — First Builders of the Western
   Hemisphere: Edwards Foundations in American History." *Journal of American His-
   tory* 5 (April): 298-99.
   Traces the Edwards family from England to America and to its "world-famous" son.

1912

*1 Bauer, Charles G. "Jonathan Edwards and His Relation to the New England Theol-
    ogy." S.T.D. dissertation, Temple University.
    Cited in *Comprehensive Dissertation Index 1861-1972*, 32: 379; also ascribed to Howard F.
    Pierce, 1912.6.

2 Cairns, William B. *A History of American Literature.* New York: Oxford University
   Press, pp. 76-81.
   Claims that Edwards had "perhaps the finest poetic sensibilities" of the colonial era, though
   he wrote no poetry, and that his diction was pure and simple, though his subjects were "dry or
   repellent."

3 Christie, Francis Albert. "The Beginnings of Arminianism in New England." In *Papers of the American Society of Church History.* Second series, 3. Edited by William
   Walker Rockwell. New York: G. P. Putnam's Sons, pp. 151-72.
   Identifies Episcopalianism, rather than Arminianism, as the real threat to Congregationalism
   that Edwards saw and feared in 1734. Edwards fought a "myth," probably created by George
   Whitefield in his "rash" denunciations of the Congregational clergy, and attacked Arminian literature, foreign, not local, in origin. Perhaps, Sereno Dwight's (1829.4) misreading of Edwards's
   letter to John Erskine, 31 August 1748, accounts for the historical confusion.

4 DeWitt, John. "Jonathan Edwards: A Study." In *Biblical and Theological Studies,* by
   the Members of the Faculty of Princeton Theological Seminary. New York: Charles
   Scribner's Sons, pp. 109-36.
   Reprints 1904.6.

5 Perry, Bliss. *The American Mind.* New York: Houghton Mifflin Co., pp. 18, 95.
   Ranks Edwards with Pascal, Augustine, and Dante.

*6 Pierce, Howard F. "Jonathan Edwards and His Relation to New England Theology."
    S.T.D. dissertation, Temple University.
    Cited in *Comprehensive Dissertation Index 1861-1972*, 32: 379; also ascribed to Charles G.
    Bauer, 1912.1.

7 Warfield, Benjamin B. "Edwards and the New England Theology." In *Encyclopaedia*

of Religion and Ethics. Edited by James Hastings. New York: Charles Scribner's Sons, 5:221-27.

> Traces Edwards's career from his early preparation at home and at Yale to his pastorate in Northampton and his theology in Stockbridge and follows his influence on doctrinal and practical matters from Joseph Bellamy to Edwards Park. Edwards was a man "of thought rather than learning," a subtle analyst who "strove after no show of originality" (save in *True Virtue*), and a "convinced defender" of standard Calvinism. It was Edwards's "misfortune" to lend his name to the "provincial" theology of his successors whose best doctrines were a "far cry" from his Calvinist teachings.

1913

1 Anon. "Famous Old Elm Gone." *New York Times,* 22 August, p. 7.
> Recounts the history of the Edwards elms and the recent loss of the last one.

2 DeJong, Ymen Peter. *De Leer den Verzoening in de Amerikaanshe Theologie.* Grand Rapids, Mich.: Eerdmans-Sevensma, pp. 21-25.
> Claims that Edwards's doctrine of disinterested benevolence detracts from God's being and virtue, that his doctrine of divine sovereignty reduces the role of Christ, and that his revival theology not only counters historical Calvinism but invites Arminianism. (In Dutch.)

3 Hendrix, E. R. "Jonathan Edwards and John Wesley." *Methodist Quarterly Review* 62 (January): 28-38.
> Draws parallels between two great revivalists, Edwards and John Wesley — both were born in the same year, both were sons of educated ministers and strong mothers, both were tutors in college, and so on — to show that the American "profoundly" influenced the Briton, that the Methodist was indebted to the Presbyterian.

4 Long, William J. *American Literature.* Boston: Ginn & Co., pp. 70-77.
> Considers Edwards "incomparably the greatest of all our early writers," in a brief survey of his life and work.

5 Mabie, Hamilton Wright. *American Ideals, Character, and Life.* New York: Macmillan Co., pp. 115-16.
> Notes the contrast between Edwards's mysticism and his harsh doctrines.

6 Santayana, G[eorge]. *Winds of Doctrine.* New York: Charles Scribner's Sons, p. 91.
> Remarks how strange Edwards's sense of sin is in modern America, in "The Genteel Tradition in America."

1914

1 Anon. "Jonathan Edwards." *Hampshire Gazette,* 9 April, p. 12.
> Notes the moral climate of Edwards's Northampton during the Awakening.

2 Collins, Varnum Lansing. *Princeton.* New York: Oxford University Press, pp. 50-52.

Doubts that Edwards would have made a successful college administrator, given his demonstrated lack of discretion and practicality at Northampton, nor that he left "any impress" on Princeton.

3 Kneeland, Harriet J. "Jonathan Edwards." In *Early Northampton*. Edited by the Betty Allen Chapter, Daughters of the American Revolution. Northampton, Mass.: Betty Allen Chapter, pp. 71-87.
Balances Edwards's "stern theology" against the "wonderful beauty" of his family life and "keen appreciation" of nature, in a brief narrative of his career in Northampton.

4 Moffett, Thomas C. *The American Indian on the New Trail: The Red Man of the United States and the Christian Gospel*. New York: Missionary Education Movement of the United States and Canada, pp. 71-72.
Notes briefly Edwards's missionary work among the Mahicans of the Housatonic.

5 Stokes, Anson Phelps. *Memorials of Eminent Yale Men: A Biographical Study of Student Life and University Influences During the Eighteenth and Nineteenth Centuries*. New Haven: Yale University Press, 1:19-29.
Recounts Edwards's life, especially those "most formative" eight years he spent as student and tutor at Yale, and reprints letters.

1915

1 Brooks, Van Wyck. *America's Coming-of-Age*. New York: B. W. Huebsch, pp. 8-14.
Typifies the rift in America between highbrow and lowbrow in the "transcendental theory" of Edwards and the "catchpenny realities" of Franklin, two philosophers who "share the eighteenth century between them." The unreality, inflexibility, aloofness, and refinement of American culture stems from Puritan piety and Edwards; flexibility, opportunism, business ethics, and American humor, from Puritan practicality and Franklin. There is no middle ground.

2 Buckham, John Wright. *Mysticism and Modern Life*. New York: Abingdon Press, pp. 81-82.
Compares Edwards, that "austere" mystic, to William Wordsworth in their shared communion with nature deeper than pantheism.

3 Riley, Woodbridge. *American Thought from Puritanism to Pragmatism*. New York: Henry Holt & Co., pp. 28-36.
Discerns in the private Edwards a poet and a mystic, a divine far different from the "pitiless professional" theologian of the public Edwards and perhaps more valuable. For Edwards there were three stages to the mystical process: "first, comes by great and violent inward struggles the gaining of a spirit to part with all things in the world; then, a kind of vision or certain fixed ideas and images of being alone in the mountains or some solitary wilderness far from all mankind; finally, a thought of being wrapt up in God in heaven, being, as it were, swallowed up in Him forever." This progression generally follows that of the "ancient manuals" — purgative, illuminative, unitive or intuitive — as well as that detailed by William James — ineffability, noetic, transiency, passivity.

1916

*1 Allison, Oscar Ethan. "Jonathan Edwards: A Study in Puritanism." Ph.D. dissertation, Boston University.
   Cited in *Comprehensive Dissertation Index 1861-1972*, 32: 379.

2 Anon. "Jonathan Edwards Vindicated." *New York Times,* 9 February, p. 10.
   Takes Roosevelt to task for the "tardy justice" he renders Edwards (1916.6). "It is a notable posthumous honor to have won approbation of our most renowned eclectic scholar and politician." (An editorial.)

3 Briggs, Charles Augustus. *History of the Study of Theology.* New York: Charles Scribner's Sons, 2:171-73.
   Considers Edwards the "father" of modern English and American religious thought: the teacher of Methodists in Great Britain and the theologian of Presbyterianism and Congregationalism in America and abroad.

4 Oviatt, Edwin. *The Beginnings of Yale (1701-1726).* New Haven: Yale University Press, pp. 415-17, 425-26.
   Details Edwards's two years as tutor at Yale (1724-1726). Although the college "decidedly prospered" under his direction, Edwards found his life among the students "somewhat irksome."

5 Redfield, Casper L. "Education Extended." *Journal of Education* 84 (19 October): [369]-71.
   Calculates the amount of education in twelve immediate ancestors of Edwards, shows the positive effect it had on his natural ability, and insists that generational improvement rests upon education only.

6 Roosevelt, Theodore. Letter to Marjorie Sterrett, 5 February 1916. *New York Tribune,* 8 February, p. 1.
   Singles out Edwards as a symbol for troubled times, in a photocopy of a letter to "little Miss Marjorie," the thirteen-year-old founder of a battleship fund. Edwards "always acted in accordance with the strongest sense of duty, and there wasn't a touch of the mollycoddle about him." (See also "Roosevelt Joins Battleship Fund," pp. 1 and 9.)

7 Waters, William O., Jr. "Yale Claims Jonathan Edwards." *New York Times,* 12 February, p. 10.
   Adds to the statement in the *Times* (1916.2): though a "'Princeton worthy,'" Edwards was a Yale man first.

1917

1 Coss, John J. "[Bibliography of] Jonathan Edwards." In *The Cambridge History of American Literature.* Edited by William Peterfield Trent et al. New York: G. P. Putnam's Sons, 1:426-38.
   Lists locations and holdings of Edwards manuscripts, collected and separate works, and over 150 items of biography and criticism.

2 Davenport, Frederick Morgan. "The New England Awakening Originating with Jonathan Edwards." *Primitive Traits in Religious Revivals.* New York: Macmillan Co.
Reprints 1905.2.

3 More, Paul Elmer. "Edwards." In *The Cambridge History of American Literature.* Edited by William Peterfield Trent et al. New York: G. P. Putnam's Sons, 1:57-71.
Regrets that Edwards's dogmatic theology kept him from being "one of the very great names in literature," though he remains a towering intellect and a master of religious psychology, in an estimate of his life and work, especially *Freedom of the Will.* (Frequently reprinted.)

4 Norris, Edwin Mark. *The Story of Princeton.* Boston: Little, Brown & Co., pp. 33-36.
Recounts Edwards's Princeton days and the influence he exerted upon the college before and after his death. Edwards was the "natural" choice to follow Aaron Burr: "no other name was even considered."

5 Platner, John Winthrop. "The Congregationalists." In *The Religious History of New England.* King's Chapel Lectures. Cambridge, Mass.: Harvard University Press, pp. 42-45 passim.
Places Edwards at the beginning of a new era in American religious history, at once evangelical and sectarian.

6 Twain, Mark. Letter to Rev. Joseph H. Twichell, February 1902. In *Mark Twain's Letters.* Edited by Albert Bigelow Paine. New York: Harper & Brothers, 2:719-21.
Reprints Mark Twain's letter concerning his reading of Edwards's *Freedom of the Will* lent him by Rev. Joseph H. Twichell. Edwards is a "drunken lunatic," a "resplendent intellect gone mad — a marvelous spectacle. . . . By God I was ashamed to be in such company."

7 Warner, Charles F. *Representative Families of Northampton: A Demonstration of What High Character, Good Ancestry and Heredity have Accomplished in a New England Town.* Northampton, Mass.: Picturesque Publishing Co., 1:19-35.
Recounts the life of Edwards (and his descendants) as an example of character building and useful citizenship.

1918

1 Dexter, Franklin Bowditch. "The Manuscripts of Jonathan Edwards." *A Selection from the Miscellaneous Historical Papers of Fifty Years.* New Haven: Tuttle, Morehouse & Taylor Co., pp. 235-46.
Reprints 1901.3.

1A Neighbor, R[obert] E[dward]. "Shall We Read Jonathan Edwards?" *Review and Expositor* 15 (January): 148-56.
Answers that it would be "decidedly advantageous" for both ministers and laymen to read Edwards — to quicken the "spiritual impulse," acquire "intellectual stimulus," and gain "theological definiteness."

2 Perry, Bliss. *The Spirit of American Literature*. New Haven: Yale University Press, pp. 48-52.

  Traces the "tragedy" of Edwards's career and the changes in his literary reputation, both the result of unforeseen events.

3 Ricker, Marilla M. *Jonathan Edwards: The Divine Who Filled the Air with Damnation and Proved the Total Depravity of God*. New York: American Freethought Tract Society, 8 pp.

  Vilifies Edwards as a mad minister who "believed in the worst God, preached the worst sermons, and had the worst religion of any human being who ever lived on this continent."

1919

1 Buckham, John Wright. *Progressive Religious Thought in America: A Survey of the Enlarging Pilgrim Faith*. Boston: Houghton Mifflin Co., pp. 6-8 passim.

  Reveals the "true American theological apostolic succession" to be Edwards, Horace Bushnell, and George Angier Gordon.

2 LeRoux, Emmanuel. "Le Développement de la Pensée Philosophique aux États-Unis." *Revue de Synthèse Historique* 29 (August): [125]-49.

  Considers Edwards "le puritanisme originel," in a short history of American philosophical thought. (In French.)

1920

1 Buckham, John Wright. "The New England Theologians." *American Journal of Theology* 24 (January): 19-29.

  Suggests that Edwards, in an effort to "square" Calvinism with reason and morality, helped define the three central metaphysical issues of New England Theology: the conflict between sovereignty and benevolence, determinism and freedom, total depravity and true virtue. It was left to his followers to reconcile these contradictory doctrines and to modern theology to withdraw from them.

2 [Cattell, J. McKeen]. "Jonathan Edwards on Multidimensional Space and the Mechanistic Conception of Life." *Science*, n.s., 52 (29 October): 409-10.

  Calls Edwards "the spiritual father" of Albert Einstein's geometry of multidimensional space because of his remarks on the similarity of the various parts of time and space in *Freedom of the Will*, Part IV, Section 8.

3 Gordon, George A. *Humanism in New England Theology*. Boston: Houghton Mifflin Co., viii, 105 pp.

  Recasts 1908.1.

4 Maxson, Charles Hartshorn. *The Great Awakening in the Middle Colonies*. Chicago: University of Chicago Press, pp. 19-20 passim.

  Contrasts Edwards's changing views on qualifications for admission to T. J. Frelinghuysen's early and continued insistence on profession, in a study of the effect of German pietism on the Awakening in the Raritan Valley and throughout the middle colonies.

5 Santayana, George. *Character & Opinion in the United States.* New York: Charles Scribner's Sons, p. 9.

   Notes that Edwards, "the greatest master in false philosophy" in America, was abandoned by his own sect in his own time.

6 Slosson, Edwin E. "Jonathan Edwards as a Freudian." *Science,* n.s., 52 (24 December): 609.

   Cites Edwards's Diary for 2 May and 10 August 1722 as instances of the psychoanalytic method. "Not only did Edwards use dream analysis for the discovery of secret sins, but he also employed the Freudian therapeutics of frank self-examination starting with random reverie and following the thread of association until he reached the complex that he desired to eradicate by confession and sublimation."

7 Van Doren, Carl. "Introduction." In *Benjamin Franklin and Jonathan Edwards: Selections from their Writings.* Edited by Will D. Howe. The Modern Students Library. New York: Charles Scribner's Sons, pp. ix-xxxiv.

   Compares Edwards and Franklin as "protagonists and symbols of the hostile movements which strove for mastery" in the eighteenth century. Generally, Franklin seems "contemporaneous, fresh, full of vitality"; Edwards seems to speak of "forgotten issues in a forgotten dialect." Yet Edwards was the better theoretical scientist, the more imaginative philosopher, an "impressive mystic" capable of a thrilling subtlety and intense power (in *Religious Affections*) or the "true lyric and elegy" of Puritanism (in *Personal Narrative*). Edwards offers illumination that lifts the spirit; Franklin offers the "indispensable wisdom" of the human experience. "They divide the world, but so do they multiply it."

1921

1 Adams, James Truslow. *The Founding of New England.* Boston: Atlantic Monthly Press, p. 82.

   Regrets that Edwards devotes the "finest" American prose to the tortures of the damned.

2 Cadman, S. Parkes. *Ambassadors of God.* New York: Macmillan Co., p. 70.

   Calls Edwards a philosopher, not a theologian, and that at another time this "misunderstood ambassador" might have become a Hume or a Kant.

3 Chrisman, Lewis H. "Jonathan Edwards." *John Ruskin, Preacher, and Other Essays.* New York: Abingdon Press, pp. 25-45.

   Considers Edwards's career a vain attempt to save a dying Calvinism and *Freedom of the Will* a "cowardly surrender" to it.

4 Hoyt, Arthur S. "Jonathan Edwards." *The Pulpit and American Life.* New York: Macmillan Co., pp. 19-39.

   Measures Edwards against the three dimensions of any preacher — personality, message, manner — and finds him "the very Doré of the pulpit." Edwards was an ascetic, an idealist, a mystic; intense and spiritual, speculative and rational. His message was a vivid, old-line Calvinism rendered "boldly and terribly" in a manner plain and direct through arguments scriptural and experiential. "This quiet, philosophic preacher had greater mastery over his audiences than Whitefield."

5 More, Paul Elmer. "Jonathan Edwards." *A New England Group and Others.* Shelburne Essays, 11th series. Boston: Houghton Mifflin Co., pp. 35-65.
    Reprints 1917.3. (Frequently reprinted in this form.)

1922

1 Anon. "Jonathan Edwards." In *Hand-Book of the Hall of Fame.* New York: Publications of the Hall of Fame, p. 23.
    Offers a brief life of Edwards, elected to the Hall of Fame in 1900 by eighty-two votes.

2 Edwards, A. J. *Short Sketches of the Life and Service of Jonathan Edwards.* Fort Worth, Tex.: A. J. Edwards, 18 pp.
    Recounts a brief life of Edwards; reprints *Sinners in the Hands of an Angry God,* a sermon "second only" to the Sermon on the Mount; and adds an "inspiring" poem, by a great-great-grandson of Edwards.

3 More, Paul Elmer. "Jonathan Edwards." In *A Short History of American Literature.* Edited by William Peterfield Trent et al. New York: G. P. Putnam's, pp. 1-15.
    Reprints 1917.3.

4 Phelps, William Lyon. "Edwards and Franklin — the Man of God and the Man of the World: A Dramatic Contrast." *Ladies Home Journal* 39 (November): 16-17, 160, 163, 164, 167.
    Contrasts "those giant contemporaries," Edwards and Franklin, the duty to God of one, the duty to man of the other; the mysticism of one, the worldliness of the other; and suggests that in the combination of the traits of both we would have the "ideal" American and in a host of such Americans, the millennium.

1923

1 Haney, John Louis. *The Story of Our Literature.* New York: Charles Scribner's Sons, pp. 18-20.
    Characterizes Edwards's style as simple, pure, and imaginative, though his subjects were often "harrowing."

2 Phelps, William Lyon. "The Man of the World and the Man of God: A Dramatic Contrast." *Some Makers of American Literature.* Boston: Marshall Jones Co., pp. 1-33.
    Reprints 1922.4.

1924

A Ball, Mary Washington. "Ye Divines of Olde New England." *Methodist Quarterly Review* 73 (April): 257-64.
Relates a brief life of Edwards — "there never was a gentleman of higher tone" — in a briefer survey of New England Puritans.

1 Harpole, Ralph Orin. "The Development of the Doctrine of Atonement in American Thought from Jonathan Edwards to Horace Bushnell." Ph.D. dissertation, Yale University.
Shows that Edwards's theory of atonement is a "natural product" of his Calvinism, mysticism, and idealism, and that it is similar to Anselm's, though more formal. But his doctrine of satisfaction by punishment and transfer of merit made the atonement "more commercial" than that of the "great" Reformed theologians.

2 Linderholm, Emanuel. *Pingströrelsen, dess forutsättningar och uppkomst.* Stockholm: Albert Bonniers, pp. 141-45.
Notes Edwards's role in the revival of 1734 and the Great Awakening, in a brief survey of the evangelical spirit in America. (In Swedish.)

3 Osgood, Herbert L. *The American Colonies in the Eighteenth Century.* New York: Columbia University Press, 3:411-17, 435-38, 448-50.
Considers Edwards a brilliant apologist for an antiquated Calvinism and, therefore, his career "a tragedy," in a detailed account of the Great Awakening and his central role in it. His *Some Thoughts* "quivers with holy passion."

4 Rowe, Henry Kalloch. *The History of Religion in the United States.* New York: Macmillan Co., pp. 46-48.
Characterizes Edwards as the apologist for a "partially humanized" Calvinism, the "apostle" against liberalism, the "prince" of Great Awakening revivalists. Combining the "severe piety" of the seventeenth-century fathers and the "mystical fervor" of an eighteenth-century prophet, Edwards clarified and spiritualized a waning Puritanism.

5 Wiggam, Albert Edward. *The Fruit of the Family Tree.* Indianapolis: Bobbs-Merrill, pp. 16-20.
Traces the genealogy of the Edwards family, notes the "splendor of the breed," and cites famous members, Grant, Cleveland, and Churchill among them.

1925

1 Anon. "Princeton Gets Old Table." *New York Times,* 4 November, p. 22.
Reports that Mrs. John W. Manning, a great-great-great-granddaughter of Edwards, gave Princeton a mahogany drop-leaf table owned by Edwards till his death.

2 Darrow, Clarence. "The Edwardses and the Jukeses." *American Mercury* 6 (October): 147-57.
Decries the "utter absurdity" of eugenics and finds amazing" that anyone would want to be

traced to Edwards. His theology was "weird and horrible," his mind "distorted and diseased." It is a "not unreasonable guess that the ancestors of the Edwardses and the Jukeses were mixed."

3 Fenn, William Wallace. "The Christian Way of Life in the Religious History of New England." In *Freedom and Truth: Modern Views of Unitarian Christianity.* Edited by Joseph Estlin Carpenter. London: Lindsey Press, pp. 249-80.

Considers *True Virtue*, with its "glorious definition" of the Christian way, to be Edwards's "preeminent" contribution to New England religious thought but that it influenced "comparatively few" churches and ministers, in a short history of Edwards's battle against Arminianism and the rise of Unitarianism.

4 Mudge, Lewis Seymour. "Jonathan Edwards and the Hall of Fame." *Presbyterian Advance* 30 (22 January): 2.

Calls for contributions totalling $3,000 to place a bust of Edwards in the Hall of Fame, New York, and offers a brief account of his career.

5 Winship, Albert E. *Heredity: A History of Jukes-Edwards Families.* Boston: [New England] *Journal of Education.*

Reprints 1900.20.

1926

1 Anon. "The Hall of Fame." *Outlook* 143 (26 May): 128.

Notes the unveiling of the bust of Edwards at the Hall of Fame of New York University on 12 May. (Illustrated.)

2 Anon. "Jonathan Edwards Honored Anew." *Hampshire Gazette,* 19 May, p. 14.

Notes Edwards's induction in the Hall of Fame in New York and a proposal to name a hotel after him in Northampton.

3 Anon. "Unveil Nine Busts of Nation's Great." *New York Times,* 13 May, p. 14.

Reports the ceremony at the Hall of Fame at which a bust of Edwards, a gift of the Presbyterian Church, was unveiled, as were those of Daniel Boone and seven others.

4 Mudge, Lewis Seymour. "Jonathan Edwards and the Hall of Fame." *Presbyterian Magazine* 32 (June): 264, 274.

Notes the installation of a bust of Edwards by Charles Grafly at the Hall of Fame on 12 May and offers a brief account of Edwards's career.

5 Mumford, Lewis. "Origins of the American Mind." *American Mercury* 8 (July): 345-54.

Calls Edwards the "last great expositor" of Calvinism in America, unfortunately caught between his love of beauty of the soul and the needs of determinism. After him, Protestantism lost its "intellectual backbone."

6 Nordell, Philip Gregory. "Jonathan Edwards and Hell Fire." *Forum* 75 (June): 860-69.

Decries Edwards's allegiance to a "false, harsh, and artificial" morality, his imprecatory sermons that "reek and seethe" with God s implacable wrath, his pitiful lack of humanity.

7 Seitz, Don C. "Jonathan Edwards, Consistent Theologian." *Outlook* 143 (30 June): 315-16.

Reads Edwards "rather casually" and concludes that at least he was a "consistent" theologian of man's depravity, but that he could have been "a rival" to Newton, Tyndall, Huxley, and Darwin.

8 Williams, Stanley Thomas. *The American Spirit in Letters.* The Pageant of America, no. 11. New Haven: Yale University Press, pp. 43-44.

Considers Edwards "the supreme Puritan," but stripped of his Calvinism, a transcendentalist. (Illustrated.)

1927

1 Adams, James Truslow. *Provincial Society, 1690-1767.* A History of American Life, no. 3. New York: MacMillan Co., pp. 282-83.

Cites the paradox of Edwards's sweetness of mind and character and his imprecatory sermons of damnation.

2 Parrington, Vernon Louis. "The Anachronism of Jonathan Edwards." *The Colonial Mind, 1620-1800. Main Currents in American Thought,* 1. New York: Harcourt, Brace & Co., pp. 148-63.

Decries Edwards's conservative stance in the midst of growing liberal tendencies, in a brief study of "the last and greatest of the royal line of Puritan mystics." Edwards's doctrine of the sovereignty of God is a return to an "absolutist past," his *Freedom of the Will* a "stifling" of New England intellectual life, his *Faithful Narrative* a collection of "repulsive records" of conversion. Ironically, reactionary Edwards hastened an end to "Puritan formalism" and old-order Presbyterian polity by espousing religious emotionalism and democratic Congregationalism. Thus Edwards, "an anachronism" in Ben Franklin's America, became "the intellectual leader of the revolutionaries." (Frequently reprinted.)

3 Wortley, George Francis. "The Status of the Child in New England Congregationalism from Jonathon [*sic*] Edwards to Horace Bushnell." Ph.D. dissertation, Hartford School of Religious Education.

Traces historically the theological status of the child from the "clear crystal" of Edwards's Calvinism to the Christian nature theory of Horace Bushnell. For Edwards, the child has a dual status, at once Adamic and parental, sinful and covenanted; for his successors, the former status is "bitterly assailed"; for Bushnell, the child is "to grow up a Christian and never know himself as otherwise."

1928

1 Anon. "Recalls Life of Edwards in City." *Hampshire Gazette,* 28 July, p. 6.
Sketches the life of Edwards, "the patron saint" of Northampton.

2 Burggraaff, Winfield. *The Rise and Development of Liberal Theology in America.* New York: Board of Publication & Bible-School Work of the Reformed Church in America, pp. 110-25 passim.

Claims that Edwards (and through him, New England Theology generally) contributed to the rise of liberal religious thought in America by shifting theological ground from the objective to the subjective. In distinguishing between natural and moral ability, he created "deserts of speculation" in which New England Theology "died" and Pelagianism was born; in shifting from God as sovereign to God as moral governor, he limited his "totality." Thus the modified Calvinism of Edwards ended in "decidedly un-Calvinistic" doctrines, preparing the way for the Arminianism of his successors.

3 Elsbree, Oliver Wendell. *The Rise of the Missionary Spirit in America, 1790-1815.* Williamsport, Pa.: Williamsport Printing & Binding Co., pp. 135-36.

Links the organization in 1792 of the Particular Baptist Society for the Propagation of the Gospel among the Heathen to the London reissue in 1789 of Edwards's *Humble Attempt.*

4 Kuiper, Herman. Appendix to his *Calvin on Common Grace.* Goes, Netherlands: Oosterbaan & Le Cointre, pp. iv-v.

Notes Edwards's distinction between common or restraining grace in natural man and saving grace in regenerate man.

5 Loud, Grover C. *Evangelized America.* New York: Dial Press, pp. 10-31.

Traces Edwards's evangelical impulse to his early life as a "spiritual hypochondriac" and to his endless concern with sin. His pastoral work during 1734-35 in Northampton heralded the Great Awakening throughout the colonies, the effects of which are still broadly felt. "He spoke little of heaven, he cared nothing for this world, but he certainly knew his hell."

6 Rowe, Henry Kalloch. "Jonathan Edwards." *Modern Pathfinders of Christianity: The Lives and Deeds of Seven Centuries of Christian Leaders.* New York: Fleming H. Revell Co., pp. 102-13.

Recounts Edwards's career as an example of a self-stimulating mind productive of original thought.

7 Seldes, Gilbert. "Jonathan Edwards." *Dial* 84 (January): 37-46.

See 1928.8 for an expanded version.

8 ———. "A Stormer of Heaven." *The Stammering Century.* New York: John Day Co., pp. 13-35.

Traces the plethora of cults, fads, reforms, movements, social crazes, and political experiments of nineteenth-century America to the revivalist spirit and method fostered by Edwards. *Sinners in the Hands of an Angry God* offers the "promise of libertarian religion" and Edwards's doctrine of direct communion with God, the hope of personal salvation. Thus Edwards undercut the authority of both minister and church and "cleared the way" for cults and madness.

9 Visser 't Hooft, Willem A. *The Background of the Social Gospel in America.* Haarlem: H. D. Tjeenk Willink & Zoon, pp. 89-97, 172-73.

Locates the center of Edwards's thought in *True Virtue,* a "thorough modification" of traditional Calvinism. In Edwards, God becomes the focus of speculation and a subject of understanding; the legal ethics of the past gives way to a mutual benevolence. Such rational theocracy, unfortunately, subordinates a mysterious and inscrutable God to human reasoning.

10 Vögelin, Erich. *Über die Form des Amerikanischen Geistes.* Tübingen: J. C. B. Mohr, pp. 109-19.

Traces the relationship of Calvinist dogma and mystical pantheism in Edwards, from "Of Being" and *Personal Narrative* to the posthumous works, and suggests links to Peirce, William James, and Santayana. (In German.)

11 Weigle, Luther A. *American Idealism.* The Pageant of America: A Pictorial History of the United States, no. 10. New Haven: Yale University Press, pp. 64-66.

Treats briefly Edwards as theologian, philosopher, mystic, and family man, and claims that he was responsible "indirectly" for religious freedom in America.

12 Williams, Stanley T. "Six Letters of Jonathan Edwards to Joseph Bellamy." *New England Quarterly* 1 (April): 226-42.

Reprints six Edwards letters in the Yale collection to Joseph Bellamy from 1741 to 1756, revealing the public man — his reading for *Freedom of the Will*, his friendship with David Brainerd, his dismissal from Northampton, his mission at Stockbridge — and the personal one — his purchase of sheep.

1929

1 Andrews, Charles M. *Jonathan Edwards.* [New Haven: Yale University Press].

Reprints part of 1929.7.

2 Bacon, Benjamin Wisner. *The Theological Significance of Jonathan Edwards.* [New Haven: Yale University Press].

Reprints part of 1929.7.

3 Billings, Thomas Henry. "The Great Awakening." *Essex Institute Historical Collections* 65 (January): 89-104.

Surveys the Great Awakening and notes that the process of conversion outlined in Edwards's *Religious Affections* becomes "stereotyped" among evangelicals throughout New England, though Salem, Massachusetts, was hardly touched by the movement or the book.

4 Brown, Charles Reynolds. "Edwards, Jonathan." *Encyclopaedia Britannica*, 14th ed., 8:19-21.

Regrets Edwards's lack of concern for the poor, the "broken-hearted," and the Indians, in a brief life and estimate, and accounts his "perpendicular piety" unfeeling and his "potent" influence surprising.

5 Burt, Struthers. "Jonathan Edwards and the Gunman." *North American Review* 227 (June): 732-18.

Offers Puritanism as a possible source for the rise in crime: gunmen "eagerly participate in the perverted remnants" of Edwards's philosophy.

6 Chandler, Thomas. Letter, 14 March 1771. In *Samuel Johnson: His Career and Writings.* Edited by Herbert W. and Carol Schneider. New York: Columbia University Press, 1:476.

Reprints a letter from Thomas Chandler to Samuel Johnson remarking his pleasure upon learning of James Dana's attack on Edwards's *Freedom of the Will* (1770.2). "If the Dissenters will confute one another, it will save us the trouble."

7 Connecticut Society of the Colonial Dames of America. *Proceedings of the Dedication of the Memorial Gateway to Jonathan Edwards at the Old Burying Ground South Windsor, 25 June 1929.* New Haven: Yale University Press, 61 pp.

Publishes the papers delivered at the dedication of a memorial gateway to Edwards at his birthplace.

Andrews, Evangeline Walker. Foreword, pp. [3]-5. Recounts the history of the Edwards memorial gateway, from the first discussions of the Landmark Committee in 1912 to the request for plans in October 1928, and describes it.

Soule, Sherrod. "The Birthplace of Jonathan Edwards," pp. [13]-14. Describes Edwards's birthplace in East Windsor.

Williams, Mrs. James S. "The Family of Jonathan Edwards," pp. [15]-23. Traces Edwards's immediate family, their marriages and their deaths.

Bacon, Benjamin Wisner. "The Theological Significance of Jonathan Edwards," pp. [24]-38. Marks the "crucifixion" by his Northampton congregation and the end of his evangelism as the beginning of the theology of Edwards. That theology was a "vital expression" of both his deep, mystical experience and his eyewitness to the conversion of others during the revivals. His significance is that "he took Paul and Calvin in deadly earnest in the midst of a generation that did not."

Andrews, Charles M. "Jonathan Edwards," pp. [39]-55. Contends that the story of Edwards is "less the history of a life than the analysis of a mind." Edwards's mind is in conflict — the logical and intellectual on one side, the emotional and mystical on the other — which he seeks to resolve by tempering Calvinism with a sense of the immediacy of God. Such is Edwards's contribution to religious thought.

8 Jordan, David Starr, and Sarah Louise Kimball. *Your Family Tree.* New York: D. Appleton & Co., pp. 235-43.

Traces Edwards's family back to Isabel de Vermandois and forward to such college presidents as Timothy Dwight and Theodore Dwight Woolsey of Yale, Sereno Dwight of Hamilton, and Merrill Edwards of Amherst, Oberlin, and Rutgers.

9 Leisy, Ernest Erwin. *American Literature: An Interpretative Survey.* New York: Thomas Y. Crowell, pp. 22-25.

Suggests that students of literature will prefer Edwards's "prose rhapsody" on Sarah Pierrepont to his polemic on free will.

10 Parkes, Henry Bamford. "New England and the Great Awakening: A study in the Theory and Practice of New England Calvinism." Ph.D. dissertation, University of Michigan.

See 1930.10.

11 Pottere, Charles Francis. "Jonathan Edwards (1703-1758) and the Great Awakening."

The Story of Religion as Told in the Lives of its Leaders. Garden City, N.Y.: Garden City Publishing Co., pp. 512-19.

Relates Sarah's religious experiences, her photistic theophany and profound ecstasy, to Edwards's sense of God-consciousness and to the psychology of religion, in a biography of "one of the shortest-lived" religious leaders, and connects the circulation of obscene books in Northampton to the emotionalism of the Great Awakening, inasmuch as revivals are often accompanied by "waves of sexual immorality."

12 White, Trentwell Mason, and Paul William Lehman. *Writers of Colonial New England.* Boston: Palmer Co., pp. 112-15.

Recounts Edward career and finds his simple and direct prose superior to the "abstruse and asinine polysyllablizing" of many colonial writers.

1930

1 Anon. Review of *Jonathan Edwards,* by Henry Bamford Parkes. *Bookman* 72 (October): 181-82.

Questions Henry Bamford Parkes's "lively" biography of Edwards (1930.10) for its "dogmatic" generalities and insufficient scholarship.

2 Brynestad, Lawrence E. "The Great Awakening in the New England and Middle Colonies. Part II." *Journal of the Presbyterian Historical Society* 14 (September): 104-41.

Conceives the influence of Edwards on the Great Awakening to be indirect and suggestive, "preparing the way" rather than shaping it, in a history of the revival, its sources and consequences, from a Presbyterian point of view. Edwards's 1734 revival had "no direct bearing" on the Awakening because it was so short, but it (and other local ones) did show that a spirit of reform was "taking root" everywhere. The Awakening itself developed a permanent schism in Presbyterianism, though the religious liberties arising from it "inspired" political liberties of union a generation later.

3 Chamberlain, John. "Jonathan Edwards, a Forebear of Modern Puritanism." *New York Times,* 28 September, Section 4, p. 4.

Reviews *Jonathan Edwards,* by Henry Bamford Parkes (1930.10) and finds that more on the river gods and less on "clerical and family bickering" would have better served the study.

4 Faust, Clarence H. "Jonathan Edwards as a Scientist." *American Literature* 1 (January): 393-404.

Questions the possibility that Edwards could have been a scientist, though there was a "thin vein" of such interest in him, because even his early "The Mind" and "Notes on Natural Science" show a "definite theological tinge." His path from the juvenile observations on flying spiders to the mature thought of *Freedom of the Will* was "surprisingly straight." What scientific promise he had has been "overestimated," for he all too frequently "disregards the truth of his premises in the enjoyment of his argument." Such is the way of the logician, not the scientist.

5 Gewehr, Wesley M. *The Great Awakening in Virginia 1740-1790.* Durham, N.C.: Duke University Press, p. 89.

Notes the efforts of Samuel Davies to persuade Edwards to settle in Virginia after his

Northampton dismissal and his failure: word came from Virginia after Edwards removed to Stockbridge.

6 Gohdes, Clarence. "Aspects of Idealism in Early New England." *Philosophical Review* 39 (November): 537-55.

Uncovers "traces" of influence of the Cambridge Platonists in the "much discussed" early idealism of Edwards. Ralph Cudworth's *The True Intellectual System of the Universe* (1678) seems to have found its way into Edwards's "The Mind," and he seems to have "frequently" borrowed from Theophilus Gale to "clinch an argument" in *Religious Affections.*

7 Hall, Thomas Cuming. *The Religious Background of American Culture.* Boston: Little, Brown & Co., pp. 148-53 passim.

Connects Edwards and the Great Awakening to the early English reformation of the fifteenth century and to John Wycliffe rather than to the Continental movement of John Calvin, even though there is no evidence that Edwards had first-hand knowledge of Wycliffe or his work. Both Wycliffe and Edwards focus upon individual redemption rather than the Church Universal and upon sermons rather than the eucharist as the agency of conversion. Edwards can "only be really understood" in a tradition of congregational Protestantism and separatist Dissent. So the Great Awakening "breathed the air" of that movement and prepared the way for revolution.

8 Kershner, Frederick D. *Pioneers in Christian Thought.* Indianapolis: Bobbs-Merrill Co., p. 299.

Refers to Edwards as the "most brilliant interpreter" of Calvin in America.

9 Meyer, Jacob C. *Church and State in Massachusetts, from 1740 to 1833: A Chapter in the History of the Development of Individual Freedom.* Cleveland: Western Reserve University Press, pp. 20-23.

Suggests that the revival in America promoted individual freedom in religion, diminished Congregationalism, and was, for Edwards at least, a reaction against the "commercialism, materialism, and rationalism" of Boston.

10 Parkes, Henry Bamford. *Jonathan Edwards: The Fiery Puritan.* New York: Menton, Balch & Co., 271 pp.

Portrays Edwards, the "father of American Puritanism," as student, parish minister, and exile, in a full-length study that details his life amid warring ministers and feuding families, his times of God's spirit and "religious lunacy," and his theology of "blight upon posterity." Edwards "rescued" Calvinism from its death through the new philosophy and rendered it "impregnable" for a century, but, in doing so, he "fastened upon the necks" of Americans a theology either "repulsive or absurd." Puritanism "satisfied his own psychological need," lending a "breathtaking sublimity" to his vision of the world, yet he "lacked the wisdom" to reject it for a kinder Christianity. And so his "baneful," posthumous influence continued through his "intolerant" and unimaginative disciples, and so this "biggest intellect" of American religious thought, this "most tragic" figure, this "fiery Puritan" is "not truly an American."

11 Riley, Woodbridge. *The Meaning of Mysticism.* New York: Richard R. Smith, pp. 90-93.

Tempers Edwards's rationalism with his mysticism: "the fetters of his iron creed were loosened by his love of nature." Edwards's reading of the Cambridge Platonists proved the "antidote" to his Calvinism and to his "sorry view" of the world and marks the distinction between his public, professional ministry and his private, personal belief.

12 Schneider, Herbert Wallace. "Jonathan Edwards." *Nation* 131 (26 November): 584-85.
Reviews *Jonathan Edwards,* by Henry Bamford Parkes (1930.10). "The facts of Edwards s life and environment which Mr. Parkes has sketched so skillfully bear little relation to the crude generalizations of the prologue and epilogue," where he traces Edwards's "blight upon posterity."

13 ———. *The Puritan Mind.* Studies in Religion and Culture: American Religion Series, 1. New York: Henry Holt & Co., pp. 102-55.
Attributes Edwards's success and failure to the private nature of his love of a sovereign God, an "individual analogue of the theocracy" of an earlier New England Puritanism and a radical departure from its public and social concerns, in an estimate of his career and thought and his role in the Great Awakening. Just as his belief in the Awakening was rooted in the efficacy of his struggle for personal conversion, so his philosophy of aesthetic idealism was "essentially the product of his own experience." But the application of that "sentimental and pathological" love of God rendered his Puritanism "impractical" in his day and "absurd" in ours.

14 Sweet, William Warren. *The Story of Religions in America.* New York: Harper & Brothers, pp. 185-90, 192-99.
Places Edwards "at the very center" of the Great Awakening and traces the effects of revivalism upon subsequent doctrinal disputes and upon church polity, the New Lights and the Old, the orthodox Congregationalists and the liberal. Although Edwards held "staunchly" to divine sovereignty, he sought "larger recognition" for man's responsibility, thus preparing the way, if inadvertently, for a permanent theological rift in New England.

1931

1 Angoff, Charles. *A Literary History of the American People.* New York: Alfred A. Knopf, 1:289-310.
Concludes, after a survey of his life and work, that Edwards was one of the "colossal tragedies" of American culture, a promising philosopher and theologian "ruined completely" by Calvinism and left a "somewhat more intelligent Cotton Mather." A "theistic idealist" and "pagan pantheist," Edwards's influence upon "enlightened American thought is nil."

2 Anon. Review of *Jonathan Edwards,* by Henry Bamford Parkes. *Saturday Review of Literature* 7 (23 May): 851.
Notes that Henry Bamford Parkes fails to give sufficient emphasis to the effect on Edwards of the Episcopal succession at Yale, in an otherwise "well-informed" biography (1930.10).

3 Blankenship, Russell. *American Literature as an Expression of the National Mind.* New York: Henry Holt & Co., pp. 120-25.
Calls Edwards "the most melancholy example in American literature of a brilliant and capable man wholly dominated by an environment that was fated soon to disappear," in a brief estimate of his life, significance, philosophy, and mysticism. Behind Edwards's "unlovely" Calvinism lay a "thorough" mystic.

4 Canby, Henry Seidel. *Classic Americans.* New York: Harcourt, Brace & Co., pp. 9-22.

Chooses Edwards as a "symbol of the dynamic force of New England intellectuality" that was to shape the American mind and considers him a "born man of letters." Through the primacy he gave to the will to be saved, the will to improve and to succeed, Edwards became the first of a long line of "strenuous uplifters" in America. And except for the practical necessity of his times and his critical Yale years, he could have turned his intuitive, mystic genius to literature.

5 Carpenter, Frederic I. "The Radicalism of Jonathan Edwards." *New England Quarterly* 4 (October): 629-44.

Discovers the radicalism of Edwards in the "quality" of his thought; his "utter pantheism"; his emphasis upon Justice or Satan as the "fourth person" of God; his psychology of the will; and, most important, his deep-grained mysticism. "All of Edwards's work was founded on a psychology of mysticism, which was radically different from the theology of Calvinism." Parallels to Walt Whitman and the Transcendentalists in the nineteenth century and Robinson Jeffers and Theodore Dreiser in the twentieth are "perhaps accidental," but those to William James are "indubitable." So, too, Edwards "unconsciously helped" the Revolution by insisting that all men were equal before a sovereign God.

6 Caskey, Ellen. "If They Were Alive Today: Jonathan Edwards — The First American Philosopher." *Thinker* 4 (October): 34-35.

Compares Edwards's insistent belief in the horrors and reality of hell with the lack of such a belief today. Perhaps we should have a "healthy fear" of more than boredom or unemployment.

7 Christie, Francis A. "Jonathan Edwards." In *Dictionary of American Biography.* Edited by Allen Johnson and Dumas Malone. New York: Charles Scribner's Sons, 6:30-37.

Traces the life of Edwards, America's "first great philosophic intelligence," and examines the major works. In his "The Mind," Edwards begins a study of excellency — "the master idea of his career" — which finds its mature expression in *True Virtue* and *End of Creation.* Perhaps Edwards delayed publication of these treatises because the aesthetic joy voiced there is "incongruous" with his rational, ethical Calvinism.

8 Dewey, Edward Hooker. "Jonathan Edwards." In *American Writers on American Literature.* Edited by John Macy. New York: Horace Liveright, pp. 13-24.

Considers Edwards "no less a poet" than a theologian, in a brief estimate of his life and work. His "admirable" phrasing and "memorable" words, his symbolic imagination breathed life into the moribund and "repellent" doctrines of Calvinism. "There is no question that American letters suffered a vital loss in Edwards's defection to his sleeveless cause."

9 Edwards, Maurice Dwight. *Richard Edwards and His Wife Catherine Pond May: Their Ancestors, Lives, and Descendants.* [St. Paul, Minn.: Webb Publishing Co.], pp. 17-21.

Outlines a life of Edwards, an "equally eminent" thinker and saint.

10 Haroutunian, Joseph G. "Jonathan Edwards: A Study in Godliness." *Journal of Religion* 11 (July): 400-19.

Details the "essentials" of Edwards's life and work — without apology for his faults — and discovers the "fundamental motif" of both to be his "supreme passion" for the glory and sovereignty of God. Holiness is a "new quality of experience": analyzable into elements; identical, like true virtue, with excellence; and, with knowledge of God, another aspect of the same experience. Although there is in Edwards "a healthy agnosticism and a genuine 'radical empiricism'" — God's love, grace, wrath, and justice are "facts" of daily life — he is not a pantheist but a "radically theocentric" Calvinist. As a doctrinal innovator Edwards is "insignificant," but his vision and type of godliness are "unique in comprehensiveness, cogency, and profundity."

11 Johnson, Thomas H. "Jonathan Edwards' Background of Reading." *Publications of the Colonial Society of Massachusetts* 28 (December): 193-222.

Traces Edwards's reading habits through his Diary, notes, and letters, but principally through his "Catalogue," a manuscript journal of forty-three brown-paper pages, begun in his early twenties and continued until within a year of his death, containing about 500 items read (and noted) or to be read. Edwards's literary interests included theology, religion — Catholic, Jewish, and Deist, as well as Protestant — contemporary philosophy, science, history, travel, and literature — fiction and poetry, but not drama — , a literary background "phenomenal" for a provincial minister. "Of all the Americans of his day — perhaps of any day — none had more notable endowments for pure scholarship or a more original metaphysical mind, yet none has left monuments so crumbled and overgrown."

12 ————. Review of *Jonathan Edwards,* by Henry Bamford Parkes. *New England Quarterly* 4 (April): 354-56.

Expresses disappointment with Henry Bamford Parkes (1930.10): because he repeats the canard of the past — Edwards was a "fiery" Puritan — and because he fails to take advantage of available biographical materials, the study is "incomplete and sensational."

13 Muirhead, John H. *The Platonic Tradition in Anglo-Saxon Philosophy: Studies in the History of Idealism in England and America.* London: George Allen & Unwin, p. 307.

Credits Edwards as the first philosophical idealist in New England, inspired probably by the "subtle air" of Malebranchean mysticism coming from England.

14 Parry, Mark H. "The Theology of the Great Awakening." Th.D. dissertation, Drew University.

Studies the life and theological views of Edwards, George Whitefield, and Samuel Davies in their relation to the evangelicalism of the Great Awakening.

15 Schneider, Herbert Wallace. *The Puritan Mind.* London: Constable & Co.

Reprints 1930.13.

16 Townsend, H. G. "An Alogical Element in the Philosophy of Edwards and Its Function in His Metaphysics." In *Proceedings of the Seventh International Congress of Philosophy.* Edited by Gilbert Ryle. Oxford: Oxford University Press, pp. 495-500.

Discovers in *End of Creation* and *True Virtue* the "synthetic principle" in Edwards to be ethics-aesthetic, more Platonic than Berkeleian, more metaphysical than epistemological. Edwards's doctrine of the divine and supernatural light or "immediate awareness" links his theory of knowledge to his metaphysics and relates existence to an otherwise abstract logic. Being and knowing unite in a principle of order that is apprehended intuitively — a theory "unique in our history."

*17 Widenhouse, Ernest Cornelius. "The Doctrine of the Atonement in the New England Theology from Jonathan Edwards to Horace Bushnell." Ph.D. dissertation, Hartford Seminary.

Cited in *Comprehensive Dissertation Index 1861-1972*, 32: 378.

1932

1 Calverton, V. F. *The Liberation of American Literature.* New York: Charles Scribner's Sons, pp. 77-79, 173-74.

Associates Edwards with a dying theology and a growing commerce. Edward's dismissal is a turning point in the mid-century crisis between the wealthy bourgeoisie and the New England clergy and marks a symbolic shift from the theocratic to the civil state.

2 Carpenter, Frederic I. Review of *Jonathan Edwards,* by Arthur C. McGiffert. *New England Quarterly* 5 (April): 395-97.

Recommends Arthur C. McGiffert's study (1932.10) for its accuracy, clarity, and insight in interpreting Edwards to the modern world.

3 Dickinson, Thomas H. *The Making of American Literature.* New York: Century Co., pp. 156-58.

Considers Edwards "a kind of anachronism," in a brief estimate.

3A Hall, Basil. Review of *Jonathan Edwards,* by Arthur C. McGiffert, Jr. *Religion in Life* 1 (Spring): 309-10.

Notes that Arthur C. McGiffert's "invigorating" study of Edwards (1932.10) was the "February first choice of the Religious Book Club."

4 Haroutunian, Joseph G. "Piety versus Morality: The Passing of the New England Theology." Ph.D. dissertation, Columbia University.

Published as 1932.5.

5 ———. *Piety versus Moralism: The Passing of the New England Theology.* Studies in Religion and Culture: American Religion Series, no. 4. New York: Henry Holt & Co., xxv, 329 pp.

Attributes the decline of New England Theology after Edwards to the lack of his "profound piety" and "intellectual vigor" in his successors and to the modifying influence of eighteenth-century political and social realities and humanitarian impulses, in a history of the shift from the theology of Edwards to the theology of the Edwardseans, from piety to moralism. Edwards erected his Calvinism upon concepts of divine sovereignty and "empirical piety," grounded in nature and Scripture, philosophical and rational, a systematic theology separate from temporal concerns and of "permanent human significance." But it was "a delicate matter" to reconcile human responsibility with theocentric piety and frequently the Edwardseans failed. The history, therefore, of New England Theology is a "history of degradation."

6 ———. Review of *Jonathan Edwards,* by Arthur C. McGiffert. *Church History* 1 (September): 174-75.

Regrets that Arthur C. McGiffert's study (1932.10) emphasizes the "mystical and practical" in

Edwards at the expense of the rational and the realistic and that it fails to explore the "essential unity" of his thought.

7 Johnson, Thomas H. "Jonathan Edwards and the 'Young Folks' Bible." *New England Quarterly* 5 (January): 37-54.
   Checks the manuscript notes of Edwards's inquiry into the reading of "'unclean'" books by certain young people of Northampton in 1744 and discovers the text to be "quite evidently" from the pseudonymous Aristotle, *The Midwife Rightly Instructed*, not some scandalous novel. Referred to mockingly as the "'young folks' Bible" by one of the accused, it was a compendium of medical information put to "pornographic uses" by young men in mixed company. Edwards's impolitic handling of the matter probably was "contributory" to his dismissal six years later.

8 Knight, Grant C. *American Literature and Culture*. New York: Ray Long & Richard B. Smith, pp. 34-41.
   Ranks Edwards the "foremost figure" in American literature before Franklin, in a short survey of his career.

9 Lewisohn, Ludwig. *Expression in America*. New York: Harper & Brothers, pp. 17-18.
   Considers Edwards properly neglected: he was a "baffled poet, a sick and corrupted soul."

10 McGiffert, Arthur Cushman, Jr. *Jonathan Edwards*. Creative Lives Series. New York: Harper & Brothers, 225 pp.
   Presents a full-length study of the "well-balanced" character and impressive thought of Edwards, "essentially a student" given to "relentless curiosity" and love of beauty, whose approach to the vexing problems of his time was that of a "historically and philosophically minded" scholar rather than a practical minister and whose reputation continues as "one of the most stimulating and forceful minds America has produced." Central to his thought is his belief, based on youthful intuition and confirmed in later observation, that God was at once "majestic and holy, beautiful and loving," the absolute sovereign, the "Supreme Connoisseur." So Edwards, in his "critical mysticism," moves from pantheism to personalism in his interpretation of God "with no apparent jolt." And Edwards, the "sacred gadfly" of Northampton, moves from the stylistic mastery of *Faithful Narrative* and from America's "most notable single discussion" of religion in *Religious Affections* to the significant, though at times "marred," works of his exile in Stockbridge. *Freedom of the Will*, for example, emphasizes the intellect at the expense of the subconscious processes of the mind and is typical of "static" eighteenth-century thought. Still Edwards remains "one of the earliest representatives of modern-mindedness" in American religious thought.

11 Mayhew, George Noel. "The Relation of the Theology of Jonathan Edwards to Contemporary Penological Theory and Practice." Ph.D. dissertation, University of Chicago.
   Published, in part, as 1935.5.

12 Parkes, Henry Bamford. "The Puritan Heresy." *Hound & Horn* 5 (January): 165-90.
   Speculates on the Catholic elements in Edwards, "the only original thinker" of Puritan New England, and traces briefly his ideas and his influence. Edwards's belief that God is beauty and is revealed in nature and his conversion experience were "Catholic and not Calvinist." And when his nineteenth-century followers denied "the Catholic solution" to nature and grace, "the Puri-

tan heresy ended in the complete disappearance of Christianity as a *religion*" and survived only as a "practical philosophy."

13 Suter, Rufus Orlando, Jr. "The Philosophy of Jonathan Edwards." Ph.D. dissertation, Harvard University.

Examines the philosophy of Edwards under two main divisions, man and the world. The first details both his psychological system about the understanding, the will, and the instincts, and his ethical theory about depravity, value, beauty, and virtue; the second deals with his metaphysics and epistemology. But in both categories Edwards is "rent" by loyalties to his Calvinism and his Neoplatonism, and the conflict creates in him a "deadlock."

14 Warfield, Benjamin Breckinridge. "Edwards and the New England Theology." *Studies in Theology.* New York: Oxford University Press, pp. 513-38.

Reprints 1912.7.

15 Warren, Austin. Review of *Jonathan Edwards,* by Henry Bamford Parkes; *Jonathan Edwards,* by Arthur Cushman McGiffert, Jr.; and "The Philosophy of Jonathan Edwards," a dissertation by Rufus Suter. *American Literature* 4 (November): 314-18.

Finds that Henry Bamford Parkes's valuable study (1930.10) is more concerned with the New England mind than the mind of Edwards; Arthur Cushman McGiffert's unpretentious study (1932.10), while it does not supersede Alexander V. G. Allen's "exhaustive" theological analysis (1889.1), reflects a Neocalvinistic admiration for Edwards's work; and Rufus Suter's "painstaking" study (1932.13) is distinctive in its emphasis on the Neoplatonism in Edwards's posthumous treatises.

1933

1 Anon. "From Jonathan Edwards Who Married Sarah Pierrepont in 1727 have Descended. . . ." *Philadelphia Evening Bulletin,* 11 August, [no pp.]

Considers Edwards's 853 male descendants, among them college presidents and professors, judges and governors, congressmen and senators, to be "the most valuable contribution to American blood."

2 Fleming, Sandford. *Children and Puritanism: The Place of Children in the Life and Thought of the New England Churches, 1620-1847.* Yale Studies in Religious Education. New Haven: Yale University Press, pp. 99-101, 163-65 passim.

Discovers no difference between Edwards's sermons to children and his sermons to adults and notes his failure (and the failure of his age) to understand children. Yet a "remarkable number" of children participated in the revivals and showed, to a great degree, the physical effects of them.

3 Shipton, Clifford Kenyon. "The New England Clergy of the 'Glacial Age.'" *Publications of the Colonial Society of Massachusetts* 32 (December): 24-54.

Cites Edwards as perhaps the "last of the very great who entered the ministry because there was no other suitable outlet for his abilities" and as an example of an impoverished clergyman in eighteenth-century New England.

1934

1 Anon. "Jonathan Edwards." *New York Times,* 30 August, p. 18.
Calls Edwards's ministry the "chief public interest" of the bicentennial celebration of the Stockbridge Congregational Church. Though cast out of Northampton and upon the frontier of Stockbridge, Edwards showed "his kindliness and beauty of soul . . . even to his primitive congregation." (An editorial.)

2 Dewey, Edward Hooker. "Jonathan Edwards." In *American Writers on American Literature.* Edited by John Macy. New York: Tudor Publishing Co.
Reprints 1931.8.

3 Horton, Walter Marshall. *Realistic Theology.* New York: Harper & Brothers, pp. 18-21.
Rests Edwards's defense of Calvinism upon his originality in responding to his time and the thought of Locke, Leibniz, Malebranche, Berkeley, and Wesley. His theology is marked by logic, piety, and mysticism.

4 Johnson, Thomas Herbert. "Jonathan Edwards as a Man of Letters." Ph.D. dissertation, Harvard University.
Traces the "literary and bibliographical history" of Edwards's prose chiefly through an examination of the methods, sources, and development of his sermon style, his effectiveness as a preacher and a polemicist, and his precocity in the juvenilia, diaries, resolutions, and notebooks. Edwards should rank higher in American letters than he does, but the "quality and scope are frequently much less than the capacity of the man."

5 Mecklin, John M. *The Story of American Dissent.* New York: Harcourt, Brace & Co., pp. 60, 213-15, 251.
Relates Edwards (and the Great Awakening) to the rising tide of political and social dissent in New England and Virginia, pointing out that his emphasis upon individual experience contained "a deadly menace" to the establishment, religious and secular.

6 Nelson, Roscoe. "Jonathan Edwards." In *Founders and Leaders of Connecticut, 1633-1783.* Edited by Charles Edward Perry. Boston: D. C. Heath & Co., pp. 147-50.
Offers a brief biography and insists that Edwards the mystic and saint will outlive his musty theology.

7 Stowe, Lyman Beecher. *Saints, Sinners and Beechers.* Indianapolis: Bobbs-Merrill, pp. 45-46.
Reports the reaction of Lyman Beecher's wife to his reading of Edwards's *Sinners in the Hands of an Angry God:* "'Dr. Beecher, I shall not listen to another word of that slander on my Heavenly father!' and swept out of the room."

8 Suter, Rufus. "The Concept of Morality in the Philosophy of Jonathan Edwards." *Journal of Religion* 14 (July): 265-72.
Underscores the importance of ethics to Edwards, "first of the American philosophers"; compares it to Kant's emphasis on ideal morality; and contrasts it to ethics as "applied sociology" of his contemporaries, as conformity to nature of Aristotle, and as pleasant sensation of Walter Pater. For Edwards, true virtue is "a sacrosanct ideal," which is rooted in faculties given

over to "a stupendously glorious emotional attachment" to being in general (God) and indistinguishable from God's love of himself. Edwards's ethical system is inextricably linked to his theology and is generally expressed in aesthetic terms.

9 ———. "The Problem of Evil in the Philosophy of Jonathan Edwards." *Monist* 44 (July): 280-95.

Claims that Edwards tried to reconcile "two violently opposed philosophies" — Calvinism, with its insistence on the depravity of man, and Platonism, with its insistence on the overflowing goodness of God — and that he "struggled heroically" with the problem of evil throughout his career. At one time or another, he suggested five different "solutions" to the problem: one, that evil is inevitable in an actual world; two, that evil is necessary to the possibility of good; three, that evil events do not exist inasmuch as consequences of those events are good; four, that evil events or things in and of themselves do not exist; five, that evil is mysteriously compatible with good because reality is rational. There is no intellectual solution to Edwards's self-created problem; "ultimately," where a solution is possible, it rests upon "an act of faith."

10 Townsend, Harvey Gates. "Jonathan Edwards." *Philosophical Ideas in the United States.* New York: American Book Co., pp. 35-62.

Considers Edwards "the first and perhaps the greatest philosophical thinker in America" by virtue of the original, systematic, and influential nature of his thought, in an analysis of his major work and principal concepts. Indebted to the Cambridge Platonists and a "sturdy" idealist from the start, Edwards found revelation and reason "inseparable" and, with Locke, rooted knowledge in sensation and reflection. Of a "sensitive aesthetic nature," Edwards is more nearly a poet than a mystic. His justly praised logical constructs are ultimately aesthetic categories, and the "real heart" of his ethics is his belief that men love God because he is beautiful. Hence the finite, ordered world tends to infinite wisdom and beauty through the divine light or love.

11 U.S. Library of Congress. *A List of Printed Materials on Jonathan Edwards, 1703-1758, to be Found in the Library of Congress Reading Room.* Washington: Office of the Superintendent of the Reading Room, 29 pp.

Lists approximately 400 Edwards items — biographies, appreciations, criticism, and fugitive references — in the Library of Congress. (Typescript.)

1935

1 Elsbree, Oliver Wendell. "Samuel Hopkins and his Doctrine of Benevolence." *New England Quarterly* 8 (December): 534-50.

Attributes Edwards's influence on Samuel Hopkins to their two years together in Northampton and the proximity of Great Barrington, where Hopkins settled, to Stockbridge. For all their theological similarities, Hopkins differs from Edwards on the extent of the atonement, the existence of free choice, and the nature of "true holiness."

2 Faust, Clarenced H. "Jonathan Edwards' View of Human Nature." Ph.D. dissertation, University of Chicago.

Reprinted as part of 1935.3 (and published separately by the University of Chicago Libraries).

3 Faust, Clarence H., and Thomas H. Johnson. "Introduction." *Jonathan Edwards:*

Representative Selections, with Introduction, Bibliography, and Notes. American Writers Series. New York: American Book Co., pp. xii-cxvii.

Examines Edwards as man, thinker, and writer in a closely argued three-part introduction to selections from the standard texts and manuscript sources and an annotated bibliography. The middle part (by Faust) deals serially with Edwards's psychological analysis of the Great Awakening, the major issues of the free-will controversy, and the coherence of his doctrines of sin, virtue, and grace — all a product of Edwards's "exalted and mystical" rendering of divine sovereignty, first experienced in conversion and later explained through logical constructs. The first part outlines Edwards's career, the third his art (both by Johnson). His rigorous logic accounts for the "severe, undilated" style of the treatises; the freedom from eccentricity accounts for the prose cadences and clarity of the sermons and makes up for any want of "conscious artistry."

4 James, Henry, Sr. Letter, 11 May 1843. In *The Thought. and Character of William James,* by Ralph Barton Perry. Boston: Little, Brown & Co., p. 47.

Remarks in a letter to Emerson that Edwards would make "the best possible reconciler and critic of philosophy" since his time.

5 Mayhew, George Noel. "The Pattern of Sovereignty in Relation to Punishment." *The Relation of the Theology of Jonathan Edwards to Contemporary Penological Theory and Practice.* Chicago: University of Chicago Libraries, pp. 47-70.

Contends that Edwards's idea of God develops from the political patterns of sovereignty inherent in feudalism and sixteenth-century monarchy and that his sense of punitive justice so derived runs counter to the more redemptive process of democratic penology "dawning in his day." Edwards deals with the problem of punishment through the Anselmic conception of sin as a violation of private right or honor and through the Grotian conception as a violation of the dignity and authority of the law. His God is ruler, lawgiver, and judge, perfect in all, for whom justice is equated with punishment and sinners with rebels. (A twenty-three page reprint of chapter 3 of 1932.11.)

6 Miller, Perry. "The Marrow of Puritan Divinity." *Publications of the Colonial Society of Massachusetts* 32 (February): 247-300.

Concludes a study of New England covenantal theology with this sentence: "It was Jonathan Edwards who went back to the doctrine from which the tradition had started; went back, not to what the first generation of New Englanders had held, but to Calvin, and who became, therefore, the first consistent and authentic Calvinist in New England." (Reprinted in 1956.8.)

1936

1 Anon. "Making Gavels from Stair Railing of Edwards House Is Idea of Rev. R. D. Scott." *Hampshire Gazette,* 25 January, pp. 1, 2.

Recounts events that led to the making of gavels from the mahogany railing recovered from the dismantled "Edwards" house on King Street.

2 Boynton, Percy H. *Literature and American Life.* Boston: Ginn & Co., pp. 84-88.

Characterizes Edwards as a "medieval mind" given to reconciling the beneficent God of *Personal Narrative* with the stern God of *Sinners in the Hands of an Angry God.*

3 Carpenter, Frederic I. Review of *Jonathan Edwards,* edited by Clarence H. Faust and Thomas H. Johnson. *New England Quarterly* 9 (March): 174-75.

Calls Clarence H. Faust and Thomas H. Johnson's introduction (1935.3) a "masterpiece of erudition" destined for the desks of scholars, not students, because of its dissertation-like qualities.

4 Crosby, C. R., and S. C. Bishop. "Aeronautic Spiders with a Description of a New Species." *Journal of the New York Entomological Society* 44 (March): 43-44.

Regrets that Edwards became a theologian of damnation instead of our first arachnologist. "It was a loss to science and a doubtful gain for religion."

5 Dean, Charles J. "Finds Whitney House and the Jonathan Edwards House Were Not the Same." *Hampshire Gazette,* 14 February, pp. 9, 13.

Describes Edwards's house in Northampton, its subsequent owners, and its razing in 1830. Josiah Dwight Whitney built a larger house on the same site, which gave rise to some local confusion about the Edwards "mansion."

6 Gerould, James Thayer. Review of *Jonathan Edwards,* edited by Clarence H. Faust and Thomas H. Johnson. *Modern Philology* 34 (August): 102-103.

Finds "illuminating" the editors' introductory remarks on Edwards's thought and style and particularly useful the bibliography (1935.3).

7 Gray, Joseph M. M. "Jonathan Edwards, His God." *Prophets of the Soul.* New York: Abingdon Press, pp. 37-61.

Counts Edwards's terrible and implacable God a misrepresentation and an "immense disservice" to man, in an estimate of his life and work. Though Edwards's stern view of divinity may explain the reality of sin and may answer a human need for authority, it lacks Christian love and misconceives Scripture. Ultimately, it yields to a more liberal faith, and God the sovereign is no longer tyrant but friend.

8 Hitchcock, Orville A. "A Critical Study of the Oratorical Technique of Jonathan Edwards." Ph.D. dissertation, State University of Iowa.

Considers Edwards "a speaker first" and analyzes 1200 sermons for their speech premises, preparation and delivery, organization, persuasion, style, and effect upon an audience of "good, honest country folk." Edwards is a prominent colonial speaker whose carefully prepared sermons were delivered in "tense, precise tones" and in a style plain and simple. "The sermons are a combination of compact, irresistible reasoning and fervent, vivid pathetic appeals."

9 Müller, Gustav E. *Amerikanische Philosophie.* Stuttgart: F. Frommann, pp. 17-39.

Calls Edwards the first and last philosophical Puritan in America whose originality and boldness stand in tragicomic incongruity to his limited education and views, in a narration of his life and an explanation of his systematic, logical, and apolitical thought. (In German.)

10 S[chneider], H[erbert] W[allace]. Review of *Jonathan Edwards,* edited by Clarence H. Faust and Thomas H. Johnson. *Journal of Philosophy* 33 (4 June): 327.

Finds only "occasional slips" — the emphasis on Edwards s mysticism in his doctrine of love of God, for instance — in Clarence H. Faust and Thomas H. Johnson's "distinguished" text (1935.3).

11 Taylor, Walter Fuller. *A History of American Letters.* Boston: American Book Co., pp. 29-36.

Suggests that *Personal Narrative* is Edwards's "enduring literary work" and mysticism his chief trait.

1937

1 Anon. "Wills of Two Famous Local Men Recalled." *Hampshire Gazette,* 6 July, p. 7.

Reprints and compares wills of two local celebrities, Edwards and Calvin Coolidge.

2 Berkhof, Louis. *Reformed Dogmatics.* Grand Rapids, Mich.: William B. Eerdmans, pp. 161-63.

Sketches Edwards's modification of Reformed views in New England in his rejection of efficiency in God's connection with the fall of man, his overemphasis of the determinate character of the will, and his adoption of the realistic theory of the transmission of sin.

3 Gambrell, Mary Latimer. *Ministerial Training in Eighteenth-Century New England.* New York: Columbia University Press, pp. 31-35 passim.

Finds typical of the clergy of the time Edwards's pastoral role in "remote" Northampton and his tutorial one to Joseph Bellamy and Samuel Hopkins at home. Though Edwards valued learning and preaching in the ministry, his *True Excellency* centers upon "mastery of doctrine."

4 Hornberger, Theodore. "The Effect of the New Science upon the Thought of Jonathan Edwards." *American Literature* 9 (May): 196-207.

Traces the influence of the new science on Edwards and suggests that he incorporated science in his theology "to save God" from seventeenth-century scientific materialists. His Yale notebooks show that science "definitely affected" his idea of God; his work of the 1730s reveal "a new synthesis" of science, philosophy, and theology; but his work during the Awakening is "singularly free" of scientific argument. The impact of science returns, however, after his dismissal. *Freedom of the Will* is "saturated" with science; *Original Sin* is "equally impregnated"; and *End of Creation,* his "final statement," demonstrates the "rather close" relationship of science to his "burning and mystical" concept of God.

5 Knöpp, Walther. "Jonathan Edwards: der Weg der Heiligung." Ph.D. dissertation, Hartford Theological Seminary.

Discovers in Edwards's doctrine of saving grace, found especially in his sermons, the key to his theology and a clue to American church history, in a study of his ideas of holiness, sovereignty, rebirth, and the coming kingdom. (In German.)

6 Lyman, Clifford H. *Northampton in the Days of Jonathan Edwards 1727-1750.* Northampton, Mass.: Metcalf Printing & Publishing Co., 14 pp.

Reviews Edwards's life "here in Northampton" and the memorials to him. There are two monuments in the Bridge Street Cemetery and a tablet in the First Church. Two other churches, the Edwards Congregational Church, Northampton, and the Edwards Congregational Church, in Davenport, Iowa, are "living memorials of this great and good man."

7   Niebuhr, H. Richard. *The Kingdom of God in America.* Chicago: Willet, Clark & Co.,
    pp. 101-103, 113-16, 135-45.
       Underscores divine sovereignty as the "explicit foundation" of Edwards's thought, from his
    conversion experience in *Personal Narrative* to his millennial hope in *History of Redemption,* in a
    survey of the Great Awakening and its impact upon the idea of the coming of the kingdom of
    God in America. Seen in the context of divine sovereignty, Edwards's hell-fire sermons represent
    an "intense awareness" of man's precarious poise between disintegration and harmony, not the
    frightening need of conventional morality often depicted. And his quickened sense of God's
    power in the revivals led him (and other ministers) to the realization of Christ's coming king-
    dom and man's "everlasting hope." That conviction is in a native, American tradition.

8   Sweet, William Warren. *Makers of Christianity from John Cotton to Lyman Abbott.*
    New York: Henry Holt & Co., pp. 75-87.
       Accounts Edwards's "personalized" Calvinism the source of "new life" in New England theol-
    ogy and the "vital spark" to religious life generally, in a survey of colonial awakeners. Edwards's
    mystical, inner experience (and Sarah's) translates the doctrines of Calvinism from a social and
    political philosophy to individual experience and searches out kindred experience in his congre-
    gation, especially in the young. Through his disciples over the next century, Edwards bequeaths
    to individuals and society "motives of great ethical value."

*9 Thomas, John Newton. "Determinism in the Theological System of Jonathan Ed-
    wards." Ph.D. dissertation, University of Edinburgh.

1938

1   Anon. "Yale Gets Collection on Jonathan Edwards." *New York Times,* 4 November,
    p. 20.
       Reports a bequest of Edwards materials — contemporary portraits, manuscript sermons, let-
    ters, and such — to Yale from the will of Eugene Phelps Edwards, of Stonington, Connecticut. "A
    Hebrew Bible printed in Amsterdam in 1753 has on the flyleaf records of the family."

2   Beardsley, Frank Grenville. *The History of Christianity in America.* New York: Ameri-
    can Tract Society, pp. 60-62 passim.
       Lists Edwards among the prominent figures of the Great Awakening — Frelinghuysen,
    Whitefield, the Tennents, and Davenport — in a general appraisal of the man and the move-
    ment.

3   Pratt, Anne Stokely. *Isaac Watts and his Gifts of Books to Yale College.* New Haven:
    Yale University Press, pp. 32-47.
       Recounts in detail the provenance of *Faithful Narrative;* the correspondence of Isaac Watts,
    Benjamin Colman, and Edwards on its publication; and the corrections Edwards made in the
    text from the English to the American edition.

4   Rice, Rebecca R. "Jonathan Edwards as a Christian Educator." Ph.D. New York Uni-
    versity.
       Traces Edwards's teaching career as a student at Yale, a pastor at Northampton, and a mis-
    sionary at Stockbridge; evaluates both the weaknesses and strengths of his Christian educational

principles (aims, agencies, leadership, techniques, and curriculum); and estimates his influence on theology, personal religion, social religion, polity, and education.

5 Rusterholtz, Wallace P. *American Heretics and Saints*. Boston: Manthorne & Burack, pp. 76-87.

Gives a brief life of Edwards and a discussion of his imprecatory sermons and contrasts his concept of God to that of the Universalist minister Hosea Ballou (1796-1861). Edwards's God was Old Testament, monarchial, thundering the law; Ballou's was New Testament, democratic, "the still small voice" of love.

1939

1 Anderson, Paul Russell, and Max Harold Fisch, eds. *Philosophy in America from the Puritans to James with Representative Selections*. The Century Philosophy Series. New York: D. Appleton-Century Co., pp. 74-82.

Suggests that for Edwards systematic philosophy was probably a "spendthrift luxury," for he early abandoned metaphysical and epistemological investigations for theological ones. Although his idealism, more Platonic than Berkeleian, is evident "from the first" and "implicit in all" his work, Edwards appears publicly an evangelist and a theologian from his first treatise to his last. Nevertheless, he often uses "the equipment of a philosopher," however apologetically, to help clarify his theology.

2 Beardsley, Frank Grenville. "Jonathan Edwards, the Great New England Divine." *Heralds of Salvation: Biographical Sketches of Outstanding Soul Winners*. New York: American Tract Society, pp. 11-24.

Recounts Edwards's career and cites the "initial impulse" he gave to the Great Awakening in the Connecticut Valley through his preaching and the publication of *Faithful Narrative*.

3 Fay, Jay Wharton. *American Psychology before William James*. New Brunswick, N.J.: Rutgers University Press, pp. 43-46 passim.

Locates the roots of Edwards's psychology in the sensationalism of Locke and the scholastic division of the operations of the mind. Psychologically, Edwards identifies the will with the inclination in *Freedom of the Will* and illustrates, as well, a logic founded upon "imperfect observation and inadequate analysis."

4 Malone, Dumas. *Saints in Action*. New York: Abingdon Press, p. 39.

Refers to Edwards as a "major saint" of American Congregationalists.

5 Miller, Perry. *The New England Mind: The Seventeenth Century*. New York: Macmillan Co., pp. 176-77.

Notes that Edward's theology, "the supreme achievement of the New England mind," differs markedly from that of the seventeenth century in its logic, metaphysics, and cosmology.

6 Sweet, William Warren. *The Story of Religion in America*. New York: Harper & Brothers.

Reprints 1930.14.

1940

1 Anon. "Precursor of Whitefield: Jonathan Edwards and his Ministry." *Times Literary Supplement*, 12 October, p. 516.
    Singles out George Whitefield's debt to Edwards in a review of Ola Elizabeth Winslow's "authorative" biography (1940.21).

2 Bates, Ernest Sutherland. "Jonathan Edwards and the Great Awakening." *American Faith: Its Religious, Political, and Economic Foundations.* New York: W. W. Norton & Co., pp. 207-17.
    Traces the career of Edwards, the "Puritan saint," and his successors in the Great Awakening. Edwards's thought hangs upon the two poles of subjectivism and idealism and neglects the "intermediate stages of social activity" for a limited theology of conscience. Unlike Roger Williams or William Penn, Edwards failed to bridge the gap between God and man. But for his mystical, personal experience, his absolute and abstract ideal would be "barren and colorless."

2A Chrisman, Lewis H. Review of *Jonathan Edwards,* by Ola Elizabeth Winslow. *Religion in Life* 9 (Summer): 471-72.
    Finds that Ola Elizabeth Winslow's "substantial" biography (1940.21) strikes "a golden mean" between the "plaster-saint school and the modern 'debunking' species."

3 Faust, C. H. Review of *Jonathan Edwards,* by Ola Elizabeth Winslow. *New England Quarterly* 13 (December): 723-26.
    Compares Ola Elizabeth Winslow's biography (1940.21) to the full-length studies of Edwards by Alexander V. G. Allen (1889.1), Arthur C. McGiffert (1932.10), and Henry Bamford Parkes (1930.10). Although none treat Edwards's personal history as "fully and precisely" as Winslow does, she reduces and blurs his system of ideas, the very arguments necessary to define him. A study is still needed to "make clear the nature of his genius by an analysis rather than a translation."

4 Gilmore, Albert F. "Miss Winslow Presents a Humanized Portrait of Jonathan Edwards." *Christian Science Monthly,* 4 May, p. 10.
    Reviews Ola Elizabeth Winslow's *Jonathan Edwards* (1940.21) and finds it an undistorted, humanized portrait of a "potent preacher."

5 Hammar, George. *Christian Realism in Contemporary Thought.* Uppsala: A. B. Lundequistska Bokhandeln, pp. 85-90.
    Explains Edwards as the "portal" figure in American church history as he sought to fuse the theocentricity of Calvin with the subjectivism of the revivals. Such a "transitional" theology was only a momentary stay against a rising individualism in America and an anthropocentric religion.

6 Hawley, C. A. "America's Unforgettable Philosopher: Review of *Jonathan Edwards,* by Ola Elizabeth Winslow." *Unity* 125 (17 June): 127.
    Predicts a wide audience for Ola Elizabeth Winslow's *Jonathan Edwards* (1940.21).

7 Johnson, Thomas H. *The Printed Writings of Jonathan Edwards 1703-1758: A Bibliography.* Princeton, N.J.: Princeton University Press, pp. vii-xiv.
    Gauges Edwards's reputation and popularity in an introduction to a descriptive bibliography

of 346 numbered items of Edwards's printed writings. The number of editions published in London, Edinburgh, and Glasgow during the eighteenth century and translated into Dutch, French, and German suggests that Edwards was "possibly better known abroad than at home," though he was not a "'leading light'" in either. About sixty items were separately printed, twenty-four of them during his lifetime. Most frequently published (exclusive of reprints) were *Life of Brainerd, Religious Affections, Faithful Narrative,* and *History of Redemption,* about thirty editions each. *Sinners in the Hands of an Angry God* went through twenty-three editions, *Freedom of the Will* twenty, *Original Sin* thirteen, and *Some Thoughts* twelve; ten works were translated, most frequently into Dutch and Welsh, but also into French, German, Arabic, Gaelic, and Choctaw. Since 1900, five works have been separately printed.

8 ————. Review of *Jonathan Edwards,* by Ola Elizabeth Winslow. *American Literature* 12 (May): 251-52.
   Recommends Ola Elizabeth Winslow's sympathetic biography (1940.21) for its "competent and lucid" judgment.

9 Miller, Perry. "From Edwards to Emerson." *New England Quarterly* 13 (December): 589-617.
   Explores continuities of the Puritan tradition by relating Edwards's perception of the "overwhelming presence" of God in the soul and in nature to Emerson's transcendentalism and by finding "implicit in the texture" of *End of Creation* mysticism and panthcism. Edwards strained his Calvinism to the "breaking point," but Emerson, without the restraints of dogma and external law, was free to conceive of man and nature as divine. (Reprinted in 1956.8 and 1959.9.)

10 ————. "Speculative Genius." *Saturday Review of Literature* 31 (30 March): 6-7.
   Considers Ola Elizabeth Winslow's biography (1940.21), though limited in its aims, "our best introduction" to Edwards.

11 Muelder, Walter G., and Laurence Sears. *The Development of American Philosophy: A Book of Readings.* Boston: Houghton Mifflin Co., pp. 2-4.
   Calls Edwards our first "real" philosopher and his idealism "largely" his own invention. Edwards grafted the new philosophy of Newton and Locke onto the old theology of Calvin and subjected both to an "intense" emotional piety.

12 Nichols, Robert Hastings. Review of *Jonathan Edwards,* by Ola Elizabeth Winslow. *Church History* 9 (June): 180-82.
   Believes Ola Elizabeth Winslow's estimate of Edwards (1940.21) would have been "truer" had she not considered his theology "a mistake and a misfortune."

13 Potter, David. "O Pioneers!" *Yale Review* 30 (Autumn): 174-79.
   Recommends Ola Elizabeth Winslow's study (1940.21) for its astute understanding and accurate rendering of Edwards, in a review of books on Ethan Allen, Daniel Boone, and others.

14 S[chnieder], H[erbert] W[allace]. Review of Jonathan Edwards, by Ola Elizabeth Winslow. *Journal of Philosophy* 37 (4 July): 390.
   Regrets that Ola Elizabeth Winslow's "excellent" biography (1940.21) "unfortunately throws little new light" on Edwards's philosophy and confuses the source of his conversion experience: it was intellectual, not mystical.

15 Shepard, Odell. Review of Jonathan Edwards, by Ola Elizabeth Winslow. *New York Times Book Review,* 10 March, p. 4.

Finds Ola Elizabeth Winslow "somewhat shy" to call Edwards a mystic, although the evidence is this "wise" book (1940.21) shows he was a mystic of "high rank."

16 Smith, Elizur Yale. "The Descendants of William Edwards." *New York Genealogical and Biographical Record* 71 (July): 217-24; (October): 323-33; 72 (January): 56-61; (April): 124-32; (July): 213-20; (October): 320-31.

Chronicles Edwards's life, his forebears and his progeny, as a persuasive example of eugenics. (See especially April, pp. 124-32.)

17 ———. Review of Jonathan Edwards, by Ola Elizabeth Winslow. *New York Genealogical and Biographical Record* 71 (April): 97-98.

Calls Ola Elizabeth Winslow's *Jonathan Edwards* (1940.21) "by far the most dynamic and absorbing of all the books on Edwards."

18 ———. Review of *The Printed Writings of Jonathan Edwards, 1703-1758,* by Thomas H. Johnson. *New York Genealogical and Biographical Record* 71 (October): 403.

Calls Thomas H. Johnson's *Printed Writings* (1940.7) "a valuable addition to the generally growing amount of data on Edwards."

19 Townsend, Harvey G. "Jonathan Edwards' Later Observations of Nature." *New England Quarterly* 13 (September): 510-18.

Inspects the manuscript of *Images or Shadows* (and by cross-references, the "Miscellanies") to show Edwards's continued, mature interest in natural science and reprints the complete index and some dozen entries. The later entries in the manuscript are "more bookish" than the early ones and stress the analogy between the material and the spiritual worlds.

20 Tufts, James H. "Edwards and Newton." *Philosophical Review* 49 (November): 609-22.

Considers the general view of the universe commonly held by Newton and Edwards and then examines in more detail Edwards's ideas of atoms, solidity, and gravitation. There can be "no doubt" about the influence of the *Principia* and the *Opticks* on Edwards: Newton's laws of nature "admirably" suited his sense of the "universal interconnection of things and events," and Newton's discoveries in color appear in his "idealistic line of thought and in his physical analyses." But in his theistic argument Edwards "went beyond" Newton (and Locke) in uniting a world of atoms and a world of ideas in the Idea and Will of God, a "swift" solution unavailable to science and philosophy since then.

21 Winslow, Ola Elizabeth. *Jonathan Edwards, 1703-1758: A Biography.* New York: Macmillan Co., xii, 406 pp.

Portrays Edwards through the "inner curve of spiritual experience" in a full-length biography that focusses upon the details of his career — his foundations at home and at Yale, his success and failure at Northampton, and his new beginnings at Stockbridge and at Princeton — rather than the details of his thought. Edwards was a lonely figure, solitary, detached, single-minded, with a sense of "inexorable justice" and "unassailable dignity"; a theologian with "mystical leanings," though not a mystic; a "compelling" preacher, though "neither Puritan nor fiery";

a religious thinker of the "vital" emotion of personal conversion (his own), though enclosed "in the husk of a dead idiom." For Edwards, to confute was "more important" than to tell; to be logical, precise, legal, discriminating, tenacious, more important than to cultivate the "delicacy of human relations." Hence, his *Farewell Sermon* is chiefly a "biographical document of importance," and *Misrepresentations Corrected,* more than his major works, illustrates the "detective quality" of his mind, his certainty and "ruthlessness." Edwards's greatness lies not in his originality — his mind was "strictly in the New England mold" — but in his "initiating and directing" the Great Awakening and in his developing New England Theology, both acts of "far reaching" consequences.

1941

1 Anon. Review of *The Printed Writings of Jonathan Edwards,* by Thomas H. Johnson. *Times Literary Supplement* 25 October, p. 536.

Finds Thomas H. Johnson's "admirable" bibliography (1940.7) follows the "exhaustive American method."

2 Cohen, I. Bernard. *Benjamin Franklin's Experiments.* Cambridge, Mass: Harvard University Press, pp. 110-11.

Remarks the similarity of Edwards's explanation of lightning in his diary to Franklin's "at about the same time" in the *Pennsylvania Gazette,* 15 December 1737.

3 Day, Richard W. "Sinner in the Hands of an Angry Logic." *Sewanee Review* 49 (July): 405-407.

Recommends Ola Elizabeth Winslow's biography (1940.21) as an "excellent introduction" to Edwards, a figure of grave importance to the development of American Christianity and to contemporary, wayward man.

4 Faust, C. H. Review of *The Printed Writings of Jonathan Edwards,* by Thomas H. Johnson. *New England Quarterly* 14 (September): 566-68.

Calls Thomas H. Johnson's bibliography (1940.7) "admirably complete and accurate" and another indication of the need for a new edition of Edwards.

5 Gohdes, Clarence. Review of *Jonathan Edwards,* by Ola Elizabeth Winslow. *South Atlantic Quarterly* 40 (January): 89-90.

Praises Ola Elizabeth Winslow's "pure" biography (1940.21), but calls for another book that deals with Edwards's thought and its place in eighteenth-century theology and psychology.

6 Hornberger, Theodore. Review of *The Printed Writings of Jonathan Edwards,* by Thomas H. Johnson. *American Literature* 13 (May): 179-80.

Judges that Thomas H. Johnson's accurate and detailed study (1940.7) supersedes John J. Coss's primary bibliography in the *Cambridge History of American Literature* (1917.1).

7 Miller, Perry. "Solomon Stoddard, 1643-1729." *Harvard Theological Review* 34 (October): 277-320.

Concludes that Edwards's grandfather, Solomon Stoddard, "had freed him from the mechanical theology of the Covenant, had brought back freshness and vigor to religion, had taught him how to manage revivals and to bring souls to conversion." For all that, Edwards failed in Northampton, not simply because he returned to an earlier way of church membership but because "the still domineering personality of Solomon Stoddard" overwhelmed him and his congregation.

8 Otto, Max C. "A Lesson from Jonathan Edwards." *Humanist* 1 (Summer): 37-40.

Fears the attention given Edwards in the last decade augurs a return to religious conservatism.

9 Parkes, Henry Bamford. "The Puritan Heresy." *The Pragmatic Test: Essays of the History of Ideas.* San Francisco: Colt Press, pp. 10-38.

Reprints 1932.12.

10 Payne, Ernest A. *The Prayer Call of 1784.* London: Baptist Laymen's Missionary Movement, pp. 4-11.

Acknowledges the influence of Edwards's *Humble Attempt* on later prayer calls, the founding of the Baptist Missionary Society, the advance of the Northampton Association, and the start of other evangelical movements.

11 Schneider, Herbert W. Review of *Jonathan Edwards,* by Ola Elizabeth Winslow. *American Historical Review* 46 (January): 417-18.

Praises Ola Elizabeth Winslow's "complete and scholarly" study (1940.21), but finds that if Edwards's career is "a chapter in the Presbyterianizing" of New England, then his pastorate in New York is more critical than his biographer allows.

12 Townsend, H. G. Review of *Jonathan Edwards,* by Ola Elizabeth Winslow. *Philosophical Review* 50 (July): 450-51.

Regrets that Ola Elizabeth Winslow's "thorough, dependable, modern" biography (1940.21) takes "little account" of Edwards's philosophy or theology.

1942

1 Atkins, Gauis Glenn, and Frederick L. Fagley. *History of American Congregationalism.* Boston and Chicago: Pilgrim Press, pp. 104-14.

Traces Edwards's career, especially in the Great Awakening, and its effects on Congregationalism. Though Edwards was "first" in a long line of important Congregational theologians, his impatience with a polity that fostered his dismissal had personal consequences for him and his "neo-orthodoxy" had profound doctrinal consequences for the church.

2 Cunningham, Charles E. *Timothy Dwight, 1752-1817: A Biography.* New York: Macmillan Co., pp. 348-51.

Draws "interesting parallels" between Timothy Dwight and Edwards — both were precocious, metaphysicians, ministers, college presidents — but notes as well "significant differences." Dwight's attack upon infidelity was "more glorious" than Edwards's upon Arminianism, and in his influence Dwight may have "surpassed the record" of Edwards.

3 Davidson, M[artin]. *The Free Will Controversy.* London: Watts & Co., pp. 55-56.

Asserts that the logic of *Freedom of the Will* would "scarcely convince the theologian in modern times" and that the conclusions Edwards draws from his assumptions of God's sovereignty and man's depravity are "repulsive."

4 Eddy, G. Sherwood. *Man Discovers God.* New York: Harper & Brothers, pp. 150-59.
Traces Edwards's career as he fulfills and terminates the mission of Calvinism, thus "opening the door to domesticating God" in America.

5 Keller, Charles Roy. *The Second Great Awakening in Connecticut.* New Haven: Yale University Press, pp. 9-31, 229-30.
Cites Edwards's influence upon Timothy Dwight and Nathaniel Taylor as a force for moderation in the Second Awakening in Connecticut.

6 Macintosh, Douglas Clyde. *Personal Religion.* New York: Charles Scribner's Sons, pp. 191-92, 196-200, 280-81.
Sketches, with distaste, the arguments of Edwards, the excesses of the Great Awakening, and the theology of his followers. Edwards is guilty of "pious blasphemy" for, among other things, suggesting disinterested love for an arbitrary and terrible God. As well, the development of Universalism may be read as a reaction to the awful vision of judgment in *Sinners in the Hands of an Angry God.*

7 Mead, Sidney Earl. *Nathaniel William Taylor, 1786-1858: A Connecticut Liberal.* Chicago: University of Chicago Press, pp. 100-108 passim.
Finds Edwards's distinction between moral and natural ability and inability in *Freedom of the Will* a "subtle tool" that enabled him to "force . . . together" as revealed facts God's sovereignty and man's freedom. In rejecting Edwards, Nathaniel Taylor (1786-1858) does not "outlogic" him but does place human reason before divine revelation, "'a rational faith of rational beings.'"

8 Payne, Ernest A. "'. . . From India's Coral Strand.'" *Christian Science Monitor,* 25 July, pp. 5, 12.
Calls Edwards, rather than John Wesley and George Whitefield, the "decisive" influence upon the founders of the Baptist Missionary Society in 1792.

9 Shipton, Clifford K. *Sibley's Harvard Graduates: Biographical Sketches of Those Who Attended Harvard College.* Vol. 6, *1713-1721.* Boston: Massachusetts Historical Society, pp. 355-56 passim.
Reports that Solomon and Elisha Williams joined together to attack their "'good Kinsman, and Brother Edwards'" on the matter of the half-way covenant, in one of many references to Edwards and the Williams family, Charles Chauncy, Thomas Clap, Joseph Dwight, David Hall, Robert Breck, and other Harvard graduates throughout subsequent volumes of the work.

10 Sweet, William Warren. *Religion in Colonial America.* New York: Charles Scribner's Sons, pp. 281-84.
Questions the primacy of Edwards in American revivalism. Priority and source belong to Theodorus Frelinghuysen and New Jersey, not Edwards and Massachusetts, to pietism not Calvinism. Still the "Great New England Awakening" begins with Edwards in Northampton in 1734, and though he was not a revivalist "in the usual sense of the word," he managed the emotional outpouring with "dignified common sense" and kept excesses to a minimum. Out of that experi-

ence came *Faithful Narrative*, probably his "most potent" work, and *Religious Affections,* "more self revealing" than any of his other writing.

11 Tsanoff, Radoslav A. *Moral Ideals of Our Civilization*. New York: E. P. Dutton, pp. 454-57.

Praises Edwards's analytical power and "mystical intimacy" and considers his later major works on theodicy and ethics to be theistic expressions of Neoplatonism. Edwards idealism persists in the "varieties" of transcendentalism in New England, especially in the thought of Emerson.

12 Winslow, Ola Elizabeth. Review of *The Printed Works of Jonathan Edwards,* by Thomas H. Johnson. *Modern Language Notes* 57 (March): 230-31.

Recommends Thomas H. Johnson's informative, accurate, and suggestive bibliography (1940.7) and wishes for a companion volume listing the "whole panorama" of criticism that Edwards's thought evoked.

13 Wright, Conrad. "Edwards and the Arminians on the *Freedom of the Will.*" *Harvard Theological Review* 35 (October): 241-61.

Suggests that "a tangle of verbal misunderstandings" about moral agency lies at the bottom of Edwards's attack on the Arminians, that his analysis of mind is really "not very different" from theirs, and that both neglect the crucial issue of original sin in their confused polemics on will. Edwards's notions about the self-determining power of the will that he ascribes to Arminians comes not from their tracts but from an anonymous book by a "Moderate Calvinist," Isaac Watts, *An Essay on Free Will* (1732); for their part, the Arminians attacked Edwards's misrepresentation in *Freedom of the Will* as if it were true. The whole controversy could have been "vastly simplified" if the Arminians had recognized that Edwards was "not wrong, but irrelevant" and if they had concentrated on original sin. "Moral necessity without total depravity loses all its sting."

1943

*1 Barnett, Das Kelley. "The Doctrine of Man in the Theology of Jonathan Edwards (1703-1758)." Th.D. dissertation, Southern Baptist Theological Seminary.

Cited in 1967.12, p. 207.

2 Beardsley, Frank Grenville. *Religious Progress Through Religious Revivals.* New York: American Tract Society, pp. 4-7.

Considers Edwards the "chief instrument" in the Great Awakening for his effective, if at times abhorrent, sermons in that lethargic age.

3 Curti, Merle. *The Growth of American Thought.* New York: Harper & Brothers, pp. 75-77.

Defines Edwards's "significant" place in American thought and disagrees that he was an anachronism, as V. L. Parrington held (1927.2). Edwards responded to the intellectual challenges of the Enlightenment, providing at once an "amazingly logical" defense of Calvinism and an important place within it for aesthetics and emotion.

4 Davis, Arthur Paul. *Isaac Watts: His Life and Works.* New York: Dryden Press, pp. 51-52.

 Calls Isaac Watts a "stout defender" of Edwards and the Awakening even though he toned down some parts of the London edition of *Faithful Narrative.*

5 Davis, Joe Lee. "Mystical Versus Enthusiastic Sensibility." *Journal of the History of Ideas* 4 (June): 301-19.

 Classifies Edwards as a mystic, not an enthusiast, in an historical analysis of the "fundamental divergencies" between mysticism and enthusiasm in Christian religious thought.

6 Hitchcock, Orville A. "Jonathan Edwards." In *A History and Criticism of American Public Address.* Edited by William Norwood Brigance. New York: McGraw-Hill Book Co., 1:213-37.

 Examines Edwards's sermons: the speaking situation; his training for them; the ideas, organization, and types of proof in them; his plain, unadorned style; his preparation and delivery; and the effect they had upon his listeners. Edwards was "a speaker first and a writer afterward," a Calvinist and a mystic who stressed logic at the expense of emotion. His language was that of his audience — the average word was four letters — and his style decidedly oral — repetitive, parallel, cumulative, direct.

7 Park, Charles Edwards. *The Beginnings of the Great Awakening.* Lancaster, Mass.: Society of the Descendants of Colonial Clergy, pp. 15-29.

 Traces the career of Edwards, a "thorough-going" mystic and a "thorough-going" Calvinist. His sense of duty to the awful power and sovereignty of God "elbowed" his mysticism out of the way but also gave rise to a "recrudesence of Puritanism" with its emphasis on moral obligation, immediate responsibility, and individual conscience. Edwards stands as both "sponsor" and symbol of the "sublime motive" of the Great Awakening.

8 Payne, Ernest A. "The Evangelical Revival and the Beginnings of the Modern Missionary Movement." *Congregational Quarterly* 21 (July): 223-36.

 Details the theological, devotional, and practical influences Edwards exerted upon the founders of the Baptist missionary movement, especially William Carey, through the widely circulated *Humble Attempt* and *Life of Brainerd.*

9 Stovall, Floyd. *American Idealism.* Norman: University of Oklahoma Press, pp. 12-15, 17-18.

 Considers Edwards's idealism to be for the self rather than for society (like Franklin's), in a short explanation of his determinism and his "cautious mysticism."

10 Wright, Charles Conrad. "Arminianism in Massachusetts, 1735-1780." Ph.D. dissertation, Harvard University.

 Includes 1942.13; revised and published as 1955.12.

1944

1 Haroutunian, Joseph G. "Jonathan Edwards: Theologian of the Great Commandment. *Theology Today* 1 (October): 361-77.

Locates the center of Edwards's theology in his passionate devotion to the beauty, excellency, and glory of God, the "clue" to his life and work and a valuable counter to the "profound indifference" to God today. Edwards's theocentricism is grounded in a distinction between creator and created: his joy arises from God's communication of his glory to man; his despair from man's blindness (his sin) to it. In a time of Calvinistic legalism and Arminian moralism, Edwards's view of man was aesthetic, asserting "the integrity of man as a thinking, feeling, willing being."

2 Henderson, C. D. "Jonathan Edwards and Scotland." *Evangelical Quarterly* 16 (January): 41-52.

Suggests that the relationship between Edwards and Scotland, based upon evangelical concerns, was intimate and reciprocal. Edwards kept in close correspondence with such Scottish theologians as John Erskine, Thomas Gillespie, and John McLaurin, and was "not uninfluenced" by them. On the other hand, Edwards's theology "undoubtedly left a permanent impression" upon the work of John McLeod Campbell, Thomas Chalmers, and George Hill.

3 Perry, Ralph Barton. *Puritanism and Democracy.* New York: Vanguard Press, pp. 75-77, 100-104 passim.

Characterizes Edwards not as a dogmatic theologian but as a "speculative genius" responsive to the past and "quickened" by the Enlightenment and explains his place in Puritanism and evangelism. Central to Edwards's thought is the sovereignty of God, apprehended in "mystical moments" and accepted without question, an expression of "authentic" Puritan piety. For Edwards, all parts of creation, from original sin to redemption, are harmonized by the whole, and, unlike covenant theologians, his God needs no justification.

4 Sweet, William Warren. *Revivalism in America: Its Origin, Growth and Decline.* New York: Charles Scribner's Sons, pp. 30-31, 78-85.

Discovers the roots of American revivalism and its emotional source in the "personalizing" of Calvinism and the pattern for it set by Edwards in his imprecatory sermons. Through his preaching and pastoral work and, especially, in his *Religious Affections,* Edwards made religious emotion "theologically and intellectually respectable. This fact is basic to any adequate understanding of the course of revivalism in America."

1945

1 DeJong, Peter Y. "Jonathan Edwards: The Half-Way Covenant Attacked." *The Covenant Idea in New England Theology, 1620-1847.* Grand Rapids, Mich.: William B. Eerdmans, pp. 136-52 passim.

Regards Edwards's attack on the half-way covenant a "turning point" in the history of Congregational thought and considers him instrumental in preparing for the "final eradication" of the covenant idea from New England religious life. By excluding all but the regenerate from church membership, Edwards effectively barred children from the covenant of grace, stressing their obligations more than their privileges. By insisting on individualism and voluntarism through revivals, Edwards left "little room" for traditional, "organic" relations, secured by covenant and maintained by Calvinists elsewhere. Thus in an attempt to revitalize a church fixed for so long in "dead formalism," Edwards unwittingly helped bring about its downfall.

2 Holbrook, Clyde Amos. "The Ethics of Jonathan Edwards: A Critical Exposition and

Analysis of the Relation of Morality and Religious Conviction in Edwardean Thought." Ph.D. dissertation, Yale University.

Claims that Edwards's objectivism produced a dogmatic theory of virtue that resulted in an "unwarranted depreciation" of natural morality. Yet his ethical theory repudiates theological utilitarianism and legalism, concentrates upon the sinful nature of man, grounds itself on the ultimately real, and couples radical subjectivism to radical objectivism, thus making the highest morality identical with religious faith.

3 Miller, Raymond Clinton. "Jonathan Edwards and His Influence upon Some of the New England Theologians." S.T.D. dissertation, Temple University.

Examines Edwards's life, world, sources, and thought to demonstrate his influence upon his pupils and associates, Joseph Bellamy and Samuel Hopkins; younger New England theologians, Stephen West, John Smalley, Nathaniel William Taylor; and later New England theologians, Bennet Tyler, Horace Bushnell, and the Oberlin group. As pastor and theologian, Edwards remains an inspiration and influence for any aspiring minister.

4 Muncy, W[illiam] L[uther], Jr. *A History of Evangelism in the United States.* Kansas City, Kan.: Central Seminary Press, pp. 7-38.

Claims Edwards's series of sermons on justification were coincidental to the spirit of God that moved Northampton into the Great Awakening.

*5 Rhoades, Donald Hosea. "Jonathan Edwards: Experimental Theologian." Ph.D. dissertation, Yale University.

See 1952.7.

6 Rudisill, Dorus Paul. "The Doctrine of the Atonement in Jonathan Edwards and his Successors." Ph.D. dissertation, Duke University.

Published as 1971.26.

7 Schrag, Felix James. "Pietism in Colonial America." Ph.D. dissertation, University of Chicago.

Traces pietism from the continent to colonial America in the revivalism of Theodorus Frelinghuysen, Gilbert Tennent, George Whitefield, and Edwards. Edwards differs from the orthodox Puritan tradition by ignoring the social and political principles of theocracy and by emphasizing the primacy of personal religious experience. Both attitudes bespeak a debt to pietism.

8 Sperry, Willard L. *Religion in America.* Cambridge, England: University Press, pp. 142-45.

Considers Edwards's work the "mature sophistication" of Calvinism in America, only "once removed" in excellence from the *Institutes.*

1946

1 Blau, Joseph L., ed. *American Philosophic Addresses, 1700-1900.* New York: Columbia University Press, pp. 517-36.

Reprints *God Glorified* and suggests that the religious individualism of Edwards and his followers sapped the congregational system, weakened the church covenant, and encouraged the Presbyterians, a group "less democratic and less philosophical" than New England Puritans.

2 Froom, Leroy Edwin. *The Prophetic Faith of Our Fathers: The Historical Development of Prophetic Interpretation.* Washington, D.C.: Review & Herald, 3:181-85.
   Explains Edwards's dating of the 1260-year reign of the papal Antichrist through the arithmetic of *Humble Attempt* and *History of Redemption.*

3 Lowell, Robert. "Mr. Edwards and the Spider" and "After the Surprising Conversions." *Lord Weary's Castle.* New York: Harcourt, Brace & Co., pp. 58-61.
   Bases two poems about Edwards upon his writing. "Mr. Edwards and the Spider" draws chiefly from "On Insects" and *Sinners in the Hands of an Angry God.* "After the Surprising Conversions" draws from the account of Joseph Hawley's suicide in Edwards's letter to Benjamin Colman.

4 Pitkanen, Allan. "Jonathan Edwards — Scourger of the Wicked." *Social Studies* 37 (October): 269-71.
   Recounts a short life of Edwards, an intellectual and moral force for eight generations but now largely unread and forgotten.

5 Schneider, Herbert W. *A History of American Philosophy.* New York: Columbia University Press, pp. 11-21.
   Characterizes the sovereignty of God as Edwards's "master passion," leading him to cast the idea of holy love into empiricist arguments and Platonic form and to attempt to reconcile Puritan grace and European pietism, in a survey of idealism and immaterialism in American philosophy. Edwards's doctrine asserts that matter and human will exist and operate in God as Being, just as it denies substance and mechanical causation. Hence the "immediate antithesis" of his idealism is Arminianism, not materialism.

6 Wertenbaker, Thomas Jefferson. *Princeton, 1746-1896.* Princeton, N.J.: Princeton University Press, pp. 42-43.
   Notes with regret the brief presidency of Edwards, an "ardent friend" of Princeton.

1947

1 Aldridge, Alfred Owen. "Jonathan Edwards and William Godwin on Virtue." *American Literature* 18 (January): 308-18.
   Reprints the dispute between Samuel Parr and William Godwin on Edwards's *True Virtue* and the place of gratitude in his scheme. Godwin acknowledged a debt to Edwards in *Political Justice* and perceived the "nihilistic tendencies" of his system; Parr argued in his *Spital Sermon* that Edwards recognized two levels of virtue. An analysis of Edwards gives comfort to both Godwin and Parr: gratitude is not a part of true virtue, but gratitude is a virtue.

2 Alexis, Gerhard Theodore. "Calvinism and Mysticism in Jonathan Edwards." Ph.D. dissertation, University of Minnesota.
   Attempts to resolve the paradox of Edwards's "clearly recognized" mysticism and his orthodox Calvinism: though they are not irreconcilable, they do oppose each other on scriptural, ec-

clesiastical, and social grounds. Yet Edwards managed to harmonize them through a process of "extension and limitation," particularly in matters of conversion and grace. For him, the mystic's way was "the way of the Christian pilgrim . . . routed through Northampton and Geneva."

3 Egbert, Donald Drew. *Princeton Portraits.* Princeton, N.J.: Princeton University Press, pp. 40-42, figs. 12-15.

Reproduces and notes four Edwards items at Princeton: a portrait by Henry Augustus Loop (1860) believed to be a copy of one by Joseph Badger (c. 1748); a bronze relief by Herbert Adams (1900); a wood statuette by Irving and Casson (1928); and a portrait, oil on wood, by John Potter Cuyler (1929).

4 Parkes, Henry Bamford. *The American Experience: An Integration of the History and Civilization of the American People.* New York: Alfred A. Knopf, pp. 78-85.

Takes Edwards to be a representative American in his repudiation of authority, confidence in the common man, exaltation of the will, and refutation of evil. Edwards "unconsciously Americanized" Calvinist theology, pitting the will against the environment and redefining conversion as a verifiable, emotional experience, in doctrines with "strongly liberal implications." Most significantly, the inner inconsistencies of Edwards's God "mirror with remarkable clarity the conflicting tendencies that run through the history of the American spirit."

5 Swaim, J. Carter. "Jonathan Edwards: The Eloquent Theologian." *Messengers upon the Mountains.* New York: Evangelism Board of National Missions of the Presbyterian Church in the U.S.A., pp. 3-5.

Recounts Edwards's life as a revivalist.

6 Townsend, Harvey G. "The Will and the Understanding in the Philosophy of Jonathan Edwards." *Church History* 16 (December): 210-20.

Deems Edwards's struggle over the relationship of the will and the understanding "as perennial as philosophy itself" and his resolution, especially to the problem of human freedom, "realistic and objective." Edwards sees human understanding and will as parts of the natural order and subject to natural laws — those of the understanding to the laws of inference, those of the will to the laws of choice. But man is limited by "the determinate nature of totality." Therefore, according to Edwards, man can understand but not perfectly, can choose but cannot determine the consequences.

7 Twitchell, Mary Edwards, and Richard Henry Edwards. *The Edwards Family in the Chenango County.* Lisle, N.Y.: Richard Henry Edwards, pp. 10-12.

Offers a brief biography and traces the later Edwards family as it moves west.

8 Witham, W. Tasker. *Panorama of American Literature.* [New York]: Stephen Daye Press, pp. 28-30.

Notes Edwards's career. (Illustrated.)

1948

1 Crabtree, Arthur Bamford. *Jonathan Edwards' View of Man: A Study in Eighteenth-Century Calvinism.* Wallington, England: Religious Education Press, 64 pp.

Locates Edwards's view of man in his concepts of the absolute sovereignty of God, the mediatorial satisfaction of Christ, and the efficacious grace of the Spirit, and concludes that he fails to solve the problem of human responsibility in a system of "rigid" determinism. Edwards's formulation of man's depravity and Adam's in *Original Sin* is "singularly ill-starred"; his failure to prove the axiom of causation in *Freedom of the Will* is but "another instance of the fallacy of *petitio principii.*" He proves that inability to do evil and human responsibility are compatible, but he does not prove the more important proposition that inability to do good and human responsibility are compatible. Like Calvin before him, Edwards's "devotion to the system" went beyond Scripture and his "very clarity [of reason] betrays a lack of that awed wonder" in the presence of divine mysteries.

2 Davidson, Frank. "Three Patterns of Living." *American Association of University Professors Bulletin* 34 (Summer): 364-74.
   Compares the autobiographical statements of Edwards, Benjamin Franklin, and John Woolman as possible models for living. Edwards's strength, unfortunately "deflected" into an apology for Calvinism, lies in his piety and spirituality, his idealism and mysticism.

3 Foster, John. "The Bicentenary of Jonathan Edwards' 'Humble Attempt.'" *International Review of Missions* 37 (October): 375-81.
   Recounts the genesis and influence of Edwards's *Humble Attempt,* a book not only "prophetic of the Missionary Awakening" but also a "main factor in the progress toward it."

*4 Holtrop, Elton. "Edwards's Conception of the Will in the Light of Calvinistic Philosophy." Ph.D. dissertation, Western Reserve University.
   Cited in *Comprehensive Dissertation Index 1861-1972,* 32: 57.

5 Johnson, Thomas H. "Jonathan Edwards." In *Literary History of the United States.* Edited by Robert E. Spiller et al. New York: Macmillan Co., 1:71-81.
   Considers Edwards "the first American Calvinist" in his rejection of the covenantal theology of his forebears and his emphasis upon divine sovereignty and the reality of sin, in an examination of the consistent and original metaphysics that gave "permanent direction to spiritual culture in America." From his early speculations in "The Mind," which attempts "to harmonize emotion and reason, mercy and justice, fate and free will," to the late treatises of the Stockbridge years, Edwards wrought a coherent, if not systematic, "living philosophy." Edwards imparted love to Calvinist dogma — his "unique contribution" — and harmonized pantheism and mysticism with it while maintaining a "tragic intensity" about sin. Both his idealism and his pessimism find their way into nineteenth-century America, in the work of Hawthorne, Melville, Emerson, Whitman, and Adams. (Frequently reprinted.)

6 Kaston, Benjamin Julian. *Spiders of Connecticut.* State Geological and Natural History Survey, Bulletin no. 70. Hartford: State of Connecticut, p. 31.
   Notes Edwards recorded the earliest observations of the ballooning or parachuting spiders in America (1715).

7 Miller, Perry. "Introduction." *Images or Shadows of Divine Things.* New Haven: Yale University Press, pp. [1]-41.
   Discovers in Edwards's typological use of nature "a revolution in sensibility" profound in its implications, in a short history and analysis of types and tropes prefatory to a reprinted manuscript notebook of 212 entries. To Edwards, the spiritualizing of nature common at the time (in

Cotton Mather's *Agricola,* for instance) falsified the world of Newton and Locke. Thus "the most sensitive stylist in American Puritanism" sought in the perception of the images or shadows of divine things a coherence of nature, Scripture, history, and mind, and a revelation of the divine intention, the "ultimate way" of knowing.

8 ———. "Jonathan Edwards on the Sense of the Heart." *Harvard Theological Review* 41 (April): 123-45.

Likens Edwards's "Miscellanies" to Pascal's *Pensées,* reprints no. 782 on the sense of the heart, and relates it to Edwards's "radical" empiricism. Edwards's fragment on spiritual knowledge "takes flight" from Locke's "Of Words" (*An Essay Concerning Human Understanding,* III, I, 1) by asserting that in regenerate man the word, naturally detached from the sensation it describes, vividly and fully identifies with the sensation. Hence Edwards's sense of the heart, distinct from the understanding of the head, is simply "a sensuous apprehension of the total situation," and thus "eternal salvation becomes possible in the midst of time."

9 ———. "Jonathan Edwards' Sociology of the Great Awakening." *New England Quarterly* 21 (March): 50-77.

Discovers hints of Edwards's social theory in "crucial" sections of three unpublished revival sermons probably written between 1734 and 1741 — on texts from Matt. 25:24-28, II Sam. 20:19, and Matt.22:9-10 — and reprints them. The first is a discussion of colonial cultural dependence; the second, a "terrifying picture" of a rural New England town; and the third, a "sociological analysis" of Northampton. Clearly, a "major premise" in Edwards's thinking is that grace operates within a social context as well as through individual psychology.

10 Savelle, Max. *Seeds of Liberty: The Genesis of the American Mind.* New York: A. A. Knopf, pp. 47-53, 64-66, 161-64 passim.

Ranks Edwards's mystical idealism as the first "great" philosophical system to have come "natively" from American soil and experience, but considers his evangelism "relatively incidental and unimportant," in an intellectual history of the United States. For Edwards, the Great Awakening was not "a democratic emotional drive for salvation" but another occasion to combat rationalism and Arminianism in his defense of Calvinist orthodoxy. Though Edwards was the intellectual leader of the revival, he was "not really of it."

11 Schneider, Herbert W. "The Puritan Tradition." In *Wellsprings of the American Spirit.* Edited by F. Ernest Johnson. Religion and Civilization Series. New York: Institute for Religious and Social Studies, pp. 1-13.

Considers that Edwards represents "only a passing phase" of Puritanism, one in which a Puritan is not a Yankee. Religion in New England had early accommodated to commerce; Edwards and the Awakening succeeded only briefly in divorcing them.

12 Squires, J. Radcliffe. "Jonathan Edwards." *Accent* 9 (Autumn): 31-32.

Closes Edwards's "American monologue," a thirty-three-line poem, with this:

> Do not open the chest
> In the attic, which is filled with something,
> Either apples or Satan. You do not wish to know.

13 Townsend, H. G. Review of *Images or Shadows of Divine Things,* edited by Perry Miller. *Philosophical Review* 57 (November): 622-23.

Questions Perry Miller's far-reaching claims for Edwards's typology in his edition of *Images or Shadows of Divine Things* (1948.7). Edwards's notes are intelligible "simply as memoranda" of an eighteenth-century New England preacher and scholar.

14 Wyckoff, D. Campbell. "Jonathan Edwards' Contributions to Religious Education." Ph.D. dissertation, New York University.

Examines Edwards 's theories of knowledge and responsibility, traces their influence (especially upon theological liberalism), and evaluates them in the light of contemporary religious education. Edwards addresses himself to the metaphysical basis, function, validity, and limits of knowledge and to man's inherent nature and its relationship to society, nature, and God, issues central to Christian education today.

1949

1 Cady, Edwin H. "The Artistry of Jonathan Edwards." *New England Quarterly* 22 (March): 61-72.

Argues that the "organic oneness" in *Sinners in the Hands of an Angry God,* achieved by blending thought and imagery, allusion and experience, "testifies" to Edwards's artistry. Although he was "addicted" to biblical allusion, Edwards's most successful images arise "natively" from his imagination and tally with those of his listeners, homely images of fire and ice and water. Probably his "freshest" images are kinesthetic not visual, expressed in symbols of tension-pressure and suspension-heaviness, most notably as he adds to the suspended sinner "a nightmarish feeling of his fatal weight." Thus Edwards finds an "'objective correlative'" to move his callous audience.

2 Chase, Mary Ellen. Review of *Jonathan Edwards,* by Perry Miller. *New York Times Book Review,* 11 December, p. 4.

Rates Perry Miller's study (1949.9) "a unique and major contribution to American letters, thought and history."

3 DeVoto, Bernard. "Our Contemporary, Jonathan Edwards." *New York Herald Tribune Book Review,* 20 November, p. 4.

Reviews Perry Miller's *Jonathan Edwards* (1949.9), a triumph of literary and philosophical criticism though it fails to examine Edwards in contemporary psychological terms.

4 Drummond, Andrew Landale. *Story of American Protestantism.* Edinburgh and London: Oliver & Boyd, pp. 107-11, 124-27 passim.

Places Edwards, an "unusual" blend of dogmatism and speculation, mysticism and logic, within the revivalist tradition in America, the "dominant" religious pattern there. A "Calvinist romanticist," Edwards was "altogether too Puritanical" to sustain the fever pitch of the Awakening. Although his theology is all but forgotten, he is remembered as the "'greatest of New England theologians'" in a stained glass procession at Mansfield College Chapel, Oxford.

5 Feaver, John Clayton. "Edwards' Concept of God as Redeemer." Ph.D. dissertation, Yale University.

Finds Edwards's concept of God as redeemer to have both a Christocentric and anthropological emphasis and to be founded upon the unresolved tensions between man's insufficiency and his ability, God's sovereignty and his holiness, and Christ's satisfaction and his beauty. Although salvation is open to all, man must actively respond to the divine offer: faith must be "inevitably accompanied" by good works. Through Christ comes redemption and the Holy Spirit, God's love and gift to man.

6 Hicks, Granville. Review of *Images or Shadows of Divine Things*, edited by Perry Miller. *New York Times Book Review*, 30 January, pp. 4, 18.

Suggests that Edwards's notes do not live up to Perry Miller's account (1948.7): if some suggest "unmistakably" a post-Newtonian universe, most are "'spiritualized commonplaces.'"

7 Horton, Rod W., and Herbert W. Edwards. *Backgrounds of American Literary Thought*. Rowayton, Conn.: Rod W. Horton & Herbert W. Edwards, p. 59.

Calls Edwards's *Sinners in the Hands of an Angry God* an "awful sermon" and his death the end of "the last great attempt" to save Calvinism.

8 Howard, Philip E., Jr., ed. "A Biographical Sketch of the Life and Work of Jonathan Edwards." In *The Life and Diary of David Brainerd*. Chicago: Moody Press, pp. 11-42.

Derives a life of Edwards from that of Samuel Miller (1837.1) and quotes a good deal from Edwards's works.

9 Miller, Perry. *Jonathan Edwards*. The American Men of Letters Series. [New York:] William Sloane Associates, xv, 348 pp.

Considers Edwards "intellectually the most modern man of his age," a speculative philosopher "infinitely more" than a theologian, a "major" artist rather, a psychologist and a poet in the native tradition, in a full-length study of the "drama of his ideas" — on inherent and objective good, Arminianism, revivalism, naturalism, conversion and communion, free will, original sin, true virtue, teleology, and history — interleaved with facts of external biography and notes on historical conditions. If Edwards's success lies in his unique ability to generalize his experience into "the meaning of America," his importance lies in his "inspired definitions," derived from Newton and Locke, and not in his often "pathetic" and unsophisticated answers. So his sermons, for example, are "immense and concentrated efforts" to define the religious life in America after Newton reduced nature to fixed laws and Locke reduced mind to vagrant sensations. In late life Edwards came to believe that the complete, eternal work of God could be perceived only in finite, successive insights in time, that the central problem was history, and that God's infinite judgment was renewed moment by moment, realized in beauty.

10 Murdock, Kenneth B. *Literature and Theology in Colonial New England*. Cambridge, Mass.: Harvard University Press, p. 183.

Notes the "transparent clarity" of Edwards's prose.

11 Niebuhr, Reinhold. "Backwards Genius." *Nation* 169 (31 December): 648.

Praises Perry Miller's "brilliant" and "artful" intellectual biography (1949.9) but finds its claim for Edwards's modernity somewhat suspect.

12 Richards, I. A. Review of *Images or Shadows of Divine Things*, edited by Perry Miller. *New England Quarterly* 22 (September): 409-11.

Uses the publication of Perry Miller's edition of *Images or Shadows* (1948.7) to indict typology (and Edwards's "*proofs* of divine design") as a limited and "self-destructive" form of metaphor. What is wrong with Edwards's mode and typology in general is "not extravagance but timidity": both refuse to "accept the responsibilities of poetic autonomy."

13 Schafer, Charles H. "Jonathan Edwards and the Principle of Self-love." *Papers of the Michigan Academy of Science, Arts, and Letters* 35: 341-48.

Contends that self-love or pride is central to Edwards's thought, from his earliest specula-tions ("The Mind") to his latest *(True Virtue)*, and important to his dismissal from Northampton. Edwards believed in "the pleasures of humility" and preached it, but when he at-tacked the self-esteem of his parishioners over the "bad book" and the new communion qualifi-cations, he was dismissed.

14 Sullivan, Frank. "Jonathan Edwards, the Contemplative Life, and a Spiritual Stutter." *Los Angeles Tidings*, 11 March, p. 27.

Cites a spiritual analogy to physical stuttering in the tension between Edwards's disposition to the contemplative life and the active life he was thrust into. *Personal Narrative* records his growing hysteria about religion — his "spiritual stutter" — as he is deprived of opportunities to meditate.

15 Suter, Rufus. "An American Pascal: Jonathan Edwards." *Scientific Monthly* 68 (May): 338-42.

Examines Edwards's "brilliantly" conceived scientific thought and regrets that, like Pascal be-fore him, a "lugubrious" religion cut short a promising career in theoretical physics. Edwards's method of inquiry was geometrical, using definitions, axioms, postulates, corollaries, lemmata, diagrams, and such; his method of proof either deductive or contradictive, proving, as he later would in theology, that the opposite proposition was untenable. His "most exciting" thought in-volves an analysis of the indiscerptibility of atoms, the conclusion that matter is solid.

16 Trinterud, Leonard J. *The Forming of an American Tradition: A Re-examination of Colonial Presbyterianism.* Philadelphia: Westminster Press, pp. 127-28, 221-27.

Refers to the loss of influence of New England Theology upon Princeton and academic Presbyterianism with the death of Edwards and the presidency of John Witherspoon.

17 Tyler, Moses Coit. *A History of American Literature.* Ithaca, N.Y.: Cornell University Press, pp. 414-26.

Reprints 1878.7.

18 Werkmeister, W[illiam] H. *A History of Philosophical Ideas in America.* New York: Ronald Press Co., p. 32.

Calls it a "strange irony" that the orthodox Edwards brought about the separation of church and state through the Great Awakening and so destroyed hopes for a Puritan theocracy in Amer-ica.

19 Winslow, Ola Elizabeth. Review of *Images or Shadows of Divine Things*, edited by Perry Miller. *William and Mary Quarterly*, 3d ser., 6 (January): 144-47.

Recommends Perry Miller's "excellent" introduction (1948.7) and welcomes these "private jottings," because during his lifetime Edwards printed "some of the wrong things." His unpub-lished work is vital to an evaluation of his contribution to religion and philosophy.

1950

1 Aijian, Paul M. "The Relation of the Concepts of Being and Value in Calvinism to Jonathan Edwards." Ph.D. dissertation, University of Southern California.

Traces the concepts of being and value from the medieval to the Calvinistic to the Edwardsean synthesis. To Edwards, divine sovereignty and power (being) are forms of good (value), which man appreciates in essentially aesthetic terms. Edwards's thought reflects a Ramist-Cambridge Platonic bent that imparts to his Calvinism a "dynamism of movement" permanently affecting American theology.

2 Aldridge, Alfred Owen. "Benjamin Franklin and Jonathan Edwards on Lightning and Earthquakes." *Isis* 41 (July): 162-64.

Claims that Edwards and Franklin did not influence each other's ideas on lightning, as I. Bernard Cohen maintained (1941.2), but that both had a common source in Ephraim Chambers's *Cyclopaedia* (London, 1728). Edwards seems the more original thinker of the two, for he does not limit himself to the theories in Chambers.

3 Baldwin, Alice M. Review of *Jonathan Edwards,* by Perry Miller. *South Atlantic Quarterly* 4 (October): 520-22.

Finds Perry Miller's study (1949.9) rewarding but not "easy" to read.

4 C., L. "Q1." *Explicator* 9 (November).

Asks for the source of Robert Lowell's "After Surprising Conversions."

5 Day, Richard Ellsworth. *Flagellant on Horseback: The Life Story of David Brainerd.* Philadelphia: Judson Press, pp. 171-201.

Contends that Edwards "blue-penciled with severity" David Brainerd's diary to hide the younger minister's "sacred" love for Jerusha from the public, to chart his spiritual ups and downs, and to reveal his abject unworthiness and total surrender to God. Edwards's life dominated Brainerd's and his *Life of Brainerd* is but an extension of his own. "For Brainerd was Edwards all over again, a sort of khaki edition of a Morocco classic."

6 Godwin, George. *The Great Revivalists.* Boston: Beacon Press, pp. 113-23 passim.

Diagnoses Edwards as a psychopath, a "spiritual quack," and the Great Awakening as a classic case of mass hysteria. Edwards was sadistic and "half insane," instrumental in bringing fear and terror, suicide and melancholia to the "simple folk" of New England. Only forced solitude kept this "self-tortured prophet" from doing even more harm.

7 Hornberger, Theodore. Review of *Images or Shadows of Divine Things*, edited by Perry Miller. *Modern Language Notes* 65 April): 292.

Finds these paragraphs of Edwards, brought together by Perry Miller (1948.7), a "fascinating study" in symbolism and psychology, because Edwards "delighted in such unnatural history as the charming powers of serpents and he had a pathological distaste for normal animal functions, not to mention pleasures."

8 Johnson, Thomas H. "Artist in Ideals." *Saturday Review of Literature* 33 (7 January): 17-18.

Praises Perry Miller's acute, deft, and sympathetic analysis of Edwards's thought (1949.9) but finds that the portrait "lacks immediacy," that Edwards's spirituality, humanity, and tragedy are "disembodied." Still, this is the first time "the artist working with ideas, emerges as a world figure."

9 Knox, R[onald] A. *Enthusiasm.* New York: Oxford University Press, pp. 494, 526.
Calls the "redoubtable" Edwards a "flinty-minded Calvinist."

10 Larrabee, Harold A. Review of *Jonathan Edwards,* by Perry Miller. *New England Quarterly* 23 (March): 106-109.
Considers Perry Miller's study (1949.9) a "masterly treatise" on colonial American culture, if a somewhat exalted view of Edwards.

11 Lewis, R[ichard] W[arrington] B[aldwin]. "The Drama of Jonathan Edwards." *Hudson Review* 3 (Spring): 135-40.
Weighs Perry Miller's "splendid," dramatic intellectual history (1949.9) against the "enormous" reservations it raises against Edwards's theology, "one of the great false philosophies." For all of Miller's art and knowledge, Edwards dwells in "learned ignorance," and his "implacably theocentric" theology invites either "immobility or excess."

12 Mead, Frank S. "Fire Under the Boiler." *Presbyterian Life* 3 (16 September): 8-10.
Claims the fiery revival sermons of the "great levellers," Edwards and George Whitefield, "planted the seeds of democracy," personalized religion, and founded colleges.

13 Miller, Perry. "Edwards, Locke, and the Rhetoric of Sensation." In *Perspectives in Criticism.* Edited by Harry Levin. Harvard Studies in Comparative Literature, no. 20. Cambridge, Mass.: Harvard University Press, pp. 103-23.
Characterizes Edwards as a "revolutionary artist" for his early and serious acceptance of Locke's theory of language — a word is an idea separable from reality or the thing itself — in a study of sensationalist psychology and rhetoric. But Edwards goes beyond Locke (and Berkeley) by insisting that an idea could be comprehended emotionally as well as intellectually, that it is "a unit of experience" sensibly apprehended. Grace becomes, for Edwards, a new simple idea learned "only from experience" and rhetoric an instrument, however inadequate, to define it. (Reprinted in 1956.8.)

14 ———. Review of Jonathan Edwards, *The Life and Diary of David Brainerd,* edited by Philip E. Howard, Jr. *New England Quarterly* 23 (June): 277.
Commends the publication of Philip E. Howard's redaction of a "classic" of evangelicals (1949.8) as testimony of the influence Edwards's text continues to have on the American character, an influence "far vaster" probably than anything else he wrote.

15 Müller, Gustav E. *Amerikanisclie Philosophie.* Stuttgart: F. Frommann.
Reprints 1936.9.

16 Roberts, Preston. Review of *Jonathan Edwards,* by Perry Miller. *Journal of Religion* 30 (October): 267-70.
Values Perry Miller's "most important" study (1949.9) but finds ambiguous his argument that Edwards based his theological insights "wholly within nature" and yet required "a transcendent reference" beyond it. How can there be a "'history *of* redemption' and yet no 'redemption *in* history'"?

17 Smith, H[ilrie] Shelton. Review of *Images or Shadows of Divine Things,* edited by Perry Miller. *American Literature* 22 (May): 192-94.

Doubts the evidence sufficient to justify Perry Miller's claim in his "brilliant" and imaginative introduction (1948.7) that Edwards intended to subordinate Scripture to nature, divine revelation to natural images.

18 Stokes, Anson Phelps. *Church and State in the United States.* New York: Harper & Brothers, 1:240-43.

Claims that the Great Awakening "aided" the cause of religious liberty and that Edwards, though he "cared little" for politics, "contributed mightily" to it. Edwards stressed the importance of individual conversion, the contrary ends of church and state, and the responsibility of man to God alone. These ideas and his return to orthodoxy in his rejection of the half-way covenant "indirectly" encouraged religious liberty by forcing a split among Congregationalists and by rendering a dominant church impossible.

19 Sweet, William Warren. *The Story of Religion in America.* New York: Harper & Brothers.

Reprints 1930.14.

20 Wach, Joachim. Review of *Images or Shadows of Divine Things,* edited by Perry Miller. *Church History* 19 (March): 66-68.

Welcomes Perry Miller's study of Edwards's aphorisms (1948.7) as a key to his hermeneutics, as a typological counter to the then current grammatico-historical interpretation of Scripture, and as an aid in understanding the Christian *kerygma* today.

21 Wade, Mason. Review of *Jonathan Edwards,* by Perry Miller. *Commonweal* 51 (27 January): 444-45.

Recommends Perry Miller's "masterly" synthesis (1949.9) to Catholics for whom Edwards is a "transitional figure" between the medieval schoolmen and Newton and Locke.

22 Wallace, Ethel. "A Colonial Parson's Wife, Sarah Pierrepont Edwards, 1710-1758, 'And a Very Eminent Christian.'" *Review and Expositor* 47 (January): 41-56.

Describes the holy affection between Edwards and his "exceptional" wife in their years together.

23 Winslow, Ola Elizabeth. Review of *Jonathan Edwards,* by Perry Miller. *William and Mary Quarterly,* 3d ser., 7 (April): 279-82.

Considers Perry Miller's "distinguished" study of the essential Edwards (1949.9) a "new chance" to measure his intellectual stature, his originality, and his modernity.

24 Wish, Harvey. *Society and Thought in Early America.* Society and Thought in America, no. 1. New York: David McKay Co., pp. 156-58, 166-67.

Attributes Edwards's methods in the Northampton revival to the German Pietists and his dismissal to this tactlessness.

1951

1 Akey, John. "Lowell's 'After Surprising Conversions.'" *Explicator* 9 (June): 53.
   Suggests that the date in Lowell's poem, 22 September, might be an oblique reference to 2 Kings 22, the text for the sermon.

2 Aldridge, Alfred Owen. "Edwards and Hutcheson." *Harvard Theological Review* 44 (January): 35-53.
   Discovers the "most pronounced" influence on the relationship between beauty and virtue in Edwards's *True Virtue* to be Francis Hutcheson's *An Inquiry into the Original of Our Ideas of Beauty and Virtue* (1725). Edwards's paper is "literally a commentary" on Hutcheson, and though he goes further than Hutcheson — putting the affections before reason and his faith almost in pantheism — he concludes "much like" Hutcheson on the prevalence in man of a sense of the basis of good and evil.

3 Brady, Mother Gertrude V. "Basic Principles of the Philosophy of Jonathan Edwards." Ph.D. dissertation, Fordham University.
   Finds the basic principles of Edwards's philosophy "rooted" in the medieval and early Christian tradition and "linked" to seventeenth- and eighteenth-century currents of thought. Such "tremendous truths" like God's immanence and imaging, historical providence, theocentrism, and Christocentrism are developed in Edwards from earlier sources in profound and brilliant ways and are "indispensable for our time."

*3A Brockway, Robert William. "The Significance of James Davenport in the Great Awakening." Ph.D. dissertation, Columbia University.
   See 1966.5.

4 Gaustad, Edwin S. "The Great Awakening in New England, 1741-1742." Ph.D. dissertation, Brown University.
   Published as 1957.6.

5 Giovanni, G. "Lowell's 'After Surprising Conversions.'" *Explicator* 9 (June): 53.
   Points to Lowell's "word-for-word copy" of Edwards's *Faithful Narrative* and identifies the suicide as Edwards's uncle, Joseph Hawley.

6 Harcourt, John B. Review of *Jonathan Edwards*, by Perry Miller. *American Quarterly* 3 (Spring): 86-87.
   Reviews six volumes in the American Men of Letters Series — Cooper, Edwards, Hawthorne, Melville, Robinson, and Thoreau — only to find that Perry Miller's study (1949.9), the "most distinguished" of them all, does not belong in the series: "Edwards was not a literary artist in any meaningful sense of the term."

6A Haroutunian, Joseph. Review of *Jonathan Edwards*, by Perry Miller. *Theology Today* 8 (January): 554-56.
   Challenges Perry Miller's view (1949.9) that Edwards was a naturalist, not a Calvinist: "Edwards was a Christian and a modern. He was not a modern posing as a Christian."

7 Johnson, Thomas H. "Jonathan Edwards." *Princeton University Library Chronicle* 12 (Spring): 159-60.

Reports on two Edwards "rarities" at Princeton: the ordination sermon for Jonathan Judd, *The Great Concern of a Watchman for Souls* (1743); and a German translation of *Faithful Narrative* 1738), "an instance of Edwards' continental reputation."

8 Leary, Lewis. Review of *Jonathan Edwards,* by Perry Miller. *American Literature* 23 (November): 382-84.

Contends that Perry Miller's *Jonathan Edwards* (1949.9) is "good intellectual biography" but "dangerous intellectual history" because it slights the background.

9 McLuhan, John, Jr. "Lowell's 'After Surprising Conversions.'" *Explicator* 9 (June): 53.

Calls Lowell's poem an "expansion" of Edwards's letter to Benjamin Colman.

*10 McCreary, Edward Daniel, Jr. "Representative Views of the Atonement in American Theology; A Study of Jonathan Edwards, Horace Bushnell, and Reinhold Niebuhr, Including the Major Trends in 18th, 19th and 20th Century American Theology." Th.D. dissertation, Union Theological Seminary in Virginia.

Cited in 1979.31: 323.

11 Marx, Leo. Review of *Jonathan Edwards,* by Perry Miller. *Isis* 42 (June): 153-56.

Characterizes Perry Miller's study (1949.9) as "a surprisingly personal book" about Edwards's "merciless dissection" of Enlightenment beliefs.

12 Miller, Perry, "The End of the World." *William and Mary Quarterly,* 3d ser., 8 (April): 171-91.

Notes that the "hidden point" of *History of Redemption* is Edwards's placement of the millennium before the apocalypse, thus refuting the mechanical-moral model of Thomas Burnet and William Whiston, in a survey of ideas about the end of the world, from Newtonians of the seventeenth century to atomic physicists of the twentieth. (Reprinted in 1956.8.)

13 Murdock, Kenneth B. "Jonathan Edwards and Benjamin Franklin." In *The Literature of the American People.* Edited by Arthur Hobson Quinn. New York: Appleton-Century-Crofts, pp. 106-23.

Explores Edwards's work and finds some of his best passages to be of "enduring literary importance" even though his "aesthetic perception often outran his stylistic capacity."

14 Nichols, James H. Review of *Jonathan Edwards,* by Perry Miller. *Church History* 20 (December): 75-82.

Considers Perry Miller's "brilliant apology" (1949.9) "not wholly satisfying" because the focus shifts from Edwards in his time to Miller in ours.

15 Pearce, Roy Harvey. "Lowell's 'After Surprising Conversions.'" *Explicator* 9 (June): 53.

Suggests that "After Surprising Conversions" views the failure of Edwards's mind, and New England Protestant thought generally, in the light of Robert Lowell's "apocalyptic Catholicism."

16 Schafer, Thomas Anton. "The Concept of Being in the Thought of Jonathan Edwards." Ph.D. dissertation, Duke Uinversity.

Isolates the "purely" ontological element in Edwards in order to examine its influence upon his theology and ethics. For Edwards, the ontological proof was a "favorite" one, central to understanding the divine outflow in *End of Creation* or the human response in *True Virtue*. And though there are unsolved problems and inconsistencies — the hierarchy of being, the ambiguous concept of causality, the conflict between benevolence and complacence, and so on — Edwards's concepts of being and excellence, at the heart of his thought, have "grandeur and beauty."

17 ———. "Jonathan Edwards and Justification by Faith." *Church History* 20 (December): 55-67.

Suggests that Edwards's doctrine of justification by faith occupies "an ambiguous and somewhat precarious place" in his thought, especially in the work of the Stockbridge years, and in the Arminian controversy. Edwards places love or consent at the center of salvation, thus bridging the gap between faith and works and avoiding the Arminian disjunction. In his later works, he departs from the early justification by faith alone by defining will to include acts of faith and obedience determined by antecedent inclination; by defining original sin as the initial inclination away from the love of God; and by defining true virtue as a new principle of love identical with God's grace.

18 Van Schelven, A. A. *Het Calvinisme Gedurende Zijn Bloeitijd: Schotland, Engeland, Noord-Amerika.* Amsterdam: Uitgeverij W. Ten Have, pp. 396-99.

Notes Edwards's role in the Awakening and his interest in spiders, contributions to the pioneer instinct of religion and science in America. (In Dutch.)

19 White, Eugene E. "Decline of the Great Awakening in New England: 1741 to 1746." *New England Quarterly* 24 (March): 35-52.

Notes that even Edwards's *Sinners in the Hands of an Angry God* (1741), "probably the most famous discourse in American homiletics," could not stay the decline of religious emotionalism in New England. In five years the Awakening was "practically dead."

1952

1 Baker, Nelson Blaisdell. "Anthropological Roots of Jonathan Edwards' Doctrine of God." Ph.D. dissertation, University of Southern California.

Discovers Edwards's anthropology rooted in his theology, which is conditioned by his familial and intellectual experience, his personal needs and religious conversion, and his observation of others in the revivals. Upon these Edwards founds his anthropological and theological judgments, namely, that he and all men were sinners in God's hands and that God is absolute and arbitrary in his saving grace. Edwards's doctrine of God reflects "both his psychological needs and the anthropological formulation of his solution."

2 Blau, Joseph L. *Men and Movements in American Philosophy.* New York: Prentice-Hall, pp. 12-27 passim.

Surveys Edwards's philosophy of Lockean-Newtonian idealism from the "teasing promise" of his "The Mind" to his mature treatises and concludes that while there is "little vitality" left in his thought, Edwards's "ingenious" use of Locke and Newton "set the pattern" of American idealism until it was supplanted by a "more sophisticated" German idealism in the nineteenth century.

Locke remained a "strong influence" upon Edwards throughout his career, but Newton left only the principle of causation and an occasional, sermonic metaphor. Edwards's psychological version of Puritanism derives from Locke *(Religious Affections)*, his ethical theory from the "durable spring" of self-interest *(True Virtue)*, and theology from the "keystone" of necessity *(Freedom of the Will)*.

2A Foster, John. "Scottish Evangelicals of the Eighteenth Century, with Especial Reference to Thomas Gillespie of Carnock." *London Quarterly and Holborn Review* 177 (October): 259-63.

Recounts briefly Edwards's relationship to Scottish evangelicals Thomas Gillespie, William M'Culloch, James Robe, and John Erskine and the source and effect of his *Humble Attempt*, in an address at the Gillespie bicentenary.

3 Leisy, Ernest E. Review of *Jonathan Edwards*, by Perry Miller. *Southwest Review* 37 (Spring): 173-74.

Praises Perry Miller's study (1949.9) of a "greatly misunderstood American," even though it stresses Edwards's debt to Locke at the expense of Calvin, in a review of five volumes in the American Men of Letters series.

4 Miller, Perry. "Jonathan Edwards and the Great Awakening." In *America in Crisis*. Edited by Daniel Aaron. New York: Alfred A. Knopf, pp. 3-19.

Contends that Edwards was the "formulator" of political and social theories of governance through his work as the "most acute definer" of the terms of the Great Awakening. By urging experiential religion — the people "*had* to speak up, or else they were lost" — and by insisting that ministers had to accommodate to the changing congregational reality, Edwards showed "in political terms" that a public leader had to adapt to "public welfare and calamity." Such propositions helped put an end to the reign of "European and scholastical" theories of social organization and authority. Americans were now free and capable to judge for themselves their welfare and threats to it. (Reprinted in 1956.8.)

4A Morey, Verne D. "American Congregationalism: A Critical Bibliography, 1900-1952." *Church History* 21 (December): 323-44.

Notes recent studies of Edwards, especially the "exciting experience" of reading Perry Miller's book (1949.9).

5 Mosier, Richard D. *The American Temper: Patterns of Our Intellectual Heritage*. Berkeley and Los Angeles: University of California Press, pp. 79-81.

Considers Edwards's "creative compromise" in *Freedom of the Will* between the sovereignty of man and the sovereignty of God a crucial statement for both Puritanism and republicanism. Edwards's defense, though couched in modern, empirical theories, rests upon aristocratic and arbitrary principles of governance. Yet he made possible at the same time "a kind of democracy in the redemption of man by which the aristocracy of Christian grace was quite effectively whittled away."

6 Patterson, Robert Leet. *The Philosophy of William Ellery Channing*. New York: Bookman Associates, pp. 10-15, 39-41 passim.

Characterizes William Ellery Channing's relationship to Edwards as one of respect but of deep disagreement. Channing studied Edwards — the many references to him bears that out —

but he was "profoundly antagonized" by Edwards on the will and his own thoughts owe little to him. Even so, Edwards's intellect and spirituality engaged Channing, and he found his mystical insight "extremely congenial."

7 Rhoades, Donald H. "Jonathan Edwards: America's First Philosopher." *Personalist* 33 (Spring): 135-47.

Summarizes the "basic" philosophy of Edwards, America's "least-known philosophical genius," into categories of being, causation, value, knowledge, and methodology. Edwards's thought, "essentially aesthetic" in nature, begins in an "idealistic monism" and becomes in his mature years a "naturalistic absolutism," where whatever is, is "ultimately" right. But his real service to both religion and philosophy lies in his "uneasy and pragmatic compound of empiricism, rationalism, and confessional symbolism in high Calvinism."

8 Roback, A. A. *History of American Psychology.* New York: Library Publishers, pp. 2-31, 105-16.

Discovers "psychoanalytical adumbrations" in Edwards and traces the two-hundred-year-old psychological debate occasioned by *Freedom of the Will* in the studies of James Dana (1770.2), Stephen West (1794.3), Thomas Upham (1834.6), Henry P. Tappan (1839.8), Jeremiah Day (1841.4), Asa Mahan (1846.3), D. D. Whedon (1864.5), Rowland Hazard (1864.3). In *Man Naturally God's Enemies*, Edwards "anticipated" Freud's notion of the Oedipal challenge to the symbolic father; in *Original Sin* he fashioned a recurrence theory "analogous" to Freud's. Like Edwards, Freud is a determinist, "the first *ever* determinist in psychology."

9 Scherman, David E., and Rosemarie Redlich. *Literary America: A Chronicle of American Writers from 1607-1952 with 173 Photographs of the American Scene that Inspired Them.* New York: Dodd, Mead & Co., pp. 20-21.

Characterizes Edwards as an all-but-forgotten creative intellect of the eighteenth century.

*10 Scott, Lee Osbourne. "The Concept of Love as Universal Disinterested Benevolence in the Early Edwardseans." Ph.D. dissertation, Yale University.

Cited in *Comprehensive Dissertation Index 1861-1972*, 32: 287.

11 Stephenson, George M. *The Puritan Heritage.* New York: Macmillan Co., pp. 50-55.

Recounts Edwards's role in the Great Awakening and notes the "terrible consistency" in his preaching, from the early *Justification by Faith Alone* to the late *Sinners in the Hands of an Angry God*.

12 Tomas, Vincent. "The Modernity of Jonathan Edwards." *New England Quarterly* 25 (March): 60-84.

Attacks Perry Miller's *Jonathan Edwards* (1949.9), "an intellectual biography written as if it were a novel," for obscuring (and falsifying) the real Edwards. For "underneath the salad dressing," when Edwards is looked at in the generic and specific characteristics of his thought, he is, despite Newton and Locke, "a medieval philosopher," not the modern empiricist Miller claims him to be. This is no more obvious than in Edwards's treatment of the "crucial" issue of the source of truth, found, for example, in *Original Sin*. It is from Scripture, not experience, that Edwards "'takes orders,'" a practice medieval, not modern.

13 Turnbull, Ralph G. "Jonathan Edwards — Bible Interpreter." *Interpretation* 6 (October): 422-35.

Details the range, use, style, structure, and effects of Edwards's sermons, expositions of the "pure gold" of Scripture. Edwards "restored" the sermon to its "primacy in the centrality" of the worship service because he held conversion to be the privilege of the elect, not the consequence of the sacraments. A "master" of approaches to the will, skilled in "soul surgery," Edwards was a passionate advocate of experimental religion then and an inspiration to evangelicals today.

1953

1 Anon. "Edwards Anniversary." *Princeton Alumni Weekly* 54 (6 November): 7-8.
Traces Edwards's career — at East Windsor, Northampton, Stockbridge, and Princeton — in a memorial exhibition at Princeton Library of his books, manuscripts, and memorabilia. But the study of his work in university classrooms two centuries after his death is his real memorial.

2 Anon. "Jonathan Edwards is Honored at Yale." *New York Times*, 17 October, p. 17.
Reports the celebration of Yale's Jonathan Edwards College of the 250th anniversary of Edwards's birth and the opening at the Library of a special exhibit, "The Life and Works of Jonathan Edwards."

3 Brauer, Jerald C. *Protestantism in America: A Narrative History.* Philadelphia: Westminster Press, pp. 49-50, 54-55.
Depicts Edwards's role in the revival of 1734 and in the Great Awakening as he "carefully guided" souls to comfort and conversion.

4 Faust, Clarence H. "The Decline of Puritanism." In *Transitions in American Literary History.* Edited by Harry Hayden Clark. Durham, N.C.: Duke University Press, pp. 22-26, 30-32, 47.
Concludes that Edwards's "heroic efforts" to halt the decline of Puritanism by revivifying Calvinism with the new philosophy failed as political, social, and economic changes swept America, in a brief survey of his thought.

5 Feidelson, Charles, Jr. *Symbolism and American Literature.* Chicago: University of Chicago Press, pp. 99-101.
Asserts that Edwards "anticipated the symbolic consciousness of Emerson" by reading nature as figuratively as he had Scripture. Edwards, a "philosophical symbolist," extended typology to the natural and empirical world of the eighteenth century, thus joining religion to science.

6 Ferm, Vergilius. "Editor's Introduction." *Puritan Sage: Collected Writings of Jonathan Edwards.* New York: Library Publishers, pp. xiii-xxvii.
Prefaces selections from Edwards, a Puritan sage who had "an inherently self-discovered wisdom," with a biography and with serial comments on his work. The "last bulwark" of Calvinism before modern thought and a practiced mystic withal, Edwards used Newton to support causation in the first and Locke to define perception in the second. His was a speculative genius haunted by "the ghost of theology."

7 ———. "Jonathan Edwards: Puritan Sage." *Christian Century* 70 (30 September): 1104-1106.
Offers a brief life and estimate of Edwards, a "puritan sage" whose God was aristocratic and

parochial and whose philosophy was built upon "a plot too narrow" for an expanding America of free men.

8 Holbrook, Clyde A. "Jonathan Edwards and His Detractors." *Theology Today* 10 (October): 384-96.

Divides Edwards's critics into those who consider him an "evil force" and those who define him as a "tragic figure," in an historical survey of his detractors over the last two hundred years. The first group indicts Edwards for his imprecatory sermons and unyielding theocentrism; the second group deals "more gently" with him, decrying the unresolved tensions within him, the scientist lost to theology, the irrelevant genius in a changing America. The fault, however, lies with his critics: either they are predisposed to a liberal theology or they are unable to meet his "flaming conviction" of divine sovereignty.

9 MacGregor, Charles P. "The Life and Service of Jonathan Edwards and His Message to the Church of Our Day." Th.D. dissertation, Boston University.

Traces Edwards's career, remarks his theology, and suggests that what he taught two hundred years ago "needs to be emphasized today."

10 Miller, Perry. *The New England Mind: From Colony to Province.* Cambridge, Mass.: Harvard University Press, pp. 343-44.

Contrasts Edwards's experience in New York with Franklin's in Boston and speculates about the New England strain in these two "archsymbols."

11 Parkes, Henry Bamford. *The United States of America: A History.* New York: Alfred A. Knopf, pp. 82-83.

Sketches Edwards as a child of the Enlightenment, a significant figure" in American cultural history.

*12 Smith, Aleck L. "Changing Conceptions of God in Colonial New England." Ph.D. dissertation, State University of Iowa.

Cited in *Comprehensive Dissertation Index 1861-1972*, 32: 418.

13 Snyder, Richard L. Letter to the Editor. *Christian Century* 70 (28 October): 1233.

Questions Virgilius Ferm's (1953.7) oversimplification of Edwards's role in America by citing Perry Miller's (1949.9) social and political reading of the matter.

14 Stowe, David M. Letter to the Editor. *Christian Century* 70 (28 October): 1233-34.

Disagrees with Virgilius Ferm's (1953.7) anthropomorphic characterization of Edwards's God. His "absolute idealism" rendered God the perfection of being, not a "gracious Christian gentleman."

1954

1 Aaron, Daniel. "Jonathan Edwards." In *The Northampton Book.* Edited by Lawrence E. Wikander et al. Northampton, Mass.: Tercentenary Committee, pp. 15-21.

Recounts Edwards's career in Northampton, an "isolated river town," for its tercentenary celebration. Edwards's difficulties there stemmed from personal and doctrinal rather than political or social differences, as is sometimes claimed. As a man he was tactless and rigid, as a thinker "uncompromising."

2 ———. "Jonathan Edwards's Finely Wrought Sermons Held Real Memorial to 'Greatest Theologian and Philosopher Yet Produced in Century.'" *Hampshire Gazette*, 2 March, p. 7.
    Recasts 1954.1.

3 Boorman, John Arthur. "A Comparative Study of the Theory of Human Nature as Expressed by Jonathan Edwards, Horace Bushnell and William Adams Brown, Representative American Protestant Thinkers of the Past Three Centuries." Ph.D. dissertation, Columbia University.
    Locates Edwards's theory of human nature in his Calvinist doctrine of absolute sovereignty and his idea of "radical" conversion, derived in part from Locke, Newton, and Hutcheson. Bushnell rejects Calvinism and so his theory is "more optimistic and moralistic" than Edwards's. Brown subscribed to Darwinism and sees progress for man through church participation.

4 Chesley, Elizabeth. "Ode to Jonathan Edwards." *Woman's Home Companion* 81 (July): 49.
    Composes nine stanzas about Edwards's view of infant damnation and closes with

    That you think them vipers may not be odd,
    But speak for yourself, John — not for God.

5 Cunliffe, Marcus. *The Literature of the United States.* London: Penguin Books, pp. 32-33.
    Refers to Edwards as an eighteenth-century philosopher with a "pantheistic tinge."

6 Flynt, William T. "Jonathan Edwards and His Preaching." Th.D. dissertation, Southern Baptist Theological Seminary.
    Studies Edwards's personality and environment as forces that affect his message and manner as a preacher; comments upon his use of Scripture, his sermonic style and structure, and the intellectual and imaginative qualities of selected sermons; and measures his contributions to religious thought, social and humanitarian movements, preaching, and modern missions.

7 Foster, Charles H. *The Rungless Ladder: Harriet Beecher Stowe and New England Puritanism.* Durham, N.C.: Duke University Press, pp. 179-84, 189-93 passim.
    Traces Edwards's influence, often contrary, upon Harriet Beecher Stowe and her work, especially *The Minister's Wooing* and *Oldtown Folks.* Edwards became a figure she struggled with, an archetype of orthodoxy in the theology of sin and grace, though it is obvious that she seriously misread his role in the intellectual history of New England.

8 Gaustad, Edwin S. "The Theological Effects of the Great Awakening in New England." *Mississippi Valley Historical Review* 40 (March): 681-706.
    Discovers in Edwards "a continuity" between the revivals of 1734 and 1741 — he was an "amazed spectator and reporter" of the first, a "vigorous apologist and leading theologian" of the second — and explores the "very significant" effects revivalism had upon his work and his school, New England Theology, in a serial history of the Awakening. Edwards's personal piety

and the many cases of conscience he witnessed and recorded made divine grace "an immediate indwelling reality" and a focus of his theology and that of his disciples, Joseph Bellamy and Samuel Hopkins. The Great Awakening, by calling attention to his theological views, "forced" Edwards to unexpected conclusions — *Religious Affections* and *Humble Inquiry,* for example — and effected a protracted defense of Calvinism and absolute sovereignty in his later years — *Freedom of the Will, Original Sin,* and *True Virtue.*

*9 Lavengood, Lawrence G. "The Great Awakening and New England Society." Ph.D. dissertation, University of Chicago.

> Cited in *Comprehensive Dissertation Index 1861-1972,* 35: 614.

10 McNeill, John T. *The History and Character of Calvinism.* New York: Oxford University Press, pp. 361-63.

> Points out that while Edwards added "humane" elements to Calvin, he thought (and preached) of hell as physical torment rather than as the spiritual alienation Calvin understood.

11 Persons, Stow. "The Cyclical Theory of History in Eighteenth-Century America." *American Quarterly* 6 (Summer): 147-63.

> Notes that Edwards's theory of history as the "unfolding revelation of divine purpose" is at odds with others in the eighteenth century.

12 Rice, Howard C., Jr. "Jonathan Edwards at Princeton." *Princeton University Library Chronicle* 15 (Winter): 69-89.

> Recounts Edwards's connections to Princeton and reprints eight Edwards letters and manuscripts and describes all other items — "waifs and strays" — acquired chiefly through gift to the College.

13 Smith, Chard Powers. *Yankees and God.* New York: Hermitage House, pp. 244-53, 259-63.

> Discusses the rise and fall of American Puritanism and distinguishes between first and second forms of it, the first tending toward Arminianism under Thomas Hooker until 1650, the second toward Antinomianism under Edwards until 1750. Edwards accepted the materialism of Newton and the sensationalism of Locke, developed an idealism in which God was "incomprehensible" to reason, and fashioned a creative aesthetic akin to the experience of grace. The "tragedy" of our first "major modern mind" was a failure to find in men an imagination comparable to his. A decade later, emotion spent, all fell before reason.

14 Smith, John E. Review of *Jonathan Edwards,* by Virgilius Ferm. *Arizona Quarterly* 10 (Spring): 83.

> Condemns the price, printing, and binding of Virgilius Ferm's "boon" to students of Edwards (1953.6).

15 Stromberg, Roland N. *Religious Liberalism in Eighteenth-Century England.* New York: Oxford University Press, pp. 114, 118, 121.

> Notes Edwards's lonely, Calvinist battle against Arminianism and the optimism of the eighteenth century and likens him to Bernard Mandeville in his denial of virtue to natural, selfish man.

16 Taylor, Robert J. *Western Massachusetts in the Revolution*. Providence: Brown University Press, pp. 45-51.

Recounts the history of opposition between the Williams family and Edwards, especially Israel Williams's role in Edwards's dismissal. With the death in 1748 of Colonel Stoddard, Williams openly challenged the minister's authority on profession and communion, put the question of church membership to a precinct meeting, and forced neighboring churches to call a council. At Williams's urging, Joseph Hawley viciously attacked Edwards at these meetings; five years later he recanted, publicly asked forgiveness from Edwards, and became a political enemy of Williams.

17 Yoder, Donald Herbert. "Christian Unity in Nineteenth-Century America." In *A History of the Ecumenical Movement, 1517-1948*. Edited by Ruth Rouse and Stephen Charles Neill. Philadelphia: Westminster Press, pp. 221-59.

Cites Edwards as an example of the "unitive influence of revivalism" through his desire for a concert of prayer and notes his influence on revival practice in the nineteenth, but not the eighteenth, century.

1955

1 Anon. "Jonathan Edwards's Works to be Published by Yale." *Hampshire Gazette*, 29 January, 1, 11.

Notes the forthcoming Yale Edwards and an earlier display of memorabilia there.

2 Anon. "Services Sunday to Mark Edwards' 252nd Birthday." *Hampshire Gazette*, 6 October, p. 21.

Notes the coming celebration of his birth at the Edwards Congregational Church, Northampton.

3 Beach, Waldo, and H. Richard Niebuhr, eds. *Christian Ethics: Sources of the Living Tradition*. New York: Ronald Press Co., pp. 380-89.

Maintains that Edwards's "primary" concern was ethical, that his unitive system of thought agrees and disagrees with naturalistic and idealistic movements of historical Christian ethics, and reprints selections from *True Virtue*. Edwards is both "radically realistic," accepting self-interest and moral relativity, and "radically idealistic," insisting upon possibilities beyond man's achievement. History, for Edwards, traces man's progress of redemption from self-love to love of being, from self-glorification to glorification of God, from parochial views of theology and politics to "wide vistas" of universal society and love of God.

4 Davies, A. Mervyn. *The Foundation of American Freedom*. New York: Abington Press, p. 196.

Notes that Edwards was the only "authentic" Calvinist of his time.

5 Lewis, R. W. B. *The American Adam: Innocence, Tragedy, and Tradition in the Nineteenth Century*. Chicago: University of Chicago Press, pp. 62-66.

Compares Edwards to the elder Henry James and Horace Bushnell on original sin and finds Edwards's doctrine "out of harmony" with his times and his scientific defense of it "too far advanced." Edwards was trying to revitalize a dying Puritanism with the theories of Locke and

Newton: he was "not trying to set the clock back, he was trying to set it right." And unlike the Edwardseans, who were precursors of the party of Memory, or their opponents, who were precursors of the party of Hope, Edwards (and James and Bushnell) had "the more flexible outlook of the *tertium quid*."

6 Morris, William Sparkes. "The Young Jonathan Edwards: A Reconstruction." Ph.D. dissertation, University of Chicago.
> Published as 1991.32.

7 Schafer, Thomas A. "Jonathan Edwards' Conception of the Church." *Church History* 24 (March): 51-66.
> Defends Edwards's ecclesiology against the charge that his revivalist impulses sundered the church by showing that his ontology, cosmology, and eschatology support its central role in redemption as the society of the elect and the body of Christ. Edwards merges the covenant of grace in the covenant of redemption, considering the visible church, with its worship, preaching, and sacraments, to be "the means by which God inducts men" into his society. A Presbyterian more than a Congregationalist in church polity, Edwards advocated church unity and ecumenical worship in his *Humble Attempt*.

8 Smith, H. Shelton. *Changing Conceptions of Original Sin: A Study in American Theology Since 1750*. New York: Charles Scribner's Sons, pp. 27-36 passim.
> Claims that Edwards's "unusually penetrating polemic" against John Taylor was instrumental in keeping the original sin controversy alive for many years, even though his "spectacular" theory of imputation and personal identity "fell flat" with his theological successors, and recounts the argument of *Original Sin*, in a survey of the doctrine over the last two centuries.

9 Spiller, Robert E. *The Cycle of American Literature: An Essay in Historical Criticism.* New York: Macmillan Co., pp. 10-12.
> Divides Edwards's work and life into three periods: the philosophical inquiries of the Yale years, the emotional sermons of the revival years, and the logical treatises of the Stockbridge years. Edwards adumbrates later American writers — Poe, Hawthorne, Melville, O'Neill, Eliot, and Faulkner — in his "structure of tragic realization," and ranks with Franklin and Jefferson as one of three "architects" of America.

10 Townsend, Harvey G. "Introduction." *The Philosophy of Jonathan Edwards from His Private Notebooks*. University of Oregon Monographs: Studies in Philosophy, no. 2. Eugene, Ore.: University Press, pp. v-xxi.
> Offers "a coherent body of the philosophical opinions" of Edwards by printing "Of Being," "The Mind," and selections from the "Miscellanies," early and private work that expresses his "radical idealism." The source for Edwards's idealism is a "long line" of Christian Platonists and John Locke, not Bishop Berkeley; the source for his rationalism and his belief in the "absolute reign of universal law," the very "basis" of his philosophy, is Isaac Newton.

11 Winn, Ralph B. "Jonathan Edwards." *American Philosophy*. New York: Philosophical Library, pp. 233-34.
> Offers a brief life of Edwards, a question about his originality, and a commendation for his polemics.

12 Wright, Conrad. "The Freedom of the Will." *The Beginnings of Unitarianism in America*. Boston: Starr King Press, pp. 91-114.
   Reprints 1942.13 (revised).

1956

1 Albert, Frank J. Review of *The Philosophy of Jonathan Edwards from His Private Notebooks*, edited by Harvey G. Townsend. *Encounter* 17 (Winter): 86-87.
   Finds that Harvey G. Townsend's book (1955.10) succeeds in establishing Edwards as an important philosopher.

2 Berg, Johannes Van Den. *Constrained by Jesus' Love: An Inquiry into the Motives of the Missionary Awakening in Great Britain in the Period between 1698-1815*. Kampen [the Netherlands]: J. H. Kok, pp. 83, 91-93 passim.
   Ascribes to Edwards a great deal of the stimulus given the missionary spirit in England and Scotland through his work in the Great Awakening and his publication of *Humble Attempt* and the *Life of Brainerd*. To Edwards as well belongs the "positive function" eschatology played in the development of missionary thought here and abroad.

3 Brown, Arthur W. *Always Young for Liberty: A Biography of William Ellery Channing*. Syracuse, N.Y.: Syracuse University Press, pp. 98-101.
   Recounts William Ellery Channing's mixed reactions to Edwards. Channing was unnerved by enthusiasm but approved Edwards's religious affections; he was impressed by his logical consistency on the will but appalled by his doctrine of necessity.

4 Clark, George Pierce. "An Unpublished Letter by Jonathan Edwards." *New England Quarterly* 29 (June): 228-33.
   Reprints a letter, 7 May 1750, from Edwards to Peter Clark, pastor at Salem Village; notes that it is quoted at length in the preface to *Farewell Sermon;* and cites its "relevancy to the controversy" of his dismissal the following month.

5 Collmer, R. G. "Two Antecedents for a Metaphor from Jonathan Edwards." *Notes and Queries*, n.s., 3 (September): 396.
   Cites two antecedents — there may be more — to Edwards's metaphor of the dangling sinner: the medieval mystic William Hinton in his *Scale of Perfection* and the counterreformer Luis de Granada in his *Of Prayer and Meditation*.

6 Gerstner, John H. Review of *The Philosophy of Jonathan Edwards from His Private Notebooks*, edited by Harvey G. Townsend. *New England Quarterly* 29 (September): 422-24.
   Considers Harvey G. Townsend's study (1955.10) "useful and essential" but cites the need for an "adequate statement" of Edwards's philosophical system.

7 Hitchcock, Orville. Review of *The Philosophy of Jonathan Edwards from His Private Notebooks*, edited by Harvey G. Townsend. *Quarterly Journal of Speech* 42 (December): 440.

Welcomes Harvey G. Townsend's collection (1955.10) for the help it affords the critics of colonial rhetoric and the student of Edwards's oratory.

8 Miller, Perry. *Errand into the Wilderness.* Cambridge, Mass.: Harvard University Press, pp. 48-98, 153-66, 167-83, 184-203, 217-39.

Reprints "The Marrow of Puritan Divinity" (1935.6); "Jonathan Edwards and the Great Awakening" (1952.4); "Edwards, Locke, and the Rhetoric of Sensation" (1950.13); "From Edwards to Emerson" (1940.9); and "The End of the World" (1951.12).

9 ————. Review of *The Philosophy of Jonathan Edwards from His Private Notebooks,* edited by Harvey G. Townsend. *American Literature* 28 (May): 236-37.

Dismisses Harvey G. Townsend's study (1955.10) for his "capricious principles of selection and his ignorance of the general bearing of the entries" in a misconceived attempt to prove Edwards a philosopher rather than "a major religious figure."

10 Oberholzer, Emil, Jr. *Delinquent Saints, Disciplinary Action in the Early Congregational Churches of Massachusetts.* New York: Columbia University Press, pp. 19-21, 23-24.

Claims that Edwards introduced "real Calvinism" to Congregational churches in Massachusetts and that he eschewed the covenant theology of his Puritan forebears.

11 Smith, H. Shelton. Review of *Jonathan Edwards,* by Virgilius Ferm. *South Atlantic Quarterly* 55 (January): 119-20.

Faults Virgilius Ferm's introduction (1953.6) for being too sketchy to be of much worth, his selections for being too short to be of much significance. Faust and Johnson's text (1935.3) is better on both counts.

12 Taylor, Walter Fuller. *The Story of American Letters.* Chicago: Henry Regnery Co., pp. 27-33.

Revises 1936.11.

13 Warren, Austin. *New England Saints.* Ann Arbor: University of Michigan Press, pp. 25-26.

Counts Edwards among "our few American saints," a philosopher, ascetic, mystic.

14 Wright, Conrad. Review of *The Philosophy of Jonathan Edwards from His Private Notebooks,* edited by Harvey G. Townsend. *William and Mary Quarterly,* 3d ser., 13 (July): 411-12.

Questions the value for scholars of Harvey G. Townsend's selections from the "Miscellanies" (1955.10), for his justification of Edwards as philosopher rather than theologian seems unnecessary and unrewarding.

1957

1 Bainton, Roland H. *Yale and the Ministry.* New York: Harper & Brothers, pp. 15-24, 52-56 passim.

Describes the effect Yale had upon the young Edwards and the influence he later exerted at

Yale. Both his knowledge of the depravity of man and the new sense of the glory of God come from his Yale years. His theology, a fusion of Calvin, Cudworth, and Newton, and "enriched" with pietism, is of that time and that place. Later, through Samuel Hopkins and Timothy Dwight, the Beechers and Horace Bushnell, Edwards found his way back to Yale.

2 Barnhouse, Donald Grey. "The Restoration of Jonathan Edwards." *Eternity* 8 (September): 4-5, 46-47.

Views with pleasure the "remarkable" restoration of Edwards, for it is part of the general movement away from liberal Christianity to a more conservative position.

3 Belknap, George N. Letter to the Editor. *American Literature* 28 (January): 525.

Corrects Perry Miller's misunderstanding of Harvey G. Townsend's comment in his *The Philosophy of Jonathan Edwards* (1955.10) on the importance of *End of Creation* and *True Virtue*.

4 Conrad, Leslie, Jr. "Jonathan Edwards' Pattern for Preaching." *Church Management* 33 (September): 45-47.

Offers Edwards's sermonic pattern to today's minister who "really means business." The pattern always begins with subject, text, and introduction but then develops into either doctrinal discussion and application or three to nine sections of argument.

5 Coombe, Jack Duncan. *Consider My Servant: A Novel Based upon the Life of Jonathan Edwards.* New York: Exposition Press, 160 pp.

Fashions a novel of the "human" Edwards in his Northampton years, from his ordination to his farewell sermon, by getting beneath "the traditional veneer of his scholarliness and Puritan composure," by taking "some liberty with the facts," and by inventing some events and characters. So Sarah never really hears the whole of his ordination sermon. "She was too much in her own secret world. Her thoughts were too sacred to be jarred by some theological discourse — even if it was from her lover." And so Samuel Sewall hears Edwards's *God Glorified* delivered in Boston 8 July 1731, though he died 1 January 1730.

6 Gaustad, Edwin Scott. *The Great Awakening in New England.* New York: Harper & Brothers, pp. 18-24, 81-101, 134-139 passim.

Narrates the struggle over the meaning of the Great Awakening by the two "great champions" of reason and faith, Charles Chauncy and Edwards, in a study of revivalism and its institutional and theological effects. To Edwards religion was an empirical affair of the heart and the Awakening "a large and timely laboratory of experience"; to Chauncy the emotion of the Awakening contradicted the reasonableness of religion. In 1741 there was "no sharp clash" theologically between the two; by 1742 their views began to harden; by 1743 their separation was "fully apparent," first expressed in Edwards's *Some Thoughts* and then answered in Chauncy's *Seasonable Thoughts.* "The intellectual bifurcation, began as a dispute over the significance and propriety of 'Shriekings and Screamings,' was soon to become a contest over the nature of God and the constitution of man."

7 Gerstner, John H. "American Calvinism until the Twentieth Century Especially in New England." In *American Calvinism: A Survey.* Edited by Jacob T. Hoogstra. Grand Rapids, Mich.: Baker Book House, pp. 13-39.

Refutes the charge that Edwards was "guilty of more or less deviation" from orthodox Calvinism and the source of New England defection and finds his work on the will, for example, "utterly Calvinistic" and that on justification "pure Calvinism." What deviation did take place was a reaction to his strict Calvinism: the Arminian reaction gave rise to Unitarianism; the Pelagian reaction led to either hyper-Calvinism or hypo-Calvinism; and the Princetonians developed a peculiar brand of Edwardsean Calvinism, that of Alexander, Hodge, Patton, and Warfield. Contrary to W. J. Burggraaff in his study of liberal theology (1928.2), Edwards was "thoroughly" Calvinistic.

8 Henderson, G. D. "Jonathan Edwards and Scotland." *The Burning Bush: Studies in Scottish Church History*. Edinburgh: Saint Andrew Press, pp. 151-62.
   Reprints 1944.2.

*9 Hoffman, Gerhard. "Seinsharmonie und Heilsgeschichte bei Jonathan Edwards." Th.D. dissertation, Göttingen University.
   Cited in James Woodress, *Dissertations in American Literature, 1891-1966* (Durham, N.C.: Duke University Press, 1968), item 641.

10 Johnson, Thomas H. Review of Jonathan Edwards, *Freedom of the Will*, edited by Paul Ramsey. *New York Times Book Review*, 23 June, p.7.
   Hopes the rest of the Yale Edwards will adhere to Paul Ramsey's standard of editing (1957.14).

11 McGraw, James. "The Preaching of Jonathan Edwards." *Preacher's Magazine* 32 (August): 9-12.
   Praises Edwards's preaching more for its thought than its eloquence, more for its logic than its rhetoric.

12 Morris, William S. "The Reappraisal of Edwards." *New England Quarterly* 30 (December): 515-25.
   Recites a short history of Edwards criticism — from the theological concerns of the eighteenth and nineteenth centuries to the philosophical ones of the early twentieth to the biographical of the last twenty-five years — and suggests that the initial volume of the Yale Edwards, Paul Ramsey's edition of *Freedom of the Will* (1957.14), is the "first evident sign" of the necessary reappraisal of Edwards, America's "greatest genius of her native intellectual heritage." Although Ramsey's introduction is strained at times and more analytical than psychological, it remains an "archetype" of editorial work, especially in the "masterly" historical analyses of the relationship of Edwards to John Locke and to the Arminians.

13 Murray, John. "The Imputation of Adam's Sin: Third Article." *Westminster Theological Journal* 19 (May): 141-69.
   Distinguishes Edwards's view of the imputation of original sin from that of New England Theology — Dwight, Emmons, Hopkins, and Taylor, and later, Hodge — as one between immediate and mediate. In *Original Sin*, Edwards held that hereditary corruption is consequent upon and is a penal consequence of Adam's sin and insisted that the sin as imputed includes, like Adam's, both the sinful disposition prior to the act and the act itself.

14 Ramsey, Paul. "Editor's Introduction." *Freedom of the Will. The Works of Jonathan Edwards*, 1. New Haven and London: Yale University Press, pp. 1-128.
   Traces the provenance, the theological issues, and the still-unresolved philosophical arguments of *Freedom of the Will* — liberty and necessity, responsibility and self-determination,

moral and natural necessity; Edwards's relationship to Locke and to his antagonists; and his effective and eloquent style, in an introduction to the first volume of the Yale Edwards. Edwards defines liberty, analyzes acts of volition, and interprets responsibility in such a way — "Edwards merely places in brackets . . . his belief in divine determination" — that he can show that universal causation applies to the will, just as every event is caused or determined, though not, he points out, compelled. Edwards's "philosophical lineage" begins in Locke's *Essay Concerning Human Understanding,* especially "Of Power," but ends in his rejection of key definitions and language, of the disjunction between faculties of the mind, and of the distinction between object and act, as Locke revised his text and Edwards's matured his thought. If "insufficient attention" has been given to the "actual" influence of Locke, still less has been given to Edwards's detailed refutation of Thomas Chubb, Daniel Whitby, and Isaac Watts, men who represented the deist, Anglican, and dissenting points of view, and regarded by Edwards as necessary to his attack upon Arminianism on all fronts.

15 Sargant, William. *Battle for the Mind: A Physiology of Conversion and Brain-Washing.* Garden City, N.Y.: Doubleday & Co., pp. 140-41, 148-52.

Culls passages from *Faithful Narrative* to illustrate the physiological mechanisins Edwards exploited in controlling thought and eliciting confessions and finds the practice reprehensible. Such methods of brainwashing and behavior modification found in Stalinist Russia are no more rigid nor intolerant than those in Edwardsean Northampton.

16 Stallknecht, Newton P. Review of Jonathan Edwards, *Freedom of the Will,* edited by Paul Ramsey. *Indiana Magazine of History* 53 (December): 449-52.

Questions the "uncritically enthusiastic" attitude of both Paul Ramsey (1957.14) and Perry Miller (1949.9) in granting Edwards philosophical significance and modernity. Edwards is, rather, a brilliant apologist who "plundered" Newton and Locke to serve his religious convictions.

17 Stewart, James A., ed. *Jonathan Edwards: The Narrative.* Grand Rapids, Mich.: Kregel Publications, 82 pp.

Interleaves comments in an abridgment of Edwards's letter to Benjamin Colman and adds a biography, the story of the Great Awakening, and case histories of conversion. *Faithful Narrative* is a "priceless document" for evangelists, a "veritable gold mine," a "helpful textbook," a "spiritual classic."

18 Webber, F. R. *A History of Preaching in Britain and America.* Milwaukee: Northwestern Publishing House, Part 3, pp. 83-90.

Lays Edwards's troubles at Northampton to his unremitting preaching of the severity of the law without the tempering influence of the gospel. Yet his effect on New England theology and on the American pulpit was lasting: both were now subject to a clergy not only intellectually trained but spiritually alive.

1958

1 Anon. "Famous Theologian's Church Honors Former Pastor Sunday; Descendant to Attend Rites." *Hampshire Gazette,* 2 October, p. 1.

Notes that Edwin Sponseller, minister of the First Church, will pay tribute to Edwards and that Edwards's great-great-great-great-great-great-granddaughter will attend.

2 Anon. "Jonathan Edwards Reinstated." *Christian Century* 75 (2 April): 397.

Notes the bicentennial tribute to Edwards at Northampton, a belated penance and reinstatement that "would not have meant too much to him."

3 Anon. "Jonathan Edwards to be Honored Today by Bay State Church that Ousted Him." *New York Times,* 9 March, p. 59.

Reports the coming memorial service for Edwards at the First Church of Christ, Congregational, in Northampton, and offers a brief life and the cause for his dismissal from the founding church. H. Richard Niebuhr will preach at a special afternoon service.

4 Beach, Waldo. "The Recovery of Jonathan Edwards: A Review." *Religion in Life* 27 (Spring): 286-89.

Welcomes the Yale edition of *Freedom of the Will* (1957.14) as an indication of the recovery of Edwards and praises Paul Ramsey's cogent, if prolix, introduction. "That the general editorial committee is headed by a Harvard professor and this volume edited by a Princeton professor is the mark of a kind of intellectual ecumenicity in the Ivy League, and of its common roots in New England Calvinism."

5 Beaver, R. Pierce. "The Concert for Prayer for Missions: An Early Venture in Ecumenical Action." *Ecumenical Review* 10 (July): 420-27.

Claims Edwards's *Humble Attempt,* instrumental in promoting world-wide prayer days in the nineteenth century, fostered common action and suggested millennial consequences.

6 Brown, Charles T. "Jonathan Edwards in 1958." *Minister's Quarterly* 14 (Summer): 34-35.

Cites the need for Edwards's "burning concept of sin" to bring contemporary man to redemption, in a notice of Edwards's death 200 years ago.

7 Faust, Clarence H. *Ideological Conflicts in Early American Books.* Syracuse, N.Y.: Syracuse University Press, pp. 13-14.

Notes that emotion mattered more to Edwards than abstract reasoning.

8 Ferm, Robert O. *Cooperative Evangelism.* Grand Rapids, Mich.: Zondervan Publishing House, pp. 49-51.

Likens the censure of Edwards as an evangelist, though not a major one, to that suffered by Billy Graham at the hands of the orthodox.

*9 Grazier, James Lewis. "The Preaching of Jonathan Edwards: A Study of his Published Sermons with Special Reference to the Great Awakening." Ph.D. dissertation, Temple University.

Cited in 1967.12: 207.

10 [Henry, Carl F. H.] "Jonathan Edwards' Still Angry God." *Christianity Today* 2 (6 January): 20-21.

Urges sinful man to heed again Edwards's still angry God, on the bicentennial of that prophet's death.

11 Hughes, Philip Edgcumbe. "Jonathan Edwards on Revival." *Christianity Today* 2 (15 September): 3-4.

Asks evangelicals, on the bicentennial of Edwards's death, to turn to his study of the revivals — *Faithful Narrative, Distinguishing Marks, Some Thoughts, Religious Affections* — for his scriptural insight is as "relevant to our day as it was to his."

12 Jones, Adam Leroy. *Early American Philosophers.* New York: Frederick Ungar Publishing Co.

Reprints 1898.5.

13 Kawerau, Peter. "Jonathan Edwards (1703-1758)." *Amerika und die Orientalischen Kirchen: Ursprung und Anfang der Amerikanischen Mission unter den Nationalkirchen Westasiens.* Berlin: Walter de Gruyter & Co., pp. 1-74.

Traces the doctrine of the divine light and its effect upon the nature of fallen man and workings of redemptive history, in a detailed examination of Edwards's view of the clergy and the revivals, covenant and sacrament, the millennium and the concert of prayer. As the old continent gave physical birth to Christ, Edwards argued, so the new continent would give spiritual birth to him through a wise and pure ministry spreading the Word. Thus the hopes of *History of Redemption* and *Humble Attempt* would be realized and America's mission fulfilled. (In German.)

*14 Long, George W., Jr. "Jonathan Edwards, 1703-1758: His Theory and Practice of Evangelism." Ph.D. dissertation, University of Edinburgh.

15 Metcalf, George Reuben. "American Religious Philosophy and the Pastoral Letters of the House of Bishops." *Historical Magazine of the Protestant Episcopal Church* 27 (March): 10-84.

Deals briefly with Edwards and Samuel Johnson as early "representative" philosophers in a history of Episcopalianism in America. Both were immaterialists and idealists, yet one was a Congregationalist and the other an Anglican.

16 Murray, Iain H. "A Memoir of Jonathan Edwards." *The Select Works of Jonathan Edwards.* London: Banner of Truth Trust. 1:13-62.

Offers a brief life of Edwards, an estimate of his publications — the "most valuable" today are *Distinguishing Marks, Religious Affections,* and *Some Thoughts* — and a plea to return to his "fearless" ministry.

17 Persons, Stow. *American Minds: A History of Ideas.* New York: Holt, Rinehart & Winston, pp. 106-109 passim.

Fits Edwards into the intellectual development of eighteenth-century America through his part in the "continuing vitality" of religion then. Religion, to the enlightened mind, was either reasonable or a fact of experience; to Edwards it was both. Though he remained "impervious" to some ideas of the time, he was not the anachronism Parrington depicts (1927.2).

18 Pratt, Glenn Ralph. "Jonathan Edwards as a Preacher of Doctrine." S.T.D. dissertation, Temple University.

Refutes the view of Edwards as an imprecatory preacher of hell-fire and finds his sermons "remarkable" for their biblical and doctrinal balance. Edwards renders doctrines from both the Old and New Testaments and balances systematically his preaching of 1,300 sermons in theology, anthropology, Christology, soteriology, ethics, ecclesiology. Of 655 sermons, 500 stress "hope, joy, and blessing"; only 155 center on damnation and hell.

19 Quince, Sheldon B., ed. *Jonathan Edwards' Sermon Outlines.* The World's Great Sermons in Outline, 5. Grand Rapids, Mich.: William B. Eerdmans, 164 pp.

Reprints thirty-five "choice" sermon outlines of Edwards and quotes with approval B. B. Warfield's dictum, "'It was in his sermons that Edwards' studies bore their richest fruit.'"

20 Riley, I. Woodbridge. "Jonathan Edwards." *American Philosophy: The Early Schools.* New York: Russell & Russell.

Reprints 1907.6.

21 Schneider, Herbert Wallace. *The Puritan Mind.* Ann Arbor: University of Michigan Press.

Reprints 1930.1.3.

22 Settle, Raymond W. "Colonial Religious Awakenings: The New England Revival, 1734." *Christianity Today* 2 (15 September): 15-17.

Recounts Edwards's efforts in 1734 to awaken religious interest among the young of Northampton, his sermon series on justification by faith, the revival's subsequent spread to nearby communities, and its development into the Great Awakening.

23 Stewart, Randall. *American Literature and Christian Doctrine.* Baton Rouge: Louisiana State University Press, pp. 8-15.

Extols Edwards as "our first Protestant American saint." Not only is he America's greatest theologian and philosopher, but in his logic and ordonnance, his tenderness and beauty, our greatest writer before the nineteenth century, a rare balance of head and heart. Edwards is an "un-Emersonian" transcendentalist whose *Divine and Supernatural Light* is the "finest statement" of experiential religion to date.

24 Turnbull, Ralph G. "Jonathan Edwards and Great Britain." *Evangelical Quarterly* 30 (April): 68-74.

Indicates that Edwards was "profoundly influenced" by such English Puritans as William Ames and William Chappell, John Preston and Richard Sibbes and that William Perkins's *The Art of Prophecying* (1618) had a "greater influence" as a literary model for his sermons than any other text. After his dismissal from Northampton, friends in Great Britain and Scotland urged Edwards to accept a settlement there.

25 ———. *Jonathan Edwards the Preacher.* Grand Rapids, Mich.: Baker Book House, 192 pp.

Insists that Edwards's theological treatises spring from the pastoral experiences and reflections of his sermons; analyzes them in outline and classifies them by types: dogmatic, imprecatory, evangelical, ethical, memorial, vocational, and pastoral; and concludes that "whereas Edwards was a staunch Calvinist on his knees, he was like an Arminianist on his feet." Edwards's sermons are the work of "an artist, a craftsman," written in a plain and modest style, limited and biblical in imagery, logical, rhythmical, and balanced, and "seldom controversial, and never contentious." They are evangelical and ethical, agencies of redemption and psalms to God's sovereignty. Edwards stands in the "first rank" of preachers throughout time, an example to other preachers and to theological students, an "evangelical mystic" who knew and felt God's spirit in the soul and who believed that "he was a voice for God."

26 ———. "Jonathan Edwards: A Voice for God." *Christianity Today* 2 (6 January): 8-9.
  Observes in Edwards the paradox of the "convinced" Calvinist and the "persuasive" Arminian, the theologian of divine sovereignty and the preacher of man's responsibility. God's foreknowledge of man's end balances his will to have ministers preach "as a means of urging" men to press into the Kingdom. Thus, Edwards is "a voice for God."

27 Weisberger, Bernard A. *They Gathered at the River: The Story of the Great Revivalists and Their Impact upon Religion in America.* Boston: Little, Brown & Co., pp. 54-57.
  Notes Edwards's role in the Great Awakening. Important as it was, *Sinners in the Hands of an Angry God* was almost Edwards's undoing: most Americans forgot the "keen psychologist" and "brilliant philosopher" for the hell-fire preacher.

28 Winslow, Ola Elizabeth. Review of Jonathan Edwards, *Freedom of the Will,* edited by Paul Ramsey. *American Literature* 30 (March): 121-22.
  Regards Paul Ramsey's "admirable" introduction (1957.14) a rare and valuable instance of reading Edwards as if he were still a contemporary.

29 Wolf, Carl J. C. "Preface" *Jonathan Edwards on Evangelism.* Grand Rapids, Mich.: William B. Eerdmans, pp. vii-xii.
  Emphasizes Edwards's theocentricism as the key to his thought, suggests that his correlation of the doctrine of divine sovereignty and experimental religion may be one of the "true secrets" of revivalism, and reprints selections from his evangelical writings.

1959

1 Buranelli, Vincent. "Colonial Philosophy." *William and Mary Quarterly,* 3d ser., 16 (July): 343-62.
  Ranks Edwards first among "genuine" (and neglected) colonial philosophers — Samuel Johnson, Cadwallader Colden, and John Witherspoon — and, with two or three others, the "greatest" American philosopher. Edwards's place derives chiefly from his emphasis upon experience and his "creative originality."

2 Duff, William Boyd. *Jonathan Edwards, Then and Now: A Satirical Study in Predestination.* Pittsburgh: Guttendorf Press, 95 pp.
  Offers a "small book" of the life and times of Edwards — with asides on Thomas Henry Huxley and Charles Darwin, Albert Einstein and Marilyn Monroe — in an attempt to define, defend, and restore Edwards's Presbyterian orthodoxy in these parlous times. So in a "ghostly interview," Edwards is made to say of Einstein, "'Rather than accept the theory of curved space, I had as soon believe that a curved mind concocted the theory.'" Later he adds, "'Communism is not a perversion but the most logical outgrowth of Darwinism.'" Hence, "the future trend" of

philosophy lies with Edwards, as does "the most nearly correct answer to the riddle of the universe."

3 Ferm, Robert O. *The Psychology of Christian Conversion*. Westwood, N.J.: Fleming H. Revell Co., pp. 113-15.
   Finds Edwards's distinction between true and false conversions a modern instance of psychological attitudes and methods in the service of religion.

4 Ferm, Vergilius, ed. *Classics of Protestantism*. New York: Philosophical Library, pp. 180-81.
   Introduces and reprints part of Edwards's *Freedom of the Will* and *Sinners in the Hands of an Angry God*.

5 Goen, C. C. "Jonathan Edwards: A New Departure in Eschatology." *Church History* 28 (March): 25-40.
   Characterizes Edwards's eschatological doctrine that a golden age of the Church and a time for earthly bliss would precede the final consummation and the coming of Christ "a radical innovation" and "counter" to commonly held Protestant opinion that unprecedented grief and darkness would usher in the millennium. Edwards argues from his belief in rational man, a just and merciful God, and an historically realized process of redemption, though the "immediate" source of his speculations was probably the Daniel Whitby-Moses Lowman exegesis. With *Humble Inquiry* and *History of Redemption* Edwards becomes our "first major post-millennial thinker," providing a religious context to manifest destiny and radical utopianism in America.

6 Hall, Thomas Cuming. *The Religious Background of American Culture*. New York: Frederick Ungar.
   Reprints 1930.7.

7 Kawerau, Peter W. "Johann Adam Steinmetz als Vermittler zwichen dem deutschen und amerikanischen Pietismus im 18. Jahrhundert." *Zetschrift für Kirchengeschichte* 70 (1-2):75-88.
   Recounts the provenance of Edwards's *Faithful Narrative* and Steinmetz's role in making the text available to a German audience. (In German.)

8 Ludwig, Richard M. "Jonathan Edwards." In *Literary History of the United States*. Edited by Robert E. Spiller et al. New York: Macmillan Co., 3:110-11.
   Supplements the bibliography in 1948.5.

9 Miller, Perry. "From Edwards to Emerson." In *Interpretations of American Literature*. Edited by Charles Feidelson, Jr., and Paul Brodtkorb, Jr. New York: Oxford University Press, pp. 114-36.
   Reprints 1940.9.

10 ———. *Jonathan Edwards*. Cleveland and New York: World Publishing Co.
   Reprints 1949.9.

11 ———. *Jonathan Edwards*. New York: Meridian Books.
   Reprints 1949.9.

12 Moulton, Charles Wells, ed. "Jonathan Edwards." In *Library of Literary Criticism of English and American Authors.* Gloucester, Mass.: Peter Smith, 3:380-95.
    Reprints 1902.10.

13 Murphy, Arthur E. "Jonathan Edwards on Free Will and Moral Agency." *Philosophical Review* 68 (April): 181-202.
    Questions Paul Ramsey's reading of *Freedom of the Will* (1957.14) — Ramsey confuses voluntary action (the effect) with the act of volition (the cause) and confounds Edwards — and suggests that the real problem lies in the relationship between the determination of the will and moral agency and Edwards's failure to solve it. By making nonsense of the Arminian position on the determination of the will, Edwards makes "equal" nonsense of moral agency, because he confuses "the language of mental causation with that of moral appraisal and justification." The will does not perform acts of mental causation, an agent does. To have it any other way destroys freedom of the will, the will itself, and man as moral agent.

13A Murray, John. *The Imputation of Adam's Sin.* Grand Rapids, Mich.: William B. Eerdmans, pp. 52-64.
    Reprints 1957.13.

14 Pickell, Charles N. "The Freedom of the Will in William Ames and Jonathan Edwards." *Gordon Review* 5 (Winter): 168-74.
    Discovers "no essential difference" between Edwards and William Ames on free will (contrary to what "many scholars" hold) and points out "noteworthy" similarities in their careers and theology. Both were "adamant" on determinism, election, and calling, but Ames stressed preparation for salvation and the means of grace in *The Marrow of Sacred Divinity* (1623), a critical text to New England Puritans, although he "studiously avoided any hint" that man might save himself. "What may appear to be theological differences between them are in reality only differences in emphasis."

15 Pierce, Richard D. "A Suppressed Edwards Manuscript on the Trinity." *Crane Review* 1 (Winter): 66-80.
    Traces the controversy surrounding the suppressed Edwards manuscripts on the Trinity (1903.25) — through contemporary newspaper accounts and the correspondence between his heirs and his editors — and posits a reason for it. Edwards accepted the Nicene doctrine of the eternal generation of the Son, a view generally abandoned and at times held in derision by later New England divines. To keep his theology in conformity with theirs, the Edwardsean custodians of his manuscripts withheld publication of his trinitarian views until forced to and then only to protect him from the charge of "even greater" heresy. In fact, the heterodoxy of the text is "slight," but it is ample testimony to fifty years of "exaggerated rumor and partisan theology."

16 Root, Robert Walter. "The Religious Ideas of Some Major Early Writers of America." Ph.D. dissertation, Syracuse University.
    Classifies Edwards as a conservative in a 1000-page study of the relation of early American religious ideas to American literature and culture.

17 Sizer, Theodore. "The Story of the Edwards Portraits." *Yale University Library Gazette* 34 (October): 82-88.

Tells of the acquisition of the Edwards portraits now at Jonathan Edwards College, Yale, in a tale of academic intrigue and the great hurricane of 1938.

18 Smith, John E. "Editor's Introduction." *Religious Affections. The Works of Jonathan Edwards,* 2. New Haven and London: Yale University Press, pp. 1-83.

Traces the provenance and historical background of *Religious Affections;* examines in detail each of the twelve signs of the affections and each of the sixteen documented sources of Edwards's reading; and comments upon the place of the affections in contemporary religion and the "remarkable literary power" of the work, in an introduction to the second volume of the Yale Edwards. Central to Edwards's view of the affections and "invariably missed" by commentators is the unitive relationship between head and heart: judgment or inclination involves both the will and the mind — it is called *will* when it is expressed through action, *heart* when it is expressed through the mind. "Affections, then, are *lively* inclinations and choices which show that man is a being with a heart." Thus Edwards contributed to his time and to ours: he restored religion to life, showed that a form of understanding was closely related to individual experience, and provided a rational means for validating piety. And his interpretation contributed in no small way to the "robust sense of activity" of American Protestantism.

19 Suter, Rufus. "A Note on Platonism in the Philosophy of Jonathan Edwards." *Harvard Theological Review* 52 (October): 283-84.

Recounts the view of Professor William Wallace Fenn, of Harvard Divinity, that Edwards was the "protagonist of a New England Tragedy" because he was self-consciously aware of being "unable to reconcile Platonism with his Calvinism."

20 Turnbull, Ralph G. Preface to his *Devotions of Jonathan Edwards.* Grand Rapids, Mich.: Baker Book House, pp. 5-6.

Reprints passages from the "riches" of Edwards's creative, experimental thought as weekly devotions.

21 Weeks, J. Stafford. A Review of *Jonathan Edwards the Preacher,* by Ralph G. Turnbull. *Church History* 28 (June): 13-14.

Considers Ralph G. Turnbull's study of a "master" preacher (1958.25) useful to today's ministers but fragmented in form and without a sense of the "profound integrity" of Edwards's sermons.

22 Williams, George Huntston. "The Wilderness and Paradise in the History of the Church." *Church History* 28 (March): 3-24.

Notes that Edwards "largely interiorized" the meaning of wilderness and held the promised land to be heaven, not a holy commonwealth, in a history of the idea of wilderness and paradise from biblical to New England times.

23 Winterich, John T. Review of *Jonathan Edwards,* by Perry Miller. *New York Herald Tribune Book Review,* 20 December, p. 9.

Reviews the paperback publication of Perry Miller's *Jonathan Edwards* (1959.11) as an "admirable presentation by a Middle Western Scholar."

1960

1 Conrad, Leslie, Jr. "The Importance of Preaching in the Great Awakening." *Lutheran Quarterly* 12 (May): 111-20.

Makes passing reference to Edwards's pulpit style in his theory that the "main benefits" of a sermon come at first hearing, not through later reflection.

1A Covey, Cyclone. "A Pilgrim in Vanity Fair." *The American Pilgrim.* Oklahoma State University Publication 57, no. 17. Stillwater: Oklahoma State University, pp. 59-90.

Concludes a study of the American pilgrimage into the wilderness — the "basic American tradition" — with the Great Awakening, when the wilderness became "home" to Americans, and Edwards's part in it. Edwards fought "anemic" Arminianism, "seeth[ed]" at the growing indifference to religion, pressed the attack in "long, slow crescendos" — *Sinners in the Hands of an Angry God* and *Future Punishment of the Wicked* — "cringed" at enthusiasm, took on the river gods. Edwards was "the least political of all the famous Puritans — and that could have been the large part of his trouble, as well as a sign of the end of the pilgrim era."

2 Dillenberger, John. *Protestant Thought and Natural Science: A Historical Interpretation.* New York: Doubleday & Co., pp. 161-62.

Slights Edwards's contribution because, while the analogy he drew between Newtonian causation and faith and regeneration was astute, it had little lasting effect.

3 Elwood, Douglas J. *The Philosophical Theology of Jonathan Edwards.* New York: Columbia University Press, xii, 220 pp.

Locates the correlation between Edwards's theology and his philosophy in his doctrine of the immediacy of God, a synthesis of elements of theism and pantheism, Calvinism and mysticism into a "third way" of describing the relationship of God and the world as one of "mutual immanence: God in the world and the world in God." Edwards reconstructs Calvinism along Neoplatonic lines, stressing the aesthetic element rather than the moral or legal one and conceiving of God as absolute power. Divine immediacy, for Edwards, becomes not only awareness but also the self-movement and self-revelation of God in creation and history as a "continuous sacrament" and represents perhaps the most "authentic" element of Puritanism in his thought. Man passively receives from God this "new sense of things" as a "new simple idea" and can then grasp the "spiritual dimension" of life, a dimension higher and deeper than that afforded the unregenerate. Thus Edwards's mysticism is an "extension" of Puritan piety, conceiving the union of the soul and God as continuous rather than fugitive and identifying grace with "the actual presence of God in the human heart." Isolated as Edwards was, such ideas were probably the product of "his own direct experience," yet they have "relevancy" to a Christian understanding of God in our time.

4 Frankena, William K., ed. Foreword to *The Nature of True Virtue.* Ann Arbor: University of Michigan Press, pp. v-xiii.

Recommends Edwards's *True Virtue* as a well-made treatise on ethics, with a special appeal to neofundamentalists and to contemporary moral philosophers, and as an important item of intellectual history, in a brief explanation of his distinction between the two moralities, their nature and source.

5 Gerstner, John H. *Steps to Salvation: The Evangelistic Message of Jonathan Edwards.* Philadelphia: Westminster Press, 192 pp.

Traces the steps to salvation in the published and unpublished sermons of Edwards, a "both/ and" theologian, both a covenant theologian and a Calvinist, both a predestinarian and an evangelist. The "keystone" to Edwards's evangelistic theory of salvation is seeking, a way for sinful man Edwards "never wearies of pleading," a doctrine Edwards preaches "insistently and repeatedly." Unregenerate man might not be able to find the salvation he sought — the two are not causal — but God might reveal it to him if he did, Edwards thought, if he prepared, especially during revivals or communion, "red-letter days for redemption." Illumination and regeneration occur simultaneously at the "sovereign pleasure" of God, bringing about true faith; justification is by faith alone but not by "the faith that is alone"; and, because the signs of salvation are so "meticulous," assurance is a "relatively rare thing." All this Edwards holds in a covenantal frame of reference, distinguishing the covenant of redemption from the covenant of grace. By insisting that a sinner can do something, Edwards agrees somewhat with the Arminians and disagrees with such Calvinists as say he can do nothing. "According to Edwards, he can do something nonsaving but promising and hopeful: namely, seek."

6 Goen, Clarence Curtis. "Revivalism and Separatism in New England, 1740-1800: Strict Congregationalists and Separate Baptists in the Great Awakening." Ph.D. dissertation, Yale University.
    Published as 1962.3.

7 Heimert, Alan Edward. "American Oratory: From the Great Awakening to the Election of Jefferson." Ph.D. dissertation, Harvard University.
    Published in part as 1966.17.

8 Hitchcock, Orville A. "Jonathan Edwards." In *A History and Criticism of American Public Address*. Edited by William Norwood Brigance. New York: Russell & Russell.
    Reprints 1943.6.

9 Holbrook, Clyde A. "Edwards Re-examined." *Review of Metaphysics* 13 (June): 623-41.
    Characterizes both Paul Ramsey's introduction to *Freedom of the Will* (1957.14) and John E. Smith's to *Religious Affections* (1959.18) "insightful and provocative," though Ramsey finds more consistency in Edwards and Smith more accuracy in his language than is so in the texts, in an essay-review.

10 Howard, Leon. *Literature and the American Tradition*. Garden City, N.Y.: Doubleday & Co., pp. 44-49.
    Places Edwards among the Cartesian logicians who rejected the Ramists and were opposed by the Baconians. His dependence on a chain of causation and his "severe" rationalism in argument exemplify his devotion to the Port-Royal logic.

11 McGinley, Phyllis. "The Theology of Jonathan Edwards." *Times Three*. New York: Viking Press, p. 19.
    Portrays Edwards's woeful congregation during an imprecatory sermon in a twenty-four-line poem and his "whimsical" deity,

    Not God the Father or the Son
    But God the Holy Terror.

12 McLoughlin, William G. "Introduction." *Lectures on Revivals of Religion,* by Charles Grandison Finney. Cambridge, Mass.: Harvard University Press, pp. x-xiii passim.

Notes critical differences between Edwards and Finney on matters of revivalism and theology, even though Finney frequently quotes from Edwards, in a history of Finney's attack on Calvinism and the "Presbygational" churches of the nineteenth century.

12A Niebuhr, H. Richard. "Reformation: Continuing Imperative." *Christian Century* 77 (2 March): 248-51.

Records an indebtedness to Edwards — "I was, as I hope to remain, closer to Calvin and Jonathan Edwards" than to the theologians of the 1930s — in an autobiographical memoir.

13 Olmstead, Clifton E. *History of Religion in the United States.* Englewood Cliffs, N.J.: Prentice-Hall, pp. 162-67, 170-71.

Distinguishes Edwards's theology from Calvin's as one more concerned with man's unworthiness than with God's sovereignty and cites his *True Virtue* as an "important" contribution to American theology. Edwards's "valiant battle" to save Calvinism and its "intellectual respectability" was bound to fail: frontier optimism was at odds with divine determinism; Arminianism was at one with a free man's responsibility. Yet Edwards's rigorous thought lent "backbone and stamina" to American theology for "generations to come."

14 Roberts, Cecil Albert, Jr. "The Apologetic Significance of Jonathan Edwards' Doctrine of Religious Experience." Th.D. dissertation, Southwestern Baptist Theological Seminary.

Examines Edwards's defense of experiential religion, the background that contributed to it and the effects that flowed from it. Edwards's apologetic for religious experience reestablished the place of emotion in religion and revitalized the regenerate church. Though it is "tragic" that Edwards had to speak through a harsh Calvinism, his belief in God's active revelation and man's appropriation of it through emotion remains a "fundamental insight."

14A Smith, Elwyn A. "The Doctrine of Imputation and the Presbyterian Schism of 1837-1838." *Journal of the Presbyterian Historical Society* 38 (September): 129-51.

Measures the "pertinence" of Edwards to the Presbyterian schism in the nineteenth century by comparing Jonathan Dickinson on the doctrine of imputation before the publication *Original Sin* with Samuel Hopkins after it.

15 Smith, H. Shelton, Robert T. Handy, and Lefferts A. Loetscher. *American Christianity: An Historical Interpretation with Representative Documents.* New York: Charles Scribner's, 1:39-40.

Reprints selections from *Religious Affections* and suggests that the "changing tone" in Edwards's four defenses of the revivals arises from excesses within the movement and criticism without. The first of these, *Faithful Narrative,* is more nearly objective and sympathetic; the last, *Religious Affections,* critical and cautionary.

16 Whitefield, George. *George Whitefield's Journals.* Edited by Iain H. Murray. London: Banner of Truth Trust, pp. 476-79.

Recounts George Whitefield's meeting with Edwards in late October 1740 — "I think I have not seen his fellow in all New England"; his stay at the family home — "A sweeter couple I have not yet seen"; and preaching to the Northampton congregation — "good Mr. Edwards wept during the whole time of exercise."

17 Winslow, Ola Elizabeth. Review of Jonathan Edwards, *Religious Affections,* edited by John E. Smith. *American Literature* 32 (November): 330-31.

> Praises John E. Smith's "enlightening" introduction to *Religious Affections* (1959.18), the "central core" of Edwards's thought.

18 Wood, A. Skevington. *The Inextinguishable Blaze: Spiritual Renewal and Advance in the Eighteenth Century.* Grand Rapids, Mich.: William B. Eerdmans, pp. 53-66.

> Connects Edwards to the 1735 revival in Wales — "part of American aid to Britain" — and considers him rather than George Whitefield the "true leader" of the Great Awakening and its "foremost" theologian, in a survey of the revival spirit in the eighteenth century.

19 Woodward, Robert H. "Jonathan Edwards as a Puritan Poet." *Exercise Exchange* 8 (October): 5-6.

> Compares Edwards's *Personal Narrative* with several poems by Edward Taylor to show another Puritan "poetic temperament" at work.

1961

1 Ahlstrom, Sydney E. "Theology in America: A Historical Survey." In *The Shaping of American Religion.* Edited by James Ward Smith and A. Leland Jamison. Religion in American Life, no. 1. Princeton, N.J.: Princeton University Press, pp. 243-51 passim.

> Characterizes Edwards as a *"Dortian philosophe,"* a Reformed theologian adapting the basic ideas of the Enlightenment to the Christian experience. Four "salient" features of his system of thought stand out: the full, scriptural rendering of the Reformed Christian message in the sermons; the empirically based apologia for the Christian faith in *Religious Affections, Freedom of the Will,* and *Original Sin;* the essentialist ontology derived from Christian Platonism in *End of Creation* and *True Virtue;* and the "ultimate mode" of expressing the meaning of Christianity in *History of Redemption.*

2 Anderson, Wallace Earl. "Mind and Nature in the Early Philosophical Writings of Jonathan Edwards." Ph.D. dissertation, University of Minnesota.

> Studies the successive stages of Edwards's development of idealism from "Of Atoms and Perfectly Solid Bodies" to notes on "The Mind" and identifies the "dominant themes" to be the immateriality of the natural world and its immediate and continuous dependence upon God. Edwards draws upon Henry More's *Immortality of the Soul,* Newton's third book of *Opticks,* and Locke's *Essay Concerning Human Understanding.*

3 Baritz, Loren. "The Idea of the West." *American Historical Review* 66 (April): 618-40.

> Notes that Edwards's eschatology was "partly determined by the idea that God faced west."

4 Burr, Nelson R. *A Critical Bibliography of Religion in America.* Religion in American Life, no. 4. Princeton, N.J.: Princeton University Press, pp. 132-37, 976-87.

> Provides a critical, bibliographical essay on Edwards in two parts: the first concerns his role in the New England Awakening, the second his reconstruction and defense of Calvinism — the

origins of his thought, his theology, his idealism and pantheism, and commentaries. There are three "major periods" in Edwards's intellectual life: his "youthful speculations" before Northampton; his "theological period" before Stockbridge; and his "systematic writing" before Princeton. "It is misleading to judge him solely by any one of these periods."

4A Cragg, Gerald R. Review of *The Philosophical Theology of Jonathan Edwards,* by Douglas J. Elwood. *Religion in Life* 30 (Summer): 476-77.
　　Finds Douglas J. Elwood's first book (1960.3) "valuable" but the medium "not perfectly mastered."

5 Horne, R. A. "The Atomic Theory of Jonathan Edwards." *Crane Review* 3 (Winter): 65-72.
　　Considers "quite novel" for his time Edwards's atomic theory in "Notes on Natural Science," anticipating as it does ideas of "collision effectiveness" and "steric hindrance," and regrets that so inventive a scientific mind fell before "sterile doctrine."

6 Illick, Joseph E., III. "Jonathan Edwards and the Historians." *Journal of the Presbyterian Historical Society* 39 (December): 230-46.
　　Compares the studies of Edwards by V. L. Parrington (1927.2), Herbert W. Schneider (1930.13), Ola Elizabeth Winslow (1940.21), Perry Miller (1949.9), and Edwin S. Gaustad (1957.6) and finds them wanting. Edwards is "somewhat mishandled," sometimes by methodology, sometimes by political or philosophical assumptions. All deny Edwards his complexity by focussing upon only one aspect of him — in American thought or in religious history, in his personal life or his intellectual one, in his contribution to the Awakening.

7 Jeanes, W. P. "Jonathan Edwards's Conception of Freedom of the Will." *Scottish Journal of Theology* 14 (March): 1-14.
　　Explicates Edwards's arguments of free agency, foreknowledge, certainty, and necessity, and contrasts the moral systems of Edwards and the Arminians. Edwards removes his theocentric concept of freedom of the will from mechanical necessity, which would preclude responsibility; from contingency, which would preclude certainty; and from a self-determined will, which would preclude reason, conscience, and inclinations. Of the moral systems, it is *"conviction"* that separates Edwards from the *"sentiment"* of the Arminians, or it is the difference between man's conviction of his duty to God's law, irrespective of his feelings, and man's sentiment (or feelings) of his ability to determine his moral state. The centrality of God in Edwards's scheme lends "stability and strength" to it, at times "stubbornness and harshness."

7A Kellaway, William. *The New England Company, 1649-1776: Missionary Society to the American Indians.* London: Longmans, pp. 274-75.
　　Considers Edwards's appointment to Stockbridge "a good one from neither the Indians' nor his own point of view," in a brief account of his time there.

8 Lasser, Michael L. "Addendum to an Exercise on Jonathan Edwards." *Exercise Exchange* 9 (November): 31.
　　Cites Edwards's "Sarah Pierrepont" as evidence of a "poetic tendency" in Edwards and suggests a useful contrast to Anne Bradstreet's "To My Dear and Loving Husband" and "A Letter to her Husband, Absent upon Public Employment."

9 MacCormac, Earl R. "Jonathan Edwards and Missions." *Journal of the Presbyterian Historical Society* 31 (December): 219-29.

Finds Edwards "vitally interested" in missions — see, for example, his post-millennial eschatology in *History of Redemption* and his doctrine of universal imputation in *Original Sin* — contrary to the "popular assumption" that a theocentric, deterministic theology like his prohibits them. While Edwards's ministry among the Mahican at Stockbridge was not impressive, he did exert considerable influence for missions upon his successors through his theology and upon others, here and abroad, through his *Life of Brainerd*.

10 McGraw, James. *Great Evangelical Preachers of Yesterday.* New York and Nashville: Abingdon Press, pp. 50-55.

Judges the strength of Edwards's preaching to rest in his thought and argument rather than his voice and manner. Edwards develops the points and major sections of his sermons in a "smooth continuity," offering few anecdotes but frequent metaphors.

11 Olmstead, Clifton E. *Religion in America.* Englewood Cliffs, N.J.: Prentice-Hall, pp. 43-45.

Recasts 1960.13.

11A Packer, J. I. "Jonathan Edwards and the Theology of Revival." In *Increasing the Knowledge of God.* Papers Read at the Puritan and Reformed Studies Conference, 20-21 December 1960. London: Evangelical Magazine, pp. 13-28.

Culls from Edwards's work "a fairly complete account" of a theology of revival for evangelicals who had rejected him as unreadable or philosophical. Though Edwards wrote about revival "piecemeal" in *Faithful Narrative, History of Redemption, Distinguishing Marks, Some Thoughts,* and *Religious Affections,* "it is, perhaps, the most important contribution" he made to theology, a "pioneer elucidation" of biblical faith.

12 Schafer, Thomas A. Review of *The Philosophical Theology of Jonathan Edwards,* by Douglas J. Elwood. *American Literature* 33 (November): 379-80.

Considers Douglas J. Elwood's explication (1960.3) "rightly centered and basically correct," though it "underplays" Edwards's rationalistic theism and gradualistic metaphysics.

13 Smith, James Ward. "Religion and Science in American Philosophy." In *The Shaping of American Religion.* Edited by James Ward Smith and A. Leland Jamison. Religion in American Life, no. 1. Princeton, N.J.: Princeton University Press, pp. 414-17.

Claims that Edwards grasped the fundamental implications of the scientific spirit, not simply the superficial adaptations of it; that his understanding was profound and mature, not experimental and puerile. All his later theology — *Religious Affections, Freedom of the Will, True Virtue* — reveals a "monumental" effort to read Calvinist axioms in terms of the "scientifically oriented philosophical spirit." That philosophical spirit remains constant in Edwards, but "the whole tone and tenor" of the Calvinist axioms do not.

14 Suter, Rufus. "The Strange Universe of Jonathan Edwards." *Harvard Theological Review* 54 (April): 125-28.

Suggests that Edwards's universe is "strange" to contemporary, liberal Protestants not because of his uncompromising biblicism but because of his stark sense of the reality of ethical concepts. The goodness of virtue, the beauty of holiness, the necessity of justice — all are real in a literal, cosmic sense, for they comprise the "warp and woof" of the universe eternally. The reality of the physical universe is secondary to them.

15 Wheatcroft, John. "Emily Dickinson's Poetry and Jonathan Edwards on the Will." *Bucknell Review* 10 (December): 102-27.

Considers Edwards's doctrine of the will to be the "mainspring" of Emily Dickinson's creative activity and his Connecticut Valley orthodoxy the cultural context of her life and work. Dickinson was "born and bred" amid Edwardseans and owes a significant part of her "inner life" to Rev. Charles Wadsworth, a "product" of New England Theology. Even the familiar opening lines of one of her "greatest" poems,

> Because I could not stop for Death
> He kindly stopped for me,

remain "dark" without Edwards's doctrine of will and necessity.

16 Williams, Daniel D. "Tradition and Experience in American Theology." In *The Shaping of American Religion*. Edited by James Ward Smith and A. Leland Jamison. Religion in American Life, no. 1. Princeton, N.J.: Princeton University Press, pp. 448-53.

Cites Edwards as a good example of the place experience holds in knowing God, the first of five categories of empiricism found in the method and content of American Christian thought. Edwards's typology attempts to find divine truths in nature and in man, to see both in a "constant interplay of challenge and adjustment," and so illustrates the very condition of experience in America. His interest in the varieties of religious experience is "not a very long step" from William James and nineteenth-century empirical theology.

17 Winslow, Ola Elizabeth. *Jonathan Edwards, 1703-1758*. New York: Collier Books.

Reprints 1940.21.

18 ———. Review of *The Philosophical Theology of Jonathan Edwards*, by Douglas J. Elwood. *New England Quarterly* 34 (June): 255-57.

Finds "exhilarating" Douglas J. Elwood's fresh approach (1960.3) and particularly "exciting" his inclusion of Edwards in the pantheon of theologians ancient and modern.

1962

1 Bacon, Martha. "Miss Beecher in Hell." *American Heritage* 14 (December): 28-31, 102-105.

Recounts the tragic "triangle" of Catherine Beecher, a leader in women's education in nineteenth-century America; Alexander Metcalf Fisher, a Yale professor; and Edwards, "the dark giant who gave shape to the American conscience." Beecher refutes Edwards in order that Fisher, a nonprofessing Christian who drowned at twenty-eight, be saved from eternal damnation.

1A Beaver, R. Pierce. "American Missionary Motivation before the Revolution." *Church History* 31 (June): 2316-26.

Attributes to the Great Awakening — and to Edwards, in particular — a new motivating factor for the American missionary movement before the Revolution and the preparation for another. Added to the three existing motives — the glory of God, Christian compassion, and the example of Catholic missionaries — was the idea of a Christian's labor for the coming of the Kingdom of God; the other was millennialism. Edwards first applied the idea of "bringing them in" to all church members, not only ministers, and set it in a "universal context" in *Humble Attempt*, a "little book" that also related Christian action to eschatological hope.

2 Faust, Clarence H., and Thomas H. Johnson. "Introduction." *Jonathan Edwards: Representative Selections.* Rev. ed. American Century Series. New York: Hill & Wang, pp. xi-cxvii.

Reprints 1935.3 with a revised and updated annotated bibliography of over 200 items by Stephen S. Webb, pp. cxix-cxlii.

3 Goen, C. C. *Revivalism and Separatism in New England, 1740-1800: Strict Congregationalists and Separate Baptists in the Great Awakening.* New Haven and London: Yale University Press, pp. 13-15, 45-46, 160-64, 209-10.

Distinguishes between Edwards's views of conversion as experience during the revivals and as profession for church membership. Edwards shaped the "normative pattern" of experiential conversion in the Great Awakening into three "well defined" stages characterized by distress, conviction, and assurance. Later, in *Humble Inquiry,* he endorsed sincere profession of faith for church membership, though he opposed the separation between professing and real saints then in vogue. His insistence upon parental profession as a prerequisite to the baptism of their children reveals a "curious blindness to history."

4 Harland, Gordon. "The American Protestant Heritage and the Theological Task." *Drew Gateway* 32 (Winter): 71-93.

Notes that Edwards and Franklin divide the Puritan soul, setting the stage for America's subsequent religious history.

5 Littell, Franklin Hamlin. *From State Church to Pluralism: A Protestant Interpretation of Religion in American History.* Garden City, N.Y.: Doubleday & Co., pp. 18-19.

Considers Edwards's career an "inevitable conflict" between evangelism and the parish system, symbolic of the transition from establishment to voluntarism. Edwards's emphasis upon conversion and grace points to "a more live initiative" of the faithful and away from the "standing order."

6 Löwe, Wolfgang Eberhard. "The First American Foreign Missionaries: 'The Students,' 1810-1820. An Inquiry into their Theological Motives." Ph.D. dissertation, Brown University.

Attributes "strong" incentives of the first American foreign missionaries for their work to particular ideas they found in Edwards, especially those on eschatology and benevolence, and to the general evangelical thrust of his theology.

7 Miller, Perry. "Benjamin Franklin — Jonathan Edwards." In *Major Writers of America.* Edited by Perry Miller et al. New York: Harcourt, Brace & World, 1:83-98.

Contends that Edwards and Franklin, "the preeminently eloquent linked antagonists in American culture," express in differing ways the Protestant ethic common to both, in a comparison of their careers and ideas introductory to a selection of their work. Though both share that code as well as an uncommon disinterestedness about personal success, the division between Edwards and Franklin is "irreconcilable," and provides "the basic and sundering theme" of American literature and our intellectual heritage.

8 Morgan, Edmund S. *The Gentle Puritan: A Life of Ezra Stiles, 1727-1795.* New Haven and London: Yale University Press, pp. 33-40 passim.

Recounts the tense relationship between Edwards and Isaac Stiles over their Yale days, the Bolton settlement, the New Haven parish, and the Great Awakening, and continuing with Stiles's son Ezra over the widow Sergeant at Stockbridge.

9 Mothersill, Mary. "Professor Prior and Jonathan Edwards." *Review of Metaphysics* 16 (December): 366-73.

Questions whether it is necessary or appropriate to seek sufficient causal conditions for contingent events as A. N. Prior suggests in his analysis (1962.13) and whether his analysis of limited and unlimited determinism is in fact an "alternative" to Edwards. "The only difference then between Edwards and Prior has to do with whether or not there are 'non-determinate' dispositions, and on this point Prior is unclear."

10 Moyer, Elgin S. "Jonathan Edwards." *Who Was Who in Church History.* Chicago: Moody Press, pp. 129-30.

Sketches the career of Edwards.

11 Newlin, Claude M. *Philosophy and Religion in Colonial America.* New York: Philosophical Library, pp. 25-31, 85-102, 135-94 passim.

Characterizes Edwards's thought as the use of "novel philosophical material to protect old theological doctrines," in a survey of his work from his Yale to his Stockbridge days, based principally upon extended quotation and brief comment and related to contemporary debates on the Awakening and Arminianism.

12 Niebuhr, H. Richard. "Ex Libris." *Christian Century* 79 (13 June): 754.

Numbers Edwards's *True Virtue* fourth among the ten books that shaped his vocation and "philosophy of life."

13 Prior, A. N. "Limited Indeterminism." *Review of Metaphysics* 16 (September): 55-61.

Contends that Edwards's inversion of approach in seeking the cause for "the beginning-to-exist of a 'thing,'" not for the event (see *Freedom of the Will,* Part II, Section III), is of "the very first importance" to his thought and argument because it assumes that the world does not consist of events but of things and that how things behave is determined partly by their natures and partly by what happens to them. Edwards distinguishes between limited and unlimited determinism dependent upon a "metaphysic of substances endowed with capacities." Hence it seems "*prima facie* possible" to distinguish between limited and unlimited indeterminism.

14 Richardson, Herbert Warren. "The Glory of God in the Theology of Jonathan Edwards (a Study in the Doctrine of the Trinity)." Ph.D. dissertation, Harvard University.

Considers Edwards the "first important modern" theologian because he attempted to join Christian doctrine to scientific doctrine in his ontology, epistemology, and trinitarian views. For Edwards, the universe and the mind of man are the "external manifestations of the internal holiness" of God; the work and the Word of God are one. Historically, Edwards, and the Reformed thought he continues, "self-consciously" bases his theological thinking on the doctrine of the Trinity.

15 Schneewind, J. B. "Comments on Prior's Paper." *Review of Metaphysics* 16 (December): 374-79.

Resolves the issue between A. N. Prior (1962.13) and Edwards into one in which Prior makes room for the *"possibility"* of limited determinism and Edwards finds such a condition a contradiction in terms. For Edwards, "occurrences of exercises of capacities" are determined by antecedent and linked causes; for Prior, exercises of capacities occur in "an utterly random fashion." If that were true, Edwards might be forced to conclude that such exercises were causeless; but, as in the case of dispositions, "it need not force him to that conclusion."

16 Smith, Elwyn Allen. *The Presbyterian Ministry in American Culture: A Study in Changing Concepts, 1700-1900.* Philadelphia: Westminster Press, pp. 61-67, 145-47 passim.

Explains Edwards's definitions of natural ability and moral inability in *Freedom of the Will* and imputation in *Original Sin* and the effect his teachings had at Princeton and on the Presbyterian clergy into the nineteenth century.

17 Tucker, Louis Leonard. *Puritan Protagonist: President Thomas Clap of Yale College.* Chapel Hill: University of North Carolina Press, pp. 136-38, 147-49 passim.

Charts the deterioration of Edwards's relationship to Thomas Clap, rector of Yale (1740-1766). Clap perceived a threat to orthodoxy and ministerial function in Edwards's (and Whitefield's) New Lightism and moved to eliminate it. *Distinguishing Marks*, the commencement address of 1741, marked the last time Edwards was invited to his alma mater.

18 Wiebe, Dallas E. "Mr. Lowell and Mr. Edwards." *Wisconsin Studies in Contemporary Literature* 3 (Spring): 21-31.

Explicates Robert Lowell's "Mr. Edwards and the Spider" and "After the Surprising Conversions" to show that the poems follow the "historical" Edwards.

1963

1 Abel, Darrel. "The Great Awakening: Jonathan Edwards." *American Literature: Colonial and Early National Writing.* Great Neck, N.Y.: Barron's Educational Series, 1:122-41.

Calls Edwards "one of the world's great figures of transition" and "an archetype of the whole intellectual and literary development of America," in an examination of his role in the Great Awakening and an explanation of *Freedom of the Will, Original Sin,* and *Images or Shadows.* From his earliest speculations on, Edwards tried to unify all knowledge by "synthesizing" the science of Newton and Locke with the theology of Calvin, though in time his interest in science became "ancillary" to his interest in theology. For us his claim to intellectual greatness rests not upon his "decadent" theology and admired logic but upon his systematic and coherent view of reality and moral man.

2 Ahlstrom, Sydney E. "H. Richard Niebuhr's Place in American Thought." *Christianity and Crisis* 23 (25 November): 213-17.

Claims H. Richard Niebuhr rescued Edwards from the "Puritan dungeon" to make his theology of theocentrism and benevolence available to twentieth-century moralists, in a eulogy for Niebuhr. Edwards is the "key" to *The Kingdom of God* and *Radical Monotheism* but not the "sole catalyst," as some have urged.

3 Baumgartner, Paul R. "Jonathan Edwards: The Theory behind His Use of Figurative Language." *Publications of the Modern Language Association* 78 (September): 321-25.

Challenges the view that figurative language for Edwards, as for Puritans generally, is an "accommodation" to fallen man or a rhetoric reluctantly used. Rather it is "natural and happy," a necessary device to enable man to apprehend by analogy beauty and truth founded in the consent to being and an "appropriate" means for God to communicate to man through the senses. Such language is consistent with Edwards's theories of sensation and religious affections and results in figures that are immediate and natural.

4 Brumm, Ursula. "Jonathan Edwards und Ralph Waldo Emerson." *Die Religiose Typologie in Amerikanischen Denken.* Studien zur Amerikanischen Literatur und Geschichte, no. 2. Leiden: E. J. Brill, pp. 73-86 passim.

Claims that Edwards finds "typical configurations" in the connection between the revivals and the eschatological hope of America and that he uses types "almost exclusively" to refer to spiritual correspondences than to traditional, concrete antitypes in Christ. Thus Edwards's mode becomes allegorical, his types symbols, and the natural world an expression and product of an analogous spiritual world in harmony with it. His world picture is "consistent and comprehensive," but it is "typico-transcendent" rather than "mechanico-causal." With Emerson, there is a "shift in accent" — nature becomes centrally important — and though "in a direct line" from Edwards, he goes "a step further" in "modifying Calvinism." (In German; translated as 1970.2.)

5 Clipsham, Ernest F. "Andrew Fuller and Fullerism: A Study in Evangelical Calvinism." *Baptist Quarterly* 20 (July): 99-114.

Cites Edwards as the "principal" theological influence on Andrew Fuller (1754-1851), the Baptist missionary, and *Freedom of the Will* as the "most powerful" book to him apart from the Bible.

6 Crabtree, Arthur Bamford. *The Restored Relationship, A Study in Justification and Reconciliation.* London: Carey Kingsgate Press, pp. 151-55.

Compares Edwards and Wesley on justification: Edwards's doctrine of faith alone is "shrouded in obscurity"; Wesley's faith that works through love has "Excellent biblical balance!"

7 Davidson, Edward H. "From Locke to Edwards." *Journal of the History of Ideas* 24 (July): 355-72.

Traces Edwards's debt to John Locke's principles of the mind and theory of language and his singular development of them, considering him "the first native American symbolist" in the "great tradition" of American literature. Edwards took Locke's notion that words were unreal forms functioning in real time and place and argued that they conveyed real ideas in the mind, that they could be communicated to others, and that they were part of "the covenanted phenomenology of God's universe" — words were willed by God. Thus the variable and potential world may be known through the experience of language, and the "vivid and nebulous association" of self and nature made real in the word (Word). Much of this is exemplified in the "masterly" *Sinners in the Hands of an Angry God.*

230

8 Duggan, Francis X. "Paul Elmer More and the New England Tradition." *American Literature* 34 (January): 542-61.

Recounts Paul Elmer More's view of Edwards's dualism: though clear and profound, it ends in a confusion of personifications and principles and illustrates the danger of joining "a rigid philosophy to a daring mythology."

9 Foster, Frank Hugh. *A Genetic History of the New England Theology*. New York: Russell & Russell.

Reprints 1907.3.

10 Foster, Mary. "Called to Her Husband." *His* 23 (February): 15-16, 21-22.

Depicts Sarah Edwards's "hidden ministry" as companion and helpmeet in spiritual things to her husband.

11 ———. "Puritan Genius." *His* 23 (January): 30-34.

Remarks the career of Edwards as theologian, philosopher, evangelist, and mystic, and quotes his dying words as the "truest summary" of his life.

12 Hofstadter, Richard. *Anti-Intellectualism in American Life*. New York: Random House, pp. 64-65.

Comments upon the combination of intellectualism, piety, and creativity in Edwards, unique among colonial ministers, and notes that the Great Awakening marked the first time the educated clergy in America was "roundly repudiated."

13 Howard, Leon. *"The Mind" of Jonathan Edwards: A Reconstructed Text*. University of California English Studies, no. 28. Berkeley and Los Angeles: University of California Press, xii, 151 pp.

Reconstructs the text of Edwards's "The Mind" to make this remarkable and "rebellious" document more comprehensible than Sereno Dwight's transcription from the manuscript (now lost) and provides an introduction, running commentary, and supplemental texts. Edwards's notes challenge the "whole intellectual system" at Yale and "consistently attack" Locke's *Essay;* they show him committed early to philosophical idealism and to logical determinism; and they prepare for his religious conversion and for his "complete conversion to Calvinism." But more important, the new arrangement of the text reveals the "developing pattern" of his rational conviction of supernatural causes and effects and of the balanced quality of the mind between the power of logic and the power of emotion.

14 Levin, David, ed. *The Puritan in the Enlightenment: Franklin and Edwards*. The Berkeley Series in American History. Chicago: Rand McNally & Co., pp. 1-2.

Suggests that selections from Edwards and Benjamin Franklin exemplify the effect of the Enlightenment on Puritanism, the contrast between piety and morality.

15 Martin, James P. *The Last Judgment in Protestant Theology from Orthodoxy to Ritschl*. Grand Rapids, Mich.: William B. Eerdmans, pp. 55-86.

Locates the source of Edwards's eschatology in his biblicism, not in Locke's sensationalism or Newton's mechanism (as Perry Miller would have it), in an examination of Orthodox, Pietist, and Puritan concepts of the millennium, judgment, and salvation. Edwards's *History of Redemption* shows "more affinity" to the New Testament than to Calvinist dogma; *End of Creation,* though orthodox in its conclusions, is a "mixture of ideas," both philosophical and biblical. Edwards "integrated" the idea of the millennium with that of the coming of the kingdom by developing an organic view of Christ's work, so that his various comings, from incarnation to parousia, are seen as divine revelation in history. The end of the world, therefore, was continuous with Christ, and the Last Judgment "could not be separated from the time process."

16 Morgan, Edmund S. *Visible Saints: The History of a Puritan Idea.* New York: New York University Press, pp. 151-52.

Notes that Edwards's *Humble Inquiry,* a return to the century-old system of admission, began a "new cycle" in the history of the idea of visible saints.

17 Plumstead, A. W. "Puritanism and Nineteenth Century American Literature." *Queen's Quarterly* 70 (Summer): 209-22.

Considers New England Puritanism "a major unifying force" in the development of American literature and Edwards's *Images or Shadows* the "most intense record" of that Puritan metaphorical mind, an artist's notebook comparable to Nathaniel Hawthorne's *American Notebook.* Edwards's poetic vision is "amazing"; his text should be "required reading" for students of American literature.

18 Robinson, Lewis Milton. "A History of the Half-Way Covenant." Ph.D. dissertation, University of Illinois.

Traces the history of the half-way covenant and compares the theory and practice of Solomon Stoddard and Edwards. Stoddard took the theory of continuity to its "logical conclusion"; Edwards contributed to the eventual abolition of the half-way covenant.

19 Schafer, Thomas A. "Solomon Stoddard and the Theology of the Revival." In *A Miscellany of American Christianity.* Edited by Stuart C. Henry. Durham, N.C.: Duke University Press, pp. 328-61.

Considers Edwards's attitude to Solomon Stoddard and to the Great Awakening one of "independence and critical appraisal," even though it is clear that Edwards followed the "general outlines" of his grandfather's evangelistic theology and practice and was undoubtedly his "main influence" upon the revivals. But Edwards's conversion experience differed markedly from the Stoddard pattern, and his ideas of spiritual light, true virtue, and divine love were attempts to resolve the dichotomy inherent in Stoddard's formula of "preparation by man and conversion by God."

20 Smith, Claude Archibald. "A Sense of the Heart: The Nature of the Soul in the Thought of Jonathan Edwards." Ph.D. dissertation, Harvard University.

Focusses upon a central concern in Edwards, his understanding of man's nature as a religious being, through an exploration of his own piety and through Locke's *Essay Concerning Human Understanding.* But Edwards goes beyond Locke and offers an empirical basis to his concept rooted in man's sense of beauty.

21 Visser't Hooft, Willem A. *The Background of the Social Gospel in America.* St. Louis: Bethany Press.

Reprints 1928.9.

22 Watts, Emily Stipes. "Jonathan Edwards and the Cambridge Platonists." Ph.D. dissertation, University of Illinois.

Traces the influence of certain Cambridge Platonists upon Edwards's philosophical and theological theories. Ralph Cudworth "certainly" influenced Edwards's idealism; John Smith "contributed" to Edwards on the affections and on the dual end of creation; and Henry More in his *Enchridion Ethicum* "may be the source" for Edwards on excellency and virtue in "The Mind."

*23 Weeks, John Stafford. "A Comparison of Calvin and Edwards on the Doctrine of Election." Ph.D. dissertation, University of Chicago.
Cited in 1967.12: 207.

24 Weeks, Romona. Review of *Jonathan Edwards*, edited by Clarence H. Faust and Thomas H. Johnson. *New Mexico Quarterly* 33 (Summer): 236-37.
Notes the extensive selections in Faust and Johnson reprinted text (1962.2).

1964

1 Aldridge, Alfred Owen. *Jonathan Edwards*. The Great American Thinkers Series. New York: Washington Square Press, 181 pp.
Locates the source of both the failure and the success of Edwards's philosophical enterprise in Calvinist dogma, which "he accepted bodily" and which he defended tirelessly, in a full-length study of the life and work of "the greatest, and virtually only, philosopher of the American colonies." What consistency there is in Edwards derives from the rigidity of Calvinism in its "last stand" and an extraordinary logic in its service; what beauty there is derives from the belief in divine sovereignty so profound that God could be realized only mystically or understood only intuitively. Reason thus became for Edwards an instrument to reveal that reason was inadequate to moral truth or inferior to it. Though Edwards provides the "most literate contemporary commentary" on eighteenth-century American theology, especially in the systematic, if not original, religious psychology of *Religious Affections*, he left "no major school and imposed no new direction." Aside from his generally anachronistic beliefs and ways, the "main trouble" with Edwards was his inability to fit his thought to common experience.

2 Anderson, Wallace E. "Immaterialism in Jonathan Edwards' Early Philosophical Notes." *Journal of the History of Ideas* 25 (April): 181-200.
Discovers in the juvenilia — "Of Atoms," "Of Being," "The Mind," "Notes on Natural Science" — a commitment by Edwards not so much to idealism as to immaterialism. The concept of solidity or resistance founded in God's action or divine power that he developed at that time underwent empirical and phenomenalistic refinement later. But Edwards never seriously questioned his initial identification of body with resistance.

3 Baritz, Loren. "Theology: Jonathan Edwards." *City on a Hill: A History of Ideas and Myths in America*. New York: John Wiley & Sons, pp. 47-89.
Examines Edwards's work for its effect on American ideas, myths, and religion. So *Sinners in the Hands of an Angry God*, the "perfect" revival sermon, does "permanent damage" to our future social history by influencing scores of mindless tub-thumpers; *Some Thoughts* manages a chiliastic nationalism "more extreme" than any before or since; and *Religious Affections*, his "gentlest" work, demands that Americans abandon formula, convention, and ritual and seek knowledge in themselves, rejecting their traditional "intellectual posture." In *Freedom of the Will* Edwards, New England's "most thoroughgoing" Calvinist, rebuilt the "entire intellectual frame-

work" of Puritanism and created a "masculine theological cosmos" devoid of "feminine mercy." This "quintessential Protestant mind," sharing with the early Puritans a "fear and hatred of person" and a love of abstraction, "helped to set both the tone and substance of much of America's future intellectual history."

4 Barth, J. Robert. "Faulkner and the Calvinist Tradition." *Thought* 34 (Spring): 100-20.

   Places William Faulkner in a "direct line" of tradition with Edwards and Cotton Mather, Nathaniel Hawthorne and Herman Melville, in his preoccupation with determinism and depravity.

5 Becker, William Hartshorne. "The Distinguishing Marks of the Christian Man in the Thought of Jonathan Edwards." Ph.D. dissertation, Harvard University.

   Surveys Edwards on ontology, excellency, Scripture, and the Christian life, principally in his work on revivals, *Faithful Narrative, Distinguishing Marks, Some Thoughts,* and *Religious Affections.* In the course of his thought, Edwards redefines Christian manhood: from his personal observation of the conversion experience to the scriptural account of the saint in heaven, from what a Christian "actually is" to what a Christian "knows he *ought* to be."

6 Bourke, Vernon J. *Will in Western Thought: An Historico-Critical Survey.* New York: Sheed & Ward, pp. 41-42, 141-43.

   Views Edwards on the will as "somewhat intellectualistic" and perhaps "no more deterministic" than Thomas Aquinas. In the nineteenth century, faculty psychologists like Bledsoe, Burton, and Day took Edwards to task for neglecting "the characteristic of activity which they thought essential to the meaning of will."

7 Claghorn, George S. "The Manuscripts of Jonathan Edwards." *Manuscripts* 16 (Spring): 38-42.

   Appeals to members of the Manuscript Society to help the Yale editors track down all letters and papers "by, to, and about" Edwards. Among the missing manuscripts are *True Grace, Faithful Narrative,* "Resolutions," and *The Mind.*

8 Clough, Wilson O. *The Necessary Earth: Nature and Solitude in American Literature.* Austin: University of Texas Press, pp. 92-94.

   Considers Edwards's introspective response to the wilderness in *Personal Narrative* typical of American "frontier innocence" and solitude and his accommodation of Locke and Newton an attempt to reconcile an inherited European tradition with a native American one through nature.

9 Davidson, Edward H. "American Romanticism as Moral Style." *Emerson Society Quarterly,* no. 35, Part 1 (Second Quarter): 10-14.

   Compares sentences by Edwards and Emerson as revealing examples of metaethics, the relation of moral thought to its expression. For Emerson, a sentence is wholly private and organizing; for Edwards, a sentence is a "steady interchange" between the private and the phenomenal. The mind comes into "exquisite conformity" with the world of substance and spirit, and the sentence becomes a moral action.

10 Gaer, Joseph, and Ben Siegel. *The Puritan Heritage: America's Roots in the Bible.* New York: New American Library of World Literature, pp. 28, 179-81.

Notes that Edwards saw "no conflict" between the Bible and the Enlightenment, between philosophy and science, but that for him, as for all Puritans, reason followed revelation.

11 Haroutunian, Joseph. *Piety versus Moralism.* Hamden, Conn.: Shoe String Press.
    Reprints 1932.5.

12 Heimert, Alan. "Perry Miller: An Appreciation." *Harvard Review* 2 (Winter): 30-48.
    Cites Perry Miller's use of Edwards as a "center of consciousness" in his attempt to understand revival phenomena, in a eulogy of Miller.

13 Jones, Howard Mumford. *O Strange New World.* New York: Viking Press, p. 200.
    Notes the complementary ethics of Edwards and Franklin.

14 Lowell, Robert. "Jonathan Edwards in Western Massachusetts." *For the Union Dead.*
    New York: Farrar, Straus & Giroux, pp. 40-44.
    Reflects upon Edwards's life and faith, in a 102-line poem:

> I love you faded,
> old, exiled and afraid
> to leave your last flock, . . .
> afraid to leave
> all your writing, writing, writing,
> denying the Freedom of the Will.

15 Miller, Perry. *Errand into the Wilderness.* Cambridge, Mass.: Harvard University Press; and New York: Harper & Row.
    Reprints 1956.8.

15A Mulder, Gerhard E. "Abraham Lincoln and the Doctrine of Necessity." *Lincoln Herald* 66 (Summer): 59-66.
    Traces Lincoln's pessimism, supernaturalism, and juxtaposition of feeling and reason to Edwards "or at least to a more or less watered-down Edwardianism."

15B Niebuhr, Richard R. *Schleiermacher on Christ and Religion: A New Introduction.* New York: Charles Scribner's Sons, pp. 142-43.
    Suggests that Friedrich Schleiermacher and Edwards share "a specific kind of empiricism" about the communion of saints.

16 Opie, John, Jr. "Conversion and Revivalism: An Internal History from Jonathan Edwards through Charles Grandison Finney." Ph.D. dissertation, University of Chicago.
    Studies the American "preoccupation" with conversion in a century of revivalism (1735-1835) led by Edwards, Joseph Bellamy, Samuel Hopkins, Timothy Dwight, Nathaniel William Taylor, Asahel Nettleton, Lyman Beecher, and Charles Grandison Finney. Conversion and revivalism mutually explain and enhance one another and give "a unique orientation" to Protestantism in America.

17 Outler, Albert C., ed. *John Wesley.* New York: Oxford University Press, pp. 15-16 passim.

Notes the Great Awakening as an effectual cause of the Wesleyan Revival and Edwards as "a major source" of John Wesley's evangelical theology, especially *Faithful Narrative* and *Distinguishing Marks.*

18 Patrides, C. A. "Renaissance and Modern Views on Hell." *Harvard Theological Review* 57 (July): 217-36.

Regrets that the undue attention given the hell-fire of Edwards (and other New Englanders) "detracts" from parallel instances of such description in earlier Western European and English literature.

19 Roback, A. A. *History of American Psychology.* New York: Collier Books.

Reprints 1952.8.

20 Savelle, Max. *The Colonial Origins of American Thought.* Princeton, N.J.: D. Van Nostrand Co., pp. 48, 56-58, 65-66 passim.

Labels Edwards an original though transitional figure in American thought whose influence upon later philosophy, particularly transcendentalism, was "enormous." Edwards achieved a "literary and philosophical synthesis" of Newton and Locke's contribution to science and philosophy in a vain defense of a dying Calvinism.

21 Sayre, Robert F. *The Examined Self: Benjamin Franklin, Henry Adams, Henry James.* Princeton, N.J.: Princeton University Press, pp. 34-39.

Discovers in Edwards's *Personal Narrative* a new form of autobiography, unconventional and typically American. Edwards's grim self-discovery is managed in the "terrifying" isolation of a desolate world. Such American loneliness differs markedly from European romanticism and demands a radical form of autobiography to deal with it. Before Franklin and Adams, Edwards used his own life as "the starting point and the ultimate test of speculation."

22 Schlaeger, Margaret Clare. "Jonathan Edwards' Theory of Perception. Ph.D. dissertation, Harvard University.

Traces Edwards's theories of perception. With his conversion experience, Edwards rejects his earlier and "vastly inferior" natural perception for his new spiritual vision, rejects the "corrupt and mutable" world of man for the "whole scheme" of God. His later, speculative work calls for the participation of human consciousness with the divine act of perception to perceive order.

23 Singer, C. Gregg. *A Theological Interpretation of American History.* Nutley, N.J.: Craig Press, pp. 26-29.

Notes that Edwards's appropriation of Lockean empiricism helped "unwittingly" in the triumph of the American Enlightenment and permanently changed Puritanism. His metaphysical idealism was "quite foreign" to Calvinism, his doctrine of benevolence a "contributing factor" in the rise of clerical liberalism after 1730.

24 Stob, Henry. "The Ethics of Jonathan Edwards." In *Faith and Philosophy: Philosophical Studies in Religion and Ethics.* Edited by Alvin Plantinga. Grand Rapids, Mich.: William B. Eerdmans, pp. 111-37.

Considers Edwards's ethics to arise from his doctrine of divine sovereignty, his "determinative intellectual conviction." Edwards "invariably" defines sovereignty in ethical terms in which God is "preeminently the ultimate and absolute moral reality, the supreme ground of moral obligation, and the final guarantor of virtue." As existence and morality are "fundamentally social" in man, so on the highest level God as triune is both absolute and social: God's perfect idea of himself is Christ, his pure act of will and love, the Holy Spirit.

25 Whittemore, Robert Clifton. "Jonathan Edwards." *Makers of the American Mind.* New York: William Morrow & Co., pp. 32-45.

> Depicts Edwards's role in the Great Awakening and the place of the religious affections. In *God Glorified*, Edwards omits mention of assurance of mercy through the covenant of grace and, therefore, reveals, in fallen man's utter dependence upon God, a God free of covenant and obligation.

26 Winslow, Ola Elizabeth. Review of *"The Mind" of Jonathan Edwards,* edited by Leon Howard. *American Literature* 36 (March): 79-81.

> Values Leon Howard's edition of *"The Mind"* (1963.13) for the light it sheds on the "originality and independence" of Edwards's early thought, the basis of "everything else" he was to write.

27 Woodward, Robert H. "Jonathan Edwards and the Sweet Life." *Fellowship in Prayer* 15 (August): 11-13.

> Urges that Edwards be known and valued for his sweetness rather than his wrath, "'ejaculatory prayer'" rather than imprecatory sermon, *Personal Narrative* rather than *Sinners in the Hands of an Angry God.*

1965

1 Ballinger, Martha. "The Metaphysical Echo." *English Studies in Africa* 8 (March): 71-80.

> Characterizes Edwards as a "terrible mouthpiece" of a wrathful God who gave his congregation a "poetic experience" and American poetry an inescapable metaphysics.

2 Barker, Shirley. *Builders of New England.* New York: Dodd, Mead & Co., pp. 68-89.

> Recounts the life of Edwards for young readers, a self-righteous logician and pious mystic.

3 Burggraaff, Winfield J. "Jonathan Edwards: A Bibliographical Essay." *Reformed Review* 18 (March): 19-33.

> Reviews selected studies of Edwards and concludes that each formulates "afresh" Edwards's contribution to theology. Since the particularly sharp attacks of liberals and Unitarians in the 1920s and 1930s, Edwards has had a "rehabilitation" and the emphasis has been upon his "positive and original" contributions to theology and letters. Yet nothing new about his genius has turned up since Perry Miller's "classic" study (1949.9).

4 Cherry, Charles Conrad. "The Nature of Faith in the Theology of Jonathan Edwards." Ph.D. dissertation, Drew University.

> Published as 1966.9.

5 ———. "The Puritan Notion of the Covenant in Jonathan Edwards' Doctrine of Faith." *Church History* 34 (September): 328-41.

> Corrects Perry Miller's misreading of both covenant theology and Edwards's doctrine of faith

(1935.6). Edwards "definitely adhered" to covenant theology and understood, as did his Puritan forebears, that the contractual agreement was simply a way of construing Revelation and did not bind God to man, for the covenant was between a sinful believer and a gracious sovereign God, not between equals. God, in Christ, promises salvation and assures his gift for which prayerful man might sue. But the "demanding act of faith" is possible only so long as God condescends to it. Edwards sought, unhappily, to mitigate the problematic nature of faith by distinguishing between a covenant of redemption and one of grace, but he always maintained that the relation of faith was a covenant-relation. He may have "narrowed" the importance of the saint's role socially and politically, but he never repudiated covenant theology.

6 Christian, Curtis Wallace. "The Concept of Life after Death in the Theology of Jonathan Edwards, Friedrich Schleiermacher, and Paul Tillich." Ph.D. dissertation, Vanderbilt University.

Compares Edwards, a "thoroughgoing teleologist," to Schleiermacher, a less overt eschatologist, and Tillich, a more "static" ontologist. Edwards's doctrine rests on the "divine creative intention" and the self illuminated by grace and arises from his idealism, pantheism, and determinism. He encounters some difficulty in reconciling the love of God with the idea of reprobation.

7 Gaustad, Edwin Scott. *The Great Awakening in New England.* Gloucester, Mass.: Peter Smith.

Reprints 1957.6.

8 Holbrook, Clyde A. "Original Sin and the Enlightenment." In *The Heritage of Christian Thought: Essays in Honor of Robert Lowry Calhoun.* Edited by Robert E. Cushman and Egil Grislis. New York: Harper & Row, pp. 142-65.

Examines Edwards's view of original sin and that of his antagonist, John Taylor, and finds that "in depth and thoroughness" Edwards's treatment has not been matched until recently. His argument from infinite sin to infinite debt to infinite punishment and his doctrines of imputation and identity are skillfully handled and apt. Whether his insights are more relevant today than those of his Enlightenment opponent "remains a question."

9 Hudson, Winthrop S. *Religion in America.* New York: Charles Scribner's Sons, pp. 64-69, 77-79.

Sees Edwards's role in the Great Awakening as a vital one and his theological contribution to the debate about the revival and its effects "most impressive." His *Faithful Narrative* not only stimulated and inspired revivals elsewhere but, more important, provided a model for subsequent revivals through its "precise and detailed" rendering of the Northampton experience.

10 Lobingier, John Leslie. *Pilgrims and Pioneers in the Congregational Christian Tradition.* Philadelphia: United Church Press, pp. 50-66.

Considers Edwards "the absentminded thinker" whose three positions at Northampton, Stockbridge, and Princeton offer an "interesting study in contrast." In all three, however, he emerges as an earnest, uncompromising, asocial, God-fearing scholar, "'the man of the century'" in American religious life.

11 Lyttle, David James. "Jonathan Edwards' Symbolic Structure of Experience." Ph.D. dissertation, Pennsylvania State University.

Analyzes Edwards's conversion experience in Freudian terms as a "victory" of superego over id and suggests analogical implications. Edwards saw correspondence between the three persons of the Trinity and the three elements of empirical experience, between a symbolic universe with a real Hell and the human personality with its equally real unconscious.

12 Mazzaro, Jerome. *The Poetic Themes of Robert Lowell.* Ann Arbor: University of Michigan Press, pp. 65-71.

Compares Edwards's phrasing to Lowell's in "Mr. Edwards and the Spider" and "After the Surprising Conversions."

13 Oliver, Robert T. *History of Public Speaking in America.* Boston: Allyn & Bacon, pp. 31-36.

Focusses upon *Sinners in the Hands of an Angry God* to explain Edwards's "totalitarian" theocracy and his manner of preaching it. He preached, without "personalized" warmth or fervor, a dying system of divine sovereignty.

13A Opie, John, Jr. "James McGready: Theologian of Frontier Revivalism." *Church History* 34 (December): 445-56.

Considers Edwards "the most likely source" of James McGready's "distinctively theological approach" to revivalism, though the western preacher may not have read the eastern one.

14 Pierce, David Clarence. "Jonathan Edwards and the New Sense of Glory." Ph.D. dissertation, Columbia University.

Traces two sorts of piety in Edwards, one founded in divine sovereignty and election, the other in the immediacy of divinity. In *Personal Narrative*, both kinds of piety are "juxtaposed" — the new sense of glory confirms God's sovereignty; in the Northampton of the Great Awakening, one "mingled" with the other; and in a Stockbridge without a church-covenant way, the new sense of glory had "the last word."

15 Rooy, Sidney H. *The Theology of Missions in the Puritan Tradition: A Study of Representative Puritans: Richard Sibbes, Richard Baxter, John Eliot, Cotton Mather, and Jonathan Edwards.* Grand Rapids, Mich.: William B. Eerdmans, pp. 285-309.

Attributes Edwards's significance for missions to his influence in the Great Awakening, to his inspiration of his later missionaries through his writings, and to his first-hand experience at Stockbridge among the Mahican. Missionary work, for Edwards, was bound to his millenarianism, expressed particularly in *History of Redemption:* the goal of misssions is the realization, in three stages, of God's purpose and the establishment of his eternal kingdom. Northampton was but an "earnest" of the growing grace that will, in time, become evident reality.

16 Savelle, Max. *Seeds of Liberty.* Seattle: University of Washington Press.

Reprints 1948.10.

17 Seldes, Gilbert. *The Stammering Century.* New York: Harper & Row.

Reprints 1928.8.

18 Shea, Daniel B., Jr. "The Art and Instruction of Jonathan Edwards's *Personal Narrative.*" *American Literature* 37 (March): 17-32.

Considers Edwards's *Personal Narrative* "a mature articulation" of his spiritual experience, an artistic account of his conversion, coherent in form, selective in detail, and affecting in language. With little of the intensity of the day-to-day struggle of the *Diary* about it, *Personal Narrative* makes its way through "heightened paradox" and a narrative technique that joins analyst to actor, reason to feeling, and instruction to autobiography. "He could scarcely have added a word to the experiential summing-up of all he ever thought on all that finally mattered." (Reprinted in 1974.21 and 1977.27.)

18A Smith, David E. "Millenarian Scholarship in America." *American Quarterly* 17 (Fall): 535-49.

Cites recent scholarship, especially that of C. C. Goen (1959.5), that makes "abundantly" clear that Edwards was "the first American postmillennialist of stature," in an outline of current studies of the millenarian tradition in America.

19 Sweet, William Warren. *Revivalism in America.* Gloucester, Mass.: Peter Smith.

Reprints 1944.4

1966

1 Aldridge, Alfred Owen. *Jonathan Edwards.* New York: Washington Square Press.

Reprints 1964.1.

2 Alexis, Gerhard T. "Jonathan Edwards and the Theocratic Ideal." *Church History* 35 (September): 328-43.

Speculates that Edwards's lack of concern for the social order or the theocratic ideal probably lies in his otherworldliness, his belief in the "eternal ostracism of the damned" and the millennial expectation of the saints. Hence in his thinking there is little to suggest that the saints would work to change the political order, none that Edwards advocates the theocratic ideal.

3 Anderson, Courtney. "Jonathan Edwards: Rational Mystic." In *Heroic Colonial Christians.* Edited by Russell T. Hirt. Philadelphia and New York: J. B. Lippincott Co., pp. 13-105.

Derives from a study of the life and works of Edwards two conclusions about the nature and genesis of his thought: first, underneath all his logic, Edwards was a mystic; second, as a theologian, Edwards was "formed almost all at once" by the time he became a minister. So his mind simply made logical what his heart felt, and so his theological formulations were "determined" by his father in the "critical first dozen years" of his life.

4 Beaver, R. Pierce, ed. *Pioneers in Mission: The Early Missionary Ordination Sermons, Charges, and Instructions.* Grand Rapids, Mich.: William B. Eerdmans, pp. 24, 78-79.

Corrects the standard view of Edwards's Stockbridge years — he was a reluctant sojourner among the Housatonics — by insisting that he was "vitally concerned about missions for many years" and by quoting from his *Life of Brainerd.*

5 Brockway, Robert. "Theological Parties in New England and the Middle Colonies in the Early Eighteenth Century." *Crane Review* 8 (Spring): 125-37.

Defines four theological parties at the time of the Great Awakening — Old Calvinist or conservative; Arminian or liberal; New Divinity or Edwardsean; and New Light Radical or antinomian — and suggests that modern American theology is "rooted" in such alternatives. "To some degree," Niebuhr's neo-orthodoxy and Tillich's existentialism are "restatements" of Edwards's New Divinity, the theologically important center of the Awakening.

6 Bushman, Richard L. "Jonathan Edwards and Puritan Consciousness." *Journal for the Scientific Study of Religion* 5 (Fall): 383-96.

Reconstructs Edwards's "dominant states of mind" in order to recover Puritan consciousness and to render it psychoanalytically, but cautions against reductive errors of the method. Edwards's cycle of depression and exhilaration is "reminiscent" of infant-mother separation and return; though his conversion experience, "on one level," may be an effort to master the Oedipal crisis by "relinquishing the ambition to overcome" the father (so common in Puritan theology), it may also be an expression of the "selfless union" of mother and child. Yet to leave it that is "grossly" to distort: unresolved is why Oedipal problems in Edwards and the Puritan consciousness were "so prominent" and "why their resolution took the form it did." (Reprinted in 1977.6.)

7 Cairns, Earle E. "Jonathan Edwards, Challenge for Evangelism Today." *Moody Monthly* 66 (January): 60-62.

Presents Edwards's evangelical work in the Great Awakening as a ministerial pattern to follow in meeting the needs of the urban masses in America today.

8 Carse, James Pearce. "The Christology of Jonathan Edwards." Ph.D. dissertation, Drew University.

Published as 1967.6.

9 Cherry, Conrad. *The Theology of Jonathan Edwards: A Reappraisal.* Garden City, N.Y.: Doubleday & Co., 270 pp.

Contends that Edwards is "first and last" a Calvinist, insisting that faith, with love at its core, is "central" to his thought and "germane" to his major work, in a full-length study of his theology in four parts: the act of faith, the reality of faith, the life of faith, and the controversy over faith. Although Edwards broadens and sometimes alters his Calvinism, he never transcends it, preferring to "feed new life" into it with the new learning. Hardly a mystic — the mantle fits him "loosely at best" — Edwards is a covenant theologian, convinced his God of faith to be "a promise-making, promise-keeping God who may be 'dealt with' in faith as a covenant partner; not the God of an inscrutable hinterland." Edwards theologized "as the occasion demanded," yet his theology is "coherent," if not systematic, resting as it does on the meaning of faith and the covenant of grace. For contemporary American Protestants, Edwards reinterprets the Puritan tradition, especially as it bears upon "his own portentous historical situation," and as it demonstrates that faith is "a vital union of heart with a sovereign, transcendent God who yet covenants in history."

10 Davidson, Edward H. *Jonathan Edwards: The Narrative of a Puritan Mind.* Riverside Studies in Literature. Boston: Houghton Mifflin Co., xii, 161 pp.

Reports the uneven battle between orthodox Calvinism and the new philosophy for the mind of Edwards, "'a Puritan baroque,'" in a full-length study of the major works. Edwards crucially apprehends the sense and disposition of light — "a metaphor of the mind" — and uses language symbolically, as he moves progressively from a world of facts to a world of ideas. In time the intellectual triumphs over the poet in Edwards — the "inevitable wastage of sensual delight" accounts for it in part — and he defines in himself the impact of Locke and Newton on a Puritan sensibility.

11 Dean, Lloyd F. "Salvation and Self-Interest: Edwards' Concept of Love and Its Relevance to Modern Evangelism." *Gordon Review* 9 (Winter): 101-10.

> Discovers the "real" Edwards for evangelicals can be found in the second sign of *Religious Affections*, namely, those affections that arise selflessly out of love for the excellencies of God. Edwards argues that sinners are elected on God's initiative alone, and he documents it with "extensive" biblical citations. This is so far a cry from the "bargain-sale" and "domesticated" process of today's conversion experience that evangelicals must "rediscover" Edwards.

12 Delattre, Roland André. "Beauty and Sensibility in the Thought of Jonathan Edwards: An Essay in Aesthetics and Ethics." Ph.D. dissertation, Yale University.

> Published as 1968.8.

13 Gaustad, Edwin Scott. *A Religious History of America.* New York: Harper & Row, pp. 61-62.

> Cites Edwards's earlier defense of the Great Awakening as the source of his later examination of the "whole question of the nature of religion itself" in *Religious Affections*.

14 Gay, Peter. *A Loss of Mastery: Puritan Historians in Colonial America.* Berkeley and Los Angeles: University of California Press, pp. 88-117.

> Marks Edwards the "greatest," perhaps the only, "tragic hero" of American Calvinism, a "brilliant scholar" whose tragedy "illuminates" the failure of the Puritan experiment and the "lost mastery" over society and whose *History of Redemption* is "reactionary and fundamentalist." For Edwards, history is a calculus of mystery and myth proving the accuracy of the Bible, not the record of a real past urged and rendered by eighteenth-century *philosophes*. Edwards uses the ideas and rhetoric of Newton and Locke simply to "confirm" long-held religious convictions. "Far from being the first modern American, therefore, he was the last medieval American — at least among intellectuals."

15 Gelpi, Albert J. *Emily Dickinson: The Mind of the Poet.* Cambridge, Mass.: Harvard University Press, pp. 57-59, 90-91 passim.

> Relates Edwards's vision (and Emerson's) to Emily Dickinson's habit of seeing "'New Englandly.'" Although there is no evidence that Dickinson read Edwards, he typifies for her the Puritan mind and heart of the fathers.

16 Griffin, Edward Michael. "A Biography of Charles Chauncy (1705-1787)." Ph.D. dissertation, Stanford University.

> Published as 1980.16 (revised).

17 Heimert, Alan. *Religion and the American Mind from the Great Awakening to the Revolution.* Cambridge, Mass.: Harvard University Press, pp. 95-158 passim.

> Contends that the evangelical religion of the Great Awakening — the "watershed in American history" — rather than the reasonable faith of eighteenth-century liberals gave impetus and shape to the Revolution and its democratic ideas; and quite frequently cites Edwards, the "most notable formal expression" of experimental Calvinism, to prosecute the argument. Evangelical religion challenged the elitist and conservative ideology of "the standing order"; Edwards, for his

part, helped provide "a radical, even democratic, social and political ideology" and helped promote American nationalism. *Some Thoughts,* for instance, was "the first national party platform in American history" and, in "a vital respect," America's declaration of independence from Europe; and *Freedom of the Will* became "the Calvinist handbook of the Revolution."

17A Ludwig, Allan I. *Graven Images: New England Stonecarving and its Symbols, 1650-1815.* Middletown, Conn.: Wesleyan University Press, pp. 37-42 passim.

> Claims that Edwards sought to replace mediate with immediate symbols in the "affairs of the religious heart," in a study of symbolic stone carving of "supposedly iconophobic" Puritans.

18 Lyttle, David. Review of *Jonathan Edwards,* by Alfred Owen Aldridge. *Seventeenth-Century News* 24 (Winter): 63-64.

> Praises A. O. Aldridge's "valuable" explications of Edwards's ethics (1964.1) but faults his insensitivity to Edwards's personality, theology, and "literary genius, which is what really keeps him alive."

19 ———. "The Sixth Sense of Jonathan Edwards." *Church Quarterly Review* 167 (January): 50-59.

> Explains that Edwards used Locke's empirical terminology of sense experience to describe orthodox grace as a new "simple idea," and so the experience of the saint is "unique" and "radically different" from that of natural man. The difference lies in the way saving ideas are held: the saint "in the depth" of the supernatural light, the natural man apart from it. The saint knows the supernatural light by a sixth sense — a spiritual, innate, non-cognitive perception — and though "utterly different" from the natural senses, unified with them in him. Thus Edwards, the empirical philosopher of Perry Miller (1949.9), is joined to Edwards, the medieval theologian of Vincent Tomas (1952.12).

20 Malefyt, Calvin Sterling. "The Changing Concept of Pneumatology in New England Trinitarianism, 1635-1755." Ph.D. dissertation, Harvard University.

> Devotes a chapter to Edwards, especially to the "impressive apologetic" for affectional evangelism found in *Religious Affections,* in a history of the role of the Holy Spirit in New England Trinitarianism and of assurance in the theory of salvation.

21 Maurer, Armand A. "Jonathan Edwards." In *Recent Philosophy: Hegel to the Present.* Edited by Etienne Gilson, Thomas Langan, and Armand A. Maurer. A History of Philosophy, no. 4. New York: Random House, pp. 559-64.

> Places Edwards's philosophical inquiries in the tradition of Hobbes and Locke on the will, Shaftesbury and Hutcheson on virtue, and the Cambridge Platonists and Newton on being. Although the source of his idealism is still in dispute, Edwards "never retracted" his early views, and they remain "implicit in much that he wrote."

22 Morgan, Edmund S. "The Historians of Early New England." In *The Reinterpretation of Early American History.* Edited by Ray Allen Billington. Essays in Honor of John Edwin Pomfret. San Marino, Cal.: Huntington Library, pp. 41-63.

> Surveys work on early New England and recommends Perry Miller's study (1949.9) and Ola Elizabeth Winslow's biography (1940.21) of Edwards, "the most creative eighteenth-century New England thinker in the Puritan tradition."

23 Pettit, Norman. *The Heart Prepared: Grace and Conversion in Puritan Life.* New Haven: Yale University Press, pp. 208-12.

Remarks Edwards's views on preparation, conversion, and assurance, and compares them to earlier doctrines and local practices. Edwards differs from the early Puritans — conversion, to him, is one of the signs of election, not the start of the process to it — and agrees with Solomon Stoddard in rejecting the concept of gradual assurance. But he would not, like his grandfather, "extend the covenant seal as a measure of pure expediency," and thus he began "a new system of theology" in New England.

24 Powers, William Jennings. "The Narrative Concept and American Consciousness." Ph.D. dissertation, University of Illinois.

Uses Franklin's *Autobiography* and Edwards's *Personal Narrative* as early instances of a continuing narrative division between the city and the self or the public and the private utterance found in the work of Thoreau, Cooper, and Hawthorne.

*25 Price, William Winfield. "The Eschatology of Jonathan Edwards." Ph.D. dissertation, University of Göttingen.

Cited in *Comprehensive Dissertation Index 1861-1972,* 29: 402.

26 Rogers, Charles A. "John Wesley and Jonathan Edwards." *Duke Divinity School Review* 31 (Winter): 20-38.

Compares Edwards and John Wesley principally to illuminate the agreements and conflicts Wesley had with doctrinaire Calvinism. On matters like election, perfection, and the perseverance of the saints the two were "unalterably opposed"; on matters like the human condition, salvation, and assurance they were "not a 'hair's-breadth' apart." Though Wesley was widely acquainted with Edwards and his work — he had much of it reprinted — Edwards had "only a single response, and that negative," to Wesley.

27 Saraceno, Chiara. "Un Pensatore Puritano del Diciottesimo Secolo: Jonathan Edwards." *Revista di Filosofia Neo-Scolastica* 58 (May): 347-55.

Traces the influence of Locke's empiricism and Newton's mechanism on Edwards's concept of experience and the problem of freedom, in an explanation of *Religious Affections* and *Freedom of the Will,* his major work. (In Italian.)

28 Sellers, James. *Theological Ethics.* New York: Macmillan Co., pp. 14, 42-43.

Suggests that Edwards's idea of benevolence to being in *True Virtue* lends ethical dimensions both to the American ethos and to the Reformation motif of justification by faith. For Edwards, every doctrine of God "implies" a doctrine of man, and so divine activity no longer contrasts with human inactivity.

29 Shea, Daniel B., Jr. "Spiritual Autobiography in Early America." Ph.D. dissertation, Stanford University.

Published as 1968.26.

30 Smith, Claude A. "Jonathan Edwards and 'The Way of Ideas.'" *Harvard Theological Review* 59 (April): 153-73.

Contends that Edwards was forced "to strike out on his own" to explain divine revelation, going beyond Locke's narrowly based empiricism. Edwards had "a more active view" of the mind than Locke, asserting that the will depends upon man's judgment as well as his apprehension of good and that through the active power of the mind man "gained access" to the materials of revelation or the knowledge of God. That active power, perceiving the data experience in an ordered or aesthetic way, "links" man to Being or God.

31 Sponseller, Edwin. *Northampton and Jonathan Edwards*. Faculty Monograph Series, no. 1. Shippensburg, Pa.: Shippensburg State College, 32 pp.

Follows the career of Edwards at Northampton, amid the "friendly mountains" of the Connecticut Valley and through the "tragic" years following the Great Awakening. The "great events" of his ministry had to do with his preparation for the revivals of 1734 and 1741; the crucial event was his rejection of the sacramentarian view of his late grandfather. Edwards, the "most brilliant son" of New England Puritanism, was "untimely born."

32 Starkey, Marion L. "The Great Awakening." *The Congregational Way: The Role of the Pilgrims and their Heirs in Shaping America*. Garden City, N.Y.: Doubleday & Co., pp. 129-56.

Traces Edwards's Congregational way from Yale to Princeton, noting the ironic role of the "newly redeemed young," instruments of both his rise and his fall.

33 Van de Wetering, John E. "The *Christian History* of the Great Awakening." *Journal of Presbyterian History* 44 (June): 122-29.

Notes that the decision to publish Thomas Prince's *Christian History* was "probably triggered" by Edwards's suggestion that the progress of the revival should be recorded fortnightly or monthly by a Boston minister "close to the press." It is "very likely" that Prince consulted Edwards before first publishing the "last major propaganda blast" of the Great Awakening.

34 Warren, Austin. *The New England Conscience*. Ann Arbor: University of Michigan Press, pp. 88-101 passim.

Examines Edwards's autobiographical writings and *True Virtue* to plumb the conscience of a New England saint. The "Resolutions" and the "Diary" reveal Edwards's strong sense of duty and discipline, in private and public matters, in intellect and in spirituality. *Personal Narrative* details the "successive deepenings" of his conversion from an emotional to an intellectual to an affectional acceptance of the sovereignty of God and ends in a new sense of glory. *True Virtue* resolves his special experience into a general love of duty, an expression of the affections and the beauty of virtue. "Only the *converted* (who, viewed from God's side are the *elect*) are capable of loving the *ought*."

35 Whittemore, Robert C. "Jonathan Edwards and the Theology of the Sixth Way." *Church History* 35 (March): 60-75.

Concludes that Edwards is neither the panentheist nor mystical realist of Douglas Elwood (1960.3), the modern empiricist of Perry Miller (1949.9), nor yet the medieval biblicist of Vincent Tomas (1952.12), but rather a Christian Neoplatonist, a "classical" theist, and a theologian of the sixth way. Of the ten ways to describe the relationship of God to the universe, Edwards offers a version of the sixth way in which God is real and the universe is God's image or shadow. Edwards is "more the medievalist than the modern" because he stresses Being to the exclusion of Becoming. Such an ontology, at one with Anselm and Aquinas, marks him "an important philosopher" as well as "an anachronism."

36 Wiley, Margaret L. "Jonathan Edwards and Eighteenth-Century Simplicity." *Creative Sceptics*. London: George Allen & Unwin, pp. 168-202.

Discovers in Edwards the "great American master of the creative paradox," a skeptic "wrestling" with experience, rejecting the simplicity of American teleology and neoclassical rationalism. Edwards reverses the standard pattern of the skeptic — nescience, dualism, paradox, and doing in order to know — and solves problems by his "overpowering conviction, wrung from the depths of bitter experience," and by his litany of belief. Thus his scriptural sense, his theological concepts (especially his trinitarian views), his philosophical speculations are characterized by "oblique insights" and cast in paradox, much in the same manner as Spenser, Bacon, and Milton, Emerson, Melville, and James.

37 Winslow, Ola Elizabeth. Foreword to her *Jonathan Edwards: Basic Writings*. New York: Signet Books, pp. vii-xxviii.

Traces Edwards's career through his publications and suggests that he is still relevant, not doctrinally, but in the "depth and dimension" of his thought, in a preface to selections from his work (with headnotes).

38 ————. Review of *Jonathan Edwards*, by Alfred Owen Aldridge. *American Literature* 38 (March): 127-28.

Praises the flawless scholarship, the sympathetic interpretation, and the lucid exposition in A. O. Aldridge's "fresh inquiry" into Edwards's place in English philosophical and theological thought (1964.1).

39 ————. Review of *Jonathan Edwards*, by Edward H. Davidson. *American Literature* 38 (November): 388-89.

Recommends, with "occasional amendments," Edward H. Davidson's narrative of Edwards's "perpetual battle" between Calvinism and the new philosophy of Locke and Newton (1966.10).

40 Wright, Conrad. "The Freedom of the Will." *The Beginnings of Unitarianism in America*. Boston: Beacon Press.

Reprints 1955.12.

1967

1 Ahlstrom, Sydney E., ed. *Theology in America: The Major Protestant Voices from Puritanism to Neo-Orthodoxy*. Indianapolis: Bobbs-Merrill Co., pp. 149-52.

Characterizes Edwards as an "apostle" to the Age of Reason, "*the* theologian of a vast international revival and the chief intellectual ornament of its American phase." Edwards synthesized the demands of the Platonic tradition and the demands of the Enlightenment — pietism and science — and made "the most impressive contribution" to Reformed theology between John Calvin and Karl Barth.

2 Anon. Review of *The Theology of Jonathan Edwards*, by Conrad Cherry. *Ethics* 77 (April): 232.

Finds that Conrad Cherry's "elaborate" study (1966.9) makes Edwards seem less remote.

3 Blanshard, Brand. "Religion and Revolt." *New York Times Book Review,* 1 January, p. 3.

Reviews *Religion and the American Mind,* by Alan Heimert (1966.17) and *The Theology of Jonathan Edwards,* by Conrad Cherry (1966.9) and finds the intellectual that Cherry writes of needed the evangelist that Heimert writes of to keep Edwards "in line."

3A Blau, Joseph L. "The North American as Philosopher." In *Naturalism and Historical Understanding: Essays on the Philosophy of John Herman Randall, Jr.* Edited by John P. Anton. Albany: State University of New York Press, pp. 134-46.

Discovers in Edwards a "genuinely philosophic inquiry emerging out of the peculiar religious problems of the American environment," in an examination of what is American about American philosophers.

4 Borges, Jorge Luis. *Introduccion a la Literatura Norte-americana.* [Buenos Aires]: Editorial Columba, pp. 11-12.

Considers Edwards a complex Calvinist, in a brief survey. (In Spanish; translated as 1971.2.)

5 Bushman, Richard L. *From Puritan to Yankee: Character and the Social Order in Connecticut, 1690-1765.* Cambridge, Mass.: Harvard University Press, pp. 209-11, 214.

Includes Edwards among the moderates of the New Lights because he believed that experimental religion could exist within the established ecclesiastical order and that ministerial authority was vital to it. His emphasis on the new birth, both the necessary evidence of it and the effective preaching to bring it about, seemed radical to some, and at first few New Lights followed him. In time, he and his followers "hammered out" concepts of experimental conversion acceptable to most, though they lost those conservatives given over to the "regeneration of reason."

6 Carse, James. *Jonathan Edwards and the Visibility of God.* New York: Charles Scribner's Sons, 191 pp.

Considers the central fact of Edwards's thought and ministry to be his rejection of the "principle of private judgment" in religious and ethical matters for the "principle of visibility," in which a communal sense of what appears to be becomes the source of action of the will. The "final validity" of Edwards's thought rests upon "a special knowledge" some men have that their greatest good lies in the visible God-man Christ and through him, God. Just as Christ is visible, so the saints, or the effects of divine grace in them, must be visible to others, and when joined to a profession of faith, something "radically revolutionary" emerges. The church becomes a community of men in the vanguard of "the long journey toward the ultimate society." Edwards preached such "radical this-worldliness" in all his sermons. He hoped that a "smaller society" of visible saints would become "the most apparent good" for the rest of civilization. But he failed, as every other "great American prophet" must fail: the "American journey is over."

7 ————. "Mr. Locke's Magic Onions and an Unboxed Beetle for Young Jonathan." *Journal of Religion* 47 (October): 331-39.

Reprints chapter 2 of 1967.6.

8 Davidson, Clifford. "Jonathan Edwards and Mysticism." *College Language Association Journal* 11 (December): 149-56.

Challenges the view that Edwards's mysticism is at odds with his reason, for he was part of a

Puritan tradition which tried to unite piety and rationalism. His Christian experience is like that of the Puritan mystic Francis Rous in his *Mysticall Marriage* (1631); his spiritual sense is like the "spiritual sensation" of the Cambridge Platonist John Smith in his "The True Way or Method of Attaining Divine Knowledge" (*Select Discourses,* 1660). Edwards's theology, then, brings together feeling and thought, pietism and orthodoxy, in a "rigid rationalistic" form.

9 Evans, W. Glyn. "Jonathan Edwards — Puritan Paradox." *Bibliotheca Sacra* 124 (January): 51-65.

Tries to explain the paradox of Edwards — scientist-revivalist, idealist-pragmatist, rationalist-emotionalist — , a "greatly gifted mind who squandered his talents on theological trifles." The answer to this "paradoxical pulpiteer" lies in his method of preaching. In those important elements of public speaking — understanding, impression, reaction, duration, and direction — Edwards was "amazingly effective," an articulate Puritan apologist and America's "greatest revivalist."

10 Foster, Mary Catherine. "Hampshire County, Massachusetts, 1729-1754: A Covenant Society in Transition." Ph.D. dissertation, University of Michigan.

Calls Edwards's dismissal an "important" turning point in the covenant society of Hampshire County. By limiting church membership to the regenerate, Edwards provoked strong opposition and a call for his removal from the social leaders, and though they succeeded in keeping the "form" of the old social covenant, they lost its "spiritual vitality."

11 [Garrett, Arthur]. "2 College Presidents: of Princeton, Yale: Jonathan Edwards and his Grandson Dwight." *AmeriChristendom.* Portland, Ore.: Graphic Arts Center, pp. 147-71.

Renders Edwards's career (and Timothy Dwight's) in a two-column folio format resembling verse.

12 Gillette, Gerald W. "A Checklist of Doctoral Dissertations on American Presbyterian and Reformed Subjects, 1912-1965." *Journal of Presbyterian History* 45 (September): 203-21.

Lists dissertations on Edwards, pp. 206-208.

13 Grant, Leonard T. "A Preface to Jonathan Edwards' Financial Difficulties." *Journal of Presbyterian History* 45 (March): 27-32.

Discovers a "yellowing" receipt of a loan from Samuel Phelps to Edwards that attests to his financial difficulties in 1742 as a result of Northampton's "disenchantment" with him and his revivals. Apparently, the town withheld his salary in an attempt to force change, but Edwards borrowed against it to sustain his family and his principles.

14 Gustafson, James Walter. "Causality and Freedom in Jonathan Edwards, Samuel Alexander, and Brand Blanshard." Ph.D. dissertation, Boston University.

Relates Edwards's concepts of causality and freedom to those of Samuel Alexander and Brand Blanshard, finds all share a theory of determined freedom, and argues that the lack of moral responsibility renders them all unsatisfactory. For Edwards, freedom is the ability to "execute decisions which are the necessary consequents of their causal antecedents."

15 Heimert, Alan, and Perry Miller. "Introduction." *The Great Awakening: Documents*

Illustrating the Crisis and Its Consequences. The American Heritage Series. Indianapolis and New York: Bobbs-Merrill Co., pp. xii-lxi.

Claims that "all of Edwards' thinking embodied both the lessons and the aspirations" of the Great Awakening, in a source book of documents — many from Edwards — touching upon the revival of 1740, the beginning of the "evolution of the American mind" and the awakening of the "spirit of American democracy." Edwards shifts the center of man's regeneration from the earlier Puritan preparation of the saint to the immediate and "undifferentiated" perception of divine excellence through the experience of conversion, from introspection and contemplation to trial and action, from self to community. Edwards "divested" Calvinism of covenant theology and construed the "ultimate test" of sainthood to be man's promotion of God's "historical program," his salvation part of a "divinely-ordered sequence" of social redemption made real in America.

16 Holbrook, Clyde A. "Edwards and the Ethical Question." *Harvard Theological Review* 60 (April): 163-75.

Challenges the radical anthropocentrism, the "unbridled human autonomy" in ethics, of such contemporary moral philosophers as P. H. Nowell-Smith, Kai Nielsen, and W. G. MacLagan with Edwards's equally radical theocentrism. Edwards adopts Francis Hutcheson's concept of benevolence and the equality of the moral sense, but he rejects his "ultimate focus" in humanity. In *True Virtue,* God, or Being in general, is the "objective criterion," the moral and aesthetic object to which man must come seeking the harmony of consent.

17 Jackson, Frank Malcolm. "An Application of the Principles of Aristotelean Rhetoric to Certain Early New England Prose." Ph.D. dissertation, University of Texas.

Applies the principles of Aristotle's *Rhetoric* to Edwards's *Sinners in the Hands of an Angry God,* one of nine early American texts examined for their persuasive intention.

17A Lamont, Corliss. *Freedom of Choice Affirmed.* New York: Horizon Press, 1967, pp. 20-21.

Cites Edwards as the "chief proponent" of the stern doctrine of determinism, in a study of freedom of choice.

18 Long, Edward Leroy, Jr. *Survey of Christian Ethics.* New York: Oxford University Press, pp. 135-38.

Compares Edwards's approach to the Christian moral impulse in *True Virtue* and *Religious Affections* to that of Augustine and Luther, but contrasts his use of philosophical categories to theirs of biblical idiom in making his argument.

19 Lovejoy, David S. "Samuel Hopkins: Religion, Slavery, and the Revolution." *New England Quarterly* 40 (June): 227-43.

Gauges Edwards's effect on Samuel Hopkins, who "lived, read, and prayed" at his Northampton home. Though his view of slavery, for instance, parallels Edwards's, his ideas on his master's disinterested benevolence undergo substantial change.

20 Lowance, Mason Ira, Jr. "Images and Shadows of Divine Things: Puritan Typology in New England from 1600 to 1750." Ph.D. dissertation, Emory University.

Relates the "transformed" types of Edwards's *Images or Shadows* to Emerson and the transcendentalists, in a detailed examination of Puritan typology and its relationship to nineteenth-century symbolism.

21 McGlinchee, Claire. "Jonathan Edwards and Benjamin Franklin, Antithetical Figures." In *Studies on Voltaire and the Eighteenth Century,* 56. Edited by Theodore Besterman. Transactions of the Second International Congress in the Enlightenment, 2. Geneva: Institut et Musse Voltaire, pp. 813-22.

Compares, in the standard way, the careers of Edwards and Benjamin Franklin, the "initial literary stylists" of America, and their influence on the Enlightenment. Edwards's influence was "limited" because he was retrospective, Franklin's "far-reaching" because he was prospective.

22 McLoughlin, William G. "The American Revolution as a Religious Revival: 'The Millennium in One Country.'" *New England Quarterly* 40 (March): 99-110.

Faults Alan Heimert's "monumental" study (1966.17) for considering the Great Awakening a "critical watershed," for the history of American life from the beginning has been a history of pietism "in various formulations," not only that of Edwards. Heimert's failure to distinguish between secular liberalism and religious liberalism undermines the "important task" he performs in reestablishing the contributions of the Edwardseans to the founding of the Republic. (An essay-review.)

23 Miller, Perry. *Jonathan Edwards.* New York: Dell Publishing Co.

Reprints 1949.9.

24 ———. "Sinners in the Hands of a Benevolent God." *Nature's Nation.* Cambridge, Mass.: Harvard University Press, pp. 279-89.

Marks the change in perception of God in America in the example of Edwards, from the grim terror of *Sinners in the Hands of an Angry God* to the ecstatic benevolence of *True Virtue.* The Enfield sermon endures as one of the "archsymbols" of its time and temper because of Edwards's "simple, unflinching, unforgettable rhetoric." *True Virtue,* a "disturbing tract" for American Protestantism, offers to sinners the hands of a benevolent God, a God who later would lead them to glorious independence and social prosperity.

25 Morgan, Edmund S. Review of *Religion and the American Mind from the Great Awakening to the Revolution,* by Alan Heimert. *William and Mary Quarterly,* 3d ser., 24 (July): 454-59.

Judges that the "enormous erudition" of Alan Heimert's study (1966.17) fails to prevent readings so wrenched from context and evidence that the world of Edwards becomes one "more of fantasy than of history."

26 O'Brien, Jon, S.J. "The Architecture of Conversion: Faith and Grace in the Theology of Jonathan Edwards." S.T.D. dissertation, Pontifical Gregorian University.

Traces Edwards's treatment of preparation, justification, and saving grace, and comments upon his doctrines of conversion from a Catholic point of view. On the theory of conversion, a Catholic would agree with Edwards that God prepares man, though the nature of grace is different; on actual conversion, a Catholic would agree about the change in man and the work faith and love in the process; on the "extent of renovation" in conversion and the absolute scheme of justification, however, a Catholic would have to disagree. Still, the "surprising agreements" between Catholics and Edwards "stand as warnings" against attributing to all American Protestants of colonial times a thorough refutation of the Council of Trent. (The final chapter of the dissertation, separately published, appears under the above title.)

27 Speare, Elizabeth George. *The Prospering.* Boston: Houghton Mifflin Co., pp. 283-331.
   Recounts Edwards's difficulties with the Williams family in Stockbridge, in a novel narrated by a fictional Elizabeth Williams: "His failure was that he was not John Sergeant," the former minister.

28 Suter, Rufus. "The Philosophy of Jonathan Edwards (1703-1758)." *Berkeley and Edwards.* Studi e Ricerche di Storia de la Filosofia, no. 85. Torino: Edizioni di Filosofia, pp. [3]-4.
   Revises the abstract of Rufus Suter's dissertation in Harvard's *Summaries of Theses,* 1932. (See 1932.13.)

29 ———. "The Word *Indiscerpible* and Jonathan Edwards." *Isis* 58 (Summer): 238-39.
   Notes that like others before him — Henry More, Isaac Newton, and Samuel Clarke — Edwards used *indiscerpible* in "Notes on Natural Science" to mean "unsplittable" as applied to the atom.

1968

1 Akers, Charles W. Review of *Jonathan Edwards and the Visibility of God,* by James Carse. *New England Quarterly* 41 (June): 302-305.
   Finds that although James Carse (1967.6) knows his subject well, he distorts Edwards for New Left purposes.

2 Clebsch, William A. *From Sacred to Profane America: The Role of Religion in American History.* New York: Harper & Row, pp. 85-86 passim.
   Underscores Edwards's appeal to the young in the Northampton revival of 1734 and suggests that he "invented" the mainstay of evangelical religion in America, the youth group.

3 Conkin, Paul K. "Jonathan Edwards: Theology." *Puritans and Pragmatists: Eight Eminent American Thinkers.* New York: Dodd, Mead, pp. 39-72.
   Considers Edwards's fusion of ethics and aesthetics in a revived piety and a sensationalist psychology "a highly original and very personal work of art" and critically important to subsequent New England philosophy, in a detailed explanation of his major work. His record and analysis of the revivals, *Freedom of the Will,* and the trilogy of his last years form "a vast intellectual homage to an overwhelming God" in an age of rising individualism, cold rationalism, and humanistic Arminianism. Edwards's notions of "temperamental determinism" and holy affections, grace and alienation, idealism and Trinitarianism, ontology and sociology, sin and virtue show "an outstanding coherence and consistency" and bear tellingly on twentieth-century existential Calvinism.

4 Cowing, Cedric B. "Sex and Preaching in the Great Awakening." *American Quarterly* 20 (Fall): 624-44.
   Argues that Edwards's revival in Northampton not only affected the young, women, and blacks, as is commonly held, but that the conversion experience was "very attractive" to men. Given the general sex ratios in New England churches then, it is "surely remarkable" that during 1729-1742 Edwards's converts were fifty percent male. Moreover, fifty of the converts over age forty were men — hardly a youthful identity crisis — and there was a dramatic increase in the

number of men confessing fornication. Whatever else the Awakening was socially or politically or theologically, by bringing men into church it "retarded the drift toward worldliness and sexual laxity."

5 Davenport, Frederick Morgan. "The New England Awakening Originating with Jonathan Edwards." *Primitive Traits in Religious Revivals.* New York: Negro Universities Press.
   Reprints 1905.2.

6 Davidson, Edward H. *Jonathan Edwards: The Narrative of a Puritan Mind.* Cambridge, Mass. Harvard University.
   Reprints 1966.10.

7 Davis, Thomas M. "The Traditions of Puritan Typology." Ph.D. dissertation, University of Missouri.
   Traces the development of typology from New Testament writers to the Puritans and finds that Edwards, though the historical traditions of that methodology cease with him, "partially utilized" typology in his symbolic rendering of nature in *Images or Shadows*.

8 Delattre, Roland André. *Beauty and Sensibility in the Thought of Jonathan Edwards: An Essay in Aesthetics and Theological Ethics.* New Haven and London: Yale University Press, xvi, 238 pp.
   Considers beauty, both primary and secondary, to be the "central clue" to the nature of reality for Edwards, especially in his theological ethics, in a full-length study that explores the relationship of beauty to being, excellence, goodness, value, order, and unity, and explains the element of beauty as divine perfection in the Trinity, creation, governance, and redemption. Reality, for Edwards, is manifest and encountered as good in forms of primary beauty of being's consent to being and as being in forms of secondary beauty of proportion and harmony. Forms of one are correlative with each other (for example, excellence, benevolence, and love in primary beauty) and coordinate to the other forms (for example, excellence and existence, benevolence and complacence, love and self-love). So, too, the understanding and the will are manifest and encountered at once as being and as good in the aesthetic-affectional self with sensibility as the "key to the quality" of both, the degree determining knowledge or ignorance in the one and consent or dissent in the other. For Edwards, the order of beauty and the order of sensibility terminate in fullness or nothingness (being and nothing, life and death) and are coordinate to the order of God or being-in-general as spiritual and moral good. Beauty is the "formulative, structural, inner first principle" of being-itself and in its fullness God manifests and communicates himself in the Trinity and in creation and, importantly, to perceiving man.

9 ———. "Beauty and Theology: A Reappraisal of Jonathan Edwards." *Soundings* 51 (Spring): 60-79.
   Considers Edwards's concept of beauty the "key" to the moral and religious life, the "central clue" to divine governance and to human freedom and responsibility. According to Edwards, God governs by his attractive power — the beauty of the apparent good — and it is by this that he is "primarily distinguished as God." Beauty, for Edwards, is objective, structural, relational, and creative and consists of primary attributes — the consent of being — and secondary attributes — harmony and proportion. What is "remarkable" in Edwards is that of the three stages in man's knowledge of God — his natural perfections, his moral perfections, and his beauty —

God's grace, goodness, and holiness may be known, yet his beauty may be "hidden from view." Such perceptions of beauty place Edwards at the beginning of an American theological tradition that reaches to H. Richard Niebuhr, Albert Hofstadter, and others.

9A Donovan, Alan B. "William Cullen Bryant: 'Father of American Song.'" *New England Quarterly* 41 (December): 505-20.

> Comments on William Cullen Bryant's "secular version" of Edwards's typology in his nature poetry.

9B Foshee, Charles N. "The Great Awakening: Pro and Con." *Radford Review* 22 (Summer): 37-59.

> Contrasts the views of Charles Chauncy and Edwards on enthusiasm and itinerancy during the Great Awakening and concludes that they came to "essential agreement" by its close.

10 Gaustad, Edwin Scott. *The Great Awakening in New England.* Chicago: Quadrangle Books.

> Reprints 1957.6.

11 Goen, C. C. Review of *Jonathan Edwards and the Visibility of God,* by James Carse. *William and Mary Quarterly,* 3d ser., 25 (October): 650-52.

> Considers James Carse's work (1967.6) "less a book than a sermon" and believes "more strait-laced scholars" will resent his "Kantian personalist-existentialist-Social Gospel activist" Edwards.

12 Goodwin, Gerald J. "The Myth of 'Arminian-Calvinism' in Eighteenth-Century New England." *New England Quarterly* 41 (June): 213-37.

> Challenges traditional interpretations of New England Puritanism that argue that Arminianism arose out of diluted or misdirected Calvinism — Anglicanism is the culprit — and that Edwards was America's "first authentic" Calvinist. Arminian-Calvinism "never existed," and Edwards's *God Glorified* is not, as some historians hold, "a crucial signpost" in American intellectual life, positing for the first time a Calvinism free of "the covenant or covert Arminianism." The Great Awakening, which Edwards had much to do with, was the "climactic demonstration" of pure, dogmatic Calvinism.

12A Harbison, Stanley L. Review of *Jonathan Edwards and the Visibility of God,* by James Carse. *Religion in Life* 37 (Winter): 640-41.

> Detects in James Carse's study of Edwards (1967.6) and William A. Clebsch's more general one (1968.2) "a special concern for American culture as a starting point."

13 Lowell, Robert. Interview with Frederick Seidel. In *Robert Lowell: A Collection of Critical Essays.* Edited by Thomas Parkinson. Englewood Cliffs, N.J.: Prentice-Hall, pp. 12-35.

> Recalls that he worked on a biography of Edwards, abandoned it when he became "numb," and wrote two poems derived from his research and Edwards's language, in Lowell's recollection of his stay at the Allen Tates'.

13A Madden, Edward H. "Oberlin's First Philosopher." *Journal of the History of Philosophy* 6 (January): 57-66.

Rehearses the critique of Edwards's *Freedom of the Will* by Asa Mahan (1846.3), Oberlin's first philosopher (and president).

14 Mead, Sidney E. "Through and Beyond the Lines." *Journal of Religion* 48 (July): 274-88.

Attacks Alan Heimert's *Religion and the American Mind* (1966.17) for its inferential methodology — exchanging facts for the shadows beyond them — and its confounding of the religious with the political. Perhaps the book may counter the neglect usually given the contribution to the Revolution of Edwards and his followers, but it has the "odor of Calvinist propaganda" about it and seems "an inordinately long doctoral dissertation that slipped past the committee."

15 Meredith, Robert. *The Politics of the Universe: Edward Beecher, Abolition, and Orthodoxy.* Nashville, Tenn.: Vanderbilt University Press, pp. 15-17, 136-37, 212.

Notes the influence Edwards's theology exerted on the Beechers — Edward, Lyman, and Charles.

16 Millar, Albert Edward, Jr. "Spiritual Autobiography in Selected Writings of Sewall, Edwards, Byrd, Woolman, and Franklin: A Comparison of Technique and Content." Ph.D. dissertation, University of Delaware.

Analyzes the autobiographical writings of Samuel Sewall, William Byrd, John Woolman, Benjamin Franklin, and Edwards and concludes that only the last wrote a "specifically designed" spiritual autobiography in his *Personal Narrative.*

17 Morris, William S. "The Genius of Jonathan Edwards." In *Reinterpretation in American Church History.* Edited by Jerald C. Brauer. Essays in Divinity, no. 5. Chicago: University of Chicago Press, pp. 29-65.

Discovers Edwards's genius in his union of the rational and the empirical, a combination of the logic of Burgersdycke and the sensationalism of Locke, in an analysis of the foundations of Edwards's method and thought. The rational in Edwards functions along Burgersdyckean (not Ramean), synthetic lines of deduction and along Lockean, analytic lines of intuition and demonstration; the empirical functions as ideas of sensation, subject to strict logic and Scripture, so that even the sense of the heart, which is immediately self-evident, must be judged by "rational norms." Edwards counters the "agnostic and skeptical tendencies" in Locke's epistemology by affirming the primacy of Being and restoring objective real essences to morality and religion. Thus his logic is "severely" metaphysical and his philosophy and theology, "spiritual realism." And thus he is "a man of his age," sharing the importance of reason but insisting it was "the subject and not the cause of man's enlightenment."

18 Nagy, Paul Joseph. "The Doctrine of Experience in the Philosophy of Jonathan Edwards." Ph.D. dissertation, Fordham University.

Considers Edwards's philosophy to be a "systematic explication" of experience, with his idea of beauty, sense of the heart, and concept of grace at its center. Edwards is an "early exponent" of an American tradition of thought emphasizing experience rather than reason.

19 Newlin, Claude Milton. *Philosophy and Religion in Colonial America.* New York: Greenwood Press.

Reprints 1962.11.

20 Parker, Gail Thain. "Jonathan Edwards and Melancholy." *New England Quarterly* 14 (June): 193-212.

Expands upon Joseph Crooker's psychological study (1890.3) by suggesting that Edwards's emphasis upon experimental religion was "clearly informed" by his knowledge of the history and disease of melancholy, a condition he explored in himself in the 1720s and in others a decade later. That store of psychological theory and experience may have been "crucial" to his health and to his interpretation of similar crises in others. In *Religions Affections,* his mature analysis of melancholy, he went "beyond" Richard Baxter and Benjamin Colman to assert that melancholy held "sinister implications for the value of rumination itself."

21 Parker, William Henry. "The Social Theory of Jonathan Edwards: as Developed in his Works on Revivalism." D.S.S. dissertation, Syracuse University.

Discerns in Edwards's works on revivalism a social theory based upon the Christian vision of a loving relationship among men, who freely subordinate their private ends to the universal Christian community, and likened to the social process outlined in George Herbert Mead's *Mind, Self and Society.* Thus in *Personal Narrative,* the saint, one of a "natural aristocracy," desires to extend his joyous experiences to the community at large in an act of love; in *Religious Affections,* the saint seeks to respond to the needs of others through trials of self-knowledge and love; and in *True Virtue,* the saint tries to reconcile diverse groups into a harmonious community through a common language of common social needs and love.

21A Paulson, Ross. "On the Meaning of Faith in the Great Awakening and the Methodist Revival." In *The Immigration of Ideas: Studies in the North Atlantic Community.* Essays Presented to O. Fritiof Ander. Edited by J. Iverne Dowie and J. Thomas Tredway. Rock Island, Ill.: Augustana Historical Society, pp. 1-13.

Evaluates Edwards's shaping of the "evangelical *content*" of revivalist theology, especially through his redefinition of faith in *Justification by Faith Alone* and its influence on John Wesley and George Whitefield.

22 Pierce, David C. "Jonathan Edwards and the 'New Sense' of Glory." *New England Quarterly* 41 (March): 82-95.

Suggests that Edwards embraced two "fundamentally contrasting" forms of piety at once in *Personal Narrative* and that this may help explain the discontinuity frequently noted in his career. The first, based on his devotion to the absolute sovereignty of God, accounts for a God of order and restraint, an elect society of limitations, a holy commonwealth; the second, based on his delight in divine omnipresence in all creation, accounts for a God of space and enlargement, a world of vastness and variety, the widening imagination of nature enthusiasm. Edwards's new sense of glory, "unique" in the Puritan tradition, involves direct and unmediated experience and stresses the heart attentive to "its own motions" rather than to "inherited paradigms." What is called Edwards's mysticism thus has a "particular historical context" in the nature enthusiasts of the "new philosophy."

23 Rees, Robert A. "Seeds of the Enlightenment: Public Testimony in the New England Congregational Churches, 1630-1750." *Early American Literature* 3 (Spring): 22-29.

Traces the history of the public profession of faith in New England and Edwards's reverting to it in the "last desperate moments of his decline and fall from ecclesiastical glory." In part the difficulty of separating the genuinely converted from the merely moved during the Great Awakening may account for his change; in part his reversion to an earlier system may have been an attempt to moderate the excesses of the revival. Ironically, the reinstitution of public profession engendered liberalism, and so the "seeds planted in the conservative New England earth had proved to be dragon's teeth."

24 Rowe, Henry Kalloch. "Jonathan Edwards." *Modern Pathfinders of Christianity.* Freeport, N.Y.: Books for Libraries Press.
Reprints 1928.6.

25 Schafer, Thomas A. "Manuscript Problems in the Yale Edition of Jonathan Edwards." *Early American Literature* 3 (Winter): 159-71.
Singles out the illegibility of the manuscripts as the "most pervasive and persistent" of all the problems facing the editors of the Yale Edwards, more troublesome than the disposition of the manuscripts, the inadequate catalogue of items, the very "size and richness" of his work. As Timothy Dwight remarked, Edwards kept "'one hand for himself, another for his friends,'" so that his "homemade" shorthand becomes, increasingly in his later years, an "almost indecipherable cryptography." Compounding the difficulty of his "well formed but very small" script is a scarcity of punctuation and a capitalization "more or less erratic."

26 Shea, Daniel B., Jr. "Jonathan Edwards and the Narrative of Conversion." *Spiritual Autobiography in Early America.* Princeton, N.J.: Princeton University Press, pp. 182-233.
Reprints 1965.18 (with additions).

27 Townsend, Harvey Gates. *Philosophical Ideas in the United States.* New York: Octagon Books.
Reprints 1934.10.

28 Tuveson, Ernest Lee. *Redeemer Nation: the Idea of America's Millennial Role.* Chicago and London: University of Chicago Press, pp. 27-30, 55-57.
Reads Edwards's *History of Redemption* as one of many American schemes for the redemption of society. Unlike Augustine, Edwards looks for redemption in this world — a kingdom of God like Utopia — in an "appointed progression" of events. His radical theory of multiple parousia hints at a continuous apocalypse and a recurrent regeneration and suggests a profound change in Protestantism.

*29 Tweet, Roald D. "Jonathan Edwards and the Affecting Style." Ph.D. dissertation, University of Chicago.
Cited in *Comprehensive Dissertation Index 1861-1972,* 29: 402.

30 Wager, Willis. *American Literature: A World View.* New York: New York University Press, pp. 8-31.
Suggests that Edwards's major work shares "common ground" with current philosophical realists.

31 Walker, Williston. "Jonathan Edwards." *Great Men of the Christian Church.* Freeport, N.Y.: Books for Libraries Press.
Reprints 1908.3.

32 Ward, Robert Stafford. "Still 'Christians,' Still Infidels." *Southern Humanities Review* 2 (Summer): 365-74.

Rescues Ralph Waldo Emerson from the charge of heresy made by the Fugitives (see 1958.23) by linking him to Edwards as a "necessary and logical outgrowth" of Puritan orthodoxy, refined of its "fundamentalist dross."

33 Williamson, Joseph Crawford. "The Excellency of Christ: A Study in the Christology of Jonathan Edwards." Ph.D. dissertation, Harvard University.

Defines Edwards's idea of excellency as "consent, expressed as love" and relates the movement of consent from God to man and from man to God through Christ, the receiver and giver of the Holy Spirit. Christ is "the supreme object and the supreme subject" of the relationship between God and man, the glorification of both man and God.

34 Winslow, Ola Elizabeth. Review of *Jonathan Edwards and the Visibility of God,* by James Carse. *American Literature* 40 (November): 400-401.

Recommends James Carse's "new slant" on Edwards (1967.6) though not all his conclusions.

35 Wood, James Playsted. *Mr. Jonathan Edwards.* New York: Seabury Press, 166 pp.

Considers Edwards "a poet, a mystic, a clear-eyed scholar, and . . . a pantheistic transcendentalist" against a background of incidental history and local politics, in a biography and appreciation designed for the young. His dismissal, for instance, is set against a background of contending factions amid Northampton's "new world of the flesh and the dollar," a world that demanded not merely victory but "his blood." And the tenor of his mind derived from a Calvinist tradition rooted in a Puritan ministerial ancestry "on both sides" and nourished in the "rural Connecticut" parish of his father. Edwards affected religion in America "lastingly, and in two different and contradictory ways": his monument of a rigid, somewhat altered Calvinism remains, and, through Emerson and his followers, his mystical, pantheistic spirit of "God as God" persists.

1969

1 Aldridge, A. Owen. Review of *Jonathan Edwards,* by Edward H. Davidson. *Seventeenth-Century News* 27 (Summer): 32, 34.

Finds Edward H. Davidson's study (1966.10) more solid and "far more credible" than Perry Miller's (1949.9).

2 Anon. "Think on These Things." *Covenant Companion* 58 (1 January): 4-5.

Reprints a shortened version of Edwards's "Resolutions" to show its spiritual force and to offer it to others.

3 Borges, Jorge Luis. "Jonathan Edwards (1703-1758)." *El otro, el mismo* [The Self and the Other]. Buenos Aires: Emecé Editors, p. 155.

Characterizes Edwards's world as a "Vessel of wrath" and his deity as "Another prisoner, God, the Spider," in a sonnet. (In Spanish; translated as 1972.4.)

4 Bormann, Ernest G. Review of *Jonathan Edwards,* by Edward H. Davidson, and *Beauty and Sensibility in the Thought of Jonathan Edwards,* by Roland A. Delattre. *Quarterly Journal of Speech* 55 (April): 202-203.

Judges Edward Davidson's book (1966.10) to be of greater relevance to rhetorical critics than Roland A. Delattre's (1968.8), though both are as difficult to understand as Edwards himself.

4A Brewer, Paul D. "The 'Sensation' in 'Sinners in the hands of an angry God.'" *Radford Review* 23 (Fall): 181-91.

Gauges the "tremendous impact" John Locke's analysis of language had on Edwards's theology, especially on his choice of the "right words" to discover affective reality in *Sinners in the Hands of an Angry God.*

4B Bumstead, J. M. "'What Must I Do to be Saved?': A Consideration of Recent Writings on the Great Awakening in Colonial America." *Canadian Association for American Studies Bulletin* 4 (Spring): 22-53.

Notes the "mixed" estimate of Edwards, in a review of recent work on the Great Awakening.

5 Bushman, Richard L. "Jonathan Edwards as Great Man: Identity, Conversion, and Leadership in the Great Awakening." *Soundings* 52 (Spring): 15-46.

Discovers in the "emotional congruities" of Edwards and the Great Awakening a compelling instance of Erik Erikson's model of the great man by reconstructing Edwards's identity and the general social condition. His father's compulsive traits, high hopes, and fear of destruction produce in Edwards an "exceedingly aggressive" conscience; three early essays reveal aspirations to succeed, "inward filthiness," and an alienating tendency to carp. But his conversion resolves or sublimates these characteristics, and his ministry channels them into acceptable forms, both public and private. Thus shaped, Edwards's psychological structure coincides with the emotional needs of his time — speculation threatens economic expansion, institutional authority clashes with personal ambition, litigation destroys friendships. Thousands of conversions testify to the coincidence. (Reprinted in 1977.7 and 1978.5.)

6 Carse, James. Review of *Jonathan Edwards,* by Edward H. Davidson. *New England Quarterly* 42 (June): 287-89.

Questions Edward Davidson's understanding of "the living center" of *Freedom of the Will* in his reissued study of Edwards (1968.6).

7 Clift, Arlene Louise. "Rhetoric and the Reason-Revelation Relationship in the Writings of Jonathan Edwards." Ph.D. dissertation, Harvard University.

Analyzes Edwards's rhetorical aims and methods as influences upon his use of Scripture. At times, Edwards uses Scripture as an appeal to reason and as a "major means" to establish doctrine; at other times, he relegates Scripture to rhetorical considerations in response to "challenges" to Calvinism. Only in his treatment of history does Edwards realize the "'ideal apprehension'" of reason and the affective mode in his rhetorical use of Scripture.

8 Collins, Edward M., Jr. "The Rhetoric of Sensation Challenges the Rhetoric of the Intellect: an Eighteenth-Century Controversy." In *Preaching in American History: Selected Issues in the American Pulpit, 1630-1967.* Edited by DeWitte Holland. Nashville, Tenn.: Abingdon Press, pp. 98-117.

Places Edwards between Charles Chauncy's reason and institutionalism and James Davenport's emotionalism and antinomianism. Edwards fused the intellect of the first with the experience of the second under grace to yield the tempered holy affections of true religion. Such "double-edged form" brought orthodoxy and revivalism to bear upon the common, crucial problem of regeneration.

9 Cowan, James C. "Jonathan Edwards' Sermon Style: 'The Future Punishment of the Wicked Unavoidable and Intolerable.'" *South Central Bulletin* 29 (Winter): 119-22.

    Offers *Future Punishment* as further testimony (see 1949.1) that in sermonic organization and imagery Edwards was a conscious stylist. Edwards uses the conventional rhetorical devices of word coupling, balance, antithesis, alliteration, and assonance found in the Puritan plain style, but his use of sensational, that is, Lockean, imagery gives his sermon "emotional power" and the cumulative, accelerated structure an "immediacy of physical fact."

10 Crozier, Alice C. *The Novels of Harriet Beecher Stowe.* New York: Oxford University Press, pp. 19-21, 74-76, 118-31 passim.

    Details the use Harriet Beecher Stowe made of her "decidedly ambiguous" relationship to Edwards. More concerned with the psychological and social consequences of his theology than with its doctrine, Stowe hated his inflexibility and rationalizing and was "enthralled" by his piety and passionate love of God, by his nobility.

11 Davidson, Edward H. Review of *Beauty and Sensibility in the Thought of Jonathan Edwards,* by Roland A. Delattre. *American Literature* 41 (May): 282-83.

    Finds Roland A. Delattre's "special kind" of study (1968.8) the "best statement" of Edwards's ontological unity and one that demonstrates affinities with contemporary radical monotheism.

12 Emerson, Everett H. Review of *Jonathan Edwards,* edited by David Levin. *Early American Literature* 4, no. 2: 109-110.

    Recommends David Levin's "intelligent" selections (1969.21).

13 Grabo, Norman S. "Jonathan Edwards' *Personal Narrative:* Dynamic Stasis." *Literatur in Wissenschaft und Unterricht* 2, no. 3:141-48.

    Examines the different structures of spiritual autobiography in Edwards's account of Abigail Hutchinson and Phebe Bartlet's conversion in *Faithful Narrative* and his own in *Personal Narrative.* The sketches in the first concentrate on the value and significance of experience rather than external events and develop linearly in Hutchinson and like "a branch erupting into blossom" in Bartlet. The second account differs from the first and from conventional forms in its use of several kinds of time simultaneously and in its circular treatment: Edwards's four periods of awakening develop into four concentric, interacting circles. Hence, by its limiting structure, *Personal Narrative* "intuitively betrays" the Great Awakening.

14 ————. Review of *Jonathan Edwards and the Visibility of God,* by James Carse. *Early American Literature* 4, no. 1:45-46.

    Finds James Carse's analysis (1967.6) at odds with Edwards's statements and the neglect of the supernatural a failure to deal with a "major dimension" of his thought.

15 Hand, James Albert. "Teleological Aspects of Creation: A Comparison of the Concept of Being and Meaning in the Theologies of Jonathan Edwards and Paul Tillich." Ph.D. dissertation, Vanderbilt University.

    Compares Edwards and Paul Tillich on spirit ontology — Edwards synthesizes rationalism and enthusiasm, Tillich idealism and existentialism — and shows that both use contemporary cultural self-interpretation. But Edwards, lacking any "dialectical process of life" in his thought, develops a theology of consciousness and Tillich one of life framed by history.

16 Helm, Paul. "John Locke and Jonathan Edwards: A Reconsideration." *Journal of the History of Philosophy* 7 (January): 51-61.

Insists that Edwards is not an empiricist and that he uses Lockean empiricism as "a *model* for religious experience," not as a theory of it, as Perry Miller mistakenly argues. For Edwards, virtue is cast in theistic paradigms of moral necessity, not only illustratively but evidentially. Though he makes use of Locke's language of "'sense,'" "'sensation,'" and "'new simple idea,'" Edwards does so to emphasize the "non-natural" character of the religious experience and to adapt, in a "radical" way, Lockean notions for purposes "entirely" his own. Any characterization of his account of the religious experience or of the "'sixth sense'" as Lockean or naturalistic is subject to "important qualifications."

17 Holbrook, Clyde A. Review of *Beauty and Sensibility in the Thought of Jonathan Edwards,* by Roland A. Delattre. *New England Quarterly* 42 (June): 310-12.

Regards Roland A. Delattre's study (1968.8) "valuable and highly persuasive," but faults its attempt to make Edwards more consistent than he is.

18 Johnson, Ellwood Gerd. "Some Versions of Individualism in American Literature and Thought." Ph.D. dissertation, University of Washington.

Relates Edwards's concept of individualism found in the psychological preparation of the heart in *Religious Affections* and *True Virtue* to later versions of that indigenous strain in Hawthorne, Emerson, Twain, Dos Passos, William James, and Faulkner.

19 Johnson, James E. "Charles Finney and a Theology of Revivalism." *Church History* 38 (September): 338-58.

Considers Edwards's awareness of conversion as "the great necessity" of the eighteenth century (and his sermons on justification) to be the foundation of the revival theology of the nineteenth century and Charles Grandison Finney's role in it.

20 Kaufman, Arnold S., and William K. Frankena. "Introduction." *Freedom of the Will.* Indianapolis and New York: Bobbs-Merrill Co., pp. ix-xl.

Analyzes Edwards's defense of "'The Compatibility Theory'" in *Freedom of the Will* by examining his linguistic method, in an introduction to a text that has only recently received "the philosophical appreciation it merits." Edwards argues for the compatibility of determinism and moral responsibility by drawing upon common sense rather than metaphysical usages of ordinary words. Though he shows "immense skill" and modernity in this method, problems persist: not only do contexts shift and meanings change, but the authority of common sense is questionable.

21 Levin, David. "Introduction." *Jonathan Edwards: A Profile*. American Profiles. New York: Hill & Wang, pp, ix-xvii, xix-xxi, 257-59.

Calls Edwards "the exemplary Puritan," fusing a rigorous intellect to a passionate piety; offers a brief biography and bibliography; and reprints selections from Samuel Hopkins's *Life* (1765.2), Williston Walker's *Ten New England Leaders* (1901.14), Henry Bamford Parkes's *The Fiery Puritan* (1930.10), Ola Elizabeth Winslow's biography (1940.21), Perry Miller's intellectual biography (1949.9), John E. Smith introduction to *Religious Affections* (1959.18), James Carse's *Visibility of*

God (1967.6), Peter Gay's *Loss of Mastery* (1966.14), and Robert Lowell's "After the Surprising Conversions" (1946.3) and "Jonathan Edwards in Western Massachusetts" (1964.14).

22 Lovejoy, David S. *Religious Enthusiasm and the Great Awakening.* American Historical Sources Series. Englewood Cliffs, N.J.: Prentice-Hall, pp. 18-21.

Views Edwards and the Great Awakening from the perspective of religious enthusiasm. Edwards mistrusted enthusiasm, as did most men of his time, and so he "exploited" Brainerd's life to distinguish the true conversion experience from the false, the lasting effect from the shortlived. The "most profound" defense of the Awakening is Edwards's *Distinguishing Marks.*

23 Lynen, John F. *The Design of the Present: Essays on Time and Form in American Literature.* New Haven and London: Yale University Press, pp. 93-119 passim.

Suggests that Edwards's "perfect harmony" of the present time of self and the eternal time of God provides the clue to his theology, style, and influence, and a measure of the effect (along with Franklin) of the single point of view. Edwards tries to resolve the duality of God as transcendence and immanence in point of view, which accounts both for his reformulation of Puritan doctrines of will, causation, and sovereignty, and for "his subtle and often confusing ambiguity." Thus Edwards's art is central to his thought: he construes theology in a world he defines "poetically" and uses language, often through exact repetition, to "dominate and transform," converting reason into feeling, harmonizing self and, nature. Edwards "clearly anticipates" Emerson, Poe, and others as a symbolist, but he regards a symbol as distinct from its meaning as well as continuous with it, as his point of view mandates.

24 Maclean, John. *History of the College of New Jersey, 1746-1854.* New York: Arno Press.

Reprints 1877.3.

25 Macphail, Andrew. "Jonathan Edwards." *Essays in Puritanism.* Port Washington, N.Y.: Kennikat Press.

Reprints 1905.4.

26 Minter, David L. *The Interpreted Design as a Structural Principle in American Prose.* Yale Publications in American Studies. New Haven and London: Yale University Press, pp. 72-77.

Contends that Edwards's *Personal Narrative* alters the pattern of Puritan spiritual autobiography by "exploiting and extending" the conventional form, by changing its tone, mood, and focus, and by interpreting, "in a radical sense," the recollected experience. Edwards "combines" the interpretation that he gives his conversion efforts (his "impotent design") with the divine judgment of it (God's "salvific design"). Each detail of his religious life forms a single pattern related to God's redemptive acts, so that for Edwards salvation becomes a "precise horizontal organization and planned vertical expansion."

27 Opie, John, Jr. "Introduction." *Jonathan Edwards and the Enlightenment.* Problems in American Civilization. Lexington, Mass.: D. C. Heath & Co., pp. v-viii.

Considers Edwards "the most acute American analyst of the achievements of the Enlightenment, far surpassing the perceptiveness of Franklin, Mayhew, Paine, and even Jefferson, in science, psychology, and philosophy," and reprints selections from Perry Miller's intellectual biography (1949.9), Vincent Tomas's "The Modernity of Jonathan Edwards" (1952.12), Clarence H. Faust's "Jonathan Edwards as a Scientist" (1930.4), Theodore Hornberger's "The Effect of the

New Science" (1937.4), Vernon Louis Parrington's "The Anachronism of Jonathan Edwards" (1927.2), Ola Elizabeth Winslow's biography (1940.21), Peter Gay's *Loss of Mastery* (1966.14), and Conrad Cherry's *The Theology of Jonathan Edwards* (1966.9).

28 Patrick, Walton R. "Melville's 'Bartleby' and the Doctrine of Necessity." *American Literature* 41 (March): 39-54.

Uses Edwards's *Freedom of the Will* and Priestley's *Necessity* to explicate a line in Herman Melville's "Bartleby" and to interpret the story.

29 Roddey, Gloria J. "The Metaphor of Counsel: A Shift from Objective Realism to Psychological Subjectivism in the Conceptual Cosmology of Puritanism." Ph.D. dissertation, University of Kentucky.

Illustrates the shift of metaphor from objective to subjective realism as a consequence of the doctrine of election in a dozen Puritans, including Edwards and Hawthorne.

30 Rupp, George. "The 'Idealism' of Jonathan Edwards." *Harvard Theological Review* 62 (April): 209-26.

Contends that the "central and indeed decisive assertion" in Edwards's early essays is that God is "coextensive" with reality and space and that his "alleged" idealism has its roots in his epistemology and his ontology. Edwards goes beyond Newton, Locke, and Berkeley in stressing the dependence of every thing, being, and event on divine energy and in connecting physics to metaphysics. Unfortunately, Edwards does not argue his case for idealism "in detail," nor does he use "adequate verbal distinctions" to differentiate between objects and ideas. Even so, there is a "measure of coherence" to his metaphysics not apparent at first glance.

31 Rutman, Darrett B. Review of *Jonathan Edwards,* by Edward H. Davidson. *American Historical Review* 74 (April): 1351-52.

Considers Edward H. Davidson's *Narrative* (1968.6, reprinted) more appropriately an exegesis of Edwards's writings and as such "commendable," but it slights the continuities between Edwards and the past.

32 Schafer, Thomas A. "The Role of Jonathan Edwards in American Religious History." *Encounter* 30 (Summer): 212-23.

Assesses Edwards's effect upon American religious history arising from his role in the Great Awakening. First, Edwards combined in himself both doctrinal correctness and vital piety "to a superlative degree," unlike earlier Puritans who kept head and heart "more or less" in balance; second, Edwards demonstrated, by precept and by example (at Stockbridge), the importance of missionary work; third, Edwards "promoted the ecumenical implications" of evangelism and fashioned a new eschatology for it; and fourth, Edwards set an "important precedent" for the voluntary principle in rejecting the communion practice of the half-way covenant and suffering dismissal for it. Yet his "chief role" in the future may well lie in theological ethics, and *Religious Affections* and *True Virtue* may become more famous than *Freedom of the Will*.

33 Waggoner, Hyatt H. "'Grace' in the Thought of Emerson, Thoreau, and Hawthorne." *Emerson Society Quarterly,* no. 54, Part 2 (First Quarter): 68-72.

Complements Perry Miller's thesis of Emerson's relation to Edwards (1940.9) by exploring similar patterns of thought in Hawthorne and Thoreau. Edwards probably would have thought all three "ultimately heretical" on the subject of grace, but in fact they were close to the "central meaning" of his divine and supernatural light, even if their language was not. Emerson's version is the "most mystical," Thoreau's the "most sensuous-aesthetic," and Hawthorne's "at once the most humanistic and commonsensical and the most 'other worldly.'"

34 Zimmerman, Lester F. "'And justify the ways . . .' — a Suggested Context." In *Papers on Milton*. Edited by Philip Mahone Griffith and Lester F. Zimmerman. University of Tulsa Department of English Monograph Series, no. 8. Tulsa, Okla.: University of Tulsa, pp. 57-66.

   Suggests that Edwards's *Personal Narrative* recounts a conversion experience similar to Adam's in Milton's *Paradise Lost*, Book X.

1970

1 Bercovitch, Sacvan. "Horologicals to Chronometricals: The Rhetoric of the Jeremiad." In *Literary Monographs*, no. 3. Edited by Eric Rothstein. Madison: University of Wisconsin Press, pp. 81-90.

   Links Edwards's eschatology to American jeremiads of the seventeenth century and finds the "gradualistic apocalypticism" of *Some Thoughts, Humble Attempt, Distinguishing Marks,* and especially *History of Redemption,* "a more effective vehicle for the old historiography." For Edwards as for his forebears, individual salvation and corporate success were counterparts of the divine work of redemption. Edwards fashioned a "new angle" to the earlier tradition by welding "the whole temporal progression into an organic whole" and, inadvertently, helped secularize millennial hope into political destiny.

2 Brumm, Ursula. "Jonathan Edwards and Ralph Waldo Emerson." *American Thought and Religious Typology.* Translated by John Hoagland. New Brunswick, N.J.: Rutgers University Press, pp. 86-108 passim.

   Translates 1963.4.

3 Buckingham, Willis J. "Stylistic Artistry in the Sermons of Jonathan Edwards." *Papers on Language and Literature* 6 (Spring): 136-51.

   Locates the strength of Edwards's sermonic style in his "controlling the movement of language." Edwards follows "closely" the Puritan homiletic tradition of restraint and decorum, a prose unadorned and plain, but adds a "peculiarly heavy kind of pacing" that gives greater weight to punctuation and achieves a certain dignity and amplitude of rhythm. Through that natural style Edwards was able to modify the "mechanical" Puritan aesthetic and bring form and content together.

4 Bumsted, J. M., ed. *The Great Awakening: The Beginnings of Evangelical Pietism in America.* Waltham, Mass.: Blaisdell Publishing Co., pp. 27, 142.

   Comments briefly on Edwards's role in the Great Awakening and reprints selections from *Faithful Narrative* and his 7 May 1750 letter to Peter Clark.

5 Bushman, Richard L., ed. *The Great Awakening: Documents on the Revival of Religion, 1740-1745.* New York: Atheneum, pp. 110, 135-36.

   Introduces and reprints selections from *Distinguishing Marks, True Virtue,* and "The Northampton Covenant, 1742."

6 Carse, James. "The Puritans, the American Dream, and the Modern Tyranny of Lei-
sure." *Presbyterian Life* 23 (1 May): 7-9, 32-33.

Uses Edwards as an example of the persistence of the American dream and an acknowledg-
ment of its failure in an essay on the current loss of faith in the young. Edwards's millennial optimism "vanished" before his congregation's "spiritual rebellion" at the coming of the Kingdom.

7 Cremin, Lawrence A. *American Education: The Colonial Experience, 1607-1783.* New
York: Harper & Row, pp. 266, 314-16.

Characterizes the Great Awakening as a "large-scale" educational movement and Edwards's
use of his church for teaching purposes as "novel."

8 Dallimore, Arnold A. *George Whitefield.* London: Banner of Truth Trust, 1:537-40.

Records the meeting between Edwards and George Whitefield, reprints supporting documents, and attributes the distance between the two not to their theological or intellectual differences so much as to Whitefield's "deep disappointment" over his proposal to Elizabeth
Delamotte.

9 Delattre, Roland A. "Beauty and Politics: Toward a Theological Anthropology." *Union Seminary Quarterly Review* 25 (Summer): 401-19.

Cites Edwards as an example of the generalization that those who are sensitive to the aesthetic in human affairs "tend to distort" the political, but suggests that his consent to being has
political as well as aesthetic relevance.

10 ———. Review of *Jonathan Edwards,* edited by David Levin. *New England Quarterly*
43 (March): 169-72.

Recommends David Levin's selection (1969.21) for its balance of biography, theology, and
criticism.

11 Dixon, John W., Jr. Review of *Beauty and Sensibility in the Thought of Jonathan Edwards,* by Roland A. Delattre. *Journal of Aesthetics and Art Criticism* 28 (Summer):
546-47.

Cautions aestheticians that Roland A. Delattre's study (1968.8) is theological ethics, not
philosophical aesthetics, and that while the first half will be of "very considerable interest" to
them, the second part — the theological consequences of Edwards's aesthetics — might not.

12 Garrison, Joseph M., Jr. "Teaching Early American Literature: Some Suggestions."
College English 31 (February): 487-97.

Suggests that only as students recognize the "other" Edwards of *Personal Narrative* will they
understand the rhetoric of the imprecatory sermons. The two voices of *Personal Narrative* —
one before conversion dominated by "I," active verbs, and images of confinement; the other after
conversion by passive verbs, "ecstatic metaphor and the language of epiphany" — differentiate
between Edwards's prideful resistance to and his selfless affirmation of God's sovereignty. Thus
Sinners in the Hands of an Angry God makes man aware not of a terrible God so much as his own
sin, finitude, and necessary submission to divine justice.

13 Haroutunian, Joseph. *Piety versus Moralism.* New York: Harper & Row.

Reprints 1932.5.

14 Hoedemaker, Libertus A. *The Theology of H. Richard Niebuhr.* Philadelphia: Pilgrim Press, pp. 33-38.

Finds in H. Richard Niebuhr's thought "a growing affinity and congruence" with major themes in Edwards based on divine sovereignty — love, beauty, order, history. The "heart" of Edwards lies in the "immediate relation" between the perception of reality and the religious affections, between divine presence and human behavior. To put it briefly, *"Edwards' anthropocentricism is built on the foundation of theocentricism."* Niebuhr's rediscovery of Edwards is "one of the aspects" of his rediscovery of God.

15 Holbrook, Clyde A. "Editor's Introduction." *Original Sin. The Works of Jonathan Edwards,* 3. New Haven and London: Yale University Press, pp. 1-101.

Traces the New England controversy about original sin and the sources of Edwards's thought; explains the arguments of *Original Sin* and the provenance of the text; and records its "mixed" reception since 1758, in an introduction to the third volume of the Yale Edwards. Edwards's defense rests on the observation that man still persists in sin, that sin results from his corrupt nature identified in Adam, and that he, not God, is the author of his deplorable state. The central doctrine, founded upon the "bedrock" of God's arbitrary and sovereign will, holds that as God unifies man's life, so he unifies the whole race of man by continuously creating him identical with Adam, imputing his sin. Thus each man recapitulates the first fall. Edwards, "haunted" by John Taylor's *The Scripture-Doctrine of Original Sin* since it first appeared on the eve of the Awakening, ended his point-by-point refutation by burying him "under an avalanche of criticism."

16 Johnson, Ellwood. "Individualism and the Puritan Imagination." *American Quarterly* 22 (Summer): 230-37.

Links Edwards's theory of the heart's preparation to the individualism of Emerson and William James, Twain and Whitman, as an instance of cultural continuity in American thought and art. Individualism, or a man's ability to become a "prime cause," is "deeply imbedded" in theocratic Puritanism and found expression "most concretely," if "rather accidentally," in Edwards's revision of the psychology of preparation for salvation. Concepts like isolation or innocence are "extensions"; terms like *affections* (Edwards), *belief* (Emerson), and *attention* (James) are "analogous." As well, each version of individualism shares a response to determinism: the Puritan to predestination, the transcendentalist to historical necessity, the pragmatist to social determinism.

17 Johnson, Thomas H. *The Printed Writings of Jonathan Edwards 1703-1758: A Bibliography.* New York: Burt Franklin.

Reprints 1940.7.

18 Laskowsky, Henry J. "Jonathan Edwards: A Puritan Philosopher of Science." *Connecticut Review* 4 (October): 33-41.

Contends that Edwards's "sophisticated" principles of causality, derived from Newton and Locke, compare favorably with modern formulations. Edwards grafted Locke's notion that physical efficient causality acts through and within the mind to Newton's mechanistic, materialistic definition of cause. And so Edwards conceptualizes the causal relationship between the physical observable world of man and the mental unobservable world of God through "certain linguistic conventions," just as modern physicists do in the unobservable world of the atom.

19 Lensing, George. "'Memories of West Street and Lepke': Robert Lowell's Associative Mirror." *Concerning Poetry* 3 (Fall): 23-26.

Cites Edwards as an example of Robert Lowell's use of others to define his "moral ambiguities and personal frailties" in his poetry.

20 Lowance, Mason I., Jr. "Images and Shadows of Divine Things: The Typology of Jonathan Edwards." *Early American Literature* 5, Part 1 (Spring): 141-81.

Discovers a "spectrum of conservative-to-liberal typological exegesis" in Edwards, from *History of Redemption* to *Images or Shadows*, from the linear and historical to the manipulated and Platonic, from type to allegory, as he tries to reconcile Nature and Scripture. In *Images or Shadows*, Edwards uses a new typology (based on Locke's empirical psychology) and endows natural objects with allegorical significance leading to spiritual truth. Such a "graduated movement" parallels the process of mystical revelation and thus accounts for calling Edwards a mystic or a pantheist.

21 Marsden, George M. *The Evangelical Mind and the New School Presbyterian Experience: A Case Study of Thought and Theology in Nineteenth-Century America.* New Haven and London: Yale University Press, pp. 31-36, 177-79.

Finds the influence of Edwards's evangelical message on nineteenth-century Presbyterian theologians to be the "moral revolution" necessary to regeneration. Particularly influential for such clergymen as Henry Boynton Smith (1815-1877) were his ideas on imputation and inability.

22 Marty, Martin E. *Righteous Empire: The Protestant Experience in America.* New York: Dial Press, pp. 79-80.

Notes Edwards's millennialist thought.

23 Miegs, James Thomas. "The Half-Way Covenant: A Study in Religious Transition." *Foundations* 13 (April): 142-58.

Connects Edwards's rebellion against the "loose system" of admission in his church and its "Arminian implications" to the Great Awakening and its response to the "radical deviation" from covenant theology, in a history of the half-way covenant. In his *Humble Inquiry*, Edwards rejects his grandfather Stoddard's and his own earlier communion practice for one limiting admission to professing Christians in complete standing. Hence his interest in a religion of self-examination is of a piece with his opposition to the half-way covenant.

24 Miller, Perry. "Edwards, Locke, and the Rhetoric of Sensation." In *Perspectives in Criticism.* Edited by Harry Levin. New York: Russell & Russell.

Reprints 1950.13.

25 Morris, William S. Review of *Jonathan Edwards,* edited by David Levin. *Church History* 39 (June): 263-64.

Finds that the "chief value" of David Levin's collection (1969.21) is Samuel Hopkins's *Life*, long out of print, and that there is little else to recommend it: Levin's introduction is careless and excessive; James Carse "manifestly falsified" Edwards on immortality and the will; and Peter Gay is "ill-informed" and "woefully wrong" about almost everything.

26 Nagy, Paul J. "Jonathan Edwards and the Metaphysics of Consent." *Personalist* 51 (Autumn): 434-46.

Considers Edward's "unique" contribution is not his synthesis of the new philosophy and the old theology but his "highly original" theories of the sense of the heart and the consent to being.

For Edwards, the "key" to all experience, to a unified view of man, nature, and God — "a new and interesting triad" — is consent realized through the heart. The world is at once physical and spiritual, utilitarian and aesthetic, material and moral, and communication (or "'conversation'") between its parts, between God and man, is experienced through holy affections. "God communicates a concrete world of value, and man responds with concrete feeling."

27 Nye, Russel B. *American Literary History: 1607-1830.* Borzoi Studies in History. New York: Alfred A. Knopf, pp. 70-73.
> Suggests that mysticism defines Edwards, sets him apart from traditional Calvinism, and accounts for the contradictions in his thought.

28 Oates, Stephen B. *To Purge this Land with Blood: A Biography of John Brown.* New York: Harper & Row, pp. 22-24.
> Claims that Edwards, particularly his imprecatory sermons, "powerfully" influenced John Brown.

29 O'Malley, J. Steven. "Edwards and the Problems of Knowledge in Protestant Tradition." *Drew Gateway* 40 (Winter): 54-79.
> Locates Edwards's epistemology within the Reformed tradition — knowledge is a public and immediate mental activity, revealed in the Word, rather than a private and interior one. Edwards goes beyond Locke by asserting that all mental activity and all externality are ideas and not real substances and that knowledge is not so much the perception of the agreement or disagreement of ideas as it is the consistency of ideas with themselves or with God. Reason, the only way to deal with things as they are, is "at the heart" of man's humanness and God intends reason to be passionate and the affections rational. Edwards developed "a cognitive basis for theology that was at once philosophically sublime and corporately meaningful, for the everyday world . . . provided the model for our knowledge of God through the Word."

30 Parkes, Henry Bamford. "The Puritan Heresy." *The Pragmatic Test.* New York: Octagon Books.
> Reprints 1932.12.

31 Patterson, Robert Leet. *A Philosophy of Religion.* Durham, N.C.: Duke University Press, pp. 92-94.
> Notes that Edwards's emphasis on the aesthetic element in the religious experience upset the Calvinist balance between subjective illumination and objective revelation.

32 Reynolds, Charles. "A Proposal for Understanding the Place of Reason in Christian Ethics." *Journal of Religion* 50 (April): 155-68.
> Cites Edwards as an example of a theologian whose ethical theory identifies God's point of view with the moral point of view and with reason. Edwards was first to use Francis Hutcheson's impartial spectator or ideal observer theory in an explicitly theological context, arguing that God acted as an impartial spectator and that his moral judgments were rational, not arbitrary. Edwards realized that the ideal observer was a "secular model" of God and that as such could analyze moral concepts because God had "conditioned meaning."

33 Rutman, Darrett B., ed. *The Great Awakening: Event and Exegesis.* New York: John Wiley & Sons, pp. 25-26, 79 passim.

Comments briefly on Edwards's role in the Great Awakening and reprints selections from *Faithful Narrative* and *Some Thoughts* and from Vernon Louis Parrington's "Anachronism" (1927.2), H. Richard Niebuhr's *Kingdom of God* (1937.7), Alan Heimert's *Religion and the American Mind* (1966.17), and Perry Miller's "Jonathan Edwards and the Great Awakening" (1952.4).

34 Searl, Stanford Jay, Jr. "The Symbolic Imagination of American Puritanism: Metaphors for the Invisible World." Ph.D. dissertation, Syracuse University.

Remarks the relationship between Edwards's prose and the symbolic process of the plain style in Bradford, Winthrop, and Hooker.

35 Simonson, Harold P. "Introduction." *Selected Writings of Jonathan Edwards.* Milestones of Thought in the History of Ideas. New York: Frederick Ungar Publishing Co., pp. 7-23.

Examines Edwards's work serially and finds that *sense* is the "all-important" word summarizing his system of thought. For Edwards, religion was an experience, a regenerative experience founded upon a sense of God's reality, at once "overwhelming, intuitive, and immediate," a sixth sense reorienting and changing the converted. Coherence lies in God — that is what God's sovereignty means — and religious certainty lies in the "direct perception" of him. Edwards's *Divine and Supernatural Light* and *Sinners in the Hands of an Angry God* "reconstruct the divine and human antipodes" of his vision, a vision corroborating our own.

36 Stearns, Monroe. *The Great Awakening, 1720-1760.* New York: Franklin Watts, pp. 14-22.

Attributes to Edwards's love of God and the Great Awakening a reversal in the spiritual (and temporal) fortunes of the politically and financially oppressed of New England. Defying the river gods and the Boston merchants, Edwards brought the "unloved" to dignity, hope, and joy through religious revival. Enfield signaled the end of medieval religious superstition and the beginning of man's responsibility for his happiness and his salvation.

37 Stephens, Bruce Milton. "The Doctrine of the Trinity from Jonathan Edwards to Horace Bushnell: A Study in the Eternal Sonship of Christ." Ph.D. dissertation, Drew University.

Traces trinitarian doctrine from Edwards to Horace Bushnell to show certain Christological developments. The tension between the doctrine of imminent Trinity and that of economic Trinity is "broken" with the rejection of the eternal sonship of Christ.

38 Stuart, Robert Lee. "The Table and the Desk: Conversion in the Writings Published by Solomon Stoddard and Jonathan Edwards during their Northampton Ministries, 1672-1751." Ph.D. dissertation, Stanford University.

Compares the function of the communion in Edwards and Solomon Stoddard and finds, though their differences were real, they were not nearly so great as Northampton or scholars have thought. Stoddard took the table and the desk to be one — the Word dramatized was the Word proclaimed — and so invited the unregenerate to communion as a converting ordinance. Edwards subordinated the table to the desk and so kept all but the regenerate from the Supper.

39 Walker, Williston. *A History of the Congregational Churches in the United States.* New York: Burt Franklin.

Reprints 1894.5.

40 Werge, Thomas. "Jonathan Edwards and the Puritan Mind in America: Directions in Textual and Interpretative Criticism." *Reformed Review* 23 (Spring): 153-56, 173-83.

Supplements W. J. Burggraaff's bibliographical essay (1965.3) by remarking serially on English and American Puritan texts, criticism, and reprints, and concludes that Edwards, not Franklin, now seems "the dominant figure" in America before the nineteenth century. Of the work on Edwards appearing since 1965, Conrad Cherry's study (1966.9) seems the "most significant," challenging Perry Miller's (1949.9) but not replacing it. Though more work will be done relating Locke and Newton to Edwards, the study of Edwards should benefit from the more general movement toward "defining the continuity" of Puritanism now underway.

1971

1 Berkouwer, G. C. *Sin.* Grand Rapids, Mich.: William B. Eerdmans, pp. 460-61.

Notes Edwards's doctrine of the double imputation of original sin.

2 Borges, Jorge Luis. *An Introduction to American Literature.* Translated and edited by L. Clark Keating and Robert O. Evans. Lexington: University Press of Kentucky, pp. 8-9.

Translates 1967.4.

3 Collins, Edward M., Jr. "The Rhetoric of Sensation Challenges the Rhetoric of the Intellect." In *Sermons in American History: Selected Issues in the American Pulpit, 1630-1967.* Edited by DeWitte Holland. Nashville, Tenn.: Abingdon Press, pp. 72-76.

Reprints Edwards's *Distinguishing Marks* and Charles Chauncy's *Enthusiasm Described and Cautioned Against* as an illustration of the polarity between religion of the heart and religion of the head in eighteenth-century America. Edwards realized, as Chauncy did not, that a synthesis of both positions was necessary to the religious experience.

4 Cook, Calvin W. *Enthusiasm Re-visited.* Grahamstown, South Africa: Rhodes University, 15 pp.

Quotes Edwards's letter to the Princeton trustees about his unsuitability to preside over the College in order to "look again at his references" as agent and apologist for revivalism. In his *Life of Brainerd*, Edwards substantiates his belief that the revival was a genuine work of God, that it overcame nature, and that it produced extraordinary results from "unlikely elements." Both Edwards and Brainerd discounted enthusiastic claims of "dreams, visions, and voices"; argued against "facile explanations" of social and psychological manipulation; and welcomed "the most shattering social implication" of divine grace in the new world: counted among the elect could be men and women of Northampton and Stockbridge, colonist and Indian.

5 Cowing, Cedric B. *The Great Awakening and the American Revolution: Colonial Thought in the 18th Century.* Rand McNally Series on the History of American Thought and Culture. Chicago: Rand McNally & Co., pp. 45-51, 64-66, 192-98 passim.

Notes Edwards's role in frontier revivalism, the New Lights controversy, and the Arminian heresy, in a survey of the Great Awakening and its relationship to the Revolution. Though Edwards was "the preeminent," yet discriminating, apologist for Calvinist evangelism, he neglected the lessons of experimental piety of the Awakening in his defense of Calvinism in *Freedom of the Will* and *Original Sin,* and "ran counter" to the growing sense of individual accountability.

6 Dodds, Elisabeth D. *Marriage to a Difficult Man: The "Uncommon Union" of Jonathan and Sarah Edwards.* Philadelphia: Westminster Press, 224 pp.

Recounts the domestic life of the Edwardses as "a parable for the befuddled woman," in a form neither scholarly (footnotes cannot explain "this intricate relationship") nor fictional ("an offense to the scrupulously truthful Edwards"). The focus is more nearly on Sarah than on Jonathan, particularly upon her emotional crisis in January 1742. Sarah emerges from that a "changed and liberated" woman, whom Jonathan, "previously her only critic, was to consider a saint." The contrast between them is remarkable: he is "socially bumbling," given to "black patches of introspection"; she is "vibrant" and "blithe." Truth to tell, "A genius is seldom an easy husband."

7 Ellis, Joseph J., III. "The Puritan Mind in Transition: The Philosophy of Samuel Johnson." *William and Mary Quarterly,* 3d ser., 28 (January): 26-45.

Identifies some commonly held philosophical points of the Puritan Edwards and the Anglican Samuel Johnson — immaterialism, idealism, causation, and so on — and their desire to infuse New England religious thought with them.

8 Emerson, Everett H. "Jonathan Edwards." In *Fifteen American Authors before 1900: Bibliographic Essays on Research and Criticism.* Edited by Robert A. Rees and Earl N. Harbert. Madison: University of Wisconsin Press, pp. 169-84.

Evaluates bibliographies, editions, and biographies of Edwards and the important criticism of the last seventy-five years and calls for "a general book" on his thought incorporating the recent and difficult work of church historians and theologians, in a bibliographical essay for students of American literature.

9 Fant, Clyde E., Jr., and William M. Pinson, eds. *20 Centuries of Great Preaching.* Waco, Texas: Word Books, 3:41-55.

Reprints several Edwards sermons, including *Sinners in the Hands of an Angry God,* the most famous of "all time," and numbers him among the great and unforgettable in the history of the American pulpit. Edwards's life was one of continued social concern, defending the unpopular Indians and championing the common folk in "their struggle with injustice and oppression."

10 Fawcett, Arthur. *The Cambuslang Revival: The Scottish Evangelical Revival of the Eighteenth Century.* London: Banner of Truth Trust, pp. 223-30 passim.

Traces the cooperative feature of the missionary movement in the second half of the eighteenth century to Edwards's *Humble Attempt* and to his suggestion for a concert of prayer in the conclusion of *Some Thoughts,* in a detailed examination of its influence among Scottish divines.

11 Grabo, Norman S. Review of Jonathan Edwards, *Original Sin,* edited by Clyde A. Holbrook. *American Literature* 43 (May): 286-87.

Welcomes Clyde A. Holbrook's "sturdy" introduction (1970.15) but faults his (and Yale's) editorial principles and practice, "living proof of Edwards's judgment of postlapsarian man."

12 Gray, Joseph M. M. "Jonathan Edwards, his God." *Prophets of the Soul.* Freeport, N.Y.: Books for Libraries Press.

Reprints 1936.7.

13 Griffin, Edward M. *Jonathan Edwards.* University of Minnesota Pamphlets on American Writers, no. 97. Minneapolis: University of Minnesota Press, 46 pp.

Focusses upon three aspects of Edwards, "man, spokesman, and symbol," in a brief biography, seriatim analysis of his chief works, and estimate of his place in American literature, and draws upon current scholarship to set the problems and solve them. Edwards's life was dramatic — "some would say tragic" — marked by "odd turns" or by the "surprising conversions" of events and actions into blessings and catastrophes. His work from *Sinners in the Hands of an Angry God* to *History of Redemption* echoes with the "keynote" of his "radical distinction" between God and man — the Great Awakening provides "a fresh appreciation" of that distinction — and affirms again and again, as the twentieth century has come to realize, that "man should not be overly optimistic about his godly propensities." His symbolic value lies in his role as "an American artist," sharing with both Herman Melville and Nathaniel Hawthorne that "cast of mind" which strikes the "uneven balance" between good and evil, and as the dramatic realization of "the pilgrim, struggling in his progress but hopeful, always hopeful, of a glorious reception in Zion."

13A Harrison, Graham. "Jonathan Edwards and the Terms of Admission to Communion." In *The Good Fight of Faith.* Papers Read at the Westminster Conference for Theological and Historical Study, 1971. London: Westminster Conference, pp. 51-71.

Traces the terms of admission to communion at Northampton from Edwards's early pastoral years to *Humble Inquiry* (1749), a work "witty," "biblical," and "devastatingly ruthless."

14 Hauck, Richard Boyd. *A Cheerful Nihilism: Confidence and "The Absurd" in American Fiction.* Bloomington: Indiana University Press, pp. 25-32.

Claims Edwards perceived the world and man's place in it as absurd. The resolution to the "dilemma of relativity" facing man lies in what Edwards calls the divine and supernatural light, an unmerited gift of God. Edwards solves the problem of the absurdist by attributing meaning to God by an act of faith, but he fails to show how to gain that faith.

15 Helm, Paul. "Introduction." *Treatise on Grace and Other Posthumously Published Writings,* by Jonathan Edwards. Cambridge and London: James Clarke & Co., pp. 1-23.

Contends, contrary to Perry Miller (1949.9) and Peter DeJong (1945.1), that Edwards's concept of grace is "a pivotal notion" in his theology and that his trinitarian views are orthodox and "quite explicitly" in the covenantal framework of Calvinism, in an historical, theological, and philosophical analysis of his *Treatise on Grace, Observations concerning the Trinity and the Covenant of Redemption,* and *An Essay on the Trinity.* Edwards offers a "modification" of covenant theology, though "clearly . . . *within*" it, because it "inadequately expresses" the immediacy and uniqueness of divine grace taught in the Bible. From his emphasis on those qualities of grace comes his opposition to the half-way covenant, his support of the revivals, his belief that the "new sense" could be tested in public, his denial of mysticism. In short, Edwards reaffirms "classic Puritan insistence on Word *and* Spirit."

16 Hofstadter, Richard. *America at 1750: A Social Portrait.* New York: Alfred A. Knopf, pp. 235-44.

Considers Edwards "a pious frontier intellectual" who became "the most subtle and formidable" apologist for the Great Awakening, though George Whitefield was its "heart and soul." In his attempt to domesticate Locke and Newton to New England needs, Edwards was not being modern so much as "trying to be up-to-date." He can hardly be said (as Perry Miller does) to be in the modernist tradition of Hume and Voltaire, Franklin and Jefferson.

17 Howard, Leon. "The Creative Imagination of a College Rebel: Jonathan Edwards' Undergraduate Writings." *Early American Literature* 5 (Winter): 50-56.

Recounts Edwards's rebellion as a Yale undergraduate — physical at first in his rejection of New Haven for Wethersfield and intellectual later in his rejection of Ramus and Locke for the Port-Royal logic — and his "extraordinary imaginative leap" from essays on spiders and rainbows to those on idealism and being. Edwards used *The Art of Thinking* rather than the categories of Ramus or the empirical induction of Locke to formulate his "greatest" intellectual achievements, "Of Being" and "Of the Prejudices of the Imagination," moving "through philosophical idealism . . . to a rationalistic concept of abstract reality" independent of Locke's theory of ideas and stirred by the passion of a "student rebel."

18 Kimnach, Wilson Henry. "The Literary Techniques of Jonathan Edwards." Ph.D. dissertation, University of Pennsylvania.

Portrays Edwards at work as a "conscious literary craftsman," in an investigation of his art and thought recorded in sermons, outlines, revisions, notebooks, and manuscript treatises. Edwards's desire for a theoretical basis for matters of style led him to important analyses of the nature of the mind, language, and communication.

19 Loud, Grover C. *Evangelized America*. Freeport, N.Y.: Books for Libraries Press, pp. 10-31.

Reprints 1928.5.

20 Miller, Glenn Thomas. "The Rise of Evangelical Calvinism: A Study in Jonathan Edwards and the Puritan Tradition." Th.D. dissertation, Union Theological Seminary.

Characterizes Edwards's evangelical Calvinism as a "development" of the preparationist-Stoddardean tradition and traces it from his juvenilia to *Religious Affections*. Early indications can be found in his idealism and his conversion experience recounted in *Personal Narrative*. Later, in the cause of evangelism, he works through ideas on immediacy, the Trinity, eschatology, and "invitational Christology." Still later, in the Great Awakening, he joins his theology of conversion to his millennialism and his typology.

21 Miller, Perry. "Jonathan Edwards and the Great Awakening." In *America in Crisis*. Edited by Daniel Aaron. Hamden, Conn.: Shoe String Press.

Reprints 1952.4.

22 Murray, Iain H. *The Puritan Hope: A Study in Revival and the Interpretation of Prophecy*. London: Banner of Truth Trust, pp. 151-52 passim.

Notes the warm reception given Edwards's *Humble Attempt* in Scotland and among the founders of the Baptist Missionary Society (1792).

23 Nagy, Paul J. "The Beloved Community of Jonathan Edwards." *Transactions of the Charles S. Peirce Society: A Quarterly Journal in American Philosophy* 7 (Spring): 93-104.

Characterizes Edwards's theology as "essentially social" rather than individual and places him "at the beginning of a speculative tradition in American social thought." Edwards seeks a dynamic reconciliation of opposites, much like Ralph Waldo Emerson's each and all, based upon the "key concept" of consent to being. Society, for Edwards, is the "instrument as well as the end" of redemption, but authentic, representative individualism, as a function of divine self-love and public affection, is the "cornerstone" of society.

24 Patterson, Robert Leet. *The Role of History in Religion.* New York: Exposition Press, pp. 24-29.

> Focusses upon Edwards's use of the "overlooked" aesthetic element in Calvin to fashion his eschatology. To Edwards, the fall, Israel, incarnation, resurrection, and judgment are connected cosmic events in time, and the spiritual enlightenment imparted by God guarantees their historicity and their beauty.

25 Rice, Daniel F. "Natural Theology and the Scottish Philosophy in the Thought of Thomas Chalmers." *Scottish Journal of Theology* 24 (February): 23-46.

> Suggests that Thomas Chalmers's reading of Edwards on philosophical necessity delivered him from the mechanistic and materialistic determinism of William Godwin's *Political Justice* to a religious piety based on an expanded vision of creation. In addition, his systematic theology is indebted to Edwards on the will, sin, holiness, and the affections.

26 Rudisill, Dorus Paul. *The Doctrine of the Atonement in Jonathan Edwards and His Successors.* New York: Poseidon Books, ix, 143 pp.

> Examines Edwards's doctrine of the atonement, its divergence from traditional, New England penal theory and its effect upon the doctrines of Joseph Bellamy, Samuel Hopkins, and Stephen West, and later Edwardseans. Edwards modifies the penal theory that Christ satisfied distributive justice by suffering "the precise quantity and the precise quality" of the elect throughout eternity by suggesting that God reconciled justice and mercy as a "precondition" to forgiveness. He abandons the quantum measure — Christ's capacity to suffer is far deeper than man's — and substitutes the nature of the passionate Christ and his relationship to God. Christ's suffering does not affect man's predicament so much as it illustrates that "all God's attributes may be effectually functional and compatible." As love, for Edwards, is the "all-controlling" attribute of God, Christ satisfies distributive justice by suffering and commutative justice by obedience. "It is scarcely possible for one to magnify and glorify the suffering of Christ more than Edwards does."

27 Sandon, Leo, Jr. "H. Richard Niebuhr's Interpretation of the American Theological Tradition." Ph.D. dissertation, Boston University.

> Finds that H. Richard Niebuhr's interpretation of the American theological tradition constitutes the single most important influence in his constructive theology and that Edwards profoundly affected his value theory, his radical monotheism, and, "quite possibly," his Christology.

28 Shea, Daniel B., Jr. Review of *Beauty and Sensibility in the Thought of Jonathan Edwards,* by Roland A. Delattre. *Early American Literature* 5 (Winter): 83-84.

> Suggests that the programmatic approach of Roland A. Delattre's study (1968.8) "unintentionally drives a wedge" between the moral and the aesthetic in Edwards.

29 Sloan, Douglas. *The Scottish Enlightenment and the American College Ideal.* New York: [Columbia] Teachers College Press, pp. 48-53, 99-101.

Recounts Edwards's relationship to Scotland, from his "close personal ties" to Scottish divines to his acquaintance with Scottish education and thought. Edwards early joined intellect and learning to a revivalist impulse — a key formulation in Scotland — and stressed understanding. Later he adapted Francis Hutcheson's study to his *True Virtue,* retaining his empirical psychology while rejecting his idea that true benevolence is possible in natural man.

30 Smith, Elwyn A. "The Voluntary Establishment of Religion." In *The Religion of the Republic.* Edited by Elwyn A. Smith. Philadelphia: Fortress Press, pp. 154-82.

Notes the influence of Edwards's concept of the voluntary upon Timothy Dwight, Lyman Beecher, and Nathaniel Taylor, the new theocrats.

31 Stein, Stephen J. "'Notes on the Apocalypse' by Jonathan Edwards." Ph.D. dissertation, Yale University.

See 1977.28.

32 Whittemore, Robert Clifton. "Jonathan Edwards." *Makers of the American Mind.* Freeport, N.Y.: Books for Libraries Press.

Reprints 1964.25.

33 Wilson, David S. "The Flying Spider." *Journal of the History of Ideas* 32 (July): 447-58.

Calls "unwarranted" the critics' claim of uniqueness for Edwards's youthful observations of flying spiders and shows his essay to be a "felicitous and precocious" example of a well-established genre in natural philosophy.

1972

1 Abelove, Henry. "Jonathan Edwards's Letter of Invitation to George Whitefield." *William and Mary Quarterly,* 3d ser., 29 (July): 487-89.

Reprints Edwards's letter of invitation to George Whitefield, 12 February 1740, a "fascinating" document of the Awakening that clarifies Whitefield's motives and reveals Edwards's temperament.

2 Ahlstrom, Sydney E. "Jonathan Edwards and the Revival of New England Theology." In his *A Religious History of the American People.* New Haven and London: Yale University Press, pp. 295-313.

Surveys Edwards's work and discovers it to be a "monumental reconstruction of strict Reformed orthodoxy." From his earliest writings on, Edwards remained "utterly captive" to the Synod of Dort, the Westminister Assembly, and Puritan thought, though freed somewhat by the new learning and by philosophical idealism. With his later, less polemical work — *True Virtue* and *End of Creation* — Edwards left Lockean psychology for the "great tradition" of Christian Platonism and a "genuine" mysticism. Perhaps always a "misunderstood stranger," he is more than any one of the five aspects others have claimed the "essential Edwards" from time to time: exegetical preacher, New England polemicist, experiential apologist, Christian ontologist, and sacred historian.

3 Bastaki, Shafikah A. A. "A Reconstruction of Jonathan Edwards' Volitional Theory in the Context of Contemporary Action Theory: An Examination of *Freedom of the Will.*" Ph.D. dissertation, University of Pittsburgh.

Reconstructs Edwards's concepts of actions and volitions, chiefly found in *Freedom of the Will*, into a "comprehensive" theory of action in the context of post-Wittgensteinian discussions. Supplemented by recent volitional and pro-attitude theories of action, Edwards proves to be "consistent" and capable of answering charges of infinite regress and circularity.

4 Borges, Jorge Luis. "Jonathan Edwards (1703-1758)." In *Selected Poems, 1923-1967*. Edited by Norman Thomas DiGiovanni. New York: Delacorte Press, pp. 168-69.
   Translates 1969.3, by Richard Howards and Cesar Rennert.

5 Colacurcio, Robert Eugene. "The Perception of Excellency as the Glory of God in Jonathan Edwards: An Essay Toward the Epistemology of Discernment." Ph.D. dissertation, Fordham University.
   Recovers Edwards's epistemology of discernment through a fugal structure of related themes. What is implied in Edwards, though "nowhere to be found in the original source," is that the "beauty of God's holiness effects an order which has its pattern virtually imaged in the perception of God's excellency." Such beauty of the living God is beyond language but is powerfully present in the heart of the believer through the medium of the virtual image.

6 Coleman, Alexander. "Notes on Borges and American Literature." *TriQuarterly* 25 (Fall): 356-77.
   Examines Jorge Borges on Edwards in prose (1967.4) and poetry (1969.3) and offers the transposition of Edwards's symbol of the spider from dangling man to entrapped God as a good example of his "literary imposition" upon American writers.

7 Davenport, Frederick Morgan. "The New England Awakening Originating with Jonathan Edwards." *Primitive Traits in Religious Revivals*. New York: AMS Press.
   Reprints 1905.2.

8 Denault, Patricia. "Jonathan Edwards, the Great Awakener." *American History Illustrated* 6 (January): 28-36.
   Recounts Edwards's career. Edwards's writing is an "atonement" for his lack of sociability, his views of the Great Awakening so singular neither side could fully accept them.

9 Fiering, Norman S. "Will and Intellect in the New England Mind." *William and Mary Quarterly*, 3d ser., 29 (October): 515-58.
   Traces the contention in the Great Awakening between Old Calvinist evangelicals like Edwards and Arminian liberals like Charles Chauncy to debates on will and intellect in the seventeenth century. There is a remarkably "close" correspondence between seventeenth-century Augustinian voluntarist ideas and those of Edwards, just as there is a similarity between seventeenth-century intellectualist ideas and those of Chauncy. (Indeed, the historical connection should temper the "exaggerated" claims of influence of Locke's sensationalism upon Edwards and others in the first half of the eighteenth century.) The Great Awakening is simply a recurrence of the "perennial opposition" of head and heart, intellect and will.

10 Gaustad, Edwin Scott. *The Great Awakening in New England*. New York: Times Books.
   Reprints 1957.6.

11 Goen, C. C. "Editor's Introduction." *The Great Awakening. The Works of Jonathan Edwards,* 4. New Haven and London: Yale University Press, pp. 1-95.

Examines the tracts and occasional pieces that show how Edwards "initially made his case" for the Great Awakening — *Faithful Narrative, Distinguishing Marks, Some Thoughts,* seven letters, and the preface to Joseph Bellamy's *True Religion* — and suggests that Edwards's analysis and pattern of the conversion experience becomes normative in America, in a survey of his role in the revivals and the controversy that ensued. By definition, revivalism is the necessary result of evangelical pietism, the very center of the Reformed movement, and Arminianism is a threat to the faith on which it rests. A "charismatic leader . . . [of] a bewildered people," Edwards clinically observed the work of God in Northampton, refracted it through Locke, and published his findings in *Faithful Narrative* (its provenance detailed fully here). But there were "premonitions" of difficulty — the reaction to Whitefield, the Tennents, and Davenport — and Edwards's *Distinguishing Marks,* an attempt to find a middle way, unintentionally polarized matters further. A "saddened" Edwards braced against the critics' onslaught, published his "most ambitious" defense in *Some Thoughts,* but only widened the "veritable chasm" between him and Charles Chauncy. His letters to correspondents here and abroad serve as a "footnote" to his devotion to revivalism; his preface to *True Religion,* written reluctantly after his dismissal, a measure of the blame he took upon himself for his lack of judgment.

12 Hall, David D. Review of Jonathan Edwards, *The Great Awakening,* edited by C. C. Goen. *New England Quarterly* 45 (September): 455-57.

Faults C. C. Goen's introduction (1972.11) for its emphasis on Edwards's challenge to Arminianism as the source of the Great Awakening in New England.

13 Hamilton, James Edward. "A Comparison of the Moral Theories of Charles Finney and Asa Mahan." Ph.D. dissertation, State University of New York at Buffalo.

Remarks the influence Edwards and Thomas Reid had on the development of nineteenth-century academic orthodoxy, especially in the moral theories of Finney and Mahan.

14 Hankamer, Ernest Wolfram. "Das Politische Denken von Jonathan Edwards." Ph.D. dissertation, University of Münich.

Published as 1972.15.

15 ———. *Das Politische Denken von Jonathan Edwards.* Münich: n.p., ix, 292 pp.

Traces Edwards's political thought from his anthropology through his ethics and predicates his *"wahre Politik"* upon passages in *True Virtue, Humble Inquiry,* and several sermons. Edwards regards man's freedom to be moral rather than social, rooted in God's grace and independent of secular guarantees of social organization or social ideology. The primary dimension of man's existence is virtue, his end is freedom; but a free life is conditional on a free heart in God. (In German.)

16 Holifield, E. Brooks. "The Renaissance of Sacramental Piety in Colonial New England." *William and Mary Quarterly,* 3d ser., 29 (January): 33-48.

Notes that the rejection of Solomon Stoddard's admissions policies by Edwards and other ministers of the Great Awakening put an end to the sacramental renaissance.

*17 Irby, Joe Ben. "Changing Conceptions of the Doctrine of Predestination in American Reformed Theology." Th.D. dissertation, Union Theological Seminary in Virginia.

Cited in *Comprehensive Dissertation Index 1861-1972*, 32:573.

18 Jones, James W. "Reflections on the Problem of Religious Experience." *Journal of the American Academy of Religion* 40 (December): 445-53.

Denies that religious experience is a function of "a sixth sense or a new faculty of sensation"; argues that it is an experiencing of "all of reality"; and compares Edwards's insights into the matter with those of Cardinal Newman, Deitrich Bonhoeffer, and Samuel Willard. For Edwards, the experience recounted in *Personal Narrative* is "the very fact" of faith realized as a new perception. His " 'new sense' " experience enables man "to live in a world of plural experiences without loss of intellectual and psychological unity."

19 Keating, Jerome Francis. "Personal Identity in Jonathan Edwards, Ralph Waldo Emerson, and Alfred North Whitehead." Ph.D. dissertation, Syracuse University.

Defines Edwards's concept of identity as both in a Lockean tradition — the mind is a passive receptor — and out of it — identity is founded in consciousness. Original sin forces Edwards to link man's identity, not to his memory as in Locke, but to his soul and to God's saving grace. Emerson illustrates the Leibnizean tradition of identity — the mind is an active participant. Whitehead combines both traditions.

20 Kolodny, Annette. "Imagery in the Sermons of Jonathan Edwards." *Early American Literature* 7 (Fall): 172-82.

Analyzes Edwards's "conscious artistic manipulation" of figurative language in three sermons — *Sinners in the Hands of an Angry God, God Glorified*, and *The Peace which Christ Gives* — and maintains that it is "characteristic of all" his sermons. Edwards uses images for "emotional persuasion" and arranges them cumulatively to emphasize divine power and to deny human power. The overall effect of the images is "to *force* the listener to go through very specific and analyzable emotional responses."

21 Lee, Brian. Review of *Jonathan Edwards*, by Edward H. Davidson; *The Interpreted Design*, by David L. Minter; and *Spiritual Autobiography*, by Daniel B. Shea. *Notes and Queries*, n.s., 19 (October): 393-95.

Compares the studies of E. H. Davidson (1966.10), D. L. Minter (1969.26), and D. B. Shea (1968.26) by focussing upon Edwards's *Personal Narrative* and finds that only Shea offers a "convincing" analysis.

22 Lee, Sang Hyun. "The Concept of Habit in the Thought of Jonathan Edwards." Ph.D. dissertation, Harvard University.

Details Edwards's concept of habit and its functions. Through it Edwards constructs a theory of experience fusing sensation and the mind's activity and a theory of reality positing being as actual and in process.

23 ———. "Jonathan Edwards' Theory of the Imagination." *Michigan Academician* 5 (Fall): 233-41.

Contends that Edwards's definition of habit, "drastically" different from Locke's, gives the mind a real and active role in experience without resorting to rationalist explanations or losing the empirical sensationalism of his epistemology. He does this by making the imaginative power of habit "a mediating principle" between the activity of the mind and the sensations it passively receives, between the intuitive or immediate mode of perception and the rational or discursive. Thus the imagination of habit of mind enables the self to achieve "unity and direction" and describes in a "fresh way" the indwelling of the Holy Spirit.

24 Logan, Samuel Talbot, Jr. "Hermeneutics and American Literature." Ph.D. dissertation, Emory University.

Contrasts, in part, Edwards's hermeneutics and Hawthorne's: Edwards restored Calvin's balanced scheme rather than continue the technologia of seventeenth- and eighteenth-century Puritans; Hawthorne failed to develop a coherent hermeneutics and ends in narrative ambiguity.

25 Long, Gary Dale. "The Doctrine of Original Sin in New England Theology from Jonathan Edwards to Edwards Amasa Park." Th.D. dissertation, Dallas Theological Seminary.

Traces the doctrinal drift on original sin from mid-eighteenth-century orthodoxy to late nineteenth-century heterodoxy; from the New Divinity School of Samuel Hopkins and Joseph Bellamy to the New Haven School, the Andover School, the Oberlin School, and New School Presbyterianism; from Edwards to Edwards Amasa Park. Early rejection of both the realistic and the representative union views of Adam and posterity resulted in semi-Pelagianism and represents a complete departure from Edwards. The error stems primarily from faulty exegesis, tactics of concealment, and ambiguous language.

26 Lowance, Mason I., Jr. "'Images or Shadows of Divine Things' in the Thought of Jonathan Edwards." In *Typology and Early American Literature*. Edited by Sacvan Bercovitch. [Amherst:] University of Massachusetts Press, pp. 209-44.

Reprints 1970.20.

27 Ludwig, Richard M., ed. "Jonathan Edwards." In *Literary History of the United States: Bibliographical Supplement II*. Edited by Robert E. Spiller et al. New York: Macmillan Co., pp. 149-50.

Updates 1959.8.

28 Lyttle, David. "Jonathan Edwards on Personal Identity." *Early American Literature* 7 (Fall): 163-71.

Defines personal identity in Edwards as "a generic unit of darkened thinking substance" and man's moral worth as part of that generic immateriality. Edwards disregards individuation and considers insignificant the uniqueness of each soul, as outlined in *Original Sin*. Man is known by his relationship to God and not, as John Locke held and Edwards rejected, by his actions.

29 Miller, Glenn T. Review of Jonathan Edwards, *The Great Awakening*, edited by C. C. Goen. *William and Mary Quarterly*, 3d ser., 29 (October): 655-57.

Values C. C. Goen's "crisp" introduction (1972.11) but finds that he "overstresses" the historical continuities of evangelicalism, thus robbing the Great Awakening of its newness, and that he "obscures the complex love-hate relationship" Edwards had with the Enlightenment.

30 Nissenbaum, Stephen, ed. *The Great Awakening at Yale College*. American History Research Series. Belmont, Cal.: Wadsworth Publishing Co., p. 54.

Comments about Edwards's career and his Yale commencement sermon, *Distinguishing*

Marks, and reprints much of that first and "major analytic" examination of the Awakening and all of his account of David Brainerd's expulsion from the College.

31 Reaske, Christopher R. "The Devil and Jonathan Edwards." *Journal of the History of Ideas* 33 (January): 123-38.

Traces and describes the devil as Edwards wrote of him from 1731 to 1750, from his "mild preoccupation" before the Great Awakening, to his "monomania" during it, to his "subdued awareness" after it. Edwards's conspicuous concern with the devil during the revival was due to his "somewhat melancholic mood," which deepened with his increased fascination. Thus the Awakening was a "catalyst," releasing the "dark part of Edwards' psyche where the devil resided." His notions of Satan, at times "unorthodox," derive from the Bible, *Paradise Lost,* and the work of John Flavel, and find expression chiefly in *Distinguishing Marks, Some Thoughts,* and *Religious Affections.*

32 ———. "An Unpublished Letter Concerning 'Sanctification' by Elisha Williams, Jonathan Edwards' Tutor." *New England Quarterly* 45 (September): 429-34.

Sees a "blurred foreshadowing" of Edwards's attack on Arminian rationalism and a "very real influence" on Edwards's views on sanctification in *Religious Affections* in an unpublished letter by Elisha Williams, Edwards's young tutor at Yale in 1719.

33 Riforgiato, Leonard R. "The Unified Thought of Jonathan Edwards." *Thought* 47 (Winter): 599-610.

Finds in Edwards a related and consistent pattern blending his early thoughts about Newtonian cosmology into his later fully developed ideas of theology. The link between the two, and at once the basis for his ontology, derives from his trinitarian model of harmonious consent: God's expressed idea of himself is consented to in love. Hence, man's conscious consent to being recapitulates creation.

34 Seldes, Gilbert. *The Stammering Century.* Gloucester, Mass.: Peter Smith.

Reprints 1928.8.

35 Serio, John N. "From Edwards to Poe." *Connecticut Review* 6 (October): 88-92.

Notes similarities between Edwards and Poe in their "emblematic reading" of the natural world, their "preoccupation" with states of guilt, and their emphasis on the moral culpability of man in a determined universe.

36 Shea, Daniel B., Jr. "Jonathan Edwards, Historian of Consciousness." In *Major Writers of Early American Literature.* Edited by Everett Emerson. Madison: University of Wisconsin Press, pp. 179-204.

Considers Edwards's thought, "not as system, but as the expression of a profound experience of the interrelatedness of things," coherent in his personality and revealed in progressive development. Thus similar ideas about true faith and false enthusiasm, for example, run through *Personal Narrative, Faithful Narrative, Some Thoughts, Life of Brainerd,* and *Religious Affections,* but in each the focus shifts — from the young Edwards to Phebe Bartlet and Abigail Hutchinson to Sarah to Brainerd to an "impersonal biography of a saint" — and yields a critical perspective on the psychology of mass movements, God's sovereignty, and man's vulnerability. Edwards understands history in "multiple dimensions" and attempts to plot the complex relationship between the regenerate soul and an emerging America. In doing so, he adumbrates later writers and contributes significantly to the "history of the American consciousness."

37 Shuffelton, Frank Charles. "Light of the Western Churches: The Career of Thomas Hooker, 1586-1647." Ph.D. dissertation, Stanford University.

Suggests Thomas Hooker's influence upon Edwards (in the final chapter).

38 Sontag, Frederick, and John K. Roth. *The American Religious Experience: the Roots, Trends, and Future of American Theology.* New York: Harper & Row, pp. 41-48.

Regards Edwards's systematic theology a failure in American terms because it had "little to do with" freedom of self-determination. Even though he combines philosophical reflection with technical theology and measures religious experience by practical tests and acts — clearly, American traits — Edwards failed to elaborate his personal compassionate experience of divinity and of the religious affections into an "'American God.'" And so his "true God remained unborn in his time."

39 Stein, Stephen J. "A Notebook on the Apocalypse by Jonathan Edwards." *William and Mary Quarterly,* 3d ser., 29 (October): 623-34.

Describes in detail Edwards's unpublished private notebook on the Apocalypse — its appearance, history, composition, and dating — and suggests its function and significance at different tunes in his life: "as a discursive commentary on the Revelation, as a copybook for transcribing authors whom he found insightful on topics related to the apocalyptic, as a scrapbook for collecting accounts from his reading in contemporary affairs and for listing evidences of progress in God's kingdom, and as a sketchbook for developing thoughts on eschatological matters."

40 Stuart, Robert Lee. "'Mr. Stoddard's Way': Church and Sacraments in Northampton." *American Quarterly* 24 (May): 243-53.

Considers Edwards's failure to note Solomon Stoddard's distinction between conversion and regeneration an "injustice" to his grandfather and a "disservice" to himself — his dismissal hinged on it — in an examination of Stoddard's "ingenious" scheme of communion.

41 Tallon, John William. "Flight into Glory: The Cosmic Imagination of Jonathan Edwards." Ph.D. dissertation, University of Pennsylvania.

Examines Edwards's modifications of the Puritan symbolic system concerning the natural world, man, God, and history. The world symbolizes the "interior reality" of God into which man tries to absorb himself. God's glory is illimitable and indefinable, and so history, as the "inevitable" fulfillment of his glory, is "meaningless" without it. "Thus the American imagination meets in Edwards a developmental dead end."

42 Thomas, Reuen. *Leaders in Thought in the Modern Church.* Freeport, N.Y.: Books for Libraries.

Reprints 1892.3.

42A Thomas, Roy R. "The Relevance of Jonathan Edwards' Thought to the Problems of Twentieth-Century America." *Potomac Review* 5 (2): 68-89.

Insists that only those who "share his beliefs" find Edwards relevant to modern America, in a survey of recent scholarship about him.

43 Townsend, Harvey G. *The Philosophy of Jonathan Edwards from his Private Notebooks.* Westport, Conn.: Greenwood Press.

Reprints 1955.10.

44 Watkins, Keith. "Original Sin." *Encounter* 33 (Spring): 203-205.

Reviews Clyde A. Holbrook's edition of *Original Sin* (1970.15); finds it "carefully edited, splendidly introduced, and handsomely printed"; sides with Edwards against John Taylor, his principal opponent in the treatise; and urges a wider audience to turn to it for it addresses our condition.

44A White, Eugene E. *Puritan Rhetoric: The Issue of Emotion in Religion.* Carbondale: Southern Illinois University Press, pp. 40-48 passim.

Considers Edwards the "culmination" of changes in Puritan rhetoric and reprints "The Future Punishment of the Wicked," *Distinguishing Marks,* and "Concerning the Nature of the Affections," in a study of emotion in American religious thought to the Great Awakening. Edwards rejected the "compartmentalization of man and the primacy of intellect" of traditional Puritanism for the "unification of man and the pervasion of the emotions," shifting from *"divine truth to divine beauty"* and bringing to the sermon, not a new structure, but "a new vitality" and "a new rhetoric."

45 White, Morton, ed. *Documents in the History of American Philosophy: From Jonathan Edwards to John Dewey.* New York: Oxford University Press, pp. 39-42.

Reprints selections from *Religious Affections* and *Freedom of the Will,* summarizes the arguments, and calls Edwards "the first American philosopher of distinction," though derivative of Locke and Calvin.

46 ———. "Jonathan Edwards: The Doctrine of Necessity and the Sense of the Heart." *Science and Sentiment in America: Philosophical Thought from Jonathan Edwards to John Dewey.* New York: Oxford University Press, pp. 30-54 passim.

Puts Edwards in the "middle band" of philosophy, combining logic in metaphysics with emotion in religion, in an examination of the dual nature of his philosophical work: the doctrine of necessity and moral judgment of the sinner in *Freedom of the Will* and the doctrine of grace and the heart of the saint in *Religious Affections.* Edwards took the theory of universal causation from Locke and Newton and rigorously applied it to the will, but he abandoned it and the "scientific mood" for the mystical one as he turned to the "superempirical" nature of grace. Thus *Freedom of the Will* shows "great intellectual power and skill," especially in distinguishing philosophical from ordinary necessity, and *Religious Affections* is "very obscure" and alogical, a pattern for transcendental thought.

1973

1 Baym, Max I. *A History of Literary Aesthetics in America.* New York: Frederick Ungar Publishing Co., pp. 1-4.

Characterizes Edwards's aesthetics as mathematical — beauty and being are perceived proportionally and numerically — and his relating physical to spiritual beauty as "close to" romantic.

2 Brumm, Ursula. *Puritanismus und Literatur in Amerika.* Darmstadt: Wissenschaftliche Buchgessellschaft, pp. 87-94.

Provides an Edwards bibliography of primary and secondary works in English and a brief estimate. (In German.)

3 Campbell, Dennis Marion. "Authority and the Renewal of Theology in America: An Historical Study and Contemporary Critique." Ph.D. dissertation, Duke University.
Published as 1976.14.

4 Cherry, Conrad. "Promoting the Cause and Testing the Spirits: Jonathan Edwards on Revivals of Religion — A Review Article." *Journal of Presbyterian History* 51 (Fall): 327-37.
Reviews *The Great Awakening*, edited by C. C. Goen (1972.11), finds Goen's "most valuable service" to be his restoration of *Faithful Narrative* from Edwards's annotated copy, but regrets the lack of "penetrating theological insights" into Edwards's critical role in the Awakening. The desk and the pulpit, theological analysis and evangelical preaching, are complementary in Edwards and are brought together in the "graphic symbol," the concrete and vivid image that moves the whole man, mind and emotion, to regeneration. After Edwards, imaginative preaching declines to the "dour dogma" of Calvinism or the "bland moral lecture" of Unitarianism, and the correlation between theology and affections disappears.

5 Clebsch, William A. *American Religious Thought: A History.* Chicago History of American Religion. Chicago: University of Chicago Press, pp. 11-68 passim.
Contends that Edwards (and Emerson and William James) exchanged the moralistic spirituality of traditional Puritanism for the aesthetic spirituality of a native American experience, "turning the sense of duty to the sense of beauty," in an examination of his theology and psychology. Edwards insists that human experience is unitive — head and heart, understanding and will are one; that God's beauty and the world's beauty are "indivisible"; that theology and the religious experience, theory and practice are one; and that "the religious life equals the good life equals the beautiful life." Neither mystic nor pantheist, Edwards "knew and taught" holy beauty, testifying to outward and empirical spirituality, no longer inward nor mysterious.

6 Davidson, James West. "Eschatology in New England: 1700-1763." Ph.D. dissertation, Yale University.
See 1977.8.

7 Davidson, Marshall B., et al. *The American Heritage History of the Writers' America.* New York: American Heritage Publishing Co., pp. 50-52.
Finds a "more engaging" Edwards in his natural observations than in his polemics, in a brief estimate and sometime comparison to Franklin. (Illustrated.)

8 Fraser, James. "Interpreters of Our Faith: Jonathan Edwards." *A.D.* 2 (August): 6-11.
Offers a brief life of Edwards and six tests of the spirit from *Religious Affections* so that a new generation might know the signs of the visibility of the Word.

9 Fulcher, J. Rodney. "Puritans and the Passions: The Faculty Psychology in American Puritanism." *Journal of the History of the Behavioral Sciences* 9 (April): 23-39.
Considers Edwards, in his adoption of Lockean empiricist psychology, a countervailing force to the divisive faculty psychology of conversion of seventeenth-century Puritans. Unlike them, Edwards fashioned a psychological theory that brought piety and intellect into balance instead of contention.

10 Griffith, John. "Jonathan Edwards as a Literary Artist." *Criticism* 15 (Spring): 156-73.

Rescues Edwards from becoming "a preserved specimen in the museum of American theology" by treating him as a literary artist, by exploring "his genius for creating psychological drama obliquely" and for manipulating distractions and logic into "figurative reality." *Personal Narrative* can be read as a "poetic fiction," a *bildungsroman* of lost youthful illusion and found mature reality, a "literary act of worship" rather than communication, with a sense of autonomy and independence about it. Likewise *True Virtue* is "a work of literary art" rather than an "outdated" religious tract, its architectonics and incantatory phrases evoking a "figurative universe" where such virtue exists. As a "symbolic paradigm of a mental universe" *True Virtue* is "a perfect work."

11 Hearn, Rosemary. "Stylistic Analysis of the Sermons of Jonathan Edwards." Ph.D. dissertation, Indiana University.

Analyzes Edwards's sermonic structure and rhetoric and finds his style somewhat inconsistent with Puritan practice, though "skillfully adapted and frequently lively." Responsive to the important issues of his time, Edwards often "manipulated" contemporary practice to suit his ends.

12 Heinemann, Robert L. "God, Man, and the Great Awakening." In *America in Controversy.* Edited by DeWitte Holland. Dubuque, Iowa: W. C. Brown Co., pp. 35-51.

Cites Edwards as an exemplar of the orthodox view in the theological, ecclesiastical, and rhetorical issues of the Great Awakening. Edwards is a "valiant" defender of the old Calvinism, a firm believer in affective rather than rational preaching. By insisting on election and experiential religion, Edwards fosters "individualistic and revolutionary" behavior, the hallmark of the Great Awakening.

13 Holbrook, Clyde A. *The Ethics of Jonathan Edwards: Morality and Aesthetics.* Ann Arbor: University of Michigan Press, ix, 227 pp.

Contends that Edwards's ethics (and much else in his thought) can best be understood as an expression of his theological objectivism — his "well-nigh overwhelming conviction of God's centrality, power, and beauty" — and rendered coherent in sermons and treatises by his "aesthetic rhetoric," in a study of the major patterns of his thought and the relationship of ethics to aesthetics, the beauty of holiness. Although Edwards escapes panentheism by his "contrived differentiation" between subject and object and sometimes turns to theological subjectivism when it suits him, the "key concept" for him remains theological objectivism with its denial of utilitarianism and its ethics of "spontaneous virtue." To Edwards, moral beauty comes from the cordial consent of beings to Being, in the same manner as the Trinity consists in the "beauty of relationships"; ethical responsibility arises from the attraction of good and beauty in being to being, not from a sense of duty. An "adventurous thinker," Edwards brings Calvinism and Neoplatonism together in a world "replete with the beauteous evidences of God's presence."

14 Jones, James W. *The Shattered Synthesis: New England Puritanism before the Great Awakening.* New Haven and London: Yale University Press, pp. 168-72, 176.

Narrows the debate between Edwards and Charles Chauncy, first, to questions about God and the world and, then, to questions about man in America. To Edwards, God was a mystery in a miraculous world; to Chauncy, God was orderly, rational, and predictable, as was the world. Edwards attacked Arminianism, in *Freedom of the Will,* not only as theology but as an expression of the American myth of the self-made man; Chauncy's defense was as political as it was moral.

15 Larson, David Mitchell. "The Man of Feeling in America: a Study of Major Early

American Writers' Attitudes toward Benevolent Ethics and Behavior." Ph.D. dissertation, University of Minnesota.

> Cites Edwards as an example of a major writer — Woolman, Franklin, Crevecoeur, H. H. Brackenridge, and Brockden Brown are the others — who adapts the man of feeling to his ethical system of benevolence, in a study of the change in sensibility in eighteenth-century America.

16 Lee, Marc Frank. "A Literary Approach to Selected Writings of Jonathan Edwards." Ph.D. dissertation, University of Wisconsin, Milwaukee.

> Examines Edwards's sermonic style and finds, though it is formal and logical, that imagery and typology often inform it. But in *End of Creation* Edwards eschews images and creates a "beauty of intellectual and metaphorical design almost as a literary by-product of the pursuit after an ever-receding truth."

16A Lee, Sang H. "Imagination and the Increasing Reality in Jonathan Edwards." In *Philosophy of Religion and Theology, 1973.* Compiled by David Griffin. Tallahassee, Fla.: American Academy of Religion, pp. 31-48.

> Discovers a "possible new interpretation" of Edwards's thought (and "an interesting alternative" to process theology) in his "realistic" concept of habit, an attempt to explain both man and nature by "one and the same principle," the ontological power of imagination.

17 Loewinsohn, Ron. "Jonathan Edwards' Opticks: Images and Metaphors in Some of His Major Works." *Early American Literature* 8 (Spring): 21-32.

> Records Edwards's debt to Newton's *Opticks* in his use of metaphors of light and suggests that such metaphors provide a "coherence" to his work unavailable through other means. Edwards distinguishes between the light of common grace and the light of special grace, marking the first in conventional eighteenth-century figures and the second in images of light and vegetation. His reading of Newton results in the "crucial" reconciliation of God and man with nature, an "even more momentous" synthesis than that of head and heart derived from Locke.

18 Lowance, Mason I., Jr. "From Edwards to Emerson to Thoreau: A Revaluation." *American Transcendental Quarterly,* no. 18, Parts 1-2 (Spring): 3-12.

> Extends the "line of continuity" between Edwards and Emerson (see 1940.9) to include Thoreau, detecting a common pattern of the perception of nature and the symbolic expression of it in all three. The transcendentalists abandon Edwards's biblical types and history for Platonic symbols and the eternal moment but retain his natural revelation, with this difference: revelation possible only to the saints in Edwards becomes available to the "transcendentally redeemed" in Emerson and Thoreau. Through the organic principle Thoreau unites symbol and idea, as earlier Edwards had through "doctrinal mysticism."

19 Lowell, Robert. "The Worst Sinner, Jonathan Edwards' God." *History.* New York: Farrar, Straus and Giroux, p. 73.

> Ends the octave of a sonnet with this:
>
> > But Jonathan Edwards prayed to think himself
> > worse than any man that ever breathed;
> > he was a good man, and he prayed with reason —
> > which of us hasn't thought his same thought worse?

20 Martin, Jean-Pierre. "Edwards' Epistemology and the New Science." *Early American Literature* 7 (Winter): 247-55.

Denies that the new philosophy of the eighteenth century materially affected Edwards's epistemology, for he was in "ever so many ways . . . behind his times." Like his speculative theology, his science was "embarrassingly conservative"; his emphasis on experimental religion was "merely" an American version of a "general European stream" of enthusiasm, shunned by the century's intellectuals. Perhaps the greatness of Edwards lies in "his effort to solve the Kierkegaardian antimony between the esthetic and theological degrees of consciousness, not by any new scientific method but by the harmonies of an inherited epistemology."

21 Miller, Perry. *Jonathan Edwards.* Westport, Conn.: Greenwood Press.

Reprints 1949.9.

22 Morsberger, Robert E. "'The Minister's Black Veil': 'Shrouded in a Blackness, Ten Times Black.'" *New England Quarterly* 46 (September): 454-63.

Suggests that, although he does not use Edwards's dramatic career in any of his fiction, Nathaniel Hawthorne deals with a "spiritual tension" in "The Minister's Black Veil" best met in Edwards.

23 Naples, Diane Clark. "The Sensible Order: An Interpretation and Critical Edition of Jonathan Edwards' *Personal Narrative.*" Ph.D. dissertation, University of California, Los Angeles.

Traces Edwards's *Personal Narrative* to his theories of spiritual epistemology and developmental psychology "implicit" in his work. The stages of his religious growth follow those detailed in "Miscellanies" no. 782 and *Religious Affections,* rather than standard Puritan conversion narratives, and may be construed in Jungian terms of centroversion.

24 Nauman, St. Elmo, Jr. *Dictionary of American Philosophy.* New York: Philosophical Library, pp. 87-97.

Offers a life and bibliography of Edwards, an "important" contributor to the philosophy and psychology of religion, metaphysics, ethics, and epistemology, despite a "barbarous" Calvinism.

25 Olsen, Wesley A. "The Philosophy of Jonathan Edwards and its Significance for Educational Thinking." Ed.D. dissertation, Rutgers University.

Uses Edwards's philosophy — particularly his psychology, aesthetics, and ethics — to gain insight into the educational thought of the Puritan period. Although no formal philosophy of education exists for his time, Edwards provides the "fundamental dispositions" toward man and nature important to it in *Freedom of the Will, True Virtue,* and *Religious Affections.* His sensational empiricism stresses individual learning; his consent to being, the unity of man and nature; and his ethics of harmony, the union of man and society.

26 Parker, William H. "Jonathan Edwards: Founder of the Counter-Tradition of Transcendental Thought in America." *Georgia Review* 27 (Winter): 543-49.

Sees Edwards's fusion of his supernaturalism, Locke's sensationalism, and Newton's empiricism as a challenge to the rationalist view of the central place of reason in human affairs. Edwards gives primacy to the reality of the religious affections at the expense of the understanding and marks the affections as the source of growth and change. Thus Edwards is a transcendentalist in the tradition of Emerson, William James, and Reinhold Niebuhr.

27 Pfisterer, Karl Dieterich. "The Prism of Scripture: Studies on History and Historicity in the Work of Jonathan Edwards." Ph.D. dissertation, Columbia University.
Published as 1975.13.

28 Scheick, William J. Review of Jonathan Edwards, *The Great Awakening*, edited by C. C. Goen. *Thought* 48 (Summer): 309-11.
Commends C. C. Goen's "reliable" text and "accurate" introduction (1972.11) but finds "somewhat misleading" his understanding of Edwards's conversion pattern. Unlike the traditional system that dwelt on means, Edwards evaluated effects of the conversion experience, thereby resolving the "problematic" issue of preparation.

29 Schultz, Joseph P. "The Religious Psychology of Jonathan Edwards and the Hassidic Masters of Habad." *Journal of Ecumenical Studies* 10 (Fall): 716-27.
Notes "remarkable similarities" between Edwards and the Habad masters of Hassidism in their attempts to join intellect to emotion in the religious experience and to distinguish "authentic religious fervor from sham enthusiasm." Although their approaches differ, their analyses of the mind, the saints, the religious experience, and the mystic way are parallel.

30 Sloan, Douglas. "Introduction." *The Great Awakening and American Education: A Documentary History.* New York: [Columbia] Teachers College Press, pp. 30-37.
Connects the shift to empiricism in American education to the experimental religion of Edwards and the Great Awakening. To Edwards, "all meaningful knowledge" combines the cognitive and affective powers of personality and draws upon sensible experience and empirical fact. His "strong pragmatic and utilitarian" thought finds its way into revivalist college curricula.

31 Slotkin, Richard. *Regeneration Through Violence: The Mythology of the American Frontier, 1600-1860.* Middletown, Conn.: Wesleyan University Press, pp. 103-106 passim.
Parallels the sensationalist psychology and rhetoric of revival sermons such as Edwards's *Sinners in the Hands of an Angry God* to that of early American myth-tales such as Mrs. Rowlandson's *A Narrative of the Captivity.*

32 Stenerson, Douglas C. "An Anglican Critique of the Early Rise of the Great Awakening in New England: A Letter by Timothy Cutler." *William and Mary Quarterly,* 3d ser., 30 (July):475-88.
Reprints a letter, 28 May 1739, from Thomas Cutler, rector at Yale, to Edmund Gibson, Bishop of London, recounting the genesis of the Great Awakening and offering this portrait of Edwards: "He is very much emaciated, and impair'd in his health, and it is doubtful to me whether he will attain to the Age of 40. He was Critical, subtil and peculiar, but I think not very solid in Disputation. Always a sober Person, but withal pretty recluse, austere and rigid." Cutler also describes the beginnings of the revival and fears the excesses inherent in it.

33 Sweet, William W. *Story of Religion in America.* Grand Rapids, Mich.: Baker Book House.
Reprints 1930.14.

34 Tattrie, George Arthur. "Jonathan Edwards' Understanding of the Natural World and Man's Relationship to It." Ph.D. dissertation, McGill University.

286

Examines Edwards's views of the natural order and man's relationship to it, a community of purpose, unity, individuality, and corporateness, subject to external authority, order, consent, and service. Such a community "participates" in Being and thus shares with man a moral quality. Edwards's "unique" concept of the natural world has significance for the "ecological debate . . . now raging."

35 Waanders, David William. "Illumination and Insight: An Analogical Study." Ph.D. dissertation, Princeton Theological Seminary.

Explores Edwards's theology for his psychological understanding of illumination — especially in his treatment of the sense of the heart and the religious affections — ; explains the analogy between insight and illumination in Edwards in terms of therapeutic, creative, and Gestalt insight; and relates data on perception, cognition, and mental health criteria to "evaluative themes in Edwards in constructing six new evaluative criteria."

36 Warch, Richard. *School of the Prophets: Yale College, 1701-1740.* The Yale Scene: University Series, no. 2. New Haven and London: Yale University Press, pp. 93-95, 204-207, 301-303 passim.

Comments briefly upon the relationship between Edwards and Yale, both as student and tutor, and the effect his training there had upon his thought and career. Only Edwards, of all Yale graduates before the Awakening, adopted the new learning and then only to "argue against its tendencies."

37 Weddle, David Leroy. "The New Man: A Study of the Significance of Conversion for the Theological Definition of the Self in Jonathan Edwards and Charles G. Finney." Ph.D. dissertation, Harvard University.

Finds the images of self in the theology of Edwards and Charles Grandison Finney reflective of their eras in American religious life. Edwards's view of personal identity, derived in part from Locke, Newton, Shaftesbury, and Puritan piety, may be called "affectional-communal"; Finney's theological anthropology, arising from nineteenth-century frontier America, may be called "volitional-individualist."

38 Wessell, Lynn R. "Great Awakening: The First American Revolution." *Christianity Today* 17 (31 August): 11-12, 21.

Argues that Edwards and the Great Awakening "helped to promote" the American Revolution by creating a "passionate sense of community love" and by liberating men and women through the doctrine of disinterested benevolence. Inner experience replaces institutional formulations, religious expressions and feelings change, and the "Americanization of pietism as a revolutionary awakening" begins. Edwards's philosophy of holy love, socially realized, is "just as democratic" as Jefferson's political thought.

39 White, Morton. "Jonathan Edwards: The Doctrine of Necessity and the Sense of the Heart." *Science and Sentiment.* London and New York: Oxford University Press.

Reprints 1972.46.

40 Wilson, Patricia Anne. "The Theology of Grace in Jonathan Edwards." Ph.D. dissertation, University of Iowa.

Characterizes Edwards's theology of grace as a departure from "prevailing" Puritan concepts and a "return" to an Augustinian-Calvinist theology influenced by the metaphysics of the Cambridge Platonists. Edwards replaces preparation, human effort, and obedience to covenant law with an absolute sovereignty of divine grace operating upon totally passive man and acting wholly for God's glorification.

41 Winslow, Ola Elizabeth. *Jonathan Edwards, 1703-1758.* New York: Octagon Books.
Reprints 1940.21.

42 Ziff, Larzer. *Puritanism in America: New Culture in a New World.* New York: Viking Press, pp. 299-311.
Weighs the effects upon the American mind and spirit of Edwards's revivalist temper and the "culture of expansion" that was Puritanism. Edwards justified revivalism, though not its anti-intellectual excesses, as a way "to lift Americans out of their sense of inconsequential provinciality by belittling the importance for their true selves of the economic and political institutions that had come to control their lives." By focussing upon a shift in psychic make-up rather than upon a rearrangement of social institutions, Edwards established the "characteristic pattern" of American rebellion against oppressive daily life. And he helped establish another pattern. Edwards stressed emotion in writing as in life; Franklin stressed reason; but neither "encouraged a confidence" in literature. American writers were to inherit this "ambivalence" and a "deep distrust" of their vocation.

1974

1 Allen, Alexander V. G. *Jonathan Edwards.* New York: Burt Franklin.
Reprints 1889.1.

2 Anderson, Wallace E. Preface to *Of Insects,* by Jonathan Edwards. New Haven: Jonathan Edwards College Press, pp. [i-ii].
Compares Edwards's earlier view of spiders as wonderful and wise in "Of Insects" to his later use of them as symbols of corruption and vileness. An edition of that work, newly transcribed from the manuscripts, supersedes that of Egbert Smyth (1890.8).

3 Bennett, Jonathan. "The Conscience of Huckleberry Finn." *Philosophy* 49 (April): 123-34.
Uses Huck Finn, Heinrich Himmler, and Edwards to show the relationship between sympathy and "bad morality" and finds Edwards's morality to be "worse than Himmler's" in his approval of eternal damnation. Of course, Edwards never actually tormented the damned, but he never found "painful" another's suffering, never bore sympathy for them.

4 Berk, Stephen E. *Calvinism versus Democracy: Timothy Dwight and the Origins of American Evangelical Orthodoxy.* Hamden, Conn.: Shoe String Press, pp. 49-54.
Traces the division in the followers of Edwards — Timothy Dwight among them — to a split in Edwards himself. In an earlier period Edwards was dominated by the heart, experiential and evangelical; in a later period by the head, rational and metaphysical. The New Divinity theologians followed either the experimental piety of the first phase or the scholasticism of the second.

5 Blight, James George. "Gracious Discoveries: Toward an Understanding of Jonathan

Edwards' Psychological Theory, and an Assessment of his Place in the History of American Psychology." Ph.D. dissertation, University of New Hampshire.

Discovers in Edwards's combination of rational-emotive and proactive and reactive principles of human nature an analogue to the multiple-processing model of contemporary information-processing theorists and applies the model to the successive stages of the conversion experience described by Edwards, in an estimate of his place in the history of American psychology from colonial times to William James.

5A Boyer, Paul, and Stephen Nissenbaum. *Salem Possessed: The Social Origins of Witchcraft.* Cambridge: Harvard University Press, pp. 27-30.

Draws parallels between Salem Village in 1692 and Northampton in 1734 — extreme anxiety, violent death, the "central role" of the young, the affected ministers — in a reading of Edwards's *Faithful Narrative.*

5B Bryant, M. Darrol. "America as God's Kingdom." In *Religion and Political Society.* Edited and translated in the Institute of Christian Thought. New York: Harper & Row, pp. 54-94.

Finds "unwarranted" the assumption of Alan Heimert (1966.17) and others that the millennial impulse was fulfilled in the Republic, "at least in relation to Jonathan Edwards," in a study of God's kingdom in America and Edwards's pre-, post-, and anti-millennialist eschatology. That assumption involves "an idolatrous confusion" of the politics of God and the politics of man: Edwards's is a spiritual not a political kingdom, even though he seems to have confused them early, which may have led to possible misreadings.

6 Cecil, Anthony C., Jr. *The Theological Development of Edwards Amasa Park: Last of the "Consistent Calvinists."* Dissertation Series, 1. Missoula, Mont.: Scholars Press, pp. 207-20 passim.

Traces the career of Edwards Amasa Park, Edwards's "last 'lineal disciple,'" as a mediating theologian in his attempt to reconcile the demands of intellect and feeling, divine sovereignty and human freedom, traditional Christianity and the modern temper, Nathaniel Taylor and Jonathan Edwards.

6A Cherry, Conrad. Review of *The Ethics of Jonathan Edwards: Morality and Aesthetics,* by Clyde A. Holbrook. *Church History* 43 (March): 118-19.

Considers Clyde A. Holbrook's study (1973.13) "a helpful guide" through the "complexities" of Edwards's ethical thought.

7 ———. *The Theology of Jonathan Edwards: A Reappraisal.* Gloucester, Mass.: Peter Smith.

Reprints 1966.9.

8 Delattre, Roland A. Review of *The Ethics of Jonathan Edwards: Morality and Aesthetics,* by Clyde Holbrook. *New England Quarterly* 47 (March): 155-58.

Calls Clyde Holbrook's study of Edwards (1973.13) "a great disappointment" for its failure to relate Edwards's ethics to his aesthetics and to accommodate both to his theological objectivism.

9 Dewey, Edward Hooker. "Jonathan Edwards." In *American Writers on American Literature.* Edited by John Macy. Westport, Conn.: Greenwood Press.

Reprints 1931.8.

10 Edwards, Jonathan, the younger. *A Dissertation Concerning Liberty and Necessity.* New York: Burt Franklin.
    Reprints 1797.1.

11 Foster, Mary C. "Theological Debate in a Revival Setting: Hampshire County in the Great Awakening." *Fides et Historia* 6 (Spring): 31-47.
    Defends Edwards's belief that the theological debate about justification by faith begun in the Connecticut Valley in November 1734 was "humanly speaking" the cause of the revival that followed a month later and suggests that the justification controversy was "much more fundamental" to the theological division following the Great Awakening than either the debates about freedom of the will and original sin or the Awakening itself. Edwards's sermons on justification were effective in removing "every hope outside of faith" for salvation and so stimulated the need for conversion experiences provided by revivals. *Religious Affections,* his "final evaluation" of the Awakening, reformulates the theology of religious experience for New England and "still clarifies" it for us today.

11A Gianakos, Perry E. "New Left Millennialism and American Culture." *Thought* 49 (December): 397-418.
    Notes that Edwards "Americanized" the Protestant millennial tradition to reflect an experience differing from a European one.

12 Holifield, E. Brooks. *The Covenant Sealed: The Development of Puritan Sacramental Theology in Old and New England, 1570-1720.* New Haven and London: Yale University Press, pp. 228-29.
    Cites Edwards's communion practice as a rejection of both Solomon Stoddard's converting ordinance and Cotton Mather's "evangelistic sacramental piety."

13 Lensing, George S. "Robert Lowell and Jonathan Edwards: Poetry in the Hands of an Angry God." *South Carolina Review* 6 (April): 7-17.
    Analyzes four Robert Lowell poems — "Mr. Edwards and the Spider" and "After the Surprising Conversions" in *Lord Weary's Castle* (1946), "Jonathan Edwards in Western Massachusetts" in *For the Union Dead* (1964), and "The Worst Sinner, Jonathan Edwards' God" in *History* (1973). Edwards's influence on Lowell is "preponderant and perplexing" and consistent over three decades of work: there is a personal affinity — the Puritan preacher is like the exhortative poet — and a "fundamental paradox." Edwards represents a stern and disastrous morality that Lowell condemns yet a theocentric, apocalyptic, and historical vision he shares.

14 Marty, Martin E. "The Edwardsean Tradition." *Christian Century* 91 (2 January): 18, 20-31.
    Reviews C. C. Goen's *The Great Awakening* (1972.11) and identifies the Edwardsean tradition in evangelism — its optimism, worldliness, and sense of community — with the Social Gospel, the Secular City, and Progressive movements and contrasts it with the tradition of Dwight Moody and Billy Sunday with its pessimism and apocalypse. Yet Edwards's pattern probably belongs more to his times than ours, a world "largely irrecoverable," and his talent for "surprises" belongs to a manner out of date.

14A Mead, Sidney E. Review of *The Ethics of Jonathan Edwards,* by Clyde A. Holbrook. *American Historical Review* 79 (June): 844-45.

Pronounces Clyde A. Holbrook's study (1973.13) "more difficult to understand than Edwards himself."

15 Mudge, Jean McClure. Review of *Marriage to a Difficult Man,* by Elizabeth D. Dodds. *Journal of Presbyterian History* 52 (Spring): 90-93.

Considers Elisabeth D. Dodds's biography of the Edwards family (1971.6) a "tract for the consecration of the domestic circle," a study in which "irrelevance joins inconsistency."

15A [Murray, Iain H.] "Jonathan Edwards 1: The Son of East Windsor." *[Tenth] Banner of Truth* no. 135 (December): 23-32.

Reprinted as part of 1987.21.

16 Parkman, Ebenezer. *The Diary of Ebenezer Parkman, 1703-1782.* First Part: 1719-1755. Edited by Francis G. Walett. Worcester, Mass.: American Antiquarian Society, p. 52 passim.

Records the first meeting with Edwards on 15 September 1738 following a Yale commencement and all subsequent meetings, conversations., readings, and notices, ending on 28 December 1754 about Edwards's months-long illness at Stockbridge. (Parkman's frequent references to Edwards's death in 1758 have not been published as yet.)

17 Schafer, Thomas A. "Edwards, Jonathan." *Encyclopaedia Britannica,* 15th ed., 6:440-42.

Considers Edwards "the greatest theologian and philosopher of American Puritanism," in a brief account of his life, works, and influence, and attributes renewed interest in him to the "cosmic sweep" of his thought with its emphasis on faith and love.

18 Scheick, William J. "Family, Conversion, and the Self, in Jonathan Edwards' *A Faithful Narrative of the Surprising Work of God.*" *Tennessee Studies in Literature* 19:79-89.

Focusses upon the family motif in *Faithful Narrative* and its relationship to Edwards's concerns for conversion and the inner self. Edwards sought to restore the early Puritan sense of the family as "a principle of order, the basic unit, the very foundation of church and state" by indicting parents for the spiritual laxity of their children and by reasserting his "parental role" as spiritual father to the communal family. The well-ordered family proved, to Edwards, the only environment for conversion and offered, in its stability and isolation, a useful symbol of the integrity of the inner self in a changing world.

19 Schultz, Joseph P. "The Lurianic Strand in Jonathan Edwards' Concept of Progress." *Judaica* 30 (September): 126-34.

Traces the gradualism in Edwards's millenarian thought to the Lurianic Kabbalah of the sixteenth century. Unlike other millenarists, Edwards believes redemption to come, not catastrophically nor miraculously, but gradually through the cumulative and ameliorative effect of the deeds of men. The Lurianic Kabbalah, "adapted to a Christian framework" and reaching Edwards through ill-defined channels, is the source for the idea of continuous progress in *History of Redemption.*

20 Selsam, Howard. "Jonathan Edwards on the Freedom of the Will." In *Boston Studies in the Philosophy of Science,* XV. Edited by R. S. Cohen, J. J. Stachel, and M. W.

Wartofsky. Scientific, Historical and Political Essays in Honor of Dirk J. Struik. Dordrecht, Holland, and Boston: D. Reidel Publishing Co., pp. 391-402.

> Characterizes Edwards as a "great philosopher almost in spite of himself" by relating his Calvinism to Marxist scientific materialism and *Freedom of the Will* to Friedrich Engels's *Anti-Duhring: Socialism, Utopian and Scientific* (1878). Edwards's "intuitively dialectical" analysis of causation, freedom, and necessity fails only in its individualistic, rather than its collective, application.

21 Shea, Daniel B., Jr. "The Art and Instruction of Jonathan Edwards' *Personal Narrative*." In *The American Puritan Imagination: Essays in Revaluation*. Edited by Sacvan Bercovitch. London: Cambridge University Press, pp. 159-72.

> Reprints 1965.18.

22 ———. "B. F. Skinner: The Puritan Within." *Virginia Quarterly Review* 50 (Summer): 416-37.

> Draws parallels between Skinner's *Beyond Freedom and Dignity* and Edwards's *Freedom of the Will* in such matters as rhetorical strategies, verbal behavior, and the "language of tropism." More broadly, both thinkers share the Puritan proclivity to "imagine utopia while suspecting the worst of human nature, and then, in the face of this dichotomy, to seek infallible controls for bringing a truculent world to moral attention." But Skinner lacks Edwards's piety and enthusiasm and substitutes verifiable works for free grace.

23 Simonson, Harold P. *Jonathan Edwards: Theologian of the Heart*. Grand Rapids, Mich.: William B. Eerdmans, 174 pp.

> Considers that the "central theme" in Edwards concerns the sense of the redeemed and sanctified heart and its preparation to experience God's glory, in a full-length study of his conversion experience, his role in the Great Awakening, his imagination and vision, his language, and his concepts of sin and salvation. That "heart-felt pietism" is at the core of the religious experience and transcends sense, reason, understanding, and aesthetics, enabling faithful man to perceive through "sanctified imagination" what is unknowable to natural man. For Edwards, religious language, an occasional rather than a sufficient cause for conversion, sets the emotional context for the experience and serves "to bridge knowledge and being, cognition and apprehension." Only through the sense of the heart, Edwards concludes, may man go beyond his tragic limitations — Edwards held that Calvinism was "experientially true" — and through Christ "come to possess all things."

24 Smith, John E. "Jonathan Edwards: Piety and Practice in the American Character." *Journal of Religion* 54 (April): 166-80.

> Examines Edwards's "fidelity" to theological empiricism, principally in *Religious Affections;* his connection of piety to practice; and his contribution to "all forms" of religion in America. By specifying the evidences of genuine religion, Edwards turned the process from a subjective and immediate affair to one objective and discursive; by making the signs of conversion part of the "total bearing" of a person, not isolated as "enclosed states" of mind, Edwards pushed empiricism to pragmatism. Religious virtues, then, could be known only in and through active expression, and private experience, subject to valid testing, could be publicly assessed. Although Edwards was the "sworn enemy" of a religion of morality and good works, his system "opened the door" to just that development in American religion at the same time that it satisfied the practical bent of the American mind.

25 Stamey, Joseph D. "Newton's Time, Locke's Ideas, and Jonathan's Spiders." *Proceedings of the New Mexico-West Texas Philosophical Society* (April): 79-87.

Compares Edwards to Marx as philosophers resolving epistemological problems not on conceptual or theoretical grounds but on practical and ideological ones with decidedly social consequences. "For Marx, one had to create the truth by creating a classless society. . . . For Edwards, one has to enact the truth in human feeling." Like Marx, Edwards tried to reconcile the themes of determinism, freedom, and providence, the impetus for Edwards arising from his New England background and his understanding of Locke's sensationalism and Newton's time.

26 Stein, Stephen J. "Cotton Mather and Jonathan Edwards on the Number of the Beast: Eighteenth-Century Speculation about the Antichrist." *Proceedings of the American Antiquarian Society* 84 (October): 293-315.

Remarks the similarities between Edwards and Cotton Mather's reception of Francis Potter's *An Interpretation of the Number 666* (1642) and concludes that, contrary to Alan Heimert's assertion that anti-Catholicism waned after the Great Awakening, such sentiments continued unabated through the Revolution. In subscribing to the myth of the Beast and Potter's square root formulas, Edwards and others like him adopted a dualistic view of history and "significantly shaped America's religious and cultural heritage."

27 ———. "Jonathan Edwards and the Rainbow: Biblical Exegesis and Poetic Imagination." *New England Quarterly* 47 (September): 440-56.

Discovers in the biblical exegesis of his later years a "delightfully different" Edwards, a creative poet quite unlike both the stereotypical logician of custom and the turgid exegete of his own day. His exegesis of the covenant of the rainbow (Genesis 9:12-17) found in No. 348 of his "Notes on Scripture" is an "excellent" example of Edwards's hermeneutics as he combines science and theology through the four-fold medieval pattern of the literal, allegorical, tropological, and analogical. For Edwards, such an exercise offers a "convenient and congenial" way of expressing dogma and provides a "synopsis of his cardinal tenets."

28 Strout, Cushing. *The New Heavens and New Earth: Political Religion in America*. New York: Harper & Row, pp. 29-45 passim.

Traces Edwards's career, focussing upon his role in the Great Awakening — "one of those notable conjunctions between private needs and public anxieties" — and remarks the social and political consequences of the revivals. Edwards's "tragic overtones of *hubris*" are matched by the special ironies of the Awakening, in which original intentions were confounded: sincerity gave way to doubt, social peace to public, legal battles, skepticism of learning to the founding of colleges, and so on. At first "profoundly nonpolitical," as Edwards understood it, the Great Awakening later "contributed to social conflict and change."

29 Weddle, David L. "Jonathan Edwards on Men and Trees, and the Problem of Solidarity." *Harvard Theological Review* 67 (April): 155-75.

Argues that Edwards uses the image of a tree and its branches as a type of the solidarity of sinners and of saints in interpreting the doctrines of original sin and the atonement and that such an organic metaphor differs "significantly" from the biological one of traditional Calvinism and the juridical one of covenant theology. For Edwards, the unity of the race arises as a "shared disposition" through a process of growth and development in history, not by Adam's infection nor by his headship; man's redemption arises through the ingrafting of Christ upon him.

Edwards identifies the common disposition as a moral act in history, and thus he makes man a moral agent, at once generic and individual, in nature and in society.

1975

1 Ahlstrom, Sydney E. "Jonathan Edwards and the Revival of New England Theology." *A Religious History of the American People.* Garden City, N.Y.: Doubleday & Co.
   Reprints 1972.2.

2 Angoff, Charles, ed. *Jonathan Edwards: His Life and Influence.* The Leverton Lecture Series. Rutherford, N.J.: Fairleigh Dickinson University Press, 65 pp.
   Publishes the papers and records the remarks at a symposium on Edwards, April 18, 1973.
   Cherry, Conrad. "Imagery and Analysis: Jonathan Edwards on Revivals of Religion," pp. 19-28. Asserts that Edwards blended theological analysis with sensible imagery to evoke both understanding and emotion during the revivals. Described in *Religious Affections* as "affectionate knowledge," this coherent use of language serves to check both unthinking enthusiasm and unfeeling reason and is clearly at odds with the anti-intellectualism of later revivalists.
   Kimnach, Wilson H. "The Brazen Trumpet: Jonathan Edwards's Conception of the Sermon," pp. 29-44. Traces the growth and direction of Edwards's sermons from the early formal ones, imitative of his father and grandfather, to those later ones given to sustained pursuit of an idea. He early masters the formula of text, doctrine, and application, and the use of rhetorical and poetic devices to pierce the heart. His later practice reflects a growing desire to divorce the hortatory from the philosophical and is best met in *Sinners in the Hands of an Angry God.* With the end of the Awakening comes few sermons; with the Stockbridge years fewer still. Yet the sermonic form pervades his major treatises, and he never found another to replace it.
   "Symposium," pp. 45-65. Ranges widely and discursively over aspects of Edwards's thought and career: his debt to Locke, his millenarianism and affections, his social and political awareness, his consistency and influence, his centrality to American intellectual history. The panel, moderated by Edward Cook, included Conrad Cherry, Wilson Kimnach, Charles Wetzel, and Donald Jones.

2A Barnes, Howard A. Review of *Jonathan Edwards,* edited by Charles Angoff. *Church History* 44 (December): 542-43.
   Finds the title of Charles Angoff's book (1975.2) "unrealized," its thought "as slim as the book itself."

3 Bercovitch, Sacvan. *The Puritan Origins of the American Self.* New Haven and London: Yale University Press, pp. 152-63 passim.
   Remarks the close relationship of natural theology to federal teleology in the rhetoric of Edwards, one of a long line of "solitary keepers" of the American dream that includes Cotton Mather and Ralph Waldo Emerson. Edwards's eschatology has a peculiarly American cast, his typology a penchant for American figures. So Edwards defines colonial progress in millennial terms and the regenerate in new world images.

4 Bogue, Carl W. "Jonathan Edwards and the Covenant of Grace." Th.D. dissertation, Free University of Amsterdam.
   Published as 1975.5.

5 ————. *Jonathan Edwards and the Covenant of Grace.* Cherry Hill, N.J.: Mack Publishing Co., xi, 312 pp.

Affirms Edwards's "rightful place" among Calvinist or Reformed theologians in his acceptance of the correlation between divine sovereignty and human responsibility acknowledged in the covenant of grace, in an examination of the Calvinist framework and Edwards's notes, sermons, and treatises. For Edwards, the covenant of grace and the covenant of redemption are aspects of the unabrogated covenant of works, but are distinctive, though not in a substantive way, in this: the covenant of grace (between Christ and man) is an "historical manifestation" of the covenant of redemption (between God and Christ) and analogous to a marriage covenant, offered now and fulfilled later. The covenant of redemption is eternal, as the Trinity is; the covenant of grace, because of man's participation, is becoming. Hence, divine sovereignty and human responsibility meet in the covenant of grace, consented to by man through faith. To see Edwards, as recent commentators have, caught in an unresolved conflict or contradiction in this is "inaccurate" and "superficial."

6 Clebsch, William A. *American Religious Thought: A History.* Chicago History of American Religion Series. Chicago: University of Chicago Press.

Reprints 1973.5.

7 Eversley, Walter Vernon Lloyd. "Christus Gloria: An Aesthetic-Teleological Investigation of Atonement." Ph.D. dissertation, Harvard University.

Attributes Edwards's use of some aesthetic-teleological ideas in his concept of the atonement to Athanasius, Anselm, and Calvin. Like them, he held the atonement to be an opportunity for man to find forgiveness of sin, but Edwards also held the atonement to be a means of "maintaining the relationship of a whole world order that contained man" and the ultimate purpose of all things to be the glory of God.

8 Fiering, Norman S. Review of *The Ethics of Jonathan Edwards,* by Clyde A. Holbrook. *William and Mary Quarterly,* 3d ser., 32 (January): 139-41.

Finds Clyde Holbrook's thesis of theological objectivism "anachronistic, irrelevant, or superfluous," his analysis of Edwards's aesthetics no more informed than that of his ethics (1973.13).

9 Gelpi, Albert. *The Tenth Muse: The Psyche of the American Poet.* Cambridge, Mass.: Harvard University Press, pp. 47-50, 229-30.

Compares Edwards's use of types and tropes, especially in *Images or Shadows,* to Edward Taylor's before him and Ralph Waldo Emerson's and Emily Dickinson's after him.

10 Hamilton, James E., and Edward H. Madden. "Edwards, Finney, and Mahan on the Derivation of Duties." *Journal of the History of Philosophy* 13 (July): 347-60.

Uses Edwards as a point of departure for examining some aspects of the moral philosophy of Charles Grandison Finney and Asa Mahan. Edwards's ethical theory in *True Virtue* is "essentially teleological" inasmuch as all duties of man are reduced to advancing being in general, and what is right is always a means, not an end, in achieving it. Though Finney rejected Edwards's Calvinistic determinism, he "followed" Edwards's teleological ethics; Mahan, on the other hand, identified Finney's view as a "variation" of utilitarianism and criticized it as such.

11 Kimnach, Wilson H. "Jonathan Edwards' Sermon Mill." *Early American Literature* 10 (Fall): 167-77.

Concludes, after inspecting 600 of his sermons, that Edwards revised them principally to meet the rhetorical demands of a different occasion or audience. Edwards was an "ingenious manipulator" of his materials, preaching some sermons (revised) as many as seven times, and kept a "carefully inventoried" sermon file and index. He used this "storehouse" to ease his pulpit burdens and the press of other work as well as to generate new sermons.

11A Laurence, David. "The Foolishness of Edwards." *Worldview* 18 (May): 49-51.
Charges that Harold Simonson's study of the self-authenticating experience in Edwards "suffers from confusion and inconsistency," in an essay-review of *Jonathan Edwards* (1974.23).

12 Martin, J. Alfred, Jr. "The Empirical, the Esthetic, and the Religious." *Union Seminary Quarterly Review* 30 (Winter): 110-20.
Lists Edwards and John Dewey among those American thinkers who approach religion empirically and who find a "strong and fruitful" affinity between the religious experience and the aesthetic. Neither Edwards nor Dewey collapse the good into the beautiful or equate the religious with the aesthetic, but both link the beautiful to the divine and express the "roots of faith" aesthetically. For Edwards the experience shows man to be a child of God, for Dewey a child of nature.

12A Mayer, Herbert T. "Rethinking Pastoral Care for a Post-Christian World." In *Gospel and Life*. Ecumenical Institute for Advanced Theological Studies Yearbook. Edited by Walter Wegner. Jerusalem: [n.p.], pp. 141-59.
Remarks Edwards's "unbalanced Christology," "barren ecclesiology," and "superficial understanding of sin," one of three case histories — others are an anonymous Syrian pastor and Ambrose of Milan — in a brief survey of pastoral care. Edwards's pastoral care "begins and ends with the sermon."

12B Murray, Iain H. "Jonathan Edwards 2: 'New dispositions and that new sense of things.'" *Banner of Truth* no. 139 (April): 7-18.
Reprinted as part of 1987.21.

12C ———. "Jonathan Edwards 3: 'Preparing to Sound the Trumpets.'" *Banner of Truth* no. 147 (December): 22-32.
Reprinted as part of 1987.21.

13 Pfisterer, Karl Dieterich. *The Prism of Scripture: Studies on History and Historicity in the Work of Jonathan Edwards*. Anglo-American Forum, no. 1. Frankfurt: Peter Lang, vi, 381 pp.
Explores Edwards's understanding of history and his use of Scripture (and exegesis) as an historiographical mode, its sources and its consequences. For Edwards, Scripture was a prism — he used "the idea if not the term" — displaying the "coherence of vision and variety," the configuration of the one and the many. As the historian of the revival, Edwards used Scripture as a prism to integrate the past and to suggest a model community; as the historian of redemption, Edwards used Scripture as a prism to develop "a theory of communication which conceptualizes the vision and variety of history ontologically as well as historically."

14 Scheick, William J. "The Grand Design: Jonathan Edwards' *History of the Work of Redemption*." *Eighteenth-Century Studies* 8 (Spring): 300-14.

Notes that Edwards considered his *History of Redemption* "innovative" because he treated history as an allegory of the conversion experience, the manifestation "in large" of the spiritual progress of the individual regenerative soul. Edwards combines nature, history, and the elect into a progressively harmonious whole and assumes for himself a prophetic *persona,* merging his private self of biography with the collective self of history, his individual covenant of grace with the historical covenant of redemption. "In a very real sense Edwards had come to think of himself as a luminary, like the prophets of old, shedding light on God's grand architectural design."

15 ————. Review of *Jonathan Edwards,* by Harold P. Simonson. *Early American Literature* 10 (Spring): 95-96.

Considers Harold Simonson's thesis about Edwards (1974.23) "unoriginal, uninspired and self-evident," a study unfit for a general or scholarly audience.

16 ————. *The Writings of Jonathan Edwards: Theme, Motif, and Style.* College Station: Texas A & M University Press, xiv, 162 pp.

Explores the "progressive interiorization" of Edwards's concerns and the implications for his theology, his quest for identity, and his art, in a chronological review of the themes and structure, the motifs and style of his writings, from the juvenilia to the major works. Particularly, Edwards uses natural images to portray the inner self's immediate and vital perception of divine reality and uses images of the family to convey "the beautiful order inherent in God's grand design," reflected in the orderly relationship of communing Christians, of the minister as spiritual father, and of the marriage between regenerate man and Christ. Edwards experiments with the sermonic form to make it a more effective means of conversion, seeking to "arouse the whole man," intellect and will, to know grace intuitively and using images of light to symbolize both the heart's intuition and God's order. But uncertainty and "spiritual unrest" mark the conversion process for Edwards, and may, in fact, be a sign of conversion. "In a sense Edwards' entire career pivoted on this inner turmoil. His study of conversion became in effect spiritual autobiography."

17 Simonson, Harold P. "Jonathan Edwards and the Imagination." *Andover Newton Quarterly* 16 (November): 109-18.

Insists that Edwards is "first and last a Christian theologian, not a literary artist," and that his theory of imagination is in keeping with Christian revelation, regardless of resemblances to Emerson, the Cambridge Platonists, or literary criticism, generally. Though he sometimes casts his theology in aesthetic terms, Edwards knew that natural imagination was inadequate to his concept of beauty and incapable of spiritual truth without the infusion of grace: "natural imagination embraces nothing unless the soul through faith first embraces God." So regenerate man sees a world not only symbolical but sacramental in a creative act of sanctified imagination.

18 Stein, Stephen J. Review of *Jonathan Edwards,* edited by Charles Angoff. *New England Quarterly* 48 (September): 443-45.

Finds Conrad Cherry's lecture "unimaginative," Wilson Kimnach's "insightful," and the symposium clichéd, in a review of Charles Angoff's gathering (1975.2).

19 Strauss, James D. "A Puritan in a Post-Puritan World — Jonathan Edwards." In *Grace Unlimited.* Edited by Clark H. Pinnock. Minneapolis: Bethany Fellowship, pp. 242-64.

Juxtaposes Edwards's "brilliant, if futile" account of free will and moral agency against modern notions of freedom in a radically determined universe in Gödel's proof, Chomsky's transformational grammar, and D. M. McKay's model of free choice. Edwards's "lethal" fallacy lies in his ambiguous definition of the determination of the will. Thus he fails both to demonstrate the necessary connection between acts and motives and to reconcile moral agency with "any form" of radical determinism.

20 Watts, Emily Stipes. "The Neoplatonic Basis of Jonathan Edwards' 'True Virtue.'" *Early American Literature* 10 (Fall): 179-89.

Suggests Thomas More's *Enchiridion Ethicum* as an early and important source for Edwards's "ultimate ethical definitions" of excellency, virtue, and justice found in his *True Virtue.* Edwards's debt to More was substantial though certainly not total: not only did Edwards have to contend with the empiricism of Locke and the moral sense philosophy of Shaftesbury in shaping his ethics, he also disagreed with More on the source of the inclination to love and on his emphasis on mind rather than sensibility.

21 Weddle, David L. "The Image of the Self in Jonathan Edwards: A Study of Autobiography and Theology." *Journal of the American Academy of Religion* 43 (March): 70-83.

Explores the relationship between the primary language of "identity" in Edwards's autobiographical writing and the secondary language of "ideology" in his theological writing (to use Erik Erikson's terms) and uncovers "a distinctive image of self," combining both the piety of obedience and the piety of adoration in a view "neither strictly legalist nor exclusively mystical." Edwards achieves a balance between the self as agent and as subject, between universal moral order and immediate divine communion, in a "personal synthesis" focussed on the divine beauty in Christ. Through his conversion experience, expressed in *Personal Narrative,* Edwards realized that his identity was of a piece with others "within a shared history," and so he broadcast that new image in his sermons and treatises. For Edwards, "religious autobiography is a form of theological argument."

22 Whaley, Howard. "The First Great Awakening." *Moody Monthly* 75 (June): 47-49.

Divides the Great Awakening, an "intercolonial, nonsectarian" movement, into three successive stages — the middle Atlantic, the New England, the Southern — and notes the role Edwards's sermons on justification played in the outpourings of God's spirit upon his church in America.

1976

1 Allen, Alexander V. G. *Jonathan Edwards.* St. Clair Shores, Mich.: Scholarly Press.

Reprints 1889.1.

2 Anderson, Quentin. "Practical and Visionary Americans." *American Scholar* 45 (Summer): 405-18.

Uses Edwards as an example of the historical development and religious roots of personal authority and its importance to other visionary Americans — Emerson, Thoreau, Whitman — and the guilt of acquisition.

3 Anon. "Sinners in the Hands of an Angry God." *Faith for the Family* 4 (July): 21-22.

Introduces and reprints selections from Edwards's *Sinners in the Hands of an Angry God.*

4   Beam, Christopher Merriman. "Millennialism in American Thought, 1740-1840." Ph.D. dissertation, University of Illinois.

   Considers Edwards's millennialism (and that of the Edwardseans) as part of a unitary force of evangelism, republicanism, and nationalism that swept over America between the Great Awakening and the Civil War in a rush of moral fervor.

5   Bledsoe, Albert T. *An Examination of President Edwards' Inquiry into the Freedom of the Will.* St. Clair Shores, Mich.: Scholarly Press.

   Reprints 1845.2.

6   ————. *A Theodicy.* New York: AMS Press.

   Reprints 1853.8.

7   Boardman, George Nye. *A History of New England Theology.* St. Clair Shores, Mich.: Scholarly Press.

   Reprints 1899.2.

8   Bogue, Carl. "Jonathan Edwards on the Covenant of Grace." In *Soli Deo Gloria: Essays in Reformed Theology.* Festschrift for John H. Gerstner. Edited by R. C. Sproul. [Nutley, N.J.]: Presbyterian and Reformed Publishing Co., pp. 134-45.

   Summarizes 1975.5.

9   Brauer, Jerald C. "Puritanism, Revivalism, and the Revolution." In *Religion and the American Revolution.* Edited by Jerald C. Brauer. Philadelphia: Fortress Press, pp. 22-23.

   Considers Edwards's vision of a new man in a new age in his *History of Redemption* an updated version of the chosen people theme and an indication of American "uniqueness and individuality" before the Revolution.

10 Bremer, Francis J. "Jonathan Edwards and the Great Awakenings." *The Puritan Experiment: New England Society from Bradford to Edwards.* New York: St. Martin s Press, pp. 226-31.

   Sees little difference between Edwards's revival in 1734 and earlier ones in Solomon Stoddard's Northampton and in John Cotton's Boston except for the "sense of expectancy" fed by Edwards's *Faithful Narrative.* Yet to understand the Great Awakening one must turn to Edwards for his "accurate and favorable" insights.

11 Bryant, Marcus Darrol. "History and Eschatology in Jonathan Edwards: A Critique of the Heimert Thesis." Ph.D. dissertation, University of St. Michaels College (Canada).

   Disputes Alan Heimert's thesis that Edwards provides a radical ideology for American nationalism, in a close analysis of *Religion and the American Mind* (1966.17) and its views of Edwards's evangelical Calvinism, eschatology, anthropology, and sociology. What Edwards does offer is a commentary and critique of "nascent forms" of American millennial thought of a heavenly, not a worldly, kind.

12 Bumsted, J. M., and John E. Van de Wetering. *What Must I Do to be Saved?: The Great*

Awakening in Colonial America. Berkshire Studies in History. Hinsdale, Ill.: Dryden Press, pp. 98-106, 118-21 passim.

Includes Edwards, as well as Thomas Prince and Jonathan Dickinson, among the "moderates" in the Great Awakening, advocates of the revival as "the logical outgrowth of the past," of the covenant of grace as "an avenue" to conversion, of "ecstatic joy" as evidence of election. But Edwards's abandonment of the traditional steps to salvation for a number of signs (in *Religious Affections*) represents "a sharp departure" from an orthodox past. Although moderates insisted defensively that there was "nothing new" theologically or religiously in the revival, both their break with past practices and their "sophisticated acceptance" of Locke and Newton — Edwards's "singular" role has been "exaggerated" — argued otherwise and threatened their position. Their critics fared no better: in his quarrel with Charles Chauncy, Edwards's uniting of affection and will represents "a truly modern" psychological view against a "medieval" faculty one.

13 Byington, Ezra Hoyt. "Jonathan Edwards, and the Great Awakening." *The Puritan as a Colonist and Reformer.* New York: AMS Press.
Reprints 1899.4.

14 Campbell, Dennis M. "Authority and the Sense of the Heart: Jonathan Edwards." *Authority and the Renewal of American Theology.* Philadelphia: United Church Press, pp. 5-19.
Characterizes Edwards's theory of the sense of the heart as "supremely dysfunctional" to the social order and a threat to traditional, hierarchal authority. Edwards couples his belief in God's sovereignty with his conviction that God revealed himself "personally, immediately, experientially" through the affections of the heart, so that man's internal awareness of God became "certain and authoritative" and the "norm and content" of theology. Such a shift in the basis of authority "frontally challenged" New England's reliance on Scripture and tradition and "knocked the props out from under" the civil governance of society.

15 Cochran, Alice Cowan. "Sin and Salvation in American Thought." *Perkins School of Theology Journal* 30 (Fall): 1-14.
Traces the evolution of American thought on sin and salvation from Edwards through the Mercersburg theologians, Horace Bushnell, and modern prophets of the social gospel. Edwards reflects the Dortian orthodoxy on election and reprobation, and his promotion of and interest in revivals comes from his conviction of man's depravity and his hope for unmerited grace. Twentieth-century theologians argue a return to an Edwardsean orthodoxy but directed outwardly as collective redemption from social immorality and achieved, as in the past, in America.

16 Conkin, Paul Keith. "Jonathan Edwards: Theology." *Puritans and Pragmatists.* Bloomington: Indiana University Press.
Reprints 1968.3.

17 Cunsolo, Ronald S. "The Return of Jonathan Edwards: A Bicentennial Reflection." *Nassau Review* 3:86-94.
Urges that Edwards be restored to the pantheon of national heroes denied him because of "denominational barriers" and his opposition to the assumptions and implications of the Enlightenment. Edwards countered the infallibility of reason, the self-sufficiency of man, and the sanctity of science with a belief in God and religion, a stand probably responsible for renewed interest in this "peerless prophet of our age."

18 D'Avanzo, Mario L. "The Ambitious Guest in the Hands of an Angry God." *English Language Notes* 14 (September): 38-42.

> Offers Edwards's *Sinners in the Hands of an Angry God* as the philosophical, moral, tonal, and linguistic "frame of reference" for Nathaniel Hawthorne's "The Ambitious Guest."

19 Emery, Allan Moore. "The Alternatives of Melville's 'Bartleby.'" *Nineteenth-Century Fiction* 31 (September): 170-87.

> Suggests Edwards's *Freedom of the Will* and *True Virtue* and Joseph Priestley's *Doctrine of Philosophical Necessity Illustrated* as glosses for Herman Melville's "Bartleby, the Scrivener."

20 Evans, W. Glyn. "Jonathan Edwards: Puritan Paradox." Profiles of Revival Leaders. Nashville, Tenn.: Broadman Press, pp. 15-31.

> Reprints 1967.9 (revised).

20A Fiering, Norman S. "The Transatlantic Republic of Letters: A Note on the Circulation of Learned Periodicals in Early Eighteenth-Century America." *William and Mary Quarterly*, 3d ser., 33 (October): 642-60.

> Includes Edwards among "uncommon" Americans — Cotton Mather, Samuel Johnson, James Logan — who kept alive their philosophical interests through the reporting in learned periodicals from abroad, his catalogue of reading "most frequently" citing the *Republick of Letters.*

21 Gardiner, Harry N., ed. *Jonathan Edwards, a Retrospect.* New York: AMS Press.

> Reprints 1901.6.

22 Gerstner, John H. "An Outline of the Apologetics of Jonathan Edwards. Part I: The Argument from Being." *Bibliotheca Sacra* 133 (January): 3-10.

> Considers Edwards "as orthodox in his view of reason as in everything else," in the first of four articles (see below) on his apologetics, perhaps "more idealistic, comprehensive, and demonstrative" than some but well within the "general" tradition of both Bible and church. Edwards explains the doctrine of the eternal cause from "an empirical a posteriori observation of the universe," seeing Eternal Being revealed as the eternal cause and proved as necessity, inasmuch as Nothing does not exist.

23 ———. "An Outline of the Apologetics of Jonathan Edwards. Part II: The Unity of God." *Bibliotheca Sacra* 133 (April): 99-107.

> Continues an outline of Edwards's apologetics, by examining his doctrine of the unitary nature of being and the implications of pantheism. Edwards distinguishes Being and being in "degree and manner, not in substance"; insists that there is only one Being, generating and glorifying itself; but does not consider all being identical. His theology is "particularistic to the core," devoted to the eternal separation of heaven and hell, in which man's being is preserved but "everlastingly and painfully aware" of its existence apart from God. Edwards was "pantheistic by implication and panentheistic by intention."

24 ———. "An Outline of the Apologetics of Jonathan Edwards. Part III: The Proof of God's Special Revelation, the Bible." *Bibliotheca Sacra* 133 (July): 195-201.

> Continues an outline of Edwards's apologetics by examining his critique of the deists — he proved them not "deficient in heart so much as soft in the head" — and his doctrine of the necessity of special revelation. For Edwards, it was foolish to expect reason to explain the Trinity,

for example, when it could not explain the external world and it was "most unreasonable" to subject the Word of God, the Bible, to the tests of reason. In addition to general or natural revelation, special revelation is necessary, if at times "unreasonable" or paradoxical, so that man might come to know God and his salvific intentions.

25 ———. "An Outline of the Apologetics of Jonathan Edwards. Part IV: The Proof of God's Special Revelation, the Bible — Continued." *Bibliotheca Sacra* 133 (October): 291-98.

Concludes an outline of Edwards's apologetics by examining his proof of God's special revelation, which culminates in Christ and which exists with right reason in the most perfect harmony." The Bible simply requires of finite man "a reasonable use of reason" to understand God's revelation. Divine light gives man "divine apprehension" of the Bible, enables him to see the excellency of doctrine, and creates, in turn, a need for even more illumination. Grace and truth "work together" in his sanctification: "The sight of God changes man into the image of God."

26 Hazard, Rowland G. "Review of Edwards on the Will." *Freedom of Mind in Willing.* New York: AMS Press.

Reprints 1864.3.

27 Hendry, George S. "The Glory of God and the Future of Man." *Reformed World* 34 (December): 147-57.

Considers Edwards's solution to the problem of God's glory and man's future, proposed in *End of Creation,* an example of a non-traditional, alternate eschatology. Edwards traces the destiny of redeemed man on an asymptotic curve, an "eternal approximation to God," as he continues through all time to approach nearer and nearer to God, finding happiness in his endless progress. Edwards avoids the "'fearful symmetry'" of Karl Barth's creature-creator annulling relationship by making man's "continuing creatureliness" compatible with the moment of his return to God. God's glory goes out from God and relates to that which is not God, the perfection of his glory returning as perfection raised to "a higher and ever higher" perfection.

28 Hindson, Edward. "Introduction." *Puritan Theology: A Reader.* Grand Rapids, Mich.: Baker Book House, pp. 249-51.

Reprints Edwards's "The Portion of the Wicked" and "The Portion of the Righteous" as illustrations of Puritan eschatology, which emphasizes judgment and eternal states but lacks speculation about "exact" fulfillment.

29 [Hopkins, Samuel]. *The Life and Character of the Late Reverend, Learned & Pious Mr. Jonathan Edwards, President of the College of New-Jersey.* New York: AMS Press.

Reprints 1804.1.

30 Hull, Aarlie J. "Sarah and Jonathan Edwards." *Herald of Holiness* 64 (1 April): 18.

Tries to account for the "generations of productive, successful" descendants of Edwards by examining the family life in Elisabeth's Dodds's *Marriage to a Difficult Man* (1971.6).

30A Kretzoi, Miklosne. *Az Amerikai Irodalom Kezdetei (1607-1750).* Budapest: Akademiai Kiado, pp. 67-72 passim.

Remarks John Locke's influence upon Edwards, in a brief appraisal of the latter's work. (In Hungarian.)

31 Laurence, David Ernst. "Religious Experience in the Biblical World of Jonathan Edwards: A Study in Eighteenth-Century Supernaturalism." Ph.D. dissertation, Yale University.

Associates Edwards's precritical biblical hermeneutics with his "peculiar perspective" of eighteenth-century currents of thought, developing his metaphysics of being out of Newton's physics and his supernaturalism out of Locke's sensationalism. The resulting visionary experience differs from Romantic expressions of the reality of spiritual truths and from Puritan preparationist models of conversion. Edwards came to believe that humiliation was an exercise of faith and that conversion was a gradual change of heart.

32 Lee, Sang Hyun. "Mental Activity and the Perception of Beauty in Jonathan Edwards." *Harvard Theological Review* 69 (October): 369-96.

Finds the "key" to Edwards's epistemology, aesthetics, and ontology in his concept of habit, defined as "an active and real tendency to behavior or event of a determinate sort." For Edwards, mental activity was a spontaneous, immediate, nondiscursive, intuitive, and creative ordering of sense experience, a relational tending toward union of the knowing mind and the unknown world, idea and reality, and beauty and being. The aesthetic sense or sense of the heart is a habit of mind integrating sensation not mechanistically but organically in the modern manner.

33 Lips, Roger Cameron. "The Spirit's Holy Errand: A Study of Continuities of Thought from Jonathan Edwards to Ralph Waldo Emerson." Ph.D. dissertation, University of Wisconsin, Madison.

Explores the connection between Edwards and Emerson in thought and in language. Both dwelt upon the natural-spiritual dichotomy of man, psychological theories of the will and the intuition, and especially the nature of the spiritual experience: religious affections, the new sense, disinterested benevolence, and the "increasing union with the divine nature." Clearly, Emerson continues to "expound the Calvinist piety of his ancestors."

34 Lloyd-Jones, D. Martyn. "Jonathan Edwards and the Crucial Importance of Revival." In *The Puritan Experiment in the New World*. Westminster Conference for Theological and Historical Study, 1976. Huntington, England: Westminister Conference, pp. 103-21.

Urges his audience, "Read Jonathan Edwards," especially on revivals — "No man is more relevant to the present condition of Christianity" — to know the essentials of the spirit, in a discursive address to the Westminster Conference, an unabashed tribute to Edwards, the "very zenith" of Puritanism, its "Mount Everest."

34A Lovejoy, David S. *Samuel Hopkins, Religion, Slavery, and the Revolution*. Philadelphia: United Church Press.

Reprints 1967.19.

35 Luisi, Miriam P. "The Community of Consent in the Thought of Jonathan Edwards." Ph.D. dissertation, Fordham University.

Considers the "basic insight" of Edwards's view of the covenant, consent, and community to be the "constitutional relatedness" of all being, in which the community of men, united through disinterested love to being in general, actively engages the self in the community of being. For Edwards, the archetype of such unity in community is the Trinity.

36 McGiffert, Arthur C., Jr. *Jonathan Edwards.* Creative Lives Series. New York: AMS Press.

Reprints 1932.10.

37 May, Henry F. *The Enlightenment in America.* New York: Oxford University Press, pp. 49-50.

Finds paradoxical Edwards's place in America: a product of the Enlightenment, he held reason "worthless" without divine light; the "greatest" figure of the Awakening, he was "least typical" of it; no founder of the American religious way of life, he "deeply" affected American culture.

38 Meyer, Donald H. "Jonathan Edwards and the Reality of the Unseen." *The Democratic Enlightenment.* New York: G. P. Putnam's Sons, pp. 18-34.

Considers Edwards "a significant representative figure" of the American Enlightenment, in an analysis of his ideas concerning the mystery of conversion *(Personal Narrative),* the nature of true religion *(Religious Affections),* and the question of human morality *(Freedom of the Will* and *True Virtue).* In a time not particularly congenial to it, Edwards tried to establish the legitimacy of the supernatural experience. In his attempt at reconciling traditional pietism and the new philosophy and at engaging in a public dialogue as a "responsible intellectual" concerned with important social issues, he was very much a part of his time.

38A Murray, Iain H. "Jonathan Edwards 4: Tutor at Yale." *Banner of Truth* no. 148 (January): 6-14.

Reprinted as part of 1987.21.

38B ———. "Jonathan Edwards 5: Northampton and Family Life." *Banner of Truth* no. 151 (April): 6-19.

Reprinted as part of 1987.21.

38C ———. "Jonathan Edwards 6: The Green Valley of Humiliation." *Banner of Truth* no. 152 (May): 28-34.

Reprinted as part of 1987.21.

38D ———. "Jonathan Edwards 7: The Breaking of the Spirit of Slumber." *Banner of Truth* nos. 154-155 (July): 15-25.

Reprinted as part of 1987.21.

39 Panosian, Edward M. "America's Theologian-Preacher." *Faith for the Family* 4 (November): 12, 42-43.

Traces the career of Edwards, a controversial figure then and now.

40 Parker, Henry Bamford. *Jonathan Edwards, the Fiery Puritan.* New York: AMS Press.

Reprints 1930.10.

40A Rivers, Cheryl. "The Jeremiad as Political Sermon." In *Amérique révolutionnaire 1975: Recueil de travaux.* Edited by Jean Béranger and Jean-Claude Barat. Talence: Maison des Sciences de l'Homme d'Acquitane, pp. 49-66.

Likens Edwards's *Sinners in the Hands of an Angry God* (1741) to the jeremiads of Samuel Willard (1682), Cotton Mather (1691), and Samuel Langdon (1775), sermons "at the center" of Puritan theology and American politics. Though Edwards's emphasis on individual rather than national redemption all but rejects that tradition, his rhetoric "plays an essential role in the turbulence of the prerevolutionary years."

41 Sandon, Leo, Jr. "Jonathan Edwards and H. Richard Niebuhr." *Journal of Religious Studies* 12 (March): 105-15.

Discovers sources for H. Richard Niebuhr's radical monotheism and his value theory in Edwards, Niebuhr's "principal mentor" in the language of sovereignty and the language of being. Without Edwardsean motifs of divine sovereignty and being-in-relation, Niebuhr's constructive theology would have been quite different, a fact "explicitly acknowledged" by him and "implicitly demonstrable."

42 Shaw, Mark R. "The Spirit of 1740." *Christianity Today* 20 (2 January): 7-8.

Singles out Edwards (and his *Faithful Narrative*) for his role in revivalism in America and suggests that what occurred in 1740 was "nothing less than an inner American revolution, a spiritual declaration of independence that made political reshuffling thirty-six years later an inevitability."

43 Smith, John E. "Jonathan Edwards as Philosophical Theologian." *Review of Metaphysics* 30 (December): 306-24.

Solves the "imposing enigma" of biblical absolutism and philosophical speculation in Edwards by showing that Edwards "never" rested his arguments on the Bible "alone," but that he "repeatedly" clinched them by philosophical concepts founded in reason and experience. His is a "subtle interweaving" of the "equally important" Augustinian (later, Cambridge Platonic) tradition and Lockean epistemology into theological empiricism. Edwards's "The Mind" and *Miscellaneous Observations* reveal "originality and critical acumen" in dealing with God's being, his existence, and man's "new sense" of glory; his *Religious Affections* reveals him as a philosophical "interpreter and mediator" of the logical and psychological elements of the emotions. In short, Edwards is "a major philosophical theologian."

43A Stein, Stephen J. "The Biblical Notes of Benjamin Pierpont." *Yale University Library Gazette* 50 (April): 195-218.

Recounts the provenance of (and reprints) the biblical notes of Benjamin Pierpont, Edwards's brother-in-law. By the end of 1730, Edwards began to use Pierpont's "blank Bible" to record "Miscellaneous Observations of the Holy Scriptures."

44 Storlie, Erik Fraser. "Grace and Works, Enlightenment and Practice: Paradox and Poetry in John Cotton, Jonathan Edwards, and Dogen Zenji." Ph.D. dissertation, University of Minnesota.

Suggests a common thought and language runs through Edwards, John Cotton, and Dogen, the Zen master (1200-1253). All expressed the union of man's finite works with infinite grace in both logical and alogical discourse and in metaphors of unity gathered from the natural world. So Edwards's sense of the heart expresses that union and is perceived in metaphors, derived from Newton and Locke, of the "flowing, unified energy in fountain, sun, and tree."

45 Stuart, Robert Lee. "Jonathan Edwards at Enfield: 'And Oh the Cheerfulness and Pleasantness. . . .'" *American Literature* 48 (March): 46-59.

Corrects the received opinion that Edwards's *Sinners in the Hands of an Angry God* is pure imprecation by analyzing the "element of comfort" at critical points in the architecture of the Enfield sermon and finds a carefully wrought tension between hope and fear there.

46 Sweet, Leonard I. "Letter from Jonathan Edwards." *Theology Today* 33 (July): 193-95.
Publishes an "unauthenticated epistle" by Edwards "from the beyond" dispelling the notion that Puritans had repressive ideas on sex and indicting the "stuffy" Victorians.

47 Waanders, David W. "The Pastoral Sense of Jonathan Edwards." *Reformed Review* 29 (Winter): 124-32.
Claims that Edwards, hardly a pastoral model, dealt chiefly with pastoral problems in his writings, most evidently in *Religious Affections* where he "penetrated to the very core" of pastoral theology. In his psychological analysis of the religious experience, Edwards considered the sense of the heart "a fundamental dimension" of religious affections — what we would call religious attitudes — , the means of apprehending theological realities, and the operative mode of grace. So Edwards designed a personality theory of religious affections where "knowledge had both an objective focus in Scripture and a subjective focus in human experience, in which understanding of human personality was essential to an understanding of genuine religion, and where Christian virtues and conduct occurred within predictable patterns of personality structure shaped by scriptural principles."

48 Weddle, David L. "The Beauty of Faith in Jonathan Edwards." *Ohio Journal of Religious Studies* 4 (October): 42-53.
Questions the view of Roland A. Delattre (1968.8) and William Clebsch (1973.5) that for Edwards beauty is an aesthetic rather than a moral category. Faith is the "vision of, and consent to, the beauty of God," perceived as his moral perfection and expressed as "'visible sanctity'" in the lives of men. Thus Edwards provides a theological gloss to Erik Erikson's discussion of basic trust and mature care in *Childhood and Society:* both thinkers point to a "fundamental congruence, or beauty, in human existence."

49 ———. "The Democracy of Grace: Political Reflections on the Evangelical Theology of Jonathan Edwards." *Dialog: A Journal of Theology* 15 (Autumn): 248-52.
Finds democratic implications in Edwards's evangelical call and millennial hope — for Americans, a new birth into a new age. The Great Awakening underscored national unity and democratic feelings by its "revolutionary" characteristics of universality, antinomianism, and pluralism. Edwards, its chief apologist, is a "test case for a revisionist interpretation of the political implications of evangelical theology."

50 Wessell, Lynn Ray. "The Relation between Religious Enlightenment and Politics in America: 1740-1840." Ph.D. dissertation, Claremont Graduate School.
Links Edwards's concept of disinterested benevolence (and his New Light successors) to the growth of communal morality during the Great Awakening and to the development of equalitarian politics before the Revolution, in a history of the religious enlightenment in America.

51 Westbrook, Robert B. "Social Criticism and the Heavenly City of Jonathan Edwards." *Soundiings* 59 (Winter): 396-412.
Suggests that Edwards's social criticism was "self-consciously normative," arising from his

millennial view that in time man's imperfect society would give way to a community of saints bound to God and each other in disinterested benevolence. His hopes for an imminent heavenly city ended with the Great Awakening, and he had to admit that he would "probably never see it."

52 Wright, Conrad. "The Freedom of the Will." *Unitarianism in America.* Hamden, Conn.: Archon.
    Reprints 1955.12.

53 Youngs, J. William T., Jr. *God's Messengers: Religious Leadership in Colonial New England, 1700-1750.* Baltimore: Johns Hopkins University Press, pp. 130-32.
    Cites Edwards as one of several ministers concerned with the role of a professional and educated clergy during and after the Great Awakening, notably in *True Excellency* (1744), *Church's Marriage* (1746), and *Christ the Great Example* (1750).

54 Zilboorg, Caroline Crawford. "The Speaking Self in American Puritan Literature: A Study in Genre and Rhetorical Continuities." Ph.D. dissertation, University of Wisconsin, Madison.
    Examines the narrative voice of self-assertion in American Puritan texts, Edwards's not-too-successful *Personal Narrative* among them, and suggests later nineteenth-century literary continuities.

1977

1 Ahlstrom, Sydney E. "The Romantic Religion Revolution and the Dilemmas of Religious History." *Church History* 46 (June): 149-70.
    Discovers the mind of a "proto-Romantic" in Edwards's reformulation of Calvinism in a natural context. Edwards took the views of nature of Descartes, Newton, and Locke, joined them to his orthodox faith, and fashioned a pantheism suggestive of Spinoza and Shaftesbury. Edwards's *Personal Narrative* is "testimony" to a rapture common to Romantics but quite unlike Puritan conversion narratives.

2 Batschelet, Margaret Susan. "Jonathan Edwards' Use of Typology: a Historical and Theological Approach." Ph.D. dissertation, University of Washington.
    Suggests that two strains of typology, the "'Pauline'" and the "'Philonic,'" culminate in Edwards and are extended through his unique formulations of perception and reality into the "new and far-reaching" typology of *Images or Shadows*. Edwards uses Philonic typology — fulfillment in the soul of the regenerate, not in Scripture — to free Pauline typology of its Old Testament-New Testament relationship and to posit a typology of the elect, God's glory revealed in natural facts. Thus Edwards frames a "unique vision" of God and creation and regenerate man through typology.

3 Berner, Robert L. "Grace and Works in America: The Role of Jonathan Edwards." *Southern Quarterly* 15 (January): 125-34.
    Attributes Edwards's dismissal to his congregation's shift from a belief in the covenant of grace to a belief in the covenant of works. That shift is simply part of the more general one in America in the eighteenth century from a belief in what men are to what men do and finds expression in the twentieth century in such works as *The Great Gatsby* and *Death of a Salesman*.

But the price of political and social equality is spiritual crisis: "our tragedy" has been that we have bought quantitative success at the expense of the quality of human experience Edwards had insisted upon.

4 Bowden, Henry Warner. "Edwards, Jonathan." *Dictionary of American Religious Biography.* Westport, Conn.: Greenwood Press, pp. 141-43.
    Stresses Edwards's mysticism rather than his doctrinal theology, in a short biography and estimate.

5 Bushman, Richard L. "Jonathan Edwards and Puritan Consciousness." In *Puritan New England: Essays on Religion, Society, and Culture.* Edited by Alden T. Vaughan and Francis J. Bremer. New York: St. Martin's Press, pp. 346-62.
    Reprints 1966.6.

6 ———. "Jonathan Edwards as Great Man." In *Encounter with Erikson: Historical Interpretation and Religious Biography.* Edited by Donald Capps et al. Missoula, Mont.: Scholars Press, pp. 217-52.
    Reprints 1969.5.

6A Carter, Everett. *The American Idea: The Literary Response to American Optimism.* Chapel Hill: University of North Carolina Press, pp. 17-23.
    Ranks Edwards "a mighty opposite" to the idea of America, the national belief in the goodness of man and nature. *Personal Narrative* and *Sinners in the Hands of an Angry God* typify "America's first alienated intellectual."

7 Conforti, Joseph A. "Samuel Hopkins and the New Divinity: Theology, Ethics, and Social Reform in Eighteenth-Century New England." *William and Mary Quarterly,* 3d ser., 34 (October): 572-89.
    Accounts Samuel Hopkins's alteration of Edwards's ethics a response to social and demographic change in mid-eighteenth-century America rather than a sterile exercise in New Divinity metaphysics as it is generally thought to be. Hopkins found "serious flaws" in *True Virtue* — Edwards mixed aesthetics and ethics, yielded to moral rationalists, lacked social dimension — and, therefore, modified it to foster social activism and "self-denying idealism" in an increasingly acquisitive, egocentric nation. His opposition to slavery and the slave trade is the simple consequence of his radical disinterested benevolence.

7A Couser, Griffith Thomas. "American Autobiography: The Prophetic Mode." Ph.D. dissertation, Brown University.
    Published as 1979.3.

8 Davidson, James West. *The Logic of Millennial Thought: Eighteenth-Century New England.* New Haven and London: Yale University Press, pp. 150-60, 166-75, 217-21 passim.
    Traces Edwards's millennial thought chiefly in *Humble Attempt*, "Notes on the Apocalypse," and *History of Redemption* and its consequences for conversion and the social order. Edwards's model for the last days changes somewhat over the years but always manages to combine gloom and hope, "central to the entire millennial rhetoric" of his time. External afflictions and inner conviction — the "crucial factor" — were "inseparable" parts of salvation, but Edwards held that

affliction might be achieved without the literal slaying of the witnesses (Revelations 11:7-12). He saw individual conversion as part of the larger, historical context of redemption — his *History* is New England's "grandest summary of the plan" — but such a view was "simply apolitical in its impact" and had little effect on social reform.

9 Delattre, Roland A. "Beauty and Politics: A Problematic Legacy of Jonathan Edwards." In *American Philosophy from Edwards to Quine*. Edited by Robert W. Shahan and Kenneth R. Merrill. Norman: University of Oklahoma Press, pp. 20-48.

Explores the political implications of Edwards's concept of beauty, discovering in *True Virtue* and *End of Creation* a pattern of divine governance appropriate to a theory of human governance. The political order, like the personal one of virtue, is a kind of beauty based upon "the affectional consent of human beings to the plurality of human beings," in which conflict and quality are resolved collectively and freedom measured by spiritual beauty. As God in creation governs by communicating his beauty and by engendering a cordial response, so men govern responsively in beauty, moving through history toward the kingdom of God. "The constitution of a genuinely political order is a humanly crucial expression of a radically monotheistic commitment and of a cordial consent to the being and the beauty and the beautification of the wider orders of reality within which the modest scope of human responsibility is set."

10 DeProspo, Richard Chris. "Nature and Spirit in the Writings of Jonathan Edwards." Ph.D. dissertation, University of Virginia.

Examines Edwards on creation, providence, and grace in order to show how he consistently reconciled the secular philosophy of the Enlightenment with the conservative theology of Calvinism "without falsifying either."

11 Douglas, Ann. *The Feminization of American Culture*. New York: Alfred A. Knopf, p. 74 passim.

Compares Edwards's strictness as a father to parental authority models a century later, in an examination of the change from the intellectual rigor of eighteenth-century Edwardseans to their popular, sentimental, and feminized nineteenth-century counterparts.

12 Ehle, Carl Frederick, Jr. "Prolegomena to Christian Zionism in America: The Views of Increase Mather and William E. Blackstone concerning the Doctrine of the Restoration of Israel." Ph.D. dissertation, New York University.

Places Edwards in an almost unbroken line of American millennialists seeking the restoration of the Jews to Palestine as a prelude to the second coming of Christ.

13 Emerson, Everett. *Puritanism in America, 1620-1750*. Twayne's World Leaders Series. Boston: Twayne Publishers, pp. 148-50.

Cites Edwards's role in the revivals, his leadership in shattering Congregational unity, and his effect upon a declining Puritanism in America. Though influenced by such Puritans as Thomas Shepard and Thomas Hooker, Edwards's thought, an amalgam of Calvinism and the Enlightenment, is "so original that it is misleading to call him a Puritan."

*14 Erdt, Terrence. "Jonathan Edwards on Art and the Sense of the Heart." Ph.D. dissertation, University of California, Santa Barbara.

Published (revised) as 1980.11.

14A Flower, Elizabeth, and Murray G. Murphey. "Jonathan Edwards." *A History of Philosophy in America*. New York: G. P. Putnam's Sons, 1:137-99 passim.

Emphasizes Edwards's early (and lasting) idealism, in a three-part examination of "the greatest American theologian and the greatest American philosopher before the Civil War." Although Edwards was "primarily" a theologian and saw philosophy as a "handmaid," he fashioned a "unique" and "impressive" philosophical synthesis out of the "unlikely combination of traditional Ramist Calvinism, Newtonian science, Cartesian logic, and Lockean epistemology." Thus Edwards's ideal world, already obvious in "The Mind," develops from Locke's theory of ideas, modified in part by Newtonian atomism and in whole by God as the only substance and the first cause. His doctrine of excellency, a corollary to his idealism and a "highly plausible aesthetic," records the moral nature of God — his being, beauty, consent, benevolence, virtue, love — and a "daring" theory of the Trinity — love of God for himself constitutes the third person. For Edwards, then, to love God was to share his excellency; to read nature (typologically) was to restore his immediacy.

15 Fye, Kenneth Paul. "Jonathan Edwards on Freedom of the Will." Ph.D. dissertation, Boston University.

Locates the central premise of Edwards's *Freedom of the Will* in his argument of the causal principle or universal determinism. In Edwards, universal determinism and absolute determinism are "functionally equivalent, equally implausible, and . . . irrevocably tied" to the Calvinism he defended against Arminian attack.

16 Greven, Philip. *The Protestant Temperament: Patterns of Child-Rearing, Religious Experience, and the Self in Early America*. New York: Alfred A. Knopf, pp. 31-34, 62-71, 75-81, 99-102, 127-33 passim.

Cites Edwards as an example of the self-suppressed evangelical, in a study of three patterns and continuities of Protestant temperament (moderate and genteel are the others) derived from modes of child-rearing and attitudes towards self, passion, power, sexuality, and piety. Like other evangelicals, Edwards abases the self and denies the body in the quest for a new birth; governs his family by authoritarian means, just as he willingly submits to the absolute sovereignty and power of God; suppresses anger and hostility beneath "a facade of compliance and obedience"; and, though he asserts the superiority of men and harbors a fear of women, implies that to be saved (as the bride of Christ) men have "to cease being masculine." And like other evangelicals, Edwards was a purist, in life, in the church and community, and in piety.

17 Hatch, Nathan O. *The Sacred Cause of Liberty: Republican Thought and the Millennium in Revolutionary New England*. New Haven and London: Yale University Press, pp. 24-36, 170-73.

Contrasts Edwards's apocalyptic expectations of the Great Awakening with the "civil millennialism" of the Revolution — the hope of conversion and religious piety of the one, the hope of victory and religious liberty of the other. Although Edwards thought the millennium would probably begin in America, the decline of piety after the Awakening led him, in *Humble Attempt*, to seek a transatlantic union and a broader apocalyptic vision through a concert of prayer. Even later millennialists like Lyman Beecher, despite their claims, show "little resemblance to Edwards's apolitical millennialism."

18 Keller, Karl. "Alephs, Zahirs, and the Triumph of Ambiguity: Typology in Nineteenth-Century American Literature." In *Literary Uses of Typology: from the Late*

Middle Ages to the Present. Edited by Earl Miner. Princeton, N.J.: Princeton University Press, pp. 274-314.

Finds Edwards's (and Cotton Mather's) use of plebeian types — allegorizing things personal or spiritualizing things natural — "at the heart" of nineteenth-century American literature. The construct of type to antitype, common in Edwards's formulation, remains in Emerson, Thoreau, Hawthorne, Melville, and Whitman, though they confuse and misuse the terms and all but abandon its theology.

19 Kimnach, Wilson H. "Jonathan Edwards' Early Sermons: New York, 1722-1723." *Journal of Presbyterian History* 55 (Fall): 255-56.

Examines Edwards's unpublished sermons of his New York stay to document his theological development and his preaching experience. The sermons, linked by their common concern for the experiential basis of the Christian life, "clearly anticipate" the work of the 1730s. Although they show a "naivete and rustic vitality," the sermons are marked by a gifted, concrete imagination and quite often the "hortatory dimension is overshadowed by the poetically evocative."

20 Lowance, Mason I., Jr. "Typology and Millennial Eschatology in Early New England." In *Literary Uses of Typology: from the Late Middle Ages to the Present.* Edited by Earl Miner. Princeton, N.J.: Princeton University Press, pp. 228-73.

Discovers in Edwards's use of typology an "original epistemology" — Scripture joined to the Book of Nature, prophecy to millennial utopianism — in an examination of Edwards's unpublished writings on types and *History of Redemption.* Edwards extends types and relationships beyond the traditional figures of the Old and New Testaments to embrace the revelation of divine images in nature and, through progressive prophetic fulfillment, in contemporary history as well. In setting the millennium before the apocalypse, Edwards provides a "radical justification" for the Great Awakening and for an emergent nationalism.

21 Manor, James. "The Coming of Britain's Age of Empire and Protestant Mission Theology, 1750-1839." *Zeitschrift für Missionswissenschaft und Religionswissenschaft* 61 (January): 38-54.

Calls Edwards a "major" influence for foreign missionary zeal in Great Britain in the late eighteenth and early nineteenth centuries. His *Humble Attempt* and *Life of Brainerd* aided in the missionary awakening early on, but succeeding generations were caught up in his eschatological vision and his insistence upon immediate conversion. "Edwards' theocentricity, known existentially, opened the way for the anthropocentrism of the later generations of evangelicals seeking to come to terms with humanistic trends of their time."

22 Marty, Martin E. *Religion, Awakening and Revolution.* Faith of Our Fathers, no. 4. Wilmington, N.C.: Consortium Books, pp. 68-69, 107 passim.

Cites Edwards's surprise, recorded in *Faithful Narrative,* to support the view that the Awakening was "largely unintended and accidental" and comments on his millennial expectations.

23 Mead, Sidney E. *The Old Religion in the Brave New World: Reflections on the Relation between Christendom and the Republic.* Berkeley: University of California Press, pp. 51-54.

Notes that the theology of Edwards (and other revivalists) "legitimated the privatization" of religion, undermined institutional churches, and inadvertently contributed to the revolution against all constituted authority. Unlike earlier Puritans, there is little in Edwards about social or political responsibility or theory.

24 Miller, Perry, ed. *Images or Shadows of Divine Things.* Westport, Conn.: Greenwood Press.

Reprints 1948.7.

24A Parker, David L. Review of *The Writings of Jonathan Edwards,* by William J. Scheick. *William and Mary Quarterly,* 3d ser., 34 (January): 169-70.

Predicts that the historian will be disappointed at the "rehashing of doctrinal issues" and the literary scholar at the lack of "sustained attention to artistic matters," in a review of William Scheick's introduction to Edwards (1975.16).

25 Pudaloff, Ross J. "The Imposition of the Garden: Nature and the Natural in Early American Literature." Ph.D. dissertation, State University of New York at Buffalo.

Cites Edwards's *Sinners in the Hands of an Angry God* as a "striking example" of an anti-pastoral, in a survey of three versions of pastoral in America, those of Byrd, Jefferson, and Thoreau.

26 Rutman, Darrett B., ed. *The Great Awakening: Event and Exegesis.* Huntington, N.Y.: Robert E. Kreiger Publishing Co.

Reprints 1970.33.

26A Schafer, Thomas A. Review of *The Writings of Jonathan Edwards,* by William J. Scheick. *Journal of Religion* 57 (July): 323-24.

Concludes that William J. Scheick's study (1975.16) "cannot be endorsed as a reliable guide to Edwards's works or interpretation of his thought."

27 Shea, Daniel B., Jr. "The Art and Instruction of Jonathan Edwards's *Personal Narrative.*" In *Puritan New England: Essays on Religion, Society, and Culture.* Edited by Alden T. Vaughan and Francis J. Bremer. New York: St. Martin's Press, pp. 299-311.

Reprints 1965.18.

28 Stein, Stephen J. "Editor's Introduction." *Apocalyptic Writings: "Notes on the Apocalypse" and An Humble Attempt. The Works of Jonathan Edwards,* 5. New Haven and London: Yale University Press, pp. 1-93.

Traces the apocalyptic tradition, the development of Edwards's "Notes on the Apocalypse" and its effect on his ministry and his millennialism, his theory of the apocalypse and his sources (Moses Lowman, Matthew Poole, and Humphrey Prideaux among them), and the provenance of the text and the related *Humble Attempt,* in an introduction to the fifth volume of the Yale Edwards. During his New York pastorate Edwards began a series of comments on Revelation in his "Theological Miscellanies"; in 1723 he started a separate notebook on the apocalypse; in 1739 he delivered a series of sermons on the redemption, "prima facie evidence" of his apocalyptic concerns; in 1743 he revealed in *Some Thoughts* a public and "atypical" commitment to millennialism; in 1748 he opened even more his private speculations on the coming of the kingdom in *Humble Attempt;* in 1757, in his letter to the Princeton trustees, he wrote of his plan for a systematic theology based in part on apocalyptic materials of a lifetime. Thus Edwards's continuing thought about the apocalypse reveals an "intriguing and complex, but sometimes contradictory," mix of a speculative, private record and a discreet, public one.

29 ———. "Quest for the Spiritual Sense: the Biblical Hermeneutics of Jonathan Edwards." *Harvard Theological Review* 70 (January): 99-113.

Finds that Edwards's biblical hermeneutics goes beyond the literal interpretation of traditional, Reformed exegesis to a "multiplicity of levels," in an investigation of the manuscript "Miscellanies" and "Blank Bible." Throughout his life Edwards "strenuously resisted" challenges to the authority and centrality of the Bible mounted by rationalists, enthusiasts, and Roman Catholics, and at his death left unfinished projects of that commitment in *History of Redemption* and *The Harmony of the Old and New Treatment*. His hermeneutics emphasizes the necessity of a spiritual, in addition to a literal, sense of the biblical text, a spiritual understanding that comes from the efficacious working of grace as process and product and results in multiple interpretations based on symbol and metaphor, typology and allegory.

30 Strout, Cushing. "Young People of the Great Awakening: The Dynamics of a Social Movement." In *Encounter with Erikson: Historical Interpretation and Religious Biography*. Edited by Donald Capps et al. Missoula, Mont.: Scholars Press, pp. 183-216.

Cites Edwards's generational status and the young converts of *Faithful Narrative* as important elements in the psychology and sociology of the revivals.

31 Tracy, Patricia Juneau. "Jonathan Edwards, Pastor: Minister and Congregation in the Eighteenth-Century Connecticut Valley." Ph.D. dissertation, University of Massachusetts.

Attributes Edwards's failure as pastor, his inability to persuade his flock "to share his vision," to his lack of ministerial training, his father's losing struggle for power, his grandfather's overwhelming example, and Northampton's (and society's) growing rejection of ministerial authority. Edwards's revivalist spirit assured his position for a time, but after 1742 his disagreement with his congregation on matters of discipline and admission was so profound that they abandoned his "vision of holiness" and forced him to leave. Published (revised) as 1980.45.

32 Wilson, John F. "Jonathan Edwards as Historian." *Church History* 46 (March): 5-18.

Uses Edwards's *History of Redemption*, "a homely but remarkable set of sermons, as an example of religious history writing and as the generic problem it presents. History, for Edwards and church historians generally, is the "basic modality of individual and collective existence," founded upon the singularly important redemptive process and meaning and couched in scriptural types and prophecies. Peter Gay and his critically antiquated Edwards (1966.14) and Perry Miller and his spiritually modern Edwards (1949.9) both do him and his *History of Redemption* "less than justice."

33 ———. "Jonathan Edwards's Notebooks for 'A History of the Work of Redemption.'" In *Reformation Conformity and Dissent: Essays in Honour of Geoffrey Nuttall*. Edited by R. Buick Knox. London: Epworth Press, pp. 239-54.

Examines the physical characteristics and the content of three notebooks Edwards arranged in preparation for his *History of Redemption* and concludes, on the basis of internal evidence, correlative material, and ink analysis, that he began "serious and concerted" work no earlier than spring 1755 and continued into summer 1757. If this is so, then three broader conclusions are possible: one, the *History* represents his "synthesized interests, resources, and issues" of the great work of the Stockbridge years; two, his letter to the Princeton trustees should be "read quite literally" as a genuine expression of his concerns and intentions; and three, the prospective work was a "theological programme" giving promise of "the fullest flowering of the English Reformed theological tradition."

34 Wilson-Kastner, Patricia. "Jonathan Edwards: History and the Covenant." *Andrews University Seminary Studies* 15 (Autumn): 205-16.

Compares Edwards's view of individual salvation and historic redemption with that of his English and American forebears and concludes that he rejects the covenant argument of the Puritans for the determinist one of Calvin. Edwards holds that grace (or the Holy Spirit) is the "sole determining factor" for salvation in the individual and that redemptive history is simply the action of grace in time: human autonomy in individuals and in history finds no place in Edwards's scheme. Just as each saint expresses the glory of God, so history is determined by it totally and particularly.

1978

1 Anon. Review of Jonathan Edwards, *Apocalyptic Writings*, edited by Stephen J. Stein. *American Literature* 49 (January): 676.

Recommends Stephen Stein's "learnedly and effectively edited" Edwards text (1977.28).

2 Banta, Martha. *Failure and Success in America: A Literary Debate.* Princeton, N.J.: Princeton University Press, pp. 124-25, 299-301.

Notes that Edwards, "God's historian of cause and effect," was able to transcend sinfulness and suffering through public profession and thus, like Henry Adams and Norman Mailer, turn failure into success.

2A Battilana, Marilla. *Il tranello diabolico: Arti visive nella letteratura americana.* Venice: Neri Pozza, pp. 61-66.

Notes Edwards's concept of beauty in his theology, in a study of the visual arts — "the devil's trap" — in American literature. (In Italian.)

3 Bercovitch, Sacvan. *The American Jeremiad.* Madison: University of Wisconsin Press.

Reprints 1978.4 (with additions).

4 ———. "The Typology of America's Mission." *American Quarterly* 30 (Summer): 135-55.

Traces Edwards's eschatology of America's mission to seventeenth-century millennialists and their union of secular history and the sacred prophecy of errand. Edwards differs from most Puritans in that he believes the apocalypse will come after a golden age rather than before it — a post-millennial idea of progress and gradual fulfillment — but, for the most part, he "simply drew out the implications" of their thought and "adopted wholesale" their vision of America. What he contributes is a logical, consistently worked-out scheme, emphasizing the corporate, not the individual, mission.

4A Berkowitz, M. S. "Religion and Irreligion in America: From Edwards to Melville." *Canadian Review of American Studies* 9 (Fall): 185-91.

Draws "almost a straight line" between Edwards and Melville on the apocalypse, in an essay-review of the fifth volume of the Yale Edwards (1977.28) and *Moby-Dick and Calvinism* (1977), by T. Walter Herbert, Jr.

4B Boller, Paul F., Jr. "Jonathan Edwards and the Free-Will Question." *Freedom and Fate in American Thought from Edwards to Dewey.* Bicentennial Series in American Studies, 7. Dallas: Southern Methodist University Press, 3-27.

Calls Edwards a necessitarian, not a fatalist, in a study of nine American writers on freedom and fate. The "main point" of *Freedom of the Will* is psychological and secular, though the last part "stresses" theology: Edwards "felt obliged to relate it to the Christian religion." Predestination was not a submissive doctrine, as his critics held, but an "animating" faith, giving to the universe structure and purpose, to life "profound meaning" and "cosmic significance."

4C Bryant, M. Darrol. "Unification Eschatology and American Millennial Traditions: Continuities and Discontinuities." In *A Time for Consideration: A Scholarly Appraisal of the Unification Church.* Edited by M. Darrol Bryant and Herbert W. Richardson. New York: Edwin Mellen, pp. 261-73.

Asserts that the millennialism "central" to Edwards and the Great Awakening shaped both an American tradition and the eschatology of the Unification Church.

4D Buell, Lawrence E. "Calvinism Romanticized: Harriet Beecher Stowe, Samuel Hopkins, and *The Minister's Wooing.*" *ESQ* 24 (3d Quarter): 119-32.

Surveys the aesthetic uses of Calvinist orthodoxy in Harriet Beecher Stowe's historical romance *The Minister's Wooing* (1859): the titular hero of the novel is Samuel Hopkins, Edwards's "most controversial" disciple; its "vital center," Hopkins's doctrine of holiness, the disinterested benevolence of Edwards's *True Virtue.*

4E Burich, Keith R. "Images of the Sun in Jonathan Edwards' Theology." In *Helios: From Myth to Solar Energy.* Compiled by M. E. Grenander. The Institute for Humanistic Studies. Albany: State University of New York, pp. 92-99.

Points out that Edwards "consistently" uses the sun — in its rising and setting, its light and heat, its progress and colors — as a type of Christ.

5 Bushman, Richard L. "Jonathan Edwards as Great Man." In *Religion in American History.* Edited by John N. Mulder and John F. Wilson. Englewood Cliffs, N.J.: Prentice-Hall, pp. 105-24.

Reprints 1969.5.

5A Cecchini, Angelo. "Jonathan Edwards' System of Theology and Its 'Contemporariness.'" *Studi filosofici e pedagogici* 2:81-106.

Recommends Edwards to contemporary readers to help them out of their existential "sad lot," in "the first really brief but thorough delineation" of his theology.

6 Crawford, Michael J. "The Invention of the American Revival: The Beginnings of Anglo-American Religious Revivalism, 1690-1750." Ph.D. dissertation, Boston University.

Traces the evolution of religious revivalism to its common evangelical sources in America,

England, and Scotland, and notes Edwards's connection to the developed "network" of revival thought and action.

6A Crumpacker, Laurie. "Esther Burr's Journal, 1754-1757: A Document of Evangelical Sisterhood." Ph.D. dissertation, Boston University.
Published as 1984.18.

7 Erdt, Terrence. "The Calvinist Psychology of the Heart and the 'Sense' of Jonathan Edwards." *Early American Literature* 13 (Fall): 165-80.
Finds in the "standard lexicon" of Calvinist piety, not in the sensationalism of Locke, the source of Edwards's sense of the heart, sweetness, and excellency. Calvin's psychology of the heart and the will informs Edwards's view of regeneration as it does those of earlier Puritans, William Ames and Thomas Hooker among them, and does so, contrary to Perry Miller, "without reduction to rationalism."

7A Fiering, Norman S. "Benjamin Franklin and the Way to Virtue." *American Quarterly* 30 (Summer): 199-223.
Argues that Edwards would be "alarmed" by Franklin's proposal of virtue founded on habit because it lacked the "divine infusion" necessary to a change of heart.

8 Gäbler, Ulrich. "Die Anfänge der Erweckungsbewegung in Neu-England und Jonathan Edwards, 1734/1735." *Theologische Zeitschrift* 34 (March): 95-104.
Attributes the beginning of revivalism in New England to Edwards's active encouragement of youthful conversions and his graphic description of them, in an account of *Faithful Narrative* and its effects. The revivals of 1734 and 1735 prepared the way for the Great Awakening five years later; fostered a spirit of unity and independence among the people, perhaps for the first time in their colonial past; and convinced Edwards of America's unique place in the scheme of redemption. (In German.)

9 Gaustad, Edwin S. Review of Jonathan Edwards, *Apocalyptic Writings,* edited by Stephen J. Stein. *Journal of American History* 65 (June): 108-109.
Praises Stephen Stein's "diligence, thoroughness, and prodigious scholarship" in his edition of Edwards's particularly difficult manuscript text (1977.28).

9A Gerstner, John H. "The Church's Doctrine of Biblical Inspiration." In *The Foundation of Biblical Authority.* Edited by James Montgomery Boise. Grand Rapids, Mich.: Zondervan, pp. 23-58.
Includes Edwards among those testifying to biblical inerrancy: "That Scripture was inerrant for Jonathan Edwards no one who has ever read his works, especially his sermons, can doubt."

9B Grabo, Norman. "Colonial American Theology: Holiness and the Lyric Impulse." In *Essays in Honor of Russel B. Nye.* Edited by Joseph Waldheim. East Lansing: Michigan State University Press, pp. 74-91.
Contends that Edwards "prepared the way" for nineteenth-century American literature by rendering the complexity of human character, by giving "theological sanction" to emotion, and by probing appearance and reality in a moral world. Following the tradition, established by Thomas Shepard and exemplified by Edward Taylor, Edwards "enunciated its psychological and aesthetic potential" for later, greater writers.

10 Gura, Philip F. "Sowing for the Harvest: William Williams and the Great Awakening." *Journal of Presbyterian History* 56 (Winter): 326-41.

Argues that William Williams, pastor at Hatfield, Massachusetts, and uncle of Edwards, "played an important part" preparing the Connecticut Valley for Solomon Stoddard's harvests and Edwards's surprising conversions through his doctrinal and evangelical work.

11 Heimert, Alan. "The Great Awakening as Watershed." In *Religion in American History: Interpretive Essays.* Edited by John M. Mulder and John F. Wilson. Englewood Cliffs, N.J.: Prentice-Hall, pp. 127-44.

Reprints excerpts from 1966.17 (editors' title).

12 Hutch, Richard A. "Jonathan Edwards' Analysis of Religious Experience." *Journal of Psychology and Theology* 6 (Spring): 123-31.

Appraises Edwards's analysis of religious experience — *Faithful Narrative, Distinguishing Marks, Some Thoughts,* and *Religious Affections* — in its cultural, historical, psychological, and theological contexts, and concludes that it is an "integrated experience of seizure," expressing itself in the inclination of the heart. True religion, for Edwards, was a matter of the affections, "a unique meeting and blending of both heat and light."

12A Jamieson, John Franklin. "Jonathan Edwards and the Renewal of the Stoddardean Controversy." Ph.D. dissertation, University of Chicago.

See 1981.18.

13 Jones, Charles Edwin. "The Impolitic Mr. Edwards: The Personal Dimension of the Robert Breck Affair." *New England Quarterly* 51 (March): 64-79.

Details the Robert Breck affair, Edwards's role in it, and the effect upon his dismission. At the behest of his uncle, William Williams, Edwards wrote a "ferocious apologetic" — *A Letter to the Author of the Pamphlet Called an Answer to the Hampshire Narrative* (1737) — in defense of that lost cause nearly two years after the fact. Nine years later, Breck, now a senior member of the ecclesiastical council called to hear the Edwards's affair, cast the decisive ballot for his dismissal.

13A Kane, J. Herbert. *A Concise History of the Christian World Mission: A Panoramic View of Missions from Pentecost to the Present.* Grand Rapids, Mich.: Baker Book House, pp. 84-87.

Cites Edwards's influence on William Carey, "the father of modern missions," and Andover Seminary, the "fountainhead" of evangelicalism in New England and missions overseas.

13B McLoughlin, William G. *Revivals, Awakenings, and Reform: An Essay on Religion and Social Change in America, 1607-1977.* Chicago History of American Religion. Chicago: University of Chicago Press, pp. 70-78 passim.

Notes the effect Edwards and the Great Awakening had upon "the powerless and the poor" and the subsequent creation of "a new social ethic," in a study of reform and revivalism in America.

14 Marini, Stephen A. Review of Jonathan Edwards, *Apocalyptic Writings,* edited by Stephen J. Stein. *New England Quarterly* 51 (September): 444-46.

Questions Stephen Stein's reading of Edwards's apocalyptic writings (1977.28) as "unconsummated intellectual passion": the texts both demonstrate Edwards's method of turning theological theory to ecclesiastical practice and explain the scriptural basis for his political vision.

14A Marsden, George. Review of *The Prism of Scripture,* by Karl Dieterich Pfisterer. *Church History* 47 (March): 87-88.
Uncovers "little that is new" in Karl Pfisterer's study of history in Edwards (1975.13).

15 Murphy, Susan. "In Remembrance of Me: Sacramental Theology and Practice in Colonial New England." Ph.D. dissertation, University of Washington.
Traces the doctrine of the covenant in New England theology from its Old Testament and Reformed sources to the half-way measures of the late seventeenth century to Edwards's communion practices, a return full-circle.

15A Nettles, Tom. Review of *The Works of Jonathan Edwards,* 1-5. *Southwestern Journal of Theology* 21 (Fall): 102-104.
Grades the first five volumes of the Yale Edwards (1957.14; 1959.18; 1970.15; 1972.11; 1977.28) "excellent from all standpoints — subject matter, scholarship, and appearance."

15B Petersen, Rodney L. Review of Jonathan Edwards, *Apocalyptic Writings,* edited by Stephen J. Stein. *Princeton Seminary Bulletin,* n.s., 1 (4): 309-11.
Values Stephen J. Stein's introduction to the fifth volume of the Yale Edwards (1977.28) as "an important chapter in the ongoing revision of Edwardsian scholarship."

16 Piper, John. "Jonathan Edwards on the Problem of Faith and History." *Scottish Journal of Theology* 31 (June): 217-28.
Considers Edwards's view on faith and history, expressed in *Religious Affections,* in terms of the current discussion of historical criticism and finds he is able to "hold together" the reasonableness and the spirituality of saving faith whereas contemporary theologians cannot. Edwards encourages historical argument for the truth of the gospel, recognizes its limitations — most men are incapable of historical analysis — but insists that faith must have "a just ground for certainty" if it is to be saving.

17 ———. "A Personal Encounter with Jonathan Edwards." *Reformed Journal* 28 (November): 13-17.
Narrates an academic theologian's three personal encounters with Edwards's work (before, during, and after seminary) and concludes that *Freedom of the Will* is "one of the world's greatest books," that *End of Creation* "captures the essence" of Edwards's theology, and that *Religious Affections* is "a very contemporary and helpful message."

17A Quinn, Philip L. "Some Problems about Resurrection." *Religious Studies* 14 (September): 343-59.
Rejects Edwards's doctrine of continuous creation in *Original Sin* because it "fails" to distinguish personal identity in time and "destroys" any hope of resurrection.

17B Sklar, Kathryn Kish. "Culture vs. Economics: A Case of Fornication in Northampton in the 1740s." *University of Michigan Papers in Women Studies* (May): 35-56.
Takes a "microscopic view" of a trial of fornication — the bastard birth within the propertied Hawley family — and Edwards's role in it. At a civil trial in May 1748, Martha Root received a set-

tlement of £155 from Elisha Hawley; later that year, the First Church voted to excommunicate him for not marrying her; but in June 1749, a Council of Ministers reversed Edwards's finding, his "innovative defense" before it that the payment was inadequate to the damage Elisha had done. That the Council's rebuff of Edwards was "thoroughly enmeshed in the politics of his dismissal" is evident in Joseph Hawley's leading part in it.

17C Spohn, William Costelloe. "Religion and Morality in the Thought of Jonathan Edwards." Ph.D. dissertation, University of Chicago.

> See 1981.32 and 1983.47.

18 Stein, Stephen J. "Providence and the Apocalypse in the Early Writings of Jonathan Edwards." *Early American Literature* 13 (Winter): 250-67.

> Locates the organizing focus of Edwards's comments on the four beasts of Revelation 4 in the theme of providence, in an examination of his early comments on the Apocalypse in "Theological Miscellanies," "Notes on Scripture," and "Notes on the Apocalypse," all written before mid-1724. The results of such an investigation of the manuscripts should caution scholars against "a monothematic portrayal" of Edwards's eschatological thought. Providence is "central" to Edwards (and to Reformed theology generally) and provides a "richer" theological construct than millennialism.

19 Stokes, Anson Phelps. *Memorials of Eminent Yale Men.* Northford, Conn.: Elliot's Books.

> Reprints 1914.5.

19A Tuveson, Ernest. Review of *The Logic of Millennial Thought*, by James West Davidson, and Jonathan Edwards, *Apocalyptic Writings*, edited by Stephen J. Stein. *William and Mary Quarterly*, 3d ser., 35 (October): 758-61.

> Remarks the "failure" of Edwards — "that archetypal millennialist thinker" — to reconcile the city of man with the city of God, in a review two works on the millennium (1977.8 and 1977.28).

19B Weber, Donald. Review of Jonathan Edwards, *Apocalyptic Writings*, edited by Stephen J. Stein. *Early American Literature* 13 (Spring): 142-44.

> Praises Stephen J. Stein's volume in the Yale Edwards (1977.28) for its "illuminating" introduction and its "scrupulous" editing.

20 ———. "The Image of Jonathan Edwards in American Culture." Ph.D. dissertation, Columbia University.

> Unravels the history of the image and meaning of Edwards for American culture by tracing the impact of his work and person on his contemporaries and "guardians" in the eighteenth century (Hopkins and Bellamy), his defenders and detractors in the nineteenth (Finney and Bancroft, Stowe and Holmes), and his rejection and restoration in the twentieth (Parrington and Miller). Edwards has "enraged and inspired" his interpreters over two centuries of American cultural history.

21 Weddle, David L. Review of Jonathan Edwards, *Apocalyptic Writings*, edited by Stephen J. Stein. *Journal of Religion* 58 (October): 437-39.

Praises Stephen Stein's "insightful" introduction to an important Edwards manuscript (1977.28).

22 Willard, Malinda Kaye. "Jonathan Edwards and Nathaniel Hawthorne: Themes from the Common Consciousness." Ph.D. dissertation, University of South Carolina.

Attributes the similarity of themes in Edwards and Hawthorne to their commonly shared New England mind, a synthesis of Augustinian piety and Calvinist dogma. Thus the reconciliation of fate and freedom is treated in both *Freedom of the Will* and *The Scarlet Letter;* the portrait of fallen man in *Original Sin* and *The Marble Faun,* of redeemed man in *Divine and Supernatural Light* and *The House of Seven Gables;* and the discrepancy between appearance and reality in man in *Religious Affections* and *The Blithedale Romance,* in nature (as symbolism) in *Images or Shadows* and the tales.

23 Wilson-Kastner, Patricia. *Coherence in a Fragmented World: Jonathan Edwards' Theology of the Holy Spirit.* Washington, D.C.: University Press of America, ix, 80 pp.

Focusses upon Edwards's unifying theology of the Holy Spirit, "a model of clarity and balance," in a study of the workings of the Spirit in his religious milieu, in conversion, and in grace, and of its effects upon personal change, social ethics, and millennial expectation. His theology demands that "we turn ourselves inside out," making God and the mystery of his relationship the center of life. Edwards held that true religion came from each man's personal relation with God, that his responsibility to all other men arose from his service to God, and that America was destined to be "a servant of God's glory in the world."

24 ———. "God's Infinity and His Relationship to Creation in the Theologies of Gregory of Nyssa and Jonathan Edwards." *Foundations* 21 (October): 305-21.

Contrasts the notions of divine infinity in Gregory of Nyssa and Edwards and their effect on the nature of God's creativity, man's freedom, and necessity, and suggests that Edwards's theological system becomes "more comprehensible" as an adaptation of Gregory's Christian Neoplatonism. Gregory's God is "absolutely satisfied in his own society"; Edwards's God is neither free nor sufficient inasmuch as his internal glory is dependent upon external exercise. Human freedom, for Edwards, is "bounded" by God's necessity to create; for Gregory a "free God" freely creates men who freely choose. Although there is no evidence to show that Edwards ever read Gregory first hand — he probably learned of him from Puritan writers, his Yale tutor, and the Cambridge Platonists — there is in Edwards a "very real, though mediated dependence" upon Gregory.

PART II

1979–1993

Introduction

In his keynote address to the Wheaton conference on Jonathan Edwards in the fall of 1984, Henry F. May cites the doubling of dissertations about him in the decades since 1940 as "intriguing" evidence of his durability (1988.17). By that calculation, Edwards is alive and well, if graying. Not surprisingly, the number of dissertations has fallen off — to fifty or so in each of the decades since the sixties from the eighty of geometric forecast — but interest has not. During the years covered by the present survey, the number of conferences on Edwards has tripled over the previous fifteen years, from one (a symposium) to three; the number of books has more than doubled, from eighteen to thirty-eight, including one in Italian (1980.9) and one in French (1987.34); and the number of volumes in the Yale definitive edition has doubled, from three to six. Such an inventory suggests that as Edwards continues to be the object of an almost relentless pursuit, he remains elusive as ever, even as the net widens. In a replay of the quarrel over Edwards's modernity, Norman Fiering binds him to British and continental moral philosophy in one remarkable study (1981.10) only to have Robert W. Jenson free him to become America's theologian in another (1988.22). The same year that Bruce Kuklick links churchmen like Edwards to philosophers like John Dewey (1985.26), R. C. DeProspo deconstructs the whole humanist enterprise attending both Edwards and "'America'" (1985.9). And, in a renewal of the dispute over territorial rights, Iain H. Murray in his long biography (1987.22) and John H. Gerstner in his longer theology (1991.10, 1992.4, and 1993.7) wrest Edwards from the academy and restore him to the church. As Professor May remarks, Edwards seems "inexhaustible and impossible to pin down."

Doctoral searches after him go on as before but, in keeping with broadening concerns, often end elsewhere. If Edwards's influence on Joseph Bellamy (1980.1 and 1985.54), Emily Dickinson (1986.38), William James (1979.30 and 1987.13), and John Wesley (1990.48) seems a twice-told tale, his connection to Mary Baker Eddy (1983.18), J. Edwin Orr (1991.33), and Friedrich Schleiermacher (1992.6) freshens the story somewhat, though a pair of dissertations on Timothy Dwight muddles it, one arguing for Edwards's influence (1983.56), the other against it (1986.12). Inquiries after his Trinitarianism continue, but now it is not a question of its orthodoxy so much as a matter of relationships, to his ecclesial ideal (1986.34) or to the mystical element of his faith (1990.41). His apocalyptic piety appears now to be part of the Franciscan tradition (1982.40), his vision of the moral life formally similar to that of Thomas Aquinas (1991.24); *Religious Affections* serves both as a comfort to a wretched New Hampshire minister (1981.39) and a model for renewal for contemporary churches (1991.3). One student discovers him among the gods and related minor deities of the Connecticut Valley (1986.43), another follows generations of Edwardses, father, son, and grandson (1988.30); others gauge his pneumatology (1988.37 and 1988.42) and soteriology (1986.49 and 1991.30); still others stretch him to embrace participative (1980.3) but not process theology (1983.3), to attribute to him the success of Particular Baptists in Britain (1991.13) as well as the failure of the ABCFM mission in Oregon (1991.25).

Of the ninety-one dissertations listed, thirteen were published, four were written by doctoral candidates abroad (Aberdeen, Keele, Pontifical Gregorian, and Strasbourg), and eighteen were the work of seminarians. Four dissertations from an earlier period were also published, one after a lapse of thirty-six years. In *The Young Jonathan Edwards: A Reconstruction* (1991.32), a Chicago dissertation of nearly 700 pages (1955.6), William Sparkes Morris explains how the young Edwards came to think what he did, from his years at home and at Yale to his months in New York, and how he integrated his theology and philosophy. Morris declares that the major part of Edwards's metaphysics derives from the Dutch scholastic Calvinists and logicians, Franciscus Burgersdicius and Adrian Heereboord. Predictably, other readers disagree.

Wallace E. Anderson and Wilson H. Kimnach track much the same development in their respective volumes of *The Works of Jonathan Edwards* and come up with different sources of influence. In *Scientific and Philosophical Writings* (1980.2), the sixth in the Yale series, Anderson traces Edwards's early speculations on natural philosophy and the structure of being, space, and mind; prints fair texts of them; and attributes the immaterialism and immediacy in them to the Cambridge Platonist Henry More, ideas which remain "fixed centers" of his philosophy, though "reshaped significantly" later on. Anderson claims that the traditional dates of Edwards's juvenilia are "quite mistaken": "Of Insects," for example, dates from 1719 or 1720, not 1715; that "The Soul" is spurious: the work of his sister Esther, as Kenneth P. Minkema has shown (1990.37); and, joining endless controversy, that his debt to John Locke's *An Essay Concerning Human Understanding* is overstated: he rejected or "consciously" modified its "express claims." In *Sermons and Discourses, 1720-1723* (1992.8), the tenth in the series, Kimnach approaches the young Edwards through the (manuscript) sermons of the New York period, recounting his early reading and its effect upon them. Though Edwards had not yet mastered the triadic form by the time he returned to Yale as tutor, the twenty-three sermons published here reveal an "intensely imaginative apprehension" of the Puritan rhetorical tradition, exemplified in the practices of his father and his grand-father Solomon Stoddard, embodied in preaching manuals like John Edwards's *The Preacher* (1702), and invigorated by the concepts, terminology, and phrasing found in *Select Discourses* (1660) by John Smith, philosopher and mathematician, Cambridge Platonist and friend of Henry More. Other influential figures, no less important to other students of the young Edwards, include William Ames (1979.11), Nicolas Malebranche (1983.25), and John Norris (1992.10).

Despite its title, nothing new about the young (or mature) Edwards turns up in Iain H. Murray's *Jonathan Edwards: A New Biography* (1987.22). A compilation of short essays published serially in the *Banner of Truth* from 1974 to 1986, Murray's evangelical life aims at the "anti-supernatural animus" of such scholars as Ola Elizabeth Winslow and her "academic" biography (1940.21) and so adds lit-tle to the record save the unabashed bias of earlier hagiographies. Of more signifi-cance is Patricia J. Tracy's *Jonathan Edwards, Pastor* (1980.45) with its account of Edwards's Northampton years in the context of local and regional changing social values and church practices. Edwards's failure, according to Tracy, results from his lack of pastoral training, his father's losing struggle for power, his grandfather's overwhelming example, and New England's growing rejection of ministerial au-thority, though, as Gregory H. Nobles proposes, his dismissal may have owed as much to the "prominent" role of the Hampshire County clergy as any of these (1983.29). Work on other parts of Edwards's life dwell on the women in it: on Sa-rah, the "centerpiece" of his defense of the Great Awakening (1980.37), the image of holy indifference in *Some Thoughts* (1984.7), and the partner who shaped his thought (1979.22 and 1983.41) and "shared" his ministry (1983.53); on Hannah and her sisters and how their acuity and resolve matched his (1992.15); and on Jerusha and the "myth" of her romance with David Brainerd, attributed, by Professor Tracy, to the need of biographers to strengthen the "Jonathan-David bond" (1985.25).

For Norman Pettit that need was Edwards's as well. In his introduction to *The Life of David Brainerd,* the seventh volume in the Yale edition (1985.46), Pettit considers Edwards's biography "a key volume" in the corpus of his work. A "model for missionary histories," the *Life* yields Edwards "a perfect example of authentic spirituality" to set beside others in *Faithful Narrative* and *Some Thoughts* and to validate observations of experimental religion in *Distinguishing Marks* and *Reli-gious Affections.* As a missionary to the Indians, Brainerd affects the question of discipline in *Humble Inquiry,* the anti-Arminianism of *Freedom of the Will* and *Original Sin,* and the life of Edwards among the Housatonics; as a personification of "the ethical man," Brainerd anticipates the disinterested benevolence of *True Virtue.* For all his deletions and alterations of the text, Edwards's publishes the "bulk" of the diary, the biography not of an individual but of a "representative" man. Aside from Pettit's remarks on Brainerd's expulsion from Yale (1986.30), Da-vid L. Weddle's on the "ambiguous" and "problematic" example Brainerd afforded

Edwards (1988.45), Joseph A. Conforti's on the nineteenth-century reception of the *Life* in America (1985.6-7), and D. Elwyn Edwards's pamphlet on its reception abroad (1989.12; in Welsh), little else greets Edwards's most popular work. Not so *Sinners in the Hands of an Angry God*, still the terrific favorite of anthologists.

From the problem of its salvific intention, which ends in our "pitying the spider and hating God" (1982.19), to the question of its "idolatrous" images (1984.34), *Sinners in the Hands of an Angry God* attracts a swarm of possibilities. At once a gloss to Nathaniel Hawthorne's "The Minister's Black Veil" (1980.7), Edgar Allan Poe's "The Pit and the Pendulum" (1980.51), and Charles Brockden Brown's *Edgar Huntly* (1983.44), it is an example of "the complete syllogism (1985.16), Kenneth Burke's theory of identification (1989.63), and neo-Aristotelian *pathé* (1991.38), as well as a "virtuoso performance" of tactility (1983.48) and the subject of a minister's journal touching upon Enfield's reaction to it (1980.30), a Connecticut village in crisis (1983.35). Of more (general) use is J. A. Leo Lemay's summary of its rhetorical strategies (1993.13). Edwards achieves an "unbearable" psychological tension, Lemay points out, by exhausting a narrow, single idea through inescapable logic, convoluted syntax, and suspenseful imagery — falling figures, dammed waters, drawn bows, dangling spiders — in "the most effective imprecatory sermon in American literature," a marked contrast to Benjamin Franklin's oddly insensitive and ineffective *A Narrative of the Late Massacres in Lancaster County*.

Lemay's paper, one of a dozen delivered at the National Conference on Edwards and Franklin at Yale in February of 1990, is the second of three to deal with the language of those "pre-eminently eloquent linked antagonists of American culture," to use Perry Miller's phrase (1962.7). The first of them, "Reason, Rhythm, and Style," David Levin's keynote address, considers Edwards and Franklin "contemporary heirs" to Puritanism and the Enlightenment in their concern for balance, clarity, and reason, in citations from *Religious Affections* and *The Way to Wealth;* the third, R. C. DeProspo's post-structuralist reading of the opening paragraphs of *Personal Narrative* and the *Autobiography,* calls for making their prose "reader-unfriendly" in hopes of saving early American literature. (For another reading of those paragraphs, see 1980.25). All three would appear to meet the criteria of the conference set by Barbara B. Oberg and Harry S. Stout, that is, to treat Edwards and Franklin as "contrapuntal" figures, not as mutually exclusive ideals of earlier studies, and to weigh their "similarities *and* differences." To a great extent the papers succeed, given old habits of mind, papers like William Breitenbach's on hypocrisy and antinomianism in these "very private public men"; A. Owen Aldridge's on the "overlapping" of the Awakening and the Enlightenment, of good works of the one and acts of charity of the other; Edwin S. Gaustad's on the "overlap" of their mutual concern for true (and useful) virtue; Elizabeth E. Dunn's on their different quests after means and ends; and Daniel Walker Howe's on their differing solutions to the dominant eighteenth-century problem of human nature and the "impressive synthesis" of them in nineteenth-century America. With the remaining essays — one, curiously, has nothing to do with Edwards — the criteria are, if anything, better met. Bruce Kuklick views "suspiciously" the project of comparing the two, ascribing it to a nineteenth-century effort to make representative men of eighteenth-century marginal figures and questioning just how "serviceable" such distinctions are, given the twentieth-century propensity for confusing ideas like Calvinism and the Enlightenment. Leonard I. Sweet rejects the traditional image of Edwards as the "sour-spirited, ill-tempered, socially-inept" pastor for one of sensitivity and "high" humor, a comic aesthetic gained through irony and satire, understatement and exaggeration, paradox and parody, word play and absurdity, "the laughter of one." And, in the last of the papers on the cultural context, Ruth H. Bloch concludes that Edwards and Franklin "played unwitting but significant parts" in the sentimental understanding of women and marriage during the middle of the eighteenth century, in a reading of their "troubled ambivalence" toward human love. Two partial, and so less convincing, readings on the question about women and love in Edwards appear elsewhere: one reprints "his treatise on marriage" ("Miscellanies," no. 37) to support his traditional, Puritan prejudice (1983.8); the other remarks his "more egalitarian" approach to gender, an aesthetic reworking of Calvinism in which he "feminized" God, religion, and moral values (1991.16). Paula M. Cooey's broader study remarks the "deeply sensual elements" in Edwards that integrate physical with divine love (1989.10).

Franklin gets notice in one paper read at the earlier Wheaton conference — the middle term in David Levin's meditation on character and reputation, "Edwards, Franklin, and Cotton Mather" — but rarely in the other thirteen (and conventionally elsewhere, 1988.36 and 1989.32; less so in 1982.1). As Nathan O. Hatch and Harry S. Stout put it, *Jonathan Edwards and the American Experience* (1988.17) tries to account for the "recent surge" in Edwards studies, particularly Perry Miller's role in it, and to pull together the "disparate strands" of recent work about the "remarkable" Edwards. Few papers venture beyond. Henry F. May recounts the "main interpretations" of Edwards in successive generations and Donald Weber his recovery at "representative junctures" of American cultural history; Norman Fiering examines the rationalist foundations of his theocentric metaphysics (absent John Locke) and John F. Wilson his postmillennialism (absent C. C. Goen); and Wilson H. Kimnach takes up his pursuit of reality in largely unpublished sermons, Harry S. Stout his Puritanism in unpublished fast and thanksgiving day sermons, and Stephen J. Stein his biblical hermeneutics in the unpublished "Harmony of the Old and New Testaments." Three papers follow Edwards into the New Divinity: William Breitenbach challenges the "betrayal interpretation" and the piety-versus-moralism paradigm of it; James Hoopes locates the causes of theological discontinuities between source and successors; and Mark A. Noll defines Edwards's place in the nineteenth century by those who appropriated, rejected, succeeded, or dismissed him. Another three papers follow a relatively uncharted course: to the theological and social issues of antinomianism and gender, in Amy Schrager Lang's study of the rhetoric of Edwards and Charles Chauncy; to the question of Edwards's "alterity," in David Laurence's "complicated theoretical reflection" on American literature; and to the dilemma of Edwards's primacy in the "confused" discipline of American philosophy, in Bruce Kuklick's reformulation of it.

Only one selection differs in kind from the others in William J. Scheick's convenient, if unexceptional, collection of reprints, *Critical Essays on Jonathan Edwards* (1980.40). "Jonathan Edwards: Textuality and the Language of Man," Wayne Lesser's previously unpublished essay, deconstructs *Personal Narrative* to uncover a self-effacing mode of introspection and "a flawed relationship" between the self and God, a point endorsed in two different approaches (1979.5 and 1979.38), though other readers posit insubstantial (1989.21) and narcissistic (1991.34) selves. Some problems about Edwards's conversion arise in connection with his "critical reevaluation" of Solomon Stoddard's preparationist model (1979.18) and with the "supremely important" images (1981.19) and the "uncertainty" of language in the narrative itself (1987.15). Stephen R. Yarbrough and John C. Adams in their *Delightful Conviction: Jonathan Edwards and the Rhetoric of Conversion* (1993.19) find that the conversion experience Edwards reported in *Personal Narrative* lacks the usual steps of preparation, especially that of legal fear; that he invariably sought the "meaning of conversion itself," not its morphology, in his writings; and that he tried to convert, not persuade, his parishioners by his sermons. Taking it a step farther, Robert Doyle Smith maintains that Edwards's emphasis on holy living qualifies the significance of conversion in his theology, when compared, for example, to John Wesley's (1990.47). On the other hand, John H. Gerstner and Jonathan Neil Gerstner insist that Edwards, like Thomas Hooker and Thomas Shepard before him, is a preparationist and traces his rationale and methodology, the theological obstacles he surmounted, and the fate his doctrine met among contemporary Edwardseans and later Calvinists, in a reading of several unpublished sermons, especially four on Eccles. 9:10 (1979.10). Checking other sources, Samuel T. Logan, Jr., contends that Edwards developed a pattern of conversion "implicitly" in *Faithful Narrative* and tallied all eight steps of the standard model "one way or another" in "The Justice of God in the Damnation of Sinners" (1984.22).

Related to the personal question of conversion for Edwards, of course, is the more public one of communion and admission to his congregation, the principal issue of *Humble Inquiry* and the proximate cause of his dismissal. As usual, much of both turns on his misgivings about Stoddardeanism, "early and persistent" (1981.18), but not apparently as a result of "practicality, purity, or church polity" (1989.46). For the most part, other familiar texts in the Edwards canon receive equally familiar treatment.

Religious Affections continues as the chief example of Edwards's "radically empirical way" in the dynamics of faith (1979.44), his "rigorous" testing of the

Holy Spirit (1981.31), especially in the twelfth sign, either a part of the changing concept for evangelicals (1990.52) or a "truly radical" theosemiotic likened to Charles Peirce's pragmatism (1993.16). Readers compare his "very sophisticated" challenge to trust one's heart to Sören Kierkegaard's (1990.3) and his ideas of "true religion" (1984.4) and gratitude (1988.23) to John Wesley's and the "common ground" of religious experience they shared (1990.6), though readers dissent to the last on matters of grace and faith (1987.6), predestination and assurance (1989.1). In a comparison of Edwards's account of the religious experience and William James's (1989.42), Wayne Proudfoot illustrates the shift from a traditional theological context to a phenomenological one. Edwards is the "more astute psychologist" than James, his analysis "thicker and more nuanced," in that he is increasingly skeptical of introspection, trusting to observed practice instead. John E. Smith, who had edited *Religious Affections* for Yale twenty-five years ago, selects "crucial points" from that text (and others) to reveal Edwards's criteria for judging piety and his critical appraisal of the Great Awakening and concludes that he "attacked the sufficiency of rationalism in religion and sought to lay hold of the truth in the piety of experience, but in the end he gave no comfort to enthusiasts or to obscurantists" (1988.38). J. I. Packer culls from many of the same sources "a fairly complete account" of Edwards's theology of revival and offers it to evangelicals who had rejected him as unreadable or philosophical (1990.39). And in an introduction to an abridgment and rewording of the text, Charles W. Colson urges Edwards's message — "the absolute primacy of biblical obedience" — upon a "crippled" western church "infected with cheap grace" and upon a "stupefied, egocentric, materialistic" and nihilistic society (1984.6). Another, more restrained, recommendation comes from John Piper's *The Supremacy of God in Preaching* (1990.43), wherein he exhorts contemporary ministers to emulate Edwards in his pulpit practice and so gain the "sweet sovereignty" of God that he enjoyed. And, by publishing ninety-nine Northampton manuscript prayer bids of the 1730s and 1740s, Stephen J. Stein reminds us that Edwards's congregation "did not reject the classic theological categories of the Reformed tradition for a new language of religious experience forged in the heat of the Great Awakening."

Still the subject of often rancorous debate (1979.7 and 1979.15), *Freedom of the Will* stands accused as the "best defense ever given to the worst theology ever conceived" (1982.9) or vindicated as the "most sustained apology ever constructed for the aristocracy of grace" (1992.19); either a failed polemic against Arminianism (1987.28) or a successful rendering of the logical problem of foreknowledge and necessity (1984.24), a problem, offers one reader, that can be solved through William of Ockham's distinction between "hard" and "soft" facts about the past (1986.32). Again useful as a gloss — to B. F. Skinner (1981.40), Ethan Frome (1983.38), and Captain Ahab (1991.20) — Edwards's celebrated treatise has "contemporary relevance" for ethical choice (1982.13) and "practical implications" for the Christian life and ministry (1982.39). Only in Allen C. Guelzo's *Edwards on the*

Will: A Century of American Theological Debate (1989.16) does a study of the text reflect one of the major concerns of current scholarship, that is, fixing Edwards in a defined context, here nineteenth-century theology. Edwards's sophisticated arguments and the corollaries of his successors — Joseph Bellamy and Samuel Hopkins, New Divinity men and some "ardent disciples" among mid-Atlantic Presbyterians — "frightened rather than consoled" Old Calvinists here and abroad, Guelzo writes. Not until Nathaniel William Taylor and New Haven Theology laid to rest the "troublesome ghost" of *Freedom of the Will* did it cease to haunt American theology. But all this seems a bit too tidy, as does *Churchmen and Philosophers: from Jonathan Edwards to John Dewey* (1985.26), Bruce Kuklick's otherwise valuable study. Broader in both time and implication than *Edwards on the Will*, *Churchmen and Philosophers* traces Edwards's intellectual development from his early philosophical speculations to his later theoretical analyses in defense of experimental religion and positions him along a continuum from the "reign" of theology to the "triumph" of philosophy, his thought instrumental for the New Divinity, his vision "congruent" with Dewey's, a questionable point at best (1985.19, 1986.47, 1987.27, and 1987.32). Kuklick engages Hopkins, Bellamy, and Taylor, as does Guelzo, but continues well into the century to Edwards Amasa Park's philosophy of religion and the end of New England Theology, "the most sustained intellectual tradition" in America. However defined, Joseph A. Conforti charges it with "cultural imperialism" for transforming the Great Awakening from a regional to a colonial event and Edwards's role in it from a local to a central one (1991.4; see also 1986.9 and 1989.8), an act of "interpretative fiction," one reader calls it (1982.5), "Calvinism's 'Great Wake,'" cries another (1984.32). For the most part, though, Hopkins, Bellamy, and the New Divinity are charged with nothing more than consistent Calvinism (1984.2), philosophical discontinuity (1988.31), or "unregenerate doings" (1982.3).

Like *Freedom of the Will* during this period, *Original Sin* is the focus of a book-length study, but unlike liberty, more readers seem drawn to sin, because, as one of them remarks, Edwards "refused to conceal or discount a feature of human existence that continues to frustrate the moral and religious life" of so many (1983.14). In *Tragedy in Eden: Original Sin in the Theology of Jonathan Edwards* (1985.53), C. Samuel Storms views Edwards's doctrine, from a biblical and theological rather than an historical perspective, in an account of his intellectual and religious development and his relation to the American Enlightenment. Though his argument about the problem of evil and identity is not without fault — "it *fails* as a theodicy," Storms says — Edwards mounts "the most lucid and convincing defense of these fundamental biblical truths since Paul penned Romans." In another assessment, Edwards "partly succeeds and partly fails" in his Augustinian defense of inherited guilt, but it is still "one of the most plausible" (1988.43); and in yet others, Edwards's "innovative" argument of divine constitution of personal identity in defense of original sin fails because it was based on "conflicting and unscriptural premises" (1990.38), succeeds as an early instance of the contemporary philosophical doctrine of temporal parts (1979.14), or, even as "an exercise in circularity," is "no less rational" a solution to the problem than, say, Alfred North Whitehead's (1984.14). Apart from these reflections about identity, Stephen R. Yarbrough perceives in *Original Sin* "two distinct notions" of time (1992.29). Before the Fall there is neither time nor self, but when one falls, that is, when one chooses, "one *begins time* — for oneself." Therefore, Yarbrough contends, "time is of the human mind, not the divine." Only through divine grace can one return to God and the aboriginal state — the ecstatic moment of conversion — "literally out of time."

In our time, much the most incisive (and sustained) commentary concerns *True Virtue.* In *Jonathan Edwards's Moral Thought and Its British Context* (1981.10), Norman Fiering traces the development of Edwards's moral thought through the "Miscellanies," *Freedom of the Will, Original Sin,* and, climactically, *True Virtue,* in the context of British and continental moralists, Francis Hutcheson and David Hume, Nicolas Malebranche and Gottfried von Leibniz, and at the expense of John Locke — "Edwards himself was no Lockean" — and Perry Miller. Yale taught Edwards the Harvard curriculum, Fiering reminds us, but Edwards was "too much of a philosopher" to be comprehended by that or New England Puritanism "alone." His was a speculative mind, wide-ranging in metaphysics and ethics, synthesizing ideas of "natural understanding," self-love, the doctrine of hell, determinism, and piety into creative structures of moral theology, "a unique work in American thought." But his theory of virtue in its aspiration toward a transcendental standard is "not strictly identified with institutionalized Christianity." Published in the same year, Fiering's *Moral Philosophy at Seventeenth-Century Harvard: A Discipline in Transition* (1981.11) locates Edwards in the voluntarist tradition and Charles Chauncy in the intellectualist tradition of the seventeenth century in their debate about the Great Awakening, an eighteenth-century example of "the perennial opposition of head and heart." While many readers are taken by Fiering's Edwards — a "large-scale corrective" (1982.14), a "quiet triumph" (1982.24), "indispensable" (1982.37), "provocative" (1983.22), "essential reading" (1983.45), and "possibly the best book on Edwards ever written" (1983.1) — others are troubled by his "cryptic implications" (1982.44), his unsympathetic treatment of Miller (1982.35), the "utterly circumstantial" influence of Malebranche (1983.58), the "underestimated" influence of Locke (1984.19), and the omission of Edwards's "most important" ethical texts (1982.7). By now the issue of Locke's influence, seized upon by Miller a generation ago (1949.9; rpt. 1981.27), has been reduced to one of limits (1980.24) and language (1983.15). Professor Fiering's missing ethical texts show up in the eighth volume of *The Works of Jonathan Edwards.*

In *Ethical Writings* (1989.44), Paul Ramsey, who had edited *Freedom of the Will* for the series in 1957, undertakes an analysis of important themes in Edwards's moral thought with only "light stress" on the times and backgrounds of *Charity and its Fruits, End of Creation,* and *True Virtue.* The first of these, Edwards's "hymn" to charity, may be read as a "systematic treatise on the Christian moral life," a parallel to the work of redemption, and a "major" account of gracious affections; the second and third (in the sequence Edwards intended, but reversed in the posthumously published *Two Dissertations*) are mirror images of each other: the end of creation "must be" the end of true virtue. Indeed, throughout his life, Edwards returned again and again to these "integrated" matters, and so it is "a grave error now or ever," Ramsey insists, to separate his philosophy from his theology, his moral philosophy from his theological ethics. Aside from Edwards's influence on William Godwin's politics (1980.43 and 1986.6) and the "democracy of the Damned" (1984.17) or his position as a "latter-day" Augustine (1981.15) and counterpart to eighteenth-century Irish philosophers (1989.3), most readers stress the relatedness of his ethical texts. William C. Spohn considers the two dissertations "parts of a single argument," a metaethics that takes the love of God as the "comprehensive context" of duty and enjoyment, morality and aesthetics (1981.32), and places Edwards firmly in the American tradition of arguing ethics from parts to the whole, not from means to ends (1986.1); Stephen G. Post, in *Christian Love and Self-Denial* (1987.26), compares Edwards's doctrine of disinterested benevolence with Samuel Hopkins's "radical" version of it, in an historical study of American theological ethics; and Virginia A. Peacock, in *Problems in the Interpretation of Jonathan Edwards' The Nature of True Virtue* (1990.42), adds *Essay on the Trinity* and the influence of Andrew Michael Ramsay to define Edwards's ideas of virtue within the "inextricably related" aspects of his theological, rather than philosophical, thought and remarks the "notable shift" in his interpretation of special and common grace in his Stockbridge years. One reader discards the whole of Edwards's "Stockbridge aesthetics" as "a gigantic failure" (1982.15). Of the other texts in *Ethical Writings,* Roland A. Delattre singles out Ramsey's explication of *Charity and its Fruits* for its "important" contribution to Edwards's radically theological and theocentric ethics (1991.7); and Linda Munk finds that in *End of Creation,* a "commentary on Creation in terms of the Incarnation," the overflowing of divine glory is not of God but of his Shekinah, "His dazzling absence" (1992.17). Finally, in a reading of the correspondence mainly between Ramsey and Miller, the first general editor of the Yale Edwards, and John E. Smith, the second, Stephen Crocco details Ramsey's use of Edwards to "sketch" the contours of Reformed ethics, to make him a "conversation partner" in discussions of contemporary ethics, and to shape the content of his own ethics (1992.2). (Several other students of Edwards have become subjects themselves: Sacvan Bercovitch, 1992.11; Norman Fiering, 1986.4; Joseph Haroutunian, 1988.6; H. Richard Niebuhr, 1986.1 and 1991.28; Herbert Schneider, 1987.30; and, of course, Perry Miller, 1981.27, 1986.4, and 1990.1.)

The same year *Ethical Writings* appeared, *A History of the Work of Redemption* (1989.59) was published, the ninth volume in the Yale series. In his introduction, John F. Wilson emphasizes the theological rather than the historical nature of what he calls Edwards's "Redemption Discourse" and examines its "unusual" composition (thirty sermons on one biblical verse, Isa. 51:8), its projected revision, and its reception, influence, and modern reclamation. The "Discourse" was "entirely congruent" with Puritan New England's preoccupation with the application of redemption and visible sainthood and was "already central" to his own work, especially in the "Miscellanies." But, Wilson goes on, he turned its sermon form "inside out" and "detached" its typological framework from Scripture to find figural patterns in "'history'" and nature. Edwards's use of a "branching" or subordination in a logical structure is an index of his theological premises and renders the work "profoundly unhistoriographical in any modern sense." Professor Wilson had addressed some of these matters in "History, Redemption, and the Millennium" at the Wheaton conference (1988.17), in large part a reply to C. C. Goen's "Jonathan Edwards: A New Departure in Eschatology" (1959.5; rpt. 1980.40), itself the center of lively debate. Now the question of Edwards's eschatology is more apt to deal with its evangelical (1981.1), missiological (1988.7), or societal ends (1985.55); his apocalyptic vision, with its "transatlantic extensions" (1984.37) and its function in the American literary imagination (1981.25, 1982.48, 1984.20, and 1991.8); and his millennialism, with its bearing on the "visionary republic" in general (1985.3) and on Samuel Hopkins (1983.9) and Aaron Burr in particular. In *Jonathan Edwards to Aaron Burr, Jr.: From the Great Awakening to Democratic Politics* (1981.13), Suzanne Geissler charts Edwards's influence upon his grandson through family "imprinting," marking parallel texts of "striking resemblance" and commonly held beliefs, so that Burr's political thought, for example, is said to derive from Edwards's millennialism, secularized. Unfortunately, the thesis wants evidence and logic. Better answers to such questions lie in Edwards's political thought apart from its practical (or lineal) consequences, an approach different from earlier, more personal accounts of the "impolitic Mr. Edwards" (1978.13; rpt. 1980.40).

One Holy and Happy Society: The Public Theology of Jonathan Edwards (1992.13), by Gerald R. McDermott, derives his political thought from his unpublished occasional sermons given on fast, thanksgiving, and election days, and argues, contrary to other studies, that Edwards's political preaching was in the tradition of the New England jeremiad, not an anthem to manifest destiny; that his millennial doctrine was "global," not tribal or provincial; and that his theories of citizenship and magistracy were "progressive" and sophisticated, not protective of a social and economic elite. Edwards achieved "a grand synthesis" of social concern and private experience, imparting dignity to the marginalized of society, women and blacks, the poor and the young. His "most important contribution," according to McDermott, "was his painstaking unfolding of the relation of private to public religion." By concentrating on four other "neglected texts" — *Humble Attempt, Life of Brainerd, Humble Inquiry,* and *Farewell Sermon* — Richard A. S. Hall limits the scope of his inquiry (1990.22) to a brief for the existence of Edwards's social and political philosophy, not an exposition of its "full range." Edwards's communal ideal of citizenship is, in Hall's words, a "radical public-mindedness" and his ethics social, in that true virtue is "loyalty to the greatest society of uncreated and created persons." Edwards wanted to implement his ideal by making his congregation into "an exclusive society of the visibly benevolent." Other neglected texts ("On the Medium of Moral Government — Particularly Conversation" and its companion piece, "The Insufficiency of Reason as a Substitute for Revelation") leads Stephen R. Yarbrough to the core of Edwards's rhetorical authority, God's grace (1986.48). Grace unifies the Word and nature, communicates God's beauty and his creation, and authorizes saints "to interpret and to teach." Yet other neglected texts, these a series of unpublished sermons, form the basis of Mark Valeri's "The Economic Thought of Jonathan Edwards" (1991.42), which recasts the image of an aloof and impractical Edwards into a preacher of a "tightly structured" order that denied the possibilities of a virtuous market economy. Edwards abandoned Puritan economic ideals early in his pastorate and attempted to reform the economic practice of Northampton's visible saints during the revivals of the 1730s and 1740s and to define external controls to remedy New England's economic ills after them. "His failure to convince his people to forego the market for the meetinghouse," Valeri concludes, "was not for lack of trying."

That Valeri and McDermott would enlist Edwards's unpublished sermons to reopen old issues reveals another important aspect of the scholarship over the past fifteen years. In *The Minister's Task and Calling in the Sermons of Jonathan Edwards* (1986.46), Helen P. Westra scours his sermons — on hearing and keeping, preaching and teaching the Word; on the ordination and installation of ministers; and on Christ as the perfect ministerial exemplar — for his theological, pastoral, and aesthetic vision of a gospel ministry. Stewards, messengers, husbandmen, lights, watchmen, proxy bridegrooms, biblical metaphors all — such are ministers in Edwards, "lively types" of Christ, Westra calls them. In another study (1990.58), she examples him as a guardian of colonial New England culture and teacher of civility, decorum, harmony, responsibility, and continuity, in a study of thirty "'domestic'" sermons on children and parents preached during the 1730s and 1740s; and in still another (1991.44), she uncovers an instance of his effort to restrain rationalist and Arminian views, in a manuscript sermon of thirty-five pages on 1 Cor. 2:11-13 at the ordination of Edward Billing in Cold Spring, Massachusetts. In "'Like Apples of Gold in Pictures of Silver'" (1985.51), Stephen J. Stein charts Edwards's "lifelong regard" for the Book of Proverbs, in an examination of more than fifty sermons (and other manuscripts). His mature readings begin in the nature of biblical language — the silver of metaphor yields the gold of sense — and ends in "a preoccupation" with God's excellency, wisdom, purity, and love, which parallels his growing concern with the divine role in man's conversion. But of all these quite revealing studies based on unpublished sermons, none is more impressive than Wilson H. Kimnach's edition of *Sermons and Discourses, 1720-1723* (1992.8).

As well as tracing Edwards's early influences (already noted), Kimnach explores the entire corpus of Edwards's sermons, his apparatus for making them, his literary theory, and the canon of printed and manuscript sermons, in "Jonathan Edwards' Art of Prophesying," the first of two introductions to the collection and, at 258 pages, the longest in the Yale series. Edwards borrows from his "formidable" and diverse notebooks to compose palm-sized sermon manuscripts for pulpit delivery and, with "conscious artistry," deploys biblical tropes, "poignant (usually visual) imagery," symbolism and typology, "chaste rhetoric," repetition and parallelism, shifts in the narrative point of view, and "tonic" words that can reverberate throughout a given text. In the second introduction, "Preface to the New York Period," Kimnach recounts Edwards's eight-month's stay as supply preacher to a separatist Presbyterian congregation in New York and recaptures the voice of an ambitious young man setting out. Edwards's contemporary "Diary" and "Resolutions," his retrospective *Personal Narrative,* and his meditative "Sarah Pierrepont" offer evidence of his struggle for personal holiness and professional identity and suggest the context for the twenty-three sermons composed largely between the summer of 1722 and the spring of the following year. Several of them bear witness to his search after hope and resolution; others rehearse the metaphors, if not the intensity, of his later imprecations; still others prefigure later (published) comforts; all brim with a "rustic vitality" and concrete imagery, each linked to each by his "definition of the Christian life in experiential terms."

Several other readers appraise the art and language of the sermons. In *Realta e immagine: L'estetica nei sermoni di Jonathan Edwards* (1980.9), Marcella DeNichilo finds in the metaphoric structures of the sermons (in print and in manuscript) connections between Edwards's aesthetics and his rhetoric, his poetics and his theology, his imagery and that of later American (Romantic) writers. Edwards modifies the plain style with the affecting style of types and tropes to awaken the unregenerate to an infinite God. His "ideal aesthetic," DeNichilo argues, integrates language, myth, and society into an "expressive organicism." Like the self, all is an "inseparable union." At the other end, William J. Scheick, in *Design in Puritan American Literature* (1992.23), locates the source of Edwards's notion of the "instability of language at the logogic site" in two kinds of knowledge, rational and affective, that often results in an "eschatological erasure" of words, in a study of images in four early sermons: *doors, gates,* and *knocking* in "Pressing into the Kingdom of God"; *family* and *journey* in "The Christian Pilgrim"; *ascent* and *descent* in "The Excellency of Christ"; and, fittingly, *mouth* in "The Justice of God in the Damnation of Sinners." Edwards breaks words as verbal icons to reveal the "concealed emptiness" at the core of all material manifestations, including language, and so renders God "unimagable, unrepresentable, and unaccountable" to all but the elect. And turning to sermons about the Great Awakening, both Harry S. Stout and Alan Heimert adjudge Edwards's style more effective than his rival Charles Chauncy's. Equal to Chauncy as a scriptural exegete, Edwards was "a master without peer" in bringing philosophy to bear upon the nature of conversion, Stout remarks, his "unexcelled" use of language particularly convincing to evangelicals, his "stock of images and metaphors" firing the hearts of clergy and laity alike (1986.42). Heimert, writing in the *Columbia Literary History of the United States* (1988.18), defines Edwards as a "consummate practitioner" of the plain style, who "revivified" Puritan sermonic practice with assonance, alliteration, repetition, and rhythmic structures and, in a "radical transformation," democratized the relationship between speaker and audience. But clearly the first issue of the unpublished sermons is theological, and John H. Gerstner has plumbed the Yale holdings to comment upon just that.

Thirty-four years ago, Gerstner found evidence enough of Edwards's Calvinist and evangelical message in the sermons (and elsewhere) to publish *Steps to Salvation* (1960.5); sixteen years later, he outlined Edwards's apologetics in a four-part series for *Bibliotheca Sacra* (1976.22-25); three years after that, he published "Jonathan Edwards and the Bible" (1979.8), certifying that Edwards "majored in God's book"; the following year, he published two studies: Edward's "great doctrine of God" (1980.13) and *Jonathan Edwards on Heaven and Hell* (1980.14), in recognition of "the greatest biblical artist ever." All of this led seven years later to the publication of *Jonathan Edwards: A Mini-Theology* (1987.8), "an introduction and nothing more than an introduction" to the "total" corpus of his writings and the "large" corpus of writings about him, a "harbinger" of a longer study. And that came four years later in the first of three volumes of *The Rational Biblical Theology of Jonathan Edwards* (1991.10). Gerstner presents Edwards's thought "systematically" — as Edwards himself had hoped to do in "A Rational Account of the Main Doctrines of the Christian Religion Attempted" — in "the first full-scale theology of Edwards ever published" and includes an account of his life, his synthesis of reason and revelation (and its subsequent breakdown), and a hundred-page outline of his theology, with extensive examples from his "indispensable" sermons and unpublished commentary. Edwards's intellectual and moral life centered on the inspired and inerrant Word, Gerstner asserts, the "sine qua non of his rational biblical theology": his preaching the Word was his theology and "his theology was his preaching." The second volume (1992.4) continues the thesis and evidence; the third (1993.7) concludes both and adds a bibliography of Edwards's reading and another of writings about him (compiled by David F. Coffin, Jr.), and appends a tribute to him. Within his nearly 2,000 pages, Professor Gerstner provides argument and text in a very alphabet of theological concerns: angels, apologetics, assurance, atonement, biblicism, covenants, creation, the church, divine sovereignty, epistemology, eschatology, evangelism, the Fall, heaven, hell, hermeneutics, imputation, the Incarnation, justification, man, metaphysics, millennialism, the ministry, ontology, perseverance, pneumatology, preaching, preparation, providence, regeneration, sacraments, sanctification, sin, and virtue. Yet it is just such serial coverage that makes the trilogy more an encyclopedia of Edwards's thought than a coherent narrative of it, and so, for all its thoroughness, a work of rather limited usefulness.

Other book-length studies aim at a part of Edwards's theology to get at the whole of it and, inevitably, meet with only partial success.

In *Theism in the Discourse of Jonathan Edwards* (1985.9), R. C. DeProspo attempts a phenomenological reading not only of Edwards but of modern interpretations of him as well, in a "stylistically dense" deconstruction of texts and critiques. What is "bedrock" in Edwards's theism — ideas of creation, providence, and grace — becomes in humanist discourse the "unstable ground" of nature, history, and psychology. Such a disparate discursive pattern, DeProspo asserts, calls into question the work of humanist scholars of Edwards and modern historiographers of "'America'" and makes it necessary to "remodel the whole corpus of American literature." Though a shrewd reader of some familiar texts, DeProspo loses sight of Edwards in another, far more different and complex, agenda. So, in a way, does Robert W. Jenson. In *America's Theologian: A Recommendation of Jonathan Edwards* (1988.22), Jenson examines the "fit" between Edwards and America, the Enlightenment and Puritanism, God and nation, in a study of Edwards's critique of religious appearances and its importance for contemporary religious, political, and social thought. A "born rationalist," Edwards resolves the clash between reason and the gospel in the beautiful harmony of the triune God, a "fugued hymn," Jenson calls it, of the elements and the community of consciousness, a "conversation" of mutuality within, but open to others without. Edwards is "America's theologian," because he "astonishingly accomplished" both a critique and a harmony, "penetrated" to that ancient dualism, and "transcended" it. But, as one reviewer points out, the Lutheran perspective of the study "make[s] Edwards into Karl Barth" (1989.31), more Jenson's theologian than America's. Though less polemical and more suggestive than Jenson, Sang Hyun Lee also uses Edwards to confront contemporary theological problems in *The Philosophical Theology of Jonathan Edwards* (1988.25). Lee finds the interpretative "key" to Edwards's "dynamic and relational" vision of reality and to the unity and modernity of his thought, not in harmony, but in the idea of habit. Edwards's concept addresses problems of ontology and epistemology and resolves questions of being and becoming, imagination and beauty, temporality and history, and the "increasing fullness" of God, the "rhythm of the becoming world." Not only does such a "highly innovative" reconception of his theological tradition make Edwards "historically important," Lee concludes, his dispositional ontology can become "an enduring source of insight" for contemporary philosophical theology as well, inasmuch as it mediates the demands of classical theism and process theology.

In two studies, the limits are self-imposed, either personal or theological. In *Profile of the Last Puritan: Jonathan Edwards, Self-Love, and the Dawn of the Beatific* (1991.2), David C. Brand reflects upon "the author's [and America's] spiritual roots" to explore Edwards's Calvinist and covenantal sources, the philosophical landscape of his time, and the development of Arminianism in New England. For Edwards, philosophy was subordinate to theology, ethics to ontology, morality to regeneration, happiness to holiness, and self-love to benevolence, the mutual love of the triune God. For him, the beatific was "basic." And in *A Comparative Study in the Theology of Atonement in Jonathan Edwards and John McLeod Campbell: Atonement and the Character of God* (1993.8), Michael Jinkins finds in Edwards's conception of the atonement, unlike Campbell's, that the forensic has "priority" over the filial, because his doctrine of God stresses the distinctiveness of the persons of the Trinity. Edwards's limited atonement, "grounded" in the limited scope of God's love, forces him into "double predestination" and the problem of ascribing the "'actual' appropriation" of the benefits of redemption to the Spirit, not to Christ.

Hardly limited by reach or intention, *La pensée de Jonathan Edwards* (1987.34) may be limited to the fortunate French. Miklós Vetö, of the University of Rennes, reconstructs Edwards's theology into a coherent and unified system of thought based on the cardinal issues of being, will, and knowledge, places it in eighteenth-century religious and philosophical historiography, and includes a concordance of six editions of his work. For Vetö, Edwards unites man's virtuous will to God's divine beauty, his spiritual perception to His gracious plentitude. (Two of Professor Vetö's earlier papers on Edwards were published in French journals: see 1979.40-41.) At another remove, two comprehensive studies of Edwards are limited by format. M. X. Lesser's *Jonathan Edwards* (1988.26) for Twayne's United States Authors Series and John E. Smith's *Jonathan Edwards: Puritan, Preacher, Philosopher* (1992.25) for the Outstanding Christian Thinkers Series both run to about 150 pages, cover Edwards's life, the corpus of his work, his debts and his influence, and fasten upon his doctrine of divine sovereignty as the signal aspect of his thought. As Professor Smith puts it, "If one were to ask, given the total body of what Edwards wrote, what one idea stands out as more important than any other, the answer would have to be the utter sovereignty of God." And yet, in spite of all these often helpful studies, Conrad Cherry's *The Theology of Jonathan Edwards: A Reappraisal* (1966.9; rpt. 1990.11) remains the essential primer to Edwards's theology.

Work on Edwards and beauty continues but, as with other elements in his thought, the emphasis shifts. Early in the period, Professor Cherry credits Edwards with a balanced, correlative view of nature, in the first of a three-part study, *Nature and Religious Imagination: From Edwards to Bushnell* (1980.6). For Edwards, nature was beautiful only as it reflected the "harmony" of all levels of being, the "symmetry" of man and God, "a whole self in a whole world." Decidedly symbolic about physical nature, Edwards perceived the natural world as "an image of an image." In *Jonathan Edwards, Art and the Sense of the Heart* (1980.11), Terrence Erdt discovers the "cornerstone" of Edwards's aesthetics, not in the sensationalism of John Locke's *Essay* but in the *sensus suavitatis* of John Calvin's *Institutes*. Though Edwards follows Calvin on regeneration and assurance, he makes a "significant modification": the saint conceives (and revives) the sense of the heart aesthetically as a response to spiritual beauty. And so images from nature, from the imagination, and from works of art can "surrogate" the sense of the heart, evoking spiritual beauty or recalling it. (For the implications of Edwards's theory of the sense of the heart for the "epistemic status" of religious belief, see 1990.55.) Diana Butler also takes "seriously" Edwards's Calvinism in order to reveal his "full" interpretation of nature, but differs from Erdt in her findings (1990.7). For Edwards (and Calvin), nature was not truth, for natural revelation condemns the fallen. But with "corrected sight," the redeemed can use nature to "teach Christian truth, see God visibly manifested, acknowledge and praise the Creator, and read the world as a book of types." Such images from nature, or the meanings Edwards attaches to them, are central to Paula M. Cooey's *Jonathan Edwards on Nature and Destiny: A Systematic Analysis* (1985.8). Since for Edwards nature communicates divine destiny, it means, variously, sensible reality and spiritual regeneration, and finds expression in his ontology, anthropology, Christology, soteriology, typology, eschatology, and epistemology. Hence, Edwards on saving grace may serve as a "paradigm" of his thought as a whole, a theocentric vision but one in which both human beings and nature play "vital" though "subordinate" roles. In *Jonathan Edwards, the Valley and Nature: An Interpretative Essay* (1987.10), Clyde A. Holbrook restores nature to its "rightful position" in Edwards's thought, in a (sometimes personal) study of the landscape of the Connecticut Valley and its "profound and determinative" influence on his philosophy, theology, and ethics. Though Edwards directly experienced the Valley at East Windsor and Northampton, his reading of continental theology and science created "a secondhand relation" to it. Thus the beauty of nature that early stirred him became the beauty of God's order and harmony, immediate sensations gave way to types and symbols, and John Locke yielded to George Berkeley. Bringing Edwards into the eighties, Richard Cartwright Austin's *Beauty of the Lord: Awakening the Senses* (1988.1) uncovers the "integrating" theme of environmental ethics in Edwards's understanding of the beauty of God, in a study that joins traditional theology to modern ecology, "sensuousness" toward God to communion with, and protection of, nature. According to Austin, Edwards left "a rich record of mistakes and accomplishments" with which to probe the Christian experience with nature. Part of that record includes *Images or Shadows of Divine Things,* first edited by Perry Miller in 1948 — to the distress of at least one reader (1980.46) — and now published, along with Edwards's other manuscripts on typology, in the eleventh volume of *The Works of Jonathan Edwards.*

In his introduction to *Typological Writings* (1993.1), the late Wallace E. Anderson traces the history of biblical typology; locates Edwards's method amid the contending claims of rationalists and deists, Catholics and Anglicans, Cabalists and Dissenters; and records his efforts to meet the challenges and objections raised by them. Begun in 1728, "Images of Divine Things" — Miller had conflated two titles Edwards gave the work — brings correspondences between the Old and New Testament into harmony with nature and history, extending traditional typology so that "the spiritual truths represented by the array of natural things comprehended the temporal unfolding of the divine plan of salvation"; the "Types" notebook, written at Northampton and Stockbridge and previously unpublished, outlines some general principles of typology usually with New Testament proofs. In his introduction to "Types of the Messiah" (or "Miscellanies," no. 1069), Mason I. Lowance, Jr., who has done significant work on typology (1979.21 and 1980.27), situates the text in the Edwards canon, especially his sermons, particularly the thirty that would become *History of Redemption*. Composed in the "dark period" between the "bad book" episode in 1744 and Edwards's dismissal in 1749, "Types of the Messiah" is not so much a prophetical scheme as an exegetical theory (with examples) in which the type is "at once a representation and an essence, precisely because it transcended time and space." Taken together, Edwards's typological writings demonstrate "a *via media*" between conservative scriptural readings and the meaning of biblical figures "recapitulated" in nature and history and made available to the elect by "the new sense of things." That "Images of Divine Things" offers clues to Edwards's theology of nature (1980.19) leads a historian of philosophy to find it in "some forms of naturalistic humanism" of later thinkers (1980.49), a Russian observer to measure it against the development of American literature (1981.21), and a student of French letters to dismiss its 212 entries as so many "sermonettes" (1987.12). In "Learning the Language of God: Jonathan Edwards and the Typology of Nature" (1991.21), Janice Knight suggests that Edwards's "own certainty" of the harmony and proportion of God's world induced him to posit a like harmony between the works of creation and redemption, nature and spirit, first principles of an "integrated" theology. He "always" joined ontological to historical types in his writing and "blurred" the traditional categories, a "paradoxical union" that mirrors (and inheres in) a dynamic, effulgent God. For Edwards, typology is "best understood as a form of divine speech," Knight says, a voice "still sounding" in nature, history, and contemporary events.

Other voices still sounding can be heard in a chorus of reprints, from Henry Philip Tappan's examination of *Freedom of the Will* (1839.8; rpt. 1979.34) to Frank Hugh Foster's history of New England Theology (1907.3; rpt. 1987.7), from Henry Bamford Parkes's *Jonathan Edwards, The Fiery Puritan* (1930.10; rpt. 1979.29) to Richard L. Bushman's "Jonathan Edwards as Great Man" (1969.5; rpt. 1980.40). Though not reprinted, Miller's "From Edwards to Emerson" (1940.9) is frequently revisited, either to modify it — through Mary Moody Emerson (1982.6 and 1986.8), Henry Whitney Bellows (1988.10), Charles Chauncy (1992.22), and the rhetoric of negation (1991.15) — or to extend it to Thoreau — through William Bartram (1983.60) and the "sacred adventure" of walking (1991.37). Revisited as well are Edwards's immaterialism (1982.42) and mysticism (1985.36); his views of continuous creation (1983.36) and justification (1984.21 and 1993.14); his links to the transatlantic community (1986.17 and 1991.6), especially the Scots (1987.29 and 1991.5); and his influence upon poets like Robert Lowell (1981.17) and novelists like William Faulkner (1980.21 and 1983.17). Connections to such disparate figures as

Thomas Carlyle (1993.3), Thomas Jefferson (1990.8), Mary Lyon (1993.4), and Josiah Royce (1983.37) appear now for the first time.

New as well are such front-page issues as crime, family, and racism. Clyde A. Holbrook, the editor of *Original Sin,* instances Edwards as a transitional figure in the shift from ecclesiastical to civil authority about crime and sin in eighteenth-century Massachusetts (1987.9). The Great Awakening "weakened" the relationship between people and pastor and between church and state, but Edwards, though lamenting civil disorder, sought God's help to rectify sinful lives, not the law's. In "The Importance of the Family: A Reformed Theological Perspective" (1986.21), Sang H. Lee uses Edwards to represent the American Reformed tradition — theocentric, trinitarian, christological — in an examination of the family, the "interplay" between creation and redemption, nature and grace. For Edwards, God's creative and redemptive works are "closely related" but "clearly distinguished": the family is the embodiment of the "self-giving love" of the Father for the Son and so a type of divine beauty. And in *Puritan Race Virtue, Vice, and Value* (1987.35), Joseph R. Washington, Jr., concentrates on the ethical writings of "New England Orthodoxy's three most influential post-theocracy definers of Puritan Piety" (Cotton Mather, Edwards, and Samuel Hopkins) in a "humanities-intensive, decisively unscientific, and probative-specific deconstructionist approach to a Christian critique of Black and White American race and religion realities." Edwards's "re-revision" of Calvinism turned piety into "private-interest ethics" that ended years later in the "caste-revering and bondage-respecting custom" denying blacks love and justice.

Also new to the period are retrospectives on the Edwards scholarly enterprise as a whole. In an introduction to his *Critical Essays on Jonathan Edwards* (1980.40), William J. Scheick summarizes material "useful in a survey of scholarship" on Edwards; in "Jonathan Edwards: the First Two Hundred Years" (1980.41), Daniel B. Shea traces the history of the "use and misuse" of Edwards to the bicentennial of his birth, in a bibliographical essay on (chiefly) nineteenth-century criticism and late twentieth-century prospects; in an introduction to his annotated bibliography, *Jonathan Edwards: A Reference Guide* (1981.22), M. X. Lesser follows the growth and direction of Edwards criticism from his assumption of the Northampton pulpit in 1729 to the recent dramatic rise of interest in him; in *Jonathan Edwards: Bibliographical Synopses* (1981.26), Nancy Manspeaker annotates over 700 items "to preserve the record" and help those "currently involved" in interpreting Edwards; and in "The Figure of Jonathan Edwards" (1983.55), Donald Weber attributes the range of new studies about him to his "variousness," concluding that Edwards is "enigmatic and slippery."

Perhaps that accounts for what must be the final calculation. In "And the Winner is . . . Jonathan Edwards?", Mark A. Noll determines that Edwards is "the most-cited figure" in the index of the *Encyclopedia of the American Religious Experience* (1989.38). His eight lines confirm that "his voice is being heard once again." From the present report, that certainly seems to be so.

An Annotated Bibliography, 1979-1993

1979

1 Berryman, Charles. *From Wilderness to Wasteland: The Trial of the Puritan God in the American Imagination.* National University Publications: Literary Criticism Series. Port Washington, N.Y.: Kennikat Press, pp. 39-66.

Views Edwards's career as a "tragic drama" and his works as a testament to a "lost cause," in a survey of the image of the Puritan God in America designed to "outrage and attract" historians, theologians, and literary critics.

2 Colacurcio, Michael J. "The Example of Edwards: Idealist Imagination and the Metaphysics of Sovereignty." In *Puritan Influences in American Literature.* Edited by Emory Elliott. Illinois Studies in Language and Literature, 65. Urbana: University of Illinois Press, pp. 55-106.

Considers Edwards, "for good or ill," a Christian philosopher with an "absolutely fundamental bias" of idealism, from his early, public, pastoral *Divine and Supernatural Light* to his late, bookish, philosophical *Original Sin.* By the 1730s Edwards can "easily swallow the gnat of sovereignty because he has already devoured the camel of pure idealism"; by the 1750s, after a "polemical delay," he returns to "the very heart of his own problems," a rational explanation of the metaphysics of sovereignty. And he fails. "Above all else, therefore, the example of Edwards provides the absolutely appropriate opportunity to observe that Christian Philosophy is valid and interesting only so long as its practitioner can keep the world from collapsing back into the mind of God."

3 Couser, G. Thomas. *American Autobiography: The Prophetic Mode.* Amherst: University of Massachusetts Press, pp. 22-27.

Compares Edwards's *Personal Narrative* to the spiritual autobiographies of Thomas Shepard and Increase Mather and finds it "by no means typical." Edwards's account is "both more private and more universal" than theirs and "radically" redefines the didactic conversion narrative to conform to his personal Calvinism and his intense mystical experience.

4 Davidson, James West. Review of Jonathan Edwards, *Apocalyptic Writings,* edited by Stephen J. Stein. *Religious Studies* 15 (March): 127-30.

Declares "definitive" Stephen J. Stein's volume in the Yale Edwards (1977.28).

5 DeProspo, R. C. "The 'New Simple Idea' of Edwards' Personal Narrative." *Early American Literature* 14 (Fall): 193-204.

Judges Edwards's *Personal Narrative* a "mature" and "sophisticated" work, a spiritual auto-biography that harmonizes John Locke's "'new simple idea'" (somewhat altered) with Puritan conversion and reconciles Edwards's theory of grace with his experience of it. That there is "nothing tangible" in the narrative; that it lacks the specifics of time, place, and person; that the imagination is not a "significant participant" in conversion is consistent with Edwards's rejection of Locke's materiality as the source of the new sense. That Edwards would write of the experience but once — and then only briefly — is consistent as well with his doubts about man's ability to know God through even the "most careful and enlightened" narrative of that experience.

6 Emerson, Everett. Review of *The Writings of Jonathan Edwards,* by William J. Scheick. *Early American Literature* 14 (Winter): 342-43.

Values William J. Scheick's "highly useful, intelligent" study (1975.16), but questions his omission of important writings — the "Treatise on Grace" and the "Miscellanies," for example — and his use of "improved" texts of Edwards's work.

7 Geisler, Norman L. "Man's Destiny: Free or Forced?" *Christian Scholar's Review* 9 (2): 99-109.

Compares the determinist views of Edwards, John Hick, and B. F. Skinner — a Calvinist, a Universalist, a behaviorist — only to conclude that C. S. Lewis offers "a more excellent way" to understand man's destiny. *Freedom of the Will* is "mistaken" in its definitions, confused in its categories, and "fallacious" in its conclusion that self-determination is a contradiction in terms.

8 Gerstner, John H. "Jonathan Edwards and the Bible." *Tenth* 9 (October): 1-71.

Examines closely Edwards's "sustained" attention to the Bible, drawn chiefly from his remarks in the "Miscellanies" and sermons and centered on the exegetical, the eschatological, and, "above all," the evangelical. Edwards's views on the Bible are "orthodox, not neo-orthodox": he held that revelation is beyond reason, that the word of God is inerrant, that the canon of Scripture is closed. In short, Edwards "majored in God's book."

9 ————. "The View of the Bible Held by the Church: Calvin and the Westminster Divines." In *Inerrancy.* Edited by Norman L. Geisler. Grand Rapids, Mich.: Zondervan, pp. 383-410.

Locates Edwards firmly within the Reformed tradition of scriptural inerrancy by citing particularly from his "Notes on the Bible" and the "Miscellanies," though it is "fully evident" in all he wrote.

10 ————, and Jonathan Neil Gerstner. "Edwardsean Preparation for Salvation." *Westminster Theological Journal* 42 (Fall): 5-71.

Insists that Edwards, like Thomas Hooker and Thomas Shepard before him, is a preparationist and traces his rationale and methodology, the theological obstacles he surmounted, and the fate his doctrine met among contemporary Edwardseans and later Calvinists, in a reading of several unpublished sermons, especially four on Eccles. 9:10. "Without moving an inch" from predestination or toward Arminianism, Edwards demanded that the fallen seek and prepare for salvation and made "strenuous striving" indispensable to it. So far, "no one has shown him wrong."

11 Gibbs, Lee W. "Introduction." *Technometry,* by William Ames. Philadelphia: University of Pennsylvania Press, pp. 51-60.

Attributes certain idealist and empiricist strains in Edwards to the "lasting influence" of Ramist logic and Puritan technologia upon both his early and later thought, in a study of the influence of William Ames's *Technometry* upon American philosophy and theology. Edwards's early essays offer "the most unambiguous witness" to an idealism founded upon the technologia taught at Yale; his later treatises — *End of Creation, True Virtue,* and *History of Redemption* — come "even closer" to Ames. Indeed, the synthesis in Edwards of idealist (Neoplatonic) metaphysics and empiricist (Aristotelian) epistemology is precisely that of Puritan technologia.

12 Gould, Timothy David. "Natural Notions, Uncommon Speech: Strands of Jonathan Edwards' Enquiry." Ph.D. dissertation, Harvard University.

Suggests that Edwards's argument from common sense and his analysis of the language of necessity found in *Freedom of the Will* might prove useful both as ways into Edwards at large and as possible modes of inquiry into contemporary philosophical criticism, such as Morton White's *Science and Sentiment* (1972.46).

13 Harlan, David Craig. "The Clergy and the Great Awakening in New England." Ph.D. dissertation, University of California, Irvine.

Published as 1980.18.

14 Helm, Paul. "Jonathan Edwards and the Doctrine of Temporal Parts." *Archiv für Geschichte der Philosophie* 61 (1): 37-51.

Discovers a "remarkable" similarity between Edwards's account of personal identity in *Original Sin* and contemporary philosophers' notion of identity: "an individual is to be understood as a succession of non-overlapping temporal parts or stages." Edwards modified John Locke by adding not only an explicitly theological stage but also another stage with "a radical twist," the doctrine of divine immediacy: an individual exists in time only by the continued re-creation of God. Thus Edwards approximates W. V. Quine, Rudolph Carnap, and R. M. Chisholm and the doctrine of temporal parts.

15 Hoitenga, Dewey J., Jr. "Norman Geisler on Man's Destiny." *Christian Scholar's Review* 9 (2): 112-16, 119-20.

Emphasizes Edwards's "startling" claim that "some form of determinism must be *consistent* with human free will," a claim Norman Geisler (1979.7) "ignores" in his "facile" interpretation of *Freedom of the Will.*

16 Keller, Karl. "A Tour of the Pit: Emily Dickinson and Jonathan Edwards." *The Only Kangaroo among the Beauty: Emily Dickinson and America.* Baltimore: Johns Hopkins University Press, pp. 67-96.

Claims that Emily Dickinson uses Edwards — particularly the Edwards of the pit, "sure of sin and damnation, beloved of a satanic God, representative of a smothering cosmic gloom" — to launch her poetry. Though parallel texts abound, they get at "nothing essential." Rather, Edwards offers Dickinson the subject of poems and provokes her "creative, aggressive" response. "It is his pit from which she sings."

17 Kenny, Anthony. *The God of the Philosophers.* Oxford: Clarendon Press, pp. 82-86.

Deems "entirely successful" Edwards's attack on the attempt to reconcile contingency with foreknowledge in *Freedom of the Will*, "less well inspired" his criticism of liberty of indifference, in an argument on the compatibility of freedom and determinism.

18 Laurence, David. "Jonathan Edwards, Solomon Stoddard, and the Preparationist Model of Conversion." *Harvard Theological Review* 72 (July): 267-83.

Traces Edwards's "critical reevaluation" of Solomon Stoddard's step-by-step preparationist model of conversion, from his experience in *Personal Narrative* to his observations in *Distinguishing Marks* and *Religious Affections*. Humiliation, for Edwards, was not the preparationist's "felt inner state" of unbelief but "the most unself-conscious form of faith" of the pilgrim, nor was an order of experience any substitute for an order of reasoning. Edwards abandoned his grandfather's "empty ritual" and its particularist argument because for him grace "transcended any of its palpable effects and had to be detected by inference and interpretation."

19 Leonard, Bill J. Review of Jonathan Edwards, *Apocalytic Writings*, edited by Stephen J. Stein. *Review and Expositor* 76 (Spring): 277-78.

Recommends Stephen J. Stein's "invaluable study" of apocalyptic thought, in a review of the fifth volume of the Yale Edwards (1977.28).

20 Lovelace, Richard F. *Dynamics of Spiritual Life: An Evangelical Theology of Renewal.* Downers Grove, Ill.: InterVarsity Press, pp. 37-43 passim.

Contends that Edwards on revival — *Distinguishing Marks, Some Thoughts,* and *Religious Affections* — is "the foundational theology of spiritual renewal in English, and perhaps in any language."

21 Lowance, Mason I., Jr. "Millennialism and the Early American Dream: Prophecy and Fulfillment in the Cycles of Early American History from the Puritans to the Civil War." *Mei-kio yen-chiu* 9 (March): 27-47.

Uncovers Puritan connections to the American dream in the typology and millennialism of seventeenth- and eighteenth-century writers, Edwards and the New Lights foremost among them. By extending types and figures beyond biblical exegesis in both *History of Redemption* and *Images or Shadows*, Edwards developed an "original epistemology," prophetic and progressive. Thus his postmillennial view of history gave rise to the "optimistic visions" of America, secular and political.

22 Mancha, Rita. "The Woman's Authority: Calvin to Edwards." *Journal of Christian Reconstruction* 6 (Winter): 86-98.

Links Edwards to John Calvin on the question of women and scriptural authority, though Edwards, unlike other Puritans, "shapes his ideas according to his wife's influence."

23 Marsden, George M. Review of Jonathan Edwards, *Apocalyptic Writings*, edited by Stephen J. Stein. *Church History* 48 (June): 226-27.

Acknowledges Stephen J. Stein's "impressively thorough" volume in the Yale Edwards (1977.28) but doubts the theological value of Edwards's apocalyptic speculations.

24 Murray, Iain H. "Jonathan Edwards 8: 'One Common Issue': The Great Awakening." *Banner of Truth* no. 187 (April): 15-29.

Reprinted as part of 1987.22.

25 ———. "Jonathan Edwards 9: Division and Disorder in New England." *Banner of Truth* no. 188 (May): 12-29.
   Reprinted as part of 1987.22.

26 ———. "Jonathan Edwards 10: The Defence of Experimental Religion." *Banner of Truth* no. 189 (June): 8-19.
   Reprinted as part of 1987.22.

27 ———. "Jonathan Edwards 10: The Defence of Experimental Religion [Continued]." *Banner of Truth* no. 190 (July): 22-26.
   Reprinted as part of 1987.22.

28 Oggel, L. Terry. "The Background of the Images of Childhood in American Literature." *Western Humanities Review* 33 (Autumn): 281-97.
   Cites Edwards's "tirade" in *Some Thoughts* as typical of the Puritan attitude toward children as sinners.

29 Parkes, Henry Bamford. *Jonathan Edwards, the Fiery Puritan.* New York: AMS Press.
   Reprints 1930.10.

30 Scott, Barbara Jean Pamela. "Faith and Chaos: The Quest for Meaning in the Writings of Jonathan Edwards and William James." Ph.D. dissertation, Syracuse University.
   Ascribes the conflict between the views of Edwards and William James to the "profound changes" in American culture between the eighteenth and nineteenth centuries, between the sense of community and the sense of the individual. Though both were affected by a youthful personal crisis and though both agreed generally about the nature of conversion, James emphasized the individual soul at the expense of the community, a stance at odds with Edwards and his time.

31 Sliwoski, Richard S. "Doctoral Dissertations on Jonathan Edwards." *Early American Literature* 14 (Winter): 318-27.
   Lists alphabetically over one hundred doctoral dissertations, American and foreign, that give "considerable attention" to Edwards.

32 Smith, John E. "Summary Report of the Progress of the Yale Edition of The Works of Jonathan Edwards." *Early American Literature* 14 (Winter): 352-53.
   Reports on the progress of the Yale Edwards, noting financial as well as editorial difficulties.

33 Stroh, Guy W. *American Ethical Thought.* Chicago: Nelson-Hall, pp. 5-25.
   Adjudges Edwards's *True Virtue* "the definitive statement" of Puritan ethics and the "real beginning" of moral philosophy in America, in a survey of American ethical thought. Though his thinking was flawed here (and in *Freedom of the Will* and *Original Sin*), Edwards gave Puritan thought its most sophisticated and subtle expression.

34 Tappan, Henry Philip. *A Review of Edwards's "Inquiry into the Freedom of the Will."* New York: AMS Press.
   Reprints 1839.8.

35 Thompson, William Oscar, Jr. "The Public Invitation as a Method of Evangelism: Its Origin and Development." Ph.D. dissertation, Southwestern Baptist Theological Seminary.

Cites Edwards as one of the contributors to the rise of public invitation during the Great Awakening.

36 Towner, W. Sibley. Review of Jonathan Edwards, *Apocalyptic Writings,* edited by Stephen J. Stein. *Interpretation* 33 (January): 107-108.

Recommends Stephen J. Stein's detailed introduction to the "fascinating" fifth volume of the Yale Edwards (1977.28), "a major event."

37 Tracy, Patricia J., R. J. Wilson, and Robert A. Gross. "Intellectuals and Society in Western Massachusetts." *Massachusetts Review* 20 (Autumn): 437-67.

Discusses the place of the intellectual in western Massachusetts in the eighteenth and nineteenth centuries.

Tracy, Patricia J. "The Pastorate of Jonathan Edwards," pp. 437-51. Charts the reciprocal relationship between Edwards and his congregation, a view more fully developed in her *Jonathan Edwards, Pastor* (1980.45).

Wilson, R. J. "Emily Dickinson and the Problem of Career," pp. 451-61. Reflects upon "some superficial similarities" between Edwards and Emily Dickinson: both had a sense of "unsatisfied yearning" and both were "locked into the present and the local," but neither "mastered the mechanisms of the professional life."

Gross, Robert A. "A Response," pp. 461-67. Considers Edwards unhappy in the pulpit and an example of the intellectual's dilemma that continues in Ralph Waldo Emerson and Emily Dickinson.

38 Unali, Lina. "La vuotezza di se nella Personal Narrative di Jonathan Edwards." *Descrizione di se: Studio sulla scrittura autobiografica del '700.* Rome: Lucarini, pp. 89-97.

Uses Edwards's *Personal Narrative* as an example of the emptied self, in a (structuralist) study of autobiography in the eighteenth century. (In Italian.)

39 Van Doren, Carl. "Introduction." In *Benjamin Franklin and Jonathan Edwards: Selections from their Writings.* Darby, Pa.: Arden Library.

Reprints 1920.7.

40 Vetö, Miklós. "La connaissance spirituelle selon Jonathan Edwards." *Revue de Theologie et de Philosophie* 111 (3): 233-51.

Probes the question of spiritual knowledge in Edwards — how to discern, distinguish, and authenticate it — in a reading of a late sermon, *True Grace, Distinguished from the Experience of the Devils* (1753), some items from the "Miscellanies," and two treatises, *Religious Affections* and *True Virtue.* (In French.)

41 ———. "La mauvaise volonte selon Jonathan Edwards." *Études Philosophiques* 34 (January): 39-54.

Recounts Edwards's argument on determinism and agency in *Freedom of the Will* and *Original Sin* and suggests a connection between the Calvinist notion of the will, the ancient (Platonic) idea of vice as habit, and the modern (Kantian) idea of uncaused morality. (In French.)

42 Viscardi, C. J. "Signs of Authenticity: A Study in the Spirituality of Jonathan Edwards." S.T.D. dissertation, Pontifical Gregorian University.

Inspects Edwards's signs of conversion in the context of the Great Awakening, distinguishing true signs from false, interior signs from exterior, and Puritan signs from Catholic.

43 Watkins, Keith. Review of Jonathan Edwards, *Apocalyptic Writings,* edited by Stephen J. Stein. *Encounter* 40 (Winter): 84-86.

Discounts the fifth volume of the Yale Edwards (1977.28) for its failure to solve "puzzles" about Edwards's "unified view" of the apocalypse.

44 Westblade, Donald. "Word and Spirit in the Theology of Jonathan Edwards." *Studia Biblica et Theologica* 9 (April): 49-60.

Asserts Edwards to be both empiricist and pietist and so "particularly appropriate" to comment upon the role of the Word and the Spirit in regeneration, in a reading of *Divine and Supernatural Light* and *Religious Affections.* God imparts to the regenerate a sense of his glory, which "alone mediates" to the understanding and "instantly evokes" the will. In this "radically empirical way," Edwards insists that in the dynamics of faith light comes before knowledge, immediacy before means.

45 Westbrook, Perry D. *Free Will and Determinism in American Literature.* Rutherford, N.J.: Fairleigh Dickinson University Press, pp. 19-22, 50-52 passim.

Cites Edwards as a "prominent" and strict Calvinist whose arguments on the will and determinism "haunted" nineteenth-century western New England and "hauntingly echo" in Ralph Waldo Emerson's "Fate."

46 Yanella, Donald, and John H. Roch, eds. *American Prose to 1820: A Guide to Information Sources.* American Literature, English Literature, and World Literatures in English, Information Guide Series, 26. Detroit: Gale Research Co., pp. 276-94 passim.

Lists over 150 books, parts of books, and articles on Edwards and briefly annotates each.

1980

1 Anderson, Michael Patrick. "The Pope of Litchfield: An Intellectual Biography of Joseph Bellamy, 1719-1790." Ph.D. dissertation, Claremont Graduate School.

Recounts Edwards's relationship to Joseph Bellamy, from the Northampton revivals to their frontier pastorates a decade later, in a study of Bellamy as a link between the first Great Awakening and the second.

2 Anderson, Wallace E. "Editor's Introduction." *Scientific and Philosophical Writings. The Works of Jonathan Edwards,* 6. New Haven: Yale University Press, pp. 1-143.

Traces the development of Edwards's scientific and philosophical thought in a detailed examination of the manuscripts from the juvenilia through the "Miscellanies" — the "spider" papers, "Natural Philosophy," "Of the Prejudices of Imagination," "Of Insects," "Of Being," "Of the Rainbow," "The Mind," among others — to establish provenance and texts, in an introduction to the sixth volume of the Yale Edwards. The traditional dates of Edwards's early writings are "quite mistaken," as are the traditional notions of his childhood interest and great skill in minute natural observation. At Yale, Edwards gained "a unique appreciation" for the "revolutionary" concepts of order of Isaac Newton; he responded to the epistemology of John Locke, if only to reject or "consciously" modify its "express claims"; and he explored the ideas of immaterialism and immediacy of Henry More, which, though "reshaped significantly" later, remained "fixed centers" of his philosophy. There is "no conflict" between Edwards's science and his theology because divine sovereignty and divine substance explain both the natural and the moral order, the physical world and the spiritual. As well, those "unshakable" doctrines explain why cognition — the knowing and perceiving of God and man — is "central" to Edwards's mature thought.

3 Belmonte, Frances Rose. "Reconciliation: A Participative Theology." Ph.D. dissertation, Joint Program of Boston College and the Andover Newton Theological School.
    Cites Edwards's experience of the kingdom of God as one of the foundations of participative theology.

4 [Boyd, J. R.] "Jonathan Edwards on Heaven and Hell." *Researcher* 10 (Summer): 14-17.
    Urges readers to "buy, beg or borrow" John H. Gerstner on Edwards (1980.14) and borrows from both.

5 Brumm, Ursula. "Jonathan Edwards and Typology." In *Early American Literature: A Collection of Critical Essays.* Edited by Michael T. Gilmore. Englewood Cliffs, N.J.: Prentice-Hall, pp. 70-83.
    Reprints 1970.2 (retitled and excerpted).

6 Cherry, Conrad. *Nature and Religious Imagination: From Edwards to Bushnell.* Philadelphia: Fortress Press, pp. 14-64 passim.
    Credits Edwards with a balanced, correlative view of nature, in the first of a three-part study of nature and the American religious imagination: nature's images (Edwards), nature's precepts (New Divinity men), and nature's symbols (Horace Bushnell). For Edwards, nature was beautiful only as it reflected the "harmony" of all levels of being, the "symmetry" of man and God, "a whole self in a whole world." Decidedly symbolic about physical nature, Edwards perceived the natural world as "an image of an image." Put another way, his doctrine of true virtue brings the beauty of the natural world, human morality, and divine benevolence into a "symbiotic" relation.

7 Colacurcio, Michael J. "Parson Hooper's Power of Blackness: Sin and Self in 'The Minister's Black Veil.'" In *Prospects: An Annual of American Cultural Studies,* 5. Edited by Jack Salzman. New York: Burt Franklin, pp. 331-411.
    Uses Edwards (and Benjamin Franklin) to gloss Nathaniel Hawthorne's "The Minister's Black Veil." Parson Hooper delivers his sermon in the "mild manner" of *Sinners in the Hands of an Angry God* and the tale itself evokes the "moral realities" of the Great Awakening.

8 Curti, Merle. *Human Nature in American Thought: A History.* Madison: University of Wisconsin Press, pp. 63-69.
    Notes Edwards's "landmark" contribution to the American discussion of human nature, for he "invigorated" Calvinist tenets with the new learning. In his view of unitive man — the interdependence of body and soul — Edwards "anticipates" transcendentalism, neo-orthodoxy, and modern psychology.

9 DeNichilo, Marcella. *Realta e immagine: L'estetica nei sermoni di Jonathan Edwards.* L'Aquila: L. U. Japadre, 360 pp.

Finds in the metaphoric structures of Edwards's sermons connections between his aesthetics and his rhetoric, his poetics and his theology, his imagery and that of later American (Romantic) writers, in a full-length study of his life, thought, and critical reception, with extended quotations from both primary and secondary sources, in print and in manuscript. His sermonic style develops from the Port-Royal logic of Antoine Arnauld and Pierre Nicolet's *The Art of Thinking,* which restored the rhetoric Peter Ramus and the New England Puritans of the seventeenth century had denied. Edwards modifies the plain style with the affecting style of types and tropes to awaken the unregenerate to an infinite God. His "ideal aesthetic" integrates language, myth, and society into an "expressive organicism," into a fixed system of correspondences between the natural world and the spiritual, between the end of nature and the end of history, between understanding and feeling. Like the self, all is an "inseparable union." (In Italian.)

10 Dickerman, David Leslie. "Family Worship in the Free-Church Tradition." D.Min. dissertation, Hartford Seminary.

Invokes the image of nurture in Edwards, in an extended definition of the inclusive church family.

11 Erdt, Terrence. *Jonathan Edwards, Art and the Sense of the Heart.* Amherst: University of Massachusetts Press, xiv, 123 pp.

Discovers the sense of the heart, the "cornerstone" of Edwards's aesthetics, not in the sensationalism of John Locke's *Essay* but in the *sensus suavitatis* of John Calvin's *Institutes.* Though Edwards follows Calvin on regeneration and assurance, he makes a "significant modification": the saint conceives (and revives) the sense of the heart aesthetically as a response to spiritual beauty. And so images from nature, from the imagination, and from works of art can "surrogate" the sense of the heart, evoking spiritual beauty or recalling it. By linking natural to spiritual beauty, Edwards's aesthetics "may have fathered" the ideas and signs of moral beauty of later American writers, "though their precise genealogy remains a mystery."

12 Gardiner, H. Norman, ed. *Jonathan Edwards, A Retrospect.* New York: AMS Press. Reprints 1901.6.

13 Gerstner, John H. "Jonathan Edwards and God." *Tenth* 10 (January): 2-71.

Derives Edwards's "great doctrine of God" from his manuscript sermons, "Miscellanies," and published work, especially *End of Creation;* parses Edwards thoughts on God's natural attributes (eternality, infinity, unity, independence, immutability, sovereignty, omniscience, personality, glory) and moral attributes (love of holiness, justice, mercy, wrath); remarks his ideas on God's happiness; and asserts his orthodox Trinitarianism "from the beginning." Edwards "resorts" to reason in his doctrine of God, but it is only the "handmaid" of revelation for him. And so "if one cannot admire the Bible, there is no way to admire Edwards (though some men keep trying)."

14 ———. *Jonathan Edwards on Heaven and Hell.* Grand Rapids, Mich.: Baker Book House, 93 pp.

Regards Edwards as "the greatest biblical artist ever" to paint the "awesome" pictures of endless heaven and endless hell, in a study chiefly of manuscript sermons and the "Miscellanies." If Edwards speaks more of hell than of heaven, if he frightens more than he comforts, then it is that the unregenerate needs stern and frequent warning, and the Bible, as often, demands it. For all that, the "truest" Edwards is the "rhapsodic seer" of divine mercy and saving grace.

15 Green, Gregory Charles. "American Eyes: The Habits of Visual Perception on a New Continent, 1620-1864." Ph.D. dissertation, Wayne State University.

Includes Edwards (and Ralph Waldo Emerson and P. T. Barnum among others) in a social history of visual perception in America.

16 Griffin, Edward M. *Old Brick: Charles Chauncy of Boston, 1705-1787*. Minnesota Monographs in the Humanities, 11. Minneapolis: University of Minnesota Press, pp. 37-46, 78-88.

Compares Edwards's treatment of Phebe Bartlet in *Faithful Narrative* with Charles Chauncy's treatment of Elizabeth Price in *Early Piety*; the image of the sinner over hell in *Sinners in the Hands of an Angry God* with the same image in *The New Creature*; and the nature and meaning of the Great Awakening in *Some Thoughts* with that in *Seasonable Thoughts*. The disorder of the Great Awakening was Chauncy's target, not Edwards.

17 Gura, Philip F. "Seasonable Thoughts: Reading Edwards in the 1980's." *New England Quarterly* 53 (September): 388-94.

Predicts that Edwards, "profoundly steeped . . . in his own historical moment," will be used to lead scholars of the 1980s to the "intellectual center of the eighteenth-century American mind," in an essay-review of the first six volumes of the Yale Edwards (1957.14, 1959.18, 1970.15, 1972.11, 1977.28, and 1980.2).

18 Harlan, David. *The Clergy and the Great Awakening in New England*. Studies in American History and Culture, 15. Ann Arbor, Mich.: UMI Research Press, pp. 1-3, 117-21.

Modifies the traditional view of the Great Awakening as a contest between Edwards and the New Lights and Charles Chauncy and the Old Lights by adding Samuel Mather and the "Regular Lights."

19 Hendry, George S. *Theology of Nature*. Philadelphia: Westminster Press, pp. 61-65.

Asserts that "No theologian devoted himself with a more sustained intensity and in a more original manner to the theme of God's work in nature than Jonathan Edwards" and offers *Images or Shadows* in evidence.

20 Hudgins, Andrew. "Awaiting Winter Visitors: Jonathan Edwards, 1749." *New Yorker*, 24 March, p. 46.

Ends a thirty-six-line poem of Edwards's reflections upon his winter season before his dismissal, "I shall retire and read St. Paul."

21 Ilacqua, Alma A. "Faulkner's *Absalom, Absalom!*: An Aesthetic Projection of the Religious Sense of Beauty." *Ball State University Forum* 21 (Spring): 34-41.

Suggests that William Faulkner "appears to translate, perhaps unconsciously," Edwards's idea of beauty to *Absalom, Absalom!*.

22 Kimball, Gayle. "Harriet Beecher Stowe's Revision of New England Theology." *Journal of Presbyterian History* 58 (Spring): 64-81.

Remarks Harriet Beecher Stowe's ambivalence towards Edwards, in a study of her reaction to New England Theology in her novels. Though "horrified" by his theology, she "inherited" his religious affections, aesthetics, sense of family, and "glorification" of New England.

23 Lang, Amy Schrager. "The Antinomian Strain in American Culture." Ph.D. dissertation, Columbia University.

Instances the debate between Charles Chauncy and Edwards on reasonable and affectionate religion as part of the antinomian conflict over the limits of self-assertion in society and theology.

24 Laurence, David. "Jonathan Edwards, John Locke, and the Canon of Experience." *Early American Literature* 15 (Fall): 107-23.

Examines Edwards's adaptation of John Locke's *Essay Concerning Human Understanding,* his effort to bend the canon of experience to the canon of Scripture. Edwards "ignored" Locke's empiricist distinctions between the material and the spiritual, positing instead a "unified" (and rational) account that links sensational psychology to spiritual illumination. And he "moved beyond" Locke with his concept of the sense of the heart, even further with his affirmation that the sense of experience was inexpressible, "shrouded in mystery."

25 Leverenz, David. "Franklin and Edwards." *The Language of Puritan Feeling: An Exploration in Literature, Psychology, and Social History.* New Brunswick, N.J.: Rutgers University Press, pp. 225-57.

Ascribes to their "assiduously sought" approval of male authority the stylistic techniques of Benjamin Franklin and Edwards, in a close reading of the first paragraphs of the *Autobiography* and *Personal Narrative.* Edwards's prose is "an exercise in disconnection," his repetition a technique to transform desire into submission, pleasure and duty into "ambiguous insecurity." His later work, marked by logic and abstraction, sacrifices the "human sensitivity and strength" of earlier Puritans for the "classically obsessive language of guilt and submission." Because such language is "overdetermined by repression of anger at several levels," Edwards's theology reveals an "awesome self-hatred."

26 Logan, Samuel T., Jr. "The Hermeneutics of Jonathan Edwards." *Westminster Theological Journal* 43 (Fall): 79-96.

Contends that Edwards "drastically expands" seventeenth-century Puritan hermeneutics into a "holistic process" involving not only the discovery of objective truth but the effect of that discovery upon the interpreting self. Edwards's practice reminds us that "hermeneutics determines homiletics," an important corrective to the imbalance of current Reformed preaching.

27 Lowance, Mason I., Jr. *The Language of Canaan: Metaphor and Symbol in New England from the Puritans to the Transcendentalists.* Cambridge: Harvard University Press.

Reprints and incorporates 1970.20, 1977.20, and 1973.18 into a record of typology in America from John Cotton to Edwards to Henry David Thoreau.

28 McGiffert, Arthur Cushman, Jr. *Jonathan Edwards.* New York: AMS Press.

Reprints 1932.10.

29 McSwain, Larry L. "Foundations for a Ministry of Community Transformation." *Review and Expositor* 77 (Spring): 253-70.

Terms Edwards "the forerunner of the Social Gospel," in a brief survey of attitudes toward community transformation in Plato, Augustine, Edwards, and Jürgen Moltmann.

30 Medlicott, Alexander, Jr. "In the Wake of Mr. Edwards's 'Most Awakening' Sermon at Enfield." *Early American Literature* 15 (Winter): 217-21.

Reprints a "detailed and graphic" description of the Enfield reaction to Edwards's *Sinners in the Hands of an Angry God,* part of the Rev. Stephen Williams's journal, published here for the first time. The village "typifies" others in the Connecticut Valley both in its initial fervor about the Great Awakening (and Edwards) and in its later skepticism.

31 Miller, Glenn T. Review of *The Prism of Scripture,* by Karl D. Pfisterer. *Catholic Historical Review* 66 (April): 250-51.

Acknowledges the importance of Karl D. Pfisterer's scriptural approach to Edwards (1975.13) but finds parts of his book "virtually unreadable."

32 Montague, Phillip. "Re-examining Huck Finn's Conscience." *Philosophy* 55 (October): 542-46.

Substitutes a scale of "blameworthiness" for one of "'bad morality,'" placing Heinrich Himmler "lower" on it than Edwards and Huck Finn off it "entirely," in another reading of an argument joining the three (see 1974.3).

33 Morgan, Edmund S. Review of *Jonathan Edwards, Pastor,* by Patricia J. Tracy. *New York Times Book Review,* 13 July, pp. 13, 38.

Questions the assumption in Patricia J. Tracy's study (1980.45) of a religious declension in Northampton after 1727 and its untoward effect on Edwards's pastorate.

34 Nettles, Tom. Review of *Jonathan Edwards on Heaven and Hell,* by John H. Gerstner. *Southwestern Journal of Theology* 23 (Fall): 109.

Commends John H. Gerstner's study (1980.14) for its "astounding volume" of citations from Edwards and for its "pithy and pertinent" remarks about them.

35 Noll, Mark A. "Moses Mather (Old Calvinist) and the Evolution of Edwardseanism." *Church History* 49 (September): 273-85.

Calls Edwards and his Calvinism "mutants" in the evolution of American theology, in a study of Moses Mather, a moderate opponent of the first Great Awakening and a probable source of the second.

36 Noyes, Richard. "The Time Horizon of Planned Social Change." *American Journal of Economics and Sociology* 39 (January): 65-77.

Cites Edwards's disagreement with John Locke over the time horizon — "the time span characteristically taken into account by an individual in the process of understanding" — in a short history of it.

37 Porterfield, Amanda. *Feminine Spirituality in America: From Sarah Edwards to Martha Graham.* Philadelphia: Temple University Press, pp. 39-48 passim.

Suggests that Edwards's marriage to Sarah Pierrepont not only typified the complementary nature of God common to Puritans but provided "experience for his theories" as well. She illustrated for him the beauty of piety and the validity of religious ecstasy, the "centerpiece" of his defense of the Great Awakening in *Some Thoughts*.

38 Przemecka, Irena. "Man and Nature in American Nineteenth-Century Poetry." *Zeitschrift für Anglistik und Amerikanistik* 28 (2): 134-38.

Divides American literature into "two distinct trends" of approach to man and nature, one derived from Edwards and alienation, the other from Ralph Waldo Emerson and union. Though nineteenth-century poets share their symbolic reading of nature, most return to Edwards's view, albeit without his theology.

39 Saucerman, James R. "A Critical Approach to Plains Poetry." *Western American Literature* 15 (Summer): 93-102.

Connects the typological use of the landscape by three western poets (Ray Young Bear, Thomas Hornsby Merril, and Clarice Short) to Edwards's practice in *Images or Shadows* and to Emerson's, "following" him.

40 Scheick, William J., ed. *Critical Essays on Jonathan Edwards.* Boston: G. K. Hall, xxv, 310 pp.

Reprints in whole or in part twenty-five selections "representative of notable commentary" on Edwards and adds an introduction and a previously unpublished essay.

Scheick, William J. "Introduction," pp. ix-xxv. Divides two hundred and fifty years of commentary on Edwards into four categories: biography (factual and interpretative): 1822.5, 1896.2, 1978.13, 1966.10, 1969.5; thought (theological, philosophical, and historical): 1750.3, 1751.3, 1873.2, 1966.9, 1889.1, 1907.6, 1950.13, 1968.9, 1959.5, 1972.39, 1975.14, 1977.20; lineage (influence on and of him): 1889.1, 1971.33, 1880.6, 1977.7, 1978.4D; and literary criticism (language and structure): 1948.1, 1965.18, 1975.2; and summarizes material "useful in a survey of scholarship" on him.

Lesser, Wayne. "Jonathan Edwards: Textuality and the Language of Man," pp. 287-304. Deconstructs Edwards's *Personal Narrative*, "the most sophisticated example of the dynamics of self-reflection in early American literature." Edwards uses a self-effacing mode of introspection to "capture the self becoming less a self and more a part of God." Less autobiographical than lexical, the "I" in the text is, by turns, passive, seeking, and choosing, and so signifies "a flawed relationship" between the self and God.

41 Shea, Daniel B. "Jonathan Edwards: the First Two Hundred Years." *Journal of American Studies* 14 (August): 181-97.

Traces the history of the "use and misuse" of Edwards to the bicentennial of his birth, in a bibliographical essay on (chiefly) nineteenth-century criticism and late twentieth-century prospects. The pattern of issues marked out early remains: Edwards as American intellectual, stern Calvinist, sometime stylist, bifurcated figure. But there is still "no wholly satisfactory" literary study of the whole of Edwards, still no synoptic study of the man and his work.

42 Scarman, Grady Temp. "The Influence of Two Theological Concepts — 'The Image of God in Man' and 'Fallen Man' — on the Thought of Selected American Protestant Religious Education Theorists." Ed.D. dissertation, University of Kansas.

Compares the influence of God's image and man's Fall on the religious educational theories of Edwards, Timothy Dwight, Horace Bushnell, and George Albert Coe.

43 Stafford, W. "Dissenting Religion Translated into Politics: Godwin's Political Justice." *History of Political Thought* 1 (Summer): 279-99.

Posits "commonplace" Calvinism rather than Edwards's *True Virtue* as the source of William Godwin's "stern insistence" on duty.

44 Stein, Stephen J. "'For Their Spiritual Good': The Northampton, Massachusetts, Prayer Bids of the 1730s and 1740s." *William and Mary Quarterly*, 3d ser., 37 (April): 261-85.

Prints ninety-nine prayer bids from the Edwards manuscript collections at Yale and Andover Newton and explains their local provenance and historical importance. Edwards saved these formal, structured prayer requests, sewing some in sermon booklets, shaping others into private notebooks. For us, they are "reminders of the bittersweet realities of daily life" in eighteenth-century New England as well as serial proof that Edwards's congregation "did not reject the classic theological categories of the Reformed tradition for a new language of religious experience forged in the heat of the Great Awakening."

45 Tracy, Patricia J. *Jonathan Edwards, Pastor: Religion and Society in Eighteenth-Century Northampton*. New York: Hill and Wang, viii, 270 pp.

Focusses on Edwards's career as a pastor — "preacher, counselor, disciplinarian" — and Northampton as an awakened community and the relation of one to the other as a paradigm of changing social values and church practices in eighteenth-century New England. His failure as pastor, his inability to persuade his flock "to share his vision," results from his lack of ministerial training, his father's losing struggle for power, his grandfather's overwhelming example, and Northampton's (and society's) growing rejection of ministerial authority. Edwards's revivalist spirit assured his position for a time, but after 1742 his disagreement with his congregation on matters of discipline and admission was so profound that they abandoned his "vision of holiness" and forced him to leave. "The tragedy of Jonathan Edwards was that he was so clearly a product of the changing patterns of authority and community life in eighteenth-century New England."

46 Wainwright, William J. "Jonathan Edwards and the Language of God." *Journal of the American Academy of Religion* 48 (December): 519-30.

Rejects Perry Miller's "overbearing" of *Images or Shadows* (1948.7) to argue that Edwards is emblematic, not symbolic, and that that implies theism. Given their Christian context, Edwards's types are hardly "subjective or capricious," scarcely rooted in John Locke's empiricism or Isaac Newton's observations. Nature, for Edwards, is "God's discourse" and its signs are "spiritual and divine realities."

47 Watts, John T. "Robert N. Bellah's Theory of America's Eschatological Hope." *Journal of Church and State* 22 (Winter): 5-22.

Scores Robert Bellah's view that Edwards's eschatological hope is at one with world civil religion: Edwards "could not accept" the non-Christian symbols of such a tradition.

48 Weber, Donald. Review of *Critical Essays on Jonathan Edwards,* edited by William J. Scheick. *Early American Literature* 15 (Winter): 281-82.

Questions some of the selections (and omissions) in William J. Scheick's "rich sourcebook" of Edwards criticism (1980.40).

49 Wohlgelernter, Maurice, ed. *History, Religion, and Spiritual Democracy: Essays in Honor of Joseph L. Blau.* New York: Columbia University Press, 375 pp.

Includes two essays touching on Edwards, in a *festschrift* for Joseph Blau.

Martin, James A., Jr. "The Esthetic, the Religious, and the Natural," pp. 76-91. Considers Edwards America's "first major spokesman" for a philosophical tradition of aesthetics in religion, a tradition including such diverse figures as George Santyana, John Dewey, and John Herman Randall, Jr. Not only was Edwards's use of tropes and types in *Images or Shadows* "radically innovative," but his theologically expressed questions also appear later in some forms of naturalistic humanism.

Madden, Edward H. "Asa Mahan and the Oberlin Philosophy," pp. 155-80. Evaluates Asa Mahan's critique of *Freedom of the Will* (1846.3).

50 Wright, Elliott. *Holy Company: Christian Heroes and Heroines.* New York: Macmillan, pp. 30-34.

Remarks the "lifelong love" of Sarah and Jonathan for each other and for God, in a summary estimate of Edwards's marriage and career.

51 Zanger, Jules. "'The Pit and the Pendulum' and American Revivalism." *Religion in Life* 49 (Spring): 96-105.

Proposes *Sinners in the Hands of an Angry God* as "a useful gloss" to "The Pit and the Pendulum," in a study of the second Great Awakening, Edwards's revivalist techniques, and Edgar Allan Poe's critical theory and fiction. Poe induced in his readers "precisely that dynamic of terror" that Edwards imbued revivalism with a century before.

1981

1 Béranger, Jean. "Interpretation et utilisation de l'Apocalypse par Jonathan Edwards." In *Le Facteur religieux en Amérique du Nord, No. 2: Apocalypse et autres travaux.* Edited by Jean Béranger. Talence: Maison des Science de l'Homme d'Aquitaine, pp. 31-47.

Examines Edwards's contribution to the literature of the Apocalypse in its historical and evangelical contexts. (In French.)

2 Bertinetti, Ilse. Review of Jonathan Edwards, *Apocalyptic Writings*, edited by Stephen J. Stein. *Theologische Literaturzeitung* 106 (January): 48-49.

Summarizes Stephen J. Stein's introduction to the fifth volume of the Yale Edwards (1977.28). (In German.)

3 Bushman, Richard L. "Jonathan Edwards as Great Man: Identity, Conversion, and Leadership in the Great Awakening." In *Our Selves/Our Past: Psychological Approaches to American History.* Edited by Robert J. Brugger. Baltimore: Johns Hopkins University Press, pp. 48-74.

Reprints 1969.5.

4 Cherry, Conrad. Review of Jonathan Edwards, *Scientific and Philosophical Writings*, edited by Wallace E. Anderson. *Church History* 50 (September): 351-52.

Values Wallace E. Anderson's "bold and persuasive" introduction to volume six of the Yale Edwards (1980.2) as a "substantial piece of philosophical reflection and historical analysis" and his texts as "authoritative transcripts."

5 Conforti, Joseph A. *Samuel Hopkins and the New Divinity Movement: Calvinism, the Congregational Ministry, and Reform in New England between the Great Awakenings.* Grand Rapids, Mich.: Christian University Press, pp. 109-24 passim.
   Reprints 1977.7 (revised).

6 Cooey-Nichols, Paula Maria. "Nature as Divine Communication in the Works of Jonathan Edwards." Ph.D. dissertation, Harvard University.
   Published as 1985.8 (revised).

7 Downey, James. "Barnabas and Boanerges: Archetypes of Eighteenth-Century Preaching." *University of Toronto Quarterly* 51 (Fall): 36-46.
   Cites Edwards as an example of the thundering evangelical preacher, "literal and graphic."

8 Dyck, Arthur J. "Moral Requiredness: Bridging the Gap between 'Ought' and 'Is' — Part II." *Journal of Religious Ethics* 9 (Spring): 131-50.
   Includes Edwards (and H. Richard Niebuhr) among Christian ethicists who characterize moral evaluations empirically, see continuity between moral requiredness and its nonmoral forms, and regard love for God as "requisite for attaining veridical moral perception," in a proposed theory of moral experiences.

9 Ellsworth, Mary Ellen Tressel. "Two New England Writers: Harriet Beecher Stowe and Mary Wilkins Freeman." Ph.D. dissertation, Columbia University.
   Notes that Edwards's theology "primarily" defines the Calvinism in Harriet Beecher Stowe's fiction.

10 Fiering, Norman. *Jonathan Edwards's Moral Thought and Its British Context.* Chapel Hill: University of North Carolina Press, xiii, 391 pp.
   Traces the development of Edwards's moral thought through the "Miscellanies," *Freedom of the Will, Original Sin,* and, climactically, *True Virtue,* in the context of British and continental moralists, particularly Francis Hutcheson and David Hume, Nicolas Malebranche and Gottfried von Leibniz, and at the expense of John Locke — "Edwards himself was no Lockean" — and Perry Miller (1949.9; rpt. 1981.27). Yale taught Edwards the Harvard curriculum — Henry More, Adrian Heereboord, Jean LeClerc, *The Art of Thinking* — but Edwards was "too much of a philosopher" to be comprehended by that or New England Puritanism "alone." His was a speculative mind, wide-ranging in metaphysics and ethics, synthesizing ideas of "natural understanding," self-love, the doctrine of hell, determinism, and piety into creative structures of moral theology, "a unique work in American thought." But his theory of virtue — disinterested benevolence and benevolence to being in general — all but loses its Christian center. "Edwards's effort, in short, kept alive a transcendental standard of virtue or, at minimum, kept alive the possibility of aspiration toward a transcendental standard of virtue that is not strictly identified with institutionalized Christianity."

11 ———. *Moral Philosophy at Seventeenth-Century Harvard: A Discipline in Transition.* Chapel Hill: University of North Carolina Press, pp. 138-46 passim.

Locates Edwards in the voluntarist tradition and Charles Chauncy in the intellectualist tradition of the seventeenth century in their debate about the Great Awakening, an eighteenth-century example of "the perennial opposition of head and heart." Edwards was "completely familiar" with William Ames, William Perkins, Petrus van Mastricht, and other exponents of Augustinian voluntarism, itself an extension of the "concursus Dei of regeneration into a broad psychological theory."

12 Gaustad, Edwin S. Review of Jonathan Edwards, *Scientific and Philosophical Writings,* edited by Wallace E. Anderson. *Christian Century* 98 (18 November): 1205-1206.

Praises Wallace E. Anderson's "library of labor" that restores "the vitality of Edwards's thought, the keenness of his observation, the scope of his imagination," in a review of the sixth volume of the Yale Edwards (1980.2).

13 Geissler, Suzanne. *Jonathan Edwards to Aaron Burr, Jr.: From the Great Awakening to Democratic Politics.* Studies in American Religion, 1. Lewiston, N.Y.: Edwin Mellen, ix, 276 pp.

Charts the influence of Edwards upon his grandson, Aaron Burr, through family "imprinting" — the boy's father was a "spiritual son" of Edwards — and through commonly held philosophical and political beliefs. Burr's early essay, "The Passions," is "strikingly similar" in its psychology to *Religious Affections;* his farewell speech to the Senate bears a "striking resemblance" to Edwards's farewell sermon fifty-five years before; and his political thought derives from Edwards's millennialism, secularized. In short, Burr tried to "live out his grandfather's interpretation of the gospel for his time."

14 Goen, C. C. Review of *Jonathan Edwards, Art and the Sense of the Heart,* by Terrence Erdt. *Journal of American History* 68 (December): 647-48.

Questions the significance of Terrence Erdt's "modest essay" on Edwards (1980.11), little more than a gloss to Perry Miller's "From Edwards to Emerson" (1940.9).

15 Gustafson, James M. *Ethics from a Theocentric Perspective: Theology and Ethics.* Chicago: University of Chicago Press, pp. 171-76.

Considers Edwards "very much" in the Reformed tradition of St. Augustine and John Calvin, sharing with them a "consistent" focus on God's sovereignty and a "common" emphasis on experimental religion. In ethics, particularly in *True Virtue,* Edwards shows himself a "latter-day" Augustine as he connects piety to morality, beauty to benevolence, harmony to consent, and all to God.

16 Hovenkamp, Herbert. Review of Jonathan Edwards, *Scientific and Philosophical Writings,* edited by Wallace E. Anderson. *Isis* 72 (June): 321.

Lauds Wallace E. Anderson's "superb analysis" of the early thought of Edwards in the sixth volume of the Yale edition (1980.2), though it scants his scientific and philosophical world view.

17 Hudgins, Andrew. "'How Will the Heart Endure?': Robert Lowell on Jonathan Edwards." *South Atlantic Quarterly* 80 (Autumn): 429-40.

Uses Robert Lowell's four poems on Edwards — "Mr. Edwards and the Spider" and "After the Surprising Conversions" (1946.3); "Jonathan Edwards in Western Massachusetts" (1964.14); and "The Worst Sinner, Jonathan Edwards' God" (1973.19) — to chart his ambivalence to Edwards and to mark the shift in his poetic stances.

18 Jamieson, John F. "Jonathan Edwards's Change of Position on Stoddardeanism." *Harvard Theological Review* 74 (January): 79-99.

Follows Edwards's "early and persistent misgivings" about Solomon Stoddard's admission practices, from his journals and sermons to his *Humble Inquiry* and dismissal, from his early theological justification to its later political expression. Edwards disapproved of the "crypto-Arminian tendencies" in Stoddardeanism and, given his role in revivalism, its rejection of experiential piety and the profession of faith.

19 Johnson, Paul David. "Jonathan Edwards's 'Sweet Conjunction.'" *Early American Literature* 16 (Winter): 270-81.

Traces four "supremely important" images in *Personal Narrative* — booth, sickness, pasture, and closet — that "crystallize" Edwards's experience from childhood to early maturity, using the model suggested by Gaston Bachelard's poetics. The images provide "visual records" of the conjunction between past and present, inner and outer, "the 'mind' of the world and the world of Edwards's mind." The image of the closet, for example, recapitulates that of the booth, but it reveals as well a shift from contemplation to action, "from the beauty of seeing to the beauty of doing."

20 Kern, Alexander. "Coleridge and American Romanticism: the Transcendentalists and Poe." In *New Approaches to Coleridge: Biographical and Critical Essays*. Edited by Donald Sultana. New York: Vision Press, pp. 113-36.

Notes parallel conceptions of the regenerate in Edwards's *Religious Affections* and Samuel Taylor Coleridge's *Aids to Reflection*.

21 Koreneva, Maiya M. "New England and American Literature." In *Problemy Stanovleniia Amerikanskoii Literatury*. Edited by Iasen N. Zasurskii. Moscow: Nauka, pp. 22-88.

Relates Edwards's natural typology, especially in *Images or Shadows*, to the development of American literature, in a survey of his work. (In Russian.)

22 Lesser, M. X. *Jonathan Edwards: A Reference Guide*. Boston: G. K. Hall, lix, 421 pp.

Annotates (chronologically) nearly 1,800 Edwards items — books, articles, dissertations, reviews, fugitive references — and includes a chronology of his works, a 45-page survey of the growth and direction of Edwards criticism from his assumption of the Northampton pulpit in 1729 to the dramatic rise of scholarly interest over the last fifteen years, and an index interleaved for author, title, and subject.

23 Lovejoy, John M. Review of *Jonathan Edwards, Pastor,* by Patricia J. Tracy. *Early American Literature* 16 (Winter): 290.

Deems Patricia J. Tracy's "challenging" study on Edwards (1980.45) "unmatched" as a social history of Northampton.

24 Main, Gloria L. "The Good Shepherd and His Wandering Flock." *Reviews in American History* 9 (December): 464-68.

Rates Patricia J. Tracy's "dual biography" of Edwards and Northampton (1980.45) "a mixed bag," better as an intellectual life of the first than as a social history of the second, in an essay-review.

25 Mani, Lakshmi. *The Apocalyptic Vision in Nineteenth-Century American Fiction: A Study of Cooper, Hawthorne, and Melville.* Washington, D.C.: University Press of America, pp. 33-38 passim.

> Outlines the apocalyptic vision of Edwards — the "greatest exponent of the millennial myth during the Great Awakening" — and traces its sources and its heirs.

26 Manspeaker, Nancy. *Jonathan Edwards: Bibliographical Synopses.* Studies in American Religion, 3. Lewiston, N.Y.: Edwin Mellen, xviii, 259 pp.

> Annotates (alphabetically) over 700 Edwards items in the bibliographies of the *Cambridge History of American Literature* (1917.1), the revised *Representative Selections* (1962.2), and other "minor" compilations — "all works in which Edwards' thought or influence is given more than incidental consideration" — and includes an introduction and a list of his published works.

27 Miller, Perry. *Jonathan Edwards.* Amherst: University of Massachusetts Press, xxxiv, 348 pp.

> Reprints 1949.9 and adds an introduction.
>
> Weber, Donald. "Perry Miller and the Recovery of Jonathan Edwards," pp. v-xxiv. Limns the "image" of Edwards in American cultural history, in an appraisal of Perry Miller's study, the "locus classicus of Edwards scholarship for a new generation." Edwards criticism shifts from rejection early in the twentieth century to renewal later on, from the cultural polarities of Van Wyck Brooks (1915.1), for example, to the neo-orthodoxy of H. Richard Niebuhr (1937.7). But Miller recovers a "usable" Edwards, a "critical realist exposing the naive doctrines of American exceptionalism in his own time," a "touchstone that could register the meaning of America."

28 Ottati, Douglas F. Review of *Jonathan Edwards, Scientific and Philosophical Writings,* edited by Wallace E. Anderson. *Interpretation* 35 (July): 332-33.

> Finds Wallace E. Anderson's introduction to the sixth volume of the Yale Edwards (1980.2) "genuinely helpful," the texts "indispensable."

29 Reynolds, David S. *Faith in Fiction: The Emergence of Religious Literature in America.* Cambridge: Harvard University Press, 21-22 passim.

> Contrasts Edwards's distrust of the "visionary ladder" with the rise of the Oriental tale in the eighteenth century.

30 Shiels, Richards D. Review of *Jonathan Edwards, Pastor,* by Patricia J. Tracy. *Catholic Historical Review* 67 (July): 489-90.

> Recommends Patricia J. Tracy's "model" study of Edwards (1980.45) to both social and intellectual historians, for it "transcends traditional categories."

31 Smith, John E. "Testing the Spirits: Jonathan Edwards and the Religious Affections." Essays in Honor of James A. Martin, Jr. *Union Seminary Quarterly Review* 37 (Fall): 27-37.

> Calls for a comprehensive view of the enigmatic Edwards, one that engages both the orthodox Calvinist of *Original Sin* and the speculative theologian of *End of Creation,* that locates him in the "great tradition of philosophically oriented theology" of the early Christian Fathers, that represents his "fusion of thought and experience." Edwards's "life-long" concern was the "rigorous" testing of the Holy Spirit followed by signs of holy practice and probably owes more to American pragmatism than to Lockean internal states of mind. Edwards has been misunder-

stood by his contemporaries and ours: religious affections are not the passions but the biblical "'fruits of the Spirit,'" love and hope and peace.

32 Spohn, William C. "Sovereign Beauty: Jonathan Edwards and the Nature of True Virtue." *Theological Studies* 42 (September): 394-421.

Considers Edwards's *True Virtue* and *End of Creation* "parts of a single argument," a metaethics that takes the love of God as the "comprehensive context" of duty and enjoyment, morality and aesthetics. Edwards argues from the twin criteria of dependence and subordination, disposition and object, benevolence and being. More important, he argues in the language of authentic religion, "an ethics of beauty based upon the love of God rather than an ethics of love of God based upon beauty."

33 Stein, Stephen J. Review of *Jonathan Edwards, Art and the Sense of the Heart,* by Terrence Erdt. *American Historical Review* 86 (October): 914-15.

Praises Terrence Erdt's study of Edwards's aesthetics (1980.11) as "an excellent example" of interdisciplinary scholarship.

34 Stephens, Bruce M. *God's Last Metaphor: The Doctrine of the Trinity in New England Theology.* American Academy of Religion: Studies in Religion, 24. Chico, Cal.: Scholars Press, pp. 1-9 passim.

Locates the source (and strength) of Edwards's Trinitarianism in the "relational experiences" of faith but finds them missing from later New England Theology.

35 Strader, Ronald Edwin. "The Chronological Development of the Spiritual-Aesthetic in the Philosophical-Theology of Jonathan Edwards and its Relationship to Seventeenth- and Eighteenth-Century British Philosophy." Ph.D. dissertation, Claremont Graduate School.

Divides Edwards's life and thought into three parts — the pre-pastoral, the pastoral, and the post-pastoral — in order to trace his aesthetics, a creative solution to "his own anxieties." To the first belongs his "mystical leanings," his reading of John Locke, and his initial exploration of beauty in "The Mind"; to the second, his rejection of mysticism and the "classic" formulation of his spiritual-aesthetic in *Religious Affections;* to the third, his solution in purely philosophical terms, the influence of Francis Hutcheson, and the "grand summary" of his aesthetic theology in *True Virtue.*

36 Vetö, Miklós. Review of Jonathan Edwards, *Scientific and Philosophical Writings,* edited by Wallace E. Anderson. *Études Philosophiques,* n.s., 1 (December): 479-80.

Recommends Wallace E. Anderson's introduction to sixth volume of the Yale edition (1980.2) to Edwards specialists, but questions the overwhelming critical apparatus. (In French.)

37 Wainwright, William J. Review of Jonathan Edwards, *Scientific and Philosophical Writings,* edited by Wallace E. Anderson. *Journal of the American Academy of Religion* 46 (September): 499-500.

Faults Wallace E. Anderson's "generally excellent" introduction (1980.2) for exaggerating Henry More's influence upon Edwards and for misreading Edwards's structure of being.

38 Westra, Helen Petter. "Jonathan Edwards' Errand into the World: The Minister as

Christ's Proxy in the Ministerial Sermons." Ph.D. dissertation, University of Notre Dame.

> Published as 1986.45.

39 Wilbur, Raymond Bernard. "Diary of the Damned: A Study in Theocentric Anxiety in Pre-Awakening New Hampshire." Ph.D. dissertation, University of New Hampshire.

> Remarks the importance of Edwards's *Religious Affections* to Joseph Moody in shaping his modified preparationist-predestinarian belief and practice, in a study of his coded Latin diary.

40 Williams, David R. "Horses, Pigeons, and the Therapy of Conversion: A Psychological Reading of Jonathan Edwards's Theology." *Harvard Theological Review* 74 (October): 337-52.

> Compares Edwards's "remarkably similar" analysis of human behavior in *Freedom of the Will* (and elsewhere) to B. F. Skinner's in *About Behaviorism*. Both Edwards and Skinner claim that human behavior results from innate inclinations responding to environmental stimuli, that habits of mind condition motives, and that the strongest motives determine will and identity. But Edwards differs "radically" from Skinner and comes "closer" to Freud and his successors when he calls for the destruction of self in order to reach regeneration.

41 Wilson, John F. Review of Jonathan Edwards, *Scientific and Philosophical Writings*, edited by Wallace E. Anderson. *Religious Studies Review* 7 (January): 90.

> Commends Wallace E. Anderson's "painstakingly" edited sixth volume of the Yale Edwards (1980.2), "an impressive achievement" that only awaits publication of the complete "Miscellanies" for confirmation.

42 ———. Review of *Jonathan Edwards, Art and the Sense of the Heart,* by Terrence Erdt. *Religious Studies Review* 7 (July): 270.

> Regards Terrence Erdt's book (1980.11) a "welcome addition" to recent studies of Edwards, especially for its literary analysis.

43 Wolf, Carl J. C., ed. *Jonathan Edwards on Evangelism.* Westport, Conn.: Greenwood Press.

> Reprints 1958.29.

1982

1 Bercovitch, Sacvan. "The Ritual of American Autobiography: Edwards, Franklin, Thoreau." *Revue Francaise d'Études Américaines* 7 (May): 139-50.

> Uncovers "persistent patterns" in three autobiographies "canonized" as representative American lives: Edwards's *Personal Narrative*, Benjamin Franklin's *Autobiography,* and Henry David Thoreau's *Walden*. All share the "distinctively American" emphasis on the individual self, yet all are "profoundly conservative and impersonal," driven by self-effacement to create archetypal selves (spiritual, civic, economic) in times of social flux and upheaval. Thus the object of "ritual" American autobiography is to "contain individualism," to "harness for social ends whatever is potentially subversive" in self-realization, and to perpetuate the "cultural continuity" of American free enterprise.

2 Berens, John F. Review of *Jonathan Edwards to Aaron Burr, Jr.,* by Suzanne Geissler. *American Historical Review* 87 (June): 848.

> Considers Suzanne Geissler's study of Edwards and Burr (1981.13) "an unfortunate example of history by assertion."

3 Breitenbach, William. "Unregenerate Doings: Selflessness and Selfishness in New Divinity Theology." *American Quarterly* 34 (Winter): 479-502.

> Labels the distinction Edwards makes between moral and natural necessity in *Freedom of the Will* the "shibboleth" of the New Divinity.

4 Budgen, Victor. "The Religious Affections and Revival Today." *Reformation Today* no. 68 (July): 21-31.

> Connects Edwards's "consistent, closely-reasoned" rejection of claimants to supernatural gifts of the spirit to his advocacy of Scripture and rigorous scrutiny and to his suspicion of "any great leader." For Edwards, the "key" passage was 1 Cor. 13, a text he turns to often, from "Notes on the Bible" to *Charity and its Fruits.* Such "splendid" scriptural exegesis is important to any assessment of the current charismatic movement.

5 Butler, Jon. "Enthusiasm Described and Decried: The Great Awakening as Interpretative Fiction." *Journal of American History* 69 (September): 305-25.

> Redefines as "regional" Edwards's role in a redefined Great Awakening, a term that "falsely homogenizes the heterogeneous."

6 Cole, Phyllis. "The Advantage of Loneliness: Mary Moody Emerson's Almanacks, 1802-1855." In *Emerson: Prospect and Retrospect.* Edited by Joel Porte. Harvard English Studies, 10. Cambridge: Harvard University Press, pp. 1-32.

> Notes Edwards's influence upon Mary Moody Emerson — she brings him "straight across the intervening generations into the nascent romantic culture of nineteenth-century Massachusetts" — and hers upon her nephew.

7 Crocco, Stephen. Review of *Moral Philosophy at Seventeenth-Century Harvard* and *Jonathan Edwards's Moral Thought and Its British Context,* by Norman Fiering. *Trinity Journal,* n.s., 3 (Fall): 244-47.

> Questions Norman Fiering's "otherwise very fine" studies (1981.11 and 1981.10) for failing to take into account the rise of deism and biblical criticism, the sixth volume of the Yale edition (1980.2), and Edwards's "most important" ethical works, *End of Creation* and *Charity and its Fruits.*

8 Dean, William. "An American Theology." *Process Studies* 12 (Summer): 111-28.

> Includes Edwards in the historical development of empirical process theology, the "distinctly, typically, and quintessentially American" movement of William James, John Dewey, Alfred North Whitehead, and the Chicago theologians, Harry Nelson Wieman, Bernard Meland, and Bernard Loomer. James's radical empiricism was "an unwitting resumption" of the epistemology of Edwards, his "intellectual grandfather."

9 Edwards, Rem Blanchard. *A Return to Moral and Religious Philosophy in Early America.* Washington, D.C.: University Press of America, pp. 1-79.

> Charts Edwards's life, times, and ideas — and those of Thomas Jefferson and Ralph Waldo

Emerson — in a brief account of early American philosophy by "a Jeffersonian democrat and freethinker." Edwards developed "the most philosophically astute version" of Puritanism, including, in *Freedom of the Will,* "the best defense ever given to the worst theology ever conceived." In him, the heretical tendency in Puritanism found "full fruition": Edwards was "always on the brink of pantheism if not totally immersed in it."

10   Fiering, Norman. Review of *Jonathan Edwards, Art and the Sense of the Heart,* by Terrence Erdt. *Journal of Presbyterian History* 60 (Spring): 92-93.
    Dismisses Terrence Erdt's study of art in Edwards (1980.11) as "a largely barren topic," for it fails to distinguish between metaphysics and aesthetics, offers questionable material in proof, and dilutes what is first-rate.

11   Gerbaud, Colette. Review of *Critical Essays on Jonathan Edwards,* edited by William J. Scheick. *Études Anglaises* 35 (June): 359-60.
    Recommends William J. Schick's collection of essays (1980.40) to Edwards specialists. (In French.)

12   Garbo, Norman S. Review of *Jonathan Edwards's Moral Thought and Its British Context,* by Norman Fiering. *American Literature* 54 (December): 608-10.
    Judges Norman Fiering's study (1981.10) an "insistent, methodical meditation" on *True Virtue* but one that "plays down" Edwards's new sense perception, his typology, his aesthetics, and his style.

13   Germander, M. E. "The Fourfold Way: Determinism, Moral Responsibility, and Aristotelean Causation." *Metamedicine* 3 (October): 375-96.
    Questions Edwards's argument in *Freedom of the Will* because it rests on efficient causation only, not Aristotle's multiple causation (material, formal, efficient, and final), in a reexamination of the relationship between necessity and moral agency. Even so, Edwards's treatise is "an extraordinary psychological document" and has "contemporary relevance" in matters of moral responsibility and ethical choice, as the goal-oriented behavior investigations of Thomas Szasz have implied.

14   Gura, Philip F. "The New England Mind Revisited." *Virginia Quarterly Review* 58 (Summer): 526-32.
    Discerns Perry Miller's "unshakable presence" but not his "gift for the felicitous phrase" in Norman Fiering's *Jonathan Edwards's Moral Thought* (1981.10) and *Moral Philosophy at Seventeenth-Century Harvard* (1981.11), in an essay-review. Fiering's "large-scale corrective" of *The New England Mind* (1939.5) and *Jonathan Edwards* (1949.9) establishes "unmistakable continuities" between Edwards and his predecessors where Miller saw none.

15   Guret, John M. "Introduction to the History of Paul's Aesthetic." In *The New Testament Student and his Field.* Edited by John H. Skilton and Curtiss A. Ladley. Phillipsburg, N.J.: Presbyterian and Reformed Publishing, pp. 260-76.
    Ascribes Edwards's "'Stockbridge aesthetic'" not to Calvin but to Augustine, to Plotinus, and to a monism "ingloriously perpetuated and enlarged," in prefatory remarks to an unfinished series of articles on Paul's aesthetics. Edwards's aesthetic, "not even an aesthetic," is "at least a gigantic failure."

16 Gustafson, James M. Review of *Jonathan Edwards, Art and the Sense of the Heart,* by Terrence Erdt. *Journal of Religion* 62 (October): 433-34.

Notes that Terrence Erdt's "significant" study (1980.11), unlike Norman Fiering's (1981.10), relies heavily on Calvin for understanding the new sense.

17 Herring, Mark Y. Review of *Jonathan Edwards,* by Nancy Manspeaker. *American Reference Book Annual,* 13. Littleton, Colo.: Libraries Unlimited, pp. 555-56.

Deems Nancy Manspeaker's bibliography (1981.26) "certainly no touchstone of Edwards scholarship, but a welcome addition."

18 Holbrook, Clyde A. Review of *Jonathan Edwards's Moral Thought and Its British Context,* by Norman Fiering. *William and Mary Quarterly,* 3d ser., 39 (October): 689-93.

Praises Norman Fiering's "magisterial command" of sources in his "exhaustive" treatment of Edwards's ethics (1981.10), but objects to the "artificial" separation of Edwards's moral philosophy from his moral theology, immorality from sin. If the documentation "almost smothers" Edwards at times, the problem of sin proves even more troublesome.

19 Jones, E. Michael. "Metaphysics as Tarbaby: Intention, Deconstruction and Absolutes." *Center Journal* 1 (Spring): 9-37.

Deals with the question of authorial intention in an Edwards sermon, a Walt Whitman poem, an Emily Dickinson poem, and, at length, essays by J. Hillis Miller, as part of an examination of the metaphysics of deconstructive criticism. The dangling spider in *Sinners in the Hands of an Angry God* "(unwittingly?) subverts" Edwards's salvific intention, and so the sermon becomes one about "helplessness and hopelessness in which we find ourselves pitying the spider and hating God."

20 Kimnach, Wilson H. "Marginalia." *Yale University Library Gazette* 57 (October): 79-82.

Describes Yale's newly acquired manuscript of Edwards's farewell sermon and its provenance.

21 Klaaren, Eugene M. Review of Jonathan Edwards, *Scientific and Philosophical Writings,* edited by Wallace E. Anderson. *Journal of Presbyterian History* 60 (Fall): 280-82.

Commends Wallace E. Anderson's introduction (1980.2) for its "careful" account of Edwards's early philosophical development, "a major contribution."

22 Leonard, Bill J. Review of *Jonathan Edwards on Heaven and Hell,* by John H. Gerstner. *Review and Expositor* 79 (Fall): 692-93.

Welcomes John H. Gerstner's study of Edwards (1980.14) for its "insight" into issues "overlooked, ignored, or sentimentalized" by ministers today, even though the interpretations are shaped by the author.

23 ———. Review of *Jonathan Edwards, Pastor,* by Patricia J. Tracy. *Review and Expositor* 79 (Summer): 548-49.

Endorses Patricia J. Tracy's study of the "human" Edwards (1980.45).

24 Levin, David. Review of *Jonathan Edwards's Moral Thought and Its British Context,* by Norman Fiering. *Journal of American History* 69 (December): 685.

    Rates Norman Fiering's study of Edwards (1981.10) "a quiet triumph" but marred by compositional methods that conflict and obfuscate.

25 Maas, David E. Review of *Jonathan Edwards, Pastor,* by Patricia J. Tracy. *Christian Scholar's Review* 11 (2): 172-73.

    Points to a "fatal flaw" in Patricia J. Tracy's "sophisticated" and "brilliant" study (1980.45): a failure to acknowledge that conversion is a spiritual experience apart from social, economic, or psychological contexts.

26 Malone, Marta Isabel Barbosa. "Dois homens — duas mensagens." *Minas Gerais, Suplemento Literario* 15 (27 March): 6-7.

    Compares two masters of the sermon, Edwards and Antonio Vieira, a seventeenth-century Brazilian Jesuit. (In Portuguese.)

27 McCartney, Lisa M. "Form and Voice in Selected American Puritan Spiritual Autobiographies." Ph.D. dissertation, University of Notre Dame.

    Places Edwards's *Personal Narrative* at the climax of American Puritan spiritual autobiographies, when compared to those of Thomas Shepard and Samuel Hopkins, because it brings to "perfect harmony" the doctrinal and experiential dimensions of the word of God.

28 McDonald, Joseph. Review of *Jonathan Edwards,* by M. X. Lesser. *American Reference Book Annual,* 13. Littleton, Colo.: Libraries Unlimited, p. 555.

    Ranks M. X. Lesser's reference guide (1981.22) "the definitive annotated bibliography" on Edwards.

29 McGreal, Ian P., and Marcus Ford. "Freedom of the Will — Jonathan Edwards." In *World Philosophy: Essay-Reviews of 225 Major Works,* 3. Edited by Frank N. Magill and Ian P. McGreal. Englewood Cliffs, N.J.: Salem Press, pp. 1061-70.

    Summarizes Edwards's *Freedom of the Will,* a masterpiece by "the first significant mind" in American philosophy, and adds critical estimates.

30 Mooney, Michael Eugene. "Millennialism and Antichrist in New England, 1630-1770." Ph.D. dissertation, Syracuse University.

    Examines Edwards on the Antichrist, in a study of millennialist thought from organicism to voluntarism, from John Cotton to Charles Chauncy.

31 Moran, Gerald F. Review of *Jonathan Edwards to Aaron Burr,* by Suzanne Geissler. *Journal of American History* 69 (September): 43.

    Doubts the "overburdened" thesis of Suzanne Geissler's study (1981.13).

32 Noll, Mark A. "The Image of the United States as a Biblical Nation, 1776-1865." In *The Bible in America: Essays in Cultural History.* Edited by Nathan O. Hatch and Mark A. Noll. New York: Oxford University Press, pp. 39-58.

    Cites Edwards's emphasis upon spiritual, not national, uses of typology, in a study of the place of the Bible in American cultural history.

33 Reynolds, Cynthia F. "Jonathan Edwards: An American Augustine." *University: A Princeton Magazine* 86 (Winter): 21-23.

Records a brief life of Edwards, third president of Princeton, and the comments of Princeton professors Paul Ramsey and John F. Wilson about editing *Ethical Writings* (1989.44) and *History of Redemption* (1989.59) for Yale.

34 Sauer, James L. Review of *Jonathan Edwards's Moral Thought and Its British Context*, by Norman Fiering. *Christianity and Literature* 31 (Summer): 96-97.

Approves Norman Fiering's "dry" study of Edwards (1981.10).

35 Schlatter, Richard. Review of *Jonathan Edwards's Moral Thought and Its British Context*, by Norman Fiering. *American Historical Review* 87 (October): 1152-53.

Questions Norman Fiering's "skillful and subtle" analysis (1981.10) for its unsympathetic treatment of Perry Miller and its failure to diagnose Edwards's psyche.

36 Simonson, Harold P. *Jonathan Edwards, Theologian of the Heart*. Macon, Ga.: Mercer University Press.

Reprints 1974.23.

37 Spohn, William C. Review of *Jonathan Edwards's Moral Thought and Its British Context*, by Norman Fiering. *Theological Studies* 43 (December): 725-26.

Adds Norman Fiering's study of Edwards (1981.10) to those of Roland Delattre (1968.8) and Clyde Holbrook (1973.13) as "indispensable" secondary sources.

38 Stephens, Bruce M. Review of *Jonathan Edwards, Art and the Sense of the Heart*, by Terrence Erdt. *Church History* 51 (September): 355.

Regards Terrence Erdt's argument about Edwards's aesthetics (1980.11) "suggestive but incomplete" and freighted with literary analysis.

39 Storms, C. Samuel. "Jonathan Edwards on the Freedom of the Will." *Trinity Journal*, n.s., 3 (Fall): 131-69.

Explores the theology of Edwards's *Freedom of the Will* and its practical implications for the Christian life and ministry, in a step-by-step recapitulation of the argument of the text. Edwards speaks to "the very heart of the Christian gospel," for the doctrines of inability and necessity are "not mere scholastic distinctions, but vocal testimony" that salvation comes from God's grace alone.

40 Thompson, Christa Marie. "Apocalyptic Piety: Franciscan Spirit and Tradition in Jonathan Edwards' Works." Ph.D. dissertation, University of Notre Dame.

Links Edwards to the apocalyptic tradition of the Franciscans in their concepts of history, nature, and mission; their reliance on sensational rhetoric and affective contemplation; and their "'lyrical eschatology.'" Edwards's views on the performative word, universal conversion, synergistic salvation, and progressive millennialism place him "firmly within" that spirit and tradition.

41 Van Leer, David M. "Rethinking the New England Mind." *Pennsylvania Magazine of History and Biography* 106 (April): 287-90.

Descries an "unusual" Edwards in Norman Fiering's *Jonathan Edwards's Moral Thought and*

Its British Context (1981.10) but finds the work "a wholly successful corrective" to earlier intellectual historians.

42 Wainwright, William J. "Jonathan Edwards, Atoms, and Immaterialism." *Idealistic Studies* 12 (January): 79-89.

Contends that Edwards's argument for immaterialism is "unsound" though plausible and original, in an analysis of "Of Atoms and Perfectly Solid Bodies" and its sources. Although he is neither as sophisticated nor as compelling as George Berkeley, Edwards is "philosophically interesting," his debt to Henry More "negligible."

43 Watson, David. Review of *Jonathan Edwards's Moral Thought and Its British Context,* by Norman Fiering. *Journal of American Studies* 16 (August): 309-10.

Terms Norman Fiering's "thorough" study (1981.10) a "major reinterpretation" of Edwards.

44 Weber, Donald. "The Question of the New England Mind." *New England Quarterly* 55 (June): 285-92.

Finds Norman Fiering's "provocative" interpretation of the complex Edwards both limiting and problematic but a "major contribution" to the history of philosophical ethics in America, in an essay-review of *Jonathan Edwards's Moral Thought and Its British Context* (1981.10) and *Moral Philosophy at Seventeenth-Century Harvard* (1981.11). Fiering's Edwards is the "antithesis" of Perry Miller's, neither modern nor Lockean, "almost a tragic figure," but in the end an uncertain one caught between "the vagaries of influence and the mystery of Fiering's cryptic implications."

45 ———. Review of *Jonathan Edwards,* by M. X. Lesser. *Analytical and Enumerative Bibliography* 6 (2): 131-32.

Considers M. X. Lesser's guide (1981.22) "a model of what a bibliography should be," but "less than complete" in collecting reviews of major studies of Edwards.

46 Wilson-Kastner, Patricia. Review of *Jonathan Edwards, Art and the Sense of the Heart,* by Terrence Erdt. *Journal of the American Academy of Religion* 50 (March): 145-46.

Takes Terrence Erdt's "avowedly literary" study of Edwards (1980.11) to be an "excellent complement" to Roland Delattre's more theoretical one (1968.8).

47 ———. Review of *Jonathan Edwards on Heaven and Hell,* by John H. Gerstner. *Church History* 51 (June): 250-51.

Concludes that John H. Gerstner's study (1980.14) "does not provide a comprehensive, analytical, or critical treatment" of Edwards's views of heaven and hell.

48 Zamora, Lois Parkinson. "The Myth of Apocalypse and the American Literary Imagination." *The Apocalyptic Vision in America: Inter-disciplinary Essays on Myth and Culture.* Bowling Green, Ohio: Bowling Green University Popular Press, pp. 97-138.

Cites the closing paragraph of Edwards's *History of Redemption* as evidence of his "very modern" understanding of the myth of the Apocalypse: chronological reality is less significant than psychological reality.

1983

1 Aldridge, A. Owen. Review of *Jonathan Edwards's Moral Thought and Its British Context*, by Norman Fiering. *Eighteenth-Century Studies* 17 (Fall): 89-92.

Ranks Norman Fiering's study (1981.10) as "possibly the best book on Edwards ever written," even though it minimizes the gulf between the Puritan Edwards and the secular moralists, between the New England theologian and the British philosophers.

2 Aycock, Martha B., and Gerald W. Gillette. "A Checklist of Doctoral Dissertations on American Presbyterian and Reformed Subjects, 1912-1982." *Journal of Presbyterian History* 61 (Summer): 257-98.

Lists sixty-one doctoral dissertations on Edwards.

3 Babcock, Edward Stanley, Jr. "A Comparison of the Divine-Human Relationship in the Writings of Jonathan Edwards and Charles Hartshorne." Ph.D. dissertation, Baylor University.

Discounts any real connection between the philosopher-theologians Edwards and Charles Hartshorne except superficial verbal ones. Because Edwards posits a sovereign God and a determined universe, his process tendencies are never fully developed, and his God, unlike Hartshorne's, acts like "the supreme puppet master" to men like "mannequins."

4 Balmer, Randall H. Review of *Jonathan Edwards, Pastor*, by Patricia J. Tracy. *Westminster Theological Journal* 45 (Fall): 471-73.

Points to "some useful" contributions in Patricia J. Tracy's study (1980.45), but it "ultimately falls prey to its own parochialism."

5 Bell, Susan. Review of *The Language of Canaan*, by Mason I. Lowance, Jr., and *Jonathan Edwards, Art and the Sense of the Heart*, by Terrence Erdt. *Journal of American Studies* 17 (April): 109-11.

Recommends both Mason I. Lowance's study of typology (1980.27) and Terrence Erdt's study of aesthetics (1980.11), but faults the first for its lack of historical continuity (between Cotton Mather and Edwards) and the second for its lack of explicit connections (between religion and both art and nature).

6 Blau, Joseph L. Review of *Jonathan Edwards's Moral Thought and Its British Context*, by Norman Fiering. *Transactions of the Charles S. Peirce Society* 19 (Winter): 83-94.

Agrees with Norman Fiering's study (1981.10) that Edwards's "true place" lies within the Augustinian, ultimately the Platonic, tradition and considers the book "a contribution of highest quality," in an essay-review.

7 Blauvelt, Martha T. Review of *Jonathan Edwards to Aaron Burr, Jr.*, by Suzanne Geissler. *Journal of Church and State* 25 (Winter): 172.

Dismisses Suzanne Geissler's claim in her study (1981.13) that Edwards or his evangelism was "a formative influence" in Aaron Burr's life.

8 ———, and Rosemary Skinner Keller. "Women and Revivalism: The Puritan and Wesleyan Traditions." In *Women and Religion in America: The Colonial and Revolu-*

tionary Periods. Edited by Rosemary Radford Ruether and Rosemary Skinner Keller. San Francisco: Harper & Row, pp. 316-67.

> Records Edwards's view of women — they are weaker, subordinate, and affectionate, not reasonable like men — and reprints "his treatise on marriage" ("Miscellanies," no. 37).

9 Bryant, M. Darrol. "From Edwards to Hopkins: A Millennialist Critique of Political Culture." In *The Coming Kingdom: Essays in American Millennialism and Eschatology.* Edited by M. Darrol Bryant and Donald W. Dayton. Barrytown, N.Y.: International Religious Foundation, pp. 25-70.

> Relates the millennial theology of Edwards to that of Samuel Hopkins and both to their redemptive effect upon American political culture.

10 Buss, Dietrich. "The Millennial Vision as Motive for Religious Benevolence and Reform: Timothy Dwight and the New England Evangelicals Reconsidered." *Fides et Historia* 16 (Fall): 18-34.

> Notes that only in the context of the contemporary debate can Edwards's eschatology be considered "nascent" postmillennialism.

11 Conforti, Joseph. Review of *Jonathan Edwards to Aaron Burr, Jr.,* by Suzanne Geissler. *William and Mary Quarterly,* 3d ser., 40 (January): 142-44.

> Questions both the thesis and the evidence in Suzanne Geissler's study of Edwards's influence (1981.13).

12 Hardman, Keith J. "The Great Awakening in New England — Jonathan Edwards." *The Spiritual Awakeners: American Revivalists from Solomon Stoddard to D. L. Moody.* Chicago: Moody Press, pp. 61-73.

> Renders a revivalist portrait of Edwards, that "awesome ambassador of the heavenly powers."

13 Hart, James D. "Edwards, Jonathan." *The Oxford Companion to American Literature.* New York: Oxford University Press, pp. 223-24.

> Sketches Edwards's life and work.

14 Holbrook, Clyde A. "Jonathan Edwards Addresses Some 'Modern Critics' of *Original Sin.*" *Journal of Religion* 63 (July): 211-30.

> Answers neo-orthodox critics of Edwards's doctrine of total depravity, its effect on reason, common morality, and human responsibility and its "less clear" connection to true virtue, in a reading of *Original Sin, Freedom of the Will,* and *True Virtue.* Unlike some moral philosophers "toying" with abstractions of little human consequence, Edwards took seriously the vexing problem of original sin: "he refused to conceal or discount a feature of human existence that continues to frustrate the moral and religious life."

15 Hoopes, James. "Jonathan Edwards's Religious Psychology." *Journal of American History* 69 (March): 849-65.

> Contends that Edwards's metaphysical idealism subverted John Locke's sensational psychology while employing his "fashionable" terminology and charges some "careless" scholars — Perry Miller (1949.9; rpt. 1981.27), Terrence Erdt (1980.11), and Norman Fiering (1981.10) — with confusing the two. Edwards's new sense "resembles" Locke's psychological empiricism "in every

possible way" though it rejects the materialist metaphysics underlying it; even John Calvin's *sensus suavitas* "only partly" accounts for it. In short, Edwards applied Locke's vocabulary to the traditional Protestant doctrine of innate grace.

16 Howe, Susan. "Part Two: Childe Emily to the Dark Tower Came." In *Code of Signals: Recent Writings in Poetics*. Edited by Michael Palmer. Berkeley: North Atlantic Books, pp. 196-218.

Claims that Edwards's consciousness "shadows and prophesies" Emily Dickinson's — his "negativity," his "disciplined" journey through despair and humiliation, his submission to an "arbitrary and absent" order — in a holistic reading of "My life had stood a loaded gun." "These two prophets of American Modernism speculated in a linguistic territory of ferocious morality."

17 Ilacqua, Alma A. "The Place of the Elect in Three Faulkner Narratives." *Christian Scholar's Review* 12 (2): 126-38.

Suggests that Edwards's religious vision of order "coincides, by intention or otherwise," with William Faulkner's artistic vision, in a reading of "That Evening Sun," "Delta Autumn," and "The Bear." Faulkner "may have been exposed" to Edwards in Phil Stone's library.

18 Johnsen, Thomas Christopher. "Christian Science and the Puritan Tradition." Ph.D. dissertation, Johns Hopkins University.

Links the Christian Science of Mary Baker Eddy to the New Light Calvinism of Edwards in its emphasis on religious affections, the "spiritual sense," and the spiritual understanding of Scripture.

19 Kimnach, Wilson H. "Realities of the Sermon: Some Considerations for Editors." *Newsletter of the Association for Documentary Editing* 5 (February): 5-10.

Distinguishes between the sermon as oral event and literary text and the editorial consequences of each in preparing Edwards's manuscript sermons for publication.

20 ———. Review of *Jonathan Edwards,* by M. X. Lesser. *Religious Studies Review* 9 (July): 265.

Calls M. X. Lesser's guide to Edwards (1981.22) "a significant work" of scholarship.

21 King, John O. "On the Effectual Work of the Word: William James and the Practice of Puritan Conscience." *Texas Studies in Literature and Language* 25 (Spring): 34-54.

Reclaims Edwards's influence on William James and *The Varieties of Religious Experience*. James read Edwards "thoroughly" and, in the Gifford Lectures, sought to "recompose" him on religious affections.

22 Laurence, David. "Moral Philosophy and New England Literary History: Reflections on Norman Fiering." *Early American Literature* 18 (Fall): 187-214.

Considers Norman Fiering's two studies "especially provocative" for the critic of early American literature, in an essay-review of *Jonathan Edwards's Moral Thought and Its British Context* (1981.10) and *Moral Philosophy at Seventeenth-Century Harvard* (1981.11). By recovering the connection between Edwards and the British moral philosophers (Hutcheson, More, and the Earl of Shaftesbury) and discounting the empirical psychologists (Locke, Berkeley, and Hume), Fiering "opens the way" to an American aesthetic (and literature) based on Platonic considerations. But the unsettled, American response to those European thinkers — America's "Janusfacedness" —

results in discontinuities in our literary history, marked by Edwards's "intensely retrospective" character and, say, Emerson's prospective one. Emerson makes poetry possible, Edwards impossible.

23 Lyttle, David. *Studies in Religion in Early American Literature: Edwards, Poe, Channing, Emerson, Some Minor Transcendentalists, Hawthorne, and Thoreau.* Lanham, Md.: University Press of America.
   Reprints 1966.19 (revised) and 1972.28.

*23A Manspeaker, Nancy. "Did Jonathan Edwards' Thought Develop?: A Comparison of his Doctrine of Love as Expressed in his First and Last Writings." Ph.D. dissertation, St. Michael's College.

24 Marini, Stephen A. "Rehearsal for Revival: Sacred Singing and the Great Awakening in America." In *Sacred Sound: Music in Religious Thought and Practice.* Edited by Joyce Irwin. Thematic Series of the Journal of the American Academy of Religion, 50. Chico, Cal.: Scholars Press, pp. 71-91.
   Notes that Edwards, at the urging of George Whitefield in 1741, forsook Psalms for the hymns of Isaac Watts without bringing "aesthetic disorder" to Northampton.

25 McCracken, Charles J. *Malebranche and British Philosophy.* New York: Oxford University Press, pp. 329-40.
   Uncovers "some striking similarities" of thought between Nicolas Malebranche and Edwards: both taught that God is being in general, that the world is an ideal one, and, "most remarkable," that God is the only and immediate cause (the doctrine of occasionalism). That the American Puritan was "in fact" influenced by the French Catholic is left "unanswered."

26 Murrin, John M. "No Awakening, No Revolution? More Counterfactual Speculations." *Reviews in American History* 11 (June): 161-71.
   Insists that the Great Awakening did not create the American Revolution, that "Edwards can in no sense be regarded as the intellectual progenitor of Jefferson and Jackson."

27 Narramore, Ruth E. "The Continuing Influence of Sarah Edwards." *Psychology for Living* 25 (May): 10-11.
   Attributes the success of Edwards's descendants to the warm, loving relationship between Jonathan and Sarah and to her godly example.

28 Niebuhr, Richard R. *Streams of Grace: Studies of Jonathan Edwards, Samuel Taylor Coleridge and William James.* The Neesima Lectures, 2. Kyoto: Doshisha University Press, pp. 1-5, 12-38.
   Links Samuel Taylor Coleridge and William James to Edwards through their common mysticism and shared convictions about being, knowledge, and responsibility. In "Of Insects," Edwards early develops a philosophy of excellency based on the dynamic relation of perception, proportion, and consent in nature, which, read aright, becomes "a grammar of spirit, a language of God." As a skilled interpreter of the religious experience, Edwards "probably has no peer" in America.

29 Nobles, Gregory H. *Division Throughout the Whole: Politics and Society in Hampshire County, Massachusetts, 1740-1775*. New York: Cambridge University Press, pp. 59-74.

Suggests that the Hampshire County clergy "ultimately played the most prominent role" in Edwards's dismissal, in an account of the personal, doctrinal, and political causes of it. Though neighboring ministers were not prime movers in the affair, they were "active accomplices," joining Joseph Hawley, Israel Williams, and Robert Breck in their personal animus to Edwards and many regional congregations in their opposition to his revised communion principles. Perceiving Edwards (and the Great Awakening) as a threat to both tradition and themselves, the Hampshire pastors acted with "a consensus they had not known in years."

30 Noll, Mark A. "Jonathan Edwards, Moral Philosophy, and the Secularization of American Christian Thought." *Reformed Journal* 33 (February): 22-28.

Submits that Norman Fiering's two "splendid" books (1981.10 and 1981.11) may help explain why Edwards's theological perspective "vanished" from American Christian thought after his death and proposes what contemporary Christians can do "to make a difference in their intellectual world" that he did in his, in an essay-review.

31 ———. Review of *Jonathan Edwards to Aaron Burr, Jr.,* by Suzanne Geissler. *Church History* 52 (June): 237.

Terms Suzanne Geissler's study of Edwards (1981.13) "not successful," its conclusions "heavy-handed," its parallels "forced," its flawed logic "fatal."

32 ———, et al. *The Search for Christian America*. Westchester, Ill.: Crossway Books, pp. 56-62 passim.

Reflects upon the political indifference of the "closest followers" of Edwards and the "misplaced" millennialism of other Christians, in a survey of the connections (or lack of them) between the Great Awakening and the American Revolution.

33 Petersen, William J. "Meet Jonathan and Sarah Edwards." *Martin Luther Had a Wife*. Wheaton, Ill.: Tyndale House, pp. 71-100.

Maintains that Edwards "shared his ministry" with his wife, in an account of their lives together.

34 Post, Stephen Garrard. "Love and Eudaemonism: A Study in the Thought of Jonathan Edwards and Samuel Hopkins." Ph.D. dissertation, University of Chicago.

Published as 1987.26 (revised).

35 Pudaloff, Ross J. "'Sinners in the Hands of an Angry God': The Socio-economic and Intellectual Matrices for Edwards' Sermon." *Mosaic* 16 (Summer): 45-64.

Locates Edwards's *Sinners in the Hands of an Angry God* (and the Great Awakening) in the social and intellectual contexts of Enfield, a Connecticut Valley town in crisis. The sermon represents "a significant, but not total, discontinuity" between the past and the future of the community, especially as its language renders the farm and agrarian way as "false and pernicious" symbols. Edwards spoke as a "radical reformer," his rhetoric undermining the assumptions of his listeners and their "normal human response to disaster."

36 Quinn, Philip L. "Divine Conservation, Continuous Creation, and Human Action."

In *The Existence and Nature of God.* Edited by Alfred J. Freddoso. Notre Dame, Ind.: University of Notre Dame Press, pp. 55-79.

Dissents from Edwards, "an important philosopher," because he denies that "created substances are persistent things," in an exploration of a theory relating divine conservation, continuous creation, and human action.

37 Ramsey, Bennett. "The Ineluctable Impulse: 'Consent' in the Thought of Edwards, James, and Royce." *Union Seminary Quarterly Review* 37 (4): 303-22.

Discovers in Edwards, William James, and Josiah Royce a common view of the religious life, one that sees the connection between the distinctive dispositions of God and man as "consent," and experiential piety and right conduct as counterparts. But the three thinkers differ as well: Edwards and James take consent to be a way to "commune with natural creation"; Royce, a way to "a community of social life." So they are caught in the "persistent dilemma" of American religious thought: nature and civilization — that "sacred pair" — frames the choice, the "ineluctable impulse" to natural creation and the compelling concern for society.

38 Rusch, Frederik L. "Reality and the Puritan Mind: Jonathan Edwards and Ethan Frome." *Journal of Evolutionary Psychology* 4 (August): 238-47.

Uses Edwards's *Freedom of the Will* as a gloss to Edith Wharton's *Ethan Frome,* the psychological and moral insights into relativity, causality, and responsibility of the treatise "amply" illustrated in the novel.

39 Schafer, Thomas A. Review of *Jonathan Edwards,* by M. X. Lesser. *Journal of Presbyterian History* 61 (Winter): 462-63.

Rates M. X. Lesser's bibliography (1981.22) "a useful handbook" for the study of Edwards.

40 ———. Review of *Jonathan Edwards's Moral Thought and Its British Context,* by Norman Fiering. *Church History* 52 (September): 382-83.

Considers Norman Fiering's "seminal" study (1981.10) "a rich gift" but one that will invite controversy, especially about Edwards's debt to Nicolas Malebranche.

41 Shea, William M. "Jonathan Edwards and Sarah Pierpont: An Uncommon Union." In *Foundations of Religious Literacy.* Edited by John V. Apczynski. Chico, Cal.: Scholars Press, pp. 107-26.

Maintains that Edwards's religious life, his pastorate, and his theology were shaped by his love for his wife (and hers for him) and offers as evidence selections from "Sarah Pierrepont," *Personal Narrative, Some Thoughts, Religious Affections,* and *True Virtue.*

42 Simonson, Harold P. "Jonathan Edwards." In *Eerdmans' Handbook to Christianity in America.* Edited by Mark A. Noll et al. Grand Rapids, Mich.: William B. Eerdmans, pp. 103-106.

Defines Edwards's religion as "the total experiential response to God's revealed truth," in a brief account of his life and work.

43 ———. "Typology, Imagination, and Jonathan Edwards." *Radical Discontinuities: American Romanticism and Christian Consciousness.* Rutherford, N.J.: Fairleigh Dickinson University Press, pp. 19-43 passim.

Reprints 1975.17 (revised).

44 Slater, John F. "The Sleepwalker and the Great Awakening: Brown's *Edgar Huntly* and Jonathan Edwards." *Papers on Language & Literature* 19 (Spring): 199-217.

Catalogues "a host of ancillary details" from Edwards's *Sinners in the Hands of an Angry God* that "reappear" in Charles Brockden Brown's *Edgar Huntly,* in a study of "apparent indebtedness." Like Edwards, Brown was "obsessed" with (spiritual) sleep and awakening, and he "mined the rich idiom" of Edwards to "shore up" his own.

45 Solberg, Winton U. Review of *Jonathan Edwards's Moral Thought and Its British Context,* by Norman Fiering. *South Atlantic Quarterly* 82 (Spring): 230-31.

Calls Norman Fiering's "superb" study of Edwards (1981.10) "essential reading" but the absence of a scientific context a "serious" omission.

46 Spires, T. Grady. Review of *Jonathan Edwards, Art and the Sense of the Heart,* by Terrence Erdt. *Christian Scholar's Review* 12 (3): 258.

Places Terrence Erdt's view of Edwards (1980.11) at the center of a controversy "sure to follow."

47 Spohn, William C. "The Reasoning Heart: An American Approach to Christian Discernment." *Theological Studies* 44 (March): 30-52.

Contends that American Protestant theologians, particularly Edwards on religious affections and H. Richard Niebuhr on biblical symbols, provide "a more adequate account" of moral discernment than does Karl Rahner's reading of Ignatius Loyola.

48 Steele, Thomas J., and Eugene R. Delay. "Vertigo in History: The Threatening Tactility of 'Sinners in the Hands of an Angry God.'" *Early American Literature* 18 (Winter): 242-56.

Applauds Edwards's "virtuoso performance upon the keyboard of the tactile sense" in *Sinners in the Hands of an Angry God,* in an analysis of the images of touch proper (dimensional and proprioceptive) and the implications of touch (spatial and temporal). Edwards "almost avoids" images of the other senses and all but the most "threatening" images of touch. Only at the end of the sermon does he use positive images (of all the senses), offering salvation and an "escape from the vertigo of history."

49 Stein, Stephen J. "Jonathan Edwards (1703-1758)." In *American Writers before 1800: A Biographical and Critical Dictionary,* 1. Edited by James A. Levernier and Douglas R. Wilmes. Westport, Conn.: Greenwood Press, pp. 507-12.

Offers an extended bibliography of Edwards's work, a brief life, critical appraisal, and suggested readings of "probably America's foremost theologian-philosopher."

50 ———. Review of *Jonathan Edwards,* by M. X. Lesser, and *Jonathan Edwards,* by Nancy Manspeaker. *Church History* 52 (December): 507-508.

Contrasts two Edwards annotated bibliographies: the one by M. X. Lesser (1981.22), "an eminently useful guide" with "a major introduction"; the other by Nancy Manspeaker (1981.26), "a rather uneven inventory."

51 Stephenson, Sally Ann. "The Ministerial and Theological Purpose of Jonathan Edwards's Thought: A Study in Source and Context." Ph.D. dissertation, University of Pennsylvania.

Locates the source of Edwards's thought in his "ministerial predecessors" — English Puritans and continental Calvinists — rather than John Locke and the Enlightenment, in a study of his "Catalogue" and Scottish correspondence.

52 Stout, Harry S. "Moral Philosophy in Colonial New England: From Early Puritan Piety to Perry Miller's Mistakes." *Fides et Historia* 15 (Spring): 97-102.

Marks Norman Fiering's analysis of Edwards and early American intellectual history a "major advance" and a "new departure" but one that "ignores" the social context, in an essay-review of *Jonathan Edwards's Moral Thought and Its British Context* (1981.10) and *Moral Philosophy at Seventeenth-Century Harvard* (1981.11). Despite his "'lapses,'" Perry Miller created "a sense of the interconnectedness of things" in early American society, a sense all but lost in Fiering's "rarified heights of formal philosophy."

53 Sweet, Leonard I. *The Minister's Wife: Her Role in Nineteenth-Century American Evangelicalism.* Philadelphia: Temple University Press, pp. 20-23.

Cites Sarah Edwards as an example of the "companion model" of a minister's wife and as the unacknowledged "paradigm" of the awakened experience in *Some Thoughts*.

54 Thomas, D. O. Review of *Jonathan Edwards's Moral Thought and Its British Context*, by Norman Fiering. *Philosophical Books* 24 (April): 79-81.

Predicts that Norman Fiering's "impressive" study (1981.10) will "accelerate" Edwards's reputation as a moral philosopher, but notes that it is "particularly hard" on Perry Miller and "over-emphasizes" the relativism of John Locke.

55 Weber, Donald. "The Figure of Jonathan Edwards." *American Quarterly* 35 (Winter): 556-64.

Attributes to Edwards's "variousness" the range of recent studies about him, in an essay-review chiefly about *Jonathan Edwards, Pastor* (1980.45), by Patricia J. Tracy, and *Jonathan Edwards's Moral Thought and Its British Context* (1981.10) and *Moral Philosophy at Seventeenth-Century Harvard* (1981.11), by Norman Fiering. Yet even with Tracy's "convincing" study of religion and society in eighteenth-century New England and Fiering's "crucial" ones about philosophical and intellectual debts here and abroad, Edwards still remains an "enigmatic and slippery" figure.

56 Wenzke, Annabelle Sassaman. "Timothy Dwight: The Enlightened Puritan." Ph.D. dissertation, Pennsylvania State University.

Published as 1989.56.

57 Wiersbe, Warren W. "Jonathan Edwards: Brilliant Mind, Burning Heart." *Good News Broadcaster* 41 (April): 26-29.

Offers a brief life and a briefer bibliography of Edwards, a "rare blend" of scholar and revivalist, head and heart.

58 Wilson, John F. "Edwards as Moralist." *Reviews in American History* 11 (June): 190-94.

Questions the "utterly circumstantial" influence of Nicolas Malebranche on Edwards posited by Norman Fiering, in a review of *Jonathan Edwards's Moral Thought and Its British Context* (1981.10), "an important word" on Edwards but certainly not the last.

59 ———. "Jonathan Edwards' A History of the Work of Redemption." *Newsletter of the Association of Documentary Editing* 5 (May): 1-3.

Recounts the "very special issues" involved in editing Yale's "'reading version'" of *History of Redemption*.

60 Ziff, Larzer. "Puritanism and Romanticism." In *Rivista di Studi Anglo-Americani*, 2. Brescia: Paideia Editrice, pp. 68-79.

Contrasts similar rhetorical expressions of Edwards and Henry David Thoreau with those of William Bartram, in a study of the shift in sensibility from the eighteenth to nineteenth century, from Puritanism through humanism to romanticism. The "truest road" between Edwards and Thoreau runs through Bartram.

1984

1 Barnsley, Richard E. "Wesley and Edwards: A Hypothesis." *Locke, Wesley, and the Method of English Romanticism.* Gainesville: University of Florida Press, pp. 215-18.

Contends that Edwards and John Wesley comprise "a single phenomenon" in their debt to John Locke, their founding of the religious enlightenment, and their roles in revivalism, in an appendix to a study of English romanticism.

2 Breitenbach, William. "The Consistent Calvinism of the New Divinity Movement." *William and Mary Quarterly,* 3d ser., 41 (April): 241-64.

Discriminates among New Divinity ministers, a "most perplexing group" of preachers, who followed Edwards in his "departures" from Puritan federal theology.

3 Campbell, David. Review of *Jonathan Edwards's Moral Thought and Its British Context,* by Norman Fiering. *Scottish Journal of Theology* 37 (1): 106-107.

Regards Norman Fiering's "rewarding" study (1981.10) not quite successful in assessing Edwards's moral thought.

4 Clapper, Gregory S. "'True Religion' and the Affections: a Study of John Wesley's Abridgement of Jonathan Edwards' *Treatise on Religious Affections.*" *Wesleyan Theological Journal* 19 (Fall): 77-89.

Analyzes what John Wesley "did, and did not, mean" by agreeing with Edwards that "'true religion, in great part, consists in holy affections,'" in a detailed account of his "ruthless" abridgement of Edwards's treatise.

5 Clarke, F. Stuart. "Christocentric Developments in the Reformed Doctrine of Predestination." *Churchman* 98 (3): 229-45.

Includes Edwards in a survey of Reformed predestinarians, finding he "seriously weakened" the Christological basis of the doctrine.

6 Colson, Charles W. "Introduction." In *Religious Affections.* Edited by James M. Houston. Classics of Faith and Devotion. Portland, Ore.: Multnomah Press, pp. xxiii-xxxiv.

> Urges Edwards's message — "the absolute primacy of biblical obedience" — upon a "crippled" western church "infected with cheap grace" and upon a "stupefied, egocentric, materialistic" and nihilistic society. Only with a deepened sense of sin, as Edwards argued, can religious affections arise and lead to practical expressions of Christian love. An editor's note, by James M. Houston, (pp. xiii-xxi) includes a brief life, commentary on (academic) misunderstandings and the "true nature" of revivals, a summary of the text, and the justification for abridging and rewording it.

7 Ellison, Julie. "The Sociology of 'Holy Indifference': Sarah Edwards' Narrative." *American Literature* 56 (December): 479-95.

> Explores the "intricate connection" between social conflict and religious experience revealed in Edwards's image of his wife (in *Some Thoughts*) and hers of him (in her account in Sereno E. Dwight's *Life of President Edwards*, 1829.4). Edwards's alienation from Northampton "stands secretly behind" his image of Sarah, a figure superior to society in her "outward deference and inward indifference to it."

8 Emerson, Everett. "Jonathan Edwards." In *Fifteen American Authors before 1900: Bibliographical Essays on Research and Criticism*. Edited by Earl N. Harbert and Robert A. Rees. Madison: University of Wisconsin Press, pp. 230-49.

> Reprints 1971.8 (updated).

9 Endy, Melvin B., Jr. "Theology and Learning in Early America." In *Schools of Thought in the Christian Tradition*. Edited by Patrick Henry. Philadelphia: Fortress Press, pp. 125-51.

> Traces the rise of parsonage seminaries in eighteenth-century America to Edwards's New Divinity or Consistent Calvinism, "the only appropriate theological tradition" for the times.

10 Gerstner, John H. "Jonathan Edwards and the Bible." In *Inerrancy and the Church*. Edited by John D. Hannah. Chicago: Moody Press, pp. 257-78.

> Reprints 1979.8 (abridged).

11 Gilpin, W. Clark. "The Seminary Ideal in American Protestant Ministerial Education, 1700-1808." *Theological Education* 20 (Spring): 85-106.

> Claims that Edwards "loosened the connections" between piety and learning by making doctrinal knowledge a necessary but not sufficient means of grace, in a survey of early American ministerial education.

12 Golding, Gordon. Review of *Jonathan Edwards to Aaron Burr*, by Suzanne Geissler. *Archives de Sciences Sociales des Religions* 29 (April): 233.

> Finds Suzanne Geissler's speculations about Aaron Burr's debt to Edwards (1981.13) to be without proof or merit. (In French.)

13 Hall, Richard Anthony Spurgeon. "The Idea of Community in the Thought of Jonathan Edwards: The Neglected Texts from Northampton." Ph.D. dissertation, University of Toronto.

> Published as 1990.22.

14 Holbrook, Clyde A. "Jonathan Edwards on Self-Identity and Original Sin." *The Eighteenth Century* 25 (Winter): 45-63.

Examines Edwards's theory of self-identity, its probable sources, and the "universal bondage in sin" that hinges upon it. Though his explanation of identity in *Original Sin* is "an exercise in circularity," his solution, based on God's continuous creation, is "no less rational" than that of recent thinkers, Alfred North Whitehead among them.

15 Holbrook, Thomas Arthur. "The Elaborated Labyrinth: The American Habit of Typology." Ph.D. dissertation, University of Maryland.

Places Edwards's natural typology in the "long exegetical tradition" of Thomas Taylor and John Flavel, part of a study of the influence of Puritan religious typology on American literary symbolism.

16 Howe, Daniel Walker. Review of *Jonathan Edwards's Moral Thought and Its British Context,* by Norman Fiering. *Journal of the American Academy of Religion* 52 (June): 381-82.

Questions Norman Fiering's view in his "convincing" study (1981.10) that Edwards's moral philosophy lacked "practical utility."

17 Hux, Samuel. "Self-Election of the Elite." *Dissent* 31 (Winter): 127-29, 141.

Counters the failure of the West to translate the doctrines of election and damnation into political terms with the soteriology of Edwards, "the richest, subtlest, and most rewarding thinker to grace America." In *True Virtue,* Edwards argues that "ordinary people, with their fractured motives and adoptive virtues, were responsible for the greater part of the moral action of the world," a "sort of democracy of the Damned."

18 Karlsen, Carol F., and Laurie Crumpacker, eds. *The Journal of Esther Edwards Burr.* New Haven: Yale University Press, pp. 6-13 passim.

Recounts Edwards's family life in Northampton.

19 Lee, Sang Hyun. Review of *Jonathan Edwards's Moral Thought and Its British Context,* by Norman Fiering. *Journal of Presbyterian History* 62 (Spring): 85-88.

Praises Norman Fiering's study (1981.10) for placing Edwards's moral thought in the mainstream of western intellectual history, but regrets that it "underestimates" John Locke's influence upon him and leaves "unargued" the connection between his theology and his ethics.

20 Lewicki, Zbigniew. *The Bang and the Whimper: Apocalypse and Entropy in American Literature.* Contributions in American Studies, 71. Westport, Conn.: Greenwood Press, pp. 13-16.

Comments on Edwards's apocalyptic writings (though they are not properly "literary" texts) and his "chiliastic inclinations," in a study of apocalypse and entropy in American literature.

21 Logan, Samuel T., Jr. "The Doctrine of Justification in the Theology of Jonathan Edwards." *Westminster Theological Journal* 46 (Spring): 26-52.

Concludes, after a careful reading of "Justification by Faith Alone" and parallel texts in *Faithful Narrative, Religious Affections, Freedom of the Will,* and *True Virtue,* that Edwards walks "the razor's edge of biblical truth" and avoids the "opposite dangers" of Arminianism and antinomianism.

22 ————. "Jonathan Edwards and the 1734-35 Northampton Revival." In *Preaching and Revival.* London: Westminster Conference, pp. 57-85.

> Reveals Edwards's morphology of conversion "developed implicitly" in *Faithful Narrative,* in a study of the 1734-35 Northampton revival, his published account of it, and a sermon he preached during it. Edwards was "primarily" an historian of the revival in *Faithful Narrative,* recalling his grandfather's harvests and reporting the work of the Spirit, but he described as well a pattern of conversion as "guidance" to the awakened and their pastors, addressing all eight steps "one way or another" in "The Justice of God in the Damnation of Sinners." At once doctrinal and affectionate, Edwards bequeathed to the Church "a superb theology of preaching."

23 Lowance, Mason I., Jr. "Jonathan Edwards." In *American Colonial Writers, 1606-1724.* Edited by Emory Elliott. Dictionary of Literary Biography, 24. Detroit: Gale Research, pp. 95-108.

> Judges the "tragic" Edwards far less successful as a parish minister than as a conscious artist of sermons and treatises, in an examination of his career as both. As a thinker and writer, he was "clearly the most important figure in the eighteenth century" and a "crucial link" between the Puritans of the seventeenth century and the transcendentalists of the nineteenth.

24 Mavrodes, George I. "Is the Past Unpreventable?" *Faith and Philosophy* 1 (April): 131-46.

> Commends Edwards for his "subtle" rendering of the logical problem of foreknowledge and necessity in *Freedom of the Will,* in an argument for an unpreventable past.

25 Miller, Stephen. "American Literature and the Idea of Equality." *This World* 8 (Spring): 111-46.

> Hears three "'voices,'" those of the Puritan Edwards, the individualist Benjamin Franklin, and the agrarian Thomas Jefferson, but especially that of Edwards, in writers lamenting the "decline of communal values" and the "bad effects" of equality, in a survey of the idea of equality in American literature.

26 Murray, Iain H. "Jonathan Edwards 11: The Troubles at Northampton." *Banner of Truth* no. 253 (October): 8-15.

> Reprinted as part of 1987.22.

27 ————. "Jonathan Edwards 11: The Troubles at Northampton (2)." *Banner of Truth* no. 254 (November): 8-15.

> Reprinted as part of 1987.22.

28 ————. "Jonathan Edwards 12: Missionary to the Indians." *Banner of Truth* no. 255 (December): 21-30.

> Reprinted as part of 1987.22.

29 Noll, Mark A. "Edwards, Jonathan." In *Evangelical Dictionary of Theology.* Edited by Walter A. Elwell. Grand Rapids, Mich.: Baker Book House, pp. 343-46.

> Comments on Edwards's theology, psychology, metaphysics, and ethics, in a short account of his thought, a "landmark for many subsequent Christians."

30 Osburg, Barbara Jean. "The Development of Metaphor in the Sermons of Jonathan

Edwards: The Individual Reflection of an Historical Progress." Ph.D. dissertation, St. Louis University.

Discovers parallels to the Puritan experience in America in the "developing pattern" of metaphors in the Northampton sermons of Edwards, who is "best understood and appreciated" as an artist of the tension between faith and experience, doctrine and imagination.

31 Porter, Roy. Review of *Jonathan Edwards's Moral Thought and Its British Context*, by Norman Fiering. *English Historical Review* 99 (July): 623-24.

Considers Norman Fiering's study (1981.10) an "authoritative if somewhat ponderous account" of Edwards's scholasticism.

32 Preus, Klemet. "Jonathan Edwards: A Case of Medium-Message Conflict." *Concordia Theological Quarterly* 48 (October): 279-97.

Reproves Edwards for failing to see that revivalism (the medium) and strict Calvinism (the message) were "culturally and inherently incompatible," for the former depending upon "individual deviation," the latter upon "corporate uniformity." Thus "America's 'Great Awakening' was Calvinism's 'Great Wake.'"

33 Quinby, Rowena Lee. "The Moral-Aesthetic Essay in America." Ph.D. dissertation, Purdue University.

Identifies Edwards's ethical writings with the emergence of moral-aesthetic discourse in the eighteenth century, in a study of the increasing formalization of the moral essay in America.

34 Randolph, Robert M. "Images of the Heart." In *Church Divinity, 1984*. Edited by John H. Morgan. Church Divinity Monograph Series, 4. Notre Dame, Ind.: Foundations Press, pp. 173-90.

Labels Edwards's *Sinners in the Hands of an Angry God* "idolatrous," because its imagery is not the "true environment" for realizing God's grace, in a study of the "complex and difficult" Second Commandment. In response, William R. Schoedel questions the unspecified terms of the definition of *idolatrous* (pp. 191-93).

35 Schafer, Thomas A. Review of *A Return to Moral and Religious Philosophy in Early America*, by Rem Blanchard Edwards. *Church History* 53 (June): 257-58.

Faults Rem Blanchard Edwards's study (1982.9) for its "out-of-date information" on Jonathan Edwards and its "around 1925" critical approach.

36 Sellers, James. "Ways of Going Public in American Theology." *Word & World* 4 (Summer): 240-47.

Denotes Edwards's practice the third and "most appropriate" way of going public in American theology, for it combines the evangelical Christianity of the first way with the social gospel of the second, joining conversion to benevolence, private to public.

37 Stein, Stephen J. "Transatlantic Extensions: Apocalyptic in Early New England." In *The Apocalypse in English Renaissance Thought and Literature: Patterns, Antecedents, and Repercussions*. Edited by C. A. Patrides and Joseph Wittreich. Ithaca, N.Y.: Cornell University Press, pp. 266-98.

Considers Edwards's "apocalyptic perspective" in his defense of the Great Awakening, *Hum-*

ble Attempt, and *History of Redemption* part of a transplanted (and transformed) English tradition, in a survey of apocalyptic thought in early New England.

38 Van Bibber, James Joe. "The Concepts of Church Membership and Ministry in the Covenantal Theology of Jonathan Edwards." Ph.D. dissertation, Southwestern Baptist Theological Seminary.

Detects in Edwards's "bilateral" covenant theology an "organizing principle" for his polity and ministry, a "harmonious relationship" among all aspects of the covenant community.

38A Vetö, Miklós. "Edwards, Jonathan." *Dictionnaire des Philosophes,* 1. Paris: Presses Universitaires de France, pp. 827-30.

Offers a brief estimate of Edwards.

39 Westra, Helen A. "Jonathan Edwards's Sermons: Search for 'Acceptable Words.'" *American Theological Library Association, Proceedings* 38: 102-16.

Sketches the "contours and progress" of recent studies of Edwards and examines ordination sermon manuscripts in the Yale collection, especially his first (6 November 1736) and last (28 May 1754), on the 250th anniversary of the surprising conversions in Northampton.

40 White, Charles E. Review of *Jonathan Edwards, Pastor,* by Patricia J. Tracy. *Fides et Historia* 16 (Spring): 108-11.

Indicts Patricia J. Tracy's "dangerous" book (1980.45) for its "errors in historical reasoning and its anti-theological bias."

1985

1 Austin, Richard Cartwright. "Beauty: A Foundation for Environmental Ethics." *Environmental Ethics* 7 (Fall): 197-208.

Builds a theory of environmental ethics upon Edwards's perceptions of consent and cordial consent in *Religious Affections* and *True Virtue* and the continuity between natural and moral beauty. For Edwards, the experience of beauty was a "saving encounter" between man and God.

2 Bell, Richard H. Review of *Jonathan Edwards's Moral Thought and Its British Context,* by Norman Fiering. *Religious Studies* 21 (December): 605-607.

Regards Norman Fiering's study (1981.10) as "brilliant" but limiting: it does not allow us to read Edwards "for ourselves."

3 Bloch, Ruth H. *Visionary Republic: Millennial Themes in American Thought, 1756-1800.* Cambridge: Cambridge University Press, pp. 16-21 passim.

Considers Edwards the "most authoritative and articulate" millennial interpreter of revivalism, in a history of the development of millennialism in late eighteenth-century America. Though Edwards was an evangelical, not a nationalist, his "intense and widespread" millennialism stirred a broadening audience with an emotional fervor that "carried over" into republican political issues.

4 Cherry, Conrad. "Symbols of Spiritual Truth: Jonathan Edwards as Biblical Interpreter." *Interpretation* 39 (July): 263-71.

Claims that Edwards, "preeminently" a biblical theologian, "anticipated" our contemporary absorption with the meaning and function of religious symbolism in his "wholehearted attention" to scriptural typology. Through his expanded hermeneutics of typology, Edwards approached the Bible, nature, and history as symbolic structures grounded in Christ made flesh, "history's central symbol."

5 Clapper, Gregory S. "'True Religion' and the Affections: A Study of John Wesley's Abridgement of Jonathan Edwards' *Treatise on Religious Affections.*" In *Wesleyan Theology Today: A Bicentennial Theological Consultation.* Edited by Theodore Runyon. Nashville, Tenn.: Kingswood Books, pp. 416-23.
Reprints 1984.4.

6 Conforti, Joseph. "David Brainerd and the Nineteenth-Century Missionary Movement." *Journal of the Early Republic* 5 (Fall): 309-29.
Stresses the popularity of Edwards's *Life of Brainerd* and its influence on the nineteenth-century missionary movement. Incorporating elements of "several genres" of popular religious literature — the conversion journal, the captivity narrative, the devotional manual — the work became "a spiritual touchstone" to missionaries, its subject "a genuine folk hero" to evangelicals.

7 ———. "Jonathan Edwards's Most Popular Work: 'The Life of David Brainerd' and Nineteenth-Century Evangelical Culture." *Church History* 54 (June): 188-201.
Notes the "important role" Edwards's *Life of Brainerd* played in nineteenth-century religious reform ethics and its place in any assessment of Edwards's contribution to American evangelical culture.

8 Cooey, Paula M. *Jonathan Edwards on Nature and Destiny: A Systematic Analysis.* Studies in American Religion, 16. Lewiston, N.Y.: Edwin Mellen, xii, 275 pp.
Delineates the several meanings Edwards attaches to nature and the contexts that govern them in order to discover "the dynamic unity" of his vision. Since for him nature communicates divine destiny, it means, variously, sensible reality and spiritual regeneration, and finds expression in his ontology, anthropology, Christology, soteriology, typology, eschatology, and epistemology. Thus Edwards on saving grace may serve as a "paradigm" of his thought as a whole, a theocentric vision, but one in which both human beings and nature play "vital" though "subordinate" roles.

9 DeProspo, R. C. *Theism in the Discourse of Jonathan Edwards.* Newark: University of Delaware Press, 292 pp.
Attempts a phenomenological reading not only of Edwards but of modern interpretations of him as well, in a "stylistically dense" deconstruction of texts and critiques. Theism, a discursive pattern based on "the ultimate duality between Creator and Creation" that continues in "hierarchical duplicities," is "systemically other" than humanism or modernism. What is "bedrock" in Edwards's theism — ideas of creation, providence, and grace — becomes in humanist discourse the "unstable ground" of nature, history, and psychology. Such a disparate discursive pattern calls into question the work of humanist scholars of Edwards and modern historiographers of "'America'" and makes it necessary to "remodel the whole corpus of American literature."

10 Engle, Peter Gregg. "Jonathan Edwards as Historiographer: An Analysis of his Schema

of Church History, Focusing on Period III of his History of Redemption." Ph.D. dissertation, Westminster Theological Seminary.

> Examines Edwards's *History of Redemption, Some Thoughts, Humble Attempt,* and his apocalyptic writings to show how the Great Awakening modified his views on church history.

11 Fiering, Norman. Review of Jonathan Edwards, *The Life of David Brainerd,* edited by Norman Pettit. *New England Quarterly* 58 (June): 295-97.

> Contends that David Brainerd's "prominent position in history was assured only by the circumstance that Jonathan Edwards believed in him," in a review of Norman Pettit's edition of the *Life of Brainerd* (1985.46).

12 Fireoved, Joseph D. "An Anthology of Colonial Sermons." Ph.D. dissertation, University of Delaware.

> Closes an anthology of ten colonial sermons of various genres with Edwards's *Sinners in the Hands of an Angry God* and an introduction to it.

13 Gerstner, John H. "Jonathan Edwards: Insights that Shaped American Thought." *Fundamentalist Journal* 4 (April): 43-44.

> Surveys the influence of the "utterly theocentric" Edwards on the Great Awakening, Baptists, and communion practice.

14 Gura, Philip F. Review of *Churchmen and Philosophers,* by Bruce Kuklick. *American Literature* 57 (December): 655-57.

> Praises Bruce Kuklick's study (1985.26) of Edwards's successors in New England Theology for its "revelation after revelation" about the history of the American mind.

15 Gustafson, James M. "A Response to Critics." *Journal of Religious Ethics* 13 (Fall): 185-209.

> Replies, in part, to Paul Ramsey's criticism of his reading of Edwards (1985.48): "My thinking is deeply informed by Edwards, . . . I think more so than is Ramsey's."

16 Hearn, Rosemary. "Form as Argument in Edwards' 'Sinners in the Hands of an Angry God.'" *CLA Journal* 28 (June): 452-59.

> Cites *Sinners in the Hands of an Angry God* as one of Edwards's best examples of "the complete syllogism as a mode of argument," in an analysis of the "simple" plan of the sermon.

17 Heimert, Alan. "The Yale Edwards." *Early American Literature* 20 (Winter): 256-70.

> Laments the pace of production of the Yale Edwards — "a major scandal in American scholarship" — but praises the "impeccable detail" of the seven published volumes and the way each "helps to cleanse and clarify the canon," in an essay-review on the publication of the latest of them, Norman Pettit's edition of the *Life of Brainerd* (1985.46).

18 ———, and Andrew Delbanco, eds. *The Puritans in America: A Narrative Anthology.* Cambridge: Harvard University Press, pp. 409-13.

> Calls Edwards's metaphoric prose "unmatched in the American canon for its intellectual vigor and its verbal architecture," in the conclusion to an anthology of Puritan writers.

19 Hewitt, Glenn A. Review of *Churchmen and Philosophers,* by Bruce Kuklick. *International Journal for Philosophy of Religion* 18 (3): 175.

Welcomes the "excellent summaries" in Bruce Kuklick's study (1985.26) but questions the influence of Edwards on John Dewey.

20 Humphries, Jefferson. "The Sorcery of Rhetoric in French and American Letters." *Massachusetts Review* 26 (Summer): 178-97.

Compares the rhetoric of Blaise Pascal to that of Edwards and finds the latter wanting, in a deconstructionist account of American letters. Edwards (and Puritans generally), "by refusing to embrace the paradoxicality of aphorism," represses the "uncontrollable underside" of rhetoric and fails to see the contradiction implicit in tropes and types.

21 Jacobs, Anton K. "Evangelicalism and Capitalism: A Critical Study of the Doctrine of Atonement in the History of American Religion." Ph.D. dissertation, University of Notre Dame.

Interprets Edwards's expression of atonement in *History of Redemption* as a justification of submission, suffering, and obedience, in a history of the doctrine of atonement in evangelical America.

22 Jenson, Robert W. "Mr. Edwards' Affections." *Dialog* 24 (Summer): 169-75.

Issues a call to Lutherans to return to Edwards — he was "a founder of American evangelicalism and remains its only theologian" — and his vision of the affections (and the Trinity) as the foundation of belief. Edwards's analysis of the affections in *Divine and Supernatural Light, Faithful Narrative,* and *Religious Affections* is "simply true."

23 Johnson, Paul. "The Almost-Chosen People." *Wilson Quarterly* 9 (Winter): 78-89.

Maintains that Edwards saw no difference between religious and political emotion, in a survey of the "organic" part religion played in the emerging American republic.

24 Jones, David C. "The Supreme Good." *Presbyterion* 11 (Fall): 124-41.

Cites Edwards on God's communicated glory in *End of Creation,* in a study of the views of theologians and philosophers on the chief end of man.

25 Kimnach, Wilson H., ed. *Three Essays in Honor of the Publication of "The Life of David Brainerd."* New Haven: Winthrop Brainerd, 36 pp.

Celebrates the publication of the Yale edition of Edwards's *The Life of Brainerd* (1985.46) with three essays.

Brainerd, Winthrop. "The Religious Influence of David Brainerd," pp. 7-22. Assesses the religious influence of David Brainerd through Edwards's use of the *Life* to further the Great Awakening and as an example of "a life lived face to face with God," in an account of Brainerd's life and times.

Pettit, Norman. "Comments on the Manuscript and Text," pp. 23-27. Suggests that Edwards revised the manuscript diaries to turn David Brainerd into "a more highly qualified opponent of Arminianism than he actually was."

Tracy, Patricia J. "The Romance of David Brainerd and Jerusha Edwards," pp. 28-36. Concludes that there is "little real evidence" that David Brainerd and Edwards's daughter Jerusha were actually betrothed, in an examination of the historical accounts of their "special relationship." Alexander V. G. Allen first suggested the engagement of the two (1889.1), a story repeated by Henry Bamford Parkes (1930.10; rpt. 1979.29), Arthur Cushman McGiffert (1932.10; rpt. 1980.28), Ola Elizabeth Winslow (1940.21), Perry Miller (1949.9; rpt. 1981.27), Alfred Owen Aldridge (1964.1), and, in the "most florid imaginative reconstruction," Elisabeth D. Dodds (1971.6). The source for this "myth" lies less with concerns about sexual propriety than with the need of Edwards biographers to strengthen the "Jonathan-David bond": the young missionary became a useful example of evangelical commitment "in the pattern prescribed" by the older pastor.

26 Kuklick, Bruce. *Churchmen and Philosophers: from Jonathan Edwards to John Dewey.* New Haven: Yale University Press, pp. 15-42 passim.

Maps Edwards's intellectual development — from his early philosophical speculations before his conversion, through his Northampton pastorate when "he laid philosophy aside," to his final years of theoretical analysis in defense of experimental religion — in a study of the growth of thought in America from the "reign" of theology to the "triumph" of philosophy, from Edwards to John Dewey. For Edwards, philosophy and theology were "intertwined," both in the Christian metaphysics of this youth and the Calvinist theology of his maturity, such that the idealism of George Berkeley and Nicolas Malabranche and the (amended) empiricism of John Locke was brought into "consonance" with the Bible and seventeenth-century Puritanism.

27 Lang, J. Stephen, ed. "Jonathan Edwards." *Christian History* 4 (November): 1-36.

Devotes a special issue to Edwards that includes selected "Resolutions," the Joseph Badger portrait, excerpts from Samuel Hopkins's *Life* (1765.2), "a gallery of family, friends, foes, and followers," a timeline, parts of two sermons, an early letter, a discussion guide, and five brief essays.

Noll, Mark A., and J. Stephen Lang. "Colonial New England: An Old Order, A New Awakening," pp. 8-10, 35. Sketches the Puritan world Edwards was born into and the world he made through the Great Awakening.

Dodds, Elisabeth S. "My Dear Companion," pp. 15-17. Recounts Jonathan and Sarah's life together.

Lovelace, Richard. "Edwards' Theology: Puritanism Meets a New Age," pp. 18-19, 22. Traces the roots of Edwards's theology and the changes he wrought.

Stout, Harry S. "The Puritans and Edwards: The American Vision of a Covenant People," pp. 23-25. Focusses on Edwards's political and social awareness and his "quintessentially Puritan notion" of a righteous city set upon a hill.

Marsden, George M. "Jonathan Edwards Speaks to Our Technological Age," pp. 26-28. Parallels the scientific revolution of Edwards's day to the technological one of ours and the need for revivalism to temper both.

28 La Shell, John K. "Imaginary Ideas of Christ: A Scottish-American Debate." Ph.D. dissertation, Westminster Theological Seminary.

Published (in part) as 1987.16.

29 Lee, Sang Hyun. Review of Jonathan Edwards, *Scientific and Philosophical Writings*, edited by Wallace E. Anderson. *Journal of Religion* 65 (January): 121-23.

Welcomes Wallace E. Anderson's "elegant" volume (1980.2) as "an important contribution" to understanding Edwards's early intellectual development and later thought.

30 Leonard, Bill J. "Getting Saved in America: Conversion Event in a Pluralistic Culture." *Review and Expositor* 82 (Winter): 111-27.

Considers Edwards "a significant force" in shaping the theology and morphology of conversion, in a brief history of both in America.

31 Lewis, John Delmas, III. "God and Time: The Concept of Eternity and the Reality of Tense." Ph.D. dissertation, University of Wisconsin-Madison.
Rejects Edwards's view of the incompatibility of divine foreknowledge and human freedom, in a study of the doctrine of eternity and the theory of tenseless time.

32 Logan, Samuel T., Jr. Review of *Moral Philosophy in Seventeenth-Century Harvard* and *Jonathan Edwards's Moral Thought and Its British Context,* by Norman Fiering. *Westminster Theological Journal* 47 (Spring): 157-66.
Regards Norman Fiering's "monumental" contribution to understanding moral thought in seventeenth- and eighteenth-century New England (1981.11 and 1981.10) flawed in that it depreciates the theological context of the issues and "distorts" Edwards's views on the noetic effects of sin.

33 Lovejoy, David S. *Religious Enthusiasm in the New World: Heresy to Revolution.* Cambridge: Harvard University Press, pp. 189-94 passim.
Recounts Edwards's "most profound defense" of the Great Awakening against charges of religious enthusiasm in *Distinguishing Marks, Religious Affections,* and *Life of Brainerd,* in a history of enthusiasm in colonial America.

34 Lyrene, Edward Charles, Jr. "The Role of Prayer in American Revival Movements, 1740-1860." Ph.D. dissertation, Southern Baptist Theological Seminary.
Evaluates Edwards's influence on prayer during the Great Awakening and through his *Humble Attempt,* in an analysis of the role of prayer in American revivalism to the Civil War.

35 Martin, John Stephen. "The Rhetoric of Grace in Jonathan Edwards' *Personal Narrative.*" In *Man and Nature: Proceedings of the Canadian Society for Eighteenth-Century Studies,* 4. Edited by David H. Jory and Charles Stewart-Robertson. Edmonton: Academic Printing and Publishing, pp. 109-27.
Reveals Edwards's rhetorical strategies in *Personal Narrative:* to render the logos of Scripture "phenomenally experiential" and to counter the "anxiety of aging" and the "loss of 'delight.'" His first conversion shows that "right doctrine" validates personal grace; his second, that the "immediate concurrence" of heart and logos authenticates supernatural grace.

36 McNerney, J. R. "The Mystical Journey of Jonathan Edwards." *Studia Mystica* 8 (Spring): 20-29.
Outlines the three stages of Edwards's "classical" mystical journey in *Personal Narrative:* natural contemplation, alteration of mind, and deepening of belief. Edwards's "total" dependence on Christ, both the "center" of his experience and the "dynamic" of his thought, is "cold, depressing, and fatalistic."

37 Meyer, William E. H., Jr. "Edwards, Emerson and Beyond: The Hyper-visual American Great Awakening." *Massachusetts Studies in English* 10 (Spring): 24-45.
Sees Edwards as an "eye-dealist," more visual than verbal, more New World than Old, in an overview of the American "'revivalist'" experience from Edwards to Ezra Pound.

38 Murray, Iain H. "Jonathan Edwards 13: At Stockbridge." *Banner of Truth* no. 256 (January): 15-21.

> Reprinted as part of 1987.22.

39 ———. "Jonathan Edwards 14: Written Ministry." *Banner of Truth* no. 258 (March): 23-27.

> Reprinted as part of 1987.22.

40 ———. "Jonathan Edwards 15: Through a Daughter's Eyes." *Banner of Truth* no. 260 (May): 15-24.

> Reprinted as part of 1987.22.

41 ———. "Jonathan Edwards 16: The First Revival at Princeton." *Banner of Truth* no. 261 (June): 22-29.

> Reprinted as part of 1987.22.

42 ———. "Jonathan Edwards 17: The Continuing Ministry." *Banner of Truth* no. 262 (July): 16-21.

> Reprinted as part of 1987.22.

43 ———. "Jonathan Edwards 18: The Generations of Readers." *Banner of Truth* no. 263 (August): 41-48.

> Reprinted as part of 1987.22.

44 Noll, Mark A. "Christian World Views and Some Lessons of History." In *The Making of a Christian Mind: A Christian World View and the Academic Enterprise.* Edited by Arthur Holmes. Downers Grove, Ill.: InterVarsity Press, pp. 29-54.

> Instances Edwards as "nearly a model case" — along with Thomas Aquinas, Martin Luther, and John Calvin — in a history of the union of faith and intellect in shaping Christian world views. "The comprehensiveness of Edwards's thought, just as much as his desire to regard all questions from a distinctly Christian perspective, makes him unusual in American Christian history."

45 Oberdiek, Hans. "Jonathan Edwards." In *American Philosophy.* Edited by Marcus G. Singer. Cambridge: Cambridge University Press, pp. 191-213.

> Concludes that while Edwards participated in eighteenth-century American thought and culture, "he was never truly of it," in a reading of his philosophy, the "handmaiden" of his theology. Edwards's errand ended in failure, not tragedy, and his greatest influence was his aesthetics.

46 Pettit, Norman. "Editor's Introduction." *The Life of David Brainerd. The Works of Jonathan Edwards,* 7. New Haven: Yale University Press, pp. 1-85.

> Considers Edwards's *Life of Brainerd* "a key volume" in the corpus of his work — an "epilogue" to his revival writings, a "prologue" to his later treatises — in a detailed account of its place in his life and thought, its provenance, historical background and figures, and textual problems and practices (including parallel columns of manuscript and edited text), in the introduction to the seventh volume of the Yale Edwards. A "model for missionary histories," Edwards's most popular work yields him "a perfect example of authentic spirituality" to set beside other case histories in *Faithful Narrative* and *Some Thoughts* and to validate observations of ex-

perimental religion in *Distinguishing Marks* and *Religious Affections.* As a missionary to the Indians, Brainerd affects the question of discipline in *Humble Inquiry,* the anti-Arminianism of *Freedom of the Will* and *Original Sin,* and the life of Edwards among the Housatonics; as a personification of "the ethical man," Brainerd anticipates the disinterested benevolence of *True Virtue.* For all Edwards's deletions and alterations of the text, he publishes the "bulk" of the diary of "a man who had recovered from the disease of enthusiasm to become a saint of sound faith," the biography not of an individual but of a "representative" man.

47 Proudfoot, Wayne. *Religious Experience.* Berkeley: University of California Press, pp. 166-69 passim.

Finds William James "mistaken" about the irrelevance to Edwards of the divine origin and cause of the religious experience: Edwards makes "exactly the opposite point" in *Religious Affections.*

48 Ramsey, Paul. "A Letter to James Gustafson." *Journal of Religious Ethics* 13 (Spring): 71-100.

Takes James M. Gustafson to task for his misreading of Edwards's *End of Creation,* in a critique of Gustafson's *Ethics from a Theological Perspective* (1981.15) and *Theology and Ethics* (1984). Edwards held the ultimate end of creation to "coincide" in God's glory and man's happiness, not simply in the first, as Gustafson claims. (See 1985.15 for Gustafson's reply.)

49 Ricard, Laura Broderick. "The Evangelical New Light Clergy of Northern New England, 1741-1755: A Typology." Ph.D. dissertation, University of New Hampshire.

Finds in Edwards's understanding of "alienating radical" behavior in the Great Awakening an apt account of extreme evangelicals, in a (corrective) study of New Light clergy in Maine and New Hampshire.

50 Shi, David E. *The Simple Life: Plain Living and High Thinking in American Culture.* New York: Oxford University Press, pp. 23-26.

Cites Edwards's early "monkish asceticism" and later "moderated" view of material comforts, in a study of the pursuit of the simple life in America.

51 Stein, Stephen J. "'Like Apples of Gold in Pictures of Silver': The Portrait of Wisdom in Jonathan Edwards's Commentary on the Book of Proverbs." *Church History* 54 (September): 324-37.

Charts Edwards's "lifelong regard" for the Book of Proverbs, from his early reflections on the figure of wisdom as proper behavior and morality to his later Christological interpretations of it as "the agent of righteousness and virtue," in an examination of his "Diary" and "Resolutions," his "Notes on Scripture" and more than fifty sermons. Edwards's mature readings begin in the nature of biblical language — the silver of metaphor yields the gold of sense — and ends in "a preoccupation" with God's excellency, wisdom, purity, and love, which parallels his growing concern with the divine role in man's conversion.

52 Storms, Charles Samuel, II. "Jonathan Edwards and John Taylor on Human Nature: A Study of the Encounter between New England Puritanism and the Enlightenment." Ph.D. dissertation, University of Texas at Dallas.

Published (in part) as 1985.53.

53 ———. *Tragedy in Eden: Original Sin in the Theology of Jonathan Edwards.* Lanham, Md.: University Press of America, xii, 316 pp.

Examines the doctrine of original sin in the thought of Edwards, chiefly from a biblical and theological rather than an historical perspective, in an account of his intellectual and religious development and his relation to the American Enlightenment; an analysis of John Taylor's Arminian assault on the traditional Calvinist position in his *The Scripture-Doctrine of Original Sin* (1738); a reconstruction and assessment of Edwards's doctrine of the Fall and the depravity of nature consequent on it; and an evaluation of his response to the three principal objections to the Calvinist rendering of the "tragedy in Eden": that original sin is incompatible with freedom of the will, that God is the author of sin, and that the imputation of Adam's sin to posterity is unjust and inequitable. Though Edwards's argument about the problem of evil and identity in *Original Sin* is not without fault — "it *fails* as a theodicy" — he mounts "the most lucid and convincing defense of these fundamental biblical truths since Paul penned Romans."

54 Valeri, Mark R. "Joseph Bellamy: Conversion, Social Ethics, and Politics in the Thought of an Eighteenth-Century Calvinist." Ph.D. dissertation, Princeton University.

Published as 1994.46.

55 ———, and John F. Wilson. "Scripture and Society: From Reform in the Old World to Revival in the New." In *The Bible in American Law, Politics, and Political Rhetoric.* Edited by James Turner Johnson. The Bible in American Culture, 4. Philadelphia: Fortress Press, pp. 13-38.

Places Edwards and the Great Awakening at the climax of the effort to "pattern political and social life according to biblical and biblically derived norms," in an account of the recovery and appropriation of the Christian Bible in the Old World and its influence on the political culture of New. Edwards fused beliefs about society and scriptural destiny with "exquisite clarity and power," especially in his *History of Redemption.*

56 Vetö, Miklós. "La pensée de Jonathan Edwards. Les fondements métaphysiques de sa théolgie." Ph.D. dissertation, University of Strasbourg.

Published as 1987.34.

57 Waters, Mary Ann. "Sermon for Jonathan Edwards." *Yankee* 49 (October): 218.

Glimpses Edwards returning home in cold October, "his greatcoat swirling," Sarah kneeling to "unpin him" of his notes, in a poem of twenty-eight lines.

58 Westra, Helen. Review of Jonathan Edwards, *The Life of David Brainerd,* edited by Norman Pettit. *Calvin Theological Journal* 20 (November): 320-25.

Hails Norman Pettit's edition of *Life of Brainerd* (1985.46) as a "scholarly landmark" and an "invaluable" aid to understanding Brainerd and Edwards, his "spiritual father."

1986

1 Anderson, Alan B., ed. *Annual of the Society of Christian Ethics,* 1985. Washington, D.C.: Georgetown University Press, pp. 19-55.

Includes two essays on the nature and influence of Edwards's ethics.

Spohn, William C. "Union and Consent with the Great Whole: Jonathan Edwards on True Virtue," pp. 19-32. Perceives in Edwards's reasoning from parts to the whole, not from means to ends, "a fertile conceptual schema for an ethics that would be both contextual and ultimate," a pattern common to American moral thought and typical of Puritans, pragmatists, and process theologians. Edwards moves from the empiricism of *Religious Affections* to the Neoplatonism of *True Virtue* and distinguishes the seemingly virtuous act of consent to part of being to the truly virtuous act of consent to the whole of it: true virtue "'unselfs' the heart by expanding its sympathies toward infinity." Edwards and H. Richard Niebuhr "stand at two ends" of the American tradition in religious ethics.

Byrnes, Thomas A. "H. Richard Niebuhr's Reconstruction of Jonathan Edwards's Moral Theology," pp. 33-55. Shows how H. Richard Niebuhr in *The Responsible Self* reconstructs Edwards's moral theology along the "pragmatic, objective, relativist lines" of John Dewey and George Herbert Mead, in a reading of the first two chapters of *True Virtue*. The Edwardsean tradition in American theology did not end with Dewey, as Bruce Kuklick maintains (1985.26), but was "transformed and revitalized" by Niebuhr.

1A Beale, Peter. "Jonathan Edwards and the Phenomena of Revival." *Congregational Studies Conference Papers.* Oswestry, Shropshire: Quinta, pp. 18-32.

Examines Edwards's comments on the phenomena of revival in *Distinguishing Marks* and *Some Thoughts* — though not *Religious Affections* — by focussing on physical manifestations and raising some questions about his treatment of them. We need Edwards's "balanced wisdom" in these "confused times" — between the "cold dead orthodoxy" that dismisses the phenomena of revival out of hand and the "naïve gullibility" that accepts without question the "signs and wonders" of them — and, above all, the pouring out of the Spirit of a "genuine" revival.

2 Becker, William H. Review of *Churchmen and Philosophers,* by Bruce Kuklick. *Theology Today* 42 (January): 543-44.

Acknowledges "affinities" between John Dewey and the Andover liberals, not the continuities with Edwards that Bruce Kuklick's study (1985.26) claims.

3 Bonomi, Patricia U. *Under the Cope of Heaven: Religion, Society, and Politics in Colonial America.* New York: Oxford University Press, pp. 158-60.

Notes Edwards's shift from a collective to an individual accounting of piety and conversion (and the place of *Humble Inquiry* in it).

4 Butts, Francis T. "Norman Fiering and the Revision of Perry Miller." *Canadian Review of American Studies* 17 (1): 1-25.

Maintains that Norman Fiering's work (1981.10 and 1980.11) complements Perry Miller's on Edwards and fails to take the "true measure" of Miller's scholarship.

5 Cairns, Earle E. *An Endless Line of Splendor: Revivals and Their Influence from the Great Awakening to the Present.* Wheaton, Ill.: Tyndale House, pp. 44-46.

Regrets that later generations of revivalists have not always held to Edwards's belief that conversion involves both head and heart.

6 Claeys, Gregory. "William Godwin's Critique of Democracy and Republicanism and its Sources." *History of European Ideas* 7 (3): 253-69.

Attributes William Godwin's rejection of patriotism to principles outlined in Edwards's *True Virtue.*

7 Clark, Stephen M. "Jonathan Edwards: The History of Redemption." Ph.D. dissertation, Drew University.

Detects in the "organizational motif" and design of the thirty sermons that make up *History of Redemption* a clue to Edwards's corpus, the "genius" of his thought, and the "driving direction" of his life. For Edwards, "biblical revelation is progressive."

8 Cole, Phyllis. "From the Edwardses to the Emersons." *CEA Critic* 49 (Winter): 70-78.

Connects Edwards to Ralph Waldo Emerson through the "social entity called the Emerson family" — ministers in the eighteenth century, Mary Moody Emerson in the nineteenth — and their "uniformly pro-Awakening" stance, in an alternative to Perry Miller's "mystical" account (1940.9; rpt. 1981.27).

9 Conforti, Joseph. "Antebellum Evangelicals and the Cultural Revival of Jonathan Edwards." *American Presbyterians* 64 (Winter): 227-41.

Charts Edwards's ascent to an "exalted place in nineteenth-century evangelical hagiography," in a study of his cultural revival in antebellum America. Edwards was "romanticized" for his piety, "memorialized" for his intellect, "resurrected" for his revivalism, "enshrined" as a founding father of America's righteous empire, and "invoked" to restrain "disquieting expressions of a democratic ethos" in religious affairs — all this as revivals again became "central" to our cultural and religious experience and Edwards's authority necessary to a "vision of individual-national regeneration."

10 Crocco, Stephen D. "American Theocentric Ethics: A Study in the Legacy of Jonathan Edwards." Ph.D. dissertation, Princeton University.

Follows Edwards's theocentric ethics from its "eclipse" in the nineteenth century to its "centrality" in the neo-orthodoxy of Joseph Haroutunian and H. Richard Niebuhr in the twentieth.

11 Diggins, John Patrick. Review of *Churchmen and Philosophers,* by Bruce Kuklick. *New Republic* 194 (28 April): 38.

Welcomes Bruce Kuklick's "exciting" study (1985.26) but finds "problematic" the relationship between Edwards and John Dewey.

12 Fitzmier, John R. "The Godly Federalism of Timothy Dwight, 1752-1817: Society, Doctrine, and Religion in the Life of New England's 'Moral Legislator.'" Ph.D. dissertation, Princeton University.

Published as 1998.12.

13 Gerstner, John H. Review of *Tragedy in Eden,* by C. Samuel Storms. *Trinity Journal,* n.s., 7 (Spring): 92-93.

Objects to the indictment of Edwards for making God the author of sin, the "tragedy" of C. Samuel Storms's "overall useful" study (1985.53).

14 Guelzo, Allen C. "Jonathan Edwards and the New Divinity: Change and Continuity in New England Calvinism, 1758-1858." In *Pressing toward the Mark.* Edited by

Charles G. Dennison and Richard C. Gamble. Philadelphia: Committee for the Historian of the Orthodox Presbyterian Church, pp. 147-67.

Claims for the New Divinity "the ideological middle movement" between Edwards and Charles G. Finney, in a study of Edwards's "intellectual agenda" and its effect upon Samuel Hopkins and Joseph Bellamy. The New Divinity was "a clarification and application" of Edwards — in the doctrine and practice of moral absolutism, church separation, and governmental atonement — and "a prescription" for revival. "For better or worse, the patterns of much of American evangelicalism were drawn from Edwards" and transmitted by New Divinity ministers.

15 ———. "The Unanswered Question: The Legacy of Jonathan Edwards's *Freedom of the Will* in Early American Religious Philosophy." Ph.D. dissertation, University of Pennsylvania.

Published as 1989.16.

16 Handy, Robert. "Some Patterns in American Protestantism." In *The Study of Spirituality.* Edited by Cheslyn Jones et al. New York: Oxford University Press, pp. 473-80.

Cites Edwards as one of three types of spirituality — Calvinist, Quaker, Episcopalian — and shows how each "enriched" Christianity.

17 Hoeveler, J. David, Jr. Review of *Churchmen and Philosophers,* by Bruce Kuklick. *Journal of American History* 72 (March): 939-40.

Judges the material and the interpretations in Bruce Kuklick's study of Edwards and New England Theology (1985.26) "familiar," the writing "insufficiently lucid."

18 Howe, Daniel Walker. Review of *Churchmen and Philosophers,* by Bruce Kuklick. *American Historical Review* 91 (February): 170.

Accounts Bruce Kuklick's rendering of Edwards's influence on nineteenth-century Congregationalism (1985.26) "the best we have."

19 Keller, Karl. "Literary Excess as Indigenous Aesthetic in Eighteenth-Century America." In *The American Revolution and Eighteenth-Century Culture: Essays from the 1976 Bicentennial Conference of American Society for Eighteenth-Century Studies.* Edited by Paul J. Korshin. AMS Studies in the Eighteenth Century, 5. New York: AMS Press, pp. 201-18.

Includes Edwards in a tour of eighteenth-century American literary "curiosities," part of an alternative aesthetic theory of early American literature. In his anti-Arminian arguments Edwards is a "fantasist of ideological intricacy," a "reactionary succeeding as a radical."

20 Ledbetter, T. Mark. "Changing Sensibilities: the Puritan Mind and the Romantic Revolution in Early American Religious Thought." In *The Interpretation of Belief: Coleridge, Schleiermacher and Romanticism.* Edited by David Jasper. London: Macmillan, pp. 176-84.

Outlines the career of Edwards, the "most outspoken proponent" of Calvinism, in an account of the shift from religious orthodoxy to liberalism in nineteenth-century America.

21 Lee, Sang H. "The Importance of the Family: A Reformed Theological Perspective."

In *Faith and Families.* Edited by Lindell Sawyers. Philadelphia: Geneva Press, pp. 115-35.

Uses Edwards to represent the American Reformed tradition (theocentric, trinitarian, Christological) in an examination of the family from a theological perspective, the "interplay" between creation and redemption, nature and grace. For Edwards, God's creative and redemptive works are "closely related" but "clearly distinguished." The family, then, is the embodiment of the "self-giving love" of the Father for the Son and so a type of divine beauty.

22 Logan, Samuel T., Jr. Review of *Tragedy in Eden,* by C. Samuel Storms. *Westminster Theological Journal* 48 (Fall): 398-404.

Values C. Samuel Storms's "excellent" book (1985.53) not only for its contribution to Edwardsean scholarship but also for its suggested ways to deal with today's challenges.

23 Meyers, Ken. "Jonathan Edwards." *Eternity* 37 (October): 37.

Regrets that Edwards is "virtually unknown in the American church," in a short account of his life and work.

24 Murray, Iain H. "Edwards on the Nature of True Religion." *Banner of Truth* no. 270 (March): 16-23.

Reprinted as part of 1987.22.

25 ———. "'Thirteen Hours, Every Day.'" *Banner of Truth* no. 271 (April): 18-25.

Reprinted as part of 1987.22.

26 Noll, Mark A. Review of *Churchmen and Philosophers,* by Bruce Kuklick. *Christian Scholar's Review* 15 (3): 271-73.

Praises Bruce Kuklick's examination of Edwards's "love-hate relationship" with European philosophy in his "signal" study (1985.26).

27 O'Brien, Susan. "A Transatlantic Community of Saints: The Great Awakening and the First Evangelical Network, 1735-1755." *American Historical Review* 91 (October): 811-32.

Suggests that Calvinist evangelicals on both sides of the Atlantic formed a close-knit group — Edwards, Benjamin Colman, and Thomas Prince in America; James Robe, Thomas Gillespie, and John Erskine in Scotland; Isaac Watts, George Whitefield, and James Doddridge in England — and locates the Great Awakening here and contemporaneous revivals abroad on a "continuum of Protestant evangelical development" from the seventeenth to the nineteenth century. Edwards's *Faithful Narrative* and *Humble Attempt* and his correspondence with several Scottish ministers were part of the "most impressive set of bilateral relations" in the revivals.

28 O'Malley, J. Steven. "Recovering the Vision of Holiness: Wesley's Epistemic Basis." *Asbury Theological Journal* 41 (Spring): 3-17.

Compares Edwards to John Wesley — they agree in joining the praxis of holiness to saving grace but differ in epistemology — in a study of Wesley's doctrine of sanctification.

29 Petersen, Rodney L. Review of *Churchmen and Philosophers,* by Bruce Kuklick. *Trinity Journal* 7 (Fall): 117-21.

Regards Bruce Kuklick's study (1985.26) intellectual history "at its best" but regrets the negative appraisal of Calvinism and Edwards's religious experience.

30 Pettit, Norman. "Prelude to Mission: Brainerd's Expulsion from Yale." *New England Quarterly* 59 (March): 28-50.

Concludes that Edwards "significantly altered" David Brainerd's diary, depicting him "more evenly balanced" than he was, in order to enlist him in the "war against Arminianism," in an examination of Brainerd's troubles at Yale and Edwards's recounting of them. In his Yale commencement address, *Distinguishing Marks*, Edwards was to have "come down hard" on the enthusiast excesses of the Great Awakening; in failing to do that, he "shared the blame" with Gilbert Tennent and James Davenport for the events that led to Brainerd's expulsion from Yale.

31 ————. "*The Life of David Brainerd:* Comments on the Manuscript and Text." *Yale University Library Gazette* 60 (April): 137-44.

Recapitulates 1985.44 and 1986.29.

31A Piper, John. *Desiring God: Meditation of a Christian Hedonist.* Portland, Ore.: Multnomah, pp. 28-29 passim.

Recounts Edwards's struggle with the doctrine of God's sovereignty in *Personal Narrative* as an example of the problem that "stands before us now," God's happiness amid misery in the world.

32 Plantinga, Alvin. "On Ockham's Way Out." *Faith and Philosophy* 3 (July): 235-69.

Resolves the problem of theological determinism in Edwards's *Freedom of the Will* by using William of Ockham's distinction between "hard" and "soft" facts about the past. Divine foreknowledge and human freedom are "not incompatible" if God's knowledge about the past is an accidental necessity, not, as in Edwards, an essential one.

33 Post, Stephen. "Disinterested Benevolence: an American Debate over the Nature of Christian Love." *Journal of Religious Ethics* 14 (Fall): 356-68.

Contrasts Edwards's view of disinterested benevolence with that of Samuel Hopkins, in a history of the debate over Christian love. Edwards thought of self-regard as "the 'joy' of consent to being"; Hopkins thought all forms of it as "raging beasts waiting to be caged." Hopkins's "radical" self-denying love — more nearly Sarah's in *Some Thoughts* than Jonathan's in *True Virtue* — remains at the center of the continuing controversy.

34 Sairsingh, Krister. "Jonathan Edwards and the Idea of Divine Glory: His Foundational Trinitarianism and Its Ecclesial Import." Ph.D. dissertation, Harvard University.

Discovers in the relational ontology of Edwards's early writings implications for his Trinitarianism and ecclesial ideal. For Edwards, the church "re-presents" the divine glory in creation, as figured in the relationship of the persons of the Trinity.

35 Schmidt, Leigh Eric. "'A Second and Glorious Reformation': The New Light Extremism of Andrew Croswell." *William and Mary Quarterly,* 3d ser., 43 (April): 214-44.

Remarks the influence of Edwards's *Life of Brainerd* on the spirituality of Andrew Croswell, a New Light extremist.

36 Shea, Daniel B. "Deconstruction Comes to Early 'America': The Case of Edwards."
   Early American Literature 21 (Winter): 268-74.
   Hails R. C. DeProspo's "discourse of antagonisms," despite its "hubris," as a "sturdy, brave
   and provocatively thoughtful" reading of Edwards and American cultural history, in an essay-
   review of *Theism in the Discourse of Jonathan Edwards* (1985.9). Still, Perry Miller (1949.9; rpt.
   1981.27) "remains the most exciting strong reader in early American studies, his brilliant misprisions the occasion of many such bright, later misprisions as this one."

37 Shea, William M. Review of *Churchmen and Philosophers*, by Bruce Kuklick. *Religion
   and Intellectual Life* 4 (Fall): 123-25.
   Finds Bruce Kuklick's otherwise "fine" study (1985.26) marred by its "patronizing" appraisal
   of *Religious Affections*, Edwards's "masterpiece."

38 Solaro, Barbara C. "The Divided Consciousness of Emily Dickinson." Ph.D. dissertation, Indiana University.
   Notes an analogue to Emily Dickinson's "fractured" consciousness — a "distinctively American" phenomenon — in Edwards.

39 Steffen, Lloyd H. *Self-Deception and the Common Life*. American University Studies:
   Theology and Religion, 11. New York: Peter Lang, pp. 335, 338-39.
   Examples Edwards as a theologian who exposes the prideful self-deception of the sinner with
   "power and sophistication."

40 Stein, Stephen J. Review of *Theism in the Discourse of Jonathan Edwards*, by R. C.
   DeProspo. *Journal of American History* 73 (September): 454-55.
   Considers R. C. DeProspo's study (1985.9) "an intellectual tease, an intentional provocation,"
   its analysis of Edwards secondary to its attack on modernist readings of American literature.
   "Despite its erudition and insight, this is not a successful book."

41 ———. Review of *Tragedy in Eden*, by C. Samuel Storms. *Church History* 55 (September): 380-81.
   Advises readers to spend time with Edwards's texts rather than with C. Samuel Storms's "not-
   so-useful commentary" (1985.53).

42 Stout, Harry S. *The New England Soul: Preaching and Religious Culture in Colonial
   New England*. New York: Oxford University Press, pp. 202-211, 228-31.
   Examines Edwards's revival debates with Charles Chauncy and the impact his sermon style
   had on evangelicals (particularly, his "unexcelled" use of language), in a history of preaching in
   colonial New England. Equal to Chauncy as a scriptural exegete, Edwards was "a master without
   peer" in bringing philosophy to bear upon the nature of conversion. And though he never prepared a preaching manual, he brought "a stock of images and metaphors" to a generation of
   ministers to fire the hearts of the laity.

43 Sweeney, Kevin Michael. "River Gods and Related Minor Deities: The Williams
   Family and the Connecticut River Valley, 1637-1790." Ph.D. dissertation, Yale University.
   Remarks the role of the Williamses in the dismissal of Edwards, their cousin, in a study of five
   generations of the family.

44 Valeri, Mark. "Church and State in America from the Great Awakening to the American Revolution." In *Church and State in America: A Bibliographical Guide,* 1. Edited by John F. Wilson. Westport, Conn.: Greenwood Press, pp. 115-50.

Remarks the influence of Edwards's theology on the formation of the new nation, in a survey of the historiography of the social and political meanings and implications the Great Awakening had for the American Revolution.

45 Ward, W. R. Review of Jonathan Edwards, *The Life of David Brainerd,* edited by Norman Pettit. *Scottish Journal of Eighteenth-Century Studies* 9 (Autumn): 275-76.

Calls Edwards's *Life of Brainerd* a "notable landmark" in the interwoven history of autobiography and biography, in a review of Norman Pettit's edition of the text (1985.46).

46 Westra, Helen. *The Minister's Task and Calling in the Sermons of Jonathan Edwards.* Studies in American Religion, 17. Lewiston, N.Y.: Edwin Mellen, xi, 370 pp.

Explores Edwards's sermons for his theological, pastoral, and aesthetic vision of a gospel ministry, in a reading of his published and unpublished work on hearing and keeping, preaching and teaching the Word, on the ordination and installation of ministers, and on Christ as the perfect ministerial exemplar. Ministers, for Edwards, are "lively types" of Christ — stewards, messengers, husbandmen, lights, watchmen, proxy bridegrooms, biblical metaphors all — and his sermons about them are literary. "In a very profound sense, Edwards's words constitute his reforming work."

47 Wright, Conrad. Review of *Churchmen and Philosophers,* by Bruce Kuklick. *New England Quarterly* 59 (June): 291-94.

Compares Bruce Kuklick's study of Edwards and his successors (1985.26) with Frank Hugh Foster's (1907.3; rpt. 1987.7) and concludes that the former, by leaving out important aspects of their thought, yields only "the most juiceless part" of New England Theology.

48 Yarbrough, Stephen R. "Jonathan Edwards on Rhetorical Authority." *Journal of the History of Ideas* 47 (July): 395-408.

Locates the center of Edwards's rhetorical authority in God's grace, in a reading of "On the Medium of Moral Government — Particularly Conversation" and its companion piece, "The Insufficiency of Reason as a Substitute for Revelation." Grace unifies the Word and nature, communicates God's beauty and his creation, and authorizes saints "to interpret and to teach."

49 Youngs, Fred William. "The Place of Spiritual Union in the Thought of Jonathan Edwards." Ph.D. dissertation, Drew University.

Adjudges Edwards's soteriology and pneumatology "similar" to John Calvin's but different from the eucharistic thought in his ecclesiology, in a study of spiritual union, "a vital element" in Edwards's thought. New Divinity ministers following Edwards fail to stress spiritual union and so fail to convey the "essential power" of his piety.

50 Zuss, Michael E. "Jonathan Edwards in the Context of Early Eighteenth-Century Moral Philosophy." Ph.D. dissertation, City University of New York.

Reveals a "new" Edwards by tracing his purely philosophical speculations chronologically. Neither the imprecatory preacher of the nineteenth century nor the Lockean empiricist of the twentieth, Edwards "adapted Calvinism to metaphysical idealism" and hence should be granted a "place of honor" in American philosophy.

1987

1 Arnal, Oscar L. Review of *Jonathan Edwards,* by John H. Gerstner. *Consensus* 13 (Fall): 94-95.

Discovers a "disembodied" Edwards in John H. Gerstner's study (1987.8), which appears to serve the "apologetic needs" of its author rather than the "splendor" of its subject.

2 Boardman, George Nye. *A History of New England Theology.* New York: Garland Press.

Reprints 1899.2.

3 Brock, Bernard L. "Jonathan Edwards." In *American Orators before 1900: Critical Studies and Sources.* Edited by Bernard K. Duffy and Halford R. Ryan. Westport, Conn.: Greenwood Press, pp. 146-53.

Labels Edwards "a paradoxical speaker" — his content was "traditional," his language "radical" — in a survey of early American orators.

4 Calhoun, David B. "David Brainerd: 'A Constant Stream.'" *Presbyterion* 13 (Spring): 44-50.

Remarks the relationship between Edwards and David Brainerd, in a reading of an 1818 edition of the *Life of Brainerd.*

5 Dayan, Joan. *Fables of Mind: An Inquiry into Poe's Fiction.* New York: Oxford University Press, pp. 20-22, 45-51.

Connects Edwards's "Of Insects," "Natural Philosophy," and "The Mind" (in Sereno E. Dwight's 1829 edition) to Edgar Allan Poe's *Eureka,* in an inquiry into Edwards's "fictions" and Poe's. Both were "obsessive" and found language "inadequate." Poe "took Calvinism seriously, read Jonathan Edwards carefully, and transplanted the 'god-possessed soul' to the perilous ground of the skeptic's 'plot of God'"; Edwards wrote "nonsense in order to make us recognize the limitations of our language."

6 Dreyer, Frederick. "Evangelical Thought: John Wesley and Jonathan Edwards." *Albion* 19 (Summer): 177-92.

Weighs the evangelical thought of Edwards against that of John Wesley — on matters of existence, faith, free will, necessity, grace, and God — and finds a "radical" opposition between them that extends to the "very fundamentals" of their faith.

7 Foster, Frank Hugh. *A Genetic History of New England Theology.* New York: Garland Press.

Reprints 1907.3.

8 Gerstner, John H. *Jonathan Edwards: A Mini-Theology.* Wheaton, Ill.: Tyndale House, 135 pp.

Offers "insights" into Edwards's "crucial affirmations" — on reason, revelation, the Trinity, the Fall, sin, atonement, regeneration, justification, sanctification, the apocalypse, hell, and heaven — in "an introduction and nothing more than an introduction" to the "total" corpus of his writings and the "large" corpus of writings about him, a "harbinger" of a longer study (see 1991.10, 1992.4, and 1993.7). The "saint of Stockbridge" gave his life to a synthesis of reason and faith and his "almost undivided" attention to the Bible. Indeed, Edwards "came closer to ascertaining the mind of God in the realm of rational reflection and biblical investigation than any other person."

9 Holbrook, Clyde A. "Crime and Sin in Puritan Massachusetts." In *Crime, Values, and Religion.* Edited by James M. Day and William S. Laufer. Norwood, N.J.: Ablex Publishing, pp. 1-22.

Instances Edwards as a transitional figure in the shift from ecclesiastical to civil authority about crime and sin in eighteenth-century Massachusetts. The Great Awakening "weakened" the relationship between people and pastor — for example, the "bad book" episode in Northampton and Edwards's dismissal — and between church and state. Though Edwards lamented civil disorder, he sought God's help to rectify sinful lives, not the law's.

10 ———. *Jonathan Edwards, the Valley and Nature: An Interpretative Essay.* Lewisburg, Pa.: Bucknell University Press, 151 pp.

Restores nature to its "rightful position" in Edwards's thought, in a (sometimes personal) study of the landscape of the Connecticut Valley and its "profound and determinative" influence on his philosophy, theology, and ethics. Though Edwards directly experienced the Valley at East Windsor and Northampton, his reading of continental theology and science created "a secondhand relation" to it. Thus the beauty of nature that early stirred him became the beauty of God's order and harmony, immediate sensations gave way to types and symbols, and John Locke yielded to George Berkeley. Whether the Valley confined or liberated him, nature for Edwards was "sensately real, typologically instructive, and scientifically and metaphysically real."

11 Hughes, Philip Edgecumbe. "Portrait of a Holy Man." *Eternity* 38 (November): 41-42.

Reviews Iain H. Murray's biography of Edwards (1987.22), "an authentic portrait of a great Christian."

12 Humphries, Jefferson. *The Puritan and the Cynic: Moralists and Theorists in French and American Letters.* New York: Oxford University Press, pp. 31-33 passim.

Charges that Edwards "virtually plagiarizes" Blaise Pascal's "Disproportion of Man" and that the texts of *Images or Shadows* read like "sermonettes," in an account of rhetoric and theology in French and American letters.

13 Jacobson, David M. "Emerson's Fate: Moving from Perspectivism to Pragmatism." Ph.D. dissertation, University of Washington.

Published (in part) as 1987.14.

14 ———. "Jonathan Edwards and the 'American Difference': Pragmatic Reflections on the 'Sense of the Heart.'" *Journal of American Studies* 21 (December): 377-85.

Contends that Edwards's logical method is closer to the pragmatism of Charles Peirce, William James, and John Dewey than to modern empiricism or idealism, in an application of Harold Bloom's rhetoric of "American difference" and Edwards's sense of the heart. Edwards, not Ralph Waldo Emerson, first develops a relational methodology for finding "the only truth relevant to human beings in the immediate effects of the full variety of human possibilities."

15 Johnson, Parker H. "Jonathan Edwards' 'Personal Narrative' and the Northampton Controversy." *Cithara* 26 (May): 31-47.

Traces Edwards's advocacy of profession of faith in *Humble Inquiry* (and the Northampton controversy over it) to his "complex attitude toward language" and the case histories in *Faithful Narrative, Personal Narrative, Religious Affections,* and elsewhere. Though Edwards knew that the expression of his own conversion was "riddled with doubt" and the "uncertainty" of language and that grace was "ultimately inexpressible," he nonetheless argued for profession and the visibility of holiness, the only valid evidence of belief for his flock.

16 La Shell, John K. "Imagination and Idol: A Puritan Tension." *Westminster Theological Journal* 49 (Fall): 305-34.
  Notes Edwards's view of imaginary ideas of Christ — "accidental concomitants of elevated affections," not necessarily idolatrous — in the Scottish debate over them, James Robe defending, Ralph Erskine attacking him.

17 Lasseter, Janice Milner. "Horrific Inspiration: The Dialogue of Faith and Reason in American Romanticism." Ph.D. dissertation, University of Alabama.
  Includes the collision between the voice of faith and the voice of reason in *Faithful Narrative,* in a study of the "crisis of voice" in Edwards, Charles Brockden Brown, Nathaniel Hawthorne, and Edgar Allan Poe.

18 Letham, Robert. Review of *Jonathan Edwards,* by Iain H. Murray. *Churchman* 101 (2): 179-81.
  Suggests that "a fraction more detachment" might help Iain H. Murray's "gripping" biography of Edwards (1987.22).

18A Lloyd-Jones, D. Martyn. "Jonathan Edwards and the Crucial Importance of Revival." In *The Puritans: Their Origins and Successors: Addresses Delivered at the Puritan and Westminister Conferences, 1959-1978.* Compiled by Mrs. D. M. Lloyd-Jones. Edinburgh: Banner of Truth, pp. 348-71.
  Reprints 1976.34.

19 Martone, John. "Augustine's Fate: Self-scripture, Conceptual Art, and the Horizons of Autobiography in America." *Southern Review* 23 (Summer): 589-604.
  Gives to Edwards's *Personal Narrative* a central place in American autobiography and the Protestant tradition of writing about self, in a study of the process of self-definition from Augustine to Nancy Kitchel. For Edwards, the "figurative sense of Scripture is finally the sense of life."

20 McKenny, Gerald. Review of *Theism in the Discourse of Jonathan Edwards,* by R. C. DeProspo. *Journal of Religion* 67 (July): 376-77.
  Considers R. C. DeProspo's study (1985.9) "a helpful corrective" to the "inconsistency thesis" of some modern studies of Edwards but one that fails to find the proper source of his consistency.

21 Minkema, Kenneth P. "A Great Awakening Conversion: The Relation of Samuel Belcher." *William and Mary Quarterly,* 3d ser., 44 (January): 121-26.
  Remarks the place of *Faithful Narrative* in the conversion narrative of Samuel Belcher, a parishioner of Edwards's father.

22 Murray, Iain H. *Jonathan Edwards: A New Biography.* Edinburgh: Banner of Truth Trust, 503 pp.

Gathers together previously published parts of a serial life of Edwards — 1974.15A, 1975.12B-C, 1976.38A-D, 1979.24-27, 1984.26-28, 1985.38-43, and 1986.24-25 — adds an introduction ("On Understanding Edwards"), four appendices, and twenty-four illustrations, in an evangelical interpretation of "this man who was, first of all, a Christian." Not since Samuel Hopkins (1765.2), Sereno E. Dwight (1829.4), and Samuel Miller (1837.1) has a biographer shared with Edwards his "basic vision for the Christian church"; in our time he has become the "preserve of academics," who, like Ola Elizabeth Winslow (1940.21) and Perry Miller (1949.9; rpt. 1981.27), are possessed of an "anti-supernatural animus." Until a "definitive and theologically dependable" life is written, this popular account may meet the "urgent need" of a new generation to read and know "one of the foremost teachers of the church."

23 Nation, Garry D. "Jonathan Edwards on Testing Your Spiritual Experiences." *Mid-America Theological Journal* 11 (Fall): 33-38.
  Enlists Edwards's help to "unravel the tangle of issues" in testing spiritual experiences, in a summary of several biblical and practical criteria (and cautions) Edwards offers in *Religious Affections.*

24 Peacock, Virginia A. "Problems in the Interpretation of Jonathan Edwards' *The Nature of True Virtue.*" Ph.D. dissertation, St. Michael's College.
  Published as 1990.42.

25 Petersen, William J. "Sarah and Jonathan Edwards: An Uncommon Union." *Partnership* 4 (May): 40-45.
  Reprints 1983.33 (retitled).

26 Post, Stephen G. *Christian Love and Self-Denial: An Historical and Normative Study of Jonathan Edwards, Samuel Hopkins, and American Theological Ethics.* Lanham, Md.: University Press of America, xiv, 124 pp.
  Compares Edwards's doctrine of Christian love in *True Virtue* with Samuel Hopkins's "radical" version of it, in an historical study of American theological ethics. Edwards put "clear limits" on self-denial and had "no tolerance" for self-damnation, a form of disinterested benevolence later popularized by Hopkins and debated at length in the nineteenth century. As a "Puritan Augustinian," Edwards appreciated the ideal of "'holy indifference'" and found a significant, but "carefully contained," place for it in a theology of love. He "consistently affirmed that God works with, not against, true self-love."

27 Ratzsch, Del. Review of *Churchmen and Philosophers,* by Bruce Kuklick. *Fides et Historia* 19 (3): 73-75.
  Remarks the "thin" evidence linking Edwards to John Dewey in Bruce Kuklick's "impressive" study (1985.26).

28 Rich, Gregory P. "Jonathan Edwards's View of the Freedom Requisite for Moral Agency." In *Religion and Philosophy in the United States of America,* 2. Edited by Peter Freese. Essen: Verlag die Blaue Eule, pp. 641-55.
  Concludes that Edwards failed to provide an "adequate" defense of Calvinism against Arminianism in *Freedom of the Will* in that he failed to show that predestination was compatible with the freedom requisite to moral agency, in a history of the theological controversy over the two. Edwards's arguments against Arminianism rest on "misinterpretations of key phrases."

What he calls "'common'" freedom is not the freedom requisite for moral agency; the freedom to choose otherwise is.

29 Simonson, Harold P. "Jonathan Edwards and His Scottish Connections." *Journal of American Studies* 21 (December): 353-76.

Uncovers "personal aspects" of Edwards's trials at Northampton in the extensive correspondence between him and six Scottish ministers — John Erskine, Thomas Gillespie, John McLaurin, William M'Culloch, James Robe, and John Willison — and remarks the "similar patterns" of the revivalist debate on both sides of the Atlantic. Not only did the Scots agree with Edwards on the primacy of religious affections, they were "heartened" by *Faithful Narrative*, fought Charles Chauncy "by proxy," endorsed *Humble Attempt*, and were first to publish *History of Redemption*.

30 Smith, John E. "Herbert Schneider on the History of American Philosophy." *Journal of the History of Philosophy* 25 (January): 169-77.

Remarks Herbert Schneider's acute understanding of the problems Edwards encountered and the solutions he proposed, in a tribute to Schneider and his *A History of American Philosophy* (1946.5).

31 Stein, Stephen J. "Edwards, Jonathan." In *The Encyclopedia of Religion*, 5. Edited by Mircea Eliade et al. New York: Macmillan, pp. 32-36.

Judges Edwards "a transitional thinker" between the Reformation and the Enlightenment, in a brief account of this life and work. "For the moment, his place is secure within the pantheon of American thinkers."

32 ———, and Henry S. Levinson. Review of *Churchmen and Philosophers,* by Bruce Kuklick. *Religious Studies Review* 13 (April): 111-17.

Offers two views of Bruce Kuklick study (1985.26). On the one hand, it is a "stimulating" and "avowedly revisionist" history of American thought, but one that is "too neat" in its estimate of Edwards (Stephen J. Stein); on the other, it is a "careful and considerate criticism" of trinitarian theology, but it avoids an important strain of American moral philosophy in neglecting Ralph Waldo Emerson, one of "'Edwards's children'" (Henry S. Levinson).

33 Turner, Eldon R. Review of *Theism in the Discourse of Jonathan Edwards,* by R. C. DeProspo. *American Studies* 28 (Spring): 102-103.

Recommends R. C. DeProspo's "difficult but interesting" study (1985.9) that "refreshes" Edwards's texts.

32 Vetö, Miklós. *La pensée de Jonathan Edwards: avec une concordance des différentes éditions.* Paris: Éditions du Cerf, ix, 363 pp.

Reconstructs Edwards's theology into a coherent and unified system of thought based on the central issues of being, will, and knowledge; traces its early and contemporary sources; and situates it in eighteenth-century religious and philosophical historiography, in an account of his life, times, reputation, and ideas — on divine being and creation, freedom of the will and sin, redemption and grace, natural and spiritual knowledge, and primary and secondary beauty — and includes a chronology, bibliography, and concordance of six editions of his work. Edwards unites man's virtuous will to God's divine beauty, his spiritual perception to his gracious plentitude. (In French.)

35 Washington, Joseph R., Jr. *Puritan Race Virtue, Vice, and Values, 1620-1820: Original Calvinist True Believers' Enduring Faith and Ethics Race Claims (in Emerging Congregationalist, Presbyterian, and Baptist Power Denominations)*. New York: Peter Lang, pp. 137-290.

Focusses on the ethical writings of "New England Orthodoxy's three most influential post-theocracy definers of Puritan Piety" — Cotton Mather, Edwards, and Samuel Hopkins — in a "humanities-intensive, decisively unscientific, and probative-specific deconstructionist approach to a Christian critique of Black and White American race and religion realities." Edwards's "re-revision" of Calvinism turned piety into "private-interest ethics" and Mather's pro-political stance into an anti-political one. Following Edwards, consistent Calvinists (and, in the twentieth century, "power parsons") honored "caste-revering and bondage-respecting custom" to deny blacks love and justice.

36 Weir, David A. Review of *Tragedy in Eden*, by C. Samuel Storms. *Journal of the Evangelical Theological Society* 30 (September): 347-48.

Calls C. Samuel Storm's "detailed and precise" book (1985.53) an "excellent contribution" to the study of Edwards and Calvinism.

37 Westra, Helen. "Jonathan Edwards and the Scope of Gospel Ministry." *Calvin Theological Journal* 22 (April): 68-90.

Reprints the first chapter of 1986.45.

38 White, B. R. Review of *Tragedy in Eden*, by C. Samuel Storms. *Themelios*, n.s., 12 (January): 63.

Recommends C. Samuel Storms's "very useful" study of Edwards (1985.53) but cautions it may be "hard going."

39 Whittemore, Robert C. "The Experimental Calvinism of Jonathan Edwards." *The Transformation of the New England Theology*. New York: Peter Lang, pp. 47-91.

Reprints 1966.35 (retitled and revised).

40 Williams, David R. *Wilderness Lost: The Religious Origins of the American Mind*. Cranbury, N.J.: Susquahanna University Press, pp. 88-110.

Reprints 1981.40 (revised), in a "new approach" to early American literature, a psychological reading of the wilderness (unconsciousness, madness) and Canaan (consciousness, God) in Puritan culture.

1988

1 Austin, Richard Cartwright. *Beauty of the Lord: Awakening the Senses*. Environmental Theology, 2. Atlanta, Ga.: John Knox, xi, 225 pp.

Discloses the "integrating" theme of environmental ethics in Edwards's understanding of the beauty of God, in a study that seeks to join traditional theology to modern ecology, "sensuousness" toward God to communion with, and protection of, nature. Edwards left "a rich record of mistakes and accomplishments" — in his "Resolutions," "Miscellanies," and *Personal Narrative;* his essays on grace and the Trinity; his treatises on *Religious Affections* and *True Virtue* — with which to probe the Christian experience with nature.

2 Brito, Emilio. Review of *La pensée de Jonathan Edwards,* by Miklós Vetö. *Laval Théologique et Philosophique* 44 (October): 416-17.

Admires the erudition of Miklós Vetö's study of Edwards (1987.34) but regrets the absence of general conclusions about influences. (In French.)

3 Burman, Ronald Sidney. "A Study of the Dynamics of Conversion and Identity in the Life and Works of Jonathan Edwards." Ph.D. dissertation, University of Minnesota.

Uses the analytic tools of history, psychology, philosophy, and stylistics to examine the crisis of identity that led to Edwards's conversion recorded in *Personal Narrative.*

4 Conforti, Joseph. Review of *Jonathan Edwards, The Valley and Nature,* by Clyde A. Holbrook. *Journal of American History* 75 (September): 594.

Suggests that Clyde A. Holbrook's "slim volume" on nature in Edwards (1987.10) may provide "a basis for future work" on him.

5 Corseri, Gary Steven. "Random Descent." Ph.D. dissertation, Florida State University.

Salutes Edwards as tonic for "this parlous era" in a thirty-nine-line poem, part of a "triptych journey" of the author's poetic psyche.

6 Crocco, Stephen. "Joseph Haroutunian: Neglected Theocentrist." *Journal of Religion* 68 (July): 411-25.

Restores Joseph Haroutunian to the "pride of place" (with H. Richard Niebuhr) as a "major" twentieth-century interpreter of Edwards's theocentric theology and ethics.

7 Davies, Ronald Edwin. "'Prepare Ye the Way of the Lord': The Missiological Thought and Practice of Jonathan Edwards (1703-1758)." Ph.D. dissertation, Fuller Theological Seminary.

Focusses on the role of missions and missionary work in Edwards, especially in *History of Redemption* (his "uncompleted Summa"), *Life of Brainerd,* and his Stockbridge years.

8 De Jong, James A. Review of *Jonathan Edwards,* by Iain H. Murray. *Calvin Theological Journal* 23 (April): 107-108.

Welcomes Iain H. Murray's "unashamedly partisan" biography of the evangelical Edwards (1987.22) as "an overdue corrective" to earlier studies.

9 Dockery, David S. Review of *Tragedy in Eden,* by C. Samuel Storms. *Grace Theological Journal* 9 (Fall): 295-96.

Considers C. Samuel Storms's "carefully documented" study (1985.53) a "significant" contribution to understanding American Christianity, New England Theology, and Edwards's complex position on original sin.

10 Duban, James. "From Emerson to Edwards: Henry Whitney Bellows and an 'Ideal' Metaphysics of Sovereignty." *Harvard Theological Review* 81 (October): 389-411.

Locates the continuity between Edwards and Emerson, not in mysticism, as had Perry Miller (1940.9; rpt. 1981.27), but in idealism, in a study of the "innovative" idealism of Henry Whitney Bellows that reconciled self-reliance with God's sovereignty. A Unitarian minister, Bellows "manipulates" the idealism of both Emerson and Edwards to strike a balance between liberal Christianity and Calvinism in what is perhaps "the most theologically sophisticated response to Edwards of any nineteenth-century writer."

11 Ehrat, Christoph. "Jonathan Edwards' *Treatise Concerning Religious Affections* and its Application to Prayer." *Crux* 24 (March): 11-16.
   Links prayer and religious affections, in a summary and synthesis of the twelve signs of Edwards's treatise.

12 Eller, Gary Steven. "Jonathan Edwards: A Study in Religious Experience and Eriksonian Psychobiography." Ph.D. dissertation, Vanderbilt University.
   Reconstructs Edwards's personality and the sources of his religious convictions as an illustration of Erik Erikson's psychobiographical life-cycle theory, including his theory of ritual applied to Edwards's dismissal and his "struggle with authority and oedipal conflicts."

13 Ellis, E. Earle. Review of *Jonathan Edwards,* by Iain H. Murray. *Southwestern Journal of Theology* 30 (Summer): 57.
   Values Iain H. Murray's biography of Edwards (1987.22) as "an inspiration" both to ministers and the Church.

14 Gerstner, John H. "Edwards, Jonathan." In *New Dictionary of Theology.* Edited by Sinclair B. Ferguson ct al. Downers Grove, Ill.: InterVarsity Press, pp. 220-21.
   Sketches Edwards's theology.

15 Guelzo, Allen C. "The Making of a Revivalist: Finney and the Heritage of Edwards." *Christian History* 7 (Winter): 28-30.
   Uncovers the roots of Charles Grandison Finney's self-made frontier theology and supposed Arminianism in Edwards's "brand" of Calvinism and the New Divinity of Samuel Hopkins, Joseph Bellamy, and Nathanael Emmons.

16 Hase, Randall Wayne. "Mainline Evangelism: A Framework for a Local Church." D.Min. dissertation, Fuller Theological Seminary.
   Explains Edwards's life and ministry in the context of Congregational history, in a study of evangelism in the life of the Church.

17 Hatch, Nathan O., and Harry S. Stout, eds. *Jonathan Edwards and the American Experience.* New York: Oxford University Press, 298 pp.
   Weaves together the "disparate strands" of Edwards's achievement in fourteen essays (and an introduction), papers first read at the Wheaton College conference on Edwards and the American experience in the fall of 1984.
   Hatch, Nathan O., and Harry S. Stout. "Introduction," pp. 3-15. Attributes to the "creative genius" of Perry Miller's *Jonathan Edwards* (1949.9; rpt. 1981.27) the surge of scholarly interest in Edwards over the last three decades; groups commentary about "this remarkable individual" under three rubrics ("Edwards and the American Imagination," pp. 19-70; "Edwards in Cultural Context," pp. 73-173; and "The Legacy of Edwards," pp. 177-287); and summarizes each.
   May, Henry F. "Jonathan Edwards and America," pp. 19-33. Suggests a "few of the main interpretations" of Edwards in successive generations, from the early devotion of his disciples through the "anguished rejection" of American Victorians to his critical rescue by modern (and

postmodern) commentators. Edwards seems "inexhaustible and impossible to pin down," and therefore worth studying.

Levin, David. "Edwards, Franklin, and Cotton Mather: A Meditation on Character and Reputation," pp. 34-49. Highlights "attractive and unattractive" resemblances of Edwards, Benjamin Franklin, and Cotton Mather rather than their differences, in a reconsideration of the character and reputation of each. Though their similar traits and actions are judged differently and though their styles differ, they are one in their intense determination to reconcile ambition and humility through "ingenious" efforts to do good in the world.

Weber, Donald. "The Recovery of Jonathan Edwards," pp. 50-70. Maps the recovery of Edwards in the uses made of him by Samuel Hopkins, Jonathan Edwards, Jr., Oliver Wendell Holmes, and H. Richard Niebuhr, in a examination of four "Edwardsian moments" that are also "representative junctures" in American cultural history. From his disciple's "filial piety" to his son's "revolutionary" rhetoric, from Holmes's "rancorous" encounter to Niebuhr's "remarkable" identification, Edwards spoke "powerfully" to those who listened, and still does.

Fiering, Norman. "The Rationalist Foundations of Jonathan Edwards's Metaphysics," pp. 73-101. Concludes that Edwards was a rationalist and had more in common with the theocentric metaphysics of Nicolas Malebranche (and John Norris and George Berkeley) than with the empiricism of John Locke, in an examination of five general (and inherited) principles of his thought: divine sovereignty, divine concurrence, divine teleology, Neoplatonic typology, and the nature of matter. "The notion that [Locke's] *Essay* played a key functional role in the development of Edwards's metaphysics is not sustainable."

Kimnach, Wilson H. "Jonathan Edwards's Pursuit of Reality," pp. 103-17. Differentiates Edwards from both Puritans and evangelicals in his "pursuit of reality" — his linking of sensation to rational conviction — in a study of his private and public papers, his "Diary" and "Resolutions," the "Miscellanies," and his (largely unpublished) sermons. In his "primary vocation," Edwards mastered the sermonic form through specificity, unity, and intensity, but his pursuit of reality was compromised by his sense of the "severe limitations of conventional language."

Stein, Stephen J. "The Spirit and the Word: Jonathan Edwards and Scriptural Exegesis," pp. 118-30. Places Edwards's scriptural exegesis between the "'precritical'" approach (described by Hans Frei) and the hermeneutical developments of his time, in a study of his biblical observations in private notebooks, sermons, published treatises, and projected work, especially "The Harmony of the Old and New Testament." In the "Harmony," Edwards focusses on prophecy, types, and doctrines, a "tripartite witness to the centrality" of Christ in both testaments and, for him, the "'genius and spirit'" of the Scriptures.

Wilson, John F. "History, Redemption, and the Millennium," pp. 131-41. Questions the claim of C. C. Goen (1959.5) and others for Edwards's "'new departure'" in eschatology, in a study of Edwards's postmillennialism, its background and appropriation. Edwards's eschatology represented "nothing remarkably new" until the Enlightenment reduced it to "literalistic formulations." His postmillennialism conformed to Puritan creedal standards but was transformed in the eighteenth century from the figural rhetoric of the seventeenth to the propositional rhetoric of the nineteenth.

Stout, Harry S. "The Puritans and Edwards," pp. 142-59. Contends that Edwards was "every bit a federal theologian that his Puritan predecessors were," in a reading of his unpublished fast and thanksgiving sermons of the 1740s and 1750s, the occasions of his temporal rhetoric. Edwards, no less than other ministers, New Lights or Old, invoked the traditional national covenant when corporate New England was threatened, especially by New France.

Lang, Amy Schrager. "'A Flood of Errors': Chauncy and Edwards in the Great Awakening," pp. 160-73. Charts the "rhetorical divide" separating Edwards and Charles Chauncy during the Great Awakening, in a study of the preface to Chauncy's *Seasonable Thoughts* and the theological and social issues of antinomianism and gender raised by him. For Edwards, words, like visible signs, were "accidental" and thus inadequate to render the experience of grace (as it was for Anne Hutchinson); for Chauncy, the inadequacy lay not in the outward signs but in the "radical mistrust" of them and the "threat it posed to the standing order."

Breitenbach, William. "Piety and Moralism: Edwards and the New Divinity," pp. 177-204. Challenges the "betrayal interpretation" of the New Divinity and the piety-versus-moralism paradigm of it, in a study of Edwards and his disciples, Joseph Bellamy and Samuel Hopkins. Edwards inherited the Puritan tradition of piety and moralism — grace and law — and occupied a middle ground between antinomianism and Arminianism. The New Divinity followed Edwards in that stance, often revealing in their work his "most creative and important contributions" to theology.

Hoopes, James. "Calvinism and Consciousness from Edwards to Beecher," pp. 205-25. Locates the theological discontinuities between Edwards and his successors — Samuel Hopkins, Nathanael Emmons, Asa Burton, Timothy Dwight, Nathaniel William Taylor, and Lyman Beecher — in their ignorance of his idealist metaphysics and their rejection of his unitary psychology, in a study of Calvinism and the structure of the mind from the eighteenth to the nineteenth century. Not only did they not know "The Mind" — it was first published in 1829 — but they believed that reconciling divine sovereignty and human moral autonomy depended upon a mind "divisible into conscious and unconscious elements."

Laurence, David. "Jonathan Edwards as a Figure in Literary History," pp. 226-45. Considers Edwards "simply one American writer," neither "outside and below" nor "outside and above" American literature, in a "complicated theoretical reflection" about literature and, more particularly, American literature. Edwards fits into an American literary history of discontinuity and "alterity" — of being "not-Europe" — and, like Ralph Waldo Emerson, Henry David Thoreau, Nathaniel Hawthorne, and Herman Melville, is not "wholly indifferent" to the historical, biographical, and regional scene.

Kuklick, Bruce. "Jonathan Edwards and American Philosophy," pp. 246-59. Calls Edwards the "foundation stone" of the history of American philosophy, in an account of the standard canon of that "confused" discipline and an alternative to it. Edwards is not the problem with "'American philosophy,'" but his primacy in it is, the product of "some unfortunate queries." His achievement, though, should survive any new formulation.

Noll, Mark A. "Jonathan Edwards and Nineteenth-Century Theology," pp. 260-87. Defines Edwards's place in nineteenth-century theology by some of those who appropriated him (Lyman Hotchkiss Atwater and Edwards Amasa Park), rejected him (Henry Philip Tappan), succeeded him (John McLeod Campbell and Thomas Chalmers), or dismissed him (George A. Gordon), in a study of the issues (and voices) raised about him from the Revolution to the First World War. Edwards may have survived "not because he anticipated the norms [that is, polarities] of nineteenth-century intellectual discourse, but because he was their foil."

18 Heimert, Alan. "Jonathan Edwards, Charles Chauncy, and the Great Awakening." In *Columbia Literary History of the United States*. Edited by Emory Elliott et al. New York: Columbia University Press, pp. 113-26.

Defines Edwards as a "consummate practitioner" of the plain style, in an assessment of his role as preacher (and antagonist of Charles Chauncy) during the Great Awakening, a "salient" episode in the intellectual life of America. Edwards "revivified" Puritan sermonic practice with assonance, alliteration, repetition, and rhythmic structures and, in a "radical transformation," democratized the relationship between speaker and audience.

19 Helm, Paul. Review of *Jonathan Edwards,* by Iain H. Murray. *Scottish Bulletin of Evangelical Theology* 6 (Spring): 58.

Finds "scarcely an adverse comment" about Edwards in Iain H. Murray's "Protestant life of a saint" (1987.22).

20 Hoffer, Peter Charles, ed. *The Marrow of American Divinity: Selected Articles on Colonial Religion.* New York: Garland Publishing.
Reprints 1948.8, 1977.7, and 1978.4.

21 Houser, William Glen. "Identifying the Regenerate: The Homiletics of Conversion during the First Great Awakening." Ph.D. dissertation, University of Notre Dame.
Delineates New Lights conversion homiletics from Old in the Great Awakening sermons of Edwards, George Whitefield, Gilbert Tennent, and Charles Chauncy. Edwards argues for both "rational order" and a "new sense" but is ambiguous about identifying the elect.

22 Jenson, Robert W. *America's Theologian: A Recommendation of Jonathan Edwards.* New York: Oxford University Press, xii, 224 pp.
Examines the "fit" between Edwards and America, the Enlightenment and Puritanism, God and nation, in a study of Edwards's critique of religious appearances and its importance for contemporary religious, political, and social thought, as seen from a Lutheran perspective. A "born rationalist," Edwards resolves the clash between reason and the gospel in the beautiful harmony of the triune God, a "fugued hymn" of the elements and the community of consciousness, a "conversation" of mutuality within, but open to others without. Edwards is "America's theologian" because he "astonishingly accomplished" both a critique and a harmony, "penetrated" to that ancient dualism, and "transcended" it.

23 Knight, Henry H., III. "The Relation of Love to Gratitude in the Theologies of Edwards and Wesley." *Evangelical Journal* 6 (Spring): 3-12.
Contrasts Edwards and John Wesley on the relationship between the love of God and gratitude, in a reading of the third part of *Religious Affections*. Wesley's search for assurance is in "sharp conflict" with Edwards, who "confuses" the entry into a Christian life with the foundations of it.

24 Koreneva, Maiya. "The Literature of the North American Colonies and the United States." *Istoriya vsemirnoi literatury w devyati tomakh*, 6. Moscow: Nauka, pp. 425-41.
Stresses the literary aspects of Edwards, in a survey of American literature in the eighteenth century. (In Russian.)

25 Lee, Sang Hyun. *The Philosophical Theology of Jonathan Edwards.* Princeton, N.J.: Princeton University Press, xiii, 248 pp.
Explicates the philosophical theology of Edwards through the idea of habit, the interpretative "key" to his "dynamic and relational" vision of reality and to the unity and modernity of his thought, in a study of the history of the idea and application of it to the corpus of his work both in print and manuscript. Edwards's concept addresses problems of ontology and epistemology raised in Isaac Newton and John Locke and resolves questions of being and becoming, imagination and beauty, temporality and history, and the "increasing fullness" of God, the "rhythm of the becoming world." Not only does such a "highly innovative" reconception of his theological tradition make Edwards "historically important," his dispositional ontology can become "an enduring source of insight" for contemporary philosophical theology as well, inasmuch as it mediates the demands of classical theism and process theology.

26 Lesser, M. X. *Jonathan Edwards.* Twayne's United States Authors Series, 537. Boston: Thayne Publishers, xi, 153 pp.

Regards Edwards's thought an extended meditation on divine sovereignty, in a primer to his published work, including a narrative (and chronology) of his life, an account of his early philosophical speculations, synopses of all his printed sermons and treatises, a review of his critical reception over more than two centuries, and a bibliography of primary sources. The "'awful sweetness'" of God's sovereignty permeates Edwards's conversion experience, his evangelical fervor, and his millennial hope, and explains, in part, his struggle with the limits of language. His doctrinal Calvinism, freshened by contemporary philosophical thought from abroad and challenged by the realities of a New England parish nearing mid-century, is at once rational and inventive, strict and lively.

27 Mains, David R. *The Sense of His Presence: Experiencing Spiritual Regenesis.* Waco, Tex.: Word Books, pp. 166-69.

Tallies instances of the eight points of Christ's presence in Edwards's writing during the Awakening, in a survey of the experience of spiritual rebirth.

28 Marini, Stephen A. "The Great Awakening." In *Encyclopedia of the American Religious Experience,* 2. Edited by Charles H. Lippy and Peter W. Williams. New York: Charles Scribner's Sons, pp. 775-98.

Cites Edwards's surprising conversions of 1734 as a model for later revivals and his theology as the "defining framework" for evangelicals for a century, in an account of the Great Awakening.

29 Marty, Martin E. Review of *Jonathan Edwards and the American Experience,* edited by Nathan O. Hatch and Harry S. Stout. *Eternity* 39 (June): 44.

Judges the "clearly reasoned updates" in Nathan O. Hatch and Harry S. Stout's collection (1988.17), "heavy going," much like Edwards's theology.

30 Minkema, Kenneth Pieter. "The Edwardses: A Ministerial Family in Eighteenth-Century New England." Ph.D. dissertation, University of Connecticut.

Charts three generations of representative New England ministers in the interconnected careers of the Edwardses (father, son, and grandson; Timothy, Jonathan, and Jonathan, Jr.), their responses to changes in religion and society in the eighteenth century, and their contributions to philosophy and ethics in the nineteenth.

31 Noll, Mark A. "The Contested Legacy of Jonathan Edwards in Antebellum Calvinism: Theological Conflict and the Evolution of Thought in America." *Canadian Review of American Studies* 19 (Summer): 149-64.

Tracks the "ghost" of Edwards to the theological conflict over antebellum Calvinism, in a study of the paper war at Princeton, Yale, and Andover and the philosophical discontinuities in the century following his death. Edwards was enlisted "both to justify and to denounce" revivalism, free will, original sin, and true virtue, in part because he had successors but no followers "at the points of his actual theological genius." Thus the controversy marks an "important intellectual transition" in America from idealism to common sense philosophy.

32 Pahl, Jon. Review of *Jonathan Edwards and the American Experience,* edited by Nathan O. Hatch and Harry S. Stout. *Christian Century* 105 (18 May): 510.

Discerns Edwards's "relentless and sublime thought" in Nathan O. Hatch and Harry S. Stout's collection of "artful" essays (1988.17).

33 Patterson, James A. Review of *Jonathan Edwards*, by John H. Gerstner. *Eternity* 39 (January): 36-37.

Questions the intended audience for John H. Gerstner's study (1987.8) but finds "commendable balance" in alerting readers to some of Edwards's "questionable arguments."

34 Post, Stephen G. Review of *Jonathan Edwards, The Valley and Nature*, by Clyde A. Holbrook. *Ethics* 99 (October): 204.

Recommends Clyde A. Holbrook's "superlative" study of Edwards's ethical thought (1987.10).

35 Schmidt, Lawrence K. "Jonathan Edwards' Idealistic Argument from Resistance." *Southwest Philosophy Review* 4 (July): 39-47.

Recounts Edwards's argument from resistance found in "The Mind" and the influence of John Locke and George Berkeley upon it.

36 Seed, David. "Exemplary Selves: Jonathan Edwards and Benjamin Franklin." In *First Person Singular: Studies in American Autobiography*. Edited by A. Robert Lee. New York: St. Martin's Press, pp. 37-56.

Balances the contrasts and similarities that link Edwards's *Personal Narrative* and Benjamin Franklin's *Autobiography* only to conclude that the first has become dated, because "bound" by its theology, while the second has been "assimilated" into American history.

37 Shaw, Nancy Joy. "Speaking for the Spirit: Cotton, Shepard, Edwards, Emerson." Ph.D. dissertation, Cornell University.

Probes Edwards's *Religious Affections* as part of a study of the doctrine of the Holy Spirit in John Cotton, Thomas Shepard, and Ralph Waldo Emerson and its "central role" in the antinomian controversy, the Great Awakening, and transcendentalism.

37A Shea, Daniel B. *Spiritual Autobiography in Early America*. Madison: University of Wisconsin Press, pp. xvii-xxi.

Reprints 1968.26 and adds a new preface suggesting that among early American spiritual autobiographies Edwards's *Personal Narrative* will "always repay study."

38 Smith, John E. "Jonathan Edwards and the Great Awakening." In *Doctrine and Experience: Essays in American Philosophy*. Edited by Vincent G. Potter. New York: Fordham University Press, pp. 7-21.

Selects the "crucial points" of *God Glorified, Divine and Supernatural Light, Distinguishing Marks, Religious Affections*, and *Some Thoughts* to reveal Edwards's conception of the Holy Spirit, his criteria for judging piety, and his critical appraisal of the Great Awakening. "Edwards attacked the sufficiency of rationalism in religion and sought to lay hold of the truth in the piety of experience, but in the end he gave no comfort to enthusiasts or to obscurantists."

39 ———. "*Religious Affections*, by Jonathan Edwards." *American Presbyterians* 66 (Winter): 219-22.

Recapitulates Edwards's *Religious Affections*, a "demanding" book that shaped American

Presbyterianism and his "most concentrated effort" to explain the Great Awakening and the role of experience in true piety.

40 Stark, Tom. Review of *Jonathan Edwards,* by John H. Gerstner. *Reformed Review* 42 (Winter): 166-67.

Welcomes John H. Gerstner's study of Edwards (1987.8), "an important introduction to a great scholar."

41 Stoever, William K. B. "The Calvinist Theological Tradition." In *Encyclopedia of the American Religious Experience,* 2. Edited by Charles H. Lippy and Peter W. Williams. New York: Charles Scribner's Sons, pp. 1039-56.

Cites Edwards as "the outstanding figure" in the American Calvinist theological tradition and briefly reviews his career.

42 Taylor, Thomas Templeton. "The Spirit of the Awakening: The Pneumatology of New England's Great Awakening in Historical and Theological Context." Ph.D. dissertation, University of Illinois at Urbana-Champaign.

Centers Edwards's work on the Holy Spirit (chiefly in *Religious Affections*) between enthusiasts like George Whitefield and rationalists like Charles Chauncy, in a history of pneumatology to the Great Awakening and beyond.

43 Wainwright, William J. "Original Sin." In *Philosophy and the Christian Faith.* Edited by Thomas V. Morris. Notre Dame Studies in the Philosophy of Religion, 5. Notre Dame, Ind.: University of Notre Dame Press, pp. 31-60.

Argues that Edwards "partly succeeds and partly fails" in his attempt at an Augustinian view of inherited guilt, in a close reading of *Original Sin.* Edwards succeeds in showing that humans are sinful, that they need a change of heart, and that their corruption is voluntary (and so subject to blame and punishment); he fails to show that Adam's sin is the source of their corruption and guilt and that God can reasonably impute Adam's guilt to them. Still, for all the misgivings about his appropriation of the Augustinian doctrine, Edwards's defense is "one of the most plausible."

44 Weber, Donald. *Rhetoric and History in Revolutionary New England.* New York: Oxford University Press, pp. 60-62.

Asserts that his manuscript sermons and notebooks show Edwards not "immune" from history but "attuned" to it, in an account of his son Jonathan's indebtedness to *History of Redemption.*

45 Weddle, David L. "The Melancholy Saint: Jonathan Edwards's Interpretation of David Brainerd as a Model of Evangelical Spirituality." *Harvard Theological Review* 81 (July): 297-318.

Contends that David Brainerd was an "ambiguous" and "problematic" example of religious experience for Edwards, in a study of his interpretation of Brainerd's "life-long" struggle with melancholy and its "pernicious" effect on evangelical spirituality. For Edwards, Brainerd's experimental piety refutes Arminianism and confirms his own doctrine of grace, but in its pathological self-concern it is "incompatible" with disinterested benevolence. In fact, Edwards's view of God is "fundamentally different" from Brainerd's.

46 Westra, Helen Petter. "Jonathan Edwards on 'Faithful and Successful Ministers.'" *Early American Literature* 23 (Winter): 281-290.

> Discovers in Edwards's first (1736) and last (1754) manuscript ordination sermons the "shifts and developments" of his ministerial vision, from celebratory to "pensive, dark, and defensive."

47 Williams, Clifford. Review of *Christian Love and Self-Denial*, by Stephen G. Post. *Ethics* 98 (April): 639-40.

> Doubts the "depth and subtlety" of Stephen G. Post's study of Edwards's theological ethics (1987.26).

1989

1 Abraham, William J. "Predestination and Assurance." In *The Grace of God, the Will of Man*. Edited by Clark H. Pinnock. Grand Rapids, Mich.: Academie Books, pp. 231-42.

> Proposes an "amicable" arrangement of mutual borrowing between Calvinists and Arminians, in an examination of Edwards and John Wesley on predestination and assurance. A "paradigm" of Calvinism, Edwards rejects the appeal to personal revelation, a "precarious enterprise" compared to Wesley's "incipient revolutionary" view. Still, Edwards on this and much else besides deserves to be "earnestly coveted," despite a vision "profoundly mistaken and deeply unscriptural."

2 Baxter, Tony. Review of *Jonathan Edwards*, by Iain H. Murray. *Evangelical Quarterly* 61 (April): 168-70.

> Finds Iain H. Murray's "invigorating" but uncritical biography of Edwards (1987.22) "very worthwhile" for the general reader but not the expert.

3 Berman, David. "Irish Philosophy and the American Enlightenment during the Eighteenth Century." *Éire-Ireland* 42 (Spring): 28-39.

> Comments on the influence of Francis Hutcheson's *Inquiry into Beauty and Virtue* (1725) on Edwards's *True Virtue*, in a "limited" examination of Irish philosophy and the American Enlightenment. "Like his Irish counterparts — [George] Berkeley, [Peter] Browne, and [William] King — Edwards uses the Enlightenment theories for Counter-Enlightenment ends."

4 Bradley, James E. Review of *Jonathan Edwards and the American Experience*, edited by Nathan O. Hatch and Harry S. Stout. *Journal of Church and State* 31 (Autumn): 554-55.

> Values Nathan O. Hatch and Harry S. Stout's collection (1988.17) for its "interdisciplinary breadth" of contemporary research on Edwards.

5 Bush, L. Russ. Review of *America's Theologian*, by Robert W. Jenson. *Southwestern Journal of Theology* 32 (Fall): 72.

> Calls Robert W. Jenson's study of Edwards (1988.22) "an excellent secondary source" for seminarians.

6 ———. Review of *Jonathan Edwards and the American Experience*, edited by Nathan O. Hatch and Harry S. Stout. *Southwestern Journal of Theology* 31 (Spring): 63.

Recommends Nathan O. Hatch and Harry S. Stout's "important" collection of essays on Edwards (1988.17) to theological libraries.

7 Coney, Charles Randolph. "Jonathan Edwards and the Northampton Church Controversy: A Crisis of Conscience?" Ph.D. dissertation, University of Texas at Arlington.

Follows Edwards's "crisis of conscience" over communion practice (and the theological basis for it) that led to his controversy with the Northampton church and his dismissal from it.

8 Conforti, Joseph. "Edwardsians, Unitarians, and the Memory of the Great Awakening, 1800-1840." In *American Unitarianism, 1805-1865*. Edited by Conrad Edick Wright. Boston: Northeastern University Press, pp. 31-50.

Contends that at no time before or after the 1830s did Edwards "bulk so large" in the minds of Edwardseans and Unitarians, in a study of the influence of the first Great Awakening on the second and the need to reassess the "direct and indirect links" between Edwards and the age of Emerson.

9 ———. "Jonathan Edwards and American Studies." *American Quarterly* 41 (March): 165-71.

Charts the shift in studies on Edwards from an earlier emphasis on his modernity to a later emphasis on his Puritan heritage, in an essay-review of Nathan O. Hatch and Harry S. Stout's collection (1988.17) and David R. Williams's *Wilderness Lost* (1987.40).

10 Cooey, Paula M. "Eros and Intimacy in Edwards." *Journal of Religion* 69 (October): 484-501.

Concludes that Edwards's concept of virtuous love is "unabashedly sensual," in a study of the complex nature of delight, complacence, and intimacy in his writings, chiefly in the notebooks and "Miscellanies," *True Virtue* and *Images or Shadows*. However abstract or formal the expression, Edwards's thought includes "deeply sensual elements" that integrate human, physical love with divine, disinterested love — *eros* and *agapé* — and offers a "refreshing alternative" to the current theological and ethical debate.

11 Dean, Kevin William. "A Rhetorical Biography of Jonathan Edwards: Beyond the Fires of Hell." Ph.D. dissertation, University of Maryland.

Constructs a rhetorical biography of Edwards, in an examination of all his published sermons to counter the minatory preacher of the many studies based solely on *Sinners in the Hands of an Angry God*.

12 Edwards, D. Elwyn. *Jonathan Edwards, 1703-1758: yn cynnwys golwg ar ei ddtlanwad ar fywyd creyfyddol Cymru a Lloeger*. Darlith Davies Series, 1989. Caernarfon: Gwasg Pantycelyn ar ran Bwrdd Darlith Davies, 40 pp.

Recounts the career of Edwards and his influence, especially through his *Life of Brainerd*, on evangelicals and missionaries in England, Scotland, and Wales. (In Welsh.)

13 Flaherty, Martin. "'The Promised Land at Princeton': Princeton and the Great Awakening, 1734-1756." *Princeton History* 8:1-21.

Notes the influence of Edwards and the Great Awakening on Princeton, a town "forged in the fires of the damned."

14 Geissler, Suzanne B. Review of *Jonathan Edwards and the American Experience,* edited by Nathan O. Hatch and Harry S. Stout. *Journal of American History* 75 (March): 1303.

> Deems Nathan O. Hatch and Harry S. Stout's collection (1988.17) "a valuable addition" to Edwards studies.

15 Gilpin, W. Clark. Review of *Jonathan Edwards, the Valley and Nature,* by Clyde A. Holbrook. *Journal of Religion* 69 (April): 250.

> Admires Clyde A. Holbrook's study (1987.10) for its explication of Edwards's idealism and the influence it had on his religious and ethical life.

16 Guelzo, Allen C. *Edwards on the Will: A Century of American Theological Debate.* Middletown, Conn.: Wesleyan University Press, xi, 349 pp.

> Concludes that Edwards's sophisticated arguments in *Freedom of the Will* and the corollaries of his successors "frightened rather than consoled" Old Calvinists here and abroad, in an account of Edwards's personal involvement with the problem of free will, a particular analysis of the text, and the varied responses and practices of Joseph Bellamy and Samuel Hopkins, New Divinity men and Old Calvinists, and some "ardent disciples" among mid-Atlantic Presbyterians. Not until Nathaniel William Taylor (1786-1858) and New Haven Theology laid the "troublesome ghost" of *Freedom of the Will* to rest did it lose its importance as a theological question in America.

17 ———. Review of *Jonathan Edwards,* by Iain H. Murray. *Fides et Historia* 21 (June): 81-83.

> Considers Iain H. Murray's life (1987.22) "hagiography" and the result "Murray's Edwards but not Jonathan Edwards."

18 Hall, Christopher. Review of *Jonathan Edwards and the American Experience,* edited by Nathan O. Hatch and Harry S. Stout. *Crux* 25 (December): 39-41.

> Praises Nathan O. Hatch and Harry S. Stout's collection (1988.17) for its "interdisciplinary approach" to Edwards, in a joint review of more general studies of religion in colonial New England by Patricia U. Bonomi (1986.3) and Harry S. Stout (1986.41).

19 Hardman, Keith. "God's Wonderful Working: The First Great Awakening in New England." *Christian History* 8 (Fall): 12-15.

> Sketches Edwards's role in the Great Awakening. (Illustrated.)

20 Holbrook, Clyde A. Review of *America's Theologian,* by Robert W. Jenson. *William and Mary Quarterly,* 3d ser., 46 (July): 611-14.

> Questions the emphasis on Edwards's Trinitarianism in Robert W. Jenson's otherwise "engaging" book (1988.22).

21 Hoopes, James. "The Thought Sign: Edwards." *Consciousness in New England: From Puritanism and Ideas to Psychoanalysis and Semiotic.* New Series in American Intellectual and Cultural History. Baltimore: Johns Hopkins University Press, pp. 64-94.

> Proposes that Edwards met the threat to traditional religion posed by the "impious implications" of the consciousness concept — that is, the self enjoys complete knowledge of its thought — by rejecting the notion of a substantial self, in a reconstructionist study of consciousness

from Puritanism to psychoanalysis. Unlike other eighteenth-century thinkers — George Berkeley and David Hume, for instance — Edwards "delighted" in the problem of personal identity and the absence of empirical evidence for a substantial soul. His metaphysical idealism posited a soul constituted of nothing but ideas in the mind of God, who might, in conversion, transform human identity and arbitrarily create a new man.

22 Jenson, Robert W. "A 'Protestant Constructive Response' to Christian Unbelief." In *American Apostasy: The Triumph of "Other" Gospels.* Encounter Series, 10. Edited by Richard John Neuhaus. Grand Rapids, Mich.: William B. Eerdmans, pp. 56-74.

Offers Edwards's critique of religious appearances as part of a "'constructive response'" to Christian unbelief, in an analysis of James Turner's *Without God, Without Creed* (1985) and the "flaws" of modern Protestantism. Edwards foresaw the need to overcome "feeble" Trinitarianism and "feeble" Christology, but American Protestantism missed the opportunity he offered and has suffered for it ever since.

23 ———. Review of *Jonathan Edwards, The Valley and Nature,* by Clyde A. Holbrook; *Jonathan Edwards,* by Iain H. Murray; and *The Philosophical Theology of Jonathan Edwards,* by Sang H. Lee. *Christian Century* 106 (5 July): 662.

Perceives in the studies by Clyde A. Holbrook (1987.10), Iain H. Murray (1987.22), and Sang H. Lee (1988.25) "an apparently ineradicable tendency of writing about Edwards: to construct some polarity — almost alien to Edwards — and then stretch him against it."

24 Jinkins, Michael. "Atonement and the Character of God: A Comparative Study in the Theology of Atonement in Jonathan Edwards and John McLeod Campbell." Ph.D. dissertation, University of Aberdeen.

Published as 1993.8.

25 Kitchens, Lester David. "An Examination of the Degree of Effectiveness of Expository Preaching in Obtaining Evangelistic Results." Th.D. dissertation, New Orleans Baptist Theological Seminary.

Examines a selection of Edwards's sermons and Gilbert Tennent's, in a survey of expository preaching and its evangelical effects.

26 Koenig, Marie-Jeanne. Review of *La pensée de Jonathan Edwards,* by Miklós Vetö. *Revue d'Histoire et de Philosophie Religieuses* 69 (January): 75-76.

Commends Miklós Vetö's book (1987.34) to French Americanists as a good starting point for the study of Edwards. (In French.)

27 Kahn, Rolf. Review of *La pensée de Jonathan Edwards,* by Miklós Vetö. *Freiburger Zeitschrift für Philosophie und Theologie* 36 (1): 220-23.

Adjudges Miklós Vetö's study of Edwards (1987.34) both important and authoritative. (In German.)

28 Kuklick, Bruce. Review of *Jonathan Edwards, the Valley and Nature,* by Clyde A. Holbrook. *International Journal for Philosophy of Religion* 26 (December): 188-89.

Faults the "amateur philosophical comments" about Edwards's metaphysical idealism in Clyde A. Holbrook's "otherwise credible" historical study (1987.10).

29 Lewis, Paul. Review of *The Philosophical Theology of Jonathan Edwards,* by Sang H. Lee. *Christian Scholar's Review* 19 (September): 90-91.
    Maintains that Sang H. Lee's study (1988.25) emphasizes the "modern elements" in Edwards at the expense of the Puritan.

30 Lippy, Charles H. Review of *America's Theologian,* by Robert W. Jenson. *Journal of American History* 76 (September): 581-82.
    Cautions that Robert W. Jenson's "solid introduction" to Edwards's thought (1988.22) presents him as a "critic of the present."

31 Marsden, George. "The Edwardsean Vision." *Reformed Journal* 39 (June): 23-25.
    Values Robert W. Jenson's *America's Theologian* (1988.22) for its "suggestive insights" but questions its attempt to "make Edwards into Karl Barth."

32 Marshall, Ian. "Taking Louisbourg by Prayer: Responses of Jonathan Edwards and Benjamin Franklin to a Military Episode in Colonial American History." *University of Dayton Review* 20 (Summer): 3-19.
    Cites two 1745 letters — one from Edwards to John McLaurin on the power of prayer, the other from Benjamin Franklin to his brother John mocking the notion — in an appraisal of public reaction to the fall of Louisbourg during the French and Indian War. Edwards saw the victory as "a convincing demonstration" of New England's faith and collective prayer; Franklin viewed the taking of Cape Breton by prayer with "non-sectarian skepticism."

33 McDermott, Gerald Robert. "One Holy and Happy Society: The Public Theology of Jonathan Edwards." Ph.D. dissertation, University of Iowa.
    Published as 1992.13.

34 ———. Review of *Jonathan Edwards,* by M. X. Lesser. *Religious Studies Review* 15 (October): 348.
    Considers M. X. Lesser's study (1988.26) "an ideal Edwards primer" for undergraduates and seminarians.

35 McKenny, Gerald P. "God the Center: Moral Objectivity in Jonathan Edwards and H. Richard Niebuhr." Ph.D. dissertation, University of Chicago.
    Published (in part) as 1991.29.

36 ———. Review of *The Philosophical Theology of Jonathan Edwards,* by Sang H. Lee. *Princeton Seminary Bulletin,* n.s., 10 (Autumn): 272-74.
    Rates Sang H. Lee's study (1988.25) "an overwhelming success" in making Edwards's difficult thought accessible to specialist and non-specialist alike.

37 Minkema, Kenneth P. Review of *America's Theologian,* by Robert W. Jenson. *Theological Studies* 50 (September): 616-17.
    Questions Robert W. Jenson's study (1988.22) for its depiction of mainline American Christianity, the "negatively pervasive" effects of the Enlightenment, and the role of Edwards in both.

38 Noll, Mark A. "And the Winner is . . . Jonathan Edwards?" *Reformed Journal* 39 (March): 5-6.

Determines that Edwards is "the most-cited figure" in the index of the *Encyclopedia of the American Religious Experience* (1988), in a survey of fifty-three individuals with at least three lines of citations each. Edwards's eight lines confirms that "his voice is being heard once again."

39 ————. Review of *American Religious Thought of the 18th and 19th Centuries*, edited by Bruce Kuklick. *Church History* 58 (June): 211-17.

Judges that the thirty-one volumes of reprints comprising *American Religious Thought of the 18th and 19th Centuries* (1988) testify to the "enduring significance" of Edwards.

40 Pahl, Jon. Review of *Edwards on the Will*, by Allen C. Guelzo. *Christian Century* 106 (19 July): 695-96.

Charges that Allen C. Guelzo study (1989.16) "barely begins" to account for the noise that greeted Edwards's book and that has marked the American question of liberty from the beginning.

41 Pauw, Amy Plantinga. Review of *The Philosophical Theology of Jonathan Edwards*, by Sang H. Lee. *Journal of American History* 76 (December): 913-14.

Prizes Sang H. Lee's "most rewarding" study (1988.25), though it omits aspects of Edwards's thought at odds with dispositional ontology.

41A Piper, John. *Desiring God: Meditation of a Christian Hedonist*. Leicester, U.K.: InterVarsity Press.

Reprints 1986.31A.

42 Proudfoot, Wayne. "From Theology to a Science of Religions: Jonathan Edwards and William James on Religious Affections." *Harvard Theological Review* 82 (April): 149-68.

Illustrates the shift in accounts of religious affections from a traditional theological context to a phenomenological one, in a comparison of Edwards's *Religious Affections* and William James's *The Varieties of Religious Experience* (1902.6). Edwards is the "more astute psychologist," his analysis "thicker and more nuanced," in that he is increasingly skeptical of introspection, trusting observed practice instead; James relies almost exclusively on "felt convictions" and tries to find common ground within the varieties of that experience.

43 Rabinowitz, Richard. *The Spiritual Self in Everyday Life: The Transformation of Personal Religious Experience in Nineteenth-Century New England*. Boston: Northeastern University Press, pp. 16-21.

Credits Edwards with imbuing evangelicals with a "fascination" for the epistemology of grace, in a study of personal religious experience in New England during the nineteenth century.

44 Ramsey, Paul. "Editor's Introduction." *Ethical Writings. The Works of Jonathan Edwards*, 8. New Haven: Yale University Press, pp. 1-121.

Undertakes an analysis of important themes in Edwards's ethical writings with only "light stress" on the times and backgrounds of them, in an introduction to the eighth volume of the Yale Edwards, and includes sections on self-love, consent to being, common morality, charity and its virtues, sources, and notes on the texts of *Charity and its Fruits*, *End of Creation*, and *True Virtue*. The first of the texts is Edwards's "hymn" to charity and may be read as a "systematic treatise on the Christian moral life," a parallel to the work of redemption, and a "major" account of gracious affections; the second and third (in the sequence Edwards intended, but reversed in the posthumously published *Two Dissertations*) are mirror images of each other: the end of creation "must be" the end of true virtue. Indeed, throughout his life, Edwards returned again and again to these "integrated" matters, and so it is "a grave error, now or ever," to separate his philosophy from his theology, his moral philosophy from his theological ethics.

45 ———. "Jonathan Edwards and the Splendor of Common Morality." *This World* 25 (Spring): 5-25.

    Reprints 1989.44, pp. 33-59.

46 Rightmire, R. David. "The Sacramental Theology of Jonathan Edwards in the Context of Controversy." *Fides et Historia* 21 (January): 50-60.

    Takes Edwards's approach to communion to be not a means of conversion, as his grandfather Solomon Stoddard held, but a "sign or seal" of the saving experience — one that confirms and sanctifies God's promise to continue the truly gracious affections in the regenerate — in a study chiefly of *Humble Inquiry* in the context of the Northampton controversy on admission. Edwards, like the Puritans before him, stressed the "internal realm" of the Spirit, not the external forms, the subjective sense, not the objective. Thus his sacramental theology has little to do with practicality, purity, or church polity.

47 Sarles, Ken L. Review of *Jonathan Edwards,* by John H. Gerstner. *Bibliotheca Sacra* 146 (January): 113-14.

    Regards John H. Gerstner's study (1987.8) an "excellent" introduction to Edwards.

48 Schick, William J. Review of *Jonathan Edwards,* by M. X. Lesser. *Early American Literature* 24 (Spring): 80-82.

    Diagnoses M. X. Lesser's study of Edwards (1988.26) a "failure of nerve" more profound than the reviewer's own (1975.16).

49 Scott, Nathan A., Jr. "The Poetry of Richard Wilbur — 'The Splendor of Mere Being.'" *Christianity and Literature* 39 (Autumn): 7-33.

    Asserts that Edwards, not Ralph Waldo Emerson, is "the great decisive strategist" of the American literary imagination, in a study of the poetry of Richard Wilbur and his delight in the "ontological amplitude" of the world.

50 Solberg, Winton U. Review of *Jonathan Edwards and the American Experience,* edited by Nathan O. Hatch and Harry S. Stout, and *Jonathan Edwards,* by Iain H. Murray. *William and Mary Quarterly,* 3d ser., 46 (January): 183-89.

    Declares that Nathan O. Hatch and Harry S. Stout's collection (1988.17) and Iain H. Murray's biography (1987.22) "complement" each other, the first "an excellent survey" of recent scholarship on Edwards, the other a "popular account" of him.

51 Spohn, William C. Review of *Christian Love and Self-Denial,* by Stephen G. Post. *Journal of Religion* 69 (April): 280-81.

    Welcomes Stephen G. Post's "insightful treatment" of Edwards (1987.26) for current discussions of Christian love.

52 Strong, Gregory Steven. "The Substance and Structure of Jonathan Edwards's Ethics in Light of his Metaphysics." Ph.D. dissertation, Drew University.

Claims that Edwards's Christian Neoplatonic metaphysics informs the two moralities of his ethics, the natural and the supernatural, and that that enables him to relate them in "a more calibrated fashion."

53 Traver, Sharon R. "An Investigation of the Bible's Influence on Colonial American Literature in Selected Content Material from a High-School American Literature Textbook." Ed.D. dissertation, Temple University.

Includes Edwards in a survey of the influence of the Bible on colonial writers in *Adventures in American Literature* (1985), a high school textbook.

54 Turner, John, and Jennifer Goetz. Review of *Jonathan Edwards,* by John H. Gerstner. *Journal of the Evangelical Theological Society* 32 (September): 410-12.

Suggests that John H. Gerstner's study (1987.8) may serve as a guide for a "first reading" of Edwards but that it lacks context, history, and balance.

55 Vetö, Miklós. Review of *America's Theologian,* by Robert W. Jenson. *Church History* 58 (December): 520-22.

Judges Robert W. Jenson's study of Edwards's theology (1988.22) "certainly the best thus far."

56 Wenzke, Anabelle S. *Timothy Dwight (1752-1817).* Studies in American Religion, 38. Lewiston, N.Y.: Edwin Mellen, pp. 113-17 passim.

Notes Edwards's theological relation to Timothy Dwight, who bequeathed a different image of God to his successors than his grandfather did to his.

57 Westblade, Donald. Review of *Jonathan Edwards,* by Iain H. Murray. *Journal of the Evangelical Theological Society* 32 (September): 408-10.

Ranks Iain H. Murray's "very partisan" biography (1987.22) "a worthy successor" to all previous ones.

58 Westra, Helen Petter. "'Above All Others': Jonathan Edwards and the Gospel Ministry." *American Presbyterians* 67 (Fall): 209-19.

Examines Edwards's ten ordination and installation sermons — four published, six in manuscript — as "performative utterances" of his pastoral theology and views of the gospel ministry. The sermons reveal a "finely detailed" picture of the ministry, a public response to shifting colonial attitudes toward it, and a series of images "tellingly" related to it. Edwards saw the design of redemption fulfilled and made visible by the "persistent, self-abnegating, Christ-reflecting love" of the ministry.

59 Wilson, John F. "Editor's Introduction." *A History of the Work of Redemption. The Works of Jonathan Edwards,* 9. New Haven: Yale University Press, pp. 1-109.

Emphasizes the theological rather than the historical nature of History of Redemption, in an introduction to the ninth volume of the Yale Edwards that examines its "unusual" composition (thirty sermons on one biblical verse, Isa. 51:8), its transmission and publication, sources and traditions, literary strategies, logical structure, and projected revision, and its reception, influence, and modern reclamation. Edwards's "Redemption Discourse" was "entirely congruent" with Puritan New England's preoccupation with the application of redemption and visible sainthood and was "already central" to his own work, especially in the "Miscellanies." But he turned its triadic sermon form "inside out" and "detached" its typological framework from

Scripture to find figural patterns in "'history'" and nature. Edwards's use of a "branching" or subordination in a logical structure is an index of his theological premises and renders the work "profoundly unhistoriographical in any modern sense."

60 ———. "Religion at the Core of American Culture." In *Altered Landscapes: Christianity in America, 1935-85.* Edited by David W. Lotz et al. Grand Rapids, Mich.: William B. Eerdmanns, pp. 373-74.

Considers Edwards's millennialism "a critical reorientation of the Christian legacy," at one with a New World culture of change over form, movement over order. For "the American Augustine," the outpourings of the Holy Spirit from Christ would rule the age before the Last Judgment.

61 ———. Review of *The Philosophical Theology of Jonathan Edwards,* by Sang H. Lee. *Theology Today* 46 (April): 101-102.

Considers Sang H. Lee's "important" book (1988.25) a "rich and imaginative" interpretation of Edwards's reconstruction of metaphysical categories.

62 Wolterstorff, Nicholas. "Liturgy, Justice, and Holiness." *Reformed Journal* 39 (December): 12-20.

Discovers a "very straightforward link" in Edwards between holiness and justice, in a study of both and liturgy. Edwards captures some of what holiness is but not the whole of it, because for him it is "all beauty — no terror."

63 Wright, Mark H. "The Role of Identification in Rhetorical Explanation." Ph.D. dissertation, Northwestern University.

Uses Edwards's *Sinners in the Hands of an Angry God* as a successful example of "association," a type of Kenneth Burke's theory of identification.

1990

1 Aldrich, Elizabeth Kaspar. "Representing and Re-Forming the Saint: The Strange Case of Jonathan Edwards." In *On Strangeness.* Edited by Margaret Bridges. Swiss Papers in English Language and Literature, 5. Tübingen: Narr, pp. 163-82.

Follows the shifts of the historical Edwards from "saint" to "demon," from "joke" to "tragic hero," in a reading of Perry Miller (1949.9; rpt. 1981.27) in the context of "strategies of estrangement." A "medieval throwback," Edwards became a "pioneering modern" in Miller's hands, a case of extreme reversal in American letters unlike any other and an instance of rhetoric which "encodes as error, and deconstructs, its own temporality."

2 Beam, Perry. "'Sarah Pierrepont' and the Gentle Side of Jonathan Edwards." *Pleiades* 10 (Winter): 38-42.

Perceives Edwards to "capsulize" his ideas of God, man, and religious affection in "Sarah Pierrepont," a piece "quite frankly" about himself.

3 Bell, Richard H. "Trusting One's Own Heart: Scepticism in Jonathan Edwards and Sören Kierkegaard." *History of European Ideas* 12 (1): 105-16.

Pursues Edwards's "very sophisticated" challenge to trust one's heart, in a comparison of his solution to trusting the experience of God and Sören Kierkegaard's. Edwards directs the regenerate to join practice to experience — outlined in the twelfth sign of *Religious Affections* — in "a kind of analogue" to Christ's self-understanding expressed in his practical actions. Thus his skepticism plays a "positive" role for understanding the grammar of religious experience.

4 Boyle, Philip John. "Paul Ramsey's Motif 'Christ Transforming the Natural Law' in Light of its Theological and Philosophical Influences." Ph.D. dissertation, St. Louis University.

Ascribes to the influence of Edwards the themes of eschatology and divine sovereignty found in Paul Ramsey's motif of transformation.

5 Brackney, William H. Review of *Jonathan Edwards and the American Experience*, edited by Nathan O. Hatch and Harry S. Stout. *Baptist Quarterly* 33 (April): 295.

Recommends Nathan O. Hatch and Harry S. Stout's collection (1988.17) to specialists, not "uninitiated" readers of Edwards.

6 Barnsley, Richard E. "The Common Ground of Wesley and Edwards." *Harvard Theological Review* 83 (July): 271-303.

Argues that Edwards and John Wesley "theologize empiricism," in a study of Wesley's abridgement of *Religious Affections* and the common ground this "charismatic diumvirate" share in their rational and sensationalist reliance on experience. Both appropriate John Locke's insights and, in their philosophical and religious epistemology, exemplify the Anglo-American imagination.

7 Butler, Diana. "God's Visible Glory: The Beauty of Nature in the Thought of John Calvin and Jonathan Edwards." *Westminster Theological Journal* 52 (Spring): 13-26.

Takes "seriously" Edwards's Calvinism in order to reveal his "full" interpretation of nature, in a comparative study of the theological purposes of nature for Edwards and John Calvin and the question of a natural theology in both. For Edwards (and Calvin), nature was not truth, for natural revelation condemns the fallen. But with "corrected sight," the redeemed can use nature to "teach Christian truth, see God visibly manifested, acknowledge and praise the Creator, and read the world as a book of types."

8 Carmody, Denise Lardner, and John Tully Carmody. "Jonathan Edwards and Human Nature." *The Republic of Many Mansions: Foundations of American Religious Thought.* New York: Paragon House, pp. 19-51.

Uses Edwards as an exemplar of Puritanism and its "sensitive and profound exploration" of human nature, one of three figures — Thomas Jefferson (the Enlightenment and religious liberty) and William James (pragmatism and the concept of truth) are the others — in a study of the foundations of American religious thought. In his life and work, Edwards figures as a cultural and historical watershed: after him, to understand Puritanism or American views of human nature or destiny, one has to "come to grips" with him.

9 Chamberlain, Mary Ava. "Jonathan Edwards against the Antinomians and Arminians." Ph.D. dissertation, Columbia University.

Considers Edwards's work more a contribution to the religious discourse in eighteenth-century Puritan New England than commentary on the European Enlightenment, in a study of the relation of nature and grace in his polemics against antinomianism in *Religious Affections* and Arminianism in *True Virtue.*

10 Cherry, Conrad. Review of *Jonathan Edwards and the American Experience,* edited by Nathan O. Hatch and Harry S. Stout. *Church History* 59 (June): 250-51.

Claims that Nathan O. Hatch and Harry S. Stout's collection (1988.17) "does not live up to the stated purpose" of its editors.

11 ————. *The Theology of Jonathan Edwards: A Reappraisal.* Bloomington: Indiana University Press, xxvi, 270 pp.

Reprints 1966.9 and adds two prefatory essays.

Stein, Stephen J. "Forward," pp. ix-xviii. Considers Conrad Cherry's study "the most instructive account available" of Edwards's Calvinism, one that "takes seriously" his theological tradition, biblicism, and Christology and is a "more sensitive" reading than Perry Miller's (1949.9; rpt. 1981.27).

Cherry, Conrad. "New Introduction," pp. xxiii-xxvi. Suggests that, if written today, his study would give "more attention to Edwards's sense of beauty and artistry, to his (humorless) personality, to the diverse influences on his thought, and to his effects on different phases of American evangelism."

12 Clairbois, M. Review of *La pensée de Jonathan Edwards,* by Miklós Vetö. *Revue Theologique de Louvain* 1 (June): 233-34.

Remarks the completeness and clarity of Miklós Vetö's exposition of Edwards (1987.34). (In French.)

13 Coleman, Robert E. "Jonathan Edwards: A Man Swallowed Up in God." *Christian Education Journal* 11 (Autumn): 87-93.

Offers a portrait of "this humble sage" to an "age of arrogant humanism," in an account of Edwards's life-long quest for holiness.

14 DeProspo, R. C. Review of Jonathan Edwards, *Ethical Writings,* edited by Paul Ramsey, and Jonathan Edwards, *A History of the Work of Redemption,* edited by John F. Wilson. *Modern Philology* 88 (November): 204-209.

Doubts whether there is an ethics in Edwards or a history, in a review of the latest volumes in the Yale Edwards — one edited by Paul Ramsey (1989.44), the other by John F. Wilson (1989.59) — and whether the project continues "not in behalf but in spite of Edwards."

15 Dunn, Elizabeth Elaine. "'The Power of a Wise Imagination': Case Studies in Value Conflict in Early Eighteenth-Century America." Ph.D. dissertation, University of Illinois at Urbana-Champaign.

Compares the values of Edwards and Benjamin Franklin in the debate over the relationship between science and religion, one of four case studies in value conflict in early eighteenth-century America.

16 Edwards, John H. "Edwards, Jonathan (1703-1758)." In *Dictionary of Christianity in America.* Edited by Daniel G. Reid et al. Downers Grove, Ill.: InterVarsity Press, pp. 380-81.

Ranks Edwards among the "greatest American theologians," in a brief estimate of his work.

17 Erwin, John Stuart. Review of *The Philosophical Theology of Jonathan Edwards*, by Sang H. Lee. *American Historical Review* 95 (April): 576.

> Places Sang H. Lee's study (1988.25) at the "pinnacle" of scholarship on Edwards.

18 Galli, Mark. "In Praise of Foolish Lovers: Why Would Martin Luther and Jonathan Edwards Make Fools of Themselves over the Return of Christ?" *Christianity Today* 34 (19 November): 35-36.

> Describes Martin Luther and Edwards as "young, impatient lovers," in a comparison of their hope for the Second Coming with the author's and his need to "fall in love again."

19 Gilpin, W. Clark. Review of *Jonathan Edwards and the American Experience*, edited by Nathan O. Hatch and Harry S. Stout. *Journal of Religion* 70 (January): 95-96.

> Praises Nathan O. Hatch and Harry S. Stout's "exceptionally well-integrated" collection (1988.17).

20 Grenz, Stanley J. Review of Jonathan Edwards, *Ethical Writings*, edited by Paul Ramsey. *Christian Century* 107 (21 March): 312-13.

> Values Paul Ramsey's introduction to the eighth volume of the Yale edition (1989.44) for unraveling Edwards's often "obtuse" reasoning.

21 Gustafson, James M. Review of Jonathan Edwards, *Ethical Writings*, edited by Paul Ramsey. *Journal of Religion* 70 (July): 479-81.

> Welcomes Paul Ramsey's "careful" editing of the eighth volume of the Yale Edwards (1989.44) but questions its lack of historical perspective and its argument that *Charity and its Fruits* is a "development" of the eschatology of *History of Redemption*.

22 Hall, Richard A. S. *The Neglected Northampton Texts of Jonathan Edwards: Edwards on Society and Politics*. Studies in American Religion, 52. Lewiston, N.Y.: Edwin Mellen, ii, 357 pp.

> Explicates four "neglected texts" from the last three years of Edwards's Northampton pastorate — *Humble Attempt, Life of Brainerd, Humble Inquiry*, and *Farewell Sermon* — to reveal his social and political philosophy, in an argument for its existence, not an exposition of its "full range." Edwards's communal ideal of citizenship is a "radical public-mindedness," his ethics social, in that true virtue is "loyalty to the greatest society of uncreated and created persons." Edwards wanted to implement his ideal by making his congregation into "an exclusive society of the visibly benevolent."

23 Harrison, Paul Vernice. "Ability and Responsibility in American Christianity from Jonathan Edwards through Charles Finney." Th.D. dissertation, Mid-America Baptist Theological Seminary.

> Examines Edwards's thought for his views on natural and moral ability (and evangelical technique), in a study of various American theologians on the "incessant conflict" between Calvinism and Arminianism on how man's innate depravity affects his responsibility to God.

24 Holifield, E. Brooks. Review of *America's Theologian*, by Robert W. Jenson. *Journal of Religion* 70 (January): 94-95.

Tempers praise for Robert W. Jenson's contemporary point of view in *America's Theologian* (1988.22) with his "insufficient attention" to Edwards's.

25 Hoopes, James. Review of *The Philosophical Theology of Jonathan Edwards,* by Sang H. Lee. *Journal of Religion* 70 (April): 258.

Questions Sang H. Lee's elegant study (1988.25) for placing a metaphysics deduced from his theology over his "explicitly" metaphysical writings.

26 Hoyt, William R. Review of *Christian Love and Self-Denial,* by Stephen G. Post. *Church History* 59 (June): 251-52.

Decides that Stephen G. Post's study (1987.26) is an "adequate" interpretation of Edwards but a "questionable" one of Samuel Hopkins.

27 Husband, Paul Edward. "Church Membership in Northampton: Solomon Stoddard versus Jonathan Edwards." Ph.D. dissertation, Westminster Theological Seminary.

Traces the conflict between Solomon Stoddard and Edwards over church membership to Reformed ideas of purity and covenant continuity — Edwards stressed the first, his grandfather, the second — and examines the narrative of grace, the "creative contribution" of New England designed to balance the two.

28 Johnson, W. Stacy. Review of *The Philosophical Theology of Jonathan Edwards,* by Sang H. Lee; *America's Theologian,* by Robert W. Jenson; and Jonathan Edwards, *Ethical Writings,* edited by Paul Ramsey. *Interpretation* 44 (April): 218.

Applauds the studies of Sang H. Lee (1988.25), Robert W. Jenson (1988.22), and Paul Ramsey (1989.44) for their "fresh insights" into Edwards's Christian vision of reality.

29 Jones, David Clyde. Review of Jonathan Edwards, *Ethical Writings,* edited by Paul Ramsey. *Presbyterion* 16 (Spring): 69-70.

Welcomes Paul Ramsey's "extremely illuminating" introduction to the eighth volume of the Yale Edwards (1989.44) and the texts that follow it.

30 Jones, Rowena Revis. "Edwards, Dickinson, and the Sacramentality of Nature." *Studies in Puritan American Spirituality* 1 (December): 225-45.

Links Emily Dickinson to Edwards "primarily" in their shared feeling of awe evoked by nature, in a comparison of her sacramental nature poems and his theory of nature. Though her poems "correspond with significant elements" in his *Personal Narrative, Divine and Supernatural Light, End of Creation,* and other writings, an "enormous distinction" separates the two: Edwards glorifies God, Dickinson, the self.

31 Leonard, Bill J. Review of *Jonathan Edwards and the American Experience,* edited by Nathan O. Hatch and Harry S. Stout. *Review and Expositor* 87 (Spring): 356-57.

Hails Nathan O. Hatch and Harry S. Stout's collection (1988.17) for its analysis of the "diverse" Edwards.

32 Manning, Susan. "After Armageddon: Jonathan Edwards and David Hume." *The Puritan-Provincial Vision: Scottish and American Literature in the Nineteenth Century.* Cambridge: Cambridge University Press, pp. 26-46.

Compares Edwards to David Hume — voices "at opposite ends of the anti-rational spectrum" of eighteenth-century thought — in a study of the evolution of Puritanism into provincialism, the nature of the prose that marks it, and the consequences of it for nineteenth-century Scottish and American literature. Edwards and Hume, both with Calvinist backgrounds, challenge John Locke's correlation of objective reality and the perception of the mind, holding that there may be "no connection whatever," the first because original sin renders mind incapable, the second because mind is "evanescent and a fiction." Edwards's problem with the "inadequacy" of language arises from his need to empty, not project, the self and suggests the "profoundly egotistical" nature of Puritan-provincial literatures.

33 Marsden, George M. *Religion and American Culture.* San Diego: Harcourt Brace Jovanovich, pp. 26-27.
Remarks Edwards's defense of theocentrism against rationalism and enthusiasm, which "anticipated" many of the trends in American Christianity for more than two hundred years.

34 ———. "Calvinist Freedom Fighters." *Reviews in American History* 18 (September): 332-36.
Charges that Allen C. Guelzo's *Edwards on the Will* (1989.16) "slants" the material to fit the central thesis that there is "no essential difference" between Edwards and the New Divinity, in an essay-review.

35 Marsh, Roger Alan. "Diminishing Respect for the Clergy and the First Great Awakening: A Study in the Antecedents of Revival among Massachusetts Congregationalists, 1630-1741." Ph.D. dissertation, Baylor University.
Cites Edwards (and Samuel Danforth and George Whitefield) for resolving the "impasse" between clergy and laity at the end of the seventeenth century by reasserting religious leadership and authority to instill "fresh zeal" toward piety and renewed interest in religion, in a study of one of several factors that led Massachusetts Congregationalists to the Great Awakening.

36 Martin, James Alfred, Jr. *Beauty and Holiness: The Dialogue between Aesthetics and Religion.* Princeton, N.J.: Princeton University Press, pp. 28-32.
Regards Edwards's formulation of beauty and holiness to be within the classical tradition of Plato, Aristotle, Augustine, and Aquinas, in a study of the relationship between aesthetics and religion.

36A McKenna, David. *New Hope for the Nineties: The Coming Great Awakening.* Downer's Grove, Ill.: InterVarsity Press, pp. 30-31.
Notes Edwards's "prophetic voice" in the history of Great Awakenings.

37 Minkema, Kenneth P. "The Authorship of 'The Soul.'" *Yale University Library Gazette* 65 (October): 26-32.
Attributes "The Soul," long considered Edwards's earliest extant work, to his oldest sister Esther, dates it between 1725 and 1729, and reprints a manuscript letter of hers as "conclusive" evidence.

38 Otto, Randall E. "The Solidarity of Mankind in Jonathan Edwards' Doctrine of Original Sin." *Evangelical Quarterly* 62 (July): 205-21.
Contends that Edwards's "innovative" argument of the divine constitution of personal identity in his defense of original sin was a failure, because it was based on "conflicting and unscrip-

tural premises," in an examination of John Taylor's *The Scripture-Doctrine of Original Sin* (1738) and Edwards's attack upon it. Rather than accepting Taylor's rationalistic presumptions, Edwards should have argued the "biblical doctrine of representation" in *Original Sin,* which "alone can satisfy the scriptural evidence, to the ultimate chagrin of reason."

39 Packer, J. I. "Jonathan Edwards and Revival." *A Quest for Godliness: The Puritan Vision of the Christian Life.* Wheaton, Ill.: Crossways Books, pp. 309-27.

Culls from Edwards's work "a fairly complete account" of a theology of revival and offers it to evangelicals who had rejected him as unreadable or philosophical. Though Edwards wrote about revival "piecemeal" — in *Faithful Narrative, History of Redemption, Distinguishing Marks, Some Thoughts,* and *Religious Affections* — it is, perhaps, his "most important contribution" to theology and biblical faith.

40 Pals, Daniel L. "Several Christologies of the Great Awakening." *Anglican Theological Review* 72 (Fall): 412-27.

Distinguishes Edwards's "novel" Christology — "an arresting blend" of traditional dogma, idealist mysticism, and divine aesthetics — from others in the Great Awakening, those of Theodore J. Frelinghausen, Gilbert Tennent, and George Whitefield. Unlike the others, Edwards moved from the "personalized" savior of individuals to the Christ of "cosmic proportions" (in both nature and history), the Christ of "transcendent beauty."

40A Pauw, Amy Plantinga. "Edwards and America." *First Things* 3 (May): 59-60.

Values Robert Jenson's *America's Theologian* (1988.22) for its "insights into Edwards's thought in itself and its alternate vision" for the church, its "elliptical" style and "agile leaps" notwithstanding.

41 ———. "'The Supreme Harmony of All': Jonathan Edwards and the Trinity." Ph.D. dissertation, Yale University.

Published as 2002.36.

42 Peacock, Virginia A. *Problems in the Interpretation of Jonathan Edwards' The Nature of True Virtue.* Studies in American Religion, 47. Lewiston, N.Y.: Edwin Mellen, ix, 176 pp.

Locates Edwards's ideas of virtue within the "inextricably related" aspects of his theological, rather than philosophical, thought, in a study of his doctrine of grace in *True Virtue, End of Creation,* and *Essay on the Trinity,* and the influence of Andrew Michael Ramsay's *Philosophical Principles of Natural and Revealed Religion,* as disclosed in the "Miscellanies." Edwards underwent a "notable shift" in his interpretation of special and common grace in his Stockbridge years. That late doctrine of grace is essential to a proper understanding and "correct" reading of *True Virtue.*

43 Piper, John. *The Supremacy of God in Preaching.* Grand Rapids, Mich.: Baker Book House, 119 pp.

Exhorts ministers to emulate Edwards in making God supreme in preaching and to follow his pulpit practice: to stir the affections, to enlighten the mind, to "saturate" with Scripture, to use analogies and images, to threaten and warn, to plead for response, to provoke the heart, to yield to the Holy Spirit, and to be brokenhearted, tenderhearted, and intense. If pastors are granted the "sweet sovereignty" of God as Edwards had been, then pulpit renewal is not only possible but inevitable.

44 Pointer, Richard W. Review of *Edwards on the Will,* by Allen C. Guelzo. *American Historical Review* 95 (October): 1285.

Declares Allen C. Guelzo's "judiciously reasoned" study (1989.16) a "solid contribution" to understanding Edwards and his legacy.

45 Pope, Robert. Review of *America's Theologian,* by Robert W. Jenson. *American Historical Review* 95 (February): 243-44.

Cautions that Robert W. Jenson's "quite successful recovery" of Edwards's theology (1988.22) becomes in time a jeremiad on contemporary America.

45A Rees, Ian. "Jonathan Edwards and the Work of the Holy Spirit." *Congregational Studies Conference Papers.* Oswestry, Shropshire: Quinta, pp. 39-48.

Analyzes two pieces of Edwards on the Holy Spirit: the first, the work of the Spirit in individuals, *Divine and Supernatural Light,* remarking what the spiritual light is and is not; the other, in groups of people, *Distinguishing Marks,* defining both negative and positive signs. If there is one thing Edwards has to teach, it is that the Spirit of God works "from time to time in glorious power" — and we should yearn for it.

46 Selement, George. Review of *Jonathan Edwards, The Valley and Nature,* by Clyde A. Holbrook. *American Historical Review* 95 (October): 1284-85.

Espies "another ripple on the sea of literature that Miller inspired" in Clyde A. Holbrook's "cogently argued" study of Edwards (1987.10).

47 Smith, Robert Doyle. "John Wesley and Jonathan Edwards on Religious Experience: A Comparative Analysis." *Wesleyan Theological Journal* 25 (Spring): 130-46.

Compares the personal religious experiences of Edwards and John Wesley and the theological formulations of them (found chiefly in their sermons), in an analysis of the "more striking" differences between the two on preparation and conversion. Both share "very similar" understandings of the religious experience, especially in acknowledging human sinfulness, but the Calvinist Edwards advocates predestination, free grace to the elect, and "growth in grace" as holiness, whereas Wesley supports foreknowledge (not foreordination), free grace to all, and "perfection in love" as holiness. Edwards adjusted his theology to accommodate holy living, qualifying the significance of the conversion experience; Wesley "re-founded" his theology in a conversion experience, qualifying the significance of growth in grace.

48 Steele, Richard Bruce. "'Gracious Affection' and 'True Virtue' in the Experimental Theologies of Jonathan Edwards and John Wesley." Ph.D. dissertation, Marquette University.

Published as 1994.43 (revised).

49 Stein, Stephen J. Review of *Jonathan Edwards,* by M. X. Lesser. *Church History* 59 (September): 408-409.

Concludes there may be "no more accessible book-length introduction available" on Edwards than M. X. Lesser's (1988.26).

50 ———. Review of *Jonathan Edwards,* Iain H. Murray. *Church History* 59 (December): 564-65.

> Rates Iain H. Murray's study of Edwards (1987.22) "a disappointing apologia for a distinguished thinker who needs no such defense."

51 ———. Review of *The Philosophical Theology of Jonathan Edwards,* by Sang H. Lee. *Church History* 59 (March): 100-102.

> Commends Sang H. Lee's "genuinely new" analysis of Edwards (1988.25) to scholars: "wrestling with it will pay dividends."

52 Stephens, Bruce M. "Changing Conceptions of the Holy Spirit in American Protestant Theology from Jonathan Edwards to Charles G. Finney." *Saint Luke's Journal of Theology* 33 (June): 209-23.

> Estimates that Edwards's pneumatology plays an important, though not dominant, role in his thought, in a study of the changing conception of the Holy Spirit in the work of his evangelical successors. For Edwards, the Holy Spirit was the "bridge" between the intellect and the affections — within the consciousness of both God and man — and could be traced in the inner life of the self and the outer life of the community.

53 Tillman, William M., Jr. Review of *Christian Love and Self-Denial,* by Stephen G. Post. *Southwestern Journal of Theology* 33 (Fall): 65-66.

> Deems Stephen G. Post's "intriguing" study (1987.26) helpful for understanding the current infrastructures of theological ethics.

54 Turner, Eldon. Review of *America's Theologian,* by Robert W. Jenson. *American Studies* 31 (Fall): 146.

> Views Robert W. Jenson's "overwrought" study (1988.22) as an "essentially homiletic assessment" of Edwards's influence.

55 Wainwright, William J. "Jonathan Edwards and the Sense of the Heart." *Faith and Philosophy* 7 (January): 43-62.

> Explores the implications of Edwards's theory of the sense of the heart for the "epistemic status" of religious belief, in a study of the philosophical and theological aspects of the regenerate's new sense of the spiritual beauty of divine things from *Personal Narrative* through the "Miscellanies" to *True Virtue.* Edwards holds spiritual beauty to be a kind of sensation or perception and defends the objectivity of the new spiritual sense. His account of how one theistic belief-producing mechanism operates may be "the right sort" to help resolve conflicts of the reliability of another.

56 Weddle, David L. Review of *America's Theologian,* by Robert W. Jenson. *Journal of the American Academy of Religion* 58 (Summer): 290-93.

> Singles out Robert W. Jenson's study (1988.22) as the one "Edwards himself would have most enjoyed reading."

57 Westblade, Donald. Review of *America's Theologian,* by Robert W. Jenson. *Journal of the Evangelical Theological Society* 33 (September): 403-405.

> Prescribes Robert W. Jenson's study (1988.22) as a "uniquely suited antidote" for American Protestant ills but questions making "a Lutheran out of Edwards."

58 Westra, Helen. "Cornerstones, Cannons, and Covenants." *Pro Rege* 19 (September): 24-31.

Examples Edwards as a guardian of colonial New England culture and teacher of civility, decorum, harmony, responsibility, and continuity, in a study of thirty unpublished "'domestic'" sermons on children and parents preached during the 1730s and 1740s. Like Puritan pastors before him, Edwards lays "cornerstones" for the family, builds communal and clerical authority and respect, and warns against subversive behavior. Like them as well, he becomes a thundering "cannon" of God and a "covenanting parent and friend."

59 Wilson, John F. Review of *Edwards on the Will,* by Allen C. Guelzo. *Church History* 59 (December): 565-66.

Judges Allen C. Guelzo's study of Edwards (1989.16) "a masterful, critical reanalysis" of the New Divinity.

60 Yaeger, D. M., ed. *The Annual of the Society of Christian Ethics,* 1990. Washington, D.C.: Georgetown University Press, pp. 249-88.

Closes with a section on teaching ethics "in an American vernacular."

Ottati, Douglas F. "Practical Believing and Personal Identity," pp. 251-56. Cites Edwards on personal and Christian identity and practice, in observations on the "affective core" of the American ethical tradition.

Crocco, Stephen. "Teaching the American Tradition in a Theological Seminary," pp. 273-76. Remarks "the pride of place" occupied by Edwards and the Puritanism he inherited and transformed, in an account of teaching the American moral tradition in a theological seminary.

1991

1 Andersen, David C. "The Lives and Ministries of Cotton Mather and Jonathan Edwards." D.Min. dissertation, Trinity Evangelical Divinity School.

Develops a model for twentieth-century pastors based on the lives and ministries of Cotton Mather and Edwards.

2 Brand, David C. *Profile of the Last Puritan: Jonathan Edwards, Self-Love, and the Dawn of the Beatific.* American Academy of Religion Series, 73. Atlanta, Ga.: Scholars Press, xi, 165 pp.

Reflects upon "the author's [and America's] spiritual roots," in a study of the beatific and the benevolent in Edwards — the "last Puritan" — and explores the Calvinist and covenantal sources of his theology, the philosophical landscape of his time, the development of Arminianism in New England, and his writings on ethics and aesthetics, benevolence and self-love, happiness and holiness. The empiricism of John Locke was not Edwards's message so much as his "idiom of expression." For him, philosophy was subordinate to theology, ethics to ontology, morality to regeneration, happiness to holiness, and self-love to benevolence, the mutual love of the triune God. For him, the beatific, with its biblical focus on divine sovereignty, was "basic."

2A Butler, Diana. "God's Visible Glory: The Beauty of Nature in the Thought of John Calvin and Jonathan Edwards." *Evangelical Review of Theology* 15 (April): 111-26.

Reprints 1990.7.

3 Childs, Robert. "Jonathan Edwards and the 'Balance' of True Religion." D.Min. dissertation, Gordon-Conwell Theological Seminary.

Bases a "model for renewal" within contemporary churches on a critical evaluation of Edwards's *Religious Affections* and his approach to pastoral problems and includes a devotional guide and a small-group Bible study series.

4 Conforti, Joseph. "The Invention of the Great Awakening, 1795-1842." *Early American Literature* 26 (Fall): 99-118.

Attributes to Edwards's New Divinity disciples the "invention" of the Great Awakening, the transformation of its place in American historical consciousness, the elevation of a "deradicalized" Edwards to a position of major cultural authority, and the "canonization" of his *Religious Affections, Life of Brainerd,* and *Personal Narrative.* The reification of the Awakening was a product of New England's cultural imperialism in which a regional event became the colonial experience, personal recollection became social memory, and Edwards became central to the American revivalist tradition — all part of a "cultural response to democratic change" during the second Great Awakening.

5 Crawford, Michael J. "New England and the Scottish Religious Revivals of 1742." *American Presbyterians* 69 (Spring): 23-32.

Cites Edwards's narrative of the Connecticut Valley revivals in particular as an influence on the Scottish revivals of 1742, in a study of transatlantic cultural exchanges. Edwards created a "new religious genre" with *Faithful Narrative* and the Scots imported it with the revivals, James Robe modelling his Kilsyth and Cambulsang account after Edwards's. It is a "mistake" to read the Great Awakening as a regional event.

6 ———. *Seasons of Grace: Colonial New England's Revival Tradition and Its British Context.* New York: Oxford University Press, pp. 124-32.

Suggests that Edwards "carried forward" the revival tradition of his Restoration predecessors, who transformed "a strain of the Puritan legacy into Reformed evangelicalism," in a study of the evolution of the idea of revivalism in its British context. Revivals subsequent to the Great Awakening confirm both Edwards's version of the dynamics of local and regional revivals in *Faithful Narrative* and his vision of the "pivotal" role of revivals in God's plan in *History of Redemption.*

7 Delattre, Roland A. "The Theological Ethics of Jonathan Edwards: An Homage to Paul Ramsey." *Journal of Religious Ethics* 19 (Fall): 71-102.

Identifies "participation in the life of God overflowing into the world" as the "essential and distinctive" element in Edwards's ethical writings, in an examination of his theological ethics and Paul Ramsey's important contribution to understanding it, especially in his reading of *Charity and its Fruits* in the eighth volume of the Yale Edwards (1989.44). Edwards's radically theological and theocentric ethics, a "complex unity" of love, happiness, and consent to being, is part of his vision of the whole drama of creation and redemption and is found at every stage of his work from *God Glorified* on. Ramsey's explication leads to "a livelier and a deeper appreciation" of Edwards's ethics and its theme of infused virtue.

8 Dewey, Joseph. *In a Dark Time: The Apocalyptic Temper in the American Novel of the Nuclear Age.* Lafayette, Ind.: Purdue University Press, pp. 21-23.

Likens the "soaring compassion" of Edwards's writings on the Apocalypse in an age of apostasy to the apocalyptic temper of American novelists in the dark time of a nuclear age, Kurt Vonnegut, Robert Coover, Thomas Pynchon, and Don DeLillo among them.

9 Egan, James Francis. "Ideology and the Study of American Culture: Early New England Writing and the Idea of Experience." Ph.D. dissertation, University of California, Santa Barbara.

Discovers parallels to the "privatization and fragmentation" of eighteenth-century geography and politics in Edwards's "poetic" conception of experience, in a study of the ideas of experience of three early New England thinkers — Anne Hutchinson and Anne Bradstreet are the others — and their alternatives to the dominant ideologies and (apparently) homogeneous culture of the time.

10 Gerstner, John H. *The Rational Biblical Theology of Jonathan Edwards*, 1. Powhatan, Va.: Berea Publications, 682 pp.

Presents Edwards's thought "systematically" — as Edwards himself had hoped to do in "A Rational Account of the Main Doctrines of the Christian Religion Attempted" — in "the first full-scale theology of Edwards ever published" and includes an account of his life; his synthesis of reason and revelation (and its subsequent breakdown); his epistemology, metaphysics, and apologetics; his biblicism and hermeneutics, with examples from his "indispensable" sermons and unpublished commentary; his preaching and the influence of his ministry; and a hundred-page outline of his theology, in the first of three volumes (see 1992.4 and 1993.7). Edwards's intellectual and moral life centered on the inspired and inerrant Word, the "sine qua non of his rational biblical theology." For Edwards, his preaching the Word was his theology and "his theology was his preaching."

10A ———. *Jonathan Edwards on the Afterlife.* Grand Rapids, Mich.: Baker Book House. Reprints 1980.14 with a changed title.

11 Goen, C. C. Review of Jonathan Edwards, *A History of the Work of Redemption,* edited by John F. Wilson. *Journal of Religion* 71 (January): 99-101.

Praises John F. Wilson's edition of Edwards's *History of Redemption* (1989.59) for its "awesome skill" and "ingenious" scheme of annotation.

12 Gunton, Colin E. "Immanence and Otherness: Divine Sovereignty and Human Freedom in the Theology of Robert W. Jenson." *Dialog* 30 (Winter): 17-26.

Remarks the relevance of Edwards to the theology of Robert W. Jenson.

13 Hayden, Roger. "Evangelical Calvinism among Eighteenth-Century British Baptists with Particular Reference to Bernard Foskett, Hugh and Caleb Evans and the Bristol Baptist Academy, 1690-1791." Ph.D. dissertation, University of Keele.

Notes that Edwards's theology "overturned hyper-Calvinism among Particular Baptists," in a study of British Baptists from 1690 to 1791.

14 Heron, Alasdair. Review of *America's Theologian,* by Robert W. Jenson. *Scottish Journal of Theology* 44 (May): 127-29.

Recommends Robert W. Jenson's "pioneering" study (1988.22) for its constructive fusion of history and dogmatics, of Edwards and Friedrich Schleiermacher and Karl Barth.

15 Hodder, Alan D. "'After a High Negative Way': Emerson's 'Self-Reliance' and the Rhetoric of Conversion." *Harvard Theological Review* 84 (October): 423-46.

Revisits Perry Miller's "From Edwards to Emerson" (1940.9) on the sesquicentennial of the publication of Emerson's "Self-Reliance" and finds affinities between "America's most famous essay" and *God Glorified,* Edwards's first publication, in a study of the rhetoric of negation, exclusion, and compensation in both. Edwards shifts from cataphasis in the earlier parts of his sermon to apophasis in the applications, from affirmative discourse to negative, from theological description to prescriptive piety, from absolute sovereignty to self-abasement. Emerson's essay "arises from the same rhetorical sources and follows essentially the same religious insight."

16 Holleman, Warren Lee. "Jonathan Edwards' Vision — as Viewed through Feminist Hindsight." *Journal of Religious Studies* 17 (1): 1-18.

Argues that Edwards "subverted" the Puritan patriarchal models of family and God, in a study of his "more egalitarian" approach to gender and the need to reinterpret the history of religion through the "lens of feminist hindsight." Edwards presents women as "positive" figures — Abigail Hutchinson and Phebe Bartlet in *Faithful Narrative,* his wife Sarah in *Some Thoughts,* and Eve in *History of Redemption* and *Original Sin* — and offers his God "replete" with feminine imagery. By locating God in beauty rather than in power and by reworking Calvinism in aesthetic terms, Edwards "feminized" God, religion, and moral values.

17 Hughes, Walter Coleman. "Models of American Charity." Ph.D. dissertation, Harvard University.

Attributes to Edwards the revival of Robert Cushman and John Winthrop's seventeenth-century model of social affection, in a study of the connection between religious charity and egalitarian democracy in America.

18 Ingram, Robert F., ed. "Jonathan Edwards." *Table Talk* 15 (June): 2-14.

Limns facets of Edwards's life and thought.

Ingram, Robert F. "Corum Deo," p. 2. Remarks the importance of holy affections in Edwards's life and work.

Sproul, R. C. "The Preacher," pp. 4-5. Locates the power of Edwards's preaching in his "acute" images and rational harmony, the "stark nudity" of his ideas and the "fruit of love" in his applications.

Gerstner, John H. "The Thinker," pp. 6-8. Considers Edwards "rational and metaphysical and biblical — all at the same time," in an account of his thought.

Logan, Samuel T., Jr. "The Life," pp. 9-11. Recounts Edwards's short but divinely purposeful life.

Bogue, Carl W. "The Man," pp. 12-13. Stresses the value of what Edwards reveals about himself and his conversion in *Personal Narrative.*

Kistler, Don. "The Pastor," p. 14. Reflects upon Edwards's courage in preaching "'the whole counsel of God.'"

19 Jinkins, Michael. Review of *America's Theologian,* by Robert W. Jenson. *Scottish Journal of Theology* 43 (January): 423-25.

Decides that Robert W. Jenson's study of Edwards (1988.22) "falls short" as historical, but "frequently succeeds" as constructive, theology.

20 Keating, Annlouise. "The Implications of Edwards' Theory of the Will on Ahab's Pursuit of Moby Dick." *English Language Notes* 28 (March): 28-35.

Uses Edwards's *Freedom of the Will* to gloss Ahab's pursuit of Moby Dick, the captain's doom "both freely willed and determined" in Herman Melville's novel.

21 Knight, Janice. "Learning the Language of God: Jonathan Edwards and the Typology of Nature." *William and Mary Quarterly*, 3d ser., 48 (October): 531-51.

Suggests that Edwards's "own certainty" of the harmony and proportion of God's world led him to posit a like harmony between the works of creation and redemption, nature and spirit, in a study of Edwards's typology within the context of the first principles of his "integrated" theology. Edwards "always" joined ontological to historical types in his writing — scriptural commentaries, *Images or Shadows*, *History of Redemption* — and "blurred" the traditional categories, a "paradoxical union" that mirrors (and inheres in) a dynamic, effulgent God. For Edwards, typology is "best understood as a form of divine speech," a voice "still sounding" in nature, history, and contemporary events.

22 Leonard, Bill J. Review of Jonathan Edwards, *A History of the Work of Redemption*, edited by John F. Wilson. *Review and Expositor* 88 (Fall): 474-75.

Praises John F. Wilson's "excellent" introduction to the ninth volume of the "outstanding" Yale Edwards (1989.59).

23 Lesser, M. X. "Edwards, Jonathan." In *The Reader's Companion to American History*. Edited by Eric Foner and John A. Garraty. Boston: Houghton Mifflin, pp. 327-28.

Recounts briefly the life and work of Edwards and the profound effect both had on the course of religious life in America.

24 Lewis, Paul Allen. "Rethinking Emotions and the Moral Life in Light of Thomas Aquinas and Jonathan Edwards." Ph.D. dissertation, Duke University.

Compares the alternative, yet "formally" similar, perspectives of Edwards and Thomas Aquinas, in a study of the relationship between emotions and the moral life in contemporary thought.

25 McCoy, Genevieve Elizabeth. "Sanctifying the Self and Saving the Savage: The Failure of the ABCFM Oregon Mission and the Conflicted Language of Calvinism." Ph.D. dissertation, University of Washington.

Attributes to the "conflicting" doctrines of Edwards and the New Divinity "profound and lifelong doubts" among Oregon missionaries about their redeemed condition, in a study of the failure of the 1846 Whitman Mission.

26 McDermott, Gerald. "Jonathan Edwards, the City upon the Hill, and the Redeemer Nation: A Reappraisal." *American Presbyterians* 69 (Spring): 33-47.

Challenges the optimistic nationalism often attributed to Edwards, in a study of fifty-four "predominantly pessimistic" occasional sermons touching upon the national covenant. Edwards seemed "obsessed" by the possibility of Northampton's destruction, speculated that God might "revoke" New England's covenant, and was "cynical" about patriotism. Though he was "bullish" on the future of God's work of redemption — if not in "'this land'" then elsewhere — over the years Edwards became convinced of a "dark future" for New England: "the most blessed, it was the most guilty."

27 McGoldrick, James E. Review of *The Supremacy of God in Preaching,* by John Piper. *Grace Theological Journal* 12 (Spring): 145-45.

    Puts "extraordinary value" on John Piper's book (1990.43) and the "'gravity and gladness'" of Edwards's preaching.

28 McKenny, Gerald P. "Theological Objectivism as Empirical Theology: H. Richard Niebuhr and the Liberal Tradition." *American Journal of Theology and Philosophy* 12 (January): 19-33.

    Shows that H. Richard Niebuhr drew upon Edwards, "the great ancestor" of American empirical theology, to criticize his liberal descendants of the 1930s, in a study of Niebuhr's indebtedness, especially to *Religious Affections.*

29 Mohler, R. Albert, Jr. Review of *The Supremacy of God in Preaching,* by John Piper. *Preaching* 6 (March): 45-46.

    Praises the "monumental content" of John Piper's small volume (1990.43) and the influence of Edwards — "America's foremost theological trophy" — on it.

30 Morimoto, Anri. "The Reality of Salvation in the Soteriology of Jonathan Edwards." Ph.D. dissertation, Princeton Theological Seminary.

    Published as 1995.35 (revised).

31 Morris, Kenneth R. "The Puritan Roots of American Universalism." *Scottish Journal of Theology* 44 (4): 457-87.

    Remarks Edwards's "difficult position" between his belief in the legitimacy of revivalism and the limited atonement of strict Calvinism, in a study of the widespread movement in late eighteenth-century America toward universal salvation. Edwards was able to "salvage" limited atonement by redefining Solomon Stoddard's open invitation as the "best method" of gathering in and sorting out the elect. But Edwards's successors in the New Divinity saw the "inconsistency" of his position and abandoned limited for general atonement.

32 Morris, William Sparkes. *The Young Jonathan Edwards: A Reconstruction.* Chicago Studies in the History of American Religion, 14. Brooklyn: Carlson Publishing, xvi, 688 pp.

    Publishes 1955.6 with an introduction.

    Bauer, Jerald C. "Editor's Preface," pp. xiii-xvi. Recommends William Sparkes Morris's thirty-six-year-old study both for its "sophisticated and finely nuanced" analysis of the thought and mind of the young Edwards and its "direct" contribution to current discussions on the nature and meaning of the Enlightenment and Edwards relationship to it.

    Morris, William Sparkes. *The Young Jonathan Edwards: A Reconstruction.* Demonstrates "as conclusively as possible" that the major part of Edwards's metaphysics derives from the Dutch scholastic Calvinists and logicians Franciscus Burgersdicius and Adrian Heereboord, in an extensive reconstruction of how Edwards came to think what he did, from his years at home and at college in Connecticut to his months at the Scots Presbyterian church in New York, and how he integrated theology and philosophy.

33 Munton, Douglas Wayne. "The Contributions of J. Edwin Orr to an Understanding of Spiritual Awakenings." Ph.D. dissertation, Southwestern Baptist Theological Seminary.

Compares the views of Edwards and Charles Grandison Finney on spiritual awakening with that of J. Edwin Orr.

34 Murray, Margaret P. "Object Relations as a Determinant in the Conversion Process." *Journal of Evolutionary Psychology* 12 (March): 174-86.

Applies Heinz Kohut's object relations to Phebe Bartlet (in *Faithful Narrative*) and David Brainerd (in the *Life*) and finds Edwards "uncannily and instinctually aware of the narcissistic line of personality development," in a psychological study of the conversion experience. Though many young men of Northampton initially met their narcissistic needs during the surprising conversions of 1735, in time they "severed their bonds" with Edwards, "their leader and self-object," because they were searching for self, he for converts.

34A Noll, Mark. Review of *Edwards on the Will*, by Allen C. Guelzo. *Journal of Religion* 71 (April): 264-65.

Reports that Allen C. Guelzo (1989.16) transforms "esoteric theological material into a compelling book."

35 Pang, Patrick. "A Study of Jonathan Edwards as a Pastor-Preacher." D.Min. dissertation, Fuller Theological Seminary.

Considers Edwards as a pastor-preacher in the context of the Great Awakening, in a study of his concept of preaching as "an agency of conversion," an examination of his plain style, and an analysis of three pastoral sermons.

36 Perkins, George, et al. "Edwards, Jonathan (1703-1758)." In *Benet's Reader's Encyclopedia of American Literature*. Edited by George Perkins et al. New York: HarperCollins, pp. 297-98.

Outlines the work of Edwards, "one of the most extraordinary men produced on the American continent."

36A Piper, John. *The Pleasures of God: Meditations on God's Delight in Being God*. Portland, Ore.: Multnomah, 328 pp.

Cites Edwards chiefly in notes, in a book about God's delight in being God.

37 Simpson, Jeffrey E. "Thoreau: The Walking Muse." *ESQ* 37 (1): 1-33.

Notes that Edwards in *Personal Narrative* and Henry David Thoreau in "Walking" treat walking as "a sacred adventure," religious enlightenment ending in epiphany.

38 Smith, Craig R., and Michael J. Hyde. "Rethinking 'The Public': The Role of Emotion in Being-with-Others." *Quarterly Journal of Speech* 77 (November): 446-66.

Examines *Sinners in the Hands of an Angry God* in light of neo-Aristotelian rhetorical criticism (or how Edwards moved his audience), in a study of *pathé* in the formation of "publics." Edwards intensified the "shared emotions" at the moment of delivery and brought about "communal catharsis." Thus in the midst of "being-with-others, a 'new' mode of publicness was 'born again.'"

39 Squires, William Harder. *The Edwardean: A Quarterly Devoted to the History of Thought in America*. Studies in American Religion, 56. Lewiston, N.Y.: Edwin Mellen, xv, 256 pp.

Reprints 1903.44 and 1904.15 and adds an introduction.

Hall, Richard. "Introduction," pp. vii-xv. Urges the rehabilitation of William Harder Squire's scholarship on Edwards inasmuch as *The Edwardean* was a "fundamental reconstruction of the philosophical enterprise of its day."

40 Stout, Harry S. *The Divine Dramatist: George Whitefield and the Rise of Modern Evangelicalism.* Grand Rapids, Mich.: William B. Eerdmans, pp. 125-27 passim.

Asserts that Edwards and George Whitefield had "little in common" other than their "shared importance" to the Great Awakening, in a study of the amalgam of preaching and acting and its effect on American religious history.

41 Unrue, Darlene Harbour. Review of *Edwards on the Will,* by Allen C. Guelzo. *Religion and Literature* 23 (Spring): 87-90.

Commends Allen C. Guelzo's "superb scholarly" study of Edwards and his successors (1989.16), in a review of three books on American Puritans.

42 Valeri, Mark. "The Economic Thought of Jonathan Edwards." *Church History* 60 (March): 37-54.

Recasts the image of an aloof and "impractical" Edwards into a preacher of a "tightly structured" order that denied the possibilities of a virtuous market economy, in a study of the development of his economic thought based on a series of unpublished sermons. Edwards abandoned Puritan economic ideals early in his pastorate and attempted to reform the economic practice of Northampton's visible saints during the revivals of the 1730s and 1740s and to define external controls to remedy New England's economic ills after them. "His failure to convince his people to forego the market for the meetinghouse was not for lack of trying."

43 Wells, C. Richard. Review of *The Supremacy of God in Preaching,* by John Piper. *Criswell Theological Review* 5 (Spring): 342-43.

Notes the "superiority" of Edwards's approach to preaching over today's practice, in a review of John Piper's study (1990.43).

44 Westra, Helen Petter. "Jonathan Edwards and 'What Reason Teaches.'" *Journal of the Evangelical Theological Society* 34 (December): 495-503.

Uncovers another instance of Edwards's effort to restrain rationalist and Arminian views in a "vigorous apologia" for divine revelation as the sole rule of faith, in a study of an unpublished sermon — a thirty-five-page manuscript on 1 Cor. 2:11-13 — on the ordination of Edward Billing in Cold Spring, Massachusetts, 7 May 1740. Edwards "repeatedly asserts" that human reason is incapable of understanding fully the mind of God and uses "sanctified reasoning" to plumb the mysteries of divine revelation. Ministers must preach, not their words, Edwards warns, but only those "'which God bids.'"

1992

1 Chironna, Paul David. "Jonathan Edwards' Ethic of Consent and the Moral Sense Theory." Ph.D. dissertation, University of Chicago.

Regards Edwards's theory of consent "a typical adumbration" of the moral sense theorists of the seventeenth and eighteenth centuries — the Earl of Shaftesbury, Francis Hutcheson, and David Hume — and, as an account of the moral life, "essentially true," in a study his ethical writings, *True Virtue,* chief among them. Though Edwards was "uncompromisingly" spiritual, he did not undervalue natural virtue, and so his Reformed ethics "embody and preserve" both the sacred sense of the religious community and the experience of the world beyond it. That there are "decisive differences" between Edwards and his moral sense contemporaries — his biblicism and theocentrism, for example — should not rule out the "family resemblances."

2 Crocco, Stephen. "Paul Ramsey and *The Works of Jonathan Edwards.*" In *The Annual of the Society of Christian Ethics,* 1992. Edited by Harlan Beckley. Washington, D.C.: Georgetown University Press, 157-73.

Details Paul Ramsey's involvement with the Yale Edwards — he edited the first volume, *Freedom of the Will* (1957.14), and the eighth, *Ethical Writings* (1989.44), a generation later — and the influence Edwards had on his ethics, in an examination of the correspondence primarily between Ramsey and Perry Miller, the first general editor of the series, and John E. Smith, the second. Putting aside his very considerable work on ethics and taking up *Charity and its Fruits, End of Creation,* and *True Virtue,* Ramsey used Edwards to "sketch" the theocentric, Christological, and ecumenical contours of Reformed ethics, to make him "a conversation partner" in discussions of contemporary ethics, and to shape the content of his own.

3 Doriani, Beth Maclay. "Emily Dickinson, Homiletics, and Prophetic Power." *Emily Dickinson Journal* 1 (2): 54-75.

Traces the structure and style of Emily Dickinson's poetry to the rhetorical strategies and forms of sermons in the Edwardsean homiletic tradition, a tradition that enabled her to speak as a prophet-preacher despite the "patriarchal temper" of her time. Edwards provided her with "an important link" to culturally authoritative voices and thus empowered her own.

4 Gerstner, John H. *The Rational Biblical Theology of Jonathan Edwards,* 2. Powhatan, Va.: Berea Publications, 527 pp.

Continues an examination of Edwards's writings both published and in manuscript — here, on the doctrine and decrees of God, the covenants, creation, angels, man, providence, the Fall, imputation, sin, the Incarnation, and atonement — in the second of three volumes on his rational biblical theology (see 1991.10 and 1993.7).

4A Hall, Richard A. Spurgeon. "Bach and Edwards on the Religious Affections." In *Johann Sebastian: A Tercentenary Celebration.* Edited by Seymour L. Benstock. Westport, Conn.: Greenwood Press, pp. 69-81.

Links Johann Sebastian Bach to Edwards as "complementary" figures in that both made room for religion and religious music "in an age that had grown impatient with both." Each stressed the "centrality of personal experience and feeling in religion" — Bach in pietism, Edwards in evangelicalism — to forge "religious affections" to music.

5 Hardy, Daniel W. Review of *Edwards on the Will,* by Allen C. Guelzo. *Journal of Theological Studies* 43 (October): 756-58.

Rates Allen C. Guelzo's study of Edwards (1989.16) "not successful" in estimating the significance of the nineteenth-century debate on American theological thought.

6 Hoggard Creegan, Nicola Anne. "The Grammar of Freedom: Edwards and Schleiermacher." Ph.D. dissertation, Drew University.

Approaches the problem of freedom of the will "indirectly" through the linguistics of Ludwig Wittgenstein and finds that both Edwards and Friedrich Schleiermacher understood freedom to be "conditioned and limited," not radical or transcendental. Edwards's ontology and eschatology envisioned a harmonious Christian community as "conversing, social, language centered."

7 Kimbrell, Cary Glynn. "An Investigation into the Changing Concepts of an Evangelist in Christian Thought and Practice." Ph.D. dissertation, New Orleans Baptist Theological Seminary.

Includes Edwards in an etymological, exegetical, and historical study of the changing concepts of an evangelist from biblical to modern times.

8 Kimnach, Wilson H. "General Introduction to the Sermons: Jonathan Edwards' Art of Prophesying" and "Preface to the New York Period." *Sermons and Discourses, 1720-1723. The Works of Jonathan Edwards,* 10. New Haven: Yale University Press, pp. 1-293.

Explores the corpus of Edwards's sermons, his literary milieu — he was steeped in the practices of his father and grandfather, Puritan preaching manuals, and the Cambridge Platonists, especially John Smith — his apparatus for making sermons, his literary theory, and the canon of printed and manuscript sermons, in the first of two introductions to the nearly 1200 extant sermons and, at 258 pages, the longest in the Yale series. Edwards borrows from his "formidable" and diverse notebooks to compose palm-sized sermon manuscripts for pulpit delivery and, with "conscious artistry," deploys biblical tropes, "poignant (usually visual) imagery," symbolism and typology, "chaste rhetoric," repetition and parallelism, shifts in the narrative point of view, and "tonic" words that can reverberate throughout a text. During his "greatest" period, that is, between his ordination and the end of the Great Awakening, Edwards's art "decisively transcended New England Puritanism." The second introduction, "Preface to the New York Period," recounts Edwards's eight-month's stay as supply preacher to a separatist Presbyterian congregation in New York and recaptures the voice of an ambitious young man setting out. Edwards's contemporary "Diary" and "Resolutions," his retrospective *Personal Narrative,* and his meditative "Sarah Pierrepont" offer clues to his struggle for personal holiness and professional identity and suggests the context for the twenty-three sermons composed chiefly between the summer of 1722 and the spring of the following year. Several of the them bear witness to his search after hope and resolution; others rehearse the metaphors, if not the intensity, of his later imprecations; still others prefigure later (published) comforts; all brim with a "rustic vitality" and concrete imagery, each linked to each by his "definition of the Christian life in experiential terms."

9 Kimura, Katsuzo. "A Study of Jonathan Edwards' *Personal Narrative.*" *Ryukokudaigaku ronshu* no. 441 (December): 2-14.

Summarizes Edwards's *Personal Narrative* and its critical reception. (In Japanese.)

10 Lowance, Mason I., Jr. "Jonathan Edwards and the Platonists: Edwardsean Epistemology and the Influence of Malebranche and Norris." *Studies in Puritan American Spirituality* 2 (January): 129-52.

Marks the shift in Edwards's perspective from an "extremely conservative," historical, biblical typology to a "more naturalistic," contemporary reading of signs and events, in a study of his debt to the Platonic epistemology of Nicolas Malebranche in *Search After Truth* and John Norris in *An Essay Towards a Theory of the Ideal and Intelligible World.* In his fusion of nature and Scripture, Edwards used reasoning and language "extremely close" to that of Malebranche; in his assessment of the real and ideal worlds, he used the "specific" language of Norris; in his description of the imagination, he used the language of both. Still, his was "an original synthesis of Scriptural and natural revelation."

11 ———. "Sacvan Bercovitch and Jonathan Edwards." *Studies in Puritan American Spirituality* 3 (December): 53-68.

Considers Edwards "possibly the most prominent spiritual Godfather" to Sacvan Bercovitch, the revisionist literary historian of the "'myth of America.'" Like Edwards in *History of Redemption,* Bercovitch "dissolves the distinction" between premillennialism and postmillennialism in *The American Jeremiad* (1978.3), adapting Edwards's methodology — a progressive, evolutionary, and prophetic historiography — to the reading of the "sacred texts" of American literature. Both dwell in a world of "prophetic symbology."

12 McClymond, Michael James. "Creation in Jonathan Edwards." Ph.D. dissertation, University of Chicago.

Examines Edwards's "consistent" theocentrism and the "subtle" interplay between the ontological and voluntaristic aspects of it, in a study principally of *End of Creation.* A force behind Edwards's "whole" philosophical enterprise, his theocentrism derives from the Reformed tradition and manifests itself in his "free exchange" of ideas with the philosophy of the Enlightenment. Edwards's theocentrism forms the core of his "unity-amid-diversity" metaphysics and provides the context for his doctrine of creation, one of the "most brilliant, most neglected, and most problematic" theological writings of the century.

13 McDermott, Gerald R. *One Holy and Happy Society: The Public Theology of Jonathan Edwards.* University Park: Pennsylvania State University, xii, 203 pp.

Derives Edwards's public theology — "his understanding of civil community and the Christian responsibility to it" — chiefly from his unpublished occasional sermons given on fast, thanksgiving, and election days, and argues, contrary to other studies, that Edwards's political preaching was in the tradition of the New England jeremiad, not an anthem to manifest destiny; that his millennial doctrine was "global," not tribal or provincial; and that his theories of citizenship and magistracy were "progressive" and sophisticated, not protective of a social and economic elite. Limited by his "capacity for self-deception," Edwards still achieved "a grand synthesis" of social concern and private experience, imparting dignity to the marginalized of society, women and blacks, the poor and the young. Edwards's "most important contribution was his painstaking unfolding of the relation of private to public religion."

14 ———. Review of *Edwards on the Will,* by Allen C. Guelzo. *American Presbyterians* 70 (Fall): 199-200.

Lauds Allen C. Guelzo's study of Edwards (1989.16), "the most concise yet incisive analysis of the New Divinity yet to appear."

15 Minkema, Kenneth P. "Hannah and her Sisters: Sisterhood, Courtship, and Marriage in the Edwards Family in the Early Eighteenth Century." *New England Historical and Genealogical Register* 146 (January): 35-56.

Revises the nineteenth-century notion that Edwards's ten sisters served as "little more than ministering angels" to him, in an account of their character, learning, and courtships drawn from their letters and journals. "If anything, Jonathan resembled his sisters for their acuity, argumentativeness, and capacity for single-minded resolve."

16 Morey, Ann-Janine. *Religion and Sexuality in American Fiction.* Cambridge Studies in American Literature and Culture. New York: Cambridge University Press, pp. 24-25, 56.

Remarks Edwards's "clear understanding of the sexual possibility of religious passion," in a brief reading of *Some Thoughts.*

17 Munk, Linda. "His Dazzling Absence: The Shekinah in Jonathan Edwards." *Early American Literature* 27 (1): 1-30.

Explicates Edwards's use of the Hebrew Shekinah in *History of Redemption* — its etymology and interpretation in Aramaic and Greek commentaries, the Targums and the Septuagint — and the metonymy for divine glory in *End of Creation.* In *History of Redemption,* Edwards conflates the post-biblical Shekinah, or divine presence, with the biblical cloud of glory that filled the Tabernacle and second Temple and identifies it as a type of Christ. In *End of Creation,* a "commentary on Creation in terms of the Incarnation," the overflowing of divine glory is not of God but of his Shekinah, "'His dazzling absence.'"

17A ———. *The Trivial Sublime: Theology and American Poetics.* New York: St. Martin's Press, pp. 136-62.

Reprints 1992.17.

18 Noll, Mark A. *A History of Christianity in the United States and Canada.* Grand Rapids: William B. Eerdmans, pp. 95-97 passim.

Regards Edwards "a theological genius" and the "most important apologist" of the Great Awakening, in a history of Christianity in North America.

19 Pahl, Jon. "'The Modern Prevailing Notions.'" *Paradox Lost: Free Will and Political Liberty in American Culture, 1630-1760.* New Studies in American Intellectual and Cultural History. Baltimore: Johns Hopkins University Press, pp. 147-61 passim.

Contends that Edwards's *Freedom of the Will* is the "first systematic treatise" in American public theology and the "most sustained apology ever constructed for the aristocracy of grace," in a study of the paradox of providence-guided freedom, "our most noble and dangerous cultural artifact." The conservative Edwards tried to demolish colonial Arminianism and preserve the anti-extremist status quo but ended up, ironically, lending legitimacy to Arminian claims and the democracy of law.

20 Pang, Patrick. "The Pastoral Preaching of Jonathan Edwards." *Preaching* 7 (January): 59-60.

Judges Edwards "at heart" a pastoral preacher and *Sinners in the Hands of Angry God* both atypical and "a pastoral document," in a note about his sermon practice.

21 Porterfield, Amanda. *Female Piety in Puritan New England: The Emergence of Religious Humanism.* Religion in America Series. New York: Oxford University Press, pp. 155-56.

Notes that Edwards argued the genderless emotional realism of traditional Puritanism rather than the emotional vulnerability (and religious humanism) associated with the imagery of female piety in New England.

22 Robinson, David. "The Road Not Taken: From Edwards, through Chauncy, to Emerson." *Arizona Quarterly* 48 (Spring): 45-61.

Links the liberal theology of Charles Chauncy — Edwards's "nemesis" — to the transcendental thought of Ralph Waldo Emerson, in a reexamination of Perry Miller's "From Edwards to Emerson" (1940.9), "one of the great acts of synthesis in American literary history."

23 Scheick, William J. "Breaking Verbal Icons." *Design in Puritan American Literature.* Lexington: University Press of Kentucky, pp. 89-119.

Locates the source of Edwards's notion of the "instability of language at the logogic site" in two kinds of knowledge, rational and affective — the postlapsarian *scientia* sanctioned by common grace and the prelapsarian *sapientia* initiated by special grace — that often ends in an "eschatological erasure" of words, in a study of images in four early sermons: *doors, gates,* and *knocking* in "Pressing into the Kingdom of God"; *family* and *journey* in "The Christian Pilgrim"; *ascent* and *descent* in "The Excellency of Christ"; and, fittingly, *mouth* in "The Justice of God in the Damnation of Sinners." Edwards breaks words as verbal icons to reveal the "concealed emptiness" at the core of all material manifestations, including language, and so renders God "unimagable, unrepresentable, and unaccountable" to all but the elect.

23A Sherry, Patrick. *Spirit and Beauty: An Introduction to Theological Aesthetics.* Oxford: Clarendon Press, pp. 13-17, 105-107 passim.

Notes that Edwards "keys" his discussion of aesthetics into a "fully developed" trinitarian theology and "explores" the Augustinian idea that the Holy Spirit is the harmony of the Trinity. In his *Essay on the Trinity,* Edwards argues that the Holy Spirit beautifies all things, sanctifies intelligent beings, and comforts and delights "the souls of God's people"; in the "Miscellanies," no. 108, he sees the Son as the image of God's glory, "manifesting His beauty." Edwards's view of the Trinity may be profitably compared to that of Hans Urs von Balthasar, "perhaps the greatest modern writer" on theological aesthetics.

24 Smith, Christopher Ralph. "Postmillennialism and the Work of Renewal in the Theology of Jonathan Edwards." Ph.D. dissertation, Boston College.

Asserts that Edwards held a "consistently postmillennnial" theology of history throughout his career — an "imminent" revival would bring about the downfall of the Antichrist and allow some of the church to "anticipate" the millennium — in a study of *History of Redemption, Distinguishing Marks, Some Thoughts, Humble Attempt,* and "Notes on the Apocalypse."

25 Smith, John E. *Jonathan Edwards: Puritan, Preacher, Philosopher.* Outstanding Christian Thinkers Series. London: Geoffrey Chapman, x, 150 pp.

Judges Edwards "unquestionably the major theologian" of American Puritanism and "the most acute philosophical thinker" in America before Charles Peirce, in a study of Edwards's life and times; his debt to the sensationalist psychology of John Locke and his dissent from it; his role in the Great Awakening and his defense of experiential religion in *Religious Affections;* his "sustained effort" to deal with both the problem of human freedom and the polemics of Arminianism in *Freedom of the Will;* his contribution to the theological controversy over innate depravity and the Enlightenment debate on the nature of man in *Original Sin;* his conception of Christian love and the holy life in *Charity and its Fruits, End of Creation,* and *True Virtue;* his "remarkable interpretation" of biblical and secular sources in *History of Redemption;* and his literary talents as preacher. "If one were to ask, given the total body of what Edwards wrote, what one idea stands out as more important than any other, the answer would have to be the utter sovereignty of God."

26 Stein, Stephen J. Review of *Edwards on the Will,* by Allen C. Guelzo. *Journal of the American Academy of Religion* 60 (Fall): 548-50.

> Praises Allen C. Guelzo's "wit and clarity" in his critical and "accessible" study Edwards's celebrated text (1989.16).

27 Stone, Jeff Jay. "The Political Philosophy of Jonathan Edwards." Ph.D. dissertation, University of Dallas.

> Uncovers Edwards's political philosophy chiefly in *A Strong Rod* (1748), the funeral sermon for his uncle Col. John Stoddard, and other sermons on moral government. Edwards finds "more problems than solutions" there and so turns to history for answers and to its end for proof of the justice of God.

28 Tanis, James R., Jr. "A Child of the Great Awakening." *American Presbyterians* 70 (Summer): 127-33.

> Notes that Gilbert Tennent's manuscript account of the spiritual awakening of a seven-year-old girl has "much in common" with Edwards's account of four-year-old Phebe Bartlet in *Faithful Narrative.*

28A Ward, W. Reginald. *The Protestant Evangelical Awakening.* New York: Cambridge University Press, pp. 275-86.

> Remarks that Edwards's kingdom of God was "more sharply perceived in Eastern Europe than in his own congregation," in a survey of revivalism in the American colonies. Edwards's targeting young people for revival, "caricatured" by one of his "favourite converts," Phebe Bartlet, proved "a broken reed": all the young men in the bad-book episode were church members, and a "large number" of young congregants voted for his dismissal several years later.

29 Yarbrough, Stephen R. "The Beginning of Time: Jonathan Edwards's *Original Sin.*" In *Early American Literature and Culture: Essays Honoring Harrison T. Meserole.* Edited by Kathryn Zabelle Derounian-Stodola. Newark: University of Delaware Press, pp. 149-64.

> Perceives in Edwards "two distinct notions" of time and identity, either of the prelapsarian "moment" or of the fallen in time, in a close reading of *Original Sin,* especially Part IV, "Containing Answers to Objections." Before the Fall there is neither time nor self; but when one falls, that is, when one chooses, "one *begins time* — for oneself." Therefore, "time is of the human mind, not the divine." Only through divine grace can one return to God and the aboriginal state — the ecstatic moment of conversion — "literally out of time."

30 Young, Arthur P., et al. *Religion and the American Experience, 1620-1900: A Bibliography of Doctoral Dissertations.* Bibliographies and Indexes in American Religion. Westport, Conn.: Greenwood Press, 496 pp.

> Lists 145 doctoral dissertations devoted in whole or in part to Edwards.

1993

1 Anderson, Wallace E., and Mason I. Lowance, Jr., with David H. Watters. "Editor's Introduction to 'Images of Divine Things' and 'Types'" and "Editor's Introduction to 'Types of the Messiah.'" *Typological Writings. The Works of Jonathan Edwards,* 11. New Haven: Yale University Press, pp. 1-48, 155-86.

Examines "Images of Divine Things," "Types," and "Types of the Messiah," their provenance and composition, their historical context, and their place in Edwards's thought, in two introductions to his typological writings. In the first, the late Wallace E. Anderson traces the history of biblical typology; locates Edwards's method amid the contending claims of rationalists and deists, Catholics and Anglicans, Cabalists and Dissenters; and records his efforts to meet such challenges and objections. "Images of Divine Things," a forty-eight-page folio of 212 entries begun in 1728, brings correspondences between the Old and New Testament into harmony with nature and history, broadening traditional typology so that "the spiritual truths represented by the array of natural things comprehended the temporal unfolding of the divine plan of salvation"; "Types," a previously unpublished twenty-page octavo booklet, outlines some general principles of typology with chiefly New Testament proofs. In the second introduction, Mason I. Lowance, Jr., situates "Types of the Messiah" (or "Miscellanies," no. 1069) in the Edwards canon, especially his sermons, particularly the thirty that would become *History of Redemption.* Composed in the "dark period" between the "bad book" episode in 1744 and Edwards's dismissal in 1749, the forty folio leaves and seventy-two entries form not so much a prophetical scheme as an exegetical theory (with examples) in which the type "was at once a representation and an essence, precisely because it transcended time and space." Together Edwards's typological writings demonstrate "a *via media*" between conservative scriptural readings and the meaning of biblical figures "recapitulated" in nature and history and made available to the elect by "the new sense of things."

2A Arkin, Marc M. "The Great Awakener." *The New Criterion* 11 (May): 59-62.

Faults John E. Smith's *Jonathan Edwards: Puritan, Preacher, Philosopher* (1992.25) for its lack of unity and "reading Edwards out of his own context."

2 Boersma, Hans. Review of *Profile of the Last Puritan,* by David C. Brand. *Westminster Theological Journal* 55 (Spring): 173-76.

Considers David C. Brand's analysis (1991.2) "a significant contribution" to the study of Edwards but vague on why he is "the last Puritan."

3 Barnsley, Richard E. *Coordinates of Anglo-American Romanticism: Wesley, Edwards, Carlyle, and Emerson.* Gainesville: University Press of Florida, pp. 1-42.

Links Edwards and John Wesley to Thomas Carlyle and Ralph Waldo Emerson, empiricism to evangelicalism, and British literature to American, in a "fully unified" study of literature, philosophy, and theology. Wesley's abridgement of Edwards's *Religious Affections* is "a bridge" between them and to John Locke's *Essay Concerning Human Understanding.* Thus their combined sensibilities are an "emblem of a binational character" and provide access to Anglo-American romanticism and the "complex entity" of nineteenth-century letters.

3A Briasco, Luca. "Jonathan Edwards." In *La litteratura americana dell'eta coloniale.* Edited by Paola Cabibbo. Rome: La Nuova Italia Scientifica, pp. 281-303.

Provides an overview of Edwards's work and influence, with a brief life and bibliography, in a study of colonial American literature. (In Italian.)

3B Bryant, M. Darrol. *Jonathan Edwards' Grammar of Time, Self, and Society: A Critique of the Heimert Thesis.* Studies in American Religion, 60. Lewiston, N.Y.: Edwin Mellen Press.

Publishes 1976.11 with an updated bibliography and footnotes.

3C Cernich, Christopher Michael. "'Salvage Lande': The Puritan Wilderness and the Preservation of the World." Ph.D. dissertation, University of Michigan.

Considers the wilderness a "conscious creation" of New England Puritans to render it "salvific," in a survey of writers from Bradford to Edwards to Thoreau.

4 Conforti, Joseph. "Mary Lyon, the Founding of Mount Holyoke College, and the Cultural Revival of Jonathan Edwards." *Religion and American Culture* 3 (Winter): 69-89.

Recognizes in Mary Lyon, founder of Mount Holyoke College, "a devoted disciple and enthusiastic supporter" of Edwards, a "case study" in his cultural revival following the second Great Awakening. By invoking the disinterested benevolence of *True Virtue* and the selflessness in *Life of Brainerd,* Lyon "socialized" her students into Edwards's traditional moral economy (opposed to an emergent free market) and "instilled" in them his evangelical piety (as prospective wives of foreign missionaries).

4A Daniel, Steven. "Paramodern Strategies of Philosophical Historiography." *Epoché: A Journal of the History of Philosophy* 1 (1): 41-63.

Regards Edwards and Berkeley not as idealists but as "simply a part of a sign system or universal text," in a study of the kinds of approaches scholars sensitive to postmodern themes might now use.

5 Daugaard, Curtis Lee. "God, Glory, and the Good: A Study in the Theological Aesthetics of Jonathan Edwards." Ph.D. dissertation, Boston University.

Argues that Edwards's theory of divine glory unites his views of aesthetics, excellence, and disposition, gives dialectical priority to value over formal structure, and comprises his major contribution, in a study of his philosophical theology and its Platonic parallels.

6 Delattre, Roland A. Review of *La Pensée de Jonathan Edwards,* by Miklós Vetö. *Church History* 62 (June): 279-80.

Recommends Miklós Vetö's "remarkably masterful" study (1987.34) as "a fine companion" to French students of Edwards.

6A Feero, Richard Lee. "Radical Theology in Preparation: From Altizer to Edwards." Ph.D. dissertation, Syracuse University.

Uses the idea of conversion as a "response to a prior act of divine grace" to explore the relationship between the Christian atheism of Thomas J. J. Altizer and the Christian theism of Edwards.

7 Gerstner, John H. *The Rational Biblical Theology of Jonathan Edwards,* 3. Powhatan, Va.: Berea Publications, 753 pp.

Concludes a three-volume study of Edwards's rational theology with chapters on evangelism, preparation for salvation, regeneration, justification, sanctification, virtue, perseverance and assurance, the church, the sacraments, eschatology, hell, and heaven; quotes extensively from his manuscript sermons; includes a bibliography of his reading and another of writings about him (1979-1991), both compiled by David F. Coffin, Jr.; and appends a tribute to him, "surely one of the greatest saints who ever wrote a sermon, now certainly in heaven." (See 1991.10 and 1992.4.)

7A Greenfield, Jane. "Notable Bindings VIII." *Yale University Library Gazette* 68 (October): 70-73.

Describes an Edwards manuscript on efficacious grace now at Yale, a small semicircular notebook of seventeen leaves assembled probably from cutoffs of fan papers painted by Sarah and perhaps her daughters.

7B Greenspan, P. S. "Guilt as an Identificatory Mechanism." *Pacific Philosophy Quarterly* 74 (March): 46-59.

Derives from Edwards's account of natural conscience in *True Virtue* a scheme for understanding guilt in terms of anger and empathy, in a study tying guilt to the self that explains its special force and pitfalls. In Edwards's "general sort of identificatory mechanism," the agent identifies with the person he harms and then combines that empathy with the agent's own sense of his contrary motives, a "*moderate* emotional reaction." Though Edwards may seem an "unpromising choice" to convince contemporary moral philosophers, it is clear that his treatment of guilt is "philosophical rather than religious."

7C Hambrick-Stowe, Charles E. Review of *The Rational Biblical Theology of Jonathan Edwards*, 1, by John H. Gerstner. *Fides et Historia* 25 (Summer): 132-34.

Commends John H. Gerstner for gathering "large amounts" of material, but his book (1991.10), obviously a "labor of love," is "manifestly not an Edwardsian systematic theology."

8 Jinkins, Michael. *A Comparative Study in the Theology of Atonement in Jonathan Edwards and John McLeod Campbell: Atonement and the Character of God.* Lewiston, N.Y.: Edwin Mellen, xii, 451 pp.

Determines that in Edwards's theology of the atonement the forensic has "priority" over the filial, as John McLeod Campbell's conception does not, in a comparative study of the soteriology of the two. Edwards's doctrine of God stresses the distinctiveness of the persons of the Trinity, derived from federal Calvinism in the context of Arminian and deistic challenges. But Edwards's limited atonement, "grounded" in the limited scope of God's love, leads him into "double predestination" and the problem of ascribing the "'actual' appropriation" of redemptive benefits to the Spirit, not to Christ.

9 ⸻. "The 'Beings of Being': Jonathan Edwards' Understanding of God as Reflected in his Final Treatises." *Scottish Journal of Theology* 46 (2): 161-90.

Traces Edwards's "theological pilgrimage" to his mature understanding of God, "the Being of beings," in a study of his late treatises — *Freedom of the Will, Original Sin, True Virtue, End of Creation,* and, especially, "Treatise on Grace" (first published in 1865) — and the foundational, anthropological, epistemological, and analogical framework of his thought. Edwards "moves well beyond" federal Calvinism in his understanding of God and the coinherence of the Trinity, although the dichotomy between God's essential love (for humanity) and his arbitrary will (in election) "tends to undermine" it. Still, his development is "substantial," his elaborate and subtle discussion of the inner life of God a "crowning" achievement.

9A Kvanvig, Jonathan L. *The Problem of Hell.* New York: Oxford University Press, pp. 33-35.

Attributes to Edwards the "most complete defense" of the claim that all sin is against God, that sinful behavior results from attachment to "private systems," not to benevolence to being in general. Because Edwards counts some "perfectly good" actions as sins against God, his argument is "flawed" and we must "look elsewhere" for a stronger defense.

10 Lesser, M. X. Review of *Delightful Conviction,* by Stephen R. Yarbrough and John C. Adams. *William and Mary Quarterly,* 3d ser., 50 (October): 825-27.

Questions the findings of Stephen R. Yarbrough and John C. Adams's study of Edwards's rhetoric (1993.19), especially in *True Grace.*

10A McGowan, A. T. B. Review of *Profile of the Last Puritan,* by David C. Brand. *Scottish Bulletin of Evangelical Theology* 11 (Summer): 52-53.

Appreciates David C. Brand's "challenging and stimulating" study (1991.2) of Edwards in an eighteenth-century philosophical context, but finds its style "convoluted and unnecessarily complex."

11 McMullen, Michael M. D. Review of *The Rational Biblical Theology of Jonathan Edwards,* 1, by John H. Gerstner. *Evangelical Quarterly* 65 (January): 58-59.

Places the first volume of John H. Gerstner's trilogy on Edwards (1991.10) "head and shoulders above most of what has gone before."

12 Noll, Mark. "God at the Center: Jonathan Edwards on True Virtue." *Christian Century* 110 (8 September): 854-58.

Considers the "major impediment" to judging Edwards's last book a religious "'classic'" is its thoroughgoing theocentrism, in a reading of Paul Ramsey's edition of *Two Dissertations* (1989.44). Both *End of Creation* and *True Virtue* affirm a "breathtaking" God-centered vision of nature and human nature, a theological vision appropriated lately by contemporary evangelicals and "a tonic" for reasonable confidence in the ways of God and man.

12A ———. "Jonathan Edwards & the Public Square." *First Things,* 34 (June): 50-53.

Commends Gerald McDermott for his "substantial contribution" in rescuing from "historical oblivion" Edwards's theological observations on public duty, in a review of *One Holy and Happy Society* (1992.13).

13 Oberg, Barbara B., and Harry S. Stout, eds. *Benjamin Franklin, Jonathan Edwards, and the Representation of American Culture.* New York: Oxford University Press, viii, 230 pp.

Publishes twelve papers delivered at the National Conference on Jonathan Edwards and Benjamin Franklin held at Yale University, February 22-24, 1990, all but one, Michael Zuckerman's "The Selling of the Self: From Franklin to Barnum," pp. 152-67, comparing the two; groups them under three heads (mind, culture, and language); and adds an introduction.

Oberg, Barbara B., and Harry S. Stout. "Introduction," pp. 3-9. Explains Edwards and Benjamin Franklin, not as the mutually exclusive ideals of earlier studies, but as "contrapuntal" figures in a comparative framework for the nineties, their "similarities *and* differences existing in creative tension," in a summary of the essays that follow.

Breitenbach, William. "Religious Affections and Religious Affectations: Antinomianism and Hypocrisy in the Writings of Edwards and Franklin," pp. 13-26. Finds Edwards's *Religious Affections* and Benjamin Franklin's *Autobiography* "remarkably similar works," for both are about conversion in a world of hypocrites — legal and evangelical ones in the first, Governor William Keith and James Ralph in the second — "where religious affections could be known only through religious affectation." Both Edwards and Franklin "tried to anchor salvation in the real world" through holy practice or good works, seeking after evidence of sanctification, warning against the lures of anti-nomianism. In a time of unfixed identities, both constructed versions of themselves and were, though in different ways, "very private public men."

Aldridge, A. Owen. "Enlightenment and Awakening in Edwards and Franklin," pp. 27-41. Locates the antithetical, though not incompatible, perspectives of the Great Awakening and the Enlightenment in the work of Benjamin Franklin and Edwards, especially *History of Redemption*, by defining their contrary responses to Poor Richard's injunction, "'Think of three Things, whence you came, where you are going, and to whom you must account.'" Thus the problem of accountability was "a rather complex matter" for Edwards involving both God and his own notions of moral conduct, but "not in the least complex" for Franklin inasmuch as he was accountable only to himself. Still, both Edwards and Franklin denied freedom of the will, acknowledged divine intervention in the nature, and shared a belief in the workings of the heart in social welfare, an illustration of the "overlapping" of the Awakening and the Enlightenment, of good works and acts of charity.

Gaustad, Edwin S. "The Nature of True — and Useful — Virtue: From Edwards to Franklin," pp. 42-57. Observes Edwards and Benjamin Franklin inhabiting "the same moral universe" but moving in "separate orbits" — one shaped by theology, faith, and presuppositions; the other by anthropology, works, and consequences — in a study of the "overlap" of their mutual concerns about virtue. Edwards in *Two Dissertations* and *Charity and its Fruits* and Franklin in (a projected) *The Art of Virtue* and the *Autobiography* agreed that virtue was more than outward conformity to rules of behavior, endorsed practice as the "ultimate test" of a redeemed or altered nature, and "respected" ordinary morality as useful, though Edwards took it as part of the divine structure and Franklin as his "major concern." And so both used some of the same names for virtue — sincerity, justice, humility — that for Edwards was "unmistakably true" and for Franklin "preeminently useful." By the time of the Revolution, such distinctions collapsed.

Dunn, Elizabeth E. "'A Wall Between Them Up to Heaven': Jonathan Edwards and Benjamin Franklin," pp. 58-74. Uncovers in the essentialism of Edwards and the functionalism of Benjamin Franklin the values each brings to the unsettling, modernizing issues of the first half of the eighteenth century in matters of science and religion, rationalism and reality, means and ends. Both used lightning as symbol and subject, for example, but Edwards saw it as the awful wrath of God, Franklin as originating in earth, not heaven; both perceived the dangers of ratiocination, but Franklin questioned its legitimacy in answering religious problems, Edwards in gaining faith. For Edwards, science and reason were means to "an inherently valuable end," the glorification of God; for Franklin "means had become ends in themselves."

Howe, Daniel Walker. "Franklin, Edwards, and the Problem of Human Nature," pp. 75-97. Charts the different solutions Edwards and Benjamin Franklin offered to the "central problem of eighteenth-century moral philosophy," the problem of human nature posed by the discrepancy between the descriptive and normative aspects of the faculties of the mind, between psychological fact and ethical imperative. Rather than "bemoaning" the failure of reason to govern emotion in human nature, each found substitutes for it, Edwards in disinterested benevolence through grace, Franklin in virtuous habits through practice. In the nineteenth century, evangelicals wrought an "impressive synthesis" of the two — mediated by the example of George Whitefield and the work of Samuel Hopkins — and created an "American tradition" of Christianity, one that joins Franklin's concern for temporal human welfare to Edwards's for church discipline and social morality.

Kuklick, Bruce. "The Two Cultures in Eighteenth-Century America," pp. 101-13. Views "suspiciously" the project of comparing Edwards and Benjamin Franklin — by all counts, a nineteenth-century effort to make representative men of eighteenth-century marginal figures — and offers a version of self as the basis for the "critical difference" between the two cultural types, Puritan and Yankee. Franklin believed in human freedom and personal autonomy, the ability of the self "to transcend circumstance"; Edwards argued, in *Freedom of the Will* (and elsewhere), that the self was not an entity hidden behind appearances but "a construct" made up of a series of "momentary engagements with the world." Franklin's notion of a self-determining power was "anathema" to Edwards, his notion of self "a nearly exact description" of Edwards's sinner. And so it remains questionable just how "serviceable" such distinctions are, given the propensity of the twentieth century to confuse ideas of self in Edwards and Franklin, Calvinism and the Enlightenment.

Sweet, Leonard I. "The Laughter of One: Sweetness and Light in Franklin and Edwards," pp. 114-33. Rejects the traditional image of Edwards as the "sour-spirited, ill-tempered, socially-inept" pastor for one of sensitivity and "high" humor — as opposed to Benjamin Franklin's folksy, bawdy, "low" humor — in an analysis of the comic mode in both. Edwards's humor was "the laughter of one," a comic aesthetic that brought "a faith-filled life to oneself" as well as nods and smiles from irony and satire, understatement and exaggeration, paradox and parody, word play and absurdity. His internal "'sense' of 'sweetness' and 'light'" enabled Edwards to write tellingly of himself to the Princeton trustees, amusingly of his last days at Northampton to his Scots correspondents, wittily of his opponents in *Farewell Sermon* and *Freedom of the Will*, and joyously of beauty and being in *Personal Narrative* and *Images or Shadows*.

Bloch, Ruth H. "Women, Love, and Virtue in the Thought of Edwards and Franklin," pp. 134-51. Concludes that Edwards and Benjamin Franklin "played unwitting but significant parts" in the sentimental understanding of women and marriage that emerged during the middle of the eighteenth century, in an examination of their "troubled ambivalence" toward human love. Edwards's thought falls into a "discernible pattern" — from an acceptance of natural as well as religious love before 1755 to an emphasis on the "direct antagonism" between them in *True Virtue* — and may have been occasioned by the "growing disaffection" of his parish and by the spiritual crisis of his wife, recounted as a genderless narrative in *Some Thoughts*. Franklin was "more straightforward," more utilitarian, linking economics to reproduction, practicality to sexuality. Even so, the omissions and inconsistencies of both on women, love, and virtue point to their "transitional" place in the century and to their evasion of what they took to be the "threatening element of human interdependence."

Levin, David. "Reason, Rhythm, and Style," pp. 171-85. Finds the rhythms of balance and parallelism heard in Benjamin Franklin and Edwards "especially appropriate" to their ideas of fitness, proportion, understanding, and reasonable judgment, and cites passages from the *Autobiography* and *The Way to Wealth* of the first and *Personal Narrative* and *Religious Affections* of the other in proof, in the keynote address of the conference. At times the "ghost of a loose pentameter" haunts Edwards's prose, at times a relentless incantation of words and phrases. Sometimes a triple anapest trips from Franklin's tongue, sometimes "irreverent" ridicule and "mocking" piety. Yet their concern for reciprocity and balance, clarity and plainness, reason and virtue, mark Edwards and Franklin as "contemporaneous heirs to both Puritanism and the Enlightenment."

Lemay, J. A. Leo. "Rhetorical Strategies in *Sinners in the Hands of an Angry God* and *A Narrative of the Late Massacres in Lancaster County*," pp. 186-203. Defines the rhetorical strategies in *Sinners in the Hands of an Angry God* and *A Narrative of the Late Massacres in Lancaster County*, Edwards's "brilliant" use of tension and suspense in "the most effective imprecatory sermon in American literature" and Benjamin Franklin's use of an ineffective, insensitive persona in his pamphlet about the Indian massacres in Pennsylvania, a "mistake" that cost him his audience at the expense of his outrage. Throughout the sermon Edwards gradually increases the sense of immediacy: of person, by shifting from *they* to *we* to *you* and from the generic *men* to the genderless *persons;* of time, by shifting from the past tense to the present, heightening the effect with a repetitive *now;* and of place, by shifting from wicked Israel to backsliding Enfield. Edwards achieves an "unbearable" psychological tension by exhausting a narrow, single idea through inescapable logic, convoluted syntax, and suspenseful imagery — falling figures, dammed waters, drawn bows, dangling spiders.

DeProspo, R. C. "Humanizing the Monster: Integral Self Versus Bodied Soul in the Personal Writings of Franklin and Edwards," pp. 204-17. Proposes that "an absolutely impermeable barrier" exists between *pneuma* and *psyche* in the personal writings of Benjamin Franklin and Edwards and tries to differentiate them from "the song of modern American selfhood," in a reading of the opening lines of the *Autobiography* on metempsychosis and of *Personal Narrative* on the booth in the swamp. Franklin in his "memoirs" — a more accurate term, because free of modern humanist presentism — reports only what the bodied soul can know *(psyche),* not what it cannot conceive or "reliably" experience *(pneuma),* not a "monstrosity" containing both. Edwards in his account of conversion — an account "neither personal nor narrative" — attempts to reconcile *psyche* with *pneuma* and constructs "a monster, a monument of, or to, asceticism, an idol of, or to, otherworldliness." Perhaps making these writings "reader-unfriendly" will make "legible" the object, not the subject, of the text, and the need to theorize about early American literature.

14 Otto, Randall E. "Justification and Justice: An Edwardsean Proposal." *Evangelical Quarterly* 65 (April): 131-45.
Observes that Edwards balances the competing doctrines of justification and justice, in a close reading of "Justification by Faith Alone." In "unmistakable boldness," Edwards argues that salvation and justification are contingent on faith and works, are "really inseparably connected." Perhaps his "more holistic" view may help mediate in the historical Reformed debate over the distinction between justice and justification.

14A Pahl, Jon. "Jonathan Edwards and the Aristocracy of Grace." *Fides et Historia* 25 (Winter): 62-72.
Explores the "ideological implications" of the Calvinist paradox of freedom and order by focussing on the evolution of Edwards's thought from the Great Awakening to *Freedom of the Will.* Edwards posited cosmic order to demolish the argument of self-determination and eternal moral order to that of indifference, hence the "inevitable rule of the saints." That he might have taken the rise of the Republic as a "revolt against good order" does not make him "any less the political thinker."

15 ———. Review of *The Theology of Jonathan Edwards,* by Conrad Cherry. *Church History* 62 (September): 405-406.
Judges Conrad Cherry's "careful and influential" study (1990.11) the starting point for any new appraisal of Edwards's theology.

15A Piggin, Stuart. "Jonathan Edwards and the Evangelical Revival Chronicles of the 1740s." *Lucas* 15 (June): 14-20.
Situates Edwards's understanding of history — that it is the "basic modality of individual and collective existence," the "primary mode for understanding the divine purpose," the "ultimate (the best) mode of expressing reality" — in the context of the use of history in revival magazines of the eighteenth century. For Edwards, the "compelling voice of God" could be heard in the common figural language of the Bible, nature, and time.

15B Reinartz, Gabriele. "Disillusionment in Eden." Ph.D. dissertation, Düsseldorf University.

> Published as 1993.15C.

15C ———. *Die amerikanische "Jeremiade" als rhetorische Strataegie im öffentlichen Diskurs: Disillusionment in Eden.* Frankfurt am Main: Peter Lang, xii, 297 pp.

> Uses as texts Edwards's *Sinners in the Hands of an Angry God,* the correspondence between John Adams and Thomas Jefferson, and James Fenimore Cooper's *The American Democrat* in a detailed analysis of the jeremiad as the rhetorical strategy of American public discourse in the eighteenth and nineteenth centuries and its influence in the twentieth. (In German.)

16 Reposa, Michael L. "Jonathan Edwards' 12th Sign." *International Philosophical Quarterly* 33 (June): 153-61.

> Links Edwards's theological empiricism to Charles Peirce's pragmatism through "theosemiotic" — the distinctively American perspective on the place of religious experience in theology — in a reading of the twelfth sign of *Religious Affections,* Christian practice. Edwards's "truly radical" theosemiotic is empiricist, aesthetic, dispositional, pragmaticistic, semiotic, and communitarian and differs "somewhat" from later theosemioticians (Peirce, Ralph Waldo Emerson, Josiah Royce, William James, Cornel West) in his emphasis on the church, the Scriptures, and the experience of conversion.

17 Rossow, Francis C. Review of *The Supremacy of God in Preaching,* by John Piper. *Concordia Journal* 19 (January): 89-90.

> Charges John Piper's book (1990.43) with a lack of focus but welcomes its "sympathetic understanding" of Edwards.

17A Smith, John E. "Jonathan Edwards: Piety and Its Fruits." In *Return of Scripture in Judaism and Christianity: Essays in Postcritical Scriptural Interpretation.* Edited by Peter Ochs. New York: Paulist Press, pp. 277-91.

> Defines Edwards's "new beginning" in philosophical theology as an attempt to apprehend the meaning of divine things in similitudes found in experience and "refined" by thought, a notion expressed with "greatest clarity" in *Religious Affections.* Edwards fastened on the scriptural "fruits of the Spirit" to assess true piety, and, in a "quite original concept," conceived of them as religious affections made available as signs. Although Edwards was aware that his term was not in the Bible, he maintained that he could "elucidate" the meaning of its fruits.

18 ———. *Jonathan Edwards: Puritan, Preacher, Philosopher.* Notre Dame, Ind.: University of Notre Dame Press.

> Reprints 1992.24.

18A Stephens, B. M. Review of *One Holy and Happy Society,* by Gerald R. McDermott. *Choice* 30 (April): 1333.

> Recommends Gerald R. McDermott's "creative and well-documented" study (1992.13) of a "neglected aspect" of Edwards's thought.

18B Sweeney, Douglas A. Review of *One Holy and Happy Society,* by Gerald R. McDermott. *Fides et Historia* 25 (Summer): 134-35.

> Contends that though Edwards emerges from Gerald R. McDermott's book (1992.13) with a

public theology "surprisingly palatable" to current tastes, it may have portrayed him "too sympathetically."

18C Van Devender, George W. Review of *Benjamin Franklin, Jonathan Edwards, and the Representation of American Culture*, edited by Barbara B. Oberg and Harry S. Stout. *Christianity and Literature* 42 (Summer): 613-14.

Finds this collection of essays (1993.13) "interesting but less than convincing," its comparison of Edwards and Franklin "obviously strained."

18D Vetö, Miklós. "Edwards, Jonathan." *Dictionnaire des Philosophes*, 1. Paris: Presses Universitaires de France, pp. 904-907.

Reprints 1984.38A.

18E Whitman, Julie. "Cotton Mather and Jonathan Edwards: Philosophy, Science, and Puritan Theology." Ph.D. dissertation, Indiana University.

Differentiates Edwards's response to divine perfection from Mather's: Edwards "went a step further" than Mather's "compendium of facts" to glorify God by formulating a religious psychology grounded in spiritual development and mental response to divine perfection.

19 Yarbrough, Stephen R., and John C. Adams. *Delightful Conviction: Jonathan Edwards and the Rhetoric of Conversion*. Great American Orators, 20. Westport, Conn.: Greenwood Press, xxiv, 176 pp.

Contends that Edwards "concentrated less on the steps toward conversion and more on the meaning of conversion itself," in a study of his sermon rhetoric, including a brief life; an outline of his concepts of conversion, the affections, will, being, and time; an examination of Northampton society in the early 1730s; an analysis of the triadic structure of *Divine and Supernatural Light*, the response of the Enfield audience to *Sinners in the Hands of an Angry God*, and the function of divine taste in *True Grace* (with reprints of the three sermons); an assessment of the causes and effects of his dismissal; and an account of Alexander Richardson's influence on Edwards — he "permeates" his thought — and Edwards's on Harriet Beecher Stowe. That Edwards's conversion reported in *Personal Narrative* lacks the usual steps of preparation, especially the experience of legal fear, results in a sermon rhetoric meant to convert his parishioners, not persuade them. That he had them in mind when he "catalogued devilish attributes" in his last published sermon shows how his dismissal "still affects him."

PART III

1994–2005

Introduction

S taid, wary Jonathan Edwards glances at a bemused Benjamin Franklin on the cover leaf of *The New York Times Book Review* of July 6, 2003. "Unmatched Americans," the legend reads, "born in New England only three years apart" three centuries ago, remarking not only the coming tercentenary of Edwards's birth but as well one of those enduring continuities of American cultural history. The popular assessment coupling Franklin and Edwards dates back at least to Harriet Beecher Stowe in *Oldtown Folks* (1869.4) — the "average New England character," she noted, combines the materiality of the one with the spirituality of the other — and was addressed yet again a century later by Perry Miller in *Major Writers of America* (1962.7) — "the pre-eminently eloquent linked antagonists," he called them. But the most sustained consideration of the pair took place at Yale over three days in 1990, "contrapuntal" figures then, their "similarities *and* differences existing in creative tension" (1993.13). The pastel portraits of the *Times* carries on the tradition with reviews of recently released biographies of both, *Benjamin Franklin: An American Life,* by Walter Isaacson, "The Many-Minded Man," and *Jonathan Edwards: A Life,* by George M. Marsden, "Soul on Fire" (2003.110).

In his opening sentence, Marsden concludes that "Edwards was extraordinary" and then spells out the terms of his study: to take "seriously his religious outlook on his own terms" — his "Calvinistic heritage" and his personal, "eternal relationship to God" — and to depict him as a "real person in his own time," at once a philosopher and a theologian, pastor and college president, missionary and family man, a "revered figure" in the "international Reformed movement" and in the "broader evangelicalism" (2003.59). Told by a historian of American culture "committed to a Christian faith" similar to Edwards's, Marsden echoed the hope of Iain H. Murray three decades earlier in his "new biography," started serially in the journal *Tenth* (1974.15A) and published thirteen years later by Banner of Truth Trust (1987.22). Murray shared with Edwards his "basic vision for the Christian church," that is, evangelical, and sought to reclaim him from the "preserve of academics" — Ola Elizabeth Winslow (1940.21) and Miller (1949.9), possessed as they were of an "anti-supernatural animus" — and to meet the "urgent need" of a new generation of readers. Marsden's work, by far the better effort and at over six hundred pages the longest of any Edwards biography, won the Bancroft Prize and the plaudits of readers — a "singular masterpiece" (2003.12), "brilliant" (2003.13), "eloquent" (2003.30), "outstanding" (2003.43), "the best book ever" about him (2003.54), "definitive" (2003.77), "*nonpareil*" (2003.94), "magnificent" (2003.100) — dissenters calling it "a chunky . . . period piece" (2003.35), at times lacking "depth of theological analysis" (2003.108), taking "some agendized liberties" with pastoral calls, Sarah Edwards's spiritual crisis, and David Brainerd's "murky" journals (2004.66), and might prove "disappointing" to some for its focus on the "very human," not the "extraordinary intellectual" Edwards (2004.79). But it seemed to settle the reclamation, even as a reviewer of several new studies cautioned evangelicals to support scholarship for the "new Edwards" lest the quadricentennial "prove not nearly so plentiful."

If the last seventy-five years of Edwards study can be divided between recovery and reclamation, the last dozen, or those surveyed here, have become increasingly evangelical and, regrettably, partisan. From the start, Edwards's evangelicalism was of a piece with the general assessment. A popular life, reprinted three times in the nineteenth century, first appeared in *Biographia Evangelica* in the late eighteenth century in London (1786.1); another biography, in two issues of the *Connecticut Evangelical Magazine* early in the nineteenth (1808.1); and a third, in *The Evangelical Succession* late in it (1884.2). A paper read before the Ministerial Association of Columbus, Ohio, during the bicentennial celebrations emphasized "his contribution to Calvinism, to evangelical theology generally" (1903.35); a more critical estimate surfaced in *Evangelized America*, twenty-five years later (1928.5); a more sympathetic one, the following year at the dedication of a memorial gate to Edwards at the Old Burial Ground in South Windsor, Connecticut, his birthplace (1929.7). In all, there were probably twenty such citations before the thirties, the onset of the recovery; twice that many before reclamation in the seventies, another forty over the next fifteen years, and twice that over the last twelve. Numbers aside, the work proved more substantial and hinted at change. During the bicentennial of his death, "The Recovery of Jonathan Edwards" appeared (1958.4) — a review of *Freedom of the Will*, the first volume of the Yale edition (1957.14) — as did two counter texts, the first volume of *The Select Works of Jonathan Edwards*, with the Banner of Truth Trust imprint and under the editorial hand of Murray, and *Jonathan Edwards on Evangelism*, put together by Carl J. C. Wolf, both based upon the aging, and flawed, Edward Hickman *Works of Jonathan Edwards* (1834.4). A battle of the books was at hand and, though not quite between ancient and modern, continues still. As Yale neared the end of its projected twenty-six volumes, the later numbers a trove of manuscripts, Banner of Truth, Soli Deo Gloria, and other houses reprinted sermon collections — *Jonathan Edwards on Knowing Christ* (1990), *The Wrath of Almighty God* (1996), *Altogether Lovely* (1997), *His Redeeming Love* (2001), *The True Believer* (2002), and *The Salva-*

tion of Souls (2002), only the last derived from manuscripts; a home library of individual works — *Sinners in the Hands of an Angry God,* "Made Easier to Read" in 1996 and rendered difficult again later that year in Paradise Valley, Arizona; and the two-volume, double-column Hickman, a facsimile edition published in Edinburgh (1974), another in Peabody, Massachusetts (1998).[1] The year the recovery essay appeared in *Religion in Life,* a review in *Christian Century* dismissed it (1958.2); *Christianity Today* urged evangelicals to read Edwards (1958.11); and *Jonathan Edwards the Preacher* held him to be an "evangelical mystic" (1958.25). Two years later, John H. Gerstner initiated a series of theological studies of Edwards with *Steps to Salvation: The Evangelical Message of Jonathan Edwards* (1960.5); a decade later, Yale issued Marsden's *The Evangelical Mind and the New School Presbyterian Experience* (1970.21), charting, in part, the influence of Edwards's evangelical message. Whatever the recovery wrought, the direction of the scholarship shifted from secular colleges and universities to religious ones, often seminaries, and affiliated ministries; from academic journals to Christian ones, in some instances from scholarship itself, readings more testimonial than analytical. Still, an inexhaustible Edwards prompted approaches in matters of historiography, of gender, slavery, and politics, of communion, salvation, and conversion, of aesthetics, ethics, and metaphysics, and questions, inevitably questions.

* * *

In something of a postscript to *A Life,* "Jonathan Edwards in the Twenty-First Century," the last paper of the last major conference of the tercentennial celebrations, gathered in early October at the Library of Congress, Marsden frames an Edwards, not of his time and place, but "especially useful for our own time," an Edwards for better understanding American culture, for his theological legacy, for his critique of enlightened modernity, his emphasis on human depravity, his lesson for evangelicals — to counter anti-intellectualism and "superficiality" — and, in closing, for his recognition of the "blazing beauty" at the center of the universe, an "overwhelming beauty that is not just a temporary escape but which is the basis for a way of life that is both practical and exhilarating." Published in *Jonathan Edwards at 300* and edited by Harry S. Stout, Kenneth P. Minkema, and Caleb J. D. Maskell (2005.35), the twelve other papers at the conference registered other measures of Edwards, the theology of history, Scripture, culture, society, and race, rehearsing the familiar at times but adding fresh lines of inquiry — Sang Hyun Lee on disposition (1995.26), Douglas A. Sweeney and Robert E. Brown on hermeneutics (1998.41 and 1999.6), Gerald R. McDermott on deism (2000.27), and Ava Chamberlain on gender (2000.5) — and also redirecting them

---

1. These, and others, are described in detail in *The Printed Writings of Jonathan Edwards* (revised, 2003.52).

— Amy Plantinga Pauw to the "uneasy coexistence" between grand and pastoral narratives on redemption, Stephen J. Stein to biblical violence, Philip F. Gura to the "discourse of sentimentalism" in American literature, Mark A. Noll to "a different story" about *Freedom of the Will*, and Mark R. Valeri to forgiveness. On the question of race, broached by Minkema (1997.25) and McDermott (1999.28) earlier and considered by them several times since (2002.28, 2005.26; 2002.26, 29, 2003.37, 2005.23), Rachel Wheeler surveys Stockbridge sources for "possible vectors" of influence between Edwards and the Mahicans to suggest that he was not "markedly shaped" by his mission work. Although his influence on them is "even harder to trace," two obscure letters by Hendrick Aupaumut, chief of the Stockbridge Indians at the end of the century, provide "tantalizing evidence" of their engagement with Christianity. And in "African American Engagements with Edwards in the Era of the Slave Trade," John Saillant considers Edwards's doctrine of disinterested benevolence the "linchpin of abolitionism" in the second half of the eighteenth century, for both black and white, both Phillis Wheatley and Samuel Hopkins. Edwards's notions of virtue, divine providence — Prince Hall wrote a thirty-five-page commentary on *History of Redemption* — free will, and typology became fundamental to their argument against slavery. "[W]hatever else early black abolitionists believed of the Bible, they believed it to be a book of types and antitypes."

Much as McDermott engaged Edwards's contention with deism at Washington, so he had at Bloomington in June 1994, remarking then Edwards's particularly vitriolic attack against Islam, the "most dangerous" of enemies of Reformed Christianity, drawing on his comments in the late "Miscellanies" transcribed in the Hickman edition and *Notes on Scripture* from Yale (1988.37). Unlike Christianity, Edwards insisted, Islam retards knowledge, preaches "sensual rewards," appeals to "base human desires," and rests on private miracles. One of twelve papers of the Indiana University conference, later published as *Jonathan Edwards's Writings: Text, Context, Interpretation* and edited by Stephen Stein (1996.46), it was part of a section on text, as was Ava Chamberlain's on the parable of the wise and foolish virgins (Matt. 25:1-12), examining Edwards's sense of the covenant of marriage and the covenant of grace; Christopher Grasso's on unpublished manuscript sermons, early and late, and rhetorical responses to *Humble Inquiry*, demonstrating how he tried to regulate public religious discourse, especially as it bore upon the communion controversy; and Kenneth Minkema's on the background and design of his "virtually unknown" 500-page manuscript, "The Harmony of the Old and New Testament," remarking his exegetical turn of mind. In the first paper in the section on context, Paul R. Lucas uncovers the sources of influence on Solomon Stoddard — and his on Edwards — during the "peculiar circumstances" of the Connecticut Valley in the late seventeenth and early eighteenth century and the "pivotal role" William Prynne, John Knox, and Samuel Rutherford played in Stoddard's thought; William K. B. Stoever explores the continuities between Thomas Shepard and Edwards on the evidence of true godliness in *The Parable of the Ten Virgins Unfolded* and Edwards's unpublished series of nineteen sermons on Matt. 25:1-13, *Religious Affections,* and *Charity and its Fruits;* Richard A. S. Hall traces the "remarkable continuities" of thought on moral sense theory between George Berkeley's *Alciphron* and Edwards's *The Nature of True Virtue;* and Wayne Proudfoot, in a reversal, doubts the parallels usually drawn between William James's *Varieties of Religious Experience* and Edwards's *Religious Affections.* The last section, that on interpretation, brings together Nathaniel William Taylor, Charles Grandison Finney, Edwards Amasa Park, and evangelical women to comment upon their impact on Edwardseans. Douglas Sweeney, for example, insists that, contrary to recent historiographical trends, Taylor did "build upon, engage, and forward" Edwards's legacy; Allen C. Guelzo challenges the conventional view of perfectionism as an "enthusiastic aberration" of Jacksonian impulses, in a study of the "complex but clear" relationship between Finney and Edwards and his New Divinity successors; Genevieve E. McCoy sets evangelical women engaged in the debates of fundamental tenets of the New Divinity descendants of Edwards in the context of prevailing attitudes about "woman's 'nature' and gender-prescribed behavior"; and, in the concluding essay, Joseph A. Conforti characterizes Edwards Park as a "major" contributor, interpreter, and "guardian" of the Edwardsean tradition in mid-nineteenth century, New England Theology.

Over another weekend in early October two years later at Philadelphia, the keynote address, "The Perennial Jonathan Edwards," ushers in eight paired essays on Edwards's contribution to contemporary religious thought — papers on nature, ethics, preaching and revival, and eschatology — and collected in *Edwards in Our Time: Jonathan Edwards and the Shaping of American Religion,* edited by Sang Hyun Lee and Allen Guelzo (1999.24). John E. Smith deals with Edwards's "most illuminating and most powerful" ideas touching recurrent problems of religion and contemporary society, his concept of the affections, rejection of nominalism, and God's method of ordering history. Lee thinks that Edwards's treatment of nature is best understood as an expression of his dispositional ontology, a "highly innovative reconception" of God's nature and his relationship to natural world; Stephen H. Daniel associates ideas in Edwards and Karl Barth to contemporary critiques of the meaning of intelligibility and its implications for the doctrine of the Trinity, a "hot topic" in postmodern theology. Roland A. Delattre cites three "formative" ideas Edwards entertained that may contribute to contemporary religious ethics, the centrality of beauty to an understanding of God and the nature of spiritual and moral life, the "joyous overflowing" of the divine being and beauty in creation, and the "cordial consent" to the being and beauty of God in Christian rebirth; and Guelzo traces the debate over free will — "our national gargoyle" — during the past two hundred and fifty years: although Edwards probably knew the "harmony" between free will and necessity was but a "workable dream," he had raised the "right questions" and thus provided for the continuing discussion of the issue, especially in its peculiarly American context. Within the section on preaching and revival, Walter V. L. Eversley theorizes that Edwards's "theological integrity actually undermined his pastoral role," as he sought to link his conversionism and sacramentalism — his revivalist impulse to his communion practice — a failed attempt that ended in his dismissal; and Helen P. Westra finds that his ideas and beliefs about the work of revivals in the "great drama" of redemption continue to influence evangelical movements "even in these post-modern times." In "The End Is Music," the first paper in the last category, Robert W. Jenson counters the suppression of eschatology in the theology of modernity, dependent as it is upon mechanism, nominalism, and the "antimony of hope," with Edwards's thoughts about end times, "a *story* of the world" within the triune story of God; and Gerald McDermott formulates his views on the possibility of the salvation of the "'heathen'" from comments in his notebooks — fully a quarter of the entries in the "Miscellanies" concern non-Christian religions — and from his voracious reading about them, travelogues, dictionaries, and encyclopedias as recorded in his "Catalogue."

Over yet another weekend, this in early March 2000 in Miami, one of fifteen papers subsequently published in *Jonathan Edwards at Home and Abroad: Historical Memories, Cultural Movements, Global Horizons,* edited by David W. Kling and Douglas Sweeney (2003.45), sketched in the necessary background to the "discourse of sentimentalism" Philip Gura later addressed at the Library of Congress. Sharon Y. Kim identifies Susan Warner's *The Wide, Wide World* as an antebellum novel that sought to "promote, not undermine" American Calvinism, unlike some other sentimental novels that characterized Edwardseans as men in black, "anachronistic, overly rational." Warner conceived and pursued "an authentic relationship" with God much as Edwards had in *Personal Narrative, Religious Affections, Some Thoughts,* and *True Virtue,* and engaged in a "meticulous specification" about Christianity reminiscent of him, thus "both influenced by Edwards and consonant with his work." In the first of the four papers on Edwards's ministry, Marsden recounts the problems confronting his biographer — the "sheer immensity" of scholarship, the "elusiveness" of his personality, locating him in his communities and traditions — and proposes that the central theme for understanding him is own phrase, "the divine and supernatural light"; Michael J. McClymond suggests that Edwards's projected *History of Redemption* was to be an expression of "'a cultural turn'" in his theology, that is, away from Anglo-American Protestantism to the divine presence in other Western cultures, in a reading of his letter to the Princeton trustees (1998.5), his notebooks for the text (1989.59), and relevant later "Miscellanies." And in a turn to Edwards's theology of children, Catherine A. Brekus examines how his "unflinching" attitude was remembered and distorted in the "new, humanitarian climate" of nineteenth-century America, Unitarians rejecting it outright, even Calvinists, who sought claimant rights to his mantle, distancing themselves from his harsh doctrines, their sentimentalized views of childhood irreconcilable with his vision of absolute divine sovereignty; the last in the group, Ava Chamberlain on the bad-book episode, reprints the published version of her paper (2002.7). In addition to Kim on women's fiction in the section on American culture, Mark Valeri reconsiders Edwards, his followers, and market culture in eighteenth-century New England, emphasizing how his ethical writings contributed to "an alliance" between evangelicals and the market economy, a "transitional figure" between his Puritan forebears and New Divinity men, though he never found "an easy or obvious" correlation between commerce and Calvinism. James D. German believes that his social and political significance might be better seen not in the political preaching of New Divinity clergy but in the moral arguments of "pious politicians," in a study of the younger Edwards, Roger Sherman, and Oliver Ellsworth; discerning a pattern of inter-racial salvation and fellowship among three "notable" Edwardseans in Revolutionary times, Charles E. Hambrick-Stowe frames Edwards's theology of revival in a new social context; and much as Valeri found Edwards a "transitional figure," so Amanda Porterfield does, but here, as one committed to the notion that a Christian life transcends ordinary human life, anticipating a "more modern," popular interpretation that religion is the "ultimate concern at the heart of individual life." In the last section, both David W. Bebbington and M. X. Lesser, the opening and closing speakers, track the contours of Edwards's international legacy, Bebbington in four phases of influence: despite lapses, he exercised "an extremely powerful influence," not least in the spread of the evangelical movement; Lesser in a publication history, appending a bibliography of over two hundred separately published texts, among them works in Dutch and German in the eighteenth century, Arabic, Choctaw, French, Gaelic, Swedish, and Welsh in the nineteenth, and Chinese, Italian, and Korean in the twentieth, as well as a "small shelf" of articles and reviews in French, German, Hungarian, Italian, Japanese, Korean, Portuguese, Russian, and Spanish. D. Bruce Hindmarsh narrows the field to early evangelicals in England: "To state it badly, the Baptists championed Edwards, the Anglican evangelicals were ambivalent, and Wesley simply corrected him"; Christopher W. Mitchell examines the "epistolary link" between Edwards and his six Scottish correspondents that opened a "new chapter" in his life, one ultimately offering "to make him a son of the Kirk"; and Andrew F. Walls labels both Edwards and Brainerd "transitional" figures in the Protestant missionary movement, acknowledging its "debt" to the one for the "impression" it retained of the other. Somewhat at odds with that perception, Stuart Piggin asserts that Edwards was "massively constitutive of modern Protestant missions," reviewing the historical record of his impact on the British missionary movement to India and the implications of his thought for missionary thinking about heathenism, especially Hinduism, the facets of his "missionary diamond" reflecting his "pervasive" evangelical legacy, his *Life of Brainerd* a "paradigm of missionary strategy."

The 1996 Philadelphia conference was sponsored jointly by *The Works of Jon-*

athan Edwards, Princeton Theological Seminary, Eastern College, Westminster Theological Seminary, the University of Pennsylvania, and The Presbyterian Church (U.S.A.), four later ones by religious organizations, the first of them the Reformed Bible Conference at the Westminister Presbyterian Church, Lancaster, Pennsylvania, in late October 2001. Its thirteen papers, published as *The Legacy of Jonathan Edwards: American Religion and the Evangelical Tradition* and edited by D. G. Hart, Sean Michael Lucas, and Stephen J. Nichols (2003.36), were grouped under vision, theology, legacy, and reflections, "no fewer than eight denominations" represented. In "Jonathan Edwards' Tri-World Vision," Harry Stout claims that Edwards had an "obsession with history" and sought to "weave" an interconnected narrative of heaven, earth, and hell into the dramatic form of history of redemption, including, though subordinate, all the major doctrines of Christian theology; Nichols takes a "close look" at Edwards's Stockbridge years, not at what he wrote, but what he did with and among the Mahicans there, in an assessment of his missionary career; Richard A. Bailey enumerates areas where he "passionately" drove his philosophy of preaching as he modified contemporary preaching patterns and prepared and proclaimed his message from the pulpit, centering his ministry on the power of the Word, drawing his flock into Christ's kingdom; and Charles Hambrick-Stowe offers *Personal Narrative* as a "fairly reliable record" of his spiritual experience and practice of piety — a "window" to his soul, his "'inward, sweet sense'" of Christ — matters "fundamental" to believers and the church still. On concerns theological, George Marsden cites Edwards's posthumous *Two Dissertations* as his "great contribution" to a critique of Enlightenment thought, *End of Creation* — "a sort of prolegomena" to all his work — and *True Virtue,* an "intellectual gem," the "most philosophical of his writings"; C. Samuel Storms uses him as a "catalyst" for a biblical and theological examination of open theism, particularly its rejection and his "unqualified endorsement" of exhaustive divine foreknowledge. Edwards's notion of reason and the noetic effects of sin, K. Scott Oliphint maintains, reveal the "substance" of a Reformed approach to apologetics; and Gerald McDermott adjudges him no different from generations of Puritan theologians in believing that New England's — and Northampton's — fortunes could be coupled to God's covenant, but that Edwards was "far too sanguine" about his own ability to unravel the meaning of every historical contingency that befell society. In reflecting on Edwards, conversion, and holy affections in the context of historic Reformed teaching on regeneration and the Christian life, Hart attempts to explain how he "unintentionally undermined" the Calvinism he sought to defend; Douglas Sweeney concentrates on New England theology, which "flourished" in the northeast in first half of the nineteenth century, part of Edwards's legacy and America's "first indigenous theological movement"; Lucas examines criticisms by southern Presbyterians of his theology in the nineteenth-century, particularly by Robert Lewis Dabney, who stood for the Reformed faith, the southern Baptists for New Divinity modes of thought, the preservers of his legacy; and George S. Claghorn recounts some of the "colorful" experiences he had both here and abroad on the "long journey" to the publication of the Yale edition of Edwards's correspondence. A "labor of love," the transcribing and editing of his "difficult hand" took thirty-five years but led to a far better understanding of a man who "walked with God," who was "focused, fearless, and faithful."

In a bibliographic essay at the end, Lucas proposes to "bridge the wide chasm" between church and academy in the reading of Edwards over the years, separating out some "important and worthy" studies for evangelical pastors and lay people from the "dizzying array" of perspectives from the academy, an effort designed to help navigate the "ever-increasing web of information" about him, some of the "most creative" scholarship in American religious studies; another, shorter essay, closing another conference (2004.61) exhorts reluctant evangelicals, *"Take up and read!"* older books and Edwards's "complicated sentences and complex thoughts." That there would be five more bibliographic essays is not surprising, given the outpouring of scholarship over the last several decades, although some compilers not only review the work but recast it. Thus, while one essay traces his foreign publications (2003.45), and two in *Religious Studies Review* take on the latest volumes of the Yale edition and the books of the eighties (1998.7 and 1998.24), a fourth creates an "Edwards for Preachers" (1998.11), and the last, by Kenneth Minkema, published in the *Journal of the Evangelical Theological Society* (2004.49), provides statistical charts — one on secondary literature in the twentieth century, another on dissertations — and sorts the whole by categories, if only to summon readers in two of them, history and theology, to a common enterprise, a more fully realized, because shared, Edwards. Conferences during the tercentennial year concentrate more nearly on theology and evangelism.

In the Congregational Studies Conference at Westminster Chapel, London, in March (2003.27), Robert E. Davis, pastor of the First Congregational Church, Millers Falls, Massachusetts, read three papers, later published as *Jonathan Edwards-His Message and Impact* (2004.75). The first of them on the nature of "true conversion" enlists *Faithful Narrative, Distinguishing Marks, Some Thoughts,* and *Religious Affections* to tally "key elements" common to all: a conviction of sin, repentance toward God, saving grace in Christ, and, the "surest sign," a changed life "perseveringly lived in the glory of God"; the second paper, a study of an Edwards "largely ignored" by scholars, shows how this "mission-minded evangelist . . . spark[ed]" the movement then and now, his *Humble Attempt* establishing the theological foundation for the expansion of the gospel throughout the world; and the third discusses the reciprocal influence of Edwards and Great Britain through his publications and correspondence, and, with "similar spiritual conditions" now, a time to join together as in his day to revive that glorious gospel work. At another, general conference in Great Britain during the tercentennial year, this at West Yorkshire and published as *Knowing the Mind of God,* two papers singled out Edwards. One, by his biographer Murray (2003.70), derives several lessons from his *"extraordinary"* life — the nature of the true Christian experience, the power of the Holy Spirit in advancing the gospel and salvation, and the need to "live to God alone"; the other, by W. Robert Godfrey (2003.34), examines his reflections on authentic spiritual experience to conclude that he cannot "escape the problematics" of his Puritan heritage. Indeed, Edwards may have "exacerbated" them with his notion of justifying faith, his writings valuable now only for their "secondary support" of assurance, their "secondary evidence" for authenticity.

In April, a Princeton Theological Seminary conference met on Edwards the theologian, all but two of its eleven papers and an panel discussion were published — the keynote address, "Edwards for Our Time: A Personal View," by Richard R. Niebuhr; "Edwards on the Trinity," by Paul Helm; and an exchange, "Edwards on Biblical Interpretation," with Douglas Sweeney, Stephen Stein, and Robert Brown — four in *The Princeton Companion to Jonathan Edwards* (2005.23), five elsewhere: Roland Delattre's "Edwards's Aesthetics and Ethics" in *Journal of Religious Ethics* (2003.111); Stephen D. Crocco's "Edwards and Princeton" in *Princeton Seminary Bulletin* (2003.26); George S. Claghorn's "Edwards behind the Scene" in *The Legacy of Jonathan Edwards* (2003.36); George Hunsinger's "Edwards's Doctrine of Justification by Faith Alone" in *Westminster Theological Journal* (2004.31); and Michael McClymond's "A Different Legacy?" in *Jonathan Edwards at Home and Abroad* (2003.45). The first paper of the nineteen in the *Companion*,[2] "A Theological Life," by Kenneth Minkema, examines Edwards's career as an effort to deal with the "changing theological currents" of his time and his "considerable critique" of them, his legacy "still felt to this day"; in the second, Peter J. Thuesen regards him as an "eclectic" thinker, torn between Puritan traditionalism and Enlightenment rationalism, premodern Western Christianity and modern skepticism, his "implicit debt" to the Reformation just that, his citations to Calvin and other sixteenth-century divines "few and far between." Richard R. Niebuhr inspects several propositions from the early Edwards representing "symbolically" the theme of being and consent "run[ning] through *much*" of his writing, that being has knowledge and consciousness, and these operations of the mind imply a complex event, "mind or proper being is plural in some sense"; Amy Plantinga Pauw links two aspects, usually "disconnected," of his theology of the Trinity, joining his "profound" metaphysical musings to his "zeal" for the church and the Christian life, his "multifaceted" articulation of beauty and excellency of the triune God retaining a "deep spiritual and theological resonance" today; and Sang Lee, the editor of the collection, elaborates several aspects of Edwards's thought on God's relation to the world, chief among them that the created world is God's "repetition outside of himself, in time and space, of his

---

2. *Another Companion,* edited by Stephen Stein, will be published by Cambridge University Press in late 2006.

prior actuality." What Christians do in the world by God's grace "matters to God," for he needs or uses the world in time and space to "exercise his dispositional essence outside of his own internal being."

In the first of the papers from the conference, Robert Jenson analyzes Edwards's Christology, one of the "more astonishing" aspects of his thought, in terms of the soteriological concerns that drove it, the metaphysical convictions that constrained it, the way of talking about Christ that it aimed at, and the conceptual means to that end; Robert Brown contends that Edwards's biblical exegesis is the "most neglected" dimension of his thought, for he devoted a "large measure" of his energies to writing about Scripture, as did the majority of eighteenth-century intellectuals, in an attempt to reconcile the ancient biblical authors' representation of the world with Newtonian astronomy and physics, using his typology in exegesis, the "most notable" aspect of his exposition; in the second paper from the conference, John E. Smith addresses the "unique synthesis" of religion, psychology, and theology of *Religious Affections,* the "most comprehensive" treatment of the subject in his writings, as he tried to show both how the affections were a "great part" of true religion and how to test the religious experience, to understand, as he said, the "sense of the heart"; and Allen Guelzo follows the reception of *Freedom of the Will* over time, examining the "exact nature" of free will and his "compatibilist" contribution to it, the "touchstone" of the New Divinity and the "great issue" to New England theology in antebellum America. Another paper by Lee, this from the conference, begins a series on doctrines associated with Edwards with one on grace, demonstrating that he reaffirms the Reformed position of the ungodly and articulates the "ontological (dispositional) grounding" of the sinner in Christian practice, in "complete agreement" with Calvin that justification and sanctification constitute a "double grace" through union with Christ; and another paper by Smith delineates Edwards on the nature of divine love and his conception of the virtuous life as they bear upon common morality, in a reading of *Charity and its Fruits* and *True Virtue.* For Edwards's ecclesiology, a part of his thought "largely unnoticed," Douglas Sweeney discovers a "paper trail" through the manuscripts dating back to his first days in Northampton and ending with *Humble Attempt,* the church for him throughout an "intimate company of God's lovers"; Janice Knight finds typology the "interpretative key" Edwards used to unlock God's revelation in nature and human history, in the created world and Scripture, a form of "divine speech" in which God communicated his intentions and his love to the saints, an "eternal dynamic" that grows stronger with the coming of the millennium. Closing the section, John F. Wilson untangles several separate but interrelated strands of his interpretation of history: the genesis and content of the 1739 sermon series "Redemption Discourse," his remarks on history in the letter to the Princeton trustees, his "broader reflections" on God's purpose in *End of Creation;* his "relatively infrequent" references to history in his writings, and modern readers' "unending conjectures and countless assertions" about his interest in the subject;

and Stephen Stein organizes his eschatology into three periods — his early reflections, from his Yale years to 1733; his involvement in revivals, from 1734 to 1748; and his most productive time, the last decade of his life, the "controlling principle" of it the connection between first and last things — divine providence governing the events between them, the Holy Spirit the "primary agent" whereby Christ's kingdom on earth advances, the forces of evil opposed to redemption impeding its progress. The final stage of the process "will not, in fact, be final," since both heaven and hell for him are "progressive" states and will continue forever — the saints in unending praise, the damned in unending punishment — both "apt reflections" of God's glory and his purpose in creation.

The last four essays consider Edwards's sermons, missions, federal theology, and legacy. Wilson H. Kimnach demonstrates that he "fully exploited" the potential of the Puritan sermon without "seriously altering" its form — text, doctrine, application — used in the seventeenth century by the great preachers of New England, noting his particular accomplishments, *Sinners in the Hands of an Angry God* among them; Gerald McDermott, the fourth of the conference papers, relates how missions to the Indians function as the "principal moving force" in his history of redemption and how Edwards's work among them shaped his ideas on indigenous religion, in time winning their affection and returning it; and Harry Stout proposes that he was more of a Puritan than Perry Miller or his revisionists concede, "every bit" the federal theologian his predecessors were, adhering "exactly" to the logic and tenets of the national covenant, reiterating them in "exactly" the same terms the New England Puritans did. In a sort of vade-mecum, Mark Noll offers a "rapid survey" of his influence on later thinkers — Protestant theologians, lay evangelicals, intellectuals — over the generations following his death, both here and abroad, on one level or another, tracing the "controversial uses" of his legacy in the nineteenth century to help understand his recovery and reclamation in the twentieth. Along with Miller's rehabilitation of the Puritans, and Edwards, in the 1930s came "fresh attention," first, from mainline Protestants and then, much later, evangelicals, his "closest" constituency. "Edwards is more comprehensively alive today than ever in own lifetime or since." Other meetings and several journals underscore that.

Christian History for February 2002, the first of seven journals devoted to Edwards, in whole or in part, published a series of thirteen short articles, edited by Chris Armstrong and reprinted as *The Warm-Hearted Genius Behind the Great Awakening* (2002.1). Beginning with "Papa Edwards," the father of evangelicalism, and ending with excerpts from "The Christian Pilgrim" and *Personal Narrative,* the papers touch upon Edwards's "mind shapers," the "exceptional" women about him, his influence here and abroad, his dismissal, his "true signs" of regeneration and defense against deism, his biblicism and delight in pursuing God's ways. In a conversation with the editor, George Marsden reminds readers that, though a "creature" of British hierarchical society, Edwards encouraged women to pursue an education, yet had a "blind spot" toward slavery, his "fingerprints" seen even now in revivalism, in American education, in the nature of religious affections, in a God-centered theology. In March of the following year, *Evangelical Magazine*, the journal of the Evangelical Movement of Wales, produced a "theme issue" on Edwards (2003.21), seven short pieces on "a biblically balanced man" defending and declaring faith all can learn from, "a complete stranger" to the separation of heart and head that often weakens evangelism. His "settled conviction" that revivals advance God's kingdom, despite the local excesses of itinerants and critics, remains a certain help in "our present desperate predicament," as does his encouragement to be "radically single-minded" to know God, to study the Bible "steadily and constantly and frequently," to "glorify God by enjoying Him forever."

Reformation & Revival Journal spent about half its summer issue on an "anniversary celebration" with half a dozen articles on Edwards's theology (2003.2). Gerald McDermott divides it into that which is familiar to "nearly all" readers, his "lifelong battle" with deism, and that which is not, the relationship between baptism and regeneration, expressed in "Miscellanies," nos. 577, 595, and 689; and Stephen Nichols offers a synopsis of his life, noting the conflicts he encountered, in his father's tenure in East Windsor, his Northampton pastorate, and his Stockbridge years, conflicts that "appeared to seek him out." Robert W. Caldwell, III, anchors Edwards's "life-long fascination" with the nature of the religious experience, indeed, his "theological vision," in the doctrine of the Holy Spirit; and Samuel Storms questions his solution to the problem of original sin, his notions of continuous creation and personal identity, since there is "*not* a legitimate correspondence" between the identity of a self and successive moments in time, and the "alleged" identity between all selves and Adam. Glenn R. Kreider explicates "The Terms of Prayer," a sermon delivered in May 1738 (2001.25), in which Edwards encouraged his people to pray because of God's "generosity" and nature, insights into prayer and the character of God that remain "timely" for us today; and Robert D. Smart cites his experimental Calvinism as a remedy to the "defective" revival experiences of New England, discovering God's love and grace without a "proportionate" discovery of God's majesty and holiness, and recommends his "wisdom and guidance" to our pastors. An interview with Michael McClymond recalls how his interest in Edwards developed — his conversion experience, his study of the Reformed tradition at Yale, his reaction to *End of Creation*, "a great book [that] moved me deeply" — the genesis of his *Encounters with God* (1998.23), and the popularity of Edwards today, "arguably, the most important writer, not only in the modern period or in Protestantism, but in all the history of the Church on the subject of spiritual discernment," surely "a Church Father for the twenty-first century." A number of snippets from his work, a review of Marsden's *A Life*, and final remarks by the editor close the account. "He understood the big-picture of God's work in the world," the editor John H. Armstrong writes, "and had an all-encompassing view of redemption that is

clearly missing today. It is a cause for real joy that Edwards celebrations have occurred all across the world in 2003!"

No less real, the celebrations brought out two dozen reprints stretching
back to mid-nineteenth century for Edwards on the atonement (1996.3) and to
the bicentennial on universal salvation (1999.48) and on his rank among *Ten New
England Leaders* (2004.77). More recent works followed: John Gerstner's *Mini-
Theology* (1996.13); John Piper's thrice revived meditation *Desiring God* (1996.44,
2003.71, 2004.59); Gerald McDermott's *Seeing God,* first in Seoul (1999.31), then
Vancouver (2000.29); from Yale a pair of readers, one of selections (1995.46), the
other of sermons (1999.21); a pair of studies central to the recovery and reclamation: from Nebraska, *Jonathan Edwards,* by Perry Miller — a "searching and
imaginative intellect" in the introduction (2005.40), "a hard-drinking atheist" in
a review (2005.33) — from Banner of Truth, Murray's *A New Biography*
(2000.30); and a pair of reprints of *Marriage to a Difficult Man,* by Elisabeth S.
Dodds, "a parable for the befuddled woman" (2003.31, 2004.19), to meet that
"rare and beautiful relationship" of *Jonathan and Sarah,* a novel by Edna Gerstner
(1995.12). More substantively, *Founders Journal* in its summer issue (2003.72)
chronicles Edwards as a "gifted servant" of the gospel for Baptists — the Southern Baptist Convention itself [was] "born, theologically" out of his writings — in
four articles. Tom J. Nettles, the editor, draws parallels between the arguments
Edwards made against the growing Arminian encroachment on Puritan New England and those Baptists made in their "exit from hyper-Calvinism"; Peter Beck
maintains that Edwards was a "consistent" Calvinist, insisting that human depravity demanded that man be changed in heart, mind, and will, holding "comfortably in tension" the doctrines of man's responsibility and God's sovereignty;
and Jeff Robinson counts him among the few in the "history of Christendom" to
offer such insights into the workings of the human heart regarding salvation as
those in *Religious Affections,* its positive signs of conversion, a "genuine experiential evangelicalism," that will shake modern readers from their "spiritual slumber." The issue closes with "Helpful Books," Nettles recommending Murray's biography (1987.22) to all "lover[s]" of Edwards, lending Marsden's *A Life* (2003.59)
to a "thoughtful non-Christian," *The Salvation of Souls* (2002.2) to the church at
large, and *The Legacy of Jonathan Edwards* (2003.36) to "provoke invigorating
thought."

That summer as well, the *Journal of Religious Ethics* (2003.111) marked the
tercentenary with five essays, 140 pages of "historical and constructive" reflection
on Edwards's theological and religious ethics. Edited by Stephen A. Wilson and
Jean Porter, "Focus: Jonathan Edwards" opens with Wilson puzzled over what Edwards's means by *virtue* "at the heart" of his ethics and the many strands of his
thought. Edwards's ethical position "resonates" with concepts from five traditions,
viz., moral sense theory, Calvinism, the Cambridge Platonists, Protestant scholasticism, and "those overlaps" between Puritanism and both Separatism and

Anabaptism, and emerges as a possible source for contemporary ethics. Yet without such a precise account of his ethics, especially as a Calvinist theologian and a theistic philosopher of the moral sense, it is "awkward" to apply his thought as a "coherent counterpoise" to current ethical problems. Gerald McDermott addresses three ways in which Edwards informs the Christian understanding of public life — in his philosophical and theological rationales for social engagement, dialectical treatment of patriotism, and use of the national covenant to "undermine" national pride — and argues that he can be important to contemporary Christians in the public square, for he resists the separation of the religious life from the public one, remarks the susceptibility of Christian life to the "deceptive accommodation" to culture, and avoids the temptation to chauvinism, demonstrating the "uncommon power" of the inextricable connection between spirituality and the public life, tools to "help deconstruct" the individual and corporate presumption in it. William C. Spohn argues that the notion of "practices" in contemporary virtue ethics can help explain the "integral connections" between moral development and spiritual transformation that Edwards describes in *Charity and its Fruits* and may offer "an antidote to the superficiality and self-absorption" to some forms of spirituality today. Drawing upon the Puritan tradition of spiritual practices and the "popular and problematic" interest in spirituality in the revivals of his own time, Edwards developed a "sophisticated" moral psychology that makes spirituality both "practical and profound" and should alert current theologians and ethicists to the "serious intellectual task" before them. Roland Delattre plays a "tricentennial riff" on Edwards's idea that beauty is both the "first principle of being and the distinguishing perfection of God" to encourage readers to think about religious ethics "outside the box." Edwards "dares" to offer God as the animating soul of the universe, governing it by the creative power of his own "beautifying life"; for him, a life of true virtue, then, is a beautifying life, "joyfully" bestowing beauty found at the "deepest reality," the beautifying life of God. "Now that could be a real turn-on!" And Philip L. Quinn comments on the four previous papers on Edwards, "quite simply, America's greatest philosophical theologian," and what can be "successfully" appropriated from him for use in contemporary ethics. While there may be a "strong cumulative" case for some elements of his thought for resources on current ethical issues, how much is "feasible" is problematic and requires "substantial revision." In fact, when incorporating Edwards as a resource for contemporary virtue theorists, we must be "highly selective" of his ethical, political, and religious views, certainly more selective than when appealing to the work of Aristotle, Aquinas, and Locke. In response, the essayists characterize Quinn's reading as, serially, offering "false alternatives," "misconstru[ing] what is there," taking "seriously" the practices of spirituality, and sowing "confusion"; for the editors, his remarks attest to Edwards's power to "generate fruitful debate on fundamental themes."

Another quarrel broke out on the pages of *Church History* in September

(2003.105) over *America's God,* by Mark Noll (2002.33), "a major moment" in the historical study of religion here, a time when, as the editor of *First Things* put it, "America was really a Christian America, and unambiguously so" (2003.73). In "Book Review Forum," Christine L. Heyrman tempers enthusiasm for Noll's "magisterial" argument for a "reconfigured" Christian theology in America with regret that it leaves out both "femininizing and masculinizing trends" at work within American Protestantism; Grant Wacker, the editor, enjoys the "rich" historiographical feast and "striking" surprises of the work but questions the absence of the Latter-day Saints from the table, the "paucity" of references to history as a sphere of divine action, and the nature of the whole: is the story ironic or "simply tragic"?; and E. Brooks Holifield weighs the differences between Noll's "remarkable" book and his, *Theology in America* (2003.39), "judgments about significance," disagreements "more interesting" than harmonies. Noll, he points out, blends theology with republicanism, an "imaginative" synthesis; he, on the other hand, substitutes denominational competition and social class for political theory, European influence for American exceptionalism, divisiveness for unity, at times violence. Noll responds to the "thoughtful" remarks of the three readers but particularly, and at length, to the "potent" criticisms of the last: on the matter of denominations, "differing narrative choices carry contrasting gains and losses"; on that of European influence, a "judgment call"; and on the notion that theological differences rarely led to violence, "I simply disagree," citing the Civil War, "the greatest collective act of violence in American history."

Coincidental with the gathering in Washington in early October, a conference held in churches in Northampton and Stockbridge included essays about current disputes on moral and political issues and, in recollection and return, a bit of poetry, prose narratives, and drama — the last poem on Edwards was published in a festschrift a dozen years ago, a Shakespearean sonnet (1991.23A); the last fiction, *Maggie's Choice* (1997.20), a novel written for young readers has more to do with its twelve-year-old heroine than the "infamous revivalist." Assembled by Richard A. S. Hall, and to be published by Mellen Press, the *Proceedings* on Edwards's life and thought includes seventeen papers ranging from M. Darrol Bryant's on his influence beyond America to Devin P. Zuber's on Emerson and Swedenborg, from Herbert Richardson on America's spiritual founding father to Ronald Story's "'Heaven Is a World of Love'" and Hall's "Edwards as Mystic." Other participants turn to Joseph Butler and John Dewey, Annie Dillard and Mary Baker Eddy, Immanuel Kant and Charles Sanders Peirce; to Satan and dystopian fiction, children and young people, Trinitarianism and the missionary movement. On the Sunday following, the *Works* staged a reading of *The Flaming Spider* in New Haven; on Tuesday, it opened a month-long exhibition with an address by Kenneth P. Minkema; on Wednesday, held a book party for the editors of recent volumes of the series and *A Life;* on Thursday, a lecture by George Marsden at the Beinecke Rare Book Library; and on Friday, another by Amy Plantinga Pauw at

Marquand Chapel, the Divinity School. That weekend in Minneapolis, the Desiring God Ministries hosted a conference on Edwards's life and legacy and lessons from his life and thought, with explications of *Original Sin, Freedom of the Will,* and *Religious Affections,* its papers published as *God Entranced Vision of All Things* and edited by John Piper and Justin Taylor (2004.61).

On the need for Edwards now, Piper decries the "ominously hollow success" of American evangelicalism and recommends his God-entranced vision as a corrective; Stephen Nichols remarks that his "ongoing" legacy has as much to do with the "depth" of his encounter with God as with the "breadth" of his writings, a life spent in the "pursuit of happiness" in and through Christ, a life still instructive 300 years later and "hopefully for years to come"; Nöel Piper outlines the "main roles" God had given Sarah Edwards, in a brief biography and time line; and J. I. Packer details how Edwards's view of God shaped his thinking about revival, but unfortunately, has "no clear meaning" for many today. Opening the second part of the program, Donald S. Whitney numbers three lessons from Edwards in pursuit of a passion for God through spiritual disciplines, but, as he would readily acknowledge, his example has value only to the extent that it "points us to his God"; in treating "how Edwards got fired," Mark Dever imparts other lessons for evangelicals today, chief among them the need of the church to be not simply "accessible and comfortable," but "pure and holy," "visibly shining," and "radiantly distinct" for God's glory; and, lastly, Sherard Burns questions how Edwards could own slaves and suggests that the only "true answer" to his "shortcomings" lies in his, and our, love of God, the sovereign over all things and events in the universe, "even the sin of slavery," and reminds us in the trials of racism that we are "not home yet." Of the three treatises under scrutiny, Paul Helm detects Edwards's "confidence" in reason throughout his three-part defense in *Original Sin;* Samuel Storms unpacks his "devastating" critique of libertarianism, reconstructs his concept of the will, marks the most "problematic" element in his theology of it, that God is the author of sin, to conclude that however "mysterious and unsettling" his treatise often proves, his reasoning and reading of Scripture is "correct"; and Mark R. Talbot contends that the "whole purpose" served by the third part of *Religious Affections* is to show that Scripture distinguishes godly affections from others, that even negative desires and emotions can be godly "in appropriate circumstances." At the site of the church Edwards attended while a student of the Collegiate School, later Yale, then in Wethersfield, the First Church of Christ met at month's end for Awakening Hearts and Minds to God, the fourth in a series of annual conferences named for him. Richard Lovelace and Stephen Macchia spoke on Edwards and the future of evangelicalism in New England and America; Glenn Sunshine shared the "Worldview, Edwards-Style"; Maggie W. Rowe presented a play, "Dear Companion: Sarah Pierpont Edwards"; and Kenneth Minkema and Harry Stout presided over a plenary session, Charles W. Colson a closing one. A 55-seat bus tour of New Haven and to the northern part of Connecticut and Northampton, a New Orleans paper reported, sold out before "dozens of additional inquiries" came in (2003.56).

At just under a hundred pages, a tribute to Edwards in *Studi di Teologia* (2003.28) at midyear centers on his theology, particularly his contributions to evangelicalism. John Gerstner's brief piece on Edwards's orthodox views of the Bible follows a somewhat longer one on his life by Michael A. G. Haykin, both in Italian translations; the editor, Leonardo De Chirico, traces Edwards's thoughts on free will; Andrea Ferrari links him, the doctrine of original sin, and preaching in postmodern times; Sergio De Blasi describes him as the theologian of the Awakening; and De Chirico compiles a bibliography of his works, adding a reprint of his distinctions between positive and negative aspects of self-love. A publication of the Istituto di Formazione Evangelica e Documentazione, *Studi di Teologia* joins the Portugeuse journal *Cultura e Informacao* (1996.39), the French *Revue d'Histoire et de Philosophie Religieuses* (1996.50), and a dozen books in several languages, either works by him or about him. In the first group appear excerpts from *Religious Affections* in Italian (1997.3), the whole of *Distinguishing Marks* in Spanish (2002.21), and both *Humble Attempt* and *Distinguishing Marks* in Korean (2004.32, 54); on the second, larger one, Anri Morimoto's Princeton dissertation (1991.30) in Japanese (1995.36); Josef Smolík's brief life and commentary in Czech in his *Kristus a jeho lid* (1997.33); Caroline Schröder's *Glaubenswahrnehmung und Selbsterkenntnis* in German (1998.34) suggesting that Edwards's experimental theology arises out of his observations of piety, the congruence of God and man; Helen K. Hosier's *The Great Awakener* (1999.17) in Finnish (2000.17); Sang Lee's *The Philosophical Theology of Jonathan Edwards* (1988.25) in Korean (2001.24); W. van Vlastuin's *De Geest van Opwekking* on his doctrine of the Holy Spirit in Dutch (2001.45); and Miklós Vetö, after an absence of several years, on Edwards and the will in his *La naissance de la volonté* in French (2003.46), later translated into Portuguese (2005.38).

Not part of the tercentennial celebrations, the last collection of the year, *Jonathan Edwards: Philosophical Theologian* (2003.37) brings together ten essays reflecting the "confluence of scholars," on Edwards's thought, a force, the editors Paul Helm and Oliver D. Crisp assert, "to be reckoned with" in both philosophy and theology. Jonathan L. Kvanvig and William J. Wainwright take up Edwards on hell, one calling his traditional view "astounding and disturbing" but as "sound a way as can be found," his defense unconvincing but yet revealing how "all of life is lived in the face of God and the justice in holding us responsible for this relationship"; the other contending that his defense is "partly successful and partly not," his permanent exclusion of some from God's presence, though consistent with God's infinite greatness and excellency, fails to show non-scriptural reasons why that exclusion be everlasting punishment and not annihilation, nor is his notion of God compatible with the rejection of "countless numbers" not fully aware of the nature of their sin or those God made not only "vessels of his hatred" but also hateful. Even though Edwards's failures are significant, his positions are not "essential" to a Christian doctrine of hell. Hugh J. McCann insists that although Edwards's perceptions are "acute," his argument about free will is "not convincing" since the ordinary concept of freedom is Arminian, not Calvinist. He is right that human freedom must be subordinated to God's will, but he is "wrong" in thinking that the operation of the will is subject to natural causation. Helm concentrates on the "interconnectedness and dislocation" of various ideas Edwards took from Locke, particularly on the question of personal identity, but in time Locke's impact was "crowded out" by other items on his agenda, "neutralized and sterilized" where it could have been useful to him, especially in *Original Sin*, where he "lost" Locke's forensic focus, the "very thing" he needed to defend the reasonableness of original sin. Crisp analyzes his metaphysical views on imputation and persistence through time and concludes that he developed an a "consistent" occasionalism "commensurate" with a form of temporal parts, a doctrine that puts Sang Lee's reading of him "in trouble." Philip Quinn explicates Edwards's philosophical argument in the first chapter of *True Virtue* in an effort to determine if it can contribute to contemporary discussions of virtue ethics and proposes that with some "fairly minor" revisions his position has "considerable plausibility" and may be offered as a "useful counterweight" to Aquinas and a "serious competitor" for the allegiance of philosophers interested in moral theory. Yet, though his argument has "philosophical plausibility," it "falls short" of the best account of true virtue available. Stephen R. Holmes engages Lee's "powerful" and "excellent" *The Philosophical Theology of Jonathan Edwards* (1988.25 and 2000.21), only to reject it as "simply wrong" and "implausible" in its main thesis, and proposes an alternative reading both historically and theologically "much less difficult to believe." Amy Plantinga Pauw judges his notion of excellency had "largely supplanted" divine simplicity as a "marker" of divine perfection in Edwards's thought, yet he seems never to have "defined it directly." Such a conviction "put him at odds" with a broad theological consensus and a distinguished tradition that linked "maximal unity with maximal existence," but it meant as well that he was "free to wrestle with" that tradition in an imaginative way, to make connections, for example, to the aesthetics of being. Gerald McDermott remarks how both Edwards and John Henry Newman, despite their doctrinal differences, shared "remarkably similar" convictions about spirituality and non-Christian religions, though they differed in some "intriguing" ways. That the "greatest Anglo-American theologians" of the eighteenth and nineteenth centuries were "similarly intrigued" by religious pluralism questions the "glib" comments about our "unprecedented" awareness of it in recent decades. And, in the last paper, Michael McClymond uncovers another odd pairing of Edwards's teaching on salvation and the Orthodox doctrine of divinization of St. Gregory Palamas, both sharing a common Platonic or Neoplatonic philosophical heritage that they "modified in analogous ways" in their understanding of the grace of

God and the experience of communion with him. Although he never mentions "the word itself," Edwards "taught a doctrine of divinization."

Closing out the season of meetings, appropriately enough at Northampton in early October a year later, sponsored once again by Mellen Press but as yet unpublished, the conference featured eight papers on Edwards's early writings, typology, and conversion, and one, by Andrea Knutson, on Edwards and "Bartleby, the Scrivener," hinting at other connections, not only earlier studies of Herman Melville's story (1969.28, 1976.19, 1991.20), but the current engagement with Emily Dickinson's poetry (2003.50, 2004.62), the reconsideration of the Jameses, father and sons (2001.15, 2002.11), and, in a recent "plea for creational theology," the bond between Edwards and both William Cowper, the eighteenth-century evangelical poet, and Gerard Manley Hopkins, the nineteenth-century Jesuit one (2005.28). On Edwards's early writing, Michael H. Niemczyk looks at his "'glistening webs'" of spiders; Jennifer Bernstein, who convened the conference, his style and imagination in "Natural Philosophy"; and Wilson N. Brissett, the beauty of logic in his *God Glorified*. On his typology, Jennifer Leader treats it as a literary device; Richard Hall, as exemplified in the Hudson school of painters; and Sandra W. Smith, as repetition in *Images or Shadows*. On the matter of conversion, Bryce Traister probes Edwards and female piety, and Daniel Riechers, his funeral sermon for David Brainerd. Three months later in Seattle at the annual conference of the American Society of Church History, a session organized by Mark Noll and chaired by Douglas Sweeney, Three Centuries of Studying Jonathan Edwards: From Samuel Hopkins to Kenneth Minkema, presented three papers — "'So the people rescued Jonathan,'" M. X. Lesser on Edwards's readers; "'We have procured one rattlesnake,'" Ava Chamberlain on his place in American social history; and "Getting Yale Excited about Its Own," Stephen Crocco on his editors — later posted on edwards.yale.edu, the website of the *Works*.

All told, these efforts account for just about half the essays published over the last dozen years, but, though they share many similar concerns, some pursue matters neither heard nor collected, the links to Robert Frost and Marianne Moore (1998.27), for instance, or Ignatius Loyola (1996.45) and Petrus Ramus (2001.14), Henry Philip Tappan (2004.1) and John Woolman (2004.24) or, more extensively, the Toronto Blessing (1995.18, 27, 1996.21, 1997.1), the last paper among those asking if Edwards is "spinning in his grave" over the "revival wars." Other papers raise other questions, not quite those of the tercentenary celebrants, questions about the "interpretative fiction" of the Great Awakening and the Northampton revival (1995.23), Edwards's legacy to Charles Finney (1997.9), his tears on hearing George Whitefield (2002.6), about Anselm and Edwards on the divine cause of sin (2003.80), prayer and contrary choice (2003.91), and, in last issue of *Church History* for 2005, enthusiasm. Douglas L. Winiarski cites "new evidence" in "Jonathan Edwards, Enthusiast?" (2005.43) intimating that Edwards may have come "uncomfortably close" to that "notoriously spirit-drenched tribe of hyperzealous New

Lights" who scandalized the Great Awakening. An extract of a contemporary letter recounts his two days of preaching and communion, counselling and conversions at Suffield, Massachusetts, just days before he delivered *Sinners in the Hands of an Angry God* across the Connecticut River at Enfield. Following his visit — ninety-six "'chiefly middle Aged'" persons were admitted to communion after the Sabbath sermon; "'Groans & Screaches,'" "'Houlings & Yellings'" ended the other — the village became a "hotbed" of radical evangelism, a form of revival he would later condemn in *Distinguishing Marks, Some Thoughts,* and *Religious Affections.* Another reader argues with little question that "certain American notions of seeing" are common to Edwards, Jefferson, and Audubon (1995.37); another brings Edwards's church chords into play (2004.53); a third, Christian hedonism (1995.43); a fourth, deification (2002.30); yet another attempts a four-part formulation of Edwards's theocentric metaphysics only to be stymied by the untimely demise of the periodical in which the first two appeared (2003.10, 2004.10). A newly minted Ph.D. from the University of London on Edwards and reprobation (2002.10), John J. Bombaro in a piece for *Westminster Theological Journal* (2003.11) reproves Anri Morimoto — and to some extent Gerald McDermott — for misreading Edwards on dispositions, and, consequently, his soteriology, in a rebuttal to the "fiction" of *Jonathan Edwards and the Catholic Vision of Salvation* (1995.35), the revised version of Morimoto's dissertation from Princeton Theological Seminary (1991.30), and "a strange, new" Edwards, in McDermott's phrase, depicted in *Jonathan Edwards Confronts the Gods* (2000.26) on deism and non-Christian faiths, both works widely reviewed, one panned as problematic (1996.7), ahistorical (1996.8), inaccurate (1996.48), and "failed" (1997.32), the other praised as "fascinating" (2001.9), "intriguing" (2001.19), "persuasive" (2001.34), and "stimulating" (2002.25). An earlier study drawn from McDermott's Iowa dissertation on Edwards's "painstaking unfolding of the relation of private to public religion" (1989.33), *One Holy and Happy Society* (1992.13) strove to make him, as one reviewer put it (1994.37), "a hero to modern church activists."

Greeted warmly for uncovering that "neglected aspect" of Edwards (1993.18B), McDermott went on to *Seeing God,* a study of Edwards's twelve reliable signs of true spirituality, three years later (1995.31); to conferences in Bloomington, Lancaster, Philadelphia, and Washington; collections of essays from them and in the *Princeton Companion, Christian History,* and *Religious Ethics;* an exchange in *Trinity Journal* (2002.13, 27); a dozen pages in his *Can Evangelicals Learn from World Religions?* (2000.25); articles on politics (1994.27), the culture wars (1995.30), discernment (1996.23), "rethinking" attitudes to Native Americans (1997.28); a cache of reviews — about thirty items in all, a grand turn of scholarship. McDermott's dissertation was one of four written and published at about the same time; twice that many were published over the last dozen years: Douglas Sweeney's Vanderbilt dissertation on Nathaniel Taylor (1995.48, 2003.97); Louis J. Mitchell's Harvard Th.D. on beauty (1995.33, 2003.66); Robert Brown's Iowa paper on Scripture (1999.5, 2002.5); Christopher W. Morgan's Mid-America Baptist, on hell (1999.35, 2004.51); Glenn R. Kreider's Dallas Theological, on hermeneutics (2000.20, 2004.36); Stephen Nichols's Westminster Theological, on apologetics (2000.31, 2003.74); William J. Danaher's Yale, on ethics (2002.9, 2004.17); and Oliver Crisp's London, on sin (2003.24, 2005.6). And although it represents but a tenth of the dissertations — there were eighty-four compared to ninety-one over the previous, longer period, a dozen during the tercentennial year alone — the roster suggests broadly theological and philosophical, not social or literary, concerns, shaped about equally in theological and secular institutions, and evidences Edwards's continuing presence abroad, dissertations for the first (and second) time at the University of London but also at Cambridge (1998.26), Queens College, Belfast (2001.4), and South Africa (2001.18); at Victoria (2002.44), Western Ontario (2002.45), and Wycliffe (1999.59) in Canada; and nearer home, at Brandeis (1999.1), Luther Northwestern (1994.19), Southeastern Baptist (2001.38), and Stanford (1997.31), among others. Two of the eight books garnered the most attention, Sweeney's *Nathaniel Taylor* and Brown's *Jonathan Edwards and the Bible,* the first at once "convincing" (2003.55) and "unconvincing" (2004.47), "an outstanding example of evangelical historiography" (2005.21); the other, twice "splendid" (2003.14, 2003.78), "first-rate" (2003.62), "fluid, complex, nuanced, and intriguing" (2003.61), yet belying its title (2003.99, 2004.57), failing to remark Edwards's "studied dismissal" of Judaism, his "uncritical animosity" to Catholicism (2003.88).

After *A Life,* probably the most widely read and admired full-length study, *Jonathan Edwards, Religious Tradition, and American Culture* (1995.7), attempts another act of restoration. The "putative neo-orthodox recovery" of Edwards in the thirties, Joseph Conforti writes, largely overlooked the "vital" nineteenth century and the cultural figure "central" to America's religious past, his writings on personal piety, conversion, revivalism, and theology appropriated by Edwardseans, Nathanael Emmons and Edwards Amasa Park, Harriet Beecher Stowe and Emily Dickinson — a time that saw the rise of seminaries and the reinvention of Edwards as a "founding father" of America's "benevolent empire"; the growth of evangelical publishing houses; the popularity of his *Life of Brainerd,* the spread of missions; and after the Civil War, recast as a "totemic figure" in colonial revivalist narratives of America's Puritan past and celebrated nationally at his bicentennial. Readers welcomed Comforti's "richly textured" portrait of the "father of our churchly soul" (1996.32) and his assessment of the "politicized reinventions of the protean" Edwards (1996.14), calling it "long needed" (1996.31), a "substantial achievement" (1996.53), a "model" of postmodern deconstuction (1997.8), although one found that it might have been "stronger" had it included commentary from "extra-theological sources" (1996.24) and another wondered whether it might also succeed in "undermining" Edwards's relevance today (1996.6). Leon Chai on Edwards and the "limits of Enlightenment philosophy" met a cooler reception, few endorsing his reading — "most original" (2000.9), at best of "mixed quality" (1998.11) — several disdaining its "unavoidable contradictions" (1999.30), "serious misconstruals" (1999.52), "misleading" title and "implausible" Edwards (2000.33). The reaction to Stephen Daniel on divine semiotics (1994.8) seemed more tentative, a study performing a "useful service" (1996.30) and opening up "new territory" (1996.16), but destined to be shelved in "academic libraries" (1996.43). Stephen Holmes on Edwards's use of "trinitarian grammar," *God of Grace and God of Glory* published in Edinburgh (2000.15), shared mixed reviews, particularly over the last chapter on reprobation, at once "invaluable" (2000.39) and "non-Christological" (2001.1), but generally for its lack of nuance (2003.47). Far fewer reviews note Edwards's appearance in chapters of books with a wider sweep, "Jonathan Edwards and the Angel of the Lord" in Linda Munk's *The Devil's Mousetrap* (1997.26), for example, or "We Are Inclined to Sin" in R. C. Sproul's *Willing to Believe* (1997.37), and even less so with the many fugitive references to him, such as those in Robert Jenson's two-volume *Systematic Theology* (1997.15, 1999.20).

A chapter in *The Creation of the British Atlantic World* (2005.44), "Jonathan Edwards, the Enlightenment, and the Formation of Protestant Tradition in America," the last of the four essays that bracket the publication of Avihu Zakai's *Jonathan Edwards's Philosophy of History* (2003.112), explores the complex interchange of British and European modes of thought on colonial America by examining Edwards's reaction to the Enlightenment and the "key role" he played in the creation both of transatlantic evangelical culture and Protestant culture in America. The first of the four, "The Conversion of Jonathan Edwards" (1998.46), traces the "crucial consequences" to Edwards's life and thought to the "signal existential moment" of his conversion described in *Personal Narrative:* the theology of God's glory, the beauty of nature, the redemptive mode of history, the "central place of revival and awakening. "Jonathan Edwards and the Language of Nature" (2002.52), the second, recognizes him as "one of the rare individuals anywhere" to take up the challenge to traditional Christian belief posed by the new science and the Enlightenment, constructing "a whole new" philosophical and theological alternative to the mechanistic interpretation of the essential nature of reality. The third, "The Ideological Context of *Sinners in the Hands of an Angry God*" (2004.81), insists that the text of probably his most famous sermon cannot be understood without the "specific ideological context" of the Great Awakening, for behind the sermon lies a "grand teleological theology of history" and the prospect of the "imminent approach" of God's impending judgment upon those refusing salvation. In the book itself, hailed as a "superb analysis" (2003.98) and a singularly "brilliant" account of *History of Redemption* (2004.56), Zakai examines Edwards's "sense of time and vision of history" and the development of his historical consciousness within the broader context of both his ideological and theological thought to account for his evangelical historiography and the "abiding importance" it has for American culture. Two years later *America's Evangelical* (2005.11), by Philip Gura, situates the "cornerstone" of his legacy to that culture in his thoughts about personal religious experience, *Faithful Narrative*, his first major publication, not his late theological treatises, "a virtual blueprint" for contemporary evangelicals and central to the "extensive" discourse of sentimentalism in antebellum America. Edwards did "nothing less than script" how evangelicals understand and embody spirituality.

That the "basic outlines" of Edwards's reflection on the Trinity was established in his notebooks and "Miscellanies" when he was twenty years old, as Amy Plantinga Pauw had earlier posited in her Yale dissertation (1990.41) and published as *"The Supreme Harmony of All"* (2002.36) — unlike the trinitarian *God of Grace*, a "beautiful theology" (2003.76), a "remarkable gift to the Christian community" (2003.83) — led, not surprisingly, to a Yale volume that numbered other "Miscellanies," the third in the series (2002.34). The first, edited by Thomas A. Schafer (1994.38), provides a table of watermarks and one of chronological parallels, Edwards's intricate table to the "Miscellanies" — his "chief means for controlling" his writing in the series and assembling materials for publication — notes on his handwriting and the varieties of ink textures, a "sophisticated" index using cross reference to and direct augmentation of earlier entries, and extended commentary on what Edwards had early called a "Rational Account." The second volume (2000.4) and the fourth (2004.72), edited, respectively, by Ava Chamberlain and Douglas Sweeney, complete the publication of this "unique source." The first of the six volumes in the series *Sermons and Discourses*, like The *"Miscellanies"* published two years earlier, opens with an introduction to the whole, though the text itself covers all but one of the sermons of Edwards's New York period, 1720-1723 (1992.8). Given his roughly 1,200 sermons — like the other manuscript sources, scheduled for the Yale website — the volumes following are necessarily more selective, publishing a representative selection from each period, those he saw through the press, those collected with varying degrees of editorial intrusion, and those made available for the first time, all read with the original manuscript at hand, edited and commented upon by Kenneth Minkema (1997.24), Mark Valeri (1999.56), M. X. Lesser (2001.25), Harry Stout, Nathan O. Hatch, with Kyle P. Farley (2003.92), and the last by the first of them, Wilson Kimnach (2006), appended to each the relevant dated and numbered sequence of sermons, a chronology devised by Schafer. Two of the remaining volumes, *Notes on Scripture* (1998.37) and The *"Blank Bible"* (2006), edited by Stephen Stein, delve into Edwards's scriptural commentary, "intriguing" in its complexity; another, *Ecclesiastical Writings* (1994.12), edited by David D. Hall, joins three published texts to an unpublished manuscript, "Narrative of Communion Controversy." Two others volumes sort through other manuscripts: for *Letters and Personal Writings* (1998.5), George Claghorn hunted down 236 of his letters, few seen before, the first to his sister Mary when he was twelve, the last to the Princeton treasurer less than a month before he died; for his *Writings on the Trinity, Grace and Faith* (2003.51) Sang Lee includes manuscript documents revealing "new aspects" of his trinitarian thought. On the golden anniversary of the first volume, *Freedom of the Will* (1957.14), the *Works* will publish the last of them, Peter Thuesen's edition of the "Catalogue," Edwards's reading list.

*   *   *

An early reader of that manuscript, Thomas H. Johnson published an essay on its "forty-three brown-paper pages" at the start of the Edwards recovery (1931.11). The following year he examined Edwards's notes on his inquiry into the "Young Folks' Bible" (1932.7); two years later he completed his Harvard dissertation, "Jonathan Edwards as a Man of Letters" (1934.4), much of it "embedded" in the introduction he shared with Clarence Faust for their *Representative Selections* (1935.3). "Edwards's ear for a prose cadence, for rise and fall and well matched vowel sounds," he wrote then, "is best seen in the sermons." At the end of the decade, working again with a "unique source," he published the poetical works of Edward Taylor, minister at Westfield, a frontier village fifteen miles southwest of Northampton, and an early opponent of Solomon Stoddard's communion practices; twenty-five years later, he edited a three-volume variorum edition of the complete poems of Emily Dickinson, born in Amherst, five miles east of Northampton and a century after Edwards assumed the pulpit there. All this is to suggest, not that editions of American poets follow hard upon the study of the manuscripts of "America's theologian," so much as that the original expression of Edwards's thought holds the promise of fresh perceptions of it.

A year after Samuel Kneeland and Timothy Green published *Distinguishing Marks* in Boston in 1741, Benjamin Franklin reprinted it in Philadelphia. The summer following, on July 28, 1743, Franklin wrote his sister Jane,

> Read the Pages of Mr. Edward's late Book entitled SOME THOUGHTS CONCERNING THE PRESENT REVIVAL OF RELIGION IN N.E. from 367 to 375; and when you judge of others, if you can perceive the Fruit to be good, don't terrify your self that the Tree may be evil, but be assur'd it is not so; for you know who has said, *Men do not gather Grapes of Thorns or Figs of Thistles.*

"Shall we read Jonathan Edwards?" the Rev. Mr. Neighbor was asked nearly a century ago. By *all* means.

An Annotated Bibliography, 1994-2005

1994

1 Cassuto, Leonard. Review of *The Trivial Sublime*, by Linda Munk. *American Literature* 66 (March): 192-93.

  Weighs the "lack of unity" in Linda Munk's study of theological language (1992.17) against the "considerable merit" of her readings of writers from Edwards to Flannery O'Connor.

2 Clayton, John. Review of *Jonathan Edwards*, by John E. Smith. *Modern Believing*, n.s., 35 (January): 49-50.

  Hopes that John E. Smith's balanced and authoritative volume (1992.25) will "help reintroduce British readers to a major thinker who at one time was more widely read here than in his own homeland."

3 Chamberlain, Ava. "Self-Deception as a Theological Problem in Jonathan Edwards's 'Treatise concerning Religious Affections.'" *Church History* 63 (December): 541-56.

  Distinguishes between Edwards's early and late responses to New Lights affectional piety, first defending it against Arminian rationalism and then attacking its "extreme radical wing" itinerants for antinomianism and enthusiasm, a "full-scale heretical movement." To Edwards, the radicals turned out "counterfeit Christians," self-deceiving hypocrites who misunderstood how justified sinners acquired assurance of salvation — not by an immediate, isolated experience but by a "repeated pattern of successful trials." Christian practice, or perseverance, was "central" to *Religious Affections*.

4 Chevreau, Guy. "A Well-Travelled Path: Jonathan Edwards and the Experiences of the Great Awakening." *Catch the Fire. The Toronto Blessing: An Experience of Renewal and Revival*. London: Marshall Pickering, pp. 70-144.

  Considers Edwards "the foremost theological architect" of the Great Awakening — like the Toronto Blessing, "another remarkable move of God" — in an encounter with his works, "one of the most helpful resources" on revival, quoting extensively from *Distinguishing Marks, Faithful Narrative, Personal Narrative, Religious Affections*, and *Some Thoughts*. Edwards's passion for religious knowledge as "*experience*, held not in the head but the heart," was known at the Airport Vineyard meetings, its manifestations "not untypical" of what he describes in *Some Thoughts* when the Spirit of God moves upon the people, their personal experiences "mirrored" in the Northampton pastor's accounts.

5 Clark, Stephen M. "Jonathan Edwards: The History of the Work of Redemption." *Westminster Theological Journal* 56 (Spring): 45-58.

Derives from *History of Redemption* three implications of "great importance" for the Edwards "agenda." First, Edwards "anticipates" the biblical-theological approach; second, the *History* is "absolutely vital" to the future of Edwards studies; and, third, the history of redemption functions as an "organizational motif" in Edwards. All other major treatises are "prolegomena."

6 Cohen, Charles L. Review of *Delightful Convictions,* by Stephen R. Yarbrough and John C. Adams. *Church History* 63 (September): 466-68.

Regrets this "highly intelligent" interpretation of Edwards's rhetoric (1993.19) "languishes amid tangential and less substantive notions" and fails to evaluate his importance in the history of elocution.

7 Cooksey, T. L. Review of *The Philosophy of Jonathan Edwards,* by Stephen H. Daniel. *Library Journal* 119 (July): 99.

Recommends Stephen Daniel's "elegant and important" study of Edwards (1994.8).

8 Daniel, Stephen H. *The Philosophy of Jonathan Edwards: A Study in Divine Semiotics.* Bloomington: Indiana University Press, ix, 212 pp.

Contrasts two fundamentally different mentalities — the classical-modern or Platonic-Aristotelian-Lockean understanding of reality (things) and the Renaissance or Stoic-Ramist understanding (communication) — placing Edwards in the latter category and explaining his philosophy through concepts developed by postmodernists Michel Foucault and Julia Kristeva. Edwards appropriates a system of signification — semiotics — in which everything is united, "signifier to signified, type to antitype," and combines ontology and logic to justify his arguments about God, the Trinity, creation, original sin, freedom, knowledge, beauty, and the figure of Christ. Edwards's semiotics distances him from the romanticism of Ralph Waldo Emerson and "draws him closer" to the American canon through Charles Sanders Peirce.

9 Doriani, Beth Maclay. Review of *One Holy and Happy Society,* by Gerald R. McDermott. *American Literature* 66 (June): 368-69.

Values Gerald R. McDermott's study of Edwards's public theology (1992.13) for its "intriguing" use of unpublished manuscripts, though its "excessive documentation makes for some labored reading."

10 Guelzo, Allen C. Review of *One Holy and Happy Society,* by Gerald R. McDermott. *American Historical Review* 99 (April): 637-38

Admires Gerald R. McDermott's "gracefully written portrait" of Edwards's public theology (1992.13), even if it "strains" at times to cast his image forward to anticipate modern concerns.

11 Gustafson, Sandra. "Jonathan Edwards and the Reconstruction of 'Feminine' Speech." *American Literary History* 6 (Summer): 185-212.

Asserts that Edwards's conversion narratives of Abigail Hutchinson and Phebe Bartlet "inaugurated an American sentimental tradition of feminine spiritual biography that flowered in the nineteenth century." *Faithful Narrative* "elevated" women in the revival culture but "muffled" the female voice; in *Some Thoughts,* five years later, Edwards removed "all traces" of gender from his wife's conversion experience, "recasting it in a nonnarrative form," a stylistic change occasioned partly by his response to the "threat to patriarchal" order inherent in "feminine erotic appeal." It was left to writers like Susan Warner and Harriet Beecher Stowe a century later to restore and transform feminine speech that Edwards "tentatively and fleetingly made available."

12 Hall, David D. "Editor's Introduction." *Ecclesiastical Writings. The Works of Jonathan Edwards,* 12. New Haven: Yale University Press, pp. 1-90.

Locates *Humble Inquiry* and *Misrepresentations Corrected* in four contexts within which the social and religious were "commingle and inseparable" — the debates and decisions about the nature of the church in Puritanism in the seventeenth and early eighteenth centuries; popular religion in Northampton as Edwards found it; Solomon Stoddard's thinking about the church; and Edwards's response to "the more radical tendencies" of the Great Awakening — reprints those treatises, and brackets them with his (unsigned) *A Letter to the Author of the Pamphlet* — about the Robert Breck affair — and "Narrative of Communion Controversy" — his account of the dispute from its inception to his dismissal. The Northampton controversy, narrow in its range, was "rooted" in the peculiar circumstances of town and church, the revivals of the 1740s, and the New England Congregational tradition. That Edwards, as a philosophical theologian, "transcended those circumstances" but was still caught up in them "cannot but remind us that he was also a person of his time and place."

13 Hall, Timothy D. *Contested Boundaries: Itinerancy and the Reshaping of the Colonial American Religious World.* Durham, N.C.: Duke University Press, x, 196 pp.

Passes over the traditional beginnings of the Great Awakening — Theodore Frelinghuysen in the 1720s and Edwards in the 1730s — to focus on George Whitefield and itinerancy. Even so, Edwards was an "exceptionally articulate, highly respected" defender of evangelical itinerancy among many such defenders and, through his *Humble Attempt,* hoped to unite Americans and Britons in a concert of prayer to revive true religion.

14 Hanley, Mark Y. *Beyond a Christian Commonwealth: The Protestant Quarrel with the American Republic, 1830-1860.* Chapel Hill: University of North Carolina Press, pp. 18-19.

Notes that Edwards "laid siege" to classical and rational assumptions in *True Virtue* and "shrilled" that to seek virtue in benevolence toward a party, nation, or creature was self-love.

15 Hardman, Keith. "Edwards: America's Greatest Theologian." *Seasons of Refreshing: Evangelism and Revivals in America.* Grand Rapids, Mich.: Baker Books, pp. 66-75.

Envisions Edwards, "standing in wig and gown behind his sacred desk," a Puritan preacher measuring the anger of a righteous God, in a brief life and estimate.

16 Jordan, Philip D. Review of *One Holy and Happy Society,* by Gerald R. McDermott. *Critical Review of Books in Religion* 7: 472-74.

Reserves a place for Gerald R. McDermott among the "important students" of Edwards for his "well-written" and "highly analytical" study (1992.13).

17 Kling, David W. Review of *Beyond a Christian Commonwealth,* by Mark Y. Hanley. *Journal of the Early Republic* 14 (Summer): 259-60.

Approves Mark Y. Hanley's "lean but ambitious revisionist" study of cultural dissent by mainline antebellum clergy (1994.14), Edwards among them.

18 Knight, Janice. *Orthodoxies in Massachusetts: Rereading American Puritanism.* Cambridge, Mass.: Harvard University Press, pp. 198-213.

Argues that Edwards's theology "significantly rehearsed" the rhetorical and doctrinal affinities of the Cambridge Brethren, chiefly Richard Sibbes and John Cotton, in a study of seventeenth-century Puritanism. Yet the correspondences between them do not constitute an argument for "meaningful continuity" as much as raise questions of the assumptions of symbolic transformations and intellectual traditions. Although Edwards articulated and experienced the voices of the Cambridge preachers, he was also "saturated" by his own time, and as such is both integral to the study and beyond it.

19 Koester, Nancy. "Enlightened Evangelicals: Benevolence in the Work of Jonathan Edwards, Charles Grandison Finney, and Samuel Simon Schmucker." Th.D. dissertation, Luther Northwestern Theological Seminary.

Reads the concept of benevolence as the "convergence" of Enlightenment ideals and evangelical commitment, the "interpretative" key to Edwards's doxology and teleology.

20 Lesser, M. X. *Jonathan Edwards: An Annotated Bibliography, 1979-1993.* Westport, Conn.: Greenwood Press, xxxi, 189 pp.

Extends an earlier annotated bibliography (1981.22) fifteen years, noting Edwards continues to be the object of "an almost relentless pursuit," yet as elusive as ever.

21 ———. Review of Jonathan Edwards, *Sermons and Discourses, 1720-1723,* ed. Wilson H. Kimnach. *New England Quarterly* 67 (June): 340-42.

Recommends Wilson Kimnach's "splendid" edition of twenty-two of Edwards's sermons (1992.8) — the first installment in the serial publication of some of the nearly 1,200 manuscript sermons in the Beinecke Library collection at Yale — its considerable introductions, "Jonathan Edwards' Art of Prophesying" and "Preface to the New York Period," testimony to his quarter century of devoted scholarship.

22 Lewis, Paul. "'The Springs of Motion': Jonathan Edwards on Emotions, Character, and Agency." *Journal of Religious Ethics* 22 (Fall): 275-97.

Sets out three contributions Edwards can make to contemporary character ethics: conceive emotions in the unity of self; construe passion as unopposed to reason; and articulate the relationship between tradition and the affective transformation of self. "Our task is . . . not to replicate his work but to emulate it."

23 Lowance, Mason I., Jr. "Biblical Typology and the Allegorical Mode: The Prophetic Strain." In *The Stowe Debate: Rhetorical Strategies in Uncle Tom's Cabin.* Edited by Mason I. Lowance, Jr., Ellen E. Westbrook, and R. C. DeProspo. Amherst: University of Massachusetts Press, pp. 159-84.

Shows how Edwards's exegetical typology (among others) helped Harriet Beecher Stowe's character formation in *Uncle Tom's Cabin,* giving specific and added "interpretive force" to figures like Uncle Tom and Simon Legree, and comments on his postmillennialism and hers.

24 Lowney, Kathleen S. Review of *Delightful Convictions,* by Stephen R. Yarbrough and John C. Adams. *Review of Religious Research* 35 (June): 365-66.

Recommends this "careful and detailed" study (1993.19) to those with an interest in Edwards and an "extensive knowledge" of eighteenth-century theology and church history.

25 MacArthur, John. *Reckless Faith: When the Church Loses Its Will to Discern.* Wheaton, Ill.: Crossway Books, pp. 162-75.

Defends Edwards and the Great Awakening — he would be "appalled" by today's laughing revival — against the "astonishing interpretation" of church history by William DeArteaga and other modern charismatics. The wailing that attended *Sinners in the Hands of an Angry God* provoked "real terror," any laughter, a joyful heart, "not just empty, spontaneous hysterics." There is "no way" Edwards can be enlisted as an apologist for modern mysticism.

26 McClymond, Michael J. "God the Measure: Towards an Understanding of Jonathan Edwards' Theocentric Metaphysics." *Scottish Journal of Theology* 47 (1): 43-59.

Demonstrates an "intimate connection" between Edwards's metaphysics and his theocentrism. His speculative thought in "The Mind" is neither "an island" among his other writings nor "an abortive project" of immaturity "abandoned" in his later work. Rather it is "a direct reflection" of what is "most permanent and enduring" in him, his "pervasive concern with the reality, centrality, and supremacy of God." As such, it "serves as a "challenge" to usual objections to the theological use of metaphysics: "The God of *this* philosopher, and the God of *this* theologian, were one and the same."

27 McDermott, Gerald R. "What Jonathan Edwards Can Teach Us about Politics." *Christianity Today* 38 (18 July): 32-35.

Registers six points of Edwards's public theology as a set of "perspectives" for contemporary evangelicals. For Edwards, the time of revival was "precisely" when the church needed to show concern and action in the public square.

28 ———. Review of *Benjamin Franklin, Jonathan Edwards, and the Representation of American Culture,* ed. Barbara B. Oberg and Harry S. Stout. *Religious Studies Review* 20 (July): 246.

Includes "some of the best current scholarship" on Edwards, Franklin, and eighteenth-century American culture (1993.13).

29 ———. Review of *Jonathan Edwards,* by John E. Smith. *Religious Studies Review* 20 (July): 247.

Calls John E. Smith's concise study (1992.25) "perhaps the best review" of Edwards for non-specialists, though he "overreaches" when he charges him with rejecting covenant theology.

30 ———. Review of Jonathan Edwards, *Sermons and Discourses, 1720-1723,* ed. Wilson H. Kimnach. *Religious Studies Review* 20 (July): 246-47.

Urges libraries to find a place for Wilson H. Kimnach's "carefully edited and elegantly written" volume (1992.8) — his general introduction "a book in itself," his decades of work on Edwards's sermons an "immeasurable service."

31 McMullen, Michael D. Review of *A Comparative Study in the Theology of Atonement in Jonathan Edwards and John McLeod Campbell,* by Michael Jinkins. *Epworth Review* 21 (January): 142-43.

Reduces the "great value" of Michael Jinkins's book (1993.8) by two "disappointing aspects" of it: it ignores changes in Edwards on limited atonement and uses him as "a straw man" for Campbell.

32 Meyer, Donald H. Review of *Benjamin Franklin, Jonathan Edwards, and the Representation of American Culture,* ed. Barbara B. Oberg and Harry S. Stout. *William and Mary Quarterly,* 3d ser., 51 (April): 330-32

Marks this "valuable" collection of essays (1993.13) as "a good starting place for deepening and revising our assessment" of Edwards and Franklin, classical figures no longer offering a "clear, transparent and unambiguous picture of our past."

33 Noll, Mark. *The Scandal of the Evangelical Mind.* Grand Rapids, Mich.: William B. Eerdmans, pp. 77-81.

Regrets that the revival tradition has "scant use for patient, comprehensive" Christian thinking, like that of Edwards, the "most intellectually subtle" reasoner in metaphysics, ethics, and epistemology in all of American evangelical history. With but few exceptions, evangelicals continue to neglect him, the "riches" of his thought virtually unknown to them, "his religious descendants."

34 Patterson, J. Daniel. Review of Jonathan Edwards, *Typological Writings,* ed. Wallace E. Anderson and Mason I. Lowance, Jr., with David H. Watters. *Early American Literature* 29 (3): 295-96.

Appreciates the "rich dialogue" between the literary scholars (Mason I. Lowance, Jr., and David H. Watters) and the academic philosopher (Wallace E. Anderson) over Edwards's typology (1993.1).

35 Pettit, Norman. Review of *Coordinates of Anglo-American Romanticism,* by Richard E. Brantley. *New England Quarterly* 67 (June): 324-28.

Leaves "open for debate" the success of Richard E. Brantley's "ambitious" study (1993.3) of links between Edwards and John Wesley.

36 Reule, Tracy Dean. "The Changing Character of New England Puritan Eschatology: 1682-1758." Ph.D. dissertation, Florida State University.

Questions some interpretations of Puritan eschatology — the work of "avid chiliasts" founded on a "millenarian core" — by noting diversity and a "measure of nuance" in the systems of Samuel Willard, Cotton Mather, and Edwards.

37 Sack, Daniel. Review of *One Holy and Happy Society,* by Gerald R. McDermott. *Pro Ecclesia* 3 (Fall): 505-507.

Contends that Gerald McDermott "enriches" Edwards scholarship (1992.13) by challenging it but is "excessively 'up-to-date'" by attempting to make him "a hero to modern church activists."

38 Schafer, Thomas A. "Editor's Introduction." *The "Miscellanies" (Entry Nos. a-z, aa-zz, 1-500). The Works of Jonathan Edwards,* 13. New Haven: Yale University Press, pp. 1-109.

Presents the first of four volumes of the complete text of the "Miscellanies" in the order in which they occur in the manuscripts, entries that span the years 1722 to 1731 — a "particularly important" time for understanding Edwards's development as a scholar and theologian — and provides a table of watermarks and one of chronological parallels, as well as Edwards's table, his "chief means for controlling" his writing in the series and assembling materials for publication, a "sophisticated" index using cross reference to and direct augmentation of earlier entries. These compositions, begun as his graduate studies at Yale ended, "preserve and reveal the genesis and incubation" of his most characteristic ideas prior to the publication of *God Glorified,* how his changing circumstances affected his writing, and how "certain fundamental convictions" arose early in his career. The "Miscellanies" invite the reader to "look over Edwards' shoulder as he improved hints, pursued clues, and penned his best thoughts." (For the remaining volumes, see 2000.4, 2002.34, and 2004.72.)

39 Schultz, Roger. Review of *Benjamin Franklin, Jonathan Edwards, and the Representation of American Culture,* ed. Barbara B. Oberg and Harry S. Stout. *Fides et Historia* 26 (Fall): 104-105.

Attributes to this "important interpretative guide" to Edwards and Franklin (1993.13) the weaknesses of such essays collections: it "sometimes" lacks coherence and becomes "too diffuse."

40 Seifrid, Mark A. Review of *One Holy and Happy Society,* by Gerald R. McDermott. *Review & Expositor* 91 (Summer): 446-47.

Accepts Gerald R. McDermott's "persuasive series of arguments" as an invitation to reevaluate Edwards's public theology (1992.13), to engage his genius "so pressingly needed at present."

41 Shea, William M. Review of *Jonathan Edwards,* by John E. Smith. *Horizons* 21 (Fall): 354-56.

Invokes John Smith's "brilliant" summary of Edwards's achievement and "historical originality" (1992.25) to explain his appeal to contemporary Americans.

42 Spencer, Stephen R., with Glenn Kreider. Review of *One Holy and Happy Society,* by Gerald R. McDermott. *Bibliotheca Sacra* 151 (October): 501-502.

Prizes Gerald R. McDermott's study of Edwards (1992.13) as a necessary "corrective" to the general misunderstanding of his public theology and "worthy of emulation" by American pastors and churches today as it was in his time.

43 Steele, Richard B. *"Gracious Affection" and "True Virtue" According to Jonathan Edwards and John Wesley.* Pietist and Wesleyan Studies, no. 5. Metuchen, N.J.: Scarecrow Press, xxv, 423 pp.

Links the lives and personal connections of the Calvinist Edwards and the Arminian John Wesley and their "extensive reciprocal influences," in a study of their "strikingly similar" experimental theologies as revealed in the five Edwards texts Wesley abridged — *Faithful Narrative, Distinguishing Marks, Some Thoughts, Religious Affections,* and *David Brainerd* — and in their "parallel" polemical writings on volition, original sin, and true virtue. Despite "obvious and significant" differences, both held that the profession of orthodox doctrine, the practice of true virtue, and the experience of gracious affection must function together in "creative and dynamic equipoise," a suffusion of elements that may serve the contemporary church much as it had theirs.

44 Stein, Stephen J. Review of *One Holy and Happy Society,* by Gerald R. McDermott. *William and Mary Quarterly,* 3d ser., 51 (January): 143-45.

Remarks "some insights" of Gerald R. McDermott's study (1992.13) but attends the "limitations" of both his method and his assumptions, particularly his "strained" reading of *Some Thoughts* and his synchronic account of Edwards's public theology.

45 Story, F. Allan, Jr. "Promoting Revival: Jonathan Edwards and Preparation for Revival." Ph.D. dissertation, Westminster Theological Seminary.

Insists that Edwards's promotion of revival depended on an "uncompromisingly Calvinistic, practical theology of preparation," a methodology "neither pragmatic nor manipulative."

46 Valeri, Mark R. *Law and Providence in Joseph Bellamy's New England: The Origins of the New Divinity in Revolutionary America.* New York: Oxford University Press, pp. 24-25.

Notes the views shared by Edwards and Bellamy on justification by faith, the distinction between public religion and genuine piety, and church membership.

47 Van Dyk, Leanne. Review of *A Comparative Study in the Theology of Atonement in Jonathan Edwards and John McLeod Campbell,* by Michael Jinkins. *Calvin Theological Journal* 29 (November): 589-91.

Commends Michael Jinkins's "fine" study (1993.8) for its "initially surprising" comparison of two "frequently misunderstood" theologians.

48 Viscardi, Christopher. Review of *Delightful Convictions,* by Stephen R. Yarbrough and John C. Adams. *Theological Studies,* 55 (March): 179-80.

Allows that Stephen Yarbrough and John Adams's scholarship on Edwards is "basically sound" and their insights "sometimes fascinating" (1993.19), but they are clearly "not conversant" with theological analysis.

49 Wainwright, William J. "The Nature of Reason: Locke, Swinburne, and Edwards." In *Reason and the Christian Religion: Essays in Honour of Richard Swinburne.* Edited by Alan Padgett. New York: Oxford University Press, pp. 91-118.

Defends the notion that reason, if "rightly disposed," is capable of knowing God by citing Edwards — the "most articulate" spokesman of the position — who places a "high value" on proofs, arguments, and inferences as well as a properly disposed heart to "see their *force.*" He believes that while reason is capable of "good rational" arguments for God's existence, defects in human nature distort it and can only be eliminated by appropriate virtues: "morally desirable character traits and rightly ordered affections." Edwards's epistemic account is "deeply embedded" in Christian tradition and should be taken "seriously" by contemporary theists; that it isn't may be ascribed, as Edwards would put, to "a failure of the heart."

50 Westerkamp, Marilyn J. Review of *Jonathan Edwards,* by John E. Smith. *Critical Review of Books in Religion* 7: 518-20.

Accounts John E. Smith's overview of Edwards's philosophy and theology (1992.25) "startlingly lucid" but finds his Northampton years "oversimplified and incomplete."

51 Westra, Helen Petter. "Confronting Antichrist: The Influence of Jonathan Edwards's Millennial Vision." In *The Stowe Debate: Rhetorical Strategies in Uncle Tom's Cabin.* Edited by Mason I. Lowance, Jr., Ellen E. Westbrook, and R. C. DeProspo. Amherst: University of Massachusetts Press, pp. 141-58.

Demonstrates that Edwards's postmillennial theology — and that of his successors, his son and grandson (Timothy Dwight), his students (Samuel Hopkins and Joseph Bellamy), and Lyman Beecher — "permeates" Harriet Beecher Stowe's *Uncle Tom's Cabin,* a novel "heavily sermonic, prophetic, and apocalyptic," its concluding paragraphs reminiscent of his imprecatory preaching. But unlike his preoccupation with anti-Christian powers in *History of Redemption,* Stowe focusses on slavery in *Uncle Tom's Cabin.* Edwards "vociferously" urged ministers to be "exemplary" Christians — "faithful collaborators in Christ's glorious work of spiritual 'redemption'" — but remained silent on the redemption of blacks from slavery.

52 Williamson, Joseph C. Review of *Benjamin Franklin, Jonathan Edwards, and the Representation of American Culture,* ed. Barbara B. Oberg and Harry S. Stout. *Theology Today* 51 (April): 190.

Values these "instructive" essays on Edwards and Franklin (1993.13), who "cast light on their own age" as well as the religion and culture of ours.

53 Ziff, Larzer. Review of *Benjamin Franklin, Jonathan Edwards, and the Representation of American Culture,* ed. Barbara B. Oberg and Harry S. Stout. *Journal of American History* 81 (September): 654-55.

Prefers those essays in the collection (1993.13) that emphasize the contrasts rather than the similarities between those "powerfully representative figures," Edwards and Franklin.

1995

1 Benfold, Gary. *God at Work? Signs of True Revival.* London: Grace Publications Trust, 94 pp.

Renders Edwards's *Distinguishing Marks* in an "easier to read and abridged" version for contemporaries who "desperately need to learn the lessons he can teach."

2 Berens, John F. Review of *Benjamin Franklin, Jonathan Edwards, and the Representation of American Culture,* ed. Barbara B. Oberg and Harry S. Stout. *Church History* 64 (June): 303-304.

Confirms that this "important" collection (1993.13) reveals "much more numerous and significant" divergences of Edwards and Franklin than convergences.

3 Brekus, Catherine A. Review of Jonathan Edwards, *The "Miscellanies," a-z, aa-zz, 1-500,* ed. Thomas A. Schafer. *Christian Century* 112 (15 November): 1089-90.

Marks this volume (1994.38) the "culmination" of Thomas A. Schafer's fifty years of work on the Edwards manuscripts, a "masterpiece of detective work."

4 Bullock, Jeffrey F. Review of *Delightful Convictions,* by Stephen R. Yarbrough and John C. Adams. *Quarterly Journal of Speech* 81 (November): 525-27.

Suggests that, though Stephen R. Yarbrough and John C. Adams's rhetorical analysis of Edwards may provide "insights" into eighteenth-century discourse (1993.19), it may have been "strengthened" by a "more substantive" link to twentieth-century literary theorists.

5 Cherry, Conrad. Review of *One Holy and Happy Society,* by Gerald R. McDermott. *American Presbyterians* 73 (Spring): 58-59.

Recommends Gerald R. McDermott's "splendid" book (1992.13), a "convincing case" for Edwards's "singular achievement for the whole of American religious history."

6 Colwell, John E. "The Glory of God's Justice and the Glory of God's Grace: Contemporary Reflections on the Doctrine of Hell in the Teaching of Jonathan Edwards." *Evangelical Quarterly* 67 (October): 291-308.

Takes to task contemporary detractors of Edwards's conception of hell, in an analysis of both their comments and his sermons. For Edwards, the justice and mercy of God are alike glorious attributes, the everlasting punishment of the wicked an "outcome and outworking" of the "ultimate triumph" of Christ. Still, his juxtaposition of God's justice and God's mercy is questionable, for in light of the Cross of Jesus, "the former is overwhelmed by the latter."

7 Conforti, Joseph A. *Jonathan Edwards, Religious Tradition, and American Culture.* Chapel Hill: University of North Carolina Press, xiv, 267 pp.

Restores Edwards to the nineteenth-century, a cultural figure "central" to America's religious past, his writings on personal piety, conversion, revivalism, and theology appropriated by Edwardseans, Nathanael Emmons and Edwards Amasa Park, Harriet Beecher Stowe and Emily Dickinson, among them. The Second Great Awakening saw the rise of seminaries and the reinvention of Edwards as a "founding father" of America's "benevolent empire," the growth of evangelical publishing houses, the popularity of *Life of Brainerd,* the spread of missions. Following the Civil War, he was recast as a "totemic figure" in colonial revivalist narratives of America's Puritan past, the Edwards celebrated nationally at his bicentennial. With his "putative neo-orthodox recovery" after a lapse of decades in the 1930s, Edwards scholarship has largely overlooked the "vital" nineteenth century.

8 Cooley, Steven D. Review of *"Gracious Affection" and "True Virtue,"* by Richard B. Steele. *Fides et Historia* 27 (Summer): 87-89.

Uncovers problems of publication, cohesion, and comprehensiveness that "impede" the "very real contributions" of Richard B. Steele's study (1994.43) of Edwards and John Wesley on the affections.

9 Davidson, Bruce W. "Reasonable Damnation: How Jonathan Edwards Argued for the Rationality of Hell." *Journal of the Evangelical Theological Society* 38 (March): 47-56.

Analyzes Edwards's doctrine of hell — that hell is consistent with God's mercy and justice, that it is an expression of God's "awesome character," that it mainly consists in the "experience of God's wrath" — and examines his responses to various objections to it. For Edwards, notions that hell neither really exists nor is merely a place of temporary suffering are "inherently illogical and self-contradictory" as well contrary to the "plain words" of Scripture. He used his doctrine to shake people out of their complacency and apathy, not by frightening them but by appealing to their reason, a treatment of hell "much more terrifying."

10 Doyle, Robert. Review of *"Gracious Affection" and "True Virtue,"* by Richard B. Steele. *Wesleyan Theological Journal* 30 (Fall): 220-22.

Questions Richard B. Steele's interpretation of the historical data concerning Edwards and John Wesley (1994.43): he "blurs" the distinctions between them to show their similarities.

11 English, John C. Review of *"Gracious Affection" and "True Virtue,"* by Richard B. Steele. *Methodist History* 33 (July): 268-69.

Parses Richard B. Steele's use of *influence* in his "thought-provoking" book (1994.43): Edwards "confirmed" certain ideas John Wesley held rather than introduced new ones to him.

12 Gerstner, Edna. *Jonathan and Sarah: An Uncommon Union. A Novel Based on the Family of Jonathan and Sarah Edwards (The Stockbridge Years, 1750-1758).* Morgan, Pa.: Soli Deo Gloria, viii, 242 pp.

Frames a novel of the "rare and beautiful relationship" between Jonathan and Sarah with the trials of their son Jonathan, from his time among the Housatonics — "No-Cry Eagle," they called the six-year-old — to the death of his wife Mary in a riding mishap and his own at fifty-six, president of Union College.

13 Gerstner, John H. *Jonathan Edwards: Evangelist.* Morgan, Pa.: Soli Deo Gloria.
    Reprints 1960.5 under a new title.

14 Grasso, Christopher. Review of *The Young Jonathan Edwards,* by William Sparkes Morris, *American Presbyterians* 73 (Spring): 59-60.
    Advises "every serious student" of Edwards to read this "erudite and meticulous" posthumous work on his early intellectual development by William S. Morris.

15 Guezlo, Allen C. "From Calvinist Metaphysics to Republican Theory: Jonathan Edwards and James Dana on Freedom of the Will." *Journal of the History of Ideas* 56 (July): 399-418.
    Remarks James Dana's commentaries on Edwards's *Freedom of the Will* (1770.2, 1773.1) — "the longest piece of sustained philosophical invective in eighteenth-century American literature" — and his sermons on republicanism as part of the discourse on the possibilities of freedom.

16 Haykin, Michael A. G. "Jonathan Edwards and His Legacy." *Reformation & Revival Journal* 4 (Summer): 65-86.
    Reduces Edwards's legacy to two issues. First, he can teach us about revival: not only did he know genuine conversion directly *(Faithful Narrative),* he had the mind and spiritual maturity to produce a "rich and profound" corpus of revival literature *(Distinguishing Marks, Some Thoughts, Humble Attempt).* Second, "and most important," he is "indispensable" to a generation largely indifferent to the glory and beauty of God *(Ruth's Resolution).*

17 ———, and Gary W. McHale. *Jonathan Edwards: The Man, His Experience, and His Theology.* Richmond Hill, Ont.: Canadian Christian Publication, 308 pp.
    Questions whether Edwards would support the Toronto Blessing, in an appraisal of his life and legacy, with extensive passages drawn chiefly from *Faithful Narrative, Distinguishing Marks, Some Thoughts,* and *Religious Affections.* That Edwards was a Calvinist, a cessationist, an "agnostic about outward manifestations," a "firm" advocate of self-control, against "holy laughter," Christ-centered, had a "high view" of preaching, and "rejoiced" in the intellect means that "the only answer that is historically accurate is 'No.'"

18 Hindmarsh, D. Bruce. "The 'Toronto Blessing' and the Protestant Evangelical Awakening of the Eighteenth Century Compared." *Crux* 31 (December): 3-13.
    Compares and contrasts the Toronto Blessing to the experience and reflections of eighteenth-century evangelicals, Edwards among them, and finds that tradition, not as something "pristine," but as a "helpful witness."

19 Jang, Kyoung-Chul. "The Logic of Glorification: The Destiny of the Saints in the Eschatology of Jonathan Edwards." Ph.D. dissertation, Princeton Theological Seminary.
    Views the saints' "active" participation in the trinitarian vision of divine glorification as communal and "healthy," in an examination of Edwards's unfolding eschatology.

20 Jinkins, Michael. "The 'True Remedy': Jonathan Edwards' Soteriological Perspective as Observed in the Revival Treatises." *Scottish Journal of Theology* 48 (2): 185-209.

Discusses Edwards's revival treatises — *Faithful Narrative, Distinguishing Marks,* and *Some Thoughts* — and his correspondence of the period as a defense against objectors and skeptics, a caution to revival participants, and a definition of his soteriology, especially the morphology of conversion, the psychology of the convert, and the pneumatology of the Spirit. The texts add "helpful insights" into his thought, as he strove to lead what he believed to be "God's 'great work' of redemption" and tried to evaluate the events around him.

21 Johnson, Ellwood. "Jonathan Edwards and the Psychology of Election." *The Pursuit of Power: Studies in the Vocabulary of Puritanism.* New York: Peter Lang, pp. 99-112.

Argues that Edwards's theology is "psychological in basis," inasmuch as everything proceeds from human nature and its limitations, both depravity and sainthood. Edwards sees behavior as "symptomatic" of sin and election, "essentially" a psychological condition, and understands the person, not the deed, is to be judged. The primary cause of behavior is the disposition of the heart, "created and affected by the divine presence," a psychological determinism.

22 ———. "Jonathan Edwards and *The Scarlet Letter.*" *The Pursuit of Power: Studies in the Vocabulary of Puritanism.* New York: Peter Lang, pp. 141-51.

Finds the psychological theories that inform Nathaniel Hawthorne's fiction "indistinguishable" from those of Edwards. Just so, the thematic ideas in *The Scarlet Letter* are "extensions" of psychological and ethical beliefs defended by Edwards in *Religious Affections* and *True Virtue,* that human nature can be defined in terms of the affections of the heart and the inclinations of the heart, sinfulness or saintliness. Still, the novel is "more radical" thematically than Edwards in that it "drifts" toward antinomianism, toward Anne Hutchinson.

23 Lambert, Frank. "The First Great Awakening: Whose Interpretive Fiction?" *New England Quarterly* 68 (December): 650-59.

Contends that eighteenth-century evangelicals — Edwards, Benjamin Colman, Thomas Prince, and John Gillies — "constructed the idea of a great and general awakening." The Northampton revival — and *Faithful Narrative* its record — became the "inspiration and model" throughout the Atlantic world of "nothing less than the second reformation, an extraordinary dispensation of grace." It was an "'interpretative fiction'" fashioned by contemporaries, not Joseph Tracy (1842.6), as Jon Butler has argued (1982.5).

24 LaShell, John K. "Jonathan Edwards and the New Sense." *Reformation & Revival Journal* 4 (Summer): 87-97.

Enlists Edwards, the "most intellectual spokesman for the revival party," to articulate the distinguishing marks of God's saving work: regeneration and justification and sanctification. Edwards saw the "organic unity" of these doctrines and added another, affection. For only through loving God, exercising benevolence towards him and taking delight in him, can we achieve a new sense of divine and spiritual things.

25 LeBeau, Bryan F. Review of *One Holy and Happy Society,* by Gerald R. McDermott. *Journal of Church and State,* 37 (Winter): 173.

Reckons Gerald R. McDermott's study (1992.13) an "impressive revisionist work well worth reading."

26 Lee, Sang Hyun. "Jonathan Edwards on Nature." In *Faithful Imagining: Essays in Honor of Richard R. Niebuhr.* Edited by Sang Hyun Lee, Wayne Proudfoot, and Albert Blackwell. Atlanta: Scholars Press, pp. 39-59.

Argues Edwards's understanding of nature in terms of his "dynamic reconception" of God and God's relation to the world; of his dispositional ontology and the special status granted nature in it; of his discrimination between nature and humanity, a relationship both mutual and distinct ; and of his theology with its "strong ecological motif" of the physical world. Nature has an "important and positive" place in Edwards's thought — from his early musings to the late "Miscellanies," from *Personal Narrative* to *End of Creation* — and may prove "helpful in the contemporary search for an ecologically responsible theology."

27 Lovelace, Richard F. "The Surprising Works of God: Jonathan Edwards on Revival, Then and Now." *Christianity Today* 39 (11 September): 28-32.

Recommends Edwards's strategy of subjecting revival to both "rigorous" criticism and extraordinary prayer, in a summary of his thought and its relevance today, especially to the Toronto renewal.

28 McClymond, Michael J. "Sinners in the Hands of a Virtuous God: Ethics and Divinity in Jonathan Edwards's *End of Creation.*" *Zeitschrift für neuere Theologiegeschichte/ Journal for the History of Modern Theology* 2 (1): 1-22.

Makes three "interrelated" claims for Edwards's *End of Creation,* among the "most brilliant" and "most neglected" theological writings of its time. First, that *End of Creation* — together with its companion piece, *True Virtue* — was Edwards's "quite innovative" response to eighteenth-century moral philosophy, especially that of Shaftesbury and Hutcheson; second, that Edwards's strategy in *Two Dissertations* consisted of "divinizing" ethics and "ethicizing" divinity; and, third, that although Edwards offers an "internally consistent perspective" on God and ethics, it rests on principles he "presupposes but does not establish." If his conclusion seems paradoxical, Edwards himself was a paradox — "at once a reasonable man of the Enlightenment age and a Calvinist of the deepest hue."

29 McCoy, Genevieve. "The Women of the ABCFM Oregon Mission and the Conflicted Language of Calvinism." *Church History* 64 (March): 62-82.

Revisits 1991.25.

30 McDermott, Gerald R. "Jonathan Edwards and the Culture Wars: A New Resource for Public Theology and Philosophy." *Pro Ecclesia* 4 (Summer): 268-80.

Proposes, contrary to "generations of scholars," that Edwards was "deeply interested" in the political and social life around him and "brimming" with ideas about Christian citizens and civil community. His ontology and social ethics mandated involvement in the life of the community "beyond the boundaries of the church." Edwards's *Nature of True Virtue* provides a "theoretical basis" for a public philosophy that provides for cooperation of Christians and non-Christians in "political projects with moral ends."

31 ———. *Seeing God: Twelve Reliable Signs of True Spirituality.* Downes Grove, Ill.: InterVarsity Press, 252 pp.

Charts the "pattern of godliness" recommended by saints over two millennia to help modern Christians regain spirituality and overcome "enduring trends" in American culture — the decline of trust in religious leaders, disenchantment with organized religion, religious pluralism, and the promotion of intellectual autonomy — borrowing chiefly from Edwards's *Religious Affections,* "the greatest work ever written on spiritual discernment." With perseverance, attention to the wisdom of masters, and trust in the grace of God, Christians today can find true spirituality as hosts of others have in ages past.

32 Meyer, William E. H., Jr. "The Unwelcomed Presupposition of American Philosophy — Eye-Epistemology: An Essay Far Beyond the Bounds of Current Interdisciplinary Scholarship." *Weber Studies* 12 (Spring): 83-94.

Cites Edwards — and Emerson — as the philosopher as "visible Christian," in an argument for the "hypervisual imperative" in American philosophy from the Puritans to the present day.

33 Mitchell, Louis Joseph. "The Experience of Beauty in the Thought of Jonathan Edwards: A Thesis." Th.D. dissertation, Harvard University.

Published as 2003.66.

34 Moore, Doreen. "Jonathan Edwards: Ministry and the Life of the Family." *Reformation & Revival Journal* 4 (Summer): 99-120.

Selects Edwards as an example of a "great" church leader who zealously served both the world and his family, in an analysis of his biblical and theological convictions that "shaped" him as a minister and husband and father. Edwards, unlike William Carey and John Wesley, left an "extraordinary" legacy to his family (and descendants) as well as to the Christian community. For Edwards, the "essence" of his duty to both was love.

35 Morimoto, Anri. *Jonathan Edwards and the Catholic Vision of Salvation.* University Park, Pa.: Pennsylvania State University, viii, 178 pp.

Claims that Edwards "learned much" from the continental Roman Catholic tradition and was "profoundly influenced" by it, in a study of the four phases of his vision of salvation — conversion, justification, sanctification, and glorification. Consistent within itself, his soteriology shows "remarkable conformity" with his general ontology, his dispositional view of reality the link between them. The strength of Edwards's soteriology is that it "fuses Protestant and Catholic concerns into one form." It is, as well, "profoundly" ecumenical.

36 ———. *Jonasan Edowazu Kenkyu: Amerika, Pyuritanizumu no Sonzai-ron to Kyusai-ron.* Tokyo: Soburisha.

Translates 1991.30. (In Japanese.)

37 New, Elisa. "Beyond the Romance Theory of American Vision: Beauty and the Qualified Will in Edwards, Jefferson, and Audubon." *American Literary History* 7 (Fall): 381-414.

Traces "certain American notions of seeing" to Edwards's *Freedom of the Will,* Thomas Jefferson's "Query IV," and selected plates from John James Audubon's *The Birds of America,* all sharing a pragmatic belief that the "experience of nature is itself a part of nature." For Edwards, "existence *is* perception," and so Being is "nowhere but in the perception of Being." The philosophy that Edwards builds on his personal theology makes attraction and fullness his "first principles," expressed in consent to beauty.

38 Noll, Mark A. "The Contested Legacy of Jonathan Edwards in Antebellum Calvinism." In *Reckoning with the Past: Historical Essays on American Evangelicalism from*

the Institute for the Study of American Evangelicals. Edited by D. G. Hart. Grand
Rapids: Baker Book House, pp. 200-17.
    Reprints 1988.31.

39 ———. Review of Jonathan Edwards, *Ecclesiastical Writings,* ed. David D. Hall. *Wil-*
liam and Mary Quarterly, 3d ser., 52 (July): 554-57
    Lauds David Hall's "nonpareil understanding of an obscure corner" of Edwards career
    (1994.12), illuminating not only his mind but also the "lives, hopes, and expectations" of his pa-
    rishioners.

40 Oliphint, K. Scott. "Jonathan Edwards: Reformed Apologist." *Westminster Theologi-*
cal Journal 57 (Spring): 165-86.
    Explicates Edwards as a Reformed apologist and incorporates his insights on ontology and
    unregenerate man into a "presuppositional or transcendental," not a classical, framework of
    apologetics. Edwards's insights can offer "stimulating applications" to the apologetics of
    Cornelius Van Til: both believed in the "noetic influence" of sin in the unbeliever and God's "re-
    velatory exigency;" both gave "full weight" to man's logical capacities; both wrote of the "abso-
    lute necessity" of God's revelation as the backdrop for "any reasoning, any thinking, any apolo-
    getic."

41 Pauw, Amy Plantinga. "'Heaven Is a World of Love': Edwards on Heaven and the
Trinity." *Calvin Theological Journal* 30 (November): 392-401.
    Plumbs Edwards's "deep fascination" with heaven and the place his doctrine of the Trinity
    has in it. The social and psychological conceptions of the Trinity come together "more harmoni-
    ously" in his reflections on heaven than anywhere else in Edwards, the psychological analogy es-
    pecially to explain "by far" his most innovative aspect of heaven, the reciprocity between the
    progressive increase of the saints' love of God and the increase of God's glory. Edwards's notions
    of heavenly dynamism appear "strangely contemporary," proof yet again of his "enduring signif-
    icance."

42 Payne, Rodger M. Review of *Benjamin Franklin, Jonathan Edwards, and the Repre-*
sentation of American Culture, ed. Barbara B. Oberg and Harry S. Stout. *Journal of*
Religion 75 (April): 281-82.
    Hopes the next comparative study of Franklin and Edwards — "these (non?) representatives"
    — will clarify issues of consensus and modernity left unresolved in this collection (1993.13).

43 Piper, John. "The Debt I Owe to Jonathan Edwards." *The Purifying Power of Living by*
Faith in Future Grace. Sisters, Ore.: Multnomah Publishers, pp. 385-99.
    Attempts to show that Christian hedonism stands in "faithful continuity" with the thinking
    of Edwards by, first, explaining Edwards's "pejorative" and "positive" uses of self-love, and, then,
    discussing at length whether *disinterested* "really mean[s]" *disinterested,* in a series of quotations
    from *True Virtue,* "rough sledding" for some readers. When Edwards writes of *disinterested* love
    to God, he means a love "grounded not in a desire for God's gifts, but in a desire for God him-
    self"; it is "*not* an anti-hedonistic word," as he uses it.

44 Ricketts, Allyn Lee. "The Primacy of Revelation in the Philosophical Theology of
Jonathan Edwards." Ph.D. dissertation, Westminister Theological Seminary.
    Affirms that, contrary to some current views, Edwards followed Puritan and Reformed tradi-

tion "without hesitation," despite lapses in language and thought that at times "clouded and obscured" his foundational faith in revelation.

45 Smith, John E. "Puritanism and Enlightenment: Franklin and Edwards." In *Knowledge and Belief in America: Enlightenment Traditions and Modern Religious Thought.* Edited by William B. Shea and Peter A. Huff. [Washington, D.C.]: Woodrow Wilson Center Press; New York: Cambridge University Press, pp. 195-226.

Considers Edwards and Benjamin Franklin "representative men" (Ralph Waldo Emerson's term), those who inherit a tradition and reinterpret it. Edwards was a preacher of "uncommon ability" (*God Glorified* and *Divine and Supernatural Light*); a polemicist on revivals and church polity *(Faithful Narrative, Religious Affections, Some Thoughts,* and *Humble Inquiry);* an apologist for Reformed doctrine *(Freedom of the Will* and *Original Sin);* a speculative thinker *(True Virtue, End of Creation,* the "Miscellanies," *Essay on the Trinity, The Mind,* and *Of Being);* and a sacred historian *(History of Redemption).* He transformed Puritanism through his idea of religious affections — the sense of things — appealing to experience and its "aesthetic overtones," combatting the "uncontrolled emotionalism" of evangelicalism. And he had a "remarkable" vision of a world community, not only of religion but also of science ("Miscellanies," no. 26, Millennium), that "definitely" places him in the modern world, a figure of the Enlightenment.

46 ———, Harry S. Stout, and Kenneth P. Minkema. "Editors' Introduction." *A Jonathan Edwards Reader.* New Haven: Yale University Press, vii-xl.

Details the contents of an anthology of the public Edwards — his printed speculations and notebooks, *Faithful Narrative,* three sermons, and his major treatises, in "essentially" chronological order — and the personal Edwards — his autobiographical writings, correspondence, and family papers, illustrative of "his humanity and the mores of [his] age" — in a volume compiled by three editors of the Yale Edwards, expressing the "range and depth" of "colonial America's greatest theologian and philosopher" and replacing the out-of-print *Representative Selections* (1935.3 and 1962.2).

47 Steele, Richard B. "John Wesley's Synthesis of the Revival Practices of Jonathan Edwards, George Whitefield, Nicholas von Zinzendorf." *Wesleyan Theological Journal* 30 (Spring): 154-72.

Details John Wesley's "hybrid" revival practice: from Edwards he "borrowed his spiritual diagnostics" and learned the value of revival narrative and spiritual autobiography.

48 Sweeney, Douglas Allen. "Nathaniel William Taylor and the Edwardsian Tradition: Evolution and Continuity in the Culture of the New England Theology." Ph.D. dissertation, Vanderbilt University.

Published (revised) as 2003.97.

49 Tiller, John. Review of *Jonathan Edwards,* by John E. Smith. *Anvil* 12 (1): 92-93.

Regrets that John E. Smith's "clear introduction" to Edwards's thought (1992.25) is the only volume of the Outstanding Christian Thinkers series not yet available in paperback.

50 Valeri, Mark R. Review of *Benjamin Franklin, Jonathan Edwards, and the Representation of American Culture,* ed. Barbara B. Oberg and Harry S. Stout. *American Studies* 36 (Spring): 145-46

Reports what this "splendid" collection of essays (1993.13) "can teach us much" about Edwards and Franklin when taken "on their terms."

51 Viscardi, Christopher J. Review of Jonathan Edwards, *Typological Writings,* ed. Wallace E. Anderson and Mason I. Lowance Jr., with David H. Watters. *Theological Studies,* 56 (March): 194-95.

Appreciates the editors' "painstaking efforts" (1993.1) to situate Edwards in a theological and historical context and their valuable introduction to the "whole question" of biblical typology.

52 Wainwright, William J. "Jonathan Edwards and the Heart." *Reason and the Heart: A Prolegomenon to a Critique of Passional Reason.* Ithaca, N.Y.: Cornell University Press, pp. 7-54.

Divides Edwards's "carefully elaborated" rational arguments for the authority of the gospels into four parts: his "ambiguous" attitudes toward reason; the "epistemic consequences" of the new heart of the converted; the moral and spiritual qualifications necessary to appreciate evidence for religious truths; and his relation to evidentialism. Although a philosophical heir of rationalism and a theological heir of a tradition that "distrusted" reason, he succeeded in "coherently" weaving these inconsistent strands together. For Edwards, one's "passional nature" is sometimes necessary to "evaluate the evidence properly" and to "assess its force accurately."

53 ———. Review of *Jonathan Edwards,* by John E. Smith. *Faith and Philosophy* 12 (April): 291-94.

Assesses John E. Smith's study of Edwards (1992.25) a "useful and generally reliable" introduction, his remarks occasionally "unclear or doubtful."

54 Westblade, Donald. Review of *One Holy and Happy Society,* by Gerald R. McDermott. *Journal of the Evangelical Theological Society* 38 (September): 453-56.

Urges "everyone" concerned about the relationship of Christians to society to read and consider Gerald R. McDermott's "impressive" study (1992.13).

1996

1 Abzug, Robert H. Review of *Jonathan Edwards, Religious Tradition, and American Culture,* by Joseph A. Conforti. *William and Mary Quarterly,* 3d ser., 53 (October): 815-17

Considers "odd" Joseph A. Conforti's "uncritical acceptance" of the concept of the Second Great Awakening in his "extremely worthwhile" study (1995.7) of the appropriation of Edwards by "religious and cultural insurgents."

2 Bozeman, T. D. Review of *Jonathan Edwards and the Catholic Vision of Salvation,* by Anri Morimoto. *Choice* 33 (March): 1152.

Notes that Anri Morimoto's attempt to promote twentieth-century ecumenical concerns in his "selective" study of Edwards's theology (1995.35) "underestimates historical confessional differences."

3 Campbell, John McLeod. *The Nature of the Atonement.* Grand Rapids, Mich.: William B. Eerdmans.

Reprints 1856.3.

4 Canup, John. Review of *The Young Jonathan Edwards,* by William Sparkes Morris. *Church History* 65 (December): 720-21.

Values William S. Morris's "most exhaustive single commentary" (1991.32) of Edwards's formative years, however "long overdue" its publication.

5 Chamberlain, Ava. Review of *Jonathan Edwards,* by M. X. Lesser. *Church History* 65 (June): 347-48.

Rates M. X. Lesser's latest bibliography (1994.20) a "useful and informative" guide to the "remarkably productive Edwards industry."

6 Chironna, Paul. "Following Edwards." *Christian Century* 113 (1 May): 491-94.

Wonders whether Joseph A. Conforti's "important contribution" may also succeed in "undermining" Edwards's relevance today, in a review of *Jonathan Edwards, Religious Tradition, and American Culture* (1995.7).

7 Conforti, Joseph A. Review of *Jonathan Edwards and the Catholic Vision of Salvation,* by Anri Morimoto. *Church History* 65 (December): 721-23.

Uncovers problems of historical interpretation in Anri Morimoto's study (1995.35), the "so-called Catholic concern" in Edwards a "creative extension" of Sang Lee's dispositional ontology applied to soteriology.

8 Daniel, Stephen H. Review of *Jonathan Edwards and the Catholic Vision of Salvation,* by Anri Morimoto. *William and Mary Quarterly,* 3d ser., 53 (October): 817-19.

Calls Anri Morimoto's use of dispositional ontology to account for Edwards's theory of salvation (1995.35) a "strength," though it is "descriptive, not explanatory."

9 Davies, Ronald E. *Jonathan Edwards and His influence on the Development of the Missionary Movement from Britain.* Cambridge: Currents in World Christianity Project, 23 pp.

Surveys Edwards's influence on the missionary movements of Baptists, Independents, Church of Scotland, Church of England, and Methodists and finds that although his influence was felt throughout denominations in Great Britain, it was felt "most powerfully" among those where Calvinism was the "dominant" theology.

10 Edwards, Rem B. Review of *The Philosophy of Jonathan Edwards,* by Stephen H. Daniel, and Jonathan Edwards, *The "Miscellanies," (Entry Nos. a-z, aa-zz, 1-500),* ed. Thomas A. Schafer. *Review of Metaphysics* 50 (December): 396-99

Terms "impressive" Stephen H. Daniel's treatment of the "almost totally neglected" aspects of Edwards's thought (1994.8) but "overly sanguine" of his successes; and "incredible" Thomas A. Schafer's account of his "herculean hermeneutical efforts" on the "Miscellanies" (1994.38) uncovering the "immense variety" of Edwards's philosophical and theological interests in an "intriguing" volume.

11 Evans, C. Stephen. "Towards a Subjective Objectivity." *Cross Currents* 46 (Winter): 567-69.

Remarks William J. Wainwright's willingness to pose "tough, critical questions" in his "careful, sympathetic" exposition of Edwards on religious truth, in a review of his *Reason and the Heart* (1995.52).

12 Evans, William Borden. "Imputation and Impartation: The Problem of Union with Christ in Nineteenth-Century American Reformed Theology." Ph.D. dissertation, Vanderbilt University.

Groups Edwards with Samuel Hopkins and Timothy Dwight as rejecting forensic imputation, defining union with Christ in terms of sanctification, and, ultimately, dispensing with union as a comprehensive theme, in a study of nineteenth-century imputation and impartation.

13 Gerstner, John H. *Jonathan Edwards: A Mini-Theology.* Morgan, Pa.: Soli Deo Gloria.

Reprints 1987.8.

14 Gould, Philip. Review of *Jonathan Edwards, Religious Tradition, and American Culture,* by Joseph A. Conforti. *American Literature* 68 (December): 849-50.

Endorses Joseph A. Conforti's "convincing" study (1995.7) of "politicized reinventions of a protean" Edwards but notes its "limitations" addressing the politics of gender in antebellum America.

15 Grasso, Christopher. "Images and Shadows of Jonathan Edwards." *American Literary History* 8 (Winter): 683-98.

Holds that Edwards "remains a profoundly engaging puzzle," in an essay-review of four books: *Typological Writings* (1993.1) reveals how "closely" tied Edwards's typological method was to his theology and metaphysics; *Benjamin Franklin, Jonathan Edwards, and the Representation of American Culture* (1993.13) avoids at times the "constraints of the compare/contrast model" to the benefit of the whole; *Delightful Conviction* (1993.19) "leap[s] too quickly" from theological division to rhetorical analogy and weakens itself by a textual problem; and *One Holy and Happy Society* (1992.13) "challenges much of current thinking about Edwards's social and political ideas."

16 ———. Review of *The Philosophy of Jonathan Edwards,* by Stephen H. Daniel. *American Literature* 68 (March): 230-31.

Notes Stephen H. Daniel's "original and provocative" study of Edwards (1994.8) other readers have missed, "dense explications" that open up "new territory" for further philosophical investigation.

17 Guelzo, Allen C. Review of *Jonathan Edwards,* by John E. Smith, and *The Neglected Northampton Texts,* by Richard A. S. Hall. *Christian Scholar's Review* 25 (4): 528-31.

Considers John E. Smith's study (1992.25) a "Michelin guide" to the Yale Edwards but one hampered by the lack of recent scholarship, a "significant defect." Richard A. S. Hall's study (1990.22) points in a "diametrically opposite direction," focussing on only four texts but often "overplaying" the neglected aspect of them. Yet it is "striking" how Perry Miller (1949.9) still sets a "large part" of the agenda of Edwardsean interpretation in both: it is time for his shadow to "dissolve."

18 ———. "(Re)Inventing Jonathan Edwards." *Harvard Divinity Bulletin* 25 (2): 18-19.

Takes pleasure in Joseph A. Conforti's "rare and delightful" cultural feast but finds Edwards himself "missing" from the table, in an essay-review of *Jonathan Edwards, Religious Tradition, and American Culture* (1995.7).

19 Hall, Dewey W. "From Edwards to Emerson: A Study of the Teleology of Nature." In *Early Protestantism and American Culture.* Edited by Michael Schuldiner. Studies in Puritan American Spirituality, 5. Lewiston, N.Y.: Mellen Press, pp. 123-47.

> Delineates how the metaphysics of Edwards and Emerson each "turns upon itself," in a study of *Images or Shadows* and *Nature* and Perry Miller's reading of both. Each reorders his system of thought within the context of his philosophy — Edwards applying biblical typology to his sense of divinity in the created world, Emerson reducing divinity and nature to a psychological scheme, the "quintessential American self" — though each "subverts and undercuts" it. The "intellectual continuity" between rests on this, not some notion of Edwards's liberalism.

20 Hambrick-Stowe, Charles E. *Charles G. Finney and the Spirit of American Evangelicalism.* Grand Rapids, Mich.: William B. Eerdmans, pp. 16-19.

> Proposes that Charles Finney's reading of Edwards, especially *Life of Brainerd,* may have "colored" his own story, but that he was "conditioned" from youth by earlier Puritan narratives of conversion.

21 Hannah, John D. "Jonathan Edwards, the Toronto Blessing, and the Spiritual Gifts: Are the Extraordinary Ones Actually the Ordinary Ones?" *Trinity Journal,* n.s., 17 (Fall): 167-89.

> Analyzes the evidence and counter-evidence for the use of Edwards as a defender of the physical manifestations of the Toronto Blessing and concludes that he should not be used to "validate" either the experiences of many or the hopes of "charismatic renewalism in end times." Edwards was neither a charismatic Christian nor a believer in extraordinary gifts for end times. His eschatological vision was based on the effusion of the Spirit, the "fruit" of gospel preaching, the triumph of godliness.

22 Holifield, E. Brooks. Review of Jonathan Edwards, *Ecclesiastical Writings,* ed. David D. Hall. *Church History* 65 (June): 285-86.

> Remarks David D. Hall's "breadth of vision and learning" in his "superb" introduction to one more "commendable" volume in the Yale edition of Edwards's writings (1994.12).

23 ———. Review of *Jonathan Edwards, Religious Tradition, and American Culture,* by Joseph A. Conforti. *Church History* 65 (December): 789-91.

> Rates the research "excellent" in Joseph A. Conforti's (1995.7), the prose "clear and attractive," the argument "thoughtful" — in all, scholarship of a "high order" indeed.

24 Ingebretsen, Edward J. Review of *Jonathan Edwards, Religious Tradition, and American Culture,* by Joseph A. Conforti. *Christianity and Literature* 45 (Spring): 437-39.

> Suggests that Joseph A. Conforti's revisionist critique of Edwards's place in American cultural history (1995.7) could have been "stronger" if it had included commentary from "extra-theological sources," Melville, Poe, Holmes, and Twain, among others.

25 Kling, David W. "The New Divinity and Williams College, 1793-1836." *Religion and American Culture* 6 (Summer): 195-223.

Recalls how on three different occasions the "powerful Williams clan challenged Edwards's convictions," in a reassessment of the influence New Divinity had on Williams College.

26 Knebel, Sven K. "Jonathan Edwards's Moral Necessity, or How to Defend Calvinism in Eighteenth-Century New England." *The Modern Schoolman* 73 (January): 129-39.

Traces the provenance of Edwards's moral necessity in *Freedom of the Will* to two Sevillan Jesuits, Diego Ruiz de Montoya and Diego Granado, and a Portuguese Franciscan, Jeronimo de Sousa. Edwards did not invent the moral necessity type of compatabilism, but as a Calvinist he was "simply better off" than his Latin sources in offering "a coherent theory": the Church "abandoned and ejected" the doctrine "just for being 'Calvinist.'"

27 Kreider, Glenn. Review of *A Jonathan Edwards Reader,* ed. John E. Smith, Harry S. Stout, and Kenneth P. Minkema. *Bibliotheca Sacra,* 153 (April): 239-40.

Approves the selection of works (1995.46) as a "manageable and affordable introduction" to Edwards for both the classroom and personal and devotional reading.

28 Lee, Sang Hyun. Review of *Jonathan Edwards,* by John E. Smith. *Journal of Theological Studies* ns 47 (October): 766-68.

Ranks John E. Smith's "brilliant and readable" slim volume (1992.25) with Perry Miller's study (1949.9) as "perhaps the two best introductory texts" to the thought of Edwards.

29 Lowance, Mason, Jr. "Jonathan Edwards: The Old and the New — Writing as Revelation." In *Making America/Making American Literature.* Edited by Robert A. Lee and W. M. Verhoeven. Amsterdam: Rodopi, pp. 59-76.

Shows the "considerable" influence of Nicolas Malebranche and the Cambridge Platonists, including John Norris and Henry More, upon Edwards's epistemological writings and articulates the connections among his contemporaries, like John Locke, in an examination of his typology of nature. Edwards transforms the authority of Scripture revelation to the "symbolic language" of the natural world, such that the type represents a "spiritual idea in a timeless fashion," as expressed in *History of Redemption,* and reveals God's divine purpose for man. He goes "far beyond" the first generation of Puritans in stressing the importance of sense perception in ways that "anticipate" the Transcendentalists, Emerson's *Nature,* for example, and Thoreau's *Walden.*

30 McClymond, Michael J. Review of *The Philosophy of Jonathan Edwards,* Stephen H. Daniel. *Journal of Religion* 76 (January): 121-22.

Allows that Stephen H. Daniel's study (1994.8) performs a "useful service" by depicting Edwards's philosophy as a "seamless garment," but it highlights typology at the expense of other aspects of it.

31 McCoy, Genevieve E. Review of *Jonathan Edwards, Religious Tradition, and American Culture,* by Joseph A. Conforti. *Fides et Historia* 28 (Summer): 98-99.

Endorses Joseph A. Conforti's "long needed assessment" (1995.7) of Edwards's influence in American religious and cultural history from a contemporary and interdisciplinary perspective.

32 McDermott, Gerald R. "Father of Our Churchly Soul." *Cross Currents* 46 (Fall): 426-28.

Counts Joseph A. Conforti's survey (1995.7) of Edwards's influence and reinvention "richly textured and engagingly written," in a review of *Jonathan Edwards, Religious Tradition, and American Culture.*

33 ———. Review of Jonathan Edwards, *Typological Writings,* ed. Wallace E. Anderson and Mason I. Lowance Jr., with David H. Watters. *Church History* 65 (March): 109-10.

Discovers in Edwards's treatises on typology "some of the most suggestive material" yet published in the Yale edition (1993.1), the editors' introductions both "lucid and learned."

34 ———. Review of *The Philosophy of Jonathan Edwards,* Stephen H. Daniel. *William and Mary Quarterly,* 3d ser., 53 (July): 658-60

Considers Stephen H. Daniel's postmodern analysis (1994.8) "provocative and at times brilliant" but questions whether Edwards was a postmodernist.

35 Miller, Gordon. "Jonathan Edwards' Sublime Book of Nature." *History Today* 46 (July): 29-35.

Locates in Edwards, influenced as he was by Isaac Newton's *Opticks* and John Locke's treatise on language in *Essay concerning Human Understanding,* a possible route to a "re-enchantment of nature." Edwards "extended and enhanced" the Puritan doctrine of the immanence of God in creation, especially in *Images or Shadows.* That kind of spiritual reading of the book of nature in the eighteenth century was taken up by the Transcendentalists and John Muir in the nineteenth.

36 Minkema, Kenneth P. Review of *Contested Boundaries,* by Timothy D. Hall. *Journal of Religion* 76 (October): 641-42.

Contends that Timothy Hall overstates the "significance" of itinerancy and so misses "nuances among moderates" — like Edwards — and the "class nature" of the conflict between laity and clergy.

37 ———. Review of *Jonathan Edwards and the Catholic Vision of Salvation,* by Anri Morimoto, and *Jonathan Edwards, Religious Tradition, and American Culture,* by Joseph A. Conforti. *Journal of American History* 83 (September): 599-601.

Finds that Anri Morimoto's ahistorical, ecumenical perspective (1995.35) leads to "misrepresentation," his concentration on Edwards's philosophical treatises to a lack of balance; Joseph A. Conforti's "valuable" historical perspective (1995.7), on the other hand, furthers our understanding of Edwards and his hold on our imagination.

38 Moser, P. K. Review of *Reason and the Heart,* by William J. Wainwright. *Choice* 33 (April): 1325.

Values William J. Wainwright's arguments (1995.52) for taking an "Edwards-style" notion of reason seriously.

39 Navone, John, S.J. "A teologia do belo segundo Jonathan Edwards." *Cultura e Informacao* (Broteria) 142 (March): 331-41.

Discloses the harmony between the teachings of St. Thomas Aquinas and Edwards on the nature of divine beauty, in a reading of the Protestant American philosopher, theologian, and pastor. (In Portuguese.)

40 Niebuhr, H. Richard. "The Anachronism of Jonathan Edwards." In *Theology, History, and Culture: Major Unpublished Writings.* Edited by William Stacy Johnson. New Haven: Yale University Press, pp. 123-33.

Rejects Vernon Louis Parrington's judgment of Edwards as an anachronism (1927.2), a judgment that persists in America, American Protestantism, and literary, academic, and even "most theological circles," in an address delivered at the First Church of Christ, Congregational, in Northampton, on 9 March 1958, to commemorate the bicentennial of his death (1958.3). "There is no really honest and consistent way of honoring Edwards at all this day except in the context of honoring, of acknowledging and renewing our dedication to his cause" — the glory of God.

41 ———. "The Anachronism of Jonathan Edwards." *Christian Century* 113 (1 May): 480-85.

Excerpts 1996.40.

42 Pahl, Jon. Review of *The Philosophy of Jonathan Edwards,* by Stephen H. Daniel. *Church History* 65 (September): 506-507.

Appreciates Stephen H. Daniel's book (1994.8) for confirming his (1992.19), as well as for illuminating Edwards's philosophy by breathing "considerable life into an eighteenth-century system of signs."

43 Pauw, Amy Plantinga. Review of *The Philosophy of Jonathan Edwards,* by Stephen H. Daniel. *Calvin Theological Journal* 31 (April): 236-37.

Consigns Stephen H. Daniel's post-structuralist analysis of Edwards's philosophy (1994.8) to "academic libraries"; those with a theological interest in signs might "more profitably" read the introduction to Edwards's *Typological Writings* (1993.1).

44 Piper, John. *Desiring God: Meditation of a Christian Hedonist.* Sisters, Ore.: Multnomah.

Reprints 1986.31A.

45 Spohn, William C. "Jonathan Edwards and Ignatius Loyola." In *Finding God in All Things: Essays in Honor of Michael J. Buckley, S.J.* Edited by Michael J. Himes and Stephen J. Pope. New York: Crossroad Publishing Co., pp. 244-61.

Compares the practical advice on judging religious experience by the two "masters" of Christian discernment, Edwards in *Religious Affections* and Ignatius Loyola in *The Spiritual Exercises.* Despite "significant differences" in their theology and traditions, the Puritan divine and the Basque mystic offer "convergent" accounts, that conversion transforms religious experience, that the affections are the center of transformation, that they are evidence of religious discernment, that they are the media of God's inspiration. Both conclude that "those who find all things in God will be able to find God in all things."

46 Stein, Stephen J., ed. *Jonathan Edwards's Writings: Text, Context, Interpretation.* Bloomington: Indiana University Press, xix, 219 pp.

Publishes a dozen essays in three parts — text: integrating unpublished manuscripts and public texts; context: interpreting texts and identifying influences; and interpretation: identifying and claiming the Edwardsean tradition — papers first delivered at Indiana University, Bloomington, 2-4 June 1994.

Stein, Stephen J. "Introduction," pp. ix-xix. Notes that the essayists in the volume share the desire to make their views "accessible to a wide audience" and take Edwards's written texts with "seriousness," in a summary of each of the papers.

Chamberlain, Ava. "Brides of Christ and Signs of Grace: Edwards's Sermon Series on the Parable of the Wise and Foolish Virgins," pp. 3-18. Argues that Edwards had both a pastoral and speculative interest in writing on the parable of the wise and foolish virgins (Matt. 25:1-12), the first of three extended sermon series — the others were published, in time, as *Charity and its Fruits* and *History of Redemption* — preached between the end of the Northampton revival and the beginning of the Great Awakening. As pastor, Edwards was responding to the economic instability and spiritual declension that followed the Northampton revival and used the text to examine the covenant of marriage and the covenant of grace, to address both domestic order and the life of faith. As a theologian, Edwards examined the anatomy of self-deception, the signs of grace, and the means of assurance in the nineteen sermons, a prolegomenon of sorts to the "final product" of such speculation almost a decade later, *Religious Affections*.

Grasso, Christopher. "Misrepresentations Corrected: Jonathan Edwards and the Regulation of Religious Discourse," pp. 19-38. Demonstrates how Edwards tried to regulate public religious discourse, especially as it bore upon the communion controversy, in an analysis of unpublished manuscript sermons, early and late, and rhetorical responses to *Humble Inquiry*. Edwards's efforts involved insisting that the minister, not the parishioners, "set the terms" of the debate; clearing away ambiguity and confusion from the diverse use of signs; defining both the meaning and the significance of "visible saints"; and restricting the use of "flattering" terms such as "God's Covenant people." Attempts by his New Divinity followers to continue controlling public religious discourse only "fueled antagonisms" between laity and clergy.

McDermott, Gerald R. "The Deist Connection: Jonathan Edwards and Islam," pp. 39-51. Considers Edwards's series of vitriolic attacks against Islam in his last decade a "foil" for deism — the "most dangerous" of enemies of Reformed Christianity — in a study of the late "Miscellanies" (and transcriptions of several in Edward Hickman's 1834 edition of the *Works*) and *Notes on Scripture* (1988.37). Edwards argues that, unlike Christianity, Islam retards knowledge, not advances it; preaches "sensual rewards," not self-denial; appeals to "base human desires," not meekness; and rests on private miracles, not public, witnessed ones — an argument common to orthodox controversialists of the eighteenth century. Elsewhere, however, Edwards held that there was "substantial and genuine truth" in non-Christian religions; but for his battle against deism, he might have "learned something from Islam as well."

Minkema, Kenneth P. "The Other Unfinished 'Great Work': Jonathan Edwards, Messianic Prophecy, and 'The Harmony of the Old and New Testament,'" pp. 52-65. Remarks the background and design of Edwards's "virtually unknown" 500-page manuscript, "The Harmony of the Old and New Testament," yet another example — "Notes on Scripture" and the "Blank Bible" are others — of his exegetical turn of mind. Within the tripartite structure — the Old Testament prophecies of the coming of Christ fulfilled in the New; the typological links between the two; and the harmony inherent in them — Edwards not only dissected words and "exhaustively" cited parallel texts to make the argument, he gathered an eclectic array authorities, ancient and modern, orthodox and non-conformist to underpin it. It was this "great work," as Edwards called it, that tempered the Princeton invitation to leave his Stockbridge study.

Lucas, Paul R. "'The Death of the Prophet Lamented': The Legacy of Solomon Stoddard," pp. 69-84. Examines the sources of influence upon Solomon Stoddard and his upon Edwards, in a study of the "peculiar circumstances" of the Connecticut Valley in the late seventeenth- and early eighteenth century and the "pivotal role" William Prynne, John Knox, and Samuel Rutherford played in his thought. Despite Edwards's rejection of "notable features" of his ministry — his instituted church, open communion, and converting ordinances — Stoddard's legacy, as much as his grandson's, "anticipates and helps explain" revivalism and evangelicalism in nineteenth-century America and the "amazing successes" of Protestant denominations. These churches shared with Stoddard a sense of nationalism, mission, and militancy, "looked again" as he had, to preaching and ordinances to convert the ungodly, to transform society.

Stoever, William K. B. "The Godly Will's Discerning: Shepard, Edwards, and the Identification of True Godliness," pp. 85-99. Explores the continuities between Thomas Shepard and Edwards on the evidence of true godliness, in a reading of Shepard's *The Parable of the Ten Virgins Unfolded* (1660) and Edwards's unpublished series of nineteen sermons on Matt. 25:1-13, *Religious Affections,* and *Charity and its Fruits.* Edwards developed his position with "conscious attention" to Shepard's, which he asserted in a "rigorous and provocative" way following the Northampton revival. But Edwards's "searching thoroughness" of the delineation of true godliness may have removed it from the "realm of practical realization."

Hall, Richard A. S. "Did Berkeley Influence Edwards?: Their Common Critique of the Moral Sense Theory," pp. 100-121. Uncovers "remarkable continuities" of thought between George Berkeley's *Alciphron, or the Minute Philosopher* (1732) and Edwards's *True Virtue* (1765) in their critique of moral sense theory, an attempt to gauge the "alleged" influence of one on the other, to frame the context of each and its public reception, and the "larger significance" of the parallels between the two. Even if the continuities are insufficient to settle the problem of influence "once and for all," they are still noteworthy: first, because they constitute a "trenchant Christian apologetics" against deists; second, because they indicate Berkeley's influence in America; and, third, because they "further embed" Edwards's thought in its European context and reveal that he is not the "theological aberration" so often portrayed. Edwards did "nothing more eccentric" than defend the faith.

Proudfoot, Wayne. "Perception and Love in *Religious Affections,*" pp. 122-36. Questions the parallel usually drawn between William James's *Varieties of Religious Experience* (1902) and Edwards's *Religious Affections* (and, in passing, his use of John Locke in it). The "sophistication," the complexity and subtlety, of Edwards's analysis of self-knowledge, self-deception and the "vagaries of the moral will," and the virtues of the saint are "more akin" to the thought of Augustine, Calvin, and Kierkegaard than to James and, as well, are sorely "lacking in much contemporary literature" on religious experience. Edwards shifts the focus from first-person accounts of the "new sense" perception of the divine to make the concept of love "central," exploring the relationship of it to its objects and manifestations. "*Religious Affections* is a treatise about love and the assessment of loves."

Sweeney, Douglas A. "Nathaniel William Taylor and the Edwardsian Tradition: A Reassessment," pp. 139-58. Insists that, contrary to recent historiographical trends, Nathaniel William Taylor did "build upon, engage, and forward" Edwards's legacy, in an account of nineteenth-century Edwardsean "enculturation" of Calvinist New England. Neither an Arminian nor an Old Calvinist, Taylor's claims of doing Edwardsean theology was "neither intentionally nor unintentionally deceptive," as he sought new ways to promote Calvinist doctrines of grace. His "pragmatic perpetuation" of this culture, although it angered more cautious Edwardsean "guardians of the past," contributed greatly to the diffusion and accessibility of Edwards's influence throughout America.

Guelzo, Allen C. "Oberlin Perfectionism and Its Edwardsian Origins, 1835-1870," pp. 159-74. Challenges the conventional view of perfectionism as an "enthusiastic aberration" of Jacksonian impulses, in a study of the "complex but clear" relationship between Charles Grandison Finney, the revivalist and professor of moral philosophy and theology at Oberlin College, and Edwards and his New Divinity successors. A "recoil from, not an embrace of" nineteenth-century democratic and sentimentalized piety, Finney's perfectionism had its intellectual roots and "distinctive architecture" in eighteenth-century New England Calvinism and was predicated on the dichotomy of natural ability and moral inability in *Freedom of the Will* and the radical disinterested benevolence in Samuel Hopkins. Oberlin perfectionism as a "living force" died with Finney.

McCoy, Genevieve. "'Reason for a Hope': Evangelical Women Making Sense of Late Edwardsian Calvinism," pp. 175-92. Discovers in Congregational and New School Presbyterian journals a number of orthodox women engaged in the debates of fundamental tenets of the New Divinity descendants of Edwards and other late-Edwardsean Calvinists, in the context of prevailing attitudes about "woman's 'nature' and gender-prescribed behavior." The "feminization" of religion during the first half of the nineteenth century was neither as anti-intellectual nor as enabling for women as some current critics would have it. Rather, conflicting orthodox Calvinist doctrine both "drew women to the forefront of the evangelical crusade and frustrated their efforts there." Most promoted God's kingdom "from the sidelines" — in concerts of prayer, in penny-a-week contributions to missions, and in hopes for their children to one day lead the crusade.

Conforti, Joseph A. "Edwards A. Park and the Creation of the New England Theology, 1840-1870," pp. 193-207. Characterizes Edwards Amasa Park, professor of sacred rhetoric and theology at Andover Seminary for forty-five years and editor of *Bibliotheca Sacra* for thirty, as a "major" contributor, interpreter, and "guardian" of the Edwardsean tradition in mid-nineteenth century, New England Theology. Park composed the first "genetic" history of that tradition; "reconciled" divine sovereignty and human accountability; offered "Consistent Calvinism" for a revivalist and evangelical culture; and promoted the neglected and misunderstood "Bartleby" of that theology, Nathanael Emmons. A creator of tradition, not an original thinker, Park was the first to "imbue the term New England theology with historical meaning."

47 Stephens, B. M. Review of *Jonathan Edwards, Religious Tradition, and American Culture,* by Joseph A. Conforti. *Choice* 33 (June): 1659.

Cites Joseph A. Conforti's "insightful survey" (1995.7) in his "important and wide-ranging" interdisciplinary study.

48 Sweeney, Douglas A. Review of *Jonathan Edwards and the Catholic Vision of Salvation,* by Anri Morimoto. *Fides et Historia* 28 (Summer): 96-98.

Criticizes Anri Morimoto's book (1995.35) for "overworking" the Catholic Edwards and for "historical inaccuracies," although it is "full of creative and compelling" interpretations.

49 Thomas, Arthur Dicken, Jr. Review of *One Holy and Happy Society* and *Seeing God,* by Gerald R. McDermott. *Crux* 32 (September): 43-44.

Predicts that Gerald R. McDermott's two works (1992.13 and 1995.31) will "do much to demonstrate the relevance" of Edwards to those unfamiliar with his "spiritual wisdom."

50 Vetö, Miklós. "Beauté et compossibilité: l'épistémologie religieuse de Jonathan Edwards." *Revue d'Histoire et de Philosophie Religieuses* 76 (October):427-58.

Develops Edwards's epistemology in terms of the holy beauty of God rendered perceptible in conversion. (In French.)

51 ———. "Spiritual Knowledge According to Jonathan Edwards." Michael J. McClymond, transl. *Calvin Theological Journal* 31 (April): 161-81.

Translates 1979.40.

52 Ward, Roger Allen. "An American Theism: Edwards, Peirce, Dewey, and the Philosophy of Return." Ph.D. dissertation, Pennsylvania State University.

Follows John Smith's proposal that the "core" of American philosophy evolves from the presence or absence of Edwards's "sense of the heart," in a study of Edwards, Charles S. Peirce, John Dewey, and Cornel West.

53 Weber, Donald. Review of *Jonathan Edwards, Religious Tradition, and American Culture,* by Joseph A. Conforti. *Early American Literature* 31 (3): 316-18.
Follows Joseph A. Conforti as he "richly maps" the vicissitudes of Edwards (1995.7) amid nineteenth-century religious controversies to become a cultural icon to generations of Americans, a study of "substantial achievement."

54 Westerkamp, Marilyn J. Review of *"Gracious Affection" and "True Virtue,"* by Richard B. Steele. *William and Mary Quarterly,* 3d ser., 53 (January): 221-22
Cites Richard B. Steele's "dual agendas of historical scholarship and Christian apologetics," a "lingering difficulty" in his study (1994.43) of the relationship between Edwards and John Wesley.

55 Youngs, Frederick W. "The Place of Spiritual Union in Jonathan Edwards's Conception of the Church." *Fides et Historia* 28 (Winter): 27-47.
Argues that the doctrine of spiritual union is not only the biblical foundation of Edwards's spirituality but the "point of contact" between his theology and his emphasis on religious experience, focussing on the doctrine in relation to the church. Edwards's notion of the church stems from his conception of the nature of God in the creation of the world, the spiritual union between God and man "an inherent part" of his purpose *(End of Creation);* the "peculiar beauty" of the church of Christ made visible in prayer and profession *(Humble Attempt* and *Humble Inquiry);* the church, the "purified, perfected" bride of Christ, in heaven, complete, without end ("Miscellanies," no. 371).

1997

1 Beverly, James A. "Jonathan Edwards: Spinning in his Grave?" *Revival Wars: A Critique of Counterfeit Revivals.* Pickering, Canada: Evangelical Research Ministries, pp. 27-42.
Plays twenty questions with four church historians — three Americans, Alan Guelzo, Kenneth Minkema, and Douglas Sweeney, and one Canadian, Ian Rennie — about Edwards and the Toronto Blessing. Several noted apologists for the revival "need to retreat from their bombastic pronouncements," for Edwards, although invaluable for historical purposes, cannot be "the way to a definitive evaluation of current controversies."

2 Bolt, John. Review of *One Holy and Happy Society,* by Gerald R. McDermott. *Calvin Theological Journal* 32 (April): 189-91.
Foresees that Gerald R. McDermott's "rich and stimulating" work (1992.13) should send many back to Edwards for "further study and reflection" as well as Christian social action.

3 Campi, Emidio, and Massimo Rubboli, eds. *Protestantesimo nei Secoli: Fonti e Documenti.* Turin: Claudiana, 2: xxv-xxvi, 290-307.
Prefaces excerpts from Edwards's letter to Benjamin Colman and *Religious Affections* with a

brief biography of that extraordinary figure of eighteenth-century American culture. (In Italian.)

4 Chamberlain, Ava. "The Grand Sower of the Seed: Jonathan Edwards's Critique of George Whitefield." *New England Quarterly* 70 (September): 368-85.

Gathers from a series of nine (manuscript) sermons preached on the parable of the sower (Matt. 13:3-8) in November 1740, shortly after George Whitefield left Northampton, Edwards's differences with him on the nature of revivals and the manner of conducting them. Edwards held a "deep ambivalence" about Whitefield's theatrical preaching and the religious hypocrisy that inevitably followed — the certainty of immediate experience, the result of a deceitful heart and untrustworthy affections — and insisted upon piety to ward off self-deception, pastoral to check personal authority. "Edwards was a revivalist, but he was also a Puritan."

5 Davies, Ronald E. "Jonathan Edwards: Missionary Biographer, Theologian, Strategist, Administrator, Advocate — and Missionary." *International Bulletin of Missionary Research* 21 (April): 60-66.

Tracks Edwards's influence on missions thorough his biography, *David Brainerd;* his years in Stockbridge preaching to the Housatonics; his *True Virtue* and its effect on Samuel Hopkins's "disinterested benevolence," a "powerful incentive" to missionaries; his *Humble Attempt* and *History of Redemption,* a theological framework for missionaries; and his "God-centered postmillennial optimism" and its importance to missionary perseverance.

6 Earls, Charles Anthony "Young John Dewey and the Call to Character." Ph.D. dissertation, Southern Illinois University at Carbondale.

Relates John Dewey's ethical theory to the American evangelical tradition "bequeathed" by Edwards.

7 Ferreira, M. Jamie. Review of *Reason and the Heart,* by William J. Wainwright. *International Philosophical Quarterly* 37 (March): 104-105

Recommends William Wainwright's study (1995.52) "most highly," its account and defense of the theory of justification in Edwards, John Henry Newman, and William James "clarifying" and "compelling."

8 Grange, Joseph. Review of *Jonathan Edwards, Religious Tradition, and American Culture,* by Joseph A. Conforti. *International Philosophical Quarterly* 37 (March): 120-22.

Calls Joseph A. Conforti's study of Edwards (1995.7) "a model of its kind," a valuable work of postmodern deconstuction *"in the hands of the right craftsman."*

9 Guelzo, Allen C. "An Heir or a Rebel? Charles Grandison Finney and the New England Theology." *Journal of the Early Republic* 17 (Spring): 61-94.

Situates Finney "precisely" within New England Theology — a movement "largely" shaped by Edwards — that he is supposedly repudiated.

10 Hall, Richard A. Spurgeon. "The Religious Ethics of Edward Bellamy and Jonathan Edwards." *Utopian Studies* 8:13-31.

Shows a "striking thematic continuity" between Edwards and Edward Bellamy in their evident philosophical individualism. But theirs was an "altruistic egoism," their moral and religious thought bound to the idea of community. Thus, in their "fundamental spiritual kinship," Edwards and Bellamy address one of the "perennial tensions" in the American experience, that between the freedom of the individual and the constraints of society.

11 Helm, Paul. "Jonathan Edwards on Original Sin." *Faith and Understanding.* Grand Rapids, Mich.: William B. Eerdmans, pp. 152-76.
   Traces Edwards's defense of original sin to his conviction that a theological truth must be philosophically cogent and consistent with empirical evidence, such that the moral objection to the doctrine — how can one be held responsible for the guilt of the actions of another? — may be best answered by contemporary notions of personal identity, those of John Locke in his *Essay Concerning Human Understanding,* and some "radical ideas" about identity "*through* time," drawn perhaps from the occasionalism of Nicolas Malebranche. Edwards used analogies derived from Locke's account of identity "coupled" with the doctrine of temporal parts to make his case; whether it is "at odds" with his other work — the causal determinism of human action in *Freedom of the Will,* for instance — may prove an inconsistency more apparent than real.

12 Holyer, Robert. Review of *Reason and the Heart,* by William J. Wainwright. *International Journal for Philosophy of Religion* 41 (April): 123-25.
   Questions William J. Wainwright's evidentialism and his argument for Edwards's sense of spiritual beauty (1995.52), in "surely one of the most important works in epistemology in recent years."

13 Howe, Daniel Walker. "Benjamin Franklin, Jonathan Edwards, and the Problem of Human Nature." *The Making of the American Self: Jonathan Edwards to Abraham Lincoln.* Cambridge, Mass.: Harvard University Press, pp. 21-47.
   Reprints part of 1993.13.

14 Jauhiainen, Peter Dan. "An Enlightenment Calvinist: Samuel Hopkins and the Pursuit of Benevolence." Ph.D. dissertation, University of Iowa.
   Investigates Samuel Hopkins's doctrine of disinterested benevolence, a synthesis of Enlightenment ideas and the teachings of Edwards, remaining "faithful to the substance" of his theology.

15 Jenson, Robert W. *Systematic Theology.* Vol. 1. New York: Oxford University Press.
   See 1999.20.

16 Jones, Virginia Pompei. "Toward a Pedagogy of Imaginative Research Writing: a Study of Collaborative Groups." Ph.D. dissertation, University of North Carolina at Greensboro.
   Predicates a study of collaborative writing on the historic antithesis of reason and imagination, citing Edwards, who "struggled to overcome this cultural dichotomy."

17 Kearney, John. "Jonathan Edwards' Account of Adam's First Sin." *Scottish Bulletin of Evangelical Theology* 15 (Autumn): 127-41.
   Challenges the prevailing view of "several" scholars that Edwards "fails" to provide an adequate and coherent account of the origin of sin. Edwards believed that God created Adam with sufficient, not efficacious, grace, a free agent with "rational" will; that sin entered the world through an "alliance" of Adam's erroneous judgment and natural appetite, a function of his "imperfection as a creature;" that sin reflects the "goodness" of God, in that it occasioned a "more

intimate relationship" between God and man in Christ. Edwards "clearly" adheres to the doctrine of *felix culpa.*

18 Landsman, Ned. *From Colonials to Provincials: American Thought and Culture, 1680-1760.* American Thought and Culture Series. New York: Twayne Publishers, pp. 105-14.

Contrasts the views of Edwards and Charles Chauncy on the nature of the Great Awakening, especially the place of enthusiasm in it, Chauncy stressing order, authority, and "decency," Edwards the effects of human nature and human psychology; Chauncy's "conservative" theology supportive of the social order, Edwards's of the marginalized in it, women and the young. Still, both were theists, both held "significant Calvinist elements," espoused the doctrine of regeneration, recognized the necessity of arguing from "observation and experience" in an age of reason, and, though sons of New England, both conducted their debate for a transatlantic audience.

19 Lucas, Paul R. "Solomon Stoddard and the Origin of the Great Awakening in New England." *The Historian* 59 (Summer): 741-58.

Suggests that the origin of the Great Awakening can be "traced back" to the theology and techniques of Solomon Stoddard and evidenced in *Faithful Narrative:* "Stoddard's formula for revival had become Edwards's formula."

20 Lutz, Norma Jean. *Maggie's Choice: Jonathan Edwards and the Great Awakening.* Uhrichsville, Ohio: Barbour Publishers, 140 pp.

Follows twelve-year-old Maggie Allerton to a revival on the Boston Common, a meeting with "kindly" Rev. Edwards, and, after hearing him, her conversion, in a novel for young readers.

21 Maddox, Randy L. Review of *"Gracious Affection" and "True Virtue,"* by Richard B. Steele. *Asbury Theological Journal* 52 (Spring): 67-68.

Claims that Richard B. Steele's "fine first contribution" (1994.43) misses the "significant difference" between Edwards and John Wesley on how regenerating grace works.

22 McClymond, Michael J. "Spiritual Perception in Jonathan Edwards." *Journal of Religion* 77 (April): 195-216.

Concludes that Edwards's teaching on the spiritual sense of divine things has a "double-sided, Janus-faced" appearance, rather than the one-sided model of most interpretations. Some readers argue for discontinuity, a "sixth sense" distinct from the five mental faculties and not part of everyday experience; others, for continuity with such experience, a "deeper vision" of reality available only to the regenerate through divine grace. Spiritual perception was one of Edwards's "most encompassing" themes, expressed throughout his writings from *Personal Narrative* to *True Virtue.*

23 McDermott, Gerald R. "Jonathan Edwards on Revival, Spiritual Discernment, and God's Beauty." *Reformation & Revival* 6 (Winter): 103-14.

Suggests that Edwards's distinctions between true and false spirituality in *Religious Affections* — a "penetrating manual of discernment" — may prove "helpful" to American evangelicals at the end of the twentieth century as they did in mid-eighteenth century. Edwards grounded Christian spirituality in the aesthetic experience, seeing — and enjoying — the beauty of God. (Adapted from *Seeing God,* 1995.31.)

24 Minkema, Kenneth P. "Preface to the Period." *Sermons and Discourses, 1723-1729. The Works of Jonathan Edwards,* 14. New Haven: Yale University Press, pp. 3-46.

Remarks Edwards's "prodigious intellectual growth" from the Fall of 1723, when he delivered *Quæstio,* part of his Yale graduate examination, to the end of 1729, when he became sole pastor at Northampton, a few months after the death of his grandfather Solomon Stoddard, in the second volume of sermons and discourses from that "little-known" period of Edwards's life — his Bolton settlement, his election as tutor at Yale, his ordination at Northampton — and appends a list of 113 sermons with the approximate date of composition from the period. From this sampling of sermons — none of the nineteen were published during his lifetime, only one posthumously, *The Day of Judgment* — some important themes and forms recur — justification by faith and the Arminian threat, light and excellency, communal strife and trinitarian harmony, the reasonableness of Christianity and the limits of language, occasional sermons and sacramental ones, terror and typology. In the years following, Edwards consolidated his pastoral relations and authority and, in time, constructed "a program of preaching on practical topics."

25 ———. "Jonathan Edwards on Slavery and the Slave Trade." *William and Mary Quarterly,* 3d ser., 54 (October): 823-31.

Reports (and reprints) a newly discovered a draft letter on the slave trade in the Edwards manuscript collection at the Andover Newton Theological School — the "only known instance" of his reflections on the issue — though there is no evidence he ever sent it. Written probably between 1738 and 1742, it also reveals both an "undercurrent of popular antislavery sentiment" in the area much earlier than was previously thought, as well as division between the clergy and the laity about it. Edwards condoned slavery — he owned four — but opposed the continuation of the slave trade.

26 Munk, Linda. "Jonathan Edwards and the Angel of the Lord: *A History of the Work of Redemption.*" *The Devil's Mousetrap: Redemption and Colonial American Literature.* New York: Oxford University Press, pp. 24-46.

Sets Edwards's theology — and that of Edward Taylor and Increase Mather — in "models of thought" drawn from Judaism and the early Church Fathers, in a close reading of his biblical typology in *History of Redemption* and "Types of Messiah," the "devil's mousetrap" of Augustine. Edwards conflates the "angel of the Lord" of the burning thorn bush in the Old Testament with the Logos of the New, a "pronounced effort" to read back into the Hebrew Bible a present and active Christ. His "radical" Christology transforms the revelations of God to Israel (theophanies) into divine acts of mercy (Christophanies), evoking the Christologies of early Christian apologists like Justin Martyr and Tertullian.

27 Novitsky, Anthony W. Review of *Jonathan Edwards and the Catholic Vision of Salvation,* by Anri Morimoto. *Journal of Ecumenical Studies,* 34 (Spring): 247-48.

Imagines with pleasure "generations of disciples" of Perry Miller immersed in the writings of Karl Rahner and Hans Küng as part of Anri Morimoto's study (1995.35) of Edwards's soteriology.

28 Pahl, Jon. Review of *A Jonathan Edwards Reader,* ed. John E. Smith, Harry S. Stout, and Kenneth P. Minkema. *Church History* 66 (March): 134-35.

Puts into an "affordable package most of the best" of Edwards (1995.46), though it omits the "famous (and eloquent)" *Farewell Sermon.*

29 Porterfield, Amanda. *Mary Lyon and the Mount Holyoke Missionaries.* New York: Oxford University Press, pp. 44-46 passim.

Remarks Mary Lyon's "enthusiasm" for Edwards's *History of Redemption,* in a study of the founder of a seminary for women at Mount Holyoke, Massachusetts, its graduates, she imagined, "cornerstones" of world redemption. She collected subscriptions for a reprinting of his text in the years prior to construction in October 1836.

30 Ross, Kenneth J. Review of *Jonathan Edwards, Religious Tradition, and American Culture,* by Joseph A. Conforti. *Journal of Presbyterian History* 75 (Summer): 135-36.
Regards Joseph A. Conforti an "able teacher," a "model study" (1995.7) of how a good scholar works, with respect to those before him and with a "passion for truth."

31 Rust, Marion. "Measuring Pleasure: Susanna Rowson and Sentimental Agency, 1754-1817." Ph.D. dissertation, Stanford University
Locates a coherent model of the self in Edwards's *Freedom of the Will,* enabling a writer like Susanna Rowson to construct female subjects who achieve freedom through "the very things" that threaten it.

32 Schlenther, Boyd Stanley. Review of *Jonathan Edwards and the Catholic Vision of Salvation,* by Anri Morimoto, and *Jonathan Edwards, Religious Tradition, and American Culture,* by Joseph A. Conforti. *Journal of American Studies* 31 (April): 136-38
Differentiates between two studies: Anri Morimoto's case (1995.35) is "tenuous," a "failed" attempt to establish affinity between Edwards and Roman Catholicism; Joseph A. Conforti's, a "generally stimulating account of the use and misuse" of him over time (1995.7), from the " 'seminary' " Edwards of the nineteenth century to the "manufactured" Edwards of the twentieth.

33 Smolík, Josef. *Kristus a jeho lid: Praktická eklesiologie.* Prague: Oikoymenh, pp. 143-47.
Comments briefly on Edwards's career and influence in America. (In Czech.)

34 Soden, Dale E. Review of *Benjamin Franklin, Jonathan Edwards, and the Representation of American Culture,* ed. Barbara B. Oberg and Harry S. Stout, and *Jonathan Edwards, Religious Tradition, and American Culture,* by Joseph A. Conforti. *Christian Scholar's Review* 27 (2): 263-65.
Holds that the collection of essays comparing Franklin and Edwards (1993.13) as well as Joseph A. Conforti's study (1995.7) of Edwards in the nineteenth century "continue to pave the way for serious students to understand better the ways in which Christian categories of thought have influenced American history."

35 Sproul, R. C. "We Are Inclined to Sin: *Jonathan Edwards.*" *Willing to Believe: The Controversy over Free Will.* Grand Rapids, Mich.: Baker Books, pp. 147-65.
Links *Original Sin* — one of Edwards's "lesser known" works — to *Freedom of the Will,* an "ancient controversy" over man's free will, his sinful nature, and biblical redemption. For Edwards, man is morally incapable of choosing unless God changes his disposition by the "immediate and supernatural" work of regeneration, and so "liberates" him from his evil inclinations. Edwards shares such views with Augustine, Luther, and Calvin.

36 Stephens, Bruce M. "Jonathan Edwards and the New Divinity: The Excellency of Christ." *The Prism of Time and Eternity: Images of Christ in American Protestant Thought from Jonathan Edwards to Horace Bushnell.* ATLA Monograph Series, 42.

Lanham, Md.: American Theological Library Association and Scarecrow Press, pp. 1-45.

Reconstructs Edwards's Christological views from published and unpublished sources, taking his doctrine of the Trinity as the point of departure. Edwards "struggled" throughout his life to read nature and history as evidences of the visibility of God, who in Christ disclosed the "excellency and beauty" of things both human and divine, whose own person is a "perfect unity" of both. As with other aspects of his thought, some of Edwards's Christology was both lost and found in his followers. (Cf. 1970.37.)

37 Stoever, William. Review of Jonathan Edwards, *Sermons and Discourses, 1720-1723,* ed. Wilson H. Kimnach, and *Sermons and Discourses, 1723-1729,* ed. Kenneth P. Minkema. *Fides et Historia* 29 (Winter): 109-11.

Praises Wilson H. Kimnach's "copious" general introduction to the sermon series and the first two volumes in it (1992.8 and 1997.24), part of the "fullest scholarly collection" of Edwards's sermon texts available.

38 Stoll, Mark. *Protestantism, Capitalism, and Nature in America.* Albuquerque: University of New Mexico Press, pp. 79-83.

Cites Edwards's solitary walks and conversations with God — and Sarah's and David Brainerd's — in a study of Protestantism, here "orthodox" Calvinism, and its attitude to nature. His understanding of creation was "thoroughly neo-Platonic," the universe a "shadow of God's ultimate glorious reality"; as a "proto-Transcendentalist," he thought of nature as "flowing continuously from the mind of God."

39 Taliaferro, Charles. Review of *Reason and the Heart,* by William J. Wainwright. *Journal of Religion* 77 (July): 488-89.

Commends William J. Wainwright for his articulation of Edwards's "appeal to beauty in his apologetic for theism" (1995.52).

40 Thuesen, Peter J. "Jonathan Edwards as Great Mirror." *Scottish Journal of Theology* 50 (1): 39-60.

Demonstrates the "multivalent" nature of Edwards's thought and suggests the "subtlety of his substance" in five categories — God, creation, religion, millennialism, and images. "[S]eeing Edwards as a Great Mirror means conceiving of him as an imposing — yet acquiescent — fixture in the cultural landscape." Put another way, "there is an Edwards for everyone," both in America's past and present.

41 Valeri, Mark. Review of Jonathan Edwards, *The "Miscellanies," a-z, aa-z., 1-500,* ed. Thomas A. Schafer. *Church History* 66 (March): 132-34.

Applauds Thomas A. Schafer (and Yale) for the first installment of Edwards's "valuable" edition of the "Miscellanies" (1994.38) and his "lucid and interesting" introduction to the text.

42 Westra, Helen Petter. Review of Jonathan Edwards, *Sermons and Discourses, 1720-1723,* ed. Wilson H. Kimnach. *Calvin Theological Journal* 32 (April): 158-64.

Regards Wilson H. Kimnach as "one of the world's foremost authorities" on Edwards's sermons, his general introduction a "comprehensive" study (1992.8) of the full sermon corpus, his preface to the New York sermons "erudite."

1998

1 Barbour, Dennis H. "The Metaphor of Sexuality in Jonathan Edwards' 'Personal Narrative.'" *Christianity and Literature* 47 (Spring): 285-94.
   Recovers the metaphor of sexuality in *Personal Narrative* as the "subconscious vehicle" for Edwards to define his relationship with Divinity and to construct a "spiritual justification for his own sexual desires." While the language of sexuality is the "closest approach" to that relationship, it became for Edwards finally unsatisfactory, for it is necessarily temporal and leads to temptation and sin. Only by following the example of Christ — selfless, pure, and loving to others — does he find a "truly satisfying" relationship with God.

2 Bushman, Richard Lyman. Review of *The Making of the American Self,* by Daniel Walker Howe. *William and Mary Quarterly,* 3d ser., 55 (July): 446-48.
   Cites Edwards's "most elemental form" of self-making in Daniel Walker Howe's rereading of familiar texts (1997.13), an analysis that "illuminates cultural phenomena in every corner of the land."

3 Chai, Leon. *Jonathan Edwards and the Limits of Enlightenment Philosophy.* New York Oxford University Press, 164 pp.
   Juxtaposes Edwards and "crucial passages" from three classic rationalist texts — John Locke's *Essay concerning Human Understanding,* Nicolas Malebranche's *Recherche de la Vérité,* and Gottfried von Leibniz's *Nouveaux Essais sur l'Entendement humain* — to uncover affinities between them and the "end or aim" of his philosophical enterprise. Edwards bases his notion of true religious experiences in *Religious Affections* on Locke's model of sensory evidences; of external objects as mental existences in "The Mind" and *True Virtue* on Malebranche's discussion of them; and his argument against Arminianism in *Freedom of the Will* on Leibniz's treatment of causation. In all, he "seems to prefer rational explanations that may ultiamtely fail the test of consistency to none at all."

4 Chamberlain, Ava. Review of Jonathan Edwards, *Sermons and Discourses, 1723-1729,* ed. Kenneth P. Minkema. *Church History* 67 (June): 406-407.
   Notes Kenneth Minkema's "unsurpassed facility" with the Edwards manuscripts in the second volume of sermons issued by Yale (1997.24).

5 Claghorn, George S. "Editor's Introduction." *Letters and Personal Writings. The Works of Jonathan Edwards,* 16. New Haven: Yale University Press, pp. 3-27.
   Transcribes the "extant locatable" letters Edwards wrote between 10 May 1716 (to his sister Mary, when he was twelve) and 28 February 1758 (to Jonathan Sergeant, Princeton College treasurer, within a month of his death) — 236 in all, fully half never before published — and appends his personal writings ("Resolutions," Diary," "On Sarah Pierpont," and *Personal Narrative*), a biographical glossary, a list of fragmentary letters, and another of letters he received. Only eight letters predate Edwards's arrival in Northampton, the last of them in 1723; a dozen years pass before his letter to Benjamin Colman about "the present extraordinary circumstances of this town." The letters that follow concern the awakenings and the aftermath, often with correspondents from abroad; the communion controversy; his tenure as missionary at Stockbridge, the bulk of the extant letters; and his college presidency. The collection shows the "many-sided Edwards mediating the worlds of thought and action with remarkable grace and fluency" as well as his "private, human" side.

6 Danaher, William J., Jr. "By Sensible Signs Represented: Jonathan Edwards's Sermons on the Lord's Supper." *Pro Ecclesia* 7 (Summer): 261-87.

Challenges the "longstanding" historiographical depiction of Edwards's sacramental theology based on *Humble Inquiry* and *Misrepresentations Corrected*, in a study of manuscript sermons on the Lord's Supper written over a lifetime. They reveal a preacher and theologian "in transition," trying to integrate his past and his present, yet with a "consistent, unified" understanding of a "'very sacred ordinance,'" participants experiencing communion, representation, and self-examination. A "complex" Edwards developed his sacramental theology within the scope of his ontology — not soteriology, as seventeenth-century Puritans had — which may have "major" implications for his ecclesiology as well.

7 Delattre, Roland A. "Recent Scholarship on Jonathan Edwards." *Religious Studies Review* 24 (October): 369-75.

Divides ten books published during the last decade into two categories — first, "Major Studies of Edwards's Thought": *The Philosophical Theology of Jonathan Edwards,* by Sang Hyun Lee (1988.25); *America's Theologian,* by Robert W. Jenson (1988.22); *La pensée de Jonathan Edwards,* by Miklós Vetö (1987.34); *One Holy and Happy Society* (1992.13), by Gerald R. McDermott; *The Philosophy of Jonathan Edwards,* by Stephen H. Daniel (1994.8); and *Jonathan Edwards,* by John E. Smith (1992.25); second, "Edwards and American Culture": *Jonathan Edwards, Religious Tradition, and American Culture,* by Joseph A. Conforti (1995.7); *Edwards on the Will,* Allen C. Guelzo (1989.16); *Jonathan Edwards and the American Experience,* ed. Nathan O. Hatch and Harry S. Stout (1988.17); and *Jonathan Edwards's Writings,* ed. Stephen J. Stein (1996.46) — and recommends those by Lee and Conforti and the essays in the Hatch and Stout volume as "the most engaging and persuasive of its kind," especially to readers unfamiliar with direction of recent scholarship on Edwards.

8 Duesing, Laurie Marie. "Restraint and Rapture: The Confessional Legacy in Late Twentieth-Century American Poetry." Ph.D. dissertation, University of California, Davis.

Includes Edwards in a survey of early confessional literature and late poetic practice.

9 Edwards, Rem B. Review of Jonathan Edwards, *Sermons and Discourses, 1723-1729,* ed. Kenneth P. Minkema. *Review of Metaphysics* 52 (September): 140-42

Terms Kenneth P. Minkema's edition of these early sermons (1997.24) a "nice job" in relating them to Edwards's philosophical and theological "ruminations" in his notebooks.

10 Ehrhard, Jim. "A Critical Analysis of the Tradition of Jonathan Edwards as a Manuscript Preacher." *Westminster Theological Journal* 60 (Spring): 71-84.

Rejects the notion that Edwards was a "boring manuscript preacher." The manuscript evidence "militates against" that traditional view: he did not preach in a monotone, the manuscript held "close to his face;" the "mere presence" of the manuscripts does not mean that he read from them; his shift to outlines "after 1741," as well as thumb notes or palm notes, argues against his reliance on manuscripts. Edwards spoke "directly" to the people with a message that "came from a Sovereign God."

11 Filson, David Owen. "Jonathan Edwards for Pastors: A Bibliographic Essay." *Presbyterion* 24 (Fall): 110-18.

Reduces an Edwards bibliography for pastors to seven secondary works — Iain H. Murray's biography (1987.22); Conrad Cherry's *Theology* (1966.9); John H. Gerstner's *Rational Theology* (vols. 1-3) and *Steps to Salvation* (1991.10, 1992.4, 1993.7, and 1960.5); and M. X. Lesser's annotated bibliography (1994.20) — and seven primary ones, in a "little trek" through his work and comments by others upon it.

12 Fitzmier, John R. *New England's Moral Legislator: Timothy Dwight.* Bloomington: Indiana University Press, pp. 24-27.

Remarks Colonel Timothy Dwight's efforts to save Edwards's "beloved pulpit." Five months after Edwards's dismissal, his fourth daughter, Mary, married Dwight's eldest son, Timothy, Jr.

13 Gatta, John. Review of *Jonathan Edwards, Religious Tradition, and American Culture,* by Joseph A. Conforti. *Religion & Literature* 30 (Spring): 99-106.

Attributes Joseph A. Conforti's "fully persuasive" study (1995.7) of Edwards to his documentary evidence and clear prose, in a review of three books on American cultural continuities.

14 Geissler, Suzanne. Review of *Jonathan Edwards, Religious Tradition, and American Culture,* by Joseph A. Conforti. *Anglican and Episcopal History* 67 (June): 261-62.

Rates Joseph A. Conforti's study (1995.7) of "nineteenth-century users" of Edwards "valuable and thought-provoking" if at times "heavy-going."

15 Gelpi, Donald L., S.J. "'Incarnate Excellence': Jonathan Edwards and an American Theological Aesthetic." *Religion and the Arts* 2:443-66.

Retrieves Edwards's Christological insights for the "significant" light it throws on the contemporary pursuit of the "foundational" theology of conversion and for the contribution it promises to make to an "inculturated" theological aesthetic. Such insights "dramatize" the sacramental character of the Christian creative imagination "simultaneously manifesting and concealing the reality of God" and illustrate the "aesthetic suggestiveness" of Edwards's vision for Christian art and literature.

16 Gerstner, John H. *Jonathan Edwards on Heaven and Hell.* Morgan, Pa.: Soli Deo Gloria.

Reprints 1980.14.

17 Godbeer, Richard. Review of *The Devil's Mousetrap,* by Linda Munk. *Journal of American History* 85 (December): 1054-55

Values Linda Munk's contextualization of Edwards's "angel-Christology" (1997.26) but questions her "refusal" to address the implications of her "tantalizing" study.

18 Goodwin, Charles H. "John Wesley's Indebtedness to Jonathan Edwards." *Epworth Review* 25 (April): 89-96.

Contends that John Wesley's "immediate reaction" on first reading *Faithful Narrative* was to accept the Northampton revival as the work of God and that the instantaneous conversion Edwards depicted there, much like his own, could be repeated on a "larger, more public scale." Edwards's descriptions of converts — and the backsliding of some — enabled Wesley to "discover himself as a popular preacher" as well to come to terms with his Luther-Moravian inspired conversion by accepting "levels of Christian regeneration," degrees of assurance, justification, and sanctification. In that, he was at liberty to pursue "his brand" of revivalism.

19 Guelzo, Allen C. "Sproul on the Will." *Christianity Today* 42 (2 March): 59-61.
Tasks R. C. Sproul for his strange reading of Edwards, in a review of his *Willing to Believe* (1997.35).

20 Gunton, Colin E. Review of *The Prism of Time and Eternity,* by Bruce M. Stephens. *Journal of Theological Studies,* n.s., 49 (October): 896-97.
Observes that Bruce M. Stephens's "chiefly descriptive" Christological study (1997.36) has more to say about Edwards and his successors than the "'modest contribution'" he claims in the introduction.

21 Imbarrato, Susan Clair. "Declaring the Self in the Spiritual Sphere: Elizabeth Ashbridge and Jonathan Edwards." *Declarations of Independency in Eighteenth-Century American Autobiography.* Knoxville: University of Tennessee Press, pp. 14-39.
Compares, in a gender-specific way, the spiritual autobiographies of the Puritan Edwards and the Quaker Elizabeth Sampson Ashbridge, *Personal Narrative* and *Some Account of the Fore Part of the Life,* "both written in the 1740s." For each of them, the spiritual autobiography "legitimatizes" the subjectivity of self-examination and develops self-awareness: for Edwards, his male quest is from "battle to surrender"; for Ashbridge, hers is from "servitude to surrender." Both texts arise in a "spiritually revolutionary" time when authority is questioned and gender roles are challenged: Edwards the more "contemplative" figure of the two, Ashbridge the more assertative, risking the displeasure of male authority.

22 Matos, Alderi Souza de. "Jonathan Edwards: Teologo do Coraqao e do Intelecto." *Fides Reformata* 3 (1): 72-87.
Focusses on the synthesis of heart and intellect in Edwards's theology, in a brief account of his life and thought. (In Portuguese.)

23 McClymond, Michael James. *Encounters with God: An Approach to the Theology of Jonathan Edwards.* New York: Oxford University Press, 194 pp.
Assesses a large portion of Edwards's corpus — *The Mind, Personal Narrative,* "Diary," *Two Dissertations,* and *History of Redemption* — to show how various texts reflect his "underlying" theological purposes, how his apologist position reflects a "complex synthesis" of Puritanism and the Enlightenment, how his notion of spiritual perception attempts to "bridge the hiatus" between Christian claims and the culture of his day. Edwards's thought "constantly shuttles back and forth" between the *"experimental manifestation"* of God and the *"cosmic integration"* of the idea of God. Situated in its historical and cultural context, Edwards's religious thought was a "brilliant exercise in 'artful theology'" — a joining together what Perry Miller separated — his artistry showing "most tellingly in his prodigious attempt" to alter and reinterpret the intellectual traditions of the eighteenth century and make them serve his Christian message, to rethink the culture of his day and turn it to the God's "advantage."

24 ———. "The Protean Puritan: *The Works of Jonathan Edwards,* Volumes 8 to 16." *Religious Studies Review* 24 (October): 361-67.
Discovers Edwards's protean character — "his ability to rethink his positions and adapt himself to shifting circumstances" — revealed in the nine volumes of his published writings and manuscripts recently issued by Yale, in a brief history of *The Works of Jonathan Edwards* — an "enduring monument" to him — and a detailed review of the texts — a "microcosm" of his corpus: *Ethical Writings,* ed. Paul Ramsey (1989.44); *A History of the Work of Redemption,* ed. John F.

Wilson (1989.59); *Sermons and Discourses, 1720-1723,* ed. Wilson H. Kimnach (1992.8); *Typological Writings,* ed. Wallace E. Anderson and Mason I. Lowance, Jr., with David H. Watters (1993.1); *Ecclesiastical Writings,* ed. David D. Hall (1994.12); *The "Miscellanies" (Entry Nos. a-z, aa-zz, 1-500),* ed. Thomas A. Schafer (1994.38); *Sermons and Discourses, 1723-1729,* ed. Kenneth P. Minkema (1997.24); *Notes on Scripture,* ed. Stephen J. Stein (1998.37); and *Letters and Personal Writings,* ed. George S. Claghorn (1998.5).

25 McKim, Donald K. Review of *The Prism of Time and Eternity,* by Bruce M. Stephens. *Reformed Review* 52 (Winter): 172-73.

Notes the "same kind of tensions" that Bruce M. Stephens (1997.36) found in Edwards in the eighteenth century to Horace Bushnell in the nineteenth afflicts contemporary Christological arguments as well.

*26 Moody, Joshua William. "Jonathan Edwards and the Enlightenment: Knowing the Presence of God." Ph.D. dissertation, Cambridge University.

Published as 2005.27.

27 New, Elisa. "Line's Eye, Lit Stream: Edwards, Jefferson, Audubon, and Thoreau" and "Work, Works, Working: Edwards, Moore, and Frost." *The Line's Eye: Poetic Experience, American Spirit.* Cambridge: Harvard University Press, pp. 53-104, 241-302.

Expands 1995.37 and extends the study to a species of American poetic practice that "measures any 'work' (the work of the poem included) against the history of Christian works," using Edwards's *Religious Affections* as the cultural expression of the Protestant tradition evident in Marianne Moore and Robert Frost. Both write poems that "know in singing not to sing" and experience that "literal lyricism of Being" that Edwards so admired in his apostrophe to Sarah Pierrepont: "'singing sweetly . . . she seems to have some one always conversing with her.'"

28 Nichols, Stephen J. Review of Jonathan Edwards, *Notes on Scripture,* ed. Stephen J. Stein, and *Letters and Personal Writings,* ed. George S. Claghorn. *Westminster Theological Journal* 60 (Fall): 352-55.

Deems *Notes on Scripture* "indispensable" to understanding Edwards's thought (1998.37) and *Letters and Personal Writings* (1998.5) an "immeasurable resource" for Edwardsean scholars, in a review of both Yale texts.

29 Oliver, John W. Review of *Charles G. Finney and the Spirit of American Evangelicalism,* by Charles E. Hambrick-Stowe. *The Historian* 61 (Fall): 157-58

Offers "high praise" for Charles E. Hambrick-Stowe's "well-written" study, emphasizing links links between Edwards and Charles Grandison Finney.

30 Pauw, Amy Plantinga. "The Church as Mother and Bride in the Reformed Tradition: Challenge and Promise." In *Many Voices, One God: Being Faithful in a Pluralistic World.* Edited by Walter Brueggermann and George W. Stroup. Louisville: Westminster John Knox Press, pp. 122-36.

Follows the "meanderings" of Reformed Church ecclesiology, a middle way between the Catholic idea of the church as a sacrament of grace and the gathered church of the Reformation — the church as both mother and bride — by examining Edwards's early appropriation of the maternal image and his later rejection of it. His ecclesiology began to shift in the wake of the "spiritual aftermath" of the Great Awakening, growing impatient with the ministerial role of "midwifing the birth of new Christians," invoking nuptial imagery in *The Church's Marriage to her Sons, and to her God* and *Religious Affections,* both published in 1746. In *Humble Inquiry* (1749), Edwards takes on the role as a "proxy bridegroom," but his congregation "broke off the engagement," dismissing him.

31 ———. "Reclaiming Jonathan Edwards." *Perspectives: A Journal of Reformed Thought* 13 (January): 9-14.

Explores Edwards's thought in *Religious Affections, True Virtue,* and the "Miscellanies" to uncover "untapped" resources for Reformed Christians concerned with justice, peace, liberation, and the "integrity of creation" and advises them to imitate his "spirit of theological adventure." If contemporary Reformed "culturalists" are to claim his "vision of the rich interplay of doctrine, religious affection, and Christian practice," they would do well to follow him, seeking "their neighbor's good as the source of their own happiness."

32 Piper, John. *God's Passion for His Glory: Living the Vision of Jonathan Edwards, with the Complete Text of The End for which God Created the World.* Wheaton, Ill.: Crossway Books, xvii, 266 pp.

Takes the reader on a "personal tour" of discovery and meaning to "at least one modern evangelical," in a study of Edwards's radical view of virtue expressed in *End of Creation* (reprinted). "Edwards's relentless God-centeredness and devotion to the Biblical contours of doctrine are profoundly needed in our day."

33 Richmond-Comins, W. Review of *The Devil's Mousetrap,* by Linda Munk. *Choice* 35 (June): 1710.

Declares Linda Munk's intertextual analysis of Puritan thinkers (1997.26) a "valuable reference" but one plagued by "numerous problems," a "frustrating" book.

34 Schröder, Caroline. *Glaubenswahrnehmung und Selbsterkenntnis: Jonathan Edwards's Theologia Experimentalis.* Göttingen: Vanderhoeck und Ruprecht, 219 pp.

Suggests that Edwards's experimental theology arises out of his observations of piety — faith perception and self realization, the congruence of God and man — and leads to psychological insights and interests not unlike those of Friedrich Schleiermacher. For Edwards, one lives every moment "corum Deo und corum hominibus" — in the presence of God and in the presence of man — drawn between an inner and an outer self, experiencing sensations of true religion, the will of God. (In German.)

35 Sharp, Douglas R. Review of *The Prism of Time and Eternity,* by Bruce M. Stephens. *Church History* 67 (December): 812.

Reports that the Christological material Bruce M. Stephens surveys from Edwards to Bushnell (1997.36), though useful, "not clearly" oriented to earlier Christological controversies.

36 Sohn, Damien Sangwoong. "Toward the Renewal of the Presbyterian Church of Korea." Ph.D. dissertation, Fuller Theological Seminary.

Evaluates the influence of Calvin, English Puritans, and Edwards as part of a study of the Presbyterian Church of Korea.

37 Stein, Stephen J. "Editor's Introduction." *Notes on Scripture. The Works of Jonathan Edwards,* 15. New Haven: Yale University Press, pp. 1-46.

Judges Edwards's scriptural commentary "intriguing" in its complexity, in the only previous edition of *Notes on Scripture* since Sereno Dwight's "seriously flawed" effort in 1830, a compendium of over five hundred entries — from his Bolton settlement in 1724 to his Stockbridge mission two years before his death — and views it in the context of the commentarial tradition and modern criticism, his "creative" approach as an exegete and his reputation. Although the text represents only a portion of his exegetical writing — he links entries to the "Blank Bible," the "Miscellanies," and other "smaller" manuscripts — it clearly documents Edwards's "consuming interest" in typology, a system that he regarded as "central" to Christianity and the foundational principle of his scriptural commentary and his public ministry — sermons, occasional writings, and major treatises. "Without this biblical element the writings of Jonathan Edwards make little sense."

38 Stelting, Donald Edd. "Edwards as Educator: His Legacy of Educational Thought and Practice." Ph.D. dissertation, University of Kansas.

Posits that Edwards's "clear and distinct educational ideal" informed his life and writings and served not only his "religious and societal purposes" but his "self-development and personal enjoyment" as well.

39 Stephens, B. M. Review of *Jonathan Edwards and the Limits of Enlightenment Philosophy,* by Leon Chai. *Choice* 36 (December): 701.

Places Leon Chai's book (1998.3) on the shelves of faculty in philosophy and religious studies, not *"beginning"* readers of secondary sources of Edwards.

40 Sweeney, Douglas A. "Edwards and His Mantle: The Historiography of the New England Theology." *New England Quarterly* 71 (March): 97-119.

Reconsiders the "classic" paper war in the 1850s over Edwards's legacy, some claimants to it — Samuel Hopkins, Nathaniel Taylor, and Edwards Amasa Park — and later characterizations of it to suggest that New England Theology might be better served if it were tested in its cultural context. "Edwardsians should no longer be measured according to their success in mass producing *his* product," not even those who took his theology with "utter seriousness": Edwards never provided "canned" answers to spiritual questions.

41 ———. "Edwards, Jonathan (1703-1758)." In *Historical Handbook of Major Biblical Interpreters.* Edited by Donald K. McKim. Downers Grove, Ill.: InterVarsity Press, pp. 309-12.

Recounts Edwards's "love affair" with the Bible, from his sermons and major treatises to unpublished notebooks — "Notes on Scripture," the "Blank Bible," and "Harmony of the Old and New Testament" — a mass of work that suggests he may be "the most prolific exegetical scholar in American history."

42 Vaughn, William Martin. "The Sublime and the Dutiful: Ethics and Excess from Edwards to Melville." Ph.D. dissertation, University of Illinois at Urbana-Champaign.

Constructs a version of the sublime to show how it can have ethical implications — "its constitutive connection to others" — in a study of early American writers, Edwards among them.

43 Westra, Helen. Review of Jonathan Edwards, *Sermons and Discourses, 1723-1729,* ed. Kenneth P. Minkema. *Calvin Theological Journal* 33 (April): 197-200.

Greets Kenneth P. Minkema's edition of Edwards's sermons (1997.24) as "good news" for readers to "deepen" their understanding of Edwards and a sign that work on the next four volumes is "moving ahead full speed."

44 Wheeler, Rachel Margaret. "Living upon Hope: Mahicans and Missionaries, 1730-1760." Ph.D. dissertation, Yale University.

Taps Edwards's "vast writings" and Moravian mission archives to investigate the "cultural encounter" of missionaries and the Stockbridge Housatonics.

45 Wilson, John F. Review of *Jonathan Edwards and the Limits of Enlightenment Philosophy*, by Leon Chai. *Church History* 67 (December): 811-12.

Considers Leon Chai's "very different" approach to Edwards (1998.3) "refreshing and salutary," an "important reminder" that this "magisterial" figure "transcends" generations of interpreters.

46 Zakai, Avihu. "The Conversion of Jonathan Edwards." *Journal of Presbyterian History* 76 (Summer): 127-38.

Traces the "crucial consequences" to Edwards's life and thought to the "signal existential moment" of his conversion described in *Personal Narrative*. From that experience come Edwards's theology of God's glory and absolute sovereignty, the coherence and beauty of creation; his "singular" redemptive mode of religious history; the "central place" he gives to revival and awakening; and the reconstruction of his religious identity and consciousness. It may also explain the difference between his theology of nature and Calvin's: for Edwards nature becomes an "important source" of revelation.

1999

1 Allison, Jennifer L. "A More Perfect Union: Garrisonian Abolitionism in American Political Thought." Ph.D. dissertation, Brandeis University.

Cites Edwards's *Freedom of the Will* as one of the "disparate" philosophical ideas that coalesced in William Lloyd Garrison's abolitionism.

2 Armstrong, John H. Review of *Edwards in Our Time*, ed. Sang Hyun Lee and Allen C. Guelzo. *Reformation & Revival Journal* 8 (Fall): 220-22.

Values Sang Lee and Allen Guelzo's collection of essays on Edwards (1999.24), "*the* major American theologian and student of true reformation and revival."

3 Baker, Jennifer Jordan. Review of *The Devil's Mousetrap*, by Linda Munk. *Criticism* 41 (Fall): 565-68.

Misses the "literary implications" of Linda Munk's "elegantly written and painstakingly researched" study of typology (1997.26) in the work of Increase Mather, Edward Taylor, and Edwards.

4 Bolt, John. Review of *God's Passion for His Glory*, John Piper. *Calvin Theological Journal* 34 (April): 263.

Owes John Piper an "enormous debt" for making available an affordable edition of *End of Creation* (1998.32) and for providing an "eminently fitting frame" to put Edwards's theology to use.

5 Brown, Robert Eric. "Connecting the Sacred with the Profane: Jonathan Edwards and the Scripture History." Ph.D. dissertation, University of Iowa.
Published as 2002.5.

6 ———. "Edwards, Locke, and the Bible." *Journal of Religion* 79 (July): 361-84.
Narrows the supposed gulf between Edwards and John Locke on their treatment of the rationality of historical religious knowledge by suggesting that they were "markedly similar." Both drew on a "shared interest" in preserving the traditional source of morality and religion in their society and in resolving the conflict between reason and revelation by maintaining the "philosophical prerogative" of the Bible for religious discourse. Edwards "reorient[ed]" his own epistemology along latitudinarian lines to identify "more closely" with Locke than with deists like Matthew Tindal who insisted that revelation be "constrained" by reason.

7 Chamberlain, Ava. "Jonathan Edwards on the Relation between Hypocrisy and the Religious Life." In *Perspectives on American Religion and Culture.* Edited by Peter W. Williams. Malden, Mass.: Blackwell, pp. 336-52.
Defends Harriet Beecher Stowe's claim in *The Minister's Wooing* that Puritans were "not morally offensive but psychologically interesting" — against Nathaniel Hawthorne's in *The Scarlet Letter* that they were hypocrites — by instancing Edwards's view that religious hypocrites primarily deceive themselves, not others, in an examination of the "incongruity" between appearance and reality in his thought. Edwards first developed his views of evangelical hypocrisy during the Great Awakening, particularly in *Religious Affections,* and of legal hypocrisy in his Stockbridge years, particularly in *True Virtue,* the language of the first common to him and "radical" New Lights, the language of the second from Frances Hutcheson, Lord Shaftesbury, and other British moral sense philosophers. For Edwards, the problem of "indiscernible counterparts" — the presence of sin after conversion — made for a "strenuous" life for saints and "frequent worry" about hypocrisy.

8 Cornett, Daryl Carter. "John Witherspoon's Moral Philosophy as an Expression of his Reformed Understanding of Human Nature." Ph.D. dissertation, Southern Baptist Theological Seminary.
Compares John Witherspoon to Edwards on human nature, in a study of the sixth president of Princeton.

9 Danaher, William J., Jr. Review of *Encounters with God,* by Michael J. McClymond. *Theological Studies* 60 (September): 552-54.
Grants Michael J. McClymond's "so-called apologetic approach" to Edwards (1998.23) but notes his interpretation is "somewhat problematic," his limited texts "somewhat troubling."

10 Davies, R. E. "Jonathan Edwards, Theologian of the Missionary Awakening." *Evangel* 17 (Spring): 1-8.
Bestows the title of "The Grandfather of Modern Missions" on Edwards, in a sketch of his importance to the missionary movement especially in Great Britain.

11 Delattre, Roland A. Review of *Jonathan Edwards and the Limits of Enlightenment Philosophy,* by Leon Chai. *American Literature* 71 (March): 175-76.
Rates Leon Chai's study (1998.3) of Edwards — and Locke, Malebranche, and Leibniz — a "mixed quality," his treatment of *Freedom of the Will* "fundamentally flawed."

12 Field, Peter. Review of *A Speaking Aristocracy,* by Christopher Grasso. *Journal of the Early Republic* 19 (Fall): 39-41.

> Recommends Christopher Grasso's six "superb case studies" (1999.14) of such public Yale figures as Edwards and Ezra Stiles, even though this study of high culture lacks an "explicit" thesis.

13 Freeberg, Bruce Allen. "The Problem of Divine Ideas in Eighteenth-Century Immaterialism: A Comparative Study of the Philosophies of George Berkeley, Samuel Johnson, Arthur Collier, and Jonathan Edwards." Ph.D. dissertation, Emory University.

> Examines different approaches to the "nature of God's ideas and their relation to human perception," in a study of eighteenth-century immaterialists, Edwards among them.

14 Grasso, Christopher. "Only a Great Awakening: Jonathan Edwards and the Regulation of Religious Discourse." *A Speaking Aristocracy: Transforming Discourse in Eighteenth-Century Connecticut.* Chapel Hill: University of North Carolina Press, pp. 86-143.

> Recounts Edwards's role in the Great Awakening and the ideological divisions and institutional developments following it, in a study of the ways learned men tried to shape the "broader culture" of eighteenth-century New England through public discourse. Edwards sought to mediate between Old and New Light extremes *(Some Thoughts)* — while distancing himself from "'spiritually proud'" Separatists *(Humble Attempt)* — and to "redefine" the nature of the Congregational Church and its communion practice *(Humble Inquiry* and *Misrepresentations Corrected).* His attempt to regulate religious discourse involved "fixing" the meaning of particular words, "controlling" the reference of religious signs, and placing this power "firmly in the hands of ministers rather than parishioners." (Reprints 1996.46 as part of it.)

15 Hansen, Wayne S. Review of Jonathan Edwards, *Letters and Personal Writings,* ed. George S. Claghorn. *Church History* 68 (March): 204-205.

> Adds George Claghorn's edition of letters (1998.5) to the list of "valuable" resources from the Yale Edwards.

16 Hinlicky, Paul R. "The Doctrine of the New Birth from Bullinger to Edwards." *Missio Apostolica* 7 (Fall): 102-19.

> Invokes Edwards's theology on the doctrine of the New Birth as it bears upon Lutheran baptismal practice. Edwards opposed the change in meaning of the New Birth — from a miraculous event to a human act of self-determination — and tried to point it back to Reformation theology, to "reground" it in the historical event of preaching Christ and to the biblically "more significant" death and resurrection. His notion differs from George Whitefield's "functional Arminianism" — and today's "neo-evangelical proponents" — and "validly criticizes" much of the practice of baptism in modern Lutheran churches.

17 Hosier, Helen K[oolman]. *Jonathan Edwards, the Great Awakener.* Uhrichsville, Ohio: Barbour Publishers, 206 pp.

> Portrays Edwards, a "giant of faith," as revivalist and theologian, pastor and missionary, beloved husband and father, in a "readable fashion."

18 Howard, Evan Bradford. "Affirming the Touch of God: A Cognitive and Philosophical Exploration of the Role of Affectivity in Christian Discernment." Ph.D. dissertation, Graduate Theological Union.

Examines Edwards's *Distinguishing Marks* and *Religious Affections* as "representative works" of spirituality, in a study of Christian discernment.

19 Jackson, Gregory S. "'The Mind's House': Literary, Philosophical, Religious, and Material Architectures of American Nationalism from Jonathan Edwards to Jacob Riis." Ph.D. dissertation, University of California, Los Angeles.

Traces the "distinctive use" of architectural tropes in American nationalism, including those in Edwards's homiletics.

20 Jenson, Robert W. *Systematic Theology.* 2 vols. New York: Oxford University Press, 1:119-20, 234-45; 2: 18-20, 39-41, 367-69.

Refers to Edwards as the eighteenth century's "only at once fully Christian and robustly constructive theologian" and cites his triune theology in two volumes: in the first, on matters of primal identity and divine beauty; in the second, on the work of redemption as the purpose of creation, on the harmony of the divine consciousness, and on the saints in heaven: "'When I would form and idea of a society in highest degree happy, I think of them . . . sweetly singing to each other.'"

21 Kimnach, Wilson H., Kenneth P. Minkema, and Douglas A. Sweeney. "Introduction." In *The Sermons of Jonathan Edwards: A Reader.* Edited by Wilson H. Kimnach, Kenneth P. Minkema, and Douglas A. Sweeney. New Haven: Yale University Press, pp. [ix]-xlviii.

Recognizes the "crucial role" sermons play in the life and art of Edwards as preacher, writer, and pastoral theologian, in a reading of fourteen sermons and discourses — his artistry in the form, their social and cultural contexts, their contents as expressions of his theological aims — texts that chart the soul's pilgrimage from earthly sin to heavenly bliss, from "The Way of Holiness" and *Sinners in the Hands of an Angry God* to *The Excellency of Christ* and "Heaven Is a World of Love."

22 Lambert, Frank. *Inventing the Great Awakening.* Princeton: Princeton Uinversity Press, pp. 62-81.

Contends that the "colonial revivalists themselves" constructed the Great Awakening, beginning in the mid-1730s in the Connecticut Valley (Northampton) and the Raritan (Freehold) and explores the "boundaries" between event and interpretation and the role of itinerants and lay people, the published accounts and the transatlantic connection. Edwards's revival and *Faithful Narrative* became the "almost exclusive center of attention of virtually every contemporary and historical account" of the Great Awakening chiefly through the guidance of Boston's Benjamin Colman and London's Isaac Watts and John Guyse. The New Jersey experience, though as dramatic as that in Massachusetts, simply lacked publicity.

23 Lee, Sang Hyun. "Jonathan Edwards's Dispositional Conception of the Trinity: A Resource for Contemporary Reformed Theology." In *Toward the Future of Reformed Theology: Tasks, Topics, Traditions.* Edited by David Willis-Watkins and Michael Welker. Grand Rapids, Mich.: William B. Eerdmans, pp. 444-55.

Argues that Edwards's dispositional reconception of God — more particularly, of the immanent Trinity — enables him to introduce an element of "becoming or potentiality" in God's being without compromising God's actuality. Such dispositional reconception results in being essentially disposed for further activities and relationships and further increases of being, and Edwards founds his notion of the divine being on just such reiteration. His recurrent emphases on time and history in his theology are "undergirded" by this dynamic conception of God and his relation to the world, "certainly one of the reasons why Edwards's remains an important resource for contemporary Reformed theology."

24 ———, and Allen C. Guelzo, eds. *Edwards in Our Time: Jonathan Edwards and the Shaping of American Religion.* Grand Rapids, Mich.: William B. Eerdmans, xvi, 214 pp.

Publishes nine papers delivered at a national conference in Philadelphia, 3-5 October 1996, in four parts (God, being, and nature; ethics; preaching and revival; and eschatology); a tenth paper, by Joseph A. Conforti, appears as "Colonial Revival: Edwards and Puritan Tradition in American Culture, 1870-1903," in his *Jonathan Edwards, Religious Tradition, and American Culture,* pp. 145-85.

Stout, Harry S. "Introduction," pp. ix-xvi. Attributes Edwards's popularity to the "artistic creativity and intellectual force of his speculations," in a summary of the essays in the volume, "remarkable evidence" of Edwards's ability to "stimulate constructive reflection" on the eve of the tercentenary of his birth.

Smith, John E. "The Perennial Jonathan Edwards," pp. 1-11. Examines Edwards's "most illuminating and most powerful" ideas touching upon recurrent problems of religion and contemporary society — his concept of the affections, his rejection of nominalism, and his idea of God's two methods of ordering history — in the keynote address to the conference. In the first, and most complex, of these, Edwards uses the affections as the basis for a "much needed objectivism" in judging value and importance and nullifies any supposed opposition of head and heart; in the second, he uses the concept of the unity of humanity to treat original sin and continuous creation; and in the third, he posits a redemptive history at once limited and broad, one of individuals repeated in time, the other of successive events tending to one effect.

Lee, Sang Hyun. "Edwards on God and Nature: Resources for Contemporary Theology," pp. 15-44. Contends that Edwards's treatment of nature can be best understood as an expression of his dispositional ontology, a "highly innovative reconception" of the nature of God and God's relationship to natural world. God is "at once actual and also eternally disposed," so that the creation of the world is an everlasting process, the repetition of God's "prior actuality," yet distinguishable from him and from humanity. As well, his reconception accounts for both the extension of his typology to include the physical world and the "strong ecological motif" in his theology. Edwards's doctrines of God and of nature "provide us with helpful insights for the theological concerns that are important to us in our own time."

Daniel, Stephen H. "Postmodern Concepts of God and Edwards's Trinitarian Ontology," pp. 45-64. Associates ideas in Edwards and Karl Barth to contemporary critiques of the meaning of intelligibility and its implications for the doctrine of the Trinity, a "hot topic" in postmodern theology. Although both thinkers take revelation and divine communication to be "central" to the semantic conditions of salvation, Edwards in particular treats God's communicative activity and the book of nature, not as metaphors, but as the "vocabulary of divine expression," and thus challenges the classical-modern notion that things, ideas, and words are intelligible apart from discursive practices. In this, Edwards's philosophy reveals its "distinctive postmodern character."

Delattre, Roland A. "Religious Ethics Today: Jonathan Edwards, H. Richard Niebuhr, and Beyond," pp. 67-85. Cites three "formative" ideas Edwards held that may contribute to contemporary religious ethics: that beauty is central to his understanding of God and of the nature of the spiritual and moral life; that the creation of the world results from the "joyous overflowing" of the being and beauty in the divine life; and that the Christian life — indeed, "any authentically religious life" — is made new by participation in the divine life, the "cordial consent" to the being and beauty of God. H. Richard Niebuhr, "powerfully" influenced by Edwards as he was, intended to "go even further" by developing his relational ethics of responsibility as a "full-blown alternative" to the standard denotological and teleological approaches to ethics. For Edwards, for Niebuhr, for us, "Beauty is our home if we ever have a home."

Guelzo, Allen C. "The Return of the Will: Jonathan Edwards and the Possibilities of Free Will," pp. 87-110. Traces the debate over free will — "our national gargoyle" — during the past two hundred and fifty years, from Edwards's time to "our current cultural crises," in an analysis of *Freedom of the Will* and the varied responses to it. Although Edwards probably knew that the "harmony" between free will and necessity was but a "workable dream" within an eighteenth-century hierarchal society, he raised the "right questions" and thus provided for the continuing discussion of the issue, especially in its peculiarly American context. "[T]he problem he poses for us is whether we are still humane enough to believe his answers."

Eversley, Walter V. L. "The Pastor as Revivalist," pp. 113-30. Suggests that Edwards's "theological integrity actually undermined his pastoral role," as he sought to link his conversionism and sacramentalism — his revivalist impulse to his communion practice — a failed attempt that ended in his dismissal from his Northampton parish. Edwards "redefined" the conditions for communion in keeping with his long held, but publicly unexpressed, belief, which put him at odds with his congregation and its open communion initiated by his grandfather Solomon Stoddard. A "disastrous political miscalculation," his experience could prove instructive to contemporary ministers. That Edwards was unable to serve "two masters" in 1750 questions "whether anyone could today."

Westra, Helen P. "Divinity's Design: Edwards and the History of the Work of Revival," pp. 131-57. Finds that Edwards's ideas and beliefs about the work of revivals in the "great drama" of redemption continue to influence evangelical movements "even in these post-modern times," in a study chiefly of six sermons from 1729 to 1749 on event-texts, scriptural texts occasioned by local happenings. Each of these sermons — on his grandfather's death, his uncle's suicide, the collapse of the meetinghouse gallery, the contentious townspeople, the seating plans for the new church, and the communion controversy — reveals the declension-revival pattern of the divine design of redemption and gains potency from Edwards's "intimate knowledge of his auditory." By addressing events and cultural circumstances in his own time and place, Edwards offers encouragement to American evangelists and revivalists today speaking to a "dramatically more fragmented, secularized society."

Jenson, Robert W. "The End Is Music," pp. 161-71. Counters the suppression of eschatology in the theology of modernity — dependent as it is upon mechanism, nominalism, and the "antimony of hope" — with Edwards's thoughts about end times. Edwards dismantled Newtonian mechanism to tell "a *story* of the world" with the triune story of God in a single dramatic narrative, a "*love* story" of the supreme harmony of the Trinity and of created persons, enabling the "meta-harmony of the infinite and the finite harmonies." Edwards identified such mutual love as music, a harmony of God's being and our love in the "divine fugue of as many voices as there are blessed creatures."

McDermott, Gerald R. "A Possibility of Reconciliation: Jonathan Edwards and the Salvation of Non-Christians," pp. 173-202. Formulates Edwards's views on the possibility of the salvation of the "'heathen'" from comments in his notebooks — fully a quarter of the entries in the "Miscellanies" concern non-Christian religions — and his voracious reading about them — travelogues, dictionaries, and encyclopedias as recorded in his "Catalogue." Edwards believed that pagans received knowledge of God's redemptive purposes, and if they failed to take advantage of it, it was, quite literally, "their own damned fault." His dispositional soteriology suggests that the only prerequisite to salvation is the "inner religious consciousness," and although this "nearly always" is a disposition to receive Christ, it could be possible without faith in him. Still, Edwards remains in "a curious tension": in most of his commentaries and sermons he took a "negative view" of the heathen, even in his Stockbridge years; at the same time, his theological speculations "opened the door" to a more hopeful salvation of them. "[T]hat God provided revelation for the majority of the heathen was sufficient to exonerate divine justice."

25 Lowance, Mason I. Review of *Jonathan Edwards's Writings,* ed. Stephen J. Stein, *American Studies* 40 (Spring): 125-27

Describes as "refreshing" Stephen J. Stein's volume of essays (1996.46) precisely because all twelve "*examine* [Edwards's] *texts closely,*" a "welcome, and healthy, antidote" to current literary criticism.

26 Lutz, Norma Jean. *Maggie's Choice.* Philadelphia: Chelsea House.

Reprints 1997.20.

27 Marchant, George. Review of *God's Passion for His Glory,* by John Piper. *Anvil* 16 (4): 328.

Suggests that John Piper's book (1998.32) may "whet the appetite for a first approach" to Edwards's theological and philosophical spirituality, but that it neither hints at nor provides the "much wider discussion" about him over the last 250 years.

28 McDermott, Gerald R. "Jonathan Edwards and American Indians: The Devil Sucks Their Blood." *New England Quarterly* 72 (December): 539-57.

Remarks the shift in Edwards's attitude towards Indians from disdain as "Satan's peculiar people" in Northampton to one more nuanced and subtle during his Stockbridge years — protecting the Housatonics against exploitive whites, pleading Boston and London for their rights to education and justice, urging the Massachusetts legislature to honor its treaty obligations to them. Edwards's "Miscellanies" reveal his "continual rethinking" of the spiritual state of the Indian, the relationship between regeneration and conversion, the traditional understanding of the limits of grace. "On this subject, in the last eight years of his life, Edwards was a work in progress."

29 ————. "Jonathan Edwards, Deism, and the Mystery of Revelation." *Journal of Presbyterian History* 77 (Winter): 211-24.

Examines Edwards's response to the Lockean and deist assertion that only reason could determine the authenticity of revelation. Edwards distinguished between fallen reason and regenerate reason, demonstrating that regenerate reason supported the authenticity of the Bible, but that the force of such an argument was "lost" on his opponents since they lacked regenerate vision. Although others in the Reformed tradition had proposed a similar distinction, Edwards drew it with "unprecedented subtlety" and left deists with an unreasonable God.

30 ————. "Unavoidable Contradictions." *Cross Currents* 49 (Summer): 270-74.

Contends that Leon Chai's use of Edwards is "incomplete," based as it is on rationality apart from its "larger theological context," in a review of his *Jonathan Edwards and the Limits of Enlightenment Philosophy* (1998.3).

31 ————. *Seeing God.* Seoul: Christian Literature Crusade.

Reprints 1995.31.

32 Minkema, Kenneth P., and Richard A. Bailey, eds. "Reason, Revelation, and Preaching: An Unpublished Ordination Sermon by Jonathan Edwards." *Southern Baptist Journal of Theology* 3 (Summer): 16-33.

Prints Edwards's unpublished sermon on a text from 1 Cor. 2:11-13 and delivered at the installation of Edward Billing in Cold Spring (later Belchertown) Massachusetts, 7 May 1740. The sermon reveals not only Edwards's conception of the ministry but his views of the relationship of reason and revelation and the Arminian threat, much of it derived "nearly verbatim" from his "Miscellanies." Unlike his "jubilant and celebratory" ordination sermons of the 1730s, this is quite polemical, a hint of the "darker, defensive" ones of the 1740s.

33 Moore, Cynthia Marie. "'Rent and Ragged Relation(s)': Puritans, Indians, and the Management of Congregations in New England, 1647-1776." Ph.D. dissertation, State University of New York at Stony Brook.

Analyzes the narratives of Indian missionaries — the experience of Edwards and his family among them — and their role in managing white New England congregations.

34 Moore, T. M. "A Brief Introduction to an Edwardsean View of Christian Instruction." *Presbyterion* 25 (Spring): 21-31.

Turns to Edwards — and Scripture — for guidance in the work of equipping "the saints for ministry" and links his writings and practice to Christian instruction: that it be goal-directed, that the goal be love, that its "satisfying and lasting" results can be realized laboring for it.

35 Morgan, Christopher William. "The Application of Jonathan Edwards's Theological Method to Annihilationism in Contemporary Evangelicalism." Ph.D. dissertation, Mid-America Baptist Theological Seminary.

Published as 2004.51.

36 Morimoto, Anri. "Salvation as Fulfillment of Being: The Soteriology of Jonathan Edwards and Its Implications for Christian Mission." *Princeton Seminary Bulletin*, n.s., 20 (1): 13-23.

Explains the concept of disposition in Edwards's ontology and its soteriological consequences in order to demonstrate its contemporary relevance to ecumenical and interfaith understanding of mission. His dispositional understanding of salvation, mission, and evangelism provides a paradigm that is "surprisingly inclusive and yet theologically responsible," consistent within itself and in his ontology. "Being provides, salvation invites, and grace achieves."

37 Munk, Linda. "Mr Edwards, Mr Lowell, and the Spider." *University of Toronto Quarterly* 68 (Summer): 790-95

Parallels several poems by Robert Lowell and Edwards's prose — the early "Spider" letter among them — in a review of *Letters and Personal Writings*, ed. George S. Claghorn (1998.5).

38 Navone, John, S.J. "Edwards and Aquinas." In *Enjoying God's Beauty*. Collegeville, Minn.: Liturgical Press, pp. 99-110.

Identifies the "unifying center" of Edwards's theology as the glory of God depicted as an active, harmonious, unfolding source of absolute Being of "supernal beauty and love," a theology of beauty that "squares" with the teaching of Thomas Aquinas. The dynamic activity of the triune God is at the "forefront" of Edwards's work — in his affectional view of reality, his understanding of a living faith, his notion of moral behavior — and testifies to his belief that beauty is God's "most distinctive characteristic," the key to man's encounter with him. Edwards shares with Aquinas the conviction that we know God through the "redemptive, transfiguring, joy-giving beauty" of his creation.

39 Nichols, Stephen J. Review of *The Devil's Mousetrap*, by Linda Munk. *Sixteenth Century Journal* 30 (Spring): 249-51.

Notes that Linda Munk makes a "positive contribution" to an understanding of Edwards's typology (1997.26), but she writes as an "outsider" — she was "trained in literature" — and her book "lacks coherence."

40 Pailin, David A. "Edwards and the Enlightenment." *Expository Times* 110 (May): 267.

Illuminates both "certain unsatisfactory features" of Edwards's theology and the limits of rationality, in a review of Leon Chai's *Jonathan Edwards and the Limits of Enlightenment Philosophy* (1998.3).

41 Pauw, Amy Plantinga. "The Future of Reformed Theology: Some Lessons from Jonathan Edwards." In *Toward the Future of Reformed Theology: Tasks, Topics, Traditions.* Edited by David Willis-Watkins and Michael Welker. Grand Rapids, Mich.: William B. Eerdmans, pp. 456-69.

Searches in Edwards for the future direction of contemporary American Reformed theology by remarking the major groups that define it: one that emphasizes correct doctrine; another, religious affections; and a third, which for the "most part" has not claimed him, the Christian life in social transformation. Edwards's *Religious Affections* focussed on the "communal nature of the earthly church," on Christian practice; his *True Virtue*, on the virtuous love among created beings derived from love to God. Thus to claim Edwards's vision of the "rich interplay" of doctrine, affection, and practice, Reformed culturalists must abandon their "bland religiosity" and seek their "neighbor's good at the source of their own happiness."

42 Pointer, Richard W. Review of *The Devil's Mousetrap*, by Linda Munk. *Fides et Historia* 31 (Summer): 146-47.

Advises readers to "begin elsewhere" for Puritan exegesis and eschatology — that is, Edwards, Increase Mather, and Edward Taylor — not in Linda Munk's "dense" book (1997.26).

43 Quinn, Philip L. "Disputing the Augustinian Legacy: John Locke and Jonathan Edwards on Romans 5:12-19." In *Augustinian Tradition.* Edited by Gareth B. Matthews. Berkeley: University of California Press, pp. 233-50.

Examines the "scriptural crux" of the doctrine of original sin — the "difficult series" of verses of Rom. 5:12-19 — in accounts of Augustine and the two "great philosophers" who wrestled with it, John Locke, in *The Reasonableness of Christianity*, and Edwards, in *Original Sin.* Edwards wrote his "powerful critique" to defend Calvinism's federal theology against Arminian assault, especially the Lockean interpretation in the work of John Taylor of Norwich, and the "metonymy gambit," charging St. Paul with equating *sinners* and *mortals.* Though Edwards's arguments are "persuasive" and the metonymy argument "fails," Christian philosophers should get more involved in the debate, engage "more closely" with biblical exegesis, and try to emulate those "exemplary" figures Locke and Edwards in the "intelligence, learning, energy, and passion" they brought to the task.

44 Sanna, Ellyn. "Introduction." *Religious Affections.* Uhrichsville, Ohio: Barbour Publishers, 1999, pp. [7-14].

Notes Edwards's "deep and unmoving" confidence in a living God, in a preface to an "abridged and updated" edition of *Religious Affections.*

45 Shea, Daniel B. Review of *Declarations of Independency in Eighteenth-Century American Autobiography,* by Susan Clair Imbarrato. *William and Mary Quarterly,* 3d ser., 56 (October): 852-54.

Sees Susan C. Imbarrato's focus (1998.21) on the movement from spiritual self-examination — Edwards, for example — to secular self-construction "not so much arguable as unfruitful"

46 Smith, M. A. Review of Jonathan Edwards, *Letters and Personal Writings,* ed. George S. Claghorn. *Journal of Ecclesiastical History* 50 (July): 604.

Remarks George S. Claghorn's "impressive" industry in gathering Edwards's letters (1998.5), an "excellent resource" for scholars and students of eighteenth-century New England.

47 Solberg, Winton U. Review of *Jonathan Edwards's Writings,* ed. Stephen J. Stein. *The Historian* 61 (Winter): 434-35

Thinks the dozen essays in Stephen J. Stein's collection (1996.46) "break new ground and offer fresh interpretations" of Edwards's thought, life, and influence.

48 Stagg, John W. *Calvin, Twisse, and Edwards on the Universal Salvation of Those Dying in Infancy.* Richmond, Va.: Presbyterian Committee of Publication.

Reprints 1902.12.

49 Stahle, Rachel Susan. "The Trinitarian Spirit of Jonathan Edwards' Theology." Ph.D. dissertation, Boston University.

Asserts that Edwards's theology is "founded upon and integrated by his own unique Trinitarianism." For him, the Trinity "unifies every aspect of reality" and finds its way in time and history, election and sanctification, religious experience and religious revival, glorification and damnation, in "every part of the implementation and fulfillment of this divine plan."

50 Stephens, Bruce M. "An Appeal to the Universe: The Doctrine of the Atonement in American Protestant Thought from Jonathan Edwards to Edwards Amasa Park." *Encounter* 60 (Winter): 55-72.

Pieces together Edwards's theory of the atonement from a number of published and unpublished sources, chief among them *Miscellaneous Observations;* remarks the place of the doctrine in the century following Edwards: Joseph Bellamy, Samuel Hopkins, Nathanael Emmons, Edwards's son, Stephen West, John Smalley, Jonathan Maxcy, Caleb Burge, and Edwards Amasa Park; and the role it played in the "ongoing discussions" about law, justice, and moral government in the early republic. In fact, atonement "took precedence" over Christology, justice and mercy over conversion and regeneration, the public sphere over the private.

51 ———. Review of *Encounters with God,* by Michael J. McClymond. *Choice* 36 (June): 1806.

Perceives Michael J. McClymond's "fresh approach" to Edwards (1998.23) yields "a sense of the whole rather than a glimpse of fragments" of recent studies of his theology.

52 Sweeney, Douglas A. Review of *Jonathan Edwards and the Limits of Enlightenment Philosophy,* by Leon Chai. *Theology Today* 56 (October): 438-43.

Holds that Leon Chai's "sophisticated" book (1998.3) both "oversimplifies" the history of modern thought and its "largely artificial juxtaposition" of Edwards and Enlightenment thinkers leads to "serious misconstruals" of him.

53 Taves, Ann. *Fits, Trances & Visions: Experiencing Religion and Explaining Experience from Wesley to James.* Princeton: Princeton University Press, pp. 34-41, 60-68.

Groups Edwards with "moderate" supporters of the transatlantic awakening — James Robe, Charles Wesley, and George Whitefield — in his encounter with the "twin dangers" of indifference and enthusiasm. Edwards, anticipating Charles Chauncy, drew upon naturalistic explanations in *Distinguishing Marks* to distinguish the "true Spirit of God from its counterfeits"; later, in *Religious Affections,* he developed the theological and psychological "underpinnings" of the distinction. He also provided four "in-depth" narratives of the religious experience, two before enthusiasm became a problem — those of Abigail Hutchinson and Phebe Bartlet in *Faithful Narrative* — and two when distinctions proved practical — Sarah Edwards in *Some Thoughts* and David Brainerd in Edwards's *Life.*

54 Taylor, Thomas T. Review of Jonathan Edwards, *Notes on Scripture,* ed. Stephen J. Stein. *Church History,* 68 (June): 491-92.

Commends to scholars Stephen Stein's "outstanding" contribution (1998.37) to the "already legendary" Yale series of Edwards.

55 Tracy, Patricia J. "Edwards, Jonathan." *American National Biography.* New York: Oxford University Press, 7:329-34.

Concludes that Edwards has become a "screen onto which each scholarly generation projects its needs to image early American thought," in a brief estimate of his life and works.

56 Valeri, Mark R. "Preface to the Period." *Sermons and Discourses, 1730-1733. The Works of Jonathan Edwards,* 17. New Haven: Yale University Press, pp. 3-44.

Follows the "overall contours" of Edwards's preaching between 1730 and 1733 — the third volume in the sermon series — by discussing the Puritan paradigm for conversion; the development of his homiletical method; the setting for preaching; his response to political and social affairs; his moral critique and doctrine of sin; and three "dominant" themes recurrent in these eighteen sermons: the theological end of human depravity, evangelical humiliation as preparation for conversion, and the necessity for a divine and supernatural light for regeneration. Edwards's homiletic powers grew the more he probed psychological and social sensibilities and learned "the language of ordinary experience." The evangelical theology that made Edwards famous emerged in his early Northampton pastorate as he reacted to local realities.

57 ———. "Religion and the Culture of the Market in Early New England." In *Perspectives on American Religion and Culture.* Edited by Peter W. Williams. Malden, Mass.: Blackwell, pp. 92-104.

Tracks religious attitudes to a market economy in early New England, enlisting Edwards as a "significant" transitional figure in the change from antipathy to acceptance, in a study of his ethics, particularly *True Virtue.* His concept of benevolence provided a framework for moral virtue "apart from the contingencies of local social relations" and would unite individuals into a "harmonious and beautiful whole," wherein God pours out his spirit to such an extant that regenerate man would "command the market as well as being pious." Still, Edwards "never displayed a fondness" for merchants or financiers.

58 Viscardi, Christopher J. Review of *Jonathan Edwards and the Limits of Enlightenment Philosophy,* by Leon Chai. *Theological Studies* 60 (March): 193-94.

> Weighs the "strongest" sections of this study (1998.3) of Edwards's affinity with the Enlightenment, his philosophical argumentation, against the "weakest" sections, his theology and spirituality.

59 Walton, Brad. "'Formerly Approved and Applauded': The Continuity of Edwards's 'Treatise concerning Religious Affections' with Seventeenth-Century Analyses of Piety, Spiritual Sensation and Heart-Religion." Th.D. dissertation, Wycliffe College.

> Reprinted (revised) as 2002.48.

60 Williams, Mark F. "The Lord's Supper and New Divinity: Post-Edwardsean Theology and Practice in the Context of the Colonial Puritan Tradition of New England." Ph.D. dissertation, Trinity Evangelical Divinity School.

> Asserts New Divinity sacramental theology was "informed by a comprehensive Edwardsean theological system," but because it was not "fully articulated," some New Divinity emphases "contrast" with those of Edwards at Northampton.

61 Wilson, Stephen A. "The Virtue of the Saints: Jonathan Edwards on the Nature of Christian Ethics." Ph.D. dissertation, Stanford University.

> Declares that Aristotlean arguments "undergird a portion" of Edwards's Christian ethics, although the Aristotlean side "never superseded" the Augustinian side of the traditional canon. That Edwards was a "dyed-in-the-wool revivalist and orthodox Calvinist warrants reevaluation."

2000

1 Armstrong, John H. Review of Jonathan Edwards, *Sermons and Discourses, 1730-1733,* ed. Mark Valeri. *Reformation & Revival Journal* 9 (Winter): 205-208.

> Remarks Mark Valeri's "extremely useful and incisive" introduction to this "wonderful," if costly, volume of Edwards's sermons (1999.56).

2 Campbell, James W. Review of Jonathan Edwards, *Sermons and Discourses, 1730-1733,* ed. Mark Valeri. *Early American Literature* 35 (2): 216-17.

> Seizes upon these early sermons (1999.56) as an opportunity — "so ably provided" by Mark Valeri — to understand what Edwards as preacher brought to the experience and texts of the Great Awakening.

3 Caldwell, Robert W. Review of *Edwards in Our Time,* ed. Sang Hyun Lee and Allen C. Guelzo. *Fides et Historia* 32 (Summer): 164-65.

> Recommends Sang Lee and Allen Guelzo's collection of essays on Edwards (1999.24) to those seeking Christianity's "rich theological past to inform contemporary reflection."

4 Chamberlain, Ava. "Editor's Introduction." *The "Miscellanies" (Entry Nos. 501-832). The Works of Jonathan Edwards,* 18. New Haven: Yale University Press, pp. 1-48.

> Remarks the emergence of Edwards as "a spokesperson for orthodox Calvinism" from late 1731 to early 1740 — the period covered by this second volume of the "Miscellanies" — as he assumed "a prominent role" in New England church politics and acquired "an international repu-

tation" as an evangelist. Five themes dominate the entries — justification by faith alone; spiritual knowledge; the rationality of the Christian religion; the history of redemption; conversion and the religious life — and record his intellectual development during those formative years, a time of his first published sermons, *God Glorified* (1731) and *Divine and Supernatural Light* (1734); his first treatise, *Justification by Faith Alone* (1738); and his first account of revival, *Faithful Narrative* (1737). Edwards's reflections upon that revival and its aftermath in Northampton "permanently transformed" his work as a theologian.

5 ———. "The Immaculate Ovum: Jonathan Edwards and the Construction of the Female Body." *William and Mary Quarterly*, 3d ser., 57 (April): 289-322.
Discovers among several entries in Edwards's "Miscellanies" theories of conception and fetal development then current in Europe, a "transitional moment" in the history of human anatomy. Edwards extends Christ's election to Mary through the notion of the immaculate ovum and to Eve through preformation and encasement, in a construction of the female body consonant with his theological commitments, Scripture and nature at one in revelation. But "remnants" of the older one-sex model of anatomy survive in Edwards, and when confronted with the bad-book episode, he found his parishioners had rejected it — and with it, him — to embrace the new two-sex paradigm.

6 ———. Review of *Encounters with God,* by Michael J. McClymond. *Church History* 69 (March): 215-16.
Welcomes Michael J. McClymond's explication of various Edwards's texts (1998.23) to identify its "apologetic purpose," but finds "problematic" his exclusion of *Freedom of the Will* and *Original Sin.*

7 Danaher, William J., Jr. Review of *Jonathan Edwards Confronts the Gods,* by Gerald R. McDermott. *Theological Studies* 61 (December): 761-62.
Ranks Gerald R. McDermott's study (2000.26) "one of the finest, most sensitive, and well-written works on Edwards available in recent years."

8 ———. Review of *Jonathan Edwards Confronts the Gods,* by Gerald R. McDermott. *Sewanee Theological Review* 44 (Christmas): 120-22.
Reprints 2000.7.

9 DeProspo, R. C. Review of *Jonathan Edwards and the Limits of Enlightenment Philosophy,* by Leon Chai. *Early American Literature* 35 (1): 97-101
Calls "most original" Leon Chai's use of Edwards (1998.3) to critique the Enlightenment, not celebrate it, as do most Americanists.

10 Gallagher, Edward J. "'Sinners in the Hands of an Angry God': Some Unfinished Business." *New England Quarterly* 73 (June): 202-21.
Focusses on "the rhythm, the beat, the sound" of Edwards's *Sinners in the Hands of an Angry God* to identify a "recurrent pulsation" inherent in it, not external to it, such as delivery. Primarily an *"auditory"* experience, the pulsation in the sermon "works broadly to destroy old ways of thought in the first half of the sermon and to build new visions in the second." Literary critics should take up the "unfinished business" of understanding the internal dynamics of his other writings.

11 Grasso, Christopher. Review of *Jonathan Edwards and the Limits of Enlightenment Philosophy,* by Leon Chai. *Journal of American History* 86 (March): 1755-56.

Decries Leon Chai's reduction of Edwards's philosophical theology (1998.3) to so many propositions and inferences "abstracted from time, place, and circumstance."

12 Guelzo, Allen C. "Self-Improvement: The Surprising Connection between American Political Theory and Cognitive Psychology." *Books & Culture* 6 (March): 28-30.

Doubts Daniel Walker Howe's reading of Edwards on self-help, in a review of his "uneven" *The Making of the American Self* (1997.13).

13 Gustafson, Sandra M. "Gender in Performance." *Eloquence Is Power: Oratory and Performance in Early America.* Chapel Hill: University of North Carolina Press, pp. 40-74.

Recasts 1994.11.

14 Hannah, John D. Review of *The Sermons of Jonathan Edwards,* ed. Wilson H. Kimnach, Kenneth P. Minkema,, and Douglas A. Sweeney. *Bibliotheca Sacra* 157 (January): 117-18.

Regards these "superbly edited" sermons (1999.21) as a "wonderfully readable" way into the practice and thought of Edwards.

15 Holmes, Stephen R. *God of Grace and God of Glory: An Account of the Theology of Jonathan Edwards.* Edinburgh: T. & T. Clark, xiv, 289 pp.

Sketches the contours of God's "divine act of self-glorification" and its significance to the Reformed tradition, in a study of how it informs Edwards's theology. Edwards uses trinitarian grammar to suggest it was an act of "divine ekstasis" — the sending of the Son and Spirit by the Father — and develops a "remarkably robust and satisfying" doctrine from it, in his teleology, metaphysics, typology, and soteriology. All of this bears directly upon our understanding of "this significant and creative theologian" and the "relationships and coherence of Christian doctrinal claims."

16 ———. "The Justice of Hell and the Display of God's Glory in the Thought of Jonathan Edwards." *Pro Ecclesia* 9 (Fall): 389-403.

Restores hell to its proper place in the writings of Edwards, a "late, and able exponent" of a homiletic tradition then "rapidly losing ground." Hell, for Edwards, was part of the "great drama" of God's actions in creation and redemption, part of the glorification of God.

17 Hosier, Helen K., and Oili Räsänen. *Jonathan Edwards: Herätyksen Mies.* Hämeenlinna: Päivä, Gummerus, 160 pp.

Translates 1999.17. (In Finnish.)

18 Howson, Barry. Review of Jonathan Edwards, *Sermons and Discourses, 1730-1733,* ed. Mark Valeri. *ARC* 28: 193-94.

Gauges Mark Valeri's introduction to Edwards's early Northampton sermons (1999.56) both "helpful and intriguing."

19 Kirk, Sandra Davis. "Revival among America's First Postmodern Generation." Ph.D. dissertation, Fuller Theological Seminary.

Develops a model based on the works of Edwards, John Wesley, and Charles Grandison Finney to "quantitatively" and "objectively" evaluate the results of postmodern revivals.

20 Kreider, Glenn Richard. "Jonathan Edwards's Interpretation of Revelation 4:1–8:1." Ph.D. dissertation, Dallas Theological Seminary.

> Published as 2004.36.

21 Lee, Sang Hyun. *The Philosophical Theology of Jonathan Edwards.* Princeton, N.J.: Princeton University Press, xv, 274 pp.

> Expands 1988.25 by adding ten pages to "state clearly that the coincidence of actuality and disposition, according to Edwards, is true for the divine being *as the Trinity.*"

22 Lukasik, Christopher. "Feeling the Force of Certainty: The Divine Science, Newtonianism, and Jonathan Edwards's 'Sinners in the Hands of an Angry God.'" *New England Quarterly* 73 (June): 222-45.

> Couples Edwards's interest in Newtonian mechanics with divine revelation and the sermonic form — the certainty of gravity with the certainty of depravity — in a study of *Sinners in the Hands of an Angry God.* As a "master rhetorician," Edwards found a way to convey the reality of divine retribution, to make the unregenerate not only feel the "terror of falling" but know the physical inevitability of it. More than a matter of metaphor, Newtonianism was for him an "integral part of a larger, ongoing intellectual project" that included his theological defense in *Freedom of the Will* and *Original Sin.*

23 Mathews, Matthew Todd. "Toward a Holistic Theological Anthropology: Jonathan Edwards and Friedrich Schleiermacher on Religious Affection." Ph.D. dissertation, Emory University.

> Explores "the centrality and nature of the religious affections and their continued importance for constructive theological thinking about the nature of the human," in a study of Edwards and Schleiermacher. Redemption "effects a Christomorphic transformation" of both distorted affection and reason and so "restores an affectional rationality" attuned to the beauty of the world.

24 McCarthy, Keely E. "'Reducing them to civilitie': Religious Conversions and Cultural Transformations in Protestant Missionary Narratives, 1690-1790." Ph.D. dissertation, University of Maryland, College Park.

> Cites Edwards's failure to "resolve the problem of cultural difference" between missionary and Indian in *Life of Brainerd,* in a study of the relationship between religion and culture in Protestant missions here and abroad.

25 McDermott, Gerald R. *Can Evangelicals Learn from World Religions? Jesus, Revelation, and Religious Traditions.* Downers Grove, Ill.: InterVarsity Press, pp. 96-108.

> Unpacks Edwards's understanding of the relation between the covenant of works of the Old Testament and the covenant of grace of the New, explains his extension of typology to history and nature, and draws out the implications for other religions. Edwards conceived of works as an outer shell, grace as the inner core, such that the gospel was "imperfectly and seldom" revealed in the one and "demonstrated fully" in the other, but that the two were actually different ways of performing a single covenant; and he held that typology was a theological way for religions outside the Judeo-Christian tradition to "affirm the possibility" of revelation. Still, Ed-

wards "never had much hope" for the salvation of heathens nor Gentiles much to teach Christians.

26 ———. "Jonathan Edwards and the Salvation of Non-Christians." *Pro Ecclesia* 9 (Spring): 208-27.
> Revisits 1999.24.

27 ———. *Jonathan Edwards Confronts the Gods: Christian Theology, Enlightenment Religion, and Non-Christian Faiths.* New York: Oxford University Press, xii, 245 pp.
> Introduces "a strange, new" Edwards, one "fascinated" by other religions, "mesmerized" by non-European and unfamiliar faiths, yet "worried" by deism, the most radical strain of Enlightenment thought and the "gravest threat" to Christianity. Edwards developed an "elaborate scheme" for the role of other religions in redemptive history and sought to "disable" deism, which rejected revelation, by proposing its definition of reason was "narrow and finally unreasonable." For deists, religion is static and moralistic; for Edwards, religion is dynamic and draws the believer into "mystical participation in the divine." But for his early death, Edwards might have published on reason, revelation, and other religions, and opened a "new perspective on the thinking of America's greatest theologian."

28 ———. Review of Jonathan Edwards, *Notes on Scripture,* ed. Stephen J. Stein. *Fides et Historia* 32 (Winter): 146-48.
> Remarks that Stephen J. Stein's first volume of Edwards's exegetical notebooks (1998.37) "opens up another dimension in the thought of America's greatest theologian."

29 ———. *Seeing God.* Vancouver: Regent College Publishers.
> Reprints 1995.31.

30 Murray, Iain Hamish. *Jonathan Edwards: A New Biography.* Carlisle, Pa.: Banner of Truth Trust.
> Reprints 1987.22.

31 Nichols, Stephen J. "'An Absolute Sort of Certainty': The Holy Spirit and the Apologetics of Jonathan Edwards." Ph.D. dissertation, Westminster Theological Seminary.
> Published (revised) as 2003.74.

32 Oh, Moontak. "The Impact of Korean Revival Movement on Church Growth of Korean Evangelical Christianity in 1903-1963." Ph.D. dissertation, Southwestern Baptist Theological Seminary.
> Examines the revival theologies of Americans such as Edwards, in study of church growth in Korea.

33 Pauw, Amy Plantinga. Review of *Jonathan Edwards and the Limits of Enlightenment Philosophy,* by Leon Chai. *Calvin Theological Journal* 35 (April): 167-68.
> Dismisses Leon Chai's study (1998.3): its title is "misleading" — the focus is on Locke, Malebrance, and Leibniz — and its treatment of Edwards "implausible" without his theology.

34 ———. Review of *Edwards in Our Time,* ed. Sang Hyun Lee and Allen C. Guelzo. *Christian Century* 117 (19 April): 477-80.

Finds "refreshing" the "creative retrieval" of Edwards's voice from tradition in Sang Lee and Allen Guelzo's collection of essays (1999.24), a "hopeful sign" of his relevance today.

35 ———. "'Where Theologians Fear to Tread.'" *Modern Theology* 16 (January): 39-59.

Reports that Edwards retained a "sturdy confidence" in the existence of angels and the devil when such a belief was waning, in a study of two "bold angelologies" — his and Karl Barth's — and their eschatological implications. Edwards's portrayal of angels is a "beautiful enhancement" of his emphasis on the centrality of love and humility of the life of faith, especially in the person and work of Christ; his depiction of the devil shifts the focus from that to the "connections between pride and hatred," Satan's fall and defeat from his "exalted calling" an enhancement of his eschatology, centered as it is in the omnipotent glory of God. But Edwards's treatment of angels and Satan provides a "counterpoint" to his eschatology with another theme in his theology — the character of God revealed in Christ — and so renders his performance "more complex."

36 Peters, Michael David. "Jonathan Edwards's Politicization of Millennialism." Ph.D. dissertation, Saint Louis University.

Argues that Edwards's politicization of millennialism encouraged his parishioners to fight against the French in King George's War as against the Antichrist so that the millennium could commence in America.

37 Plantinga, Alvin. *Warranted Christian Belief.* New York: Oxford University Press, pp. 294-309.

Questions Edwards, a "peerless student" of the religious affections, about the relationship between affection and belief, both on the priority of the will or the intellect in the work of the affections and on the nature of the affirmation of faith. Edwards "seems to endorse" the priority of the intellect: the believer "first *sees*" the beauty and amiability of God, the affections following. As well, one either perceives the divine beauty in the "great things of the gospel" — the Trinity, incarnation, atonement, and so on — and infers they are from God and so believes; or one sees the divine beauty of them in the gospel and *"immediately"* believes them to be true and from God. The second proposition is the "stronger."

38 Reid, Jasper William. "Early Eighteenth-Century Immaterialism in Its Philosophical Context." Ph.D. dissertation, Princeton University.

Differentiates Edwards's version of immaterialism from George Berkeley's, in a study of the intellectual milieu in the first quarter of the eighteenth century. Although both had "a strongly Platonist flavor," Edwards drew on earlier theories of incorporeal extension and divine substance to fashion "a clearer conception" of the divine ideas than Berkeley.

39 Schillinger, Jamie A. Review of *Encounters with God,* by Michael J. McClymond. *Journal of Religion* 80 (October): 683-85.

Calls Michael J. McClymond's book (1998.23) an "edifying approach" and a "significant contribution" to the study of Edwards but lacks a "philosophical edge."

40 ———. Review of *Jonathan Edwards and the Limits of Enlightenment Philosophy,* by Leon Chai. *Journal of Religion* 80 (April): 347-48.

Regrets that Leon Chai's study (1998.3) holds together "somewhat uneasily" — too many thinkers in too short a space, explications of texts "often unique" to each thinker — that sections of it "tend to wander."

41 Schmidt, Bernard. "The Purchase Theme in Jonathan Edwards's *A History of the Work of Redemption*." *South Carolina Review* 33 (Fall): 114-23.

Uncovers the "critical" center of Edwards's definition of redemption — "a significant contribution" to western theology and religion — in the purchase theme evident in each of the three periods of *History of Redemption*. Not only his purchase theme but his concept of history continue in the words of Karl Barth: "the old master finds a stalwart modern representative."

42 Sproul, R. C. "Introduction." In *The Spirit of Revival: Discovering the Wisdom of Jonathan Edwards*. Edited by Archie Parrish. Wheaton, Ill.: Crossway Books, pp. 17-39.

Revisits *Distinguishing Marks*, Edwards's "map" to the Great Awakening, in order help contemporary evangelicals discern the presence of an "authentic" revival, in an introduction to a simplified, "modernized" edition of the text, including William Cooper's preface and a discussion guide.

43 Vaughan, David J. *Jonathan Edwards*. Minneapolis: Bethany House Publishers, 127 pp.

Finds the key to Edwards to be "knowing the power of consecration," his "ultimate vindication" the influence he continues to exert both in his "godly example" to average Christian men and women and through his writings, published in a definitive edition by his alma mater — "fallen prey to liberalism and secularism" — in a brief account of his life and work.

44 Viscardi, Christopher J. Review of *The Sermons of Jonathan Edwards*, ed. Wilson H. Kimnach, Kenneth P. Minkema, and Douglas A. Sweeney. *Theological Studies* 61 (March): 190.

Rates the collection (1999.21) "a major step in the advancement" of Edwards scholarship, an "excellent" introduction to the artistry, the social and cultural context, and the theological thrust of his sermons.

45 Ward, Roger. "Experience as Religious Discovery in Edwards and Peirce." *Transactions of the Charles S. Peirce Society* 36 (Spring): 297-309.

Observes that Charles Sanders Peirce "maybe the one thinker" like Edwards to warrant comparison, in a study of the architectonics of experience as religious discovery revealed in Edwards's 1746 treatise, *Religious Affections*, and Peirce's 1868 essay, "Some Consequences Four Incapacities Claimed for Man." Both affirm the "natural discovery of transcendent conclusions" and the religious worth of them; both insist the religious experience cannot be separated from the "character of the objects that orient their thought." Such a dialect may enable American thinkers to better evaluate religious claims for experience.

46 ———. "The Philosophical Structure of Jonathan Edwards's *Religious Affections*." *Christian Scholar's Review* 29 (Summer): 744-68.

Maintains that Edwards's twelve distinguishing signs of gracious and holy affections in the third part of *Religious Affections* reflect a "discrete arrangement" and constitute an "architectonic structure" of conversion. For Edwards, conversion was an ordered process that brought order to religious experience and practice and was "central" to his experimental religion. Its complex structure has the potential to provide "continuing ground" for reconciliation between God's demand on humanity and human efforts to respond to it.

47 Wilson, Kenneth. Review of *The Sermons of Jonathan Edwards,* ed. Wilson H. Kimnach, Kenneth P. Minkema, and Douglas A. Sweeney. *Epworth Review* 27 (October): 75-76.

Suggests that attending to Edwards's sermons (1999.21) "will not come amiss, even if the literary style is archaic and the circumstances so apparently different" from our own.

48 Withrow, Brandon G. "An Empty Threat: Jonathan Edwards on Y2K and the Power of Preaching." *Reformation & Revival Journal* 9 (Winter): 69-92.

Differentiates between Edwards's vision of the future and the doomsday anticipated by today's theologians. Edwards taught that Christ "transforms culture," that Christianity "slowly fills the world" with the truth of the gospel, and that preaching it raises the culture into "one holy and happy society." Even in dark times, Edwards held, "God still works revival and reformation in the progress of redemption."

49 ———. Review of Jonathan Edwards, *Letters and Personal Writings,* ed. George S. Claghorn. *Fides et Historia* 32 (Summer): 162-64.

Gains an "invaluable look" into Edwards's life and relationships perusing George Claghorn's "insightful" volume of letters (1998.5).

2001

1 Armstrong, John H. Review of *God of Grace and God of Glory,* by Stephen R. Holmes. *Reformation & Revival Journal* 10 (Summer): 189-92.

Agrees with Stephen R. Holmes until his last chapter (2000.15), where he suggests that Edwards's view of reprobation is "non-Christological."

2 ———. Review of Jonathan Edwards, *Letters and Personal Writings,* ed. George S. Claghorn. *Reformation & Revival Journal* 10 (Spring): 166-69.

Gains a "unique insight" into Edwards's private life, as well as his thoughts on slavery, his dismissal, and his Stockbridge years, through this "amazing" collection of letters (1998.5).

3 Ayabe, John. "A Search for Meaning: Principles of Literal and Spiritual Exegesis in Jonathan Edwards's 'Notes on Scripture.'" Ph.D. dissertation, Trinity Evangelical Divinity School.

Identifies the principles that guided Edwards's exegetical thought — a mixture of both literal and spiritual interpretations, historical and typological — as recorded in *Notes on Scripture.*

4 Baird, Allen Robert. "The 'Psychological Analogy' of the Doctrine of the Trinity: A Comparative Study." Ph.D. dissertation, Queen's University of Belfast.

Analyzes the "singular" texts of Augustine, Anselm, and Edwards to provide an "approved and authentic ancestry" to Cornelius Van Til's controversial "psychological analogy" doctrine of the Trinity.

5 Bebbington, David W. Review of *Edwards in Our Time*, ed. Sang Hyun Lee and Allen C. Guelzo. *Journal of Ecclesiastical History* 52 (October): 762-63.

Contends that Edwards is "too little appreciated" outside America and that scholars would "profit from fuller attention" to such essays found in Sang Lee and Allen Guelzo's collection (1999.24).

6 Bolt, John. "America as God's Kingdom: Abraham Kuyper and Jonathan Edwards." *A Free Church, a Holy Nation: Abraham Kuyper's American Public Theology.* Grand Rapids, Mich.: William B. Eerdmans, pp. 187-225.

Provides "ample evidence" of the difficulty of constructing an American evangelical public theology, in a "reflective" comparison of Abraham Kuyper and Edwards and their views on America's place in providential history, their interpretations of John's Apocalypse, and the ontological foundations of their public theologies on trinitarian beauty and common grace. When they both invoke the "covenantal link" between Israel and America — or the Netherlands — it seems all too "facile," but their ontological correctives and universal perspectives on the cosmic work of the Holy Spirit are "essential building blocks" for an American public theology, and together Edwards and Kuyper remain "essential guides" in the project.

7 Brekus, Catherine A. "Children of Wrath, Children of Grace: Jonathan Edwards and the Puritan Culture of Child Rearing." In *The Child in Christian Thought.* Edited by Marcia J. Bunge. Grand Rapids, Mich.: William B. Eerdmans, pp. 300-28.

Cites the conversion of Phebe Bartlet as an illustration of Edwards's view of children: "indelibly tainted" with original sin but capable of "genuine faith." Although he defended the traditional Calvinist and Puritan notion of infant damnation, Edwards "subtly undermined" it with his belief in the "essential humanity" of the young and took "seriously" their religious thoughts and questions. Influenced by the intellectual currents of his time and place, he has bequeathed an "ambivalent legacy" to future Christians in search of a theology of childhood.

8 Carpenter, John Berry. "Globalization and the 'City upon a Hill': The Puritan Economic Ethic and the Fate of New England Puritanism." Ph.D. dissertation, Lutheran School of Theology.

Notes that Edwards's writings helped "touch off" the great century of missions.

9 Chamberlain, Ava. Review of *Jonathan Edwards Confronts the Gods*, by Gerald R. McDermott. *Journal of the American Academy of Religion* 69 (September): 713-16.

Concludes that while Gerald R. McDermott "succeeds in exploring a fascinating and virtually unknown aspect" of Edwards's thought (2000.26), he attributes to him a notion of the salvation of the heathen that "clearly goes beyond" the means of grace Edwards argued throughout his career.

10 Clark, David Edward. "Leveling Mountains, Drying up Rivers: Jonathan Edwards' Historiography Applied." Ph.D. dissertation, Westminster Theological Seminary.

Takes Edwards's historiography to be "the most important factor in his life, work, and career," focussed on millennial anticipation, expectation, and realization. Through it he transformed his doctrine of preparation and developed a "new model" of Christian experience and assurance.

11 Crocco, Stephen D. Review of *Jonathan Edwards Confronts the Gods*, by Gerald R. McDermott. *Journal of Presbyterian History* 79 (Winter): 294-95.

Credits Gerald R. McDermott with "significant new insights" into Edwards's attitudes towards non-Christian faiths (2000.26) but questions whether he has "read too much" into the "American Augustine."

12 Danaher, James P. "David Hume and Jonathan Edwards on Miracles and Religious Faith." *Southwest Philosophy Review* 17 (July): 13-24.

Determines that, although it is difficult to know Hume's "actual convictions" about Christianity, he took as its basis the same kind of miracles Edwards endorsed, in a reading of Hume's "Of Miracles," in his *An Inquiry Concerning Human Understanding,* and Edwards's *Religious Affections.* Both Edwards and Hume "caution us away" from the miraculous, pointing rather to an inward experience that "neither man is able to describe."

13 Daniel, Stephen H. "Berkeley's Pantheistic Discourse." *International Journal for Philosophy of Religion* 49 (June): 179-94.

Links Edwards — and Henry More, Joseph Raphson, and John Toland — to Berkeley's notion of God as "absolute space," citing "Of Being" among other texts.

14 ———. "Edwards, Berkeley, and Ramist Logic." *Idealistic Studies* 31 (Winter): 55-72.

Argues that Edwards and Berkeley are not metaphysical idealists but semantic realists, relying on the logic of Petrus Ramus (1515-1572) and his followers, not on Aristotelian subject-predicate logic or substance metaphysics. Although both describe the laws of nature as ordered sense experience attributable to the "direct activity" of God and describe that as communication or discourse, by "reframing" the discussion of mind and body, spirit and matter, as "discursive places," both engage the "rhetorical ontology" of Ramus. Instead of thinking of Edwards and Berkeley in idealist or immaterialist terms, it might be "more useful" to think of their philosophies by the "mentality that informs them."

15 Duban, James. *The Nature of True Virtue: Theology, Psychology, and Politics in the Writings of Henry James, Sr., Henry James, Jr., and William James.* Madison, N.J.: Fairleigh Dickinson University Press, 261 pp.

Suggests that Henry James, Sr., "systematically appropriated" Edwards's theology — chiefly *True Virtue,* but as well *Religious Affections, Freedom of the Will, Original Sin,* and *End of Creation* — and that it "resonates" in the work of his "illustrious" sons, the novels of Henry, Jr., and the philosophy of William. Edwards's notion of "benevolence to Being in general" appealed to the elder James in the construction of his theological socialism and proved compatible with his "reconfigured" spiritualism of Emmanuel Swedenborg, the usually cited source of his thought. Edwards's categories of benevolence — the differences between true virtue and specious appearance — have "vital implications" for Henry's characters in *The Ambassadors* and *The Wings of the Dove,* for example, as much as Edwards's equation of disinterested benevolence and true virtue are a "vital component" of William's psychology and the world of experience.

16 Gilman, James Earl. *Fidelity of Heart: An Ethic of Christian Virtue.* New York: Oxford University Press, pp. 46-49.

Draws on the work of Edwards, who "perhaps as much as any modern theologian understood the central role dispositions and emotions play in Christian life," especially *Religious Affections.*

17 Hambrick-Stowe, Charles E. Review of Jonathan Edwards, *Sermons and Discourses, 1730-1733,* ed. Mark Valeri, and *The Sermons of Jonathan Edwards,* ed. Wilson H.

Kimnach, Kenneth P. Minkema, and Douglas A. Sweeney. *Journal of Ecclesiastical History* 52 (October): 763-65

Notes the introductions to both books "reliably describe" the religious and political context of Edwards's preaching and the connection between his theology and evangelicalism: the first collection (1999.56) "opens a window" to his thoughts before the Northampton revival, the second (1999.21) reveals the "full range" of his talent, from his sermons as a young graduate to those as missionary to the Stockbridge Indians.

18 Herbert, Brook Bradshaw. "Resurrection of Beauty for a Postmodern Church." Th.D. dissertation, University of South Africa.

Examines the work of Thomas Aquinas, Edwards, and Gerard Manley Hopkins to define the concept of beauty consistent with Christian belief and to reassert its "fundamental and essential" value for the postmodern church.

19 Hinlicky, Paul R. Review of *Jonathan Edwards Confronts the Gods,* by Gerald R. McDermott. *Pro Ecclesia* 10 (Summer): 368-72.

Takes the occasion of Gerald R. McDermott's "intriguing" account of Edwards's response to the Enlightenment and other religions (2000.26) to address the "unsatisfactory positions" between exclusivism and pluralism of Christianity today, in an essay-review.

20 Holmes, Stephen R. *God of Grace and God of Glory.* Grand Rapids, Mich.: William B. Eerdmans.

Reprints 2000.15.

21 Isenberg, Nancy. Review of *Eloquence Is Power,* by Sandra M. Gustafson, *American Studies* 42 (Summer): 155-56

Remarks Sandra M. Gustafson's "new" reading of Edwards, in her "careful and intelligent" study of the "changing protocols" of formal and spontaneous speech in early America (2000.13).

22 Kuklick, Bruce. "Calvinism and Jonathan Edwards." In his *A History of Philosophy in America, 1720-2000.* New York: Oxford University Press, pp. 6-25.

Opens a history of American philosophy with an essay on Edwards and his "coming to terms" with the formulas of Calvinism, from his Yale years and his ministerial career to his major treatises, *Religious Affections* and *Freedom of the Will* chief among them. Already well known abroad at the time of his death, Edwards bequeathed to succeeding generations of American thinkers "the central question" of moral freedom. But in "clinging" to Calvinism, when the intellectual life of nineteenth-century America was moving into realms even Edwards did not anticipate, his followers were left "almost helpless."

23 ———. "Review Essay: An Edwards for the Millennium." *Religion and American Culture* 11 (Winter): 109-17.

Discerns in five volumes in the Yale series — *Ecclesiastical Writings,* ed. David D. Hall (1994.12); *The "Miscellanies," (Entry Nos. a-z, aa-zz, 1-500),* ed. Thomas A. Schafer (1994.38); *Sermons and Discourses, 1723-1729,* ed. Kenneth P. Minkema (1997.24); *Notes on Scripture,* ed. Stephen J. Stein (1998.37); and *Letters and Personal Writings,* ed. George S. Claghorn (1998.5) — three "overlapping" themes "critical to our comprehension" of Edwards — his significance as a revivalist preacher, as a "potent systematic thinker," and as a biblical exegete. Taken together, they suggest that the "most fruitful" path for scholars is one that views him in a popular religious tradition, that places him "more centrally in the provincial theological culture of premodern New England."

24 Lee, Sang Hyun, and Yong-sang No. *Chonadan Edwoju ui Ch'olhak Chok Sinhak.* Seoul: Han'guk Changnogyo Ch'ulp'ansa, 328 pp.

Translates 1988.25. (In Korean.)

25 Lesser, M. X. "Preface to the Period." *Sermons and Discourses, 1734-1738. The Works of Jonathan Edwards,* 19. New Haven: Yale University Press, pp. 3-36.

Suggests that at no time in a preaching career that spanned more than thirty-five years did Edwards sustain such mastery of the sermon form than during the five years between 1734 and 1738 — the scope of this fourth volume in the sermon series — a period covering the Northampton awakening and the publication of *Five Discourses,* the only collection he saw through the press. Edwards preached probably four hundred sermons — only half survive — during that time, touching upon youth and piety, the justice of God and the excellency of Christ, salvation and declension, "practical" sermons and occasional ones, a sequence on the ten virgins and another the fruits of charity, strife and dissension, earthquakes and pews. If Edwards's earlier sermons "hint at promise" and "often at fulfillment," the thirty-two here disclose not only "bright success but the type and end of his homiletic talent and the direction it would eventually take him."

26 Lutz, Norma Jean. *Jonathan Edwards: Colonial Religious Leader.* Philadelphia: Chelsea House Publishers, 78 pp.

Presents a life of Edwards for juvenile readers, in large type and difficult words in boldface.

27 Maddux, Harry Clark. "Ramist Rationality, Covenant Theology, and Puritan Poetics." Ph.D. dissertation, Purdue University.

Indicates that Ramist pedagogies found in the work of Anne Bradstreet, Michael Wigglesworth, and Edward Taylor tend towards Edwards's "philosophical theology of cosmic excellence" and influences in "identifiable ways" the rhetoric of the Great Awakening and nineteenth-century evangelicals.

28 McClymond, Michael J. Review of *Jonathan Edwards Confronts the Gods,* by Gerald R. McDermott. *Journal of Religion* 81 (July): 478-80.

Compares Gerald R. McDermott's "well-documented and clearly written" book (2000.26) to Edwards's unfinished notebooks that inspired it: it "tantalizes and leaves the reader thirsting for more."

29 McLean, Kate. Review of *Jonathan Edwards,* by Norma J. Lutz. *School Library Journal* 47 (May): 168-69.

Faults Norma J. Lutz (2001.26) for failing to "make clear the full significance" of Edwards in American history, an "attractive" volume designed for grades five to seven.

30 Minkema, Kenneth P. "Old Age and Religion in the Writings and Life of Jonathan Edwards." *Church History* 70 (December): 674-704.

Probes Edwards's earliest unpublished writings (and Northampton church records) to reveal that he shared a common attitude of the time towards the elderly and harbored a prejudice against them that "verged on outright hostility." From the beginning, and especially in his efforts at revival, Edwards focussed on young people and women, "threatening the church's aged-based, patriarchal hierarchy." Stirred by his antipathy and complaints that they failed to support the Great Awakening, older church members played an important role in the disputes that ended in Edwards's dismissal in 1750.

31 Nichols, Stephen J. *Jonathan Edwards: A Guided Tour of His Life and Thought.* Phillipsburg, N.J.: P & R Publishing, 247 pp.

Guides the reader on a tour of Edwards's "vast and rewarding" life, thought, and writings, not as a substitute for his texts, but as a help with them. Edwards's life was "intriguing," a "prince of pastors," a thorough student on a "wide variety" of subjects, a perennial figure with a "wholistic devotion" to God, a deep sense of his beauty and excellency. The tour includes a brief biography, his role as churchman and revivalist, his theological and philosophical studies, his pulpit presence, and a sketch of the various editions of the primary texts and a "few beneficial" secondary works.

32 ———. Review of Jonathan Edwards, *The "Miscellanies," (Entry Nos. 501-832),* ed. Ava Chamberlain. *Westminster Theological Journal* 63 (Spring): 202-205.

Cites Ava Chamberlain's "careful" presentation and "insightful" introduction to the second volume of the "Miscellanies (2000.4)," a "welcome new edition" to the Yale series of Edwards's work.

33 Nichols, William C. *Seeking God: Jonathan Edwards' Evangelism Contrasted with Modern Methodologies.* Ames, Iowa: International Outreach, iv, 564 pp.

Lays out Edwards's methodology of evangelism in detail and contrasts it with contemporary ones, in a series of introductions to seventeen manuscript sermons. This "greatest evangelist this country has ever produced" reignited the fires of hell to remind what "truly awaits" sleeping sinners. He taught — and contemporaries must learn — the character of God, the depravity of man, true and false conversion, and, especially, man's moral inability: to change his heart he must seek God.

34 Pauw, Amy Plantinga. Review of *Jonathan Edwards Confronts the Gods,* by Gerald R. McDermott. *Church History* 70 (September): 580-82.

Accounts "persuasive" Gerald R. McDermott's analysis of Edwards's fascination with heathens (2000.26), though it elides the "ambiguities" of Edwards's pastoral experience in Northampton.

35 Reid, Jasper. "Thomas Daniel: An Unknown Philosopher of the Mid-Eighteenth Century." *History of European Ideas* 27 (3): 257-72.

Suggests that Edwards's immaterialism "bear[s] some resemblance" to Thomas Daniel's, both inspired by Newton and "probably" Malebranche.

36 Rosengarten, Richard A. Review of *Declarations of Independency,* by Susan C. Imbarrato. *Journal of Religion* 81 (October): 703-704.

Pits the "richness" of Susan Imbarrato's analysis of "fascinating" texts (1998.21) — Edwards's *Personal Narrative,* for example — against its "struggle to conceptualize" such details into an "overarching paradigm."

37 Schmidt, Leigh E. "The Edwards Revival: or, The Public Consequences of Exceedingly Careful Scholarship." *William and Mary Quarterly,* 3d ser., 58 (April): 480-86.

Reviews volumes 13-18 of the "solid, enduring, proudly untrendy" Yale Edwards — *The "Miscellanies" (Entry Nos. a-z, aa-zz, 1-500)*, ed. Thomas A. Schafer (1994.38); *Sermons and Discourses, 1723-1729*, ed. Kenneth P. Minkema (1997.24); *Notes on Scripture*, ed. Stephen J. Stein (1998.37); *Letters and Personal Writings*, ed. George S. Claghorn (1998.5); Mark R. Valeri, *Sermons and Discourses, 1730-1733* (1999.56); and Ava Chamberlain, *The "Miscellanies," (Entry Nos. 501-832)* (2000.4) — and "one of the most interesting and important works on Edwards in the last decade," *Jonathan Edwards Confronts the Gods*, by Gerald R. McDermott (2000.26). Each of the Yale introductions amounts to a "critical monograph in itself," an exercise in "seemingly dispassionate" scholarship. Even so, the edition has become a "prominent bulwark" to current evangelical theology and philosophy, McDermott's study a "subtle" example of the connection between the public availability of Edwards's manuscripts and the "neo-evangelical renaissance."

38 Schofield, James Christopher. "A Study of the Interface of Prayer and Evangelism as They Relate to the Theme of Mission in the Acts of the Apostles." Ph.D. dissertation, Southeastern Baptist Theological Seminary.

Remarks how Edwards (among other "historical characters") linked prayer with evangelism, a "vital component" of missions in Acts.

39 Slater, Graham. "Exploring Jonathan Edwards." *Expository Times* 113 (December): 104.

Directs non-specialists to the final chapter, an "invaluable *Baedeker* for travel in difficult and unfamiliar theological terrain," in a review of Stephen R. Holmes's *God of Grace and God of Glory* (2000.15).

40 Strout, Cushing. "William James and the Tradition of American Public Philosophers." *Partisan Review* 68 (Summer): 432-45.

Notes that Edwards is one of three public philosophers — the other two are Ralph Waldo Emerson and William James — to give voice to the spiritual life of the American people.

41 Studebaker, Steve. Review of *Jonathan Edwards Confronts the Gods*, by Gerald R. McDermott. *Pneuma* 23 (Spring): 166-68.

Commends Gerald R. McDermott's "detailed analysis" of Edwards in an Enlightenment context (2000.26) but argues that his theology is left "undeveloped," his doctrine of justification misinterpreted.

42 ———. Review of *Edwards in Our Time*, ed. Sang Hyun Lee and Allen C. Guelzo. *Journal of the Evangelical Theological Society* 44 (June): 365-66.

Considers Sang Lee and Allen Guelzo's collection of essays (1999.24) a "snapshot" of Edwards's relevance to contemporary theological and philosophical thought.

43 Talbot, Mark R. "Sex in the Christian Life: Godly Emotions." *Modern Reformation* 10 (November): 32-37.

Cites Part I of Edwards's *Religious Affections* — and a good deal of Scripture — that "*all* true religion" consists of strong emotions.

44 Vaughn, William. "Orality, Divinity, Sublimity: Jonathan Edwards and the Ethics of Incorporation." *College Literature* 28 (Winter): 127-43.

Defines Edwards's ethics of incorporation — and compares its influence to that of Martin

Heidegger's — in a reading of *Personal Narrative, Religious Affections,* and *True Virtue.* Edwards interweaves history, ontology, and phemonology, through tropes of taste, incorporation, and the sublime and seeks to "negotiate the crucial distance between community and individual." Thus, his ethics attempted a reconciliation of God, self, and community, an incorporative ethics not premised on self or self-interest.

45 Vlastuin, W. van. *De Geest van Opwekking: Een Onderzoek narr de Leer van de Heilige Geest in de Opwekkingstheologie van Jonathan Edwards (1703-1758).* Heerenveen: Groen, 389 pp.

Outlines the Edwards's doctrine of the Holy Spirit, in an historical and systematic study of the theologian of revival, his preparation for the Great Awakening in *Faithful Narrative;* the conflicts that surrounded it in *Distinguishing Marks, Some Thoughts,* and *Religious Affections;* and his work after it in *Humble Attempt, Humble Inquiry,* and *Life of Brainerd.* The key to his revival theology is his pneumatology, and although Calvin and Edwards agree on fundamentals — the Trinity, election and reprobation, the perseverance of the saints — Edwards is the more radical and focussed, affording deeper insights into the power of the Spirit. (In Dutch.)

46 Ward, R. Review of *Jonathan Edwards Confronts the Gods,* by Gerald R. McDermott. *Choice* 38 (February): 1099.

Recommends Gerald R. McDermott's "thorough" investigation Edwards's challenge to deism (2000.26), a worthy addition to his "excellent" *One Happy and Holy Society* (1992.13).

47 Webber, Richard M. "The Trinitarian Theology of Jonathan Edwards: an Investigation of Charges Against its Orthodoxy." *Journal of the Evangelical Theological Society* 44 (June): 297-318.

Contends that Edwards's trinitarian theology is "certainly a departure" from Reformed formulations but at the same time "entirely orthodox," in an essay on his "voluminous output" on the subject, not a limited selection. Edwards considered the immanent Trinity of the Father, Son, and Spirit as part of the economic Trinity, the ontological relationships among them. Although he did not presume to "grasp fully" the mysteries of the triune God, he made "clear statements" of his orthodoxy: each person of the Trinity is to be "equally glorified" in the work of redemption, a mutual relationship of infinite love, a love "shed forth upon the saints."

48 Wilson, Stephen A. "The Possibility of a Habituation Model of Moral Development in Jonathan Edwards's Conception of the Will's Freedom." *Journal of Religion* 81 (January): 49-77.

Includes Edwards as a resource for the contemporary debate over Christian ethics of virtue — the others are Aristotle and Aquinas — and finds, in an examination of *Freedom of the Will,* the habitation model of moral development akin to Aristotle's. Although extracting the possibility of a virtue ethic from Edwards is a "difficult task" and contains significant challenges, it may prove useful to argue his "unique place" in intellectual history and work from a Reformed perspective. Edwards offers a kind of counsel in "closer proximity" to modern moral theory that Aquinas cannot.

2002

1 [Armstrong, Chris, et al.] *Jonathan Edwards: The Warm-Hearted Genius Behind the Great Awakening*. Carol Stream, Ill.: Christian History, 47 pp.

Collects thirteen short essays on Edwards, with illustrations and selections from his works, first published as Issue 77, *Christian History* 22 (1): 1-47.

Armstrong, Chris. "'Papa Edwards,'" pp. 7-8. Places Edwards at the "very root" of the Protestant family tree, the "'father of evangelicalism,'" his *Faithful Narrative*, a "sort of evangelical Baedeker's, Hoyle's, and *Joy of Cooking* rolled into one."

The Editors. "A Modern Puritan," p. 9. Configures Edwards as a "child" of the Puritans and a "brother" of the Enlightenment, conferring the riches of the one on the world created by the other.

Holmes, Stephen R. "A Mind on Fire," pp. 10-15. Scans Edwards's notebooks from the Stockbridge years for hints of the "towering" work to come from them — *Freedom of the Will, Original Sin,* and *Two Dissertations* — the fruit of a lifetime of "fervent thinking" about God, man, and nature, in a brief biography and estimate.

Bailey, Richard A. "Devoted Disciplinarian," pp. 16-18. Remarks how Edwards mixed "assurances" of God's love for his covenanted people with "stern reminders" of the requirements that it bestowed upon them, in an account of his Northampton pastorate.

Armstrong, Chris. "The Trouble with George," p. 19. Notes Edwards's critique of George Whitefield in a series of sermons during and after the visit to Northampton. (Adapted from 1997.4)

Nichols, Stephen J. "The Mind Shapers," pp.20-22. Traces the influence of four figures on Edwards's thought and work: John Calvin for his doctrine of the "new sense"; Solomon Stoddard for his "affectionate" preaching and five seasons of "harvests"; William Ames for *The Marrow of Theology;* and John Locke for his empirical approach to philosophy.

Nichols, Heidi. "Those Exceptional Edwards Women," pp. 23-25. Numbers the remarkable women in Edwards's life, among them, his mother Esther Stoddard, his wife Sarah Pierrepont, his sister Hannah, his daughter Jerusha, and Abigail Hutchinson and Phebe Bartlet of *Faithful Narrative*.

Noll, Mark. "Passing the Torch," pp. 26-28. Constructs a time line of Edwards's influence here and abroad, from the New Divinity to the Second Great Awakening, from missionaries in England to theologians in Scotland, from twentieth-century academics to twentieth-century evangelicals.

Edwards, Jonathan. "Pilgrim's Paradise," p. 29. Reprints an excerpt on heavenly bliss from "The Christian Pilgrim," a sermon on Heb. 11:13-14.

Kling, David W. "Testing the Spirits," pp. 30-34. Follows Edwards's search for the signs of those "truly regenerated" by the Spirit of God from *Faithful Narrative, Distinguishing Marks,* and *Some Thoughts* to *Religious Affections,* differentiating between those uncertain signs and the twelve signs of the true Christian, especially the last of them, which "'seals and crowns all other signs,'" Christian practice, and includes excerpts from William James's *The Varieties of Religious Experience* and Edwards's *Personal Narrative*.

Guelzo, Allen. "The Northampton Eviction," pp. 35-37. Outlines the events that led to Edwards's dismissal from his Northampton pastorate. In the end, he found himself "too distant from his congregants at too many points to salvage his relationship with them."

McDermott, Gerald R. "Holy Pagans," pp. 38-39. Lists three strategies Edwards developed to defend Reformed orthodoxy against deism — *prisca theologica,* typology, and "'disposition'" — the last "better evidence" of regeneration than explicit knowledge of Christ. His Stockbridge letters and notebooks suggest that the last category might include Indians, "holy pagans."

Nichols, Stephen J. "Thunderstorms & Flying Spiders," pp. 40-41. Recalls that Edwards was "a person of two books," the Bible and nature, in a brief account of *Personal Narrative* and the spider papers.

Sweeney, Douglas A. "Expect Joy!" pp. 42-43. Counters the image of the dour Edwards with his teachings of the sweetness and delight in pursuing God's ways, the happiness in the loving union with him.

[The Editors.] "On His Own Terms: A Conversation with George Marsden," pp. 44-46. Responds to questions about Edwards as a "cold fish": he was a "serious" person, but had a "lot of warmth and genuine concern for others"; as an "elitist": though a "creature" of British hierarchical society, he encouraged women to pursue an education, yet had a "blind spot" toward slavery; as a figure for today: his "fingerprints" are seen in revivalism, in American education, in the nature of religious affections, in a God-centered theology — a "loving God who stands at the center of reality."

Armstrong, Chris. "Recommended Resources: Jonathan Edwards," p. 47. Offers further readings of Edwards.

2 Bailey, Richard A., and Gregory A. Wills. "Introduction." *The Salvation of Souls: Nine Previously Unpublished Sermons on the Call of Ministry and the Gospel by Jonathan Edwards.* Wheaton, Ill.: Crossway, pp. 15-26.

Takes Edwards's "pervasive vision" and "central task" of the ministry and the church to be the "rescuing of the lost," in an introduction to eight manuscript sermons and another, "Ministers to Preach not their own Wisdom but the Word of God," recently published.

*3 Bombaro, John J. "Beautiful Beings: The Function of the Reprobate in the Philosophical Theology of Jonathan Edwards." Ph.D. dissertation, University of London.

4 Broome, J. R. *In Search of Souls: New England in the Eighteenth Century: Jonathan Edwards and David Brainerd.* Harpenden, Hertfordshire: Gospel Standard Trust, 107 pp.

Offers biographies — and brief selections — of Edwards and Brainerd, both used by God "as instruments in His hands" for the spread of revivals and the blessing of Indians in eighteenth-century New England.

5 Brown, Robert E. *Jonathan Edwards and the Bible.* Bloomington: Indiana University Press, xxi, 292 pp.

Addresses the manner and degree that the historical process of biblical narrative "permeated" Edwards's theological reflections and writings, one of the "most comprehensive and systematic" treatments of the matter in the colonial period. Edwards's approach accommodated the new learning in "significant ways," taking "seriously" the contributions of philology, history, epistemology, and natural science; yet there is "simply no way" to remake him as a modern thinker. Without taking into account his critical biblical interpretation, every other aspect of his thought — his doctrine, epistemology, historiography, typology, comparative religions, constructive theology, public discourse — would remain "largely unintelligible."

6 Carton, Evan. "What Feels an American?: Evident and Alienable Emotions in the New Man's World." In *Boy's Don't Cry?: Rethinking Narratives of Masculinity and Emotion in the U.S.* Edited by Millette Shamir and Jennifer Travis. New York: Columbia University Press, pp. 23-43.

Compares Edwards's and Franklin's "personal encounters" with George Whitefield — Edwards wept, Franklin did not — in an examination of the process of self-becoming in eighteenth-century America (and its internal resistances in St. John de Crèvecoeur's *Letter from an American Farmer*). Both confront the "vexed relationship between affect and identity," a contrast "most striking and significant" in the "emotional and sensory experience" in *Personal Narrative*, and its "virtual absence" in the *Autobiography*.

7 Chamberlain, Ava. "Bad Books and Bad Boys: The Transformation of Gender in Eighteenth-Century Northampton, Massachusetts." *New England Quarterly* 75 (June): 179-203.

Reassesses the bad book affair to suggest that it was less a manifestation of Edwards's declining ministerial authority than one of underlying social forces in eighteenth-century New England, chiefly a profound shift in gender relations from the "premodern world view" of the Puritans to the "laissez-faire approach of male sexual ethics" in the 1740s. Earlier such an affair would have generated "little debate" — and the offenders disciplined — for the sexes were then considered "spiritually equal." But Edwards presided during a time (and a congregation) in transition, and the conviction of gender difference made it "extremely difficult" for him to hold out against the changed position of a growing majority of his parishioners.

8 Cunliffe, Christopher. Review of *Jonathan Edwards Confronts the Gods*, by Gerald R. McDermott. *Journal of Theological Studies*, n.s., 53 (April): 400-402

Senses a "somewhat pedestrian feel" to Gerald R. McDermott's discussion of deism in an otherwise "thorough and painstaking" rendering of Edwards's views on non-Christian religion (2000.26).

9 Danaher, William Joseph, Jr. "The Trinitarian Ethics of Jonathan Edwards." Ph.D. dissertation, Yale University.

Published as 2004.17.

10 Davies, Ron. "Jonathan Edwards (1703-1758): Eschatology and Mission." *A Heart for Mission: Five Pioneer Thinkers*. Fearn, Scotland: Christian Focus, pp. 79-96.

Includes the hellfire preacher Edwards — an "unlikely candidate" for a book on missionaries — because he was a "missionary theologian" (throughout his life), "missionary biographer" (*Life of Brainerd*), "missionary trainer" (John Sergeant), "missionary strategist" (*Humble Attempt*), "missionary administrator" (Stockbridge), "missionary advocate" (*History of Redemption*) — and a "missionary" (to the Indians)!

11 Duban, James. "John Walker and the Early Edwardsianism of Henry James, Sr." *New England Quarterly* 75 (June): 276-85.

Connects "points of compatibility" of Edwards and the Irish Calvinist John Walker to Henry James, Sr., in a reading of the work of the three: Edwards's *God Glorified, Religious Affections*, and *True Virtue;* Walker's *Essays and Correspondence, Chiefly on Scriptural Subjects;* and James's *The Gospel Good News to Sinners.* James eventually used Edwsardsean ideas of true virtue to "frame [his] socialistic discourse," ideas that figure in the fiction of his son Henry as well.

12 Gelinas, Helen Kay. "'The Great Business of Religion': Conversion, Commerce, and Ambiguity in the Writings of Jonathan Edwards." In *Millennial Thought in America:*

Historical and Intellectual Contexts, 1630-1860. Edited by Bernd Engler, Joerg O. Fichte, and Oliver Scheiding. Tubingen: Wissenschaftlicher, pp. 187-214.

Contends that Perry Miller (1949.9 and 1956.8) and Sacvan Bercovitch (1975.3 and 1978.3) misread Edwards's postmillennialism, creating a "great divide" between his texts and their application of his eschatology to social and political developments in America, the "historical unravellings" following the Great Awakening. In his 1748 funeral oration for his uncle John Stoddard, *A Strong Rod,* a "superb outline" of the conflict of values between the people of Northampton and their pastor and a "wonderfully symbolic illustration" of his advocacy for theocratic rule at the expense of democracy, Edwards draws the line between commerce and conversion, private interest and public trust, regeneration and sham, distinctions rooted in his doctrine of salvation by faith, not works. His proposal to alter communion practice issued within a year, *Humble Inquiry,* sought to "clarify" his position — and prompted his dismissal.

13 Gilbert, Greg D. "'The nations will worship': Jonathan Edwards and the Salvation of the Heathens." *Trinity Journal,* n.s., 23 (Spring): 53-76.

Questions whether Edwards may be "properly conscripted" to the defense of inclusivism — first proposed by Anri Morimoto in *Jonathan Edwards and the Catholic Vision of Salvation* (1995.35) and advanced by Gerald R. McDermott in *Jonathan Edwards Confronts the Gods* (2000.26) — and concludes he neither "embraced" it nor does his system of theology allow for it. For McDermott, the idea that "unevangelized people may be saved apart from explicit knowledge" of or faith in Christ rests on Edwards's revision of *prisca theologia;* for Morimoto, dispositional soteriology. Far from being the spokesman for inclusivism, Edwards was "a clear voice" for orthodoxy, that salvation comes through conscious faith in Christ through hearing and understanding the gospel. (For McDermott's reply, see 2002.27.)

14 Gilpin, W. Clark. "'Inward, Sweet Delight in God': Solitude in the Career of Jonathan Edwards." *Journal of Religion* 82 (October): 523-28.

Develops a theology of solitude from *Personal Narrative,* the convergence of "solitary spiritual disciplines" — long hours of reading and study, intimate spiritual conversation, devotional seclusion, mental images of solitary presence before God — that shaped Edwards's career. These disciplines interact with "visionary images" of solitude in nature and, through the act of writing, "bridge" piety and his intellectual project as a theologian. The discipline of solitude allowed him to "compose and unify his vocation and accept as beautiful and fitting, and with all humility, the course of events into which his life had been cast."

15 ———. "Protestantism, American Style." *Christian Century* 119 (4 December): 40-41.

Tasks Mark A. Noll's "notable achievement" (2002.33) with dealing insufficiently with "two crucial features" of American Protestantism — personal piety and religious vitality outside the church — in a review of *America's God.*

16 Hannah, John D. "The Homiletical Skill of Jonathan Edwards." *Bibliotheca Sacra* 159 (January): 96-107.

Enumerates four points of Edwards's homiletics — the primary means of glorifying God, the inadequacy of finite language to convey the infinite, the vehicle for revealing and exalting Christ to the people, and the "enormous effort" required to bring it all about — an activity that joined his "deep passion for knowledge of God with his sincere love of God." Preachers today would do well to emulate Edwards: "Every preacher should so minister that he too can affirm the same steadfast commitment to the task of preaching Christ."

17 ———. "Jonathan Edwards and the Art of Effective Communication." *Reformation & Revival Journal* 11 (Fall): 109-131.

Calls "significant and tragic" the famine of the Word in evangelical pulpits and suggests Edwards's preaching as remedy. First, Edwards proclaimed the mind and will of God; second, he practiced the art of speaking and understood how people "most profitably" receive the Word; and, third, he presented a "beautiful" Christ for people to see and believe in. "I have sought out acceptable words," he said in leaving his Northampton parishioners, "that if possible I might prevail upon you" to forsake sin, turn to God, and accept Christ.

18 Henry, Caleb Barton. "Jonathan Edwards as Lockean Puritan?: Epistemology and Natural Law in Jonathan Edwards." Ph.D. dissertation, Claremont Graduate University.

Concludes that Edwards's "manipulation" of Calvin and Locke resulted in a political theory "much more Lockean" than usually assumed and a "substantial change" from earlier Puritan convenental thought.

19 Holmes, Stephen R. "Strange Voices: Jonathan Edwards on the Will." *Listening to the Past: The Place of Tradition in Theology.* Grand Rapids, Mich.: Baker Academic, pp. 86-107.

Demands that readers take "seriously" Edwards's *Freedom of the Will,* listen to his "diagnosis in all its strangeness," and challenge the "almost universal" Arminianism of modern churches, a doctrine so "deeply illogical, utterly inimical" to the gospel. Edwards is interested in ethics — the "moral agency, virtue and vice, reward and punishment" of the title — and freedom, the freedom found only in God, who orders all things and calls the community of morally responsible creatures to the "true freedom" found only in relationship with him. Hardly the "sad anachronism" of his day or ours, Edwards saw with "more clarity than most" the alternative notions.

20 Huffer, Mary Lee Stephenson. "Emily Dickinson's Experiential Poetics: 'Not precisely knowing/and not precisely knowing not.'" Ph.D. dissertation, University of Florida.

Places Dickinson within the context of the Westminister Confession and Edwards's works but proposes that her experiential poetics "within and against changing orthodoxy" are "best revealed" in the sermons of her contemporary, Charles Wadsworth.

21 Klassen, Ernie, ed. *Caracteristicas de un Autentico Avivamiento Presentando a Jonathan Edwards al Contexto Latino.* Lima, Peru: Grafitec, pp. xliii, 176 pp.

Translates Edwards's *Distinguishing Marks* (and *Personal Narrative*), with introduction and commentary, and adds brief remarks by several others. (In Spanish.)

22 Kreider, Glenn R. Review of *Jonathan Edwards Confronts the Gods,* by Gerald R. McDermott. *Bibliotheca Sacra* 159 (October): 503-504.

Takes Gerald McDermott's "outstanding analysis" of Enlightenment religion (2000.26) as evidence of his "passion for history, theology, and mission."

23 Lamborn, James Spencer. "Blessed Assurance? Depraved Saints, Philosophers, and the Problem of Knowledge for Self and State in New England, 1630-1820." Ph.D. dissertation, Miami University.

Considers Edwards (among other divines and philosophers) in an examination of the doctrine of assurance and the problem of human depravity.

24 Larsen, Dale, and Sandy Larsen. *Jonathan Edwards — Renewed Heart: 6 Studies for Individuals or Groups with Study Notes.* Christian Classics Bible Studies. Downers Grove, Ill.: InterVarsity Press, 63 pp.

Correlates six facets of the heart with Edwards texts — surrendered: *Excellency of Christ;* trusting: *God Glorified;* trained: *The Importance and Advantage of a Thorough Knowledge of Divine Truth;* warm: *Religious Affections;* peaceful: *The Peace which Christ Gives his True Followers;* and forgiving: *Farewell Sermon* — in a Bible study guide.

25 Maclean, Iain S. Review of *Jonathan Edwards Confronts the Gods,* by Gerald R. McDermott. *Anglican Theological Review* 84 (Spring): 428-29.

Views Gerald McDermott's "surprising and stimulating" work of historical theology (2000.26) an important correction to "popular misconceptions" of both Edwards and his thought.

26 Matless, Sally Ingalls. "Jonathan Edwards' Relational Metaphysics of Love." Th.D. dissertation, Harvard University.

Affirms that Edwards's relational metaphysics of love evolves from his earliest philosophical speculations, in a chronological study of his work, an "authentic and lively organicism." Thus *Two Dissertations,* the late expression of his metaphysics, ontology, aesthetics, and morality, arises out of the "continuous pattern of inter-relational development" evident throughout the canon.

27 McDermott, Gerald R. "Response to Gilbert: 'The nations will worship': Jonathan Edwards and the Salvation of the Heathens." *Trinity Journal,* n.s., 23 (Spring): 77-80.

Argues that Greg Gilbert "eliminated" ambiguity and nuance from Edwards's private notebooks, making him into a "tidy Calvinist" of the seventeenth century, in a quest to disprove his inclusivism. Edwards recognized "abnormal cases" — Old Testament saints were saved but did not explicitly know Christ; elect infants; New Testament saints such as Cornelius, "holy pagans" such as Job's three friends. Although Edwards did not finally resolve the "great question" of Christ and the religions, "let us not try to resolve it for him."

28 Minkema, Kenneth P. "Jonathan Edwards's Defense of Slavery." *Massachusetts Historical Review,* 4: 23-59.

Narrates Edwards's involvement in the slave trade and reproduces the bill of sale for his first slave, the thirteen-year-old Venus, and reprints a description of the conversion of an "African Woman," Rose Binney Salter, his former slave. Although Edwards tried to be a "just and Christian" slave master and deplored the cruelty of others, he recognized as early as his New York pastorate that slavery "prevented individuals from fulfilling their religious duties." By the 1740s he could invoke the image of Exodus to describe slavery, but he could not reach the conclusion of the later abolitionists and remained "an unapologetic defender of slavery" and slaveholder.

29 Moorhead, James H. Review of Jonathan Edwards, *Sermons and Discourses, 1734-1738,* ed. M. X. Lesser. *Journal of Presbyterian History* 80 (Summer): 122-23.

Welcomes the latest volume of sermons in the Yale Edwards (2001.25), a "reminder of the extraordinary richness" of thought of America's greatest theologian.

30 Mosser, Carl. "The Greatest Possible Blessing: Calvin and Deification." *Scottish Journal of Theology* 55 (1): 36-57.

Contends that, while it is not a "prominent" theme, deification is present in Calvin as it is in other "fountainheads" of Western theology, Edwards among them.

31 Munk, Linda. "Jonathan Edwards: Types of the Peaceable Kingdom." In *Millennial Thought in America: Historical and Intellectual Contexts, 1630-1860*. Edited by Bernd Engler, Joerg O. Fichte, and Oliver Scheiding. Tubingen: Wissenschaftlicher, pp. 215-28.

Makes an "extreme case" of one aspect of Edwards's millennial rhetoric, his use of biblical typology to promote his belief in an earthly messianic kingdom, the peaceable reign of the saints on earth. Edwards's disposes of scriptural proof texts in three categories: types pointing to the first advent of Christ (David); types of the messianic kingdom (Solomon); and prophecies of the heavenly kingdom. Coincident with the end of the papacy and the conversion of the Jews will be the opening of "the Messiah days," around the year 2000, when the world will enjoy a "thousand-year sabbath."

32 Nicholls, Jason Andrew. "'Certainty' with 'Power to the Contrary': Nathaniel William Taylor (1786-1858) on the Will." Ph.D. dissertation, Marquette University.

Highlights "underlying similarities" between Taylor and Edwards on the will to "salvage" him as a "modified" Edwardsean.

33 Noll, Mark A. *America's God: from Jonathan Edwards to Abraham Lincoln*. New York: Oxford University Press, pp. 22-25, 42-50, 271-77.

Contextualizes Christian theology from Edwards to Lincoln — a period when theology played an "extraordinarily important" role in American thought, when Protestant evangelical theology was "decisively shaped" by republican convictions and commonsense moral reasoning — and briefly outlines the body of Edwards's work, its "remarkable" cohesion, "brilliant renovation" of Calvinism, and the "long shadow" it cast over the nineteenth century.

34 Pauw, Amy Platinga. "Editor's Introduction." *The "Miscellanies" (Entries Nos. 833-1152). The Works of Jonathan Edwards*, 20. New Haven: Yale University Press, pp. 1-39.

Documents the "eventful and tumultuous" years between 1740 and 1751 — the period of this third volume of the "Miscellanies" — a time of the Great Awakening and its decline, of international celebrity and local hostility, of *Sinners in the Hands of an Angry God* and *Distinguishing Marks, Some Thoughts* and *Religious Affections, Humble Attempt* and *Humble Inquiry*, of trial and dismissal. Some entries reflect his "creative engagement" with issues of the moment: heaven's glory and hell's torments, saving faith and holy practice, true religion and the Trinity; others prepare for "larger apologetic works": long excerpts from the "ancient heathens" and his arguments against heterodoxies. These notebooks served as an "intellectual refuge" for Edwards: there are few allusions to his pastoral difficulties or millennial interests, the subjects of his contemporary sermons and publications.

35 ———. Review of *God of Grace and God of Glory*, by Stephen R. Holmes. *Interpretation* 56 (April): 220.

Values Stephen R. Holmes's study for its "trinitarian amplification" of Edwards's idealist ontology (2000.15) but questions his Barthian reading of Edwards's Christology.

36 ——. *"The Supreme Harmony of All": The Trinitarian Theology of Jonathan Edwards.* Grand Rapids, Mich.: William B. Eerdmans, x, 196 pp.

Focusses on the "harmonious interiority" of Edwards's trinitarian reflection, its "basic outlines" established in his notebooks and "Miscellanies" when he was twenty years old, an interest that "never flagged" throughout his life, though there is "scant evidence" of it in some of his polemical works. Edwards assumed that the Trinity was at the "center" of Christian faith, showing connections between God's communal love and religious experience, ecclesiology, and eschatology, modulating between two distinct models, one emphasizing divine unity, the other relationality, depending on the "immediate" theological and cultural context of his writing. Although his treatment provides an "important link" between disparate areas of his thought, the pervasiveness of Edwards's reflection reveals as well the "unsystematic, situational" character of his theology, notably through his "flexible array" of images of the Godhead and the role of the Holy Spirit, "the most original and the most problematic" aspect of his thought. Edwards's "largely untapped" work deserves a place amid the "tremendous renewed interest" of contemporary western theologians in the doctrine of Trinity.

37 Rée, Jonathan. "Absolutely Pragmatic." *Times Literary Supplement* no. 5198 (15 November): 27.

Questions the notion of "aligning philosophical cultures with national boundaries," in a review of Bruce Kuklick's otherwise "exemplary" *A History of Philosophy in America 1720-2000* (2001.23)

38 Reid, Jasper. "The Trinitarian Metaphysics of Jonathan Edwards and Nicolas Malebranche." *Heythrop Journal* 43 (April): 152-69.

Draws out both similarities and differences between the trinitarian views of Edwards and Nicholas Malebranche, their ontological theories "largely in conformity," their epistemological theories "significantly" different. Although "fundamentally in agreement" on morality, Edwards's "chief interest" lay with the Third Person, Malebranche with the Second, a difference reflective of their characters and their intellectual/religious objectives. Both are "conspicuous" among early modern philosophers in that their account of the Trinity is at once theologically orthodox and "absolutely central" to their respective metaphysical systems.

39 Rothchild, Jonathan. Review of *Fidelity of Heart,* by James Earl Gilman. *Journal of Theological Studies,* n.s., 5 (April): 418-19.

Uncovers "entirely too many" editorial mistakes in James Earl Gilman's "provocative" study of the cognitive character of emotions in Edwards, among others.

40 Sederholm, Carl Hinckley. "Dormant Talismans: Reconceiving America's Spiritual and Occult Notions of Identity." Ph.D. dissertation, University of Utah.

Notes Edwards's failed attempt to "divide" the spiritual from the occult, in a study of the narrative means of representing personal identity and religious faith in early American literature.

41 Sholl, Brian K. "On Robert Jenson's Trinitarian Thought." *Modern Theology* 18 (January): 27-36.

Contrasts briefly Edwards's trinitarian thought to that of Robert Jenson's in his *Systematic Theology.* For Edwards, "God as Trinity cannot be known as a repeatable object of knowledge reflected within human consciousness . . . , but as a non-identical repetition of eternal love to which univocal categories do not apply."

42 Sinitiere, Phillip L. Review of *The Sermons of Jonathan Edwards,* ed. Wilson H. Kimnach, Kenneth P. Minkema, and Douglas A. Sweeney. *Journal of the Evangelical Theological Society* 45 (December): 738-40.

> Remarks the "great service" rendered by the editors of Edwards's sermons (1999.21), restoring him to his "primary vocation," uncovering some of his exegetical and hermeneutical "innovation and brilliance."

43 Stein, Stephen J. "American Millennial Visions: Towards Construction of a New Architectonic of American Apocalypticism." In *Imagining the End: Visions of Apocalypse from the Ancient Middle East to Modern America.* Edited by Abbas Amanat and Magnus Bernhardsson. London: I. B. Tauris, pp. 187-211.

> Juxtaposes the "unlikely pair" of Jonathan Edwards, of Northampton, and David Koresh, of Waco, to illustrate the complexity of American apocalyptic ideas over the past four hundred years, in a survey of the shift of scholarly concern with millennial issues from mainstream figures and groups to marginal ones. Edwards spent two decades of "persistent private" study of apocalyptic exegesis, believed that revivals were the "start of something special," perhaps an "earnest" of the millennium itself, and was "quite mainstream," quite within the Anglo-American Puritan tradition. Koresh and the Branch Davidians decidedly were not.

44 Stewart, Carole Lynn. "Conversion, Revolution, and Freedom: The Religious Formation of an American Soul in Edwards, Melville and Du Bois." Ph.D. dissertation, University of Victoria.

> Singles out Edwards's "structure of conversion" in pre-Revolutionary Northampton, in a study of the notion of civil religion and the American self to Reconstruction.

45 Vanderspek, Dennis Randolph John. "From Edwards to Dillard: Puritan Mysticism and the Typology of American Nature Writing." Ph.D. dissertation, University of Western Ontario.

> Proposes that Edwards's use of typology "instantiated a nature structured by a textual economy of erasure, suppression, and revelation," in a study of mysticism in American nature writing.

46 Vetö, Miklós. "La volonté en elle-même: Jonathan Edwards." In his *La naissance de la volonté.* L'Ouverture Philosophique. Paris: Harmattan, pp. 151-80.

> Recasts "La mauvaise volonté salon Jonathan Edwards" (1979.41) and part of *La pensée de Jonathan Edwards* (1987.34) on the will. (In French.)

47 Wainwright, William J. "Jonathan Edwards and the Hiddenness of God." In *Divine Hiddenness: New Essays.* Edited by Daniel Howard-Snyder and Paul K. Moser. Cambridge: Cambridge University Press, pp. 98-119.

> Examines Edwards's views of revelation and noetic failure to frame a response to John Schellenberg's argument in *Divine Hiddenness and Human Reason* that a perfectly loving God does not exist. Edwards held that there is sufficient evidence available to believe in God's existence and goodness in everyone "capable of such belief," although sin has "blinded" us to its force. While Edwards's claims are not "novel," his treatment of them is "interesting and illuminating" and, more to the point, "defensible."

48 Walton, Brad. *Jonathan Edwards, Religious Affections, and the Puritan Analysis of True*

Piety, Spiritual Sensation, and Heart Religion. Lewiston, N.Y.: E. Mellen Press, vi, 256 pp.

Appraises Edwards's *Religious Affections* as a "conservative extension" of standard seventeenth-century Puritan pietism, not, as "much of scholarly literature" holds, a departure from it. *Religious Affections* is "heavily indebted" to that tradition for its analysis of religious sincerity and hypocrisy, its signs of regeneration, and its psychological model. Edwards inherited the "heart language" as well, rearticulating and giving it "more precise and coherent" expression than it earlier had, much as he developed not only a more systematic "consistency and exhaustiveness" of religious affectivity but also a more "polemical and defensive" posture than the Puritans.

49 Weber, Richard Martin. "'One-Step' Salvation: The Knowledge of God and Faith in the Theology of Jonathan Edwards." Ph.D. dissertation, Marquette University.

Insists that Edwards's soteriology "permeated" his work, that salvation resulted from a "single divine work of grace," and that all facets of it "united" in an illuminating work of the Holy Spirit.

50 Withrow, Brandon. "Jonathan Edwards and Justification by Faith [1]." *Reformation & Revival Journal* 11 (Spring): 93-109.

Proposes that Edwards's doctrine of justification by faith can contribute much to the "current debate" of evangelicals over the language of justification and its relation to the rest of the order of salvation, in a two-part essay. For Edwards, though not for traditional Protestant thinkers, the salvation process joins rather than separates regeneration from justification: a saving disposition contains the faith uniting one to Christ and declared righteousness.

51 ———. "Jonathan Edwards and Justification by Faith [2]." *Reformation & Revival Journal* 11 (Summer): 98-111.

Concludes a two-part essay. Unlike the contemporary discussion of justification, Edwards describes a person's righteousness as infusion rather than inherent; conflates the terms *regeneration, sanctification,* and *justification;* emphasizes the real as the foundation of the legal; challenges the understanding of the will and the disposition; argues perseverance as natural, not moral, fitness; gives love a "prominent position" as the object from which faith flows; and "undermines" the assumption that all theologians argue justification in a like manner. Edwards offers a "creative" soteriological view necessary for an ecumenical exchange.

52 Zakai, Avihu. "Jonathan Edwards and the Language of Nature: The Re-Enchantment of the World in the Age of Scientific Reasoning." *Journal of Religious History* 26 (Fall): 5-41.

Recognizes Edwards as "one of the rare individuals anywhere" to take up the challenge to traditional Christian belief posed by the new science and the Enlightenment, in a study of his early scientific and philosophical writings and late *End of Creation.* Edwards constructed "a whole new" philosophical and theological alternative to the mechanistic interpretation of the essential nature of reality by reconstituting the glory of God's sovereignty and divine presence — a "re-enchantment" of the natural world — by, first, claiming that God created the world so that things natural would represent things divine and, second, by invoking the notion of a hierarchal universe, a great chain of being of spiritual, not material, things. For Edwards, the whole creation is the "overflowing of divine being" and depends "moment by moment" on divine activity, thus restoring God's transcendence and immanence.

2003

1 Anderson, Douglas A. "Awakening in the Everyday: Experiencing the Religious in the American Philosophical Tradition." In *Pragmatism and Religion: Classical Sources and Original Essays.* Edited by Stuart E. Rosenbaum. Urbana: University of Illinois Press, pp. 142-52.

   Locates the "heart" of the American religious experience, not in a particular belief or set of beliefs but in an "ongoing process" of conversions or awakenings, first "fully articulated" by Edwards and expressed later by Thoreau and John Dewey. His diary and *Personal Narrative* disclose not only ecstatic conversion but an "undercurrent of frustration" about its incompleteness, the necessity of further awakenings. The "central irony" of his religious experience is that he "kept questing and seeking when his doctrines told him explicitly that there was not need to do so."

2 Armstrong, John H., ed. "Jonathan Edwards: An Anniversary Celebration." *Reformation & Revival Journal* 12 (Summer): 7-204.

   Celebrates Edwards tercentenary in nearly two hundred pages of an issue of *Reformation & Revival Journal.*

   Armstrong, John H. "Introduction," p. 7. Welcomes readers to a "good-sized dose" of Edwards.

   McDermott, Gerald R. "Jonathan Edwards, Theologian for the Church," pp. 11-23. Divides Edwards's theology into that which is familiar to "nearly all" readers — his "lifelong battle" with deism — and that which isn't — the relationship between baptism and regeneration, expressed in "Miscellanies," nos. 577, 595, and 689. Edwards's understanding of baptism rested on his conception of the covenant, a sacrament of initiation into the church and a possible sign and seal of regeneration. The church, according to Edwards, receives the baptized into God's family, who are "'as it were'" redeemed and justified: the eternal benefits are "*presumptively* promised" on condition of the perseverance of faith, the final determination at Judgment.

   Nichols, Stephen J. "Heaven Is a World of Love, Congregations Can Be Full of Strife: The Life of Jonathan Edwards and Handling Conflict," pp. 25-42. Offers a synopsis of Edwards's life, focussing on the conflicts he encountered — during his father's tenure in East Windsor, his Northampton pastorate, his Stockbridge years — conflicts that "appeared to seek him out." "Heaven as a World of Love," the last sermon of his series on 1 Cor. 13 — in time *Charity and its Fruits* — was "quite incarnational," for it grew out of those conflicts and struggles. Rather than the "classic" *Sinners in the Hands of an Angry God,* that sermon reflects Edwards's thought and preaching, his vision and the "standard by which he gauged his own life."

   Caldwell, Robert W., III. "The Holy Spirit as the Bond of Union in the Theology of Jonathan Edwards," pp. 43-58. Anchors Edwards's "life-long fascination" with the nature of the religious experience — indeed, his "theological vision" — in the doctrine of the Holy Spirit. Edwards conceived of the Holy Spirit as the "personal divine love" binding Father and Son, a union of love communicated to created beings binding them to God, Christians to Christ. For Edwards, Christians honor the Holy Spirit as the "third *person*" of the Trinity, a communion of Father and Son.

   Storms, C. Samuel. "Is Imputation Unjust? Jonathan Edwards on the Problem of Original Sin," pp. 61-69. Questions Edwards's solution to the problem of original sin — his notions of continuous creation and personal identity — for there is "*not* a legitimate correspondence" between the identity of a self and successive moments in time, and the "alleged" identity between all selves and Adam. Although his theories "may well be correct," Edwards fails to provide a "cogent basis" for responding to objections brought by John Taylor and others on the morality of imputation. Perhaps, Edwards should have left it as God's determination, instead of attempting to "*prove*" it based on philosophical and theological theories.

Kreider, Glenn. "'God Never Begrutches His People Anything They Desire': Jonathan Edwards and the Generosity of God," pp. 71-91. Explicates the text, doctrine, and application of Edwards's sermon on Ps. 21:4, "The Terms of Prayer," delivered in May 1738 (and published for the first time in the Yale Edwards, 2001.25). Edwards encouraged his people to pray because of God's "generosity," because of his nature. Edwards's insights into prayer and the character of God remain "timely" for us today.

Helm, Paul. [Quotation], p. 92. Notes Edwards's use of Locke.

Jenson, Robert W. [Quotation], p. 93. Offers eschatology as the organizing principle of Edwards's unwritten *summa*.

Smart, Robert D. "Jonathan Edwards' Experimental Calvinism: Pastors Learning Revival Harmony of Theology and Experience from a Leader in the Great Awakening," pp. 95-106. Cites Edwards's experimental Calvinism as a remedy to the "defective" revival experiences of New England — discovering God's love and grace without a "prorportionate" discovery of God's majesty and holiness, leading to pride and presumption; or the reverse, leading to unbelief and oppression — and recommends his "wisdom and guidance" to today's pastors. Edwards's published narratives and sermons on the revival experience "countered this polarization" of God's excellencies, proportioning one to another, tempering them together in harmony.

"A *Reformation & Revival Journal* Interview with Michael J. McClymond," pp. 109-40. Records how Michael McClymond's interest in Edwards developed — his conversion experience, his reading of Louis Berkhof's *Systematic Theology*, his study of the Reformed tradition at Yale, his reaction to *End of Creation*, "a great book [that] moved me deeply" — the genesis of *Encounters with God* (1998.23), and the popularity of Edwards today. "I think Edwards is, arguably, the most important writer, not only in the modern period or in Protestantism, but in all the history of the Church on the subject of spiritual discernment, . . . a Church Father for the twenty-first century."

McDermott, Gerald R. [Quotation], p. 160. Corrects readers' notions of Edwards's interests.

Helm, Paul. [Quotation], p. 161. Remarks Edwards's trove of manuscript material.

Smart, Robert D. Review of *Jonathan Edwards,* by George M. Marsden, pp. 163-69. Appreciates George Marsden's *Life* (2003.59) for its "symmetry and proportion" and "highly" recommends it, but is "troubled" by some of its "interpretative assumptions."

Armstrong, John H. "Final Remarks," pp. 201-204. Finds "cause for real joy" in the Edwards celebrations across the world.

3 Baird, William. "A Calvinist Precursor: Jonathan Edwards (1703-58)." *From Jonathan Edwards to Rudolf Bultmann. History of New Testament Research,* v. 2. Minneapolis : Fortress Press, pp. 6-10.

Cites Edwards's theological use of the New Testament in *Original Sin* and his fascination with the book of Revelation, but regards him as "perhaps the greatest philosophical mind America has produced," not "primarily" a New Testament scholar.

4 Barker, William S., and Samuel T. Logan. *Sermons that Shaped America: Reformed Preaching from 1630 to 2001.* Phillipsburg, N.J.: P & R Publishing, pp. 58-62.

Prefaces a reprint of *Distinguishing Marks* (pp. 62-119) with praise: Edwards was "the greatest pastor/theologian that America has yet seen," and the "greatest intellect of any American thinker, Christian or otherwise"; indeed, "no human being can be more helpful to us," as Christians in a pluralistic society, than he.

5 Beach, J. Mark. Review of *God of Grace and God of Glory,* by Stephen R. Holmes. *Mid-America Journal of Theology* 14: 173-78.

Approves Stephen R. Holmes's reading of Edwards's theology within the "wider" orthodox

Reformed tradition (2000.15) but finds he "clutters" his analysis with his "own Barthian agenda" and "mars" the entire project.

6 ───────. Review of *"The Supreme Harmony of All,"* by Amy Platinga Pauw. *Mid-America Journal of Theology* 14: 204-209.

Commends Amy P. Pauw (2002.36) for her "irenic treatment" of Edwards's Trinitarianism and its relevance to the present, though her "own theological agenda" gets in the way of placing it "within his own theological scheme."

7 Bernstein, Jennifer. "American Antinomianisms from Anne Hutchinson to Pragmatism." Ph.D. dissertation, City University of New York.

Traces antinomianism from Hutchinson to William James; for Edwards, no epistemological system "could grant the human mind a permanent grasp of the 'precise and stable idea in God's mind.'"

8 Bolt, John. Review of *God of Grace and God of Glory,* by Stephen R. Holmes, and *The Supreme Harmony of All,* by Amy Platinga Pauw. *Calvin Theological Journal* 38 (November): 383-86.

Appreciates the studies of Stephen R. Holmes (2000.15) and Amy P. Pauw's (2002.36) for taking "seriously" Edwards's trinitarian theology: hers "elegantly and clearly" written, the more "circumspect" and "focused" of the two, though her discussion of divine simplicity and covenant of works is "less persuasive"; his a "sprawling synthetic overview" of "daunting thoroughness," yet it fails in its analysis of reprobation and eternal judgment.

9 ───────. Review of *Jonathan Edwards,* by Stephen J. Nichols. *Calvin Theological Journal* 38 (November): 397-98.

Judges Stephen Nichols's guided tour of Edwards the "best general introduction" to the man and his thought for the beginning student.

10 Bombaro, John J. "The Formulation of Jonathan Edwards' Theocentric Metaphysics: Part 1 of 4." *Clarion Review* 1 (October): 8-19.[1]

Claims that a theocentric metaphysics of "finality" — not as Sang Hyun Lee has it, dispositions (1988.25) — as the "bedrock" of Edwards's vision of reality and affected the way he thought of "'everything' from cosmology to causality, from matter to man." Although Edwards's metaphysical "reconception" of reality was not prominent in his intellectual agenda from the start, after his conversion it became "pervasive." With his idea of being in general, Edwards "ontologically links" all existences to that necessary and encompassing existence, God. The pantheistic implications of that is the subject of the next part of this exposition of Edwards's theocentric metaphysics.

11 ───────. "Jonathan Edward[s]'s Vision of Salvation." *Westminster Theological Journal* 65 (Spring): 45-67.

Reproves Anri Morimoto (1995.35) — and to some extent Gerald McDermott (2000.26) — for misinterpreting Edwards on dispositions, and consequently, his soteriology, in a rebuttal of the "fiction" of his Catholic vision of salvation. Although Edwards's theory is a "complex laby-

---

1. "Available" in October 2003, this part later appeared in the first issue of *Clarion Review* in January 2004; the second part followed, a printer's symbol instead of the month later that year (2004.10). The journal seems to have ceased publication with that issue.

559

rinth" of innovations, it "clearly" shows affinities with Geneva and Westminster, not Rome and Trent. Morimoto "wrongly imposes a Thomist and Tridentine template onto [his Lombardian soteriology], the result of which leaves much of Edwards's telic-theocentrism neglected and his philosophy of dispositions misappropriated."

12 ———. Review of *Jonathan Edwards*, by George M. Marsden. *Catholic Historical Review* 89 (October): 812-14.

Judges George M. Marsden's biography (2003.59) a "singular masterpiece," a "meticulously documented, truly captivating, occasionally speculative, and always instructive" account of Edwards.

13 Bratt, James D. "Edwards Unbound." *Perspectives: A Journal of Reformed Thought* 18 (October): 18-20.

Praises George M. Marsden's "brilliant success" in *Jonathan Edwards* (2003.59), the result of his "consumate craft" as a historian and his "commitments" to Reformed Christianity.

14 Breitenbach, William. Review of *Jonathan Edwards and the Bible*, by Robert E. Brown. *Journal of American History* 90 (December): 993-94.

Appreciates Robert E. Brown's "splendid" study (2002.5) for "reattaching" Edwards's writing about the Bible to the corpus of his work, the very "heart" of his theology.

15 Bryant, David. "Introduction." Jonathan Edwards, *A Call to United, Extraordinary Prayer . . . [Humble Attempt]*. Ross-shire, Scotland: Christian Heritage, pp. 7-25.

Recalls a first encounter with *Humble Attempt* more than twenty years ago — "*It changed my life forever!*" — and hails this publication as the "perfect time," in the midst of the international ferment for prayer, to revisit Edwards's "wisdom and pragmatism."

16 Bush, Michael David. "Jesus Christ in the Theology of Jonathan Edwards." Ph.D. dissertation, Princeton Theological Seminary.

Sets Edwards's "unsystematic" Christology in the "parabolic pattern of emanation and return" as formulated in his letter to the Princeton trustees, the "structuring principle" of *End of the Creation* and *History of Redemption* and the "golden thread" between God and the saints.

17 Caldwell, Robert W., III. "The Holy Spirit as the Bond of Union in the Theology of Jonathan Edwards." Ph.D. dissertation, Trinity Evangelical Divinity School.

Demonstrates the "strong trinitarian shape" of Edwards's theology and the "continuities" between the inner-trinitarian and economic operations of the Holy Spirit, the paradigm for "all other holy unions" in his work.

18 ———, and D. A. Sweeney. "Edwards, Jonathan (1703-1758)." In *Biographical Dictionary of Evangelicals*. Edited by Timothy Larsen et al. Downers Grove, Ill.: InterVarsity Press, 201-205.

Calculates that Edwards's historical and theological influence has been "immense," as is his appeal and challenge to "a wide variety of evangelicals," in a short account of his life and work.

19 Carstensen, John Allen. "Just Cause: Determinism and Moral Responsibility." Ph.D. dissertation, Fuller Theological Seminary.

Appropriates Edwards's "bold contention" in *Freedom of the Will* that indeterminism rather than determinism entails amorality to argue the "rational superiority" of determinist theory of moral agency.

20 Chang, Chul Tim. "Toward a Model of Renewal: An Analysis of Korean Baptist Churches in the United States." Ph.D. dissertation, Fuller Theological Seminary.

Instances Edwards (and others) for a "developed biblical and historical model of renewal," in a study of the Korean church in America from 1902 to 2001.

21 Clark, Stephen, ed. "Theme Issue: Jonathan Edwards (1703-1758)." *Evangelical Magazine* 42 (March): 2-20, 26-28.

Includes seven short pieces on Edwards and excerpts from his work, a tercentenary tribute to him in the journal of the Evangelical Movement of Wales.

Clark, Stephen. "Editorial: What We Can Learn from Jonathan Edwards," pp. 2-4. Finds Edwards "a biblically balanced man" — defending and declaring faith, relating evangelism and revival, remarking holiness in the church and the individual, giving as much thought to death and dying as to life and living — a "remarkable example" all can learn from.

Fielder, Geraint. "Jonathan Edwards, the Man," pp. 5-6. Notes that Edwards was "a complete stranger" to the separation of heart and head that often weakens evangelism, in a brief biography.

Davies, Andrew. "Jonathan Edwards and the Sovereignty of God," pp. 7-8. Derives from four early sermons by Edwards — on Rom. 9:18, Ps. 46:10, 1 Cor. 1:31 *(God Glorified)*, and Matt. 16:17 *(Divine and Supernatural Light)* — the truth of what divine sovereignty is "meant to do for us."

Olyott, Stuart. "Fuel and Fire: The Preaching of Jonathan Edwards," pp. 9-10. Composes a letter about a visit to Northampton in 1741 to hear Edwards — "a touch of holiness on his life and on his lips" — on the subject "all his sermons and writings are about," redemption.

Harrison, Graham. "Jonathan Edwards on Revival," pp. 11-13. Remarks Edwards's "settled conviction" that revivals advance God's kingdom — despite the local excesses of itinerants like James Davenport and critics like Charles Chauncy — in a reading of *Distinguishing Marks* and *Some Thoughts*. A study of Edwards would surely help in "our present desperate predicament."

Bombaro, John J. "Defender of the Faith," pp. 14-16. Considers Edwards a "worthy recipient" of the title "Defender of the Faith" for his point-by-point response to the deist threat to biblical orthodoxy. Edwards moved away from his defense based upon rationality — *Distinguishing Marks, Some Thoughts, Religious Affections* — to one based upon biblical prophecy and redemptive history — the Stockbridge treatises and *History of Redemption*.

Piper, John. "Lasting Legacy," pp. 17-19. Numbers four exhortations from Edwards to encourage understanding, holiness, and faithfulness: be "radically single-minded" to know God; study the Bible "steadily and constantly and frequently"; study for "heartfelt worship and for practical obedience"; and "glorify God by enjoying Him forever."

Vine, Keith. "Lessons from the Young Edwards," pp. 19-20. Derives from seventeen "Resolutions" Edwards's desire to live in a "thoroughly biblical way" and suggests that such discipline is necessary in "every aspect of the life of a Christian."

[Clark, Stephen, ed.] "Resolutions of Jonathan Edwards," pp. 26-27. Reprints thirty-four of Edwards's "Resolutions" and a comment by Sereno Edwards Dwight.

[Clark, Stephen, ed.] "PS," p. 28. Reprints a passage on Christian practice from *Religious Affections*.

22 Colson, Charles W. "Introduction." In *Religious Affections: A Christian's Character before God.* Edited by James M. Houston. Vancouver: Regent College Publishers.

Reprints 1984.6 under a new title.

23 Crisp, Oliver D. "Jonathan Edwards on Divine Simplicity." *Religious Studies* 39 (March): 23-41.

Assesses Edwards's "innovative and idiosyncratic" version of the doctrine of divine simplicity and concludes that it results from his idealism and trinitarian thought. His approach leads to "serious" problems, chief among them his metaphysics of property attribution and the way he goes about "individuating" the divine persons and "reorganizing" the divine perfections. In short, it is a question of whether Edwards's ontology is "sufficiently fine-grained enough" to distinguish the persons of the Godhead while maintaining their essential simplicity.

24 ———. "The Metaphysics of Sin in the Philosophical Theology of Jonathan Edwards. Ph.D. dissertation, University of London.

Published as 2005.6.

25 ———. "On the Theological Pedigree of Jonathan Edwards's Doctrine of Imputation." *Scottish Journal of Theology* 56 (3): 308-27.

Defends Edwards's doctrine of imputation against the "aberrant" readings of nineteenth- and twentieth-century commentators on it. Edwards picks his way through the complexities of the doctrine to forge a *"media via"* between Augustinian realism and Calvinist federalism, using the real union of Adam and his posterity of the one and the representational notion — Adam as first man — of the other. In response to the charge that "I am punished for the sins of another," Edwards can claim that "it is not his sin, but *ours.*"

26 Crocco, Stephen D. "Jonathan Edwards and Princeton." *Princeton Seminary Bulletin,* n.s., 24 (3): 328-42.

Details Edwards's last days — the six weeks he spent in Princeton — and his earlier association with the College of New Jersey before he assumed its presidency — the expulsion of David Brainerd from Yale in 1743 ("arguably Princeton's first student"), his commencement address in 1752, his son Timothy's enrollment that year, his "close ties" to Jonathan Dickinson (first president) and Aaron Burr (second president and son-in-law). During the last fifteen years of his life, Edwards "honored the school with his prayers, writings, conversations, correspondence, and his children."

27 Davis, Robert E. *Jonathan Edwards — His Message and Impact.* Oswestry, Shropshire: Quinta Press, 72 pp.

Publishes three papers delivered by Rev. Robert E. Davis, First Congregational Church, Millers Falls, Massachusetts, at the Congregational Studies Conference, Westminster Chapel, London, March 2003, in celebration of the Edwards tercentenary.

"'What Must I Do to Be Saved?' Jonathan Edwards and the Nature of True Conversion," pp. 7-27. Gathers Edwards's answer to the question — itself the sum of four others: what is the nature of man that makes necessary divine redemption?; what is the nature of the new life brought to saving faith in Christ?; how can one know the genuine marks of the new life?; and how can others discern them? — from *Faithful Narrative, Distinguishing Marks, Some Thoughts,* and *Religious Affections.* For Edwards, certain "key elements" must always be present — a conviction of sin, true repentance toward God, and saving grace in Christ — and the "surest sign" of true conversion, a changed life, "perseveringly lived in the glory of God." Ministers must preach to the conscience, as Edwards did, trusting to the Holy Spirit to bring the sinner to conviction, "saved by the Lord's marvellous, matchless grace."

"Jonathan Edwards: A Father of the Modern Mission Movement," pp. 29-58. Turns to a study of Edwards "largely ignored" by scholars, the "mission-minded evangelist," from his early pastoral years in the "frontier village" of Northampton to his missionary years in Stockbridge, his writings and practices "sparks" to the missionary movement then and now. Edwards's *Life of Brainerd* became the "principal model of early missionary spirituality"; his *Humble Attempt* — "in part, a call to prayer for missions" — set the theological foundation for the expansion of the gospel throughout the world. Not only did Edwards impact the content and motivation of the missionary enterprise, he set the form as well, preaching to settlers and Indians alike.

"Jonathan Edwards and Britain: 18th Century Trans-Atlantic Networking," pp. 61-68. Remarks the reciprocal influence of Edwards and Great Britain: Edwards molded by English Puritans (Perkins, Owen, and Sibbes), Britain through his works (*Faithful Narrative, Distinguishing Marks, Life of Brainerd,* and *Humble Attempt*), and, in frequent correspondence with Scots (Erskine and Chalmers). Now, when America and Britain are again in "similar spiritual conditions," it may be time to join together as in Edwards's day to revive God's glorious gospel work.

28 De Chirico, Leonardo, ed. "Jonathan Edwards." *Studi di Teologia* 15 (1): 1-97.
Devotes an issue of an Italian journal to Edwards.
De Chirico, Leonardo. "Jonathan Edwards: Introduzione a questo numero della Revista," pp. 1-2. Dedicates a monograph to Edwards and his theology — particularly, his contributions to evangelicalism — on the tercentenary of his birth.
Haykin, Michael. "Un profilo biografica di Jonathan Edwards," pp. 3-17. Relates a brief life of Edwards.
Gerstner, John. "Edwards e la Bibbia," pp. 18-24. Examines Edwards's orthodox views on the Bible.
De Chirico, Leonardo. "La libertia dello volunia nel pensiero di Edwards," pp. 25-37. Traces free will in the thought of Edwards.
Ferrari, Andrea. "Edwards, il peccato originale e la predicazione nell eta postmoderna," pp. 38-53. Links Edwards, the doctrine of original sin, and preaching in postmodern times.
De Blasi, Sergio. "Jonathan Edwards, teologo del resveglio," pp. 54-71. Centers on Edwards as the theologian of the Awakening.
De Chirico, Leonardo. "Le opere di Jonathan Edwards," pp.72-77. Compiles a bibliography of Edwards's works.
Edwards, Jonathan. "L'amore e contrario ad uno spirito egoista," pp. 78-97. Reprints Edwards on the positive and negative aspects of self-love. (In Italian.)

29 Dennison, James T., Jr. "The Odyssey of Jonathan Edwards [1703-1758]." *The Outlook* 53 (October):6-10.
Finds Edwards "a classic Calvinist . . . with profound insights into historic Reformed truths," in a biographical sketch and postscript on biographies, finding a "sleeper" (1988.26) among them.

30 D'Evelyn, Thomas. "America's First Superstar Preacher." *Christian Science Monitor,* 6 March, p. 18.
Rates George Marsden's life of the pious, complex, and "unruly" Edwards (2003.59) both "conscientious and eloquent."

31 Dodds, Elisabeth D. *Marriage to a Difficult Man.* Laurel, Miss.: Audubon Press.
Reprints 1971.6.

32 Durnin, Richard G. *Jonathan Edwards: 300th Anniversary of his Birth: Third President* *of the College of New Jersey.* Princeton, N.J.: Rare Book Collectors, Friends of the Princeton University Library, 8 pp.

Sketches a life of Edwards.

33 Friesen, Paul H. Review of *Jonathan Edwards, Religious Affections and the Puritan Analysis of True Piety,* by Brad Walton. *Journal of the Canadian Church Historical Society* 45 (Spring): 100-102.

Calls on other theologians and historians to take up the "wider challenge" implied by Brad Walton's "helpful" book (2002.48).

34 Godfrey, W. Robert. "Jonathan Edwards and Authentic Spiritual Experience." In *Knowing the Mind of God: Papers Read at the 2003 Westminster Conference.* Mirfield, West Yorkshire: Westminster Conference, pp.25-45.

Examines Edwards's reflections on authentic spiritual experience — conversion in *Personal Narrative,* church membership in *Humble Inquiry,* revival in *Some Thoughts,* and the "latter day glory" of the church in *Religious Affections* — and concludes that he cannot "escape the problematics" of his Puritan heritage. Indeed, Edwards may have "exacerbated" them with his notion of justifying faith, his writings valuable only for their "secondary support" of assurance, their "secondary evidence" for authenticity. On such matters, "Calvin and the Westminster Larger Catechism remain better guides."

35 Guelzo, Allen C. "Piety and Intellect: America's Theologian." *Christian Century* 120 (4 October): 30-31, 34-35.

Questions the focus of George Marsden's "chunky new biography" (2003.59) — not the Edwards of the eighteenth century but the evangelicals of the twenty-first — a work that will be remembered "less as a biography and more as a period piece" of our times.

36 Hart, D. G., Sean Michael Lucas, and Stephen J. Nichols, eds. *The Legacy of Jonathan Edwards: American Religion and the Evangelical Tradition.* Grand Rapids, Mich.: Baker Academic, 255 pp.

Publishes thirteen essays on Edwards in an effort to understand his place in the past and the present, papers first delivered at the Reformed Bible Conference, Westminister Presbyterian Church, Lancaster, Pa., 26-28 October 2001, and grouped under vision, theology, legacy, and reflections.

Hart, D. G., Sean Michael Lucas, and Stephen J. Nichols. "Introduction," pp. 19-24. Summarizes the essays and celebrates the variety of views on Edwards — "no fewer than eight denominations" are represented here — and how he continues to "impact the life and thought of the church."

Stout, Harry S. "Jonathan Edwards' Tri-World Vision," pp. 27-46. Contends that Edwards had an "obsession with history" and sought to "weave" an interconnected narrative of heaven, earth, and hell into dramatic form — including, though subordinate, all the major doctrines of Christian theology — a history of redemption. He used the history of earth and earthly time as the "spine" of his narrative and interleaved the worlds of heaven and hell into it, the end of creation the self-glorification of God, not the happiness of his creatures. For Edwards, redemption *"required"* the fact of sin to generate salvation; hence, the fall, not creation, was the actual starting point for his narrative.

Nichols, Stephen J. "Last of the Mohican Missionaries: Jonathan Edwards at Stockbridge," pp. 47-63. Takes a "close look" at Edwards's Stockbridge years, not at what he wrote, but what he did with and among the Housatonics there, in an assessment of his missionary career. Edwards became involved in the politics of "Indian affairs" in the eighteenth century and in the struggles over the missionary school, the sermons at the church, and the "little-known" statements of faith he wrote for the converted among them. He and his family were the first settlers to live on "the plain," among the Indians, his son Jonathan at school and play with them, Edwards himself sensitive to the issues of their culture and the importance of "the land to their identity."

Bailey, Richard A. "Driven by Passion: Jonathan Edwards and the Art of Preaching," pp. 64-78. Enumerates three areas where Edwards's passion drove his philosophy of preaching: first, he argued against Enlightenment thought about the relationship between divine revelation and human reason; second, he sought to encourage the onset of the millennium and to fulfill his "divine commission," modifying contemporary preaching patterns; third, he "passionately prepared and proclaimed" his message from the pulpit. Edwards "anchored" his sermons in the objective, special revelation of God, centering his ministry on the power of the Word, drawing his flock into Christ's kingdom.

Hambrick-Stowe, Charles. "The 'Inward, Sweet Sense' of Christ in Jonathan Edwards," pp. 79-95. Argues that Edwards's *Personal Narrative* offers a "fairly reliable record" of his spiritual experience and practice of piety, a "window" to his soul. Throughout his pastoral career Edwards strove to share with others the "'inward, sweet sense'" of Christ he had known and later recorded elsewhere: Sarah's "remarkable experience" in *Some Thoughts* and David Brainerd's in his published *Life*. But his effort to make Northampton a "purer community of believers" able to testify to that indwelling sense led to his dismissal and to Stockbridge, where he would "flesh out" in treatises his understanding of true religion. The issues Edwards "wrestled" with and gave meaning to his life in the eighteenth century remain "fundamental" to believers and the church in the twenty-first.

Marsden, George M. "Challenging the Presumption of the Age: The Two Dissertations," pp. 99-113. Cites Edwards's posthumous *Two Dissertations* — *End of Creation* and *True Virtue* — as his "great contributions" to a critique of Enlightenment thought. The first, "a sort of prolegomena" to all his work, insists that the ultimate end in creation is the union between God and loving creatures, a God-centered universe in which the saints share divine happiness; the second, the "most philosophical of his writings" — it does not quote any Scripture — addresses eighteenth-century moral philosophy, particularly that of Shaftesbury and Hutcheson, and argues that true love identifies our interest with others and derives from our union with God. We learn to love all that God loves, and so act justly and with benevolence, do good for its own sake, for its beauty. An "intellectual gem," *True Virtue* challenges the project that dominated Western thought for the next two centuries and revealed the "emptiness of its highest hopes."

Storms, C. Samuel. "Open Theism in the Hands of an Angry Puritan: Jonathan Edwards on Divine Foreknowledge," pp. 114-30. Uses Edwards as a "catalyst" for a biblical and theological examination of open theism, particularly its rejection and his "unqualified endorsement" of exhaustive divine foreknowledge (EDF). Contemporary open theism argues that if human choices are necessary, and so unavoidable, they are not worthy of reward or punishment; if morally relevant choices are contingent, and so unknowable antecedents to their being chosen, then God cannot have EDF of the choices of free moral agents. Edwards, however, demonstrates that there is ample exegetical evidence that God infallibly foreknows human volitions for which the individual is morally accountable. As well, in *Freedom of the Will*, a treatise that has "yet to be successfully refuted," he holds that the necessity "logically entailed" by EDF is perfectly compatible with moral accountability.

Oliphint, K. Scott. "Jonathan Edwards on Apologetics: Reason and the Noetic Effects of Sin," pp. 131-45. Looks at Edwards's notion of reason and the noetic effects of sin to show that his thought reveals the "substance" of a Reformed approach to apologetics. The pervasiveness of sin in God's creatures and the necessity of his revelation for apologetics serves to "locate" Edwards in that approach and the function of reason within it. Edwards gives "full weight" to our logical and noetic capacities without destroying sin's effects and so maintains the "absolute necessity" of God's revelation as the "backdrop" for any true, sensible reasoning or thinking.

McDermott, Gerald R. "Jonathan Edwards and the National Covenant: Was He Right?" pp. 147-57. Points out that Edwards was no different from generations of Puritan theologians in believing that New England's — and Northampton's — fortunes could be explained by reference to God's covenant, but that he was "far too sanguine" about his own ability to discern the meaning of every historical contingency that befell society. Though we, like him, are "inordinately inclined to self-deception," we should begin work on a "sensitive and responsible" theology of discernment of historical meaning. Edwards's use of the national covenant can suggest to us that the church is to continue to participate in the prophetic ministry of Christ; that Edwards's priestly ministry brought God's blessing and comfort in a time of war suggests as well the need for a theology of public discernment today.

Hart, D. G. "Jonathan Edwards and the Origins of Experimental Calvinism," pp. 161-80. Explores Edwards on conversion and holy affections in the context of historic Reformed teaching on regeneration and the Christian life, in an attempt explain how he "unintentionally undermined" the Calvinism he sought to defend. Edwards and the form of piety he promoted may have led to the neglect of a "churchly Reformed faith" because he thought it ineffective to forward piety. By elevating the solitary soul's "subjective agonies and struggles" over a church-centered and catechetical faith, Edwards and experimental Calvinism triumphed over the "grand and glorious" objectives of the Reformed tradition.

Sweeney, Douglas A. "Taylorites, Tylerites, and the Dissolution of the New England Theology," pp. 181-99. Focusses on the consequences of the Taylorite-Tylerite controversy on Edwards's legacy and its significance for the later history of New England theology. New England theology "flourished" in the northeast in the first half of the nineteenth century, becoming America's "first indigenous theological movement," but the Edwardseans grew so large and diverse that they "tore themselves apart," leaving them "too weak to sustain a vital tradition." The movement declined because its leaders had become "self-absorbed," lost in internal strife over control and resources, not because of the culture wars at the time, a conflict they "hardly entered" at all.

Lucas, Sean Michael. "'He Cuts Up Edwardsism by the Roots': Robert Lewis Dabney and the Edwardsian Legacy in the Nineteenth-Century South," pp. 200-214. Examines Edwards's legacy in the nineteenth-century South by focussing on the criticisms of his theology by southern Presbyterians, particularly by Robert Lewis Dabney. Dabney stood for the Reformed faith, best summarized by the Presbyterian confessional standards, and against "innovation(s)" such as his — on divine causation, freedom of the will, personal identity, imputation of sin, and true virtue — and those who embraced them. It was southern Baptists, "free to adopt and adapt" New Divinity modes of thought, who preserved Edwards's legacy, not Dabney and his brethren, who sought to "'cut up Edwardsism by the roots.'"

Claghorn, George S. "Transcribing a Difficult Hand: Collecting and Editing Edwards Letters over Thirty-five Years," pp. 217-27. Recounts some of the "colorful" experiences, both here and abroad, on the "long journey" to the publication of the Yale edition of Edwards's correspondence, a collection of 236 of his letters, almost half of them never before published. A "labor of love," the transcribing and editing of Edwards's "difficult hand" took thirty-five years, but it led to a far better understanding of a man who "walked with God," who was "focused, fearless, and faithful." Such personal rewards — and the "riches" of Edwards's work — are now available for all to share.

Lucas, Sean Michael. "Jonathan Edwards between Church and Academy: A Bibliographic Essay," 228-47. Proposes to "bridge the wide chasm" between church and academy in the reading of Edwards over the years by pointing out, first, some "important and worthy" studies for evangelical pastors and lay people, and, second, a selection from the "dizzying array" of perspectives from the academy, in a bibliographic essay of both primary and secondary works designed to help navigate the "ever-increasing web of information" about him, some of the "most creative" scholarship in American religious studies.

37 Helm, Paul, and Oliver D. Crisp, eds. *Jonathan Edwards: Philosophical Theologian.* Burlington, Vt.: Ashgate, xvi, 165 pp.

Helm, Paul, and Oliver D. Crisp. "Introduction," pp ix-xvi. Brings together ten essays reflecting the "confluence of scholars" in philosophy and theology on Edwards's thought, essays on his doctrines of hell, free will, virtue, original sin, and divine simplicity, on his occasionalism, ontology, soteriology, and Neoplatonism. With renewed interest in him over the last half century, Edwards is again a "force to be reckoned with" in both philosophy and theology.

Kvanvig, Jonathan L. "Jonathan Edwards on Hell," pp. 1-11. Argues that Edwards not only preached a doctrine of hell in "astounding and disturbing" ways but addressed theoretical questions about it in as "sound a way as can be found." Edwards held to the traditional Christian notion of hell, that all sin is against God and that each person consigned to hell receives the same infinite punishment, and, in keeping with this "strong" view, that those in hell exist forever in that state, that at least some people will end up in there, that there is no escape from it, and that all deserve to be there. Even though his defense is unconvincing, especially as it depends on the different status between God and his creatures, it reveals how "all of life is lived in the face of God and the justice in holding us responsible for this relationship."

Wainwright, William J. "Jonathan Edwards and the Doctrine of Hell," pp. 13-26. Contends that Edwards's traditional defense of hell is "partly successful and partly not." Given certain assumption about the "disvalue" of offending God, the "fittingness" of retributive punishment, and value of God's "self-manifestation," Edwards has shown that the permanent exclusion of some from God's presence is consistent with God's infinite greatness and excellency; but he fails to show non-scriptural reasons why that exclusion be everlasting punishment and not annihilation. Nor is his notion of God compatible with the rejection of "countless numbers" not fully aware of the nature of their sin or those God made not only "vessels of his hatred" but also hateful. Even though Edwards's failures are significant, his positions are not "essential" to a Christian doctrine of hell.

McCann, Hugh J. "Edwards on Free Will," pp. 27-43. Insists that although Edwards's perceptions are "acute," his argument about free will is "not convincing" since the ordinary concept of freedom is Arminian, not Calvinist. Edwards is right that human freedom must be subordinated to God's will, but he is "wrong" in thinking that the operation of the will is subject to natural causation. If he cast his argument of volition as a product of God's sovereign will as creator — and his view of continuous creation "fits nicely" into that proposition — then Edwards "gets his way," and so do his opponents.

Helm, Paul. "A Forensic Dilemma: John Locke and Jonathan Edwards on Personal Identity," pp. 45-59. Concentrates on the "interconnectedness and dislocation" of various ideas Edwards took from Locke, particularly on the question of personal identity. In time, Locke's impact was "crowded out" by other items on Edwards's agenda, "neutralized and sterilized" where it could have been useful to him, especially in *Original Sin*. Stressing divine immediacy, Edwards "lost" Locke's forensic focus, the "very thing" he needed to defend the reasonableness of original sin; indeed, the idea of divine immediacy and continuous creation is "fundamentally at odds" with his doctrine of imputation.

Crisp, Oliver D. "How 'Occasional' was Edwards's Occasionalism?", pp. 61-77. Analyzes Edwards's metaphysical views on imputation and persistence through time, his doctrine of divine creation and conservation, in order to place him among three candidate theories — a strong conservation thesis, a continuous creation thesis, and an occasionalistic thesis — and concludes he was a "defender" of the last. That Edwards developed an occasionalism "commensurate" with a form of temporal parts doctrine puts Sang Hyun Lee's reading of him (1988.25 and 2000.21) "in trouble." What Edwards held in *Original Sin*," Miscellanies," no. 1263 (a frequently cited text), and elsewhere was not a "modified" but a "consistent" occasionalism.

Quinn, Philip L. "The Master Argument of *The Nature of True Virtue*," pp. 79-97. Explicates Edwards's philosophical argument in the first chapter of *True Virtue* in an effort to determine if it can contribute to contemporary discussions of virtue ethics. In the following chapter, the technical terms "Being in general" and "Being simply considered" refer to God "among other things," but it is not a "presupposition or assumption" in the argument of the first chapter. With but some "fairly minor" revisions, Edwards's position has "considerable plausibility" and may be offered as a "useful counterweight" to Aquinas and a "serious competitor" for the allegiance of philosophers interested in moral theory. Still, although Edwards's argument has "philosophical plausibility," it "falls short" of the best account of true virtue available.

Holmes, Stephen R. "Does Jonathan Edwards Use a Dispositional Ontology? A Response to Sang Hyun Lee," pp. 99-114. Engages Sang Hyun Lee's "powerful" and "excellent" study, *The Philosophical Theology of Jonathan Edwards* (1988.25 and 2000.21), only to reject it as "simply wrong" and "implausible" in its main thesis, suggesting an alternative reading both historically and theologically "much less difficult to believe." Given Edwards's consciously chosen theological conservatism, it is "extremely unlikely" that he would adopt a novel doctrine of God that would "undermine" the basic features of his account of God based on Reformed orthodoxy. Edwards neither needed dispositional ontology nor used it.

Pauw, Amy Plantinga. "'One Alone Cannot be Excellent': Edwards on Divine Simplicity," 115-25. Argues that excellency "largely supplanted" divine simplicity as a "marker" of divine perfection in Edwards's thought, yet he seems never to have "defined it directly." Although there remained "traces" of divine simplicity in Edwards's theology, from his early notebooks *(The Mind)* to his mature writing, his notion of excellency was "at the core" of his reflections on the divine reality, on the Trinity, on religious affections, true virtue, and God's end in creation. Such convictions "put him at odds" with a broad theological consensus and a distinguished tradition that linked "maximal unity with maximal existence"; but it meant as well that Edwards was "free to wrestle with" that tradition in an imaginative way, to make connections, for example, to the aesthetics of being.

McDermott, Gerald R. "Jonathan Edwards, John Henry Newman and non-Christian Religion," pp. 127-37. Remarks how both Edwards and John Henry Newman, despite their doctrinal differences, shared "remarkably similar" convictions about spirituality and non-Christian religions. Edwards used three models — *prisca theologia*, typology, and dispositional soteriology — to understand the role of the religions in the history of the work of redemption, the first two to show deists that the biblical God had "*not* limited" revelation to a minority of humankind, the third how God might save those who had not heard the gospel. Still, Edwards and Newman differed in some "intriguing" ways: Newman stressed continuities between Christian and other faiths more than Edwards; he saw more "pagan influence" in Christianity than Edwards; and he was more willing to "talk about saved pagans" than Edwards. That the "greatest Anglo-American theologians" of the eighteenth and nineteenth centuries were "similarly intrigued" by religious pluralism questions the "glib" comments about our "unprecedented" awareness of it in recent decades.

McClymond, Michael J. "Salvation as Divinization: Jonathan Edwards, Gregory Palamas and the Theological Uses of Neoplatonism," 139-59. Uncovers a "wide area of overlap" between Edwards's teaching on salvation and the Orthodox doctrine of divinization of St. Gregory Palamas. Both share a common Platonic or Neoplatonic philosophical heritage that they "modified in analogous ways" in their understanding of the grace of God and the experience of communion with him. Although Edwards never mentions "the word itself," using instead a "rich vocabulary" of terms and phrases — *communication, emanation, participation, partaking,* and *uniting;* creatures referred to as *of, in,* and *to* God; believers *swallowed up* in God, the world as God *diffused himself* — he "taught a doctrine of divinization." The two traditions may not be as "far apart" in their understanding of salvation as is "commonly assumed."

38 Holifield, E. Brooks. "America's God: *Review Essay.*" *Journal of the Historical Society* 1 (March): 81-90.

Weighs the differences between Mark Noll's "remarkable" book (2002.33) and Holifield's *Theology in America* (2003.39), "judgments about significance," the disagreements "more interesting" than the harmonies. Noll blends theology with republicanism, an "imaginative" synthesis; Holifield substitutes denominational competition and social class for political theory, European influence for American exceptionalism, divisiveness for unity, at times violence.

39 ———. "Jonathan Edwards." *Theology in America: Christian Thought from the Age of the Puritans to the Civil War.* New Haven: Yale University Press, pp. 102-26.

Considers Edwards a typical New England theologian — a "Calvinist concerned about piety in a local congregation" — yet one of unequalled intellectual depth and enduring influence, in an appraisal of his theology, its roots and dimensions. A philosopher and exegete, Edwards sought to "preserve" the Calvinist balance between reason and revelation but "recast" conventional categories, his notions of excellency affecting the way he thought about "almost everything," rationality, ethics, metaphysics, and biblical interpretation. That theme of excellency — expressed variously as consent, harmony, symmetry, proportion, and fitness — would lead him in "new directions," but it "split" his congregation as well and helped "fracture" American Reformed theology "for almost a century."

40 Hunt, Richard. "Refiguring an Angry God: The Nature of Jonathan Edwards." *Interdisciplinary Literary Studies* 4 (Spring): 21-35.

Focusses on *Images or Shadows* and *Sinners in the Hands of an Angry God* to show the development of Edwards's typology of nature from science to religion. Edwards "opens a door into a new sense of equivalence" between God and the natural world, using natural typology to define elements of the natural world as "examples of *God's* plan, not the devil's." For all its "revolutionary" character, Edwards's contribution has not been "widely acknowledged" even today.

41 James, Sharon. "Sarah Edwards (1710-1758)." *In Trouble and in Joy: Four Women who Lived for God — With Selections from their Writings.* Auburn, Mass.: Evangelical Press, pp. 67-113.

Remarks how Edwards "looked to" his wife to describe the religious experience characteristic of revival times, in a portrait of Sarah drawn from her writings (and his).

42 Jeffery, Peter. "Jonathan Edwards." *Lights Shining in the Darkness: Men of Faith.* Auburn, Mass.: Evangelical Press, pp. 70-83.

Remarks Edwards's contribution to biblical Christianity "immense," his place among theologians "Mount Everest," in a brief biography.

43 Johnson, Paul. "That Old-Time Religion." [London] *Sunday Telegraph,* 25 May, p. 10.

Considers "outstanding" George Marsden's life of Edwards (2003.59), the "most articulate spokesman" of the "most valuable and attractive aspects of the American character."

44 Kang, Kevin Woongsan. "Justified by Faith in Christ: Jonathan Edwards' Doctrine of Justification in Light of the Union with Christ." Ph.D. dissertation, Westminster Theological Seminary.

Takes Edwards's formulation of union with Christ as the "method and framework" of his doctrine of justification within the history of redemption, a "unified perspective" and possible approach to systematic theology.

45 Kling, David W., and Douglas A. Sweeney, eds. *Jonathan Edwards at Home and Abroad: Historical Memories, Cultural Movements, Global Horizons.* Columbia: University of South Carolina Press, xxiii, 330 pp.

Gathers together fifteen papers delivered at an international conference on Edwards held 9-11 March 2000 in Miami.

Kling, David W., and Douglas A. Sweeney. "Introduction," pp. xi-xxii. Charts the reasons for the "relative neglect" of Edwards's legacy, summarizes the essays addressing those concerns, and remarks the "un-Edwardsian" site of the conference, in a comprehensive introduction to the three parts of the volume — "Remembering Edwards's Ministry," "Edwards and American Culture," and "Edwards around the World."

Marsden, George M. "The Quest for the Historical Edwards: The Challenge of Biography," pp. 3-15. Recounts the problems confronting a biographer of Edwards — the "sheer immensity" of scholarship, the "elusiveness" of his personality, locating him in his communities and traditions — and proposes that the central theme for understanding him is own phrase, "'the divine and supernatural light.'" Edwards's "favorite" metaphor, light is regenerating grace, awakening, God's love, uniting the theological and the practical, the personal and the global. As much as Edwards is part of eighteenth-century culture, he left a legacy that "transcends his time and place."

McClymond, Michael. "A Different Legacy?: The Cultural Turn in Later Notebooks and the Unwritten *History of the Work of Redemption,*" pp. 16-39. Argues that Edwards's projected *History of Redemption* was to be an expression of "'a cultural turn'" in his theology, that is, away from Anglo-American Protestantism to the divine presence in other Western cultures, in a reading of his letter to the Princeton trustees (1998.5), his notebooks for the text (1989.59), and relevant later "Miscellanies." Had he finished it, Edwards's "possible" legacy might have added to the stimulus of his *Life of Brainerd* "a model of cultural engagement" for the missionary movement; offered a "different character" to the Social Gospel; altered the place of America in the "grand narrative" of redemption; occasioned a "nonfundamentalistic" theological style; and anticipated a number of major intellectual movements "long before they arrived."

Brekus, Catherine A. "Remembering Jonathan Edwards's Ministry to Children," pp. 40-60. Examines how Edwards's "unflinching" theology of children was remembered and distorted in the "new, humanitarian climate" of nineteenth-century America. Unitarians rejected it outright, but even Calvinists, who sought claimant rights to his mantle, distanced themselves from his harsh doctrines, their sentimentalized views of childhood irreconcilable with his vision of absolute divine sovereignty. "[I]n a world where 'Little Eva,' not Phebe Bartlet, had won the battle for America's religious imagination, few wanted to remember his theology of childhood."

Chamberlain, Ava. "Bad Books and Bad Boys: The Transformation of Gender in Eighteenth-Century Northampton, Massachusetts," pp. 61-81. Reprints 2002.7.

Valeri, Mark. "Jonathan Edwards, the Edwardsians, and the Sacred Cause of Free Trade," pp. 85-100. Reconsiders Edwards, his followers, and market culture in eighteenth-century New England, emphasizing how his ethical writings contributed to "an alliance" between evangelicals and the market economy. A "transitional figure" between his Puritan forebears and New Divinity men, Edwards brought the "moral language" of Calvinism into the ethical discourse of the transatlantic market. Even so, Edwards never found "an easy or obvious" correlation between Calvinism, the new philosophical idiom, and commerce.

German, James D. "The Political Economy of Depravity: The Irrelevance (and Relevance) of Jonathan Edwards," pp. 101-20. Argues that the social and political significance of Edwards's thought might be better seen not in the political preaching of New Divinity clergy but in the moral arguments of "pious politicians," in a study of the younger Edwards, Roger Sherman, and Oliver Ellsworth. Edwards's critique of Francis Hutcheson's ethics "ironically opened the door" to naturalistic political economy — one premised on "the reality of self love rather than the possibility of true virtue" — and led Edwardseans to render supernaturalism in theology and ethics "irrelevant" to public life.

Hambrick-Stowe, Charles E. "All Things Were New and Astonishing: Edwardsian Piety, the New Divinity, and Race," pp. 121-36. Discerns a pattern of inter-racial salvation and fellowship among three "notable" Edwardseans in Revolutionary times — Samuel Hopkins, trained for the ministry by Edwards and his first biographer; Sarah Osborne, a prolific writer, popular leader, and teacher; and Lemuel Haynes, the first black to be ordained in America — framing Edwards's theology of revival in a new social context. The New Divinity movement connected the gospel of salvation with "the single most crucial — and in their day neglected — issue of American history, the status of African Americans in this society."

Kim, Sharon Y. "Beyond the Men in Black: Jonathan Edwards and Nineteenth-Century Woman's Fiction," pp. 137-53. Focusses on Susan Warner's *The Wide, Wide World* (1850) as an example of nineteenth-century woman's fiction that sought to "promote, not undermine" American Calvinism, unlike some other sentimental novels that characterized Edwardseans as men in black, "anachronistic, overly rational." Warner conceived and pursued "an authentic relationship" with God in *The Wide, Wide World* much as Edwards did in *Personal Narrative, Religious Affections, Some Thoughts,* and *True Virtue,* and engaged in a "meticulous specification" about Christianity reminiscent of him. In her most famous novel — it was translated into four languages — Warner portrayed a Christian belief "both influenced by Edwards and consonant with his work."

Porterfield, Amanda. "Gary Marshall's *Runaway Bride* in Light of *The Religious Affections* and *The Nature of True Virtue:* Reflections on Popular American Culture," pp. 154-74. Interprets *Runaway Bride* in light of the problem of hypocrisy that concerned Edwards, as did the "inherent connection" between virtue and happiness, preparation and love — see *True Virtue* and *Religious Affections* — in an essay on the expression of feeling in American popular culture that "some followers of Edwards might call spiritual." Edwards is a "transitional figure": committed to the notion that a Christian life transcends ordinary human life, he anticipates a "more modern" interpretation that religion is the "ultimate concern at the heart of individual life."

Bebbington, David W. "Remembered around the World: The International Scope of Edwards's Legacy," pp. 177-200. Sketches four phases of Edwards's legacy outside America — first, among contemporaries in England, Scotland, and the Netherlands, especially through John Erskine; second, from 1770 until well into the nineteenth century among "shapers of opinion," William Godwin, Dugald Stewart, John Ryland, Andrew Fuller, Thomas Chalmers, and others; third, a period overlapping the second, when his reputation was "challenged and declined" through a shift in sentiment; and fourth, in the twentieth century in a "series" of revivals, the final one in the late 1950s with the first volume of the Yale edition — and suggests that, despite lapses, Edwards exercised "an extremely powerful influence," not least in the spread of the evangelical movement.

Hindmarsh, D. Bruce. "The Reception of Jonathan Edwards by Early Evangelicals in England," pp. 201-21. Analyzes the reception of Edwards in England by the early evangelical communities, surveying Armenian Methodists through John Wesley; Particular Baptists and their Congregationalist counterparts through John Ryland, Andrew Fuller, and John Sutcliff, and Edward Williams; and moderate Calvinist Anglicans through John Newton, Thomas Scott, and Joseph Milner. "To state it badly, the Baptists championed Edwards, the Anglican evangelicals were ambivalent, and Wesley simply corrected him."

Mitchell, Christopher W. "Jonathan Edwards's Scottish Connection," pp. 222-47. Examines the "epistolary link" between Edwards and his six Scottish correspondents — John Erskine, of Edinburgh; Thomas Gillespie, of Carnock; John MacLaurin, of Glasgow; William McCulloch, of Cambuslang; James Roby, of Kilsyth; and John Willison, of Dundee — that opened a "new chapter" in his life. Not only did they promote his work, seek his counsel, and enlist his help, they, in turn, became some of his "most loyal friends, his most ardent supporters," enhancing his ministry and intellect, providing "a steady stream of books," ultimately tendering "to make him a son of the Kirk."

Walls, Andrew F. "Missions and Historical Memory: Jonathan Edwards and David Brainerd," pp. 248-65. Considers both Edwards and Brainerd "transitional" figures in the Protestant missionary movement, its historical memory acknowledging its "debt" to Edwards for the "impression" it retained of Brainerd's life, work, and death as presented in *Life of Brainerd*, not to Edwards the theologian. Even so, the Brainerd remembered was not Edwards's — "a Christian minister whose ministerial charge happened to be among Native Americans" — but a pioneer of the maritime age of missions, linking the revival in Christendom with the evangelizing of the non-Western world and the way the movement became the "learning experience" of Western Christianity.

Piggin, Stuart. "The Expanding Knowledge of God: Jonathan Edwards's Influence on Missionary Thinking and Promotion," pp. 266-96. Concludes that Edwards was "massively constitutive of modern Protestant missions," in a review of the historical record of his impact on the British missionary movement to India and the implications of his thought for missionary thinking about heathenism, especially Hinduism. Edwards's "missionary diamond" of seven facets — theology, history, philosophy, pragmatics, practice, spirituality, aesthetics — reflects his "pervasive" evangelical legacy, his *Life of Brainerd* a "paradigm of missionary strategy."

Lesser, M. X. "'An Honor Too Great': Jonathan Edwards in Print Abroad," pp. 297-319. Traces the publication history of Edwards's works abroad, from the London and Edinburgh editions of *Faithful Narrative* in 1737 — a year before the first Boston issue — to a Spanish translation of *Sinners in the Hands of an Angry God* in Léon in 2000; comments upon publishing houses and editorial emendations; and appends a bibliography of over two hundred separately published texts. Edwards was translated into Dutch and German in the eighteenth century, Arabic, Choctaw, French, Gaelic, Swedish, and Welsh in the nineteenth, and Chinese, Italian, and Korean in the twentieth; as well, a "small shelf" of articles and reviews appeared in French, German, Hungarian, Italian, Japanese, Korean, Portuguese, Russian, and Spanish.

46 Kloosterman, Nelson D. "The Use of Typology in Post-Canonical Salvation History: An Orientation to Jonathan Edwards' *A History of the Work of Redemption*." *Mid-America Journal of Theology* 14: 59-96.

Suggests some ways Edwards's exegetical-theological approach to salvation history may help "shed light" on the continuing debate within Reformed exegesis, theology, and homiletics, particularly on the post-canonical history and his use of typology to retain "harmony and unity," in a reading of sermons 18, 20, and 21 of his *History of Redemption*. Edwards extended the "grammar" of typology to include the fulfillment, in post-biblical history, of prophecies and patterns given in Scripture, and so was a "forerunner" of presuppositional theology. In his notion that the Holy Spirit uses typology in post-canonical salvation history, Edwards "properly relates" *historia salutis* to *ordo salutis,* an approach both "comprehensive and integrative."

47 Kreider, Glenn R. Review of *God of Grace and God of Glory,* by Stephen R. Holmes. *Bibliotheca Sacra* 160 (October): 502-504.

Faults Stephen R. Holmes's "strongly worded" argument (2000.15) for its lack of nuance and interaction with the "vast secondary literature" on Edwards.

48 ———. Review of *Jonathan Edwards,* by Stephen J. Nichols. *Bibliotheca Sacra* 160 (January): 124-25.

   Urges students of Edwards, "Buy your tickets and join" Stephen J. Nichols, a "competent and engaging" guide.

49 ———. Review of *The Spirit of Revival,* ed. Archie Parrish and R. C. Sproul. *Bibliotheca Sacra* 160 (October): 504-505.

   Recommends this "reader-friendly" version of Edwards's *Distinguishing Marks* for its "valuable" introduction.

50 Leader, Jennifer Lynn. "'A house not made with hands': Natural Typology in the Work of Jonathan Edwards, Emily Dickinson and Marianne Moore." Ph.D. dissertation, Claremont Graduate University.

   Links Dickinson and Moore's representations of nature to a "common source," Edwards's Calvinist typological hermeneutics.

51 Lee, Sang Hyun. "Editor's Introduction." *Writings on the Trinity, Grace, and Faith. The Works of Jonathan Edwards,* 21. New Haven: Yale University Press, pp. 1-106.

   Highlights the nature and significance of this "unprecedented" collection of essays and notebooks of "key doctrines" of Edwards's theological vision — the Trinity, grace, and faith — and incorporates other writings that touch upon them. Edwards's theology represents a "fundamental reconception" of God, essentially a dispositional being "completely actualized within his trinitarian life," a view unlike much of traditional Western theology. For Edwards, God in a sense is "'internally,' not just 'externally'" related to the world, his self-communicating to his creatures the exercise of his "original dispositional essence."

52 Lesser, M. X. *The Printed Writings of Jonathan Edwards, 1703-1758: A Bibliography,* by Thomas H. Johnson. Revised edition. Princeton: Princeton Theological Seminary, xiv, 250 pp.

   Extends the reach of Thomas H. Johnson's bibliography of Edwards's work almost seventy years, adds "substantially" to its list — eighty or so entries before 1940, half again as many since then — and alters markedly the appearance of the text — the title page of each item attempts a quasi-facsimile transcription with bracketed descriptives for rules, borders, ornaments, and publishers' devices — in a revision of *The Printed Writings of Jonathan Edwards* (1940.7). Each entry details the contents of the text, including collected editions, and notes publication anomalies among different copies.

53 Levesque, George G., ed. *Jonathan Edwards Tercentennial Exhibition: Selected Objects from the Yale Collection, 1703-2003.* New Haven, Conn.: Jonathan Edwards College, Yale University, 46 pp.

   Catalogues (and comments upon) items from the Edwards collection at Yale, in an exhibition on the tercentenary of his birth, 7-31 October 2003.

   Minkema, Kenneth P. "Jonathan Edwards, America's Theologian: A Commemorative Yale Exhibition," pp. 5-27. Sketches the life and legacy of Edwards — "America's often ambivalent, though rich, relationship" with him — and remarks the provenance of several portraits, objects, manuscripts, and books.

   Levesque, George G. "Jonathan Edwards at Yale," pp. 29-41. Follows Edwards's career at the "fledgling" school — it was founded in 1701 — as student and tutor, reprints his Latin valedictory on justification, and appends an English translation.

54 Logan, Samuel T., Jr. Review of *Jonathan Edwards,* by George M. Marsden. *Westminster Theological Journal* 65 (Fall): 373-82.

Opens and closes an essay-review of George M. Marsden's *Life* (2003.59) with, "this is the best book ever written about America's (and perhaps the world's) greatest theologian," adding at the end "because it helps us see the beauty of the redemptive love of Christ." Although Marsden's study lets Edwards off "too easily" on the matter of slavery, he is "superb" on the bad book incident (but for his handling of it), "extraordinary" on the church membership controversy, and reveals Edwards's strengths — and his own — "superbly" in explications of *True Virtue* and *End of Creation* among other texts. "Jonathan Edwards would be delighted!"

55 Lucas, Sean Michael. Review of *Nathaniel Taylor,* by Douglas A. Sweeney. *Westminster Theological Journal* 65 (Spring): 151-54.

Concludes that Douglas A. Sweeney's "breathtaking and convincing" study of Taylor (2003.97) should become the "standard" for students of American religious history, especially New England theology.

56 Macdonald, G. Jeffrey. "Theologian Still Drawing a Crowd." [New Orleans] *Times Picayune,* 25 October, p. 6.

Reports the "most notorious Puritan" is back in the public eye at a two-day conference, "Awakening Hearts and Minds to God," in First Church of Christ, Wethersfield, Conn., 25-26 October. A 55-seat bus tour of New Haven, northern Connecticut, and Northampton sold out before "dozens of additional inquiries" came in.

57 Maddux, H. C. "Ruling Passion: Consent and Covenant Theology in Westfield, Massachusetts, August 1679." *Early American Literature* 38 (1): 9-29.

Suggests that Edward Taylor "foreshadows" Edwards, "while remaining distinct from him," in an analysis of the documents Taylor prepared in 1679 concerning the Foundation Day of his Westfield church.

58 Maffly-Kipp, Laurie F. "Book Review Essay." *Church History* 72 (September): 634-38.

Predicts that Mark A. Noll's study (2002.33) will be an "indispensable reference tool for the study of American theology for many years to come" but questions his insistence on "orthodox Calvinism as the 'core' of theological expression," thus limiting his narrative and leaving Lincoln a "puzzle," in a review of *America's God* (and *In Search of American Catholicism,* by Jay P. Dolan).

59 Marsden, George M. *Jonathan Edwards: A Life.* New Haven: Yale University Press, xxi, 615 pp.

Concludes in the opening sentence of the first full-length biography in nearly two decades that "Edwards was extraordinary" and takes "seriously his religious outlook on his own terms" — his "Calvinistic heritage" and his personal, "eternal relationship to God" — to depict him as a "real person in his own time," at once a philosopher and a theologian, pastor and college president, missionary and family man, a "revered figure" in the "international Reformed movement" and in "broader evangelicalism," told by a historian of American culture "committed to a Christian faith" similiar to his. Edwards, an instance of "a perennial American story," illustrates the role of religion "always . . . near the center" of the American experience, his eighteenth-century evangelicalism "prominent" in subsequent American history. His world of personal relationships — God's love and creatures' responses — "challenges the commonsense view of our culture that the material world is the 'real' world."

60 ————. "Jonathan Edwards, the Missionary." *Journal of Presbyterian History* 81 (Spring): 5-17.

Maintains that Edwards kept good relations with the Housatonics both through his ministry to them and his "even-handed ways of judging all people by the same spiritual standards," in an account of his missionary years in Stockbridge. Edwards preached sermons with strong narrative strains and vivid metaphors, not simpler versions of earlier ones, sermons not only of terror, but increasingly of divine love, God's compassion and mercy in allowing his own to suffer and die. Although the Edwardses shared many of the prejudices of the time, they could be "genuinely more approving" of a spiritual Indian than a "profane English gentleman."

61 McClymond, Michael J. Review of *Jonathan Edwards and the Bible,* by Robert E. Brown. *Church History* 72 (June): 416-18.

Applies to Robert Brown's book (2002.5) his analysis of the state of biblical interpretation in the early modern period — "fluid, complex, nuanced, and intriguing."

62 McDermott, Gerald R. Review of *Jonathan Edwards and the Bible,* by Robert E. Brown. *Catholic Historical Review* 89 (April): 336-37.

Labels Robert Brown's study (2002.5) "first-rate intellectual history" for demonstrating how Edwards "fully engaged" biblical critics and how that encounter affected both his understanding of the Bible and the history of salvation.

63 ————. "The Eighteenth-Century American Culture War: Thomas Jefferson and Jonathan Edwards on Religion and the Religions." *Litteraria Pragensia: Studies in Literature and Culture* 15 (29): 48-63.

Compares Edwards and Thomas Jefferson, two of the "most influential" thinkers on the culture war that "*most* divided" eighteenth-century America, the nature of God and the nature of goodness and justice. Jefferson — and all deists — started with abstract reason and proceeded to conclusions about goodness, justice, and God, a humanocentric devotion to morality; Edwards started with tradition — the testimony of previous religious thinkers — and countered that unregenerate reason was incapable of seeing the "aesthetic center" of true religion and so misunderstood true moral virtue, a theocentric devotion to a transcendent God, for whom morality was "probative not constitutive." Although neither religious vision prevailed, their debate "set the agenda" for American theology in the centuries following and reverberates still.

64 McKenna, George. "A Conservative Innovator." *First Things* 136 (October): 61-66.

Characterizes George M. Marsden's "painstaking" work (2003.59) on the life and times of Edwards as "the prolegomena to any future intellectual biography," in a review of *Jonathan Edwards.*

65 McMullen, Michael D., ed. *The Blessing of God: Previously Unpublished Sermons of Jonathan Edwards.* Nashville, Tenn.: Broadman and Holman, ix, 390 pp.

Transcribes twenty-two Edwards manuscript sermons drawn from both the Old Testament and the New, brief sermons and long, evangelical sermons and doctrinal; adds a "representative sample" of periodical titles (and years) in which an article about him appears; remarks the past and present interest in him; and concludes that this "labor of love" is an attempt to counter the "heavily criticized, but hardly ever read" Edwards.

66 Mitchell, Louis Joseph. *Jonathan Edwards on the Experience of Beauty.* Studies in Reformed Theology and History, 9. Princeton, N.J.: Princeton Theological Seminary, x, 115 pp.

Posits the language of beauty as the framework for Edwards to express his understanding of "genuine religious experience," an experience of God's beauty made manifest individually in the accounts of saints — David Brainerd, Sarah Edwards, and in *Personal Narrative* — and corporately in revivals. For Edwards, beauty was "the very structure of being" — the triune God "a society of love and beauty," all of creation the "overflow of God's inner-trinitarian beauty" — and so provided him with a category sufficient to achieve a "unique integration" of his most important philosophical and theological ideas, in his notebooks, his sermons, and his treatises.

67 ————. Review of *Edwards in Our Time*, ed. Sang Hyun Lee and Allen C. Guelzo. *Princeton Seminary Bulletin*, n.s., 24 (1): 145-47.

Remarks the "vitality" of scholarship in the collection (1999.24) in applying Edwards thought to modern theological concerns but "weakness" in treating him as preacher and pastor.

68 ————. Review of *God of Grace and God of Glory*, by Stephen R. Holmes. *Princeton Seminary Bulletin*, n.s., 24 (1): 162-63.

Recommends Stephen Holmes's "useful" introduction to Edwards (2000.15) though it may be a "bit intramural and tangential" for most readers.

69 Moore, T. M. "Introduction." *Growing in God's Spirit.* Jonathan Edwards for Today's Reader, 1. Phillipsburg, N.J.: P & R Publishers, pp. 1-7.

Describes Edwards's works as "urgent, compelling, gracious, [and] profound," in an introduction to three sermons — *Divine and Supernatural Light, Christian Knowledge,* and *The Christian Pilgrim* — the first volume in a series of reprints based on the recent Banner of Truth Issue, derived from Edward Hickman's 1834 two-volume edition.

70 Murray, Iain H. "Lessons from the Extraordinary Life of Jonathan Edwards." In *Knowing the Mind of God: Papers Read at the 2003 Westminster Conference.* Mirfield, West Yorkshire:: Westminster Conference, pp. 7-24.

Justifies Edwards's life as *"extraordinary"* — he was dismissed after twenty-three years of notable service; he met with "contradictory evaluations" during his lifetime; he brought on extraordinary differences about the central theme of his thought; he was the source of "two different streams of influence," metaphysical and evangelical; and, though dying at fifty-four, he left so much written material — and derives four lessons from it, viz., the nature of the true Christian experience; a framework for understanding history and the future, the "key" to understanding Edwards; the power of the Holy Spirit in advancing the gospel and salvation; and the need to "live to God alone."

71 Piper, John. *Desiring God: Meditation of a Christian Hedonist.* Sisters, Ore.: Multnomah.

Reprints 1986.31A.

72 Nettles, Tom J., ed. *Founders Journal: Committed to Historic Southern Baptist Principles* no. 53 (Summer): [i-iii], 1-33.

Celebrates the Edwards tercentenary with an issue devoted to him and his influence on Baptists.

Nettles, Tom J. "Jonathan Edwards: An Appreciation," pp. [i-iii]. Regards Edwards a "gifted servant" for the gospel and, more particularly, for Baptists, in a summary of his life and the papers about him in this issue. No one spoke "so profoundly and searchingly" on the realities of God's absolute sovereignty and the devastating effects of human sin than Edwards: the Southern Baptist Convention was "born, theologically," out of his writings.

Nettles, Tom J. "Edwards and His Impact on Baptists," pp. 1-18. Draws parallels between the arguments Edwards made against the growing Arminianism encroachment on Puritan New England and those Baptists made in their "exit from hyper-Calvinism," as well their common refutation of Arminianism itself, particularly in Isaac Backus, John Dagg, and Basil Manly. With Edwards "so deeply connected" to the beginnings of Southern Baptists — in his understanding of grace, will, and the glory of God — it may be time to return to "our original missionary vision" as it was his.

Beck, Peter. "Awakening an Interest in Evangelism and Edwards," pp. 19-24. Maintains that Edwards was a "consistent" Calvinist, holding the view that human depravity demanded that man be changed in heart, mind, and will. But that "necessitates intervention," both the evangelistic sermon that leads to the "door of mercy" and the divine and supernatural light that "truly moves the heart, changes the mind, and alters the will." Thus Edwards "held comfortably in tension" the doctrines of man's responsibility and God's sovereignty.

Edwards, Jonathan. [An excerpt from *Excellency of Christ*], p. 24.

Robinson, Jeff. "*Religious Affections*: Sorting the Wheat from the Chaff," pp. 25-30. Counts Edwards among the few in the "history of Christendom" to offer such insights into the workings of the human heart regarding salvation. In his "sustained and careful" *Religious Affections*, Edwards first "unpacks" the false marks of conversion from the true, exploding "common delusions" about authentic assurance and then the positive signs, a "genuine experiential evangelicalism." One of Edwards's most "readable" and "sobering" works, *Religious Affections* will shake modern readers from their "spiritual slumber."

[Nettles, Tom J.] "Helpful Books," pp. 31-33. Reviews four books on Edwards — *Jonathan Edwards*, by Iain Murray (1987.22); *Jonathan Edwards*, by George M. Marsden (2003.59); *The Salvation of Souls*, edited by Richard A. Bailey and Gregory A. Wills (2002.2); and *The Legacy of Jonathan Edwards*, edited by D. G. Hart, Sean M. Lucas, and Stephen J. Nichols (2003.36) — and recommends the first to all "lover[s]" of Edwards; lending the second to a "thoughtful non-Christian"; the third to the church at large: preachers, staff, and congregants; and the fourth to "provoke invigorating thought."

73 Neuhaus, Richard John. "When America Was Christian." *First Things* 136 (May): 82-85.

Meditates on Mark Noll's "big and important" book (2002.33) — "when America was really a Christian America, and unambiguously so" — in a review of *America's God*.

74 Nichols, Stephen J. *An Absolute Sort of Certainty: The Holy Spirit and the Apologetics of Jonathan Edwards*. Phillipsburg, N.J.: P & R Publishing, x, 202 pp.

Elucidates Edwards's apologetics, focussing on doctrines related to the Holy Spirit, especially assurance, which provides an "absolute sort of certainty" regarding the truth of Christianity. In doing so, Edwards counters deism and non-Christian religions and contributes to the postmodern critique of knowledge and the idea of "proper epistemic function and warrant." Thus his apologetics unifies and complements his roles as theologian, philosopher, and pastor and offers a "paradigm" for interpreting the "entire Edwardsean corpus."

75 Nichols, William C. *Knowing the Heart: Jonathan Edwards on True and False Conversion.* Ames, Ia.: International Outreach, vii, 435 pp.

Probes what the Bible and Edwards teach about man's depravity, the "windings and turnings" of the heart, and the differences between the regenerate and unregenerate, in brief commentaries on thirteen sermons, all but one previously unpublished.

76 Noll, Mark A. "Beautiful Theology." *Christian Century* 120 (8 March): 38-39.

Admires Amy P. Pauw's "skillful" historical and theological arguments in her "coruscating" volume (2002.36), though being a modern theologian may at times "obscure" coherence in Edwards, in a review of *"The Supreme Harmony of All."*

77 Oakes, Edward T., S.J. "The Great Awakener." *Commonweal* 130 (6 June): 24-26.

Hails George Marsden's "definitive" Edwards (2003.59): it fulfills "magnificently" the need for a new biography of this "quintessential American figure" and "reads like a novel."

78 Pauw, Amy Plantinga. Review of *Jonathan Edwards and the Bible,* by Robert E. Brown. *Christian Century* 120 (9 August): 35.

Welcomes Robert Brown's "splendid" book (2002.5) but suggests his focus of biblical criticism tends to "overshadow" Edwards's other writings, especially his expressions of God's beauty.

79 Reid, Jasper. "Jonathan Edwards on Space and God." *Journal of the History of Philosophy* 41 (July): 385-403.

Charts Edwards's notion of the relationship of absolute space to the divine substance, from his earliest expression of it to his later rejection, and places it within the broader context of seventeenth- and eighteenth-century European philosophy. Edwards's remarks in the three initial paragraphs of "Of Being" (1721), though made with "remarkable capability," are little more than a "juvenile intellectual exercise," and are abandoned as early as 1724 as he sought to construct his ontological system. The mature Edwards still believed that bodies existed *in* God, not "*locally* in God's *immensity,*" as he had first argued, but "*virtually* in God's *will.*"

80 Rogers, Katherin A. "Does God Cause Sin? Anselm of Canterbury versus Jonathan Edwards on Human Freedom and Divine Sovereignty." *Faith and Philosophy* 20 (July): 371-78.

Argues that God does not cause sin, along the lines first advanced by Anselm, and, *contra* Edwards, that if he did so, he would be blameworthy. Edwards's attempts to salvage that position are "unsuccessful," his defense of divine sovereignty a "failure" as well. Edwards suggests that "God *needs* evil choices to accomplish His ends."

81 Schröder, Caroline. "Jonathan Edwards (1703-1758)." In *Key Thinkers in Christianity.* Edited by Adrian Hastings and Alistair Mason. New York: Oxford University Press, pp. 85-91.

Traces the life and work of Edwards — "considered by some the greatest theologian" of his time — one of twenty-three brief assessments of Christian thinkers from Irenaeus to Hans Urs von Balthasar.

82 Scott, David Hill. "From Boston to the Baltic: New England, Encyclopedics, and the Hartlib Circle." Ph.D. dissertation, University of Notre Dame.

Counts Edwards among the "neoteric thinkers" behind the encyclopedic tradition.

83 Shaw, Ross. Review of *"The Supreme Harmony of All,"* by Amy Platinga Pauw. *International Journal of Systematic Theology* 5 (March): 120-122.

> Receives Amy P. Pauw's "remarkable gift to the Christian community" (2002.36) with some misgivings: the influence of Augustine on Edwards's trinitarian thought was "more extensive" than she allows, that of Richard of St. Victor "extremely scant and circumstantial."

84 Sinitiere, Phillip L. Review of *The Salvation of Souls,* ed. Richard A. Bailey and Gregory A. Wills. *Reformed Review* 57 (Winter): 23.

> Hopes that Edwards's sermons, like those collected here (2002.2), inspire today's ministers to "shepherd faithfully the souls entrusted to their care."

85 Smith, Andrew Michael. "Regeneration through Photography: Invention and Identity in Pre-Twentieth-Century United States Literature." Ph.D. dissertation, University of New Mexico.

> Features the science writings of Edwards and Benjamin Franklin as "a kind of proto-photography" before the invention of the daguerreotype.

86 Smith, John E., Harry S. Stout, and Kenneth P. Minkema, eds. *A Jonathan Edwards Reader.* New Haven: Yale Nota Bene.

> Reprints 1995.46.

87 Stackhouse, Max L. "Edwards for Us." *Christian Century* 120 (4 October): 32-33.

> Recommends to those "drifting through life" and fearful of a "profound religious commitment" the Edwards of love and glory, "his sense of the beauty of God."

88 Stein, Stephen J. Review of *Jonathan Edwards and the Bible,* by Robert E. Brown. *Journal of Religion* 83 (July): 462-64.

> Accounts the "many virtues" of Robert E. Brown's "important" book (2002.5) as well as its "tensions," those "uncomplimentary" aspects of Edwards's approach to the Bible — his "studied dismissal" of Judaism, his "uncritical animosity" to Roman Catholicism.

89 Stetina, Karin Spiecker. "The Biblical-Experimental Foundations of Jonathan Edwards' Theology of Religious Experience, 1720-1723." Ph.D. dissertation, Marquette University.

> Stresses the "fundamental importance" of Scripture and personal faith in the development of Edwards's theology, in an examination of his earliest sermons and writings.

90 Stickel, George W. "Jonathan Edwards." In *American Philosophers before 1950.* Edited by Phillip B. Demetteis and Leemon B. McHenry. Farmington Hills, Mich.: Thomson Gale, pp. 89-102.

> Sums up a survey of Edwards's life and works — "the most prolific writer of the American colonial period" — as the "first pragmatist," rather than the "last Puritan."

91 Storms, C. Samuel. "Prayer and the Power of Contrary Choice: Who Can Pray and Cannot Pray for God to Save the Lost?" *Reformation & Revival Journal* 12 (Spring): 53-67.

Cites Edwards's *Freedom of the Will* as the most "convincing critique" of libertarian freedom, in an essay on the consequences of it for intercessory prayer.

92 Stout, Harry S. "Preface to the Period." *Sermons and Discourses, 1739-1742.* Edited by Harry S. Stout and Nathan O. Hatch, with Kyle P. Farley. *The Works of Jonathan Edwards,* 22. New Haven: Yale University Press, pp. 3-47.

Situates the sermons from 1739 to 1742 — the fifth volume of Edwards's sermons and discourses that covers the Great Awakening — in the context of a series of thirty sermon-lectures on Isa. 51:8 he delivered between March and August of that first year, a series "unique" in his preaching and published in Edinburgh and London fifteen years later as *A History of the Work of Redemption.* The themes developed in that discourse "occupied him directly or indirectly" in many of the sermons preached during the period, sermons on heaven — "They Sing a New Song," for example — on earth — "Like Rain upon Mown Grass" — and, "a central component" in his redemptive narrative, on hell — "Sinners in Zion" and, a half year later, *Sinners in the Hands of an Angry God.* As Edwards wrote the trustees of Princeton in 1757, it was a study that he "long ago began," and has "swallowed up my mind, and been the chief entertainment and delight of my life."

93 Strange, Alan D. "Jonathan Edwards on Visible Sainthood: The Communion Controversy in Northampton." *Mid-America Journal of Theology* 14: 97-138.

Considers Edwards's notion of visible sainthood in the communion controversy, first, by looking at the "wider context" of visible sainthood in the Reformed tradition and its New England expression; second, by explicating it in the context of communion qualifications; next, by examining the half-way covenant and Solomon Stoddard's modifications of it; then, by remarking Edwards's revisions of those ideas; and, finally, by discussing the several factors that led to his dismissal by his Northampton congregation. Denied to preach on communion practice, Edwards published *Humble Inquiry* and later defended it against Solomon Williams in *Misrepresentations Corrected.* Although Edwards "failed pastorally," his people failed as well, refusing to give his arguments "even a respectful hearing."

94 ———. Review of *Jonathan Edwards,* by George M. Marsden. *Mid-America Journal of Theology* 14: 189-94.

Urges readers to "run, not walk" to buy George M. Marsden's "*nonpareil*" biography of Edwards (2003.59).

95 Studebaker, Steven Michael. "Jonathan Edwards's Social Augustinian Trinitarianism: A Criticism of and an Alternative to Recent Interpretations." Ph.D. dissertation, Marquette University.

Published (in part) as 2003.96.

96 ———. "Jonathan Edwards's Social Augustinian Trinitarianism: An Alternative to a Recent Trend." *Scottish Journal of Theology* 56 (3): 268-85.

Counters the threeness-oneness paradigm of contemporary interpretations of the Trinity — an "overgeneralized" understanding of trinitarian traditions and "unsuitable" template for Edwards — with the Augustinian mutual love model, a reflection of his "continuity" with both the dominant Western tradition and early Enlightenment apologetics for it. Although Edwards "clearly used" social language to discuss the immanent trinitarian relations, it was in the context of Augustinian Trinitarianism. His emphasis on the Trinity of the Godhead does not mean that he shared in the criticism of late twentieth-century social trinitarians that the Western tradition was "unduly concerned with the oneness of God."

97 Sweeney, Douglas A. *Nathaniel Taylor, New Haven Theology, and the Legacy of Jonathan Edwards.* New York: Oxford University Press, xi, 255 pp.

Depicts Nathaniel William Taylor, professor of didactic theology at Yale from 1822 to 1858, as a "symbol of the vitality" of Edwardsean Calvinism during the first half of the nineteenth century and charts his role in the "modification, diversification, and ultimate dissolution" of that tradition, contributing "mightily" to the intellectual culture of evangelical America. Although Taylor "fractured" the ranks of Edwards's heirs, he also "set loose" the forces of Edwardsean spirituality to the culture at large. Taylor perpetutated Edwards's legacy in a manner "unprecedented" among New England theologians, a legacy since appropriated in "countless arenas" here and around the world through revival and conversion.

98 ———. "A Plentiful Harvest." *Books & Culture* 9 (November): 16, 40-42.

Reaps a harvest of recent studies of Edwards, in a review of *Jonathan Edwards and the Bible,* by Robert E. Brown (2002.5) — "a masterful treatment"; *Jonathan Edwards's Philosophy of History,* by Avihu Zakai (2003.112) — a "superb" analysis; "*The Supreme Harmony of All,*" by Amy Platinga Pauw (2002.36) — "a treasure trove"; and *Jonathan Edwards,* by George M. Marsden (2003.59) — the "crowning achievement" to appear during the tercentenary. These books, among others, and the supporting texts of the Yale edition, especially those of unpublished manuscripts, have "revolutionize[d]" the study of Edwards. No longer an anachronism transcending his age, Edwards was a genius of his time, "an engaged intellectual in the Christian tradition." But unless evangelicals support scholarship for the "new Edwards," the harvest will "prove not nearly so plentiful at 400."

99 ———. Review of *Jonathan Edwards and the Bible,* by Robert E. Brown. *Theology Today* 60 (April): 100-102.

Ranks Robert E. Brown's study (2002.5) the "best work ever written on Edwards's response to the rise of biblical higher criticism," even though it "fails to deliver in full" on its title.

100 Thompson, Damien. "Dangling over the Pit of Hell." [London] *Daily Telegraph,* 21 June, p. 4.

Contends that George Marsden's "magnificent" biography of Edwards (2003.59) leaves the modern reader "baffled" about America's greatest theologian but that Christians can draw inspiraton from him, even if the American academy "no longer gives a hoot" for his ideas.

101 Thurber, Jane Bradford. *Orthodoxy or Liberalism: Never the Twain shall Meet: Contrasting Orthodox Preaching and Liberal Preaching.* Lynchburg, Va.: Author, 189 pp.

Contrasts Edwards and Harry Emerson Fosdick in education and family, doctrine and use of Scripture, general preaching and particular sermons in an effort to persuade young evangelical scholars and preachers not to "compromise or quibble" about biblical inerrancy nor to apply "supposedly higher criticism." Edwards's "whole being was centered in Scripture"; Fosdick's liberalism, on the other hand, had the "deadening effect of an emasculated humanistic gospel."

102 Tolson, Jay. "The New Old-Time Religion." *U.S. News & World Report* (8 December): 36-44.

Imagines Edwards as witness to the great outpouring of contemporary American evangelicals, in an overview of his possible reactions to it on the tercentenary of his birth — caution about their excesses, praise for their seriousness about religion and the "authenticity of their faith."

103 Trigsted, Mark. "Meet Jonathan Edwards (1703-1758)." *Jonathan Edwards: His Greatest Sermons.* Gainesville, Fla.: Bridge-Logos, pp. 1-3.

Remarks Edwards's pulpit manner — "His eyesight was poor, so [his] face was nearly in his papers as he read" — in the preface to a collection of eight sermons, "rewritten and updated."

104 Trumbull, Ralph G., and Don Kistler, comps. *Devotions from the Pen of Jonathan Edwards.* Morgan, Pa.: Soli Deo Gloria, 120 pp.

Adds sixteen new entries to Ralph G. Trumbull's 104 *Devotions of Jonathan Edwards* (1959.20) to "get people to read Jonathan Edwards, and then to read *more* of Jonathan Edwards!"

105 Wacker, Grant, ed. "Book Review Forum: Mark A. Noll, *America's God: from Jonathan Edwards to Abraham Lincoln.*" *Church History* 72 (September): 617-33.

Discusses *America's God,* by Mark A. Noll (2002.33), a book that marks "a major moment" in the historical study of religion in America.

Heyrman, Christine Leigh. "Mark Noll's Master Synthesis," pp. 617-20. Tempers enthusiasm for Mark Noll's "magisterial" argument for a "reconfigured" Christian theology in America with regret that it leaves out both "femininizing and masculinizing trends" at work within American Protestantism.

Wacker, Grant. "How America's God Became, Well, America's God," pp. 620-24. Enjoys the "rich" historiographical feast and "striking" surprises of Mark Noll's work but remains puzzled by the absence of the Latter-day Saints from the table, the "paucity" of references to history as a sphere of divine action, and the nature of the whole: is the story ironic or "simply tragic"?

Holifield, E. Brooks. "Republican Dialect or European Accents? The Sound of American Theology," pp. 624-30. Reprints 2003.30 under a different title.

Noll, Mark. "Response to Critiques of *America's God: From Jonathan Edwards to Abraham Lincoln,*" pp. 630-33. Responds serially to the "thoughful" remarks of the three readers but particularly — and at length — to the "potent" criticisms of the last: on the matter of denominations, "differing narrative choices carry contrasting gains and losses"; on the matter of European influence, a "judgment call"; and on the remark that theological differences rarely led to violence, "I simply disagree," citing the Civil War, "the greatest collective act of violence in American history."

106 Walhout, Clarence. "Inexpressible Sweetness: Jonathan Edwards' History with God." *Perspectives: A Journal of Reformed Thought* 18 (October): 8-13.

Characterizes Edwards's *Personal Narrative* as a "show-and-tell" demonstration of what Reformed theology means, what constitutes genuine Christian experience. Because Edwards's "ineffable encounter" with God renders language inadequate, it becomes oxymoronic and analogical, his experience of prayer and closeness to heaven and Christ "rare moments of mystical experience." Edwards's "poignant wrestle" with God reveals the kinds of experiences in the life of the true believer.

107 Westra, Helen. Review of *Sermons and Discourses, 1739-1742,* ed. Harry S. Stout and Nathan O. Hatch, with Kyle P. Farley. *Calvin Theological Journal* 38 (November): 372-75.

Remarks the "brilliant clarity and depth" of Edwards's sermons in the latest Yale edition (2003.92), a "worthy subject" of study in seminary and literature classes for a "vivid glimpse of one of the liveliest" times in America's religious history.

108 Whaling, Frank. "Book of the Month." *Expository Times* 115 (October): 15-18.
Considers that George M. Marsden (2003.59) provides a "fuller critical biography of Edwards than has ever been possible before," although it sometimes lacks the "depth of theological analysis," and contends that it is "open to obvious question" to rank him with Augustine or Aquinas or as America's greatest theologian.

109 Wheeler, Rachel. "'Friends to Your Souls': Jonathan Edwards' Indian Pastorate and the Doctrine of Original Sin." *Church History* 72 (December): 736-65.
Traces the "oddly egalitarian" text of *Original Sin* to Edwards's preaching to the Indians, in an examination of "long-neglected" manuscript sermons of his Stockbridge years. Emphasizing those "encouraging aspects" of Calvinism — the total depravity of *all* humanity, the unconditional election of members of *all* nations and social ranks — Edwards conveyed to them doctrines suited to their "special circumstances," a congregation "radically different" from the one he left in Northampton and encountered again on the frontier. Yet both shared the "absolute necessity" of divine revelation to acquire true religion, the river gods no less than the Housatonics.

110 Wills, Garry. "Soul on Fire." *New York Times Book Review,* 6 July, p. 10.
Acknowledges George M. Marsden's "convincing case" for Edwards's greatness and speculates what effect he would have had on James Madison and the young Aaron Burr had he lived on at Princeton, in a review of *Jonathan Edwards* (2003.59).

111 Wilson, Stephen A., and Jean Porter, eds. "Focus: Jonathan Edwards." *Journal of Religious Ethics* 31 (Summer): 181-321.
Wilson, Stephen A., and Jean Porter. "Focus Introduction: Taking the Measure of Jonathan Edwards for Contemporary Religious Ethics," pp. 183-99. Marks the tercentenary of his birth with a collection of five essays of "historical and constructive" reflection on Edwards's theological and religious ethics, examines his main texts — *True Virtue, End of Creation, Religious Affections,* and *Charity and its Fruits* — and summarizes each of the essays.
Wilson, Stephen A. "Jonathan Edwards's Virtue: Diverse Sources, Multiple Meanings, and the Lessons of History for Ethics," pp. 201-28. Notes that the puzzle of what Edwards means by *virtue* is "at the heart" of his ethics and the many strands of his thought. Edwards's ethical position "resonates" with concepts from five traditions — moral sense theory, Calvinism, the Cambridge Platonists, Protestant scholasticism, and "those overlaps" between Puritanism and both Separatism and Anabaptism — and emerges as a possible source for contemporary ethics. Yet without such a precise account of his ethics — especially as a Calvinist theologian and a theistic philosopher of the moral sense — it is "awkward" to apply Edwards's thought as a "coherent counterpoise" to current ethical problems.
McDermott, Gerald R. "Poverty, Patriotism, and National Covenant: Jonathan Edwards and Public Life," pp. 229-51. Addresses three ways in which Edwards informs the Christian understanding of public life — by providing philosophical and theological rationales for social engagement; by his dialectical treatment of patriotism; and by his use of the national covenant to "undermine" national pride — and notes how he can be important to Christians today in the public square. Edwards resists the separation of the religious from the public life (as his consideration of poverty reveals), demonstrates the susceptibility of Christian life to the "deceptive accomodation" to culture, and avoids the temptation to chauvinism. Edwards shows the "un-

common power" of the inextricable connection between spirituality and public life and thus provides contemporary Christians with the tools to "help deconstruct" the individual and corportate presumption in public life.

Spohn, William C. "Spirituality and Its Discontents: Practices in Jonathan Edwards's *Charity and its Fruits*," pp. 253-76. Argues that the notion of "practices" in contemporary virtue ethics, chiefly developed by Alasdair MacIntyre and Pierre Hadot, can help explain the "integral connections" between moral development and spiritual transformation that Edwards describes in *Charity and its Fruits* and may offer "an antidote to the superficiality and self-absorbtion" to some forms of spirituality today. Edwards is a "cogent example" of both the spiritual and the religious: drawing upon the Puritan tradition of spiritual practices and the "popular and problematic" interest in spirituality in the revivals of his own time, he developed a "sophisticated" moral pyschology that makes spirituality both "practical and profound." Edwards's theological reflections should alert current theologians and ethicists to the "serious intellectual task" before them.

Delattre, Roland A. "Aesthetics and Ethics: Jonathan Edwards and the Recovery of Aesthetics for Religious Ethics," pp. 277-97. Plays a "tricentennial riff" on Edwards's idea that beauty — the "quintessential subject" of aesthetics — is both the "first principle of being and the distinguishing perfection of God" to encourage readers to think about religious ethics "outside the box." Edwards "dares" to offer God as the animating soul of the universe, governing it by the creative power of his own "beautifying life"; affirms primary beauty (the cordial consent of being to being); and also gives secondary beauty (harmony and proportion) a "constructive and practical" role in the conduct of life. For Edwards, a life of true virtue, then, is a beautifying life, "joyfully" bestowing beauty found at the "deepest reality," the beautifying life of God. "Now that could be a real turn-on!"

Quinn, Philip L. "Honoring Jonathan Edwards," 299-314. Comments on the four previous papers on Edwards — "quite simply, America's greatest philosophical theologian" — and what can be "successfully" appropriated from him for use in contemporary ethics. While there may be a "strong cumulative" case for some elements of Edwards's thought for resources on current ethical issues, how much is "feasible," what "assistance" might be gained is problematic and requires "substantial revision." In fact, when incorporating Edwards as a resource for contemporary virtue theorists, we must be "highly selective" of his ethical, political, and religious views, certainly more selective than when appealing to the work of Aristotle, Aquinas, and Locke.

"Responses to Philip Quinn," pp. 315-21. Characterizes Philip Quinn's reading of the four essays as, serially, offering "false alternatives," "misconstru[ing] what is there," taking "seriously" the practices of spirituality, and sowing "confusion"; for the editors, his remarks attest to Edwards's power to "generate fruitful debate on fundamental themes."

112 Zakai, Avihu. *Jonathan Edwards's Philosophy of History: The Reenchantment of the World in the Age of Enlightenment.* Princeton, N.J.: Princeton Uinversity Press, xvii, 348 pp.

Examines Edwards's "sense of time and vision of history," in an analyis of the development of his historical consciousness — in the early "Miscellanies" and *History of Redemption* — and his philosophy of salvation history within the broader context of both his ideological and theological thought — in *Sinners in the Hands of an Angry God, Distinguishing Marks,* and *Some Thoughts* — and the emergence in the Enlightenment of a secular conception of history emphasizing human agency. Edwards's evangelical historiography had an "abiding importance" for American Protestant culture, for it signified that the "heart" of history was revival — the "crucial element" in the drama of salvation and redemption — and that the process of history depended "entirely and exclusively" on God's redemptive activity manifested in a series of revivals throughout time. "Edwards looked for the reenthronement of God as the author and Lord of history, the reenchantment of the historical world."

2004

1 Adams, Todd L. "Tappan vs. Edwards on the Freedom Necessary for Moral Responsibility." *Transactions of the Charles S. Peirce Society* 40 (Spring): 319-33.
   Presents the analysis of *Freedom of the Will* by Henry Philip Tappan, the "most important and successful" of commonsense critics of Edwards's compatabilism, the attempt to make freedom and determinism compatible with moral responsibility. Tappan accepts Edwards's position "as is," focusses on his definition of liberty, and concludes that his scheme will not work because the agent is not active but passive. "It is futile to claim one could have done otherwise if he had willed otherwise which in fact he could not have willed otherwise."

2 Anderson, Douglas. "Idealism in American Thought." In *The Blackwell Guide to American Philosophy*. Edited by Armen T. Marsoobian and John Ryder. Malden, Mass.: Blackwell Publishing, pp. 22-34.
   Marks Edwards as the "most forceful and persuasive" proponent of objective idealism in the early colonial era, an idealism "embedded" in Calvinism. Edwards's idealism, following Berkeley and Newton, was a "creative synthesis" of the ideas available to him, but New England found it inadequate, challenging it experientially, and turned elsewhere.

3 Armstrong, John H. "Introduction." In *Praying Together for True Revival*. Edited by T. M. Moore. Jonathan Edwards for Today's Reader, 2. Phillipsburg, N.J.: P & R Publishers, pp. 1-10.
   Contends that Edwards's "little book has done more to spark prayer for true revival than any other book in human history, besides the Holy Scriptures," in an introduction to a reprinting of *Humble Attempt*.

4 Atchison, Thomas F. "Towards Developing a Theology of Christian Assurance from 1 John with Reference to Jonathan Edwards." Ph.D. dissertation, Trinity Evangelical Divinity School.
   Investigates the birth imagery of assurance in the First Epistle and sets it in the context of Edwards's Trinitarianism.

5 Bangley, Bernard. "Introduction." *Awakening: The Essential Writings of Jonathan Edwards*. Edited and modernized by Bernard Bangley. Brewster, Mass.: Paraclete Press, pp. vii-xiv.
   Reduces the "effort and pain" of reading Edwards with "simplified paraphrases" and modernized texts — Edwards did not give "much attention to his *style* of writing" — in a brief selection from his work.

6 Barnhart, Joe E. Review of *Jonathan Edwards*, by George M. Marsden. *Journal of the American Academy of Religion* 72 (March): 269-72.
   Praises George M. Marsden's "scholarly, balanced, fair-minded, and highly readable" biography (2003.59) and recommends to seminarians this "vivid account of Edwards's shining integrity and glaring flaws as a pastor."

7 Beal, Jane. "Jonathan Edwards." In *The Oxford Encyclopaedia of American Literature*. Edited by Jay Parini. New York: Oxford University Press, 1: 432-41.

Centers on Edwards's prose style and his influence on American culture — including a "surprising number of important poets and prose authors" — in a brief account of his life and works.

8 Beilby, James. "Divine Aseity, Divine Freedom: A Conceptual Problem for Edwardsian-Calvinism." *Journal of the Evangelical Theological Society* 47 (December): 647-58.

Considers whether the Calvinist's understanding — more particularly, Edwards's in *End of Creation* — of why God created the world is consistent with the assertation of his independence and self-sufficiency, or his aseity. Edwards's "enormously influential" and comprehensive treatment of God's sovereignty in creation "fails" because it implies the denial of divine aseity. It may be that Edwards has paid God "too many theological compliments."

9 Bombaro, John J. "Dispositional Peculiarity, History, and Edwards's Evangelistic Appeal to Self-love." *Westminster Theological Journal* 66 (Spring): 121-57.

Doubts the vision of "'A Strange, New Edwards'" advanced by Anri Morimoto (1995.35) and Gerald McDermott (2000.26) — a "surprising" difference between his public treatises and private notebooks — with a new soteriological paradigm built on dispositional ontology, which engaged non-Christian religions and was "potentially" salvific. Rather, Edwards was "collating materials," not for a reassessment of Christian particularism or a pluralistic eschatology, but for a body of divinity, as he put it, "'in an entire new method," called *A History of the Work of Redemption*, translating his theocentric notion of reality into a concrete, accessible, and meaningful narrative. Edwards laid out no new paradigm but attempted to buttress "his own restrictivist tradition" against the deist assault on redemption and damnation.

10 ———. "God in Us, Us in God: Part Two of Four: The Formulation of Jonathan Edwards' Theocentric Metaphysics." *Clarion Review* 2 (§): 7-16.

Determines that Edwards's "miscellanies" that culminate in *End of Creation* signals the "second and final" shift in the formulation of his theocentrism, in the second essay of four (see 2003.10). The first shift occurred with his conversion — a "generic" theocentrism of religion, of "origins" — the final expression, a theocentricism of "ends," the divine nature and essence are "inseparable," an "intrinsically" moral propensity. As Edwards's thought develops, it incorporates concepts of God, the Trinity, Christ, the Spirit, and redemption in his theocentricism.

11 Bratt, James D. "Edwards for his Time — and Ours: A Historian's View." *Fides et Historia* 36 (Summer): 126-29.

Reprints, in large part, 2003.13.

12 Brown, Robert E. Review of *The Legacy of Jonathan Edwards,* ed. D. G. Hart and Sean Michael Lucas. *Sixteenth Century Journal* 35 (Winter): 1129-30.

Deems the scholarship in this collection of essays (2003.36) "impressive" and the issues covered "notable," evidence yet again that Edwards remains a "vital resource" for theological reflection.

13 Campagna-Pinto, Stephen Thomas. "'The workshop of being': Religious Affections and Pragmatic Value in the Thought of Jonathan Edwards and William James." Ph.D. dissertation, Harvard University.

Assesses the relationship between Edwards's experiential religion and James's radical empiricism: both carry out a similar purpose of inspiring a charitable community.

14 Crampton, W. Gary. *Meet Jonathan Edwards: An Introduction to America's Greatest Theologian/Philosopher.* Edited by Don Kistler. Morgan, Pa.: Soli Deo Gloria Publications, viii, 147 pp.

Offers a brief biography and critique of Edwards's work, including his views on knowledge, special revelation, the Bible, God, Christ, and the Christian experience.

15 Curtis, Finbarr. "Locating the Revival: Jonathan Edwards's Northampton as a Site of Social Theory." In *Embodying the Spirit: New Perspectives on North American Revivalism.* Edited by Michael J. McClymond. Baltimore: The Johns Hopkins University Press, pp. 47-66.

Probes the theological dimensions of whether a revival "'really' happened" — whether there was an authentic outpouring of the Holy Spirit — in an appraisal of Edwards's Northampton during revival. Edwards developed a methodology to discern the real presence of the Spirit — the notion of a "spiritual sense" beyond the empirical — which resulted in "a crisis of signification," a crisis "ultimately irresolvable," his confidence declining as he moved from the "aggressive" authentication of *Faithful Narrative* to the "more cautious" *Religious Affections,* the "common thread" in them that the Spirit "resisted" any external or linguistic form. This crisis of signification makes revivalism interesting to social theory: Edwards's challenge — to consider the role of "experiential aesthetics" — could "reinvigorate social life."

16 Danaher, William J., Jr. Review of *Jonathan Edwards and the Bible,* by Robert E. Brown. *Theological Studies* 65 (March): 189-91.

Finds Robert Brown's insights "significant," but questions his assertion that Edwards's biblical interpretation affected every other aspect of this thought (2002.5).

17 ———. *The Trinitarian Ethics of Jonathan Edwards.* Louisville, Ky.: [Westminster] John Knox Press, xi, 324 pp.

Identifies the "distinctive points" in Edwards's trinitarian theology — the central analogies that serve as "vehicles" for his moral reflections — and the "distinctive contributions" his works offer to contemporary ethics, in a reading of *Religious Affections, Freedom of the Will, Original Sin, True Virtue, End of Creation,* and *Charity and its Fruits.* Edwards's psychological analogy discloses not only the triune processions but that the moral life "hinges" on the participation in the divine nature through the Holy Spirit; his social analogy discloses not only the love among the divine persons but that the church's identity rests in communion with the triune God, the moral life of members embodying its eschatological destiny. Missing from Edwards's theological ethics are two presuppositions from postmodernity, alterity and tragedy, but what is left "exudes a vitality," a quality largely missing from contemporary theology and ethics.

18 Dean, William D. "Religion." In *The Blackwell Guide to American Philosophy.* Edited by Armen T. Marsoobian and John Ryder. Malden, Mass.: Blackwell Publishing, pp. 325-42.

Acknowledges Edwards's "enormous importance" to American philosophers of religion, but denies he was "anything approximating" an American Augustine. Though his radical empiricism is a "distinctively" American element in religious thought, Edwards lacks the others: a sense of the heart — his is "vague and highly fallible" — and religious thought commensurate with the growth of society — his was "inadequate," content in settled theological verities. Charles Sanders Peirce and William James add to Edwards's "accomplishment."

19 Dodds, Elisabeth D. *Marriage to a Difficult Man*. Laurel, Miss.: Audubon Press.
Reprints 2003.31.

20 Dyrness, William A. "Jonathan Edwards: The World as Image and Shadow." *Reformed Theology and Visual Culture: The Protestant Imagination from Calvin to Edwards*. Cambridge: Cambridge University Press, pp. 240-99.
Attributes to Edwards's "radical dependence" upon God both the strength and the weakness of his aesthetic. For Edwards, beauty was communicated by God through special grace to the believer, leaving the unregenerate "at one remove" from it. Although Edwards's religious affections, taken out of its theological context, "played a role" in eighteenth-century aesthetics, it did not serve to encourage a "broader cultural vision," for it failed to allow for any forms other than "human life itself" to express it. And while experiential religion had a profound impact on a developing popular culture unanticapated by theologians like Edwards, even elite culture in time "cut ties" with his vision and its "imaginative reordering of life."

21 Gatta, John. "Intimations of an Environmental Ethic in the Writings of Jonathan Edwards: From Edwards to Aldo Leopold." In his *Making Nature Sacred: Literature, Religion, and Environment in America from the Puritans to the Present*. New York: Oxford University Press, pp. 55-70.
Links Edwards's "protoecological vision" to Aldo Leopold's land ethic (*A Sand County Almanac*, 1949), in a study of his environmental ethics. In his early years, Edwards responded to the "distinctive topography" of the Connecticut River valley — rainbows, flying spiders, the "epiphantic wonder" of physical creation in *Personal Narrative* — but his theocentrism rendered physical nature unequal to scriptural revelation, even in an expanded typology. In later years, in *True Virtue*, Edwards "explored the ethical ramifications" of his vision in *End of Creation*, but failed to address "social and political issues raised by a land ethic."

22 Goren, Joshua Abram. "Religion between the Testaments: Biblical Reconciliation in Antebellum-American Literature and Thought." Ph.D. dissertation, Columbia University.
Cites Edwards's typology as a unifying cultural force in the eighteenth century, in a study of the reconciliation of biblical hermeneutics in selected writings of Joseph Smith, Fenimore Cooper, Harriet Beecher Stowe, and John Brown.

23 Guelzo, Allen C. "Learning Is the Handmaid of the Lord: Jonathan Edwards, Reason, and the Life of the Mind." In *The American Philosophers*. Midwest Studies in Philosophy, 28. Edited by Peter A. French and Howard K. Weinstein. Boston: Blackwell, 1-18.
Reconfigures Edwards as an eighteenth-century pietist, imbued with scholastic rationalism, not Enlightenment reason, more the product of Ramist logic than Lockean sensationalism. Usually credited with being "a major architect of evangelical revivalism" through his revival treatises, after the Awakening he concluded that "truth lay in action" and spiritual knowledge and understanding in practice. In this, there are "structural" and, for some, "disturbing" similarities to the pragmatism of William James and Charles Sanders Peirce. Edwards may not have com-

mitted to the "need of an evangelical mind," but may well be "the very reason why American religion is where it is today."

24 Gura, Philip F. "Jonathan Edwards in American Literature." *Early American Literature* 39 (1): 147-66.

Reevaluates Edwards's place in literary history as a "particularly American writer," in an essay-review of the first twenty-two volumes of the Yale edition. His self-consciousness about language is evident in the volumes of the "Miscellanies"; his "compositional habits" in the volumes of sermons; his devotion to clarity of thought in "The Mind" and *Freedom of the Will;* his appreciation for aesthetics in *End of Creation.* Edwards's "immense presence" in antebellum culture makes for an "immense contribution" to the "discourse of sentimentalism" — the mode of Hawthorne, Melville, Whitman, Stowe — though not with his late treatises, but with his widely circulated texts in the nineteenth century, *Religious Affections, Life of Brainerd,* "Conversion of President Edwards," and "Account of Abigail Hutchinson." "[H]is influence is everywhere."

25 Han, Chae-Dong. "Tradition and Reform in the Frontier Worship Tradition: A New Understanding of Charles G. Finney as Liturgical Reformer." Ph.D. dissertation, Drew University.

Focusses on Charles Grandison Finney's relationship with Edwards (and John Wesley), in a study of the frontier liturgical tradition and reform.

26 Harris, Dana M. Review of *Nathaniel Taylor,* by Douglas A. Sweeney. *Trinity Journal,* n.s., 25 (Spring): 118-20.

Numbers among the strengths of Douglas Sweeney's book on Edwards and Nathaniel Taylor (2003.97) its "lucid" writing and its theological and historical competence, a "fascinating read."

27 Hirrel, Leo. Review of *Nathaniel Taylor,* by Douglas A. Sweeney. *American Historical Review* 109 (February): 178.

Contends that though Douglas Sweeney displays "impressive knowledge" in his study (2003.97), he "short circuits" how Edwards's followers "subtly undermined the visionary aspects" of his theology.

28 Holifield, E. Brooks. Review of *Jonathan Edwards,* by George M. Marsden. *American Historical Review* 109 (February): 177-78.

Avers that George M. Marsden's life of Edwards (2003.59) will "endure as the standard account," a book "informed by mastery" of the time and place.

29 Holmes, Stephen R. "Jonathan Edwards." In *The Blackwell Companion to Protestantism.* Edited by Alister E. McGrath and Darren C. Marks. Malden, Mass.: Blackwell, pp.180-88.

Attributes the continued interest in Edwards not just to his "undoubted genius" but to his "fruitful location," in a brief survey of his life and thought. A "theologian of modernity," Edwards's rendering of Reformed Christianity remains "powerful and astonishing relevant" in our time.

30 ———. "Religious Affections by Jonathan Edwards (1703-1758)." In *The Devoted Life: An Invitation to the Puritan Classics.* Edited by Kelly M. Kapic and Randall C. Gleason. Downers Grove, Ill.: InterVarsity Press, pp. 283-97.

Uncovers the significance of *Religious Affections* in Edwards's "high vision" of the Christian calling, a "humble, cheerful love" for God, unlike the "carnal and emaciated" living in our churches today. Edwards challenges the work of the Spirit as "warm fuzzy feelings while singing" — God has given us "immeasurably" more than that — as he traces Scripture with "care and clarity" in this Puritan classic.

31 Hunsinger, George. "Dispositional Soteriology: Jonathan Edwards on Justification by Faith Alone." *Westminster Theological Journal* 66 (Spring): 107-20.

Parses "Justification by Faith Alone" to find that, although Edwards "clearly understood" the intention of standard Reformation doctrine of justification, he contradicted three "basic tenets" of it. First, as Francis Turretin put it, "'what is inherent is opposed to what is imputed'"; second, as stressed by Martin Luther, "'the whole procedure of justification is passive'"; and last, as John Calvin "emphasized powerfully," participation in Christ's righteousness entails participation with his person, a mystical union and a "giving himself." Edwards's later distinction between primary and secondary saving righteousness "unfortunately" fits in with a version of justification by works and crosses the "fine line" laid down by the Reformation.

32 Hwang, Hyon-gi. *Gido Hapjuhoe.* Seoul: Buhung gwa Gaehyoksa, 202 pp.

Translates *Humble Attempt.* (In Korean.)

33 Kidd, Thomas S. "'The Very Vital Breath of Christianity': Prayer and Revival in Provincial New England." *Fides et Historia* 36 (Summer): 19-33.

Demonstrates the "crucial importance" of prayer in the theology of revival in eighteenth-century New England, in an examination of the practices of prayer during the period, how the emphasis on prayer in revival developed in the first half of the century, and the theological context of Edwards's call for a concert of prayer in *Humble Attempt.* Edwards noted, in the *History of Redemption,* that prayer accompanied all great outpourings of the Holy Spirit, and believed that a great movement of prayer, such as that of the Great Awakening, might bring the Kingdom of God. That, in turn, led him to promote the transatlantic concert of prayer, that the saints in New England might unite in prayer with England and Scotland and introduce the "last great dispensation of God's Holy Spirit."

34 Kling, David W. Review of *Jonathan Edwards and the Bible,* by Robert E. Brown. *Review of Biblical Literature* 6: 551-54.

Views Robert E. Brown's "brilliantly crafted" study (2002.5) "a prolegomenon" to Edwards's use of the Bible, more theoretical than exegetical.

35 Kostis, Russell D. "A Loss of Will: 'Arminianism,' Nonsectarianism, and the Erosion of American Psychology's Moral Project, 1636-1890." Ph.D. dissertation, University of New Hampshire.

Examines Edwards's *Freedom of the Will,* one of four texts — the others were William Ames's *Marrow of Theology,* Thomas C. Upham's *Mental Philosophy,* and William James's *Principles of Psychology* — that dominated American moral psychology for nearly three centuries.

36 Kreider, Glenn R. *Jonathan Edwards's Interpretation of Revelation 4:1–8:1.* Lanham, Mass.: University Press of America.

Numbers more than fifteen books on Edwards over the last twenty years that avoid any treatment of the Bible — the very "heart" of his life and thought — in a "first study" of his interpretation of a passage of Scripture, Rev. 4:1–8:1. Edwards's hermeneutical methodology there and elsewhere is "explicitly" a Christological typology — "the language of God" — in which the Bible, the natural world, and history are linked. A "man of his time," he was dependent on exegetes in "every age," his interpretation changing in the face of "compelling" evidence to do so.

37 ———. Review of *Jonathan Edwards and the Bible,* by Robert E. Brown. *Bibliotheca Sacra* 161 (July): 377-79.

Measures Robert Brown's book (2002.5) as but an "initial step" in understanding Edwards's biblicism: it encourages others to attend it and provides an example of his value to contemporary evangelicals.

38 ———. Review of *"The Supreme Harmony of All,"* by Amy Platinga Pauw. *Bibliotheca Sacra* 161 (April): 251-52.

Refers "all students of the history of theology" to Amy Pauw's "excellent" work (2002.36) on Edwards's Trinitarianism both itself and its relevance to the "contemporary conversation" on the Trinity.

39 Lane, Belden C. "Jonathan Edwards on Beauty, Desire, and the Sensory World." *Theological Studies* 65 (March): 44-72.

Relates Edwards's "richly sensual, almost sacramental" view of the natural world to contemporary discussions of beauty, ecology, and moral practice. Edwards understood the contemplation of nature as an "exercise in prayer," the physical world a "mirror of God's glory, participating it what it reflects." As such, his work is "highly compatible" with the environmental concerns of Catholics and Protestants alike.

40 Larm, Terry A. "A Grammar of Conversion." Ph.D. dissertation, Fuller Theological Seminary.

Refers to Edwards on the affections as part of the theological underpinning for conversion narratives of a number of people in a Methodist church in southern California.

41 Lovelace, Richard F. "Afterword: The Puritans and Spiritual Renewal." In *The Devoted Life: An Invitation to the Puritan Classics.* Edited by Kelly M. Kapic and Randall C. Gleason. Downers Grove, Ill.: InterVarsity Press, pp. 298-309.

Looks briefly at Edwards — and Cotton Mather — as an exemplar of the English Puritan model of the Christian experience in America, the "great theologian" of the Great Awakening. Like the Puritans, Edwards was "relentlessly God-centered," his early account of the Northampton revival their kind spiritual illumination and "thoroughly biblical."

42 Lowery, Kevin Twain. "Constructing a More Cognitivist Account of Wesleyan Ethics." Ph.D. dissertation, University of Notre Dame.

Examines the way that John Wesley appropriates Edwards on the affections, in a study of Wesley's doctrines of assurance and Christian perfection.

43 Lucas, Sean Michael. "'A man just like us': Jonathan Edwards and Spiritual Formation for Ministerial Candidates." *Presbyterion* 30 (Spring): 1-10.

Derives the process of Edwards's spiritual formation from his years at Yale, as a supply minister in New York, and a candidate in Bolton, Connecticut, expressed in his diary, resolutions, sermons, and "Miscellanies" of the time. To become like him, today's ministers who seek the presence of God must give themselves "wholeheartedly to God out of a passionate love for God and others, the evidence of which will be a humble reliance upon God's sovereign grace and a gentle spirit with God's people."

44 Maclean, Iain S. Review of *Nathaniel Taylor,* by Douglas A. Sweeney. *Calvin Theological Journal* 39 (April): 228-30.

Marks Douglas Sweeney's work (2003.97) a "valuable contribution," its notes providing "numerous directions for readers and scholars wishing to trace Edwards's disappearing influence."

45 Macquarrie, John. "Eighteenth Century: Jonathan Edwards, John Woolman." *Two Worlds Are Ours: An Introduction to Christian Mysticism.* London: SCM Press, pp. 199-214.

Justifies the inclusion of Edwards among Christian mystics chiefly through the "mystical vision" he describes in *Personal Narrative.* Still, there is the "difficult question" of how he "reconciled" this mystical tendency with his orthodox Calvinism. Had he lived longer he might have resolved "some of the inconsistencies" in his thought.

46 Marsden, George M. Review of *Nathaniel Taylor,* by Douglas A. Sweeney. *Theology Today* 60 (January): 602-605.

Values Douglas Sweeney's work (2003.97) as both "intelligent and engaging," although it tends to overdevelop Taylor's Edwardseanism.

47 McClymond, Michael J. Review of *Nathaniel Taylor,* by Douglas A. Sweeney. *Journal of the Early Republic* 24 (Winter): 699-701.

Remarks Douglas Sweeney's "engaging" picture of early nineteenth-century ministerial collegiality (2003.97), but finds his evidence of Taylor's theology "frequently ambiguous," his arguments "unconvincing."

48 McMullen, Michael D., ed. *The Glory and Honor of God: Volume 2 of Previously Unpublished Sermons of Jonathan Edwards.* Nashville, Tenn.: Broadman and Holman, ix, 387 pp.

Adds twenty transcriptions of manuscript sermons to an earlier volume, *The Blessing of God* (2003.65), to remark Edwards's achievement in preaching. The "clear truth" in his preaching is that redemption involves all three persons of the Trinity; that the glorious Christ cannot be separated from his gracious work (incarnation and atonement); that "our ascension lies in Christ's condescension"; that Christ is "incomplete" without the church; and that Christ's work is "genuinely" offered to all and to reject it is "inexcusable."

49 Minkema, Kenneth P. "Jonathan Edwards in the Twentieth Century." *Journal of the Evangelical Theological Society* 47 (December): 659-87.

Tracks the interpretation and appraisal of Edwards during the twentieth century within the "professional academic culture," that is, scholarship arising out of secular research universities and theological schools and seminaries; categorizes the secondary literature (homiletics, revivalism, missiology, ethics, literary and cultural criticism, philosophy, theology); discusses some current topics in Edwards studies; reflects upon the relationship between the academy and the church in the effort ("history vs. theology, history and theology"); and concludes with an extensive, if "by no means an exhaustive," bibliography of primary and secondary sources.

50 Moore, Doreen. "The Legacy of Jonathan Edwards." *Good Christians, Good Husbands? Leaving a Legacy in Marriage & Ministry: Lessons from the Marriages & Ministries of Elizabeth & George Whitefield, Sarah & Jonathan Edwards, Molly & John Wesley.* Fearn, Ross-shire, Scotland: Christian Focus, pp. 97-127.

Gleans from Edwards's writings his convictions regarding the role as minister, husband, and father, a man "wholly devoted to the labor of love for the eternal well-being of others," both his family and his people.

51 Morgan, Christopher W. *Jonathan Edwards and Hell.* Fearn, Scotland: Christian Focus Publications, 171 pp.

Defends the historic doctrine of the conscious, endless punishment of unbelievers in hell against the annihilationists in contemporary evangelicalism by invoking Edwards's theological method, a "careful synthesis" of linguistic, exegetical, philosophical, and polemical arguments, drawn from his sermons, treatises, and "Miscellanies." Central to Edwards's response to annihilationism then — and now — is his "particular" understanding of the biblical doctrines of God and sin.

52 Moss, Daniel K. "Jonathan Edwards." *American Writers: A Bibliography with Indexes and Vignettes.* New York: Nova Science Publishers, pp. 93-95.

Lists thirteen items in a bibliography of Edwards, an American preacher evoking "equal parts" of adulation and fear from his "passionate beliefs in scrupulous Calvinism."

53 Music, David W. "Jonathan Edwards and the Theology and Practice of Congregational Song in Puritan England" and "Jonathan Edwards's Singing Lecture Sermon." In *From Anne Bradstreet to Abraham Lincoln: Puritanism in America.* Edited by Michael Joseph Schuldiner and Roxanne Harde. Studies in Puritan American Spirituality, 8. Lewiston, N.Y.: Mellen Press, pp. 103-33, 135-46.

Rehearses Edwards's "principal philosophical discussions of sacred music" in three sermons: a thanksgiving sermon preached on 7 November 1734 (Rev. 14:2); a sermon "for a singing meeting" preached in June 1736 (Col. 3:16), and reprinted here; and "Christian Cautions; or, The Necessity of Self-Examination" preached September 1733 (Ps. 139:23-24), published posthumously. Like others before him, Edwards related the act of singing to heavenly worship, exhorting his congregants that they are part of " 'the same society with those who are praising God in heaven,' " in the first sermon; pointing out in the second that public singing is an " 'ordinance instituted by Christ,' " especially appropriate for the Northampton at the time of its awakening; and asking them in the third, " 'Do you not live in sin, in living in the neglect of singing God's praises?' "

54 No, Byong-gi. *Songryng ui yoksa bunbyol bangbop.* Seoul: Buhung gwa Gaehyoksa, 206 pp.

Translates *Distinguishing Marks.* (In Korean.)

55 Noll, Mark A. *The Rise of Evangelism: The Age of Edwards, Whitefield, and the Wesleys.* Downers Grove, Ill.: InterVarsity Press, pp. 75-80 passim.

Chronicles a series of events abroad between Edwards's Northampton revival in late 1734 and late 1735: the emigration of a group of Moravians to Georgia; the spiritual struggles of George Whitefield, at Oxford, Howell Harris and Daniel Rowland, in Wales; the unsettled plans of the Wesleys; the desire of John Guyse and Isaac Watts, of London, to print Edwards's letter to

Benjamin Colman about it. *Faithful Narrative* (1737), more than the sermons he preached during the revival, "fired the evangelical imagination" and became "an instant classic."

56 Pauw, Amy Plantinga. Review of *Jonathan Edwards's Philosophy of History*, by Avihu Zakai. *Theology Today* 61 (October): 420-21.

Submits that "no one has given a more brilliant account" of Edwards's *History of Redemption* than Avihu Zakai, his "impressive" book (2003.112) illuminating Edwards's life and writings "in new ways."

57 Pettit, Norman. Review of *Jonathan Edwards and the Bible*, by Robert E. Brown. *New England Quarterly* 77 (June): 333-34.

Uncovers stylistic "flaws" in Robert E. Brown's work (2002.5), a study that belies its title and does little more than "touch upon" Edwards's biblical commentary.

58 Piggin, Stuart, and Dianne Cook. "Keeping Alive the Heart in the Head: The Significance of 'Eternal Language' in the Aesthetics of Jonathan Edwards and S. T. Coleridge." *Literature and Theology: An Internatioanl Journal of Religion, Theory, and Culture* 18 (December): 383-414.

Explores the "surprising congruity" of thought and vision of Edwards and Samuel Taylor Coleridge, not only in parallel ideas, but in a similarity of "philosophical sympathy, of detail, intellectual ability, intensity of spiritual conviction, and sense of the artist's vocation." Both agree that divine truths are communicated in creation; that creation contains signs of the spiritual within the material; that the meaning of these signs is grasped through aesthetic vision and intuition, "'the heart living in the head.'" In their typological world, the preacher and the poet recreate a vision of divine truth with the "warmth and light of spiritual awakening."

59 Piper, John. *Desiring God. Meditation of a Christian Hedonist.* Leicester, U.K.: InterVarsity Press.

Reprints 1986.31A.

60 ———. *The Supremacy of God in Preaching.* Grand Rapids, Mich.: Baker Book House.

Reprints 1990.43.

61 ———, and Justin Taylor, eds. *God Entranced Vision of All Things: The Legacy of Jonathan Edwards.* Wheaton, Ill.: Crossway Books, 287 pp.

Gathers together ten papers on Edwards first delivered at a Minneapolis conference hosted by Desiring God Ministries, 10-12 October 2003. (A shorter version — 46 pages — under the same title published in 2003 includes parts of papers here and others from 2002.1.)

Taylor, Justin. "Introduction," pp. 13-18. Offers an overview of the collection grouped under three headings — his life and legacy, lessons from his life and thought, and expositions of *Original Sin, Freedom of the Will*, and *Religious Affections* — appending "an Edwardsean sermon" and some resources for reading Edwards today.

Piper, John. "A God-Entranced Vision of All Things: Why We Need Jonathan Edwards 300 Years Later," pp. 21-34. Decries the "ominously hollow success" of American evangelicalism and recommends Edwards's God-entranced vision of all things as a corrective. What Edwards saw in God and in God's universe, through Scripture, was "breathtaking," his vision of an absolutely sovereign God, self-sufficient, infinite in holiness, perfectly glorious, "infinitely beautiful in all his perfections." A vision such as Edwards's is "rare and necessary."

Nichols, Stephen J. "Jonathan Edwards: His Life and Legacy," pp. 35-53. Explains that Edwards's "ongoing" legacy has as much to do with the "depth" of his encounter with God as with the "breadth" of writings. Edwards had, first, a thorough understanding of the gospel, balancing a "deep and abiding" sense of our sin with an exaltation of "joy in Christ and delight in God"; second, a vision of the beauty of God in nature and at work in the Word and the world; and, third, "unlike any other," he portrayed life as a "relishing" in the gifts and world of the triune God. Edwards spent his life in the "pursuit of happiness" in and through Christ, a life still instructive 300 years later and "hopefully for years to come."

Piper, Nöel. "Sarah Edwards: Jonathan's Home and Haven," pp. 55-78. Outlines the "main roles" God had given Sarah Edwards, in a brief biography and timeline. The "supporter and protector and home-builder" for her husband, Sarah was a "godly mother and example" to their eleven children; a "hostess and comforter and encourager" to Samuel Hopkins, David Brainerd, and others; an "example" to George Whitefield; and a child of God, who from early on experienced "sweet, spiritual" communion with him, grew in grace, and at least once was "very dramatically visited by God in a way that changed her life."

Packer, J. I. "The Glory of God and the Reviving of Religion: A Study of the Mind of Jonathan Edwards," pp. 81-108. Details how Edwards's view of God shaped his thinking about revival, glancing, first, at similarities and differences between him and John Wesley — the other evangelical celebrating a tercentenary — and, then, distinguishing his understanding from the "more general ideas" of renewal of the church's corporate life. Unfortunately, Edwards's concept of a reviving of religion — a "deepening and energizing" of personal communion with God according to Scripture; an enjoying of God in Christ, "framed by the struggles of a life of repentance" — has "no clear meaning" for many today. To fully realize religion as Edwards described it, contemporary evangelicals must "seek for ourselves" and pray for revival.

Whitney, Donald S. "Pursuing Passion for God Through Spiritual Learning from Jonathan Edwards," pp. 109-28. Numbers three lessons from Edwards in pursuit of a passion for God through spiritual disciplines: through the "full range" of them in Scripture; through them "regardless of our intellect or abilities"; through them "equally" with head and heart. But, as Edwards — a "spiritual hero," a "genius" — would readily acknowledge, his example has value only to the extent that it "points us to his God": in Christ alone is "endless fascination, satisfaction, the forgiveness of sins, and eternal life."

Dever, Mark. "How Jonathan Edwards Got Fired, and Why It's Important to Us Today," pp. 129-44. Derives from Edwards's dismissal by his Northampton congregation in 1750 several lessons for evangelicals today. Edwards understood better than his grandfather Solomon Stoddard — and his idea of communion as a converting ordinance — that spiritual life and discipline had to be reflected in the church, that the church had to be visible for the glory of God. To that end, evangelicals need to recover Edwards's vision, that the church be not simply "accessible and comfortable," but "pure and holy," that it be "visibly shining" and distinct from the world, "radiantly distinct" for God's glory.

Burns, Sherard. "Trusting the Theology of a Slave Owner," pp. 145-71. Questions how Edwards, with his "intellect and theological understanding and love of God," could own slaves, in a reading of his "Draft Letter on Slavery." Had he understood the atrocities of the slave trade, Edwards would have "changed his position" on slavery, much as would have seen the "hypocrisy" in the Revolution, freedom for some but not for all. Still, the only "true answer" to the question of his "shortcomings" lies in his — and our — love of God, the sovereign over all things and events in the universe, "even the sin of slavery." By placing history in its "right context" — that is, as "subservient" to the God's will and decrees — the trials of slavery and racism, as of all sin, are reminders that we are "not home yet."

Helm, Paul. "The Great Christian Doctrine *(Original Sin)*," pp. 175-200. Detects Edwards's "confidence" in reason in his three-part defense in the doctrine of original sin — from the empirical evidence of human evil, from Scripture, and from reason itself — each part "complementing" the others. Drawing these strands of argument together, Edwards provides a "powerful cumulative case" for the imputation of sin, that sin through Adam is "race-deep" — not, as with contemporary Christians, where the focus is on the individual sinner — and cure only through union with "the last Adam, Jesus Christ." That Edwards may have pushed theological rationalism in *Original Sin* to the "breaking point" suggests his attempt was both "heroic and tragic."

Storms, Sam. "The Will: Fettered Yet Free *(Freedom of the Will)*," pp. 201-20. Unpacks Edwards's "devastating" critique of libertarianism, reconstructs his concept of the will, and remarks the most "problematic" element in his theology of it — that God is the author of sin — in an essay on *Freedom of the Will*. Edwards appears "unwilling to explain how Adam fell," although his deterministic concept of human volition must trace "every effect" in the universe, every act of will, to the "ultimate, all-sufficient, uncaused cause, the eternal Deity." Still, however "mysterious and unsettling" his treatise often proves, Edwards's reasoning and reading of Scripture is "correct."

Talbot, Mark R. "Godly Emotions *(Religious Affections)*, pp. 221-36. Contends that the "whole purpose" of Part Three of Edwards's *Religious Affections* serves is to show that Scripture distinguishes godly affections from others, that even negative desires and emotions — jealousy, hatred, anger, indignation, fear — can be godly "in appropriate circumstances." Reading that "treasure trove" of Edwards's great book will enlighten the mind, warm the heart, and bring truths, shedding "joy from now throughout eternity."

Piper, John. "'A Divine and Supernatural Light Immediately Imparted to the Soul by the Spirit of God': An Edwardsean Sermon (2 Corinthians 3:18–4:7)," pp. 257-65. Reprints Edwards's sermon, delivered at the close of the conference, as an answer to Objection #6 raised in the first paper of this volume and comments upon it.

Taylor, Justin. "Reading Jonathan Edwards: Objections and Recommendations," pp. 267-72. Exhorts reluctant evangelicals, *"Take up and read!"* older books and Edwards's "complicated sentences and complex thoughts," and appends a short bibliography.

62 Qin, Dongxin. "The Critique of Symbolic Representation in Emily Dickinson's Poetry: Seeing Things in Themselves." Ph.D. dissertation, Binghamton University, State University of New York.

Suggests Edwards's influence upon Emily Dickinson's poetry, and includes translations of Chinese poems and prose.

63 Rowe, William L. "Jonathan Edwards on Divine and Human Freedom." *Can God be Free?* New York: Oxford University Press, pp. 54-73.

Uses Edwards's "penetrating" discussion in *Freedom of the Will* to distinguish the Calvinist from the Arminian understanding of human and divine freedom. In his "brilliant" effort, Edwards sought to reconcile human freedom and moral responsibility with causal determination and divine predestination. In his dispute with the Arminians, Edwards is "victorious" in showing that God necessarily wills to do what he sees to be best, but there are "sufficient grounds for rejecting" his position that moral inability is irrelevant to the agent's moral responsibility.

64 Ryan, Michael C., ed. *Living in Colonial America.* Exploring Cultural History Series. Farmington Hills, Mich.: Greenhaven Press, pp. 87-92.

Illustrates a moral role model in Puritan society with quotations from Edwards's July 1736 sermon on Matt. 5:14, "A City on a Hill" (2001.25, pp. 539-59).

*65 Saldine, Kristin Emery. "Preaching God Visible: Geo-rhetoric and the Theological Appropriation of Landscape Imagery in the Sermons of Jonathan Edwards." Ph.D. dissertation, Princeton Theological Seminary.

66 Scheick, William J. Review of *Jonathan Edwards,* by George M. Marsden. *Early American Literature* 39 (1): 195-201.
Balances George Marsden's "masterfully" achieved life-and-times biography (2003.59) against "some agendized liberties" taken with such matters as Edwards's decision on pastoral calls, Sarah's spiritual crisis, and his "murky" handling of David Brainerd's journal.

67 Schillinger, Jamie Andrew. "Triangulating Faith, Virtue, and Reason: An Edwardsean Account." Ph.D. dissertation, University of Chicago.
Describes the interdependence of faith, virtue, and reason in its effect upon Edwardsean epistemology and religious pluralism, exemplified by Edwards and David Brainerd in the success (and failure) of their missions to the Indians.

68 Shook, John R. "Jonathan Edwards' Contribution to John Dewey's Theory of Moral Responsibility." *History of Philosophy Quarterly* 21 (July): 299-312.
Asserts that the John Dewey of *Ethics* (1908) and *Human Nature and Conduct* (1922) upheld the Edwardsean criticisms of free will he had "absorbed" as a young man, the New Divinity tradition of his native Vermont. Dewey's arguments in his earlier works, "Ego and Cause" and *The Study of Ethics* (1894), are "strongly reminiscent" of Edwards's agent-centered theory of moral responsibility, Dewey's argumentative tactics those of *Freedom of the Will.* Although he could not follow Edwards's Calvinistic Christianity, Dewey's "useful and robust compromise" carried Edwards's thought into the progressive movement of the twentieth century.

69 Simonson, Harold, ed. *Selected Writings of Jonathan Edwards.* Long Grove, Ill.: Waveland Press.
Reprints 1970.35.

70 Stephens, B. M. Review of *Jonathan Edwards at Home and Abroad,* ed. David W. Kling and Douglas A. Sweeney. *Choice* 42 (July): 2062.
Admires this "fine collection" of essays on Edwards's historical influence, an important, if "neglected," contribution to the "proliferation of works" on him.

71 Storms, Sam. *One Thing: Developing a Passion for the Beauty of God.* Fearn, Ross-hire, Scotland: Christian Focus, 188 pp.
Struggles to find words to describe the "pervasive impact" of the nineteen-year-old Edwards's "Miscellanies," no. 3, "Happiness Is the End of the Creation," in a testament to God's "ineffable" beauty, explaining the "catalytic" power of the divine encounter — and its "ever-increasing" intensity in heaven — and drawing upon manuscripts, sermons, treatises, and letters in the Yale Edwards as well as other sources.

72 Sweeney, Douglas A. "Editor's Introduction." *The "Miscellanies" (Entry Nos. 1153-1360). The Works of Jonathan Edwards,* 23. New Haven: Yale University Press, pp. 1-36.

Outlines the ways these "Miscellanies" fit into Edwards's "vocational agenda" and remarks his acute concern over the lack of faith among European intellectuals and their neglect of revelation, showing himself to be a "uniquely *modern* supernaturalist," refuting the "'generous doctrine'" of natural religion, infusing Reformed orthodoxy with new meaning — an "Enlightenment Calvinist." The fourth volume in the series covers Edwards's final years at Stockbridge — shedding new light on his regular routine as an Indian missionary — and confirms his assertion to the Princeton trustees in October 1757 that his studies had "swallowed up" his mind. From 1751 to 1755, Edwards wrote about 100 entries, from 1756 to 1758, eighty; the first covered 145 folio pages, the second, 560 octavo — "double the output in less than half the time."

73 Talbot, Mark R. "Edwards for his Time — and Ours: A Philosopher's View." *Fides et Historia* 36 (Summer): 121-25.

Points out that George M. Marsden has not "thought through" carefully enough issues of divine sovereignty and human freedom to represent Edwards "accurately," in an essay-review of *Jonathan Edwards* (2003.59), a "great read!"

74 Van Der Weele, Steve J. Review of *Jonathan Edwards,* by George M. Marsden. *Calvin Theological Journal* 39 (April): 218-21.

Counts George Marsden (2003.59) "uniquely qualified" as an historian of American culture to correct the "flawed" biographies by Ola Winslow (1940.21) and Perry Miller (1949.9) and to appropriate Edwards's world to ours, situating him both in traditional Christianity and its New England variant, "exegeting" his major works.

75 Vogan, Matthew. Review of *Jonathan Edwards — His Message and Impact,* edited by Robert E. Davis. *Evangelical Times* 38 (September): 23.

Finds the "real meat" of the collection in a paper on Edwards as "a father of the modern missionary movement."

76 Waddington, Jeffrey C. "Jonathan Edwards's 'Ambiguous and Somewhat Precarious' Doctrine of Justification." *Westminster Theological Journal* 66 (Fall): 357-72.

Questions Thomas A. Schafer's reading of Edwards on justification (1951.17) — he grounds the "*legal* imputation" of Christ's righteousness in the believer's "*real* union" with Christ; he places "sanctification *before* justification"; he uses the notion of "*formed* faith" — and concludes that Schafer "failed to make his case," chiefly because he neglected the Reformed context of Edwards's formulation. Although he was "creative and unique" and his language perhaps too "fluid," Edwards "stands well within" Reformed orthodoxy and brings "clear insight and depth" to his discussion. *Contra* Schafer, Edwards neither compromises the doctrine of justification nor puts it in "a tenuous position."

77 Walker, Williston. *Ten England Leaders.* Eugene, Ore.: Wipf and Stock.

Reprints 1901.14.

78 Ward, Roger A. "The Philosophical Structure of Jonathan Edwards's *Religious Affections.*" In his *Conversion in American Philosophy: Exploring the Practice of Transformation.* New York, N.Y.: Fordham University Press, pp. 1-28.

Reprints 2000.46.

79 Wilson, John F. Review of *Jonathan Edwards*, by George M. Marsden. *Theology Today* 60 (January): 588-90.

Contends that George Marsden's "great gift" (2003.59) will "entirely supplant" Ola Winslow's life (1940.21) and put in "helpful perspective" Perry Miller's (1949.9) but will "disappoint" some readers with its emphasis on the "very human" Edwards, not the "extraordinary intellectual."

80 Young, Malcolm Clemens. "One World at a Time: Henry David Thoreau's Religious Practices." Th.D. dissertation, Harvard University.

Uncovers important continuities between Thoreau's perception of nature and Edwards's, in a study of religious influences on Thoreau's thought.

81 Zakai, Avihu. "The Ideological Context of *Sinners in the Hands of an Angry God*." *Fides et Historia* 36 (Summer): 1-18.

Insists that the text of probably Edwards's most famous sermon cannot be understood without the "specific ideological context" of the Great Awakening, viz., his apocalyptic and eschatological interpretation of the revivals that swept New England in the early 1740s. Behind the sermon lies a "grand teleological theology of history" and, for Edwards, the prospect of the "imminent approach" of God's impending judgment upon those refusing salvation. Not an isolated text, *Sinners in the Hands of an Angry God* cannot be separated from the "rhetoric of history" nor from Edwards's "developed interpretation" of revival in *Distinguishing Marks*, two months later, and *Some Thoughts*, the year following.

2005

1 Boyden, Michael. "The Institutional Origins of American Literary History." *Comparative American Studies* 3 (June): 173-88.

Illustrates the important role institutions play in literary history with Perry Miller's "From Edwards to Emerson" (1940.9), a genealogy connecting Puritans to Transcendentalists. Miller's successful taxonomy reflects "institutional myopia . . . *because the connection already existed*"; as earlier histories of American literature make clear, it was "firmly ingrained" in academic discourse before his article appeared. Still, Miller managed to turn Edwards into *"common property"* and Transcendentalism into a "central *American* movement," and so contributed to the creation of a national literary tradition.

2 Capps, Donald. "Jonathan Edwards: Decline and Failure within a Stable Structure." In his *Young Clergy: A Biographical-Developmental Study*. Binghamton, N.Y.: Haworth Pastoral Press, pp. 67-99.

Applies Daniel J. Levinson's developmental paradigm (*The Seasons of a Man's Life*, 1978) to Edwards representing decline and failure in a stable life, one that came to a "frustrating end," in a study that includes Phillips Brooks, Orestes Brownson, John Henry Newman, and John Wesley. The very features of Edwards's stable life — his long-term pastorate, his secure family life (Sarah and their children), his extended family — "contributed" as well to his decline in his late thirties, for example, his decision to "dissociate" himself from his grandfather's position on church membership. But if that "most dramatic controversy" was the proximate cause for his failure, his manipulation of the young in the bad-book episode was the "recurrent issue," one the young Edwards discovered in his study of spiders: "the urge to manipulate the object of one's attention becomes irresistible when [it] threatens to drift away."

3 Chamberlain, Ava. Review of *Jonathan Edwards and the Bible,* by Robert E. Brown. *Modern Theology* 21 (January): 183-85.

Demurs from Robert Brown's claim (2002.5) that Edwards was "'preeminently concerned with the rationalist critique regnant within deism,'" but agrees that he was concerned about the implications that historical disciplines had for theology throughout his career.

4 Clark, Stephen M. "Jonathan Edwards: The Assurance of Salvation and the Care of the Church." In *The Assembling of Ourselves Together: Ecclesiology in the Twenty-First Century.* Edited by John L. Vance. Rock Tavern, N.Y.: WPC Books, pp. 17-37.

Frames the question of salvation with two events that "intrude offensively" into Edwards's career — his uncle's suicide that ended the revival in Northampton and his nephew's role in the council that ended in his dismissal — linking both to the issue of assurance. The elder Joseph Hawley "latched upon" it at the height of the awakening, his son — and uncle Solomon Williams — upon it in the argument over church membership and public profession. Although *Religious Affections* confronts the issue "head on," the twelve distinguishing signs of gracious affections Edwards spells out applied to sanctification, not assurance; only professors of Jesus as savior were "assured of salvation."

5 Colson, Charles W. "Introduction." In *Faith beyond Feelings: A Christian's Character before God.* Edited by James M. Houston. Colorado Springs, Col.: Victor Books

Reprints 1984.6 under a new title.

6 Crisp, Oliver D. *Jonathan Edwards and the Metaphysics of Sin.* Burlington, Vt.: Ashgate Publishing, [viii], 146 pp.

Assesses Edwards's "highly original" contributions to hamartiology — the metaphysics of the fall, original sin, guilt, and the imputation of sin — in the context of the "increasing interest" in philosophical theology. Although his thinking took him "beyond the boundaries" of the Reformed tradition, it was not so much a departure from it as a "reformulation"; and, although he failed to reconcile his different views of sin into "one coherent whole," he raised the standard of discussion to a "new level of limpidity and philosophical acuity." Philosophers and theologians would do well to take Edwards's doctrine of sin "a great deal more seriously."

7 Crompton, Samuel Willard. *Jonathan Edwards.* Spiritual Leaders and Thinkers. Philadelphia: Chelsea House, x, 124 pp.

Sums up Edwards as, first, a man of God; second, a man of tradition; third, a man who believed in books; fourth, a man who believed in the "covenant of the New Englanders with God"; and fifth, a man of "extraordinary single-mindedness," in a biography for young readers, and reprints in part *Sinners in the Hands of an Angry God* and *Wicked Men Useful in their Destruction Only,* adding a chronology, glossary, and bibliography.

8 Delaney, Harold D., and Carlo C. DiClemente. "Psychology's Roots: A Brief History of the Influence of Judeo-Christian Perspectives." In *Judeo-Christian Perspectives on Psychology: Human Nature, Motivation, and Change.* Edited by William R. Miller and Harold D. Delaney. Washington, D.C.: American Psychological Association, pp. 31-54.

Sketches Edwards's psychology revealed in *Religious Affections, Freedom of the Will,* and "The Mind," notions more in keeping with the "predominant" view of modern psychology in his determinism than earlier Christian writers.

9 Filson, David Owen. "Fit Preaching: 'Fitness' in the Preaching of Jonathan Edwards." *Presbyterion* 31 (Fall): 89-100.

Explores "fitness" — the relationship between two aspects of the same theological operation — as a homiletical and soteriological concept in Edwards's preaching, in *Divine and Supernatural Light* and *Justification by Faith Alone,* for example. In the first, Edwards argues that there is a "relationship of concurrence" between the Word preached and saving grace, between the sermon and faith; in the second, he uses fitness to describe the "unique" conditions between the nature of Christ and the nature of redemption, the two "conjoin[ed]" in justification. Fitness for Edwards, then, is not only a homiletic device but a polemic tool as well in his fight against the "dangers of Romanism, Arminianism, and even antinomianism."

10 Garrett, Paula K. "A Splinter off the 'Sound Old Theological Block': Grace Greenwood's Humorous Revision of the American Jeremiad." *Studies in American Humor* 3d ser., no. 12 : 17-43.

Delights in Grace Greenwood's "hilarious preaching" on the pages of the *New York Times* in the late nineteenth century, Edwards's "'prodigal'" great-granddaughter, calling herself a "'small splinter'" off the "'sound old theological block.'"

11 Gura, Philip F. *Jonathan Edwards: America's Evangelical.* New York: Hill and Wang, xx, 282 pp.

Situates the "cornerstone" of Edwards's legacy and importance to American culture in his writings about personal religious experience, not his late theological treatises — *Faithful Narrative* "a virtual blueprint" for contemporary evangelicals and central to the "extensive" discourse of sentimentalism in antebellum America — in a biographical portrait of the "chief exponent" of American revivalism. Edwards did "nothing less than script" how evangelicals understand and embody spirituality, grasping, as he himself had in *Personal Narrative,* "the new simple idea of man's utter insufficiency without the divine." Edwards's "immense" cultural presence in the nineteenth century appears "most vibrantly" in Harriet Beecher Stowe, Maria Cummins, and Susan Warner, in Nathaniel Hawthorne, Herman Melville, and Walt Whitman.

12 Hart, D. G. "The Church in Evangelical Theologies, Past and Future." In *The Community of the Word: Toward an Evangelical Ecclesiology.* Edited by Mark Husbands and Daniel J. Treier. Downers Grove, Ill.: InterVarsity Press, pp.23-40.

Cites Edwards as one of the "rare evangelical worthies" who was a regular, settled pastor, in an account of prominent evangelicals on the "church question," John Nevin, George Whitefield, Charles Finney, and Charles Hodge, among them. Edwards identified true religion with personal experience and, in attempting to gauge it, thought the church "superfluous." In *Humble Inquiry,* his reflections on communion and church membership, Edwards's concern was "not what the church ministers in the sacrament but what qualifications believers need to manifest for participation."

13 Haykin, Michael A. G. *Jonathan Edwards: The Holy Spirit in Revival: The Lasting Influence of the Holy Spirit in the Heart of Man.* Darlington, U.K.: Evangelical Press, xix, 227 pp.

Appreciates Edwards's reflections on revival — his "meticulous and minute" observations, his heart devoted to the "pursuit of the glory of God" — in a study of *Faithful Narrative, Religious Affections,* and *Humble Attempt,* the morphology of revival and the work of the Holy Spirit. A "reliable mentor" to evangelicals and a "skillful navigator" of the spiritual experience, Edwards is "still of immense value," now when the Christian world is "deeply interested" in revival and spirituality.

14 Hewitson, James Kenneth. "Mechanization and the Transformation of Millennial Discourse: Jonathan Edwards and Nathaniel Hawthorne." Ph.D. dissertation, University of Toronto.

> Excavates the history of the "dark" postmillennialism in American culture through an analysis of Edwards's use of the "master metaphor" of the machine of rotating wheels and gears to express God's work of redemption, then in Nathaniel Hawthorne and Herman Melville, Ken Kesey and Thomas Pynchon.

15 Holifield, E. Brooks. Review of *Jonathan Edwards at Home and Abroad,* ed. David W. Kling and Douglas A. Sweeney. *American Historical Review* 110 (February): 123-24.

> Applauds the "salutary tendency" of studies of American religion placed in an international context so "nicely exemplified" by the editors and essayists here.

16 Hopkins, Philip. O. "Missions for the Glory of God: An Analysis of the Missionary Theology of John Piper." Ph.D. dissertation, Southeastern Baptist Theological Seminary.

> Notes the impact of Edwards (among others) on John Piper's theology and missions.

17 Johnson, Ellwood. *The Goodly Word: The Puritan Influence in American Literature from Jonathan Edwards to William James.* Toronto: Clements Academic.

> Reprints 1995.21-22 under a new title.

18 [Klein, Patricia.] "Preface." *Sermons of Jonathan Edwards.* Peabody, Mass.: Hendrickson Publishers, pp. xi-xxvii.

> Introduces a "fine sampling" of twenty Edwards's sermons — some revival, some pastoral, some instructional, all "brilliant" — with a brief life and estimate of that "murky figure" to most twenty-first-century Americans.

19 Kreider, Glenn R. Review of *An Absolute Sort of Certainty,* by Stephen J. Nichols. *Bibiliotheca Sacra* 162 (April): 251-52.

> Regards Stephen Nichols's treatment of Edwards's apologetics (2003.74) as "helpful" if "overstated."

20 ———. Review of *The Blessing of God,* ed. Michael D. McMullen. *Bibiliotheca Sacra* 162 (October): 504-505.

> Recommends "reading and rereading" sermons like those collected here (2003.65) because it is "difficult to overstate the importance and value" of Edwards to American Christianity.

21 ———. Review of *Nathaniel Taylor,* by Douglas A. Sweeney. *Bibiliotheca Sacra* 162 (April): 250.

> Calls Douglas Sweeney's "impressive" study (2003.97) an "outstanding example of evangelical historiography."

22 ———. Review of *The Salvation of Souls,* ed. Richard A. Bailey and Gregory A. Wills. *Bibiliotheca Sacra* 162 (January): 127-28.

Singles out "The Kind of Preaching People Want," one of nine unpublished ministerial sermons by Edwards (2002.2), as "especially relevant to the contemporary American church."

23 Lee, Sang Hyun, ed. *The Princeton Companion to Jonathan Edwards*. Princeton, N.J.: Princeton University Press, xxviii, 331 pp.

Lee, Sang Hyun. "Introduction," pp. xi-xix. Describes briefly each of the nineteen essays on Edwards's major theological ideas and the through three approaches used — relational, doctrinal, constructive — in a volume designed to promote "more vigorous discussion" of his thought.

Minkema, Kenneth P. "Chronology of Edwards' Life and Writings," pp. xx-xxviii. Compiles a detailed chronology of Edwards's life and work, often dating events and items by month and day to reveal meaningful relationships between them.

Minkema, Kenneth P. "Jonathan Edwards: A Theological Life," pp. 1-15. Examines Edwards's career as an effort to deal with the "changing theological currents" he was born into, a New England Calvinist orthodoxy in tension. At times conforming to those currents, often drawing upon them for "his own purposes," Edwards also constructed a "considerable critique" of them. Although his defense of Calvinism "may have failed" — even given the "innovative and forceful" arguments in his published treatises and in the promise of his *Harmony of the Old and New Testament* — by mounting it, he left a legacy "still felt to this day."

Thuesen, Peter J. "Edwards' Intellectual Background," pp. 16-33. Considers Edwards an "eclectic" thinker, torn between Puritan traditionalism and Enlightenment rationalism, premodern Western Christianity and modern skepticism, in a study of his intellectual development. For all his "implicit debt" to the Reformation, citations to Calvin and other sixteenth-century divines are "few and far between"; rather, as his "Catalogue" of over 700 books suggests, the Enlightenment was his "reference point." Edwards read largely contemporary texts, immersed in the eighteenth-century transatlantic culture of print, borrowing and "creatively refashioning" what he found there.

Niebuhr, Richard R. "Being and Consent," pp. 34-43. Cites several propositions from the early Edwards — "The Mind," "Of Being," and "Of Atoms" — that "symbolically" represents the theme of being and consent that "runs through *much*" of his writing. From this come two points later elaborated and modified by Edwards: first, that being has knowledge and consciousness and that these operations of the mind imply that "mind or proper being is plural in some sense," a complex event, and bring about consequences, such as excellency and love; second, that despite his use of "shadow language" about natural phenomena, Edwards's interest is "intense," derived as it is from the mind's passionate "appetite" for knowledge. Even the posthumous *True Virtue* can be "illuminated" by "The Mind" and, in turn, can reflect "additional light" upon that early manuscript.

Pauw, Amy Plantinga. "The Trinity," pp. 44-58. Links two aspects, usually "disconnected," of Edwards's theology of the Trinity, joining his "profound" metaphysical musings to his "zeal" for the church and the Christian life. For Edwards, the ultimate reality was the "dynamics of union" and the "paradigm" for it the Trinity: "God is like a mind that knows and loves itself, and God is like a society or family of three." If Edwards's arguments appear "quaint or even outlandish" today, his "confident" assumption of the centrality of the Trinity to Christian faith and his "multifaceted" articulation of beauty and excellency of the triune God retain a "deep spiritual and theological resonance."

Lee, Sang Hyun. "God's Relation to the World," pp. 59-71. Elaborates on several points of Edwards's thought on God's relation to the world, chief among them that the created world is God's "repetition outside of himself, in time and space, of his prior actuality." Thus what God does in time and history is part of his own life and, since that involves an "element of becoming" in God's being, according to Edwards, creatures in the realm of becoming can participate in God's life. In short, what Christians do in the world by God's grace "matters to God." For Edwards, God needs or uses the world in time and space to "exercise his dispositional essence outside of his own internal being."

Jenson, Robert W. "Christology," pp. 72-86. Discusses Edwards's Christology — one of the "more astonishing" aspects of his thought — in terms of the soteriological concerns that drove it, the metaphysical convictions that constrained it, the way of talking about Christ that it aimed at, and the conceptual means to that end. For modern (or post modern) society, with little to replace its failed faith in "secularized reason," Edwards's "drastic" discourse about the Christ, as both the Logos and the man Jesus, can have "moral or political bite" in late modernity and may be just the kind "urgently demanded" by the church's present historical situation. Indeed, Edwards's language of spirits and their various communions can serve as a "splendid model" for it.

Brown, Robert E. "The Bible," pp. 87-102. Contends that Edwards's biblical interpretation is the "most neglected" aspect of his thought. Edwards devoted a "large measure" of his energies to writing about Scripture — as did the majority of eighteenth-century intellectuals — in an attempt to reconcile the ancient biblical authors' representation of the world with Newtonian astronomy and physics, using his typology in exegesis, the "most notable" aspect of his exposition. Although he "clearly occupies the conservative end" of commentaries of the period, Edwards's biblical interpretation was "some kind of composite" of traditional views and modern canons of historical investigation.

Smith, John E. "Religious Affections and the 'Sense of the Heart,'" pp. 103-14. Concludes that Edwards produced a "unique synthesis" of religion, psychology, and theology in *Religious Affections*, the "most comprehensive" treatment of the subject in his writings. Edwards tried to show both how the affections were a "great part" of true religion and how to test the religious experience, to understand, as he said, the "sense of the heart." But he was also "caught between two fires" in the attempt: those opposed to the importance of the affections yet approved testing for error and excess, like Charles Chauncy, and those sympathetic to heart religion yet were "not particularly pleased" with the twelve signs, believing religious fervor self-authenticating.

Guelzo, Allen C. "Freedom of the Will," pp. 115-29. Examines the "exact nature" of free will and Edwards "compatibilist" contribution to it, in a history of the publication of and response to *Freedom of the Will*. The book became the "touchstone" of the New Divinity and the "great issue" to New England theology in antebellum America, but with the rise of pragmatism at the end of the century fell into "philosophical limbo" and remained largely ignored by Edwards's readers. Although Paul Ramsey's introduction to the Yale edition was a "turning point" in interpretation, the text "still suffers" from inattention. Perhaps with renewed interest in various forms of philosophical determinism, Edwards's "greatest" work may yet prove relevant.

Lee, Sang Hyun. "Grace and Justification by Faith Alone," pp. 130-46. Demonstrates that Edwards reaffirms the Reformed doctrine of the justification of the ungodly and articulates the "ontological (dispositional) grounding" of the sinner in Christian practice. Edwards is in "complete agreement" with Calvin that justification and sanctification constitute a "double grace" through union with Christ. By adding disposition to the sanctified life, Edwards "carefully expanded" the Reformed doctrines of regeneration and sanctification. Such a view of faith as "infused disposition," however, makes his doctrine of justification neither "practically" Roman Catholic, as some have claimed, nor similar to the "created grace" of Thomas Aquinas. "Edwards is Protestant and Reformed."

Smith, John E. "Christian Virtue and Common Morality," pp. 147-66. Delineates Edwards's views on the nature of divine love and his conception of the virtuous life as they bear upon common morality, in a reading of *Charity and its Fruits* and *True Virtue*. Edwards held that the "main ingredients" of common morality — secondary beauty, self-love, conscience, and kindly affections — do not have the "essence" of true virtue and have been mistaken for it. Although these natural principles of common morality further human life and enhance its quality, Edwards is "at pains" to explain how they profoundly differ from true virtue, the consent of beings to Being in general, that is, God.

Sweeney, Douglas A. "The Church," pp. 167-89. Gleans Edwards's writings, especially the manuscript sources, for his ecclesiological views, a part of his thought "largely unnoticed" by scholars. Edwards viewed the church as an "intimate company of God's lovers" — the unity and beauty of the mystical body of Christ — and delineated between spiritual and carnal Christians, "the hearts confession and that of the lips." That he would call for stricter standards of membership during and after the Great Awakening follows from what he perceived as an "alarming number" of hypocrites in his church at the time, a cacophony in the "symphony of saints." Edwards labored "long and hard" on the purity of his church, *Humble Attempt* but the end of a "paper trail" dating back to his first days in Northampton.

Knight, Janice. "Typology," pp. 190-209. Considers typology the "interpretative key" Edwards uses to unlock God's revelation in nature and human history, in the created world and Scripture. Edwards understood typology as a form of "divine speech" in which God communicated his intentions and his love to the saints, an "eternal dynamic" that grows stronger with the coming of the millennium — a calculus of an increasing mass with diminishing distance — his discourse embracing more and more the "idioms of everyday life." For Edwards, the immortal glory of God himself resides in his "ceaseless desire" to communicate through all time and all creation.

Wilson, John F. "History," pp. 210-25. Untangles several separate but interrelated strands of Edwards's interpretation of history: the genesis and content of the 1739 sermon series "Redemption Discourse," published posthumously as *A History of the Work of Redemption;* his remarks on history in the letter to the Princeton trustees; his "broader reflections" on God's purpose in *End of Creation;* his "relatively infrequent" references to history in his writings; and modern readers' "unending conjectures and countless assertions" about his interest in the subject. Although Edwards was a figure of his own time, "indelibly imprinted" with seventeenth-century Anglo-American salvation history, his exposition of a new redemptive framework, predicated on the "proximity of the presumed completion" of history, seems to have "heralded" the nineteenth-century view of the American future. Thus understood, Edwards turns out more a creature of history than the creator of a new historiography.

Stein, Stephen J. "Eschatology," pp. 226-42. Organizes Edwards's eschatological ideas into three periods: his early reflections, from his Yale years to 1733; his involvement in revivals, from 1734 to 1748; and his most productive time, the last decade of his life. From his "random and occasional" comments scattered throughout his private and public writings comes an adumbrated, not a systematic, eschatology: the "controlling principle" of it is the connection between first and last things, divine providence governing the events between them; the Holy Spirit is the "primary agent" whereby Christ's kingdom on earth advances, the forces of evil opposed to redemption impeding its progress; and the final stage of the process "will not, in fact, be final." For Edwards, both heaven and hell are "progressive" states and will continue forever — the saints in unending praise, the damned in unending punishment — both "apt reflections" of God's glory and his purpose in creation.

Kimnach, Wilson H. "The Sermons: Concept and Execution," pp. 243-57. Suggests that Edwards "fully exploited" the potential of the Puritan sermon without "seriously altering" its form — text, doctrine, application — used in the seventeenth century by the great preachers of New England, in an analysis his general sermonic practice and particular accomplishments, including *Sinners in the Hands of an Angry God.* Over time, he not only developed a "surer" sense of movement with the form but also employed it "more artfully" than any other American preacher, revising his sermons with great deftness and economy. For Edwards, the sermon was the "essential literary form," both in his pastoral homiletics and in "virtually all" his major treatises.

McDermott, Gerald R. "Missions and Native Americans," pp. 258-73. Relates how missions to the Indians function as the "principal moving force" in Edwards's history of redemption and how his work among the Housatonics shaped his ideas on indigenous religion, in time winning their affection and returning it. Edwards came to believe that what God was doing among Native Americans was "tangible evidence" that the great work of his Spirit may have begun, dramatic previews of the "final act" of redemption. Edwards's direct experience at Stockbridge and, to a far greater extent, his depiction of David Brainerd's at Crossweeksung in *Life of Brainerd* — "probably the first full missionary biography ever published" — had an enormous impact on Anglo-American missions and missionaries over the last two centuries.

Stout, Harry S. "The Puritans and Edwards," 274-91. Proposes that Edwards was more of a Puritan than Perry Miller or his revisionists concede, "every bit" the federal theologian his predecessors were. Edwards adhered "exactly" to the logic and tenets of the national covenant, reiterating them in "exactly" the same terms the New England Puritans did, as his fast-day and thanksgiving-day sermons attest. In fact, the federal covenant was a "taken-for-granted reality" in eighteenth-century New England society, a special people with a messianic destiny, a city on a hill. Such a "dazzling" vision of a redeemer nation was inescapable for Edwards, and has yet to fade for many Americans.

Noll, Mark. "Edwards' Theology after Edwards," pp. 292-308. Offers a "rapid survey" of Edwards's influence on later thinkers — Protestant theologians, lay evangelicals, intellectuals — over the generations following his death, both here and abroad, on one level or another, tracing the "controversial uses" of his legacy in the nineteenth century to help understand his recovery and reclamation in the twentieth. The "great struggle" to control Reformed Calvinism between New England theologians and mid-Atlantic Presbyterians in the nineteenth century involved Edwards's theology, the controversy, his evangelicalism. Along with Miller's rehabilitation of the Puritans — and Edwards — in the 1930s came "fresh attention" first from mainline Protestants and, much later, evangelicals, his "closest" constituency. "In the breadth of his learning, piety, and intellectual rigor, Edwards is more comprehensively alive today than ever in own lifetime or since."

24 Macquarie, John. "Eighteenth Century: Jonathan Edwards, John Woodman." *Two Worlds Are Ours: An Introduction to Christian Mysticism.* Minneapolis: Fortress Press, pp. 199-214.
Reprints 2004.45.

25 Minkema, Kenneth P. "Foreword." William Sparkes Morris, *The Young Jonathan Edwards: A Reconstruction.* New Haven: Jonathan Edwards Center at Yale University; Eugene, Ore.: Wipf & Stock, pp. v-vi.
Speculates that had William Sparkes Morris's dissertation (1955.6) been published earlier it may have provided a "corrective" to Perry Miller's critical biography (1949.9), anticipated in part Norman Fiering's *Jonathan Edwards's Moral Thought and Its British Context* (1981.10), and underscored the importance of Edwards's unpublished manuscripts, in the preface to the inaugural volume of Yale's Jonathan Edwards Classic Studies Series. (Reprints 1991.32.)

26 ———, and Harry S. Stout. "The Edwardsean Tradition and the Antislavery Debate, 1740-1865." *Journal of American History* 92 (June): 47-74.
Traces the different approaches of the New Divinity and later Edwardseans in the antislavery

debate to the "conflicted influence" of Edwards: "so at home" with domestic slavery — he owned a number of slaves — Edwards "balked" at continuing the slave trade — slavery could never be a converting ordinance that would bring "captured Africans" into Christianity voluntarily. Antislavery sentiment among Edwards's disciples "reached its apex" in the revolutionary period but "largely lost" its moral sense of urgency thereafter.

27 Moody, Josh. *Jonathan Edwards and the Enlightenment: Knowing the Presence of God.* Latham, Md.: University Press of America, vii, 203 pp.

Characterizes Edwards's response to the Enlightenment as "active, conscious," in an analysis of his epistemology, his theology, and his practice of "'knowing the presence of God'" within that context. Of "prime importance" in his response to the Enlightenment is the issue of spiritual epistemology — the "axis around which Edwards' globe spins" — more important to him than the historical criticism of the Bible that arose then, more important than evidentialist apologetics, though he engaged both. "[F]ar from being solely cerebral," Edwards's response to the Enlightenment served a practical contemporary need as well, combatting a certain "moral looseness" not before seen in New England and promoting a spiritual awakening.

28 Moore, T. M. *Consider the Lilies: A Plea for Creational Theology.* Phillipsburg, N.J.: P & R Publications, pp. 125-82.

Draws upon Edwards — and the poetry of William Cowper (1731-1800) and Gerard Manley Hopkins (1844-1889) — to explain and represent creational theology, in a challenge to contemporary Christians to take "seriously" the revelation of God in creation and to discover and celebrate his glory there. Edwards, "the greatest creational theologian of all time," made "extensive use" of the doctrine of general revelation in his Northampton ministry and can be a guide in its practice now. His example and recommendations can "enhance our efforts to know the Lord and deepen our sense of happiness."

29 Noll, Mark A. *America's God.* New York : Oxford University Press, xiii, 622 pp.

Reprints 2002.33.

30 Norris, Robert M. "Introduction." *Pursuing Holiness in the Lord: Jonathan Edwards.* Edited by T. M. Moore. Jonathan Edwards for Today's Reader, 3. Phillipsburg, N.J.: P & R Publishing, pp. 1-10.

Notes the continuing impact Edwards's preaching makes on "every generation," in an introduction to three sermons — "The Character of Paul an Example to the Christians," "Hope and Comfort Usually Follow Genuine Humiliation and Repentance," and "The Preciousness of Time and the Importance of Redeeming It."

31 Pederson, Randall J., and Joel R. Beeke. "Introduction." In *Day by Day with Jonathan Edwards.* Edited by Randall J. Pederson. Peabody, Mass.: Hendrickson Publishers, pp. 1-5.

Prefaces daily selections from the "treasures" of Edwards's pen with a brief life, "one of America's best and last Puritans."

32 Sasser, Daryl. Review of *The Salvation of Souls,* ed. Richard A. Bailey and Gregory A. Wills. *Interpretation* 59 (January): 97-98.

Regards this collection of sermons (2002.2) a "fine illustration" of Edwards's perception of the minister's role and duties, even if they were not intended as such.

33 Schmidt, Leigh E. "The Great Reckoning." *Bookforum* 12 (Summer): 18-19.

Reproves Perry Miller — "a hard-drinking atheist" — and his "notorious" essay "From Edwards to Emerson" and Philip Gura — "a winsome scholar" — for placing Edwards "within the pale" of Emerson's universalism, in a review of a reprint of Miller's *Jonathan Edwards* (2004.79) and Gura's *Jonathan Edwards* (2005.11).

34 Steensen, Sasha. "Wanderings (Back) Toward a Poetic Historiography." Ph.D. dissertation, State University at New York at Buffalo.

Discusses Edwards as one of three early American writers (the others are Mary Rowlandson and Henry Thoreau) using wandering to represent non-linear indeterminate movements as the historical context for three modern poets, William Carlos Williams, Charles Olson, and Susan Howe.

35 Stout, Harry S., Kenneth P. Minkema, and Caleb J. D. Maskell, eds. *Jonathan Edwards at 300: Essays on the Tercentenary of His Birth.* Latham, Md.: University Press of America, xvii, 175 pp.

Publishes thirteen papers delivered at an Edwards tercentennial celebration held 3-4 October 2003 at the Library of Congress.

Stout, Harry S., Kenneth P. Minkema, and Caleb J. D. Maskell. "Introduction," pp. v-xvii. Charts the direction of interest in Edwards over the last century — "one of the most studies figures in American history and *the* most studied figure in the colonial period" — and summarizes the essays in the collection, grouped under six headings: theology of history, Scripture, culture, society, race, and biography.

Lee, Sang Hyun. "Does History Matter to God? Jonathan Edwards's Dynamic Reconception of God's Relation to the World," pp. 1-13. Answers the question affirmatively, in a discussion of Edwards's "dispositional re-conception" of divine being — God's temporality and spatiality — chiefly in his doctrine of the Trinity and *End of Creation.* Such a reconception has a "profound impact" on Edwards's theology as a whole, his emphasis upon Christian practice, for instance, repeating God's "intra-trinitarian acts in time and space," much as his eschatology reveals a "heightened importance" of both. For Edwards, God's relation to the world makes what happens in time and history "a participation in God's own life."

Pauw, Amy Plantinga. "Edwards as American Theologian: Grand Narratives and Pastoral Narratives," pp. 14-24. Complements Edwards's grand narrative of God's overarching presence, *History of Redemption,* with his pastoral narrative "much closer" to the quotidian life of the church, the "ruts and bumps" in the lives of his parishioners. Intertwined as they were in his writing, the grand narrative and the pastoral had "an uneasy co-existence" in his thought — witnessed in his early ministry in Northampton among English settlers and his missionary work among the Housatonics near the end of it — though Edwards's "most enduring" theology reconciles them. In this, Edwards was, indeed, "an American theologian," his grand vision tempered by a "frank recognition" of national and religious failings.

Sweeney, Douglas A. "'Longing for More and More of It'? The Strange Career of Jonathan Edwards's Exegetical Exertions," pp. 25-37. Decries the neglect of modern scholars of Edwards's biblicism — his world "revolved around" the Word of God — and attributes it to their denigration of biblical theology and to the "spirit of mainstream American culture," its liberation from external authority, its independence. Yet Edwards's biblical theology has exerted "more spiritual force" in America since its founding than before, his evangelical reach now global. "Perhaps it is time to pay due attention to Edwards's vast exegetical writings."

Brown, Robert E. "The Sacred and the Profane Connected: Edwards, the Bible, and Intellectual Culture," pp. 38-53. Cites two instances from Edwards's biblical hermeneutics — the authorship of the Pentateuch and the nature of hell — of how his commentary points to "a complex interpretative context," the first illustrating a connection of Scripture to the new history, the second to the new physics. In the first, Edwards anticipates the sort of rationalist apologetics popular in nineteenth-century America, the "confident assertion of the harmony of the Bible and secular knowledge"; in the second, he reverses the paradigm, insisting on "a looser association," taking the biblical characterizations of hell "metaphorically." In attempting to connect these narratives, Edwards is as "important and creative a thinker" on these issues as any in early America.

Stein, Stephen J. "Jonathan Edwards and the Cultures of Biblical Violence," pp. 54-64. Explores Edwards's "disturbing" reactions to a variety of biblical accounts of violence, a celebration "central" to his religious perspective and his theology, part of a "larger tradition" of Christian theology and ambivalence about it. For Edwards, the contemplated sacrifice of Isaac (Genesis 22), for example, was "appropriate and religiously meaningful," much as the massacre of the young children in Bethlehem by Herod (Matthew 2:16) "a just punishment" for their inhumanity to Mary and the infant Jesus. While these texts expose Edwards's "anti-Jewish perspective," the one culture of biblical violence that "most occupied" him was Catholicism — an "antichristian force subject to the will of the Antichrist," the pope — his apocalyptic vision calling for its defeat and destruction.

McDermott, Gerald R. "Franklin, Jefferson, and Edwards on Religion and the Religions," pp. 65-85. Compares Edwards, Franklin, and Jefferson on the issues that "most *divided*" eighteenth-century Americans — religion and the religions — a disagreement, not on whether God existed, but on the nature of goodness and justice, that is, the nature of God. Deists, like Franklin and Jefferson, stripped religion of "extraneous trappings" — mystery and special revelation — reducing it to a "basic core," at once reasonable and moral; Edwards countered that special revelation was necessary, for "unregenerate reason was incapable of seeing the aesthetic center" of true religion and true moral virtue. Although neither vision prevailed, their debate "helped set the agenda" for American theology over the next two centuries.

Gura, Philip F. "Lost and Found: Recovering Edwards for American Literature," pp. 86-97. Traces Edwards's "position of centrality" in the American canon until the mid-1970s, attributing the loss of interest in him to a shift in literary studies — post-structuralism, linguistics, and comparative literature — to a decline in "theological literacy," and to misrepresentative selections in anthologies. To reclaim Edwards, early Americanists need to focus on his "'influence'" on antebellum writers, on his "hypnotic" prose style, his aesthetics, and, particularly, his contribution to the "discourse of sentimentalism," in Harriet Beecher Stowe, Maria Cummins, and Susan Warner, Hawthorne, Melville, and Whitman. Edwards's "practical divinity" — *Religious Affections,* for example, *Life of Brainerd*, his conversion narrative, and Abigail Hutchinson's — not his "lengthy theological treatises," are the source-texts for that influence, and "his influence is there, everywhere."

Noll, Mark. "Jonathan Edwards's *Freedom of the Will* Abroad," pp. 98-110. Tells "a different story" from the negative American reaction to Edwards's *Freedom of the Will* — by James Dana, Charles Grandison Finney, Oliver Wendell Holmes, and Mark Twain — to the varied British reception — by Lord Kames, Andrew Fuller, William Godwin, and Thomas Chalmers — a "singular set of testimonies to the genius" of the work. Fuller, Godwin, and Chalmers praised the "clarity" of Edwards's reasoning; Kames complimented him by "stealing [his] arguments." It was a mark of the "radical dislocation of the age" that these four Britons could agree with Edwards's view of the human will but did not "parse the world" as he did.

Chamberlain, Ava. "Jonathan Edwards and the Politics of Sex in Eighteenth-Century New England," pp. 111-22. Illustrates the changing dynamics of sex, legal standards, and clerical authority in eighteenth-century New England, in a case of fornication involving twenty-year-old

Elisha Hawley, whose father's suicide put an end to Northampton's little awakening, and whose brother helped end Edwards's pastorate. By 1748, a "double standard" allowed men to escape legal responsibility for fornication — a standard evangelical ministers objected to — and Edwards moved to excommunicate Elisha as visibly unregenerate, his position in *Humble Inquiry.* Unfortunately, Edwards could not sustain in his church "a unity the wider society was no longer willing to accept."

Valeri, Mark. "Forgiveness and the Party of Humanity in Jonathan Edwards's World," pp. 123-30. Remarks Edwards's spirited defense of evangelical Calvinism against charges that it was "irrational and morally dubious," in a reading of three sermons on forgiveness — on Matt. 5:44, early 1730s; Matt. 12:7, January 1740; and Ps. 119:56, September 1740 — the last on the (brief) return of Eunice Williams after thirty-six years of living among Catholic, French-allied Indians near Montreal. Edwards stressed the importance of forgiveness not only for the public reputation of revivals but as a sign to those outside New England that "piety promoted the common good," that evangelical morality exceeded the "quotient of benevolence" recommended by the English and Scottish Enlightenment — Lord Shaftesbury, Francis Hutcheson, David Hume, and Adam Smith.

Wheeler, Rachel. "Lessons from Stockbridge: Jonathan Edwards and the Stockbridge Indians," pp. 131-40. Surveys Stockbridge sources for "possible vectors" of influence between Edwards and the Mahicans — *Freedom of the Will, True Virtue, Original Sin,* and about two hundred sermons, on the one hand, missionary records, letters, petitions, and deeds, on the other. A few references to the Stockbridge Indians in *Original Sin* — scarcely any in the other treatises — and a difference in tone between sermons preached to them and to the settlers suggest that Edwards was not "markedly shaped" by his mission work. Although Edwards's influence on the Mahicans is "even harder to trace," two obscure letters by Hendrick Aupaumut, chief of the Stockbridge Indians at the end of the century, provide "tantalizing evidence" of their engagement with Christianity.

Saillant, John. "African American Engagements with Edwards in the Era of the Slave Trade," pp. 141-51. Considers Edwards's doctrine of disinterested benevolence the "linchpin of abolitionism" in second half of the eighteenth century, both black and white, both Phillis Wheatley and Samuel Hopkins. Edwards's notions of virtue, divine providence — Prince Hall wrote a thirty-five-page commentary on *History of Redemption* — the will, and typology became fundamental to their argument against slavery. "[W]hatever else early black abolitionists believed of the Bible, they believed it to be a book of types and antitypes."

Marsden, George M. "Jonathan Edwards in the Twenty-First Century," pp. 152-64. Offers an Edwards, not of his time and place — as in *A Life* (2003.59) — but an Edwards "especially useful for our own time": for better understanding American culture, the balance of the secular and the religious; for his theological legacy, "a dynamic loving God of personal relationships"; for his critique of enlightened modernity, the premise that the triune God "defines whatever is good"; for his emphasis on human depravity; for his lesson for evangelicals, to counter anti-intellectualism and "superficiality"; and for his recognition that "blazing beauty" is at the center of the universe, an "overwhelming beauty that is not just a temporary escape but which is the basis for a way of life that is both practical and exhilarating."

36 Sweeney, Douglas A. *The Evangelical Story: A History of the Movement.* Grand Rapids, Mich.: Baker Academic, pp. 44-49 passim.

Asserts that Edwards proved "the single most important evangelical in America," in a brief life. The "theological genius" of the Great Awakening, Edwards "cleared the way" for people to back the revival and to evangelize outside their churches and ethnic groups.

*37 Vermaire, Mark. Emotions of the God-shaped Heart: the Religious Affections for a Twenty-first Century Church. D.Min. dissertation, Fuller Theological Seminary.

38 Vetö, Miklós. "A vontade em si mesma: Jonathan Edwards." In his *O nascimento da vontade*. Translated by Alvaro Lorencini. Sao Leopoldo, Brazil: Usisinos Publishing, pp. 144-72.

> Translates 2003.46. (In Portuguese.)

39 Wallace, Dewey D., Jr. Review of *America's God,* by Mark A. Noll. *Interpretation* 59 (April): 204-206.

> Regards Mark Noll's book (2002.33) a "must-read" for those concerned with the relation of religion to American cultural and political life, a "major work of great erudition."

40 Wilson, John F. "Introduction." *Jonathan Edwards,* by Perry Miller Lincoln: University of Nebraska Press, pp. v-x.

> Traces Perry Miller's lifelong engagement with colonial history and literature, culminating in his intellectual biography of Edwards — an "outsized figure among scholars" on an "outsized" figure in American culture — in an introduction to a reissue of *Jonathan Edwards* (1949.9). Even if Miller "indulged in overreaching," such leaps served his larger point: to offer to moderns, not the provincial revivalist preacher, but the "searching and imaginative intellect" of his time who "wrestled with issues relevant" to ours.

41 Wilson, Stephen A. "A Question of Balance: Evangelical Revivalism, Calvinist Theology, and Enlightenment Philosophy in George M. Marsden's *Jonathan Edwards: A Life.*" *Connecticut History* 44 (Spring): 158-62.

> Contends that the "surfeit of edification" in two areas — the evangelical movement and the doctrine of divine sovereignty — "creates deficits" in others, in a review of George M. Marsden's *Jonathan Edwards* (2003.59). "Edwards remains more impressive than even his most impressive biographer can tell in even a lengthy volume."

42 ———. *Virtue Reformed: Rereading Jonathan Edwards's Ethics.* Boston: Brill, xxv, 406 pp.

> Documents how features of the Aristotlean-Neoplatonic virtue tradition "latent" in Protestant scholasticism and "corroborated" in the English Reformation reinforce one another in Edwards's ethics. In *Two Dissertation* and *Religious Affections*, Edwards examines the role of Christian love in the assurance of salvation, the "inherent" conception of Christian righteousness, "the agency behind the power of the habit of charity"; in *Freedom of the Will,* he argues the freedom remaining to the regenerate; in *Life of Brainerd,* he lays out the "most extended case study" of the post-conversion search for assurance. "[T]easing out what Edwards thought about ethics requires the deliberate effort to restore the pastness to the past."

43 Winiarski, Douglas L. "Jonathan Edwards, Enthusiast? Radical Revivalism and the Great Awakening in the Connecticut Valley." *Church History* 74 (December): 683-739.

> Questions whether Edwards was an enthusiast, citing "new evidence" that suggests he may have come "uncomfortably close" to that "notoriously spirit-drenched tribe of hyperzealous New Lights" who scandalized the Great Awakening. An extract of a contemporary letter (attached) recounts Edwards's two days of preaching and communion, counselling and conversions

at Suffield, Massachusetts, just days before he delivered *Sinners in the Hands of an Angry God* across the Connecticut River at Enfield, 8 July 1741. Following his visit — ninety-six "'chiefly middle Aged'" persons were admitted to communion after the Sabbath sermon; "'Groans & Screaches,'" "'Houlings & Yellings'" ended the other — the village became a "hotbed" of radical evangelism, a form of revival Edwards would later condemn in *Distinguishing Marks, Some Thoughts,* and *Religious Affections.*

44 Zakai, Avihu. "Jonathan Edwards, the Enlightenment, and the Formation of Protestant Tradition in America." In *The Creation of the British Atlantic World.* Edited by Elizabeth Mancke and Carole Shammas. Baltimore: Johns Hopkins University Press, pp. 182-208.

Explores the complex interchange of British and European modes of thought on colonial America by examining Edward's reaction to the Enlightenment — particularly its theories of ethics and history — and the "key role" he played in the creation both of transatlantic evangelical culture and Protestant culture in America. Edwards was "among the first" to raise serious objections to those Enlightenment modes of thought well before the Revolution, and, due to his "brilliance as a theologian and philosopher," was able to "inaugurate" an American Protestant tradition. In his reaction to the "new science" of ethics and history, Edwards's "genius" forged a novel tradition "most adapted" to the American mind, a "powerful influence" little diminished over time and evident still in "many spheres" of American life and thought.

Index of Authors and Titles

Aaron, Daniel 1954.1, 2
Abel, Darrel 1963.1
Abelove, Henry 1972.1
"Ability and Responsibility in American Christianity" 1990.23
"'Above All Others': JE and the Gospel Ministry" 1989.58
Abraham, William J. 1989.1
"Abraham Lincoln and the Doctrine of Necessity" 1964.15A
"'An Absolute Sort of Certainty'" 2000.31
An Absolute Sort of Certainty 2003.74 [2005.19]
"Absolutely Pragmatic" 2002.37
Abzug, Robert H. 1996.1
"An Account of the Author's Life and Writings" 1808.1; 1844.1
An Account of the Conduct of the Council which Dismissed the Rev. Mr. Edwards 1750.1
Account of the Life and Writings of John Erskine, D.D. 1818.3
"Accounts of the Revival of Religion in Boston" 1744.2
Adams, James T. 1921.1; 1927.1
Adams, John C. 1993.19
Adams, Todd L. 2004.1
"Addendum to an Exercise on JE" 1961.8
Addison, Daniel D. 1900.1
An Address, Delivered at Northampton 1855.1
"Address of Welcome" 1903.17
"The Advantage of Loneliness" 1982.6
"Advertisement," *Faithful Narrative* 1808.4
"Advertisement," *Humble Inquiry* 1790.1

"Advertisement by the Editor," *Life of Brainerd* 1822.2
"Aeronautic Spiders with a Description of a New Species" 1936.4
"Aesthetics and Ethics" 2003.111
"Affirming the Touch of God" 1999.18
"African American Engagements with Edwards" 2005.35
"'After a High Negative Way'" 1991.15
"After Armageddon: JE and David Hume" 1990.32
"After the Surprising Conversions" 1946.3
"Afterword: The Puritans and Spiritual Renewal" 2004.41
Ahlstrom, Sydney E. 1961.1; 1963.2; 1967.1; 1972.2 (1975.1); 1977.1
Aijian, Paul M. 1950.1
Akers, Charles W. 1968.1
Akey, John 1951.1
Albert, Frank J. 1956.1
Albro, John A. 1847.1
Aldrich, Elizabeth K. 1990.1
Aldrich, P. Emory 1879.1
Aldridge, Alfred O. 1947.1; 1950.2; 1951.2; 1964.1 (1966.1); 1969.1; 1983.1, 1993.13
"Alephs, Zahirs, and the Triumph of Ambiguity" 1977.18
Alexander, Archibald 1852.A
Alexander, James W. 1839.1
Alexis, Gerhard T. 1947.2; 1966.2
"All Things Were New and Astonishing" 2003.45
Allen, Alexander V. G. 1889.1 (1889.2; 1890.1; 1896.1; 1899.1; 1901.6; 1974.1; 1976.1; 1980.12, 40)

Index of Subjects

ABCFM Oregon mission 1991.25; 1995.29

Absurdist 1971.14

Adams, John 1993.15C

Admission 1750.1; 1751.2; 1790.1; 1920.4; 1963.16; 1970.32; 1971.13A; 1972.16; 1977.31; 1980.45; 1981.18; 1989.46. *See also* Communion, *Humble Inquiry*

Aesthetics 1931.16; 1934.8; 1968.8-9; 1970.9; 1971.24; 1973.1, 5, 14; 1975.12; 1976.32, 48; 1977.9; 1978.2A, 9B; 1980.9, 11, 22, 40, 49; 1981.32, 35; 1982.15; 1985.45; 1990.36, 40; 1991.2; 1993.5; 1998.15; 2003.111; 2004.20, 58. *See also* Beauty, Ethics, *True Virtue*

Affections 1999.24; 2000.37

"After the Surprising Conversions" 1981.17

Aids to Reflection 1981.20

Alciphron 1996.46

Ambiguity 2002.12

American culture 1995.30; 1995.7; 1997.40; 2002.33; 2003.45, 63

American Enlightenment 1964.23; 1976.37-38; 1985.53; 1989.3

American Revolution 1902.2; 1904.11; 1905.2; 1927.2; 1948.10; 1950.18; 1952.4; 1966.17; 1983.26, 32; 1985.54; 1986.44

Ames, William 1959.14; 1979.11; 1981.11

Angelology 2000.35

Anglicanism 1903.35; 1968.12; 1971.7; 1993.1

Anselm 1896.8; 1924.1; 1935.5; 1966.35; 1975.7; 1987.39; 2003.80

Anthropology 1863.1; 1900.14; 1943.1; 1948.1; 1949.5; 1952.1; 1954.3; 1967.16; 1970.14; 1972.15; 1976.11; 1977.21

Antichrist 1946.2; 1974.26; 1982.30; 1992.24

Antinomianism 1928.8; 1954.13; 1980.23; 1984.21; 1988.17, 37; 1990.9; 1993.13

Apocalypse 1972.39; 1977.28; 1978.18; 1980.40; 1981.1, 25; 1982.40, 48; 1984.20, 37; 1985.10; 1987.8; 1988.20; 1991.8; 2001.6; 2002.43. *See also* Antichrist, Eschatology, Millennialism

Apologetics 1960.14; 1976.22-25; 1991.10; 1995.40; 2003.36, 74

Aquinas, Thomas 1868.2; 1896.8; 1964.6; 1966.35; 1985.44; 1987.39; 1990.36; 1991.24; 1996.39; 1999.38; 2001.48

Aristotle 1853.6; 1935.8; 1982.13; 1990.36

Arminianism 1793.6; 1912.3; 1928.2; 1942.13; 1968.12; 1979.10; 1981.18, 27; 1984.21; 1985.25, 46, 53; 1986.19, 30; 1987.2, 28; 1988.15, 17, 45; 1990.9, 23; 1991.2, 44; 1992.19, 25; 1993.8

Art. *See* Style

The Art of Thinking 1977.17; 1980.9; 1981.10

The Art of Virtue 1993.13

Aseity 2004.8

Ashbridge, Elizabeth S. 1998.21

Assurance 1960.5; 1962.3; 1964.25; 1966. 20, 22; 1980.11; 1988.23; 1989.1; 1993.7; 1994.3; 2003.74; 2005.4

Atonement 1856.3; 1859.5; 1860.4; 1924.1; 1931.17; 1951.10; 1971.26; 1975.7; 985.21; 1986.14; 1987.8; 1989.24; 1991.31; 1993.8; 1999.50

Atheism 1770.1; 1793.6; 1845.2

Atwater, Lyman H. 1988.17

Audubon, John J. 1995.37; 1998.27

Augustine 1868.2; 1879.4; 1896.8; 1968.28; 1972.9; 197340; 1976.43; 1978.22; 1980.29; 1981.15; 1982.15; 1987.19; 1990.36; 2004.18

1986.27, 30, 44; 1987.9, 21; 1988.17, 18, 21, 28, 38-39, 42; 1989.8, 13, 19; 1990.35, 36A, 40; 1991.4, 35, 40; 1992.18, 25, 28; 1993.13; 1994.25; 1995.23; 1999.14, 22. *See also* Evangelicalism, Revivalism

Gregory of Nyssa 1978.24

Half-way covenant 1884.5; 1892.5; 1904.14; 1945.1; 1963.18; 1970.23. *See also Humble Inquiry,* Stoddard

Hall, Robert 1832.4

Hamartiology 2005.6. *See also* Sin

"The Harmony of the Old and New Testament" 1977.29; 1988.17; 1996.46

Haroutunian, Joseph 1986.10; 1988.6

Hartshorne, Charles 1983.3

Harvard 1840.4; 1942.9; 1981.11

Hassidism 1973.29

Hawley, Joseph 1983.29

Hawthorne, Nathaniel 1904.12; 1969.33; 1972.24; 1973.22; 1976.18; 1978.22; 1980.7; 1987.17; 1988.17; 1995.22

Heereboord, Adrian 1955.6; 1981.10; 1991.32

Heidegger, Martin 2001.44

Hell 1859.1; 1934.9; 1964.18; 1965.11; 1980.14; 1981.10; 1987.8; 1991.39; 1993.9A; 1995.6, 9; 2000.16; 2003.37; 2004.51

Hermeneutics 1972.24; 1974.27; 1976.31; 1977.29; 1979.21; 1980.17, 26, 40; 1982.4; 1988.17; 2004.36; 2005.35. *See also* Biblicism

Hick, John 1979.7

Hiddenness 2002.46

Himmler, Heinrich 1980.32

Historiography 1975.13-14; 1977.32; 1985.10; 1992.11; 1993.4A; 2003.36. *See also History of Redemption*

History of Redemption 1774.3; 1775.1; 1827.2; 1951.12; 1965.15; 1966.14; 1968.28; 1970.20; 1975.13-14; 1977.32-33; 1979.11, 21; 1980.27, 40; 1982.33, 48; 1983.59; 1984.37; 1985.10, 21, 55; 1986.7; 1987.29; 1988.7, 44; 1989.59; 1990.39; 1991.6, 16, 21, 39; 1992.11, 17, 24, 25; 1993.1, 13; 1994.5; 1997.26; 1998.23; 2000.41; 2003.45-46, 112; 2005.23. *See also* Millennialism

Hofstadter, Albert 1980.40

Holy Spirit 1978.23; 1981.31; 1986.49; 1988.38, 42; 1989.60; 1990.43, 52; 2001.45; 2003.2; 2005.13

Holmes, Oliver Wendell 1988.17

Homiletics 1970.3; 1980.26; 1988.21; 1992.3; 2002.16

Hooker, Thomas 1897.8; 1972.37; 1979.10

Hopkins, Samuel 1852.8; 1935.1; 1967.19; 1977.7; 1980.40; 1982.27; 1983.9, 34; 1986.14, 33; 1987.7, 26, 35; 1988.15, 17, 20; 1989.16; 1993.13; 1997.14

Housatonics. *See* Stockbridge mission

Humble Attempt 1798.1; 1928.3; 1941.10; 1943.8; 1948.3; 1958.5; 1971.10; 1984.37; 1985.10, 34; 1986.27; 1987.29; 1990.22; 1992.24; 2004.3. *See also* Missions

Humble Inquiry 1749.1; 1750.2; 1751.3; 1867.2; 1884.5; 1962.3; 1970.23; 1971.13A; 1980.40; 1981.18; 1985.46; 1986.3; 1987.15; 1989.46; 1990.22; 1994.12; 1998.6, 30; 2003.15, 93. *See also* Communion

Hume, David 1898.5; 1981.10; 1983.22; 1989.21; 1990.32; 1991.39; 1992.1; 2001.12

Hutcheson, Francis 1951.2; 1967.16; 1970.32; 1971.29; 1980.10, 35; 1983.22; 1989.3; 1992.1. *See also True Virtue*

Hutchinson, Abigail 1991.16

Hutchinson, Anne 1988.17; 1991.9

Hypocrisy 1999.7

Idealism 1888.2; 1897.7; 1899.7; 1900.12; 1930.6; 1943.9; 1946.5; 1952.2; 1955.10; 1961.2; 1963.13; 1966.21; 1969.30; 1977.14A; 1979.2, 11; 1980.12, 40; 1983.15, 25; 1985.26; 1986.50; 1987.14; 1988.10, 17, 35; 1989.21; 2004.2. *See also* Neoplatonism

Identity 1888.3; 1972.19; 1973.37; 1974-29; 1975.21; 1979.14; 1980.40; 1981.40; 1983.23; 1984.14; 1985.54; 1988.3; 1989.21; 1990.38, 60; 1992.8; 29

Idolatry 1984.34; 1987.16

Imagery 1970.12; 1972.20; 1973.17; 1974.29; 1975.2, 16; 1976.44; 1978.4E; 1980.9, 11, 15, 40, 42; 1984.34; 1991.16; 1992.8, 17, 21; 1993.13. *See also* Style

"Images of Divine Things" 1993.1

Images or Shadows 1940.19; 1948.7; 1963.17; 1967.20; 1970.20; 1979.21; 1980.19, 27, 39, 46, 49; 1981.21; 1987.12; 1989.10; 1991.21; 1993.1, 13 1996.35. *See also* Typology

Imagination 1972.23, 41; 1973.16A; 1975.17; 1981.6, 9, 40; 1982.36; 1984.30; 1987.16;

Index of Additions